W9-BVR-394

HANDBOOK OF INDUSTRIAL ORGANIZATION

VOLUME I

HANDBOOKS IN ECONOMICS

10

Series Editors

KENNETH J. ARROW
MICHAEL D. INTRILIGATOR

NORTH-HOLLAND
AMSTERDAM • NEW YORK • OXFORD • TOKYO

EHEHEHEHEHEHEHEHEHEHEHEHEHEHEHEHEHEHEHEHEHEHEHE

HANDBOOK OF INDUSTRIAL ORGANIZATION

VOLUME I

Edited by

RICHARD SCHMALENSEE
Massachusetts Institute of Technology

and

ROBERT D. WILLIG
Princeton University

1989

NORTH-HOLLAND

AMSTERDAM · NEW YORK · OXFORD · TOKYO

ISBN North-Holland for this set 0 444 70436 1
ISBN North-Holland for this volume 0 444 70434 5

Publishers
ELSEVIER SCIENCE PUBLISHERS B.V.
P.O. Box 1991
1000 BZ Amsterdam
The Netherlands

Sole distributors for the U.S.A. and Canada
ELSEVIER SCIENCE PUBLISHING COMPANY, INC.
655 Avenue of the Americas
New York, N.Y. 10010
U.S.A.

Library of Congress Cataloging-in-Publication Data

Handbook of industrial organization/edited by Richard Schmalensee and Robert Willig.
p. cm.—(Handbooks in economics; 10)
Includes bibliographies.
ISBN 0-444-70434-5 (v. 1). ISBN 0-444-70435-3 (v. 2). ISBN 0-444-70436-1 (set)
1. Industrial organization (Economic theory)—Handbooks, manuals, etc. I. Schmalensee, Richard. II. Willig, Robert D., 1947– III. Series: Handbooks in economics; bk. 10.
HD2326.H28 1988
338.6—dc19 88-25138
CIP

PRINTED IN THE NETHERLANDS

INTRODUCTION TO THE SERIES

The aim of the *Handbooks in Economics* series is to produce Handbooks for various branches of economics, each of which is a definitive source, reference, and teaching supplement for use by professional researchers and advanced graduate students. Each Handbook provides self-contained surveys of the current state of a branch of economics in the form of chapters prepared by leading specialists on various aspects of this branch of economics. These surveys summarize not only received results but also newer developments, from recent journal articles and discussion papers. Some original material is also included, but the main goal is to provide comprehensive and accessible surveys. The Handbooks are intended to provide not only useful reference volumes for professional collections but also possible supplementary readings for advanced courses for graduate students in economics.

CONTENTS OF THE HANDBOOK

VOLUME I

PART 1 – DETERMINANTS OF FIRM AND MARKET ORGANIZATION

PART 2 – ANALYSIS OF MARKET BEHAVIOR

PREFACE TO THE HANDBOOK

Purpose and motivation

The *Handbook of Industrial Organization* aims to serve as a source, reference, and teaching supplement for industrial organization (or industrial economics), the broad field within microeconomics that focuses on business behavior and its implications both for market structures and processes, and for public policies towards them.[1] Our purpose has been to provide reasonably comprehensive and up-to-date surveys of recent developments and the state of knowledge in the major areas of research in this field as of the latter part of the 1980s, written at a level suitable for use by non-specialist economists and students in advanced graduate courses.

We feel that the preparation and publication of the *Handbook of Industrial Organization* is particularly timely due to the confluence of several exciting trends in this field of economics. First, industrial organization is a primary locus of the recent and ongoing revolution that is re-examining all microeconomic phenomena as strategic interactions with explicitly-specified (and often asymmetric) information structures. This trend alone has generated an unprecedented burst of theoretical research on industrial organization, with new answers to old questions rivalled in quantity only by the volume of new answers to new questions.

Second, new waves of empirical and experimental work in industrial organization are gathering momentum, driven by clarified views of the limitations of the previous focus on cross-sectional interindustry studies, and by the profusion of new hypotheses and possibly testable conclusions produced by the explosion of theoretical work

Third, the boundaries between historically distinct fields of economics, such as international trade and macroeconomics, and industrial organization, have recently become blurred. The perfectly competitive model traditionally central to other fields is being replaced by explicit models of imperfect competition derived from industrial organization. As a consequence, important new results are being generated in these fields, and significant new issues for the field of industrial organization are emerging.

[1]This Handbook attempts to cover only those themes and issues that have been prominent in what de Jong (1986) has called "Anglo-Saxon thinking" in industrial organization. He presents an interesting overview of the rather different continental European tradition.

Finally, a bevy of significant policy issues squarely in the domain of industrial organization has been at the forefront of public and political attention in recent years. Takeover and merger activity, the movement towards deregulation, increasing globalization of competition, and concerns about national competitiveness have all been powerful stimuli to theoretical, empirical, and policy research, and have increased awareness of the magnitude of the work still to be done in industrial organization.

These trends both make the field of industrial organization exciting and enhance the value that this Handbook can provide by communicating the state-of-the-art in that field to those who seek to contribute to it or to apply it to their own concerns. This potential value has motivated us as editors and has induced the authors of the chapters that follow to contribute so generously of their enormously productive efforts.

Organization

The organization of the *Handbook of Industrial Organization* reflects our perspectives on the principal topics in the field that have recently received intensive research attention or that otherwise are most needful of a new integrative survey. Each of the chapters in the Handbook can be read independently, though they are organized into Parts with some logic, and many pairs are close complements.

Part 1 begins the Handbook with four chapters on the firm. In much of economics, the firm has been viewed as just a black box that maximizes profits subject to an exogenous production or cost function. Because firm behavior is so important in industrial organization, scholars in this field have been productively working to open that box. John Panzar (Chapter 1) focuses on the impact of costs and technology on the organization of production among firms in an industry. He surveys the body of theoretical results on the connections between detailed properties of multiproduct cost functions and details of firm and market structure, and discusses methods of applying these results in empirical analyses of such industries as electric power and telecommunications.

Bengt Holmstrom and Jean Tirole (Chapter 2) consider the implications of imperfect information for the behavior of firms viewed as organizations of self-interested owners, managers, and employees. They summarize the burgeoning body of research that formally analyzes from this perspective the existence, scope, financing, internal structure, control, and objectives of firms. In a complementary chapter, Oliver Williamson (Chapter 3) analyzes the consequences of the minimization of transactions costs for the structures of firms and for the locations of boundaries between firms and markets. Martin Perry (Chapter 4) focuses on vertical integration as an important dimension of firm structure. His presentation surveys the long line of research on the incentives for and effects of vertical integration, and connects this body of work to the perspectives of transactions costs and information asymmetries.

A solid understanding of the firm is a logical prerequisite to answering what has long been the central research question in industrial organization: "How can behavior and performance in a market be understood and predicted on the basis of observable data?" Scholars who attempt to answer this question generally deal also with its sequel: "Can government policy somehow improve market performance?" Parts 2–5 of this Handbook concentrate on these questions. Antitrust policy issues are discussed as they arise in the chapters in Parts 2–4 (and in several of the chapters in Part 1); Part 5 focuses on economic and social regulation.

Part 2 is devoted to the theoretical literature on market behavior and performance, which has grown explosively in the last decade and a half, and to the implications of this research for antitrust policy.[2] Much of this work draws on recent developments in noncooperative game theory, especially the theory of dynamic games of incomplete or imperfect information. Drew Fudenberg and Jean Tirole (Chapter 5) present an overview of the game-theoretic tools that have been most widely applied in this spate of new research, and employ representative models as examples of the analytic techniques.

The next two chapters provide complementary analyses of the determinants of the intensity of rivalry among sellers in a market. Carl Shapiro (Chapter 6) integratively summarizes the state of oligopoly theory, running the gamut from the classical models of Cournot and Bertrand to the latest models set in the context of repeated games with imperfect information. Alexis Jacquemin and Margaret Slade (Chapter 7) consider related theoretical work focusing on cartels, explicit and implicit collusion, and mergers, and the implications of this work for antitrust policy.

The following two complementary chapters are concerned with the process of market entry. Richard Gilbert (Chapter 8) focuses on structural barriers to entry and mobility, bridging the gaps between the classical treatments of Bain and Stigler and the recent treatments that formally model the strategic incentives of both incumbents and potential entrants. Janusz Ordover and Garth Saloner (Chapter 9) emphasize rational strategic behavior designed to prevent or remove competition and use this theory to analyze antitrust policy towards "predatory" business behavior.

The next four chapters in Part 2 cover economic models of the "Four P's" of traditional marketing textbooks: Product, Price, Promotion (mainly advertising), and Place (distribution). Hal Varian (Chapter 10) summarizes and integrates the

[2] The reader interested in theoretical work in industrial organization should also consult Tirole (1988). One could argue that this Part might have contained a chapter on the theory of auctions and bargaining, which has advanced rapidly in recent years.

large literature on price discrimination, describes how a wide variety of selling practices are analytically equivalent when viewed through the lens of price discrimination, and contrasts the results of welfare analyses of such pricing with its treatment by antitrust policy. Michael Katz (Chapter 11), in a chapter that complements several of the chapters in Part 1, analyzes contracts between manufacturing firms and the wholesalers and retailers who distribute their wares. The formal treatment covers a host of vertical restraints and practices and their welfare effects. Curtis Eaton and Richard Lipsey (Chapter 12) survey models of product choice and product differentiation, focusing on the positive and normative implications unavailable from less structured models of oligopoly. Joseph Stiglitz (Chapter 13) focuses on the consequences of imperfectly informed buyers for the way that markets work, with specific attention to the implications for pricing, advertising, and other modes by which information is conveyed in market equilibria.

The last two chapters in Part 2 are concerned with issues of great empirical and policy importance that have recently begun to receive serious theoretical attention. Jennifer Reinganum (Chapter 14) provides a survey of game-theoretical work on competition in the processes of R&D and the dissemination of its technological fruits, focusing on both analytical technique and on the economic meaning of assumptions and results. Dennis Carlton (Chapter 15) considers evidence on price rigidity, industrial organization theories that are consistent with that evidence, and the associated implications for macroeconomics.

Part 3 contains four surveys of market-oriented empirical studies that bear on the issues raised in Part 2.[3] Until the start of this decade, industry-level cross-section studies of profitability differences dominated empirical work in industrial organization. Richard Schmalensee (Chapter 16) provides an overview of these and related studies, assessing the underlying methodologies and highlighting the robust regularities found in the data. Timothy Bresnahan (Chapter 17) contributes an integrative treatment of the tools and results that are emerging from the rapidly expanding stream of research devoted to building and testing structural models of firm behavior in individual markets. Wesley Cohen and Richard Levin (Chapter 18) survey the broad, interdisciplinary empirical literature on the determinants of technical progress. Their chapter is a natural complement to Chapter 14. Charles Plott (Chapter 19) concludes this Part of the Handbook with an overview of the methods, results, and analyses of the new wave of laboratory experiments designed to test industrial organization hypotheses.

[3] We had hoped that Part 3 would contain a chapter on the theoretical and empirical tools from modern finance theory that have proven valuable in industrial organization. For a useful discussion of one important aspect of the relation between these fields, see Schwert (1981). Some other aspects of this relation are discussed by Bengt Holmstrom and Jean Tirole in Chapter 2.

Part 4 consists of two chapters that take an explicitly global view of industrial organization. Paul Krugman (Chapter 20) describes recent theoretical work on imperfect competition in open economies. His analysis, relating closely to several chapters in Part 2, shows how the theory of international trade can be enriched with foundations drawn from the field of industrial organization, and how the international context raises new issues of theory and application for the field. Richard Caves (Chapter 21) explores the use of international comparisons in empirical research. This chapter, closely related to Chapter 16, shows the value of a broader perspective on industrial organization issues than is provided by the experience of any single nation.

Part 5 provides overviews of theoretical and empirical studies of regulatory policy.[4] Roger Noll (Chapter 22) contributes a chapter on the economic analysis of the political–economic determination of regulatory policies and other government interventions in the marketplace. The next three chapters consider economic regulation of price, entry, and conditions of sale, regulation which is nominally intended to limit the exercise of monopoly power. Ronald Braeutigam (Chapter 23) reviews and interprets the literature on optimal pricing for natural monopolies (whether regulated or publicly owned). David Baron (Chapter 24) provides an overview of recent formal research on the design of optimal regulatory mechanisms and institutions when information is asymmetric, connecting this literature to the classical treatment of rate-of-return regulation. Paul Joskow and Nancy Rose (Chapter 25) survey and critique the voluminous empirical literature on the effects of economic regulation. Howard Gruenspecht and Lester Lave (Chapter 26) conclude the *Handbook of Industrial Organization* with an overview of the economic rationales and effects of social regulatory policies directed at health, safety, environmental, and related problems.

Historical overviews

Because most of the individual chapters in the *Handbook of Industrial Organization* provide historical overviews of the topics they cover, it seems redundant to provide a general overview here. For additional discussions of the historical development of the field of industrial organization, see Scherer (1980), Bresnahan and Schmalensee (1987), Hay and Morris (1979), Schmalensee (1982, 1988), and Roberts (1987).

[4]We must again note a gap in coverage; we had hoped that this Part would contain an overview and analysis of competition (antitrust) policies and their enforcement.

Acknowledgements

Our primary debt is, of course, to the authors of the chapters in the *Handbook of Industrial Organization*. We appreciate the care, skill, and imagination with which they carried out their assignments, their willingness to take our comments seriously, and their efforts to meet our deadlines. Many also provided us with useful advice and comments. We are also indebted to Louis Phlips for his many hours of work on this project; it is our fault and the reader's loss that he is not among the Handbook authors.

RICHARD SCHMALENSEE
Massachusetts Institute of Technology

ROBERT D. WILLIG
Princeton University

References

Bresnahan, T.F. and R. Schmalensee (1987) 'The empirical renaissance in industrial economics: An overview', *Journal of Industrial Economics*, 35:371–378.

Hay, D.A. and D.J. Morris (1979) *Industrial economics: Theory and evidence*. Oxford: Oxford University Press.

de Jong, H.W. (1986) 'European industrial organization: Entrepreneurial economics in an organizational setting', in: H.W. de Jong and W.G. Shepherd, eds., *Mainstreams in industrial organization, Book I*. Boston: Kluwer.

Roberts, D.J. (1987) 'Battles for market share: Incomplete information aggressive strategic pricing, and competitive dynamics', in: T. Bewley, ed., *Advances in economic theory, Fifth World Congress*. Cambridge: Cambridge University Press.

Scherer, F.M. (1980) *Industrial market structure and economic performance*, 2nd edn. Chicago: Rand McNally.

Schmalensee, R. (1982) 'The new industrial organization and the economic analysis of modern markets', in: W. Hildenbrand, ed., *Advances in Economic Theory*. Cambridge: Cambridge University Press.

Schmalensee, R. (1988) 'Industrial economics: An overview', *Economic Journal*, 98:643–681.

Schwert, G. W. (1981) 'Using financial data to measure the effects of regulation', *Journal of Law and Economics*, 24:121–158.

Tirole, J. (1988) *The theory of industrial organization*. Cambridge: MIT Press.

CONTENTS OF VOLUME I

PART 2 – ANALYSIS OF MARKET BEHAVIOR

Chapter 13

Imperfect Information in the Product Market

JOSEPH E. STIGLITZ

PART 1

DETERMINANTS OF FIRM AND MARKET ORGANIZATION

Chapter 1

TECHNOLOGICAL DETERMINANTS OF FIRM AND INDUSTRY STRUCTURE

JOHN C. PANZAR*

Northwestern University

Contents

*I would like to thank Avner Greif for his research assistance, Bobby Willig for helpful comments, and the National Science Foundation, SES 8409171, for partial research support. Any errors are, of course, solely my responsibility.

Handbook of Industrial Organization, Volume I, Edited by R. Schmalensee and R.D. Willig

1. Introduction

The title of this volume is the *Handbook of Industrial Organization*. The literal interpretation of the term "industrial organization" has, in large part, receded from the surface when the noun or adjective "IO" is used. As many of the subsequent chapters in this volume indicate, the field has moved far beyond the mere description of how industries are organized. Yet it is at this basic level that the discussion must begin. For the very name of the field alerts one to the fact that we are dealing with questions that do not even arise in the traditional Marshallian framework. There the industry, itself, was the unit of analysis. Its internal organization, while perhaps of anecdotal interest, was not viewed as being at all important for answering the important positive or normative questions of value theory. Thus, the distinguishing feature of research in industrial organization is that, for some reason or other, it is not fruitful to employ the classical perfectly competitive model to analyze the problems of interest. This chapter explores the technological conditions that may make it necessary to abandon the competitive model: there simply may not be "enough room" in the market for a sufficiently large number of firms to give credence to the assumption of price-taking behavior.

The chapter is organized in the following manner. Section 2 introduces the cost concepts required for analyzing the role of technology in the determination of firm and industry structure. The emphasis is on the general multiproduct case, although important single product aspects of the problem are also discussed. Section 3 presents an analysis of the role these cost concepts play in determining efficient industry structure. Section 4 addresses some issues that must be dealt with in any empirical study of technology and industry structure, as well as presenting selective surveys of such studies of the telecommunications and electric power industries. Section 5 ends the chapter with some concluding observations.

2. The multiproduct cost function[1]

The most basic concept with which to characterize the productive technology available to the firm is the technology set T, a list of the combinations of inputs and outputs that are available to the firm. Thus, let x denote a vector of r inputs

[1]The material in this section is based upon the discussion in Baumol, Panzar and Willig (1982). Most formal proofs have been included in order to make this discussion of important multiproduct cost concepts as self-contained as possible.

available to the firm and $\boldsymbol{y}$ a vector of possible outputs that may be selected from the set $N = \{1, 2, \ldots, n\}$. Then the technology set is formally defined as

Definition 1. The technology set

$T = \{(\boldsymbol{x}, \boldsymbol{y})\colon\ \boldsymbol{y} \text{ can be produced from } \boldsymbol{x}\}.$

In the familiar single output case, T can be directly related to the simple production function $y = f(\boldsymbol{x})$. Assuming free disposal, the technology set can be characterized as $T = \{(\boldsymbol{x}, y)\colon\ y \le f(\boldsymbol{x})\}$. While this definition of T is intuitively quite clear, more structure must be assumed in order to facilitate mathematical analysis. The following weak regularity condition is commonly employed:

Regularity condition R1

Input vectors $\boldsymbol{x}$ are elements of the compact set $X \subset R^r_+$ and output vectors $\boldsymbol{y}$ are elements of the compact set $Y \subset R^n_+$. The technology set T is a nonempty closed subset of $X \times Y$, with the additional properties that (i) $(\boldsymbol{0}, \boldsymbol{y}) \in T$ iff $\boldsymbol{y} = \boldsymbol{0}$, and (ii) If $(\boldsymbol{x}, \boldsymbol{y}) \in T$, $(\boldsymbol{x}^1, \boldsymbol{y}^1) \in X \times Y$, $\boldsymbol{x}^1 \ge \boldsymbol{x}$, and $\boldsymbol{y}^1 \le \boldsymbol{y}$, then $(\boldsymbol{x}^1, \boldsymbol{y}^1) \in T$.

$R1$(i) states that positive inputs are required to produce positive outputs. $R1$(ii) is a "free disposal" axiom that assures that the production process is at least weakly monotonic, i.e. an increase in input use makes possible at least a weak increase in output.

Given $R1$, there exists a continuous production transformation function $\varphi(\boldsymbol{x}, \boldsymbol{y})$ that is nondecreasing in $\boldsymbol{x}$ and nonincreasing in $\boldsymbol{y}$ such that $\varphi(\boldsymbol{x}, \boldsymbol{y}) \ge 0$ iff $(\boldsymbol{x}, \boldsymbol{y}) \in T$.[2] The production transformation function provides a convenient functional representation of the set of feasible input/output combinations. It is directly related to the familiar single output production function. For example, if $y = f(\boldsymbol{x})$ is the production function, then $\varphi(\boldsymbol{x}, y) = f(\boldsymbol{x}) - y$ is a well-defined production transformation function.

Since most of the analysis of this chapter will be carried out under the assumption that the firms in the industry are price takers in input markets, it is more convenient to work with the cost function representation of the technology. Therefore define the multiproduct minimum cost function:

$$C(\boldsymbol{y}, \boldsymbol{w}) = \min_{\boldsymbol{x}} \{\boldsymbol{w} \cdot \boldsymbol{x}\colon (\boldsymbol{x}, \boldsymbol{y}) \in T\} = \boldsymbol{w} \cdot \boldsymbol{x}^*(\boldsymbol{y}, \boldsymbol{w}),$$

[2] See McFadden (1978).

where $\boldsymbol{x}^*(\boldsymbol{y}, \boldsymbol{w})$ is an efficient, cost-minimizing input vector for producing the output vector $\boldsymbol{y}$ when factor prices are given by $\boldsymbol{w}$.

It will be convenient (and sometimes essential) to assume that this central analytic construct has the following smoothness property:

Regularity condition R2

For all $i \in N$, if $y_i > 0$, then $C_i \equiv \partial C/\partial y_i$ exists.

This simply assumes that marginal cost is well defined for any output that is produced in strictly positive quantity. It is not desirable to assume that the cost function is globally differentiable, because that would rule out the possibility that additional fixed or startup costs may occur when production of another output begins. (Mathematically, such possibilities would require the presence of jump discontinuities along the various axes.) At this point it is also appropriate to introduce a regularity condition defined on the transformation function $\varphi(\boldsymbol{x}, \boldsymbol{y})$ that suffices for $R2$:

Regularity condition R3

T can be characterized by a transformation function, $\varphi(\boldsymbol{x}, \boldsymbol{y})$, that is continuously differentiable in $\boldsymbol{x}$ and in y_i, for $y_i > 0$, at points $(\boldsymbol{x}, \boldsymbol{y})$ where $\boldsymbol{x}$ is cost-efficient for $\boldsymbol{y}$.

A particularly convenient and reasonably general[3] specification of a cost function satisfying $R2$ is as follows. Let $C(\boldsymbol{y}) = F\{S\} + c(\boldsymbol{y})$, where c is continuously differentiable, $c(0) = 0$, $S = \{i \in N\colon\ y_i > 0\}$ and $F\{\varnothing\} = 0$.[4] A simple two-product example will serve to illustrate the usefulness of this construction:

$$C(y_1, y_2) = \begin{array}{lll} F^{12} + c_1 y_1 & + c_2 y_2, & \text{for } y_1 > 0,\ y_2 > 0, \\ F^1 + c_1 y_1, & & \text{for } y_1 > 0,\ y_2 = 0, \\ F^2 + & + c_2 y_2, & \text{for } y_1 = 0,\ y_2 > 0, \end{array} \tag{1}$$

[3]This formulation is not completely general, however. In particular, it does not allow for the possibility that the magnitude of the jump discontinuity that result when a new product is introduced may depend upon the quantities of the outputs in the existing product mix as well as the composition of that mix.

[4]Here, and wherever it will not lead to confusion, the vector $\boldsymbol{w}$ will be suppressed as an argument of the cost function.

with $0 < F^1, F^2 < F^{12}$ and $C(0,0) = 0$. Thus, in this example, starting up production of y_1 only requires incurring the fixed cost F^1. If the firm then begins production of y_2 as well, additional fixed costs of $F^{12} - F^1$ are incurred. The important role in the determination of industry structure played by such product specific fixed costs will be discussed below.

2.1. Economies of scale

The technological limits to competitive market structures have long been attributed to the presence of economies of scale.[5] Later we shall discuss its importance in the determination of firm and industry structure in great detail. But what, precisely, is meant by the term "economies of scale"? The most natural intuitive characterization in the single product case is: Given a proportional increase in all input levels, does output increase more or less than proportionately? While this technological definition is often used in undergraduate textbooks,[6] it is not useful for current purposes, because it does not bear the desired relationship to the properties of the firm's cost curves.

To understand why, suppose that in a small neighborhood of the output level $y = f(\mathbf{x})$, it is the case that $f(k\mathbf{x}) = k'y$. Then the above definition would say that returns to scale were increasing, constant, or decreasing as k' is greater than, equal to, or less than k. It is easy to see that increasing returns to scale, by this definition, implies that average costs are lower at $k'y$ than they are at y.[7] However, the converse is not necessarily true. The reason is that if the firm wishes to increase output by the factor k', the cheapest way to do so is not necessarily a proportionate increase in all input levels. Thus, even if per unit expenditure does not fall when output is increased by expanding all inputs proportionately (i.e. $k > k'$), it may decrease when inputs are chosen in a cost-minimizing manner. Part of the conceptual difficulty is due to the need to relate economies of scale concepts, defined in terms of properties of the productive technology without reference to factor prices, to the cost conditions facing the firm. For, as we shall see, it is the latter that play a key role in determining firm and industry structure.

Fortunately, assuming that regularity condition $R3$ holds, it is possible to define a technologically based measure of the degree of scale economies that also serves to characterize important properties of firms' cost functions.

[5]See Scherer (1980, ch. 4) for an extended factual and intuitive discussion of the sources of and limits to economies of scale in a manufacturing setting.

[6]See, for example, Hirshleifer (1984, p. 329).

[7]*Proof*: $AC(k'y, \mathbf{w}) \leq k\mathbf{w} \cdot \mathbf{x}/k'y = (k/k')\mathbf{w} \cdot \mathbf{x}/y = (k/k')AC(y, \mathbf{w}) < AC(y, \mathbf{w})$.

Definition 2. Technological economies of scale

The degree of technological scale economies at $(\boldsymbol{x}, \boldsymbol{y}) \in T$ is defined as $\tilde{S}(\boldsymbol{x}, \boldsymbol{y}) = -\{\sum x_i(\partial\varphi/\partial x_i)\}/\{\sum y_i(\partial\varphi/\partial y_i\}$. Returns to scale are said to be (locally) increasing, constant or decreasing as $\tilde{S}$ is greater than, equal to or less than 1.

For the single output case, this definition reduces to the familiar concept known as the elasticity of scale.[8] That concept is defined as the elasticity with respect to t of $f(t\boldsymbol{x})$, evaluated at $t = 1$. That is,

$$e(t\boldsymbol{x}) \equiv t[\mathrm{d}f(t\boldsymbol{x})/\mathrm{d}t]/f(t\boldsymbol{x}) = t\left[\sum x_i f_i(t\boldsymbol{x})\right]/f(t\boldsymbol{x}),$$

where $f_i \equiv \partial f/\partial x_i$. Thus, $e(\boldsymbol{x}) = \sum x_i f_i(\boldsymbol{x})/f(\boldsymbol{x})$. To see that this is exactly equal to $\tilde{S}$, note that in the single output case, $\varphi(\boldsymbol{x}, y) = f(\boldsymbol{x}) - y$. Thus, $\partial\varphi/\partial x_i = \partial f/\partial x_i$ and $\partial\varphi/\partial y = -1$. Substituting into Definition 1 yields the result that $\tilde{S} = \sum x_i f_i/y = \sum x_i f_i/f = e(\boldsymbol{x})$.

Now consider an alternative measure of economies of scale that is defined in terms of the firm's cost function:

Definition 3. Cost function economies of scale

The degree of cost function scale economies enjoyed by the firm at any output vector $\boldsymbol{y}$ when facing factor prices $\boldsymbol{w}$ is defined as $S(\boldsymbol{y}, \boldsymbol{w}) = C(\boldsymbol{y}, \boldsymbol{w})/[\sum y_i C_i(\boldsymbol{y}, \boldsymbol{w})]$. Again, returns to scale are said to be (locally) increasing, constant or decreasing as S is greater than, equal to or less than 1.

Of course, for the single product case, S reduces to $C/yC' = AC/MC$, the ratio of average cost to marginal cost. Since $\mathrm{d}AC/\mathrm{d}y = (MC - AC)/y$, this means that the firm enjoys increasing, constant or decreasing returns to scale as the derivative of average cost with respect to output is negative, zero or positive.

Note that it is not quite correct to replace this characterization with one that determines the presence or absence of scale economies based upon whether AC is decreasing or increasing. Consider, for example, the cost function $C(y) = y[2 - (y - 1)^3]$. At $y = 1$, $MC = AC = 2$ and $S(1) = 1$. However, $AC = [2 - (y - 1)^3]$ is clearly decreasing at $y = 1$, since $AC(1 + \varepsilon) = 2 - \varepsilon^3 < AC(1) = 2 < 2 + \varepsilon^3 = AC(1 - \varepsilon)$ for any small, positive ε. This establishes

Proposition 1

Locally, economies of scale are sufficient but not necessary for the firm's average cost curve to be declining in the single output case.

[8] See, for example, Varian (1984, ch. 1) and Ferguson (1969).

At first, it is difficult to see the connection between the technology based definition of scale economies $\tilde{S}(x, y)$ and the cost based definition $S(y, w)$. Both are local concepts, possibly taking on different values at every point in their domain. Because $\tilde{S}$ is a property of a point in input/output space, while S is a property of the cost function, it is not obvious that they are closely related. In fact, however, they are equivalent!

Proposition 2

Given $R1$ and $R3$, $\tilde{S}(x^*(y, w), y) = S(y, w)$, i.e. when outputs are produced in a cost efficient manner, the degree of scale economies is the same, whether it is measured using the transformation function or the cost function.

Proof

The cost function results from minimizing $w \cdot x$ subject to $x \geq \mathbf{0}$ and $\varphi(x, y) \geq 0$. Letting λ denote the value of the Lagrange multiplier at the optimum, the Kuhn–Tucker necessary conditions for this problem are

$$w_i - \lambda \partial\varphi/\partial x_i \geq 0,$$

$$x_i^*[w_i - \lambda \partial\varphi/\partial x_i] = 0, \tag{2}$$

$$\varphi(x^*, y) \geq 0, \quad \lambda \geq 0 \quad \text{and} \quad \lambda\varphi(x^*, y) = 0. \tag{3}$$

Summing (2) over all inputs and using the fact that $C(y, w) \equiv w \cdot x^*(y, w)$, yields:

$$C(y, w) = \lambda \sum x_i^* \partial\varphi/\partial x_i. \tag{4}$$

The Lagrangian expression for this problem evaluated at the optimum is given by

$$C(y, w) \equiv w \cdot x^* - \lambda\varphi(x^*, y).$$

Thus, from the Envelope Theorem, we have:

$$C_j = -\lambda \partial\varphi/\partial y_j. \tag{5}$$

Multiplying (5) through by y_j and summing over all outputs, using (4), yields:

$$S(y, w) = -\left[\lambda \sum x_i^* \partial\varphi/\partial x_i\right] / \left[\lambda \sum y_j \partial\varphi/\partial y_j\right] = \tilde{S}(x^*(y, w), y),$$

as long as $\lambda \neq 0$. But $\lambda = 0$ and (2) would imply $\boldsymbol{x}^* = \boldsymbol{0}$, which, given (3), would violate $R1$. Q.E.D.

Thus, we have succeeded in developing a technologically based measure of the degree of scale economies that can be directly related to properties of the firm's multiproduct cost function.

In the subsequent discussion, I shall often adopt the assumption that the cost function exhibits increasing returns to scale at small output levels that are eventually exhausted, followed by a region of decreasing returns as output levels become ever larger. In the single product case, this just the traditional assumption that average cost curves are U-shaped, although the flat and rising portions of the U may lie beyond the range of experience. In this case, it is also well understood that the output level at which average cost attains its minimum plays a particularly important role in the determination of industry structure. However, in the multiproduct case, it is not clear what will fulfill this role, for average cost is not a clearly defined concept when the firm produces more than one product.

Fortunately, it is not average cost itself that plays this crucial role, but rather that the shape of the AC curve indicates the output level at which economies of scale become exhausted. This concept does translate directly to the multiproduct world, and the easiest way to make this clear is to reduce n dimensions down to one by fixing the proportions in which the various outputs of the firm are produced. It is then possible to study the behavior of costs as a function of the (scalar) number of such fixed proportion bundles. Geometrically, this is equivalent to studying the behavior of total costs as production is varied along a ray through the origin in output space. Therefore, consider

Definition 4. Ray average cost

The ray average cost of producing the output vector $\boldsymbol{y} \neq \boldsymbol{0}$, $RAC(\boldsymbol{y})$ is defined to be $C(\boldsymbol{y})/\boldsymbol{a} \cdot \boldsymbol{y}$, $\boldsymbol{a} > \boldsymbol{0}$. Ray average cost is said to be increasing (decreasing) at $\boldsymbol{y}$ if $RAC(t\boldsymbol{y})$ is an increasing (decreasing) function of the scalar t, at $t = 1$. Ray average cost is said to be minimized at $\boldsymbol{y}$ if $RAC(\boldsymbol{y}) < RAC(t\boldsymbol{y})$ for all positive $t \neq 1$.

The vector of positive weights $\boldsymbol{a}$ in this definition is, of course, completely arbitrary, as are the units in which each output level is measured. However, this somewhat artificial construction of a denominator for this multiproduct average cost construct makes it possible to formally relate the slope of the RAC curve at a point in output space to the degree of scale economies experienced by the firm, just as in the single product case.

Proposition 3

The derivative with respect to t of $RAC(ty)$, evaluated at $t = 1$, is negative, zero or positive as the degree of scale economies $S(y)$ is greater than, equal to, or less than 1.

Proof

Since $RAC(ty) = C(ty)/\boldsymbol{a} \cdot (ty)$, $\mathrm{d}[RAC(ty)]/\mathrm{d}t = [t(\boldsymbol{a} \cdot y)(y \cdot \nabla C(ty) - (\boldsymbol{a} \cdot y)C(ty)]/t^2(\boldsymbol{a} \cdot y)^2 = [1 - S(ty)]/[t^2(\boldsymbol{a} \cdot y)(y \cdot \nabla C(ty)]$. Therefore, when $t = 1$, $\text{sign}\{\mathrm{d}RAC/\mathrm{d}t\} = -\text{sign}\{S(y) - 1\}$. Q.E.D.

Hence, just as in the single product case, the firm enjoys increasing, constant or decreasing returns to scale depending upon whether the derivative of ray average cost with respect to the level of (a fixed bundle of) output is negative, zero or positive.

It is now possible to make precise the above presumption that returns to scale are first increasing, then constant and, eventually, decreasing, i.e. RAC curves are U-shaped. The only complication in the multiproduct case is that the size of the output bundle at which economies of scale are exhausted will tend to vary with the composition of the bundle. Thus, instead of a single point of minimum efficient scale at which scale economies are first exhausted, as in the scalar output case, in higher dimensions there will be a locus (surface, hypersurface) of such points: the M-locus. As depicted in Figure 1.1, the M-locus connects all the

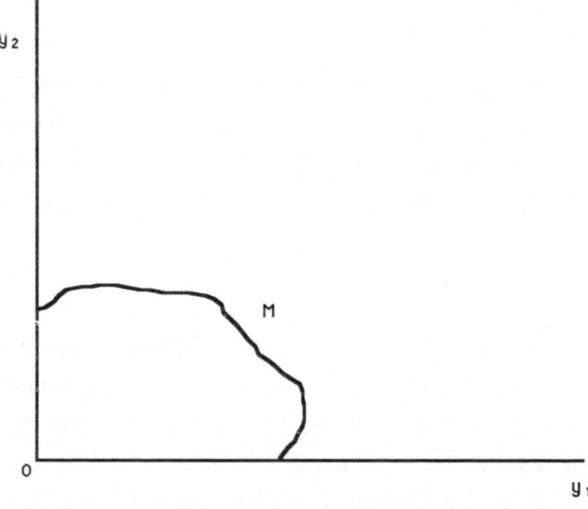

Figure 1.1

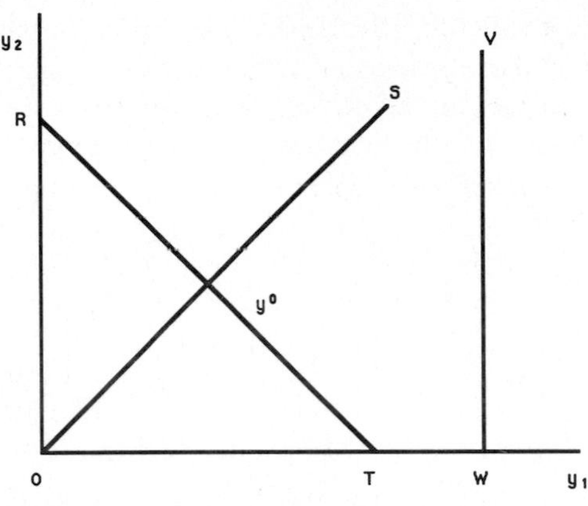

Figure 1.2

minima of the RAC curves corresponding to different output proportions.[9] The points of the M-locus on the axes represent the minimum points of the average cost curves in stand alone production of the various products.

2.2. *Product specific economies of scale*[10]

Our discussion of multiproduct economies of scale revealed that that important property of the technology pertains to the change in costs resulting from proportional variations in output, i.e. as output moves along a ray through the origin. In terms of Figure 1.2, if one envisions the cost surface plotted in the vertical dimension, then economies of scale are characterized by the behavior of RAC as output varies along a ray such as OS. However, when one refers to a firm "increasing" its scale of operations, one might just as easily have in mind an upward movement along WV as an outward movement along OS. That is, the change in costs resulting from a proportional increase in one product (or a subset of products) holding other output levels constant, also has important implications for firm and industry structure.

To begin to discuss this matter requires us to precisely define the incremental cost of product i as the change in the firm's total cost caused by its introduction

[9] If the cost function is twice continuously differentiable, except at the axes, then M will be smooth, if irregular, in the interior of output space.

[10] This term seems to have first been used in Scherer et al. (1975) and Beckenstein (1975) to refer to a concept similar in spirit, but less useful for the present analysis. The discussion here closely follows that in Baumol, Panzar and Willig (1982, ch. 4).

at the level y_i, or, equivalently, the firm's total cost of producing y minus what that cost would be if the production of good i were discontinued, leaving all other output levels unchanged. More formally, we have

Definition 5. Incremental cost of a single product

The incremental cost of the product $i \in N$ at y is $IC_i(y) \equiv C(y) - C(y_{\hat{i}})$, where $\hat{i} = \{j \in N: j \neq i\}$, the complement of i in N, and $y_{\hat{i}}$ is a vector with a zero component in place of y_i and components equal to those of y for the remaining products. The average incremental cost of product i is defined as $AIC_i(y) \equiv IC_i(y)/y_i$.

For example, for $y_2 > 0$, the incremental cost of y_1 in the generalized affine cost function of equation (1) above is given by

$$IC_1 = F^{12} - F^2 + c_1 y_1,$$

and the average incremental cost of y_1 by

$$AIC_1 = c_1 + (F^{12} - F^2)/y_1.$$

Contrast these formulae with those that would result if the cost function were given by the simple affine function $C = F + c_1 y_1 + c_2 y_2$ for $(y_1, y_2) \neq (0,0)$. In that case, for $y_2 > 0$, $IC_1 = c_1 y_1$ and $AIC_1 = c_1$. The difference stems from the fact that there are product specific fixed costs of $F^{12} - F^2$ in the first case and none in the second. (All the fixed costs are incurred as soon as any positive amount of either product is produced.) These product specific fixed costs give rise to decreasing average incremental costs in the first case and constant average incremental costs in the second. By analogy to the single product case, it is natural to describe the former example as one that exhibits increasing product specific returns to scale. More precisely, we have

Definition 6. Scale economies specific to a single product

The degree of scale economies specific to product i at output level y is given by $S_i(y) = IC_1(y)/y_i C_i(y) = AIC_i/MC_i$. Returns to the scale of product i at y are said to be increasing, decreasing or constant as $S_i(y)$ is greater than, less than, or equal to 1.

Since it is quite possible to envision a proportional expansion of a proper subset of the firm's products (i.e. more than 1 but less than n), it is useful to generalize Definitions 5 and 6 to describe the properties of the cost function in such cases.

Definition 7. Incremental cost

The incremental cost of the product set $T \subset N$ at y is given by $IC_T(y) = C(y) - C(y_{\hat{T}})$. Again, $\hat{T}$ is the complement of T in N and $y_{\hat{T}}$ is that vector with components equal to y for products in the set $\hat{T}$ and zero for products in the set T.

Using the same technique as for $RAC(y)$, it is possible to unambiguously define the average incremental costs of a product set:

Definition 8. Average incremental cost

The average incremental cost of the product set T at y is $AIC_T(y) \equiv IC_T(y)/\boldsymbol{a} \cdot y_T$. The average incremental cost of the product set T is said to be decreasing (increasing) at y if $AIC_T(ty_T + y_{\hat{T}})$ is a decreasing (increasing) function of t at $t = 1$.

We can now define a measure of the degree of product set specific scale economies that is consistent with both the scalar and multiproduct measures developed so far.

Definition 9. Product specific economies of scale

The degree of scale economies specific to the product set $T \subset N$ at y is given by $S_T(y) \equiv IC_T(y)/y_T \cdot \nabla C(y)$. Product set specific economies of scale are said to be increasing, decreasing or constant at y as $S_T(y)$ is greater than, less than, or equal to 1.

This definition is identical to $S(y)$ when $T = N$ and equals the product specific measure of Definition 6 when $T = \{i\}$. Also, the same arguments employed to establish Proposition 3, can be used to establish that the sign of $\mathrm{d}AIC_T(ty)/\mathrm{d}t$, evaluated at $t = 1$, is the same as the sign of $1 - S_T(y)$. Thus, just as in the scalar and n product cases, the degree of economies of scale can be defined in terms of the derivative of the (appropriately defined) average cost curve. Note also that $S_T(y) > 1$ implies $DAIC_T(y)$ (decreasing average incremental costs of the product set T at y), but, as in the scalar case, not conversely.

Having explored the concept of product specific economies of scale it is interesting to examine the relationship between the overall degree of scale economies $S(y)$ and the degree of scale economies that pertain to a subset of products T and its complement $\hat{T}$. Using Definitions 7 and 9 yields:

$$S = \{\alpha_T S_T + (1 - \alpha_T) S_{\hat{T}}\} / \{(IC_T + IC_{\hat{T}})/C\}, \tag{6}$$

where $\alpha_T = y_T \cdot \nabla C / y \cdot \nabla C$. If the denominator of this expression were 1, then the overall degree of scale economies would be a simple weighted average of that of any subset of products and its complement. Indeed, if the production processes used in producing T and $\hat{T}$ were completely separable, that denominator would be 1. Substituting using the definition of incremental cost allows us to write the denominator of (6) as

$$[C(y) - C(y_{\hat{T}}) + C(y) - C(y_T)]/C(y)$$

or

$$1 + [C(y) - C(y_{\hat{T}}) - C(y_T)]/C(y). \tag{7}$$

If the production processes for product sets T and $\hat{T}$ were truly independent, then the total costs of producing all n products would be exactly equal to the sum of the stand-alone costs of the subsets T and $\hat{T}$ [i.e. $C(y_T)$ and $C(y_{\hat{T}})$]. However, if economies of joint production are present, total costs will be less than the sum of the stand-alone costs. Then (7) will be less than 1, and the overall degree of scale economies will exceed the weighted sum of the two product specific measures. The next section discusses these *economies of scope* in detail.

2.3. *Economies of scope*

The multiproduct cost constructs discussed in the previous sections have described the behavior of the cost surface over conveniently chosen cross sections of output space. This section discusses a cost concept that is crucial to our understanding of firm and industry structure, yet cannot be characterized directly in terms of such a "slice" of the cost surface.

In addition to the intuitively familiar economies deriving from the shear size or scale of a firm's operations, cost savings may also result from the production of several different outputs in one firm rather than each being produced in its own specialized firm. That is, the *scope* of the firm's operations may give rise to economies as well. More formally, consider

Definition 10. Economies of scope

Let $P = \{T_1, \ldots, T_m\}$ denote a nontrivial partition of $S \subseteq N$. That is, $\cup T_i = S$, $T_i \cap T_j = \emptyset$ for $i \neq j$, $T_i \neq \emptyset$, and $m > 1$. Then there are economies of scope at

y_S with respect to the partition P if $\sum_i [C(y_{Ti})] > C(y_S)$. There are said to be weak economies of scope if this inequality is weak rather than strict, and diseconomies of scope if the inequality is reversed.

For example, in the simplest two product case, $N = \{1,2\}$ and $P = \{1,2\}$. Then economies of scope are present at the output vector (y_1, y_2) if $C(y_1, y_2) < C(y_1, 0) + C(0, y_2)$. In the generalized affine example of equation (1), there are economies of scope if and only if $F^{12} < F^1 + F^2$.

In order to study the relationship between economies of scope and the measures of economies of scale derived above, the following quantitative description is useful:

Definition 11. Degree of scope economies

The degree of economies of scope at y relative to the product set T and the partition $P = \{T, \hat{T}\}$ is defined as $SC_T(y) \equiv [C(y_T) + C(y_{\hat{T}}) - C(y)]/C(y)$.

The degree of economies of scope measures the percentage increase in cost that would result from dividing the production of y into product lines T and $\hat{T}$. Breaking up the firm along these lines increase, decreases, or leaves total costs unchanged as SC_T is greater than, less than, or equal to zero.

If all products have positive incremental costs, it is easy to show that the degree of economies of scope must be less than 1 for any binary partition. Rearranging terms, Definition 11 can be rewritten as

$$SC_T(y) = 1 - [IC_T(y) + IC_{\hat{T}}(y)]/C(y) < 1. \tag{8}$$

Equation (8) allows us to examine the role of economies of scope in relating the degrees of product specific and overall scale economies. Using (8), equation (6) can be rewritten as

$$S(y) = [\alpha_T S_T + (1 - \alpha_T) S_{\hat{T}}]/[1 - SC_T(y)].$$

Thus, it is the presence of economies of scope that "magnifies" the extent of overall economies of scale beyond what would result from a simple weighted sum of product specific levels.

As mentioned briefly above, the literature abounds with discussions of the technological, "engineering" sources of economies of scale. Since economies of scope has a much briefer life as a precise analytic construct,[11] it is desirable to

[11]The term "economies of scope" was introduced and precisely defined in Panzar and Willig (1975).

spend some time describing, in intuitive terms, the properties of the productive technology that give rise to its presence as a property of the multiproduct cost function. The natural place to begin the search for sources of economies of scope is the Marshallian notion of joint production. Intuitively, it must clearly be cheaper to produce pairs of items such as wheat and straw, wool and mutton, and beef and hides in one firm than in two specialized firms. Therefore, I shall construct a formal model of technological joint production and derive its relationship between that concept and economies of scope.

Joint production, in the Marshallian sense, arises because one or more factors of production are public inputs. That is, once acquired for use in producing one good, they are costlessly available for use in the production of others.[12] Assume that there are n production processes:

$$y_i = f_i(z^i, K), \quad i = 1,\ldots,n,$$

where z^i is a vector of inputs that are directly attributable to the production of products i and K is the amount available of the pure public input. It is more convenient to work with the variable cost representation of the productive technology which expresses the minimized level of attributable costs, V^i, of producing product i as a function of y_i, K and the vector w of the prices of the private inputs. That is,

$$V^i(y_i, K, w) = \min\{z^i \cdot w\colon f(z^i, K) \leq y_i\}, \quad i = 1,\ldots,n.$$

Assuming that the public input is at least weakly productive, it must be the case that

$$V^i(y_i, K_1) \leq V^i(y_i, K_2), \quad \text{for } K_2 \leq K_1,\ i = 1,\ldots,n. \tag{9}$$

If, in addition, the public input is strictly productive in the weak sense that any positive amount of the public input is better than none at all, then it is also true that

$$V^i(y_i, K) < V^i(y_i, 0), \quad \text{for all } y_i,\ K > 0,\ i = 1,\ldots,n. \tag{10}$$

Finally, assume for simplicity that units of the public input are available at the constant price β. Then we can state the following result:

[12] The clearest examples are to be found in the peak load pricing literature: see, for example, Clark (1923), Demsetz (1973) and Panzar (1976). In Marshall's agricultural examples, the plant or animal in question can be viewed as the public input.

Proposition 4

The multiproduct minimum cost function $C(y, w, \beta)$ that is dual to a set of multiproduct production techniques employing a public input (as described above) exhibits economies of scope.

Proof

A firm that produces at minimum cost any subset of products Tj at output levels y_{Tj} solves the program: $\min_k\{\sum_{i \in Tj}[V^i(y_i, K) + \beta K]\}$. Let $\tilde{K}_{Tj}$ solve this program. Then the multiproduct minimum cost function has the property that

$$C(y_{Tj}, w, \beta) = \sum_{i \in Tj} \left[V^i\left(y_i, w, \tilde{K}_{Tj}\right)\right] + \beta \tilde{K}_{Tj}.$$

Now let $\{T_1, \ldots, T_k\}$ constitute a nontrivial partition of N and define the feasible cost function:

$$\bar{C}(y, w, \beta) = \sum_{j=1}^{k} \sum_{i \in Tj} V^i(y_i, w, \bar{K}) + \beta \bar{K},$$

where $\bar{K} = \max_j\{\tilde{K}_{Tj}\}$, $j = 1, \ldots, k$. Then

$$\bar{C}(y) - \sum_j C(y_{Tj}) = \sum_j \sum_{i \in Tj} \left[V^i\left(y_i, \bar{K}\right) - V^i\left(y_i, \tilde{K}_{Tj}\right)\right] + \beta\left[\bar{K} - \sum_j \tilde{K}_{Tj}\right].$$

Given (9) and (10), both terms on the right-hand side of this expression are nonpositive, with at least one strictly negative. Because $C(y)$ is defined to be the minimum cost function, we know that $C(y) \le \bar{C}(y)$. Therefore,

$$C(y) - \sum_j C(y_{Tj}) \le \bar{C}(y) - \sum_j C(y_{Tj}) < 0. \tag{11}$$

But for $y > \mathbf{0}$, the inequality in (11) is precisely the definition of economies of scope.

Q.E.D.

The public input model analyzed above illustrates one technological source of economies of scope. Proposition 4 has demonstrated that the presence of a public input is sufficient for the existence of economies of scope. However, it is far from necessary. This is fortunate, since cases of joint production involving pure public inputs do not seem numerous enough to account for the ubiquity of multiproduct firms that presumably enjoy economies of scope. There is another tradition in the literature[13] that explains the existence of economies of scope as a result of the presence of inputs that, perhaps because of indivisibilities, are easily shared by the production processes of several different outputs.

In order to investigate this type of phenomenon more precisely, consider a micro model of the sharing of "overhead" between n otherwise independent production processes. For ease of exposition, assume that there is only one such input, called "capital". Let $\psi(\boldsymbol{k}, \boldsymbol{\beta})$ denote the cost of acquiring the vector $\boldsymbol{k} = (k_1, k_2, \ldots, k_n)$ of capital services used in production processes 1 through n when the relevant input prices are $\boldsymbol{\beta}$. If ψ is strictly subadditive in $\boldsymbol{k}$ (i.e. $\psi(\boldsymbol{k}^0 + \boldsymbol{k}^1, \boldsymbol{\beta}) < \psi(\boldsymbol{k}^0, \boldsymbol{\beta}) + \psi(\boldsymbol{k}^1, \boldsymbol{\beta})$), then it is natural to describe k as a quasipublic input, since its services can be shared by two or more product lines at a lower total cost than would be incurred if each obtained its capital services independently. An extreme example is the pure public input case considered above, in which $\psi(\boldsymbol{k}, \beta) = \beta \max_i[k_i]$. Another benchmark case is when capital is a pure private input obtainable at a constant price per unit, so that $\psi(\boldsymbol{k}, \beta) = \beta \sum k_i$ is only weakly subadditive in k. It is also possible to envision situations in which the production processes impede one another, so that ψ is actually superadditive in $\boldsymbol{k}$, e.g. $\psi(k_1, k_2, \beta) = a(\boldsymbol{\beta})(k_1 + k_2)^2$.

Perhaps more common might be a situation in which capital services are private inputs in the sense that a given total capacity K can be exhaustively allocated across product lines (e.g. $k_1 + k_2 \leq K$), but there are regions of increasing and decreasing returns to scale in the installation of K. For example, consider the case in which $\psi(k_1, k_2, \boldsymbol{\beta}) = \Phi(k_1 + k_2, \boldsymbol{\beta}) = a_0(\boldsymbol{\beta}) + a_1(\boldsymbol{\beta})(k_1 + k_2)^2 = a_0(\boldsymbol{\beta}) + a_1(\boldsymbol{\beta})K^2$. Here, it can be shown that Φ and ψ are subadditive for $k_1 + k_2 = K \leq \sqrt{2a_0/a_1}$.

Thus, economies of shared inputs (subadditivity of ψ) may arise either because the input in question is public or quasipublic or because there are economies of scale in its acquistion. In any event, there is an intimate connection between the acquisition cost properties of shared inputs and the presence or absence of economies of scope at the final output level:

[13]Consider, for example, Hicks (1935/1952, p. 372): "... almost every firm does produce a considerable range of different products. It does so largely because there are economies to be got from producing them together, and these economies consist largely in the fact that the different products require much the same overhead." See also, Clemens (1950/1958, p. 263): "It is a commonplace of business practice that the production and sales managers work hand in hand to devise new products that can be produced with the company's idle capacity.... What the firm has to sell is not a product, or even a line of products, but rather its capacity to produce."

Proposition 5

For any nontrivial partition of N, there are economies (diseconomies) of scope if and only if ψ is strictly subadditive (superadditive) in the relevant range.

Proof

The multiproduct minimum cost function associated with the above micro model of the technology is given by

$$C(y_S, \boldsymbol{w}, \boldsymbol{\beta}) = \min_{\boldsymbol{k}} \left\{ \sum_{i \in S} V^i(y_i, \boldsymbol{w}, k_i) + \psi(\boldsymbol{k}, \boldsymbol{\beta}) \right\}. \tag{12}$$

Let the vector $\tilde{\boldsymbol{k}}(y, \boldsymbol{w}, \boldsymbol{\beta})$ denote the argmin of program (12) for $S = N$, i.e. the cost minimizing vector of capital services for the production of the output vector y. Assuming that capital services are an essential input into each production process implies that $\tilde{k}_i > 0$ for $y_i > 0$, while, if ψ is nondecreasing, $\tilde{k}_i = 0$ if $y_i = 0$. Now let $\{T_1, \ldots, T_l\}$ be a nontrivial partition of N and let $\hat{\boldsymbol{k}} = \sum_j [\tilde{\boldsymbol{k}}(y_{Tj})]$, the sum of the optimal capital services vector for each product subgroup if it were produced in isolation. Then from (12) and the definition of $\hat{\boldsymbol{k}}$, it follows that

$$\sum_{i \in N} V^i(y_i, \tilde{k}_i(y)) + \psi(\tilde{\boldsymbol{k}}(y)) = C(y) \le \sum_{i \in N} V(y_i, \hat{k}_i) + \psi(\hat{\boldsymbol{k}}) \tag{13}$$

and

$$\sum_{i \in Tj} V^i(y_i, \tilde{k}_i(y)) + \psi(\tilde{\boldsymbol{k}}_{Tj}(y)) \ge C(y_{Tj})$$

$$= \sum_{i \in Tj} V^i(y_i, \tilde{k}_i(y_{Tj})) + \psi(\tilde{\boldsymbol{k}}(y_{Tj})). \tag{14}$$

Summing (14) over $j = 1, \ldots, l$ and subtracting (13) yields:

$$\psi(\tilde{\boldsymbol{k}}(y)) - \sum_{j=1}^{l} \psi(\tilde{\boldsymbol{k}}_{Tj}(y)) \le C(y) - \sum_{j=1}^{l} C(y_{Tj})$$

$$\le \psi(\hat{\boldsymbol{k}}) - \sum_{j=1}^{l} \psi(\tilde{\boldsymbol{k}}(y_{Tj})). \tag{15}$$

The conclusions follow since the leftmost (rightmost) term in equation (15) is positive (negative) if and only if ψ is strictly superadditive (subadditive) over the relevant range. Q.E.D.

This micro model of the firm's production process establishes the intimate connection between the existence of economies of scope and the presence of inputs that may be effectively shared among production processes. While the focus of the above discussion may have seemed to have been directed exclusively toward technological, engineering considerations, a broader interpretation is certainly possible. For example, the shareable inputs might include managerial expertise, a good financial rating, a sales staff, and so forth.[14]

The foregoing discussion has analyzed the sources of economies of scope at the micro level, in effect, deriving that property of the multiproduct cost function on the basis of assumptions about the way that the firm's production processes interact with one another. While this may provide an intuitive understanding of the factors responsible for economies of scope, it is not terribly useful for empirically testing for their presence. It is difficult to envision obtaining the data that would be required to estimate ψ and evaluating whether or not it is subadditive. Therefore, it is useful to have available a condition defined in terms of properties of the multiproduct cost function that can be used to infer the presence of economies of scope. The following multiproduct cost concept will prove useful in this quest:

Definition 12. Weak cost complementarities

A twice-differentiable multiproduct cost function exhibits weak cost complementarities over the product set N, up to the output level y, if $\partial^2 C(\hat{y})/\partial y_i \partial y_j \equiv C_{ij}(\hat{y}) \leq 0$, $i \neq j$, for all $\mathbf{0} \leq \hat{y} \leq y$, with the inequality strict over a set of output levels of nonzero measure.

The presence of weak cost complementarities implies that the marginal cost of producing any one product does not increase with increases in the quantity of any other product. According to Sakai (1974), this is a normal property of joint production. Note that, because C_{ii} is allowed to be positive, Definition 12 does not impose the strong condition that all of the individual product marginal cost curves C_i are decreasing. The following result is true:

[14]See Teece (1980) for a discussion of such less easily quantifiable sources of economies of scope.

Proposition 6

A twice-differentiable multiproduct cost function that exhibits weak cost complementarities over N up to output level y exhibits economies of scope at y with respect to all partitions of N.

Proof

Since any partition of N can be obtained by a sequence of binary partitions, it suffices to demonstrate the result for the partition $T, \hat{T}$, where $N \neq T = \varnothing$. Rearrange terms so that the condition to be demonstrated is

$$[C(y_T + y_{\hat{T}}) - C(y_T)] - [C(y_{\hat{T}}) - C(\mathbf{0})] < 0.$$

The first term in brackets can be rewritten as $\int_{\Gamma} \sum_{i \in \hat{T}} [C_i(y_T + x_{\hat{T}})\,\mathrm{d}x_i]$ and the second bracketed term as $\int_{\Gamma} \sum_{i \in \hat{T}} [C_i(x_{\hat{T}})\,\mathrm{d}x_i]$, where Γ is any smooth monotonic arc from $\mathbf{0}$ to $y_{\hat{T}}$. Since these are line integrals along the common path Γ, their difference can be written as

$$\int_{\Gamma} \sum_{i \in \hat{T}} [C_i(y_T + x_{\hat{T}}) - C_i(x_{\hat{T}})]\,\mathrm{d}x_i$$

$$= \int_{\Gamma} \sum_{i \in \hat{T}} \int_{\Lambda} \sum_{j \in T} C_{ij}(z_T + x_{\hat{T}})\,\mathrm{d}zjx_i < 0,$$

where Λ is a smooth monotonic arc from $\mathbf{0}$ to y_T. Q.E.D.

The only problem with this sufficient condition for economies of scope is that it requires that the cost function be twice differentiable everywhere, even at the origin and along the axes. As discussed earlier, this is overly restrictive, since it rules out the presence of overall and product specific fixed costs. Fortunately, the result can be easily extended to deal with this important complication. Without loss of generality, any multiproduct cost function can be expressed as $C(y) = F\{S\} + c(y)$, where $S = \{i \in N\colon\ y_i > 0\}$. This formulation allows for $C(\cdot)$ to exhibit discontinuities along the axes even if $c(\cdot)$ is smooth. Thus, Proposition 6 can be generalized to:

Proposition 7

If $c(\cdot)$ is a twice-differentiable function that exhibits weak complementarities over N up to output level y, and if F is not superadditive – i.e. $F\{S\} + F\{T\} \geq F\{S \cup T\}$ for all $S, T \subseteq N$ – then the cost function exhibits economies of scope at $y > \mathbf{0}$ with respect to all partitions of N.

Proof

The proof is the same as that of Proposition 6, with $c(\cdot)$ replacing $C(\cdot)$, so that the above equations also contain the expression $F\{N\} - F\{T\} - F\{\hat{T}\}$. This term is nonpositive by hypothesis. Q.E.D.

Proposition 7 reveals that a multiproduct cost function may exhibit economies of scope because of complementarities in either "fixed" or "variable" components. Clearly, economies of scope may occur even in cases in which $c_{ij} > 0$, as long as $F\{\cdot\}$ is sufficiently subadditive. For example, the cost function introduced in Section 2 exhibits global economies of scope even though $c_{12} = 0$ at all output levels. This follows from the fact that $C(y_1, y_2) - C(y_1, 0) - C(0, y_2) = F^{12} - F^1 - F^2 < 0$ for all $y \neq \mathbf{0}$. Similarly, suppose $C(y_1, y_2) = F + a(y_1 + y_2)^2$ for $y \neq \mathbf{0}$. This cost function never exhibits cost complementarities, as $C_{12} = 2a(y_1 + y_2) > 0$. Yet it exhibits economies of scope for all output vectors such that $y_1 y_2 < F/2a$.[15]

2.4. *Cost subadditivity and natural monopoly*

There has been a long tradition of government regulation of "monopolies" in the United States, and, recently, a wave of deregulation in industries that were once thought to be characterized by substantial monopoly attributes. Thus, much of the empirical work on firm and industry structure to be discussed below has focused upon trying to determine the extent of "natural monopoly" in various regulated industries. Somewhat surprisingly, until fairly recently there was considerable confusion as to what, precisely, is meant by the term "natural monopoly".[16] Therefore this subsection will provide a precise definition of this important concept and a discussion of the properties of the cost function that ensure its presence.

Definition 13. Strict subadditivity

A cost function $C(y)$ is strictly subadditive at y if for any and all output vectors $y^1, y^2, \ldots, y^k$, $y^i \neq y$, $i = 1, \ldots, k$, such that $\sum y^i = y$, it is the case that $C(y) < \sum C(y^i)$.

[15]*Proof*: Economies of scope are present whenever the cost of producing both outputs together, $F + a(y_1 + y_2)^2$, is less than the total cost of producing each product in a separate firm, $[Fay_1^2] + [F + ay_2^2]$, i.e. when $2ay_1 y_2 < F$.

[16]Baumol (1977) provided the first rigorous discussion of this issue in the multiproduct setting. The discussion that follows is based primarily on that in Baumol, Panzar and Willig (1982, ch. 7). See also Sharkey (1982, ch. 4).

Intuitively, then, subadditivity of the cost function at y ensures that that output vector can be produced more cheaply by a single firm than by any group of two or more firms. Thus, subadditivity of the cost function can be taken as the obvious criterion for natural monopoly.

Definition 14. Natural monopoly

An industry is said to be a natural monopoly if the cost function is strictly subadditive over the entire relevant range of outputs. An industry is said to be a natural monopoly through output level y if $C(y')$ is strictly subadditive at all $y' \leq y$.

It is important to note that subadditivity is a local concept in that it refers to a particular point on the cost surface. However, determining whether or not costs are subadditive at any such point requires knowledge of the cost function at all smaller output levels. That is to say, in order to know whether single-firm production of y is or is not cheaper than its production by any combination of smaller firms, one must know the level of cost that would be incurred by any smaller firm, i.e. one must know $C(y^*)$ for every $y^* \leq y$.

In the "familiar" single product case, natural monopoly has been associated with the presence of increasing returns to scale and falling average costs. However, this characterization is imprecise at best and can be seriously misleading. In order to examine this issue, we need

Definition 15. Declining average costs

Average costs are strictly declining at y if there exists a $\delta > 0$ such that $C(y')/y' < C(y'')/y''$ for all y' and y'' with $y - \delta < y'' < y' < y + \delta$. Average costs are said to decline through output y if $C(y')/y' < C(y'')/y''$ for all y' and y'' such that $0 < y'' < y' \leq y$.

In nontechnical discussions, the notion of falling average costs and natural monopoly are often confused. The following result clarifies the relationship between the two for the single output case.

Proposition 8

Decreasing average cost through y implies that the cost function is subadditive at y, but not conversely.

Proof

Let $y^1, \ldots, y^k$ be any nontrivial way of dividing y among two or more firms, so that $\sum y^i = y$ and $y > y^i > 0$. Because average cost is declining and because $y^i < y$, $C(y)/y < C(y^i)/y^i$, so that $(y^i/y)C(y) < C(y^i)$. Summing over i yields $\sum C(y^i) > \sum (y^i/y)C(y) \equiv C(y)$, which is the definition of subadditivity. To prove that the converse is not true requires only a counterexample. Consider a cost function such that $C(y) = a + cy$ for $0 < y < y^0$ and $C(y) = a + b + cy$ for $y \geq y^0$, with $a > b > 0$. This cost function is clearly globally subadditive, since $C(y) \leq a + b + cy < 2a + cy \leq C(y^1) + \cdots + C(y^k)$ for all $k > 1$ and $y^i > 0$ such that $\sum y^i = y$. Yet there is a region in which average costs are increasing, since $AC(y^0 - \delta) = a/(y^0 - \delta) < (a + b)/(y^0 + \delta) = AC(y^0 + \delta)$ for $0 < \delta < y^0$. Q.E.D.

If one wishes to maintain the presumption that all AC curves are, ultimately, U-shaped, then another counterexample is required. (The AC curve in the counterexample in the above proof is falling almost everywhere, with a discontinuous upward jump at y^0.) Consider the cost function given by $C(y) = F + ay^2$ for $y > 0$. It is easy to see that average costs are U-shaped: falling for $0 < y < \sqrt{F/a} \equiv y_m$ and increasing for $y > \sqrt{F/a}$. Yet this cost function remains subadditive through $y = \sqrt{2F/a} \equiv y_s$. To see this, first note that, when there are rising marginal costs, any industry output y is divided in positive portions most cheaply among k different firms if each firm produces the same amount, y/k. Then (minimized) total industry costs for a k firm industry are $kC(y/k) = kF + ay^2/k > F + ay^2$ for all $y < y_s$.

The foregoing discussion has revealed that the relationship between economies of scale and natural monopoly is nontrivial, even in the single product case. In the multiproduct world things are even more complicated. In fact there exists no logical connection between the two concepts in the multiproduct world!

Proposition 9

Economies of scale is neither necessary or sufficient for natural monopoly.

Proof

Non-necessity was proven as part of Proposition 8. To see that economies of scale is not sufficient for natural monopoly, consider the cost function $C(y_1, y_2) = \sqrt{y_1 + y_2}$. This function exhibits economies of scale everywhere, as $S(y_1, y_2) = 2$. Yet it is *super*additive for all $(y_1, y_2) > (0,0)$, since $C(y_1, 0) + C(0, y_2) = \sqrt{y_1} + \sqrt{y_2} < \sqrt{y_1 + y_2} = C(y_1, y_2)$. Q.E.D.

The proof of Proposition 9 has revealed that one reason that the presence of economies of scale does not suffice for natural monopoly is that economies of scale do *not* imply economies of scope. Economies of scope is clearly necessary for natural monopoly, since one way of viewing its definition is as a requirement that the cost function be subadditive for all *orthogonal* divisions of the output vector $\mathbf{y}$. Clearly, this requirement is subsumed in those of Definition 13. More simply, if single firm production is to be less costly than *any* multifirm alternative, it must involve less costs than those that would result if the firm were split up along product lines.

Therefore it should not be surprising that economies of scope must always be assumed as part of (or be implied by) any set of conditions that are sufficient for subadditivity. What is somewhat surprising is that economies of scale and economies of scope, together, do not imply subadditivity!

Proposition 10

Economies of scale and economies of scope do not suffice for subadditivity.

Proof[17]

Consider the cost function given by

$$C(y_1, y_2) = 10v + 6(x - v) + z + \varepsilon,$$

$$\text{for } (y_1, y_2) \neq (0,0) \text{ and } C(0,0) = 0, \quad (16)$$

where $x \equiv \max[y_1, y_2]$, $v \equiv \min[y_1, y_2]$, $z \equiv \min[v, x - v]$, and ε is an arbitrarily small positive number.[18] This function would be linearly homogeneous (exhibiting globally constant returns to scale) were it not for the presence of the fixed cost $\varepsilon > 0$. Therefore it exhibits increasing returns to scale everywhere. For the case of stand-alone production, $C(y_i) = 6y_i + \varepsilon$, so that

$$C(y_1, 0) + C(0, y_2) = 6y_1 + \varepsilon + 6y_2 + \varepsilon = 6(x + v) + 2\varepsilon.$$

[17]The following counterexample is from Baumol, Panzar and Willig (1982, ch. 7, pp. 173–74 and ch. 9, pp. 249–251). Another can be found in Sharkey (1982, ch. 4, pp. 68–69).

[18]An intuitive interpretation might go as follows. A farmer is in the business of producing "meat" and "fiber". The technologies available to him include raising sheep, raising chickens and growing flax. Raising sheep costs \$10 per animal and yields one unit of meat and one unit of fiber. Raising chickens (woolless sheep) costs \$6 per unit of meat obtained and growing flax (meatless sheep) cost \$6 per unit of fiber obtained. However, since sheep will destroy the flax crop, the farmer must fence in the *smaller* of these operations at a cost of \$1 per unit. When combined with a setup cost of ε, these options give rise to the stated *minimized* cost function.

Subtraction of equation (16) yields:

$$C(y_1, 0) + C(0, y_2) - C(y_1, y_2) = 2v - z + \varepsilon \geq v + \varepsilon > 0,$$

which demonstrates that this cost function exhibits economies of scope everywhere. Without loss of generality, assume that $x = y_2 > y_1 = v$ and consider dividing the production of (y_1, y_2) between two firms with output levels (y_1, y_1) and $(0, y_2 - y_1)$. This division results in total costs of

$$C(y_1, y_1) + C(0, y_2 - y_1) = 10v + \varepsilon + 6(x - v) + \varepsilon.$$

Subtracting this from (16) yields:

$$C(y_1, y_2) - C(y_1, y_1) + C(0, y_2 - y_1) = z - \varepsilon - \min[y_1, y_2 - y_1] - \varepsilon.$$

Since ε can be chosen as small as desired without violating the properties of global economies of scale and scope, it is always possible to choose a positive $\varepsilon < y_2 - y_1$ so that the above expression is positive. Thus, the cost function is not subadditive for $y_1 \neq y_2$.[19] Q.E.D.

In view of this result, it is clear that a stronger set of sufficient conditions is required to guarantee subadditivity of costs. Intuitively, this strengthening can be accomplished in one of two ways. We can strengthen the assumptions concerning the savings achieved as the scale of the firm's operations increases, or we can strengthen the assumptions about the extent of production cost complementarities. First, we consider the former option. The discussion in Subsection 2.3 suggests how to proceed. Instead of requiring only that the cost function exhibit economies of scale with respect to the firm's entire product line, we assume that the cost function exhibit decreasing average incremental costs with respect to *each* product line. That this will, in general be a more stringent requirement can be seen from equation (6), which reveals that it is quite possible for the cost function to exhibit overall economies of scale at $\mathbf{y}$ even though there may be decreasing product specific returns to scale for one (or both) of the product lines involved.

Proposition 11

Decreasing average incremental costs through $\mathbf{y}$ for each product $i \in N$ and (weak) economies of scope at $\mathbf{y}$ imply that the cost function is subadditive at $\mathbf{y}$.

[19] This "vanishing ε" can easily be dispensed with. Without it, the cost function exhibits globally constant returns to scale and economies of scope but is strictly superadditive everywhere except on the diagonal $(y_1 = y_2)$, where it is additive.

Proof

For clarity and notational convenience, the proof presented here will be for the two output case.[20] The key to the argument is the fact that *DAIC* in a product line implies that *that product line* must be monopolized if industry costs are to be minimized. Consider an output vector $y = (y_1, y_2)$ and divide it into two batches, $\hat{y} + \tilde{y} = y$, with both $\hat{y}_1$ and $\tilde{y}_1 > 0$. Then the following lemma is true:

Lemma

If $DAIC_1(y)$ holds, then either

$$C(\hat{y}_1 + \tilde{y}_1, \tilde{y}_2) + C(0, \tilde{y}_2) < C(\hat{y}) + C(\tilde{y}) \tag{17}$$

or

$$C(\hat{y}_1 + \tilde{y}_1, \tilde{y}_2) + C(0, \hat{y}_2) < C(\hat{y}) + C(\tilde{y}). \tag{18}$$

To establish the lemma, assume without loss of generality that the average incremental cost of shifting the production of $\tilde{y}_1$ from one firm to the other is no greater than the cost of shifting the production of $\hat{y}_1$, i.e.

$$[C(\hat{y}_1 + \tilde{y}_1, \hat{y}_2) - C(\hat{y})]/\tilde{y}_1 \leq [C(\hat{y}_1 + \tilde{y}_1, \hat{y}_2) - C(\tilde{y})]/\hat{y}_1. \tag{19}$$

From the *DAIC* assumption we have

$$[C(\hat{y}_1 + \tilde{y}_1, \tilde{y}_2) - C(0, \tilde{y}_2)]/(\hat{y}_1 + \tilde{y}_1) < [C(\tilde{y}) - C(0, \tilde{y}_2)]/\tilde{y}_1.$$

Cross-multiplying and adding and subtracting $\tilde{y}_1 C(\tilde{y})$ on the left-hand side yields:

$$[C(\hat{y}_1 + \tilde{y}_1, \tilde{y}_2) - C(0, \tilde{y}_2)]/\hat{y}_1 < [C(\tilde{y}) - C(0, \tilde{y}_2)]/\tilde{y}_1.$$

Along with (19) this implies:

$$C(\hat{y}_1 + \tilde{y}_1, \hat{y}_2) < C(\hat{y}) + C(\tilde{y}) - C(0, \tilde{y}_2),$$

which completes the proof of the lemma. Now to complete the proof of the proposition suppose, without loss of generality, that (17) holds. Now applying the lemma again tells us that consolidating the production of product 2 will also

[20]The proof for the *n* output case can be found in Baumol, Panzar and Willig (1982, pp. 176–77, 186).

reduce industry costs, i.e. either

$$C(\hat{y}_1 + \tilde{y}_1, \hat{y}_2 + \tilde{y}_2) + C(0,0) < C(\hat{y}) + C(\tilde{y}) \tag{20}$$

or

$$C(\hat{y}_1 + \tilde{y}_1, 0) + C(0, \hat{y}_2 + \tilde{y}_2) < C(\hat{y}) + C(\tilde{y}). \tag{21}$$

If (20) holds, subadditivity is established immediately. If (8) holds, then (weak) economies of scope establishes the result, since, then

$$C(y) \leq C(\hat{y}_1 + \tilde{y}_1, 0) + C(0, \hat{y}_2 + \tilde{y}_2) < C(\hat{y}) + C(\tilde{y}). \quad \text{Q.E.D.}$$

Not only does this result establish sufficient conditions for an industry to be a natural monopoly, the lemma itself provides important information for understanding industry structure. This important result bears restating.

Proposition 12

If the cost function exhibits Declining Average Incremental Costs for product i ($DAIC_i$) through y, then industry cost minimization requires that production of good i be consolidated in a single firm.

It is clear why this result was important in establishing the sufficient conditions for natural monopoly set forth in Proposition 11, since if $DAIC_i$ holds across all products, the addition of economies of scope implies that all product lines must be monopolized together. However, Proposition 12 is more generally applicable, since it establishes a condition that suffices for any single product to be efficiently monopolized, regardless of the overall presence or absence of natural monopoly. As we shall see, this has important implications for public policy toward industry structure in cases in which there economies of scale in one product that shares scope economies with another for which economies of scale are exhausted at relatively small output levels.

Proposition 11 has set forth sufficient conditions for subadditivity of costs based upon economies of scope and a strengthened version of multiproduct economies of scale. Next, consider the alternative response to the problem posed by Proposition 10: maintaining the assumption of multiproduct economies of scale, while strengthening the accompanying cost complementarity condition. To do this requires the following multiproduct cost concept:

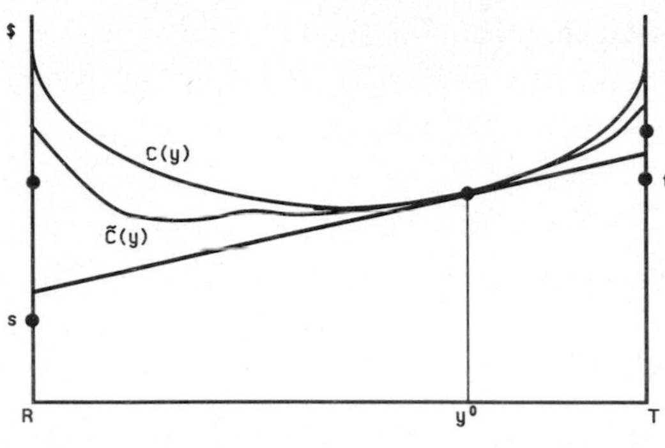

Figure 1.3

Definition 16. Trans-ray supportability

A cost function $C(y)$ is trans-ray supportable at y^0 if there exists at least one trans-ray direction above which the cost surface is supportable. That is, there is a trans-ray hyperplane $H \equiv \{ y \geq \mathbf{0}\colon \boldsymbol{a} \cdot y = \boldsymbol{a} \cdot y^0\}$, $\boldsymbol{a} > \mathbf{0}$, for which there exists a constant v_0 and a vector $\boldsymbol{v}$ such that $C(y) \geq v_0 + \boldsymbol{v} \cdot y$ for all $y \in H$.

This powerful condition is difficult to interpret intuitively. It can be made clearer with the aid of Figure 1.3, in which the vertical axis measures total cost and the horizontal axis coincides with the base RT of the trans-ray slice in Figure 1.2. Consider a point y^0 on this ray. If a straight line can be drawn through $C(y^0)$ that nowhere rises above $C(y)$ over RT, then the cost function C has a support at y^0 over the trans-ray hyperplane $H = RT$. Now consider all possible trans-rays through y^0 in the y_1, y_2 plane. If the cost function C has such a support above any *one of them*, then it is said to be trans-ray supportable at y^0. This brings us to a basic set of sufficient conditions for subadditivity:

Proposition 13

If $C(y)$ is trans-ray supportable at y^0 and exhibits decreasing ray average costs along all rays through the origin *up to* H, the hyperplane of trans-ray supportability for y^0, then C is strictly subadditive at y^0.

Proof

Let $y^1 + \cdots + y^k = y^0$, with $y^i \neq \mathbf{0}$ and $0 < \boldsymbol{a} \cdot y^i < \boldsymbol{a} \cdot y^0$, where $\boldsymbol{a} > \mathbf{0}$ is the vector of coefficients that defines H. Then the vector $(\boldsymbol{a} \cdot y^0/\boldsymbol{a} \cdot y^i)y^i \equiv \alpha^i y^i \in H$

is well defined. Letting the vector $\boldsymbol{v}$ contain the coefficients of the hyperplane that supports C at y^0, by hypothesis, $C(\alpha^i y^i) \geq \boldsymbol{v} \cdot (\alpha^i y^i) + v_0$. Dividing by α^i yields:

$$C(\alpha^i y^i)/\alpha^i \geq \boldsymbol{v} \cdot y^i + v_0/\alpha^i. \tag{22}$$

Since $\alpha^i > 1$, declining ray average costs ensure that

$$C(y^i) > C(\alpha^i y^i)/\alpha^i. \tag{23}$$

Putting (22) and (23) together yields $C(y^i) > \boldsymbol{v} \cdot y^i + v_0/\alpha^i$. Summing over all i yields

$$\sum_i C(y^i) > \boldsymbol{v} \cdot \sum_i y^i + \left[\boldsymbol{a} \cdot \sum_i y^i/(\boldsymbol{a} \cdot y^0)\right] v_0 = \boldsymbol{v} \cdot y^0 + v_0 = C(y^0).$$

Q.E.D.

The logic behind this proof is as follows. Let $k = 2$, so that $y^1 + y^2 = y^0$ in Figure 1.2. Now extend rays from the origin through y^1 and y^2 to H, the hyperplane along which the cost function is trans-ray supportable, i.e. to the points $\alpha_1 y^1$ and $\alpha_2 y^2$. By declining ray average costs, the unit cost of each of these commodity bundles is thereby reduced. Now, since y^0 can be expressed as a weighted sum of $\alpha_1 y^1$ and $\alpha_2 y^2$, trans-ray supportability ensures that the cost of producing it is less than or equal to a similarly weighted sum of the costs of those output vectors. Thus, both steps in the procedure which makes it possible to compare $C(y^0)$ to $C(y^1) + C(y^2)$ serve to reduce the former relative to the latter.

This combination of declining ray average cost and trans-ray supportability is another set of sufficient conditions for natural monopoly. A whole class of stronger sufficient conditions is immediately available, since any cost complementarity condition that implies trans-ray supportability will, when combined with *DRAC*, yield subadditivity. These stronger conditions may prove easier to verify on the basis of the parameter values of empirically estimated cost functions. Two conditions that guarantee that the cost function has a support in at least one trans-ray direction are *trans-ray convexity* of the cost function and quasiconvexity of the cost function.

The concept of trans-ray convexity, developed in Baumol (1977), requires that the cost function be convex on the trans-ray hyperplane in question, e.g. line RT in Figure 1.2. Since a convex function can be supported at any point in its domain, trans-ray convexity of the cost function with respect to any hyperplane immediately implies trans-ray supportability. Quasiconvexity can be shown to imply that the cost function has a support over the trans-ray hyperplane defined by the gradient of the cost function at the point in question.[21] There is one more issue that must be discussed in connection with this set of sufficient conditions for subadditivity and natural monopoly. Trans-ray supportability (unlike trans-ray convexity) does not rule out the presence of product specific fixed costs. In Figure 1.3, these would show up as jump discontinuities above R and T. As with the cost function $\tilde{C}$, it may still be possible to support the cost function above a point such as y^0. If, however, product specific fixed costs were greater, so that the single product cost levels dropped to s and t, then none of the cost functions depicted could be supported over the trans-ray in question. Yet it seems intuitively clear that the degree of economies of scale and the extent of natural monopoly can only be enhanced by increases in fixed costs, since they would seem to increase the advantage of single firm production over that of any multifirm alternative. Therefore, let us again use the formulation introduced above, writing $C(y) = F\{S\} + c(y)$, where S is the set of outputs produced in strictly positive quantities. Then we can state the following result:

Proposition 14

If $c(y)$ is strictly (weakly) subadditive at y^0 and $F\{S\}$ is weakly (strictly) subadditive in the sense that $F\{S \cup T\} \leq (<) F\{S\} + F\{T\}$, $\forall S, T \subset N$, then $C(y)$ is strictly subadditive at y^0.

Proof

Consider the nonzero output vectors $y^1, y^2, \ldots, y^k$ s.t. $\sum y^s = y^0$. Then

$$\sum_{s=1}^{k} C(y^s) = \sum_{s=1}^{k} F\{S^s\} + \sum_{s=1}^{k} c(y^s),$$

where $S^s = \{i \in N: y_i^s > 0\}$. Using the weak (strict) subadditivity of F, we have

$$\sum_{s=1}^{k} C(y^s) \geq (>) F\{S\} + \sum_{s=1}^{k} c(y^s),$$

where $N \supseteq S = \{i \in N: \sum y_i^s \equiv y_i^0 > 0\}$. The result then follows from the strict (weak) subadditivity of $c(\cdot)$. Q.E.D.

[21] The proof of both of these assertions can be found in Baumol, Panzar and Willig (1982, ch. 4, appendix I, p. 91).

This completes the present discussion of sufficient conditions for subadditivity. Additional sets of sufficient conditions can be found in Baumol, Panzar and Willig (1982, ch. 7) and Sharkey (1982, ch. 4).

3. Industry configurations[22]

Thus far we have examined the properties of the cost function of the firm that are important determinants of firm and industry structure. However, in order to gain a complete understanding of market structure, it is necessary to understand the interactions between the determinants of firm size and the size of the market. The former is, as I have argued, determined in large part by the position of the cost function. The latter is determined by the position of the market demand curve. The interaction between these two exogenously given constructs places bounds on the structure of the industry, i.e. limits on the number and size distribution of firms that can be present in equilibrium.

In a private enterprise economy any industry structure that persists in the long run must yield the firms in the industry at least zero economic profits. This places certain restrictions on the relative locations of the cost and demand curves. Thus, at a minimum, it must *not* be the case that the market demand curve lies entirely to the left of the firm average cost curve. For in such a circumstance the firm and industry could not break even unless it had recourse to some form of discriminatory pricing policies or a subsidy. Note that this is true even though it may well be the case that the industry in question *ought* to produce because the total benefits to consumers, as approximated by the area under the market demand curve, exceed the total cost of providing, say, W units of output in Figure 1.4.

Thus, a minimal requirement for inclusion in the set of industries relevant to the student of Industrial Organization, is that there exist some industry configurations that are *feasible* in the sense that the firms involved in the industry at least break even. It will prove useful to precisely define the terms to be used in this discussion:

Definition 17. Industry configuration

An industry configuration is a number of firms, m, and associated output vectors $\boldsymbol{y}^1, \boldsymbol{y}^2, \ldots, \boldsymbol{y}^m$ such that $\sum \boldsymbol{y}^i = \boldsymbol{Q}(\boldsymbol{p})$. Here, $\boldsymbol{p}$ is the vector of market prices and $\boldsymbol{Q}(\boldsymbol{p})$ is the system of market demand equations.

[22] The discussion in this section is based upon that in chapter 5 of Baumol, Panzar and Willig (1982), which, in turn, built upon Baumol and Fischer (1978).

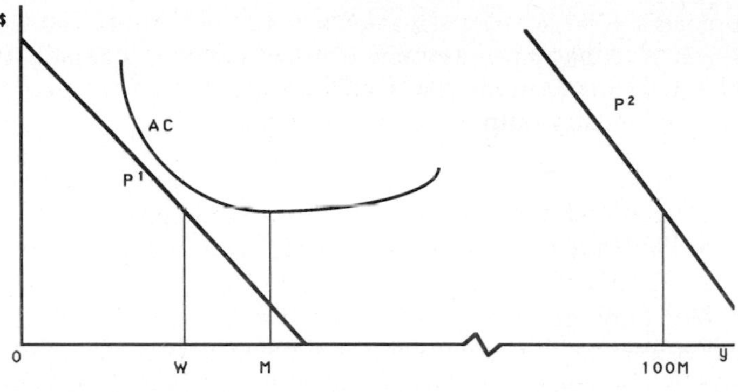

Figure 1.4

Definition 18. Feasible industry configuration

An industry configuration is said to be feasible if, in addition, it is the case that $\boldsymbol{p} \cdot \boldsymbol{y}^i \geq C(\boldsymbol{y}^i)\ \forall i$. If, alternatively, we use the system of market inverse demand relationships, $\boldsymbol{P}(\boldsymbol{y}^I)$, this condition becomes $\boldsymbol{P}(\boldsymbol{y}^I) \cdot \boldsymbol{y}^i \geq C(\boldsymbol{y}^i)$, where $\boldsymbol{y}^I = \sum \boldsymbol{y}^i$ is the industry output level.

Since the primary focus of this analysis is on long-run industry structure, the first definition limits attention to industry situations in which supply equals demand and the second requires that *each firm* earns non-negative profits from its market activities. One must go further than this, of course. For there are situations in which there may exist feasible industry configurations containing one, four, or a hundred firms. The industry demand curve $P^2(y^1)$ in Figure 1.4 illustrates such a situation, if one imagines that the average cost curve rises, but only imperceptibly, beyond M. While competitive, monopoly or oligopoly market structures may all be *feasible* for this industry, common sense and standard practice suggest that this industry be classified as naturally competitive. Thus, another important characteristic of an industry configuration is its *efficiency*.

Definition 19. Efficient industry configuration

$\{y^1, y^2, \ldots, y^m\}$ is an efficient industry configuration if and only if

$$\sum_{j=1}^{m} C(y^j) = \min_{m,\, y^1, \ldots, y^m} \sum_{j=1}^{m} C(y^j) \equiv C^I(y^I),$$

where $y^I \equiv \sum y^j$ is total industry output and $C^I(y^I)$ is the *industry cost function*. Thus, an industry configuration is efficient if and only if it consists of a number of firms and a division of output that yield the lowest possible total industry costs of producing the industry output vector in question.

The analysis that follows will focus on the determination of the number of firms that can constitute a feasible and efficient industry configuration for the relevant set of industry output levels.[23] This focus does not mean that it is logical to presume that only efficient industry configurations can be observed in real world industries. Rather, it is an attempt to determine an unambiguous standard for determining the maximum amount of concentration that is *required* by considerations of productive efficiency. Thus, as the analyses of later chapters in this Handbook indicate, there may be strategic considerations that cause an industry to remain a monopoly even if it is structurally competitive. However, it is important to recognize that this type of "market failure" argument can go only one way. If, for example, only one or few firms can be part of feasible and efficient industry configurations, that industry simply *cannot* be structurally competitive.

3.1. *Feasible and efficient single product industry configurations*

I shall now relate the above constructs to the standard textbook practice of making inferences about market structure from the relative positions of the market demand curve and the average cost function of the firm. Suppose the firm's average cost curve is as depicted in Figure 1.5. If the market inverse demand curve is given by $P^1(y)$, then the industry has been traditionally classified as a "natural monopoly".[24] Alternatively, if the market inverse demand curve is given by $P^2(y)$, so that it intersects the competitive price level p_c at an output level, C, that is a large multiple of M, the industry is classified as structurally competitive. Finally, if C is a small multiple, then the industry is

[23] The determination of the relevant set of industry output levels can be a nontrivial exercise, especially in the multiproduct case. In the single product examples depicted in Figure 1.5, the relevant set of industry outputs for the industry whose inverse demand curve is given by $P^2(y)$ is the compact interval $[W, 100M]$. For output levels smaller than W, there exists no price at which even a monopolist could break even. For outputs greater than $100M$, consumers' willingness to pay is less than the lowest possible unit cost achievable by the industry. For the industry facing the inverse demand curve given by $P^1(y)$, the set of relevant output levels is empty.

[24] Of course the subadditivity analysis of the previous section has revealed that the natural monopoly region will typically also include some output levels to the right of the minimum point of the average cost curve.

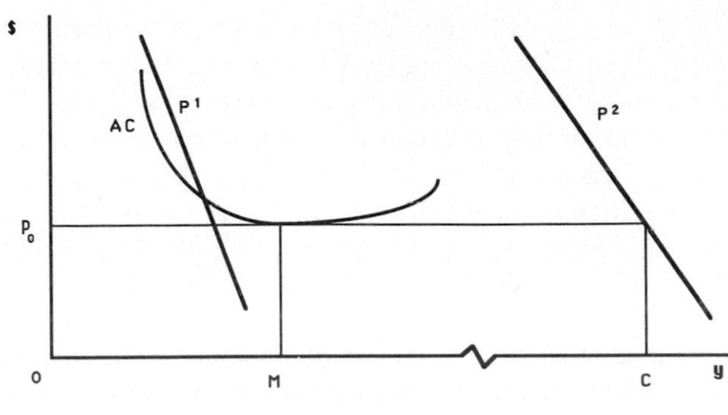

Figure 1.5

traditionally considered as likely to be an oligopoly. The following propositions make this standard practice precise.[25]

Proposition 15

Assume that the average cost function $C(y)/y$ has a unique minimum at y^M, is strictly decreasing for $0 < y < y^M$, and is strictly increasing for $y > y^m$. Then the cost-minimizing number of firms for the production of the industry output y^I is exactly y^I/y^M if that number is an integer. In this case, $C^I(y^I) = (y^I/y^M)C(y^M) \equiv y^I \cdot AC^M$. If y^I/y^M is not an integer, then the cost-minimizing number of firms is either the integer just smaller or the integer just larger than y^I/y^M.

This result formalizes the intuitive notion that, with U-shaped average cost curves, the most efficient way to produce any given industry output is to divide it up equally among the required number of minimum efficient scale firms. It goes beyond this, however, in that it addresses the case in which the required number is not an integer. This turns out to be a nontrivial extension that requires the hypothesis that the average cost curve be monotonically decreasing (increasing) for outputs smaller (greater) than y^M.

Similarly, it is possible to rigorously justify the standard practice of determining industry structure using the relative positions of the market demand and average cost curves.

[25]These results, which are stated here without proof, are from Baumol, Panzar and Willig (1982). Proposition 15 has also been proved by Ginsberg (1974) under more restrictive conditions.

Proposition 16

Assume that the average cost function has a unique minimum at y^M, is strictly decreasing (increasing) for $0 < y < (>) y^M$. Let $[x]$ denote the smallest integer at least as large as x. Then no more than $[Q[AC^M]/y^M]$ firms can participate in a feasible and efficient industry configuration and there always exists a feasible and efficient industry configuration containing $[Q[AC^M]/y^M] - 1$ firms.

This result instructs the analyst to find the quantity demanded at the price equal to unit cost at y^M. Next, divide that quantity by y^M, the quantity that minimizes average cost, to determine the critical number $Q[AC^M]/y^M \equiv m^*$. The proposition establishes that no feasible and efficient industry configuration has more than $[m^*]$ firms and that there *does* exist a feasible and efficient industry configuration of $[m^*] - 1$ firms. Note that this test requires quantitative information about the cost function only at y^M.

Thus, if m^* is large, the industry is structurally competitive, because there are feasible and efficient industry configurations with as many as $[m^*] - 1$ firms. If $0 < m^* < 1$, the industry is a natural monopoly, since there can exist no feasible and efficient configurations of more than one firm. However, in this case, one cannot be sure that there exist *any* feasible configurations. That depends upon whether the demand curve intersects the average cost curve or not, as in the case of $P^1(y)$ in Figure 1.4. That cannot be determined from cost information only at y^M.

Before leaving the single product world, it is important to modify the above results to deal with an important departure from the assumption that average cost curves are strictly U-shaped. Conventional wisdom holds that average costs in many industries decline for a range of outputs, attain their minimum at

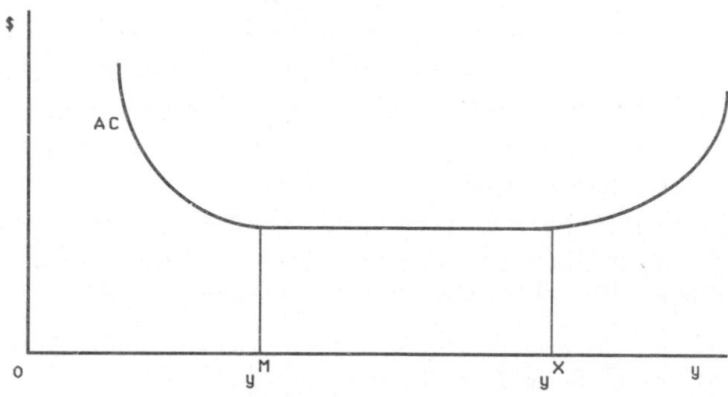

Figure 1.6

minimum efficient scale, and then remain constant for a considerable range of output levels.[26] Figure 1.6 depicts such a situation, with minimum efficient scale being achieved at y^M and average cost remaining constant through output level y^X, the point of *maximum efficient scale*, and rising thereafter.[27]

If average costs are constant up to an output level at least twice as large as minimum efficient scale (i.e. $y^X \geq 2y^M$), the set of market structures that are consistent with feasible and efficient industry configurations is greatly expanded. This means that Propositions 15 must be modified:

Proposition 17

When $y^X \geq 2y^M$, an efficient industry configuration for industry output levels $0 < y^I < 2y^M$ can involve only one firm, and for larger industry outputs at least $\underline{m}$ firms and at most $\overline{m}$ firms are required, where $\underline{m}$ is the smallest integer greater than or equal to y^I/y^X and $\overline{m}$ is the largest integer less than or equal to y^I/y^M.

Thus, if y^M is large relative to $Q(AC^M)$, a competitive industry structure is inconsistent with industry cost minimization. Similarly, if $Q(AC^M)/y^X$ is small, a concentrated industry does not result in any loss of *productive efficiency*, though, of course, there may be welfare losses from oligopolistic pricing.

3.2. *Efficient multiproduct industry configurations*

The problem of establishing bounds on the number of firms that can participate in an efficient industry configuration is considerably more complicated in the multiproduct case. First, when there are two or more products, any given industry output vector $\mathbf{y}^I$ can be apportioned among firms in ways that may involve some or all of the firms producing different output mixes, i.e. operating on different output rays. Second, as noted earlier, the size of firm at which economies of scale are first exhausted may differ across output rays, so that the set of outputs at which there are locally constant returns to scale will be a locus rather than a single point. Therefore, in order to get any results at all, it is necessary to assume that all ray average cost curves are strictly U-shaped, so that all points inside (outside) the M-locus depicted in Figure 1.7 exhibit increasing (decreasing) returns to scale. Also, since economies of scale do not ensure

[26]See Bain (1954) and the discussion in chapter 4 of Scherer (1980).

[27]Of course this latter region may never be observed, since no firm would be operating there under most reasonable notions of industry equilibria.

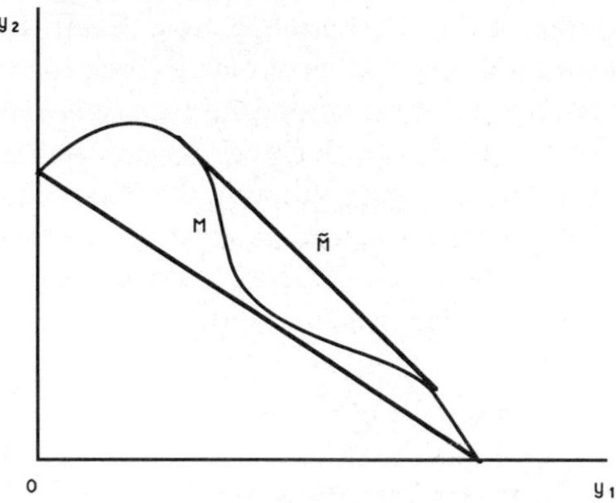

Figure 1.7

subadditivity in the multiproduct case, it is necessary to *assume* that the firm cost function $C(y)$ is strictly subadditive "inside" the M-locus.[28]

Next, let $\tilde{M}$ denote the convex hull of the M-locus, as illustrated in Figure 1.7. Then, for any given industry output vector y^I, let $\bar{t}(y^I) = \max\{t\colon ty^I \in \tilde{M}\}$ and $\underline{t}(y^I) = \min\{t\colon ty^I \in \tilde{M}\}$. Then the following result is true:[29]

Proposition 18

The cost-minimizing number of firms for the production of industry output vector y^I, $m(y^1)$, satisfys the following conditions: (i) $m(y^I) > 1/2\bar{t}(y^I)$ and $m(y^I) \geq [1/2\bar{t}(y^I)]$; (ii) $m(y^I) = 1$ if $\underline{t}(y^I) \geq 1$, otherwise, $1 \leq m(y^I) < 2/\underline{t}(y^I)$ and $1 \leq m(y^I) \leq [2/\underline{t}(y^I)] - 1$.

These upper and lower bounds on the cost-minimizing number of firms tell us, in effect, that the "average-sized" firm in the industry must be sufficiently close to the M-locus. Also, it is clear that these bounds are not nearly as "tight" as those in the single product case. Nevertheless, they are the tightest bounds available, as it is possible to construct examples in which they are exactly satisfied.[30]

[28]In the single product case subadditivity was implied by the assumption that average cost was decreasing up to y^M. Actually, this assumption is required only for output vectors inside the convex closure of M, a concept to be defined below.

[29]Baumol, Panzar and Willig (1982, proposition 5F1). The proof is given in appendix III to chapter 5.

[30]Baumol, Panzar and Willig (1982, pp. 119–120).

There is another issue in the multiproduct case. Even if the lower bound on $m(y^I)$ is large, that would not be sufficient to conclude that the industry is likely to be competitive. For such a finding would indicate only that one could expect a large number of firms involved in producing *all* the industry's products, not a large number of firms producing *each* product, which is required for the *industry* to be competitive. Thus, it is necessary to modify Proposition 18 in order to calculate bounds on the number of firms producing any particular product or subset of products in an efficient industry configuration:[31]

Proposition 19

Let $m_S(y^I)$ denote the number of firms producing products in the subset S in an industry configuration efficient for the production of y^I, and let $M_S \equiv \{y_S\colon\ y \in M\}$ denote the projection of the M-locus in the subspace corresponding to the product subset S, with $\tilde{M}_S$ its convex hull. Then $m_S(y^I) > 1/2t^S(y^I)$ and $m_S(y^I) \geq [1/2t^S(y^I)]$, where $t^S(y^I) \equiv \max\{t\colon\ ty_S^I \in \tilde{M}_S\}$.

The implications of Proposition 19 are illustrated in Figure 1.8 for the case of a two-product industry. If the object of the investigation is to determine whether or not the industry is a candidate for pure competition, then it is necessary to place large lower bounds on the number of producers of *both* products required in an efficient industry configuration producing $y^I > \mathbf{0}$. Specializing Proposition 19 to the case of $S = \{i\}$, the relevant lower bounds are $m_i(y^I) > y_i^I/2\tilde{y}_i$, and $m_i(y^I) \geq [y_i^I/2\tilde{y}_i]$, where $\tilde{y}_i = \max\{y_i\colon\ y \in M\}$. Note that it is the maximum value of y_i over the entire projection of the M-locus, rather than $\hat{y}_i$, the output that achieves minimum efficient scale in stand-alone production, that is used to calculate the lower bounds. When, as drawn, the M-locus is "bowed out" from the axes, $\tilde{y}_i$ may be considerably larger than $\hat{y}_i$. Also note that these are the relevant bounds even if the ray through y^I intersects the M-locus at output levels for each product that are small relative to $\tilde{y}_i$, i.e. even when an industry of "average" size firms would be relatively unconcentrated.

The above discussion indicates the important role played by the shape of the M-locus in determining the lower bounds on the number of firms producing in an efficient industry configuration. Given this, it is important to know what shape the M-locus is "likely" to be, based upon properties of the multiproduct cost function. Unfortunately, the answer here is discouraging. Under most plausible scenarios, the M-locus will tend to have the "bowed out" shape shown in Figure 1.8. This is true even if the two production processes are completely independent! To see this, consider the rectangle formed by $\hat{y}_1$, $\hat{y}_2$, $\hat{y}$, and the origin. At any point on, say, the right border of this rectangle, $S_1 = 1$ and $S_2 > 1$. But, from

[31] Baumol, Panzar and Willig (1982, proposition 5G1, p. 123).

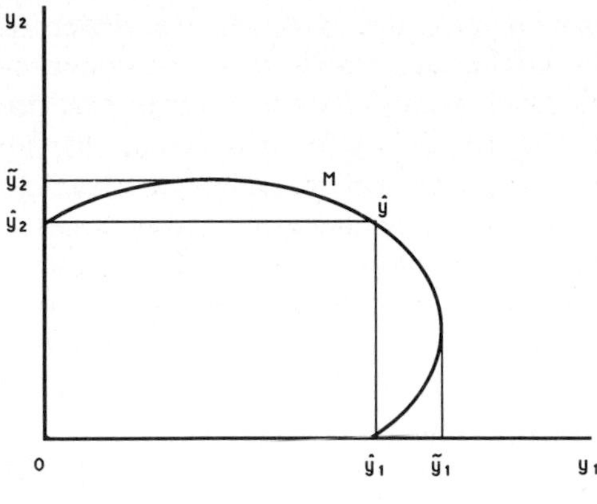

Figure 1.8

equation (6), we know that S is simply a weighted sum of S_1 and S_2 when the products are produced independently. Therefore S must be greater than 1. When ray average costs are U-shaped, this means that one must proceed outward along the ray from the origin before S falls to 1. This effect is increased when there are economies of scope, for then S *exceeds* the weighted average of S_1 and S_2. Finally, when there are product specific fixed costs, the M-locus is discontinuous at the axes, so that $\hat{y}_1$ and $\hat{y}_2$ lie *inside* the points where the M-locus reaches the axes.[32] Without assuming diseconomies of scope, only the limiting case in which (at least some) inputs are perfectly transferable between outputs can one expect the M-locus not to be concave to the origin. In that case, the cost function can be written as $C(y) = \sum c_i y_i + \Phi[\sum a_i y_i]$ and the M-locus is a hyperplane (e.g. the outer border of the rectangle in Figure 1.8) characterized by $\{ y\colon \sum a_i y_i = k \}$, where $k\Phi'(k) = \Phi(k)$.[33]

This completes the discussion of the theoretical results underlying the role played by technology in the determination of industry structure. The next section examines the extent to which practice has kept up with theory in this area.[34]

4. Empirical issues

The remainder of this chapter is devoted to a discussion of issues that arise in attempting to give empirical content to the theory developed in the previous two sections. The first two subsections discuss general methodological problems that

[32]See Baumol, Panzar and Willig (1982, figure 9C3, p. 255).

[33]Baumol, Panzar and Willig (1982, pp. 129–130).

[34]As is usual, practice tends to follow theory only with a lag. This is especially true with respect to the material of this section. For an exception, see Wang Chiang and Friedlaender (1985).

often arise in empirical applications. The final two subsections discuss empirical cost function studies in electric power and telecommunications. I will not be concerned with econometric methodology, but rather with the extent to which the cost functions estimated are useful for addressing the questions of industry structure that, presumably, provided the initial motivation for such empirical studies. For as Nerlove (1963) remarked (p. 409) in his pioneering study of electricity supply, "the first question one must ask is 'To what use are the results to be put?' ". The bulk of the discussion of empirical studies will be devoted to those that have been published in the last few years, since surveys by Gold (1981) and Bailey and Friedlaender (1982) in the *Journal of Economic Literature* cover the earlier literature in some detail.

4.1. Aggregation and the hedonic approach[35]

In most real world industries, firms are likely to be producing a large number of distinct products. Thus, in attempting to estimate cost functions econometrically, the analyst will usually be forced to aggregate the output data in some way in order to reduce the parameters to be estimated to a manageable number. Until fairly recently, the typical approach was to construct a single, scalar measure of output, $Y \equiv \sum a_i y_i$, were $\boldsymbol{a} > \boldsymbol{0}$ is some vector of weights, often based on output prices. However, this procedure imposes the implicit restriction that the multiproduct cost function can be written as $C(y) = \tilde{C}(Y)$. Unfortunately, this imposes severe restrictions on the important multiproduct cost constructs developed earlier in this chapter. Of course, in principle, it is possible to test the validity of such restrictions, but such tests usually require that sufficient data is available to render such restrictions unnecessary in the first place.[36]

Of course, if there is reason to believe that the true multiproduct cost function can be written in this simple form, all of the important multiproduct cost constructs discussed above can be calculated from the estimated parameters of $\tilde{C}$. However, there is also a situation in which it is possible to reliably infer something about the properties of C from estimates of $\tilde{C}$. Suppose all of the output vectors in the sample lie on or close to the same ray, i.e. firms in the sample always produced essentially the same output mix. Then the single product measure of economies of scale calculated from the parameters of $\tilde{C}$ will correctly measure the degree of multiproduct scale economies *along the ray in question*. In particular, the intersection of that ray with the M-locus, at which returns to scale are locally constant, can be correctly identified. It is important to note, however,

[35] Most of this section is drawn from the discussion in Baumol, Panzar and Willig (1982, pp. 446–448).

[36] See Blackorby, Primont and Russell (1977) or Denny and Fuss (1977) for discussions of econometric aggregation tests.

that it is *not* generally valid to extrapolate those measures to output mixes outside the sample. As the discussion of the previous section indicates, knowledge of the *entire* M-locus is generally required when calculating bounds on the number of firms in an efficient industry configuration for *any* output mix.

During the last decade, estimates of *hedonic cost functions* have become common in the literature. These represent a compromise between the estimation of scalar aggregate and multiproduct product cost functions. This approach was pioneered by Spady and Friedlaender (1978) in their analysis of trucking firms. Rather than attempt to estimate costs as a function of the (large) number of different types of freight carried over a (very large) number of origin and destination pairs, they specified costs as a function of aggregate ton-miles and hedonic variables such as the average length of haul. Formally, a hedonic cost function can be expressed as $\tilde{C}(Y, Z_1, \dots, Z_k)$, where Y is, again, a scalar measure of aggregate output and $\boldsymbol{Z}$ are hedonic measures of the output mix. Of course, if enough such hedonic measures are included, then the output vector $\boldsymbol{y}$ could be reconstructed from Y and $\boldsymbol{Z}$, so that there would exist a hedonic cost function representation equivalent to the true multiproduct cost function. However its estimation would, in general, require estimating the same number of parameters.

Use of hedonic cost functions enables the investigator to, in effect, perform often unavoidable aggregation based upon informed judgements about characteristics that are likely to have important impacts upon the costs associated with producing a given aggregate output vector. If the resulting hedonic cost function is judged to be good approximation of the true multiproduct cost function, the multiproduct cost characteristics developed above can be computed from its parameter estimates and employed in an analysis of industry structure. This last step requires some care in interpretation, however, even if the specified hedonic cost function is assumed to reflect the true multiproduct cost structure.

For example, consider the recent study of airline cost by Caves, Christensen and Tretheway (1984). They estimate a cost function for airlines as a function of, inter alia, aggregate output (e.g. revenue passenger miles, RPM) and P, the number of points served by the firm. Therefore, assume that the true cost function can be written as $C(y) = H\{G(Y), P\}$, where Y is aggregate output and P is the number of points served. Caves et al. define two cost concepts to be used in describing the cost characteristics of airline networks, returns to density, $RTD = H/YG'$ and "returns to scale", $RTS = H/[PHp + YG']$. RTD measures the proportional increase in output made possible by a proprotional increase in all inputs, with points served (and other hedonic measures) held constant. RTS measures the proportional increase in output and points served made possible by a proportional increase in all inputs, ceteris paribus. At the sample mean, they found significant returns to density ($RTD \approx 1.2$), but essentially constant "returns to scale" ($RTS \approx 1.0$).

How do these cost concepts relate to those that have been shown to be important for the determination of industry structure earlier in this chapter? In order to examine this question, it is necessary to relate Caves et al.'s hedonic cost function more directly to an underlying multiproduct cost function. For expository purposes, it is convenient to assume a simple structure for H, i.e. $H = cY + rP$, where c and r are positive constants. Then the underlying multiproduct cost function can be written as

$$C(y) = c \cdot \sum_{i \in T} y_i + rP = c \cdot Y + rP = H\{G(Y), P\},$$

where T is the set of markets served and P is the cardinality of T.[37] Now it is easy to see that returns to density are precisely equal to (what has been previously defined to be) the degree of multiproduct economies of scale! That is, $RTD = [(c \cdot Y + rP)/c \cdot Y] = C(y)/\nabla C(y) \cdot y \equiv S$. Also, in this example it is easy to see that Caves et al.'s measure of "returns to scale" is always equal to 1. Unfortunately, it is also easy to see that that fact is not particularly relevant for the analysis of industry structure described in Sections 2 and 3.

Examining this example in terms of the cost concepts developed above, reveals globally increasing returns to scale, both with respect to the entire product set and any subset of products. That is, S and S_T both exceed 1 at all output levels and for all subsets of markets T. There are no economies of scope in this example. However, the more general hedonic specification is consistent with either economies or diseconomies of scope. These would be determined by the returns to scale properties of G and of H with respect to P. The extent of economies of scope would, of course be useful in determining efficient firm size. However, measures of economies of scope were not computed.

Industries characterized by network technologies are disproportionately represented in econometric cost studies. There are two related reasons for this. First, network technologies are usually thought to be characterized by economies of scale. This has resulted in most of them being regulated over the years, which, in turn, has meant much better than average data availability for cost function estimation. Furthermore, the opening of such industries to competitive entry has often focused important policy debates on the extent of scale economies that may or may not be present. Unfortunately, their network structure makes the aggregation problem under discussion particularly severe. If point-to-point transportation (or transmission) movements are viewed as the true cost-causitive outputs of the firm, a firm operating even a relatively small network must be viewed as producing an astronomical number of products. The hedonic approach has, in large part, arisen as an attempt to deal with the problem of networks.

[37]For ease of exposition, I am ignoring the network aspects of airline costs, so that the number of economically distinct outputs is the same as the number of points served, as in a simple star-shaped network.

In an important recent paper, Spady (1985) proposes an innovative solution to this problem. By assuming that the cost of production on each link of the network are quadratic, he is able to construct a multiproduct cost function that is econometrically parsimonious, yet a true aggregate of the underlying production processes. All that is required, in addition to aggregate data, are estimates of the first and second moments of the distribution of the links' traffic and technological characteristics. This exciting approach has, to my knowledge, yet to be empirically implemented.

4.2. Long-run and short-run measures of returns to scale

The discussion in this chapter has focused on the properties of the *long-run* cost function and the role that they play in determining equilibrium industry structure. However, in an empirical application that attempts to estimate the cost function of an individual firm, the data available may be better suited for estimating a *short-run* cost function: a specification that assumes that only some of the inputs available to the firm are set at their cost-minimizing levels. For example, if a cost function were to be estimated using monthly data, it would be unrealistic to assume that the firms capital inputs were adjusted to the cost-minimizing level associated with each month's rate of output. In that case, it might be appropriate to estimate a *variable cost* function representation of the technology. Conceptually, this is done by dividing the vector of inputs available to the firm into two categories: $\boldsymbol{x} = (\boldsymbol{v}, \boldsymbol{k})$. The *variable inputs* $\boldsymbol{v}$ are assumed to be observed at their cost-minimizing levels but the *fixed inputs* $\boldsymbol{k}$ may or may not be. Then $V(\boldsymbol{y}, \boldsymbol{k}, \boldsymbol{s})$ is defined as the minimum expenditure on variable inputs $\boldsymbol{v}$ required to produce the output vector $\boldsymbol{y}$, given the availability of the fixed inputs at level $\boldsymbol{k}$, provided that $\boldsymbol{y}$ can be produced from $\boldsymbol{k}$. That is, $V(\boldsymbol{y}, \boldsymbol{k}, \boldsymbol{s}) = \min_{v}\{\boldsymbol{s} \cdot \boldsymbol{v}\colon (\boldsymbol{v}, \boldsymbol{k}, \boldsymbol{y}) \in T\}$, where $\boldsymbol{s}$ is the vector of variable input prices. Examples of empirical cost studies that estimate variable cost functions include the telecommunications study by Christensen, Cummings and Schoech (1983) and the railroad study of Friedlaender and Spady (1981).

Once estimates of the parameters of a variable cost function are obtained, however, how does one calculate the degree of economies of scale to be used for policy purposes? For example, Braeutigam and Daughety (1983) present the following measure of economies of scale:

$$\hat{S} = \left\{V - \sum_i (\partial V/\partial k_i) k_i\right\} \Big/ \left\{\sum_j (\partial V/\partial y_j) y_j\right\}.$$

This measure of economies of scale is defined as a function of variable input prices, output levels and fixed input levels, i.e. $\hat{S} = \hat{S}(\boldsymbol{y}, \boldsymbol{k}, \boldsymbol{s})$. Clearly, this measure differs from both $S(\boldsymbol{y}, \boldsymbol{w})$ and $\tilde{S}(\boldsymbol{y}, \boldsymbol{x})$, the measures discussed in

Subsection 2.1. However, the relationships between these measures should be clear. $\hat{S}$ is a hybrid of the technological and cost function measures of economies of scale. $\tilde{S}$ reflects a fundamental property of the productive technology and can be calculated at every point in input/output space, $X \times Y$. S measures the elasticity of costs with respect to output(s). By construction, it pertains only to cost-efficient input/output combinations.

If one assumes, instead, that only a subset of inputs is selected optimally, $\hat{S}$ is the resulting measure of economies of scale. In fact, using the same argument that established Proposition 2, it is possible to show that $\tilde{S}(y, \hat{v}(y, k, s), k) = \hat{S}(y, k, s)$, where $\hat{v}$ is the argmin of the above variable cost-minimization problem. Thus, the technological and variable cost measures of the degree of scale economies coincide at those input/output points at which the variable inputs are chosen optimally. Similarly, it is also the case that $\hat{S}(y, k^*(y, r, s), s) = S(y, w)$, where r is the vector of fixed input prices, so that $w = (r, s)$.

Given that it is sometimes necessary and/or desirable to estimate a variable cost function, there remains the question of how to use the estimates to provide the most appropriate information regarding economies of scale. As Braeutigam and Daughety (1983) point out, one would not expect $\hat{S}$ and S to be equal unless the fixed inputs happen to be at their cost-minimizing levels or the technology is homothetic.[38] Furthermore, they show that it is generally not possible to make any inferences about the relative magnitudes of S and $\hat{S}$ for any given y and s. Thus, if one wishes, for policy purposes, to determine the extent of economies of scale *in the long run*, there is no alternative but to use the variable cost function estimates and the vector of fixed input factor prices to derive the long-run cost function $C(y, s, r)$, which can be used to calculate S.[39] Of course, this eliminates one of the perceived advantages of the variable cost function approach, the ability to obtain estimates without observations on the prices of fixed factors. This issue is particularly important for studies in which the "fixed factor" is actually some accounting measure of assets for which it is difficult to impute a price.

4.3. *Empirical studies of electric power*

Nerlove (1963) provided a pioneering study of economies of scale in electricity generation based upon modern duality theory. Using data from 1955, he estimated a cost function that included factor prices as arguments. His basic

[38] In this context the appropriate multiproduct version of homotheticity requires that the transformation function can be written as $\varphi(v, k, y) = F(h(v, k), y)$, with h linearly homogeneous. That is, there exists a natural aggregate of inputs that can be used to produce any desired output mix. In that case, $\tilde{S}$, the technological measure of economies of scale, is constant along any isoquant.

[39] This is the method used by Friedlaender and Spady (1981) in their study of rail and trucking costs.

estimation equation was a Cobb–Douglas log-linear specification of the cost function:

$$\ln C = K + (1/S)\ln y + (1/S)\sum a_i[\ln p_i].$$

Here S is the (single product) degree of scale economies, the p_i refer to the prices of labor, fuel and capital, and $\sum a_i$ is constrained to equal unity. Two variants of this model yielded estimates of $S \approx 1.4$ [Nerlove (1963, tables 3 and 4)]. To put this in perspective, this would mean that the utility's costs would exceed its revenues by forty percent if its output were priced at marginal cost.

As Nerlove recognized, this functional form has the disadvantage of imposing the condition that the degree of returns to scale is the same for all output levels and factor prices. And, indeed, examination of the residuals from this basic regression equation revealed that the true relationship of costs to output could not be log-linear. Therefore he tried various techniques to allow for the intuitively plausible possibility that the degree of scale economies decreases as output increases. Dividing the sample into five output categories yielded estimates (depending on the treatment of the price of capital) ranging from $S > 2.5$ at small output levels to $S \approx 0.95$ for the largest output category. This suggested that economies of scale were exhausted at large plant sizes.

In order to examine the robustness of these results, Nerlove then estimated equations based upon what he referred to as the hypothesis of "continuous neutral variations in returns to scale". That is, he assumed that the degree of economies of scale depended upon the output level of the firm but not upon the factor prices it faced. (It is easy to show that this implies that the underlying production function must be homothetic.) The estimated equations were of the form:

$$\ln C = K + \alpha[\ln y] + \beta[\ln y]^2 + \sum a_i[\ln p_i].$$

These estimates also yielded the result that the degree of economies of scale declined with output. However, in this case, economies of scale persisted throughout, with estimates ranging from $S \approx 3.0$ at low output levels to $S \approx 1.7$ for the largest plants in the sample. [However, Christensen and Greene (1976) point out an error in Nerlove's calculation of the degree of scale economies from his estimated parameter values. When corrected, the results of this regression equation also show that economies of scale are exhausted by firms with the largest output levels.]

Nerlove's pioneering study was important because it clearly established the cost function, with its factor price arguments, as the proper framework in which to study the returns to scale experience of public utilities and because it demonstrated that economies of scale tend to decline with output, thereby setting the stage for the application of more flexible function forms better suited to capture this effect empirically.

Christensen and Greene (1976) studied economies of scale in the electric power industry using data from 1970. They employed the translog cost function:

$$[\ln C] = K + \alpha Y + \beta Y^2 + \sum a_i P_i + \sum\sum b_{ij} P_i P_j + \sum \gamma_i Y P_i, \tag{24}$$

where capital letters denote the natural logarithms of the independent variables y and the p_i. In order for (24) to represent a proper cost function, it is required that $\sum a_i = 1$, $\sum \gamma_i = 0$ and $\sum_i b_{ij} = \sum_j b_{ij} = \sum\sum b_{ij} = 0$. This functional form allowed them to encompass all of the equations estimated by Nerlove as special cases and statistically test the validity of the implied restrictions. For example, if one restricts $\beta = b_{ij} = \gamma_i = 0$, equation (24) reduces to the homogeneous Cobb–Douglas function, with a degree of scale economies $(1/\alpha)$ that is constant overall output ranges and unaffected by changes in factor prices. Allowing for $\beta \neq 0$ yields Nerlove's homothetic model in which the degree of scale economies varies with output $(S = 1/(\alpha + 2\beta Y))$ but not factor prices, and retains the property that the elasticity of substitution between factors of production is fixed at unity.

Christensen and Greene found it possible to reject the hypotheses of homogeneity, homotheticity and unitary elasticities of substitution in the generation of electric power, both for their own 1970 data and Nerlove's 1955 data. They also found that maintaining the hypothesis of homogeneity results in estimates of global economies of scale, whereas more flexible representations again reveal that economies of scale are exhausted at very large scales of operation. One implication of their estimates that they do not discuss is the effects of factor price changes on the degree of scale economies. Based on the parameter values reported in their table 4, an increase in the price of labor (fuel) results in a small ($\approx$ 2 percent), but statistically significant, increase (decrease) in the degree of scale economies enjoyed by firms in both 1955 and 1970. Changes in the price of capital appear to have no effect on the degree of scale economies. (The coefficients are extremely small and insignificant for both years.)

Christensen and Greene conclude their article with an illuminating presentation of the average cost curves based on the estimates of the translog model. One interesting finding was that, while the representative average cost curve had shifted downward considerably, the shape of the average cost curve did not change. Thus, since firms had expanded their output levels considerably, far fewer firms were operating with substantial unexploited economies of scale: the figures for steam-generated electric power were 48.7 percent in 1970 versus 74.1 percent in 1955. Finally, while the estimated translog average cost curve was U-shaped, there was a large segment that was approximately flat. This range of output levels – from 19 to 67 billion kWh – was produced by firms producing 44.6 percent of total output.

The papers by Nerlove, and Christensen and Greene, established standards for rigor, thoroughness and precision in the empirical study of economies of scale. However, they did not even begin to deal with the multiproduct nature of the world inhabited by the firms that they study. Electric utilities often sell natural gas as well. Electricity produced at peak times of the day or seasons of the year may cause the firm to incur much greater costs than electricity generated off peak. If the peak/off peak mix varies across firms (i.e. they are not on the same output ray), estimates of single output cost functions will be biased. And what of the costs of transmission and distribution, and the interrelationship between those costs and the costs of generation? Empirical work addressing such *multiproduct* issues did not really begin until the theoretical constructs discussed in previous sections had been developed.

Mayo (1984) attempted to extend the Christensen and Greene (1976) type of analysis of the efficiency of industry structure in the case of regulated public utilities to the case of multiple outputs, electricity (kilowatt hours) and natural gas (cubic feet). He estimated two forms of the quadratic (in outputs) cost function for electric and gas utilities using data from 1979. In his single intercept equation, Mayo found that the estimated coefficient of the electricity–gas interaction term was positive. This guaranteed that diseconomies of scope would eventually set in, despite the positive estimate of the intercept (fixed cost) term. What is somewhat surprising is that the magnitude of the estimated coefficients are such that diseconomies of scope set in at very small output levels. The estimated coefficient of the quadratic electricity term was also positive, which, in the single intercept case, ensures that there are globally decreasing electricity specific returns to scale. Mayo's estimates also yielded the result that overall returns to scale were exhausted at rather small electricity output levels for all of the gas electricity product mixes considered. This was true despite the negative estimated coefficient of the quadratic gas term (and the resulting global gas specific economies of scale).

Using 1981 data for the same sample, but leaving out utilities that generate more than 10 percent of their electricity using nuclear plants, Chappell and Wilder (1986) obtained estimates of the parameters of the single intercept quadratic cost function that yielded significantly different measures of scale and scope economies. That is to say, their estimated coefficients yielded measures of multiproduct, electricity specific and gas specific economies of scale that were not exhausted by even the largest firms in the sample, and economies of scope prevailed over most of the sample. They attributed the difference between their results and Mayo's to the fact that the relatively larger nuclear utilities had considerably higher ex post cost levels. In response, Mayo (1986) argued that nuclear generation of electric power is a different technique but not a different *technology*, and therefore firms that employ it should not be excluded from the sample on a priori grounds. I agree with his position in principle, but the fact that the presence of a relatively few large, high cost firms can dramatically alter the range over which economies of scale and scope pertain is clearly a weakness of the simple quadratic cost specification.

From a methodological point of view, these studies dismiss too readily the use of multiple dummy variables in attempting to measure the fixed costs of the firms in the sample. The use of a single intercept term in a quadratic cost specification is overly restrictive because it assumes away product specific fixed costs and reduces the determination of scope economies to the interplay between the level of fixed costs and the magnitude of the coefficient of the quadratic interaction term. In the two-output case, it is possible to use dummy variables to attempt to measure the fixed costs associated with all possible product sets. That is, it is a simple matter to estimate the function $F\{S\}$ $\forall S \subseteq N$. What is more, it is possible to do this using only two dummy variables. Mayo did this in his Flexible Fixed Cost Quadratic (FFCQ) model. Unfortunately, he decided to favor the single intercept quadratic model on questionable statistical grounds.

Recall what it is one hopes to accomplish via the use of dummy variables. Under the maintained hypothesis that variable costs are a quadratic function of electricity and gas output levels, the object of using dummy variables is to distinguish the intercept (fixed cost) terms of the cost functions of three types of firms: those producing gas only, electricity only, and both electricity and gas. Let *FG*, *FE* and *FB*, respectively, denote the true intercept terms of these three cost functions. Then an appropriate estimating equation would be given by

$$C = \beta_0 + \beta_1 E + \beta_2 B + c.$$

Here, $E(B)$ are dummy variables that take on a value of 1 if electricity only (both electricity and gas) are produced by the firm and zero otherwise and c is a quadratic function of gas and electricity output levels. If this equation is estimated appropriately, the stand-alone fixed cost of gas production, *FG*, is estimated by the estimated value of the parameter β_0, *FE* by β_1, and *FB* by β_2.

Now consider the cost function estimating equation Mayo used:

$$C = \alpha_0 + \alpha_1 E + \alpha_2 G + c.$$

In this equation, $E(G)$ are dummy variables that take on a value of 1 whenever electricity (gas) is produced by the firm and zero otherwise, and c is a quadratic function of gas and electricity output levels. This specification directly estimates the incremental fixed costs of electricity and gas production as α_1 and α_2, respectively. Thus, FG is measured by $\alpha_0 + \alpha_1$, FE by $\alpha_0 + \alpha_2$, and FB by $\alpha_0 + \alpha_1 + \alpha_2$.

Mayo performed an F-test that indicated that one could not reject the hypothesis that $\alpha_1 = \alpha_2 = 0$. However, the fact that one cannot be 90 percent or 95 percent certain that a coefficient is *not* zero does not make it appropriate to treat it as zero in one's calculations. (The estimate of α_0 in Mayo's Quadratic model is not significantly greater than zero, yet he uses its positive value in computing the degrees of scale and scope economies.)

4.4. *Empirical studies of telecommunications*

The U.S. Department of Justice filed an antitrust suit against the Bell System in 1974, seeking divestiture of the Bell Operating Companies, AT & T Long Lines, Western Electric and Bell Telephone Laboratories. Although it was not the main focus of the legal case raised by the DOJ, a part of AT & T's initial defensive position was that the break-up of the Bell System's "natural monopoly" would result in a loss of economic efficiency. This issue was also at least implicit in the policy debate concerning the entry of MCI and others into AT & T's long-distance monopoly markets. The Bell System's position was that these long-distance markets were natural monopolies and that wasteful duplication of facilities would result if competitive entry were permitted and protected.

Thus, empirically determining the extent of economies of scale in the telecommunications industry became more than a mere academic exercise. As in the case of railroads and trucking, the presence or absence of empirically estimated economies of scale was thought to be vitally important for public policy purposes. However, in the case of telecommunications, it was recognized rather early on that the multiproduct nature of the technology should play an important role in the empirical work. Unfortunately, none of the studies conducted during the late 1970s and early 1980s using U.S. data attempted to shed light upon the multiproduct cost concepts developed earlier in this chapter. However, multiproduct cost studies were made employing data from Bell Canada. All of this work is discussed in detail in an important survey article by Fuss (1983). The discussion that follows draws heavily from that source.

The studies covered by Fuss's survey include Fuss and Waverman (1981), Denny et al. (1981), Nadiri and Shankerman (1981), Breslaw and Smith (1980), Denny and Fuss (1980), and Christensen et al. (1983). All of these are translog-based studies. The survey restricts its attention to these papers because the maintained hypotheses (homogeneity, constant elasticities of substitution, Hicks-neutral technical change, etc.) in earlier studies were statistically tested and rejected using the more flexible translog specification. Of course, it is not immediately clear that flexibility of the cost function with respect to *input* prices is the most important criterion to use when attempting to evaluate empirical estimates of its multiproduct *cost* properties.

The first issue that must be faced when using the translog flexible functional form to characterize a multiproduct cost function is how to handle observations which contain zero values for one or more output variables. The translog cost function is undefined at such points, since it is a quadratic function of the logarithms of the independent variables. This issue does not arise in the estimation of the traditional single product translog cost function, since the independent variables (output and factor prices) could take on only strictly positive values. Even if all output levels are strictly positive throughout the sample, calculation of important multiproduct cost measures such as the degrees of economies of scope or product specific economies of scale require evaluating the cost function at points at which one or more output levels are zero.

Fuss and Waverman (1981) circumvent that problem by employing a Box–Cox transformation of the output variables: $\hat{y}_i = (y_i^\theta - 1)/\theta$. Here, θ is a parameter to be estimated and $\hat{y}_i$ replaces [log y_i] in the translog estimation equation. Since $\hat{y}_i$ approaches [ln y_i] as θ approaches 0, the translog specification can be approximated arbitrarily closely by a sufficiently small value of θ. Similarly, when $\theta = 1$, a linear specification results. Thus, for θ in the unit interval, this *hybrid translog* cost function can be thought of as a mixture of linear and log-linear functional forms.

Even when the problems posed by zero output levels are solved, there remains the difficulty of calculating and interpreting the multiproduct cost constructs obtained from the estimated equations. For flexible functional forms, measures of economies of scale and other multiproduct cost constructs depend upon output levels as well as the values of estimated parameters. This is a desirable property, since one intuitively expects that the degree of economies scale or scope decline with size. However, this poses a difficult problem for the researcher attempting to summarize his results concisely, since the degrees of economies of scope and (various types of) economies of scale will be different at each point in the sample. The standard technique employed in practice is to normalize the data by dividing the values of each observed variable by its sample mean. Since both [log y_i] and $\hat{y}_i$ are zero when $y_i = 1$, most of the coefficients of second-order terms in the formulae for the degree of economies of scale and scope are eliminated when these measures are evaluated at the sample means. Thus, it has become standard to summarize regression results by reporting the magnitudes of interest at the sample mean of the variables in the regression equation. However, it is important to remember that this normalization in no way eliminates the substantial variation in, say, the degree of scale economies that may in fact be present over the range of output levels in the sample.

Using this approach, it is straightforward to show that, for both the translog and hybrid translog cost functions, the degree of multiproduct economies of scale evaluated at the sample mean is given by $S = 1/[\Sigma\beta_i]$. In order to measure the extent of economies of scope or product specific economies of scale, it is necessary that the cost function specified be defined when one or more output levels are zero. Thus, these magnitudes cannot be measured from an estimated translog cost function. However, for the hybrid translog cost function, the degree of scale economies specific to output i evaluated at the sample mean, for example, is given by

$$S_i = \{\exp[\alpha_0] - \exp[\alpha_0 - \beta_i/\theta + \delta_{ii}/2\theta^2]\}/\{\alpha_i \cdot \exp[\alpha_0]\}.$$

Summarizing the results of the translog studies referred to above, the estimates of overall economies of scale, evaluated at sample means, range from 0.94 for Fuss and Waverman's (1981) hybrid translog to Nadiri and Shankerman's (1981) estimate of 2.12, with all studies except the former yielding estimates significantly greater than 1.[40] Since the calculation of the degrees of economies of scope or product specific economies of scale requires that the cost function in question be defined for zero output levels, only the Fuss and Waverman (1981) hybrid translog study could provide empirical tests for the presence or absence of these economies. They find no evidence of economies of scope in the operations of Bell Canada. They did find evidence of product specific increasing returns to scale for private line services at the sample mean. However, they determined that these increasing returns would be exhausted if Bell Canada were to serve the entire Canadian private line market in 1980. Thus, the strictures of Proposition 12 do not hold, and one *cannot* conclude that industry cost minimization requires that all private line services be provided by Bell Canada.

The two studies that yielded the upper and lower extremes of the estimates of the degree of overall scale economies also raise two important issues in empirical cost function studies: the treatment of technological change and the specification of the functional form to be estimated. The Nadiri and Shankerman (1981) study was focused on assessing technological change and the growth of total factor productivity in the Bell System. They obtained the highest estimate of the degree of overall scale economies. As mentioned above, the Fuss and Waverman study was the only one of the group employing the hybrid translog cost function. They obtained the lowest estimate of overall economies of scale.

Nadiri and Shankerman's study differed from the others under discussion in two primary respects: they used R&D expenditures to characterize technological change and they used U.S. rather than Canadian data. [Interestingly, the study of Christensen et al. (1983) shared these two characteristics and produced estimates of overall economies of scale nearly as large: 1.73.] While it may be the case that economies of scale are simply greater in the United States than in Canada, the

[40]See Fuss (1983, table 4, p. 19).

larger size of the U.S. telecommunications system would suggest exactly the opposite, i.e. that there should be more unexploited scale economies in Canada. Thus, it would be wise to give some weight to the possibility that the differing treatment of technological change played a determining role in the results.

Why is the specification and measurement of technological change such an important issue when attempting to estimate the degree of economies of scale experienced by a firm? In an industry (like telecommunications) that is experiencing *both* rapid technological change *and* demand growth, there are two effects that are lowering observed unit costs over time: technological advances that shift down the cost curve and output growth that moves the firm down along a falling average cost curve. When a cost function is to be estimated using time series data, it is important to separate the two effects in order to get an accurate estimate of the magnitude of either. For example, when output is growing, data that indicate a downward trend in unit costs could result from a downward shift over time of a constant average cost curve. Alternatively, such observations could be the result of output expansion over time down a stable falling average cost curve. Without careful measurement and specification of a measure of the state of technological progress, it is impossible to separate the two effects.

Even the beginning student of econometrics is continually reminded of the fact that any hypothesis tests or parameter estimates resulting from his analysis are conditional on the validity of the functional form specified for the estimating equation. That is why there has been considerable emphasis of late on the estimation of so-called flexible functional forms such as the translog which reduce to more restrictive functional forms (e.g. Cobb–Douglas) for certain parameter values. With respect to the empirical studies of the telecommunications industry under discussion, it should be remembered that, here, the translog is the restrictive functional form, being one limiting value of the hybrid translog. Fuss and Waverman tested the implied restriction and were able to reject it. It is interesting to note that their unrestricted estimate of the degree of overall scale economies of 0.92 is substantially below the next lowest estimate [Breslow and Smith's (1980) 1.29] and the modal estimate of about 1.45. However, when estimated over their sample, the translog specifications yields an estimate of the degree of overall economies of scale of 1.43, in line with the results of the other studies.

This evidence suggests that imposing the translog specification on the data may lead to an upward bias of the estimate of the degree of scale economies. That is the same conclusion reached by Guilkey and Lovell (1980) in their Monte Carlo study.

Throughout this discussion, the thoughtful reader will have noted that the policy issue motivating the discussion – i.e. whether or not telecommunications is a natural monopoly – has been addressed only tangentially. For the analysis presented in Subsection 2.5 points out that overall economies of scale are neither necessary nor sufficient for a multiproduct industry to be a natural monopoly. Even when combined with evidence on economies of scope and product specific economies of scale, as in Fuss and Waverman, to reach definitive conclusions on the presence or absence of natural monopoly requires more than point estimates of such economies at the sample mean.

Evans and Heckman (1984) were the first to attack the problem directly. They test the subadditivity of a two output (toll and local) translog cost function estimated using time series data from the Bell System. The approach that they take is straightforward. A cost function is subadditive for some output level if it is cheaper to produce the quantity in question with a single firm than with any multifirm alternative. Thus, as noted in Subsection 2.5, in order to establish that a cost function is subadditive over some output region it is necessary to perform this calculation for each output level in the region and for each multifirm alternative industry structure. However, as Evans and Heckman recognize, to show that a cost function is *not* subadditive requires only that this test fails for *some* output level in the region for *one* multifirm alternative.

Evans and Heckman's strategy was to perform this test for all possible two firm alternatives to observed Bell System output levels that lie in their "admissible region". This region is defined by the intuitive notion that any output vector assigned to a firm in a hypothetical multifirm alternative must be at least as large (in both dimensions) as that of the smallest sample point and comprise a ratio of local to toll no smaller (larger) than the smallest (largest) actually observed in the sample used to estimate the cost function. This enabled them to avoid the problems caused by extrapolation outside the sample used to estimate the underlying cost function.

Their results can be summarized as follows. There were 20 data points, 1958–77, for which it was possible to find two firm alternatives in the admissible region. For *all* of these, Evans and Heckman found that there existed a two firm alternative industry configuration that would have resulted in a lowering of industry costs; often a statistically significant lowering.[41] These results enabled them to conclude, directly, that the *necessary* conditions for the subadditivity of the estimated Bell System cost function could not be satisfied, and that, therefore, the Bell System was not a natural monopoly. Note that Evans and Heckman were able to obtain their results even though the translog cost function they employed could not have been used to test for many of the *necessary* (economies of scope) or *sufficient* (economies of scope plus declining average incremental costs) conditions for cost subadditivity derived in Subsection 2.4. That is an important advantage of their direct approach when attempting to *disprove* subadditivity.

[41]See Evans and Heckman (1984, table 1).

5. Concluding remarks

The last decade has seen considerable advances in both theoretical and empirical work on the technological determinants of firm and industry structure. In particular, there has been a dramatic increase in the number of empirical studies that take explicit account of the intrinsic multiproduct nature of most real world industries. In addition to the papers discussed above, the Bibliography offers a (nonexhaustive) selection of empirical cost studies of hospitals, insurance firms, banks, airlines, railroads, motor carriers, automobile producers, to cite just a few examples.

Bibliography

Allen, B.T. (1983) 'Concentration, scale economies and the size distribution of plants', *Quarterly Review of Economics and Business*, 23(4):6–27.

Atkinson, S.E. and Halvorsen, R. (1984) 'Parametric efficiency test, economies of scale, and input demand in U.S. electric power generation', *International Economic Review*, 25(3):647–662.

Bailey, E.E. (1985) 'Airline deregulation in the United States: The benefits provided and the lessons learned', *International Journal of Transportation Economics*, 12(2):113–144.

Bailey, E.E. and Friedlaender, A.F. (1982) 'Market structure and multiproduct industries', *Journal of Economic Literature*, 20:1024–1041.

Bain, J. (1954) 'Economies of scale, concentration and entry', *American Economic Review*, 44:15–39.

Baumol, W.J. (1977) 'On the proper cost tests for natural monopoly in a multiproduct industry', *American Economic Review*, 67:43–57.

Baumol, W.J. and Fischer, D. (1978) 'Cost-minimizing number of firms and the determination of industry structure', *Quarterly Journal of Economics*, 92:439–467.

Baumol, W.J., Panzar, J.C. and Willig, R.D. (1982) *Contestable markets and the theory of industry structure*. New York: Harcourt Brace Jovanovich.

Beckenstein, A.R. (1975) 'Scale economies in the multiplant firm: Theory and empirical evidence', *Bell Journal of Economics*, 6:644–664.

Berechman, J. (1983) 'Costs, economies of scale, and factor demands in bus transport', *The Journal of Transport Economics and Policy*, 17(1):7–24.

Blackorby, C., Primont, D. and Russell, R. (1977) 'On testing separability restrictions with flexible functional forms', *Journal of Econometrics*, 5:195–209.

Braeutigam, R. and Daughety, A.F. (1983) 'On the estimation of returns to scale using variable cost functions', *Economic Letters*, 11:25–31.

Braeutigam, R.R. and Pauly, M.V. (1986) 'Cost function estimation and quality bias: The regulated automobile insurance industry', *Rand Journal of Economics*, 17:606–617.

Braeutigam, R.R., Daughety, A.F. and Turnquist, M.A. (1982) 'The estimation of a hybrid cost function for a railroad firm', *Review of Economics and Statistics*, 64:394–404.

Braeutigam, R.R., Daughety, A.F. and Turnquist, M.A. (1984) 'A firm specific analysis of economies of density in the U.S. railroad industry', *Journal of Industrial Economics*, 33:3–20.

Breslaw, J. and Smith, J. (1980) 'Efficiency, equity and regulation: An econometric model of Bell Canada', final report to the Canadian Department of Communications.

Bruning, R.E. and Olson, R.E. (1982) 'The use of efficiency indexes in testing for scale economies in the motor carrier industry', *Journal of Transport Economics and Policy*, 16(3):227–293.

Caves, D., Christensen, L. and Swanson, J. (1980) Productivity in U.S. railroads 1951–1974', *Bell Journal of Economics*, 11(1):166–181.

Caves, D.W., Christensen, L.R. and Swanson, J.A. (1981a) 'Economic performance in regulated environments: A comparison of U.S. and Canadian railroads', *Quarterly Journal of Economics*, 96:559–581.

Caves, D.W., Christensen, L.R. and Swanson, J.A. (1981b) 'Productivity growth, scale economies and capacity utilization in U.S. railroads, 1955–74', *American Economic Review*, 71:994–1002.

Caves, D.W., Christensen, L.R. and Tretheway, M.W. (1980) 'Flexible cost functions for multiproduct firms', *Review of Economics and Statistics*, 62(3):477–481.

Caves, D.W., Christensen, L.R. and Tretheway, M.W. (1984) 'Economies of density versus economies of scale: Why trunk and local service airline costs differ', *Rand Journal of Economics*, 15:471–489.

Chappell, Jr., H.W. and Wilder, R.P. (1986) 'Multiproduct monopoly, regulation, and firm costs: Comment', *Southern Economic Journal*, 52(4):1168–1174.

Christensen, L. and Greene, W. (1976) 'Economies of scale in U.S. electric power generation', *Journal of Political Economy*, (4):655–676.

Christensen, L., Cummings, D. and Schoech, P. (1983) 'Econometric estimation of scale economies in telecommunications', in: L. Courville, A. de Fontenay and R. Dobell, eds., *Economic analysis of telecommunications: Theory and applications*. Amsterdam: North-Holland.

Clark, J.M. (1923) *Studies in the economics of overhead costs*. Chicago: University of Chicago Press.

Clemens, E. (1950–1951) 'Price discrimination and the multiproduct firm', *Review of Economic Studies*, 19(4):1–11; reprinted in: R. Heflebower and G. Stocking, eds., *Readings in industrial organization and public policy*. Homewood, Ill.: Irwin, 1958, 262–276.

Cowing, T.G. and Holtmann, A.G. (1983) 'Multiproduct short run hospital cost functions: Evidence and policy implications from cross-section data', *Southern Economic Journal*, 50:637–653.

Daly, M.J. and Rao, P.S. (1985) 'Productivity, scale economics, and technical change in Ontario Hydro', *Southern Economic Journal*, 52(1):167–180.

Daly, M.J., Rao, P.S. and Geehan, R. (1985) 'Productivity, scale economics and technical progress in the Canadian life insurance industry', *International Journal of Industrial Organization*, 3(3): 345–361.

De Borgen, B.L. (1984) 'Cost and productivity in regional bus transportation: The Belgian case', *Journal of Industrial Economics*, 33:37–54.

Demsetz, H. (1973) 'Joint supply and price discrimination', *Journal of Law and Economics*, 16(2):389–405.

Denny, M. and Fuss, M. (1977) 'The use of approximation analysis to test for separability and the existence of consistent aggregates', *American Economic Review*, 67:404–418.

Denny, M. and Fuss, M. (1980) 'The effects of factor prices and technological change on the occupational demand for labour: Evidence from Canadian telecommunications', Institute for Policy Analysis working paper no. 8014, University of Toronto.

Denny, M., Everson, C., Fuss, M. and Waverman, L. (1981) 'Estimating the effects of diffusion of technological innovations in telecommunications: The production structure of Bell Canada', *Canadian Journal of Economics*, 14:24–43.

Doherty, N.A. (1981) 'The measurement of output and economies of scale in property-liability insurance', *Journal of Risk and Insurance*, 48:390–402.

Evans, D.S., ed. (1983) *Breaking up Bell*. New York: North-Holland.

Evans, D.S. and Heckman, J.J. (1984) 'A test for subadditivity of the cost function with application to the Bell system', *American Economic Review*, 74:615–623.

Evans, D.S. and Heckman, J.J. (1986) 'A test for subadditivity of the cost function with application to the Bell system: Erratum', *American Economic Review*, 76:556–558.

Fare, R., Jansson, L. and Knox Lovell, C.A. (1985) 'Modelling scale economies with ray-homothetic production functions', *Review of Economics and Statistics*, 67:624–636.

Ferguson, C.E. (1969) *The neoclassical theory of production and distribution*. Cambridge: Cambridge University Press.

Friedlaender, A.F., Winston, C. and Wang, K. (1983) 'Costs, technology and productivity in the U.S. automobile industry', *Bell Journal of Economics*, 14:1–20.

Friedlaender, A.F. and Spady, R. (1981) *Freight transport regulation: Equity, efficiency and competition in the rail and trucking industries*. Cambridge, Mass.: MIT Press.

Fuss, M.A. (1983) 'A survey of recent results in the analysis of production conditions in telecommunications', in: L. Courville, A. de Fontenay and R. Dobell, eds., *Economic analysis of telecommunications: Theory and applications*. Amsterdam: North-Holland.

Fuss, M.A. and Waverman, L. (1981) 'The regulation of telecommunications in Canada', final report to the Economic Council of Canada.
Gillen, D.W. and Oum, T.H. (1984) 'A study of the cost structure of the Canadian intercity motor coach industry', *Canadian Journal of Economics*, 17(2):369–385.
Gilligan, T. and Smirlock, M. (1984) 'An empirical study of joint production and scale economies in commercial banking', *Journal of Banking and Finance*, 8:67–77.
Gilligan, T., Smirlock, M. and Marshall, W. (1984) 'Scale and scope economies in the multiproduct banking firm', *Journal of Monetary Economics*, 13:393–405.
Ginsberg, W. (1974) 'The multiplant firm with increasing returns to scale', *Journal of Economic Theory*, 9:283–292.
Gold, B. (1981) 'Changing perspectives on size, scale and returns: An interpretive survey', *Journal of Economic Literature*, 19:5–33.
Gort, M. and Wall, R.A. (1984) 'The effect of technical change on market structure', *Economic Inquiry*, 22(4): 668–675.
Guilkey, D. and Lovell, C.A.K. (1980) 'On the flexibility of the translog approximation', *International Economic Review*, 21:137–148.
Harmatuck, D.J. (1981) 'A motor carrier joint cost function', *The Journal of Transport Economics and Policy*, 15(2):135–153.
Harmatuck, D.J. (1985) 'Short run motor carrier cost functions for five large common carriers', *The Logistics and Transportation Review*, 21(3):217–237.
Harris, R.G. and Winston, C. (1983) 'Potential benefits of rail merger: An econometric analysis of network effects on service quality,' *Review of Economics and Statistics*, 65:32–40.
Hicks, J.R. (1935) 'Annual survey of economic theory: Monopoly', *Econometrica*, 3:1–20; reprinted in: G. Stigler and K. Boulding, eds., *Readings in price theory*. Chicago: Irwin, 1952, 361–383.
Hirshleifer, J. (1984) *Price Theory and Applications*, 3rd ed. Englewood Cliffs, N.J.: Prentice-Hall.
Kellner, S. and Matthewson, G.F. (1983) 'Entry, size distribution, scale, and scope economies in the life insurance industry', *Journal of Business*, 56(1):25–44.
Kim, H.Y. and Clark, R.M. (1983) 'Estimating multiproduct scale economies: An application to water supplies', U.S. Environmental Protection Agency, Municipal Environment Research Laboratory, Cincinnati, Ohio.
Kott, P.S. (1983) 'Return to scale in the U.S. life insurance industry: Comment', *Journal of Risk and Insurance*, 50(2):506–507.
Mayo, J.W. (1984) 'Multiproduct monopoly, regulation, and firm costs', *Southern Economic Journal*, 51(1):208–218.
Mayo, J.W. (1984) 'The technological determinants of the U.S. energy industry structure', *Review of Economics and Statistics*, 66:51–58.
McFadden, D. (1978) 'Cost, revenue and profit functions', in: M.A. Fuss and D. McFadden, eds., *Production economics: A dual approach to theory and applications*. Amsterdam: North-Holland.
Murray, J.D. and White, R.W. (1983) 'Economies of scale and economies of scope in multiproduct financial institutions: A study of British Columbia credit unions', *Journal of Finance*, 38:887–901.
Nadiri, M.I. and Shankerman, M. (1981) 'The structure of production, technological change and the rate of growth of total factor productivity in the Bell system,' in: T. Cowing and R. Stevenson, eds., *Productivity measurement in regulated industries*. New York: Academic Press.
Nerlove, M. (1963) 'Returns to scale in electricity supply', in: C. Christ, ed., *Measurement in economics: Studies in mathematical economics and econometrics in memory of Yehuda Grunfeld*. Stanford: Stanford University Press.
Pagano, A.M. and McKnight, C.E. (1983) 'Economies of scale in the taxicab industry: Some empirical evidence from the United States', *The Journal of Transport Economics and Policy*, 17(3):299–313.
Panzar, J.C. (1976) 'A neoclassical approach to peak load pricing', *Bell Journal of Economics*, 7:521–530.
Panzar, J.C. and Willig, R.D. (1975) 'Economies of scale and economies of scope in multi-output productions', Bell Laboratories economic discussion paper no. 33.
Panzar, J.C. and Willig, R.D. (1981) 'Economies of scope', *American Economic Review*, 71(2):268–272.
Praetz, P. (1980) 'Returns to scale in the United States life insurance industry', *The Journal of Risk and Insurance*, 47:525–533.

Praetz, P. (1983) 'Returns to scale in the United States life insurance industry: Reply', *The Journal of Risk and Insurance*, 50(2):508–509.

Praetz, P. and Beattie, M. (1982) 'Economies of scale in the Australian general insurance industry', *Australian Journal of Management*, 7(2):117–124.

Sakai, Y. (1974) 'Substitution and expansion effects in production theory: The case of joint production', *Journal of Economic Theory*, 9(3):255–274.

Scherer, F.M. (1980) *Industrial market structure and economic performance*, 2nd ed. Chicago: Rand McNally.

Scherer, F.M., Beckenstein, A.R., Kaufer, E. and Murphy, R.D. (1975) *The economics of multiplant operation: An international comparison study*. Cambridge, Mass.: Harvard University Press.

Sharkey, W.W. (1982) *The theory of natural monopoly*. Cambridge U.K.: Cambridge University Press.

Sickles, R.C. (1985) 'A nonlinear multivariate error components analysis of technology and specific factor productivity growth with an application to the U.S. airlines', *Journal of Econometrics*, 27:61–78.

Skogh, G. (1982) 'Returns to scale in the Swedish property-liability insurance industry', *The Journal of Risk and Insurance*, 49(2):218–228.

Spady, R. (1985) 'Using indexed quadratic cost functions to model network technologies', in: A.F. Daughety, ed., *Analytical studies in transport economics*. Cambridge, U.K.: Cambridge University Press.

Spady, R. and Friedlaender, A.F. (1978) 'Hedonic cost functions for the regulated trucking industry', *Bell Journal of Economics*, 9(1):159–179.

Sueyoshi, T. and Anselmo, P.C. (1986) 'The Evans and Heckman subadditivity test: Comment', *American Economic Review*, 76:854–855.

Talley, W.K., Agarwal, V.B. and Breakfield, J.W. (1986) 'Economies of density of ocean tanker ships', *The Journal of Transport Economics and Policy*, 20(1):91–99.

Tauchen, H., Fravel, F.D. and Gilbert, G. (1983) 'Cost structure and the intercity bus industry', *The Journal of Transport Economics and Policy*, 17(1):25–47.

Teece, D.J. (1980) 'Economics of scope and the scope of the enterprise', *Journal of Economic Behavior and Organization*, 1:223–247.

Varian, H. (1984) *Microeconomic analysis*. New York: Norton.

Victor, P.A. (1981) 'A translog cost function for urban bus transit', *Journal of Industrial Economics*, 23:287–304.

Wang Chiang, S.J. and Friedlaender, A.F. (1984) 'Output aggregation, network effects, and the measurement of trucking technology', *Review of Economics and Statistics*, 66:267–276.

Wang Chiang, J.S. and Friedlaender, A.F. (1985) 'Truck technology and efficient market structure', 67:250–258.

White, L.J., (1979) 'Economics of scale and the question of "natural monopoly" in the airline industry', *Journal of Air Law and Commerce*, 44:545–573.

Winston, C., et al. (1987) *Blind intersection? Policy and automobile industry*. The Brookings Institution, Washington D.C.

Chapter 2

THE THEORY OF THE FIRM

BENGT R. HOLMSTROM

Yale University

JEAN TIROLE*

Massachusetts Institute of Technology

Contents

*Support from NSF and the Sloan Foundation is gratefully acknowledged. We would like to thank Jeff Borland, Joel Demski, Bob Gibbons, Oliver Hart, Paul Milgrom, John Moore and Richard Schmalensee for very helpful comments on an earlier draft.

Handbook of Industrial Organization, Volume I, Edited by R. Schmalensee and R.D. Willig

1. Introduction

The theory of the firm has long posed a problem for economists. While substantial progress has been made on the description and analysis of market performance, firm behavior and organization have remained poorly understood. Typically, the firm has been treated in no more detail than the consumer; indeed, the standard textbook analysis of production corresponds closely to the analysis of consumption. In the light of scale differences, equal treatment is plainly peculiar. The volume of trade within firms is probably of the same order as market trade. Large firms are substantial subeconomies of their own with thousands of participants. This alone warrants more attention to non-market modes of transaction.

The nature of decision-making within firms is of a different kind than individual choice in markets. Firm members act as agents for their superiors rather than themselves. In the aggregate, firm behavior is the result of a complex joint decision process within a network of agency relationships. One can justly ask what forces ensure that the process will maximize profits as postulated in the neoclassical theory. Thus, the question of firm organization is not an independent appendix to value theory. It could well have ramifications for market analysis.

Yet another reason for studying firms – perhaps the most important one – is that firms have, as ever-developing institutions, played a central role in the growth and prosperity of a country's economy. In tandem with technological innovations, innovations in firm organization (as well as other institutions) have enhanced welfare greatly. It would seem essential to understand the underlying forces behind such institutional dynamics, both for a proper appreciation of how institutions have conditioned economic development and for policy decisions that relate to institutional change. To analyze institutional legislation purely from a market perspective, as has commonly been the case (cf. anti-trust analysis), is narrow at best.

It is our purpose to discuss analytical models of the firm that go beyond the black-box conception of a production function. Today economists are groping for a deeper understanding based on a contractual view. The firm is seen as a contract between a multitude of parties. The main hypothesis is that contractual designs, both implicit and explicit, are created to minimize transaction costs between specialized factors of production. This follows Coase's original hypothesis that institutions serve the purpose of facilitating exchange and can best be understood as optimal accommodations to contractual constraints rather than production constraints.

The premise that institutions are optimal solutions to various exchange programs warrants a comment. The approach assumes rationality of a high order.

How an efficient arrangement will be found is rarely if ever detailed. Yet, it is easy to envision problems with locating organizational improvements, because of substantial externalities in experimenting with new organizational forms. Few things are as easy to imitate as organizational designs. Information is a public good and patents that would prevent imitation have to our knowledge never been awarded.[1] The fact that organizational innovations often look like fads (witness today's take-over rush) is evidence in point. These doubts notwithstanding, the Coasian postulate lends substantial discipline to the methods of organizational analysis. It is an empirical matter to find out how closely the predictions line up with evidence and, if necessary, to elaborate later on the detailed processes of organizational change and the possible problems that informational externalities present.

A prime source of transaction costs is information. For technological reasons it pays to have people become specialized as specialization vastly expands the production potential. But along with specialization comes the problem of coordinating the actions of a differentially informed set of experts. This is costly for two reasons. Processing information takes time and effort even when parties share organizational goals. More typically, individuals have differing objectives and informational expertise may permit them to pursue their own objectives to the detriment of the organization as a whole. The organization must succeed in capturing the returns from informational expertise by alleviating the exchange hazards that inevitably accompany asymmetric information.

Consequently, much of recent analytical work on organizations has centered on an improved understanding of how one goes about contracting when people know different pieces of information of relevance for the organization as a whole. With the advent of information economics in the early 1970s, the door was opened for these studies. Our survey is chiefly directed towards reporting on the progress of these research efforts.

Oliver Williamson, Chapter 3 in this Handbook and elsewhere, has discussed at length the transaction cost point of view and some of its ramifications. Our efforts are complementary. Analytical models that attempt to articulate contractual problems are useful insofar that they succeed in offering a firmer test of our intuition and logic. They are not meant as competing alternatives to less formal theorizing, but rather as supportive exercises. For those looking for a broader view of the firm we recommend reading Williamson's chapter as well as the related chapter by Martin Perry (Chapter 4) on vertical integration.

With all young and immature fields of inquiry, a survey is made difficult by the limited vision and generality of the initial research efforts. This is particularly true when it comes to modelling the firm. The theory of the firm addresses a wide

[1]Problems with appropriating the returns from organizational innovations are somewhat alleviated by consulting firms.

range of questions. At the highest level of aggregation, one is interested in the firm's behavior towards markets. From there one goes down all the way to individual labor contracts and the organization of work in the smallest units of production. Obviously, no single model or theory will capture all elements of the puzzle. Nor is it clear where one most appropriately begins the analysis. As a consequence, modelling efforts have been all over the map, often with more attention paid to the methodological side than to the economic side of the analysis.

Trying to organize these fragments of a theory into a coherent economic framework is difficult. Indeed, an easier task would have been to present the material either choronologically or from a methodological point of view. There has been a distinct line of development in modelling approaches. But, we have tried to face the challenge of looking at present models from the perspective of issues rather than methodology. We hope this will reveal gaps in the overall structure of research on the firm and thereby direct future efforts. Our discussion will not be instructive for those seeking to learn about methods and techniques. For a more methodological perspective on much the same material the reader may find the survey paper by Hart and Holmstrom (1987) useful. [See also Chapter 24 in this Handbook by David Baron on optimal regulation regimes, which contains a detailed discussion of related modelling techniques, as well as Caillaud et al. (1988).]

The chapter is organized around four issues. The first concerns the limits and nature of firms. What determines a firm's boundaries and what explains its existence? The second issue is the financing of firms. What determines a firm's capital structure? The third issue concerns the role of management. How does separation of ownership and control affect a firm's objectives? The last issue is the internal organization of the firm. How is the firm's hierarchy structured and what arc the rules of decision-making and the nature of rewards within that hierarchy?

Needless to say, these four issues are interrelated and strains arise when one tries to deal with them separately. Moreover, many models, being so abstract and methodologically oriented, say a little about all the issues rather than a lot about just one. The reader will encounter, if not the same arguments, at least very similar ones in separate places of the chapter.

2. The limits of integration

What is the purpose of firms and what determines their scale and scope? These are two basic questions that a theory of the firm must address. Yet, satisfactory answers have proved very difficult to come by. The challenge is to offer a genuine trade-off between the benefits and costs of integration. One needs to explain both why firms exist as well as why all transactions are not organized within a single firm. While it is relatively easy to envision reasons for integration, it is substantially harder to articulate costs of increased size.

Williamson (1975, 1985) has phrased the problem sharply. He asks why could one not merge two firms into one and, by *selective intervention*, accomplish more in the integrated case than in the decentralized case. In other words, let the two firms continue as before and interfere (from the top) only when it is obviously profitable. The fact that there are limits to firm size must imply that selective intervention is not always feasible. Trying to figure out why this is so provides a useful focus for theorizing about the nature of the firm.

Traditional theories of firm size – beginning with Viner's (1932) classical analysis of long-run average cost curves – are technology based. Scale economies explain concentrated production while minimum average costs determine the optimal size. More substance can be added by specifying particular cost structures. Baumol et al. (1982) offer a considerably extended version of scale choice in their analysis of contestable markets (see Chapter 1 by John Panzar's in this Handbook).[2] Lucas (1978) and Kihlstrom and Laffont (1979) focus on cost-minimizing allocations of scarce managerial inputs (talent and risk tolerance, respectively), identifying firms with managers. In Geanakopolos and Milgrom (1985) firm size is determined by pairing the benefits of coordination with the costs of communication and acquiring information. There are also dynamic models – beginning with Lucas (1967) – which center on adjustment costs with the objective of explaining finite growth rates rather than absolute limits to firm size. A natural source of adjustment costs is imperfect knowledge either about the technology [Jovanovic (1982), Lippman and Rumelt (1982) and Hopenhayn (1986)] or about worker–job matches [Prescott and Visscher (1980)].

These technological models offer interesting insights into the role of firms but none is able to address the costs of selective intervention. They all fail to provide a genuine trade-off between integration and non-integration. This suggests that firm limits are determined by contracting costs. For the rest of this section we will focus on the contractual avenue, with particular attention paid to incomplete contracting.

2.1. *Incomplete contracts*

We begin with a brief description of Alchian and Demsetz's (1972) theory of the firm, which is contractual, but nevertheless fails to draw clear organizational

[2] Vassilakis (1985) is another notable contribution. His model provides a theory of vertical integration, derived from the tension between competition for rents and the desire to exploit scale economies.

boundaries, at least as originally envisioned. The same type of failure is common to most early contracting work. The problem can be remedied within the framework of incomplete contracting, which also suggests a reinterpretation of the Alchian–Demsetz theory.

Alchian and Demsetz's theory centers on the incentive problems of joint production. Suppose it takes two workers to perform a given task and assume initially that the workers form a partnership. The design problem amounts to choosing a reward structure for each of the partners. How should the partners divide the proceeds from the joint output? If the inputs can be observed and contracted upon, the answer is simple. Pay one the cost of his input and let the other receive the residual. Then it will be in each partner's interest to set input levels in a way that is socially efficient.

But what if inputs cannot be verified so that rewards must be based on joint output alone? This leads to a free-rider problem. There is no way of dividing the joint output in such a way that each worker receives his social marginal product in equilibrium. To see this, suppose the technology is given as $y = f(a_1, a_2)$, where a_1 and a_2 are the effort levels of the two workers, measured in effort cost units. The efficient choice of effort would occur where the partial derivatives $f_1 = f_2 = 1$. Now, let $s_1(y)$ and $s_2(y) = y - s_1(y)$ be the rules by which the joint output is divided between the two partners. Assume for simplicity that these rules are differentiable. In a non-cooperative equilibrium, workers would choose input levels so that $s_1'f_1 = s_2'f_2 = 1$. For this equilibrium to coincide with the efficient choice of inputs, it must be that $s_1' = s_2' = 1$. But that cannot be, because $s_2' = 1 - s_1'$.

The problem is that cheating cannot be detected. Based on joint output alone, either of the two workers could be responsible for a suboptimal outcome. A natural solution would be to introduce some monitoring and this is what Alchian and Demsetz propose. They argue for an organizational change in which a monitor is brought in to measure inputs and mete out appropriate rewards. Of course there may be a problem with the monitor not having the incentive to monitor – after all, there is still joint production, this time with three workers. To solve this dilemma, it is suggested that the monitor is given the residual rights to output. He pays the input factors fixed amounts (contingent upon proper input supply) and keeps the difference. In the tradition of identifying ownership with the rights to the residual income stream, the monitor in this story also becomes the owner of the firm.

The limited extent of partnerships and cooperatives in our economy lends some support to the owner-monitor model, since free-riding could be a big problem in these organizations. The importance of monitoring is also evident quite generally. Firms invest in elaborate control systems joined with complex reward structures, implicit and explicit. Without monitoring, the problem of paying individual rewards so as to equate marginal and social products, even approximately, would be overwhelming.

Yet, the simple story of the owner-monitor has its problems. First, those who do the monitoring in firms are rarely the residual claimants. Except for small entrepreneurial firms, owners hardly monitor management, at least not for the purpose of separating individual contributions. In fact, it has frequently been suggested that one of the major problems with corporate organization is the limited interest it creates for a diverse ownership to monitor management (see Section 4). Second, horizontal mergers are hard to understand from a monitoring perspective. One would have to argue that there are scale economies in monitoring, which seems implausible.[3] Third, monitoring is not the distinguishing feature of corporations. Partnerships and cooperatives certainly have supervision as well. One might argue, in line with what was said above, that the distinctive feature of corporations is the separation of ownership and active participation in firm decisions. This point is elaborated on in Holmstrom (1982a), where it is shown that separation (budget-breaking) may be desirable from an incentive perspective.

The main problem, however, is that the monitoring story (as told) does not offer an explanation of firm boundaries. Nothing would preclude the monitor from being an employee of a separate firm with a service contract that specifies his reward as the residual output. Similarly with the workers. They could be monitored and paid as independent agents rather than employees.

The problem with organizational anonymity can be traced to the nature of contracts considered. Most contractual models have the property that contract execution is independent of the institutional setting in which it is placed. (Alchian and Demsetz make a point of erasing the distinction between employment and service relationships.) Contracts which are *comprehensive* in the sense that they will never need to be revised or complemented, are of this kind. If parties can agree today to a contract that needs no changes in the future, then it does not matter what affiliations the parties have and hence where the contract is embedded organizationally. Governance structures become important only insofar as the evolution of the contract varies with the organizational setting.[4]

Williamson (1975, 1985) has argued for a long time that comprehensive contracting analyses are misguided and that an incomplete contract perspective is essential for explaining the relative merits of governance implied by different organizational forms. He emphasizes the problems caused by incomplete contracting in relationships where parties make irreversible investments. His standard paradigm is one in which partners are locked into a relationship ex post

[3]One paper that does develop the theme of monitoring economies is Diamond (1984). He argues that banks as creditors may perform the task of monitoring more effectively than a diverse ownership. However, the logic is quite different from Alchian and Demsetz's theory.

[4]We use the term comprehensive rather than complete in order to avoid a mistaken association with Arrow–Debreu contracts. Contracts that are not comprehensive are called incomplete, despite a potential confusion with the traditional meaning of incomplete contracts. The term is so widely used that it is likely to resist change.

because of investments that have substantially higher value within the relationship than outside of it. To the extent that one cannot specify ex ante how the surplus should be divided between the two, i.e. if one cannot write a comprehensive contract, the division will depend on ex post bargaining positions. Bargaining positions in turn will depend on the organizational context. Where relationship-specific investments are large, Williamson argues against the use of market exchange, because parties will fear that they will be unable to appropriate the returns from their investments in an ex post non-competitive bargaining environment. Bringing the transaction within a firm will offer safeguards against opportunistic behavior. [See also Klein et al. (1978).]

Grossman and Hart (1986) have sharpened the argument by suggesting that the crucial difference between governance structures resides with their implied residual decision rights. Residual decision rights are those rights to control that have not been explicitly contracted for beforehand. In Grossman and Hart's framework, the allocation of residual decision rights is identified with the ownership of assets. Thus, ownership defines the default options in an incomplete contract.[5] A transaction within the firm (concerning the firm's assets) is controlled by the owner of the firm (or the manager, if he has been delegated the authority) in those situations where the contract does not specify a unique course of action. In contrast, a market transaction must be resolved through negotiation between relevant asset owners if the contract is incomplete. These two modes of transaction will imply a different division of the surplus from the relationship ex post and therefore lead to different levels of investment in relationship specific capital ex ante. Let us illustrate this with a simple example.

Example

Consider a buyer and a seller who have signed a contract for exchanging a unit of a good tomorrow at a specified price. They are aware of the possibility that a technological innovation may make the present design redundant, but they cannot foresee the nature of the innovation and hence cannot make the contract contingent on a change in design [e.g. assume there is always a costless but non-improving change in design that the court cannot distinguish from a real change so that it would be fruitless to index the contract merely on a design change; see Hart and Moore (1988) for an analysis of contingent contracting].

[5]Grossman and Hart's definition of ownership is essentially the same as the legal notion, though the law, of course, recognizes a variety of different ownership and institutional modes. For instance, the employment relationship has its own set of defaults that distinguishes it from a sale of services by somebody outside the firm. Simon's (1951) seminal paper on the employment relationship makes a similar observation. More recently, the implications of different legal blueprints on the organization and operation of firms has been elaborated on by Masten (1986b).

Denote the buyer's benefit from a design change by v and the seller's cost of implementing the design change by c. These figures are net of benefits and costs from the present design. The values of v and c are uncertain today; tomorrow their actual values will be realized. Both the buyer and the seller will be able to observe the realized values of v and c, but in order to preclude the possibility of contracting on the realization, assume that the values cannot be verified by a third party.

For concreteness assume there are only two possible values for v: 20 and 40; and two for c: 10 and 30. The buyer can influence the outcome of v by making an unobserved investment today. Let $x = \text{Prob}(v = 40)$ represent the buyer's investment decision and assume the cost is $10x^2$. Similarly, the seller makes a relationship specific investment $y = \text{Prob}(c = 10)$ at a cost $10y^2$.

Ownership determines who has the right to veto a design change. There are three cases of interest. In *non-integration* both sides can block a change. In *buyer-integration* the buyer can implement a change by fiat and in *seller-integration* the reverse is true. In addition one needs to specify what happens to cost and benefit streams under the different regimes. In Grossman and Hart's original analysis benefits and costs were inalienable. In our context it would mean that the seller bears the costs y and c and the buyer bears the cost x and receives the benefit v, irrespective of ownership structure. We will assume instead that v and c (and later x and y as well) get transferred with ownership. In reality most financial streams get transferred. However, one needs to explain why these streams cannot be transferred by contract rather than ownership change. Our argument is that separating the return streams of the productive assets from the decision rights of these assets is not feasible, because the return streams cannot be verified. Put differently, the owner of the asset can use the asset to generate returns for his own benefit, which cannot for reasons of verifiability be appropriated by the owner of the return stream. (For example, a contract that specifies that the buyer pays the costs of the seller if a design change is implemented is subject to misuse by the seller – he can load costs onto the buyer which are unrelated to the design change.) Thus, incomplete contracting explains the joining of decision rights concerning asset use with the title to residual return streams.[6]

Let us first analyze the non-integrated case. There are four possible outcomes for the pair (v, c). In three of them $v > c$. Assuming that bargaining is costless, these three situations will lead to the implementation of the new design since

[6]In general, of course, parts of the return stream as well as the decision rights can and will be contracted for. Incentive contracts are examples of the first kind, while leasing contracts and delegation of authority are examples of the second kind. Note though that even in these cases there is typically a connection between the right to decide and the financial responsibility for the outcome of the decision.

both sides can observe v and c and implementation is efficient. Only if $v = 20$ and $c = 30$ will the new design not be implemented.

Assume that both sides have equal bargaining power so that it is reasonable to predict an equal division of the surplus from implementation of the new design. For example, if $v = 40$ and $c = 10$, the price of the change will be negotiated so that both sides gain an additional 15 (buyer pays seller 25 for the change). With this rule for dividing the surplus the marginal return to the buyer from investing x is $5y + 5$, where y is the forecasted level of investment of the seller; and symmetrically for the seller. The Nash equilibrium in investment choices will then be $x = 1/3$ and $y = 1/3$, considering the marginal costs of investment: $20x$ and $20y$, respectively. The social surplus, net of investment costs, is $50/9 = 5.6$ for the non-integrated form of organization.

Consider next, buyer integration. The buyer's net return in the second period is $v - c$ by our earlier arguments. The seller will merely cover his labor costs and hence earn zero returns in the second period. Consequently, he will have no incentive to invest in the relationship ($y = 0$). The cost of implementing the new design will therefore equal 30 for certain. The buyer's returns from investing x are $10x - 10x^2$ (if the value of the new design is 40 it will be implemented and the buyer will receive the total gain of 10). Thus, the buyer will choose $x = 1/2$. The social surplus, net of investment costs, is in this case 2.5.

The third case of seller integration is symmetric to the previous one and therefore yields the same social surplus.[7]

Since the buyer and the seller can divide the social surplus in any desired way by a transfer payment in the first period it is reasonable to assume that they will agree on implementing the socially efficient organizational form. We conclude that with the particular parameter values chosen here, buying and selling would be conducted under separate ownership.

The example demonstrates that with incomplete contracts the allocation of residual decision rights via ownership can affect investments in relationship-specific capital and thereby efficiency. In particular, this mode of analysis offers a reason why selective intervention is not possible and therefore why integration may not be desirable. The prerequisite is that initial investments are not contractible and comprehensive contracts are infeasible; it is not possible to sign a contract today that will be effective in all contingencies tomorrow.

In the example, specific conclusions about the desirability of integration obviously depend on parameter values. For instance, suppose the high cost is 11

[7]The fact that the two forms of integration are identical is an artifact of symmetry. In general, they will be different. This is interesting since the literature on integration has commonly taken for granted that it does not matter who takes over whom. There are only two modes: integration and non-integration.

instead of 30. Then buyer integration is best because reducing costs becomes less important than increasing value. Similarly, changes in the costs of relationship-specific investments would affect the optimal design. Such comparative static exercises are rather naive in this overly simple setting, but nevertheless point to possibilities in deriving testable hypotheses.

More interestingly, we note that the organizational design is quite sensitive to the nature of assets involved. In particular, the role of human capital as an inalienable asset is important. The ownership of human capital cannot legally be transferred and hence places particular constraints on contracting. Going back to the example, the assumption was made that investment costs were borne by the investing persons irrespective of ownership structure – in other words, non-transferable human assets were used, and their services could not be compensated for by incentive contracts because of enforcement problems. Incentives could only be affected by a change in ownership of physical assets. However, suppose instead that the investments are financial outlays, necessarily borne by the owner (for reasons explained above). Now the seller-employee under buyer integration would have no objections to incurring those costs, because the money would not be out of his pocket. Consequently, buyer integration (or seller integration) would lead to first-best and be superior to non-integration.

Notice that only this version of the example matches Williamson's vision of the benefits of integration. Here integration does reduce opportunistic tendencies, while in the earlier version it was just the reverse. Apparently the value of integration is quite sensitive to the nature of assets being used for investment as well as to the limitations in contracting that relate to return streams. Our two variations fit the common claim that human capital investment and use is best encouraged by independent ownership, while coordination of capital investments is better accomplished by joint ownership.

Although the example was inspired by Williamson's central theme that ex post contracting hazards distort ex ante investments and that changes in ownership affect outcomes via a change in bargaining positions, we want to stress that this scenario is not the only one in which ownership plays a role. It could also be the case that bargaining costs are affected directly by a change in ownership.[8] For instance, suppose that information about v and c remains private to the buyer and seller, respectively. Neither can observe the other's parameter value. Also, suppose as before that the nature of the design innovation cannot be envisioned in period one so a mechanism for communicating the private information cannot

[8]Milgrom and Roberts (1987) have emphasized the role of bargaining costs more generally. They note that incomplete contracting need not lead to inefficiencies if bargaining is costless and there is no unobservable specific investment. [See also Fudenberg et al. (1986), Malcomson and Spinnewyn (1988), Masten (1986a) and Rey and Salanié (1986) on gains to long-term contracting.] Crawford (1986) is an early contribution to the role of bargaining under incomplete contracting. Crawford shows that ex ante underinvestment is not always implied by non-integration. Tirole (1986a) provides reasonable conditions under which underinvestment will occur, for instance, in the context of procurement contracting.

be set up today. Then, assuming that bargaining under asymmetric information is costly (any of a number of models of bargaining deliver this; either through costly delays or through incomplete trading),[9] we would typically conclude that ownership would matter for the outcome of the bargaining process.

The simplest case is the following. Departing from our earlier parameterization, assume that v is always greater than c. Then integration will always lead to an immediate implementation of the design change. By contrast, non-integration will lead to costly negotiations on how to split the surplus, which carries only social costs and no benefits. Buyer integration is clearly superior, because it will prevent needless delays in decision-making.[10] Presumably, the value of authority is frequently one of resolving conflicting private interests in an expedient fashion. One would expect that authority relationships are more prevalent, the more costly are the delays (as is the case in an army in a wartime economy, or in a complex hierarchy when conflicts between two individuals hinders the proper functioning of the organization).

Let us finally return to the Alchian–Demsetz theory with which we began this section. We have emphasized that changes in ownership may imply inevitable transfers of return streams, because of incomplete contracting. Therefore ownership may be the only means by which proper financial incentives can be provided. Consider joint production in this light. Suppose that one worker's marginal product is more easily (though imperfectly) assessed than the other's. This is not possible in the original Alchian–Demsetz model, because the joint product was assumed observable, which implies that knowing one of the marginal products tells the other. But if we accept that the joint product is not always observed or contractable (actual returns will be revealed only in the long run, say), then the distinction makes sense and ownership will matter. Ownership should go with the input factor whose marginal contribution is hardest to assess (relative to the value of that factor). Reinterpreted this way, the Alchian–Demsetz theory can be read as suggesting that the monitor is the owner because his product is important but diffuse (cf. discussion in Subsections 5.2 and 5.3).

We do not subscribe to this revised version of the monitoring story either, because it is rare to see owners monitor the firm's operations. We believe it is more likely that the contribution of capital is hardest to measure, because capital is easy to misappropriate. Consequently, capital should hold title to the residual return stream. This idea deserves further elaboration. Our main point here is that the allocation of return streams via ownership can be a significant component in understanding which factor becomes the owner. This is overlooked in the model provided in Grossman and Hart (1986). Indeed, the authors stress the importance

[9]See, for instance, Fudenberg and Tirole (1983), Sobel and Takahashi (1983), Cramton (1984) and Admati and Perry (1987).

[10]Milgrom and Roberts (1987) make the same observation. The idea goes back at least to Weitzman (1974) who noted that centralized decision-making can be much more effective than decentralization in delivering an urgently needed service, which is known to be socially desirable.

of not confusing return streams with ownership of physical assets. This contrasts with the older property rights literature, which identified ownership expressly with the right to a residual return stream [see De Alessi (1983) for a recent survey].

Our view is that these two definitions really should be subsumed in one: ownership provides residual rights to all kinds of assets, physical as well as financial. The right to a residual return stream is after all nothing more than a right to decide how to spend the firm's money, which has not been explicitly contracted for.

2.2. Information flows and incomplete contracts

Williamson (1985, p. 134) has taken issue with the notion that firms are primarily distinguished by their implied residual decision rights. He wants to place corresponding emphasis on the fact that organizational changes imply concomitant changes in information flows. Certain information that is available at one cost before integration may no longer be available at the same cost after integration. Assuming for the moment that this is true, it is a short step to conclude that organizational design can influence performance, since information is used both in decision-making and in the construction of incentive schemes.

It remains to argue why the set of feasible information systems would depend on organizational structure. Grossman and Hart (1986) expressly take the view that this is not the case. Differences in information flows are endogenously chosen, not exogenously conditioned by the choice of organizational form.

Consider a concrete example. Two publicly traded firms merge. Typically, one of the stocks will be withdrawn from trading as a consequence. This elimination of a variable that is crucial for managerial incentives would seem to validate Williamson's position. But one must really ask why the firm could not continue to trade both stocks. In fact, it can and sometimes it will. When General Motors bought EDS, a new GM–E stock carrying no voting right was created, the value of which was tied to EDS performance.[11] Presumably this was done to maintain an independent outside monitor of EDS. As it happens, this arrangement has run into difficulties in a way that suggests why it may be infeasible or ineffective to trade stocks on pieces of a company. EDS and the rest of GM have had a hard time agreeing on transfer prices. Apparently they are trying to resolve contractual disputes arising from an incomplete contract. Indeed, brief thought would suggest that as long as GM has substantial control rights in the transfer of goods – and by definition it will as soon as unspecified contingencies arise – the GM–E stock will to some extent be manipulable by GM. This itself does not render the stock valueless. The stock can be protected by covenants and in the

[11] We are grateful to Mark Wolfson for bringing this example to our attention.

GM–EDS case it was. However, as soon as covenants are necessary and/or the presence of GM–E stock causes distortions in transfers, the costs of replicating the old pre-merger stock information are higher than before or – more likely – the information simply cannot be replicated.

The loss of a stock measure is but one instance of a change in information flow associated with a transfer of authority. Centralized procurement provides another example. For instance, at GM, managerial compensation at the division level is based to a significant extent on division as well as on corporate profits. Centralized procurement of materials and parts (which is meant to exploit returns to scale in procurement and increase GM's bargaining power with suppliers) has generated little enthusiasm [see Corey (1978)]. This is partly because the division manager loses control over the cost of inputs that represent a non-negligible fraction of his budget. The measure of his performance becomes garbled by centralized procurement.

We conclude that organizational changes affect the cost of information flows. Interestingly, the argument for how this comes about must apparently rely on an incomplete contract somewhere in the chain of logic. Thus, the information paradigm and the incomplete contract paradigm are not competitors at all. Incomplete contracting provides the proper framework in which to discuss implications on information flows due to ownership change.

Milgrom (1988) offers a somewhat related discussion. In looking for limits on firm size, he is led to the idea of "influence costs". By influence costs he means undesired employee activities that are intended to change a superior's actions to the sole benefit of the employee. (The emphasis is on "undesired", since subordinates are continuously invited to influence decision-making in constructive ways.) He argues that non-market organizations are particularly susceptible to influence costs, because of their authority structure and the quasi-rents associated with jobs within the hierarchy. Stringent rules and bureaucratic inflexibility can be understood as rational responses, intended to limit the scope of authority and the returns to influence activity.

An important case of costly influence activity arises, because employees are concerned with their careers. They do things with an eye on how their actions will change their superior's (or other evaluators', like the market's) perceptions about their qualifications for future (more desirable) jobs. Such a career concern model is presented in Holmstrom (1982b). The analysis shows that a labor market, which rationally learns (makes inferences) about ability from past performance, can induce employees to exert excess effort early in their careers as well as force managers to make wrong investment decisions [see also Narayanan (1985) and Stein (1987)]. In order to reduce these costs, it may be desirable to change managerial incentives through explicit contracts [Holmstrom and Ricart i Costa (1986)], limit the manager's exposure in the labor market [Gibbons (1985)] or make other organizational adjustments. The fact that young professionals tend to join established firms before going on their own may be explained, in part, as a way of limiting market exposure that would otherwise lead to distorting influence activities.

Thus, influence activities are pursued both in markets and in hierarchies; indeed, in all situations where individuals care about their careers. As information flows unavoidably change with the organizational form (because of contractual incompleteness), the returns from influence activities differ across organizations. This may provide a basis for a partial theory of organizational choice.

2.3. Reputation

Another theory of the firm that takes as its starting point the inability or the cost to sign comprehensive contracts has been offered by MaCaulay (1963), Williamson (1975, pp. 107–108) and most explicitly by Kreps (1984) and Cremer (1986a). In this theory the soul of the firm is its reputation. Reputation is an intangible asset that is beneficial for transacting in environments where one frequently encounters unforseen contingencies. Reputation offers an implicit promise for a fair or reasonable adjudication process when events occur that are uncovered by contract. The more faith the firm's trading partners have in the firm's ability and willingness to fill in contractual voids in a reasonable (efficient) manner, the lower the costs of transacting. Thus, establishing and nurturing a good reputation is of much strategic significance.

Kreps argues that "corporate culture" is a main vehicle in this process. It serves two purposes: it conditions and synchronizes the employees' behavior in accordance with desirable reputational objectives and it sends a message to its transacting partners, which informs about expectations of the trading relationship. Thus, the firm's corporate culture acts as the language for telling "how things are done and how they are meant to be done".

As an example, IBM's policy not to lay off employees (in the absence of misdemeanor) is part of its corporate culture. It is not a guarantee that comes in the form of a written or even oral contract. It is a principle that has been established by the historic record. This distinction is crucial. If it were a written contract it would not be as flexible. One can imagine that under some yet to be seen event there will be a need to back out of the pattern and lay workers off. With a contract this would trigger expensive negotiations and perhaps lead to a distribution of surplus that if foreseen would interfere with a smooth and efficient employment policy today. With only a principle and an implicit promise, the adjudication process can be less straining and give a division of surplus that is more conducive to efficient trading today. This of course assumes that IBM can be relied upon. It is crucial for IBM to portray an image of reliability by not laying off anybody except under extreme circumstances. In consequence, today's workers are partly protected by the threat of IBM losing the value of its investment in reputation.[12]

The management of reputation capital is affected by the allocation of decision rights. It is important to note that only those with residual decision rights can establish a reputation. The other parties will simply follow prescribed conditions in the contract, which signal nothing about future intentions.[13] Thus, parties with significant interest invested in acquiring a reputation should typically be given residual decision rights, assuming that the potential loss of reputation will assure a more efficient and fair adjudication process in the event of the unforeseen.[14] For instance, in transactions between firms and single individuals, one would expect the firm to have the authority to fill contractual gaps if the firm is more visible in the market and transacts more frequently. [Another reason is that the firm has the relevant information; Simon (1951).]

A central ingredient in a reputational theory of the firm is the mechanism for transferring reputation capital from one generation of managers to the next. Both Cremer (1986a) and Kreps (1984) offer overlapping-generations models in which transfers are feasible. They show that there are supergame equilibria in which reputations will be maintained. In Kreps's model, managers own the firm and thereby the title to future income streams. These can be sold to future managers, who buy themselves into a favorable supergame equilibrium and continue to play it. In Cremer's model the reputation asset is not sold explicitly. It is simply the case that new managers enter into the hierarchy over time and become recipients of as well as contributors to the favorable equilibrium returns.

One problem with the reputation story, taken as the defining characteristic of firms, is that it leaves unexplained why firms could not simply be labels or associations that carry the requisite reputation capital. At present the theory does not make a distinction between the firm as a label and the firm as a collection of physical and human capital assets.

Another dimension that deserves elaboration is the joint responsibility for reputation in a firm with many employees. After all, reputations are in the end attached to individuals and their actions. The incentives of individuals not to milk the firm's reputation has not been clarified; it must be the case that somehow the incentives of the stock-holding layer trickles down through the rest of the hierarchy. The internal organization models studied in Section 5 may have something to say about this.

[12]A recent article in the *Wall Street Journal* (8 April 1987) provides a corroborative account of IBM's corporate culture.

[13]Note also that reputation can only be built if explicit contracting is costly or incomplete. Else there would be no cost to defaulting on an implicit promise; one could costlessly continue with an explicit contract after the default.

[14]A concern for reputation need not always be good. Managers overly concerned about their reputation may not always be trusted with authority. [See Holmstrom and Ricart i Costa (1986).]

A more technical point is that reputation is viewed as a bootstrap phenomenon; its formalization relies on supergames, which permit many outcomes. Reputation may, but need not, arise in equilibrium. An alternative theory of reputation was offered by Kreps and Wilson (1982) and Milgrom and Roberts (1982). The reputation of a firm in such a model could refer, for instance, to the outsiders' beliefs that the firm's managers may be intrinsically honest or that their cost of reneging on an implicit contract may be sufficiently high to discourage unfriendly behavior [Hart and Holmstrom (1987)]. The way intrinsic honesty is transmitted would be technological in the second case, and sociological in the first (intrinsically honest managers would only choose successors with the same attitude towards business).

2.4. Concluding remark

In discussing the limits of firm organization we have heavily advertised the incomplete contracting paradigm and the attendant idea of allocating residual decision rights via ownership. It is the only approach we have seen that succeeds in resolving the selective intervention puzzle raised by Williamson. Obviously, the incomplete contracting framework is not in itself a theory of the firm or its limits. It is merely a tool – an extremely useful one – for articulating, in a clear and consistent way, specific hypotheses about the determinants of firm size. It is in this spirit that we offered the elaborations in Subsections 2.2 and 2.3.

The questions of selective intervention and the nature of the firm are of interest in their own right. One can hardly be satisfied with a theory of the firm that does not understand its main purpose. However, one should not overlook the equally important consideration that, eventually, there is a need to tie the logical arguments for firm limits to the empirical facts about size distribution. Industries show systematic differences in this regard. Also, the finding that firms grow roughly in accordance with Gibrat's Law [growth rates are independent of size; see Mansfield (1962) and Evans (1986)] must be attended to. It remains to be seen how successful the incomplete contracting paradigm will be in addressing itself to real data.

3. Capital structure

Work on the capital structure of the firm was paralyzed for two decades upon discovery of Modigliani and Miller's (1958, 1963) famous irrelevance propositions. Their finding that the value of the firm in a frictionless and tax-free capital market was in fact independent of the mix of equity and debt, as well as changes in dividend policy, stunned the profession. Yet, their reasoning was simple. If the firm's value could be changed by altering the financial mix, this would imply a pure arbitrage opportunity. An entrepreneur could come in and purchase the firm, repackage the return stream to capitalize on the higher value and yet assure himself of the same risk by arranging privately an identically leveraged position.

The elegant logic of arbitrage proved extremely useful in the development of finance in general, but troubling in the context of capital structure. As Ross (1977) notes, if capital structure does not matter, how can one explain the substantial amount of time and resources corporate treasurers and investment bankers spend on decisions concerning financing? And although the empirical evidence on debt–equity patterns is quite inconclusive [see papers in the volume by Friedman (1985)], it is hard to escape the casual impression that regularities do exist both cross-sectionally and over time. Capital structure does not appear to be a matter of indifference, either on the input side or the output side of the decision.

Efforts to introduce a role for financial decision making have focused on challenging the major premise in the MM-logic, namely that the firm's return stream (or more generally the market perception of the return stream) is unaffected by capital structure. Indeed, the basic logic says that no matter how one divides up a *given* return stream, either over time or across states, the total value stays the same, provided that the capital market offers linear pricing of the pieces (which free arbitrage will imply).

But it is quite possible that the return stream itself may be altered by the financial decision. (Social) bankruptcy costs and non-neutral tax treatment provide one line of reasoning which was pursued early on as an amendment to the MM-theory. Taxes favor debt financing, while equity reduces expected bankruptcy costs. However, this trade-off is not compelling, because debt–equity ratios have been a concern much longer than taxes have existed.

We will discuss three more recent theories of capital structure that also turn on the idea that perceived or real return streams are affected by the firm's financing decision. One argument is based on incentive reasoning. The capital structure is part of an incentive scheme for management; if it is changed the incentives for management – and hence the return stream – are changed. A second argument rests on signalling. If the firm (or its management) is better informed about the return stream, then capital structure may signal information and alter market perceptions about future returns. Finally, a third line takes note of the fact that changes in capital structure involve changes in control rights, which in a world of imperfect information and incomplete markets have ramifications for decision-making.

3.1. The incentive argument

Jensen and Meckling (1976) originated the incentive argument. They developed a theory of the firm, with specific emphasis on capital structure, based on the notion that firms are run by self-interested agents. The separation of ownership and control gives rise to agency costs. Articulating what these agency costs are, gives the theory its operational content.

According to Jensen and Meckling, there are agency costs associated with both equity financing and debt financing. When "outside" equity is issued (equity not held by those in control), it invites slack. If 50 percent of the firm is owned by outsiders, manager-entrepreneurs realize that each wasted dollar will cost them only fifty cents. Cost-reducing activities will not be pursued to the point where social marginal benefits equal social marginal costs; instead, they will be chosen to equalize private benefits and costs, with resulting excess slack. Of course, the less of a claim on the firm that managers have, the weaker will be the incentives to reduce slack. Thus, from a "shirking" point of view, the firm should be fully owned by management with no outside equity at all. To the extent that there is a need for outside capital it should all be in the form of debt.

Having managers own 100 percent of the firm is not efficient for other reasons. First, managers may want to diversify their portfolio for risk-spreading reasons. Second, financially constrained managers need to raise debt to finance a large holding in the firm. But debt financing incurs agency costs as well. Jensen and Meckling elaborate on the traditional theme that debt and equity holders will not share the same investment objectives. Typically, a highly leveraged firm controlled by the equity holder will pursue riskier investment strategies than debt holders would like (because of bankruptcy).

Pitting the agency cost of equity against the agency cost of debt produces the desired trade-off. The optimal capital structure minimizes total agency costs. The debt–equity ratio is set so that marginal agency cost of each category is equalized. Of course, measurement problems are enormous and Jensen and Meckling offer little guidance for quantification. One qualitative prediction they note is that firms with significant shirking problems – ones in which managers can easily lower the mean return by "theft, special treatment of favored customers, ease of consumption of leisure on the job, etc.", for example restaurants – will have little outside equity. On the other hand, firms which can alter significantly the riskiness of the return – for example conglomerates – will, according to Jensen and Meckling, rely relatively more on equity financing.

Obviously, the above account of agency costs is terse. Jensen and Meckling elaborate on alternative safeguards that can limit both types of agency costs. These include monitoring as well as explicit contracting. We will take up some of these arguments in the next section in connection with managerial incentives.

Grossman and Hart (1982) work out a formal agency model with a slightly different emphasis. In their model a professional manager with little or no stake in the firm (presumably because of limited wealth) controls the allocation of funds raised, either through equity or debt, from the capital market. The manager's allocation decision is very simple. He has to decide how much to invest in a project with uncertain returns and how much to spend on himself. Funds diverted to private consumption should be interpreted as a stream of benefits (perks, status, etc.) that come from investments (or distortions in investment) that are not valued by shareholders.

The manager does not want to spend all the money on himself, because if the firm goes bankrupt and he is fired, he will no longer be able to enjoy the stream of benefits that he has set up for himself. The trade-off is between a higher stream of private benefits versus a higher risk of bankruptcy and a consequent loss of all perks (it is assumed that more funds invested in the real project will lower bankruptcy risk). Since the actual model has only one period, the allocation decision must of course precede the realization of the investment return or else the manager would always take out the residual, leaving nothing for equity owners.

The key point of the paper is that since the manager has to bear bankruptcy costs, debt financing can be used as an incentive device. Debt acts as a bond which the manager posts to assure equity holders that their funds will not be completely misappropriated. The choice of debt is influenced by its incentive effect as well as the risk that the manager will have to carry. Too much debt will imply excessive risk, while too little will encourage fund diversion.

If there is no uncertainty, then the firm must be financed by debt alone, because the manager can pocket all excess returns.[15] A less trivial conclusion is that increased project risk will increase the market value of equity and reduce the market value of debt. Unfortunately, the model analysis is so complicated that much more cannot be said economically.[16]

The major shortcoming of these and other incentive arguments is that they beg the question: Why should capital structure be used as an incentive instrument, when the manager could be offered explicit incentives that do not interfere with the choice of financing mode? For an unexplained reason both Jensen and Meckling, as well as Grossman and Hart, assume that the only way to influence the manager is via changes in capital structure. But this is true only if the manager's compensation contract remains fixed. If the contract can be varied,

[15]A related argument is in Diamond (1984) and Gale and Hellwig (1985). These papers establish that, if the entrepreneur is the only one who can observe the outcome of the return and therefore appropriate all residual income, then the only feasible investment contract is a standard debt contract. The distinguishing feature of the Grossman–Hart model is that diversion of funds occurs before returns are in.

[16]The idea of debt as a bonding device can be exploited in other directions. Jensen (1986) has recently suggested a Free Cash Flow theory of the firm's capital structure, which argues that debt financing reduces managerial incentives to misallocate funds, because it commits management to return cash to the capital market. Thus, leverage lowers agency costs and raises the value of the firm in cases where mismanagement of free cash is a serious concern. Jensen points to the oil industry, which received windfall profits in the wake of the oil crises, as an example. He argues that the restructuring that followed was partly due to a free cash flow problem further aggravated by the paucity of profitable oil exploration projects. In general, declining industries that are being (or should be) milked are likely to face this type of incentive problem.

then one could presumably provide the same incentives under rather different capital structures. Thus, the challenge for future work is this: to explain why changes in capital structure cannot be undone by corresponding changes in incentive schemes. Without a satisfactory answer to this question, the incentive arguments can only be consistent with the MM-propositions they were designed to dispel. This criticism applies equally to the signalling models we turn to next.

3.2. The signalling argument

Several models have been developed that suggest the debt–equity ratio signals information about the return distribution. We begin with a simple model by Leland and Pyle (1977).

Leland and Pyle consider an entrepreneur who has identified a valuable project with an uncertain return. The entrepreneur is better informed about the distribution of returns. For concreteness, let the return be $x = \mu + \theta$, and assume that $E(\theta) = 0$ and only the entrepreneur knows μ. The structure of the technology and the information is common knowledge.

Because the manager is risk averse and/or because he has limited wealth, he would like to share the project with investors. His problem is to convince investors about the project's true value, μ. Talking does not help. However, a credible communication device is available. The entrepreneur can vary his own stake in the project and use that as a signal of the project's quality.

The formal analysis involves solving for a rational expectations (signalling) equilibrium in which the entrepreneur's *share* of the equity investment (i.e. the ratio of inside equity to outside equity) fully reveals his beliefs about the mean return of the project, μ.[17] Firm debt is determined as the residual amount necessary to finance the project (this could alternatively be private debt to the entrepreneur). For simplicity it is assumed that such debt is riskless. As is typical for signalling models, there is a continuum of equilibria; Leland and Pyle give a selection argument for singling out a particular one. As one would expect, this equilibrium has the property that a higher entrepreneurial share signals a higher project value, μ.[18]

The debt–equity ratio is uniquely determined in this equilibrium. It is shown that the value of debt (its face value because it is riskless by assumption) will fall

[17]The paper does not consider the possibility that the entrepreneur first takes a large position in order to signal a favorable investment return and then resells the shares. This would complicate the analysis.

[18]An interesting feature of the equilibrium is that all projects with positive net present value (accounting for the relevant risk) will be undertaken. This is explained by the fact that a risk averse person is risk neutral for small enough gambles and hence willing to invest a bit in any project with positive net return. Consequently, investment decisions are efficient. The social cost of asymmetric information manifests itself in an inefficient distribution of risk. The entrepreneur will have to carry more risk than he would like to in a world of symmetric information.

with increased risk. Also, an unconditional regression between the value of debt and the value of the firm would reveal a positive correlation; more debt will raise the value of the firm. However, as they are quick to point out, this is not a causal relationship, but rather a statistical property of equilibrium, which comes about because a higher amount of debt goes hand in hand with a higher share of equity held by the entrepreneur. The ratio of debt to equity should not matter in a regression conditioned on the entrepreneur's share.[19] The MM-proposition reappears in a conditional regression.

Myers and Majluf (1984) have analyzed a model closely related to that of Leland and Pyle. The main distinguishing feature is that the firm seeking capital is already established. Its shares are publically traded and its operations are controlled by a manager.

The basic point of the paper is to argue that, because of adverse selection, there are severe problems in raising outside equity. Suppose the market is less informed about the value of shares than the manager of the firm and assume for the moment that there is no new investment to undertake. Then no new equity (from new shareholders) can be raised, if the manager is acting in the interest of old shareholders. He will be willing to issue new shares only if the shares are overvalued, but of course no one would want to buy under those circumstances. Just as in the famous lemon's market of Akerlof (1970), adverse selection will preclude any trade (except in the lowest value state).

Now, suppose capital is needed for an investment. Extending the argument above, Myers and Majluf show that debt financing is preferred to equity financing even when debt is not riskless. Most of the paper, however, focuses on the case where debt is not a feasible option (for reasons outside the model) and new projects have to be financed by issuing equity. This is of course unrealistic, but it leads to an interesting insight. The logic of adverse selection implies that the stock price will always decline in response to a new issue – a result that has empirical support. This may appear paradoxical. How could it be worthwhile to take an action that lowers stock price? The explanation is that a new project is undertaken only if the firm was overvalued *given the manager's private information*. The manager's action is in the best interest of the present shareholders. At the same time it reveals the bad news that the old price was too high in light of his information.[20] Another way of reaching the same conclusion is to note that if the share price were to increase with a new issue then it would always pay to raise equity irrespective of the project's value (assuming the proceeds could be rein-

[19] However, in this model there are no additional error terms to make such a regression meaningful.

[20] It is assumed that the market is aware that there is a potentially valuable investment and that no debt is available. Also, the manager has private information about the value of the investment, which varies sufficiently for the decision to be sensitive to this information. If the investment were so good that it would always be undertaken, then issuing equity would not signal any information and the price would remain unaffected.

vested in the market rather than in the project if its net present value is negative). An uncontingent increase in the share price is, of course, inconsistent with market equilibrium.

A major weakness with the signalling approach to capital structure is that the qualitative conclusions are quite sensitive to what is being signalled. If it is the mean of the return distribution, then equity financing is bad news, as discussed above. On the other hand, if the manager's private information pertains to the riskiness of the project (but not the mean) then debt financing would be bad news. Debt would indicate that the variance is high rather than low. It is difficult to build discipline into a theory which depends on something as inherently unobservable as the nature of the information that the manager possesses.

A weakness with the Myers–Majluf model is the treatment of the manager's preferences. One would assume that the manager is driven by his own financial interests, induced by an incentive scheme of some kind, but this dimension is omitted. Ross (1977), who pioneered the signalling approach with Leland and Pyle, was sensitive to this question and went on to study the ramifications of having an endogenously determined managerial incentive scheme [Ross (1978)]. A key observation is that the manager's incentive scheme will signal information jointly with the choice of the firm's capital structure. In fact, the relevant information is really the manager's choice within the set of "securities" that the incentive scheme permits (as the debt–equity ratio is varied). Generally, there are several different pairs of incentive scheme/capital structure that will lead to precisely the same signalling information and the same value of the firm. Thus, very different financial packages could be consistent with the same outcome in reduced form. (This conclusion is partly due to the assumption that managers are risk neutral.)

Ross also shows that (theoretically at least) very rich signals may be communicated through complex managerial incentive schemes. The idea is that, by structuring lotteries that are favorable only in one of the manager's information states, he, as a risk neutral person, can be induced to reveal his precise knowledge. This observation pushes the signalling idea to an extreme conclusion: by constantly changing managerial incentives and capital structure the market can be provided with perfect information. This is obviously unrealistic, but one is then left wondering what determines permanence in incentives and debt–equity ratios. While some form of signalling through debt–equity ratios seems plausible, its strength and relevance is quite open to further research.[21]

[21]A very interesting aspect of signalling arises when there is more than one "audience" who is interested in the signal. This has recently been studied by Gertner, Gibbons and Scharfstein (1987). For instance, signalling that the firm has a high value is valuable for the capital market, but it may lead to more difficult and costly labor negotiations.

3.3. The control argument

The finance literature has traditionally ignored the fact that a share does not merely confer a right to a residual return stream. It also gives a vote. Likewise, loan contracts confer some contingent control rights either implicitly through bankruptcy threats, or explicitly through covenants. As we discussed in Section 2, the distribution of control rights is important for incentives if contracting is incomplete, which certainly is the empirically relevant case. Thus, interest in the distribution of control could well be a key part of the capital structure puzzle. This point has recently been pursued in a paper by Aghion and Bolton (1986).

The ultimate objective of this line of reasoning is to explain why equity and debt are chosen as financing instruments in the first place. The presumption of course is that financing with equity and debt is optimal in some economic environments. It should be noted that optimality in this context refers to more than the nature of the return streams. One also needs to explain why the typical debt contract is linked to a bankruptcy mechanism and the equity contract to a right to run the firm as long as it remains solvent. In other words, one needs to construct a model in which the efficient form of financing is found by maximizing over return streams as well as control rights, with the result that debt and equity – both in terms of their financial and their control characteristics – emerge as optimal.

Aghion and Bolton provide a model which goes some way towards meeting these ambitious objectives. Their primary focus is on explaining features of the bankruptcy mechanism in a debt contract. In a multi-period world they show that it may be optimal to shift control rights to the lender contingent upon unfavorable, publicly observed return information.[22] The argument requires a reason for differences in objectives between the lender and the equity holder (without reference to differences driven by the return characteristics of equity and debt, since these could be contractually altered). In one version of the model the difference in objectives comes from different prior beliefs; the lender is pessimistic about future returns contingent upon low intermediate profit reports, while the investor is not. In another version objectives are different because of moral hazard. The difference in objectives explains why the two parties do not simply coinvest in the project using equity, though the return characteristics in Aghion and Bolton's solution need not coincide with those of standard debt and equity contracts.

Two features of their analysis are notable. Their model clarifies the distinction between preferred stock (or non-voting shares) and debt. This would not be

[22] Interpreting this control shift as a bankruptcy mechanism overlooks of course many of the intricacies of actual bankruptcy laws. In particular, the firm could file for protection under Chapter 11, permitting management to reorganize the firm.

evident in a model which focused on return streams alone. Also, in their model bankruptcy does not necessarily imply liquidation. In some events in which the lender gets control liquidation occurs, and in other events the lender merely uses his decision rights to reorganize the firm. This accords with reality and is in stark contrast with earlier economic analyses of bankruptcy.

3.4. *Concluding remark*

The debt–equity ratio has been an enigma in the theory of finance for a long time. As we have discussed, there are models that suggest a role for capital structure based on signalling and screening arguments. These models are not very powerful predictively and consequently have been subjected to little empirical testing. They also have theoretical weaknesses, as we have indicated. The problem is probably that we have not looked deeply enough at the question of capital structure. Rather than taking debt and equity as given instruments, we may get a better understanding of both their role and their determinants by asking why particular instruments are used in the first place. The paper by Aghion and Bolton is a start [see also Grossman and Hart (1987) and Harris and Raviv (1987)]. It seems clear that the most fruitful direction of research at this stage is to pursue further the notion that different instruments imply different control rights. They protect different sources of capital in different ways. In the language of Jensen and Meckling (1976), an optimal capital structure is one that minimizes agency costs, some of which arise from separation of ownership and control, some of which stem from conflicts of interest between different sources of capital.

4. The separation of ownership and control

In reality, firms are mostly controlled by managers. The typical owner will have very little if any influence on the course that the firm takes. Even though there is a formal channel of influence and monitoring through the board of directors, anecdotal evidence suggests that boards rarely take a very active role in running the firm. Also, the choice of directors is often influenced more by management than shareholders. [On these matters, see Mace (1971).]

This raises the question: What keeps management from pursuing its own goals and, if it does, how will the firm actually behave? Some, like Galbraith (1967), are convinced that managerial capitalism (management in effective control of decision-making with few constraints from owners) is a distinct peril for our economy and that the objectives of the firm are far removed from those of a profit-maximizing price taker. That specter may be overly grim. As Alchian (1968) has noted, it is a marvel that millions of people willingly hand billions of their money over to managers against very limited explicit assurances their investments will be handled responsibly. This could not be going on each day without some strong forces that keep management in check.

We will describe some of the reasons why management may behave despite potential incentive problems. These include the use of explicit incentive schemes as well as the indirect policing forces of the labor market, the capital market and the product market. We will also consider the implications that a managerial theory of the firm has on the objectives that the firm pursues. In this connection we will touch on the more traditional discussions of the objective function of the firm in incomplete markets.

4.1. Internal discipline

Increasing attention is paid to the design of executive compensation plans. Of particular concern are their incentive properties. A good plan should support the strategic objectives of the firm as well as motivate the manager to excel. Contingent compensation constitutes a substantial fraction of a top manager's remuneration. It is not uncommon that over half of the yearly income of an executive derives from stock or option plans and bonus schemes.[23]

Principal–agent models offer a more theoretical paradigm within which managerial incentive problems can be studied. In the principal–agent abstraction, owners are viewed as a homogeneous group, a syndicate to use Wilson's (1969) terminology, which can be represented by the preferences of a single person, the principal. The top manager is the agent. The rest of the firm is represented by a stochastic technology, which the manager operates. The manager's compensation scheme is designed by the principal to maximize firm value subject to the constraint that the manager's opportunity cost is covered; or equivalently, the scheme maximizes the manager's expected utility subject to a minimum welfare level for the principal. Either way, the design will be Pareto optimal relative to incentive constraints.

The presumption that the relationship between stockholder and management can be adequately described in a principal–agent paradigm is not innocuous. In the next section we will argue that a stochastic technology of the kind typically used in principal–agent models is generally inadequate for describing the rest of the firm, even if viewed as black-box. More importantly, perhaps, legal scholars, notably Clark (1985), have criticized the agency notion for overlooking the fiduciary nature of management. Both officers and directors are fiduciaries rather

[23]The popular press has often questioned the incentive role of stock and option plans, citing evidence that there really is no connection between pay and performance. The data do not support such claims. See Murphy (1984) for a study which indicates that pay and performance are related when all forms of contingent compensation are accounted for properly.

than agents with respect to the corporation and its shareholders. This distinction is important in an incomplete contract framework. For instance, the board of directors – not shareholders – has the right to intervene in the firm's operation. Were the directors agents, the shareholders would retain the ultimate right to control and could, if they wished, impose their preferred policy on the directors and the company.

The independence of directors raises several issues. First, they must be given incentives to exert supervisory effort. Second, they must not collude with the manager and permit him to divert funds for joint benefits. There is substantial evidence [Mace (1971)] that directors have close ties to management and are therefore unlikely to be too critical about inadequate performance. The main option that shareholders have is to sue directors or the management for violating their fiduciary duties (such lawsuits have been more successful recently). Another incentive is that directors are frequently large shareholders of the company (or represent a firm that is a large shareholder). Also, like management, directors may have a reputation to protect. But unlike management, directors are rarely (though sometimes) paid contingent fees for their services. The role of directors as a control layer between the shareholders and management is an important issue that has not been studied theoretically as far as we know.[24]

These considerations notwithstanding, the principal–agent paradigm is a first step towards modelling how control is exercised in a company and how agency costs are kept within manageable limits.

In order for any managerial incentive problem to arise, it is of course essential that preferences do not coincide. It would seem easy to come up with reasons why a manager would not want to pursue the objectives of owners, say value maximization. The manager may want to divert company funds for private consumption; he may want to expand the business for reasons of prestige; he may cater to the tastes of other stakeholders like employees in order to enjoy an easier life within the organization; he may prefer leisure to work; and so on. Yet, to build a disciplined theory, one cannot formulate models with too much flexibility in the choice of preferences for the manager. One needs to derive his behavior from a narrower set of basic assumptions. For this reason a lot of extant agency models have been based on the notion that the agent is averse both to risk and to work. Aversion to work gives a primitive and obvious reason for incentive problems, but it may not be the most realistic assumption. Managers seem to be quite industrious by inclination ("workaholics"). An alternative, and possibly

[24]To our knowledge, there also has been little empirical work on the control exercised by the board of directors. An exception is Hermalin and Weisbach (1987) who find that: (i) firms with poor performance tend to add outsiders to the board; (ii) new CEOs put more outsiders on the board; and (iii) large shareholdings of top management are a strong predictor of the proportion of insiders on the board.

more attractive hypothesis, which we will come back to later, is that the manager is driven by concerns for his career and its implied lifetime income stream.

Differences in preferences alone are not sufficient to explain why there is a serious incentive problem with management. One also needs to explain why incentive alignment carries costs. An obvious reason is asymmetric information. Managers are experts who know more about the relevant aspects of decision-making. They also supply unobserved inputs like effort, which cannot be accurately inferred from output. It is the presence of private information that prevents inexpensive contractual solutions and provides a potential opportunity for the manager to pursue his own objectives rather than the owner's.

Let us elaborate on this theme with some examples, which will illustrate the kinds of models that have been analyzed. Suppose the technology is of the form $x = x(a, \theta)$, where x is output, a is the manager's effort and θ is a stochastic term. Assume that the manager is risk and work averse, so effort is costly. Furthermore, assume that both sides agree on the probability distribution of the stochastic term. The manager's effort cannot be observed, nor can it be inferred with certainty from the jointly observed and contractible variable, x. This means that θ cannot be observed either, or else the effort could be inferred from the knowledge of θ and x, assuming x is increasing in a.

An incentive scheme is a sharing rule $s(x)$. The owner's design problem can be viewed as one of instructing the manager to take a particular action, a, and finding a sharing rule that will make the manager obey that instruction. A Pareto optimal design $\{a, s(x)\}$ maximizes the owner's welfare subject to the constraints that the manager gets a minimum level of expected utility and the design pair is incentive compatible, i.e. $s(x)$ induces the manager to choose a.

This is an example of a *moral hazard* problem. Its characteristic feature is that there is symmetric information at the time of contracting. The economic trade-off in the model is between risk sharing and incentive provision. An optimal design will have to compromise between these two conflicting objectives, offering some incentives without exposing the manager to excessive risk. The significance of risk sharing is underscored by noting that if the manager is risk neutral (which implies unlimited access to funds) there is a costless solution: let the manager rent or purchase the technology from the owner.

A common variation of moral hazard is obtained by assuming that the manager observes θ before taking the action a (but after contracting). This enriches the manager's strategic options. His strategy is now a contingent decision rule $a(\theta)$ rather than a single choice a. More options for the manager is bad from the point of view that he is more difficult to control (more incentive constraints), but good from the point of view that information about the technology before an action is taken expands the production set. The net value of information could have either sign.

When there is asymmetric information at the time of contracting, the situation is labeled *adverse selection*. For instance, assume the manager observes θ before he begins negotiating a contract. This case is different than the one just discussed, because the manager's information changes his bargaining position. Now the owner does not know what the manager's reservation utility is and the manager will be able to use this to extract informational rents. One implication is that even with a risk neutral manager, the problem has a non-trivial solution. The rental solution that works for moral hazard does not work here, because the proper rental price is not common knowledge. A more complicated solution, e.g. a royalty scheme, which uses the outcome x as a signal about the value of the technology can reduce managerial rents and be preferred by the owner [Sappington (1984)].

Adverse selection is studied in detail in Chapter 24 by David Baron in this Handbook. Here I will constrain myself to discuss some features of moral hazard solutions, most of which are relevant also for adverse selection.[25]

In reduced form all moral hazard models have the manager choose a distribution over contractible as well as payoff relevant variables. For instance, in the example introduced above, the manager, by his choice of effort, picks a distribution over output x, induced by the distribution of θ. Note that this is true whether he chooses his effort before or after θ is realized. The feasible set of distributions available if he chooses effort after observing θ is larger, but conceptually the two cases are equivalent. To indicate the dependence of the distribution on effort, one may write the manager's distribution choice as $F(x|a)$ [or $F(x|a(\theta))$]. As an example, if $x(a, \theta) = a + \theta$ and θ is distributed normally with zero mean, then $F(x|a)$ is normal with mean a. The simplest possible case is one in which the manager has only a choice between two distributions, $H(x)$ and $L(x)$. Say, he can work hard or be lazy. What can we say about the optimal contract in that case (assuming that it is desirable to have the manager work hard)?

The solution is quite intuitive. Relative to a first-best contract which provides optimal risk sharing, the manager is paid more the more strongly the outcome x conforms with the view that he worked hard. Conversely, he is paid less if the signal x indicates that he did not work hard. Technically, the optimal sharing rule is a function of the likelihood ratio of the two distributions, i.e. the ratio of the density functions $h(x)/l(x)$. This statistical connection is notable in that no inferences really are made; the principal knows the manager's action given the incentive scheme.[26]

[25] Moral hazard models have been analyzed extensively. See, for instance Spence and Zeckhauser (1971), Mirrlees (1974, 1976), Stiglitz (1975), Harris and Raviv (1979), Holmstrom (1979, 1982a), Shavell (1979) and Grossman and Hart (1983). Similar models were earlier studied by Wilson (1969) and Ross (1973). For surveys of agency theory, see MacDonald (1984) and Arrow (1985).

[26] For a more detailed discussion, see Hart and Holmstrom (1987).

The statistical intuition is in fact the central feature of the basic model. It has both good and bad implications. The most problematic feature is that the shape of the optimal scheme is extremely sensitive to the distributional assumptions, because shape is determined by the likelihood ratio, which varies with the minute informational details of the model. The model can be made consistent with almost any shape of the sharing rule by altering the information technology suitably. The mapping from distribution choices to sharing rules is intuitive, but not useful for explaining regularities about shape. Linear schemes, for instance, are used across a wide range of technologies, so it is clear that they cannot possibly derive from statistical properties of the environment. Yet the simple model could explain linearity only on the basis of the information content of the output signal.

Holmstrom and Milgrom (1987) argue that the failure to explain shape is due to the fact that simple agency models do not capture an important piece of reality: real world schemes need to be robust. It is not enough that a scheme performs optimally in a limited environment. It must also perform reasonably as circumstances change, since constant updating of schemes is not feasible. The schemes that are optimal in simple agency models are fine-tuned to a specific environment. They tend to be complex, because they exploit, unrealistically, every bit of information provided by the output signal.

The great virtue of linear schemes is probably their robustness. They perform well across a wide range of circumstances. They also prevent arbitrage, which often would be possible with non-linear schemes. Robustness is hard to capture in a Bayesian model. Holmstrom and Milgrom show, however, that one can construct Bayesian models in which linear schemes arise out of a richer set of distributional options for the agent than is typically assumed. In particular, they consider a model in which the agent can choose his effort over time, conditioning his choice on how well he has done up to that time. Technically, the agent, who has an exponential utility function over consumption, controls the drift rate of a Brownian motion over a fixed time period. In this environment linear rules are optimal, because they provide the agent with the same incentive pressure irrespective of how he has done in the past. The agent will choose the same level of effort throughout the period and the optimal linear scheme can be solved from a static model in which the agent picks the mean of a normal distribution (constraining the principal to linear rules). Paradoxically, a complex model is needed to provide a simple and computationally tractable solution.[27]

While simple moral hazard models say little of predictive value about shape because of a strong statistical connection, the statistical intuition is very powerful

[27]A linearity result in the adverse selection context is found in Laffont and Tirole (1986). [See also McAfee and McMillan (1987), Laffont and Tirole (1987a), Picard (1987) and Chapter 24 by David Baron in this Handbook.]

in predicting what information sharing rules should depend on. The main result states that optimal sharing rules should be based on sufficient statistics about the manager's actions [Holmstrom (1979) and Shavell (1979)]. For instance, suppose that there is a signal y that the parties can contract on in addition to output x. Then y should be included in the contract if and only if x is not a sufficient statistic for the pair $\{x, y\}$ with respect to the manager's action a. The reason is that the likelihood ratio mentioned earlier, which determines the sharing rule, depends both on x and y precisely when x is not a sufficient statistic.

The most interesting implication of the sufficient statistic result relates to relative performance evaluation [Baiman and Demski (1980) and Holmstrom (1982a)]. Managerial performance should to some extent be measured against the competition as well as against general economic circumstances. Performance in a bad year ought to be valued more highly than the same performance in a good year. The rationale for relative comparisons is that they filter out uncontrollable risk. In some cases, the filter is simple. Suppose, for instance, that managerial technologies take the form $x_i = a_i + \theta + \varepsilon_i$, where i is an index for manager i, a_i is his effort, θ is an economy wide shock and ε_i is an idiosyncratic noise term. Then, a weighted sum $\sum \tau_j x_j$, where τ_j is the precision (the inverse of the variance) of the noise term ε_j will be a sufficient statistic if distributions are normal. The optimal scheme for manager i can be based on the difference between his output and this sufficient statistic.

Relative performance evaluation is common in managerial compensation. Promotions are presumably based on relative merit. (The literature on tournaments discusses this type of incentive; see Subsection 5.3). The newest innovations in executive compensation plans also move towards the use of explicit relative measures. Schemes which explicitly compare management performance with competitors are becoming more popular. The fact that competitors constitute the comparison set is in agreement with the notion that closely related technologies are more informative (cf. the weights in the sufficient statistic above). Also, indexed stock options have been introduced. In these the exercise price is contingent on industry or economy wide circumstances.

Antle and Smith (1986) offer more systematic evidence. They study the extent to which executive compensation reflects relative performance, either explicitly or implicitly. Their tests pick up statistically significant evidence that relative evaluations are present. However, the use of relative performance measures is not as extensive as one would expect from the basic agency theory. One reason could be that executives can protect themselves against systematic risk through private market transactions. A more important reason is that relative evaluations distort economic values and thereby decision making. For instance, an executive who is completely insulated from market risk (i.e. whose compensation depends only the firm's deviation from overall market performance) will care little about factors that affect the market or the industry as a whole. This could obviously lead to very misguided investment or production decisions.[28] Effort-based agency models overlook such implications, because they typically do not include investment or production decisions. This is a variation on the earlier robustness theme and suggests that models with a richer action space for the agent would be desirable to explore.

We have been vague about the nature of the performance measure x, except to say that it should incorporate all informative signals. The most natural measure of performance is profit. However, this variable can be garbled by manipulating accounts. Furthermore, current profit is a poor measure of the manager's true performance, which is equal to the increment in the expected present discounted value of profits (which cannot be measured from accounting data). For instance, investments (in capital or reputation) lower the firm's current profit. This brings us to the standard rationale for giving the manager stock options: the firm's valuation ought to incorporate the present discounted value of the investments that are observable by the market, so that the presence of large stock options in the manager's portfolio aligns his and the owners' preferences.

There are limits to the use of stock options. First, the principal–agent theory emphasizes that incentives conflict with insurance: large stock options conflict with the manager's portfolio diversification. Second, stock options do not necessarily create incentives to make investments, that have benefits that are imperfectly observed by the market. To encourage such investments the manager should be forced to hold stock options after his tenure on the job. But this policy has other problems. It creates a free-rider problem of the type discussed in Subsection 2.1: the manager's return on the stock option depends not only on his performance but also on his successor's performance. Also, the firm and the manager have an incentive to renegotiate when the manager leaves his job so as to let the manager sell his stock options and diversify his portfolio (because his investments are sunk, the stock option imposes ex post inefficient risk on the manager). The problem implied by overlapping generations of management and delayed performance measurement are important, but have received little attention in the agency literature.

One extension of agency models that deserves comment is dynamics. Some models seem to suggest that repetition will alleviate moral hazard problems. The idea is that repetition will offer better monitoring capabilities. This notion appears substantiated by results that show that in an infinitely repeated agency model (the agent faces the same technology with independent shocks infinitely often) with no discounting, the agency costs are reduced to zero. The first best can be supported as a self-enforcing equilibrium [Rubinstein (1979) and Radner

[28] Imagine the decision-making of an oil executive, whose compensation neutralizes the effects of changes in oil price.

(1981)]. Moreover, with little discounting one can come close to first best [Radner (1985)].

The interpretation of these results, as due to better monitoring, may be misleading. Fudenberg et al. (1986) show that in a similar repeated model, the optimal long-term contract coincides with the sequence of optimal short-term contracts, assuming that the agent has free access to the capital market.[29] Thus, repetition offers no additional gains. What explains the first-best result is that little discounting will offer the agent a degree of self-insurance such that he will behave essentially as a risk neutral person.

4.2. *Labor market discipline*

Fama (1980) has suggested that the incentive problems of management that are the focus of agency theory may be greatly exaggerated because dynamic effects are ignored. Fama has in mind the disciplining powers of the managerial labor market. He argues that a manager who misbehaves will show a poor performance and consequently his human capital value will deteriorate. The labor market will settle up ex post by paying the manager his perceived marginal product, which will reflect past performance. A concern for reputation alone will take care of any deviant incentives. There is no real need for explicit incentives.

This conclusion is optimistic. Holmstrom (1982b) provides a model explicating Fama's intuition. The essential ingredient in the model is that the manager's productivity is unknown. It pays to work hard, because that influences the market's perception about the unknown productivity. Of course, in equilibrium no one is fooled. Instead, the manager is caught in a rat race where he has to work to prevent an adverse evaluation. However, there is no presumption that returns to reputation coincide with periodic returns from output. A manager may well work excessively in the early periods of developing his reputation and slack off later. If productivity is not fixed forever, but subject to periodic shocks, then a stationary equilibrium will support a level of effort that is positively related to the signal-to-noise ratio (how accurately the market can observe output relative to the variance in productivity) and positively related to the discount factoral. With little discounting one comes close to first best.

The model shows that the labor market can induce effort without explicit contracts, but that there is little reason to believe that supply will be optimal. More interestingly, if one introduces other decisions like investment, the manager's choice need not be well guided by reputation concerns. In fact, the presence of a

[29]See also the closely related work by Malcomson and Spinnewyn (1988). For repeated principal–agent models without free access to the capital market, see Lambert (1983) and Rogerson (1985).

longer horizon may be the very source of divergent investment preferences even assuming that the manager is naturally industrious. The manager will choose investments that maximize his human capital returns (his reputation) while owners want to maximize the financial value of the firm. These two investment returns can be quite unrelated. Depending on the technology and the uncertainties involved, the manager may choose too much or too little risk. For a particular model specification, Holmstrom and Ricart i Costa (1986) show how contracting can align preferences. The optimal contract in this model is an option on the value of the manager's human capital, which in some cases is well approximated by an option on the value of the firm.

It is quite possible that the real problems with managerial incentives derive from the conflicts that arise due to managerial career concerns rather than effort choice as commonly considered in agency theory. This dimension deserves further investigation.

Wolfson (1985) has done an interesting empirical study of the disciplinary powers of reputation. He investigated the market for limited partnerships in oil-drilling ventures. Because of the tax code, which allows limited partners to deduct initial drilling expenses from their income tax, the contract between the general partner and limited partners is designed so that limited partners bear the main exploratory expenses while the general partner bears the main costs of completing the well. Since both share in the returns if a well is completed, the contract gives the general partner an incentive to complete fewer wells than limited partners desire. However, new ventures come up frequently and new partnerships are formed. One would expect this to have an effect on the general partner's behavior, and it does. Wolfson finds that the general partner completes more wells than myopic behavior would dictate. But the reputation effect is not strong enough to remove all incentive problems; Wolfson finds that share prices of limited partnerships reflect residual incentive problems. This accords broadly with the predictions from the reputation model above. The labor market exerts disciplinary influence, but is not sufficient to alleviate all problems.

4.3. Product market discipline

It is an old theme that the real costs of monopoly may derive more from organizational slack than price distortions [e.g. Leibenstein (1966)]. The easy life of a monopolist may be the greatest benefit of running a monopolistic firm. By implication, then, competition will provide discipline and reduce managerial incentives to slack off.

Jensen and Meckling (1976) take exception with this inefficiency hypothesis. They claim that agency costs are no less in competitive industries than in monopolistic industries. Since the easy life is enjoyed by the manager and his associates rather than the owners, the owners of monopolistic firms should be as interested in curbing agency costs as the owners of competitive firms.

This reasoning misses one important distinction between competitive and monopolistic industries. In the former there is more information about the circumstances in which the manager operates. In line with the rationale for using relative evaluations, competitive markets provide a richer information base on which to write contracts.

The value of competition is obvious if one imagines explicit incentive schemes in which the manager is compared with other firms in his market. We know that relative evaluations will allow some reduction in the uncontrollable risk that the manager has to bear and this will reduce agency costs.[30]

It is also easy to see that competition can reduce slack via a concern for reputation. For instance, the model in Holmstrom (1982b) has the feature that a sharper signal about performance will automatically lead to an increased level of effort in equilibrium (since effort responds positively to the signal-to-noise ratio). Observing competitors' performance is one way in which signal strength is increased.

A somewhat subtler channel of incentives is provided by the price mechanism. Suppose costs are uncertain but correlated. Then any rule of price formation will carry information about the other firms' costs and thereby be useful as a signal. An incentive contract that uses price as an index would help in reducing agency costs and possibly slack.

Hart (1983a) has developed a model to study a variation of this argument. In his model there is a continuum of firms. Some are run by managers and therefore subjected to control problems, others are run by the owners themselves. The degree of "competition" is measured by the ratio of entrepreneurial firms to managerial firms. Slack occurs, by assumption, only in managerial firms.

The marginal cost of all firms is the same. Managers are rewarded solely as function of their own profits. Price, which in this case reveals fully the marginal cost, is not a contractual variable by assumption. This hypothesis may be hard to rationalize empirically. One could argue that in some cases the industry is so poorly circumscribed that it is hard to identify which price to look at. Also, prices do reflect other variables like quality. Yet, even weakly correlated price signals should be valuable in contracting. The best argument therefore is a methodological one: one wants to study in isolation the indirect effects of competition through profits. In other words, how effective is the price systems as an implicit incentive scheme?

Hart's model has some special features. Managerial effort is a direct substitute for input costs. More critically, managers only care about reaching a subsistence

[30]However, risk reduction does not necessarily lead to less managerial slack in all agency models, though this may be a peculiarity of specific models more than anything else.

level of consumption. Consumption above this level has no value; consumption below it is catastrophical. The implication is that managers, who observe input costs before acting, will always work hard enough to achieve a profit level that will allow them to consume the minimum necessary for subsistence. An increase in productivity translates directly into slack.

With this structure it is intuitive that competition will reduce slack. Competition drives price down. If the manager were to slack the same amount as without competition, he would not be able to reach a sufficiently high profit level to collect the minimum reward that he needs. Hence, he has to work harder.

The complete argument is more complicated, because one has to consider changes in the incentive schemes in response to competition. The particular preference structure that Hart uses plays a critical role here. This was pointed out by Scharfstein (1988a), who considered a more standard preference structure. He found that when managers are more responsive to monetary incentives, Hart's conclusion is precisely reversed: competition increases slack. Apparently, the simple idea that product market competition reduces slack is not as easy to formalize as one might think.

4.4. Capital market discipline

Take-overs are presumed to be the ultimate weapon against managerial misconduct. Take-over threats are often suggested as a rationale for the neoclassical assumption that managers will maximize firm value. A naive argument is that if managers do not maximize value, then somebody can take over the firm, install a new value maximizing management and realize an arbitrage profit. Thus, incumbent management can do nothing less than maximize firm value.

Some authors, like Scherer (1980), have questioned the strength of take-overs as a disciplinary device. He notes that take-overs are quite costly and therefore it seems likely that if there is managerial misconduct it has to be substantial before there is an incentive for somebody to intervene.

There are other problems with the take-over argument. Why can present owners not effect the same change as the raider can? Apparently, the value of a take-over must rest either on private information that a raider holds or on special benefits that the raider, but not the shareholders at large, can capture (or perhaps both). Even so, one must ask: Why would the new management behave any better than the old one? If not, why does the old management have to leave? And if it does not, why would take-over threats change the behavior of present managers?

One of the notable contributions of formal take-over models is the discovery that take-overs by an outsider cannot easily be explained by private information alone. Grossman and Hart (1980) provide the following rationale for why such tender offers might not succeed. Suppose that the raider knows privately how to improve the performance of the firm. For instance, he may have identified a better management team. If he makes a tender offer that will benefit him if he succeeds, then it must be that his gain comes at the expense of those who tendered. The mere knowledge that a tender offer is valuable to the raider should lead present shareholders to conclude that it is not to their advantage to tender. It is a dominant strategy to hold on to one's shares, assuming that these shares are marginal. (It would be different of course if one held so many shares that tendering them could swing the outcome.)

Another way of expressing the take-over dilemma is in terms of free-riding. Present share holders can free-ride on the raider's efforts to improve the firm. The scenario outlined above is the extreme one in which the raider would have to give away all gains in order to take over. Thus, he has no incentive to take over nor to invest any resources in identifying improvements.

So what explains the occasional success of tender offers? There are several possible changes in the simple story. One is that the raider values the firm differently than the present owners in a subjective sense (ignoring private information). He may desire to run the firm. Or some other firms that he owns could benefit from the take-over. Closely related to this is the possibility that the raider could exploit minority shareholders if he succeeds. In fact, it may be in the interest of shareholders to write a charter that explicitly permits such dilution, because that will make take-over easier, encourage raiders to invest effort into identifying poorly run firms and thereby indirectly provide managers with incentives to act in the interest of its ownership (assuming that a take-over is costly to the manager and hence something to be avoided).

The question of the optimal design of dilution rights is precisely what Grossman and Hart focus on. They prove, in a stylized model, that higher rights to dilute will drive the manager closer to maximizing firm value. Take-over threats will act as an incentive scheme as postulated in less formal accounts. Dilution is not costless for present shareholders, because it will lower their return in case a take-over occurs as well as lower the price at which the raider can successfully bid for the company. The trade-off is between better management and a higher frequency of take-overs versus a lower bid price and less residual income. This determines the optimal dilution rights of the charter. Uncertainty about potential benefits as well as costs for the raider are key factors in the calculation.[31]

[31] For two recent, very interesting entries on the role of the corporate charter in influencing take-overs, see Grossman and Hart (1987) and Harris and Raviv (1987). Both papers try to explain why it might be optimal to have one share/one vote. The main argument is that an equal distribution of voting rights (rather than multiple classes of stock) will place all competitors for corporate control in the same position. An unequal distribution, by contrast, can favor those for whom the private benefits from control are high while the social benefits are not. Thus, one share/one vote may provide for the right transfer of control.

Dilution rights are important in inducing take-overs by forcing the shareholders to tender. Yet they need not cost present shareholders much, if there is more than one bidder. Present takeover regulations (in particular, Williams Amendment from 1968) encourage multiple bids by requiring a minimum number of days before target shares can be purchased and by permitting tendered shares to be withdrawn if a higher bid arrives. The role of multiple bids is discussed in Bradley et al. (1987). They provide empirical evidence showing that take-over bids are frequently front-end loaded and hence coercive, but nevertheless give present shareholders the bulk of the synergistic gains (about 95 percent of the joint increase in firm values). Their study suggests that multiple bids are quite common as well as important for a proper understanding of take-overs.

Dilution is not the only way to provide incentives for a take-over. An alternative explanation for why tender offers can succeed is that the raider holds a substantial share of the firm at the time of the offer [Shleifer and Vishny (1986a)]. In that case he can offer a price which is high enough to compensate present owners for the expected increase in firm value and still be left with a surplus. In other words, the minority shareholders free-ride, but the raider's gains are big enough that free-riding does not hinder a take-over. (Present regulations require that stockholdings (and intent) be disclosed once more than 5 percent of the firm is acquired. However, due to a permitted lag in filing, the initial stake of raiders is on average above 10 percent by the time the tender offer becomes public.) Thus, the prospect of take-overs, hence market monitoring of management, could be substantially improved by the presence of large shareholders. In contrast, one might hypothesize that if management holds a large enough proportion of shares, then take-overs are unlikely to succeed. Of course, management interest in the firm should reduce incentives to slack in accordance with standard moral hazard reasoning [see our discussion of Jensen and Meckling (1976) in Subsection 3.1]. There is a potential trade-off. A small management share will act as a good incentive. A larger share will prevent the market for corporate control from operating effectively. Morck, Shleifer and Vishny (1986) provide preliminary evidence that the best incentives are supported by an intermediate managerial stake (in the range of 5–20 percent).

The models mentioned so far say little about the actual mechanism by which take-overs police management. Scharfstein (1988b) has elaborated considerably on this dimension.[32] He analyzes a model in which the manager would want to put less effort into managing if he could. The manager has an opportunity to slack, because he, but not the owners, knows the potential productivity of the firm.

Scharfstein assumes that with an exogenously given probability there is a raider who can observe the change in the technology. If he takes over, he can implement a new and better contract. There is no argument given for why the

[32]A related model is in Demski, Sappington and Spiller (1987).

raider might be in the unique position of learning about technology. Ideally, one would like to study the incentives for the raider to invest effort in monitoring the firm.

The problem for present shareholders is to design a optimal contract for the manager, given the knowledge that technology may change and that this may trigger a take-over. Dilution is a parameter in the design. To make matters simple, Scharfstein assumes that dilution is determined by a commitment on behalf of the shareholders to tender their shares if and only if the raider's offer is above a given price. Also to be determined is the severance pay to the manager in the event of a take-over and a loss of the job.

The optimal program is relatively complicated despite the simplifying assumptions. Scharfstein shows, however, that the potential of a raid is helpful in disciplining the manager. Also, in accordance with Grossman and Hart (1980), shareholders will commit to a price that is below the potential value of the firm in order to encourage take-overs. From this he goes on to conclude that efforts to curb a manager's ability to fight take-overs have value, both socially and for incumbent ownership.

Defensive tactics have been a hotly debated legal issue in recent years.[33] Shleifer and Vishny (1986b) argue that it is not always against the interests of present shareholders to prevent defense mechanisms. They focus on greenmail whereby the manager buys out the raider in exchange for a promise not to attempt a take-over for a given period of time. The idea is that excluding a bidder may be a way of inviting even better offers from other bidders later. In their model, by assumption, the manager acts purely in the interest of the shareholders, yet greenmail occurs.

Another rationale for defensive tactics is that the threat of take-overs may induce managers to behave myopically. One could conceive of situations in which take-overs are desirable ex post, but undesirable ex ante, because of the distortions in decision-making that they induce. Thus, if the threat can be reduced by poison pills and the like, or alternatively, if the likelihood of take-overs can be altered by golden parachutes or other compensation schemes, this may be socially good. Laffont and Tirole (1987b) have studied a model of efficient managerial turnover and optimal defense tactics in case managerial quality is uncertain (management can be either good or bad ex ante). The second-best (screening) contract makes transfer of control less likely than under full information and it also provides for time-increasing (incentive) stock plans. Both serve to make the manager value the future more. [Two other papers, investigating managerial myopia and take-overs, are Hermalin (1987) and Stein (1988).]

[33] Defensive tactics include altering the debt-equity ratio [see Harris and Raviv (1985)], invitation of a "White Knight", selling off assets of value to the potential acquirer, acquiring assets that may make the merger illegal on anti-trust grounds as well as litigation of other forms.

The preceding discussion has studied the private incentives to favor or fight take-overs. In conclusion, we note that we have not said much about the social benefits of take-overs. First, the optimal corporate charter from the point of view of initial shareholders may lead to socially too few take-overs (this is akin to monopoly pricing; a similar argument is made in a related context by Aghion and Bolton (1987)). Second, it may be the case that there are too many take-overs, because the latter may simply redistribute rents (away from labor unions, say), as has recently been suggested by Shleifer and Summers (1988).

4.5. Implications for firm behavior

It should be clear by now that many forces operate to discipline management. But what are the implications of these disciplinary measures on firm behavior? In what ways will the neoclassical treatment of the firm be altered?

We discussed in Section 3 one important decision which may be influenced by agency considerations: the choice of financing mode. Here we will focus on investment and production decisions.

Regarding investment choice we note first that the objective function of the firm is typically ill-defined as soon as markets are incomplete, even without separation of ownership and control. Only under exceptional circumstances will shareholders agree on which investment and production decisions the firm should take. Since the question of unanimity has been explored rather exhaustively in the literature by now, with several good summaries available [see, for example, Grossman and Hart (1977)], there is no reason for us to reiterate the findings here.[34]

Two implications are, however, worth noting. The first is that the question, does the manager maximize profits (or the value of the firm)? is not always a meaningful one, particularly in connection with investment choice. The second implication is that there is little reason to expect that owners will agree on the manager's incentive structure when markets are incomplete. Thus, the abstraction employed throughout, that the owners can be represented by a single principal who designs a scheme for the manager, can well be questioned. Perhaps a better approach, as well as a more realistic one, would be to see the corporate control problem in a political perspective. Grossman and Hart (1977) mention this. They

[34]We know of little empirical evidence concerning the importance of incomplete markets. Some would argue that with the multitude of instruments presently available, securities markets are effectively complete. Thus, shareholders should not disagree for reasons of market incompleteness about a firm's investment plans. This is not in conflict with the apparent fact that markets for human capital are seriously incomplete. Claims on human capital cannot be sold (slavery is forbidden) and services for human capital face trading impediments for moral hazard and adverse selection reasons as we have discussed.

envision that all corporate decisions are determined by majority rule. More generally we can envision a constituent theory in which managers act much like politicians. Managerial decisions are guided by a concern for constituent support, in particular from owners, but they are not directly controlled by ownership. The voting power of the owners is primarily vested in the right to oust management.

Let us go back to our original question. The implications of incentive problems on investment choice are ambiguous if one looks at general managerial models. This is hardly surprising and partly a modelling problem. For more specific models, sharper predictions can be made. For instance, consider a moral hazard model in which the manager's incentive scheme is linear such as that of Holmstrom and Milgrom (1987). In this model the slope of the manager's incentive scheme is negatively related to the size of risk (the variance of the technology), while the overall agency costs are positively related to risk. Consequently, scale decisions, which increase riskiness in the sense that they make it harder to identify the manager's contribution, entail increased agency costs. Scale will be smaller than in a world with symmetric information.

A more interesting scale effect is present in models where managers can use capital (or any other input, like labor) as a substitute for their own effort and the owner cannot determine whether the manager is asking for capital because prospective returns are high or because the manager intends to slack [see, for example, Hart (1983b) or Holmstrom and Weiss (1985)]. The nature of an incentive compatible scheme in this case is such that the manager is not given as much capital as he would get if the owner could verify the information the manager has. Agency costs manifest themselves in underemployment of capital, because one wants to discourage managers with a high return potential from pretending that it is low.

These findings may have macroeconomic consequences. For instance, one can construct models in which economy-wide resources are underemployed [Grossman, Hart and Maskin (1983)] as well as models in which swings in aggregate economic variables get amplified due to managerial slack [Holmstrom and Weiss (1985)].

Portfolio choice is also influenced by agency considerations. The normative implications of standard portfolio analysis, for instance the capital asset pricing model, are simple. A publicly held firm should only consider contributions to systematic risk in deciding on an optimal portfolio. Idiosyncratic risk should not matter, because investors can diversify in the market. Moreover, all firms should judge projects the same way (assuming of course that the return characteristics are independent of the firm undertaking the investment). In contrast, once agency costs are incorporated, idiosyncratic risk may come to play an important role. The reason is that the manager must bear some idiosyncratic risk, because that is precisely the risk that is informative about the effort he put in. In fact, with relative performance evaluation one may in some cases completely want to eliminate the systematic risk component from the manager's reward structure.[35] This will imply that in making investment decisions, the firm should consider idiosyncratic risk an important factor, which indeed seems to be the case in reality.

Because idiosyncratic risk will have to be borne, diversification by the firm may become desirable. The argument is a bit more delicate than one might think, though, because one has to explain why, instead of diversifying, the firm could not use relative performance evaluation as a substitute. Aron (1988) has studied the problem in more detail.

Quite generally, portfolio choice in a managerial model is influenced by a desire to specialize for technological reasons versus a desire to use a common technology for incentive reasons. As a manifestation of this tension, consider the choice of how much correlation to seek with the market. Agency theory puts a premium on being technologically closer to other firms for the purpose of being able to control the manager better. Thus, firms should bunch together more than they would in a world under symmetric information. Consequently, the social portfolio will be riskier. More interestingly, if the managers feel that they are directly and indirectly compared to the competition, that may lead to bandwagoning effects (the mistakes in loaning extensively to the LDC countries could be one example). Managers, in fear of being too exposed, will choose their activities close to each other. This has not been extensively analyzed, though it is easy to see how it may come about, for instance, in reputational models. We suspect that the racing aspects present in career pursuits may in the end be the ones that have the most profound effects on managerial behavior.

Next, consider implications for output decisions. Will the manager set output so as to maximize firm profits? The answer depends very much on the technology. Suppose managerial effort only affects marginal cost and, somewhat unrealistically, suppose marginal cost can be observed and contracted on. Then it is obvious that the manager will be quite happy to choose the quantity that maximizes profit, *conditional on cost*. In a sense, cost acts as a sufficient statistic and nothing additional is learned from quantity choice. Hence, incentives should not be connected with quantity choice and the profit maximization paradigm remains valid in spite of agency problems. In contrast, of course, if quantity decisions, directly or indirectly, provide additional information for contracting, then distortions will occur in its choice.

Managerial incentives also affect product market competition. Indeed, if the contract between the manager and owner is observed by competitors, the contract should be designed to influence competitor behavior. For instance, in an

[35] This is true if the technology takes the form $x = a + \theta + \varepsilon$, where a is the manager's effort, and the manager cannot privately decide on investments. But recall our earlier observation that if the manager can control investments, then relative evaluations may be less desirable.

oligopoly game, a manager can be given incentives not to lower price or not to increase sales. The agency relationship allows owners to commit to a price in a way that may be infeasible otherwise.[36] The effect is that competitors will also raise their price. However, it can be shown [Fershtman et al. (1986) and Katz (1987)] that if the manager's *actions* can be contracted on and managerial contracts are mutually observed, a "Folk Theorem"-like result will obtain: the oligopoly equilibrium is indeterminate. By contrast, if actions cannot be contracted for directly, but rather must be induced via a *performance* plan, agency will matter and need not lead to indeterminacy [Fershtman and Judd (1986)].

The strategic aspects of agency have also been studied when performance-based contracts are impossible, but some contractual choice is still feasible [see Bonanno and Vickers (1986), Mathewson and Winter (1985) and Rey and Stiglitz (1986), all on vertical restraints; see also Brander and Lewis (1986) on debt contracts]. If managerial contracts are not mutually observed, say because they are implicit or entail side-contracting, then agency does not matter if the manager is risk neutral (the owners offer to sell their firm to the manager), but may matter if the manager is risk averse; see Katz (1987). (For instance, risk-sharing provisions may make the manager a tougher bargainer.)

The effect of agency on competition (as well as the feedback of competition on agency contracts) is an interesting topic. Much seems to depend on variations in assumptions such as: Are contracts observed by competitors? Can contracts depend on the agent's action or just his performance? Can contracts be linked to those of competitors? A lot more work remains to be done on the subject.

4.6. *The hazards of a black-box view of the firm*

In Subsection 4.5 we presented an example of a firm whose manager slacks, and yet the firm is observationally indistinguishable from a profit-maximizing firm. This leads us to consider more generally whether the firm can be represented by a single objective function such as profit maximization, or, as was presumed by the older literature on managerial theories of the firm, a utility function increasing with the firm's profit, size, growth or expenses [see, for instance, Baumol (1959), Penrose (1959) and Williamson (1964)].

Many models have assumed that the firm's managers maximize the firm's size subject to "capital market constraints", which guarantee the owners a minimum profit. Such reduced forms beg the question of why managers care about size. The literature commonly offers psychological reasons. No doubt, managers enjoy the power associated with a large number of subordinates. But it also seems

[36] The use of agents for purposes of commitment, and hence an improved strategic position, is widespread.

important to investigate whether size concerns could be explained economically. For example, we could identify economic reasons which emanate from the traditional principal–agent model in which the manager has private information about productivity, and in which his effort to obtain a given output target decreases with the productivity parameter and the number of subordinates (a larger number of subordinates may reduce on-the-job pressure, etc.). In such a model, the manager cares about size (the number of his subordinates) *not per se*, but because a large workforce allows him to enjoy an easy life (exert low effort). The size of the firm then exceeds the optimal size (obtained when the owners have perfect information about productivity). Other – more conjectural – economic explanations for the size concern come to mind. (1) The size of one's staff may influence the labor market's perception of one's ability. (2) A large staff may make a manager's function harder to suppress (because relocation or layoff of the staff are more costly). (3) In a framework in which managerial compensation is based on the performance of competitors, it may pay to expand beyond the profit-maximizing point if competitors are on the same product market and are thus hurt by one's expansion. (4) In a dynamic setting, a manager may want the firm to grow to secure promotion opportunities for his subordinates.

These more "primitive" explanations could be read as supporting the general assumption that managers care about size, and interpreted as vindicating the reduced form approach. This is missing the point. Reduced forms are not robust to structural changes. Only a careful consideration of the structural form will indicate whether profit maximization or size maximization are good approximations for positive or normative analysis. It is clear, for instance, that the five "explanations" above of why managers care about size have diverse implications concerning the firm's behavior in the product market. We feel strongly that there is a need to study where black-box representations of the firm's objective yield appropriate approximations of its behavior.

4.7. Concluding remark

Agency considerations affect the behavior of the firm quite generally. As the attentive reader must have noticed, however, there is a significant dilemma in that most of the changes in firm behavior are hard to observe. The modeller sees everything that goes on inside his model, but to an outside observer much of it will go unnoticed. For instance, the fact that the manager chooses more or less risky investments than would be the case without an incentive problem is hardly an observable implication. The same can be said about scale and output decisions. We believe this problem (which is not entirely unique to agency theory) has received way too little attention in the literature to date. One reason is that agency models are rarely incorporated into an economically richer environment, because such extensions tend to be complicated.

5. Internal hierarchies

The previous section identified the firm with a manager (or a group of perfectly colluding managers), whom shareholders and creditors tried to control through a variety of mechanisms. The rest of the firm was viewed as a black box described by a stochastic technology that transforms the manager's actions and characteristics into an outcome (e.g. profit). We now open this black box and take a look at internal organization. Before addressing the relevant issues, we make two methodological points.

The two-tier capitalist-management model creates the potentially misleading impression that the internal hierarchy (below management) can be summarized in reduced form by an exogenous random production function. To see why this need not be the case, consider a three-tier structure: owner/manager/worker. The manager faces an incentive scheme $s_1(\cdot)$ that is contingent on observable variables and picks some unobservable action a_1 (related to production, supervision, etc.); similarly, the worker faces an incentive scheme $s_2(\cdot)$ and picks an action a_2. In general, the optimal action $a_i(=1,2)$ does not only depend on $s_i(\cdot)$, but also on $a_j(j=1,2;\ j\neq i)$. For instance, the manager and the worker may form a productive team in which the manager picks the technology (a_1), the worker produces using this technology (a_2) and hence output x depends on both sides' actions. Assuming that both sharing rules are tied to output, each party's decision to act depends on what the other party intends to do.[37] The outcome will be a solution to a non-cooperative game. Consequently, even if the incentive contracts for the rest of the hierarchy are taken as given, one cannot write a reduced form technology for the firm, $F(x\mid a_1)$, that maps the manager's effort into a probability distribution over output, and then proceed as in a standard one-agent model (cf. Subsection 4.1). The mistake is in assuming that the manager's action can be described by a maximization over his expected utility given his sharing rule, when in fact it will be determined by the outcome of a non-cooperative game, where the expectation of the worker's action plays a central role. Another way of expressing this is to say that the technology controlled by the manager cannot be defined independently of his incentive scheme as in one-agent models.

[37]To give another example, suppose that x depends only on a_2, and that a_1 represents supervisory effort, which provides an estimate of a_2. Assuming that the sharing rule depends on the supervisory evidence found by the manager (as well as on x, if the latter is verifiable), the hierarchical structure yields a supervision game, in which, again, each party's optimal structure depends on the other party's action.

Our second methodological point concerns the distinction between single comprehensive contracting and multi-lateral contracting. The former assumes that the owners impose a grand contract upon the entire hierarchy, preventing side (or delegated or sequential) contracting between its members. In the context of the previous example, a grand contract, chosen by the owner, would determine $s_2(\cdot)$ and $s_1(\cdot)$ simultaneously, assuming recontracting between the manager and the worker is prohibited. A grand contracting approach is employed in the unified, abstract models of Laffont and Maskin (1982) and Myerson (1984). For instance, Myerson views an organization as a centralized communication system in which at each date a mediator receives information from the various agents and, in turn, tells each agent the minimal amount necessary to guide the agents' actions at that date. Most other work on multi-agent models assumes likewise that the principal can design contracts for all agents without the agents being able to recontract or communicate among themselves.

Clearly, if preventing side-contracts is costless, there is no loss in employing a grand contract design. In fact, one would typically gain strictly by controlling all contract options. Unfortunately, preventing side-contracts is costly or infeasible, which suggests considering the polar case of unlimited side-contracting. Side-contracting will usually add costly constraints to the owners' optimization problem.[38] Obviously, both the grand contract design and the unlimited side-contracting model are caricatures, and the reality must lie somewhere in between; we would actually argue that the amount of side-contracting that takes place in organizations is an important aspect of the overall design problem.

Below, we will discuss hierarchies in terms of the services that they provide. Information systems are taken up in Subsection 5.1 and supervision in 5.2. Associated incentive features are discussed in Subsection 5.3. Subsection 5.4 considers the implications of learning on promotion and task assignment as well as on wage structures. Subsection 5.5 looks at how hierarchies limit the costs of side-contracting. We finish with two subsections – one on authority, the other on organizational forms – which make little reference to models for the simple reason that there is almost no formal work on these subjects. Our remarks here are correspondingly more philosophical and intended to bring attention to a big gap in formal theorizing about the firm.

5.1. Hierarchies as information systems

As we have noted before, information is valuable for at least two reasons. It improves decision-making and it permits better control of a subordinate's ac-

[38]These additional constraints bring technical complications. In a grand design, the optimal contract that implements action a_i by agent i only depends on what the other agents are asked to do, not on what contracts they are on. In contrast, such a partial decomposition is not possible when side-contracting must be considered.

tions. Thus, there is both a decision-making demand and an incentive demand for information, both of which have been well recognized by accountants studying the properties of internal information systems. To isolate the decision-making demand, one can study organizations under the simplifying assumption that all members share the same objective. This is the approach taken in team theory [Marschak and Radner (1972)].

A team theoretic study begins by postulating an underlying organizational decision problem. For instance, the problem could concern how much to produce and distribute to separate markets, each with an uncertain demand. Information about demand is collected by different members. How much information should they collect and how should they communicate with each other? This problem is approached in two stages. In the first stage the value of a given information system is established by solving for the optimal organizational decision rule (which consists of the set of decision rules for its team members) under that particular information structure. One of the central results of team theory is that the optimal decision rule coincides with a person-by-person satisfactory rule under standard concavity assumptions. This means that the overall optimal decision rule is one in which each team members' rule is optimal for that member alone taking the other members' rules as given. (In game theoretic language, person-by-person satisfactory is equivalent to a Bayesian Nash equilibrium, which obviously is a necessary condition for optimality.)

Equipped with a characterization of optimal decision rules, the second stage compares alternative information systems. These correspond to stylized communication structures that might be observed in the real world. The problem is usually too complicated to derive the best information structure given costs of information acquisition and communication. Therefore, most of the theory is focused on discrete comparisons of the benefits, leaving the costs to be evaluated separately. An exception is a recent paper by Geanakopolos and Milgrom (1985) which formalizes information and communication costs in a tractable way and derives closed form solutions for the optimal hierarchical design. The cost of communication is interpreted as stemming from delays in decision-making. One interesting implication is that the optimal hierarchy is finite in size, because the benefits from adding coordinating layers of management eventually go to zero.

One general result on the comparison of information systems emerges from team theory: an information system x is more valuable than information system y if it is more informative in the sense of Blackwell (1953). Loosely speaking, x is more informative than y if it is less garbled, that is the distribution of signal y can be construed as arising from the signal x plus additional noise. This is closely related to the notion that x is a sufficient statistic for y. What this result shows is that Blackwell's analysis of one-person decision problems extends to multi-person settings, assuming that objectives are shared.

In fact, recalling our discussion about information in agency problems in Subsection 4.1, Blackwell's result also extends to situations in which objectives are not shared. A more informative information system is not only more valuable for decision-making, but also for writing incentive contracts. A quite general treatment of these questions, covering both decision-making and incentive demand for information, is provided in Gjesdal (1982).

These results all have bearing on problems in accounting, particularly managerial accounting. Accountants have taken a keen interest in the information economic literature and developed it for their own needs [see, for instance, Demski and Feltham (1976) and Baiman (1982)]. The informativeness criterion gives us some feel for what type of information is worth recording in an accounting system. Elaborations are provided in several papers. Antle and Demski (1987) view accounting rules as providing a numerical representation of some coarsening of the information and analyze when these rules (in the context of revenue that must be recognized over time) involves a loss of (useful) information. Demski and Sappington (1986), analyze line-item reporting and ask when there are strict gains to auditing one more variable. Holmstrom and Milgrom (1987) rationalize the use of time-aggregated accounts. Caillaud, Guesnerie and Rey (1986) and Melumad and Reichelstein (1986) study gains to communication in an organization in which coordination is not required; communication serves the purpose of selecting a desirable incentive contract from a menu of choices (participatory management). Maskin and Riley (1985) compare the values of alternative information structures, assuming that high measurement costs make them mutually exclusive. For instance, is it better to monitor a worker's output or her input (use of capital, raw materials or possibly labor)? Crampes (1983) offers a similar analysis in a regulatory context.

The central question in accounting is how to aggregate information. Accounting systems aggregate information to a substantial degree. The explanation offered by Blackwell-type results is that nothing is lost from aggregating information into a sufficient statistic. However, it is clear that accounting systems go well beyond such limited aggregation. The obvious explanation is that information is costly to process and communicate. Information of marginal value is not worth including in contracts nor worth communicating further within the organization. Unfortunately, neither team theory nor agency theory have been able to incorporate information costs very effectively. Partly this is due to severe problems in quantifying information. For instance, trying to measure information in terms of "bits" transmitted or processed has met with limited success economically.

It appears that further progress on information costs will require a better understanding of the nature of information and its role in decision-making. In particular, one must come to grips with the difficult concept of bounded rationality. Bounded rationality manifests itself on two levels in organizational decision-making. On an individual level, a decision-maker must (i) isolate the relevant part of the available information and (ii) find the optimal decision. The first step is not a trivial one; we all know that having too much information is as bad as having no information at all if, as is often the case, we do not have the time to sort out the decision-relevant part. Indeed one of the functions of accounting systems is to aggregate information so that decision-makers can focus on a small number of key variables. The second step is also time-consuming (the typical example is a chess decision, which to be even nearly optimal would require extremely long backward induction computations). In both steps, the decision-maker must trade-off the quality of information and decision-making against the costs (time or other) of improving them. This tradeoff, particularly emphasized by Simon (1957, 1976), is of crucial importance in practice, but little formal progress has been made on examining it or its implications for organizational behavior.

Bounded rationality is important not only on the individual level, but also on the organizational level. An organization cannot afford to remember extensive and detailed information. Instead it attempts to codify information in the form of standardized rules that are meant to help the organization to adapt quickly and relatively efficiently to changes in the environment. Several authors [for instance, Arrow (1974), Nelson and Winter (1982), Kreps (1984), Schein (1984) and Cremer (1986b)] have tried to bring content to the notion of organizational memory. The interesting question of what happens when the environment changes more dramatically, outdating present agendas, operating rules and organizational memory, is largely unexplored, though it must be of considerable importance. This relates closely to the problem of modelling unforeseen contingencies under incomplete contracts, mentioned earlier. Both issues would benefit greatly from a successful formalization of bounded rationality and complexity.

5.2. *Supervision in hierarchies*

The complexity of the two-tier agency structure may well account for the fact that studies of higher-order hierarchies have been rare. Very special assumptions must be made in order to be able to solve the optimal contract associated with a complex hierarchy. Interesting insights have nevertheless been obtained by Williamson (1967), Calvo and Wellisz (1978, 1979), Rosen (1982) and Keren and Levhari (1983) among others. As an illustration, we will give a simplified exposition of the Calvo–Wellisz model (1978).

Suppose that the firm is organized according to a familiar pyramidal structure. Level 1 forms the productive tier of the firm (workers). Level 2 consists of managers supervising level 1 workers. Because the quality of supervision is a function of the number of workers being supervised, there may be many level 2 supervisors. These in turn need to be monitored by a third level and so on. The top level consists of a single agent (or unit), who is the residual claimant of the firm's profit, net of wage and input payments. For instance, level 3 could be the shareholders (respectively, the executive officers) and level 2 the executive officers (respectively, the division officers). Note that the numbering of levels is from bottom to top. One of the main questions is how many supervision layers to build above the productive workers on level 1. What determines the size of the firm? What constrains it from growing indefinitely? Potentially, the answer could be a deterioration of supervisory effort as envisioned in Williamson (1967).

Calvo and Wellisz consider the following simple technology. Employees can either work (0) or shirk (1). The monetary disutility of work is g. Supervision involves "checking" a subordinate (employees on the immediately lower level) with some probability. Checking reveals the subordinate's activity without error.[39] If the employee could be punished sufficiently for not working, then the agency problem could be solved costlessly (the threat to punish would act as a sufficient threat at a minimal level of supervision, i.e. probability of checking). To avoid this, one assumes limited liability (or infinite risk aversion below some threshold income if there is any possibility of a monitoring mistake) so that the punishments are restricted. Then the optimal punishment is to bring the employee to her reservation utility (normalized to zero).

If the employee is not checked, or if she works when being checked, she gets a wage w. If p is the probability of being checked, the employee works if and only if $wp \geq g$. Thus, the "efficiency wage" equals g/p. Note that it decreases with the probability of monitoring. Also, the employee earns rents because of limited punishments; the rent is $w - g = g(1 - p)/p$. The supervision technology is described as follows: the probability of being checked is a decreasing function of the total number s of employees supervised by her supervisor; for instance, $p = 1/s$. The employee at the top of the pyramid is exogenously supposed to choose $e = 1$ (presumably because of the labor or capital market incentives discussed in Section 4). Note that this is an Alchian–Demsetz-type model in which monetary incentives based on individual performance are infeasible and control must rest on supervision of input supply.

In the optimal contract, all employees work (shirking at any level implies shirking at all lower levels of the hierarchy). Suppose that a level-k employee together with the employees under her, brings profit Π_k (where $\Pi_1 = x$ is the output per worker). Π_k is defined gross of the wage required to induce the employee to work. A level-$k+1$ employee should supervise n_k level-k employees, where n_k maximizes $n_k(\Pi_k - gn_k)$; so $n_k = \Pi_k/2g$. And $\Pi_{k+1} = \Pi_k^2/4g$. Given this, the top manager is willing to add a $(k+1)$th layer of employees (pushing herself to the $(k+2)$th layer) only if $\Pi_{k+2} > \Pi_{k+1}$ or $\Pi_{k+1}^2/4g > \Pi_k^2/4g$, that is, $\Pi_{k+1} > \Pi_k$.

In this model, we thus obtain an optimal firm size equal to either one (self-employment) or infinity. This is not very satisfactory, but the conclusion is very sensitive to the supervision technology specified; see Calvo and Wellisz

[39] For an interesting analysis of imperfect monitoring, see Baiman and Demski (1980).

(1978). More interesting is the observation that the span of control increases with the rank in the hierarchy; because $\Pi_{k+1} > \Pi_k$, $n_{k+1} > n_k$. This implies that the wage also increases with the rank in the hierarchy, even though all employees are identical, and all jobs equally hard to perform.

An important question for owners of a private firm or supervisors of public enterprises is how incentives extend down the hierarchy. Top managers form only a small part of the organization; indeed, much of the productive work is done by layers that have limited financial incentives and whose rewards are not determined directly by the owners (engineers, marketing staff, product analysts, and especially production workers). Top managers are crucial because a failure in their supervisory, coordination and arbitration functions has severe consequences for how the rest of the organization behaves. This is well illustrated in the Calvo–Wellisz model, where lack of supervision by one manager implies shirking by all employees below her. The way in which lower units, and therefore the performance of the firm, respond to changes in the upper units' incentive schemes is an important question that hierarchical models of the kind just described could shed useful light on.

Let us turn next to some other questions concerning supervision. As mentioned in Section 2, technological non-separabilities and the concomitant problem of identifying individual performance, create a problem of moral hazard in teams.[40] Monetary incentives based on joint performance, which involve a source that breaks the budget balancing constraint, may work in some circumstances [Holmstrom (1982a)]. This solution may be limited by coalition formation and risk aversion.[41]

An alternative is to obtain further measures of individual performance by establishing the input supply (effort) of each agent. Supervision serves that role. We would expect supervision to be more prevalent in parts of the firm where individual contributions to output would otherwise be hard to measure.

The type of evidence that the supervisor collects is of central importance. One must distinguish between hard evidence, which is data that can be verified in case of a dispute and soft data, which cannot be verified. Examples of hard data include accounting information and information about the number of units that an employee has produced. Hard data can be used in explicit incentive schemes such as piece rates.

More often the supervisor can only obtain soft data by judging the employee's performance by direct observation. The supervisor must then be trusted to report findings in an honest fashion. This can pose special problems. Honest reporting

[40] "Team" here has a different meaning from the one given in Subsection 5.1. Parties in a team do have conflicts of interest in this subsection.

[41] The agents may collude against the source by coordinating to produce beyond the non-cooperative level. See Eswaran and Kotwal (1984).

may not be in the supervisor's interest for several reasons. First, to induce her to exert supervisory effort, she may be paid according to the number of mistakes or failures she records; she may thus have an incentive to overstate the frequency of shirking. Second, a supervisor is often a member of the team herself through her non-supervisory activities (coordination, management, communication). Hence, she may be tempted to assert facts that reflect poorly on the other members in order to emphasize her own contribution to the team's performance.

There are mechanisms that can "harden" soft information (make it more reliable). Suppose the supervisor monitors many agents (or a single agent over time). A "quota" system entitles the supervisor to distribute a given number (or maximum number) of sanctions or rewards among the agents. She still has the authority to announce which agents shirked and which did well, but now she cannot influence sanctions or rewards as freely. Examples of quota systems include a coach who picks the players for a game, or a school teacher who decides who should enter the next grade. The point of a quota is that it circumscribes the supervisor's ability as well as desire to misrepresent facts.

This important observation originated in the tournament literature [Bhattacharya (1983), Carmichael (1983) and Malcomson (1984)]. Tournaments, in which a set of prizes are distributed to team members based on rank-order performance, can be viewed as a variation on the quota system. The essential characteristic is that the sum of prizes is constant, which has desirable incentive properties for the principal. She cannot escape payment by distorting observations. Furthermore, when there is a large number of agents in the team, optimal tournaments may approximate closely optimal general incentive schemes [Green and Stokey (1983)]. (Note, however, that the large numbers case has the drawback of yielding a large span of control and therefore a poor quality of supervision.) We will return to tournaments in the next subsection.

The use of quotas has potential drawbacks. It may have perverse effects on the supervisor's incentive to exert supervisory effort. Why should she care about whether Mr. A did better than Mr. B? This problem is partly curbed by the supervisor's reputation. To take an analogy, consider the case of a policeman handing out tickets for speeding. The policeman's word is trusted by authorities (police department or courts) over the driver's. Presumably, this is only because the policeman has a more frequent relationship with the authorities than the driver, and therefore is more able to develop trust with those authorities. And, indeed, if too many drivers complained of unfair ticketing by the same policeman, the authorities would become suspicious and would launch an inquiry. Similar considerations may be important in firms.[42]

[42] Note that this mechanism is similar to allowing a maximum number of complaints over some length of time.

5.3. *Hierarchies as incentive structures*

Hierarchies can act as incentive structures by inducing competition among agents. We will discuss two channels through which members of a hierarchy may be led to compete with each other. First, an agent's performance may be usefully compared to the other agent's performance for monitoring purposes when agents face correlated shocks (this will be referred to as yardstick competition). Second, the agents may be induced to compete in the same market.

The tournament literature has discussed an interesting incidence of yardstick competition [Lazear and Rosen (1981), Green and Stokey (1983), Nalebuff and Stiglitz (1983), Mookererjee (1984) and Shleifer (1985)]. Tournaments compare agents by rank, which provides both insurance and flexibility. Agents will have to carry less risk, because their performance rank is insensitive to common uncertainties (cf. our earlier discussion of relative performance evaluation; Subsection 4.1). They will also be induced to adapt more efficiently to common changes in the environment. In special cases, tournaments duplicate optimal insurance as well as work effort despite non-variable changes in circumstances. The fact that rewards are paid based on ordinal rather than cardinal measures can be a further advantage when measurement costs are high or when measures are hard to quantify (for instance, because they are based on supervisory judgement; see the discussion above). Indeed, tournaments are commonplace in firms. A prize for "the most valuable employee of the month" is a quite explicit example. More importantly, promotions induce a tournament or a sequence of tournaments.

The optimal design of prizes as well as the composition of agents in a tournament have been analyzed in this literature. One question of interest is the following: Can the strongly skewed distribution of earnings across ranks commonly observed in firms [Lydall (1968)] be explained as an optimal tournament design? Lazear and Rosen (1981) find that single tournaments do not yield sufficient skewness. Subsequently, Rosen (1986) has reconsidered the question in a model of elimination tournaments. He notes that most top managers come through the ranks and that the process may be similar to sports contests in which players are eliminated in each round. In sports (e.g. tennis) the distribution of prize money is very skewed as well. Rosen finds that sequential tournaments can explain skewness better. The intuition is that managers who come close to the top of the hierarchy see their advancement opportunities shrink (assuming that the size of the hierarchy is fixed). To preserve their work incentives higher rewards must be provided.

The tournament literature provides other interesting insights into the design of hierarchies. We think one should be cautious, however, in interpreting a hierarchy as designed uniquely for the purpose of providing agents with an incentive structure. Why should job assignment be part of the reward system? Why not let the supervisor distribute prespecified monetary rewards instead? It seems more likely that promotions primarily serve the purpose of moving people to tasks where their comparative advantage is highest and that incentive properties are derivative. On the margin promotion rules could be influenced by incentive considerations, but incentives could hardly be the driving force. [In fact, promotions with associated large wage increases could have rather detrimental effects on the continued incentives for losers; see Dye (1984).][43] In the next subsection we will discuss learning models of job assignment and provide independent reasons why wages might be attached to jobs. It would be desirable to mix the adverse selection/job assignment literature with the moral hazard/tournament literature to obtain a more consistent theory of hierarchical mobility as an incentive device. [For a start, see MacLeod and Malcomson (1985).]

We turn next to product market competition. When an agent's incentives cannot be based on a reliable measure of performance, product market competition can supplement imperfect compensation schemes and act as an implicit incentive device. We describe two examples, in which the principal may want to induce product market competition between the agents (this contrasts with the literature reviewed in Subsection 4.3, in which the market structure is exogenous).

Rey and Tirole (1986) offer a model of retailers serving a given geographical area or more generally a market (within a firm, one might think of competing salespersons, divisions, or marketing teams). The retailers (agents) sell the goods produced by a monopolist supplier (principal). They may either compete throughout a geographical area or market, or alternatively be allocated a territory or market segment over which they have a local selling monopoly (exclusive territories). Their performance is not directly observable. Competition on the product market (in the price or services) has the advantage of partly insuring the agents. A shock on demand or retail cost is likely also to affect one's competitors and therefore gets partly absorbed through the competitive mechanism (cf. our earlier discussion in Subsection 4.3). By contrast, under exclusive territories, no such compensatory mechanism exists, and the agents are therefore more exposed to demand and cost fluctuations.

Competition has desirable insurance properties similar to general relative performance schemes. And, analogously, in the course of providing insurance it acts as an incentive device. There is, however, a flip-side to competition. It constrains the way agents can exploit monopoly power in the product market. As is usual in industrial organization, strategic behavior to appropriate monopoly rents destroys some in the process. By contrast, an agent who is granted a monopoly through exclusive territories, is free of strategic constraints and can

[43]Another problem with tournaments is that they are detrimental to cooperation [Lazear (1986)]. This relates closely to the problem with relative performance evaluation raised in Section 4; managers may be led to make wrong production and investment decisions if relative values are distorted.

exploit his monopoly power fully. Hence, product market competition may or may not be optimal.[44]

Farrell and Gallini (1988) and Shepard (1987) introduce another reason why product market competition may be desirable. In their models, competition acts as a commitment to supply non-contractible quality. Recall the buyer/seller paradigm of Subsection 2.1, in which the buyer must make some specific investment before the seller delivers. Suppose that the value of this investment depends on the ex post quality chosen by the seller, and that this quality is observable but not verifiable. With only one seller (source), he has an incentive to choose ex post the minimum quality he can get away with legally. This quality is in general much too low, and alternative incentives must be provided to yield an efficient level of quality. The mechanism envisioned by Farrell and Gallini, and Shepard, is licensing by the upstream firm to create a competitor. Upstream competition for the downstream market yields an ex post incentive to supply acceptable quality. This explanation seems to fit some licensing practices (like Intel in the semi-conductor industry).[45]

Tournaments and product market competition are just two ways in which incentives are structured so that information about relative performance gets exploited. The same principles can be applied to explore job structures more generally. One implication is that it may be desirable to design jobs so that they overlap even though such overlap is technologically wasteful. Consultants on organizations have occasionally emphasized the use of job duplication without seeing the economic merits in it [Peters and Waterman (1982)]. A theoretical analysis of a similar phenomenon has been provided in the context of second sourcing (use of two suppliers) by Demski et al. (1987).

Closely related to job duplication is the question of job rotation. Having the same employee perform one task for a long time may be technologically desirable, but the longer he does the job, the harder it may become to know whether he is performing to the potential of that job. Also, setting standards for such an employee may become problematic because of the well-known ratchet effect. In fear of raised standards in the future, the employee may underperform deliberately today [see, for instance, Weitzman (1980), Freixas et al. (1985) and Laffont and Tirole (1988)]. Job rotation provides some relief. The knowledge that the job is temporary induces the employee to perform harder – the cost of higher

[44]Similar effects arise for other competition-reducing restraints, for instance resale price maintenance, when these are feasible. Caillaud (1986) formalizes the effect of unregulated product market competition on the control of a regulated firm.

[45]Unlike the previous model, competition does not have any direct costs in the Farrell–Gallini–Shepard theory. In order to have a single upstream production unit, Shepard introduces increasing returns to scale. One might also be able to construct models in which quality competition would have some drawbacks; for instance, if quality is measured by several attributes, competition may well yield a mix of attributes that is not optimal from the point of view of exploiting monopoly power.

standards will not be borne by him. Also, job rotation offers an alternative source of information about potential. Against these benefits one has to weigh, of course, the costs of training and learning about the task, as well as the intertemporal free-rider problems that may emerge [Fudenberg et al. (1986)].

Finally, we want to mention that incentive concerns influence organizational design in other ways as well. Task assignment can change the opportunity cost of agents. For instance, doing a job at home can be more costly incentive-wise than doing it on the job, because the temptation to slack is greater. The use of time-cards, which permit flexible working hours, which are more sensitive to opportunity costs are another example. The agency literature has paid scant attention to these issues.

5.4. Hierarchies as internal labor markets

Hierarchies are composed of a variety of jobs. An important task of labor management is to assign the right employees to the right jobs. In this subsection we will briefly review the literature on internal labor markets that deals with job assignment and its implications for the wage structure. For the most part, jobs are taken as given here. A related and important question is the design of an efficient job structure, which has received little attention in this literature.

The simplest case of job assignment is one in which job and worker characteristics are known and the environment is static (one period). A basic question is the following: Is it optimal to assign the most able employees to the top of the hierarchy? This need not always be the case. Counter-examples are provided in the communication models studied by Geanakopolos and Milgrom (1985). There is reason to believe, however, that talent is commonly valued more highly at the top, because of the pyramidal structure of the hierarchy. Paraphrasing Rosen (1982), if a soldier makes a mistake he may die, if a colonel makes a mistake his division may be captured, but if the general makes a mistake the whole war can be lost. In other words, the value of correct decision-making multiplies as one goes up the hierarchy and with it the marginal product of ability. This logic carries through in an extension of the supervision model of Subsection 5.2 that incorporates different abilities [see Calvo and Wellisz (1979)].

An interesting implication of matching higher level jobs with higher ability is that it skews the earnings profile. Suppose output in job level i is $x_i = \rho a_i + b_i$, where ρ is a measure of worker ability and a_i is a measure of the importance of the job level. In each job level, more able workers earn more because they are more productive – the relationship is linear in our example. But if it is also the case that higher ability workers are assigned to higher level jobs, the difference in productivity is magnified. The overall relationship between wage and ability becomes convex. This is emphasized by Rosen (1982) and is also a feature of the Calvo–Wellisz model.

Static models overlook important questions of job mobility. Mobility is of interest only if worker or job characteristics are imperfectly known. This brings us to learning models in which the hierarchy acts as an information acquisition filter. The problem is intricate, because the question is not just to match workers with jobs in a myopic fashion based on currently available information, but also to consider the implications of current assignments on what might be learned for the benefit of future assignments. Obviously, organizations are well aware of this dynamic dimension. Careers are partly designed with learning about ability in mind. A lot of experimentation goes on, particularly with young workers. Correspondingly, older workers may never be given a chance to prove themselves; they may get stuck in jobs that are below their true potential.[46]

Learning models in which workers are merely passive participants – "pawns" moved around by the company – have been studied by Prescott and Visscher (1980), MacDonald (1982) and Waldman (1984) among others. As an illustration, let us give some details of the Waldman model, because it brings out some interesting strategic aspects of job assignment.

Waldman introduces the idea that what is observable to outside firms is not the same as what the present employer learns. Specifically, in his model the worker's performance (output) can be observed internally, while the outside market only can observe the worker's job assignment and wage. He sets up a two-period model in which a worker performs a routine job in the first period, which reveals ability. The firm, based on this information, decides whether to promote the worker to a job in which output grows with ability.

Ignoring the market, the optimal promotion policy would be to assign a worker whose ability is above a cut-off level ρ^* to the ability-contingent job and leave him in the routine one otherwise. But one has to consider the fact that the market can bid away the worker contingent on the promotion, which reveals partial information about ability. Assuming that the worker can quit without penalty (because involuntary servitude is prohibited, including the posting of bonds), a promotion implies a wage increase as well to meet the outside bid. Consequently, a worker whose ability turns out to be just above the cut-off level ρ^* is not worth promoting, because of the implied (discrete) wage increase.

[46]The so-called two-armed bandit models [Rothschild (1974)] can explain why some workers may not reach their optimal level. In these models one stops experimenting before the true value is learned with certainty. It is commonly claimed that the reverse phenomenon – known as "Peter's Principle" – is true. This empirical principle states that everybody eventually rises to a level at which s/he is incompetent. Learning models provide a natural vehicle for studying Peter's Principle, but we are unaware of any work on this. One of the biggest problems such a model would have to address is why workers, who are found incompetent in their present task, are not demoted. Are the reasons sociological or can an economic rationale be found?

The equilibrium in this model will therefore exhibit fewer promotions than would be optimal if ability information were symmetric.[47] Actual wage patterns depend on contractual options. Waldman considers two cases: one-period contracts (spot wage) and long-term contracts. The most interesting feature, present in both cases, is that wages are attached to jobs, not to ability. The literature on internal labor markets has made frequent note of this important empirical regularity [Doeringer and Piore (1971)]. The rationale here is that discrete (and sometimes substantial) wage increases accompany promotions, because promotions involve considerable changes in market beliefs. This works in tandem with Rosen's idea, described above, that task assignment magnifies productivity differences due to ability.

In the models discussed so far, the employees do not act strategically. Ricart i Costa (1986) has analyzed a variation of Waldman's model in which the employee also learns his ability, but can use this information to solicit better job offers. The market offers a menu of output-contingent wage contracts in the second period, such that the employee's choice reveals his true ability. The present employer will foresee this and offer a matching wage. The upshot is that wages will be somewhat sensitive to ability in addition to jobs.[48]

Another strategic aspect of importance is that employees, whose promotions will depend on inferences about ability obtained from performance, may change their behavior to influence perceptions. That was already mentioned in Subsections 2.2 and 4.2. Career concerns can be beneficial in inducing effort to excel [Holmstrom (1982b)] as well as detrimental, because they may lead to undesirable influence activities [Milgrom (1988)] or to undesirable investment, production and other decisions [Holmstrom and Ricart i Costa (1986)]. Promotion policies can have a profound impact on employee behavior in this regard. Policies which place relatively larger weight on seniority (the alleged practice in Japan), remove a built-in pressure to compete and may be desirable, because they reduce unwanted influence activity.

From the notion that promotion policies have significant effects on the process of learning as well as employee behavior, it is a short step to realize that job design should be guided by these considerations. Even when employees act non-strategically, job structure matters for learning. Sociologists [e.g. Jacobs (1981)] have argued that the depth of the job hierarchy may reflect the need to become informed about the true characteristics of workers. For instance, in

[47]In a similar spirit, Milgrom and Oster (1984) argue that employers may bias promotion policies in favor of "visible" employees, whose characteristics are better known to the market for some other reason (so that the act of promoting the employee has a lower information content). They suggest that women earn less than men, because they are less visible publicly.

[48]Strategic use of information by the employee has also been investigated in the large labor literature on screening, though most of it makes no reference to hierarchies. [See, for instance, Spence (1973), Guasch and Weiss (1980).] A recent interesting paper on screening is Hermalin (1986.)

activities where errors are rare, but disastrous when they occur, a long career path is implied (e.g. airline pilots). These questions could well be addressed more formally with the learning apparatus we already have in place.

A related design question is the degree to which tasks are performed by groups. Sharing of praise or blame changes individual preferences in career models, possibly in an advantageous way. Obviously, there are many other reasons why team work is efficient. But the point is that individual performance measurement, which is prescribed by all effort-based agency models, need not be necessary, nor even desirable when career concerns are considered. This has been overlooked in the past and deserves more attention.

5.5. *The hierarchy as a nexus of contracts*

The grand mechanism design envisioned in the introduction to this subsection, as well as in Subsections 5.2 through 5.4, is appealing from the point of view of tractability. If it were feasible and costless to design a single contract for the whole organization, it would also be optimal. However, the single-contract paradigm is obviously a fiction. Organization theorists [see, for example, Cyert and March (1963) and Nelson and Winter (1982)] have emphasized the multilateral nature of contracting in real world hierarchies suggesting that the firm is a nexus of contracts [Jensen and Meckling (1976)].

There are many reasons why contracting is necessarily multi-lateral. For instance, all relevant parties cannot meet at the same time. This is clearly the case when contracting takes place across generations. Future workers cannot be part of a labor contract until they enter the firm (certainly not before they are born). More generally, it is hard to envision who the future partners will be even if they are acting agents in the economy at present. It is also true that, by choice, parties may decide to use short-term contracts if informational asymmetries are present [Hermalin (1986)]. Incomplete contracting, which will require subsequent updating and renegotiation, does not fit the single-contract paradigm either if new parties will enter later.

A major reason for multi-lateral contracting is that agents can enter into side-contracts with each other. On an informal basis this is commonplace in all organizations. Personal relationships and the like fall in this category.[49] More generally, reciprocation in the conduct of tasks represents side-contracting that cannot fully be controlled by a comprehensive contract. The most explicit form of side-transfers are bribes. They may be paid as monetary compensation for services or they may take more subtle forms – a promotion in exchange for another favor, for instance. It has been alleged that auditing firms occasionally

[49]Such indirect transfers have been emphasized by the Human Relations School; see Etzioni (1964).

obtain favorable contracts from their clients in exchange for good audits. Civil servants are known to have received lucrative job offers after they have quit their government jobs. The list could be extended. The point is that side-contracting in the form of bribes, personal relationships and promises of reciprocation are prevalent. How does this affect the design of incentives and tasks in a hierarchy?

This question, which is truly a major one, has hardly been studied at all, partly because of the analytical complexity. The grand contract design leads to a tractable optimization program, with a manageable set of constraints. By contrast, side-contracting will involve subdesigns by the agents, which generally complicate the analysis considerably. Some headway has been made recently, however, in certain simple agency settings. The approach that is taken is to view the side-contracts as incorporated into the grand design. The principal designs the contract outright so that it leaves no opportunity for the agents to engage in further side-transfers. This approach is not meant to be descriptive of the real situation. Typically, the principal will not be able to control information flows to the extent required for exhausting side-contracting opportunities. However, it is a useful technical device and provides an initial evaluation of the costs of side-contracting. The very fact that there are additional restrictions on the design makes it clear that side-contracting is, in general, costly.

Tirole (1986b) considers side-contracting between an owner, a supervisor and a worker.[50] The structure is the following. The worker observes the productivity of the technology (which can take only two values) after the contract is drawn. Depending on a random event, the supervisor may or may not observe the productivity. Thus, there are four information states. The owner designs a contract for both the worker and the supervisor, but cannot prevent his two employees from colluding via a side-contact (the owner could also collude with an employee, but this is proved to be worthless in the optimal contract). The owner's contract specifies that the worker and the supervisor report the productivity and as a function of the reports, payments are made and production is ordered.

[50]Cremer and Riordan (1986) is another paper using a similar approach. They consider a special case in which side-contracting can be made innocuous by a judicious organizational design. In their first model (their analysis holds for more complex hierarchical models), a group of downstream firms contract with an upstream supplier for the procurement of some input. Over the course of their relation the supplier becomes privately informed about its production cost while each customer gets private information about its value for the input. All parties are risk neutral. Cremer and Riordan solve for the optimal grand design, and show that by using expected externality payments, the optimal contract is immune to side-contracting. The intuition is that such payments force each party to internalize the externality imposed by its decisions on the other parties. By adding payments, a group internalizes the externality imposed by its decisions on the rest of the organization.

Demski and Sappington (1984) consider a model in which agents can collude about which equilibrium to play. No side-contracts are involved, because both prefer a different equilibrium than the principal desires. This triggers a design change, which is costly for the principal. However, see Ma and Moore (1985) and Turnbull (1985) on mechanisms that can avoid the problem costlessly.

It is shown that the optimal contract indeed looks different than if the supervisor and agent could be prevented from side-contracting. The contract provides for efficient production in all states, except the one in which the worker alone is aware that productivity is low. Thus, the supervisor is useful. To prevent side-contracting, information rents have to be shared between the worker and the supervisor. Most interestingly, the solution can be interpreted as one in which the worker and the supervisor collude so that the latter acts as an advocate for the former towards the owner. This is a phenomenon that is not surprising to observers of firms. It also points to the general idea that collusion occurs at the nexus of informed parties: shared secrets act as a catalyst for collusion.

The importance of collusion and side-contracting is heavily documented in the sociology literature [e.g. Crozier (1963) and Dalton (1959)]. Collusion is partly issue-dependent and is argued to be conditioned by the structure of information in the way indicated by the supervision model in Tirole (1986b).

To alleviate problems with side-contracting, the organization can try to curb transfers in various ways. This is routinely done for monetary transfers by direct prohibition. Limiting personal relationship (through isolation) is sometimes used as well, but it has obvious drawbacks. Functional transfers are often restricted; the threat of collusion may provide an explanation for limited use of supervisory reports, or for the widespread use of rough and inflexible bureaucratic rules and referral to a superior authority who resolves conflicts due to unforeseen contingencies (bureaucracies are organizations mainly run by rules). This points to some costs of using a grand contract that is coalition-proof, that is, which eliminates the incentives to collude. Supervision and flexibility may be lost in the process.

Finally, the organization can try to restrict reciprocity by promoting short-run relationships between its members through mobility. For instance, consider the extensive use of consulting firms, independent boards, anonymous refereeing or frequent permutations in the civil service and diplomatic corps. Of course, promoting such short-run relationships has drawbacks. They may prevent specific investments in work relationships or the development of trust that is so crucial for cooperation [Tirole (1986b)]. More work needs to be done to formalize how these internal reciprocity games interfere with efficient organizational behavior and how they influence the organizational design.

Side-contracting is a special case of multi-lateral contracting. An interesting multi-lateral contracting problem occurs when one agent works for many principals. This case has been studied by Bernheim and Whinston (1985, 1986). They assume that each principal contracts independently with the common agent; contracts between principals are excluded. The main issue is efficiency of the agent's action, as a result of the efforts of the principals to influence his choice. They show that if the agent is risk neutral, the efficient action is selected. Intuitively, the agent can be made the residual claimant for each of the principals' interests. When the agent is risk averse, however, bilateral contracting generally leads to an inefficient action. (The aggregate incentive scheme is efficient conditional on the choice of action.) For this result to obtain it is critical that principals know enough to forecast each others' incentive schemes (in a Nash equilibrium). It would be interesting to consider the case in which other parties' incentives are not known.

Bernheim and Whinston have opened a useful alley of research. Common agency is an important phenomenon, which can be found in wholesaling, government, and central service functions of firms, to name but a few examples.[51] It is also of interest in view of the recent organizational trend towards matrix management in firms. In matrix management subordinates are responsible to several superiors simultaneously. It remains to be seen how well such organizations can cope with the emerging problems of common agency.

5.6. The hierarchy as an authority structure

As in the two-tier case, a major obstacle in designing contracts for a complex organization is the impossibility or the high cost of specifying all the relevant future contingencies. Contracts will necessarily be incomplete and as new contingencies arise, gaps in the contract must be filled through bargaining. One role of authority within the organization is to constrain the bargaining process by designating a decision-maker in case of disagreement. Authority – its scope and entitlements – is a rather elusive concept. For instance, consider scope. Because contingencies are not precisely specified in an initial contract, neither is the exact set of decisions from which the party with the authority can choose. An engineer may have the authority to introduce a new technology for workers, but at the same time he may be prevented from choosing exhausting or potentially dangerous technologies.

The rights of authority at the firm level are defined by ownership of assets, tangible (machines or money) or intangible (goodwill or reputation). The distribution of authority rights comes from the delegation of the owner's authority to lower level functions (managers, foremen, etc.), usually in a nested fashion (one manager can delegate forward within his set of rights). A production manager or foreman is free, within limits, to reorganize his shop to adjust to new circumstances. A production worker can decide on how he carries out a task. The

[51]Baron (1985) analyzes a common agency problem arising from the regulation of a public utility by the Environmental Protection Agency (EPA) as well as a public utility commission. He shows that in a non-cooperative equilibrium, the EPA chooses more stringent abatement standards and maximum allowable emission fees than those which the two regulators would choose in a cooperative equilibrium. The PUC, which must provide the firm with a fair return, chooses higher prices than in the cooperative equilibrium.

allocation of decision rights within the firm is obviously a central issue and one could envision an approach to hierarchies based on the analysis of incomplete contracts. At this point in time such a theory is still to emerge. Hence, we will restrict ourselves to comments on some features of authority that can be expected to play an important role in any analysis.

The notion of authority through asset ownership is more distinct than delegated authority. The former has a fairly clear-cut legal meaning and is conferred by written document. By contrast, delegated authority is in most cases conferred orally and is revocable by simple declaration. The legal implications of delegated authority have been discussed by some legal scholars [Conrad et al. (1982)]. The very purpose of delegated authority may well be to avoid constant recourse by third parties to the principal. This implies that third parties must be able to transact with the agent with a minimum of inquiry as to her authority. The delegation is thus based on a common understanding of how the organization works, which must be shared by the principal, the agent and the third party. Because incomplete contracts are the basis for authority, we must look for a rule that gives legitimacy to non-contractible actions taken by the agent on behalf of the principal. Legal systems generally define authority by usage: either the authority is implied by the position or it is circumstantial; in both cases, authority is thought to be legitimate if it corresponds to good practice or prevailing customs.[52] Of course, this common usage definition of authority is still ambiguous, as witnessed by the courts' very diverse interpretations of the powers of a CEO.

The struggle for a clear legal definition of delegated authority has its counterpart in corporate organizations, where internal arbitration may replace the judicial system. Making all members understand who is deciding what in yet unforeseen circumstances is a perilous, but important, exercise in organization behavior, and its outcome can be seen as a part of corporate culture or organizational capital. If a common understanding fails, disagreements, conflicts of authority, and noncommitant delays and use of upper-managerment time result. An important aspect of authority within an organization is its vertical structure. Most conflicts between divisions or employees are solved by higher authorities, for instance chief executives, rather than by courts. Williamson (1975), in particular, has emphasized the superiority of internal organization in dispute settling matters.

This leads us to enquire about the requisite qualities of an arbitrator (be she a court or a superior). First the arbitrator must have a good knowledge of the situation to try to duplicate the outcome of the missing optimal comprehensive contract. Second, she must be independent. With respect to the first quality,

[52] The German procura system goes much further and allows the agent to bind the principal in all transactions but transfers of real estate.

external arbitrators, like courts, are likely to incur a cost of becoming informed. This cost also exists for superiors in an organization; in particular, in large firms the chief executives may be overloaded with decisions to arbitrate between their subordinates and have little a priori knowledge of each case; but because of everyday interaction, as well as a past familiarity with various jobs within the firm, internal arbitrators may incur a lower information cost. The second quality, independence, requires that the arbitrator not be judge and party, so as to value aggregate efficiency beyond the interest of any party. Side-contracting with the arbitrator must be prevented. Independence may fail, for instance, when the arbitrator has kept close ties with one of the involved divisions. More generally, arbitrators must have a reputation for settling disputes "fairly" (understand: "efficiently").

5.7. *Organizational forms*

As mentioned in the Introduction, organizational forms are related to several factors. At a given point of time, a firm's organization is meant to promote communication and incentives. The capital structure, the outside visibility of managers, the internal job market, the auditing and supervisory designs, the structure of competition between agents are all geared to this purpose. The organizational model is also conditioned by the current knowledge of how various types of organization work. The cost of experimenting (associated with both the possibility of mistake and the cost of training employees to learn the new rules of the game) explains both the predominant role of history and the existence of fads in organizational innovations. Last, the organizational model depends on the economic environment, including factor prices, and on the growth of the firm.

Examples of organizational innovations are the apparition of the U- and M-forms documented by Chandler (1966) and Williamson (1975). A reading of these innovations in the light of our survey might go as follows.

The U-form (unitary form) gathers activities according to their function within the firm: for example, auditing, marketing, finance, materials procurement, production. The Viner-like rationale for this gathering is to avoid a duplication of costs associated with each function.

The drawback of the U-form is, of course, the team problems (à la Alchian and Demsetz) that it may create. The performance of a product in a market depends on its design (R&D department), the quality of manufacturing (production), post-sale services (maintenance department), marketing efforts (marketing department), and so on. The difficulty of measuring individual performance is that it requires careful supervision and a good understanding of each functional division by the CEO and top managers. The latter become easily overloaded as the firm grows. And, indeed, the U-form collapsed with the horizontal expansion of firms [Chandler (1966)]. It was replaced by the M-form (multidivisional form), which resembles a collection of scaled-down U-form structures. In the M-form, divisions are organized so that their performance can be reliably measured. Distinction by product categories is most likely to achieve this goal. The role of the top management is then reduced to advising, auditing and allocating resources between the competing divisions. Within a division, by contrast, the supervisory mode is more prevalent and allows some assessment of the relative contributions of functional subdivisions.

As can be seen, the switch from the U-form to the M-form was partly triggered by a changing environment. A more recent example of this phenomenon is the matrix organization. Among other things, matrix organizations try to promote horizontal communication and decision-making (for instance, between marketing, R&D and production managers). The need for joint decision-making was made more acute by the gradual shortening of the life-cycle of products. In an industry where products become obsolete within a year, firms must be particularly quick at finding the right market niches. One may predict that future organizational innovations will follow. Already some discontent has been recorded concerning, for instance, the high number of authority conflicts between the joint decision-makers, which creates a high demand for time-consuming arbitration by top executives. [For an account of recent organizational developments, see Piore (1986) and Piore and Sabel (1985).] We are unaware of formal, agency-related work modelling these organizational forms.

6. Conclusion

This chapter has been deliberately issue-oriented. Rather than recapitulating existing techniques and results, we outlined the main lines of research and unveiled many open questions. Despite the tremendous progress made by organization theory over the last fifteen years, we still have a weak understanding of many important facets of organizational behavior.

There are at least three outstanding problems that need attention. A first (theoretical) step is to develop and apply techniques that deal with non-standard problems such as incomplete contracts, bounded rationality and multi-lateral contracting. The second step ought to integrate observations from neighboring fields such as sociology and psychology – in a consistent (not ad hoc) way into the theoretical apparatus. The third step will be to increase the evidence/theory ratio, which is currently very low in this field. While informational asymmetries, contractual incompleteness or imperfect communication will typically be hard to measure, empirical research such as Joskow's (1985) (applying Williamson's ex-post bilateral monopoly problem to contracts between coal mines and electric utilities) or Wolfson's (1985) (applying incentive theory to oil drilling) raise hopes that the economic approach to organizations will be more carefully tested in the near future.

References

Admati, A. and Perry, M. (1987) 'Strategic delay in bargaining', *Review of Economic Studies*, 54:345–364.

Aghion, P. and Bolton, P. (1986) 'An 'incomplete contracts' approach to bankruptcy and the optimal financial structure of the firm', University of California, Berkely, mimeo.

Aghion, P. and Bolton, P. (1987) 'Contracts as a barrier to entry', *American Economic Review*, 77:388–401.

Akerlof, G. (1970) 'The market for 'lemons': Quality and the market mechanism', *Quarterly Journal of Economics*, 84:488–500.

Alchian, A. (1968) 'Corporate management property rights', in: *Economic policy and the regulation of securities*. Washington, D.C.: American Enterprise Institute.

Alchian, A. and Demsetz, H. (1972) 'Production, information costs, and economic organization', *American Economic Review*, 62:777–795.

Antle, R. and Demski, J. (1987) 'Revenue recognition', Yale University, mimeo.

Antle, R. and Smith, A. (1986) 'An empirical investigation of the relative performance evaluation of corporate executives', *Journal of Accounting Research*, 24:1–39.

Aron, D. (1988) 'Ability, moral hazard, firm size and diversification', *Rand Journal of Economics*, 19:72–87.

Arrow, K. (1974) *The limits of organization*. New York: Norton.

Arrow, K. (1985) 'The economics of agency', in: J. Pratt and R. Zeckhauser, eds., *Principals and agents: The structure of business*. Boston: Harvard Business School Press, 37–51.

Baiman, S. (1982) 'Agency research in managerial accounting: A survey', *Journal of Accounting Literature*. 1:154–213.

Baiman, S. and Demski, J. (1980) 'Economically optimal performance evaluation and control systems', *Journal of Accounting Research*, 18(Supplement):184–220.

Baron, D. (1985) 'Noncooperative regulation of a nonlocalized externality', *Rand Journal of Economics*, 16:553–568.

Baumol, W. (1959) *Business behavior, value and growth*. New York: Macmillan.

Baumol, W., Panzer, J. and Willig, R. (1982) *Contestable markets and the theory of industry structure*. New York: Harcourt Brace Jovanovich.

Bernheim, D. and Whinston, M. (1985) 'Common marketing agency as a device for facilitating collusion,', *Rand Journal of Economics*, 16:269–281.

Bernheim, D. and Whinston, M. (1986) 'Common agency', *Econometrica*, 54:932–942.

Bhattacharya, S. (1983) 'Tournaments and incentives: Heterogeneity and essentiality', research paper no. 695, Graduate School of Business, Stanford University.

Blackwell, D. (1953) 'Equivalent comparisons of experiments'. *Annals of Mathematical Statistics*, 24:265–272.

Bonanno, G. and Vickers, J. (1986) 'Vertical separation', Nuffield College, Oxford, mimeo.

Bradley, M., Desai, A. and Kim, E. (1987), 'Synergistic gains from corporate acquisitions and the division between the stockholders of target and acquiring firms," *Journal of Financial Economics*, forthcoming.

Brander, J. and Lewis, T. (1986) 'Oligopoly and financial structure: The limited liability effect', *American Economic Review*, 76:956–970.

Caillaud, B. (1986) 'Regulation, competition and asymmetric information', *Journal of Economic Theory*, forthcoming.

Caillaud, B., Guesnerie, R. and Rey, P. (1986) 'Noisy observation in adverse selection models', INSEE, mimeo.

Caillaud, B., Guesnerie, R., Rey, P. and Tirole, J. (1988) 'Government intervention in production and incentives theory: A review of recent contributions', *Rand Journal of Economics*, 19:1–26.

Calvo, G. and Wellisz, S. (1978) 'Supervision, loss of control, and the optimal size of the firm', *Journal of Political Economy*, 86:943–952.

Calvo, G. and Wellisz, S. (1979) 'Hierarchy, ability, and income distribution', *Journal of Political Economy*, 87:991–1010.

Carmichael, L. (1983) 'Firm-specific human capital and promotion ladders', *Bell Journal of Economics*, 14:251–258.

Chandler, A. (1966) *Strategy and structure*. New York: Doubleday and Company (Anchor Book Edition).

Clark, R. (1985) 'Agency costs versus fiduciary duties', in: J. Pratt and R. Zeckhauser, eds., *Principals and agents: The structure of business*. Cambridge, Mass.: Harvard Business School Press.

Conrad, A., Knauss, R. and Spiegel, S. (1982) *Enterprise organization*, 3rd ed. Foundation Press.

Corey, R. (1978) 'Should companies centralize procurement?' *Harvard Business Review*, 56:102–110.

Crampes, C. (1983) 'Subventions et régulations d'une enterprise privée', *Annales de l'INSEE*, 51:47–63.

Cramton, P. (1984) 'Bargaining with incomplete information: An infinite horizon model with two-sided uncertainty', *Review of Economic Studies*, 51:529–593.

Crawford, V. (1986) 'Long term relationships governed by short term contracts', working paper no. 205, Industrial Relations Section, Princeton University.

Cremer, J. (1986a) 'Cooperation in ongoing organizations', *Quarterly Journal of Economics*, 101:33–50.

Cremer, J. (1986b) 'Corporate culture: Cognitive aspects', Virginia Polytechnic Institute, mimeo.

Cremer, J. and Riordan, M. (1986) 'On governing multilateral transactions with bilateral contracts', discussion paper no. 134, Studies in Industry Economics, Stanford University.

Crozier, M. (1963) *Le phenomene bureaucratique*. Paris: Editions du Seuil; (translated by Crozier as *The bureaucratic phenomenon*, University of Chicago Press, 1967).

Cyert, R. and March, J. (1963) *A behavioral theory of the firm*. Englewood Cliffs, N.J.: Prentice-Hall.

Dalton, M. (1959) *Men who manage*, New York: Wiley.

De Alessi, L. (1983) 'Property rights, transaction costs, and X-efficiency', *American Economic Review*, 73:64–81.

Demski, J. and Feltham, G. (1976) *Cost determination: A conceptual approach*. Ames, Iowa: The Iowa University Press.

Demski, J. and Sappington, D. (1984) 'Optimal incentive contracts with multiple agents', *Journal of Economic Theory*, 17:152–171.

Demski, J., and Sappington, D. (1986) 'Line item reporting, factor acquisition and subcontracting', *Journal of Accounting Research*, 24:250–269.

Demski, J., Sappington, D. and Spiller, P. (1987) 'Managing supplier switching', *Rand Journal of Economics*, 18:77–97.

Diamond, D. (1984) 'Financial intermediation and delegated monitoring', *Review of Economic Studies*, 51:393–444.

Doeringer, P. and Piore, M. (1971) *Internal labor markets and manpower analysis*. Lexington, Mass.: Heath.

Dye, R. (1984) 'The trouble with tournaments', *Economic Inquiry*, 22:147–149.

Eswaran, M. and Kotwal, A. (1984) 'The moral hazard of budget-breaking', *Rand Journal of Economics*, 15:578–581.

Etzioni, A. (1964) *Modern organizations*. Englewood Cliffs, N.J.: Prentice-Hall.

Evans, D. (1986) 'Tests of alternative theories of firm growth', research report no. 86-36, C.V. Starr Center for Applied Economics, New York University.

Fama, E. (1980) 'Agency problems and the theory of the firm', *Journal of Political Economy*, 88:288–307.

Farrell, J. and Gallini, N. (1986) 'Second-sourcing as a commitment: Monopoly incentives to attract competition', *Quarterly Journal of Economics*, forthcoming.

Fershtman, C. and Judd, K. (1986) 'Strategic incentive manipulation in rivalous agency', IMSSS TR 496, Stanford University.

Fershtman, C., Judd, K. and Kalai, E. (1986) 'Cooperation and the strategic aspect of delegation', Northwestern University, mimeo.

Freixas, X., Guesnerie, R. and Tirole, J. (1985) 'Planning under incomplete information and the ratchet effect', *Review of Economic Studies*, 52:173–191.

Friedman, B. (1985) *Corporate capital structures in the United States*. Chicago: University of Chicago Press.
Fudenberg, D. and Tirole, J. (1983) 'Sequential bargaining with incomplete information', *Review of Economic Studies*, 50:221–247.
Fudenberg, D., Holmstrom, B. and Milgrom, P. (1986) 'Short term contracts and long term agency relationships', School of Organization and Management, Yale University, draft.
Galbraith, K. (1967) *The new industrial state*. Boston: Houghton Mifflin.
Gale, D., and Hellwig, M. (1985) 'Incentive compatible debt contracts: The one period problem', *Review of Economic Studies*, 52:647–664.
Geanakopolos, J. and Milgrom, P. (1985) 'A theory of hierarchies based on limited managerial attention', Cowles Foundation paper no. 775, Yale University.
Gertner, R., Gibbons, R. and Scharfstein, D. (1987) 'Simultaneous signalling to the capital and product markets', Massachusetts Institute of Technology, mimeo.
Gibbons, R. (1985) 'Optimal incentive schemes in the presence of career concerns', Massachusetts Institute of Technology, mimeo.
Gjesdal, F. (1982) 'Information and incentives: The agency information problem', *Review of Economic Studies*, 49:373–390.
Green, J. and Stokey, N. (1983) 'A comparison of tournaments and contests', *Journal of Political Economy*, 91:349–364.
Grossman, S. and Hart, O. (1977) 'On value maximization and alternative objectives of the firm', *Journal of Finance*, 32:389–440m.i.t.2.
Grossman, S. and Hart, O. (1980) 'Takeover bids, the free rider problem, and the theory of the corporation', *Bell Journal of Economics*, 11:42–64.
Grossman, S. and Hart, O. (1982) 'Corporated financial structure and managerial incentives', in: J. McCall, ed., *The economics of information and uncertainty*. Chicago: Univeristy of Chicago Press, 107–137.
Grossman, S. and Hart, O. (1983) 'An analysis of the principal–agent problem', *Econometrica*, 51:7–45.
Grossman, S. and Hart, O. (1986) 'The costs and benefits of ownership: A theory of vertical and lateral integration', *Journal of Political Economy*, 94:691–719.
Grossman, S. and Hart, O. (1987) 'One share/one vote and the market for corporate control', working paper, Department of Economics, Massachusetts Institute of Technology.
Grossman, S., Hart, O. and Maskin, E. (1983) 'Unemployment with observable aggregate shocks', *Journal of Political Economy*, 91:907–928.
Guasch, L. and Weiss, A. (1980) 'Wages as sorting mechanisms in competitive markets with asymmetric information: A theory of testing', *Review of Economic Studies*, 47:653–664.
Harris, M. and Raviv, A. (1979) 'Optimal incentive contracts with imperfect information', *Journal of Economic Theory*, 20:231–259.
Harris, M. and Raviv, A. (1985) 'Corporate control contests and capital structure', working paper, Northwestern University.
Harris, M. and Raviv, A. (1987) 'Corporate governance: Voting rights and majority rules', working paper, Department of Finance, Northwestern University.
Hart, O. (1983a) 'The market mechanism as an incentive scheme', *Bell Journal of Economics*, 74:366–382.
Hart, O. (1983b) 'Optimal labour contracts under asymmetric information: An introduction', *Review of Economic Studies*, 50:3–35.
Hart, O. and Holmstrom, B. (1987) 'The theory of contracts', in: Trueman Bewley, ed., *Advances in economic theory, Fifth World Congress*. Cambridge: Cambridge University Press.
Hart, O. and Moore, J. (1988) 'Incomplete contracts and renegotiation', *Econometrics*, 56:755–786.
Hermalin, B. (1986) 'Adverse selection and contract length', Massachusetts Institute of Technology, mimeo.
Hermalin, B. (1987) 'Adverse effects of the threat of takeovers', Massachusetts Institute of Technology, mimeo.
Hermalin, B. and Weisbach, M. (1987) 'The determinants of board composition', Massachusetts Institute of Technology, mimeo.
Holmstrom, B. (1979) 'Moral hazard and observability', *Bell Journal of Economics*, 10:74–91.

Holmstrom, B. (1982a) 'Moral hazard in teams', *Bell Journal of Economics*, 13:324–340.

Holmstrom, B. (1982b) 'Managerial incentive problems – A dynamic perspective', in: *Essays in economics and management in honor of Lars Wahlbeck*. Helsinki: Swedish School of Economics.

Holmstrom, B., and Milgrom, P. (1987) 'Aggregation and linearity in the provision of intertemporal incentives', *Econometrica*, 55:303–328.

Holmstrom, B. and Ricart i Costa, J. (1986) 'Managerial incentives and capital management', *Quarterly Journal of Economics*, 101:835–860.

Holmstrom, B. and Weiss, L. (1985) 'Managerial incentives, investment and aggregate implications: Scale effects', *Review of Economic Studies*, 52:403–426.

Hopenhayn, H. (1986) 'A competitive stochastic model of entry and exit to an industry', University of Minnesota, mimeo.

Jacobs, D. (1981) 'Towards a theory of mobility and behavior in organizations: An inquiry into the consequences of some relationships between individual performance and organizational success', *American Journal of Sociology*, 87:684–707.

Jensen, M. (1986) 'Agency costs of free cash flow, corporate finance and takeovers', *American Economic Review*, 76:323–329.

Jensen, M. and Meckling, W. (1976) 'Theory of the firm: Managerial behavior, agency costs, and capital structure', *Journal of Financial Economics*, 3:305–360.

Joskow, P. (1985) 'Vertical integration and long term contracts: The case of coal-burning electric generating plants', *Journal of Law, Economics and Organization*, 1:33–80.

Jovanovic, B. (1982) 'Selection and the evolution of industry', *Econometrica*, 50:649–670.

Katz, M. (1987) 'Game-playing agents: Contracts as precommitments', Princeton University, mimeo.

Keren, M. and Levhari, D. (1983) 'The internal organization of the firm and the shape of average costs', *Bell Journal of Economics*, 14:474–486.

Kihlstrom, R. and Laffont, J.-J. (1979) 'A general equilibrium entrepreneurial theory of the firm based on risk aversion', *Journal of Political Economy*, 87:719–748.

Klein, B., Crawford, R. and Alchian, A. (1978) 'Vertical integration, appropriable rents and the competitive contracting process', *Journal of Law and Economics*, 21:297–326.

Kreps, D. (1984) 'Corporate culture and economic theory', Graduate School of Business, Stanford University, mimeo.

Kreps, D. and Wilson, R. (1982) 'Reputation and imperfect information', *Journal of Economic Theory*, 27:253–279.

Laffont, J.-J. and Maskin, E. (1982) 'The theory of incentives: An overview', in: W. Hildenbrand, ed., *Advances in economic theory*. New York: Cambridge University Press.

Laffont, J.-J. and Tirole, J. (1986) 'Using cost observation to regulate firms', *Journal of Political Economy*, 94:614–641.

Laffont, J.-J. and Tirole, J. (1987a) 'Auctioning incentive contracts', *Journal of Political Economy*, 95:921–937.

Laffont, J.-J. and Tirole, J. (1987b) 'Repeated auctions of incentive contracts, investment and bidding parity, with an application to takeovers', discussion paper no. 463, Massachusetts Institute of Technology.

Laffont, J.-J. and Tirole, J. (1988) 'The dynamics of incentive contracts', *Econometrica*, September.

Lambert, R. (1983) 'Long-term contracting and moral hazard', *Bell Journal of Economics*, 14:441–452.

Lazear, E. (1986) 'Pay equality and industrial politics', Hoover institution, Stanford University, mimeo.

Lazear, E. and Rosen, S. (1981) 'Rank-order tournaments as optimum labor contracts', *Journal of Political Economy*, 89:841–864.

Leibenstein, H. (1966) 'Allocative efficiency as '*X*-efficiency'', *American Economic Review*, 56:392–415.

Leland, H. and Pyle, D. (1977) 'Information asymmetries, financial structure, and financial inatermediaries', *Journal of Finance*, 32:371–387.

Lippman, S. and Rumelt, R. (1982) 'Uncertain imitability: An analysis of interfirm differences in efficiency under competition', *Bell Journal of Economics*, 13:418–438.

Lucas, R. (1967) 'Adjustment costs and the theory of supply', *Journal of Political Economy*, 75:321–339.

Lucas, R. (1978) 'On the size distribution of business firms', *Bell Journal of Economics*, 9:508–523.

Lydall, H. (1968) *The structure of earnings*. New York: Oxford University Press.

Ma, C. and Moore, J. (1985) 'Stopping agents cheat', working paper, London School of Economics.

MaCaulay, S. (1963) 'Nob-contractual relations in business', *American Sociological Review*, 28:55–70.

MacDonald, G. (1982) 'Information in production', *Econometrica*, 50:1143–1162.

MacDonald, G. (1984) 'New directions in the economic theory of agency', *Canadian Journal of Economics*, 17:415–440.

Mace, M. (1971) 'Directors: Myth and reality'. Graduate School of Business Administration, Harvard University.

MacLeod, B. and Malcomson, J. (1985) 'Reputation and hierarchy in dynamic models of employment', Queen's University, mimeo.

Malcomson, J. (1984) 'Work incentives, hierarchy, and internal labor markets', *Journal of Political Economy*, 92:486–507.

Malcomson, J. and Spinnewyn, F. (1988) 'The multiperiod principal agent problem', *Review of Economic Studies*, 55:391–408.

Mansfield, E. (1962) 'Entry, Gibrat's law, innovation and the growth of firms', *American Economic Review*, 52:1023–1051.

Marschak, J. and Radner, R. (1972) *Economic theory of teams*. New Haven: Yale University Press.

Maskin, E. and Riley, J. (1985) 'Input vs. output incentive schemes,' *Journal of Public Economics*, 28:1–23.

Masten, S. (1986a) 'Institutional choice and the organization of production: The make-or-buy decision', *Journal of Institutional and Theoretical Economics*, 142:493–509.

Masten, S. (1986b) 'The institutional basis for the firm', working paper no. 473, Graduate School of Business Administration, The University of Michigan.

Mathewson, F. and Winter, R. (1985) 'Is exclusive dealing anticompetitive?', working paper no. 8517, University of Toronto.

McAfee, P. and McMillan, J. (1987) 'Competition for agency contracts', *Rand Journal of Economics*, 18:296–307.

Melumad, N. and Reichelstein, S. (1986) 'Value of communication in agencies', Graduate School of Business, Stanford University, mimeo.

Milgrom, P. (1988) 'Employment contracts, influence activities and efficient organization design', *Journal of Political Economy*, 96:42–60.

Milgrom, P. and Oster, S. (1987) 'Job discrimination, market forces and the invisibility hypothesis', *Quarterly Journal of Economics*, 102:453–476.

Milgrom, P. and Roberts, J. (1982) 'Predation, reputation and entry deterrence', *Journal of Economic Theory*, 27:280–312.

Milgrom, P. and Roberts, J. (1987) 'Bargaining and influence costs and the organization of economic activity', research paper no. 934, Graduate School of Business, Stanford University.

Mirrlees, J. (1974) 'Notes on welfare economics, information and uncertainty', in: M. Balch, D. McFadden and S. Wu, eds., *Essays in economic behavior under uncertainty*. Amsterdam: North-Holland, 243–258.

Mirrlees, J. (1976) 'The optimal structure of authority and incentives within an organization', *Bell Journal of Economics*, 7:105–131.

Modigliani, F. (1963) 'Corporate income taxes and the cost of capital: A correction', *American Economic Review*, 53:433–443.

Modigliani, F. and Miller, M. (1958) 'The costs of capital, corporation finance, and the theory of investment', *American Economic Review*, 48:261–297.

Mookerjee, D. (1984) 'Optimal incentive schemes with many agents', *Review of Economics Studies*, 51:433–446.

Morck, R., Shleifer, A. and Vishny, R. (1986) 'Ownership structure and corporate performance: An empirical analysis', NBER: Cambridge, Mass., mimeo.

Murphy, K. (1984) 'Incentives, learning and compensation: A theoretical and empirical investigation of managerial labor contracts', *Rand Journal of Economics*, 17:59–76.

Myers, S. and Majluf, N. (1984) 'Corporate financing and investment decisions when firms have information that investors do not have', *Journal of Financial Economics*, 13:187–221.

Myerson, R. (1984) 'Multistage games with communication', discussion paper no. 590, CMSEMS, Northwestern University.

Nalebuff, B. and Stiglitz, J. (1983) 'Prizes and incentives: Towards a general theory of compensation and competition', *Bell Journal of Economics*, 14:21–43.

Narayanan, M.P. (1985) 'Managerial incentives for short-term results', *Journal of Finance*, 40(5):1469–1484.

Nelson, R. and Winter, S. (1982) *An evolutionary theory of economic change*. Cambridge, Mass.: Harvard University Press.

Penrose, E. (1959) *The theory of the growth of the firm*. New York: Wiley.

Peters, T. and Waterman, R. (1982) *In search of excellence*. New York: Warner Books.

Picard, P. (1987) 'On the design of incentive schemes under moral hazard and adverse selection', *Journal of Public Economics*, 33:305–332.

Piore, M. (1986) 'Corporate reform in American manufacturing and the challenge to economic theory', Massachusetts Institute of Technology, mimeo.

Piore, M. and Sabel, C. (1985) *The second industrial divide*. New York: Basic Books.

Prescott, E. and Visscher, M. (1980) 'Organization capital', *Journal of Political Economy*, 88:446–461.

Radner, R. (1981) 'Monitoring cooperative agreements in a repeated principal–agent relationship', *Econometrica*, 49:1127–1148.

Radner, R. (1985) 'Repeated principal–agent games with discounting', *Econometrica*, 53:1173–1198.

Rey, P. and Salanié, B. (1986) 'Long term, short term, and renegotiation', INSEE, mimeo.

Rey, P. and Stiglitz, J. (1986) 'The role of exclusive territories in producers' competition', Princeton University, mimeo.

Rey, P. and Tirole, J. (1986) 'The logic of vertical restraints', *American Economic Review*, 76:921–939.

Ricart i Costa, J. (1986) 'Managerial task assignment and promotions', Universitat Autonoma de Barcelona, mimeo.

Rogerson, W. (1985) 'Repeated moral hazard', *Econometrica*, 53:69–76.

Rosen, S. (1982) 'Authority, control, and the distribution of earnings', *Bell Journal of Economics*, 13:311–323.

Rosen, S. (1986) 'Prizes and incentives in elimination tournaments', *American Economic Review*, 76:701–715.

Ross, S. (1973) 'The economic theory of agency: The principal's problem', *American Economic Review*, 63:134–139.

Ross, S. (1977) 'The determination of financial structure: The incentive signalling approach', *Bell Journal of Economics*, 8:23–40.

Ross, S. (1978) 'Some notes on financial incentive signalling models, activity choice and risk preferences', *Journal of Finance*, 33:777–792.

Rothschild, M. (1974) 'A two-armed bandit theory of market pricing', *Journal of Economic Theory*, 9:185–202.

Rubinstein, A. (1979) 'Offenses that may have been committed by accident – An optimal policy of retribution', in: S. Brahms, A. Shotter and G. Schrodiauer, eds., *Applied game theory*. Wurtzburg: Physica-Verlag, 406–413.

Sappington, D. (1984) 'Incentive contracting with asymmetric and imperfect precontractual knowledge', *Journal of Economic Theory*, 34:52–70.

Scharfstein, D. (1988a) 'Product market competition and managerial slack', *Rand Journal of Economics*, 19:147–155.

Scharfstein, D. (1988b) 'The disciplinary role of takeovers', *Review of Economic Studies*, 55:185–200.

Schein, E. (1984) 'Coming to a new awareness of organizational culture', *Sloan Management Review*, 25:3–16.

Scherer, F. (1980) *Industrial market structure and economic performance*, 2nd edn. Chicago: Rand McNally College Publishing Company.

Shavell, S. (1979) 'Risk sharing and incentives in the principal and agent relationship', *Bell Journal of Economics*, 10:55–73.

Shepard, A. (1987) 'Licensing to enhance demand for new technologies', *Rand Journal of Economics*, 18:360–368.

Shleifer, A. (1985) 'A theory of yardstick competition', *Rand Journal of Economics*, 16:319–327.

Shleifer, A. and Summers, L. (1988) 'Hostile takeovers and breaches of trust', in: A. Auerbach, ed., *Corporate takeovers: Causes and consequences*. Chicago: The University of Chicago Press, 33–56.

Shleifer, A. and Vishny, R. (1986a) 'Large shareholders and corporate control', *Journal of Political Economy*, 94:461–488.
Shleifer, A. and Vishny, R. (1986b) 'Greenmail white knights and shareholders' interest', *Rand Journal of Economics*, 17:293–309.
Simon, H. (1951) 'A formal theory of the employment relationship', *Econometrica*, 19:293–305.
Simon, H. (1957) *Models of man*. New York: Wiley.
Simon, H. (1976) *Administrative behavior*, 3rd edn. London: Macmillan.
Sobel, J. and Takahashi, I. (1983) 'A multistage model of bargaining', *Review of Economic Studies*, 50:411–426.
Spence, M. (1973) 'Job market signalling', *Quarterly Journal of Economics*, 87:355–374.
Spence, M. and Zeckhauser, R. (1971) 'Insurance, information and individual action', *American Economic Review Papers and Proceedings*, 61:380–387.
Stein, J. (1987) 'Efficient stock prices, inefficient firms: A signal-jamming model of myopic corporate behavior', Harvard Business School, mimeo.
Stein, J. (1988) 'Takeover threats and managerial myopia', *Journal of Political Economy*, 96:61–80.
Stiglitz, J. (1975) 'Incentives, risk and information: Notes towards a theory of hierarchy', *Bell Journal of Economics*, 6:552–579.
Tirole, J. (1986a) 'Procurement and renegotiation', *Journal of Political Economy*, 94:235–259.
Tirole, J. (1986b) 'Hierarchies and bureaucracies', *Journal of Law, Economics and Organization*, 2:181–214.
Turnbull, S. (1985) 'The revelation principle and the 'principal pet' in multiple agency problems', working paper, the Ohio State University.
Vassilakis, S. (1985) 'On the division of labor', Johns Hopkins University, mimeo.
Viner, J. (1932) 'Cost curves and supply curves', *Zeitschrift für National-ökonomie*, 3:23–46.
Waldman, M. (1984) 'Job assignments, signalling, and efficiency', *Rand Journal of Economics*, 15:255–270.
Weitzman, M. (1974) 'Prices versus quantities', *Review of Economic Studies*, 41:477–491.
Weitzman, M. (1980) 'The 'ratchet principle' and performance incentives', *Bell Journal of Economics*, 11:302–308.
Williamson, O. (1964) *The economics of discretionary behavior: Managerial objectives in a theory of the firm*. Englewood Cliffs, N.J.: Prentice–Hall.
Williamson, O. (1967) 'Hierarchical control and the optimal firm size, *Journal of Political Economy*, 75:123–138.
Williamson, O. (1975) *Markets and hierarchies: Analysis and antitrust implications*. New York: Free Press.
Williamson, O. (1985) *The economic institutions of capitalism*. New York: Free Press.
Wilson, R. (1969) 'The structure of incentives of decentralization under uncertainty', in: M. Guilbaud, ed., *La decision*. Paris: CNRS.
Wilson, R. (1986) 'The theory of syndicates', *Econometrica*, 36:119–132.
Wolfson, M. (1985) 'Empirical evidence of incentive problems and their mitigation in oil and tax shelter programs', in: J. Pratt and R. Zeckhauser, eds., *Principals and agents: The structure of business*. Boston: Harvard Business School Press, 101–125.

Chapter 3

TRANSACTION COST ECONOMICS

OLIVER E. WILLIAMSON*

University of California, Berkeley

Contents

*The author is Professor of Economics, Transamerica Professor of Corporate Strategy, and Professor of Law, University of California, Berkeley. The chapter benefited from the Sloan Foundation grant to Yale University to support research on the Economics of Organization. Helpful comments on an earlier draft from Erin Anderson, Henry Hansmann, Bengt Holmstrom, Roberta Romano, and Robert Willig are gratefully acknowledged.

Handbook of Industrial Organization, Volume I, Edited by R. Schmalensee and R.D. Willig

1. Introduction

Recent and continuing headway notwithstanding, transaction cost economics maintains that our understanding of the economic institutions of capitalism – firms, markets, hybrid modes – is very primitive. It subscribes to the following modest research objective: "to organize our necessarily incomplete perceptions about the economy, to see connections that the untutored eye would miss, to tell plausible ... causal stories with the help of a few central principles, and to make rough quantitative judgments about the consequences of economic policy and other exogenous events" [Solow (1985, p. 329)].

Transaction cost economics adopts a contractual approach to the study of economic organization. Questions such as the following are germane: Why are there so many forms of organization? What main purpose is served by alternative modes of economic organization and best informs the study of these matters? Striking differences among labor markets, capital markets, intermediate product markets, coporate governance, regulation, and family organization notwithstanding, is it the case that a common theory of contract informs all? What core features – in human, technology, and process respects – does such a common theory of contract rely on? These queries go to the heart of the transaction cost economics research agenda.

As compared with other approaches to the study of economic organization, transaction cost economics (1) is more microanalytic, (2) is more self-conscious about its behavioral assumptions, (3) introduces and develops the economic importance of asset specificity, (4) relies more on comparative institutional analysis, (5) regards the business firm as a governance structure rather than a production function, (6) places greater weight on the ex post institutions of contract, with special emphasis on private ordering (as compared with court ordering), and (7) works out of a combined law, economics and organization perspective. The basic transaction cost economics strategy for deriving refutable implications is this: assign transactions (which differ in their attributes) to governance structures (the adaptive capacities and associated costs of which differ) in a discriminating (mainly transaction cost economizing) way.

The background out of which transaction cost economics works is sketched in Section 2. The operationalization of transaction cost economics is discussed in Section 3. Vertical integration, an understanding of which serves as a paradigm for helping to unpack the puzzles of complex economic organization more generally, is the subject of Section 4. Other applications of the transaction cost approach are examined in Section 5. Some empirical tests of the transaction cost hypotheses are briefly summarized in Section 6. Public policy ramifications are developed in Section 7. Concluding remarks follow.

2. Background

Transaction cost economics traces its origins to seminal contributions in law, economics, and organization that were made in the 1930s. Leading economic contributions were made by Commons (1934) and Coase (1937). Llewellyn (1931) added key legal insights, and Barnard (1938) offered an organization theory perspective.

Commons urged that the transaction was and should be made the basic unit of analysis. A contractual point of view was adopted and attention was focused on the importance of crafting institutions that serve to harmonize trading between parties with otherwise adversarial interests. Coase likewise adopted a microanalytic perspective and insisted that the study of firms and markets proceed comparatively, with emphasis on transaction cost economizing. Llewellyn maintained that the study of contract should focus less on legal rules than on the purposes to be served. Much more attention to private ordering (efforts by the parties to align their own affairs and devise mechanisms to resolve differences) with correspondingly less weight being assigned to legal centralism (dispute resolution under the legal rules evolved by the courts and adopted by the state) was thus indicated. And Barnard urged that the powers and limits of internal organization be brought more self-consciously to the fore.

2.1. Main case

Economic organization services many purposes. Among those that have been ascribed by economists are monopoly and efficient risk bearing. Power and associational gains are sometimes held to be the main purposes of economic organization, especially by noneconomists. And some hold that "social institutions and arrangement...[are] the adventitious result of legal, historical, or political forces" [Granovetter (1985, p. 488)].

The study of complex systems is facilitated by distinguishing core purposes from auxiliary purposes. Transaction cost economics subscribes to and develops the view that economizing is the core problem of economic organization. Frank Knight's remarks are apposite [Knight (1941, p. 252; emphasis added)]:

> ...men in general, and within limits, wish to behave economically, to make their activities *and their organization* "efficient" rather than wasteful. This fact does deserve the utmost emphasis; and an adequate definition of the science of economics...might well make it explicit that the main relevance of the discussion is found in its relation to social policy, assumed to be directed toward the end indicated, of increasing economic efficiency, of reducing waste.

Main case frameworks do not purport to be exhaustive but are designed to go to the fundamentals.[1] Especially in an area where opinions proliferate, of which the economics of organization is one, insistence upon refutable implications is needed to sort the wheat from the chaff. This is the touchstone function to which Georgescu-Roegan refers. Thus, although "the purpose of science in general is not prediction but knowledge for its own sake" [Georgescu-Roegan (1971, p. 37)], prediction is nevertheless "the touchstone of scientific knowledge".

2.2. Behavioral assumptions

Many economists treat behavioral assumptions as unimportant. This reflects a widely held opinion that the realism of the assumptions is unimportant and that the fruitfulness of a theory turns on its implications [Friedman (1953)]. But whereas transaction cost economics is prepared to be judged (comparatively) by the refutable implications which this approach uniquely affords, it also maintains that the behavioral assumptions are important – not least of all because they serve to delimit the study of contract to the feasible subset.

Knight insisted that the study of economic organization needed to be informed by an appreciation for "human nature as we know it" (1965, p. 270), with special reference to the condition of "moral hazard" (1965, p. 260). And Bridgeman reminded social scientists that "the principal problem in understanding the actions of men is to understand how they think – how their minds work" [Bridgeman (1955, p. 450)]. Coase more recently remarked that "modern institutional economics should start with real institutions. Let us also start with man as he is" [Coase (1984, p. 231)]. Coase urges in this connection that the view of man as a "rational utility maximizer" should be abandoned (1984, p. 231), but the salient attributes of "man as he is" otherwise remain undescribed.

I have previously argued that contracting man is distinguished from the orthodox conception of maximizing man in two respects. The first of these is the condition of bounded rationality. Second, contracting man is given to self-interest seeking of a deeper and more troublesome kind than his economic man predecessor.

Although it is sometimes believed that Herbert Simon's notion of bounded rationality is alien to the rationality tradition in economics, Simon actually

[1]Agreement on the main case does not imply that extensions to the main case, to make allowance, for example, for monopoly purposes (where the appropriate preconditions hold), cannot be made. But this is very different from making monopoly the main case – to which economizing is an added wrinkle.

enlarges rather than reduces the scope for rationality analysis. Thus, the economic actors with whom Simon is concerned are "*intendedly* rational, but only *limitedly* so" [Simon (1961, p. xxiv)]. Both parts of the definition warrant respect. An economizing orientation is elicited by the intended rationality part of the definition, while the study of institutions is encouraged by acknowledging that cognitive competence is limited: "It is only because individual human beings are limited in knowledge, foresight, skill, and time that organizations are useful investments for the achievement of human purpose" [Simon (1957, p. 199)].

Transaction cost economics pairs the assumption of bounded rationality with a self-interest-seeking assumption that makes allowance for guile. Specifically, economic agents are permitted to disclose information in a selective and distorted manner. Calculated efforts to mislead, disguise, obfuscate, and confuse are thus admitted. This self-interest-seeking attribute is variously described as opportunism, moral hazard, and agency.

It is noteworthy that Niccolo Machiavelli's efforts to deal with "men as they are" [Gauss (1952, p. 14)] makes prominent provision for opportunism. Upon observing that humans have a propensity to behave opportunistically, Machiavelli advised his prince that "a prudent ruler ought not to keep faith when by so doing it would be against his interest, and when the reasons which made him bind himself no longer exist.... [L]egitimate grounds [have never] failed a prince who wished to show colorable excuse for the promise" [Gauss (1952, pp. 92–93)]. But reciprocal or pre-emptive opportunism is not the only lesson to be gleaned from an awareness that human agents are not fully trustworthy. Indeed, that is a very primitive response. As discussed below, the wise prince is one who seeks both to give and to receive "credible commitments".[2]

Bounded rationality and opportunism serve both to refocus attention and help to distinguish between feasible and infeasible modes of contracting. Both impossibly complex and hopelessly naive modes of contracting are properly excluded from the feasible set. Thus:

(1) Incomplete contracting. Although it is instructive and a great analytical convenience to assume that agents have the capacity to engage in comprehensive ex ante contracting (with or without private information), the condition of bounded rationality precludes this. All contracts within the feasible set are incomplete. Accordingly, the ex post side of a contract takes on special economic importance. The study of structures that facilitate gapfilling, dispute settlement, adaptation, and the like thus become part of the problem of economic organiza-

[2]Critics of transaction cost economics sometimes characterize it as "neo-Hobbesian" because it assumes that economic agents are given to opportunism (in varying degrees). See, for example, Bowles and Gintis (1986, p. 201). Note, however, that the bilateral design of credible commitments (as well as other forms of private ordering) is a very non-Hobbesian response.

tion. Whereas such institutions play a central role in the transaction cost economics scheme of things, they are ignored (indeed, suppressed) by the fiction of comprehensive ex ante contracting.[3]

(2) Contract as promise. Another convenient concept of contract is to assume that economic agents will reliably fulfill their promises. Such stewardship behavior will not obtain, however, if economic agents are given to opportunism. Ex ante efforts to screen economic agents in terms of reliability and, even more, ex post safeguards to deter opportunism take on different economic significance as soon as the hazards of opportunism are granted. Institutional practices that were hitherto regarded as problematic are thus often seen to perform valued economizing purposes when their transaction cost features are assessed.

Inasmuch as alternative theories of contract with different behavioral assumptions support different definitions of the feasible set, rival theories of contact can, in principle, be evaluated by ascertaining which of the implied feasible sets is borne out in the data.

2.3. Legal centralism versus private ordering

It is often assumed, sometimes tacitly, that property rights are well defined and that the courts dispense justice costlessly. The mechanism design literature expressly appeals to the efficacy of court ordering [Baiman (1982, p. 168)]. Much of the legal literature likewise assumes that the appropriate legal rules are in place and that the courts are the forum to which to present and resolve contract disputes.

[3]Note, moreover, that impossibly complex contracting processes cannot be saved by invoking economic natural selection arguments. Natural selection applies only to the set of viable practices and cannot be used to extend the domain. Alchian's (1950, p. 218) claim that "the economist, using the present analytical tools developed in the analysis of the firm under certainty, can predict the more adoptable or viable types of economic interrelationships that will be induced by environmental change even if individuals themselves are unable to ascertain them", is both prescient and provocative. But the argument needs to be invoked with care [Nelson and Winter (1982)]. Thus, whereas it is plausible to invoke natural selection to support an efficient factor proportions outcome in a competitively organized industry [Becker (1962)], since the choice of efficient proportions – by accident, insight, or otherwise – by some subset of firms is entirely feasible, to invoke natural selection to support a vaguely described process of "ex post settling up", whereby managers are purportedly paid their individual marginal products [Fama, (1980)], is highly problematic. Unless and until *feasible process mechanics* are described, ex post settling up, at least in its stronger forms, looks like and performs the functions of a deus ex machina.

This is not, however, to say that natural selection plays no role in the study of contract. To the contrary, transaction cost economics maintains that those forms of organization that serve to economize on bounded rationality and safeguard transactions against the hazards of opportunism will be favored and will tend to displace inferior modes in these respects. But transaction cost economics insistently deals only with feasible modes. Within this subset it focuses analytic attention on those properties of organization that have economizing and safeguarding features.

The attractions of legal centralism notwithstanding, this orientation was disputed by Llewellyn (1931). He took exception to prevailing contract law doctrine, which emphasized legal rules, and argued that more attention should be given to the purposes served. Less concern with form and more with substance was thus indicated – especially since being legalistic could stand in the way of getting the job done. A rival conception of "contract as framework" was advanced. Llewellyn thus described contract as "a framework highly adjustable, a framework which almost never accurately indicates real working relations, but which affords a rough indication around which such relations vary, an occasional guide in cases of doubt, and a norm of ultimate appeal when relations cease in fact to work" [Llewellyn (1931, p. 737)].

If, as Galanter has subsequently argued, the participants to a contract can often "devise more satisfactory solutions to their disputes than can professionals constrained to apply general rules on the basis of limited knowledge of the dispute" [Galanter (1981, p. 4)], then court ordering is better regarded as a background factor rather than the central forum for dispute resolution. Albeit useful for purposes of ultimate appeal, legal centralism (court ordering) gives way to private ordering. This is intimately connected to the incomplete contracting/ex post governance approach to which I refer above.

3. Operationalizing transaction cost economics

As reported above [and elaborated elsewhere by Williamson (1985, pp. 2–7)], the decade of the 1930s recorded striking insights – in law, economics, and organization – on which transaction cost economics has subsequently built. A thirty-five year interval elapsed, however, during which time the transaction cost approach to economic organization languished and the applied price theory approach to Industrial Organization ruled the day [Coase (1972, pp. 63–64)]. The significant accomplishments of the firm-as-production-function approach notwithstanding, orthodox analysis ignored both the internal organization of the firm and the private ordering purposes of contract. As a consequence, "very little [was known] about the cost of conducting transactions on the market or what they depend on; we know next to nothing about the effect on costs of different groupings of activities within firms" [Coase (1972, p. 64)].

Lack of progress with transaction cost economics notwithstanding, the intuition that the leading institutions of economic organization had transaction cost origins was widely shared. As Arrow observed, "market failure is not absolute, it is better to consider a broader category, that of transaction costs, which in general impede and in particular cases completely block the formation of markets" [Arrow (1969, p. 48)]. It was not, however, obvious how to operationalize this insight. Lacking definition, transaction cost arguments acquired a "well deserved bad name" [Fisher (1977, p. 322, n. 5)].

3.1. The technology of transacting

Adopting Commons' proposal that the transaction be made the basic unit of analysis, attention is focused on economizing efforts that attend the organization of transactions – where a transaction occurs when a good or service is transferred across a technologically separable interface. One stage of activity terminates and another begins. With a well-working interface, as with a well-working machine, these transfers occur smoothly. In mechanical systems we look for frictions: do the gears mesh, are the parts lubricated, is there needless slippage or other loss of energy? The economic counterpart of friction is transaction cost: for that subset of transactions where it is important to elicit cooperation,[4] do the parties to the exchange operate harmoniously, or are there frequent misunderstandings and conflicts that lead to delays, breakdowns, and other malfunctions? Transaction cost analysis entails an examination of the comparative costs of planning, adapting, and monitoring task completion under alternative governance structures.

Assessing the technology of transacting is facilitated by making the transaction the basic unit of analysis. The central question then becomes: What are the principal dimensions with respect to which transactions differ? Refutable implications are derived from the hypothesis that transactions, which differ in their attributes, are assigned to governance structures, which differ in their costs and competencies, in a discriminating – mainly transaction cost economizing – way.

The principal dimensions on which transaction cost economics presently relies for purposes of describing transactions are (1) the frequency with which they recur, (2) the degree and type of uncertainty to which they are subject, and (3) the condition of asset specificity. Although all are important, many of the refutable implications of transaction cost economics turn critically on this last.

3.1.1. Asset specificity

Asset specificity has reference to the degree to which an asset can be redeployed to alternative uses and by alternative users without sacrifice of productive value. This has a relation to the notion of sunk cost. But the full ramifications of asset specificity become evident only in the context of incomplete contracting and went

[4] The genius of neoclassical economics is that there are large numbers of transactions where conscious cooperation between traders is not necessary. The invisible hand works well if each party can go its own way – the buyer can secure product easily from alternative sources; the supplier can redeploy his assets without loss of productive value – with little cost to the other. Transaction cost economics is concerned with the frictions that obtain when bilateral dependency intrudes. This is not a trivial class of activity.

unrecognized in the pre-transaction cost era [Williamson (1975, 1979a), Klein, Crawford and Alchian (1978)].

Interestingly, Marshall (1948, p. 626) recognized that idiosyncratic human capital could sometimes accrue during the course of employment. Becker (1962), moreover, made express provision for human capital in his examination of labor market incentive schemes. Marschak expressly took exception with the readiness with which economists accept and employ assumptions of fungibility. As he put it, "There exist almost unique, irreplaceable research workers, teachers, administrations; just as there exist unique choice locations for plants and harbors. The problem of unique or imperfectly standardized goods...has indeed been neglected in the textbooks" [Marschak (1968, p. 14)]. Polanyi's (1962) remarkable discussion of "personal knowledge" further illustrates the importance of idiosyncratic knowledge and working relations.

Transaction cost economics accepts all of the foregoing and moves the argument forward in three respects: (1) asset specificity can take many forms, of which human asset specificity is only one; (2) asset specificity not only elicits complex ex ante incentive responses but, even more important, it gives rise to complex ex post governance structure responses; and (3) the study of economic organization in all of its forms – industrial organization, labor, international trade, economic development, family organization, comparative systems, and even finance – becomes grist for the transaction cost economics mill.

Without purporting to be exhaustive, asset specificity distinctions of five kinds have been made: (1) site specificity, as where successive stations are located in a cheek-by-jowl relation to each other so as to economize on inventory and transportation expenses; (2) physical asset specificity, such as specialized dies that are required to produce a component; (3) human asset specificity that arises in a learning-by-doing fashion; (4) dedicated assets, which are discrete investments in general purpose plant that are made at the behest of a particular customer; and (5) brand name capital. As discussed in Sections 4 and 5, below, the organizational ramifications of each type of specificity differ. Additional predictive content arises in this way.

3.1.2. Uncertainty

Koopmans (1957, p. 147) described the core problem of the economic organization of society as that of facing and dealing with uncertainty. He distinguished between primary and secondary uncertainty in this connection, the distinction being that whereas primary uncertainty is of a state-contingent kind, secondary uncertainty arises "from lack of communication, that is from one decision maker having no way of finding out the concurrent decisions and plans made by others" – which he judges to be "quantitatively at least as important as the primary uncertainty arising from random acts of nature and unpredictable changes in consumer's preferences" (pp. 162–163).

Note, however, that the secondary uncertainty to which Koopmans refers is of a rather innocent or nonstrategic kind. There is a lack of timely communication, but no reference is made to strategic nondisclosure, disguise, or distortion of information. Such strategic features are unavoidably presented, however, when parties are joined in a condition of bilateral dependency. A third class of uncertainty – namely, behavioral (or binary) uncertainty – is thus usefully recognized.[5]

The distinction between *statistical risks* and *idiosyncratic trading hazards* is pertinent in this connection. This is akin to, but nonetheless different from, Knight's (1965) distinction between risk and uncertainty. Hazards are due to the behavioral uncertainties that arise when incomplete contracting and asset specificity are joined. Of special importance to the economics of organization is that the mitigation of hazards can be the source of mutual gain. The language of governance, rather than statistical decision theory, applies.

3.1.3. The fundamental transformation

Economists of all persuasions recognize that the terms upon which an initial bargain will be struck depend on whether noncollusive bids can be elicited from more than one qualified supplier. Monopolistic terms will obtain if there is only a single highly qualified supplier, while competitive terms will result if there are many. Transaction cost economics fully accepts this description of ex ante bidding competition but insists that the study of contracting be extended to include ex post features. Thus, initial bidding merely sets the contracting process in motion. A full assessment requires that both contract execution and ex post competition at the contract renewal interval come under scrutiny.

Contrary to earlier practice, transaction cost economics holds that a condition of large numbers bidding at the outset does not necessarily imply that a large numbers bidding condition will obtain thereafter. Whether ex post competition is fully efficacious or not depends on whether the good or service in question is supported by durable investments in transaction specific human or physical assets. Where no such specialized investments are incurred, the initial winning bidder realizes no advantage over nonwinners. Although it may continue to supply for a long period of time, this is only because, in effect, it is continuously meeting competitive bids from qualified rivals. Rivals cannot be presumed to operate on a parity, however, once substantial investments in transaction specific assets are put in place. Winners in these circumstances enjoy advantages over

[5]The recent paper by Helfat and Teece (1987) examines vertical integration with reference to this condition.

nonwinners, which is to say that parity at the renewal interval is upset. Accordingly, what was a large numbers bidding condition at the outset is effectively transformed into one of bilateral supply thereafter. The reason why significant reliance investments in durable, transaction specific assets introduce contractual asymmetry between the winning bidder on the one hand and nonwinners on the other is because economic values would be sacrificed if the ongoing supply relation were to be terminated.

Faceless contracting is thereby supplanted by contracting in which the pairwise identity of the parties matters. Not only is the supplier unable to realize equivalent value were the specialized assets to be redeployed to other uses, but the buyer must induce potential suppliers to make similar specialized investments were he to seek least-cost supply from an outsider. The incentives of the parties to work things out rather than terminate are thus apparent. This has pervasive ramifications for the organization of economic activity.

3.2. *A simple contractual schema*

3.2.1. *The general approach*

Assume that a good or service can be supplied by either of two alternative technologies. One is a general purpose technology, the other a special purpose technology. The special purpose technology requires greater investment in transaction-specific durable assets and is more efficient for servicing steady-state demands.

Using k as a measure of transaction-specific assets, transactions that use the general purpose technology are ones for which $k = 0$. When transactions use the special purpose technology, by contrast, a $k > 0$ condition exists. Assets here are specialized to the particular needs of the parties. Productive values would therefore be sacrificed if transactions of this kind were to be prematurely terminated. The bilateral monopoly condition described above and elaborated below applies to such transactions.

Whereas classical market contracting – "sharp in by clear agreement; sharp out by clear performance" [Macneil (1974, p. 738)] – suffices for transactions of the $k = 0$ kind, unassisted market governance poses hazards whenever nontrivial transaction-specific assets are placed at risk. Parties have an incentive to devise safeguards to protect investments in transactions of the latter kind. Let s denote the magnitude of any such safeguards. An $s = 0$ condition is one in which no safeguards are provided; a decision to provide safeguards is reflected by an $s > 0$ result.

Figure 3.1 displays the three contracting outcomes corresponding to such a description. Associated with each node is a price. So as to facilitate comparisons

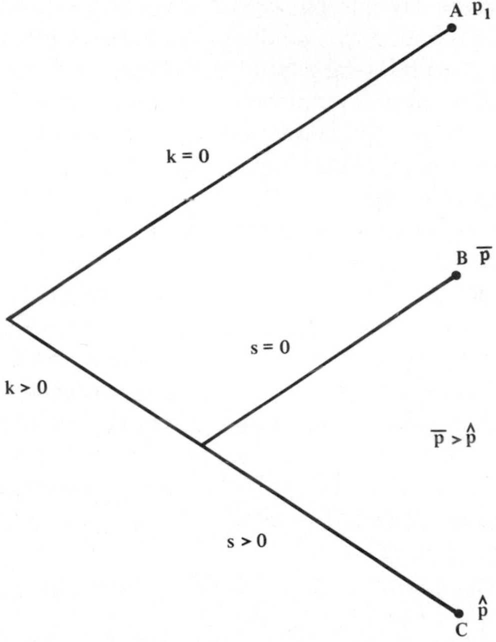

Figure 3.1. A simple contracting schema.

between nodes, assume that suppliers (1) are risk neutral, (2) are prepared to supply under either technology, and (3) will accept any safeguard condition whatsoever so long as an expected breakeven result can be projected. Thus, node A is the general purpose technology ($k = 0$) supply relation for which a break-even price of p_1 is projected. The node B contract is supported by transaction-specific assets ($k > 0$) for which no safeguard is offered ($s = 0$). The expected breakeven price here is $\bar{p}$. The node C contract also employs the special purpose technology. But since the buyer at this node provides the supplier with a safeguard, ($s > 0$), the breakeven price, $\hat{p}$, at node C is less than $\bar{p}$.[6]

The protective safeguards to which I refer normally take on one or more of three forms. The first is to realign incentives, which commonly involves some type of severance payment or penalty for premature termination. Albeit important and the central focus of much of the formal contracting literature, this is

[6]Specialized production technologies commonly afford steady-state cost savings over general purpose production technologies. But since the former are less redeployable than the latter, stochastic disturbances may reverse the cost advantage (whether p_1 is greater than or less than $\hat{p}$ requires that stochastic factors be taken into account). See Williamson (1985, pp. 169–175).

a very limited response. A second is to supplant court ordering by private ordering. Allowance is expressly made for contractual incompleteness; and a different forum for dispute resolution (of which arbitration is an example) is commonly provided.[7] Third, the transactions may be embedded in a more complex trading network. The object here is to better assure continuity purposes and facilitate adaptations. Expanding a trading relation from unilateral to bilateral exchange – through the concerted use, for example, of reciprocity – thereby to effect an equilibration of trading hazards is one illustration. Recourse to collective decision-making under some form of combined ownership is another.

This simple contracting schema applies to a wide variety of contracting issues. It facilitates comparative institutional analysis by emphasizing that technology (k), contractual governance/safeguards (s) and price (p) are fully interactive and are determined simultaneously. It is furthermore gratifying that so many applications turn out to be variations on a theme. As Hayek (1967, p. 50) observed: "whenever the capacity of recognizing an abstract rule which the arrangement of these attributes follows has been acquired in one field, the same master mould will apply when the signs for those abstract attributes are evoked by altogether different elements".

By way of summary, the nodes A, B, and C in the contractual schema set out in Figure 3.1 have the following properties:

(1) Transactions that are efficiently supported by general purpose assets ($k = 0$) are located at node A and do not need protective governance structures. Discrete market contracting suffices. The world of competition obtains.

(2) Transactions that involve significant investments of a transaction-specific kind ($k > 0$) are ones for which the parties are effectively engaged in bilateral trade.

(3) Transactions located at node B enjoy no safeguards ($s = 0$), on which account the projected breakeven supply price is great ($\bar{p} > \hat{p}$). Such transactions are apt to be unstable contractually. They may revert to node A [in which event the special purpose technology would be replaced by the general purpose ($k = 0$) technology] or be relocated to node C (by introducing contractual safeguards that would encourage use of the $k > 0$ technology).

(4) Transactions located at node C incorporate safeguards ($s > 0$) and thus are protected against expropriation hazards.

(5) Inasmuch as price and governance are linked, parties to a contract should not expect to have their cake (low price) and eat it too (no safeguard). More generally, it is important to study *contracting in its entirety*. Both the ex ante terms and the manner in which contracts are thereafter executed vary with the investment characteristics and the associated governance structures within which transactions are embedded.

[7]See Williamson (1985, pp. 164–166) and Joskow (1985, 1987).

3.2.2. *An illustration*

Klein and Leffler (1981) argue that franchisees may be required to make investments in transaction-specific capital as a way by which to safeguard the franchise system against quality shading. As Klein (1980, p. 359) puts it, franchisers can better

> ...assure quality by requiring franchisee investments in specific...assets that upon termination imply a capital loss penalty larger than can be obtained by the franchisee if he cheats. For example, the franchiser may require franchisees to rent from them short term (rather than own) the land upon which their outlet is located. This lease arrangement creates a situation where termination can require the franchisee to move and thereby impose a capital loss on him up to the amount of his initial nonsalvageable investment. Hence a form of collateral to deter franchisee cheating is created.

The arrangement is tantamount to the creation of hostages to restore integrity to an exchange.

That logic notwithstanding, the use of hostages to deter franchisees from exploiting the demand externalities that inhere in brand name capital is often regarded as an imposed (top down) solution. Franchisees are "powerless"; they accept hostage terms because no others are available. Such power arguments are often based on ex post reasoning. That the use of hostages to support exchange can be and often is an efficient systems solution, hence is independent of who originates the proposal, can be seen from the following revised sequence.

Suppose that an entrepreneur develops a distinctive, patentable idea that he sells outright to a variety of independent, geographically dispersed suppliers, each of which is assigned an exclusive territory. Each supplier expects to sell only to the population within its territory, but all find to their surprise (and initially to their delight) that sales are also made to a mobile population. Purchases by the mobile population are based not on the reputation of individual franchisees but on customers' perceptions of the reputation of the system. A demand externality arises in this way.

Thus, were sales made only to the local population, each supplier would fully appropriate the benefits of its promotional and quality enhancement efforts. Population mobility upsets this: because the cost savings that result from local quality debasement accrue to the local operator while the adverse demand effects are diffused throughout the system, suppliers now have an incentive to free ride off of the reputation of the system. Having sold the exclusive territory rights outright, the entrepreneur who originated the program is indifferent to these unanticipated demand developments. It thus remains for the collection of independent franchisees to devise a correction themselves, lest the value of the system deteriorate to their individual and collective disadvantage.

The franchisees, under the revised scenario, thus create an agent to police quality or otherwise devise penalties that deter quality deterioration. One possibility is to return to the entrepreneur and hire him to provide such services. Serving now as the agent of the franchisees, the entrepreneur may undertake a program of quality checks (certain purchasing restraints are introduced, whereby franchisees are required to buy only from qualified suppliers; periodic inspections are performed). The incentive to exploit demand externalties may further be discouraged by requiring each franchisee to post a hostage and by making franchises terminable.

This indirect scenario serves to demonstrate that it is the *system* that benefits from the control of externalities. But this merely confirms that the normal scenario in which the franchiser controls the contractual terms is not an arbitrary exercise of power. Indeed, if franchisees recognize that the demand externality exists from the outset, if the franchiser refuses to make provision for the externality in the original contract, and if it is very costly to reform the franchise system once initial contracts are set, franchisees will bid less for the right to a territory than they otherwise would. It should not therefore be concluded that perceptive franchisers, who recognize the demand externality in advance and make provision for it, are imposing objectionable ex ante terms on unwilling franchisees. They are merely taking steps to realize the full value of the franchise. Here, as elsewhere, contracts must be examined in their entirety.

3.3. The measurement branch

Most of the foregoing and most of this chapter deal with the governance issues that arise in conjunction with asset specificity. There is, however, another branch that focuses on problems of measurement. The treatment of team organization by Alchian and Demsetz (1972) in the context of technological nonseparabilities is one example. Barzel's (1982) concerns with product quality is another.

All measurement problems are traceable to a condition of information impactedness – which is to say that either (1) information is asymmetrically distributed between buyer and seller and can be equalized only at great cost or (2) it is costly to apprise an arbiter of the true information condition should a dispute arise between opportunistic parties who have identical knowledge of the underlying circumstances [Williamson (1975, pp. 31–37)]. Interestingly, measurement problems with different origins give rise to different organizational responses. Thus, whereas team organization problems give rise to supervision, the classical agency problem elicits an incentive alignment response. Reputation effect mechanisms are responses to quality uncertainty, and common ownership is often the device by which concerns over asset dissipation are mitigated. Plainly, an integrated treatment of governance and measurement is ultimately needed.[8] Such efforts are just beginning [Williamson (1986b), Milgrom and Roberts (1987)].

4. The paradigm problem: Vertical integration

The leading studies of firm and market organization – in 1937 and over the next thirty-five years – typically held that the "natural" or efficient boundaries of the firm were defined by technology and could be taken as given. Boundary extension was thus thought to have monopoly origins.[9]

Coase (1937) took exception with this view in his classic article on "The Nature of the Firm". He not only posed the fundamental question: When do firms choose to procure in the market and when do they produce to their own requirements?, but he argued that comparative transaction cost differences explain the result. Wherein, however, do these transaction cost differences reside?

The proposition that asset specificity had significant implications for vertical integration was first advanced in 1971. A comparative institutional orientation was employed to assess when and for what reasons market procurement gives way to internal organization. Given the impossibility of comprehensive contracting (by reason of bounded rationality) and the need to adapt a supply relation through time (in response to disturbances), the main comparative institutional alternatives to be evaluated were between incomplete short-term contracts and vertical integration. Problems with short-term contracts were projected "if either (1) efficient supply requires investment in special-purpose, long-life equipment, or (2) the winner of the original contract acquires a cost advantage, say by reason of 'first mover' advantages (such as unique location or learning, including the acquisition of undisclosed or proprietary technical and managerial procedures and task-specific labor skills)" [Williamson (1971, p. 116)].

4.1. A heuristic model

The main differences between market and internal organization are these: (1) markets promote high-powered incentives and restrain bureaucratic distortions more effectively than internal organization; (2) markets can sometimes aggregate demands to advantage, thereby to realize economies of scale and scope; and (3) internal organization has access to distinctive governance instruments.

[8]Alchian (1984, p. 39) joins the two as follows: "One might...define the firm in terms of two features: the detectability of *input* performance *and* the expropriability of quasi-rents of [transaction specific] resources".

[9]The main monopoly emphasis was on the use of boundary extension to exercise economic muscle [Stigler (1951, 1955), Bain (1968)]. McKenzie (1951) and others have noted, however, that vertical integration may also be used to correct against monopoly-induced factor distortions. Arguments of both kinds work out of the firm-as-production-function tradition. For a much more complete treatment of vertical integration, see Chapter 4 by Martin Perry in this Handbook.

Consider the decision of a firm to make or buy a particular good or service. Suppose that it is a component that is to be joined to the mainframe and assume that it is used in fixed proportions. Assume, furthermore, that economies of scale and scope are negligible. Accordingly, the critical factors that are determinative in the decision to make or buy are production cost control and the ease of effecting intertemporal adaptations.

Although the high-powered incentives of markets favor tighter production cost control, they impede the ease of adaptation as the bilateral dependency of the relation between the parties builds up. The latter effect is a consequence of the fundamental transformation that occurs as a condition of asset specificity deepens. For a fixed level of output (say $X = \bar{X}$), let $B(k)$ be the bureaucratic costs of internal governance and $M(k)$ the corresponding governance costs of markets, where k is an index of asset specificity. Assume that $B(0) > M(0)$, by reason of the above-described incentive and bureaucratic effects. Assume further, however, that $M' > B'$ evaluated at every k. This second condition is a consequence of the comparative disability of markets in adaptability respects. Letting $\Delta G = B(k) - M(k)$, the relation shown in Figure 3.2 obtains.

Thus, market procurement is the preferred supply mode where asset specificity is slight – because $\Delta G > 0$ under these circumstances. But internal organization is favored where asset specificity is great, because the high-powered incentives of markets impair the comparative ease with which adaptive, sequential adjustments to disturbances are accomplished. As shown, the switchover value, where the choice between firm and market is a matter of indifference, occurs at $\bar{k}$.

The foregoing assumes that economies of scale and scope are negligible, so that the choice between firm and market rests entirely on the governance cost differences. Plainly that oversimplifies. Markets are often able to aggregate diverse demands, thereby to realize economies of scale and scope. Accordingly, production cost differences also need to be taken into account.[10]

[10]The argument assumes that the firm produces exclusively to its own needs. If diseconomies of scale or scope are large, therefore, technological features will deter all but very large firms from supplying to their own needs.

Plausible though this appears, neither economies of scale nor scope are, by themselves, responsible for decisions to buy rather than make. Thus, suppose that economies of scale are large in relation to a firm's own needs. Absent prospective contracting problems, the firm could construct a plant of size sufficient to exhaust economies of scale and sell excess product to rivals and other interested buyers. Or suppose that economies of scope are realized by selling the final good in conjunction with a variety of related items. The firm could integrate forward into marketing and offer to sell its product together with related items on a parity basis – rival and complementary items being displayed, sold, and serviced without reference to strategic purposes.

That other firms, especially rivals, would be willing to proceed on this basis, is surely doubtful. Rather than submit to the strategic hazards, some will decline to participate in such a scheme [Williamson (1975, pp. 16–19; 1979b, pp. 979–980)]. The upshot is that *all* cost differences between internal and market procurement ultimately rest on transaction cost considerations. Inasmuch, however, as the needs of empirical research on economic organization are better served by making the assumption that firms which procure internally supply exclusively to their own needs, whence technological economies of scale and scope are accorded independent importance, I employ this assumption here.

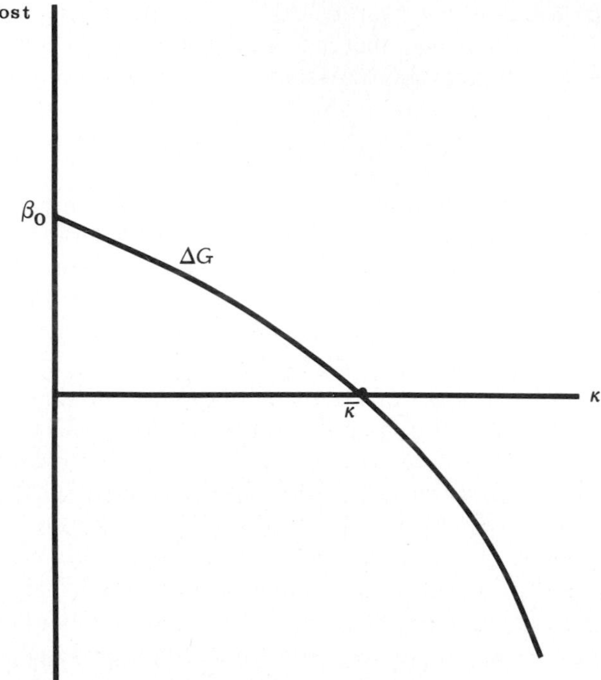

Figure 3.2. Comparative governance cost.

Again it will be convenient to hold output unchanged. Let ΔC be the steady-state production cost difference between producing to one's own requirements and the steady-state cost of procuring the same item in the market. (The steady-state device avoids the need for adaptation.) Expressing ΔC as a function of asset specificity, it is plausible to assume that ΔC will be positive throughout but will be a decreasing function of k.

The production cost penalty of using internal organization is large for standardized transactions for which market aggregation economies are great, whence ΔC is large where k is low. The cost disadvantage decreases but remains positive for intermediate degrees of asset specificity. Thus, although dissimilarities among orders begin to appear, outside suppliers are nevertheless able to aggregate the diverse demands of many buyers and produce at lower costs than can a firm that produces to its own needs. As goods and services become very close to unique (k is high), however, aggregation economies of outside supply can no longer be realized, whence ΔC asymptotically approaches zero. Contracting out affords neither scale nor scope economies in those circumstances. The firm can produce without penalty to its own needs.

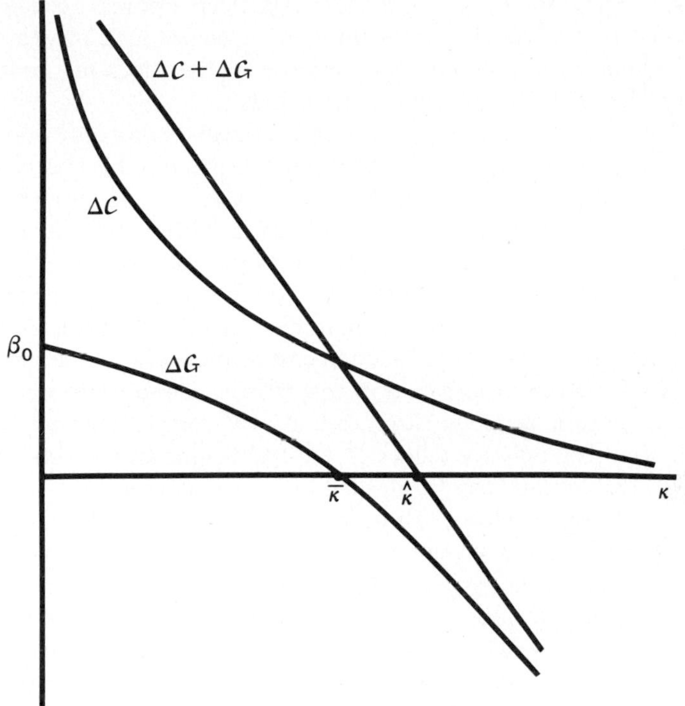

Figure 3.3. Comparative production and governance costs.

This ΔC relation is shown in Figure 3.3. The object, of course, is not to minimize ΔC or ΔG taken separately but, given the optimal or specified level of asset specificity, to minimize the sum of production and governance cost differences. The vertical sum $\Delta G + \Delta C$ is also displayed. The crossover value of k for which the sum $(\Delta G + \Delta C)$ becomes negative is shown by $\hat{k}$, which value exceeds $\bar{k}$. Economies of scale and scope thus favor market organization over a wider range of asset specificity values than would be observed if steady state production cost economies were absent.

More generally, if k^* is the optimal degree of asset specificity,[11] Figure 3.3 discloses:

(1) Market procurement has advantages in both scale economy and governance respects where optimal asset specificity is slight ($k^* \ll \hat{k}$).

[11]Reference to a single "optimal" level of k is an expository convenience: the optimal level actually varies with organization form. This is further developed in Subsection 4.2, below.

(2) Internal organization enjoys the advantage where optimal asset specificity is substantial ($k^* \gg \hat{k}$). Not only does the market realize little aggregation economy benefits, but market governance, because of the "lock-in" problems that arise when assets are highly specific, is hazardous.

(3) Only small cost differences appear for intermediate degrees of optimal asset specificity. Mixed governance, in which some firms will be observed to buy, others to make, and all express "dissatisfaction" with their procurement solution, are apt to arise for k^* in the neighborhood of $\hat{k}$. Accidents of history may be determinative. Nonstandard contracts of the types discussed briefly above and developed more fully in Subsection 4.2 below may arise to serve these.

(4) More generally, it is noteworthy that, inasmuch as the firm is everywhere at a disadvantage to the market in production cost respects ($\Delta C < 0$ everywhere),the firm will never integrate for production cost reasons alone. Only when contracting difficulties intrude does the firm and market comparison support vertical integration – and then only for values of k^* that significantly exceed $\hat{k}$.

Additional implications may be gleaned by introducing quantity (or firm size) and organization form effects. Thus, consider firm size (output). The basic proposition here is that diseconomies associated with own production will be everywhere reduced as the quantity of the component to be supplied increases. The firm is simply better able to realize economies of scale as its own requirements become larger in relation to the size of the market. The curve ΔC thus everywhere falls as quantity increases. The question then is: What happens to the curve ΔG? If this twists about $\bar{k}$, which is a plausible construction,[12] then the vertical sum $\Delta G + \Delta C$ will intersect the axis at a value of k that progressively moves to the left as the quantity to be supplied increases. Accordingly:

(5) Larger firms will be more integrated into components than will smaller, ceteris paribus.

Finally, for reasons that have been developed elsewhere [Williamson (1970)], the bureaucratic disabilities to which internal organization is subject vary with the internal structure of the firm. Multidivisionalization, assuming that the M-form is feasible, serves as a check against the bureaucratic distortions that appear in the unitary form (U-form) of enterprise. Expressed in terms of Figure 3.3, the curve ΔG falls under multidivisionalization as compared with the unitary form organization. Thus, assuming $\Delta C$is unchanged:

(6) An M-form firm will be more integrated than its U-form counterpart, ceteris paribus.

[12]Assume that $I(k, X) = I(k)X$ where $I(0) > 0$ and $I(k)$ is the internal governance cost per unit of effecting adaptations. Assume, furthermore, that $M(k, X) = M(k)X$ where $M(0) = 0$ and $M(k)$ is the corresponding governance cost per unit of effecting market adaptations. Then $\Delta G = [I(k) - M(k)]X$, and the value at which ΔG goes to zero will be independent of X. The effect of increasing X is to twist ΔG clockwise about the value of k at which it goes to zero.

4.2. A combined neoclassical–transaction cost treatment

A unified framework is herein employed to formalize the arguments advanced above.[13] It is in the spirit of Arrow's remark that new theories of economic organization take on greater "analytic usefulness when these are founded on more directly neoclassical lines" [Arrow (1985, p. 303)]. The spirit of the analysis is consonant with that of economics quite generally: use more general modes of analysis as a check on the limitations that inform more specialized types of reasoning.

The heuristic model assumes that both firm and market modes of supply produce the same level of output and that the optimal level of asset specificity is the same in each. These are arbitrary constraints, however. What happens when both are relaxed? This is examined below in the context of a combined production and transaction cost model that is itself highly simplified – in that it (1) deals only with polar firm or market alternatives, (2) examines only one transaction at a time, and (3) employs a reduced form type of analysis, in that it ascribes rather than derives the basic production and governance cost competencies of firms and markets.

It will facilitate the argument to assume initially that firm and market employ the identical production cost technology. This assumption is subsequently relaxed.

4.2.1. Common production technology

Revenue is given by $R = R(X)$, and production costs of market and internal procurement are assumed to be given by the relation:

$$C = C(X, k; \alpha); \quad C_X > 0; C_k < 0; C_{Xk} < 0,$$

where the parameter α is a shift parameter, a higher value of α yielding greater cost reducing consequences to asset specificity:

$$C_{k\alpha} < 0; \qquad C_{X\alpha} < 0.$$

Asset specificity is assumed to be available at the constant per unit cost of γ. The neoclassical profit expression corresponding to this statement of revenue and production costs is given by

$$\pi^*(X,k; \alpha) = R(X) - C(X, k; \alpha) - \gamma k.$$

Governance costs are conspicuously omitted from this profit relation, there being no provision for such costs in the neoclassical statement of the problem.

[13]The argument is based on Riordan and Williamson (1985). See also Masten (1982).

Assume that this function is globally concave. At an interior maximum the decision variables X^* and k^* are determined from the zero marginal profit conditions:

$$\pi_X^*(X, k; \alpha) = 0; \qquad \pi_k^*(X, k; \alpha) = 0.$$

Consider now the governance costs of internal and market organization. Let the superscripts i denote internal and m denote market organization. Governance cost expressions congruent with the cost differences described above given by

$$G^{\mathrm{i}} = \beta + V(k); \quad \beta > 0; V_k >= 0,$$

$$G^{\mathrm{m}} = W(k); \quad W_k > 0,$$

where $W_k > V_k$, evaluated at common k.

The corresponding profit expressions for internal market procurement in the face of positive governance costs are

$$\pi^{\mathrm{i}} = R(X) - C(X, k; \alpha) - \gamma k - (\beta + V(k)),$$

$$\pi^{\mathrm{m}} = R(X) - C(X, k; \alpha) - \gamma k - W(k).$$

The zero marginal profit conditions for internal procurement are

$$\pi_X^{\mathrm{i}} = R_X - C_X = 0,$$

$$\pi_k^{\mathrm{i}} = -C_k - \gamma - V_k = 0.$$

Those for market procurement are

$$\pi_k^{\mathrm{m}} = R_X - C_X = 0,$$

$$\pi_k^{\mathrm{m}} = -C_k - \gamma - W_k = 0.$$

In each instance, therefore, optimal output, given asset specificity, is obtained by setting marginal revenue equal to the marginal costs of production, while optimal asset specificity, given output, is chosen to minimize the sum of production and governance costs.

Given that $\pi_{Xk}^* = -C_{Xk} > 0$, the neoclassical locus of optimal output given asset specificity and the corresponding locus of optimal asset specificity given output will bear the relations shown by $\pi_X^* = 0$ and $\pi_k^* = 0$ in Figure 3.4. The corresponding loci for internal and market organization are also shown. Inasmuch as the zero marginal profit expressions for output for all three statements

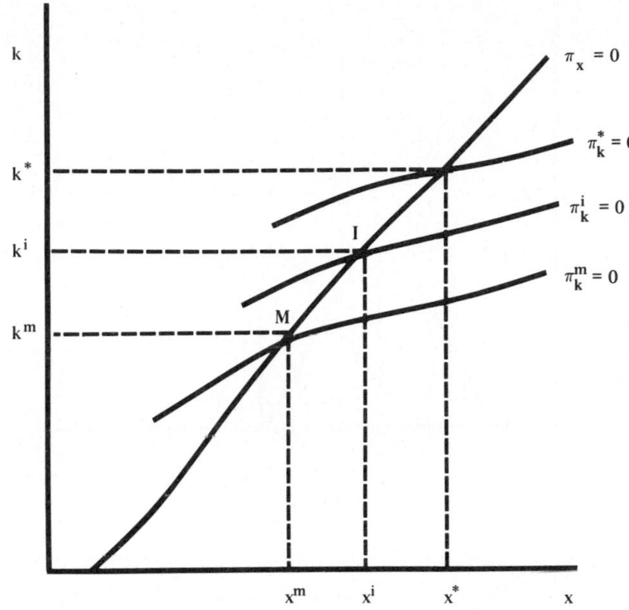

Figure 3.4. For π_{Xk}.

of the maximand are identical, the loci $\pi_X^{\mathrm{i}} = 0$ and $\pi_X^{\mathrm{m}} = 0$ track $\pi_X^* = 0$ exactly. The zero marginal profit expressions for asset specificity, however, differ. Given that $W_k > V_k > 0$, the locus $\pi_k^{\mathrm{m}} = 0$ is everywhere below $\pi_k^{\mathrm{i}} = 0$, which in turn is below $\pi_k^* = 0$. Accordingly, profit maximizing values of X and k for these three statements of the optimization problem bear the following relation to each other: $X^* > X^{\mathrm{i}} > X^{\mathrm{m}}$ and $k^* > k^{\mathrm{i}} > k^{\mathrm{m}}$. The output effects are indirect or induced effects, attributable to shifts in the zero marginal profit asset specificity loci.

Of course, the X^* and k^* choices are purely hypothetical since, in reality, a zero transaction cost condition is not a member of the feasible set. The relevant choices thus reduce to using input combinations I under internal procurement or M under market procurement. An immediate implication is that if the firm were operating in two identical markets and was constrained to buy in one and to make in the other, it would sell more goods of a more distinctive kind in the region where it produced to its own needs.

Ordinarily, however, the firm will not be so constrained but will choose to make or buy according to which mode offers the greatest profit in each region. Figure 3.5 shows profit as a function of asset specificity, the choice of output assumed to be optimal for each value of k. Whereas there is a family of π^{i} curves, one for each value of the bureaucratic cost parameter β, there is only a single π^{m}

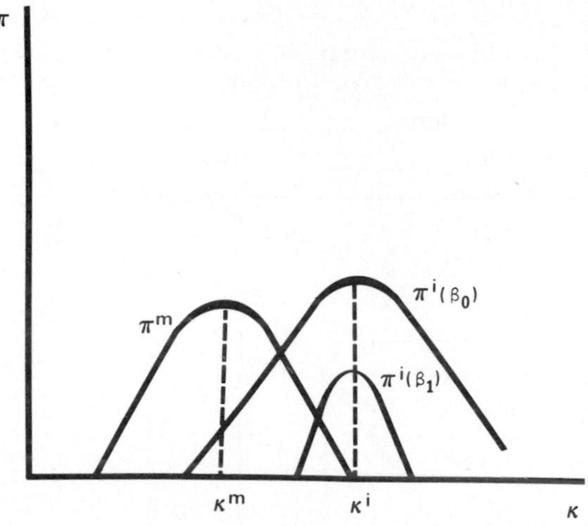

Figure 3.5

curve. Which mode is favored depends on which has the highest peak. This is the internal mode for $\beta = \beta_0$ but the market mode for $\beta = \beta_1$, where $\beta_1 > \beta_0$. The optimal values of k and X depend only on the mode selected and not on β, however, since β does not influence the marginal conditions.

The comparative statics ramifications of the production cost parameter α are more central. Applications of the envelope theorem reveal that

$$\pi_\alpha^{\mathrm{m}} = -C_\alpha(X^{\mathrm{m}}, k^{\mathrm{m}}; \alpha),$$
$$\pi_\alpha^{\mathrm{i}} = -C_\alpha(X^{\mathrm{i}}, k^{\mathrm{i}}; \alpha).$$

Inasmuch as $X^{\mathrm{i}} > X^{\mathrm{m}}$ and $k^{\mathrm{i}} > k^{\mathrm{m}}$, it follows from our earlier production cost assumptions that $\pi_\alpha^{\mathrm{i}} > \pi_\alpha^{\mathrm{m}}$. In other words, as asset specificity has greater cost reducing impact, internal organization is progressively favored.

4.2.2. Production cost differences

Consider now the case, to which earlier reference was made and is arguably the more realistic, where the firm is unable to aggregate demands and sell product that exceeds its own demands without penalty. Let $H(X, k)$ denote the production cost disadvantage per unit of output associated with internal organization. The production costs of the two modes then are

$$C^{\mathrm{m}} = C(X, k; \alpha),$$
$$C^{\mathrm{i}} = C(X, k; \alpha) + H(X, k)X.$$

Assume that $H_X < 0$ and $H_k < 0$ but that $H(X, k)X$ is positive and asymptotically approaches zero as X and k approach infinity. Denote the marginal production cost disadvantage by $M(X, k) = H_X(X, k)X + H(X, k)$.

The analysis depends on the way in which the total production cost disadvantage experienced by internal organization changes for outputs within the relevant range. At low levels of output, decreasing unit cost disadvantages will normally be attended by an increasing total cost, whence $M(X, k) > 0$. Beyond some threshold level of output, however, the total production cost disadvantage of internal organization will begin to decline. Indeed, as the firm progressively increases in relation to the size of the market, the production cost disadvantage presumably approaches zero – since firm and market have access to identical economies of scale as a monopoly condition evolves. Accordingly, $M(X, k) < 0$ once this threshold is crossed.

The main results are strengthened within the (large output) range where $M(X, k) < 0$: $X^{\mathrm{m}} < X^{\mathrm{i}}$; $k^{\mathrm{m}} < k^{\mathrm{i}}$; and $\pi_\alpha^{\mathrm{i}} > \pi_\alpha^{\mathrm{m}}$. Within the (small output) range, however, where $M_X > 0$, the marginal production cost disadvantage of internal organization and the marginal governance cost disadvantage of market procurement operate in opposite directions. An unambiguous ordering of optimal output and asset specificity is not possible in terms of the above-described qualitative features of the problem in this instance. An anomaly thus arises that was not evident in the heuristic presentation above.

5. Other applications

The underlying transaction cost economizing theme repeats itself, with variation, almost endlessly. Three applications are sketched here: to nonstandard commercial contracting, career marriages, and corporate finance.[14] The systems' ramifications of organizational innovation are also noteworthy. These are examined with reference to "Full Functionalism" [Elster (1983)].

5.1. *Nonstandard commercial contracting*

Many nonstandard contracting phenomena are explained with the aid of one of two models: the hostage model and the oversearching model.

5.1.1. *The hostage model*

The hostage model described below is a member of the family of models dealing with credible commitments [Telser (1981), Klein and Leffler (1981), Williamson

[14]Applications to labor market organization and comparative economic systems are developed in Williamson (1985, chs. 9 and 10).

(1983)]. Although the particulars differ, all of these models feature intertemporal contracting, uncertainty, and investments in transaction specific assets. The treatment here follows Williamson (1983).

Assume that either of two production technologies can be used. The first technology uses general purpose inputs and is variable cost intensive. The second employs special purpose inputs of a more durable kind. The costs of production under the second technology are lower than the first, assuming that plant is utilized to design capacity. Idle plant, however, cannot be economically shifted to other uses, whence the producer will be holding unproductive assets should buyers defect from the agreement under the second technology. If buyers can invoke a technicality and easily defect whenever it suits their purposes, producers will either demand some assurance against breach or will add a defection premium if the second technology is put in place. Assurance can be provided by offering hostages. Interestingly, hostages can be used both as an ex ante screening device and to discourage "irresponsible" ex post breach.

The ex ante screening argument is a variant of the argument by Rothschild and Stiglitz (1976) that it may be possible to offer insurance on discriminating terms such that good and poor risks sort themselves appropriately across policies. The use of hostages can similarly be used to discourage buyers with poorer prospects, but who cannot by inspection be distinguished from those with better prospects, to self-select out of the market.

The ex post execution argument is somewhat more involved. Assume that buyers wish to procure product from producers who use the low cost (asset specific) technology and that it is not feasible (or perhaps is too hazardous) for buyers to make up-front payments that will cover the costs of the dedicated asset investments made by producers in support of each buyer's prospective needs. The question then is how to design a contract such that (1) the efficient technology is selected and (2) product is exchanged in all states of the world for which demand price (net of marketing costs) exceeds the marginal costs of production.

Assume that there are two periods. Dedicated assets are committed in the first. Demand is stochastic and demand realizations occur in the second. Production, if any, also occurs in the second. Assume that there are many potential risk neutral suppliers who will produce to any contract for which an expected break-even condition can be projected. Consider two contracting alternatives:

(a) the producer makes the specific asset investment himself and receives a payment of $\bar{p}$ in the second period if the buyer places an order but nothing otherwise; and

(b) the producer makes the specific asset investment himself and receives $\hat{p}$ from the buyer if an order is placed, is paid $\alpha h, 0 < \alpha < 1$, if no second period order is made, while the buyer pays $\hat{p}$ upon placing an order and experiences a reduction in wealth of h if no order is placed.

The second scenario can be thought of as one where the buyer posts a hostage that he values in amount h, which hostage is delivered to the producer, who values it in amount αh, if no order is placed.

Producers will be indifferent with respect to (e.g. will break-even on) each contract only if $\bar{p} > \hat{p}$. It can furthermore be shown that product will be exchanged on marginal cost terms if h is set equal to the amount of the investment in specific assets (say k) and α is equal to unity. Indeed, contract (b) precisely replicates a vertical integration supply relation assuming that there are no problems of valuing and transferring hostages.

The argument that buyers can effect the terms and technology of supply by offering (or refusing to offer) hostages has ramifications for the enforcement of the Robinson–Patman Act, for franchising, and for an understanding of reciprocal trading. The franchising story has already been set out in Subsection 4.2.2, above. Consider, therefore, Robinson–Patman and reciprocity.

The Robinson–Patman Act has been interpreted as an effort "to deprive a large buyer of [discounts] except to the extent that a lower price could be justified by reason of a seller's diminished costs due to *quantity* manufacture, delivery, or sale, or by reason of the seller's good faith effort to meet a competitor's equally low price".[15] Plainly, that $\hat{p}$ is less than $\bar{p}$ in the hostage model has neither quantity nor meeting competition origins. Neither is it contrary to the public interest. Indeed, it would be inefficient and unwarranted for a producer to charge the same price to two customers who order an identical amount of product, but only one of which offers a hostage, if (1) investments in specialized assets are required to support the transactions in question, or (2) if, because of a refusal to make a credible commitment, transactions of the second kind are produced with general purpose (but high cost) technology.

The missing ingredients, plainly, are the differential commitment to buy (as reflected by the willingness to offer hostages) and the differential incentives to breach once hostages have been posted. The confusion is explained by the propensity to employ conventional (steady-state) microtheory to the neglect of transaction cost aspects. Rectifying this involves examination of the microanalytics of transactions, with special reference to asset specificity and the hazards thereby posed, and evaluating alternative contracts with respect to a *common reference condition* – prospective break-even being a useful standard. Once this is done, a different understanding of many nonstandard or unfamiliar contracting practices, many of which are held to be presumptively unlawful, frequently emerges.[16]

[15] *FTC v. Morton Salt Co.*, 334 U.S. 37 (1948); emphasis added.

[16] Note that the argument applies only to $\hat{p}$ vs. $\bar{p}$ comparisons in trades where specific assets are involved. The efficiency properties of customer price differentials that do not have these origins are not reached by the argument in this chapter.

Reciprocity is also believed to be a troublesome practice. Reciprocity transforms a unilateral supply relation – whereby *A* sells *X* to *B* – into a bilateral one, whereby *A* agrees to buy *Y* from *B* as a condition for making the sale of *X* and both parties understand that the transaction will be continued only if reciprocity is observed. Although reciprocal selling is widely held to be anticompetitive [Stocking and Mueller (1957), Blake (1973)], others regard it more favorably. Stigler offers the following affirmative rationale for reciprocity:[17]

> The case for reciprocity arises when prices cannot be freely varied to meet supply and demand conditions. Suppose that a firm is dealing with a colluding industry which is fixing prices. A firm in this collusive industry would be willing to sell at less that the cartel price if it can escape detection. Its price can be reduced in effect by buying from the customer-seller at an inflated price. Here reciprocity restores flexibility of prices.

Inasmuch, however, as many industries do not satisfy the prerequisites for oligopolistic price collusion [Posner (1969), Williamson (1975, ch. 12)] and as reciprocity is sometimes observed among these, reciprocity presumably has other origins as well. Tie breaking is one of these. A second is that reciprocity can have advantageous governance structure benefits. These two can be distinguished by the type of product being sold.

The tie-breaker explanation applies where firm *B*, which is buying specialized product from *A*, asks that *A* buy standardized product from *B* on the condition that *B* meets market terms. Other things being equal, procurement agents at *A* are apt to accede. Scherer (1980, p. 344) notes that "Most of the 163 corporation executives responding to a 1963 survey state that their firms' purchases were awarded on the basis of reciprocity only when the price, quality, and delivery conditions were equal".

The more interesting case is where reciprocity involves the sale of specialized product to *B* conditioned on the procurement of specialized product from *B*. The argument here is that reciprocity can serve to equalize the exposure of the parties, thereby reducing the incentive of the buyer to defect from the exchange – leaving the supplier to redeploy specialized assets at greatly reduced alternative value. Absent a hostage (or other assurance that the buyer will not defect), the sale by *A* of specialized product to *B* may never materialize. The buyer's commitment to the exchange is more assuredly signaled by his willingness to accept reciprocal exposure of specialized assets. Defection hazards are thereby mitigated.

Lest the argument be uncritically considered to be a defense for reciprocal trading quite generally, note that it applies only where specialized assets are

[17]President's Task Force Report on Productivity and Competition, reprinted in Commerce Clearing House *Trade Regulation Reporter*, 24 June 1969, No. 419, p. 39.

placed at hazard by both parties. Where only one or neither invests in specialized assets, the practice of reciprocity plainly has other origins.

Shepard (1986) has recently developed another interesting application of transaction cost reasoning that involves not the creation but the release of a hostage. The puzzle to be explained is the insistence by buyers that semiconductor producers license their design of chips to others. One explanation is that this averts delivery failures attributable to idiosyncratic disruptive events at the parent company (earthquakes, labor strife, and the like). If, however, exposure to geographic hazards and supply interruptions due to company-wide bargaining were the only concerns, then subcontracting would afford adequate relief. Since the parent company could retain full control over total production via subcontracting, and since such control offers the prospect of added monopoly gains, licensing is evidently a poorly calibrated – indeed, in relation to the above described economic purposes, it is an excessive – response.

The possibility that the demand for licensing has other origins is thus suggested. The transaction cost rationale for insistence upon licensing is that buyers are reluctant to specialize their product and production to a particular chip without assurance of "competitive" supply. The concern is that a monopoly seller will expropriate the buyer when follow-on orders are placed – which is after the buyer has made durable investments that cannot be redeployed without sacrifice of productive value. The insistence on licensing is thus explained by the fact that access to several *independent* sources of supply relieves these expropriation hazards.[18]

5.1.2. Oversearching

Most of the applications of transaction cost economics have dealt with governance issues. Transaction cost economics also deals, however, with measurement problems [Barzel (1982)]. One manifestation of this is oversearching.

Kenney and Klein (1983) address themselves to several such cases. One is a reinterpretation of the *Loew's* case,[19] where Kenney and Klein take exception to Stigler's interpretation of block-booking as an effort to effect price discrimination. They argue instead that block-booking economizes on measurement costs for motion picture films the box-office receipts of which are difficult to estimate ex ante.

A more interesting case is their interpretation of the market for gem-quality uncut diamonds. Despite classification into more than two thousand categories, significant quality variation in the stones evidently remains. How can such a market be organized so that oversearching expenses are not incurred and each

[18]This is akin to, though slightly different from, Shepard's (1986) explanation.
[19]*United States v. Loew's Inc.*, 371 U.S. 38 (1962).

party to the transaction has confidence in the other? The "solution" that the market evolved and which Kenney and Klein interpret entailed the assembly of groups of diamonds – or "sights" – and imposing all-or-none and in-or-out trading rules. Thus, buyers who refuse to accept a sight are thereafter denied access to this market.

These two trading rules may appear to "disadvantage" buyers. Viewed in systems terms, however, they put a severe burden on de Beers to respect the legitimate expectations of buyers. Thus, suppose that only an all-or-none trading rule were to be imposed. Although buyers would thereby be denied the opportunity to pick the better diamonds from each category, they would nonetheless have the incentive to inspect each sight very carefully. Refusal to accept would signal that a sight was over-priced – but no more.

Suppose now that an in-or-out trading rule is added. The decision to refuse a sight now has much more serious ramifications. To be sure, a refusal could indicate that a particular sight is egregiously over-priced. More likely, however, it reflects a succession of bad experiences. It is a public declaration that de Beers is not to be trusted. In effect, a disaffected buyer announces that the expected net profits of dealing with de Beers under these constrained trading rules is negative.

Such an announcement has a chilling effect on the market. Buyers who were earlier prepared to make casual sight inspections are now advised that there are added trading hazards. Everyone is put on notice that a confidence has been violated and to inspect more carefully.

Put differently, the in-or-out trading rule is a way of encouraging buyers to regard the procurement of diamonds not as a series of independent trading events but as a long-term trading relation. If, overall, things can be expected to "average out", then it is not essential that an exact correspondence between payment made and value received be realized on each sight. In the face of systematic underrealizations of value, however, buyers will be induced to quit. If, as a consequence, the system is moved from a high to a low trust trading culture, then the costs of marketing diamonds increase. de Beers has strong incentives to avoid such an adverse outcome – whence, in a regime which combines all-or-none with in-or-out trading rules, will take care to present sights such that legitimate expectations will be achieved. The combined rules thus infuse greater integrity of trade.

5.2. Economics of the family

Transaction cost economics has been brought to bear on the economics of family organization in two respects: the one deals with family firms and productive relations; the other deals with "career marriages".

5.2.1. *Family firms*

Pollak's (1985) recent examination of families and households actually addresses a broader subject than family firms. I nevertheless focus these remarks on the family firm issue.

Pollak (1985, pp. 581–582) introduces his article with the following overview of the literature:

> The traditional economic theory of the household focuses exclusively on observable market behavior (i.e., demand for goods, supply of labor) treating the household as a "black box" identified only by its preference ordering. The "new home economics" takes a broader view, including not only market behavior but also such nonmarket phenomena as fertility, the education of children, and the allocation of time. The major analytic tool of the new home economics is Becker's household production model, which depicts the household as combining the time of household members with market goods to produce the outputs or "commodities" it ultimately desires.
>
> The new home economics ignores the internal organization and structure of families and households. Although this may surprise noneconomists who tend to believe that the internal organization and structure of an institution are likely to affect its behavior, economists find it natural. For the economist the most economical way to exploit the fundamental insight that production takes place within the household is to apply to households techniques developed for studying firms. Since neoclassical economics identifies firms with their technologies and assumes that firms operate efficiently and frictionlessly, it precludes any serious interest in the economizing properties of the internal structure and organization of firms. The new home economics, by carrying over this narrow neoclassical view from firms to households, thus fails to exploit fully the insight of the household production approach. ... [By contrast,] the transaction cost approach which recognizes the significance of internal structure provides a broader and more useful view of the economic activity and behavior of the family.

Pollak then goes on to examine the strengths and limitations of the family in governance structure and technological respects and identifies the circumstances where family firms can be expected to enjoy a comparative advantage. The advantages of the firm are developed under four headings: incentives, monitoring, altruism, and loyalty. The main disadvantages of the family as a production unit are conflict spillover from nonproduction into production activities, a propensity to forgive inefficient or slack behavior, access to a restricted range of talents, and possible diseconomies of small scale. He concludes that the strongest case for the family firm is "in low-trust environments (that is, in societies in which nonfamily members are not expected to perform honestly or reliably) and in sectors using relatively simple technologies" [Pollak (1985, p. 593)].

5.2.2. Career marriages

Career marriages of two kinds can be distinguished. One of these involves the marriage of a manager with a firm. The other involves cohabitation by two people, usually but not always of the opposite sex. The analysis here deals with the latter, but much of the argument carries over to marriages of manager and firm with minor changes.

I examine career marriages in the context of the contracting schema set out in Figure 3.1. Career being the entire focus, the parties are assumed to contract for marriage in a wholly calculative way.

Recall that node A corresponds to the condition where $k = 0$. Neither party in these circumstances makes career sacrifices in support of, or at the behest of, the other. This is strictly a marriage of convenience. Each party looks exclusively to his/her own career in deciding on whether to continue the marriage or split. If, for example, a promotion is offered in a distant city to one but not both, the marriage is severed and each goes his/her own way. Or if one job demands late hours or weekends and this interferes with the leisure time plans of the other, each seeks a more compatible mate. A wholly careerist orientation is thus determinative. Nothing being asked or given, there are no regrets upon termination.

The case where $k > 0$ is obviously the more interesting. Nodes B and C here describe the relevant outcomes.

A $k > 0$ condition is one in which one of the parties to the marriage is assumed to make career sacrifices in support of the other. Let X and Y be the parties, and assume that X subordinates his/her career for Y. Thus, X may help Y pay for his/her education by accepting a menial job that pays well but represents a distinctly inferior promotion track. Or X may agree to specialize in nonmarket transactions called "homemaking". Or X may agree to be available to Y as a companion. Not only are career sacrifices incurred, but X's homemaking and companionship skills may be imperfectly transferable if Y has idiosyncratic tastes.

Whatever the particulars, the salient fact is that X's future employment prospects are worsened by reason of career sacarifices made on behalf of Y.[20] The interesting question is: How will the life styles of such career marriages differ depending on whether Y offers a marriage safeguard to X or refuses one?

[20]This ignores the possibility that Y is a "celebrity" and that having been married to Y carries cachet. X then realizes an immediate status gain upon marriage. Career sacrifices by X can then be interpreted as "payment" for the status gain. But Y, under these circumstances, is the vulnerable party.

A node B outcome obtains if Y refuses (or is unable) to provide a safeguard to X. Under the assumption that contracts are struck in full awareness of the hazards, X will demand up-front pay for such circumstances. This is the condition to which Carol Channing had reference in the line "diamonds are a girl's best friend".

If, however, Y is willing and able to offer a safeguard, a node C outcome can be realized. Since X has better assurance under these circumstances that Y will not terminate the relation except for compelling reasons (because Y must pay a termination penalty), X's demands for current rewards (diamonds, dinner, travel, etc.) will be reduced.

This raises the question, however, of what form these safeguards can or do take. There are several possibilities, some of which are dependent on the prevailing legal rules.

Children provide a safeguard if the prevailing legal rules award custody to X and severely limit Y's visitation rights (place these rights under X's control). The award of other assets that Y is known to value also perform this function.

Dividing the property accumulated in the marriage and making alimony conditional on the magnitude of X's career sacrifice is another type of safeguard. In effect, such legal rules deny node B outcomes. If X is awarded wealth and income protection under the law, then Y will be deterred from terminating.

As with most deterrrents, however, there are side-effects. Thus, Y can squander assets in contemplation of termination. And Y may refuse to work or flee if alimony payments are thought to be punitive.

A third possibility is to develop a reciprocal career dependency. This may not be easy, but it may be done (at some sacrifice, usually) in certain complementary career circumstances. A pair of dancers with a highly idiosyncratic style is one illustration. Lawyers with complementary specialties and idiosyncratic knowledge of a particular class of transactions (say, of a particular corporation) is another. An artist and his/her agent is a third possibility.

5.3. *Corporate finance*

The Modigliani–Miller theorem that the cost of capital in a firm was independent of the proportion of debt and equity revolutionized modern corporate finance. It gave rise to an extensive literature in which a special rationale for debt in an otherwise equity-financed firm was sought. The first of these, unsurprisingly, was that debt had tax advantages over equity. But this was scarcely adequate. Further and more subtle reasons why debt would be used in preference to equity even in a tax-neutral world were also advanced. The leading rationales were: (1) debt could be used as a signal of differential business prospects [Ross (1977)]; (2) debt could be used by entrepreneurs with limited resources who were faced with new

Table 3.1

Governance feature	Financial instrument	
	Debt	Equity
Contractual constraints	Numerous	Nil
Security	Pre-emptive	Residual claimant
Intrusion	Nil	Extensive

investment opportunities and did not want to dilute their equity position, thereby to avoid sacrifice of incentive intensity [Jensen and Meckling (1976)]; and (3) debt could serve as an incentive bonding device [Grossman and Hart (1982)].

The Modigliani–Miller theorem and each of the debt rationales referred to above treats capital as a composite and regards the firm as a production function. By contrast, transaction cost economics maintains that the asset characteristics of investment projects matter and furthermore distinguishes between debt and equity in terms of their governance structure attributes. The basic argument is this: the investment attributes of projects and the governance structure features of debt and equity need to be aligned in a discriminating way. The key governance structure differences between debt and equity are shown in Table 3.1.

The transaction cost approach maintains that some projects are easy to finance by debt and *ought to be financed by debt*. These are projects for which physical asset specificity is low to moderate. As asset specificity becomes great, however, the pre-emptive claims of the bondholders against the investment afford limited protection – because the assets in question have limited redeployability. Not only does the cost of debt financing therefore increase, but the benefits of closer oversight also grow. The upshot is that equity finance, which affords more intrusive oversight and involvement through the board of directors (and, in publicly held firms, permits share ownership to be concentrated), is the preferred financial instrument for projects where asset specificity is great.

Although this sketch oversimplifies greatly,[21] it nevertheless captures the flavor of the transaction cost approach to corporate finance and advances the refutable hypothesis that the capital structure of the firm ought to reflect rational transac-

[21] A major puzzle that is not addressed is what I have referred to elsewhere as "dequity": Why cannot a new financial instrument be devised which permits "selective intervention"? Thus, the constraints on managerial discretion that are attributable to debt are everywhere observed except when these prevent the firm from realizing added value, in which event they are (selectively) waived. Since selective intervention appears to dominate either pure security type, wherein does it break down?

I have examined this and related issues elsewhere [Williamson (1988)]. The puzzle of selective intervention in corporate finance is, unsurprisingly, closely related to my discussion of selective intervention in the vertically integrated firm [Williamson (1985, ch. 6)].

tion cost economizing principles. Assuming, for argument, that the approach has merit, it ought, among other things, to have ramifications for leveraged buyouts.

Thus, consider a firm that is originally financed along lines that are consistent with the debt and equity financing principles set out above. Suppose that the firm is successful and grows through retained earnings, whence the debt–equity ratio falls as a consequence. And suppose, further, that many of the assets in this now expanded enterprise are of a kind that could have been financed by debt.

Added value, in such a firm, can be realized by substituting debt for equity. This argument applies, however, selectively. It only applies to firms where the efficient mix of debt and equity has gotten seriously out of alignment. These will be firms that combine (1) a very high ratio of equity to debt with (2) a very high ratio of redeployable to nonredeployable assets.

Interestingly, many of the large leveraged buyouts in the 1980s displayed precisely these qualities.[22] The following features of leveraged buyouts are pertinent:

(1) The major lenders are finance companies and banks and insurance companies. The finance companies specialize in shorter term inventory and receivable financing, where they have an advantage over the banks in policing the collateral, and will lend up to 85 percent of the liquidation value. Banks and insurance companies specialize in intermediate and longer term financing, usually at a lower lending percentage of liquidation value [Colman (1981, p. 539)].

(2) The cash flow and asset-based financing approaches are distinguished by the fact that under "the conventional approach, the lender wanted protection primarily via cash flow", whereas under "the asset-based approach... the lender ties all or at least part of his loan to the liquid value of the borrower's assets..., [and realizes protection by] taking a security interest in the assets..., [establishing] a lending formula on the basis of the liquid value, and... [obtaining] periodic information on the nature and size of those assets" [Colman (1981, p. 542)].

Plainly, the shift from cash-flow to asset-based financing lines up rather closely with the transaction cost economics rationale for secure transactions.[23]

[22]Robert Colman's examination of leveraged buyouts disclosed that "only an existing firm with a small amount of debt is able to support" a leveraged buyout and that a "frequent characteristic of the leveraged buyout company is that the firm has a high proportion of its total assets in tangible property" [Colman (1981, p. 531)]. Although the tangible–intangible distinction is not identical to the redeployability test herein suggested, there is plainly a correlation.

[23]In fact, of course, the condition of asset specificity is only one important attribute of an investment project. Among other things, the time profile of expected cash flows also matters [Jensen (1986)]. Thus, redeployable assets with deferred cash flows require greater equity funding at the outset than those with earlier cash flows, ceteris paribus. More generally, the investment attribute approach to project financing stands in need of elaboration and refinement. I nevertheless conjecture that redeployability will remain the key feature of an extended asset attribute approach to corporate finance.

5.4. *The modern corporation*

Transaction cost economics appeals to the business history literature for the record and description of organizational innovations.[24] The work of Alfred Chandler, Jr. (1962, 1977) has been especially instructive. Among the more notable developments have been the invention of the line and staff structure by the railroads in the mid-nineteenth century, the *selective* appearance of vertical integration (especially forward integration out of manufacturing into distribution) at the turn of the century, and the appearance in the 1920s and subsequent diffusion of the multidivisional structure.

Transaction cost economics maintains that these innovations are central to an understanding of the modern corporation. The study of such organizational innovations requires, however, that the details of internal organization be examined. That technological and monopoly conceptions of the corporation ruled in an earlier era is precisely because the details of internal organization were passed off as economically irrelevant.

From a transaction cost point of view, the main purpose of studying internal organization is to better understand the comparative efficacy of internal governance processes. What are the ramifications – for economizing on bounded rationality; for attenuating opportunism; for implementing a program of adaptive, sequential decisionmaking – of organizing the firm this way rather than that? The shift from the functionally organized (U-form) structure by large corporations that began in the 1920s is especially noteworthy.

The M-form innovation began as an effort to cope. Chandler's statement of the defects of the large U-form enterprise is pertinent [Chandler (1966, pp. 382–383)]:

> The inherent weakness in the centralized, functionally departmentalized operating company... became critical only when the administrative load on the senior executives increased to such an extent that they were unable to handle their entrepreneurial responsibilities efficiently. This situation arose when the operations of the enterprise became too complex and the problems of coordination, appraisal, and policy formulation too intricate for a small number of top officers to handle both long-run, entrepreneurial, and short-run operational administrative activities.

Bounds on rationality were evidently reached as the U-form structure labored under a communication overload. Moving to a decentralized structure relieved some of these strains.

[24]Arrow (1971, p. 224) observes that "truly among man's innovations, the use of organization to accomplish his ends is among both his greatest and earliest". And Cole (1968, pp. 61–62) asserts that "if changes in business procedures and practices were patentable, the contributions of business change to the economic growth of the nation would be as widely recognized as the influence of mechanical innovations or the inflow of capital from abroad".

But there was more to it than this. The M-form structure served not only to economize on bounded rationality, but it further served (in comparison with the U-form structure which it supplanted) to attenuate subgoal pursuit (reduce opportunism). This is because, as Chandler (1966, p. 382) puts it, the M-form structure "clearly removed the executives responsible for the destiny of the entire enterprise from the more routine operational activities, and so gave them the time, information, and even psychological commitment for long-term planning and appraisal".

The upshot is that the M-form innovation (X), which had mainly bounded rationality origins, also had unanticipated effects on corporate purpose (Y) by attenuating subgoal pursuit. Benefits of two kinds were thereby realized in the process.

There were still further unexpected consequences in store, moreover. Once the M-form organization had been perfected and extended from specialized lines of commerce (automobiles; chemicals) to manage diversified activities, it became clear that this structure could be used to support takeover of firms in which managerial discretion excesses were occurring (Z). A transfer of resources to higher valued purposes arguably obtains [Williamson (1985, pp. 319–322)].

The spread of multidivisionalization through takeover thus yields the *reproductive link* that Elster (1983, p. 58) notes is normally missing in most functional

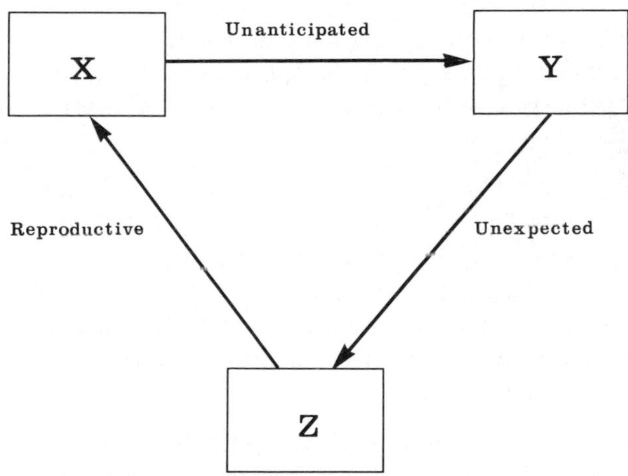

Figure 3.6. Full functionalism.

arguments in social science. The requisites of full functionalism are evidently satisfied.

Indeed, there is an additional process of spreading the M-form that ought also to be mentioned: mitosis. The large and diversified M-form structure may discover that the benefits associated with new activities or acquisitions do not continue indefinitely. Acquired components or diversified parts may therefore be divested. To the extent that these are spun-off or otherwise divested as discrete multidivisional units themselves, propagation through cell division may be said to exist. This quasi-biological process would also presumably qualify as a reproductive link and thereby contribute to successful functional explanation. Figure 3.6 summarizes the argument.

6. The evidence

Transaction cost economics operates at a more microanalytic level of analysis than does orthodoxy. Whereas prices and quantities were thought to be the main if not the only relevant data in the orthodox scheme of things [Arrow (1971, p. 180)], transaction cost economics looks at the attributes of transactions and the maintains that the details of organization matter. Additional data thus come under review. Simon's (1984, p. 40) remarks on econometric testing are pertinent:

> In the physical sciences, when errors of measurement and other noise are found to be of the same order of magnitude as the phenomena under study the response is not to try to squeeze more information out of the data by statistical means; it is instead to find techniques for observing the phenomena at a higher level of resolution. The corresponding strategy for economics is obvious: to secure new kinds of data at the micro level.

Although it may be possible, as Kreps and Spence (1985, pp. 374–375) observe, "to divine the correct 'reduced form' for the behavior of the organization without considering the micro-forces within the organization", this requires an exceptionally keen intuition. There are some conditions, the study of complex organization arguably being among them, for which there is no substitution for direct observations (and even direct experience) whereby the relevant microanalytics are engaged or at least brought under review.[25]

Although the costs of such data collection can be great, resolution gains of the kind referred to by Simon are frequently realized. Recent microanalytic studies in

[25]To be sure, transaction cost economics operates at a semi-microanalytic rather than a fully microanalytic level of analysis. An appreciation for the relevant semi-microanalytics is nonetheless promoted by pushing deeper. The study of process (of which the Fundamental Transformation is an example) is frequently implicated.

which transaction costs are featured include:

(1) Statistical models (utilizing, for example, probit techniques) in which the attributes of transactions are associated with organization form. The study of vertical integration in the automobile industry by Monteverde and Teece (1982) is an example.

(2) Bivariate tests for association between attributes of transactions and contracting modes. The studies of defense contracting by Masten (1984) and of transportation contracting by Palay (1984, 1985) are examples.

(3) The examination of contractual vignettes, some of which arise in antitrust proceedings. My assessment of petroleum exchanges in the context of what, under a neoclassical interpretation, appear to be "incriminating" internal company documents is an illustration [Williamson (1985, ch. 8)].

(4) Focused case studies, of which franchise bidding for CATV is an example [Williamson (1985, ch. 13)], and focused industry studies, of which Stuckey's (1983) remarkable treatment of vertical integration and joint ventures in the aluminum industry is especially noteworthy.

(5) Studies of the contractual features and governance structures of long-term contracts, of which recent studies of long-term coal contracts [Goldberg and Erickson (1982), Joskow (1985, 1987)] and take-or-pay provisions in the contracting nexus between natural gas producers and pipelines [Masten and Crocker (1985), Mulherin (1986)] are examples.

(6) Studies of vertical integration in which financial economics (the capital asset pricing model) and asset specificity features are joined [Spiller (1985), Helfat and Teece (1987)].

(7) Studies of the multinational enterprise, where technology transfer and production issues are addressed by examining whether the attributes of transactions and the use of licensing and foreign direct investment (of both partial and full ownership kinds) are aligned in a discriminating way [Teece (1977), Gatignon and Anderson (1986)].

(8) An examination of changing organization practices as reported in the business history literature. Chandler's (1962, 1977) work, a summary and interpretation of which is reported elsewhere [Williamson (1985, ch. 5)], is especially noteworthy.

(9) Studies of corporate governance and securities regulation, where Romano (1985, 1986) has done pathbreaking work.

(10) Studies of the organization and structure of labor unions in which power versus transaction cost hypotheses are tested [Weakliem (1987)].

In addition to the above studies of contract and organization, the majority of which were done by economists, an empirical literature in marketing has been developing in which sales compensation practices and choice of distribution channels are examined in transaction cost terrms. The first of these was done by Anderson and Schmittlein (1984), who examine the organization of the sales force in the electronic components industry. They report that "integration is associated with increasing levels of asset specificity, difficulty of performance evaluation, and the combination of these factors", but frequency and uncertainty measures did not turn out to be significant [Anderson and Schmittlein (1984, p. 385)]. The empirical results on distribution channels obtained by Lilien (1979, pp. 197–199), in his influential paper on the marketing mix decision, are broadly consistent with transaction cost reasoning [Anderson (1985, p. 165)]. John and Weitz (1986) also examine forward integration into distribution in industrial markets and report that asset specificity favors forward integration – as does added uncertainty (of both market variability and measurement kinds). The manner in which manufacturers' agents attempt to safeguard specific assets by bonding themselves to their customers is investigated by Heide and John (1986). They not only demonstrate that bonding is a discriminating response, but they further contrast the transaction cost and resource dependence perspectives. As they put it, the key resource dependence measures are "*numbers* of exchange partners and the *distribution* of transactions across the partners. The idea is that the concentration of exchange constitutes dependence" [Heide and John (1988, p. 13)]. The characteristics of the assets, rather than the concentration of exchange, is what matters from a transaction cost viewpoint. The data corroborate the latter: "concentration of exchange by itself does not induce an agency to strengthen its bonds with other exchange partners.... It is the presence of specific assets at risk or the nature of the investments that prompts the action" [Heide and John (1988, p. 24)].

Thus, although empirical studies and tests of transaction cost economics are still few in number and many are crude, the main implications are borne out and/or fare well in comparison with the leading alternatives. The crudeness to which I refer has two sources. First, transaction cost theory and models are still very primitive. Only gross predictions are usually available. Secondly, severe measurement problems are posed. Both limitations will be mitigated as better models and better data become available.

Albeit real, current data limitations ought not to be exaggerated. Empirical researchers in transaction cost economics have had to collect their own data. They have resolved the trade-off of breadth (census reports; financial statistics) for depth (the microanalytics of contract and investment) mainly in favor of the latter. In the degree to which a subject becomes a science when it begins to develop its own data, this data switch is a commendable response.

7. Public policy ramifications

Transaction cost economics can be brought to bear on a wide variety of public policy issues. Although most of the applications have dealt with matters of microeconomic policy, the transaction cost economics perspective can also help to inform public policy toward stagflation.

7.1. Microeconomics

Microeconomic applications include regulation and antitrust. Consumer protection is another possibility.

7.1.1. Regulation / deregulation

Monopoly supply is efficient where economies of scale are large in relation to the size of the market. But, as Friedman (1962, p. 128) laments, "There is unfortunately no good solution for technical monopoly. There is only a choice among three evils: private unregulated monopoly, private monopoly regulated by the state, and government operation."

Friedman characterized private unregulated monopoly as an evil because he assumed that private monopoly ownership implied pricing on monopoly terms. As subsequently argued by Demsetz (1968b), Stigler (1968), and Posner (1972), however, a monopoly price outcome can be avoided by using ex ante bidding to award the monopoly franchise to the firm that offers to supply product on the best terms. Demsetz (1968b, p. 57) advances the franchise bidding for natural monopoly argument by stripping away "irrelevant complications" – such as equipment durability and uncertainty. Stigler (1968, p. 19) contends that "customers can auction off the right to sell electricity, using the state as an instrument to conduct the auction.... The auction... consists of [franchise bids] to sell cheaply." Posner agrees and furthermore holds that franchise bidding is an efficacious way by which to award and operate cable TV franchises.

Transaction cost economics recognizes merit in the argument but insists that both ex ante and ex post contracting features be examined. Only if competition is efficacious at *both* stages does the franchise bidding argument go through. The attributes of the good or service to be franchised are crucial to the assessment. Specifically, if the good or service is to be supplied under conditions of uncertainty and if nontrivial investments in specific assets are involved, the efficacy of franchise bidding is highly problematic. Indeed, the implementation of a franchise bidding scheme under those circumstances essentially requires the progressive elaboration of an administrative apparatus that differs mainly in name rather than in kind from the sort associated with rate of return regulation.

This is not, however, to suggest that franchise bidding for goods or services supplied under decreasing cost conditions is never feasible or to imply that extant regulation or public ownership can never be supplanted by franchise bidding with net gains. Examples where gains are in prospect include local service airlines and, possibly, postal delivery. The winning bidder for each can be displaced without posing serious asset valuation problems, since the base plant (terminals, post office, warehouses, and so on) can be owned by the government, and other assets (planes, trucks, and the like) will have an active second-hand market. It is not, therefore, that franchise bidding is totally lacking in merit. On the contrary, it is a very imaginative proposal. Transaction cost economics maintains, however, that all contracting schemes – of which franchise bidding for natural monopoly is one – need to be examined microanalytically and assessed in a comparative institutional manner. The recent examination of alternative modes for organizing electricity generation by Joskow and Schmalensee (1983) is illustrative.

7.1.2. Antitrust

The inhospitality tradition maintains the rebuttable presumption that nonstandard forms of contracting have monopoly purpose and effect. The firm-as-production function theory of economic organization likewise regards vertical integration skeptically. Integration that lacks technological purpose purportedly has monopoly origins [Bain (1968, p. 381)]. The argument that "vertical integration loses its innocence if there is an appreciable degree of market power at even one stage of the production process" [Stigler (1955, p. 183)] – a 20 percent market share being the threshold above which market power is to be inferred [Stigler (1955, p. 183)] – is in this same spirit.

Transaction cost economics views integration differently. It maintains the rebuttable presumption that nonstandard forms of contracting, of which vertical integration is an extreme form, have the purpose and effect of economizing on transaction costs. It thus focuses on whether the transactions in question are supported by investments in specific assets. It furthermore examines monopoly purpose in the context of strategic behavior.[26]

Consider, in this connection, two stages of supply – which will be referred to generically as stages I and II (but for concreteness can be thought of as production and distribution). If the leading firms in a highly concentrated stage I were to integrate into an otherwise competitive stage II activity, the nonintegrated sector of the market may be so reduced that only a few firms of efficient size can service the stage II market. Then, entry would be deterred by the potential entrant's having to engage in small-numbers bargaining with those few nonintegrated stage II firms. Furthermore, the alternative of integrated entry will be less attractive because prospective stage I entrants that lack experience in

[26]Strategic behavior has reference to efforts by established firms to take up advance positions in relation to actual or potential rivals, to introduce contrived cost disparities, and/or respond punitively to new rivalry. These matters are examined in detail by other chapters in this Handbook. Suffice it to observe here that strategic behavior is interesting only in an intertemporal context in which uncertainty and specific assets are featured.

stage II activity would incur higher capital and start-up costs were they to enter both stages themselves. If, instead, stages I and II were of low or moderate concentration, a firm entering either stage can expect to strike competitive bargains with either integrated or nonintegrated firms in the other stage, because no single integrated firm can enjoy a strategic advantage in such transactions, and because it is difficult for the integrated firms to collude. Except, therefore, where strategic considerations intrude – namely, in highly concentrated industries where entry is impeded – vertical integration will rarely pose an antitrust issue.

Whereas the original 1968 Guidelines reflected pre-transaction cost thinking and imposed severe limits on vertical integration (the vertical acquisition of a 6 percent firm by a 10 percent firm was above threshold), the revised Guidelines are much more permissive. The 1982 Guidelines are congruent with the policy implications of transaction cost economics in three respects. First, the 1982 Guidelines express concern over the competitive consequences of a vertical merger only if the acquired firm is operating in an industry in which the HHI exceeds 1800. The presumption is that nonintegrated stage I firms can satisfy their stage II requirements by negotiating competitive terms with stage II firms where the HHI is below 1800. The Guidelines thus focus exclusively on the monopolistic subset, which is congruent with transaction cost reasoning. Second, the anticompetitive concerns in the Guidelines regarding costs of capital, (contrived) scale diseconomies, and the use of vertical integration to evade rate regulation are all consonant with transaction cost reasoning. Finally, the Guidelines make express reference to the importance of asset specificity, although the analysis is less fully developed than it might be. Also, whereas the 1982 Guidelines make no provision for an economies defense, the 1984 Guidelines take this further step – which provision is especially important where asset specificity is demonstrably great.

7.2. Macroeconomics: Stagflation

Martin Weitzman's recent treatment of stagflation in his influential book *The Share Economy* mainly works out of a monopolistic competition framework. Weitzman augments the standard monopolistic competition apparatus, however, by distinguishing between redeployable and nonredeployable assets. Thus, he regards labor as redeployable while intermediate product is not: a "coalminer and a fruitpicker are infinitely closer substitutes than the products they handle. Rolled sheet and I-beams ... are virtually inconvertible in use" [Weitzman (1984, p. 28)]. Unfortunatley, this is a technological rather than a transactional distinction.

Such a technological view leads to a much different assessment of the contracting process than does a contractual view. Thus, whereas Weitzman regards labor market contracting as unique and flawed by rigidities, transaction cost economics maintains that labor markets and intermediate product markets are very similar and puts a different construction on rigidities. In particular, an examination of the governance needs of contract discloses that the full flexibility of wages and prices advocated by Weitzman would pose a serious threat to the integrity of contracts that are supported by durable investments in firm-specific assets. The lesson is that macroeconomics needs to come to terms with the study of contracting of a more microanalytic kind.[27]

8. Conclusions

Friction, the economic counterpart for which is transaction costs, is pervasive in both physical and economic systems. Our understanding of complex economic organization awaits more concerted study of the sources and mitigation of friction. What is referred to herein as transaction cost economics merely records the beginnings of a response.

Refinements of several kinds are in prospect. One is that many of the insights of the transaction cost approach will be absorbed within the corpus of "extended" neoclassical analysis. The capacity of neoclassical economics to expand its boundaries is quite remarkable in this respect. Second, transaction cost arguments will be qualified to make allowance for process values such as fairness that now appear in a rather ad hoc way. [As Michelman (1967) has demonstrated, however, fairness and efficiency considerations converge when an extended view of contracting in its entirety is adopted. This insight is important and needs further development.] Third, numerous phenomena have yet to be brought under the lens of transaction cost reasoning. Recent experience suggests that new insights and new models are both in prospect. Fourth, a more carefully and fully developed theory of bureaucracy is greatly needed. Among other things, the powers and limits of alternative forms of internal organization with respect to reputation effects, internal due process, complex contingent rewards, auditing, and life cycle features need to be assessed. Finally, empirical research on transaction cost issues has just begun.

References

Akerlof, G.A. (1970) 'The market for 'lemons': Qualitative uncertainty and the market mechanism', *Quarterly Journal of Economics*, 84:488–500.

Alchian, A. (1950) 'Uncertainty, evolution and economic theory', *Journal of Political Economy*, 58:211–221.

Alchian, A. (1961) *Some economics of property*, RAND D-2316, Santa Monica, Calif.: RAND Corporation.

Alchian, A. (1965) 'The basis of some recent advances in the theory of management of the firm', *Journal of Industrial Economics*, 14:30–41.

Alchian, A. (1984) 'Specificity, specialization, and coalitions', *Journal of Economic Theory and Institutions*, 140:34–39.

[27]The argument is elaborated in Williamson (1986a).

Alchian, A. and Demsetz, H. (1972) 'Production, information costs, and economic organization', *American Economic Review*, 62:777–795.
Anderson, E. (1985) 'Implications of transaction cost analysis for the management of distribution channels', in: R.E. Spekman, ed., *Proceedings: A strategic approach to business marketing*. Chicago: American Marketing Association, 160–168.
Anderson, E. and Schmittlein, D. (1984) 'Integration of the sales force: An empirical examination', *The Rand Journal of Economics*, 15:385–395.
Aoki, M. (1983) 'Managerialism revisited in the light of bargaining-game theory', *International Journal of Industrial Organization*, 1:1–21.
Arrow, K.J. (1969) 'The organization of economic activity: Issues pertinent to the choice of market versus nonmarket allocation', in: *The analysis and evaluation of public expenditure: The PPB system*, Vol. 1, U.S. Joint Economic Committee, 91st Congress, 1st Session. Washington, D.C.: U.S. Government Printing Office, 59–73.
Arrow, K.J. (1971) *Essays in the theory of risk-bearing*. Chicago: Markham.
Arrow, K.J. (1985) 'Informational structure of the firm', *American Economic Review*, 75:303–307.
Azariadis, C. and Stiglitz, J. (1983) 'Implicit contracts and fixed price equilibria', *Quarterly Journal of Economics*, 94:1–22.
Baiman, S. (1982) 'Agency research in managerial accounting: A survey', *Journal of Accounting Literature*, 1:154–213.
Bain, J. (1956) *Barriers to new competition*. Cambridge, Mass.: Harvard University Press.
Bain, J. (1958) *Industrial organization*. New York: Wiley.
Bain, J. (1968) *Industrial organization*, 2d edn. New York: Wiley.
Barnard, C. (1938) *The functions of the executive*, 15th printing (1962). Cambridge: Harvard University Press.
Barzel, Y. (1982) 'Measurement cost and the organization of markets', *Journal of Law and Economics*, 25:27–48.
Becker, G.S. (1962) 'Irrational behavior and economic theory', *Journal of Political Economy*, 70:1–13.
Berle, A.A. and Means, G.C. (1932) *The modern corporation and private property*. New York: Macmillan.
Bewley, T. (1986) 'A theory of layoffs, strikes and wage determination', Cowles Foundation, unpublished research proposal.
Blake, H.M. (1973) 'Conglomerate mergers and the antitrust laws', *Columbia Law Review*, 73:555–592.
Bowles, S. and Gintis, H. (1986) *Democracy and capitalism*. New York: Basic Books.
Bridgemen, P. (1955) *Reflections of a physicist*, 2d edn. New York: Philosophical Library.
Buchanan, J. (1975) 'A contractarian paradigm for applying economic theory', *American Economic Review*, 65:225–230.
Caves, R. and Bradburg, R. (1988) 'The empirical determinants of vertical integration', *Journal of Economic Behavior and Organization*, 9:265–280.
Chandler, A.D., Jr. (1962) *Strategy and structure*. Cambridge, Mass.: MIT Press; subsequently published (1966), New York: Doubleday and Co.
Chandler, A.D., Jr. (1977) *The visible hand: The managerial revolution in American business*. Cambridge, Mass.: Harvard University Press.
Coase, R.H. (1937) 'The nature of the firm', *Economic*, 4:386–405; reprinted in: G.J. Stigler and K.E. Boulding, eds., *Readings in price theory*. Homewood, Ill.: Richard D. Irwin.
Coase, R.H. (1960) 'The problem of social cost', *Journal of Law and Economics*, 3:1–44.
Coase, R.H. (1972) 'Industrial organization: A proposal for research', in: V.R. Fuchs, ed., *Policy issues and research opportunities in industrial organization*. New York: National Bureau of Economic Research, 59–73.
Coase, R.H. (1984) 'The new institutional economics', *Journal of Institutional and Theoretical Economics*, 140:229–231.
Cole, A.H. (1968) 'The entrepreneur: introductory remarks', *American Economic Review*, 63:60–63.
Colman, R. (1981) 'Overview of leveraged buyouts', in: S. Lee and R. Colman, eds., *Handbook of mergers, acquisitions and buyouts*. Englewood Cliffs, NJ: Prentice-Hall.
Commons, J.R. (1934) *Institutional economics*. Madison: University of Wisconsin Press.
Dahl, R.A. (1970) 'Power to the workers?' *New York Review of Books*, November 19, 20–24.
Demsetz, H. (1967) 'Toward a theory of property rights', *American Economic Review*, 57:347–359.
Demsetz, H. (1968a) 'The cost of transacting', *Quarterly Journal of Economics*, 82:33–53.

Demsetz, H. (1968b) 'Why regulate utilities?', *Journal of Law and Economics*, 11:55–66.
Demsetz, H. (1969) 'Information and efficiency: Another viewpoint', *Journal of Law and Economics*, 12:1–22.
Director, A. and Edward, L. (1956) 'Law and the future: trade regulation', *Northwestern University Law Review*, 10:281–317.
Dodd, E.M. (1932) 'For whom are corporate managers trustees?', *Harvard Law Review*, 45:1145–1163.
Elster, J. (1983) *Explaining technical change*. Cambridge: Cambridge University Press.
Fama, E.F. (1980) 'Agency problems and the theory of the firm', *Journal of Political Economy*, 88:288–307.
Fama, E.F. and Jensen, M.C. (1983) 'Separation of ownership and control', *Journal of Law and Economics*, 26:301–326.
Fisher, S. (1977) 'Long-term contracting, sticky prices, and monetary policy: Comment', *Journal of Monetary Economics*, 3:317–324.
Friedman, M. (1953) *Essays in positive economics*. Chicago: University of Chicago Press.
Friedman, M. (1962) *Capitalism and freedom*. Chicago: University of Chicago Press.
Furubotn, E. and Pejovich, S. (1974) *The economics of property rights*. Cambridge, Mass.: Ballinger.
Galanter, M. (1981) 'Justice in many rooms: Courts, private ordering, and indigenous law', *Journal of Legal Pluralism*, 19:1–47.
Gatignon, H. and Anderson, E. (1986) 'The multinational corporation's degree of control over foreign subsidiaries: An empirical test of a transaction cost explanation', unpublished.
Gauss, C. (1952) 'Introduction' to Machiavelli (1952), 7–32. (Machiavelli, N., *The prince*. New York: New American Library.)
Georgescu-Roegen, N. (1971) *The entropy law and economic process*. Cambridge, Mass.: Harvard University Press.
Goldberg, V. and Erickson, J.E. (1982) 'Long-term contracts for petroleum coke', working paper series no. 206, Department of Economics, University of California, Davis.
Gower, E.C.B. (1969) *Principles of modern company law*. London: Stevens and Sons.
Granovetter, M. (1985) 'Economic action and social structure: The problem of embeddedness', *American Journal of Sociology*, 91:481–510.
Grossman, S. and Hart, O. (1982) 'Corporate financial structure and managerial incentives', in: J. McCall, ed., *The economics of information and uncertainty*. Chicago: University of Chicago Press, 107–137.
Hayek, F. (1967) *Studies in philosophy, politics, and economics*. London: Routledge and Kegan Paul.
Heide, J.B. and John, G. (1988) 'Safeguarding transaction-specific assets in conventional channels: The role of offsetting investments', *Journal of Marketing*, 52:20–35.
Helfat, C. and Teece, D. (1987) 'Vertical integration and risk reduction', *Journal of Law, Economics and Organization*, 3:47–68.
Jensen, M. (1983) 'Organization theory and methodology', *Accounting Review*, 50:319–339.
Jensen, M. (1986) 'Agency costs and free cash flow, corporate finance, and takeovers', *American Economic Review*, 76:323–329.
Jensen, M. and Meckling, W. (1976) 'Theory of the firm: managerial behavior, agency costs, and capital structure', *Journal of Financial Economics*, 3:305–360.
John, G. and Weitz, B.A. (1986) 'Forward integration into distribution: An empirical test of transaction cost analysis', unpublished.
Joskow, P.L. (1985) 'Vertical integration and long-term contracts', *Journal of Law, Economics, and Organization*, 1:33–80.
Joskow, P.L. (1987) 'Contract duration and transactions specific investment: Empirical evidence from the coal markets', *American Economic Review*, 77:168–183.
Joskow, P.L. and Schmalensee, R. (1983) *Markets for power*. Cambridge, Mass.: MIT Press.
Kenney, R. and Klein, B. (1983) 'The economics of block booking', *Journal of Law and Economics*, 26:497–540.
Klein, B. (1980) 'Transaction cost determinants of 'Unfair' contractual arrangements', *American Economic Review*, 70:356–362.
Klein, B. and Leffler, K. (1981) 'The role of market forces in assuring contractual performance', *Journal of Political Economy*, 89:615–641.
Klein, B., Crawford, R.A. and Alchian, A.A. (1978) 'Vertical integration, appropriable rents, and the competitive contracting process', *Journal of Law and Economics*, 21:297–326.

Knight, F.H. (1941) 'Review of M.J. Herskovits' 'Economic Anthropology',' *Journal of Political Economy*, 49:247–258.
Knight, F.H. (1965) *Risk, uncertainty and profit*. New York: Harper and Row.
Koopmans, T. (1957) *Three essays on the state of economic science*. New York: McGraw-Hill.
Kreps, D. and Spence, A.M. (1985) 'Modelling the role of history in industrial organization and competition', in: G. Feiwel, ed., *Issues in contemporary microeconomics and welfare*. London: MacMillan, 340–379.
Lilien, G.L. (1979) 'Advisor 2: Modelling the market mix decision for industrial products', *Management Science*, 25:191–204.
Llewellyn, K.N. (1931) 'What price contract? An essay in perspective', *Yale Law Journal*, 40:704–751.
Macneil, I.R. (1974) 'The many futures of contract', *Southern California Law Review*, 47:691–816.
Marschak, J. (1968) 'Economics of inquiring, communicating, deciding', *American Economic Review*, 58:1–18.
Marshall, A. (1948) *Principles of economics*, 8th edn. New York: Macmillan.
Mason, E. (1958) 'The apologetics of managerialism', *Journal of Business*, 31:1–11.
Masten, S. (1982) 'Transaction costs, institutional choice, and the theory of the firm', Unpublished Ph.D. dissertation, University of Pennsylvania.
Masten, S. (1984) 'The organization of production: Evidence from the aerospace industry', *Journal of Law and Economics*, 27:403–418.
Masten, S. and Crocker, K. (1985) 'Efficient adaptation in long-term contracts: Take-or-pay provisions for natural gas', *American Economic Review*, 75:1083–1093.
McKenzie, L. (1951) 'Ideal output and the interdependence of firms', *Economic Journal*, 61:785–803.
Meade, J.E. (1971) *The controlled economy*. London: Allen and Unwin.
Michelman, F. (1967) 'Property, utility and fairness: Comments on the ethical foundations of 'Just Compensation' Law', *Harvard Law Review*, 80:1165–1257.
Milgrom, P. and Roberts, J. (1987) 'Bargaining costs, influence costs, and the organization of economic activity', unpublished.
Monteverde, K. and Teece, D. (1982) 'Supplier switching costs and vertical integration in the automobile industry', *Bell Journal of Economics*, 13:206–213.
Mulherin, J.H. (1986) 'Complexity in long term contracts: An analysis of natural gas contractual provisions', *Journal of Law, Economics and Organization*, 2:105–118.
Nelson, R. and Winter, S. (1982) *An evolutionary theory of economic change*. Cambridge, Mass.: Harvard University Press.
Nozick, R. (1974) *Anarchy, state and utopia*. New York: Basic Books.
Olson, M. (1965) *The logic of collective action*. Cambridge, Mass.: Harvard University Press.
Ouchi, (1980) 'Markets, bureaucracies, and clans', *Administrative Science Quarterly*, 25:120–142.
Palay, T. (1984) 'Comparative institutional economics: The governance of rail freight contracting', *Journal of Legal Studies*, 13:265–288.
Palay, T. (1985) 'The avoidance of regulatory constraints: The use of informal contracts', *Journal of Law, Economics and Organization*, 1:155–175.
Polanyi, M. (1962) *Personal knowledge: Towards a post-critical philosophy*. New York: Harper and Row.
Pollak, R. (1985) 'A transaction cost approach to families and households', *Journal of Economic Literature*, 23:581–608.
Posner, R.A. (1969) 'Natural monopoly and its regulation', *Stanford Law Review*, 21:548–643.
Posner, R.A. (1972) 'The appropriate scope of regulation in the cable television industry', *The Bell Journal of Economics and Management Science*, 3:98–129.
Posner, R.A. (1979) 'The Chicago School of antitrust analysis', *University of Pennsylvania Law Review*, 127:925–948.
Riordan, M. and Williamson, O. (1985) 'Asset specificity and economic organization', *International Journal of Industrial Organization*, 3:365–368.
Romano, R. (1985) 'Law as a product: Some pieces of the incorporation puzzle', *Journal of Law, Economics and Organization*, 1:225–284.
Romano, R. (1986) 'The state competition debate in corporate law', unpublished.
Ross, S. (1977) 'The determinants of financial structure: The incentive signaling approach', *Bell Journal of Economics*, 8:23–40.
Rothschild, M. and Stiglitz, J. (1976) 'Equilibrium in competitive insurance markets', *Quarterly*

Journal of Economics, 80:629–650.
Salop, S. and Scheffman, D. (1983) 'Raising rival's costs', *American Economic Review*, 73:267–271.
Scherer, F.M. (1980) *Industrial market structure and economic performance*. Chicago: Rand McNally.
Shepard, A. (1986) 'Licensing to enhance demand for new technologies', Yale University, unpublished.
Simon, H.A. (1957) *Models of man*. New York: Wiley.
Simon, H.A. (1961) *Administrative behavior*, 2nd ed. New York: Macmillan.
Simon, H.A. (1984) 'On the behavioral and rational foundations of economic dynamics', *Journal of Economic Behavior and Organization*, 5:35–56.
Smith, V. (1974) 'Economic theory and its discontents', *American Economic Review*, 64:320–322.
Solow, R. (1985) 'Economic history and economics', *American Economic Review*, 75:328–331.
Spiller, P. (1985) 'On vertical mergers', *Journal of Law, Economics and Organization*, 1:285–312.
Stigler, G.J. (1951) 'The division of labor is limited by the extent of the market', *Journal of Political Economy*, 59:185–193.
Stigler, G.J. (1955) 'Mergers and preventive antitrust policy', *University of Pennsylvania Law Review*, 104:176–185.
Stigler, G.J. (1966) *Theory of price*. New York: Macmillan.
Stigler, G.J. (1968) *The organization of industry*. Homewood, Ill.: Richard D. Irwin.
Stocking, G.W. and Mueller, W.F. (1957) 'Business reciprocity and the size of firms', *Journal of Business*, 30:73–95.
Stuckey, J. (1983) *Vertical integration and joint ventures in the aluminum industry*. Cambridge, Mass.: Harvard University Press.
Summers, C. (1982) 'Codetermination in the United States: A projection of problems and potentials', *Journal of Comparative Corporate Law and Security Regulation*, 155–183.
Teece, D.J. (1977) 'Technology transfer by multinational firms', *Economic Journal*, 87:242–261.
Telser, L. (1981) 'A theory of self-enforcing agreements', *Journal of Business*, 53:27–44.
Wachter, M. and Williamson, O.E. (1978) 'Obligational markets and the mechanics of inflation', *Bell Journal of Economics*, 9:549–571.
Weakliem, D. (1987) 'Explaining the outcomes of collective bargaining: Transaction cost and power approaches', University of Wisconsin, Madison, unpublished.
Weitzman, M. (1984) *The share economy*. Cambridge, Mass.: Harvard University Press.
Williamson, O. (1967) 'Hierarchical control and optimum firm size', *Journal of Political Economy*, 75:123–138.
Williamson, O. (1970) *Corporate control and business behavior*. Englewood Cliffs, N.J.: Prentice–Hall.
Williamson, O. (1971) 'The vertical integration of production: Market failure considerations', *American Economic Review*, 61L:112–123.
Williamson, O. (1975) *Markets and hierarchies*: *Analysis and antitrust implications*. New York: Free Press.
Williamson, O. (1979a) 'Transaction-cost economics: The governance of contractual relations', *Journal of Law and Economics*, 22:233–261.
Williamson, O. (1979b) 'Assessing vertical market restrictions', *University of Pennsylvania Law Review*, 127:953–993.
Williamson, O. (1983) 'Credible commitments: Using hostages to support exchange', *American Economic Review*, 73:519–540.
Williamson, O. (1985) *The economic institutions of capitalism*. New York: Free Press.
Williamson, O. (1986) 'A microanalytic assessment of 'the share economy'', *Yale Law Journal*, 95:627–637.
Williamson, O. (1988) 'Corporate finance and corporate governance', *Journal of Finance*, 43:567–591.

Chapter 4

VERTICAL INTEGRATION: DETERMINANTS AND EFFECTS

MARTIN K. PERRY*

Rutgers University
and Bell Communications Research, Inc.

Contents

*This survey was done while the author was a member of the Economic Research Group at Bell Communications Research. This survey represents the views and assumptions of the author and not necessarily those of Bell Communications Research.

Handbook of Industrial Organization, Volume I, Edited by R. Schmalensee and R.D. Willig

"If you want something done right, do it yourself!"
– A theory of vertical integration –
Benjamin Franklin?

1. Introduction

The theory of vertical integration is situated at the intersection of the theory of the firm, the theory of contracts, and the theory of markets. Thus, the literature has developed from several different perspectives. I will discuss the differing perspectives, and comment upon what seem to be the most interesting pieces of the literature. The focus will be on theoretical work, but I will also mention case studies and empirical work when they relate to specific theories. Finally, I will attempt to point out areas of controversy and suggest directions for future research.

1.1. What is vertical integration?

A firm can be described as vertically integrated if it encompasses two single-output production processes in which either (1) the *entire* output of the "upstream" process is employed as *part or all* of the quantity of one intermediate input into the "downstream" process, or (2) the *entire* quantity of one intermediate input into the "downstream" process is obtained from *part or all* of the output of the "upstream" process. This includes the more restrictive criterion that the *entire* output of the upstream subsidiary be employed as *all* of the quantity of one intermediate input into the downstream process. However, both characterizations rule out the case in which *most* of the output of the upstream process is employed as *most* of the input in the downstream process. This case is best described as "partial" vertical integration because some of the output of the upstream process is sold to other buyers and some of the intermediate input for the downstream process is purchased from other suppliers.

Thus, inherent in the notion of vertical integration is the elimination of contractual or market exchanges, and the substitution of internal exchanges within the boundaries of the firm. Suppose that the upstream subsidiary of a firm sold *all* its output to other buyers, and the downstream subsidiary purchased *all* of this intermediate input from other suppliers. We would not describe this firm as being vertically integrated, even if some of the input sold by the upstream subsidiary was eventually resold to the downstream subsidiary. There are no internal exchanges, only contractual or market exchanges. Instead, this is a vertical "combination".

Although internal exchange provides the observational content of vertical integration, it does not fully capture the essence of vertical integration. Vertical integration also means the ownership and complete control over neighboring stages of production or distribution. In particular, a vertically integrated firm would have complete flexibility to make the investment, employment, production, and distribution decisions of all stages encompassed within the firm. Indeed, the focus of neoclassical models of vertical integration is how these decisions by integrated firms differ from those which would be made by disintegrated firms, or from those which would be socially optimal.

Grossman and Hart (1986) have recently argued that vertical integration is the ownership and thus complete control over "assets". Indeed, they take the position that the nature of the firm's relationship with labor is not relevant for distinguishing vertical integration. The workers could be employees or independent contractors without altering the degree of vertical integration. On the other hand, Williamson (1975) and other authors [see also Cheung (1983)] have emphasized the relationship with labor in discussing vertical integration. For these authors, vertical integration would encompass the switch from purchasing inputs to producing those inputs by hiring labor. The requisite capital, such as buildings and equipment, could be owned or leased without altering the degree of vertical integration. Leasing of capital can allow control of production without ownership. Each view would have certain appeal for specific industries. However, neither view alone provides a complete description of vertical integration. Vertical integration is control over the entire production or distribution process, rather than control over any particular input into that process.

Vertical "controls" characterize vertical relationships between the two extremes of vertical integration and anonymous spot market exchange. A vertical control arises from a contract between two firms at different stages which transfers control of some, but not all, aspects of production or distribution. Examples of vertical controls are resale price maintenance and exclusive territories. Vertical "quasi-integration" is a term coined by Blois (1972) to define financial relationships between firms in neighboring stages. These relationships need not involve additional control of production and distribution decisions. Examples include equity investments, loans or loan guarantees, leases on real estate or capital, and inventory credits.[1] Porter (1980) argues that these arrangements may create a community of interest which can achieve some of the benefits of vertical integration. Vertical control and quasi-integration are intimately

[1]Two specific examples illustrate quasi-integration. IBM has a substantial equity interest in Intel, a leading manufacturer of semiconductors used in IBM products. The major oil refiners often own the service stations that are leased to their franchise dealers.

related to vertical integration. However, since they are the subject of Chapter 11 by Michael L. Katz in this Handbook, we will confine our attention to vertical integration.

Vertical integration may arise in a number of ways. Vertical "formation" describes vertical integration which occurs at the time the firm is created. Vertical "expansion" describes vertical integration which occurs as a result of internal growth of the firm, creating its own new subsidiaries in the neighboring stages. Vertical "merger" describes vertical integration which occurs through the acquisition by one firm of an existing firm in a neighboring stage. In both theoretical and empirical work, the term vertical integration may be used to describe any one of these three patterns. However, the pattern by which vertical integration arises may be intertwined with the determinants and effects of vertical integration.

1.2. Determinants of vertical integration

There are three broad determinants of vertical integration: (1) technological economies, (2) transactional economies, and (3) market imperfections.

Vertical integration may arise from technological economies of integration. In particular, less of the other intermediate inputs may be required in order to obtain the same output in the downstream process when the firm has integrated one of the upstream processes. A typical example is the energy savings from not having to reheat steel in the production of steel sheet. Even though the downstream production process has a well-defined production frontier given a set of intermediate inputs purchased through contracts or markets, a more efficient frontier exists when the set of inputs is broadened to include primary inputs. Vertical integration not only replaces some intermediate inputs with primary inputs, but it also reduces the requirements of other intermediate inputs. This is the sense in which technological economies of integration give rise to vertical integration.

Technological economies may be an important determinant of vertical integration in some industries. However, they will not be a central topic of this chapter. In the theoretical discussions, we will generally presume that firms have integrated so as to internalize technological economies. This allows us to focus upon the more interesting economic reasons for vertical integration. Indeed, Williamson (1975, 1985) has forcefully argued that the costs and hazards of contracting are real reason why "cheek-by-jowl" production processes are generally performed by integrated firms.

Vertical integration may also arise from transactional economies. Transaction costs are different from production costs in that they are associated with the process of exchange itself. However, there is a conceptual analogy to technological economies. One could define the resources consumed in the exchange of intermediate "technological inputs" as intermediate "exchange inputs" of the downstream production process. Transactional economies could then be defined in exactly the same fashion as technological economies. In particular, vertical integration into the production of intermediate technological inputs would reduce the requirements of intermediate exchange inputs.[2]

Transactional economies are an important determinant of vertical integration. Transactional issues will be prominent in a number of the discussions in this chapter, but only Section 5 will be completely devoted to the "transaction cost economics" of vertical integration. Thus, many of the theoretical discussions will presume that firms have integrated so as to internalize transactional economies. A more general treatment of transaction cost economics is contained in Chapter 3 by Oliver E. Williamson in this Handbook.

Finally, vertical integration can arise from imperfections in markets. Imperfect competition is the most notable example, but other market imperfections also give rise to vertical integration. For example, we will discuss imperfections caused by externalities and imperfect or asymmetric information. How is this distinguished from transaction cost economics?

In transaction cost economics, the primary determinant of vertical integration is "asset specificity" in one or both of the production processes. Asset specificity means that an upstream or downstream firm has made investments such that the value of an exchange is greatest when it occurs between these two firms rather than with other firms. Thus, transaction-specific assets create bilateral monopoly. One cannot then talk about a market for the intermediate input existing between the two firms. Neither firm would necessarily have the ability to set the price or choose the quantity unilaterally. Price, quantity, and any other important dimension of the good (such as quality and delivery) would be determined by negotiation and embodied in a contract. Thus, in transaction cost economics "contractual" exchanges are the relevant alternative to "internal" exchanges. The choice between the two depends upon differences in the cost of "governing" the contractual relationship.

What then is meant by a "market" exchange? These are exchanges which require no negotiations or governance of a continuing relationship. Rather, they are take-it-or-leave-it exchanges in which the price, quantity, and other dimensions of the good are each set by one firm or the other.[3] For example, an upstream manufacturer may set the price and quality, while the downstream

[2]Intermediate exchange inputs could also be integrated, for example by hiring the lawyers necessary for making contracts. However, the economies from such probably arise from the reduced requirement of other exchange inputs, such as expenses for outside legal counsel, rather than technological inputs.

[3]Motty Perry (1986) has recently examined the game theoretic underpinnings of take-it-or-leave-it exchange in a bilateral bargaining situation. With costs of making offers or counter-offers, he finds that the player with the lowest such cost makes the initial offer while the other player accepts or rejects depending upon whether the offer yields a net surplus and does not make a counter-offer.

retailer chooses the quantity to purchase and the delivery schedule. We call this "market" exchange because it is the natural extension of price-taking behavior by firms.

This distinction between contractual exchange and market exchange is artificial and stylized, but it provides a useful method of contrasting transaction cost economics with the neoclassical analysis of vertical integration. The transaction cost analysis of vertical integration discusses the relative advantages of contracts versus internal organization for the joint determination and enforcement of exchange. Various contractual arrangements bridge the gap between vertical integration and anonymous spot markets. The focus is upon the exchange process. On the other hand, the neoclassical analysis of vertical integration assumes that all the relevant dimensions of the good are chosen unilaterally by either upstream firms or downstream firms. The firms make choices so as to maximize their individual profits, rather than the joint profits. Vertical controls then bridge the gap between vertical integration and anonymous spot markets. In this way, the neoclassical analysis of vertical integration or control avoids the bargaining issues of bilateral monopoly by assigning the choice of any particular dimension to the firms at some stage. The focus is upon the production and distribution choices themselves.

Even if firms are integrated to internalize both technological and transactional economies, market imperfections remain an important determinant of vertical integration. Vertical integration in response to technological or transactional economies would generally increase welfare. As a result, transaction cost economics is primarily interested in explaining and predicting patterns of vertical integration. On the other hand, vertical integration in response to market imperfections may increase or decrease welfare. Thus, public policy questions become the primary interest.

1.3. Outline

Sections 2 and 3 discuss neoclassical models in which imperfect competition is the determinant of vertical integration. Section 2 examines forward integration by a monopolist and backward integration by a monopsonist into competitive industries. The incentives for integration are variable proportions, price discrimination, rent extraction, and barriers to entry. Section 3 examines forward integration by a monopolist into a monopolistically competitive industry. The incentives for integration are the elimination of successive markups, internalization of the choice of product diversity, and internalization of service externalities.

Section 4 discusses neoclassical models in which imperfect or asymmetric information is the determinant of vertical integration. The incentives for integration are diversification, assurance of supply, acquisition of information, and reduction of agency problems.

Section 5 switches to a discussion of vertical integration from the perspective of transaction cost economics. The incentive for vertical integration arises from reducing the transaction costs of bilateral exchange. Evidence for the transaction cost analysis is also summarized and contrasted with the neoclassical interpretations discussed in the previous sections.

Section 6 discusses the theory of incomplete contracts. We first discuss the legal content of an "incomplete" contract, as that term is used by economists. We then examine some recent models which focus upon investments made prior to a bilateral exchange. These models formalize some aspects of the literature on transaction cost economics, and provide a forum for discussing the theoretical distinction between vertical integration and long-term contracts.

Section 7 discusses several related models of "vertical equilibrium". In the same fashion that a horizontal equilibrium defines the output of each firm, a vertical equilibrium would define the stages in which each firm operates. This analysis is at an early stage, so it offers some interesting and challenging questions for research.

Section 8 discusses empirical measures of vertical integration. These measures have been employed to examine aggregate and industry trends in the extent of vertical integration in U.S. manufacturing during the twentieth century. We also discuss some historical cases which shed light upon the pattern of vertical integration prior to the twentieth century.

Section 9 concludes with a discussion of public policy. We summarize the history and current state of antitrust law toward vertical integration in the United States. In the process, we discuss the economic theories which have been the basis for the antitrust challenges to vertical integration. Finally, we briefly discuss public policy toward vertical integration in the United Kingdom and the European Economic Community.

2. Monopoly and monopsony

Imperfect competition at a single stage gives rise to several incentives for the imperfectly competitive firms to integrate into the neighboring competitive stages. These incentives arise from three sources: (1) the internalization of the efficiency losses from the imperfect competitive behavior, (2) the ability to extract inframarginal rents from the competitive stage, and (3) the ability to price discriminate within the competitive stage. We discuss these incentives for both a monopolist integrating forward and a monopsonist integrating backward. However, the insights should clearly apply to oligopolists integrating forward and oligopsonists integrating backward.

2.1. Monopoly and variable proportions

One of the most extensively discussed incentives for vertical integration is that of an upstream monopolist into a competitive downstream industry which employs the monopolist's product in variable proportions with other intermediate inputs. The basic insight is clear. The price set by a monopoly manufacturer leads downstream fabricators to substitute away from the monopoly input toward the other inputs which are competitively supplied. The resulting efficiency loss in downstream production can be converted into profit for the manufacturer when it integrates into the fabrication stage and expands the usage of its input to the efficient level. Note that no such incentive exists when the manufacturer's product is used in fixed proportions with other inputs by a constant cost downstream stage. In this case, the final demand is simply mirrored to the manufacturer by the competitive downstream stage, and the manufacturer can maximize industry profits without forward integration.[4]

The incentive created by variable proportions was first discussed by McKenzie (1951). However, a brief graphical illustration by Vernon and Graham (1971) triggered a steady stream of research on this model since then. The driving force in this literature has been the welfare question of whether vertical integration by the monopoly manufacturer will increase or decrease welfare. The loss from inefficient production is eliminated and captured by the manufacturer in the form of profits. The size of this gain depends upon the elasticity of substitution in production. However, the integrated manufacturer may increase the retail price of the fabricated product and thereby reduce consumer welfare. This loss depends in part upon the elasticity of demand. Thus, there are two issues. First, when is the retail price higher after integration? And second, if the retail price is higher, is it so high that total welfare (consumer plus producer surplus) actually decreases?

Schmalensee (1973) showed that the retail price rises when the retail production function is Cobb–Douglas and demand has a constant elasticity (greater than unity). But even in this case, he was not able to draw any general conclusions about the direction of total welfare. Using a constant elasticity of substitution (CES) production function, Hay (1973) showed that the retail price rises for many values of the elasticity of substitution. In particular, the retail price rises if the elasticity of substitution exceeds the elasticity of demand. Computations by Warren-Boulton (1974) indicated that even if this condition is not satisfied, the retail price may still rise. Warren-Boulton also found that welfare could increase even though the retail price rises. But the welfare increases

[4]Quirmbach (1986a) demonstrates that there can be "scale" incentives for the manufacturer to forward integrate if the downstream stage is composed of firms with U-shaped average cost curves. The monopoly price of the input alters the minimum efficient scale of downstream firms and causes a distortion in the number of firms. Forward integration by the manufacturer can correct this.

are relatively small and occur only for values of the elasticity of substitution less than some value itself less than unity. This would appear to be counterintuitive in that the efficiency gains increase with the elasticity of substitution (up to a point). But the increase in the retail price also becomes more significant when the elasticity of substitution is larger. The substitution possibilities at the retail stage are an important constraint on the wholesale pricing of the manufacturer.

Other authors have generalized this model in some fashion. Mallela and Nahata (1980) re-examine the CES production function and derive the condition necessary for the final price to decline when the elasticity of substitution is less than unity. Westfield (1981) employs a more general framework to summarize all of the retail price results. He finds specific cases in which the retail price falls when the elasticity of substitution is less than unity. Waterson (1982) employs the CES production function, but assumes that the downstream industry is a Cournot oligopoly rather than competitive. Finally, Quirmbach (1986b) assumes a competitive fringe at the upstream stage and examines forward integration by the now dominant firm.

This literature generates a few policy conclusions. First, Westfield's summary suggests that we should not expect the retail price to fall when manufacturers integrate into subsequent fabrication stages of the industry. Second, the incentive to integrate is relatively strong in that the manufacturer increases its profits both by internalizing the efficiency gain and by setting a higher retail price. But third, the reduction in total welfare will be relatively small. Although Warren-Boulton did not calculate the percentage welfare loss, his results seem to suggest that it is less than a couple of percent. Moreover, oligopoly would generate smaller losses than monopoly. Thus, it is not clear that variable proportions raises a major policy issue on vertical integration.

Vertical integration in response to variable proportions is a relatively drastic solution to what is primarily a pricing problem. Blair and Kaserman (1983) have shown that tying arrangements, output or sales royalties, and lump-sum entry fees can all be used by the monopolist to eliminate and internalize the efficiency loss from simple monopoly pricing. Warren-Boulton (1977) examines the use of these alternatives by the United Mine Workers Union, the monopolist over the supply of labor to a competitive mining industry. Thus, the variable proportions model is probably a better description of some observed vertical controls than of vertical integration.

2.2. *Monopoly and price discrimination*

The separation of downstream markets for price discrimination is perhaps a more important incentive for forward integration by manufacturers. Wallace (1937) seems to have been aware of this point in his pioneering case study of Alcoa, but Stigler (1951) clearly stated the basic argument [see also Gould (1977)].

Suppose a monopoly manufacturer is selling its product to two competitive fabrication stages, one with an elastic derived demand and one with an inelastic derived demand. If the manufacturer fully integrated both downstream stages, he would contract input employment in the inelastic stage and expand input employment in the elastic stage. But the manufacturer could also duplicate this outcome by integrating into only the elastic stage. He would expand input employment in that stage while raising the input price to the monopoly price of the inelastic stage. This strategy results in a "price squeeze" against independent fabricators in that the manufacturer's downstream subsidiary lowers the price of fabrications while raising the market price of the input.[5] Because of this, the monopolist can effectuate price discrimination by vertical expansion rather than vertical merger.

If the manufacturer reversed this strategy by integrating into the inelastic stage, resale and free entry would prevent the manufacturer from achieving price discrimination. The manufacturer could not contract input employment in the inelastic stage while lowering the input price intended for the elastic stage. The higher retail price in the inelastic stage would be undercut by new entrants who obtain the input at the lower market price either from the manufacturer (if he cannot identify buyers) or from the fabricators in the elastic stage on resale.

Although price discrimination is an important determinant of vertical integration, no clear policy conclusions can be drawn from this analysis. Third-degree price discrimination may increase or decrease total welfare depending upon the nature of the derived demands of the downstream industries.[6]

The price discrimination story becomes more interesting if the manufacturer faces some competition at his stage of production. Perry (1978a) discusses the simplest such case. There are many competitive fabrication stages, and they can obtain the necessary input from either the dominant manufacturer or from a competitive fringe of small manufacturers. Perry then examines the extent to which the dominant manufacturer can still price discriminate in the presence of the fringe. By the previous reasoning, the optimal strategy for dominant manufacturer is to integrate into a set of stages which have more elastic derived demands than the remaining non-integrated stages. Since these are the stages with the lower monopoly prices, the stages can be ordered by their monopoly prices. Let $\hat{R}_j$ be the monopoly price of the jth fabricating stage, such that $\hat{R}_1 < \hat{R}_2 < \cdots < \hat{R}_m$. When the dominant manufacturer integrates into one of the stages, that demand is eliminated from the input market in which the fringe

[5]Carlton and Perloff (1981) examine the implications of this theory for depletion of a natural resource when the monopolist is the sole owner of the resource.

[6]See Schmalensee (1981) and Varian (1985).

manufacturers compete. As a result, the dominant manufacturer optimally resets the open market price of its product, taking into account (1) the lower but less elastic demand and (2) the unchanged supply curve of the fringe manufacturers. Let $\hat{P}_j$ be profit-maximizing open market price when all industries $i > j$ are not integrated.

If the fringe is not too large, $\hat{P}_0 > \hat{R}_1$ since $\hat{P}_0$ is the dominant firm's price to all the downstream industries while $\hat{R}_1$ is the monopoly price to the industry with the least elastic demand. For small j, $\hat{P}_j$ increases because the market demand is less elastic. But for large j, $\hat{P}_j$ decreases because the market demand is small relative to the fringe supply. Perry then defines the industry $\xi = \max\{j\colon \hat{R}_j < \hat{P}_j\}$. The dominant firm can integrate the downstream industries up to and including the ξth industry without creating resale possibilities at the profit-maximizing prices. However, forward integration beyond the ξth industry requires the dominant firm to contract open market sales in order to keep the open market price above the profit-maximizing internal prices of the additional integrated industries. Otherwise, new entrants could undercut the final price in these industries. Perry shows that the gains from setting the monopoly price in an industry $j > \xi$ are more than offset by the reduction in profits from open market sales. Thus, ξ is the maximum number of downstream industries over which the dominant firm can price discriminate. Moreover, ξ decreases with outward shifts in the supply curve of the competitive fringe.[7]

Perry (1980) applies this theoretical analysis to the forward integration by Alcoa prior to 1930. Alcoa was the only domestic producer of primary aluminum during this period, but there existed several foreign producers whose exports to the United States were subject to a tariff which varied over the period. Thus, the industry arguably approximated the dominant firm model, raising the question whether the observed pattern of forward integration into domestic fabrication stages by Alcoa was consistent with the motive of price discrimination. Consider four of the major uses for aluminum during this period: (1) cooking utensils, (2) electric cable, (3) automobile parts, and (4) aircraft parts. Using rough judgments, Perry estimates that the derived demand for aluminum by each of these industries. The derived demand was very elastic for the electric cable industry, and very inelastic aircraft industry. However, the elasticity varied for different products in the cooking utensil and automobile part industries depending upon the other materials which were good substitutes (primarily iron and steel, but also secondary aluminum).

[7]Oligopolists could also price discriminate by forward integration in the same fashion. But it is not clear whether dominant oligopolists would be able to integrate more or less of the elastic industries than a dominant firm. The oligopoly input price is lower, but the oligopoly final prices in the integrated industries would also be lower. The oligopolists could obviously do even better if they could each fully integrate and individually monopolize a subset of the elastic industries.

The pattern of forward integration by Alcoa appears to be roughly consistent with price discrimination. There was complete integration into the fabrication of aluminum cable, very little integration into the production of aircraft parts, and selective integration into those cooking utensils and automobile parts which were most subject to competition from other materials.[8] These conclusions are crude, but they raise questions about the traditional explanation that Alcoa integrated forward only after it was unable to persuade independent metal fabricators to use aluminum in the production of their goods.[9]

McNicol (1975) has a related story of vertical integration and price discrimination. McNicol argues that a manufacturer who is partially integrated into one of the downstream industries with an inelastic demand may increase its profits by rationing the intermediate input to the independent firms in that downstream industry. The manufacturer cannot explicitly raise the price of the intermediate input to such industries, but he can raise the final price of such industries by rationing the independent producers. Partial integration into these industries then allows the manufacturer to share in their higher profits. But the increase in profits of the downstream subsidiary must dominate the reduced profits on sales to the independent firms at the unchanged market price of the intermediate input. McNicol calls this "quantity discrimination". Unlike price discrimination, quantity discrimination implies that producers would partially integrate into those industries with inelastic demands, rather than the industries with elastic demands.[10] But like price discrimination, quantity discrimination results in a "supply squeeze" of independent fabricators.

Vertical integration for quantity discrimination has problems which are not present in vertical integration for price discrimination. If resale is costless, it would limit the ability of a producer to effectively ration independent fabricators in an industry with an inelastic demand. Independent fabricators could obtain the input on the spot market. But suppose resale is costly. If the manufacturer can identify buyers, as he must in order to ration any particular industry, then why cannot the producer price discriminate with a different input price to each downstream industry? The Robinson–Patman Act may be a barrier to such explicit price discrimination. Alternatively, McNicol may be implicitly assuming

[8]Alcoa's forward integration into aluminum sheet, cookware, and automobile parts was investigated by the FTC during most of the 1920s. Independent firms in those industries frequently alleged that they were unprofitable and went out of business because of Alcoa's integration and subsequent price squeeze. See Wallace (1937).

[9]See Peck (1961) for a discussion of the traditional explanation forward integration by aluminum producers. Silver (1984, ch. 12) disputes Perry's conclusions and argues in favor of the traditional explanation.

[10]Curiously, McNicol argues that the copper wire industry had important substitution possibilities, suggesting that its demand was elastic. However, this fabricating industry was partially integrated and rationed by the copper producers during the period 1946–70.

that the producer is only one member of an upstream oligopoly and that oligopoly pricing inhibits price discrimination.

These models posit forward integration as an implicit method of achieving price discrimination. However, Katz (1987) points out that the threat of backward integration may be the cause of explicit price discrimination in intermediate good markets. Katz examines a model in which a retail chain competes with local firms in geographically separated markets. The chain and the local retailers purchase inputs from an upstream monopolist. Because of scale economies in upstream production, the chain has a stronger incentive to integrate backward. If the upstream monopolist cannot price discriminate, this threat results in lower input prices for both the chain and its local competitors. However, if the upstream monopolist can price discriminate, it can increase its profit by charging a higher input price to the local firms. This will benefit the chain by giving it a cost advantage over its local competitors. As a result, the upstream monopolist can even raise the input price to the chain slightly without inducing it to integrate backward. The threat of backward integration makes the derived demand of the chain infinitely elastic at some price. This suggests that implicit price discrimination could also be effectuated by a vertical merger between the upstream monopolist and the retail chain.

2.3. *Monopsony and backward integration*

Incentives also exist for backward integration by a monopolist into an upstream competitive stage. McGee and Bassett (1976) discuss the basic efficiency incentive. Consider a manufacturer who is the sole buyer of a raw material which is supplied by competitive firms but subject to a rising supply price. Because of the rising supply price, the expenditure of the manufacturer for an additional unit of the raw material exceeds the supply price. Thus, the manufacturer employs too little of the raw material. Vertical integration eliminates this monopsony inefficiency. Industry profits and welfare obviously increase.

Perry (1978c) expands this model to include the process of vertical merger by the monopsonist. Backward integration by the manufacturer requires that the assets of the raw material suppliers be acquired at some price exceeding the rents they were earning. The manufacturer could initially acquire all of the suppliers, paying them the rents earned under monopsony. However, the manufacturer can actually extract some of these initial rents by acquiring the suppliers one at a time. Cost minimization by a partially integrated manufacturer results in an expansion in the production of the subsidiaries and a reduction in the purchases from the remaining independent suppliers. This reduces the market price of the raw material and the rents to independent suppliers. Thus, the manufacturer can acquire new subsidiaries at a lower price. Moreover, such an acquisition strategy is credible because the manufacturer is maximizing profits at each point. With an optimal acquisition program, the manufacturer can substantially reduce the cost of integration. This extraction of rents is a form of imperfect price discrimination which enhances the manufacturer's incentive to integrate backward.

Backward integration by a dominant manufacturer may also create a barrier to entry so as to preserve its dominance. Bain (1956) popularized the concept of barriers to entry and also discussed the importance of potential competition. Bain argued that vertical integration creates a capital barrier to entry by forcing potential entrants to contemplate entry at two stages of production rather than just one. In addition, he pointed out that vertical merger also eliminates one of the most natural potential entrants into each stage. Indeed, these two theories are complements. It is difficult to argue that firms in neighboring stages are the most likely entrants without also believing that entry at both stages is more difficult than entry at one stage.

Similarly, a dominant firm may also use vertical integration to raise the costs of its competitors. Salop and Scheffman (1983) have discussed vertical integration as one device which can be used to "raise rivals' costs".[11] An extreme example is the acquisition of essential inputs or facilities which would genuinely foreclose competitors.[12] The opportunity cost of holding such resources may be less than the risk of reduced profits from new competition. A dominant firm need not acquire all of the scarce resource in order to effectively raise the costs of its actual or potential rivals. By leaving the open market thin, competitors may be unable to expand without significantly driving up the input price, they may be subject to higher prices set by the fewer remaining suppliers, or they may incur higher transaction costs from having to negotiate contracts with suppliers.

In an attempt to illustrate the second of these three possibilities, Ordover, Saloner and Salop (1987) examine a model of successive duopoly with price-setting. By acquiring one of the upstream firms, a downstream firm can disadvantage and reduce the profits of its competitor by forcing it to rely on an upstream monopolist for the input. Moreover, the integrated firm can prevent its competitor from merging with the upstream monopolist by continuing to offer the input for sale at some appropriate price less than the monopoly price. However, if both downstream firms can bid to acquire one of the upstream firms, a prisoner's

[11] Such devices would also include vertical controls such as exclusive dealing, or horizontal restraints such as exclusionary contracts or product standards. They would also include political and regulatory activity. Such devices can be less costly than acquiring competitors or engaging in predatory pricing to drive them out of business.

[12] The most notable historical example was the formation of the Terminal Railroad Association of St Louis to monopolize the ferry and bridges across the Mississippi River connecting eastern and western railroad lines. The facilities were for exclusive use of the member railroads. The Supreme Court held the combination to be a violation of the Sherman Act, and required the Association to admit members and set prices in a non-discriminatory fashion. *U.S. v. Terminal Railroad Association* (1912, 224 U.S. 383).

dilemma arises in that the winning bid makes the integrated firm less profitable than it was when both downstream firms were disintegrated.

It is useful to consider the early domestic steel and aluminum industries in light of these alternative theories of backward integration.

Mancke (1972) examined the rapid backward integration into iron ore production by Carnegie and the other large steel producers during the period 1896–1900 before the formation of U.S. Steel. In 1896, two-thirds of the iron ore consumed in the United States came from the Lake Superior region. Of the more than one hundred iron ore suppliers in this region, only one produced as much as 10 percent of the ore. Moreover, only Carnegie Steel had an interest in any of these suppliers, and that interest was insignificant. But by 1900, eight steel producers completely controlled almost three-quarters of this region's output, each becoming self-sufficient in iron ore. Moreover, this backward integration coincided with declining prices for both iron ore and iron ore properties. Mancke concludes that the steel producers were less pessimistic about the trend of future iron ore prices than the owners of iron ore properties. Iron ore prices did rise abruptly thereafter. In 1901, U.S. Steel was formed by a merger of Carnegie Steel and other major steel producers. As its predecessors, U.S. Steel continued to acquire iron ore properties. Parsons and Ray (1975) document these events and argue that control of iron ore deposits by U.S. Steel inhibited domestic entry and preserved the dominance of U.S. Steel longer than would have been the case otherwise. Given the rapid increase in concentration during this period, subsequent backward integration by the steel producers is also not inconsistent with the monopsony theory.

During its early years as the domestic monopolist of primary aluminum, Alcoa was completely integrated into the extraction of bauxite and the generation of electricity for refining alumina into aluminum. By 1910, Alcoa had acquired most of the bauxite lands in Arkansas, shipping the ore to its sole alumina plant in East St. Louis. When the Arkansas ore began to deplete, Alcoa turned to South America acquiring or leasing nearly all the deposits in the Guianas by the end of World War I. Alcoa built and operated hydroelectric power stations near its refineries in the United States. These acquisitions are perhaps a classic example of Alcoa erecting entry barriers in light of the expiration of the domestic patents on the aluminum reduction process. However, they are also consistent with the monopsony theory.

Crandall (1968) proposes an interesting model to explain backward integration into the production of automobile parts by the automobile manufacturers. The argument could apply to the assembly stage of any industry in which there would be demand for replacement parts on the durable final good. If the assembler could not integrate backward, a competitive parts industry increases the demand for the final good by lowering the price of replacement parts for consumers. However, if the assembler can integrate backward and monopolize the parts industry, then he would clearly charge a higher price to consumers for replacement parts even though it caused some reduction in demand for the durable good. This would price discriminate against consumers who use the durable good more intensively. This is the common explanation for tying arrangements [see Burstein (1960)]. Thus, backward integration allows price discrimination in the sense of optimal pricing of complementary goods [see Telser (1979)].

The assembler can certainly integrate the production of parts for assembly of the durable good. But because of the high price of replacement parts, other vertical controls would generally be necessary to prevent entry into parts. Crandall discusses some of the practices used by the automobile assemblers to inhibit such entry. Crandall then finds that the automobile assemblers are highly integrated into a number of components. Moreover, the assemblers seem to make very high returns on the replacement parts. This strategy would not be available for replacement parts, such as tires, which consumers clearly recognize as not being specialized to their automobile.

3. Monopolistic competition

In this section we focus upon the incentives created by successive stages of imperfect competition. Price remains an important dimension of the analysis. However, we focus upon the problems raised by new dimensions such as product differentiation and retail service externalities. Imperfect competition with the disintegrated structure prevents the industry from achieving the profit-maximizing price, diversity, or service. Vertical integration corrects these choices for the industry but it need not increase total welfare.

Consider the simplest case of successive monopolists, first examined by Spengler (1950) and Machlup and Taber (1960). A manufacturer sells to regional wholesalers who sell to local retailers. The retailers have local monopolies, the wholesalers have regional monopolies, and the manufacturer has a national monopoly. With constant marginal costs of distribution, the marginal revenue function of a retailer becomes that retailer's inverse demand function to the wholesaler. Similarly, the marginal revenue function of a wholesaler's aggregate inverse demand function is the manufacturer's inverse demand function from that wholesaler. Thus, each monopoly stage rotates the inverse demand function downward and causes the upstream monopolist, here the manufacturer, to produce an output less than the output that would maximize industry profits. Vertical integration by the manufacturer into all stages of distribution would reduce the final price, thereby increasing industry profits and consumer welfare.[13]

[13]The analysis and results would obviously be identical for forward integration by upstream oligopolists into a downstream oligopoly. See Greenhut and Ohta (1976), the comments by Perry (1978b) and Haring and Kaserman (1978), reply by Greenhut and Ohta (1978), and subsequent correction by Greenhut and Ohta (1979).

3.1. *Monopolistic competition at the retail stage*

The price effects of successive monopoly provide a clear prescription for vertical integration when the product is homogeneous and the wholesalers or retailers have isolated monopolies. However, successive monopoly raises a more interesting and difficult issue when the retail stage is monopolistically competitive. When retailers are differentiated and compete for consumers at the margin, we are concerned not only with the final price but also with the number of retailers. The ease of access to a retailer or the diversity in the choice among retailers affect consumer welfare. Thus, we must examine the impact on the number of retailers before we can prescribe vertical integration as a remedy for successive monopoly. This issue has been discussed in recent work by Dixit (1983), Mathewson and Winter (1983), and Perry and Groff (1985).

The models posit a manufacturer whose product is distributed to consumers by a retail stage. The manufacturer is a simple monopolist, but the retail stage is monopolistically competitive. The product of each retailer is differentiated, but free entry increases the number of retailers to the point where each earns no profit. Dixit (1983) and Mathewson and Winter (1983) employ the spatial model of retail differentiation, popularized by Salop (1979). On the other hand, Perry and Groff (1985) employ the CES model of retail differentiation, introduced by Spence (1976) and Dixit and Stiglitz (1977).

In the spatial model of Salop (1979), L consumers are uniformly distributed along a circular market of unit length, and must incur a travel cost t per unit distance in order to reach a retailer. Each retailer has a fixed cost f, but its only variable cost is the wholesale price r of the manufacturer's good. The manufacturer is a monopolist and has a constant cost c of producing the good. Salop assumes that consumers purchase only one unit of the good, and that they have a reservation price v. Consumers then purchase the good from the retailer with the lowest full price (retail price plus transportation costs) as long as that full price is less than their reservation price. Thus, the price set by each of two neighboring retailers will determine the market boundary where consumers are just indifferent between the two retailers. As a result, each retailer faces a locally linear demand function, given the price set by the two retailers on either side. In particular, a lower price reduces the retailer's full price to all consumers, causing consumers at the boundaries to shift their purchases to him. This is the sense in which each retailer is a monopolist, differentiated from its neighboring retailers, yet in direct price competition with them.

Given a low wholesale price, a Nash equilibrium can be defined in which each retailer sets its price assuming that the prices of neighboring retailers will remain unchanged. Free entry then determines the total number of retailers n. This is Salop's "competitive equilibrium", and all consumers clearly purchase the good from some retailer. At some higher wholesale price this "competitive equilibrium" will not exist. Instead, free entry drives the industry to the highest price and lowest output such that the profits of all retailers are just non-negative. This is Salop's "kinked equilibrium". Finally, at a sufficiently high wholesale price, $r_m = v - [2 \cdot t \cdot f/L]^{1/2}$, there remains only one such price–output combination which enables retailers to earn non-negative profits. This is Salop's "monopoly equilibrium", so called because it occurs at the output where the monopoly price of a retailer equals its average cost.

At wholesale prices above r_m, retailers cannot earn non-negative profits at any price, and sales of the good fall to zero. Ignoring the integer problem on the number of retailers, free entry insures that all consumers purchase the good in each equilibria with $r < r_m$. Thus, the derived demand facing the manufacturer is perfectly inelastic up to the wholesale price r_m, which then becomes the profit-maximizing wholesale price. The monopoly equilibrium prevails and the number of retailers is $n_m = [tL/2f]^{1/2}$. Since all consumers purchase the good, there is no efficiency loss caused by successive monopoly pricing, and thus no corresponding incentive for the manufacturer to vertically integrate. The free entry number of retailers is also the number that would be chosen by an integrated manufacturer.[14] Thus, there is no distortion in the retail diversity from the monopoly equilibrium, and therefore no diversity incentive for vertical integration.

Salop's model generates no price or diversity incentive for forward integration by the manufacturer. The reason is that the derived demand facing the manufacturer reflects the perfectly inelastic demand of each consumer up to the reservation price. Dixit (1983) avoids this degeneracy by assuming that retailers actually produce the final good using the manufacturer's product in variable proportions with other inputs. If the elasticity of substitution is sufficiently high, the profit-maximizing wholesale price will be less than r_m. This would then leave the retail stage in a kinked or competitive equilibrium with a higher final price and a larger number of retailers than the monopoly equilibrium. The manufacturer now has an incentive to integrate, and welfare will increase with vertical integration. Vertical integration eliminates the inefficient production at the retail stage. Moreover, the integrated manufacturer reduces the number of retailers to n_m, which is closer to the optimal number of retailers n^*. Moreover, since consumption of the final good remains unchanged, any change in the retail price is merely a transfer with no deadweight loss.

Mathewson and Winter (1983) maintain fixed proportions in retailing, and instead generalize consumer demand. They assume that each consumer has an

[14] To see this, consider the profit function of the integrated manufacturer. Since the manufacturer would either increase the number of retailers or decrease the retail price in order to sell his good to all consumers, we can let $p = v - t/2n$, and write the manufacturer's profit function solely in terms of n as $\Pi(n) = (v - t/2n - c) \cdot L - n \cdot f$. The number of retailers that maximize this profit function is n_m, the same number of retailers as in the monopoly equilibrium with r_m as the wholesale price.

exponential demand for the good. But in so doing, they must also assume that the transportation cost t is per unit of the product purchased as well as per unit distance traveled. An alternative interpretation is that the consumers at each location still demand only one unit of the good, but that they have different reservation prices which would aggregate to an exponential demand. Let p_j be the price of the jth retailer and p be the price of the neighboring retailers. The demand function facing the jth retailer can be expressed as

$$x_j(p_j, p, n) = (2v/t) \cdot [1 - \mathrm{e}^{(p_j - p - t/n)/2}] \cdot \mathrm{e}^{-p_j}. \tag{1}$$

The derived demand facing the manufacturer at any given wholesale price is obtained from the free entry Nash equilibrium in prices at the retail stage. The profit-maximizing wholesale price will result in both a pricing distortion and a diversity distortion.

Vertical integration allows marginal cost internal pricing to the retail subsidiaries. This results in a lower final price, eliminating the pricing distortion and increasing welfare. However, vertical integration also reduces the number of retailers, by allowing the manufacturer to internalize the entry externality. Without integration, a potential entrant into retailing would ignore the reduction in the profits of other retailers when making its decision to enter. But the integrated manufacturer will take this reduction into account when considering a new retailer. As a result, the integrated manufacturer will always reduce the number of retailers from that which would arise in the free entry disintegrated equilibrium. The resulting welfare evaluation of vertical integration will then depend upon whether there is a welfare loss from the reduction in diversity, and if so, how large that welfare loss is.

In the spatial model used by Dixit, the free entry equilibrium yields excessive retail diversity, and vertical integration produces a welfare gain by reducing the number of retailers. However, this is not the case in the spatial model used by Mathewson and Winter. Their simulations indicate that the optimum ($p = c$) and the constrained optimum ($r = c$) both call for *more* retailers than the free entry Nash equilibrium under wholesale pricing. Thus, vertical integration generates a welfare loss from reduced retail diversity. However, this welfare loss is dominated by the welfare gain from eliminating successive markups. Mathewson and Winter discover small welfare gains from vertical integration.

The welfare conclusion of Mathewson and Winter can be reversed when a non-spatial model of retail differentiation is used. Perry and Groff (1985) examine a convenient non-spatial model. In particular, they employ the constant elasticity of substitution (CES) benefit function introduced by Spence (1976) to generate the derived demands for retailers. If x_i is the output of the ith retailer, a composite commodity y can be defined as $y = \sum \alpha \cdot x_i^{\beta}$, where $\alpha > 0$ and $0 < \beta < 1$. The benefit function is then specified as $U(\cdot) = y^{\theta}$, where $0 < \theta < 1$. Since the elasticity of substitution is $\sigma = 1/(1 - \beta)$, $\beta < 1$ insures that the retailers are differentiated. Assuming no income effects, the inverse demand function facing the kth retailer can be expressed as

$$p_j(x_1,\ldots,x_n) = \alpha\beta\theta \cdot \left\{ \sum_{i=1}^{n} \alpha \cdot x_i^{\beta} \right\}^{\theta-1} \cdot x_j^{\beta-1}. \tag{2}$$

With this demand structure, Perry and Groff define a free entry "monopolistically competitive" equilibrium in which each retailer chooses its quantity assuming that the weighted average of all outputs remains unchanged. This equilibrium generates a derived demand for the manufacturer's good. The profit-maximizing wholesale price of the manufacturer generates both a price and a diversity distortion. Vertical integration by the manufacturer eliminates the wholesale markup and lowers the retail price. Vertical integration also reduces the number of retailers, moving the retail stage farther from the optimum number of retailers. But unlike the Mathewson and Winter model, the welfare loss to consumers from reduced retail diversity now dominates the gains from eliminating the wholesale markup for all values of the parameters. Thus, vertical integration reduces welfare. This also occurs when there are oligopolists at the manufacturing stage. Oligopoly only lessens the severity of the welfare loss.

These models make it clear that the welfare assessment of vertical integration by a manufacturer depends upon the nature of consumer demand facing the monopolistically competitive retail stage. Consider two differences between the spatial and CES models. First, competition is "localized" in the spatial model, but "generalized" in the CES model. In (1), the quantity demanded from the jth retailer depends only upon the price p charged by the neighboring retailers. On the other hand, the demand price for the jth retailer in (2) depends upon the quantity sold by all other retailers. Thus, each retailer competes equally with all other retailers in the CES demand model. This suggests that we might expect more entry in the spatial model, implying that the free entry equilibrium may not perform too badly with respect to retail diversity. Second, new retailers "crowd" the market in a spatial model, whereas they create a new dimension to the product space in the CES model. In other words, entry does not increase total demand in the spatial model, but it does in a CES model. This suggests that the spatial model would place a lower value on retail diversity than the CES model. These two considerations may account for the fact that reduced retail diversity does not prevent vertical integration from increasing welfare in the model of Mathewson and Winter, but it does in the model of Perry and Groff.

3.2. Monopolistic competition and externalities at the retail stage

The welfare assessment of vertical integration by a manufacturer into retailing will also depend upon yet other non-price characteristics of the retail stage that enter into consumer benefits. In particular, Mathewson and Winter (1984, 1986) and Perry and Porter (1986) provide further extensions of the spatial and CES models to address advertising or service by retailers. The primary purpose of these papers is to examine vertical controls, but they also have important implications for vertical integration.

Mathewson and Winter (1984) use the same spatial model as their previous paper, but introduce the additional complication that retailers must advertise in order to inform consumers about the existence of the product. An increase in the advertising of one retailer will inform more consumers in that retailer's market area, but it will also inform consumers in the market areas of other retailers. This advertising spillover dulls the incentive of retailers to advertise, primarily to the detriment of the manufacturer. Thus, vertical integration will increase advertising. Mathewson and Winter (1986) are not able to make definitive conclusions about the retail price and the number of retailers, but some calculations indicate that vertical integration generally reduces the number of retailers, but does not necessarily reduce the retail price. Moreover, their calculations indicate that welfare increases with vertical integration, as in their model without the externality. Since advertising is purely informative and brings new consumers into the market, it would seem that the increased retail advertising would benefit both the manufacturer and consumers.

Similarly, Perry and Porter (1986) generalize the CES model of Perry and Groff (1985) to allow for service externalities in retailing. The composite commodity y is modified so that it depends upon both the quantity purchased, x_i, and the service received, z_i. In particular, $y = \sum z_i^{\alpha} \cdot x_i^{\beta}$, where $\alpha + \beta < 1$. Service can be thought of as presale non-appropriable information. However, the service received by a consumer is assumed to be a linear combination of the service of the retailer from whom the good is purchased and the average level of service by all retailers, i.e. $z_i = \lambda \cdot s_i + (1 - \lambda) \cdot \bar{s}$, where $0 \leq \lambda \leq 1$. Thus, there is an externality which reduces the incentive of retailers to perform service. This reduces the derived demand for the manufacturer's good and limits the profits that can be achieved with wholesale pricing. Vertical integration allows the manufacturer to internalize the externality, increase the retail service, and increase profits. However, welfare need not increase. Since vertical integration reduces welfare in the model of Perry and Groff without a service externality, it is not surprising that Perry and Porter find that vertical integration still reduces welfare when the service externality is not too strong. But as the externality becomes stronger, consumer losses increase because of the reductions in retail service. Thus, vertical integration will increase welfare at some point when the service externality becomes strong. There are three separate welfare effects of vertical integration. The reduction in retail diversity works to decrease welfare. On the other hand, eliminating the wholesale markup and internalizing the service externality both work to increase welfare.

In summary, a complete welfare evaluation of vertical integration requires an examination of the relevant non-price dimensions of competition. The problem is that such models become very cumbersome, even with convenient parameterizations and assumptions.

4. Uncertainty and information

In this section we discuss the vertical integration caused by the presence of uncertainty or private information.

4.1. *Diversification*

When all intermediate markets are competitive without imperfections such as rationing, firms are still subject to fluctuations in the prices which result from exogenous shifts in supply or demand at any point in the system. However, vertical integration cannot insulate the firm from such uncertainties. To illustrate this point, consider the simple model by Perry (1982). Consumers purchase the final good from retailers who in turn obtain the good from an intermediate market supplied by manufacturers. There is also an external net demand for the good from intermediate market. This can be thought of as foreign demand or supply of the manufactured good. Finally, manufacturers purchase the factor inputs necessary to produce the good from factor markets. Exogenous random events can impinge upon the final domestic market through shifts in consumer demand, upon the intermediate market through shifts in net foreign demand, or upon the factor market through shifts in the factor supply.

The manufacturers and retailers can vertically integrate in the sense of joint ownership, but the integrated firm cannot and will not want to avoid the price fluctuations in these markets. Even if the integrated firm refused to participate in the intermediate market, thereby synchronizing its manufacturing and retailing subsidiaries, it would still be directly subject to shifts in consumer demand or factor supply, and indirectly subject to shifts in net foreign demand in the intermediate market through its impact upon the factor and final prices.[15] Moreover, the integrated firm should optimally continue to participate in the intermediate market just as if its subsidiaries were independent firms. The price in the intermediate market is the relevant opportunity cost for each of the

[15] Bernhardt (1977) examines the extent to which forward integration and synchronization allows the manufacturer to reduce the variability of its demand. When the source of the fluctuations is consumer demand, integration cannot reduce demand variability for the manufacturer. However, when the source of the fluctuations is random purchasing behavior by retailers, integration can reduce demand variability.

subsidiaries [see Porter (1980)]. Thus, if the intermediate price is high, the manufacturing subsidiary should expand production while the retail subsidiary should contract domestic sales.[16]

Since no real production decisions are affected,[17] why then should vertical integration arise? Diversification of the firm's returns is the only possible incentive. Even this requires that capital markets be imperfect in that investors cannot adequately diversify against these fluctuations in their portfolios. When the source of the fluctuations is exogenous shifts in final demand, the returns of the manufacturers and retailers are positively correlated. This increases the fluctuation in profits and diversification would favor vertical disintegration. However, when the source of the fluctuations is exogenous shifts in foreign net demand in the intermediate market, the returns of the manufacturers and retailers are negatively correlated if the elasticity of final demand exceeds the elasticity of substitution in retail production. This would create a diversification incentive for vertical integration.[18]

4.2. *Rationing and assurance of supply*

The traditional business explanation for vertical integration is that firms want to assure their supply of inputs and their market for outputs [see Porter (1980)]. This typically means much more than mere avoidance of purely random fluctuations in the intermediate market.[19] Moreover, it must mean more than simply acquiring inputs at low prices or selling outputs at high prices. In particular, the notion of "assuring supplies or markets" entails the inability to obtain the quantity of inputs that the firm would wish to purchase at the prevailing input prices or the inability to sell the quantity of output that the firm would wish at the prevailing output prices. In other words, the market is not clearing at prevailing prices because of some imperfection.

[16]Of course, this assumes no economies from synchronization of production. See Subsection 7.4 for a vertical equilibrium model with such economies. Moreover, this assumes no costs of participation in an intermediate market subject to price fluctuations. Wu (1964) discusses such costs in suggesting that integration and synchronization is more profitable.

[17]Blair and Kaserman (1978) examine a model in which final demand is uncertain but that retailers must make their output decisions prior to the revelation of the uncertainty. Risk aversion will distort the output decision of the firms, inducing forward integration by a risk neutral manufacturer.

[18]When the source of the fluctuations is exogenous shifts in factor supply, it is not clear whether to expect the returns of the manufacturers and the retailers to be positively or negatively correlated. Levin (1981) finds that vertical integration into crude production reduced the variance in profits for oil refiners from 1948 to 1972. Mitchell (1976) argues that the cost of capital (S & P stock rating) is lower for integrated oil refiners.

[19]In 1981, Du Pont acquired Conoco stating that this would "reduce the exposure of the combined companies to fluctuations in the price of energy and hydrocarbons" [see Buzzell (1983)]. However, the fluctuations in oil prices during the 1970s were hardly random so that one expects that other presumed risks were being avoided by this merger.

Stigler (1951) pointed out that rationing induced by regulated prices would provide a powerful force for vertical integration. In a vertical equilibrium model by Green (1974), rationing results in an inflexible intermediate good price and provides an incentive for integration. But to understand the argument for "assuring supplies", one must account for rationing in a model with unregulated optimizing firms. Carlton (1979) has provided such a model.

In Carlton's model there are many consumers who demand a perishable good produced by the manufacturers. However, there is a retail stage and each consumer must seek the good only by presenting his demand function to a single retailer in each market period. Aggregate consumer demand is random, but all production and pricing decisions must be made before demand is observed. At the preset retail price, retailers attempt to satisfy the demands of their consumers, first from their own production of the good, i.e. vertical integration, and then by purchases in the wholesale market. But like consumers, retailers can frequent only one manufacturer in each market period. Thus, if a manufacturer has not produced a sufficient amount of the good prior to entering the market period, then some retailers will not be able to obtain enough of the good to satisfy all of their customers.

The production cost of the good, for either manufacturers or integrated retailers, is a constant c. However, demand uncertainty creates an additional cost from the risk that produced goods may go unsold. Thus, the equilibrium wholesale price set by the independent manufacturers, p_{int}, must exceed the marginal production cost c. Now, if a retailer were certain that at least one consumer would show up at his store, he could increase his profits by producing the good himself at the cost c rather than purchasing the good from a manufacturer. Thus, each retailer will partially integrate backward if the probability of no consumers showing up, Pr(0), is sufficiently low. This occurs when the cost of production, c, is less than the expected cost of having to enter the wholesale market to obtain one unit of the good, $[1 - \Pr(0)] \cdot p_{\text{int}}$. This incentive is reinforced by the probability that the retailer may also be rationed by the manufacturer and thus be forced to forgo the sale altogether.[20]

A vertical equilibrium will exist in which retailers partially integrate to satisfy the demand which will arise with high probability, and use the wholesale market to satisfy any greater demand which arises with low probability. This is the sense in which the model captures the notion of "assuring supplies". The traditional arguments did not account for why input supplies were unreliable, and appealed only to lost sales as the reason for seeking reliability through vertical integration.

[20]Carlton's model could also account for differing incentives to integrate. In particular, suppose the manufacturers sold an intermediate input which was employed by fabricators in differing consumer goods industries. The fabricators in some industries may have more certain demands, and thus have a greater incentive to integrate.

Not only is rationing endogenous in Carlton's model, but the insight behind partial integration is more appealing than the traditional arguments.

Vertical integration does not improve welfare in Carlton's model. As a result of integration, retailers now bear some risk of excess production. However, retailers are less efficient than manufacturers in bearing this risk. Since there are more retailers than manufacturers, the retailers have to produce a greater quantity of the good in order to satisfy the same fraction of consumers. Thus, vertical integration by the retailers, full or partial, will reduce the expected utility of the market equilibrium. Industry costs will be higher, prices will probably be higher, and consumers will incur a lower probability of obtaining the good.[21]

Carlton's model illustrates the incentive that rationing provides for vertical expansion. The retailers do not acquire manufacturers, but set up their own manufacturing subsidiaries. However, if we considered vertical merger in Carlton's model, we would discover a strong incentive for the manufacturers to acquire the retailers. The retailers owned by a given manufacturer would funnel their demands directly to him. In this way, the manufacturers could aggregate the demands of their retailers and the larger number of retailers would no longer interfere with efficient provision of the good to consumers by the smaller number of manufacturers. Exclusive dealing could also generate this outcome. It is also important to note that rationing in this model creates a strong incentive for horizontal merger among either the retailers or manufacturers.

4.3. *Information and agency problems*

Arrow (1975) posits a model in which vertical integration allows the acquisition of valuable private information. Downstream fabricators must make investment decisions prior to knowing the price of the intermediate input. Moreover, there is uncertainty about the intermediate price because the output of each upstream supplier is affected by the realization of a random variable. In general, the random variables will be correlated across suppliers. Backward integration enables a fabricator to learn the output of the acquired supplier prior to making its investment decision. Since the intermediate market is competitive, there is no rationing nor any incentive to internally transfer the input at other than the market price. Thus, backward integration enables the fabricator to obtain a better prediction of the intermediate price and make a more profitable investment decision.

Although the model does illustrate the acquisition of information, the upstream firms have no incentive to conceal their information. The upstream firms

[21]Carlton was unable to prove that the final price was always higher under partial integration. However, he was able to demonstrate that consumers would be worse off even if the price fell because of the lower probability of obtaining the good.

obtain knowledge about their supply prior to the investment decisions of the downstream firms, but Arrow assumes that the information is not revealed until aggregated into the equilibrium price. Since upstream firms are competitive, they cannot benefit from concealing their private information. Instead, they can benefit by simply revealing the information and improving the investment decisions of the downstream firms. Thus, vertical integration is not necessary. Downstream firms could buy the information from individual upstream firms or, better yet, an independent agency could collect and disseminate the aggregate supply information.

Crocker (1983) illustrates the acquisition of private information in a principal–agent model which avoids the degeneracy inherent in Arrow's model. The retailer (the agent) has private information about whether the final demand price is high or low. The manufacturer (the principal) then maximizes his expected profits by choosing a contract which specifies the quantity and the wholesale price as a function of the retailer's report. In order to induce the retailer to correctly reveal the final price, the contract offered by the manufacturer yields quasi-rents for the retailer when the final price is high, and results in less than the ex post optimal quantity when the final price is low. The retailer has no independent incentive to reveal its private information about the demand price since the strategic use of that information yields quasi-rents. Forward integration eliminates the inefficiency by enabling the upstream firm to directly observe the joint profits. The integrated firm can then induce the downstream subsidiary to reveal the correct price by rewarding the downstream subsidiary only when the optimal quantity for the reported price is consistent with the observed joint profits.

The inefficiency which arises from the profit-maximizing contract in the Crocker model is an example of the costs in using contractual exchange. However, there are no corresponding disadvantages of vertical integration. Vertical integration is posited as necessary to obtain the private information, but it creates no new problems such as attenuated incentives on the part of the downstream subsidiary to lower costs. Note also that this inefficiency could also be eliminated with more complex payment schemes designed into the contract [see Riordan (1984)].

Riordan and Sappington (1987) have a more complex model of vertical integration and private information. The model can be interpreted as having three vertical stages. Research and development determines the quality of the final good and the developer is endowed with private information about the unit cost of quality. The manufacturer of the final good has private information about the unit cost of production. Finally, the retailer merely sells the product at a known demand price. The retailer is the principal and the developer is the agent, but either can do the manufacturing and both are equally adept as such. Thus, the principal must decide whether to manufacture the product himself or let the agent do the manufacturing. Whoever does the manufacturing observes the unit cost of production. When the cost realizations are positively correlated, the developer's incentive to overstate the cost of quality is accentuated when he is also manufacturing. As a result, the retailer's expected profit is lower when the developer manufactures the product than when the retailer himself does the manufacturing. Thus, the retailer would vertically integrate into manufacturing. Conversely, when the cost realizations are negatively correlated, the developer's incentive to overstate the cost of quality is dampened when he is also manufacturing. It may then be best for the retailer to have the developer do the manufacturing.

As in the models of Arrow and Crocker, vertical integration in the model of Riordan and Sappington enables the principal or the agent to observe valuable private information, the true unit cost of production (once the quality decision is observed). Moreover, like Arrow's model, the value of the information revealed by backward integration is that it may be correlated with the private information held by the agent, the cost of quality. However, unlike Arrow, there is no independent incentive to reveal the private information without vertical integration. And unlike Crocker, vertical integration by the principal does not eliminate the principal–agent problem and the associated inefficiencies.

It is not clear that vertical integration should be characterized as automatically revealing valuable information. The parties in the new integrated firm would often remain unchanged, and they would still have individual objectives apart from the firm's interest in profit maximization.[22] If private information is not revealed by vertical integration, a principal–agent problem remains within the firm. This raises the question of who should then be the principal within the integrated firm, the upstream subsidiary or downstream subsidiary. One might think that the acquiring firm, the principal, should be the one whose private information is the most valuable to the exchange and the most costly to obtain by internal incentives.

The literature also raises a broader conceptual problem concerning the nature of vertical integration. Should vertical integration mean an increase in the decision-maker's control over production and distribution or an increase in his information about the parameters of production and distribution? The two may seem inseparable. For example, in the model of Riordan and Sappington, backward integration into manufacturing enables the retailer to use the information about manufacturing costs to write a contract with the developer which improves its control over the quality of the product. However, it would seem more natural to define vertical integration as directly augmenting control, yet recognizing that control then facilitates revelation of private information. The

[22] Evans and Grossman (1983) take the extreme position that the multidivisional management of large vertically integrated companies via transfer prices does not reduce the information and agency problems encountered in arm's-length contracting.

new controls which come with vertical integration would enable the decision-maker to write new types of contracts. As such, backward integration in the model of Riordan and Sappington can be thought of as allowing the retailer to write a contract directly with the developer.

Williamson (1975) and others have argued that vertical integration enables new monitoring mechanisms which are more effective in obtaining private information (or in obtaining it sooner). For example, Alchian and Demsetz (1972) discuss the problem "shirking" in team production where the productivity of individual inputs is difficult to measure. They argue that firms arise because an owner-employer can subjectively evaluate the performance of individual workers and discipline individual team members. Similar arguments may be applicable to vertical integration which imparts control over the inputs of the neighboring stages. The controls of a disintegrated firm using contracts or market exchanges are weaker because they are restricted to measurable outputs rather than the inputs themselves. For example, Anderson and Schmittlein (1984) find that the difficulty in evaluating the performance of salesmen is a significant factor in accounting for the fact that electrical equipment manufacturers frequently employ a direct sales force rather than sell through independent sales representatives. This suggests that models of vertical integration and information need to focus upon the exact mechanisms by which integration enables information to be discovered, and how this differs from the mechanisms available in contracts or markets.

Even if vertical integration does not enable specific new monitoring mechanisms, it could reduce the agency problem in other ways. Vertical integration should increase the likelihood and duration of exchange between the two subsidiaries. This assurance of a continued relationship could facilitate the discovery or transfer of information. For similar reasons, Malmgren (1961) argues that vertical integration simply requires less information than using contracts or markets. By committing itself to internal exchange, the integrated firm need not incur the costs of following market developments and investigating alternative sources of inputs or outlets for its products. Such a commitment presumably incurs a corresponding cost of possibly missing advantageous external opportunities.

4.4. *Prices versus quantities*

If private information cannot be discovered by vertical integration, the existence of private information does have implications for the organization of an integrated firm. Consider the literature on "prices versus quantities" initiated by Weitzman (1974). Weitzman is concerned with the problem of a "planner" who wishes to maximize expected surplus in light of private information which is too costly to elicit from the parties through revelation incentives. But this is also the problem facing the manager of an integrated firm with upstream and downstream subsidiaries. The upstream subsidiary has private information about a parameter that affects its costs, while the downstream subsidiary has private information about a parameter that affects its revenues.

If quantity is the internal decision variable, the manager sets the transfer quantity so as to maximize expected joint profit with respect to his distributions on the private information. Call this option 1, or the quantity option. On the other hand, if price is the internal decision variable, then there are two decentralized options. In option 2, the manager sets the price to maximize expected joint profit given that the downstream subsidiary chooses quantity to maximize its profits at that price. In option 3, the manager sets the price to maximize expected joint profit given that the upstream subsidiary chooses quantity to maximize its profits at that price. Since joint profit is the objective function for all three integrated options, they dominate decentralized bilateral monopoly outcomes. Thus, the question is which option generates the highest expected joint profits for the integrated firm. Assuming that the random variables characterizing private information affect only the marginal costs and revenues, Laffont (1976) shows that one of the pricing options dominates the quantity option, but that the quantity option then dominates the other pricing option. Option 1 dominates option 2 when the revenue function of the downstream subsidiary is more concave than the cost function of the upstream subsidiary is convex. This means that information about revenues is more valuable to the planner than information about the costs.

Flaherty (1981) discusses the vertical integration in this framework. In some sense, option 1 is "more" integrated than option 2 because it involves quantity controls rather than price controls. Thus, the tone, if not the intent, of Flaherty's discussion is that when the revenue and cost functions are such that option 1 is preferred to option 2, that we should expect firms to be vertically integrated. This ignores option 3 which Laffont has shown dominates both options 1 and 2 in these circumstances. But even so, this makes too fine of a distinction between what are essentially three forms of internal organization for a vertical integrated firm. However, this literature remains relevant to the theory of vertical integration because the incentive to integrate is enhanced when the internal organization of the firm is optimally configured to deal with undiscoverable private information.

5. Transaction cost economics

Coase (1937) argued that the key to understanding vertical integration would come not so much from understanding the vertical production relationships, but rather from understanding vertical exchange relationships. Like production, exchange is costly. Moreover, vertical integration is simply one method of effectuating a bilateral exchange. Thus, an analysis of the costs of alternative methods of exchange is the required in order to understand vertical integration. Viewed from the transaction cost framework, the neoclassical focus on market imperfections has limited value because it ignores the costs of exchange. Since the primary alternative to vertical integration is contractual exchange, transaction cost economics examines the relative costs of contractual versus internal exchange.

Oliver E. Williamson is the leading proponent of transaction cost economics, and his many writings on the subject are summarized in his two books *Markets and Hierarchies* (1975) and *The Economic Institutions of Capitalism* (1985). I cannot do justice to the richness and complexity of transaction cost economics in this chapter. However, I will briefly summarize the theoretical and empirical analysis as it applies to vertical integration.

5.1. Asset specificity

Bilateral monopoly between a buyer and seller arises because gains from trade are enhanced by investments in assets which are specialized to their exchange. Williamson calls this "asset specificity". Asset specificity may arise from investments in (1) specific physical capital, (2) specific human capital, (3) site specific capital, (4) dedicated capital, or (5) brand name capital. Such transaction specific assets give rise to what Klein, Crawford and Alchian (1978) call "appropriable quasi-rents", which are the difference between the value of the asset in this use and the value in its next best use. When the environment is complex and uncertain, the transaction costs of negotiating and enforcing contracts make it prohibitively costly to write long-term contracts which specify all obligations under all contingencies. The resulting bilateral relationships fail to define the terms of performance for the parties in all or certain states of nature. In such states, either party may engage in "opportunistic" behavior, attempting to extract the quasi-rents of the other party by threatening to dissolve the relationship unless price concessions are forthcoming. Goldberg (1976) calls this the "hold-up" problem. Opportunistic behavior involves costs of haggling, and may result in the failure to maximize joint profits.[23]

Some of these problems can be mitigated by provisions in long-term contracts designed to govern the exchange. These would include requirements clauses, price indexing clauses, cost-plus pricing clauses, liquidated damages, and arbitration

[23]Fellner (1947) discusses bilateral monopoly, and Machlup and Taber (1960) point out the obvious incentive to integrate if the bilateral monopolists fail to maximize joint profits.

provisions.[24] However, when asset specificity is substantial, contractual governance over opportunism may become very costly. Internal organization of this exchange through vertical integration may then be a more efficient governance structure. Of course, the hierarchical structure of internal organization gives rise to other costs such as attentuated incentives and bureaucratic distortions. Thus, given the degree of asset specificity, the relative costs of governance dictate the choice between contractual exchange and vertical integration. If asset specificity is weak, contractual exchange is preferable; whereas if asset specificity is strong, vertical integration is preferable.

Williamson (1985) complements this analysis of relative governance costs with relative production costs. For example, as the supplier invests in assets more specific to this particular buyer, it loses economies of scale or scope because of its inability to make sales to other buyers. Thus, contractual exchange has an additional production cost advantage for a given degree of asset specificity. This extends the range of asset specificity over which contractual exchange is preferable.

Riordan and Williamson (1985) enhance Williamson's analysis by making the degree of asset specificity a choice variable for the buyer and seller. The degree of asset specificity and the quantity exchanged are both greater with vertical integration than with contractual exchange. Thus, the choice between vertical integration and contractual exchange involves a comparison of joint profits at the optimally chosen quantity and asset specificity. Riordan and Williamson also specify production cost advantages of contractual exchange and design benefits of vertical integration, both of which yield the expected effects.

Riordan and Williamson specify, rather than derive, the production and governance costs relationships. Asset specificity is treated like capital in a variable cost function. It reduces the total and marginal costs of production, and is available at a constant marginal cost itself. The governance cost functions for contractual exchange and vertical integration are chosen to generate the interrelationships postulated by the theory. These specifications allow them to focus immediately upon the comparative statics of the Williamson analysis. Moreover, arbitrary specifications may be unavoidable for certain nebulous governance costs. However, once asset specificity becomes a choice variable rather than an exogenous technological condition, it would be preferable to have a model which directly derives the benefits and costs of asset specificity. In so doing, one would also need to determine how to parameterize the specificity of assets.

The production cost or design advantages of asset specificity raise market issues beyond the pure transaction costs issues of contractual exchange. The

[24]Goldberg and Erickson (1987) discuss such provisions in the long-term contracts used in the petroleum coke industry. Joskow (1985) does the same for the long-term contracts between coal mines and utilities with coal-burning electric generating plants.

supplier is forgoing sales to other buyers in the input market by investments in a specialized input for this buyer. Similarly, the buyer's demand for the specialized input is derived from investments in the differentiation of its product in the final market. These observations raise issues of economies of scale and scope on the supplier side of the exchange and issues of product differentiation on the buyer side of the exchange. Thus, the market alternatives surrounding the buyer and seller become important in determining the choices of asset specificity. The exchange remains bilateral, but it is circumscribed by the surrounding markets. Production and demand considerations as well as transaction costs become intertwined in an equilibrium specificity of the assets.

Porter and Spence (1977) examine a simple model with design specificity and market alternatives. Standardization of intermediate inputs widens the market for any given supplier, and potentially allows the suppliers to achieve greater economies of scale. On the other hand, a specialized input may enhance the value to consumers of the buyer's final product. The specialized input increases revenues for an integrated buyer. But his average cost for the input will be higher than the market price because the fixed costs of producing the input cannot be spread over other buyers. Larger buyers will integrate and smaller buyers will employ the standardized input. Porter and Spence do not characterize the equilibrium price for the standardized input. But this price would determine a vertical equilibrium in that buyers above a certain size would find it optimal to integrate. Despite the fact that standardization may maximize welfare, buyers may vertically integrate because they fail to take into account their impact on increasing the price of the standardized input when they switch to a specialized input.

Porter and Spence do not discuss contracting. If contracting were possible, suppliers would have a choice about producing a standardized input at the market price or producing a specialized input for one buyer. This would then introduce a discrete choice on design specificity. The number of bilateral contracting situations would be dependent upon the market alternatives for both the supplier and the buyer. Moreover, these markets would affect negotiating positions of the parties and thus the nature of the contracts.

5.2. *Evidence*

Teece (1976) discusses vertical integration by petroleum refiners using the transaction cost framework outlined by Williamson (1975). Teece argues that although there are many crude oil producers, transaction problems arise from the high cost to refiners of a shortage or interruption in their flow of crude oil [see also McLean and Haigh (1954)]. Teece then finds that the major oil companies are integrated, producing between 50 and 90 percent of their crude requirements.

Similarly, the refiners have integrated into pipelines since they are the specialized investment linking refineries to the crude producers.

Levin (1981) challenges these findings with some regression results that yield no significant relationship between the profitability of oil companies and their degree of self-sufficiency in crude production. Levin also argues that since the divestiture of Standard Oil in 1911 there has been a wide variation in the degree of self-sufficiency among oil companies and no clear industry trend toward greater self-sufficiency. This conclusion also raises questions about the received business history that the offspring of Standard Oil who were left without crude properties subsequently reintegrated into crude production [see Johnson (1976)]. Since Standard Oil made investments based upon its monopoly and monopsony position, these investments probably differed from those that would have arisen under a competitive industry structure. Moreover, the size, location, and specificity of the investments were chosen within the context of the integrated structure of Standard Oil. Both of these considerations could have distorted post-divestiture markets, encouraging the vertical integration which occurred. If there is an ideal degree of self-sufficiency in crude oil, one might expect that refiners below that degree would be engaging more heavily in exploration than refiners above that degree.[25]

Teece (1976) also argues that forward integration by the refiners into marketing can be explained in terms of transaction cost considerations. However, the arguments involve retail diversity and service externalities similar to the neoclassical models discussed in Section 3. The forward integration of refiners into retailing has ebbed and flowed. Refiner owned and operated stations were predominant in the 1920s, but franchise stations emerged in the 1930s. However, refiner stations still constitute about 20 percent of the retail market.[26] If forward integration is an avenue of competition among refiners, we might expect more refiner operated stations during periods in which crude is plentiful and refiner capacity is underutilized. This suggests a model with vertical externalities that cannot be internalized by refiner price reductions.

These and other case studies [see deChazeau and Kahn (1959)] suggest that vertical integration by the major oil refiners is "tapered" both backward and

[25]It is interesting to note that Standard Oil produced less than 30 percent of its requirements of crude oil prior to the divestiture [see Johnson (1976)]. This fact seems inconsistent with both the monopsony incentive discussed by Perry (1978c) and the transaction cost arguments of Teece (1976).

[26]Refiner relationships with gasoline stations has always been a sensitive policy issue. In *Standard Oil Co. of California v. U.S.* (1949, 337 U.S. 293), the exclusive dealing contracts between refiners and their franchisees were held to be a violation of §3 of the Clayton Act. As a result, franchisees have the right to sell other brands. However, few do so. In *Exxon Corp. v. Governor of Maryland* (1978, 437 U.S. 117), the Supreme Court rejected a Commerce Clause challenge to a Maryland statute prohibiting refiners from operating retail service stations. The statute was enacted in response to evidence that refiner-owned stations had received preferential treatment during the 1973 oil embargo.

forward from the refining stage. The typical major refiner is substantially integrated into transportation of crude and wholesaling of refined products, but only partially integrated into crude production and retailing. Porter (1980) discusses tapered integration as a means of obtaining many of the benefits of vertical integration while avoiding many of the costs. In particular, Porter argues that partial integration allows the firm to adequately coordinate flows of intermediate inputs while providing both a competitive check on the integrated subsidiaries and a bargaining advantage with respect to the independent firms in these stages. In contradiction, Buzzell (1983) examined a large dataset of manufacturing firms, and concluded that tapered integration is less profitable than either no or full integration.

Stuckey (1983) examined vertical integration in the aluminum industry and argues that backward integration into bauxite and alumina by the refiners of aluminum can be explained by transaction cost considerations. Bilateral monopoly arises for three main reasons. First, efficient refining of alumina and aluminum requires large plants relative to the size of the market. Second, bauxite deposits are scattered around the world and refining involves a substantial reduction in volume. Thus, there are considerable transportation cost savings from locating the refining near the mining. Third, Stuckey points out that both bauxite and alumina are heterogeneous materials. For example, bauxite deposits differ in their alumina and silica content, while alumina may be either sandy or floury in composition. Other characteristics of bauxite affect the design of aluminum refineries.

Backward integration into automobile parts by the assemblers has also been explained by transaction cost considerations. Klein, Crawford and Alchian (1978) attribute the merger of General Motors and Fisher Body in 1928 to their close bilateral relationship and the inability to settle their disputes in the context of a long-term contract [see also Weiss (1987) for a discussion of the 1953 merger of Chrysler and Briggs Manufacturing]. Monteverde and Teece (1982a) use engineering effort in the design of components to measure transaction-specific skills, and find it highly significant in accounting for backward integration by GM and Ford. In related work, Monteverde and Teece (1982b) measure the quasi-rents in automobile components by calculating the cost of converting the tooling to its next best use. They then find that this measure is significantly related to the probability that assemblers own the tooling equipment. Since the equipment is employed by independent suppliers to produce the components, the arrangement is one of vertical quasi-integration. These explanations for backward integration in the automobile industry are in sharp contrast with the price discrimination explanation of Crandall discussed in Subsection 2.3. White (1971) presents a more complete picture of vertical integration by the U.S. automobile manufacturers. As with the petroleum industry, White concludes that tapered integration has been common for many components.

Using FTC data on mergers,[27] Spiller (1985) examines vertical mergers to test the transaction cost theory. Spiller estimates the gains from mergers using stock price information, and finds that they are negatively related to the distance between vertically related plants, a measure of transaction-specific assets. This provides some support for site specificity and vertical coordination as explanations of vertical mergers. Levy (1985) uses a distance measure as one of the explanatory variables for the ratio of value-added to sales for 69 manufacturing firms. It is intended to capture site specificity, but it is insignificant. However, Levy finds that the ratio of R&D expenditures to sales is significant, and argues that this supports the transaction cost theory since R&D is a proxy for specialized inputs. Armour and Teece (1980) argue that vertical integration increases the returns to R&D by facilitating communication between stages of production. They examine the U.S. petroleum industry from 1954 to 1975 and find a positive relationship between the number of stages in which firms participate and their expenditures on R&D.

Helfat and Teece (1987) argue that vertical integration enables the firm to better adapt to uncertainty and complexity, and that this should reduce the relative response of the firm's return to general economic uncertainties, measured by β in the CAPM model of financial markets. They examine 14 vertical mergers and find that the actual β of the merged firm is smaller (relative to a control group) than a predicted β derived from the premerger β's of the two merger partners. Weiss (1987) argues that the transaction specificity of two firms can be measured by observing that their stock returns are more highly correlated with each other than with other firms in the same industry. Using FTC data on mergers, Weiss finds that the returns of vertical merger partners prior to the merger were indeed more correlated. As Weiss points out, it remains difficult to explain why contractual alternatives became unsatisfactory at the point of merger.

Masten (1984) found a strong relationship between vertical integration by aerospace firms into the production of components and a measure of design specificity. The measure of design specificity was constructed from survey responses on whether the component could be adapted for use by other aerospace firms or by other industries. Anderson and Schmittlein (1984) examine the marketing decision by the producers of electrical components to use either a direct sales force or a system of manufacturer's representatives. They construct a transaction-specific human capital variable from survey responses, and find it to be a significant factor in explaining the use of direct sales forces. More generally, a direct sales force enables a firm to provide incentives such as security and promotion which may be better at eliciting specific human investments than the monetary rewards which are typical for representatives or franchisees. This is a

[27] The FTC has classified mergers involving assets in excess of 10 million dollars into horizontal, vertical, and conglomerate.

good example of vertical integration defined in terms of the firm's relationship to labor.

5.3. Cases from business history

Case studies in business history have been used by Williamson and others to illustrate various transactional reasons for forward integration. Chandler (1977) has employed such case studies to infer an intriguing link between mass production and vertical integration. Technological and organizational innovations during the nineteenth century permitted a smaller workforce to produce a higher rate of output. This was accomplished by a finer division of tasks to which specialized machinery was applied. Vertical integration was then required to synchronize the intermediate input flows between these stages of production within the firm. Technological or transactional reasons could account for the "economies of synchronization" which induce this integration within the production stage.[28] However, Chandler extends the argument to explain forward integration beyond production into wholesaling and retailing. Forward integration arose from the inability of traditional marketing channels to respond to the pressure created by the greatly increased volume of goods from manufacturers taking advantage of the economies of scale at the production stage.

Chandler's argument has its greatest appeal for the cases involving perishables. Swift developed and owned a fleet of refrigerated railroad cars and wholesale houses in major cities in order to distribute beef dressed in its midwestern meat-packing plants. This system replaced the delivery of beef on-the-hoof to eastern markets. Similarly, United Fruit owned banana plantations, a fleet of refrigerated steamships, and wholesale houses in major cities for ripening the bananas [see Porter and Livesay (1971) and Chandler (1977)]. These cases have been cited as illustrations of transaction-specific investments where failure to synchronize the flows imposes large costs on one party or another. However, the assets at each stage of these industries were specific to the producers primarily because the producers were monopolists. Assets specialized for a particular use become effectively transaction-specific when a neighboring stage is monopolized. Thus, integration into specialized transportation and wholesaling may not have been necessary if there had been more producers. Independent transportation and wholesaling companies could have switched producers in response to opportunism by one.

[28]McLean and Haigh (1954) focused upon this theme is explaining the backward integration by oil refiners into crude production. Unit costs increase rapidly with refinery operations below capacity, while the costs of maintaining inventories of crude are non-trivial. They argue that integration insures the optimal flow. Of course, long-term contracts may achieve similar results. In Goldberg and Erickson (1987), the costs of storing hazardous petroleum coke was a key consideration in long-term contracts for its disposal by oil refiners.

The industries which Chandler cites for the pure application of his coordination argument are tobacco, matches, grain milling, canning, soap, and photography. The manufacturers in these industries set up sales offices and warehouses in major cities to distribute their products. These offices often sold directly to large retailers. The manufacturers also initiated product differentiation by the advertising of new branded products. Thus, the traditional role of merchant wholesalers was substantially diminished. Chandler argues that forward integration and the switch to branded rather than generic products was a consequence of the need to market the greatly increased volume of output from the new continuous-process technologies employed in manufacturing. An alternative view is that branding was a marketing innovation independent of the technological innovations. Under this view, forward integration by manufacturers could have been the efficient method of distribution for the new branded products, or a temporary measure to deal with the sluggish response by the traditional distribution channels.

The experience in these industries could be also be understood as a tradeoff between economies of scale and scope. With indivisibilities in wholesaling, a substantial volume of sales would be necessary to justify setting up sales offices, even if such offices had coordination and promotional advantages. Otherwise, the economies of scope in wholesaling different products to the same retailers would dominate. In discussing the tobacco industry, Porter and Livesay (1971) point out that the manufacturers continued to use independent jobbers for distribution to small retailers in urban markets and to rural retailers. These jobbers could capture economies of scope by distributing a range of grocery and drug products.

Chandler also discusses forward integration into retailing by the manufacturers of consumer durables. These products required specialized services such as information, repair, and credit. He argues that existing distribution channels were unable or unwilling to provide these services. For example, Singer and the other major sewing machine companies set up branch offices for demonstrations, sales, and repair. Similarly, McCormick sold farm machinery through exclusive franchise dealers and had regional offices to handle repair and supervise advertising and credit by the dealers. Although Chandler discusses the inventory problems that arise with independent wholesalers and retailers, the synchronization of flows is not the most natural explanation for this forward integration. Incentive and externality problems seem more likely explanations. The incentive problem concerns the best compensation arrangement for generating sales and service effort. Sales and service may be done by independent distributors, by franchised distributors, or by employees. The externality problem concerns the spillovers and resulting incentives to free-ride in the provision of non-appropriable presale services.[29]

[29]Vertical quasi-integration and vertical controls are often employed to deal with incentive and externality problems in retailing. For example, see Mathewson and Winter (1984) and Perry and Porter (1986).

Williamson has used these cases as an example of forward integration motivated by human asset specificity. The argument is that manufacturers require sales and service people specifically trained to handle the complex differentiated products. This may have been true when these products were originally introduced. However, with growth and maturity, these and similar industries have attained a higher sales volume, a stable set of producers, and some standardization. These developments have given rise to independent service firms, most notably in the automobile industry. This suggests that human asset specificity may be more a consequence of product novelty rather than product complexity or differentiation.

The overwhelming aspect of the cases from American industry prior to 1900 is that the industries were built around new products as well as new technologies. Thus, to fully assess of Chandler's arguments, we need the entire case histories rather than case studies at the particular point in time when these new products were introduced.

6. Incomplete contracts

In this section we discuss the recent theoretical literature on "incomplete contracts" and the relevance of this work for understanding vertical integration. To a large extent, this literature is a theoretical response to transaction cost economics where the inability to write complete contracts allows opportunistic ex post bargaining. However, the models have no explicit transactions costs, nor any costs associated with the governance of a long-term contractual relationship. Rather, the losses arise from inefficiencies in the ex ante investments or the ex post exchange.

6.1. *Contract law*

An incomplete contract has been defined by economists as a contract that either fails to specify performance obligations for the parties in all states of nature, or fails to specify the nature of the performance itself [see the survey by Hart and Holmstrom (1986)]. The first case occurs because it is costly to enumerate the future states of nature or costly to agree about the performance obligations in a given state. The second case occurs because it is costly to agree on or specify clearly the performance obligations, irrespective of the state of nature. In addition, either case can also occur if it is impossible for a third party such as a court to verify the occurrence of a state of nature or identify a performance obligation.

When a contract is incomplete, economists may implicitly assume that the contract is not longer relevant for determining the nature of the exchange in the first case or for determining some dimension of the exchange in the second case. If so, the contract fails to circumscribe the bargaining and reduce opportunism. This favors vertical integration as the preferable form of exchange. A summary of contract law will demonstrate that this is a narrow and inaccurate conception of contracting. In the process, we will clarify some issues which are relevant for theoretical work.

The term "incomplete contract" has no independent meaning in contract law. However, the economic notions of incompleteness do have legal analogies. A contract which specifies performance obligations only for certain states of nature would be a contract "with conditions precedent". A "condition precedent" is an event, other than the lapse of time, which must occur before a performance obligation arises.[30] A contract with conditions precedent will then have no performance obligations in the unspecified states of the world. For example, contracts between a general contractor and a subcontractor are typically contingent upon the general contractor winning his bid. If exchange is to occur in the unspecified states, a new contract must be negotiated.

Contracts which fail to specify the nature of performance are called "indefinite contracts". Contracts may be so indefinite that they would have no legal force. In early contract law, any indefiniteness about a material term such as quantity, quality, price, delivery, or payment would invalidate the contract. Williamson (1979) refers to this as "classical" contracting. However, modern contract law governed by the *Uniform Commercial Code*[31] (*UCC*) will attempt to "fill the gaps" of an indefinite contract, and invalidate it only if a court could not fashion a remedy upon breach.[32] In supplying the unspecified terms, called "open" terms, the courts will examine the course of dealing by the parties on prior contracts, the course of performance by the parties on this contract, or the customary practice in the trade (*UCC* 1-205). A court will even infer a "reasonable" price for a contract which fails to mention price [*UCC* 2-305 (1)(a)]. Note that the reasonable price need not be the market price.

The parties may purposely leave the performance obligations indefinite by "agreeing to agree" at a future time before performance is due. But, like indefinite contracts, a court will substitute a "reasonable" performance if the parties fail to agree. The parties may also leave the performance obligations indefinite by allowing one party to decide certain terms at a future time. The

[30] See Calamari and Perillo (1977, ch. 11). The party to whom the performance obligation is due must prove the occurrence of the condition.

[31] The *UCC* is a codification of contract law and has been adopted with minor variations in every state but Louisiana.

[32] *UCC* 2-204(3) states that "even if one or more terms are left open a contract for sale does not fail for indefiniteness if the parties have intended to make a contract and there is a reasonably certain basis for giving an appropriate remedy". Of course, the cost of enforcing a contract with more gaps would increase for the non-breaching party.

most common example is a long-term requirements contract in which either the buyer (or seller) can choose the quantity exchanged in each future period within some bounds [*UCC* 2-306 (1)]. Indeed, the *UCC* even allows contracts in which either party can set the price for a future exchange [*UCC* 2-305 (2)]. Open terms of performance assigned to one party would seem to be an invitation to opportunism, but the *UCC* requires that these terms be set in "good faith". If the open terms are not set in good faith, a court will again substitute "reasonable" performance.

This discussion is not intended to suggest that opportunistic bargaining cannot arise under a contract with indefinite or open terms of performance. Rather, the point is that such terms do not nullify performance obligations as if a contract never existed. Thus, unlike contracts with conditions precedent, indefinite contracts create performance obligations for each party in all states of nature. If a dispute arises as to the nature of the performance, its resolution will be negotiated in light of the rights and remedies under contract law. Of course, the legal positions of the parties may be uncertain, and there are costs of enforcing those rights and remedies. But the bargaining position on an indefinite contract would generally be different from the bargaining position on a contract with a condition precedent.[33] Indeed, one should expect that even indefinite contracts are intended to circumscribe the range of bargaining outcomes and thereby reduce the potential for subsequent opportunism.

Even if a contract has no conditions precedent and no open terms of performance, renegotiation can occur in response to contingencies. Parties to a contract have the right to not perform their contractual obligations, i.e. breach the contract. But the breaching party is then subject to money damages sufficient to compensate the non-breaching party for his expected value under the contract. Breach and the payment of damages enables the parties to avoid an exchange which has become inefficient under realized states of nature not specified as conditions precedent. Even if the exchange remains efficient, one party may incur a loss under the contract for some states of nature. Since a contract can be renegotiated and modified even though the performance obligations of only one party are reduced (*UCC* 2-209), the right to breach could also trigger renegotiation in this case.

Shavell (1984) points out that money damages for breach and renegotiation are legal substitutes for conditions precedent in contracts. This is particularly true if the conditions precedent would not be verifiable by a third party such as a court or arbitrator, and thus are not contractable. Since all that can be observed is non-performance, a court must fashion a remedy which is independent of the

[33]There could be dispute about the occurrence of an event which would trigger performance obligations in a contract with conditions precedent. If so, the bargaining positions would be based upon a combination of the legal and economic positions.

state of the world that triggered the breach. Renegotiation would then prevent the breach of an efficient contract (if there are no costs of enforcement).

When there are legal costs of enforcing the payment of damages, an opportunistic party can extract some quasi-rents from the other party by threatening to breach even if it would not incur a loss on the contract. Renegotiation to reach a performance or monetary settlement may be better than going to court for the non-breaching party. Thus, renegotiation can occur in the context of a complete contract so that performance differs from that specified in the initial contract. However, the bargaining between the parties over the new performance obligation is still circumscribed by the legal rights and remedies under the initial contract.

In summary, a contract alters the ex post bargaining positions of the parties when there are no explicit conditions precedent to performance. The economic positions of the parties in the realized state of nature remain relevant in that they define the gains from exchange. However, the contract performance specified by the parties or by the law alters the positions of the parties if exchange fails to occur. Unless the costs of enforcement are very large, the remedies for breach of the contract replace the pure economic positions of the parties as the threat point for ex post bargaining.

6.2. *Models of incomplete contracts*

The incentive for pre-performance investments is a crucial issue in evaluating vertical integration relative to contractual exchange. Such investments widen the gains from trade by increasing the value of the exchange to the buyer, v, or decreasing the costs of production to the seller, c.

Tirole (1986) discusses the pre-performance investment problem. The seller's costs of performance in the second period decline with an investment in the first period and depend upon a random variable which he learns at the beginning of the second period. The value of the exchange cannot be enhanced by investments on the part of the buyer, and thus it depends only upon a random variable which he learns at the beginning of the second period.

Vertical integration might be thought of as the symmetric information complete contract in which the seller chooses the level of investment which maximizes the discounted expected net value of exchange in the second period minus the cost of investment in the first period. Since only the ex post efficient exchanges are consummated in the second period, performance in various states of nature need not be specified in the first period. Williamson (1975) calls such a process "adaptive sequential decision making". In this sense, vertical integration avoids advance specification of any contingencies.

Tirole then focuses upon the short-term contractual alternative. At the beginning of the first period, the buyer and seller cannot contract on the price in the second period. However, if the investment is observable and verifiable, they can contract on the level of investment and its financing. The price is then determined by bargaining in the second period subject to the private information of the parties.[34] Thus, the contract is incomplete in the sense that it does not specify price or performance in the second period. There is not even an agreement to agree since the bargaining process need not result in an exchange (and surely not if costs c exceed the value v). The buyer can only bargain for the investment by the seller in the first period.

Tirole finds that the investment contracted for need not be less than the optimal level of investment. The buyer may bargain for overinvestment by the seller because the resulting cost reduction can soften the seller's behavior in the second period bargaining process.[35] Thus, if vertical integration is interpreted as the symmetric information complete contract, the investment under the short-term contract is non-optimal and may actually exceed the investment under vertical integration.

It is surely inappropriate to interpret Tirole's symmetric information complete contract as vertical integration. As such, vertical integration allows full use of all the information of both the buyer and the seller in the second period. Instead, vertical integration might be defined as one party choosing both the level of investment in the first period, and whether exchange takes place in the second period. However, in deciding whether exchange takes place, the integrating party would not have access to the other party's private information. Vertical integration would only enable him to structure incentives for obtaining private information. This would capture the notion of a long-term relationship without assuming the acquisition of information. Since some probability of an inefficient exchange would then exist, the investment could be non-optimal under vertical integration.

Tirole does not examine long-term contracts for which the price in the second period is contracted in the first period. This limits what can be inferred about vertical integration because long-term contracts are the best alternative to vertical integration. Hart and Moore (1988) focus upon such a contract and allow renegotiation in light of the right to breach and pay damages. At the beginning of the first period, the buyer and seller agree to a contract price for exchange in the second period. The buyer and seller can then take actions such as investments in the first period which will respectively increase the value v or reduce the cost c of

[34] If investment is unobservable and thus non-contractable, a weak assumption on the bargaining process implies that the seller will choose a level of investment less than the optimal level chosen under vertical integration. The bargaining solution prevents the seller from reaping the full reward of his investment activity.

[35] With symmetric information, efficient bargaining in the second period enables the buyer to contract for the optimal investment in the first period.

the exchange. However, these investments are not observable and thus cannot be contracted for themselves. As a result, Hart and Moore do not examine vertical integration which would have an impact upon these investments.[36]

The state of nature is realized at the beginning of the second period revealing the value and the cost to both the buyer and seller. Renegotiation then occurs to prevent one party from breaching if the exchange is efficient, i.e. $v > c$. The compensation to the party who would breach under the contract price is increased to make him just willing to make the exchange. The other party than absorbs the surplus $v - c$ of the exchange. Note that this particular bargaining solution is only triggered by the certainty of breach. As such, it implicitly assumes that specific enforcement of the contract is costless. Thus, there is no real opportunistic bargaining in the second period. However, this division of surplus in the second period still produces too little investment in the first period.[37]

Hart and Moore have designed their bargaining model around the existence of a long-term contract in which the contractual obligations can be costlessly enforced. Thus, the model does not capture all the bargaining issues inherent in renegotiation of a long-term contract. If there are costs of enforcement, a bargaining game of renegotiation could involve opportunistic rent extraction up to the amount of these costs. The ability of the non-breaching party to obtain specific performance upon incurring these legal costs prevents any greater rent extraction. However, money damages rather than specific performance is the typical remedy in commercial contracts not involving real estate. If the damage measure is less than the ex post net value to the non-breaching party, the potential rent extraction for the breaching party could be greater than the legal costs of enforcement.[38] Thus, even a long-term contract does not eliminate opportunistic renegotiation. However, it does place constraints upon bargaining outcomes which are different than those which exist when there is no contract.

The model of Tirole suggests directions toward defining vertical integration, while the model of Hart and Moore suggests directions toward defining long-term contracts. Grossman and Hart (1986) examine a related model in order to

[36] In a similar model, Riordan (1986) defines a contract which maximizes expected joint surplus. This contract involves a delegation scheme which may resemble how an integrated firm would function in this setting.

[37] If there is no probability that the exchange will be inefficient, a two-price long-term contract can be constructed which will generate the optimal investments. Hart and Moore do not compare the levels of investment with and without the long-term contract.

[38] Under a pure *expectation measure* of damages, the non-breaching party would receive the ex ante expected value of the bargain, $E(v) - p - I_b$ for the buyer or $p - E(c) - I_s$ for the seller. Of course, the actual damage awards by a court could deviate from these measures in that realized values or costs might be taken into account. Under a pure *reliance measure* of damages, the non-breaching party would simply receive his investment expenses. See Shavell (1984) for a discussion of damage measures.

explicitly discuss vertical integration. The two firms to an exchange can make pre-performance investments, but vertical integration is not defined in terms of control over these investments. Vertical integration is defined as control of subsequent production decisions.

The manufacturer must make his investment in the first period prior to a production decision about the quality or quantity in the second period. Similarly, the retailer must make his investment in the first period prior to a production decision about sales effort or service in the second period. Product-specific advertising is an example of an investment that might be undertaken by either the manufacturer or the retailer. There is no uncertainty or private information. Thus, without the sequencing of decisions, the manufacturer and retailer should be able to reach an efficient agreement in the first period on both investments and production decisions. However, Grossman and Hart assume that the production decisions are sufficiently complex that this complete contract is not possible.

Unlike the previous models, Grossman and Hart circumscribe the bargaining in the second period by introducing "residual rights of control" over the production decisions. In the absence of a contract in the second period, the manufacturer and the retailer each make their respective production decisions. Vertical integration is then defined as transferring these residual rights of control over the production decision exclusively to either the manufacturer or the retailer. Vertical integration does not transfer any rights to control the investments, and thus cannot directly solve the problem of inefficient investments. For this reason, their definition might be better interpreted as a contract which assigns vertical control to either the manufacturer or the retailer.

Without vertical control, the residual rights prevail. The Nash equilibrium in production decisions can then be defined for the given investments. This will be an inefficient solution in that it will not maximize joint profits. As a result, Grossman and Hart allow the production decisions to be contractable after the investments are made. The Nash equilibrium in the production decisions then becomes the threat point for a Nash bargaining outcome in those decisions. The investments in the first period are then chosen non-cooperatively in a Nash equilibrium with full recognition of the Nash bargaining outcome in the second period. Since neither firm internalizes the full incremental benefits in the second period from their investments in the first period, both firms underinvest.

With vertical control, the production decisions are vested solely with either the retailer or the manufacturer. Given the investments, the firm in control chooses both production decisions, so as to maximize his benefit as if no recontracting would occur. This choice again serves as the threat point for a Nash bargaining solution in the second period. Again, the Nash equilibrium for investments in the first period can be defined with full recognition of the Nash bargaining outcome in the second period. In general, the investments will be inefficient for the same reason as in the case of of no vertical control.

Grossman and Hart then compare these three alternatives. No vertical control is preferable when the production decision of each firm has only a small impact upon the benefits of the other firm. Vertical control by the manufacturer would result in a retail production decision which ignores the benefits to the retailer, while generating no offsetting benefits for the manufacturer. This can then produce a very inefficient investment by the retailer. In this sense, the model captures the notion of "opportunism" by the manufacturer. On the other hand, vertical control will dominate in certain circumstances. If the benefits of the retailer are relatively insensitive to either production decision, while the benefits of the manufacturer are sensitive to both production decisions, then vertical control by the manufacturer is preferable. Vertical control by the manufacturer in the second period insures a more efficient investment by the manufacturer in the first period. Either of the other alternatives could produce a very inefficient investment by the manufacturer. The analysis is identical when the roles of the retailer and the manufacturer are reversed.[39]

The model of Grossman and Hart has no long-term contracts with performance obligations. The investments are never contractable, and the production decisions are only contractable in the second period as a short-term contract. However, there is a long-term contract which allocates the rights to control the production decisions if negotiation of a short-term contract in the second period should fail. Such long-term contracts are indefinite contracts in which the terms of performance are left to be decided by the assigned party. But since the indefinite terms are chosen on the basis of self-interest rather than in good faith, these contracts have the flavor of ownership as well as control. This is the sense in which the model addresses vertical integration.

There are two reasons why this is an unusual definition of vertical integration. First, the production choices of the integrated firm merely serve as the threat point for the Nash bargaining outcome. As a result, vertical integration does not allow the integrating firm to internalize the full benefits of its choice of production variables. Moreover, this resembles renegotiation of an initial contract concerning vertical control, rather than integration. Second, the investment decisions cannot be directly affected by vertical integration. Vertical integration need not provide the direct control and information necessary to choose the optimal investments. This contrasts sharply with the transaction cost literature which views vertical integration as a means to alleviate opportunism and the resulting underinvestment. Even a neoclassical model of vertical integration would have the integrating firm exercise some control over the investments of the acquired firm in the neighboring stage. Indeed, vertical integration could occur by

[39] Note that these results are predicated upon an assumption that the investments of both firms are equally important to the outcome. If not, then vertical control by the firm whose investment is most important would generally be preferable.

having a third party owning the upstream and downstream subsidiaries but involving itself only in the investment decisions of these subsidiaries. The subsidiaries would make production decisions, dealing with each other at arm's length but subject to corporate rather than market incentives.[40]

7. Vertical equilibrium

When we examine the patterns of vertical integration, we not only find differences across industries, but we also find considerable differences among firms within an industry. This section discusses some models which attempt to account for these observations. In so doing, we introduce the notion of a "vertical equilibrium".

7.1. Vertical equilibrium

Coase (1937) outlined the equilibrium condition for vertical integration by an individual firm. Transactions are integrated when the internal cost of exchange is less than the external cost of exchange, either the cost of using markets or the cost of contracting. For Coase, this first-order condition for minimizing the costs of exchange defines the optimal size of the firm.[41] However, it seems more natural to interpret the Coase condition as the first-order condition on the extent of vertical integration of the firm, with the size of the firm remaining indeterminant.

The costs and benefits of vertical integration by a given firm would in general depend upon the extent of vertical integration by other firms in the industry. This suggests that firms in the same industry need not be equally integrated into the various stages of production. A "vertical equilibrium" would define a pattern of integration in the industry such that no firm would alter its choice of the stages in which it operates. As a result, firms may sort themselves, either by integrating or by specializing in certain stages of production. When combined with the existing models of "horizontal equilibrium" (competitive, oligopolistic, or collusive), a vertical equilibrium could complete the conceptual picture of the industry.

7.2. The Young model

In the *The Wealth of Nations* (Book 1, chs. 1–3), Adam Smith (1776) introduced the concept of "division of labor" and how it is necessarily limited by the "extent

[40] This would be a multi-divisional corporate structure of the integrated firm. See Williamson (1975, 1985).

[41] The Coase tradition, viewing the theory of the firm in terms of transaction costs, is in contrast with the neoclassical tradition of defining the firm in terms of a production function.

of the market". The insight of Smith is that a greater quantity of production will enable and induce a greater refinement of tasks within the firm. The growth in demand for a firm's product stimulates specialization by workers in that each worker performs fewer of the tasks required to produce the good. This reinvestment and specialization of tasks allows a greater quantity to be produced in a shorter time with less labor. Each worker becomes more skilled at this task and avoids losing time from switching tasks. Moreover, specialization stimulates each worker to devise better methods of performing his task. These new methods generally involve the application of machinery. In these ways, Smith argues that the division of labor is an important source of industrial progress.

Young (1928) agrees that growth in demand generates a refinement and specialization of tasks within the firm. However, he points out that the division of labor also applies to the development and production of machinery for the refined tasks. Thus, he argues that industrial progress arises both from applying specialized machinery to the refined tasks within the firm and from refining and specializing the tasks in the production of the machinery itself.

Vassilakis (1986) attempts to capture the Young story with a vertical equilibrium model. The final good can be produced from any one of a continuum of intermediate goods indexed by $v > 0$. Production "roundaboutness" is represented by higher v, and has implications for both labor cost and productivity. More roundabout production involves higher fixed costs of labor, $\gamma(v)$, where $\gamma'(v) > 0$, but lower marginal costs of labor, $c(v)$, where $c'(v) < 0$. The fixed costs increase as labor is employed to build new equipment, but the marginal costs of producing the intermediate good are lower because the new equipment requires less labor to operate. In addition, an intermediate good with a higher index may be more effective in producing the final good. If $\delta(v)$ is the number of units of the intermediate good v required to produce one unit of the final good, fewer units are required when production is more roundabout, i.e. $\delta'(v) \leq 0$.

The model has a fixed number of firms, each endowed with a unit of labor. The "specialist firms" are downstream firms which produce the final good from purchased units of whatever intermediate good is offered. Integrated firms produce the intermediate good both for sale to the specialist downstream firms and for production of the final good by their own downstream subsidiaries. Given final demand, general equilibrium in the labor and intermediate markets generates an equilibrium degree of production roundaboutness. This determines the boundary between the two stages of production. When the equilibrium wage rate is high relative to the equilibrium price of the intermediate good, production becomes more roundabout as labor is employed to create new equipment and thereby reduce the labor operating costs of producing the final good. The equilibrium number of integrated firms is then determined by the tradeoff between economies of scale in the production of the intermediate good and imperfectly competitive behavior by the integrated firms in the market for the intermediate good. If there were only a few integrated firms, the intermediate good price would be high making these firms very profitable. Entry would then occur by downstream firms integrating into the production of the intermediate good, both to supply their own downstream production (avoiding the oligopoly markup) and to profit from sales to the remaining specialist downstream firms. Thus, the sorting of firms is determined simply by the relative profitability of being integrated or being specialized. With a larger economy (a larger number of firms/agents), the fixed labor costs and imperfect competition become less relevant. Thus, the degree of roundaboutness and the ratio of downstream to integrated firms both increase.

The model of Vassilakis is very intriguing, but it has some conceptual limitations. First, it only determines the boundary between two stages of production. As such, it does not have the full flavor of the Young story in which industrial progress results in *more* stages of production, i.e. a refinement of the producers' goods industries. This problem could be remedied by having a series of these models generating differing types of downstream firms using different intermediate goods. But this raises a second issue. A downstream firm which uses an intermediate product from a more roundabout production process is not more integrated itself because it is not really performing any of the intermediate stages. Thus, even if there were different types of downstream firms, this could not naturally be interpreted as differing degrees of integration. There would remain only one type of integrated firm. Finally, there would still be no specialized upstream firms, only integrated firms and specialized downstream firms. Once a firm is producing the intermediate good, there is no disadvantage of then producing the final good.

7.3. The Stigler model

The classic paper by Stigler (1951) not only provided the first review of the literature on vertical integration, but also introduced a novel theory of vertical disintegration in growing industries. Applying Adam Smith's theorem that the division of labor is limited by the extent of the market, Stigler first argued that infant industries would be composed of integrated firms because the level of production at any one stage is too small to support specialized firms and intermediate markets. However, as demand grows for the final good of the industry, stages subject to increasing returns would be spun off. At first there would be monopoly in these stages, but with continued industry growth, oligopoly and then competition would arise. Specialization drives vertical disintegration as the industry matures. Conversely, vertical integration would occur in declining industries. Stigler clearly envisioned a vertical equilibrium intertwined with the horizontal equilibria at each stage of production. Moreover, the vertical equilibrium is derived from the production technology at the two stages, and not the exchange technology between them.

The Stigler model is concerned with the impact of industry growth upon the industry equilibrium. In contrast, it has been commonly argued that individual firms integrate when they have grown sufficiently at their primary stage in order to capture the scale economies at neighboring stages. This scenario implicitly requires that the diseconomies of scale at the primary stage be relatively minor, and that there be at least some economies of integration between the stages. To the extent that firm growth results from industry growth, the prediction of integration is in sharp contrast with the Stigler model. However, our interest in the Stigler model stems from the fact that it explicitly attempts to consider the interactions with other firms.

The difficulty with the Stigler model occurs from trying to capture the notion of specialization. If specialization means only that the production process of the upstream stage is subject to economies of scale, then the vertical equilibrium will degenerate irrespective of the size of the industry. As soon as demand has grown to the point that two downstream firms are more efficient than one, the upstream stage would be spun off. Vertical disintegration would prevail thereafter. Economies of synchronization could prevent this degeneracy, but Stigler assumes none.

This does not mean that the upstream stage could immediately set the monopoly price because downstream firms still have the option to reintegrate. Thus, the upstream monopolist would set a limit price. Further growth in demand would generally cause the input price to decline. First, demand could shift outward such that the monopoly price fell below the limit price. Second, even if the monopoly price remained above the limit price, the upstream stage could become so profitable as to induce entry of a second firm. The duopolists could charge the limit price or some equilibrium price less than the limit price. Thus, the only issue raised by growth in demand is the exact nature of the free entry equilibrium in the upstream stage, i.e. the price and number of firms.

An alternative view of specialization is that there are economies from doing a limited set of activities, rather than economies of scale from simply doing a lot of any one activity. These notions are inversely related if the firm is fixed in overall size, but they are distinct when we are explicitly discussing the size and boundaries of the firm. Specialization would mean diseconomies of scope across vertically related production processes.[42] Thus, both economies of scale and diseconomies of vertical scope would be necessary to generate large specialized firms as suggested by Adam Smith.

[42] Baumol, Panzar and Willig (1982) have discussed the difference and relationship between economies of scale and scope in the context of production processes which are not vertically related. With both types of economies, large diversified firms would arise.

Perry and Groff (1982) have constructed a model which resembles the verbal model of Stigler. The model avoids the degeneracy inherent in defining specialization as economies of scale. However, it does not possess true diseconomies of vertical scope. In particular, it is not more costly for a given firm to operate in both stages rather than operate in each stage separately. However, the notion of specialization is captured in a related, though ad hoc, fashion. Each firm is endowed with a separate cost function for each stage, but firms which are more efficient (lower costs at any output) in upstream production are less efficient in downstream production. In upstream production, there is a constant marginal cost for all firms, but the more efficient firms have a lower fixed cost. In downstream production, firms have linear rising marginal costs (and no fixed costs), but the marginal costs of more efficient firms rise more slowly. Thus, as posited by Stigler, there are economies of scale in the upstream stage and diseconomies of scale in the downstream stage. But since the cost function of the integrated firm is the sum of the upstream and downstream costs, there are no diseconomies of vertical scope for a given firm.

The cost functions are defined so that the integrated firms all have the same minimum average cost. But even though all firms are equally efficient in integrated production, many firms will specialize into either upstream or downstream production based upon their relative advantage. The firms with low fixed costs become specialist firms upstream, while the firms with flatter marginal costs become specialist firms downstream. This process is driven by imperfect competition at the upstream stage. The oligopoly equilibrium among the upstream firms generates a price above marginal cost. Firms with high fixed costs in upstream production pay this price for the input and specialize in downstream production. But firms with moderate fixed costs remain integrated in order to avoid the upstream markup. Given a linear final demand, a vertical equilibrium can be defined in which firms sort themselves into upstream, integrated, or downstream firms by the profitability of each alternative.

It is not surprising that firms would sort themselves according to their relative cost advantages. But the goal is to use this simple vertical equilibrium to examine Stigler's hypothesis that growing industries will disintegrate. Perry and Groff computationally examine the comparative statics of this vertical equilibrium for shifts in the demand parameters. Indeed, the Stigler hypothesis is confirmed for one very plausible set of circumstances. If demand shifts outward horizontally around a constant intercept (by decreasing the slope parameter) and if the total number of firms increases in the same proportion, then the equilibrium integrated sector decreases so that proportionately more firms specialize in either upstream or downstream production. However, the Stigler hypothesis is not confirmed when the number of firms does not increase with demand.

There is some empirical evidence in support of the Stigler model. Levy (1984) examined Census data for 38 industries from 1963, 1967, and 1972. He found that demand growth, measured as the ratio of current to past sales, was significantly and positively related to the degree of vertical integration, measured as the ratio of value-added to sales. This is consistent with the Stigler hypothesis in that young industries are growing faster and are thus more integrated than mature industries. Tucker and Wilder (1977) examined 54 manufacturing firms using an adjusted value-added to sales ratio and found a U-shaped relationship of vertical integration to the age of the firm. This is consistent with the Stigler hypothesis if the reason why firms are young (old) is that they are in industries which are young (old) and thus have low demand. On the other hand, Stuckey (1983) argues that the increased forward integration by aluminum refiners into fabrications during 1955–78 is inconsistent with the Stigler hypothesis in light of the general growth of the aluminum market.

7.4. Models with demand fluctuations

Perry (1984) builds upon a point made by Oi (1961) to construct a very simple vertical equilibrium. Assume that price fluctuations occur in an intermediate good market because of random exogenous net demand. Oi pointed out that when competitive buyers or sellers can respond ex post to price fluctuations, their expected profits exceed the profits they would earn at the expected price. Buyers cut their losses by reducing purchases of the input and reducing production of the final good when the input price is high; whereas, they profit by increasing input purchases and production when the input price is low. Sellers behave in the opposite fashion. Thus, both buyers and sellers can increase their profits by riding the highs and lows of the market. Even if firms were averse to fluctuating returns, that aversion would have to be very strong in order to overcome the increase in expected profits from price fluctuations. To generate the price fluctuations, Perry makes the simplifying assumption that there is an exogenous random net demand for the input. To further simplify the model, the net demand is assumed to be independent of the input price with an expected value of zero.

From the Oi insight, a buyer and seller would reduce their combined profits if they mutually agreed to exchange a fixed quantity of the input and not otherwise participate in the input market. Thus, there must be economies from the synchronization of production in order for any buyer and seller to vertically merge. These economies might be production economies from coordinating the two stages and eliminating the identity of the intermediate input. They might also arise from reductions in transaction costs as a result of not participating in the input market. Perry simply assumes that these economies augment the profits of integrated firms in the form of a fixed subsidy.

This structure can produce a vertical equilibrium in which some buyers and sellers merge together as integrated firms, while the other buyers and sellers remain independent. Assume the gains from integration are large enough to induce the first buyer and seller to merge. In the process, they respectively withdraw their stable demand and supply from the open market in the input. As a result, the random exogenous net demand becomes a relatively larger factor in the input market. This amplifies the price fluctuations and increases the expected profits of the independent buyers and sellers. Additional buyers and sellers merge until the gains from synchronization no longer dominate the expected increment in profit from riding the highs and lows of the input market. Thus, even though all buyers and sellers are identical, some will choose to vertically merge while others will remain independent. This finding is not easily reversed by generalizations such as risk aversion and costly storage.

This vertical equilibrium suggests a partial explanation of the more general observation that many industries have a fringe of specialized firms which operate at only one stage. Such firms often adopt more flexible production technologies in order to be more responsive to volatile intermediate good markets. For example, most petroleum products move through integrated channels, but the industry also contains very successful independent crude producers and gasoline retailers. Szenberg (1971) describe a similar story in his case study of the Israeli diamond industry. Although the cutting and polishing of diamonds is primarily handled by integrated firms, subcontractors are employed in the various stages partially to absorb fluctuations in demand.

Green (1974) posits a model of vertical equilibrium with an interesting contrast to the Perry model. A fluctuating exogenous demand and an inflexible price in the intermediate market causes rationing for either upstream or downstream firms. As a result, these firms would like to integrate with one another. However, Green assumes diseconomies of integration. These could arise from either diseconomies of vertical scope or diseconomies of firm size. If the rationing is severe enough, the first upstream and downstream firms will integrate despite these diseconomies. However, this amplifies the severity of the rationing for the other independent firms. This process eventually causes the other upstream and downstream firms to integrate. Thus, the vertical equilibrium is either no integration by any firms or complete integration by all firms. No internal vertical equilibrium exists.

Although there is no explanation for the fixed intermediate price, rationing makes the intermediate market unstable in an undesirable way. This is consistent with the informal stories about vertical integration being a method of avoiding the risks of using the market. Green needs diseconomies of integration so that vertical integration does not automatically arise. The intermediate market in Perry's model is also unstable. But in contrast with Green's model, this is a benefit for disintegrated firms because they can adjust their production. Moreover, Perry needs economies of integration in order to generate the vertical equilibrium.

8. Measurement and trends

8.1. Input measures

We can recognize vertical integration in the context of a specific firm. However, if vertical integration could be measured, then we could also compare firms in the same industry, compare industries with one another, or examine firms and industries over time. The literature on the measurement of vertical integration has developed separately from the theoretical literature previously discussed. The reason for this is that the theory has typically focused upon forward or backward integration by a single firm, while the measurement literature has typically focused upon broader questions concerning the trends of vertical integration.

In Section 1, vertical integration was characterized in terms of the *quantities* transferred internally by a firm operating in two stages of production. Quantity measures are feasible in some industries, the best example being the self-sufficiency ratio used to measure backward integration into crude production by petroleum refiners. However, it is frequently difficult to obtain information on the internal and market exchanges of firms. Thus, other measures have been developed using information that is publicly available. In particular, input measures based upon either capital or labor have been suggested.

Chapman and Ashton (1914) examined the textile industry in both England and other countries. They obtained data from published directories on textile firms. The manufacture of cloth was composed of two distinct stages of production: spinning and weaving. Spindles were employed in the upstream stage for spinning, and looms were employed in the downstream stage for weaving. The data consisted of the number of spindles and looms in each firm. Chapman and Ashton were then able to examine the size distributions of firms which do only spinning, do only weaving, and do both. Thus, physical capital is the measure of vertical integration.

The data indicate that there was a "typical ratio of looms to spindles". This would suggest a synchronization of the output of spindles to the input of looms. However, it is not clear that firms which combined spinning and weaving were integrated in the sense of substituting internal exchange for market exchange. The data represent the equipment stocks of firms, and not the "counts" of yarn transferred from the spinning stage to the weaving stage. Moreover, Chapman and Ashton report that "not infrequently" a combined firm would sell the output of yarn from its spinning and buy the input of yarn for its weaving. Thus, some textile firms may have been simply vertical combinations. This illustrates the potential problem of measuring vertical integration by using the extent to which firms participate in the various stages of production and distribution.

Gort (1962) measures vertical integration in terms of employment rather than equipment. Gort defines the "major" activity of a firm as the one with the most employment. "Auxiliary" activities are the other activities in neighboring stages of production or distribution. The measure of integration is the ratio of employment in auxiliary activities to total employment. From his sample of 111 manufacturing firms in 1954, he finds differences in the degree of integration across 13 manufacturing sectors. The petroleum industry stands out with two-thirds of its employment in auxiliary activities outside of refining, while all of the other sectors were below one-third. This measure has the same potential problem as an asset measure in that it does not necessarily reflect internal transfers.

The measure of quantities transferred internally is certainly the appropriate measure if we are considering vertical integration which arises from technological or transactional economies. However, it may not be an ideal measure in models based upon market imperfections. The reason is that vertical integration in these models leads to different production decisions, thereby confounding the definition with the effects. As a result, input measures can be useful in some theoretical models, as long as it is also assumed that the intermediate input is transferred internally.[43]

8.2. Measures and trends in the twentieth century

The historical discussions of the vertical integration and the growth of modern industry must often rely upon an informal assessment of the extent to which firms participate in various stages. Thorp (1924) and Crowder (1941) classified firms in major industrial groups by their "functions" or types of activities. Several of the classifications involve the combination of vertically related activities within firms. Although this work provided only a picture of U.S. industry at particular points in time, it was the predecessor to later classification schemes designed to examine trends in vertical integration.

Livesay and Porter (1969) examined over 100 major manufacturing firms and classified them according to whether they were integrated backward into the extraction of raw materials or integrated forward into wholesaling or retailing. This procedure has the problem of deciding when partial integration becomes

[43]For example, in Perry (1978c), the monopsonist who partially integrates backward by acquiring suppliers would expand production of the input from these subsidiaries and contract purchases from independent suppliers. Thus, the percentage of input usage from the subsidiaries exceeds the percentage of ownership over the suppliers of the input. It would then seem that ownership of the sources of supply is the relevant measure of integration, and that the percentage of input usage from internal sources is simply a consequence of that vertical integration. This issue is not apparent in most models because only complete integration is examined.

integration for the purpose of classification. Moreover, if the extent to which the industry is integrated is measured by the percentage of its firms which are operating in the other stages, then the impact of decisions by small firms is weighed too heavily relative to those by large firms. Livesay and Porter claim that "variations in integration levels which do exist within industry groups are not, in general, proportionate to the size of firms in the group". As such, their classifications for 6 years in the period 1899–1948 do suggest a trend toward forward integration into wholesaling for a number of manufacturing groups and a trend toward forward integration into retailing for the automobile related groups (petroleum, rubber, and transportation equipment).

Adelman (1955) proposed measuring vertical integration by the ratio of value-added to sales. Value-added equals sales less the costs of materials and intermediate inputs, or equivalently the payments to labor and capital. This measure would partially reflect the difference between integration and combination. The value-added would be the same in both cases, but the sales revenue would be larger under vertical combination because of the sales of the intermediate input. Unfortunately, vertical combination does increase the ratio as if some vertical integration had occurred.[44] But if vertical combination is not prevalent, the ratio of value-added to sales can be useful in comparing the extent of integration between similar firms in a given industry at a particular point in time (also using the same technology and facing the same factor prices). This is the primary emphasis of Adelman's research.

When used for measuring aggregate trends in vertical integration, the value-added to sales ratio has other theoretical problems.[45] However, Adelman presents some illustrative calculations for the entire manufacturing and corporate sector of the economy. He finds that the ratio exhibits no trend for vertical integration. Laffer (1969) confirms this finding for broad subsectors of manufacturing over the period 1929–65. In contrast, Tucker and Wilder (1977) find a small but statistically significant trend toward integration in the weighted ratios of 377 four-digit SIC manufacturing industries over the period 1954–72.

Maddigan (1981) objects to the characterization of vertical integration in terms of sequential stages of production. Instead, she proposes a measure derived from a Leontief input–output matrix for the U.S. economy. Each firm is classified into the various industries in which it participates. The measure of integration is then designed to increase when the firm either (1) participates in more industries

[44]Consider Adelman's example (p. 282) in which the primary producer and the manufacturer each contribute the same value-added. The manufacturer alone would have a ratio of 0.5, while the integrated manufacturer would have a ratio of 1.0. However, a simple combination of the primary producer and manufacturer would have a ratio of 0.67.

[45]Profitability is an important component of value-added, but it varies considerably over the business cycle. See Barnes (1955). To remedy this problem, Tucker and Wilder (1977) suggest an adjusted index which deletes net income and income taxes from the numerator and denominator of the ratio.

having input or output flows between each other or (2) participates in industries having greater input or output flows between themselves. Although creative, this approach cannot capture differences in integration between firms unless they operate in different sets of industries. Moreover, this approach does not allow an independent measure of integration for an entire industry. Indeed, Maddigan must use the average of the measures over the sample of firms in order to conclude that there has been some trend toward integration over the period 1947–72.

If the data were available on the quantities of internal versus external exchanges, one could construct measures of vertical integration similar to the of measures of horizontal integration [see Dirrheimer (1980)]. A vertical Herfindahl–Hirschman Index has recently been introduced into the *Vertical Restraint Guidelines* (1985) issued by the Antitrust Division of the Department of Justice. This index is simply a Herfindahl–Hirschman Index on the firms in an industry which are employing a vertical control. Some problems would arise in applying this measure to vertical integration. In particular, it may be difficult to handle partial integration or to deal with industries having multiple inputs into which firms can integrate.

8.3. Trends prior to the twentieth century

Porter and Livesay (1971) argue that vertical integration in the United States prior to the Civil War was generally backward integration by merchants into the new manufacturing industries. This thesis is based upon the observations that wealth during this period resided with the merchants and that capital markets were non-existent or very imperfect. Thus, backward integration was the source of financing for industrial development. Before examining the evidence produced by Porter and Livesay, we briefly point out that their thesis may have also been accurate in European history.

International trade virtually ceased after the fall of the Roman Empire. Saracen pirates controlled the Mediterranean while Norse raiders dominated the Atlantic coast. But beginning in the eleventh century, merchants arose in the coastal cities to resume international trade.[46] The first merchant cities were Venice on the Mediterranean and Bruges in Flanders on the Atlantic. The merchants amassed wealth from the profits on the local products exported to other lands. Thus, the development of a local extractive or manufacturing industry became an important element of the success of local merchants. For example, Venetian merchants exported wheat, wine, wood, and salt from the surrounding areas of Italy.[47] Merchants often financed the local industries in a

[46]See Pirenne (1974, p. 90).
[47]See Pirenne (1974, pp. 85–87).

form of early banking. But merchants also became more directly involved in local industries by acquiring machinery, hiring local craftsmen, and managing production.

The textile industry is replete with examples of merchants integrating into the production of export products. Local craftsmen from rural areas were attracted to the cities to produce export products. For example, the merchants of Bruges imported wool from England and produced fine woven dyed cloths for export.[48] The Venetian merchants also imported wool and then financed and supervised the production of cloth through a putting-out system. This pattern apparently continued into the sixteenth century in many parts of Western Europe. Flemish merchants continued to produce worsted yarn spun from long-staple wool, and the merchants of Lyon produced silk fabric from imported raw silk.[49]

We now turn to the historical evidence of Porter and Livesay (1971). During the early 1800s, merchants in the United States specialized in the export of specific commodities. Most notably, certain merchants specialized in the export of cotton. Although these merchants did not directly produce cotton, they usually advanced credit to the planters. Other merchants specialized in the distribution of imported textiles. Some of these merchants then financed the New England textile industry. Typically, the merchants funded the construction of the mills and engaged a British manufacturing expert to manage the operations. The merchants would then set up a selling house to distribute the textiles produced by their mills. The selling house provided working capital and took the risk of unsold production.[50]

In the iron industry, specialized merchants served as the intermediaries between the producers of pig iron located near the ore deposits and either the foundries located near cities of the rolling mills located near water power. However, prior to the Civil War, the pig iron furnaces were integrated with the rolling mills into new companies financed by the iron merchants of Pennsylvania.[51] The new companies supplied rail for the rapidly growing railroad industry, and became the forerunners of the current steel corporations.

[48]See Pirenne (1974, pp. 153–155).

[49]Silver (1984, pp. 98–103) cites several other examples.

[50]Porter and Livesay (1971) cite the example of Francis Cabot Lowell who founded the Boston Manufacturing Company in 1813 along with other Boston textile merchants. The company constructed and operated mills on the Merrimack River. Later in 1828, B.C. Ward and Company was formed as a selling house for the entire output of the mills. See also Temin (1987) for a detailed examination (with an extensive bibliography) of vertical integration in the early textile industry of both Great Britain and the United States. Temin takes issue with some transaction cost explanations of this history, and suggests that one alternative explanation for vertical integration was the existence of capital in the more mature neighboring stages of production.

[51]Coal was substituted for charcoal as fuel for the furnaces, and steam power was substituted for water power.

These and other examples lead Porter and Livesay to conclude that the vertical integration of distribution into manufacturing in early American business was a consequence of the primitive state of capital markets. Capital resided with merchants prior to the Civil War, but the investment opportunities were in the manufacturing of new products. Financial institutions such as banks and insurance companies were generally unwilling to make loans without collateral such as government bonds or real estate. With the exception of the railroads, manufacturers could not generally raise money by public offerings of securities. Thus, merchants became direct participants in the new enterprises, merging the source of investment funds with the capital collateral.

During the Civil War, manufacturers prospered and were able to end their dependence upon merchant distributors for either investment or working capital. Indeed, the profits from manufacturing in the late nineteenth century were an important source of investment funds. Porter and Livesay discuss many cases during this period in which manufacturers integrated either backward into extraction or forward into distribution (see Subsection 5.3). But the question remains to what extent this integration was determined by the need for financing. On the one hand, the nineteenth century witnessed the gradual development of capital markets and contract law.[52] These developments should have reduced the financial motive for vertical integration, in that firms could contract for independent financing. On the other hand, the case studies indicate that vertical integration did not cease and was typically initiated by the stage with the largest and most profitable firms, manufacturers or large retailers. Moreover, vertical quasi-integration developed as a form of retail financing. Thus, the importance of retained earnings as a determinant of modern vertical integration remains an intriguing question.

9. Public policy

Vertical expansion has not been generally found to be a violation of the U.S. antitrust laws. On the other hand, vertical merger has been viewed much less favorably, at least until recently. Although neither has been held to be an unreasonable restraint of trade in violation of §1 of the Sherman Act, both have been held to be exclusionary practices in monopolization cases under §2. But the primary difference in treatment arises from §7 of the Clayton Act which condemns vertical mergers that substantially lessen competition.

[52] Horwitz (1977, ch. VI) examines the symbiotic development of capital markets and contract law during the nineteenth century.

9.1. *Section 2 of the Sherman Act*

Vertical expansion by dominant firms has been condemned in a few cases as an exclusionary practice in the acquisition or maintenance of monopoly at the primary stage of production. Alcoa's pre-emptive backward integration into bauxite and electric power generation was found to be an exclusionary practice in that it created barriers to entry protecting Alcoa's monopoly at the refining stage.[53] However, no vertical divestiture was ordered. A & P was also held to have violated §2 for exclusionary practices related to its backward integration into wholesale food production and distribution.[54] A & P was said to have abused its buying power by threats to boycott suppliers or to integrate into processing. In addition, its upstream buying subsidiary discriminated against independent grocers in favor of A & P stores in supplying produce.[55] Other cases are similar to A & P in that vertical integration occurred in conjunction with exclusionary practices such as refusals to deal or price discrimination. Thus, despite *Alcoa*, vertical expansion is probably not a sufficient exclusionary practice by itself for antitrust liability under §2.

Vertical divestiture was the horizontal remedy in two major monopolization cases under §2. The Standard Oil Trust was ordered to divest in 1911.[56] The corporate members severed from the Trust were generally specialized in crude production, pipeline transportation, refining, or marketing. More recently, the Bell System has been vertically divested as a consequence of a 1982 consent decree settling the antitrust suit initiated by the Justice Department in 1972.[57] AT & T divested the Bell operating companies supplying local service but continues to supply long-distance service and produce equipment.[58]

Several cases under §2 deal with forward integration as an extension of upstream monopoly into downstream stages of distribution. The upstream monopoly may be legal or unchallenged so that the §2 violation is monopolization of the downstream stage. These cases present less deference toward vertical integration by a monopolist, but one important reason is that they involve vertical acquisitions as well as vertical expansion. An early example is Kodak's forward integration into the distribution of its photographic supplies by acquiring whole-

[53] *U.S. v. Aluminum Company of America* (2nd Circuit, 1945, 148 F.2d 416).

[54] *U.S. v. New York Great Atlantic and Pacific Tea Co.* (7th Circuit, 1949, 173 F.2d 79).

[55] Adelman (1949b) thoroughly criticizes the economic analysis employed by the Justice Department and adopted by the court. The case has also been severely criticized by legal scholars. Although A & P was the largest grocery chain, its national market share was only 10 percent. The Justice Department eventually abandoned its attempt to split A & P into seven regional grocery chains.

[56] *Standard Oil Co. of New Jersey v. U.S.* (1911, 221 U.S. 1).

[57] *U.S. v. AT & T Co.* (D.D.C., 1982, 552 F.Supp. 131).

[58] The offspring of Standard Oil partially reintegrated into the other stages [see Johnson (1976)]. Similarly, the Bell operating companies are seeking court permission to re-enter the long distance and equipment markets, and AT & T is attempting to re-enter certain types of local service.

sale houses in 1910. Kodak's tactic of discontinuing the usual wholesale discounts to an independent distributor who had refused to be acquired was held to be an illegal attempt to monopolize the distribution stage.[59]

Forward integration into exhibition by the major producers of motion pictures was challenged by the Justice Department in 1938 as a conspiracy to monopolize the distribution of feature films. The Supreme Court stated that vertical integration can violate §2 of the Sherman Act "if it was a calculated scheme to gain control over an appreciable segment of the market and to restrain or suppress competition, rather than an expansion to meet legitimate needs".[60] Other exclusionary practices against independent theaters were also examined in the case, but the key remedy ordered in 1949 was vertical divestiture.[61]

More recently, Otter Tail Power, an electric power company, was held to have violated §2 by refusing to sell power at wholesale or to transmit power from other sources to retail municipal electric systems within its territory.[62] These exclusionary practices forced over 90 percent of the municipalities to grant Otter Tail the franchise to perform retail distribution within their boundaries. Vertical divestiture was not essential because by enjoining the exclusionary practices, a municipality could acquire Otter Tail's retail distribution system when the franchise expired.

In each of these cases, a price or supply squeeze was used to either acquire or maintain a dominant position in the downstream stage. The price squeeze is a necessary consequence of forward integration to effectuate price discrimination (see Subsection 2.2). But in these Sherman Act cases, the price squeeze is viewed as a device to extend an existing upstream monopoly into a downstream stage. Bork (1978) argues that there is no additional welfare loss from the mere extension of monopoly or oligopoly into neighboring stages. Indeed, vertical integration can achieve some efficiencies. This view was reflected in a recent Court of Appeals decision which rejected a §2 challenge to forward integration by a monopoly newspaper. The Kansas City Star discontinued distributing its newspaper through independent contract carriers, and began delivering the newspaper itself. The court recognized that forward integration would eliminate the successive monopoly problem inherent in the territorial arrangements with independent carriers.[63]

The requirement of substantial market share prevents §2 from being an effective method of challenging vertical integration by firms in less concentrated

[59] *Eastman Kodak Co. of New York v. Southern Photo Materials Co.* (1927, 273 U.S. 359).

[60] *U.S. v. Paramount Pictures* (1948, 334 U.S. 131).

[61] Block booking and circuit renting were also enjoined in order to force picture-by-picture, theater-by-theater rentals. *U.S. v. Paramount Pictures* (S.D.N.Y., 1949, 85 F.Supp. 881).

[62] *Otter Tail Power Co. v. U.S.* (1973, 410 U.S. 366).

[63] *Paschall v. The Kansas City Star Co.* (8th Circuit, 1984). Note that maximum resale price maintenance, an alternative solution to the successive monopoly problem, was held to be a violation of §1 in a similar newspaper case. See *Albrecht v. Herald Co.* (1968, 390 U.S. 145).

markets. In 1946, U.S. Steel, through its West Coast subsidiary Columbia Steel, acquired Consolidated Steel, a West Coast steel fabricator with 11 percent of the regional market. The merger would have given U.S. Steel 24 percent of the regional market in fabricated steel products. The Justice Department argued that the acquisition would foreclose Consolidated's demand for rolled steel from the competitors of U.S. Steel. The Supreme Court responded that "vertical integration, as such without more, cannot be held violative of the Sherman Act".[64] The market foreclosure must "unreasonably restrict the opportunities of competitors to market their product", probably meaning it must rise to the level of monopolization.

9.2. *Section 7 of the Clayton Act*

Prior to 1950, §7 of the Clayton Act did not apply to vertical vergers. But the concern over mergers after World War II and the *Columbia Steel* limitations on the Sherman Act lead to the Celler–Kefauver amendments to §7 in that year. Vertical mergers became illegal "where in any line of commerce..., the effect of such acquisition may be substantially to lessen competition, or to tend to create a monopoly". Both of these criteria are weaker than the judicial requirements under §2 of the Sherman Act. Thus, since 1950, vertical mergers have been challenged under the Clayton Act rather than the Sherman Act.

The predominant legal theory employed to challenge vertical mergers is market foreclosure.[65] Under the market foreclosure theory, vertical merger harms competition in both stages by denying competitors access either to one of their suppliers or to one of their buyers. Market foreclosure was employed in the three major vertical merger cases to reach the Supreme Court after 1950.

The Court condemned the 23 percent stock interest that duPont had held in General Motors since 1919.[66] During the 1950s, General Motors manufactured about 50 percent of the automobiles in the domestic market, while duPont supplied as much as two-thirds of the finishes and half of the fabrics used by General Motors. Thus, the actual foreclosure was significant. This was not true for the acquisition of Kinney by Brown Shoe in 1955. Brown Shoe accounted for only 5 percent of the domestic shoe production, while Kinney's chain of family shoe stores accounted for only 1 percent of the domestic shoe sales. A trend toward vertical integration and foreclosure were employed by the Court to condemn this merger.[67] Finally, foreclosure was a consideration in condemning

[64] *U.S. v. Columbia Steel Co.* (1948, 334 U.S. 495).
[65] Adelman (1949a) has a nice discussion of the early antitrust fallacies concerning vertical integration.
[66] *U.S. v. E.I. duPont de Nemours & Co.* (1957, 353 U.S. 586).
[67] *Brown Shoe Co. v. U.S.* (1962, 370 U.S. 294).

Ford's acquisition of Electric Autolite, a spark plug manufacturer, in 1961.[68] Ford had 25 percent of the domestic automobile market, while Electric Autolite manufactured 15 percent of the domestic spark plugs.

In the late 1960s and early 1970s, the Federal Trade Commission employed §7 to block or dissolve a number of vertical acquisitions of ready-mix concrete firms by cement manufacturers. In 1966, an FTC staff report argued that these vertical acquisitions foreclosed markets and caused a "chain reaction" of defensive vertical mergers. The effect of these vertical mergers was to increase the barriers to entry and concentration in the cement industry.[69] The numerous comments on the FTC report focused upon the excess capacity in the cement industry as the key factor explaining the subsequent forward integration.[70] This excess capacity arose not from the construction of more plants having the same size and efficiency, but rather from the construction of larger plants which reduced the average cost per barrel by at least 50 percent [see Peck and McGowen (1967)]. Between 1950 and 1964, the demand for cement much less than doubled while the minimum efficient scale of a cement plant at least tripled. This suggests a rationalization of the cement industry in which vertical acquisition was employed by new efficient firms to hasten the inevitable trend and by old inefficient firms in a futile attempt to prevent it. If so, the vertical acquisitions were a substitute for price competition in reducing the market share of smaller inefficient plants, and should have had no long-run efficiency or strategic significance.[71] Similarly, McBride (1983) has argued that the vertical acquisitions and foreclosure were non-price competition strategically designed to increase capacity utilization and market share in the short run while postponing price competition among the cement oligopolists.[72]

The original Department of Justice *Merger Guidelines* (1968) incorporated the foreclosure theory, but not to the extent of the *Brown Shoe* case. The *Guidelines* suggested that vertical mergers between an upstream firm with more than 10 percent of its market and a downstream firm with more than 6 percent of its market would be challenged by the government. However, the foreclosure theory has been strongly criticized by both economists and lawyers.[73] The basic point is that vertical foreclosure is a definition rather than a theory. Since vertical

[68] *Ford Motor Co. v. U.S.* (1972, 405 U.S. 562).

[69] See Mueller (1969). Whalen (1969) questioned this strategic theory of vertical foreclosure because of the ease of entry into the production of ready-mix concrete. Allen (1971) questioned the profitability of vertical foreclosure by the cement manufacturers.

[70] Peck and McGowen (1967) argued that forward integration by cement manufacturers was a natural investment opportunity given the excess capacity and a falling rate of return on cement during the early 1960s. Wilk (1968) pointed out that excess capacity would only explain why cement manufacturers did not reinvest in their own stage of production.

[71] Inefficiencies could arise in the short-run if the cement manufacturers with suboptimal size plants were able to survive longer as a result of vertical acquisitions.

[72] McBride provides some empirical evidence of short-run rigidity in the price of cement.

[73] See Comanor (1967), Peltzman (1969), and Bork (1978).

integration is the substitution of internal exchange for market or contractual exchange, foreclosure would naturally occur if either partner dealt with other firms prior to the merger. This and other criticisms have made an impact on recent decisions in some Circuit Courts of Appeal. For example, the Second Circuit refused to enforce an FTC divestiture order of Fruehauf, the largest manufacturer of truck trailers with 25 percent of the market, from Kelsey-Hayes which had 15 percent of the market for truck and trailer wheels.[74] The court rejected the foreclosure theory absent very high market concentration in one of the two stages.

Criticism of the foreclosure theory has also resulted in a change in enforcement policy by the Department of Justice. Under Assistant Attorney General William Baxter, the Antitrust Division of the Department of Justice revised its *Merger Guidelines* in 1982 and abandoned the market foreclosure theory. Bork (1978), Posner (1976), Baxter, and others have argued that vertical mergers often generate important efficiencies and can present no competitive problem unless one stage is highly concentrated. The current *Merger Guidelines* (1984) now reflect this approach. The Department is unlikely to challenge the vertical merger by a firm unless its stage of the industry has a Herfindahl–Hirschman Index above 1800. Even then, the Department may decline to challenge a vertical merger when there is evidence of substantial economies such as better coordination of production and distribution.

The *Guidelines* also fail to recognize a merger "trend" as being relevant for challenging any given vertical merger in an industry. The legislative history and language of §7 demonstrate some concern about industry trends, i.e. the issue of "incipient" monopoly. Moreover, a perceived trend of vertical mergers was an important factor in condemning the merger in the *Brown Shoe* case and the mergers in the cement industry. Although it may be difficult to incorporate such considerations into the *Guidelines*, it does seem that there is a valid economic concern. The first firms to integrate into neighboring stages reduce the number of alternative sources for other firms at either stage. This "thinning" of the market can increase the costs of market or contractual exchange (see Subsection 2.3). Subsequent integration by other firms then becomes more likely. This raises two issues. First, it may be inaccurate to formulate public policy from economic theories that focus only upon the production, exchange, or market problems of a particular buyer and seller. Second, the private incentives for vertical merger may not generate a vertical industry structure which is socially optimal. This is another reason why research on vertical equilibrium should be enlightening (see Section 7).

[74]The actual foreclosure of this merger was less than 6 percent. *Fruehauf Corp. v. FTC* (2nd Circuit, 1979, 603 F.2d 345).

The *Guidelines* have clearly reduced the likelihood of a Justice Department challenge to a vertical merger. For example, the 1981 vertical merger of the chemical company duPont and the petroleum company Conoco would not have been challenged under the *Guidelines*. Unlike the 1950s and 1960s, current vertical merger enforcement is much closer to the deference accorded vertical expansion. However, the standards articulated in the *Guidlines* have not been incorporated into court decisions to narrow the existing precedents under §7.[75] The *Ford Motor* case remains the relevant precedent. In that case, the Supreme Court condemned Ford's acquisition of Electric Autolite on the basis that it would increase barriers to entry in the spark plug industry and eliminate Ford as a major potential entrant. Even though the automobile market was concentrated, it seems unlikely that this merger would have triggered the criteria for challenge under the *Guidelines*.

The *Guidelines* do recognize three major competitive problems of vertical mergers in concentrated industries. First, forward mergers into retailing may facilitate collusion at the manufacturing stage by making it easier to monitor prices or by eliminating a "disruptive buyer". Second, vertical mergers may enhance barriers to entry into the primary industry if entrants must operate at both stages in order to be competitive with existing firms and if entry at both stages is substantially more difficult than entry at one stage. Finally, vertical mergers may have an adverse competitive impact by eliminating specific potential entrants who could integrate by vertical expansion rather than merger. Each of these avenues of challenge are further circumscribed by market structure conditions which narrow their force.

9.3. Public policy in the United Kingdom and the European Economic Community

Similar to U.S. antitrust law, European "competition" law makes a distinction between vertical expansion and vertical merger. We illustrate the parallels with a brief discussion of the United Kingdom (U.K.) and the European Economic Community (EEC). The discussion relies heavily upon Merkin and Williams (1984).[76]

In the United Kingdom, complaints about violations of the competition laws are investigated by the Office of Fair Trading (OFT). The Director General of the

[75]Private parties can challenge vertical mergers but they must also prove a private injury (for damages) or a threat of private injury (for an injunction). Moreover, the private injury must be of the type which the antitrust laws were designed to prevent and which flows from the anticompetitive consequences of the merger. These requirements limit the ability of private parties to challenge mergers which would have anticompetitive consequences for consumers. See *Brunswick Corp. v. Pueblo Bowl-O-Mat, Inc.* (1977, 429 U.S. 477) and *Cargill, Inc. v. Monfort of Colorado, Inc.* (1986, 479 U.S. 104).

[76]See also Korah (1982).

OFT may then refer a case to the Monopolies and Mergers Commission (MMC) which has the responsibility for evaluating monopolies, mergers, and most vertical practices.[77] The MMC employs a "public interest" standard to promote price and non-price competition. The non-price considerations include product quality and variety, the development of new techniques and products, and entry. The MMC will report to the Secretary of State (Department of Trade and Industry) on whether the laws were violated and will make recommendations concerning the remedies which should be sought.

In the European Economic Community, competition law arises from Articles 85 and 86 of the Treaty of Rome creating the EEC in 1957. Vertical integration is covered by Article 86 which prohibits "abuse of a dominant position".[78] The European Commission is the executive body of the EEC, and the administration of competition policy is implemented by one of its departments (Directorates-General IV). The DG IV investigates possible violations, and the Commission can issue cease and desist orders or impose fines. The firms subject to these penalties can then appeal to the European Court of Justice.

In the U.K., vertical expansion by a dominant firm has been challenged when it results from a vertical price or supply squeeze. The MMC carefully investigated the complaints of independent bakers concerning a price squeeze by the dominant millers of flour. The millers were forward integrated into baking, but the MMC found no proof of a squeeze designed to increase the market share of their baking subsidiaries.[79] In a similar case, the MMC investigated British Oxygen, the dominant manufacturer of machinery used to produce oxygen. British Oxygen was forward integrated into the production of oxygen, and the MMC criticized the company for limiting the supply of machinery available to independent producers of oxygen.[80]

In the EEC, vertical expansion has been condemned if it results from a refusal to deal. Commercial Solvents Corporation (CSC) had a dominant position in the world production of aminobutanol, an input in the production of certain drugs. Zoja manufactured ethambutol from aminobutanol, and had purchased the latter from CSC until switching suppliers in 1970. CSC unsuccessfully attempted to takeover Zoja, and thereafter began producing ethambutol itself. When Zoja lost its alternative sources of aminobutanol, CSC refused to sell the input to Zoja. The European Court of Justice held that this was an abusive practice in violation

[77]The Fair Trading Act of 1973 vests jurisdiction over monopolies and mergers, while the Competition Act of 1980 vests jurisdiction over most vertical practices. Horizontal agreements and resale price maintenance are referred to the Restrictive Practices Court.

[78]Article 85 is concerned with horizontal agreements and practices.

[79]*Flour and Bread (1976–77)* H.C. 412.

[80]Procedural reasons prevented the MMC from recommending remedial measures. *Industrial and Medical Gases (1956–57)* H.C. 13.

of Article 86.[81] In a related case, a manufacturer of cash registers refused to supply spare parts for its products to an independent service firm. The Advocate General, an assistant to the Court, agreed with the Commission that this practice was abusive. However, the Court expressed no opinion on this substantive issue after finding that interstate trade was not affected, as required by Article 86.[82] These cases suggest that vertical expansion is clearly not sufficient to violate the competition laws unless it also involves practices designed to disadvantage or exclude competitors. This is similar to the prevailing view of vertical expansion in the United States under §2 of the Sherman Act. Vertical integration is not illegal itself, but rather it provides an opportunity and maybe an incentive for other practices deemed undesirable.

European competition law with respect to vertical mergers is less developed and apparently less controversial than in the United States. Indeed, in the EEC, it is unresolved whether vertical mergers are subject to Article 86.[83] In the U.K., OFT investigations of vertical mergers typically examine the issue of foreclosure. However, the MMC has recognized the weaknesses of the foreclosure theory and has not employed it to condemn vertical mergers. Berisford, the dominant distributor of sugar in the U.K., proposed to acquire British Sugar, the leading U.K. producer of sugar. Tate and Lyle, the only other producer of sugar, objected to the possible foreclosure of its distribution channel. The MMC approved the merger, but subject to the condition that Berisford continue to distribute Tate and Lyle products.[84]

The MMC has rejected a vertical merger on the grounds that it would eliminate a potential entrant into R&D. Boots, a pharmaceutical company with an R&D laboratory, attempted to acquire Glaxo Group, a pharmaceutical manufacturer with a major R&D laboratory. This was viewed as a backward merger, and was disallowed by the MMC on the grounds that Boots might develop its own R&D capability.[85] Since this case also reflects a strong interest in encouraging R&D in the U.K., it is not clear that it reflects a strong precedent for challenging other types of vertical mergers. However, the focus upon potential competition, rather than foreclosure, is similar to the modern analysis of vertical mergers in the United States.

[81] *Instituto Chemioterapico Italiano and Commercial Solvents v. Commission*. Cases 6 and 7/73 (1974) E.C.R. 707.

[82] *Hugin Kassaregister v. Commission*. Case 22/78 (1979) E.C.R. 1869. In the U.K., an identical practice was prevented by an OFT investigation. A manufacturer of catering equipment had refused to supply independent service firms with spare parts for its equipment. See *Still* (OFT, July 1982).

[83] The European Court of Justice has held that horizontal mergers are subject to Article 86. See *Europembellage and Continental Can Co. v. Commission*. Case 6/72 (1972) E.C.R. 157.

[84] *Berisford Ltd. and British Sugar Corporation Ltd. (1980–81)* H.C. 241.

[85] *The Boots Company Ltd. and Glaxo Group Ltd. (1971–72)* H.C. 341.

References

Adelman, M.A. (1949a) 'Integration and antitrust policy', *Harvard Law Review*, 63:27–77.
Adelman, M.A. (1949b) 'The A & P case: A study in applied economic theory', *Quarterly Journal of Economics*, 63:238–257.
Adelman, M.A. (1955) 'Concept and statistical measurement of vertical integration', in: G.J. Stigler, ed., *Business concentration and price policy*. Princeton, N.J.: Princeton University Press.
Alchian, A.A. and Demsetz, H. (1972) 'Production, information costs, and economic organization', *American Economic Review*, 62:777–795.
Allen, B.T. (1971) 'Vertical integration and market foreclosure: The case of cement and concrete', *Journal of Law and Economics*, 14:251–274.
Anderson, E. and Schmittlein, D. (1984) 'Integration of the sales force: An empirical examination', *The Rand Journal of Economics*, 15:385–395.
Areeda, P. (1981) *Antitrust analysis*. Boston: Little, Brown and Company.
Armour, H.O. and Teece, D.J. (1980) 'Vertical integration and technological innovations', *Review of Economics and Statistics*, 62:490–494.
Arrow, K.J. (1975) 'Vertical integration and communication', *Bell Journal of Economics*, 6:173–183.
Bain, J.S. (1956) *Barriers to new competition*. Cambridge, Mass.: Harvard University Press.
Barnes, I.R. (1955) 'Concept and statistical measurement of vertical integration: Comment', in: G.J. Stigler, ed., *Business concentration and price policy*. Princeton, N.J.: Princeton University Press.
Baumol, W.J., Panzar, J.C. and Willig, R.D. (1982) *Contestable markets and the theory of industry structure*. New York: Harcourt Brace Jovanovitch.
Bernhardt, I. (1977) 'Vertical integration and demand variability', *Journal of Industrial Economics*, 25:213–229.
Blair, R.D. and Kaserman, D.L. (1978) 'Vertical integration, tying, and antitrust policy', *American Economic Review*, 68:397–402.
Blair, R.D. and Kaserman, D.L. (1983) *Law and economics of vertical integration and control*. New York: Academic.
Blois, K.J. (1972) 'Vertical quasi-integration', *Journal of Industrial Economics*, 20:253–272.
Bork, R. (1978) *The antitrust paradox*. New York: Basic Books.
Burstein, M. (1960) 'The economics of tie-in sales', *Review of Economics and Statistics*, 42:68–73.
Buzzell, R.D. (1983) 'Is vertical integration profitable?', *Harvard Business Review*, 61:92–102.
Calamari, J.D. and Perillo, J.M. (1977) *Contracts*. St. Paul, Minn.: West Publishing.
Carlton, D.W. (1979) 'Vertical integration in competitive markets under uncertainty', *Journal of Industrial Economics*, 27:189–209.
Carlton, D.W. and Perloff, J.M. (1981) 'Price discrimination, vertical integration and divestiture in natural resource markets', *Resources and Energy*, 3:1–11.
Chandler, A.D. (1977) *The visible hand: The managerial revolution in American business*. Cambridge, Mass.: Harvard University Press.
Chapman, S.J. and Ashton, T.S. (1914). 'The sizes of businesses, mainly in the textile industries', *Journal of the Royal Statistical Society*, 77:469–549.
Cheung, S.N.S. (1983) 'The contractual nature of the firm', *Journal of Law and Economics*, 26:1–21.
Cipolla, C.M. (1980) *Before the industrial revolution: European society and economy*, 1000–1700. New York: Norton.
Coase, R. (1937) 'The nature of the firm', *Economica*, 4:386–405.
Comanor, W.S. (1967) 'Vertical mergers, market power, and the antitrust laws', *American Economic Review*, 57:254–265.
Crandall, R. (1968) 'Vertical integration and the market for repair parts in the United States automobile industry', *Journal of Industrial Economics*, 16:212–234.
Crocker, K.J. (1983) 'Vertical integration and the strategic use of private information', *Bell Journal of Economics*, 14:236–248.
Crowder, W.F. (1941) *The integration of manufacturing operations*. Washington, D.C.: T.N.E.C. monograph no. 27.
deChazeau, M.G. and Kahn, A.E. (1959) *Integration and competition in the petroleum industry*. New Haven: Yale University Press.

Department of Justice, Antitrust Division (1984) 'Merger guidelines', in: M. Handler, H.M. Blake, R. Pitofsky and H.J. Goldschmid, eds., *Trade regulation, 1985 supplement*. Mineola, N.Y.: Foundation Press.

Department of Justice, Antitrust Division (1985) 'Vertical restraint guidelines', in: M. Handler, H.M. Blake, R. Pitofsky and H.J. Goldschmid, eds., *Trade regulation, 1985 supplement*. Mineola, N.Y.: Foundation Press.

Dirrheimer, M.J. (1980) 'Vertical integration: Transaction cost advantages versus market power disadvantages', International Institute of Management, Berlin.

Dixit, A. (1983) 'Vertical integration in a monopolistically competitive industry', *International Journal of Industrial Organization*, 1:63–78.

Dixit, A. and Stiglitz, J.E. (1977) 'Monopolistic competition and optimum product diversity', *American Economic Review*, 67:297–308.

Evans, D.S. and Grossman, S.J. (1983) 'Integration', in: D.S. Evans, ed., *Breaking up Bell*. New York: North-Holland.

Federal Trade Commission (1966) *Economic report on mergers and vertical integration in the cement industry*. Washington: U.S. Government Printing Office.

Fellner, W. (1947) 'Prices and wages under bilateral monopoly', *Quarterly Journal of Economics*, 61:503–509.

Flaherty, M.T. (1981) 'Prices versus quantities and vertical financial integration,' *Bell Journal of Economics*, 12:507–525.

Goldberg, V.P. (1976) 'Regulation and administered contracts', *Bell Journal of Economics*, 7:426–448.

Goldberg, V.P. and Erickson, J.R. (1987) 'Quantity and price adjustment in long term contracts: A case study of petroleum coke', *Journal of Law and Economics*, 30:369–398.

Gort, M. (1962) *Diversification and integration in American industry*. Princeton, N.J.: Princeton University Press.

Gould, J.R. (1977) 'Price discrimination and vertical control: A note', *Journal of Political Economy*, 85:1063–1071.

Green, J.R. (1974) 'Vertical integration and assurance of markets', discussion paper no. 383, Harvard Institute of Economic Research.

Greenhut, M.L. and Ohta, H. (1976) 'Related market conditions and interindustrial mergers', *American Economic Review*, 66:267–277.

Greenhut, M.L. and Ohta, H. (1978) 'Related market conditions and interindustrial mergers: Reply', *American Economic Review*, 68:228–230.

Greenhut, M.L. and Ohta, H. (1979) 'Vertical integration of successive monopolists', *American Economic Review*, 69:137–141.

Grossman, S.J. and Hart, O.D. (1986) 'The costs and benefits of ownership: A theory of vertical and lateral integration', *Journal of Political Economy*, 94:691–719.

Gunther, G. (1980) *Cases and materials on constitutional law*. Mineola, N.Y.: Foundation Press.

Hale, R.D. (1967) 'Cookware: A study in vertical integration', *Journal of Law and Economics*, 10:169–179.

Handler, M., Blake, H.M., Pitofsky, R. and Goldschmid, H.J. (1983) *Trade regulation*. Mineola, N.Y.: Foundation Press.

Haring, J.R. and Kaserman, D.L. (1978) 'Related market conditions and interindustrial mergers: Comment', *American Economic Review*, 68:225–227.

Hart, O. and Holmstrom, B. (1986) 'The theory of contracts', in: T. Bewley, ed., *Advances in Economic Theory*. Cambridge University Press.

Hart, O. and Moore, J. (1988) 'Incomplete contracts and renegotiation', *Econometrica*, 56:755–785.

Hay, G. (1973) 'An economic analysis of vertical integration', *Industrial Organization Review*, 1:188–198.

Helfat, C.E. and Teece, D.J. (1987) 'Vertical integration and risk reduction', *Journal of Law, Economics, and Organization*, 3:47–67.

Horwitz, M.J. (1977) *The transformation of American law, 1780–1860*. Cambridge, Mass.: Harvard University Press.

Hovenkamp, H. (1985) *Economics and federal antitrust law*. St. Paul, Minn.: West Publishing.

Johnson, A.M. (1976) 'Lessons of the Standard Oil divestiture', in: E.J. Mitchell, ed., *Vertical integration in the oil industry*. Washington, D.C.: American Enterprise Institute.

Joskow, P.L. (1985) 'Vertical integration and long-term contracts: The case of coal-burning electric generating plants', *Journal of Law, Economics, and Organization*, 1:33–80.

Kaserman, D.L. (1978) 'Theories of vertical integration: Implications for antitrust policy', *Antitrust Bulletin*, 23:483–510.

Katz, M.L. (1987) 'The welfare effects of third degree price discrimination in intermediate good markets', *American Economic Review*, 77:154–167.

Klein, B., Crawford, R.G. and Alchian, A.A. (1978) 'Vertical integration, appropriable rents, and the competitive contracting process', *Journal of Law and Economics*, 21:297–326.

Korah, V. (1982) *Competition law of Britain and the Common Market*. The Hague: Martinus Nijhoff Publishers.

Laffer, A.B. (1969) 'Vertical integration by corporations: 1929–1965', *Review of Economics and Statistics*, 51:91–93.

Laffont, J.J. (1976) 'More on prices vs. quantities', *Review of Economic Studies*, 43:177–182.

Levin, R.C. (1981) 'Vertical integration and profitability in the oil industry', *Journal of Economic Behavior and Organization*, 2:215–235.

Levy, D.T. (1984) 'Testing Stigler's interpretation of "The division of labor is limited by the extent of the market"', *Journal of Industrial Economics*, 32:377–389.

Levy, D.T. (1985) 'The transactions cost approach to vertical integration: An empirical examination', *Review of Economics and Statistics*, 67:438–445.

Livesay, H.C. and Porter, P. (1969) 'Vertical integration in American manufacturing', *Journal of Economic History*, 29:494–500.

Machlup, F. and Taber, M. (1960) 'Bilateral monopoly, successive monopoly, and vertical integration', *Economica*, 27:101–119.

Maddigan, R.J. (1981) 'The measurement of vertical integration', *Review of Economics and Statistics*, 63:328–335.

Mallela, P. and Nahata, B. (1980) 'Theory of vertical control with variable proportions', *Journal of Political Economy*, 88:1009–1025.

Malmgren, H.B. (1961) 'Information, expectations, and the theory of the firm', *Quarterly Journal of Economics*, 75:339–421.

Mancke, R.B. (1972) 'Iron ore and steel: A case study of the economic causes and consequences of vertical integration', *Journal of Industrial Economics*, 21:220–229.

Mancke, R.B. (1982) 'The petroleum industry', in: W. Adams, ed., *The structure of American industry*. New York: Macmillan.

Masten, S.E. (1984) 'The organization of production: Evidence from the aerospace industry', *Journal of Law and Economics*, 27:403–417.

Mathewson, G.F. and Winter, R.A. (1983) 'Vertical integration by contractual restraints in spatial markets', *Journal of Business*, 56:497–517.

Mathewson, G.F. and Winter, R.A. (1984) 'An economic theory of vertical restraints', *Rand Journal of Economics*, 15:27–38.

Mathewson, G.F. and Winter, R.A. (1986) 'The economics of vertical restraints in distribution', in: J.E. Stiglitz and G.F. Mathewson, eds., *New developments in analysis of market structures*. Cambridge, Mass.: MIT Press.

McBride, M.E. (1983) 'Spatial competition and vertical integration: Cement and concrete revisited', *American Economic Review*, 73:1011–1022.

McGee, J.S. and Bassett, L.R. (1976) 'Vertical integration revisited', *Journal of Law and Economics*, 19:17–38.

McKenzie, L.W. (1951) 'Ideal output and the interdependence of firms', *Economic Journal*, 61:785–803.

McLean, J.G. and Haigh, R.W. (1954) *The growth of integrated oil companies*. Boston, Mass.: Harvard Business School.

McNicol, D.L. (1975) 'The two price system in the copper industry', *Bell Journal of Economics*, 6:50–73.

Merkin, R. and Williams, K. (1984) *Competition law: Antitrust policy in the U.K. and the EEC*. London: Sweet and Maxwell.

Mitchell, E.J. (1976) 'Capital cost savings of vertical integration', in: E.J. Mitchell, ed., *Vertical integration in the oil industry*. Washington, D.C.: American Enterprise Institute.
Monteverde, K. and Teece, D.J. (1982a) 'Supplier switching costs and vertical integration in the automobile industry', *Bell Journal of Economics*, 13:206–213.
Monteverde, K. and Teece, D.J. (1982b) 'Appropriable rents and quasi-vertical integration', *Journal of Law and Economics*, 25:321–328.
Mueller, W.F. (1969) 'Public policy toward vertical mergers', in: J.F. Weston and S. Peltzman, eds., *Public policy toward mergers*. Pacific Palisades, California: Goodyear Publishing Company.
Oi, W.Y. (1961) 'The desirability of price instability under perfect competition', *Econometrica*, 29:58–64.
Ordover, J.A., Saloner, G. and Salop, S.C. (1987) 'Equilibrium vertical foreclosure', Department of Economics, New York University.
Parsons, D.O. and Ray, E. (1975) 'The United States Steel consolidation: The creation of market control', *Journal of Law and Economics*, 18:181–219.
Peck, M.J. (1961) *Competition in the aluminum industry 1945–1958*. Cambridge, Mass.: Harvard University Press.
Peck, M.J. and McGowan, J.J. (1967) 'Vertical integration in cement: A critical examination of the FTC Staff Report', *Antitrust Bulletin*, 12:505–531.
Peltzman, S. (1969) 'Public policy toward vertical mergers,' in: J.F. Weston and S. Peltzman, eds., *Public policy toward mergers*. Pacific Palisades, California: Goodyear Publishing Company.
Perry, M. (1986) 'An example of price formation in bilateral situations: A bargaining model with incomplete information', *Econometrica*, 54:313–321.
Perry, M.K. (1978a) 'Price discrimination and forward integration', *Bell Journal of Economics*, 9:209–217.
Perry, M.K. (1978b) 'Related market conditions and interindustrial mergers: Comment', *American Economic Review*, 68:221–224.
Perry, M.K. (1978c) 'Vertical integration: The monopsony case', *American Economic Review*, 68:561–570.
Perry, M.K. (1980) 'Forward integration by Alcoa: 1888–1930', *Journal of Industrial Economics*, 29:37–53.
Perry, M.K. (1982) 'Vertical integration by competitive firms: uncertainty and diversification', *Southern Economic Journal*, 49:201–208.
Perry, M.K. (1984) 'Vertical equilibrium in a competitive input market', *International Journal of Industrial Organization*, 2:159–170.
Perry, M.K. and Groff, R.H. (1982) 'Vertical integration and growth: An examination of the Stigler story', Bell Laboratories economic discussion paper no. 257.
Perry, M.K. and Groff, R.H. (1985) 'Resale price maintenance and forward integration into a monopolistically competitive industry', *Quarterly Journal of Economics*, 100:1293–1311.
Perry, M.K. and Porter, R.H. (1986) 'Resale price maintenance and exclusive territories in the presence of retail service externalities', Department of Economics, State University of New York at Stony Brook.
Pirenne, H. (1974) *Medieval cities: Their origins and the revival of trade*. Princeton, N.J.: Princeton University Press.
Porter, M.E. (1980) *Competitive strategy*. New York: Free Press.
Porter, M.E. and Spence, A.M. (1977) 'Vertical integration and differentiated inputs', discussion paper no. 576, Harvard Institute of Economic Research, Harvard University.
Porter, P. and Livesay, H.C. (1971) *Merchants and manufacturers*. Baltimore: Johns Hopkins Press.
Posner, R.A. (1976) *Antitrust law*. Chicago: University of Chicago Press.
Posner, R.A. and Easterbrook, F.H. (1981) *Antitrust*. St. Paul, Minn.: West Publishing.
Quirmbach, H.C. (1986a) 'Vertical integration: Scale distortions, partial integration, and the direction of price change', *Quarterly Journal of Economics*, 101:131–147.
Quirmbach, H.C. (1986b) 'The path of price changes in vertical integration', *Journal of Political Economy*, 94:1110–1119.
Riordan, M.H. (1984) 'Uncertainty, asymmetric information and bilateral contracts', *Review of Economic Studies*, 51:83–93.
Riordan, M.H. (1986) 'A note on optimal procurement contracts', *Information Economics and Policy*,

2:211–219.
Riordan, M.H. and Sappington, D.E.M. (1987) 'Information, incentives and organizational mode', *Quarterly Journal of Economics*, 102:243–263.
Riordan, M.H. and Williamson, O.E. (1985) 'Asset specificity and economic organization', *International Journal of Industrial Organization*, 3:365–378.
Salop, S.C. (1979) 'Monopolistic competition with outside goods', *Bell Journal of Economics*, 10:141–156.
Salop, S.C. and Scheffman, D.T. (1983) 'Raising rivals' costs', *American Economic Review*, 73:267–271.
Schmalensee, R. (1973) 'A note on the theory of vertical integration', *Journal of Political Economy*, 81:442–449.
Schmalensee, R. (1981) 'Output and welfare implications of monopolistic third-degree price discrimination', *American Economic Review*, 71:242–247.
Shavell, S. (1984) 'The design of contracts and remedies for breach', *Quarterly Journal of Economics*, 99:121–148.
Silver, M. (1984) *Enterprise and the scope of the firm*. Oxford, England: Martin Robertson and Company.
Smith, A. (1776) *The wealth of nations*. London: J.M. Dent and Sons, 1910.
Spence, A.M. (1976) 'Product selection, fixed costs, and monopolistic competition', *Review of Economic Studies*, 43:217–236.
Spengler, J.J. (1950) 'Vertical integration and antitrust policy', *Journal of Political Economy*, 53:347–352.
Spiller, P.T. (1985) 'On vertical mergers', *Journal of Law, Economics, and Organizations*, 1:285–312.
Stigler, G.J. (1951) 'The division of labor is limited by the extent of the market', *Journal of Political Economy*, 59:185–193.
Stuckey, J.A. (1983) *Vertical integration and joint ventures in the aluminum industry*. Cambridge, Mass.: Harvard University Press.
Sullivan, L.A. (1977) *Handbook of the law of antitrust*. St. Paul, Minn.: West Publishing.
Szenberg, M. (1971) *The economics of the Israeli diamond industry*. New York: Basic Books.
Teece, D.J. (1976) *Vertical integration and vertical divestiture in the U.S. oil industry*. Institute for Energy Studies, Stanford University.
Telser, L.G. (1979) 'A theory of monopoly of complementary goods', *Journal of Business*, 52:211–230.
Temin, P. (1987) 'Transactions costs and vertical integration: An historical test', *Journal of Economic History*, forthcoming.
Thorp, W. (1927) *The integration of manufacturing operation*. Washington, D.C.: U.S. Printing Office.
Tirole, J. (1986) 'Procurement and renegotiation', *Journal of Political Economy*, 94:235–259.
Tucker, I.B. and Wilder, R.P. (1977) 'Trends in vertical integration in the U.S. manufacturing sector', *Journal of Industrial Economics*, 26:81–94.
Varian, H.R. (1985) 'Price discrimination and social welfare', *American Economic Review*, 75:870–875.
Vassilakis, S. (1986) 'Increasing returns and strategic behavior', Ph.D. dissertation, Department of Economics, Johns Hopkins University.
Vernon, J. and Graham, D. (1971) 'Profitability of monopolization by vertical integration', *Journal of Political Economy*, 79:924–925.
Wallace, D.H. (1937) *Market control in the aluminum industry*. Cambridge, Mass.: Harvard University Press.
Warren-Boulton, F.R. (1974) 'Vertical control with variable proportions', *Journal of Political Economy*, 82:783–802.
Warren-Boulton, F.R. (1977) 'Vertical control by labor unions', *American Economic Review*, 67:309–322.
Warren-Boulton, F.R. (1978) *Vertical control of markets: Business and labor practices*. Cambridge, Mass.: Ballinger Publishing Company.
Waterson, M. (1980) 'Price-cost margins and successive market power', *Quarterly Journal of Economics*, 94:135–150.
Waterson, M. (1982) 'Vertical integration, variable proportions and oligopoly', *Economic Journal*, 92:129–144.
Weiss, A. (1987) 'Firm-specific physical capital: An empirical analysis of vertical mergers', Ph.D. dissertation, Department of Economics, University of Chicago.

Weitzman, M.L. (1974) 'Prices vs. quantities', *Review of Economic Studies*, 41:477–491.
Westfield, F.M. (1981) 'Vertical integration: Does product price rise or fall?', *American Economic Review*, 71:334–346.
Whalen, T.J., Jr. (1969) 'Vertical mergers in the concrete industry', *Antitrust Law and Economics Review*, 1:113–124.
White, J.J. and Summers, R.S. (1980) *Uniform commercial code*. St. Paul, Minn.: West Publishing.
White, L.J. (1971) *The automobile industry since 1945*. Cambridge, Mass.: Harvard University Press.
Wilk, D. (1968) 'Vertical integration in cement revisited: A comment on Peck and McGowan', *Antitrust Bulletin*, 13:619–647.
Williamson, O.E. (1971) 'The vertical integration of production: Market failure considerations', *American Economic Review*, 61:112–123.
Williamson, O.E. (1975) *Markets and hierarchies: Analysis and antitrust implications*. New York: Free Press.
Williamson, O.E. (1979) 'Transaction cost economics: The governance of contractual relations', *Journal of Law and Economics*, 22:233–261.
Williamson, O.E. (1985) *The economic institutions of capitalism*. New York: Free Press.
Wu, S.Y. (1964) 'The effects of vertical integration on price and output', *Western Economic Review*, 2:117–133.
Young, A.A. (1928) 'Increasing returns and economic progress', *Economic Journal*, 38:527–542.

PART 2

ANALYSIS OF MARKET BEHAVIOR

Chapter 5

NONCOOPERATIVE GAME THEORY FOR INDUSTRIAL ORGANIZATION: AN INTRODUCTION AND OVERVIEW

DREW FUDENBERG

Massachusetts Institute of Technology

JEAN TIROLE*

Massachusetts Institute of Technology

Contents

*The authors would like to thank Alfredo Kofman, Jennifer Reinganum, John Roberts, and the editors for helpful comments on a previous draft. Financial support from NSF Grants SES 88-08204 and SES 97619 is gratefully acknowledged.

Handbook of Industrial Organization, Volume I, Edited by R. Schmalensee and R.D. Willig

1. Introduction

Noncooperative game theory is a way of modelling and analyzing situations in which each player's optimal decisions depend on his beliefs or expectations about the play of his opponents. The distinguishing aspect of the theory is its insistence that players should not hold arbitrary beliefs about the play of their opponents. Instead, each player should try to predict his opponents' play, using his knowledge of the rules of the game and the assumption that his opponents are themselves rational, and are thus trying to make their own predictions and to maximize their own payoffs. Game-theoretic methodology has caused deep and wide-reaching changes in the way that practitioners think about key issues in oligopoly theory, much as the idea of rational expectations has revolutionized the study of macroeconomics. This chapter tries to provide an overview of those aspects of the theory which are most commonly used by industrial organization economists, and to sketch a few of the most important or illuminating applications. We have omitted many interesting game-theoretic topics which have not yet been widely applied.

2. Games, strategies, and equilibria

This section introduces the two formalisms used to represent noncooperative games, and then discusses what we might mean by a "reasonable prediction" for how a game will be played. This will lead us to the ideas of Nash and subgame-perfect equilibria.

2.1. The extensive and normal forms

There are two (almost) equivalent ways of formulating a game. The first is the *extensive* form.[1] An extensive form specifies: (1) the order of play; (2) the choices available to a player whenever it is his turn to move; (3) the information a player has at each of these turns; (4) the payoffs to each player as a function of the moves selected; and (5) the probability distributions for moves by "Nature".

The extensive form is depicted by a "game tree", such as those in Figures 5.1 and 5.2. Game trees are the multi-player generalization of the decision trees used in decision theory. The open circle is the first or initial node. The tree's structure says which nodes follow which, and the numbers at each node indicate which

[1] The following description is freely adapted from Kreps and Wilson (1982a).

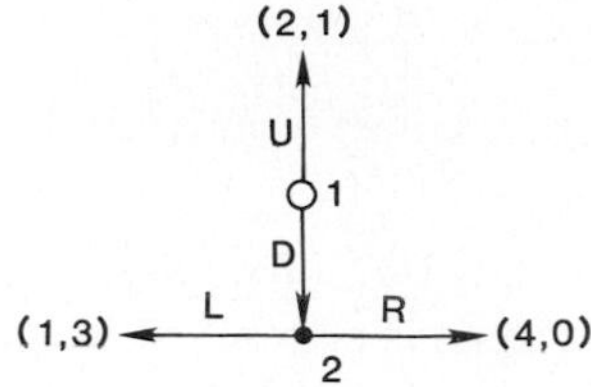

Figure 5.1

player has the move there. [Part of what is meant by "tree" is that this structure is an ordering – two distinct nodes cannot have the same successor. Thus, for example in chess, two different sequences of moves which lead to the same position on the board are assigned different nodes in the tree. See Kreps and Wilson (1982a) for a more formal discussion of this and other details of extensive form games. See also the classic book by Luce and Raiffa (1957) which addresses most of the topics of this section.] The dotted line connecting two of player 2's nodes in Figure 5.2 indicates that these two nodes are in the same "information set", meaning that player 2 cannot tell which of the two actions has occurred when it is his turn to move. Players must know when it is their turn to move, so different players' information sets cannot intersect, and players must know which choices are feasible, so all nodes in the same information set must allow the same choices. We will restrict attention throughout to games of *perfect recall*, in which each player always knows what he knew previously, including his own previous actions. This implies an additional restriction on the information sets.

Players are assumed to maximize their expected utility, given their beliefs about the actions of their opponents and of "Nature". The payoffs corresponding to each sequence of actions are depicted at the terminal nodes or "outcomes" of the tree; (x, y) at a terminal node means that player 1 gets x and player 2 gets y. The different initial nodes in Figure 5.3 correspond to different moves by Nature, i.e. different "states of the world". (Note that this is a one-player game.) There is

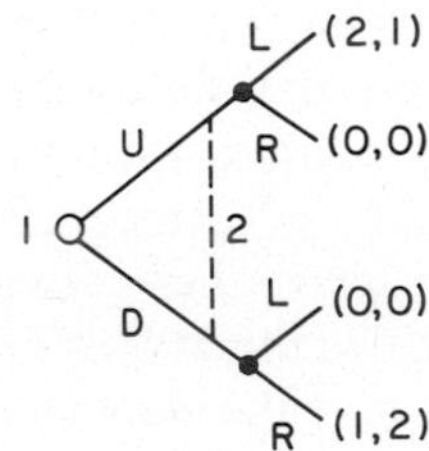

Figure 5.2

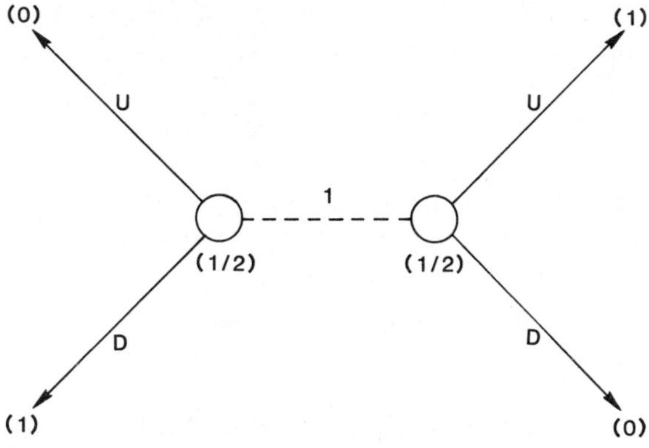

Figure 5.3

no loss in generality in placing all of Nature's moves at the start, because players need not receive information about these moves until later on. The initial assessment p is a probability measure over the initial nodes. The formal models we will discuss will always assume that this assessment, the terminal payoffs, and the entire structure of the tree is "common knowledge", meaning that all players know it, and they know that their opponents know it, and so on. This does not mean that all players are perfectly informed, but rather that we have explicitly depicted all the differences in information in our tree.[2] The extensive form will be taken to fully describe the real situation – all possible moves and observations will be explicitly specified. For example, if the "same game" is played three times, the "real game" to be analyzed is the three-fold replication. The idealized situation we have in mind is that, possibly after some "pre-play communication", players are in separate rooms. They are informed of the course of play only by signals corresponding to the information structure of the tree, and push various buttons corresponding to the feasible actions at their various information sets. Once play begins, players cannot explicitly communicate, except as provided by the rules of the game. (In many situations, it is difficult to explicitly model all the possible means of communication. This has spurred interest in shorthand descriptions of the effects of communication. See our discussion of correlated equilibrium.) A *behavioral* strategy for player i is a map that specifies for each of his information sets, a probability distribution over the actions that are feasible at that set. A behavioral pure strategy specifies a single action at each information set, as opposed to a probability mixture. (Later we will discuss whether it might be reasonable for a player to randomize.) A given specification of behav-

[2]See Aumann (1976) and Brandenburger and Dekel (1985a) for a formal treatment of common knowledge, and also the Mertens and Zamir (1985) paper we mention in Section 4.

ioral strategies and an initial assessment generates a probability distribution over terminal nodes, and thus over payoffs, in the obvious way.

The distinguishing feature of game theory is that each player's beliefs about his opponents' actions are not arbitrarily specified. Instead, each player is assumed to believe that his opponents are "rational", and to use that information in formulating his predictions of their play. Any predictions that are inconsistent with this presumed, but vaguely specified, rationality are rejected.

To help clarify what we mean, let us return to the game depicted in Figure 5.1. Is there a reasonable prediction for how this game should/will be played? One way to look for a prediction is to apply backwards induction. If player 2's information set is reached, and the payoffs are as specified, then 2 should play L. Then if player 1 knows that player 2 will play L, player 1 should play U. Is this a good prediction? If all is as in Figure 5.1, player 2 should not expect player 1 to play D. What should 2 tell himself if D is nevertheless observed? If the payoffs are guaranteed to be as specified, the only possible explanation is that player 1 made a "mistake" – he meant to play U but somehow he failed to do so. This analysis falls apart if we take Figure 5.1 as a shorthand description for a game which is probably as depicted, but might not be, so that playing D could convey information to player 2. We will say more about this in Section 5. The key for now is that the game must be taken as an exact description of reality for our arguments to be sound.

In Figure 5.1, all (both) the information sets are singletons, so that each player knows all previous actions at each of his turns to move. Games like this are called "games of perfect information". The backwards induction argument used above is called "Kuhn's algorithm" [Kuhn (1953)]. It always "works" (yields a conclusion) in finite games of perfect information, and yields a unique conclusion as long as no two terminal nodes give any player exactly the same payoff. Backwards induction will not yield a conclusion in games of imperfect information, such as that in Figure 5.2. Player 2's optimal choice at his information set depends on player 1's previous move, which player 2 has not observed. To help find a reasonable prediction for this game we introduce the idea of the *normal* form.

The normal form representation of an extensive game condenses the details of the tree structure into three elements: the set of players, I; each player's strategy space, which is simply the set of his behavioral pure strategies; and a payoff function mapping strategy selections for all of the players to their payoffs. We will use S_i to denote player i's strategy space, S to be the product of the S_i, and $\pi^i: S \to R$ to be player i's payoff function. A triple (I, S, π) completely describes a normal form.

Normal forms for two-player games are often depicted as matrices, as in Figure 5.4. The left-hand matrix is the normal form for Figure 5.1, while the right-hand one corresponds to Figure 5.2. Note that different extensive forms can

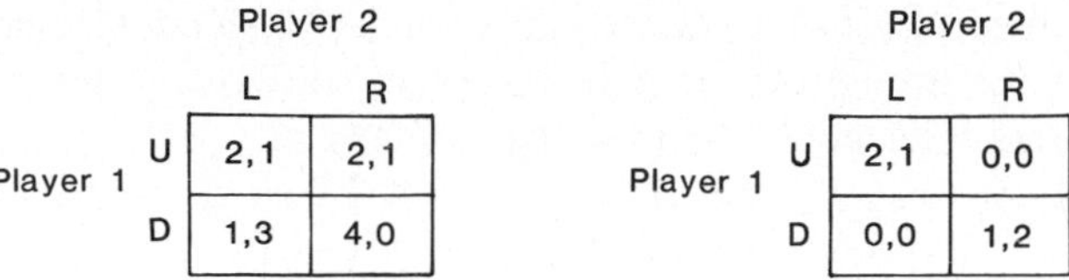

Figure 5.4

have the same normal form. For example, Figure 5.2 is a "simultaneous-move" game, in which neither player observes his opponent's action before choosing his own. We could represent this game equally well with an extensive form in which player 2 moved first.

A *mixed strategy* is a probability distribution over the normal-form strategies. Payoffs to mixed strategies are simply the expected value of the corresponding pure-strategy payoffs. We will denote mixed strategies by Σ, and the space of player i's mixed strategies by Σ_i. Although different mixed strategies can give rise to the same behavior strategies, Kuhn showed that the two concepts are equivalent in games of perfect recall – any probability distribution over outcomes that can be generated using one kind of randomization can be duplicated by using the other.[3]

In the normal form corresponding to Figure 5.1, choosing L gives player 2 at least as high a payoff as choosing R regardless of player 1's choice, and gives strictly more if player 1 plays D. In such a case we say that L is a (weakly) dominant strategy for player 2. (Strict dominance means that the strategy is strictly better for all choices by opponents.) It seems reasonable that no player should expect an opponent to play a dominated strategy, which means that 1 should expect that 2 will play L. This is just rephrasing our backwards induction argument. The analogy of rolling backwards through the tree is the iterated elimination of dominated strategies: making optimal choices at the last nodes is simple dominance, folding back one step is first-order iterated dominance, and so on. (Actually iterated dominance is a more general technique, as it can be applied to games of imperfect information.)

2.2. *Nash equilibrium*

The normal form for Figure 5.2 does not have dominant strategies. Here to make predictions we will have to accept a weaker notion of "reasonableness", that

[3]Two strategies for a player which differ only at information sets which follow a deviation by that player yield the same probability distribution over outcomes for any strategy selections of the other players. Some authors define the normal form as identifying such equivalent strategies.

embodied in the concept of a *Nash* equilibrium. A Nash equilibrium is a strategy selection such that no player can gain by playing differently, given the strategies of his opponents. This condition is stated formally as

Definition

Strategy selection s^* is a pure-strategy Nash equilibrium of the game (I, S, π) if for all players i in I and all s_i in S_i,

$$\pi^i(s^*) \geq \pi^i(s_i, s^*_{-i}). \tag{1}$$

Here, the notation (s_i, s^*_{-i}) represents the strategy selection in which all players but i play according to s^*, while i plays s_i. Note that s^* can be an equilibrium if there is some player i who is indifferent between s_i^* and an alternative, s_i. We view Nash equilibrium as a minimal requirement that a proposed solution must satisfy to be "reasonable". If a strategy prediction is not a Nash equilibrium and the prediction is known to all players, then all players know that some player would do better not to play as the selection specifies. If "reasonable" is to mean anything, it should rule out such inconsistent predictions. Not all Nash equilibria are reasonable, as is revealed by examining the extensive and normal forms of Figure 5.5. The backwards-induction equilibrium (D, L) is a Nash equilibrium, but so is (U, R). We will soon discuss the idea of a "perfect equilibrium", which is designed to formalize the idea that (U, R) is not reasonable. The perfection notion and other refinements of Nash equilibrium do not help with the following problem. Consider a game like that in Figure 5.6. The only Nash equilibrium is (U, L), yet is this a reasonable prediction? It depends on whether the players are sure that the payoffs are exactly as we have specified, and that their opponents are "rational". If player 1 plays U against L, his payoff is 5, which is better than the 4.9 that 1 gets from D. However, playing D guarantees that 1 gets 4.9, while if the outcome is (U, R) then 1 gets 0. And similarly, player 2 can guarantee 4.9 by playing R. Yet if player 1's not sure that player 2 might not prefer R to L,

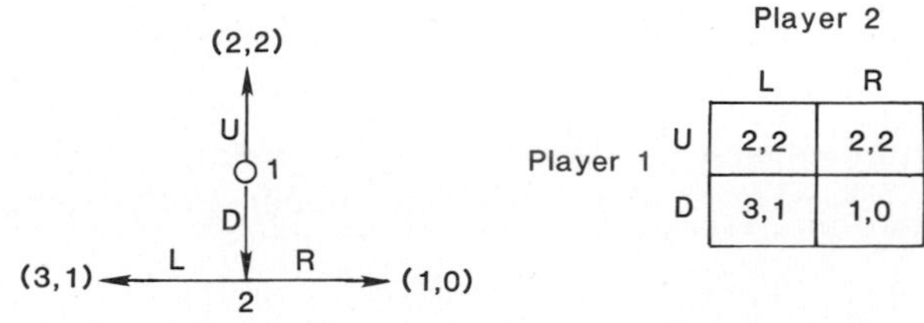

Figure 5.5

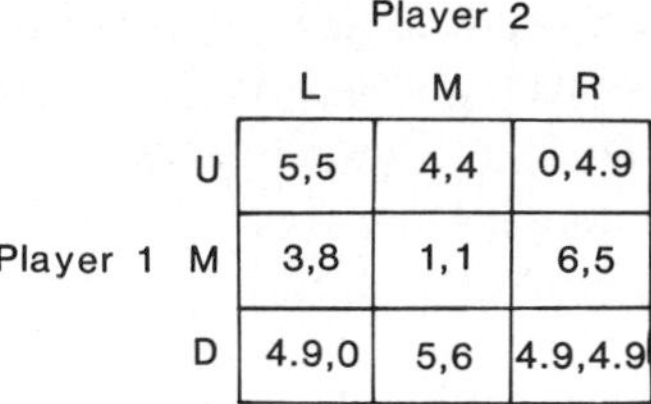

Player 1 \ Player 2	L	M	R
U	5,5	4,4	0,4.9
M	3,8	1,1	6,5
D	4.9,0	5,6	4.9,4.9

Figure 5.6

then D could be attractive. And even if player 1 is sure of player 2's payoffs, if player 1's not sure that player 2 knows player 1's payoffs, then player 1 might still fear that player 2 will play R. The point is that the logic of Nash equilibrium relies on every player knowing that every player knows that . . . the payoffs are as specified. Technically, the payoffs should be "common knowledge" (as should the Nash concept itself.) The closer the payoffs guaranteed by D and R come to the equilibrium payoffs, the more we need to insist on the common knowledge. Ideally, equilibria should be subjected to this sort of informal check or "sensitivity analysis".

Finally, game theory lacks a convincing argument that players will in fact predict a Nash equilibrium outcome. This problem is particularly acute when more than one equilibrium exists, as in the game of Figure 5.2. Here there are two pure strategy equilibria, (U, L) and (D, R). If there is a reasonable outcome in this game, both players must be able to predict it, and predict that their opponents will predict it, and so on. If players cannot so coordinate their expectations, there is no reason to expect observed play to correspond to either equilibrium – for example, we might see the outcome (U, R). Not all games have reasonable solutions, and on the data given so far this could be one. However, Schelling's (1960) theory of "focal points" suggests that in some "real life" situations players may be able to coordinate on a particular equilibrium by using information that is abstracted away in the standard game formulation. For example, the *names* of the strategies may have some commonly understood "focal" power. An example is two players who are asked to name an exact time, with the promise of a reward if their choices match. Here "12 noon" is focal, while "1:43" is not. The payoffs may also help coordinate expectations. If *both* players did better with (U, L) then (D, R), then (U, L) seems a natural outcome to expect one's opponent to expect that. . . . Some authors (including us!) have argued that if there is a unique Pareto optimum among the set of equilibria, it should be a focal point. While this intuition seems sound for two-player games, a recent example of Bernheim, Peleg and Whinston (1985) shows that with more than two players the intuition is suspect. In response, they have introduced the concept of "coalition-proofness", which we discuss at the end of this section.

The idea of a Nash equilibrium is implicit in two of the first games to have been formally studied, namely the Cournot and Bertrand models of oligopoly. Let us emphasize that despite the common practice of speaking of *Cournot and Bertrand* equilibrium, the models are best thought of as studying the Nash equilibria of two different simultaneous move games. In the Cournot model, firms simultaneously choose quantities, and the price is set at the market-clearing level by a fictitious auctioneer. In the Bertrand model, firms simultaneously choose prices, and then must produce to meet demand after the price choices become known. In each model, firms choose best responses to the anticipated play of their opponents.

For concreteness, we remind the reader of the Cournot model of a duopoly producing a homogeneous good. Firm 1 and firm 2 simultaneously choose their respective output levels, q_1 and q_2, from feasible sets F_i. They sell their output at the market-clearing price $p(Q)$, where $Q = q_1 + q_2$. Firm i's cost of production is $c_i(q_i)$, and firm i's total profit is then $\pi^i(q_1, q_2) = q_i p(Q) - c_i(q_i)$. The feasible sets F_i and the payoff functions π^i determine the normal form of the game; the reader should check that he/she knows how to construct an equivalent extensive form. The "Cournot reaction functions" $R^1(q_2)$ and $R^2(q_1)$ specify each firm's optimal output for each fixed output level of its opponent. If the π^i are differentiable and strictly concave, and the appropriate boundary conditions are satisfied, we can solve for these reaction functions using the first-order conditions. The intersections of the two reaction functions (if any exist) are the Nash equilibria of the Cournot game: neither player can gain by a change in output, given the output level of its opponent.

The Cournot game is often contrasted to the situation in which one firm, say firm 1, is a "Stackelberg leader" and the other firm is the "Stackelberg follower". The Stackelberg leader moves first, and chooses an output which is observed by the follower before the follower makes its own choice. Thus, the Stackelberg game is one of perfect information. In the backwards induction (i.e. "perfect" – see below) equilibrium to this game, firm 2's output is along its reaction curve. Knowing this, firm 1 chooses its own output to maximize its payoff along the graph of R^2. The first-order condition for this choice is that

$$\partial\pi^1\big(q_1, R^2(q_1)\big)/\partial q_1 + \big(\partial\pi^1\big(q_1, R^2(q_1)\big)/\partial q_2\big)\big(\mathrm{d}R^2(q_1)/\mathrm{d}q_1\big) = 0.$$

The backwards-induction equilibrium to the Stackelberg game is called the "Stackelberg equilibrium". This terminology can be confusing to the beginner. The Stackelberg equilibrium is *not* an alternative equilibrium for the Cournot game, but rather a shorthand way of describing an equilibrium of an alternative extensive form. While the prevailing terminology is too well established to be changed, the student will do well to keep this distinction in mind.

The Cournot and Bertrand models are all static games, in which firms make their choices once and for all. Subsection 3.1 discusses a dynamic version of these games. Also, even as static games the Cournot and Stackleberg models must be thought of as reduced forms, unless one literally believes in the existence of the price-setting auctioneer. Kreps and Scheinkman (1983) have shown that the auctioneer in the Cournot model can be replaced by a second period in which firms choose prices, taking their production as fixed (at least if the rationing scheme is "efficient" and the demand function is concave). Thus, in both models firms choose both prices and outputs; the difference is in the timing of these two decisions. [See Gertner (1985a) for simultaneous choices.]

2.3. *Existence of Nash equilibria*

We will now take up the question of the existence of Nash equilibria. Not all games have pure-strategy Nash equilibria. A simple example is "matching pennies": players 1 and 2 simultaneously announce either "heads" or "tails". If the announcements match, then player 1 gains a util, and player 2 loses one. if the announcements differ, it is player 2 who wins the util, and player 1 who loses. If the predicted outcome is that the announcements will match, then player 2 has an incentive to deviate, while player 1 would prefer to deviate from any prediction in which announcements do not match. The only "stable" situation is one in which each player randomizes between his two strategies, assigning equal probability to each. In this case each player is completely indifferent between his possible choices. A mixed-strategy Nash equilibrium is simply a selection of mixed strategies such that no player prefers to deviate, i.e. the strategies must satisfy equation (1). Since expected utilities are "linear in the probabilities", if a player uses a nondegenerate mixed strategy (one that puts positive weight on more than one pure strategy) then that player cannot strictly prefer not to deviate – the inequality in (1) must be weak. (For the same reason, it suffices to check that no player has a profitable pure-strategy deviation.) This raises the question of why a player should bother to play a mixed strategy, when he knows that any of the pure strategies in its support would do equally well. In matching pennies, if player 1 knows that player 2 will randomize, player 1 has a zero expected value from all possible choices. As far as his payoff goes, he could just as well play "heads" with certainty, but if this is anticipated by player 2 the equilibrium disintegrates. Some authors have suggested that for this reason there is no "reasonable" prediction for matching pennies, or, equivalently, that all possible probability mixtures over outcomes are equally reasonable. [See, for example, Bernheim (1984) and Pearce (1984).] Harsanyi (1973) followed by Aumann et al. (1981) and Milgrom and Weber (1986) have offered the defense that the "mixing" should be interpreted as the result of small, unobservable variations in the players' payoffs. Thus, in our example, sometimes player 1 might prefer matching on T to matching on H, and conversely. Then for each value of his payoff player 1 would play a pure strategy. This "purification" of mixed-strategy equilibria is discussed in Subsection 4.2. Despite some controversy, mixed strategies have been widely used both in "pure" game theory and in its applications to industrial organization.

One reason is that, as shown by Nash (1950), mixed-strategy equilibria always exist in finite games (games with a finite number of nodes, or, equivalently, a finite number of normal-form pure strategies per player and a finite number of players).

Theorem (Nash)

Every finite n-player normal form game has a mixed-strategy equilibrium.

This can be shown by applying the Kakutani fixed-point theorem to the players' reaction correspondences, as we now explain. A good reference for some of the technical details involved is Green and Heller (1981).

Define player i's reaction correspondence, $r^i(\sigma)$, to be the correspondence which gives the set of (mixed) strategies which maximize player i's payoff when his opponents play σ_{-i}. This is just the natural generalization of the Cournot reaction functions we introduced above. Since payoffs are linear functions of the mixing probabilities, they are in particular both continuous and quasiconcave. This implies that each player's reaction correspondence is nonempty valued and convex valued. Moreover, we can show that the reaction correspondences are "upper hemi-continuous": If $\sigma^n \to \sigma$ and $\sigma_i^n \in r^i(\sigma^n)$, then there is a subsequence of the σ_i^n which converges to a $\sigma_i \in r^i(\sigma)$. Now define the correspondence r to be the Cartesian product of the r_i. This correspondence satisfies the requirements of the Kakutani fixed-point theorem: it maps a compact convex subset of Euclidean space (the relevant probability simplex) into its subsets, and it is nonempty valued, convex valued, and upper hemi-continuous. Hence, r has a fixed point, and by construction the fixed points of r are Nash equilibria.

Economists often use models of games with an uncountable number of actions. Some might argue that prices or quantities are "really" infinitely divisible, while others that "reality" is discrete and the continuum is a mathematical abstraction, but it is often easier to work with a continuum of actions rather than a large finite grid. Moreover, as Dasgupta and Maskin (1986) argue, when the continuum game does not have an equilibrium, the equilibria corresponding to fine, discrete grids could be very sensitive to exactly which finite grid is specified. These fluctuations can be ruled out if the continuum game has an equilibrium. The existence of equilibria for infinite games is more involved than for finite ones. If payoffs are discontinuous there may be no equilibria at all. If the payoffs are continuous, then the Fan (1952) fixed-point theorem can be used to show that a mixed-strategy equilibrium exists. If payoffs are quasiconcave as well as continuous, then there exist equilibria in pure strategies, as shown by Debreu (1952) and Glicksberg (1952).

Theorem (Debreu, Glicksberg, Fan)

Consider an n-player normal form game whose strategy spaces S_i are compact convex subsets of an Euclidean space. If the payoff functions $\pi^i(s)$ are continuous in s, and quasiconcave in s_i, there exists a pure-strategy Nash equilibrium.

The proof here is very similar to that of Nash's theorem: we verify that continuous payoffs imply nonempty, upper hemi-continuous reactions, and that quasiconcavity in own actions implies that reactions are convex valued.

Theorem (Glicksberg)

Consider an n-player normal form game (I, S, π). If for each i, S_i is a compact convex subset of a metric space, and π is continuous, then there exists a Nash equilibrium in mixed strategies.

Here the mixed strategies are the (Borel) probability measures over the pure strategies, which we endow with the topology of weak convergence.[4] Once more, the proof applies a fixed-point theorem to the reaction correspondences. One point to emphasize is that the mixed-strategy payoffs will be quasiconcave in own actions even if the pure-strategy payoffs are not. With infinitely many pure strategies, the space of mixed strategies is infinite-dimensional, so a more powerful fixed-point theorem is required. Alternatively, one can approximate the strategy spaces by a sequence of finite grids. From Nash's theorem, each grid has a mixed-strategy equilibrium. One then argues that since the space of probability measures is weakly compact, we can find a limit point of the sequence of these discrete equilibria. Since the payoffs are continuous, it is easy to verify that the limit point is an equilibrium.

There are many examples to show that if payoffs are discontinuous, equilibria need not exist. Dasgupta and Maskin (1986) argue that this lack of existence is sometimes due to payoffs failing to be quasiconcave, rather than failing to be continuous. They show if payoffs are quasiconcave, then a *pure strategy* equilibrium will exist under a very weak condition they call "graph continuity". They also provide conditions for the existence of mixed-strategy equilibria in games

[4] Fix a compact metric space A. A sequence of measures μ^n on A converges "weakly" to a limit μ if $\int f \, d\mu_n \to \int f \, d\mu$ for every real-valued continuous function f on A.

without quasiconcave payoffs. The idea of their result is to provide conditions ensuring that the limits of the discrete-grid equilibria do not have "atoms" (non-negligible probability) on any of the discontinuity points of the payoff functions. Simon (1985) relaxes their condition by requiring only that at least one limit has this no-atoms property, instead of all of them.

A sizeable literature has considered the existence of pure strategy equilibrium when payoffs are not quasiconcave, particularly in the Cournot model. Without quasiconcave payoffs, the reaction functions can have "jumps". To prove existence of equilibrium in this setting one must show that the jumps "do not matter". Roberts and Sonnenschein (1977) showed that "nice" preferences and technologies need not lead to quasiconcave Cournot payoffs, and provided examples of the nonexistence of pure-strategy Cournot equilibrium. McManus (1962) and Roberts and Sonnenschein (1976) show that pure-strategy equilibria exist in symmetric games with real-valued actions if costs are convex. The key is that the convex-cost assumption can be shown to imply that all the jumps in the reaction functions are jumps up. Novshek (1985) has shown that pure-strategy equilibria exist in markets for a homogeneous good where each firm's marginal revenue is decreasing in the aggregate output of its opponents, for any specification of the cost functions. Topkis (1970) and Vives (1985) use a fixed-point theorem for nondecreasing functions due to Tarski (1955) to prove the existence of pure-strategy equilibria in games where the reactions are increasing. Tarski (1955) also proved that a function from $[0,1]$ to $[0,1]$ which has no downward jumps has a fixed point, even if the function is not everywhere nondecreasing. Vives uses this result to give a simple proof of the McManus/Roberts–Sonnenschein result. (Each firm's reaction function depends only on the sum of its opponents' actions, and in symmetric equilibria all firms have the same reaction function. Thus, if the actions are real-valued the second of the Tarski results can be applied.)

The converse of the existence question is that of the characterization of the equilibrium set. Ideally one would prefer there to be a unique equilibrium, but this is only true under very strong conditions. When several equilibria exist, one must see which, if any, seem to be reasonable predictions, but this requires examination of the entire Nash set. The reasonableness of one equilibrium may depend on whether there are others with competing claims. Unfortunately, in many interesting games the set of equilibria is difficult to characterize.

2.4. Correlated equilibria

The Nash equilibrium concept is intended to be a minimal necessary condition for "reasonable" predictions in situations where the players must choose their actions "independently". Let us return to our story of players who may have

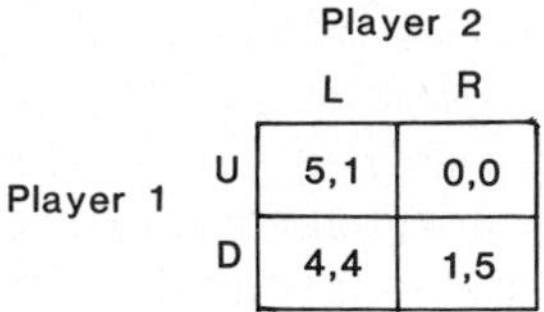

Figure 5.7

pre-play discussion, but then must go off to isolated rooms to choose their strategies. In some situations, both players could gain if they could build a "signalling device" that sent signals to the separate rooms. Aumann's (1974) notion of a correlated equilibrium captures what could be achieved with any such signals. [See Myerson (1983) for a fuller introduction to this concept, and for a discussion of its relationship to the theory of mechanism design.]

To motivate this concept, consider Aumann's example, presented in Figure 5.7. This game has three equilibria: (U, L), (D, R), and a mixed-strategy equilibrium that gives each player 2.5. If they can jointly observe a "coin flip" (or sunspots, or any other publicly observable random variable) before play, they can achieve payoffs $(3, 3)$ by a joint randomization between the two pure-strategy equilibria. However, they can do even better (still without binding contracts) if they can build a device that sends different, but correlated, signals to each of them. This device will have three equally likely states, A, B, and C. Player 1's information partition is $(A, (B, C))$. This means that if A occurs, player 1 is perfectly informed, but if the state is B or C, player 1 does not know which of the two prevails. Player 2's information partition is $((A, B), C)$. In this transformed game, the following is a Nash equilibrium: player 1 plays U when told A, and D when told (B, C); player 2 plays R when told C, and L when told (A, B). Let us check that player 1 does not want to deviate. When he observes A, he knows that 2 observes (A, B), and thus that 2 will play L; in this case U is player 1's best response. If player 1 observes (B, C), then conditional on his information he expects player 2 to play L and R with equal probability. In this case player 1 will average 2.5 from either of his choices, so he is willing to choose D. So player 1 is choosing a best response; the same is easily seen to be true for player 2. Thus, we have constructed an equilibrium in which the players' choices are correlated: the outcomes (U, L), (D, L), and (D, R) are chosen with probability one-third each, while the "bad" outcome (U, R) never occurs. In this new equilibrium the expected payoffs are $3\frac{1}{3}$ each, which is better than in any of the equilibria of the game without the signalling device. (Note that adding the signalling device does not remove the "old" equilibria: since the signals do not influence payoffs, if player 1 ignores his signal, player 2 may as well ignore hers.)

If we had to analyze each possible signalling device one at at time, we would never be done. Fortunately, if we want to know what could be done with all possible devices, we can dispense with the signals, and work directly with probability distributions over strategies. In our example, players need not be told about the states A, B, and C. They could simply be given recommended strategies, as long as the joint distribution over recommendations corresponds to the joint distribution over outcomes that we derived. Player 1 could be told "play D" instead of (B, C), as long as this means there is a 50–50 chance of player 2 playing L.

Definition

A *correlated equilibrium* is any probability distribution $p(s)$ over the pure strategies $S_1 \times \cdots \times S_n$ such that, for every player i and every function $d_i(s_i)$ that maps S_i to S_i,

$$\pi^i(p) \geq \Sigma p(s) \pi^i(d_i(s_i), s_{-i}).$$

That is, player i should not be able to gain by disobeying the recommendation to play s_i if every other player obeys the recommendations.

A pure-strategy Nash equilibrium is a correlated equilibrium in which the distribution $p(s)$ is degenerate. Mixed-strategy Nash equilibria are also correlated equilibria: just take $p(s)$ to be the joint distribution over actions implied by the equilibrium strategies, so that the recommendations made to each player convey no information about the play of his opponents.

Inspection of the definition shows that the set of correlated equilibria is convex, so the set of correlated equilibria is at least as large as the convex hull of the Nash equilibria. Since Nash equilibria exist in finite games, correlated equilibria do too. Actually, the existence of correlated equilibria would seem to be a simpler problem than the existence of Nash equilibria, because the set of correlated equilibria is defined by a system of linear inequalities, and is therefore convex. Recently, Hart and Schmeidler (1986) have provided an existence proof that uses only linear methods (as opposed to fixed-point theorems.) One might also like to know when the set of correlated equilibria differs "greatly" from the convex hull of the Nash equilibria, but this question has not yet been answered.

We take the view that the correlation in correlated equilibria should be thought of as the result of the players receiving correlated signals, so that the notion of correlated equilibrium is particularly appropriate in situations with pre-play communication, for then the players might be able to design and implement a procedure for obtaining correlated, private signals. However, we should point out that Aumann (1986) and Brandenburger and Dekel (1985b) argue that the correlated equilibrium notion is more "natural" than the Nash one from the point of view of subjective probability theory.

2.5. Coalition-proof equilibria and strong equilibria

While no single player can profitably deviate from a Nash equilibrium, it may be that some coalition could arrange a mutually beneficial deviation. If players can engage in pre-play communication, then some coalitions of players might hope to arrange for *joint* deviations from the specified play. The notion of a "strong equilibrium" [Aumann (1959)] requires that no subset of players, taking the actions of the others as given, could jointly deviate in a way that benefits all of its members. As this requirement applies to the grand coalition of all players, strong equilibria are Pareto-efficient. Because no restrictions are placed on the play of a deviating coalition, the conditions for a strong equilibrium are quite stringent, and these equilibria fail to exist in many games of interest for industrial organization, such as, for example, Cournot oligopoly. Recently, Bernheim, Peleg and Whinston (1985) (B-P-W) have proposed the idea of a "coalition-proof" equilibrium, which, they argue, is a more natural way to take account of coalitional deviations.

The best way to explain their concept is to use their example, which also serves the important function of showing why the criterion of Pareto-dominance may not be a good way to select between equilibria when there are more than two players. In Figure 5.8, player 1 chooses rows, player 2 chooses columns, and player 3 chooses matrices. This game has two pure-strategy Nash equilibria, (U, L, A) and (D, R, B) and an equilibrium in mixed strategies. B-P-W do not consider mixed strategies, so we will temporarily restrict attention to pure ones. The equilibrium (U, L, A) Pareto-dominates (D, R, B). Is (U, L, A) then the obvious focal point? Imagine that this was the expected solution, and hold player 3's choice fixed. This induces a two-player game between players 1 and 2. In this two-player game, (D, R) is the Pareto-dominant equilibrium! Thus, if players 1 and 2 expect that player 3 will play A, and if they can coordinate their play on their Pareto-preferred equilibrium in matrix A, they should do so, which would upset the "good" equilibrium (U, L, A).

The definition of a coalition-proof equilibrium proceeds by induction on the coalition size. First one requires that no one-player coalition can deviate, i.e. that the given strategies are a Nash equilibrium. Then one requires that no two-player

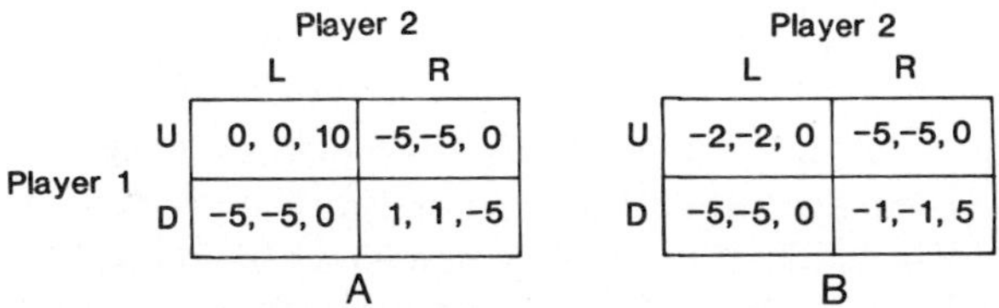

Figure 5.8

deviation can deviate, given that once such a deviation has "occurred", either of the deviating players (but none of the others) is free to deviate again. That is, the two-player deviations must be Nash equilibria of the two-player game induced by holding the strategies of the others fixed. And one proceeds in this way up to the coalition of all players. Clearly, (U, L, A) in Figure 5.8 is not coalition-proof; brief inspection shows that (D, R, B) is. However, (D, R, B) is not Pareto-optimal, and thus is not a strong equilibrium; no strong equilibrium exists in this game.

The idea of coalition-proofness is an interesting way to try to model the possibility of coalitional deviations. However, the assumption that only subsets of the deviating coalitions can be involved in further deviations can be questioned, and the general properties of the concept are unknown. For these reasons, and because coalition-proof equilibria need not exist (even with mixed strategies), we feel that at this time the B-P-W paper is more important for the issues it raises than for its solution concept. We should mention here that Bernheim and Whinston (1985) apply coalition-proofness to several well-known games with interesting results.

3. Dynamic games of complete information

Most of the examples in the previous section were static games: each player's choice of actions was independent of the choices of his opponents. Many of the interesting strategic aspects of the behavior of firms are best modelled with dynamic games, in which players can observe and respond to their opponents' actions. This is true not only of inherently dynamic phenomena such as investment, entry deterrence, and exit, but also of the determination of price and output in a mature market. Section 3 discusses a few special kinds of dynamic games that have been frequently used in the study of oligopoly theory. These are all games of *complete information*, i.e. the payoff functions are common knowledge. Section 4 discusses games of incomplete information, which have become increasingly common in the literature.

3.1. Subgame perfection

In dynamic games a question arises that is not present in static ones: What beliefs should players have about the way that their current play will affect their opponents' future decisions? Recall that the game in Figure 5.5 had two Nash equilibria, (U, R) and (D, L). We argued that (U, R) was unreasonable, because R was dominated by L for player 2. Alternatively, we arrived at (D, L) as our prediction by working backwards through the tree. Another way of putting this is that player 1 should not be deterred from playing D by the "threat" of player 2 playing R, because if player 2's information set was actually reached, 2 would back off from his "bluff" and play L. This approach is useful for thinking about situations in which backwards induction and/or weak dominance arguments do not give sharp conclusions. Selten's (1965) notion of a *subgame-perfect equilibrium* generalizes the backwards-induction idea to rule out empty threats in more general situations.

Subgame-perfect equilibrium strategies must yield a Nash equilibrium, not just in the original game, but in every one of its "proper subgames". Loosely speaking, a proper subgame is a subset of the initial game tree which: (1) is closed under succession – if a node is in the subgame, so are all of its successors; (2) "respects information sets", which means roughly that all of the information sets of the subgame are information sets of the initial game; and (3) begins with an information set that contains only one node. This last requirement is in a general sense very restrictive, which is one of the motivations for the various refinements of the perfection concept. However, most of the games we discuss in this section are "deterministic multi-period games", which have a very simple structure that makes subgame-perfection a useful tool. These games have extensive forms that can be divided into periods so that: (1) at the start of the kth period all play in periods 1 through $(k-1)$ is common knowledge (the initial information sets in each period are all singletons); and (2) no information set contained in the kth period provides any knowledge of play within that period. Any game of perfect information is a multi-period game: just take all the successors of the initial nodes to belong to period 1, their successors to period 2, and so on. The Cournot and Bertrand models are one-period games. If the same players play a Cournot game twice in a row, and all players observe the "first-period" quantities before making their second choice, we have a two-period game.

In a multi-period game, the beginning of each period marks the beginning of a new subgame. Thus, for these games we can rephrase subgame-perfection as simply the requirement that the strategies yield a Nash equilibrium from the start of each period. The reader should note that applying subgame perfection to games where each player moves in several periods involves an implicit assumption that was not required in the game of Figure 5.5; namely that whether a player has previously deviated from predicted play should not alter the way his opponents predict his future moves. We discuss this point further in Subsection 5.5.

Figure 5.5 is actually the game Selten used to introduce subgame-perfection. Here there are two proper subgames: the whole game, and the game beginning in the second "period" if 1 played D. In this subgame, the only Nash equilibrium is for player 2 to choose L, so that any subgame-perfect equilibrium must prescribe this choice, and only (D, L) is subgame-perfect. More generally, in any game of perfect information subgame-perfection yields the same answer as backwards induction. In finite-period simultaneous move games, subgame-perfection does "backwards induction" period by period: at the last period, the strategies must yield a Nash equilibrium, given the history. Then we replace the last period with the possible last-period equilibria, and work backwards. For example, a subgame-perfect equilibrium of a two-period Cournot model must yield Cournot equilibrium outputs in the second period, regardless of first-period play. *Caution*: if there are several Cournot equilibria, then which of them prevails in the second period *can* depend on first-period play. We will say more about this when we discuss Benoit and Krishna (1985).

3.2. Repeated games and "implicit collusion"

3.2.1. Infinitely repeated games

Chamberlain (1956) criticized the Cournot and Bertrand models of oligopoly for assuming that firms were myopic. He argued that in an industry with few, long-lived firms, firms would realize their mutual interdependence and thus play more "cooperatively" than the Cournot and Bertrand models suggested. The theory of *repeated games* provides the simplest way of thinking about the effects of long-term competition.

This theory shows that, under the proper circumstances, Chamberlin's intuition can be partially formalized. Repetition can allow "cooperation" to be an equilibrium, but it does not eliminate the "uncooperative" static equilibria, and indeed can create new equilibria which are worse for all players than if the game had been played only once. Thus, to complete the Chamberlin argument, one must argue that the "cooperative" equilibria are "reasonable".

In an infinitely repeated game, players face the same constituent game in each of infinitely many periods. There is no direct physical link between the periods; each period's feasible actions and per-period payoffs are exactly as in the constituent game. This rules out important phenomena such as investment in productive machinery, so few interesting industries can be modelled exactly as repeated games. Nevertheless, if the history-dependent aspects of the industry are not too important, the repeated game model may be a reasonable approximation. Also, many of the qualitative predictions about the importance of repeated play and the nature of equilibria are useful in thinking about more general dynamic games, as we discuss in Subsection 3.3. Of course, the main reason that repeated games have received so much attention is their simplicity.

The constituent game

g is a finite n-player game in normal form, (I, Σ, π) where Σ_i is the probability distributions over a finite set S_i of pure strategies. In the repeated version of g, each player i's strategy is a sequence of maps $(\sigma_i(t))$ mapping the previous actions of all players to a $\sigma_i \in \Sigma_i$. Let us stress that it is the past *actions* that are observable, and not past choices of *mixed strategies*.

Players maximize the average discounted sum of their per-period payoffs with common discount factor δ. (We use the average discounted sum rather than simply the sum so that payoffs in the one-shot and repeated games are comparable – if a player receives payoff 5 every period his average discounted payoff is 5, while the discounted sum is, of course $5/(1-\delta)$.)

Player i's *reservation utility* is

$$v_i^* \equiv \min_{\sigma_{-i}} \max_{\sigma_i} \pi^i(\sigma_i, \sigma_{-i}).$$

In any equilibrium of the repeated game, player i's strategy must be a best response to the strategies of his opponents. One option player i has is to play myopically in each period, that is to play to maximize that period's payoff, ignoring the way this influences his opponents' future play. This static maximization will give player i at least v_i^* in each period, so that in any equilibrium, player i's expected average payoff must be at least v_i^*. A payoff vector v is *individually rational* if for all players $v_i > v_i^*$.

Notice that the equilibria of the constituent game (the "static equilibria") remain equilibria if the game is repeated: if each player's play is independent of the past history, then no player can do better than to play a static best response. Notice also that if the discount factor is very low, we would expect that the static equilibria are the *only* equilibria – if the future is unimportant, then once again players will choose static best responses. (This relies on g being finite.)

The best-known result about repeated games is the celebrated "folk theorem". This theorem asserts that if the game is repeated infinitely often and players are sufficiently patient, then "virtually anything" is an equilibrium outcome. By treating the polar case of extreme patience, the folk theorem provides an upper bound for the effects of repeated play, and thus a benchmark for thinking about the intermediate case of mild impatience.

The oldest version of the folk theorem asserts that if players are sufficiently patient (the discount factors are near enough to one), then any feasible individually rational payoffs are supportable by a *Nash* equilibrium. The idea of the proof is simple: any deviation from the prescribed path by player i leads the other players to play to "minmax" him (i.e. using the strategies that attain the minimum in the definition of v_i^*) for the rest of the game. In a repeated Cournot game, this would correspond to all players choosing the largest possible output forever. Given this threat, players will indeed choose not to deviate as long as

(1) never deviating yields more than v_i^*, and

(2) the discount factor is large enough that the gains to any one-period deviation are outweighed by the never ending ("grim") punishment.

The strategies sketched above clearly need not be subgame perfect – no firm would choose to produce a huge amount if the market price were zero! However, the "perfect folk theorem" shows that the same outcome can be enforced by a perfect equilibrium, so that restricting attention to perfect equilibria does not reduce the limit set of equilibrium *payoffs*. (It does, of course, rule out some Nash equilibria.)

Friedman (1971) proved a weaker version of this theorem which showed that any payoffs better for all players than a Nash equilibrium of the constituent game are the outcome of a *perfect* equilibrium of the repeated game, if players are sufficiently patient. The desired play is enforced by the "threat" that any deviation will trigger a permanent switch to the static equilibrium. Because this "punishment" is itself a perfect equilibrium, so are the overall strategies. This result shows, for example, that patient, identical, Cournot duopolists can "implicitly collude" by each producing one-half the monopoly output, with any deviation triggering a switch to the Cournot outcome. This would be "collusive" in yielding the monopoly price. The collusion is "implicit" (or "tacit") in that the firms would not need to enter into binding contracts to enforce their cooperation. Instead, each firm is deterred from breaking the agreement by the (credible) fear of provoking Cournot competition. If this equilibrium is suitably "focal", as it might be with two identical firms, then the firms might be able to collude without even communicating! This possibility has grave implications for anti-collusion laws based on observed conduct. How could two noncommunicating firms be charged with conspiracy?

Whether collusion can be enforced in a particular oligopoly then depends on whether the "relevant" discount factor is sufficiently large. This discount factor measures the length of the observation lag between periods, as well as the player's impatience "per unit time". In a market where orders are large but infrequent, a single order might represent several years of full-time production. Here the short-run gains to cheating might well outweight the costs of (greatly delayed) punishments. In the other extreme, with frequent, small orders, implicit collusion is more likely to be effective.

The Friedman result is weaker than the folk theorem because of its requirement that both players do better than in a static equilibrium. As a Stackelberg follower's payoffs are worse than a Cournot duopolist's, Friedman's result does not show that the Stackelberg outcome can be enforced in a repeated Cournot game. That this is however true is shown in the "perfect folk theorems" of Aumann and Shapley (1976), Rubinstein (1979), and Fudenberg and Maskin (1986a). Aumann–Shapley and Rubinstein consider the no-discounting models in which players are "completely" patient. Fudenberg–Maskin show that, under a mild "full-dimensionality" condition, the result continues to hold if the discount factors are sufficiently close to one. They also strengthen earlier results by allowing players to use mixed strategies as punishments. Aumann–Shapley and Rubinstein had restricted attention to pure strategies, which leads to higher individually-rational payoff levels, and thus a weaker theorem. For example, consider the game "matching pennies", where player 1 wins $1 if both players announce H or both announce T, and player 1 loses $1 otherwise. Here player 1's minmax value is $1 if player 2 is restricted to pure strategies, while his minmax value is 0 when mixed strategies are allowed. (The Aumann–Shapley and Rubinstein papers can also be interpreted as allowing mixed strategies as long as the mixing probabilities themselves, and not just the actions actually chosen, are observable at the end of each period.)

One might wish to characterize the set of perfect equilibria when there is "substantial" impatience. Abreu (1986, 1988) provides a tool for this purpose. [See also Harris (1986), who gives a clearer exposition and simpler proofs of Abreu's results.] Call strategies "simple" if they have the following form: there is an "equilibrium path" and n "punishment paths", one for each player. Play follows the equilibrium path as long as no one has deviated. If player i was the most recent player to deviate, and did so at period t, then play at period $(t + k)$ is given by the kth element of the "punishment path" corresponding to player i. (What happens if two or more players deviate simultaneously is irrelevant.)[5] The force in the restriction to simple strategies is that player i's punishment path is independent of the history before i's deviation and also of the nature of the deviation itself.

It is easy to see that any perfect equilibrium path that can be enforced with some perfect equilibrium punishments can be enforced by the threat that if player i deviates play will switch to the equilibrium $w(i)$ in which player i's payoff is lowest, provided such an equilibrium exists. Note that these strategies are simple in Abreu's sense. Thus, simple strategies are sufficient to enforce all possible equilibrium paths provided that there is a worst equilibrium for each player, which will be the case if the set of equilibrium payoffs is closed. For games with a finite number of actions per period, Fudenberg and Levine (1983) show that the set of equilibrium payoffs is closed by proving that the set of equilibrium strategies is closed as well. Abreu shows that the set of equilibrium payoffs is closed for games with a continuum of actions per period. Because the

[5]Simultaneous deviations can be ignored, because in testing for Nash or subgame-perfect equilibria, we ask only if a player can gain by deviating *when his opponents play as originally specified*.

strategy spaces are then not compact in a natural topology, proving closedness requires a more subtle proof.

Given that worst equilibria exist the next problem is to construct them. In general this may be difficult, but the worst symmetric equilibria of symmetric games are more easily characterized. [*Caution*. Symmetry here requires not only that the payoffs along the equilibrium path be identical, but that the payoffs be identical in the punishment phases as well.] Abreu's thesis (1983) finds the worst symmetric equilibria of repeated Cournot games and uses them to construct the set of symmetric equilibria. Shapiro's chapter in this Handbook (Chapter 6) explains this characterization in detail.

Another case in which the lowest perfect equilibrium payoffs can be pinned down is when equilibria can be constructed that hold players to their reservation values. Fudenberg and Maskin (1987) provide conditions for this to be true for a range of discount factors between some δ and 1. Because the reservation values are of course the worst possible punishments, any equilibrium outcome (Nash or perfect) can be enforced with the threat that deviations will switch play to an equilibrium in which the deviator is held to his reservation value.

3.2.1. Repeated games with imperfect monitoring

One drawback of repeated games as a model of collusion is that they do not predict price wars (although they are not inconsistent with them). This lack motivated the Green and Porter (1984) model of "Noncooperative Collusion under Imperfect Price Information". The Green–Porter model is an infinitely repeated quantity-setting game in which firms do not observe the outputs of their opponents. Instead, firms only observe the market price, $p(Q, \theta)$, which is determined by aggregate output Q and a stochastic disturbance, θ. The θ's in the different periods are identically and independently distributed according to a density $f(\theta)$, which is such that the set of possible prices [the support of $p(Q, \theta)$] is independent of Q. All firms are identical, and there is a symmetric ("Cournot") equilibrium of the constituent game in which each firm produces output q^c. As with ordinary repeated games, one equilibrium of the repeated game is for all firms to produce q^c each period. Could the firms hope to improve on this outcome if they are patient?

Green and Porter show that they can, by constructing a family of "trigger-price" equilibria of the following form: Play begins in the "cooperative" phase, with each firm producing some output q^*. Play remains in the cooperative phase as long as last period's price exceeded a trigger level p^*. If the price falls below p^*, firms switch to a "punishment phase" in which each firm produces output q^c. Punishment lasts for T periods, after which play returns to a cooperative phase. For a triple (q^*, p^*, T) to generate a Nash equilibrium, each firm must prefer not to cheat in either phase. Since q^c is a static equilibrium, no firm will cheat in the punishment phases, so we need only check the cooperative phase. Setting $q^* = q^c$ results in a trivial trigger-price equilibrium. If the firms are somewhat patient they can do better by setting $q^* < q^c$. In such an equilibrium, p must be high enough that punishment occurs with positive probability. Otherwise, a firm could increase its output slightly in the cooperative phase without penalty. Thus, punishment will occur *even if no firm has deviated*. On seeing a low price, all firms expand their output *not* out of concern that an opponent has cheated, but rather in the knowledge that *if* low prices did not sometimes trigger punishment, then their collusive scheme would not be self-enforcing. [See Rotemberg and Saloner (1986) for a repeated game model with perfect monitoring in which price wars are voluntary.]

The trigger-price equilibria constructed by Green and Porter have an appealing simplicity, but they need not be optimal – other equilibria may yield higher expected payoffs (for the firms). Abreu, Pearce and Stacchetti (1986) investigated the structure of the optimal symmetric equilibria in the Green–Porter model. In the process, they develop the concept of self-generation, which is useful for analyzing all repeated games with imperfect monitoring.

Self-generation is a sufficient condition for a set of payoffs to be supportable by equilibria. It is the multi-player generalization of dynamic programming's principle of optimality that provides a sufficient condition for a set of payoffs, one for each state, to be the maximal net present values obtainable in the corresponding states. Abreu, Pearce and Stacchetti's insight is that the "states" need not directly influence the player's payoffs, but can instead reflect (in the usual self-confirming way) changes in the play of opponents. Imagine, for example, that in the Green–Porter model there are only three possible values of the market price – $p_1 > p_2 > p_3$. Price p_i occurs with probability $m_i(Q)$, where Q is total industry output. Note that past prices do not directly influence current payoffs or transition probabilities. Nevertheless, we can construct equilibrium strategies that use the realized prices to determine the transitions between "fictitious" states.

For example, imagine that we are told that there are two fictitious states, a and b, with associated payoffs for both firms of u_a and u_b. (We will look at symmetric equilibria; otherwise we would need to specify each firm's payoffs.) We are also given the following transition rule: the state switches from a to b if p_3 occurs, remaining at a if $p = p_1$ or p_2. State b is absorbing: once it is reached, it prevails from then on. As we will see, state b corresponds to an infinite "punishment phase" in Green and Porter. The values u are self-generating if, in each state $i = \mathrm{a, b}$, when players believe that their future payoffs are given by $\{u_a, u_b\}$, there is an equilibrium s_i in current actions with average (over current and future payoffs) payoff u_i. In the language of dynamic programming, this says that for each player the payoff u_i is unimprovable, given the specified continuation payoffs and his opponents' current actions. To show that self-generating payoffs are sustainable by Nash equilibria, we first must define strategies for the players. To do this, trace out the succession of single-period equilibria. If play begins in state a, and p_1 occurs in the first period, the state is still a, so the second-period outputs are again given by the s_a. By construction, no player can gain by deviating from strategy s_i in state i for one period and then reverting to them thereafter. The standard dynamic programming argument then shows that unimprovability implies optimality: by induction, no player can improve on u_a or u_b by any finite sequence of deviations, and the payoff to an infinite sequence of deviations can be approximated by finitely many of them. In our example, since state b is absorbing, for (u_a, u_b) to be self-generating, u_b must be self-generating as a singleton set. This means that u_b must be the payoffs in a static equilibrium, as in Green and Porter's punishment phase. In state a, today's outcome influences the future state, so that players have to trade off their short-run incentive to deviate against the risk of switching to state b. Thus, state a corresponds to a "cooperative" phase, where players restrict output to decrease the probability of switching to the punishment state.

The self-generation criterion not only provides a way of testing for equilibria, it also suggests a way of constructing them: one can construct state spaces and transition rules instead of working directly with the strategy spaces. Fudenberg and Maskin (1986b) use this technique to investigate when "folk theorems" obtain for repeated games with imperfect monitoring.

Returning to the topic of implicit collusion in oligopolies, what lessons do we learn from the study of repeated games? First, repetition matters more, and (privately) efficient outcomes are more likely to be equilibria, when the periods are short. Second, more precise information makes collusion easier to sustain, and lowers the costs of the occasional "punishments" which must occur to sustain it. Third, firms will prefer "bright-line" rules which make "cheating" easy to identify. For example, firms would like to be able to respond to changes in market conditions without triggering "punishment". Scherer (1980) suggests that the institutions of price leadership and mark-up pricing may be responses to this problem. [See also Rotemberg and Saloner (1985), who explain how price leadership can be a collusive equilibrium with asymmetrically-informed firms.]

While most applications of repeated games have been concerned with games with infinitely lived players, "implicitly collusive equilibria" can arise even if all the players have finite lives, as long as the model itself has an infinite horizon. Let us give two examples. First, a finitely lived manager of a firm becomes the equivalent of an infinitely lived player if he owns the firm, because the latter's value depends on the infinite streams of profits [as in Kreps (1985)]. Second, overlapping generations of finite lived players can yield some cooperation between the players. A player who cheats early in his life will be punished by the next generation, which in turn will be punished by the following generation if it does not punish the first player, etc. [Cremer (1986)].

We conclude this subsection with three warnings on the limitations of the repeated game model. First, by focusing on stationary environments, the model sidesteps the questions of entry and entry deterrence. These questions can in principle be studied in games whose only time-varying aspect is the number of entrants, but serious treatments of the entry process more naturally allow for factors such as investment. Second, because repetition enlarges the set of equilibria, selecting an equilibrium becomes difficult. If firms are identical, an equal division of the monopoly profits seems an obvious solution; however, if one complicates the model by, for instance, introducing a prior choice of investment, most subgames are asymmetric, and the quest for a focal equilibrium becomes harder. However, the selection criterion of picking a date-zero Pareto-optimal equilibrium outcome is not "meta-perfect": date-zero Pareto-optimal outcomes are typically enforced by the threat of switching to a non Pareto-optimal outcome if some player deviates. Just after the deviation, the game is formally identical to the period-zero game, yet it is assumed that players will not again coordinate on the focal Pareto-optimal outcome. Third, implicit collusion may not be enforceable if the game is repeated only *finitely* many times. What then should we expect to occur in finite-lived markets?

3.2.2. Finite-horizon games

Infinite-horizon repeated games are used as an idealization of repeated play in long-lived markets. Since actual markets are finite-lived, one should ask whether the infinite-horizon idealization is sensible. One response is that we can incorporate a constant probability μ of continuing to the next period directly into the utility functions: the expected present value of ten utils tomorrow, if tomorrow's units are discounted by δ, and tomorrow arrives with probability μ, is simply $\delta\mu$.

Then if both δ and μ are near to one, the folk theorem applies. This specification implies that the game ends in finite time with probability one, but there is still a positive probability that the game exceeds any fixed finite length. Thus, one may ask what the theory predicts if the game is certain to end by some very far-distant date. It is well known that in some games the switch from an infinite horizon to a long finite one yields dramatically different conclusions – the set of equilibrium payoffs can expand discontinuously at the infinite-horizon limit. This is true, for example, in the celebrated game of the "prisoner's dilemma", which is depicted in Figure 5.9. When played only once, the game has a unique Nash equilibrium, as it is a dominant strategy for each player to "fink." "Never fink" is a perfect equilibrium outcome in the infinitely-repeated game if players are sufficiently patient.

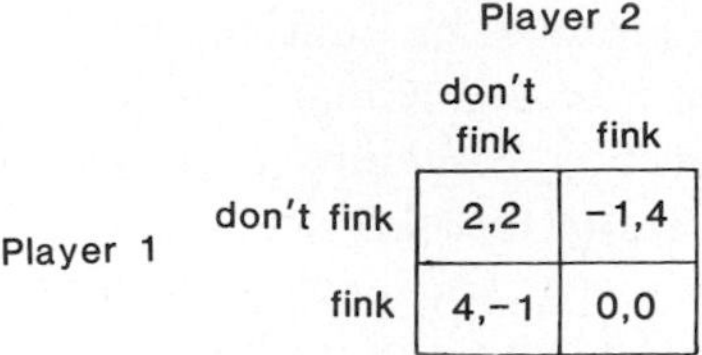

Figure 5.9

With a finite horizon, cooperation is ruled out by an iterated dominance argument: finking in the last period dominates cooperating there; iterating once, both players fink in the second period, etc. The infinite-horizon game lacks a last period and so the dominance argument cannot get started. Should we then reject the cooperative equilibria as technical artifacts, and conclude that the "reasonable solution" of the finitely-repeated prisoner's dilemma is "always fink"? Considerable experimental evidence shows that subjects do tend to cooperate in many if not most periods. Thus, rather than reject the cooperative equilibria, we should change the model to provide an explanation of cooperation. Perhaps players derive an extra satisfication from "cooperating" beyond the rewards specified by the experimenters. While this explanation does not seem implausible, it seems a bit too convenient. Other explanations do not add a payoff for cooperation per se, but instead change the model to break the backwards-induction argument, which is argued to be unreasonable. One way of doing this is developed in the "reputation effects" models of Kreps, Milgrom, Roberts, and Wilson, which we discuss in Section 4. These models assume, not that all players prefer cooperation, but that each player attaches a very small prior probability to the event that his opponent does.

Radner (1980) provides another way of derailing the backwards induction in the finitely-repeated game. He observes that the best response against an opponent who will not fink until you do, but will fink thereafter (the "grim" strategy) is to cooperate until the last period, and then fink. Moreover, as the horizon T grows, the *average* gain (the gain divided by T) to playing this way instead of always cooperating goes to zero. Formally, in an ε-equilibrium, a player's strategy gives him within ε of his best attainable payoff (*over the whole horizon*); in a subgame-perfect ε-equilibrium this is true in every subgame. Radner shows that cooperation is the outcome of a perfect ε-equilibrium for any $\varepsilon > 0$ if players maximize their average payoff and the horizon is sufficiently long. This is because one-period gains become small in terms of *average* payoff (compared to the fixed ε) as the horizon grows.

Fudenberg and Levine (1983) show that if players discount the future then the ε-equilibrium, finite horizon approach gives "exactly" the same conclusions as the infinite-horizon one: the set of infinite-horizon (perfect) equilibria coincides with the set of limit points of finite-horizon (perfect) ε-equilibria, where ε goes to zero as the horizon T goes to infinity. That is, every such limit point is an infinite-horizon equilibrium, and every infinite-horizon equilibrium can be approximated by a convergent sequence of finite-horizon ε-equilibria. Fudenberg and Levine define the "limits" in the above with respect to a topology that requires the action played to be uniformly close in every subgame. In finite-action games (games with a finite number of actions per period) this reduces to the condition that $s_n \to s$ if s_n and s exactly agree in the first k_n periods for all initial histories, where $k_n \to \infty$ as $n \to \infty$. Harris (1985a) shows that this simpler convergence condition can be used in most games, and dispenses with a superfluous requirement that payoffs be continuous.

With either of the Fudenberg–Levine or Harris topologies, the strategy spaces are compact in finite-action games, so that the limit result can be restated as follows. Let $\Gamma(\varepsilon, \mathrm{T})$ be the correspondence yielding the set of ε-equilibria of the T-period game. Then Γ is continuous at $(0, \infty)$. This continuity allows one to characterize infinite-horizon equilibria by working with finite-horizon ones. Backwards induction can be applied to the latter, albeit tediously, but not to the former, so that working with the finite horizon ε-equilibria is more straightforward. The continuity result holds for discounted repeated games, and for any other game in which players are not too concerned about actions to be taken in the far-distant future. (It does not hold in general for the time-average payoffs considered by Radner.) Specifically, preferences over outcome paths need not be additively separable over time, and there can be links between past play and future opportunities. In particular the result covers the nonrepeated games discussed later in this section. The intuition is simply that if players are not too concerned about the future, the equilibria of the infinite-horizon game should be similar to the equilibria of the "truncated" game in which no choices are allowed after some terminal time T. So for any equilibrium s of the infinite-horizon game and $\varepsilon > 0$, by taking T long enough, the difference in each player's payoff between the play prescribed by s and that obtained by truncating s at time t will be of order ε.

We should point out that the "epsilons" are not always needed to ensure continuity at the infinite-horizon limit. One example is Rubinstein's (1982) bargaining game, which, even with an infinite horizon, has a unique perfect equilibrium. (Rubinstein allows players to choose from a continuum of sharing rules between 0 and 1. With a finite grid of shares, the uniqueness result requires that each player prefers the second-largest partition today to the largest one tomorrow, so that the grid must be very fine if the discount factors are near to one.) Benoit and Krishna (1985) provide conditions for continuity to obtain in the "opposite" way, with the set of finite-horizon equilibria expanding as the horizon grows, and approaching the limit set given by the folk theorem.

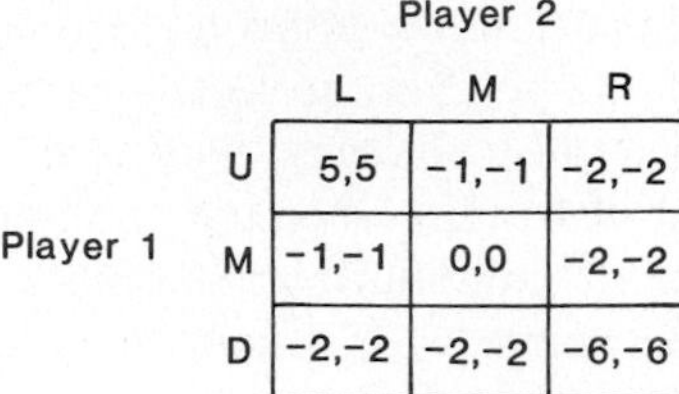

Player 1 \ Player 2	L	M	R
U	5,5	−1,−1	−2,−2
M	−1,−1	0,0	−2,−2
D	−2,−2	−2,−2	−6,−6

Figure 5.10

[Friedman (1984) and Fraysse and Moreaux (1985) give independent but less complete analyses.] For *Nash* equilibria this is true as long as the static equilibria give all players more than their minmax values. Then any individually-rational payoffs can be enforced in all periods sufficiently distant from the terminal date by the threat that any deviation results in the deviator being minmaxed for the rest of the game. Such threats are not generally credible, so proving the analogous result for perfect equilibria is more difficult. Benoit and Krishna show that the result *does* hold for perfect equilibria if each player has a strict preference for one static equilibrium as opposed to another (in particular there must be at least two static equilibria) and the Fudenberg–Maskin full dimensionality condition is satisfied. The construction that Benoit and Krishana use to prove this is too intricate to explain here, but it is easy to see that there can be perfect equilibria of a finitely-repeated game which are not simply a succession of static equilibria. Consider the game in Figure 5.10.

There are two pure-strategy static equilibria, (U, L) and (M, M). In the twice-repeated game (without discounting, for simplicity) there is an equilibrium with total payoffs $(-1, -1)$. These payoffs result from the strategies "play (D, R) in the first period; play (U, L) in the second iff (D, R) was played in the first, otherwise, play (M, M)".

3.3. Continuous-time games

Frequently, continuous-time models seem simpler and more natural than models with a fixed, non-negligible period length. For example, differential equations can be easier to work with than difference equations. As in games with a continuum of actions, continuous-time games may fail to have equilibria in the absence of continuity conditions. More troublesome, there are deep mathematical problems in formulating general continuous-time games.

As Anderson (1985) observes, "general" continuous-time strategies need not lead to a well-defined outcome path for the game, even if the strategies and the outcome path are restricted to be continuous functions of time. He offers the example of a two-player game where players simultaneously choose actions on the unit interval. Consider the continuous-time strategy "play at each time t the limit as $r \to t$ of what the opponent has played at times r previous to t". This limit is the natural analog of the discrete-time strategies "match the opponent's last action". If at all times before t the players have chosen matching actions, and the history is continuous, there is no problem in computing what should be played at t. However, there is not a unique way of extending the outcome path beyond time t. Knowing play before t determines the outcome at t, but is not sufficient to extend the outcome path to any open interval beyond t. As a result of this problem, Anderson opts to study the limits of discrete-time equilibria instead of working with continuous time.

Continuous-time formulations are fairly tractable when strategies depend on a "small" set of histories. This is the case in stopping-time games, open-loop games, and in situations where players use "state–space" strategies. These games or strategies are not restricted to continuous time, and discrete-time versions of all of them have been used in the industrial organization literature.

3.4. State–space or Markov equilibria

Consider games in which players maximize the present value of instantaneous flow payoffs, which may depend on state variables as well as current actions. (The feasible actions may also depend on the state.) For example, current actions could be investment decisions, and the state could be the stocks of machinery. Or current actions could be expenditures on R & D, with the state variables representing accumulated knowledge. The strategy spaces are simplified by restricting attention to "state–space" (or "Markov") strategies that depend not on the complete specification of past play, but only on the state (and, perhaps, on calendar time.) A *state–space or Markov equilibrium* is an equilibrium in state–space strategies, and a perfect state–space equilibrium must yield a state–space equilibrium for every initial state. Since the past's influence on current and future payoffs and opportunities is summarized in the state, if one's opponents use state–space strategies, one could not gain by conditioning one's play on other aspects of the history. Thus, a state–space equilibrium is an equilibrium in a game with less restricted strategies. The state–space restriction can however rule out equilibria, as shown by the infinitely-repeated prisoner's dilemma. Since past play has no effect on current payoffs or opportunities, the state–space is null, and all state–space strategies must be constants. Thus the only state–space equilibrium is for both sides to always fink. (*Caution*. This conclusion may be due to a poor model, and not to the wrong equilibrium concept. Subsection 5.5 shows how the conclusion is reversed in a slightly different model.)

Maskin and Tirole (1988), using the Markov restriction, obtain collusion in a repeated price game in which prices are locked in for two periods. They argue that what is meant by "reaction" is often an attempt by firms to react to a state that affects their *current* profits; for instance, when facing a low price by their opponents, they may want to regain market share. In the classic repeated-game model, firms move simultaneously, and there is no physical state to react to. If, however, one allows firms to alternate moves, they can react to their opponent's price. [Maskin and Tirole derive asynchronicity as the (equilibrium) result of two-period commitments.] The possibility of reaction leads to interesting Markov equilibria. However, although equilibrium payoffs are bounded away from the competitive levels (in contrast to the folk theorem approach), they are still many equilibria (Maskin and Tirole use renegotiation-proofness to select one which exhibits the classic "kinked demand curve"). Gertner (1985b) formalizes collusion with Markov strategies when commitment (inertia) takes the form of a fixed cost of changing prices.

The literal definition of a state says that strategies can depend "a lot" on variables with very little influence on payoffs, but they cannot depend at all on strategies that have no influence. This can generate rather silly discontinuities. For example, we can restore the cooperative equilibria in the repeated prisoner's dilemma by adding variables that keep track of the number of times each player has finked. If these variables have an infinitesimal effect on the flow payoffs, the cooperative equilibria can be restored.

The state–space restriction does not always rule out "supergame"-type equilibria, as shown in Fudenberg and Tirole (1983a). They reconsidered a model of continuous-time investment that had been introduced by Spence (1979). Firms choose rates of investment in productive capacity. The cost of investment is linear in the rate up to some upper bound, with units chosen so that one unit of capital costs one dollar. If firms did not observe the investment of their rivals, each firm would invest up to the point where its marginal productivity of capital equaled the interest rate. The capital levels at this "Cournot" point exceed the levels the firms would choose if they were acting collusively, because each firm has ignored the fact that its investment lowers its rivals' payoffs. Now, if firms observe their rivals' investment (in either discrete or continuous time) they could play the strategy of stopping investment once the collusive levels are reached. This "early stopping" is enforced by the (credible) threat that if any firm invests past the collusive level, all firms will continue to invest up to the "Cournot" levels. The state–space restriction seems to have little force in this game. There are no general results on when the restriction is likely to have a significant impact.

State–space games closely resemble control problems, so it is not surprising that they have been studied by control theorists. Indeed, the idea of perfection is just the many-player version of dynamic programming, and it was independently formulated by Starr and Ho (1967) in the context of non zero-sum differential games. The differential games literature restricts attention to state–space equilibria in which the equilibrium payoffs are continuous and almost everywhere differentiable functions of the state. These conditions obtain naturally for control problems in smooth environments, but they impose significant restrictions in games: it might be that each player's strategy, and thus each player's payoff, change discontinuously with the state due to the self-fulfilling expectation that the other players use discontinuous strategies. This was the case in the "early-stopping" equilibria of the previous paragraph, so those equilibria would not be admissible in the differential-games setting. Perhaps the continuity restriction can be justified by the claim that the "endogenous discontinuities" that they prohibit require excessive coordination, or are not robust to the addition of a small amount of noise in the players' observations. We are unaware of formal arguments along these lines.

The technical advantage of restricting attention to smooth equilibria is that necessary conditions can then be derived using the variational methods of optimal control theory. Assume that player i wishes to choose a_i to maximize the integral of his flow payoff π^i, subject to the state evolution equation:

$$\dot{k}(t) = f(k(t)),\ k(0) = k_0. \tag{2}$$

Introducing costate variables λ_i, we define H_i, the Hamiltonian for player i, as

$$H_i = \pi^i(k, a, t) + \lambda_i f(k(t)). \tag{3}$$

A state–space equilibrium $a(t)$ must satisfy:

$$a_i = a_i(k, t) \text{ maximizes } H_i(k, t, a, \lambda_i) \tag{4}$$

and

$$\dot{\lambda}_i = -\partial H_i/\partial k_i - \sum_{j \neq i} \partial H_i/\partial a_j\ \partial a_j/\partial k_i \tag{5}$$

along with the appropriate transversality condition.

Notice that for a one-player game the second term in (5) vanishes, and the conditions reduce to the familiar ones. In the n-player case, this second term captures the fact that player i cares about how his opponents will react to changes in the state. Because of the cross-influence terms, the evolution of λ is determined by a system of partial differential equations, instead of by ordinary differential equations as in the one-player case. As a result, very few differential games can be solved in closed form. An exception is the linear-quadratic case, which has been studied by Starr and Ho among others. Hanig (1985) and Reynolds (1985) consider a linear-quadratic version of the continuous-time investment game. (Their model is that of Spence–Fudenberg–Tirole, except that the cost of investment increases quadratically in the rate.) They show that the "smooth" equilibrium for the game has higher steady-state capital stocks and so lower profits, than the static "Cournot" levels. Is this a better prediction than the collusive levels? We do not know.

Judd (1985) offers an alternative to the strong functional form assumptions typically invoked to obtain a closed-form solution to differential games. His method is to analyze the game in the neighborhood of a parameter value that leads to a unique and easily computed equilibrium. In his examples of patent races, he looks at patents with almost zero value. Obviously if the patent has exactly zero value, in the unique equilibrium players do no R & D and have zero values. Judd proceeds to expand the system about this point, neglecting all terms over third order in the value of the patent. Judd's method gives only local results, but it solves an "open set" in the space of games, as opposed to conventional techniques that can be thought of as solving a lower-dimensional subset of them.

3.5. *Games of timing*

In a game of timing, each player's only choice is when and whether to take a single pre-specified action. Few situations can be exactly be described this way, because players typically have a wider range of choices. For example, firms typically do not only choose a time to enter a market, but also decide on the scale of entry, the type of product to produce, etc. This detail can prove unmanageable, which is why industrial organization economists have frequently abstracted it away to focus on the timing question in isolation.

We will not even try to discuss all games of timing, but only two-player games which "end" once at least one player has moved. Payoffs in such games can be completely described by six functions $L_i(t)$, $F_i(t)$, and $B_i(t)$, $i = 1, 2$. Here L_i is player i's payoff if player i is the first to move (the "leader"), F_i is i's payoff if j is the first to move (the "follower"), and B_i is i's payoff is both players move simultaneously. This framework is slightly less restrictive than it appears, in that it can incorporate games which continue until both players have moved. In such games, once one player has moved, the other one faces a simple maximization problem, which can be solved and "folded back" to yield the payoffs as a function of the time of the first move alone. A classic example of such a game is the "war of attrition", first analyzed by Maynard Smith (1974): two animals are fighting for a prize of value v; fighting costs one util per unit time. Once one animal quits, his opponent wins the prize. Here $L(t)$ is $-t$, and $F(t)$ is $v - t$.

With short time periods $B(t)$ will turn out to not matter much; let us set it equal to $v/q - t$, $q \geq 2$. If $q = 2$, then each player has probability 1/2 of winning the prize if both quit at once; if $q = \infty$, this probability is zero. Let us solve for a symmetric equilibrium of the discrete-time version with period length Δ. Let p be the probability that either player moves at t when both are still fighting. For players to use stationary mixed strategies, the payoff to dropping out, pv/q, must equal that to fighting one more period and then dropping out, $pv + (1 - p) pv/q - \Delta$. Equating these terms yields:

$$p = \left(1 - (1 - 4\Delta/qv)^{1/2}\right)q/2.$$

[Dropping out with probability p per period is a "behavioral strategy"; the corresponding mixed strategy is an exponential distribution over stopping times.]

Let us note that as $\Delta \to 0$, $p \to \Delta/v$, independent of q. More generally, a war of attrition is a game of "chicken", in which each player prefers his opponent to move ($F(t) > L(t)$), and wishes that he would do so quickly (F and L decrease over time). Weiss and Wilson (1984) characterize the equilibria of a large family of discrete-time wars of attrition; Hendricks and Wilson (1985a) do the same for the continuous-time version. Section 4 describes some of the many incomplete-information wars of attrition that have been applied to oligopoly theory.

Preemption games are the opposite case, with $L(t) > F(t)$, at least over some set of times. One example of a preemption game is the decision of when and whether to build a new plant or adopt a new innovation, when the market is only big enough to support one such addition. (If each firm will eventually build a plant, but the second mover would optimally choose to wait until long after the first one, we can "fold back" the second mover's choice to get the payoffs as a function of the time of the first move alone.)

The relationship between L and F can change over time, and the two players may have different "types" of preferences, as in Katz and Shapiro (1984). No one has yet attempted a general classification of all games of timing. Because the possible actions and histories are so limited, it is easy to formulate continuous-time strategies for these games, in a way that permits a well-defined map from strategies to outcomes. We develop these strategies below. However, we will see that the simplicity of this formulation is not without cost, as it is not rich enough to represent some limits of discrete-time strategies. That is, there are distributions over outcomes (who moves and when) that are the limits of distributions induced by discrete-time strategies, but which cannot be generated by the "obvious" continuous time strategies.

The usual and simple continuous-time formulation is that each player's strategy is a function $G_i(t)$ which is nondecreasing, right-continuous, and has range in

[0, 1]. This formulation was developed in the 1950s for the study of zero-sum "duels", and was used by Pitchik (1982), who provides several existence theorems. The interpretation is that G_i is a distribution function, representing the cumulative probability that player i has moved by time t conditional on the other player not having moved previously. These distribution functions need not be continuous; a discontinuity at time t implies that the player moves with nonzero probability at exactly time t. Where G is differentiable, its derivative $\mathrm{d}G$ is the density which gives the probability of a move over a short time interval. With this notation, player 1's payoff to the strategies G_1, G_2 is

$$V^i(G_1, G_2) = \int_0^{\infty} \left[L(s)(1 - G_j(s))\,\mathrm{d}G_i(s) + F(s)(1 - G_i(s))\,\mathrm{d}G_j(s)\right] + \sum \alpha_i(s)\alpha_j(s)B(s),$$

where $\alpha_i(s)$ is the size of the jump in G_i at s.

This formulation is very convenient for wars of attrition. In these games there are "nice" discrete-time equilibria in which the probability of moving in each period is proportional to the period length. In the example computed above, the equilibrium strategies converged to the continuous-time limit $G(t) = 1 - \exp(-t/v)$. [For the case $q = 2$, the *sum* of the two players' payoffs is upper hemi-continuous, and the fact that the equilibria converge is a consequence of theorem 5 of Dasgupta and Maskin (1986).] More complex wars of attrition can have continuous-time equilibria with "atoms", ($\alpha_i(t) > 0$ for some t), but as the periods shrink these atoms become isolated, and again admit a nice continuous-time representation.

Pre-emption games are markedly different in this respect, as shown in Fudenberg and Tirole (1985). Consider the discrete-time "grab-the-dollar" game: $L(t) = 1$, $F(t) = 0$, and $B(t) = -1$. The interpretation is that "moving" here is grabbing a dollar which lies between the two players. If either grabs alone, he obtains the dollar, but simultaneous grabbing costs each player one. There is a symmetric equilibrium in which each player moves with (conditional) probability $1/2$ in each period. Note well that the intensity of the randomization is independent of the period length. The corresponding payoffs are (0, 0), and the distribution over outcomes is that with identical probability $(1/4)^{(t+1)}$ either player 1 wins (moves alone) in period t, or player 2 wins in period t, or both move at once at t. As the length of the period converges to zero, this distribution converges to one in which the game ends with probability one at the start, with equal probabilities of $1/3$ that player 1 wins, that player 2 does, or that they both move at once. This distribution cannot be implemented with the continuous-time strategies described above, for it would require a correlating device à la Aumann. Otherwise, at least one player would move with probability one at the start, which would make it impossible for this opponent to have a 1/3 probability of winning. The problem is that a great many discrete-time strategies converge to a continuous-time limit in which both players move with probability one at time zero, including "move with probability 1/2 each period", and "move with probability one at the start". The usual continuous-time strategies implicitly associate an atom of size one with an atom of that size in discrete time, and thus they cannot represent the limit of the discrete-time strategies. Fudenberg and Tirole offered an expanded notion of continuous-time strategies that "works" for the grab-the-dollar game and a class of pre-emption games, but they did not attempt a general treatment of what the strategy space would need to handle all games of timing.

The moral of this story is that while continuous time is often a convenient idealization of very short time periods, one should keep in mind that a given formulation of continuous time may not be adequate for all possible applications. When confronted with, for example, the nonexistence of equilibria in a seemingly "nice" continuous-time game, it can be useful to think about discrete-time approximations. Simon and Stinchcombe (1986) provide a general analysis of when the usual continuous-time strategies are in fact appropriate.

3.6. *Discrete vs. continuous time, and the role of period length*

The discussion above stressed that one must be careful that a given continuous time model is rich enough to serve as the "appropriate" idealization of very short time periods. Now we would like to point out that new equilibria can arise in passing to continuous time, and that these should *not* be discarded as pathological. The simplest, and oldest, example of this fact is the Kreps–Wilson (1982a) stopping-time version of the prisoner's dilemma. In this version, players begin by cooperating, and once either finks they both must fink forever afterwards. Thus, the only choice players have is when to fink if their opponent has not yet done so. In discrete time with a finite horizon, the familiar backwards-induction argument shows that the only equilibrium is to both fink at once. However, the gain to finking one period ahead of one's opponent is proportional to the period length, and in the continuous-time limit there is no gain to finking. Thus, cooperation is an equilibrium in the continuous-time game.

The analogy with the finite-to-infinite horizon limit is more than suggestive. In a generalization of their earlier work, Fudenberg and Levine (1986) showed that, in cases such as stopping-time games and state–space games where the continuous time formulation is not too problematic, any continuous-time equilibrium is a limit of discrete-time epsilon-equilibria, where the epsilon converges to zero with the length of the period.

Little is known in general about the effect of period length on equilibrium play, but several examples have been intensively studied. The best known is the work of Coase (1972), Bulow (1982), Stokey (1981), and Gul, Sonnenschein and Wilson (1986) who argue with varying degrees of formality that the monopolistic producer of a durable good loses the power to extract rents as the time period shrinks, thus verifying the "Coase conjecture". [See also Sobel and Takahashi (1983) and Fudenberg, Levine and Tirole (1985).]

3.7. *Open-loop equilibria*

The terms "open loop" and "closed loop" refer to two different information structures for multi-stage dynamic games. In an open-loop model, players cannot observe the play of their opponents; in a closed-loop model all past play is common knowledge at the beginning of each stage. Like "Cournot" and "Bertrand" equilibria, open- and closed-loop equilibria are shorthand ways of referring to the perfect equilibria of the associated model. (*Caution*. This terminology is widespread but not universal. Some authors use "closed-loop equilibrium" to refer to all the Nash equilibria of the closed-loop model. We prefer to ignore the imperfect equilibria.) Open and closed loop models embody different assumptions about the information lags with which players observe and respond to each other's actions, and thus about the length of time to which players can "commit" themselves not to respond to their opponents. In an open-loop model, these lags are infinite, while in a closed-loop model, a player can respond to his opponents. Because dynamic interactions are limited in open-loop equilibria, they are more tractable than closed-loop ones. For this reason, economists have sometimes analyzed the open-loop equilibria of situations which seem more naturally to allow players to respond to their opponents. One possible justification for this is that, if there are many "small" players, so that no one player can greatly affect the others, then optimal reactions should be negligible. When this is true, the open-loop equilibria will be a good approximation of the closed-loop ones. Fudenberg and Levine (1988) explore this argument.

4. Static games of incomplete and imperfect information

4.1. *Bayesian games and Bayesian equilibrium*

Players in a game are said to have *incomplete information* if they do not know some of their opponents' *characteristics* (objective functions); they have *imperfect information* if they do not observe some of their opponents' *actions*. Actually, the distinction between incomplete and imperfect information is convenient, but artificial. As Harsanyi (1967–68) has shown, at a formal level, one can transform a game of incomplete information into a game of imperfect information. The idea is the following: let the original game be an n-player game with incomplete information. Assume that each player's characteristic is known by the player, but, from the point of view of the $(n - 1)$ other players, is drawn according to some known probability distribution. (See below for a discussion of this representation.) Harsanyi's construction of a transformed game introduces nature as a $(n + 1)$st player, whose strategy consists in choosing characteristics for each of the n original players at the start of the game, say. Each player observes his own characteristic, but not the other players'. Thus, he has *imperfect* information about nature's choice of their characteristics. (One can endow nature with an objective function in order for it to become a player. One way of doing so is to assume that nature is indifferent between all its moves. To recover the equilibria of the original game (i.e. for given initial probability distributions), one takes the projection of the equilibrium correspondence for these probability distributions).

The notion of "type". In Harsanyi's formulation, the "type" of a player embodies everything which is relevant to the player's decision-making. This includes the description of his objective function (fundamentals), his beliefs about the other players' objective functions (beliefs about fundamentals), his beliefs about what the other players believe his objective function is (beliefs about beliefs about fundamentals), etc. Since this is a bit abstract, it is helpful to begin with Harsanyi's simple representation (this representation is used in virtually all applications). Suppose that in an oligopoly context, each firm's marginal cost c_i is drawn from an "objective" distribution $p_i(c_i)$. (N.B. we will write probability distributions as if the number of potential types were finite. Continuous type spaces are also allowed; summation signs should then be replaced by integral signs.) c_i is observed by firm i, but not by the other firms; p_i is common knowledge; everybody knows that c_i is drawn from this distribution; that everybody knows that c_i is drawn from this distribution, etc. ...[6] In this case firm i's type is fully summarized by c_i: because the probability distributions are common knowledge, knowing c_i amounts to knowing everything known by firm i. By abuse of terminology, one can identify firm i's type with the realization of c_i.

[6]Aumann (1976) formalizes common knowledge in the following way. Let (Ω, p) be a finite probability space and let P and Q denote two partitions of Ω representing the informations of two players. Let R denote the meet of P and Q (i.e. the finest common coarsening of P and Q). An event E is common knowledge between the two players at $\omega \in \Omega$ if the event in R that includes ω is itself included in E.

More generally, Harsanyi assumed that the player's types $\{t_i\}_{i=1}^n$ are drawn from some objective distribution $p(t_1, \ldots, t_n)$, where t_i belongs to some space T_i. For simplicity, let us assume that T_i has a finite number $|T_i|$ of elements. t_i is observed by player i only. $p_i(t_{-i}|t_i)$ denotes player i's conditional probability about his opponents' types $t_{-i} = (t_1, \ldots, t_{i-1}, t_{i+1}, \ldots, t_n)$ given his type t_i.

To complete the description of a Bayesian game, we must specify an action set A_i (with elements a_i) and an objective function $\Pi_i(a_1, \ldots, a_n, t_1, \ldots, t_n)$ for each player i. The action spaces A_i, the objective functions Π_i and the probability distribution p are common knowledge (every player knows them, knows that everybody knows them, ...). In other words, everything which is not commonly known is subsumed in the type.

The Harsanyi formulation looks restrictive in that it presumes a single "type" for each player describes all the player's information: That is, a type for player i describes his beliefs about player j's type, his beliefs about player j's beliefs about his type, and so on. If we start from the idea that a "type" is an infinite hierarchy of beliefs, beliefs about beliefs, and so on, one might ask when these hierarchies can be summarized by "types" in the Harsanyi fashion. Mertens and Zamir (1985) and Brandenburger and Dekel (1985a) show that one can construct a "universal type space" that meets Harsanyi's conditions whenever the underlying hierarchies of beliefs satisfy a "common knowledge of coherency".

In this section we consider only one-shot simultaneous move games of incomplete information. The n players first learn their types and then simultaneously choose their actions (note that the game is also a game of imperfect information). The game is static in that the players are unable to react to their opponents' actions. The inference process as to the other players' types is irrelevant because the game is over at the time each player learns some signal related to his opponents' types. Section 5 considers dynamic games and the associated updating process.

Each player's optimal choice may depend on his information, i.e. his type. For instance, a high-cost firm chooses a high price. Let $a_i(t_i)$ denote the action chosen by player i when his type is t_i (this could also denote a mixed strategy, i.e. a randomization over actions for a given type). If he knew the strategies adopted by the other players $\{a_j(t_j)\}_{j \neq i}$ as a function of their types, player i would be facing a simple decision problem; given his type t_i, he ought to maximize:

$$\Sigma_{t_{-i}} p_i(t_{-i}|t_i) \Pi_i(a_1(t_1), \ldots, a_i, \ldots, a_n(t_n), t_1, \ldots, t_i, \ldots, t_n).$$

Harsanyi extended the idea of a Nash equilibrium by assuming that each player correctly anticipates how each of his opponents behaves as a function of his type:

Definition

A *Bayesian equilibrium* is a set of (type-contingent) strategies $\{a_i^*(t_i)\}_{i=1}^n$ such that $a_i^*(t_i)$ is player i's best response to the other strategies when his type is t_i:

$$a_i^*(t_i) \in \arg\max_{a_i} \Sigma_{t_{-i}} p_i(t_{-i}|t_i)$$
$$\cdot \Pi_i(a_1(t_1),\ldots,a_i,\ldots,a_n(t_n),t_1,\ldots,t_i,\ldots,t_n).$$

Thus, the Bayesian equilibrium concept is a straightforward extension of the Nash equilibrium concept, in which player recognizes that the other players' strategies depend on their types.

Proving *existence* of a Bayesian equilibrium turns out to involve a simple extension of the proof of a Nash equilibrium. The trick is the following: since player i's optimal action depends on type t_i, everything is as if player i's opponents were playing against $|T_i|$ different players, each of these players being drawn and affecting his opponents' payoffs with some probability. Thus, considering different types of the same player as different players leads to transform the original game into a game with $\{\Sigma_{i=1}^n |T_i|\}$ players. Each "player" is then defined by a name *and* a type. He does not care (directly) about the action of a player with the same name and a different type (another incarnation of himself), but he does care about the other players' actions. If a_{i,t_i} denotes the action chosen by player $\{i, t_i\}$, player $\{i, t_i\}$'s objectives is to maximize over a:

$$\Sigma_{t_{-i}} p_i(t_{-i}|t_i)\Pi_i(a_{1,t_1},\ldots,a,\ldots,a_{n,t_n},t_1,\ldots,t_i,\ldots,t_n).$$

Thus, existence of a Bayesian equilibrium of a game with $|T_i|$ players stems directly from the existence of a Nash equilibrium for a game with $\{\Sigma_i|T_i|\}$ players, as long as the numbers of players and types are finite.

With a continuum of types, some technicalities appear about whether there exists a measurable structure over the set of random variables [Aumann (1964)]. One is then led to define a mixed strategy as a measurable function from $[0,1] \times T_i$ into A_i. Or, equivalently, one can define it, as Milgrom and Weber (1986b) do, as a measure on the subjects of $T_i \times A_i$ for which the marginal distribution on T_i is p_i. Milgrom and Weber give sufficient conditions for the existence of an equilibrium in such settings.

Example 1

Consider a duopoly playing Cournot (quantity) competition. Let firm i's profit be quadratic: $\Pi_i = q_i(t_i - q_i - q_j)$, where t_i is the difference between the intercept of the linear demand curve and firm i's constant unit cost ($i = 1, 2$) and q_i is the quantity chosen by firm i ($a_i = q_i$). It is common knowledge that, for firm 1, $t_1 = 1$ ("firm 2 has complete information about firm 1", or "firm 1 has only one potential type"). Firm 2, however, has private information about its unit cost. Firm 1 only knows that $t_2 = 3/4$ or $5/4$ with equal probabilities. Thus, firm 2 has two potential types, which we will call the "low cost type" ($t_2 = 5/4$) and the "high cost type" ($t_2 = 3/4$). The two firms choose their outputs simultaneously. Let us look for a pure strategy equilibrium. Firm 1 plays q_1, firm 2 plays q_2^{L} (if $t_2 = 5/4$) or q_2^{H} (if $t_2 = 3/4$). Let us start with firm 2:

$$q_2(t_2) \in \arg\max_{q_2} \{ q_2(t_2 - q_2 - q_1)\} \Rightarrow q_2(t_2) = (t_2 - q_1)/2.$$

Let us now consider firm 1, which does not know which type it faces:

$$q_1 \in \arg\max_{q_1} \{ \tfrac{1}{2} q_1 (1 - q_1 - q_2^{\mathrm{H}}) + \tfrac{1}{2} q_1 (1 - q_1 - q_2^{\mathrm{L}})\}$$

$$\Rightarrow q_1 = (1 - \mathrm{E} q_2)/2,$$

where $\mathrm{E}(\cdot)$ denotes an expectation over firm 2's types. But $\mathrm{E}q_2 = \frac{1}{2}q_2^{\mathrm{H}} + \frac{1}{2}q_2^{\mathrm{L}} = (\mathrm{E}t_2 - q_1)/2 = (1 - q_1)/2$. One thus obtains $\{q_1 = 1/3,\ q_2^{\mathrm{L}} = 11/24,\ q_2^{\mathrm{H}} = 5/24\}$ as a Bayesian equilibrium (one can prove this equilibrium is unique). This simple example illustrates how one can compute the Bayesian equilibrium as a Nash equilibrium of a three-player game ($|T_1| = 1$, $|T_2| = 2$).

Example 2

Consider an incomplete-information version of the war of attrition discussed in Subsection 3.5. Firm i chooses a number a_i in $[0, \infty)$. Both firms choose simultaneously. The payoffs are:

$$\Pi_i = \begin{cases} -a_i, & \text{if } a_j \geq a_i, \\ t_i - a_j, & \text{if } a_j < a_i. \end{cases}$$

t_i, firm i's type, is private information and takes values in $[0, +\infty)$ with cumulative distribution function $P_i(t_i)$ and density $p_i(t_i)$. Types are, as in Example 1, independent between the players. t_i is the price to the winner, i.e. the highest bidder. The game resembles a second-bid auction in that the winner pays the second bid. However, it differs from the second-bid auction in that the loser also pays the second bid.

Let us look for a Bayesian equilibrium of this game. Let $a_i(t_i)$ denote firm i's strategy. Then, we require:

$$a_i(t_i) \in \arg\max_{a_i} \left\{ -a_i \operatorname{Prob}\big(a_j(t_j) \geq a_i\big) + \int_{\{t_j | a_j(t_j) < a_i\}} (t_i - a_j) \right\}.$$

A few tricks make the problem easy to solve. First, one can write the "self-selection constraints": by definition of equilibrium, type t_i prefers $a_i(t_i)$ to $a_i(t_i')$, and type t_i' prefers $a_i(t_i')$ to $a_i(t_i)$. Writing the two corresponding inequalities and adding them up shows that a_i must be a nondecreasing function of t_i. Second, it is easy to show that there cannot be an atom at $a_i > 0$, i.e. $\operatorname{Prob}(a_j(t_j) = a_i > 0) = 0$. To prove this, notice that if there were an atom of types of firm j playing a_i, firm i would never play in $[a_i - \varepsilon, a_i)$ for ε small: it would be better off bidding just above a_i (the proof is a bit loose here, but can be made rigorous). Thus, the types of firms that play a_i would be better off playing $(a_i - \varepsilon)$, because this would not reduce the probability of winning and would lead to reduced payments.

Let us look for a strictly monotonic, continuous function $a_i(t_i)$ with inverse $t_i = \Phi_i(a_i)$. Thus, $\Phi_i(a_i)$ is the type that bids a_i. We then obtain:

$$a_i(t_i) \in \arg\max_{a_i} \left\{ -a_i\big(1 - P_j(\Phi_j(a_i))\big) + \int_0^{a_i} (t_i - a_j) p_j\big(\Phi_j(a_j)\big) \Phi_j'(a_j)\, \mathrm{d}a_j \right\}.$$

By differentiating, one obtains a system of two differential equations in $\Phi_1(\cdot)$ and $\Phi_2(\cdot)$ [or, equivalently, in $a_1(\cdot)$ and $a_2(\cdot)$]. Rather than doing so, let us take the following intuitive approach. If firm i, with type t_i, bids $(a_i + \mathrm{d}a_i)$ instead of a_i, it loses $\mathrm{d}a_i$ with probability 1 (since there is no atom), conditionally on firm j bidding at least a_i (otherwise this increase has no effect). It gains t_i $(= \Phi_i(a_i))$ with probability $\{ p_j(\Phi_j(a_i))\Phi_j'(a_i)/(1 - P_j(\Phi_j(a_i)))\}\, \mathrm{d}a_i$. Thus, in order for firm i to be indifferent:

$$\Phi_i(a_i) p_j\big(\Phi_j(a_i)\big) \Phi_j'(a_i) = 1 - P_j\big(\Phi_j(a_i)\big).$$

We leave it to the reader to check that, for a symmetric exponential distribution $P_i(t_i) = 1 - e^{-t_i}$, there exists a symmetric equilibrium: $\Phi_i(a_i) = \sqrt{2a_i}$, which corresponds to $a_i(t_i) = t_i^2/2$ [as Riley (1980) has shown, there also exists a continuum of asymmetric equilibria:

$$\Phi_1 = K\sqrt{a_1} \quad \text{and} \quad \Phi_2 = \frac{2}{K}\sqrt{a_2}, \quad \text{for } K > 0].$$

Let us now give an industrial organization interpretation of the game. Suppose that there are two firms in the market; they both lose 1 per unit of time when they compete; they make a monopoly profit when their opponent has left the market, the present discounted value for which is t_i (it would make sense to assume that the duopoly and monopoly profit are correlated, but such a modification would hardly change the results). The firms play a war of attrition. a_i is the time firm i intends to stay in the market, if firm j has not exited before. At this stage, the reader may wonder about our dynamic interpretation: if firms are free to leave when they want and are not committed to abide by their date-zero choice of a_i, is the Bayesian equilibrium "perfect"? It turns out that the answer is "yes"; the dynamic game is essentially a static game (which is the reason why we chose to present it in this section). At any time a_i, either firm j has dropped out (bid less then a_i) and the game is over, or firm j is still in the market and the conditional probability of exit is the one computed earlier. Thus, the equilibrium is perfect as well.[7]

4.2. *Using Bayesian equilibria to justify mixed strategy equilibria*

In Section 2 we saw that simultaneous move games of *complete* information often admit mixed strategy equilibria. Some researchers are unhappy with this notion because, they argue, "real world decision-makers do not flip a coin". However, as Harsanyi (1973) has shown, mixed strategy equilibria of complete information games can often be vindicated as the limits of pure strategy equilibria of slightly perturbed games of incomplete information. Indeed, we have already noticed that in a Bayesian game, once the players' type-contingent strategies have been computed, each player behaves as if he were facing mixed strategies by his

[7] The war of attrition was introduced in the theoretical biology literature [e.g. Maynard Smith (1974), Riley (1980)] and has known many applications since. It was introduced in industrial organization by Kreps and Wilson (1982a). [See also Nalebuff (1982) and Ghemawat and Nalebuff (1985).] For a characterization of the set of equilibria and a uniqueness result with changing duopoly payoffs and/or large uncertainty over types, see Fudenberg and Tirole (1986). See also Hendricks and Wilson (1985a, 1985b).

opponents (nature creates uncertainty through its choice of types rather than the choice of the side of the coin).

To illustrate the mechanics of this construction, let us consider the one-period version of the "grab-the-dollar" game introduced in Section 3. Each player has two possible actions: investment, no investment. In the complete information version of the game, a firm gains 1 if it is the only one to make the investment (wins), loses 1 if both invest, and breaks even if it does not invest. (We can view this game as an extremely crude representation of a natural monopoly market.) The only symmetric equilibrium involves mixed strategies: each firm invests with probability 1/2. This clearly is an equilibrium: each firm makes 0 if it does not invest, and $\frac{1}{2}(1) + \frac{1}{2}(-1) = 0$ if it does not. Now consider the same game with the following type of incomplete information. Each firm has the same payoff structure except that, when it wins, it gets $(1 + t)$, where t is uniformly distributed on $[-\varepsilon, +\varepsilon]$. Each firm knows its type t, but not that of the other firm. Now, it is easily seen that the symmetric pure strategies: "$a(t < 0)$ = do not invest, $a(t \geq 0)$ = invest" form a Bayesian equilibrium. From the point of view of each firm, the other firm invests with probability 1/2. Thus, the firm should invest if and only if $\frac{1}{2}(1 + t) + \frac{1}{2}(-1) \geq 0$, i.e. $t \geq 0$. Last, note that, when ε converges to zero, the pure strategy Bayesian equilibrium converges to the mixed strategy Nash equilibrium of the complete information game.

As another example, the reader may want to study the symmetric war of attrition. Under complete information and symmetric payoffs, it is easily shown that in a symmetric equilibrium, each player's strategy is a mixed strategy with exponential distribution over possible times.[8] The symmetric incomplete information equilibrium (computed in Subsection 4.1) converges to this mixed strategy equilibrium when the uncertainty converges to zero (see Milgrom and Weber for the case of a uniform distribution).

Milgrom and Weber (1986b) offer sufficient (continuity) conditions on the objective functions and information structure so that the limit of Bayesian equilibrium strategies when the uncertainty becomes "negligible", forms a Nash equilibrium of the limit complete information game. (*Note*. The war of attrition does not satisfy their continuity conditions; but as Milgrom and Weber show, the result holds anyway.) They also identify a class of (atomless) games for which there exists a pure strategy equilibrium.

We must realize that games of complete information are an idealization. In practice, everyone has at least a slight amount of incomplete information about the others' objectives; Harsanyi's argument shows that it is hard to make a strong

[8]Letting t denote the common payoff to winning, waiting $\mathrm{d}a$ more yields $(x(a)t)\,\mathrm{d}a$, where $x(a)\,\mathrm{d}a$ is the probability that the opponent drops between a and $(a + \mathrm{d}a)$. This must equal the cost of waiting: $\mathrm{d}a$. Thus, $x(a) = 1/t$ is independent of time a.

case against mixed strategy equilibria on the grounds that they require a randomizing device.

5. Dynamic games of incomplete information

We now study games in which, at some point of time, a player bases his decision on a signal that conveys information about another player. This type of game is dynamic in that a player reacts to another player's move. The tricky aspect of it is that, under incomplete information, the former must apply Bayes' rule to update his beliefs about the latter's type. To do so, he uses the latter's choice of action (or a signal of it) and equilibrium strategy, as we shall see shortly. The equilibrium notion for dynamic games of incomplete information is naturally a combination of the subgame-perfect equilibrium concept that we discussed earlier and Harsanyi's (1967–68) concept of Bayesian equilibrium for games of incomplete information. In this section we consider the simplest such notion, that of the perfect Bayesian equilibrium concept, as well as some easy-to-apply (and sometimes informal) refinements. In the next section we will discuss more formal refinements of the perfect Bayesian equilibrium concept for finite games.

The notion of a perfect Bayesian equilibrium was developed under various names and in various contexts in the late 1960s and the 1970s. In economics, Akerlof's (1970) and Spence's (1974) market games and Ortega-Reichert's (1967) analysis of repeated first-bid auctions make implicit use of the concept. In industrial organization the first and crucial application is Milgrom and Roberts' (1982a) limit pricing paper, followed by the work of Kreps and Wilson (1982b) and Milgrom and Roberts (1982b) on reputation. In game theory, Selten (1975) introduced the idea of trembles to refine the concept of subgame-perfect equilibria in games of imperfect information. (If each player's type is private information, the only proper subgame is the whole game, so subgame perfection has no force.) Kreps and Wilson's (1982a) sequential equilibrium is similar, but, in the tradition of the economics literature, it emphasizes the formation of beliefs, which makes the introduction of refinements easier to motivate. We should also mention the work of Aumann and Machler (1967) on repeated games of incomplete information.

We start this section with the simplest example of a dynamic game of incomplete information, the signalling game. This is a two-period leader–follower game in which the leader is endowed with private information that affects the follower. We give some examples of such games and introduce some refinements of the equilibrium concept. As the principles enunciated here for signalling games generally carry over to general games, we do not treat the latter in order to save on notation and space.

5.1. The basic signalling game

As mentioned earlier, the simplest game in which the issues of updating and perfection arise simultaneously has the following structure. There are two players; player 1 is the leader (also called "sender", because he sends a signal) and player 2, the follower (or "receiver"). Player 1 has private information about his type t_1 in T_1, and chooses action a_1 in A_1. Player 2, whose type is common knowledge for simplicity, observes a_1 and chooses a_2 in A_2. Payoffs are equal to $\Pi_i(a_1, a_2, t_1)$ $(i = 1, 2)$. Before the game begins, player 2 has prior beliefs $p_1(t_1)$ about player 1's type.

Player 2, who observes player 1's move before choosing his own action, should update his beliefs about t_1 and base his choice of a_2 on the posterior distribution $\tilde{p}_1(t_1|a_1)$. How is this posterior formed? As in a Bayesian equilibrium, player 1's action ought to depend on his type; let $a_1^*(t_1)$ denote this strategy (as before, this notation allows a mixed strategy). Thus, figuring out $a_1^*(\cdot)$ and observing a_1, player 2 can use Bayes' rule to update $p_1(\cdot)$ into $\tilde{p}_1(\cdot|a_1)$. And, in a rational expectations world, player 1 should anticipate that his action would affect player 2's also through the posterior beliefs. Thus, the natural extension of the Nash equilibrium concept to the signalling game is:

Definition

A perfect Bayesian equilibrium (PBE) of the signalling game is a set of strategies $a_1^*(t_1)$ and $a_2^*(a_1)$ and posterior beliefs $\tilde{p}_1(t_1|a_1)$ such that:

(P$_1$) $$a_2^*(a_1) \in \arg\max_{a_2} \sum_{t_1} \tilde{p}_1(t_1|a_1)\Pi_2(a_1, a_2, t_1);$$

(P$_2$) $$a_1^*(t_1) \in \arg\max_{a_1} \Pi_1(a_1, a_2^*(a_1), t_1);$$

(B) $\tilde{p}_1(t_1|a_1)$ is derived from the prior $p_1(\cdot)$, a_1 and $a_1^*(\cdot)$ using Bayes' rule (when applicable).

(P$_1$) and (P$_2$) are the perfectness conditions. (P$_1$) states that player 2 reacts optimally to player 1's action given his posterior beliefs about t_1. (P$_2$) demonstrates the optimal Stackelberg behavior by player 1; note that he takes into account the effect of a_1 on player 2's action. (B) corresponds to the application of Bayes' rule. The qualifier "when applicable" stems from the fact that, if a_1 is not part of player 1's optimal strategy for some type, observing a_1 is a zero-probability event and Bayes' rule does not pin down posterior beliefs. *Any* posterior beliefs $\tilde{p}_1(\cdot|a_1)$ are then admissible. Indeed, the purpose of the refinements of the perfect Bayesian equilibrium concept is to put some restrictions on these posterior beliefs.

Thus, a PBE is simply a set of strategies and beliefs such that, at any stage of the game, strategies are optimal given beliefs and beliefs are obtained from equilibrium strategies and observed actions using Bayes' rule. Two features of the concept developed thus far should be emphasized:

First, a PBE has a strong fixed point flavor. Beliefs are derived from strategies, which are optimal given beliefs. For this reason, there exists no handy algorithm to help us construct equilibria. Remember that for games of complete information, Kuhn's algorithm for *backward* induction gave us the set of perfect equilibria. Here we must also operate the Bayesian updating in a *forward* manner. This makes the search for equilibria rely on a few tricks (to be discussed later) rather than on a general method.

Second, we have not imposed enough structure on the type and action spaces and on the objective functions to prove existence of a PBE. Existence theorems are available only for games with a finite number of types and actions (see Subsection 5.5). Most applications, however, involve either a continuum of types or/and a continuum of actions. Existence is then obtained by construction, on a case-by-case basis.

For more general games than the signalling game, the definition of PBE given above is quite weak, as it, for example, allows a player's deviation to be treated as though it conveyed information the deviator himself did not know. Fudenberg and Tirole (1987) develop a more restrictive notion of PBE.

Let us now give simple examples of PBE in signalling games. From now on, we delete the subscript on player 1's type, as there is no possible confusion.

5.2. Examples

Example 1: A two-period reputation game

The following is a much simplified version of the Kreps–Wilson–Milgrom–Roberts reputation story. There are two firms ($i = 1,2$). In period 1, they are both in the market. Only firm 1 (the "incumbent") takes an action a_1. The action space has two elements: "prey" and "accommodate". Firm 2 (the "entrant")'s profit is D_2 if firm 1 accommodates and P_2 if firm 1 preys, such that $D_2 > 0 > P_2$. Firm 1 has one of two potential types t: "sane" and "crazy". When sane, firm 1 makes D_1 when it accommodates and P_1 when it preys, where $D_1 > P_1$. Thus, a sane firm prefers to accommodate rather than to prey. However, it would prefer to be a monopoly, in which case it would make M_1 per period. When crazy, firm 1 enjoys predation and thus preys (its utility function is such that it is always worth preying). Let p_1 (respectively, $(1 - p_1)$) denote the prior probability that firm 1 is sane (respectively, crazy).

In period 2, only firm 2 chooses an action a_2. This action can take two values: "stay" and "exit". If it stays, it obtains a payoff D_2 if firm 1 is actually sane, and P_2 if it is crazy (the idea is that unless it is crazy, firm 1 will not pursue any predatory strategy in the second period because there is no point building or keeping a reputation at the end. This assumption can be derived more formally from the description of the second-period competition.) The sane firm gets D_1 if firm 2 stays and $M_1 > D_1$ if firm 2 exits. We let δ denote the discount factor between the two periods.

We presumed that the crazy type always preys. The interesting thing to study is thus the sane type's behavior. From a static point of view, it would want to accommodate in the first period; however, by preying it might convince firm 2 that it is of the crazy type, and thus induce exit (as $P_2 < 0$) and increase its second-period profit.

Let us first start with a taxonomy of potential perfect Bayesian equilibria. A *separating* equilibrium is an equilibrium in which firm 1's two types choose two different actions in the first period. Here, this means that the sane type chooses to accommodate. Note that in a separating equilibrium, firm 2 has complete information in the second period:

$$\tilde{p}_1(t = \text{sane} | a_1 = \text{accommodate}) = 1 \quad \text{and} \quad \tilde{p}_1(t = \text{crazy} | a_1 = \text{prey}) = 1.$$

A *pooling* equilibrium is an equilibrium in which firm 1's two types choose the same action in the first period. Here, this means that the sane type preys. In a pooling equilibrium firm 2 does not update its beliefs when observing the equilibrium action: $\tilde{p}_1(t = \text{sane} | a_1 = \text{prey}) = p_1$. Last, there can also exist *hybrid or semi-separating equilibria*. For instance, in the reputation game, the sane type may randomize between preying and accommodating, i.e. between pooling and separating. One then has

$$\tilde{p}_1(t = \text{sane} | a_1 = \text{prey}) \in (0, p_1) \quad \text{and}$$

$$\tilde{p}_1(t = \text{sane} | a_1 = \text{accommodate}) = 1.$$

Let us first look for conditions of existence of a separating equilibrium. In such an equilibrium, the sane type accommodates and thus reveals its type and obtains $D_1(1 + \delta)$ (firm 2 stays because it expects $D_2 > 0$ in the second period). If it decided to prey, it would convince firm 2 that it is crazy and would thus obtain $P_1 + \delta M_1$. Thus, a necessary condition for the existence of a separating equilibrium is:

$$\delta(M_1 - D_1) \leq (D_1 - P_1). \tag{6}$$

Conversely, suppose that (6) is satisfied. Consider the following strategies and beliefs: the sane incumbent accommodates, and the entrant (correctly) anticipates that the incumbent is sane when observing accommodation; the crazy incumbent preys and the entrant (correctly) anticipates that the incumbent is crazy when observing predation. Clearly, these strategies and beliefs form a separating PBE.

Let us now look at the possibility of a pooling equilibrium. Both types prey; thus, as we saw, $\tilde{p}_1 = p_1$ when predation is observed. Now, the sane type, who loses $(D_1 - P_1)$ is the first period, must induce exit. Thus, it must be the case that

$$p_1 D_2 + (1 - p_1) P_2 \leq 0. \tag{7}$$

Conversely, assume that (7) holds, and consider the following strategies and beliefs: both types prey; the entrant has posterior beliefs $\tilde{p}_1 = p_1$ when predation is observed and $\tilde{p}_1 = 1$ when accommodation is observed. The sane type's equilibrium profit is $P_1 + \delta M_1$, while it would become $D_1(1 + \delta)$ under accommodation. Thus, if (6) is violated, the proposed strategies and beliefs form a pooling PBE [note that if (7) is satisfied with equality, there exists not one, but a continuum of such equilibria]. So the equilibrium is that the entrant never enters and the incumbent never preys.

We leave it to the reader to check that if both (6) and (7) are violated, the unique equilibrium is a hybrid PBE (with the entrant's randomizing when observing predation).

Remark

The (generic) uniqueness of the PBE in this model is due to the fact that the "strong" type (the crazy incumbent) is assumed to prey no matter what. Thus, predation is not a zero probability event and, furthermore, accommodation is automatically interpreted as coming from the sane type if it belongs to the equilibrium path. The next example illustrates a more complex and a more common structure, for which refinements of the PBE are required. Example 2, which, in many respects, can be regarded as a generalization of Example 1, also involves several cases resembling those in Example 1.

Example 2: The limit-pricing game

As mentioned earlier, the paper which introduced signalling games into the industrial organization field is Milgrom and Roberts' (1982a) article on limit pricing. Let us take the following simple version of their two-period model. Firm 1, the incumbent, has in the first period a monopoly power and chooses a first-period quantity $a_1 = q_1$. Firm 2, the entrant, then decides to enter or to stay out in the second period (thus, as in the previous game, $a_2 = 0$ or 1 or $\in [0, 1]$ if we allow mixed strategies). If it enters, there is duopolistic competition in period 2. Otherwise, firm 1 remains a monopoly.

Firm 1 can have one of two potential types: its constant unit production cost is "high" (H) with probability p_1 and "low" (L) with probability $(1 - p_1)$. We will denote by q_m^t the monopoly quantities for the two types of incumbent ($t = \mathrm{H, L}$). Naturally, $q_m^{\mathrm{H}} < q_m^{\mathrm{L}}$. We let $M_1^t(q_1)$ denote the monopoly profit of type t when producing q_1; in particular, let $M_1^t = M_1^t(q_m^t)$ denote type i's monopoly profit when it maximizes its short-run profit. We assume that $M_1^t(q_1)$ is strictly concave in q_1.

Firm 1 knows t from the start; firm 2 does not. Let D_2^t denote firm 2's duopoly profit when firm 1 has type t (it possibly includes entry costs). To make things interesting, let us assume that firm 2's entry decision is influenced by its beliefs about firm 1's type: $D_2^{\mathrm{H}} > 0 > D_2^{\mathrm{L}}$. The discount factor is δ.

Let us look for separating equilibria. For this, we first obtain two necessary conditions: that each type does not want to pick the other type's *equilibrium* action ("incentive constraints"). We then complete the description of equilibrium by choosing beliefs off-the-equilibrium path that deter the two types from deviating from their equilibrium actions. Thus, our necessary conditions are also sufficient, in the sense that thc corresponding quantities are equilibrium quantities. In a separating equilibrium, the high-cost type's quantity induces entry. He thus plays q_m^{H} (if it did not, he could increase his first-period profit without adverse effect on entry). Thus, he gets $\{M_1^{\mathrm{H}} + \delta D_1^{\mathrm{H}}\}$. Let q_1^{L} denote the output of the low-cost type. The high-cost type, by producing this output, deters entry and obtains $\{M_1^{\mathrm{H}}(q_1^{\mathrm{L}}) + \delta M_1^{\mathrm{H}}\}$. Thus, a necessary condition for equilibrium is:

$$M_1^{\mathrm{H}} - M_1^{\mathrm{H}}\left(q_1^{\mathrm{L}}\right) \geq \delta\left(M_1^{\mathrm{H}} - D_1^{\mathrm{H}}\right). \tag{8}$$

The similar condition for the low-cost type is:

$$M_1^{\mathrm{L}} - M_1^{\mathrm{L}}\left(q_1^{\mathrm{L}}\right) \leq \delta\left(M_1^{\mathrm{L}} - D_1^{\mathrm{L}}\right). \tag{9}$$

To make things interesting, we will assume that there is no (separating) equilibrium in which each type behaves as in a full-information context; i.e. the low-cost type would wish to pool:

$$M_1^{\mathrm{H}} - M_1^{\mathrm{H}}\left(q_m^{\mathrm{L}}\right) < \delta\left(M_1^{\mathrm{H}} - D_1^{\mathrm{H}}\right). \tag{10}$$

To characterize the set of q_1^{L} satisfying (8) and (9), one must make more specific assumptions on the demand and cost functions. We will not do it here, and we refer to the literature for this. We just note that, under reasonable conditions, (8) and (9) define a region $[\tilde{q}, \tilde{\tilde{q}}_1]$, where $\tilde{q}_1 > q_m^{\mathrm{L}}$. Thus, to separate, the low-cost type must produce sufficiently above its monopoly quantity so as to make pooling very costly to the high-cost type. A crucial assumption in the derivation of such an interval is the Spence–Mirrlees (single-crossing) condition:

$$\frac{\partial}{\partial q_1}\left(M_1^{\mathrm{L}}(q_1) - M_1^{\mathrm{H}}(q_1)\right) > 0.$$

$\tilde{q}_1$ is such that (8) is satisfied with equality; it is called the "least-cost" separating quantity, because, of all potential separating equilibria, the low-cost type would prefer the one at $\tilde{q}_1$.

Let us now show that these necessary conditions are also sufficient. Let the high cost type choose q_m^{H} and the low-cost type choose q_1^{L} in $[\tilde{q}_1, \tilde{\tilde{q}}_1]$. When a quantity that differs from these two quantities is observed, beliefs are arbitrary. The easiest way to obtain equilibrium is to choose beliefs that induce entry; this way, the two types will be little tempted to deviate from their presumed equilibrium strategies; so let us specify that when q_1 does not belong to $\{q_m^{\mathrm{H}}, q_1^{\mathrm{L}}\}$, $\tilde{p}_1 = 1$ (firm 2 believes firm 1 has high cost); whether these beliefs, which are consistent with Bayes' rules, are "reasonable", is discussed later on. Now, let us check that no type wants to deviate. The high-cost type obtains its monopoly profit in the first period and, thus, is not willing to deviate to another quantity that induces entry. He does not deviate to q_1^{L} either from (8). And similarly for the low-cost type. Thus, we have obtained a continuum of separating equilibria.

Note that this continuum of separating equilibria exists for any $p_1 > 0$. By contrast, for $p_1 = 0$, the low-cost firm plays its monopoly quantity q_m^{L}. We thus observe that a tiny change in the information structure may make a huge difference. *A very small probability that the firm has high cost may force the low-cost firm to increase its production discontinuously to signal its type*. Games of incomplete information (which include games of complete information!) are very sensitive to the specification of the information structure, a topic we will come back to later on.

Note also that Pareto dominance selects the least-cost separating equilibrium among separating equilibria. [The entrant has the same utility in all separating equilibria (the informative content is the same); similarly, the high-cost type is indifferent. The low-cost type prefers lower outputs.]

The existence of pooling equilibria hinges on whether the following condition is satisfied:

$$p_1 D_2^{\mathrm{H}} + (1 - p_1) D_2^{\mathrm{L}} < 0. \tag{11}$$

Assume that condition (11) is violated (with a strict inequality – we will not consider the equality case for simplicity). Then, at the pooling quantity, firm 2 makes a strictly positive profit if it enters (as $\tilde{p}_1 = p_1$). This means that entry is not deterred, so that the two types cannot do better than choosing their (static) monopoly outputs. As these outputs differ, no pooling equilibrium can exist.

Assume, therefore, that (11) is satisfied so that a pooling quantity q_1 deters entry. A necessary condition for a quantity q_1 to be a pooling equilibrium quantity is that none of the types wants to play his static optimum. If he were to do so, it would at worse induce entry. Therefore, q_1 must satisfy (9) and the analogous condition for the high-cost type:

$$M_1^{\mathrm{H}} - M_1^{\mathrm{H}}(q_1) \leq \delta\left(M_1^{\mathrm{H}} - D_1^{\mathrm{H}}\right). \tag{12}$$

Again, the set of outputs q_1 that satisfy both (9) and (12) depends on the cost and demand functions. Let us simply notice that, from (10), there exists an interval of outputs around q_m^{L} that satisfy these two inequalities.

Now it is easy to see that if q_1 satisfies (9) and (12), q_1 can be made part of a pooling equilibrium. Suppose that whenever firm 1 plays an output differing from q_1 (an off-the-equilibrium path action), firm 2 believes firm 1 has a high cost. Firm 2 then enters, and firm 1 might as well play its monopoly output. Thus, from (9) and (12), none of the types would want to deviate from q_1.

We leave it to the reader to derive hybrid equilibria (the analysis is very similar to the previous ones). We now investigate the issue of refinements.

5.3. Some refinements

Games of incomplete information in general have many PBEs. The reason why this is so is easy to grasp. Consider the basic signalling game and suppose that one wants to rule out some action a_1 by player 1 as an equilibrium action. If, indeed, a_1 is not played on the equilibrium path, player 2's beliefs following a_1 are arbitrary. In most games there exists some type t such that if player 2 puts all the weight on t, it takes an action that is detrimental for all types of player 1 (for instance, t is the high-cost type in the limit pricing game; it induces entry). As playing a_1 produces a bad outcome for player 1, not playing a_1 on the equilibrium path may be self-fulfilling. Some authors have noted that, while noncredible actions are ruled out by the perfectness part of the PBE, players could still " threaten" each other through beliefs. This subsection and Subsection 5.4 discuss refinements that select subsets of PBEs.

Often, however, the very structure of the game tells us that some beliefs, while allowable because of off-the-equilibrium path, "do not make sense". Over the years intuitive criteria for the selection of beliefs have been developed for each particular game. We mention here only a few of these criteria. These criteria, which apply to all types of games (including games with a continuum of types or actions), are sometimes informal in that they have not been designed as part of a formal solution concept for which existence has been proved. But most of them are, for finite games, satisfied by the Kohlberg and Mertens (1986) concept of stable equilibria, which are known to exist (see Subsection 5.5 below). Last, we should warn the reader that the presentation below resembles more a list of cookbook recipes than a unified methodological approach.

5.3.1. *Elimination of weakly dominated strategies*

In the tradition of Luce and Raiffa (1957), Farquharson (1969), Moulin (1979), Bernheim (1984), and Pearce (1984), it seems natural to require that, when an action is dominated for some type, but not for some other, the posterior beliefs should not put any weight on the former type. This simple restriction may already cut on the number of PBE considerably. Consider the limit-pricing game. Quantities above $\tilde{q}_1$ are dominated for the high-cost type [if this type chooses q_m^{H}, its intertemporal profit is at least $M_1^{\mathrm{H}} + \delta D_1^{\mathrm{H}}$; if it chooses q_1, this profit does not exceed $M_1^{\mathrm{H}}(q_1) + \delta M_1^{\mathrm{H}}$; from the definition of $\tilde{q}_1$, the second action is weakly dominated for $q_1 \geq \tilde{q}_1$]. Thus, when q_1 belongs to $[\tilde{q}_1, \tilde{\tilde{q}}_1]$, the entrant should believe that the incumbent's cost is low, and should not enter. Thus, the low-cost incumbent need not produce above $\tilde{q}_1$ to deter entry. We thus see that we are left with a single separating PBE instead of a continuum (this reasoning is due to Milgrom and Roberts).

A small caveat here: playing a quantity above $\tilde{q}_1$ is dominated for the high-cost type only once the second period has been folded back. Before that, one can think of (nonequilibrium) behavior which would not make such a quantity a dominated strategy. For instance, following q_m^{H}, the entrant might enter and charge a very low price. So, we are invoking a bit more than the elimination of dominated strategies. A quantity above $\tilde{q}_1$ is dominated conditional on subsequent equilibrium behavior – a requirement in the spirit of perfectness. More generally, one will want to iterate the elimination of weakly dominated strategies.

Note that, in the limit-pricing game, the elimination of weakly dominated strategies leaves us with the "least-cost" separating equilibrium, but does not help us select among the pooling equilibria. This is because the equilibrium pooling quantities are not dominated for the high-cost type.

5.3.2. *Elimination of equilibrium weakly dominated strategies (intuitive criterion)*

The next criterion was proposed by Kreps (1984) to identify an intuitive property satisfied by the more stringent stability requirement of Kohlberg and Mertens (1986). The idea is roughly to extend the elimination of weakly dominated strategies to strategies which are dominated *relative to equilibrium payoffs*. So doing eliminates more strategies and thus refines the equilibrium concept further.

More precisely, consider the signalling game and a corresponding PBE and associated payoffs. Let a_1 denote an *out-of-equilibrium* action which yields for a subset J of types payoffs lower than their equilibrium payoffs *whatever* beliefs player 2 forms after observing a_1.

More formally, let $\Pi_1^*(t)$ denote player 1's equilibrium payoff when he has type t. Let

$$\mathrm{BR}(\tilde{p}_1, a_1) = \arg\max_{a_2 \in A_2} \{\Sigma \tilde{p}_1(t) \Pi_2(a_1, a_2, t)\}$$

denote player 2's best response(s) when he has posterior beliefs $\tilde{p}_1(\cdot)$; and let

$$\mathrm{BR}(I, a_1) = \bigcup_{\{\tilde{p}_1 : \tilde{p}_1(I)=1\}} \mathrm{BR}(\tilde{p}_1, a_1)$$

denote the set of player 2's best responses when his posterior beliefs put all the weight in a subset I of types.

Suppose that there exists a subset J of T such that:

(1) for all t in J and for all a_2 in $\mathrm{BR}(T, a_1)$, $\Pi_1(a_1, a_2, t) < \Pi_1^*(t)$; and

(2) there exists a type t in $T - J$ such that for all a_2 in $\mathrm{BR}(T - J, a_1)$, $\Pi_1(a_1, a_2, t) > \Pi_1^*(t)$.

From condition (1), we know that no type in J would want to deviate from his equilibrium path, whatever inference player 2 would make following the deviation. Kreps argues that player 2 does not put any weight on types in J. But, one would object, no type outside J may gain from the deviation either. This is why condition (2) is imposed. There exists some type outside J that strictly gains from the deviation. The intuitive criterion rejects PBE that satisfy (1) and (2) for some action a_1 and some subset J.

One immediately sees that this criterion has most power when there are only two potential types (see below for an application to the limit-pricing game). The subset J and $T - J$ of the criterion are then necessarily composed of one type each. Thus, the requirement "for all a_2 in $\mathrm{BR}(T - J, a_1) \ldots$" in condition (2) is not too stringent, and the criterion has much cutting power. With more than two types, however, there may exist many a_2 in $\mathrm{BR}(T - J, a_1)$ and, therefore, the requirement that some type prefers the deviation for all a_2 in $\mathrm{BR}(T - J, a_1)$ becomes very strong. The refinement then loses some of its power.

Cho (1986) and Cho and Kreps (1987) invert the quantifiers in condition (2), which becomes:

(2′) For each action a_2 in $\mathrm{BR}(T - J, a_1)$, there exists t such that $\Pi_1(a_1, a_2, t) > \Pi_1^*(t)$.

In other words, whatever beliefs are formed by player 2 which do not put weight on J, there exists some type (in $T - J$) who would like to deviate. Condition (2′) may be more appealing than condition (2), since if (2′) is satisfied, the players cannot think of any continuation equilibrium which would satisfy (1) and induce no type to deviate from equilibrium behavior. In contrast, condition (2), except in the two-type case, does not rule out the possibility that for any continuation equilibrium satisfying (1), some type in $T - J$ would want to deviate.

Cho and Cho–Kreps' "communicational equilibrium" is a PBE such that there does not exist an off-the-equilibrium action a_1 and a subset of types J that satisfy (1) and (2′). Banks and Sobel (1987) identify a condition that is closely related to (2′); they require (among other things) that player 2's off-the-equilibrium-path beliefs place positive probability only on player 1's types who might not lose from a defection. They go on to define the concept of "divine equilibrium". A divine equilibrium thus satisfies the Cho–Kreps criterion and, for finite games, exists (because it is stable).

We should also mention the work by Farrell (1984) and Grossman and Perry (1986) who offer a criterion similar to, but stronger than, the intuitive criterion. In a signalling game their criterion *roughly* says that, if there exists a deviation a_1 and a set of types J such that if the posterior beliefs are the same as the prior truncated to $(T - J)$, types in J [respectively, in $(T - J)$] lose (respectively, gain) relative to their equilibrium payoffs, the initial equilibrium is not acceptable. This requirement is stronger than the Cho–Kreps criterion because, in particular, it does not allow any leeway in specifying posterior beliefs within the support $(T - J)$. The refinement, however, is so strong that equilibrium may not exist; so it is restricted to a given (and yet unknown) class of games.

Let us now apply the intuitive criterion to the limit-pricing game. As the intuitive criterion is stronger than iterated elimination of weakly dominated strategies, we get at most one separating equilibrium. The reader will check that this least-cost separating equilibrium indeed satisfies the intuitive criterion. Let us next discuss the pooling equilibria (when they exist, i.e. when pooling deters entry). Let us show that pooling at $q_1 < q_m^{\mathrm{L}}$ does not satisfy the intuitive criterion: consider the deviation to q_m^{L}. This deviation is dominated for the high-cost type ("$J = \mathrm{H}$"), who makes a lower first-period profit and cannot increase his second-period profit. Thus, posterior beliefs after q_m^{L} should be $\tilde{p}_1 = 0$, and entry is deterred. But, then the low-cost type would want to produce q_m^{L}. This reasoning, however, does not apply to pooling equilibria with $q_1 \geq q_m^{\mathrm{L}}$. Deviations to produce less are not dominated for any type. Thus, one gets a (smaller) continuum of pooling equilibria [the intuitive criterion here has less cutting power than in the Spence signalling game – see Kreps (1984)].

One can restrict the set of pooling equilibria that satisfy the intuitive criterion by invoking Pareto dominance: the pooling equilibrium at q_m^{L} Pareto dominates pooling equilibria with $q_1 > q_m^{\mathrm{L}}$ (both types of player 1 are closer to their static optimum, and player 2 does not care). But, we are still left with a separating and a pooling equilibria which cannot be ranked using Pareto dominance (player 2 prefers the separating equilibrium). For further refinements in the context of limit pricing, see Cho (1986).

5.3.3. Guessing which equilibrium one is in [McLennan (1985)]

McLennan's idea is that a move is more likely if it can be explained by a confusion over which PBE is played. He calls an action "useless" if it is not part of some PBE path. Posterior beliefs at some unreached information set must assign positive probability only to nodes that are part of *some* PBE, if any (i.e. to actions which are not useless). One thus obtains a smaller set of PBE, and one can operate this selection recursively until one is left with "justifiable equilibria" (which, for finite games, are stable).

5.3.4. Getting rid of out-of-equilibrium events

As we explained, the indeterminacy of beliefs for out-of-equilibrium events is often a factor of multiplicity. The previous criteria (as well as the one presented in the next section) try to figure out what posterior beliefs are reasonable in such events. An alternative approach, which was pioneered by Saloner (1981) and Matthews and Mirman (1983), consists in perturbing the game slightly so that these zero-probability events do not occur. The basic idea of this technique is to let the action chosen by an informed player be (at least a bit) garbled before it is observed by his opponents. For instance, one could imagine that a firm's capacity choice is observed with an error or that a manufacturer's price is garbled at the retail level. By introducing noise, all (or most) potentially received signals are equilibrium ones and, thus, refinements are useless. Although the class of games to which this technique can be applied is limited (the noise must represent some reasonable economic phenomenon), this way of proceeding seems natural and is likely to select the "reasonable" equilibria of the corresponding ungarbled game in the limit (as Saloner, for instance, shows in the limit-pricing game).

5.4. Finite games: Existence and refinements in finite games

We now informally discuss refinements that are defined only for finite games. Some of these refinements (Selten, Myerson) rest on the idea of taking the limit of equilibria with "totally mixed strategies". One basically considers robustness of each PBE to slight perturbations of the following form: each agent in the game tree is forced to play all his potential actions with some (possibly small) probability, i.e. to "tremble". This way, Bayes' rule applies everywhere (there is no off-the-equilibrium-path outcome). To be a bit more formal, assume that an agent is forced to put weight (probability) $\sigma(a)$ on action a where $\sigma(a) \geq \varepsilon(a) > 0$ (for each action a). Then the agent can maximize his payoff given these constraints and pick a best perturbed strategy. A refined equilibrium is a PBE which is the limit of equilibria with totally mixed strategies, where the limit its taken for a given class of perturbations. The other two refinements we discuss (Kreps–Wilson, Kohlberg–Mertens) employ somewhat similar ideas. We shall present the refinements in an increasing-strength order.

General existence results for equilibria of dynamic games with incomplete information have been provided only for games with a finite number of actions and types, starting with Selten. We sketch the proof of existence of a trembling hand equilibrium below. Proofs of existence for alternative refinements are similar.

5.4.1. Sequential equilibrium [Kreps and Wilson (1982)]

Kreps and Wilson look at PBE which satisfy a *consistency* requirement. The set of strategies and beliefs at each information set of the game must be the limit of a sequence of sets of strategies and beliefs for which strategies are always totally mixed (and beliefs are thus pinned down by Bayes' rule). Moreover, the beliefs on all players are derived as the limit corresponding to a *common* sequence of strategies. The perturbed strategies and beliefs are not a priori required to form a (constrained) PBE of a perturbed game in contrast with the Selten criterion discussed below. So, the check is purely mechanical; given a PBE, it suffices to show that it is or is not the limit of a sequence of totally mixed strategies and associated beliefs.

In the signalling game considered above, any beliefs can be generated by the appropriate choice of trembles for player 1, so the consistency requirement has no bite, and every PBE is sequential. Sequential equilibrium has more cutting power in more complex games because it imposes consistent beliefs between the players (or agents) off the equilibrium path. For instance, if there are two receivers in the signalling game (players 2 and 3), these two players should form the same beliefs as to player 1's type when observing the latter's action. This property comes from the fact that at each stage of the converging sequence, players 2 and 3's Bayesian updating uses the same trembles by player 1 and, thus, reach the same conclusion. Similarly, sequential equilibrium requires consistency of a player's beliefs over time. [See Fudenberg and Tirole (1987) for examples of the other restrictions imposed by the consistency requirement.] Kreps and Wilson have shown that for "almost all" games, the sequential equilibrium concept coincides with the perfect equilibrium concept (see below). For the other (non-generic) games, it allows more equilibria. Selten requires the strategies in the perturbed game to be optimal given the perturbed strategies. But, unless the payoff structure exhibits ties, this condition has no more bite than the consistency requirement of Kreps and Wilson.

5.4.2. Trembling-hand perfect equilibrium [Selten (1975)]

In developing his notion of "trembling-hand" perfection Selten begins by working with the normal form. An equilibrium is "trembling-hand perfect in the normal form" if it is the limit of equilibria of "ε-perturbed" games in which all strategies have at least an ε probability of being played. That is, in an ε-perturbed game, players are forced to play action a with probability of at least $\varepsilon(a)$,

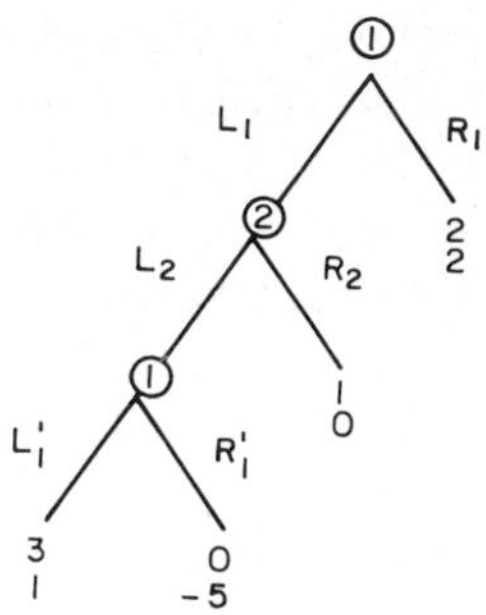

Figure 5.11

where the $\varepsilon(a)$ are arbitrary as long as they all exceed ε. The $\varepsilon(a)$ are called "trembles". The idea of introducing trembles is to give each node in the tree positive probability, so that the best responses at each node are well defined. The interpretation of the trembles is that in the original game if a player unexpectedly observes a deviation from the equilibrium path he attributes this to an inadvertent "mistake" by one of his opponents.

To see how the trembles help refine the equilibrium set, let us once again consider the game in Figure 5.5 which Selten used to motivate subgame perfectness.

The Nash equilibrium $\{U, R\}$ is not the limit of equilibria with trembles: if player 1 plays D with some probability, player 2 puts as much weight as possible on L.

However, Selten notes that his refinement is not totally satisfactory. Consider Figure 5.11, which is a slight variation on the previous game. Player 1 moves at "dates" 1 and 3.

The only subgame-perfect equilibrium is $\{L_1, L_2, L_1'\}$. But the subgame-imperfect Nash equilibrium $\{R_1, R_2, R_1'\}$ is the limit of equilibria with trembles. To see why, let player 1 play (L_1, L_1') with probability ε^2 and (L_1, R_1') with probability ε. Then player 2 should put as much weight as possible on R_2, because player 1's probability of "playing" R_1' conditional on having "played" L_1 is $\varepsilon/(\varepsilon + \varepsilon^2) \simeq 1$ for ε small. The point is that in perturbing the normal form, we have allowed there to be correlation between a player's trembles at different information sets. In the above example, if a player "trembles" onto L_1, he is very likely to tremble again.

To avoid this correlation, Selten introduces a second refinement, based on the "agent normal form". The idea is to treat the two choices of player 1 in Figure 5.11 as made by two different players, each of whom trembles independently of the other. More precisely, the agent normal form for a given game is constructed by distinguishing players not only by their names (i) and their types (t_i), but also by their location in the game tree. So, for instance, player 1 with type t_1 playing at date 1 is not the same agent as player 1 with type t_1 playing at date 3; or player 1 with type t_1 playing at date 3 should be considered as a different agent depending on his (her) information at that date. In the agent normal form, each information set represents a different agent/player. However, different agents of a same player i with type t_i are endowed with the same objective function. A "trembling-hand perfect" equilibrium is a limit of equilibria of ε-perturbed versions of the *agent* normal form.

It is clear that a trembling-hand perfect equilibrium is sequential: we can construct consistent beliefs at each information set as the limit of the beliefs computed by Bayes' rule in the perturbed games, and the equilibrium strategies are sequential given these beliefs. One might expect that the (constrained) optimality requirement along the converging sequence adds some cutting power. However, the arbitrariness of the $\varepsilon(a)$ makes perfectness a weak refinement, as shown by Kreps and Wilson's result that the sets of the sequential and perfect equilibria coincide for generic extensive-form payoffs.

Let us now sketch the proof of existence of a trembling-hand perfect equilibrium. Remember that the proof of existence of a Bayesian equilibrium consists of considering $\{\sum_i |T_i|\}$ players (i.e. in introducing one player per type), and applying standard existence theorems for Nash equilibrium. More generally, the proof for trembling-hand perfect equilibrium uses existence of a Nash equilibrium in the agent normal form. Consider the perturbed game in which the agents are forced to play trembles [i.e. to put weight at least equal to $\varepsilon(a)$ on action a]. The strategy spaces are compact convex subsets of a Euclidean space. Payoff functions are continuous in all variables and quasiconcave (actually, linear) in own strategy. So there exists a Nash equilibrium of the agent normal form of the perturbed game. Now consider a sequence of equilibrium strategies when ε tends to zero. Because the strategy spaces are compact, there is a converging subsequence. The limit of such a subsequence is called a trembling-hand perfect equilibrium.[9]

We should also note that Selten works with the normal form or the agent normal form; so do the next two refinements. Thus, beliefs are left implicit. Kreps and Wilson's paper is the first pure game theory article to put emphasis on the extensive form and on beliefs. While we believe that this approach has been fruitful, there is currently a debate about whether the normal form on the extensive form is the most appropriate framework for studying equilibrium refinements. At this time, the refinements that are easily applicable to industrial organization models put constraints on beliefs. (See the previous section.)

[9] Note that because payoffs are continuous, the limit is automatically a Nash equilibrium. But the converse, of course, is not true (for instance, for games of perfect information, a trembling-hand equilibrium is subgame perfect, as is easily seen).

5.4.3. *Proper equilibrium* [Myerson (1978)]

Myerson considers perturbed games in which, say, a player's second-best action(s) get at most ε times the weight of the first-best action(s), the third-best action(s) get at most ε times the weight of the second-best action(s), etc. The idea is that a player is "more likely to tremble" and put weight on an action which is not too detrimental to him; the probability of deviations from equilibrium behavior is inversely related to their costs. As the set of allowed trembles is smaller, a proper equilibrium is also perfect. (With such an ordering of trembles, there is no need to work on the agent's normal form. The normal form suffices.)

To illustrate the notion of proper equilibrium, consider the following game (due to Myerson) (Figure 5.12):

Player 1 \ Player 2	L	M	R
U	1, 1	0, 0	-9, -9
M	0, 0	0, 0	-7, -7
D	-9, -9	-7, -7	-7, -7

Figure 5.12

This game has three pure strategy Nash equilibria: (U, L), (M, M), and (D, R). Only two of these are perfect equilibria: D and R are weakly dominated strategies and therefore cannot be optimal when the other player trembles. (M, M) is perfect. Suppose that each player plays M with probability $1 - 2\varepsilon$ and each of the other two strategies with probability ε. Deviating to U for player 1 (or to L for player 2) increases this player's payoff by $(\varepsilon - 9\varepsilon) - (-7\varepsilon) = -\varepsilon < 0$. However, (M, M) is not a proper equilibrium. Each player should put much more weight (tremble more) on his first strategy than on his third, which yields a lower payoff. But if player 1, say, puts weight ε on U and ε^2 on D, player 2 does better by playing L than by playing M, as $(\varepsilon - 9\varepsilon^2) - (-7\varepsilon^2) > 0$ for ε small. The only proper equilibrium in this game is (U, L).

5.4.4. *Stable equilibrium* [Kohlberg and Mertens (1986)]

Ideally, one would wish a PBE to be the limit of some perturbed equilibrium for *all* perturbations when the size of these perturbations goes to zero. Such an equilibrium, if it exists, is labelled *truly perfect*. Unfortunately, true perfection may be out of this world (truly perfect equilibria tend not to exist). Kohlberg and Mertens, to obtain existence, settled for "stability." Stability is a complex criterion, which encompasses the intuitive criterion mentioned in the previous section and other features as well. Let us give an example of the description of a stable equilibrium in the *signalling game* [this introduction follows Kreps (1984)]. Consider two *totally mixed* strategies, $\tilde{\sigma}_1$ and $\tilde{\sigma}_2$, for players 1 and 2, and two strictly positive numbers, ε_1 and ε_2. A $\{\varepsilon_i, \tilde{\sigma}_i\}_{i=1}^2$ perturbation of the original game is such that, when player i chooses strategy σ_i, the strategy which is implemented for him is σ_i with probability $(1 - \varepsilon_i)$ and $\tilde{\sigma}_i$ with probability ε_i. Let (σ_1, σ_2) be a PBE of the perturbed game. A subset E of PBE of the original game is stable if, for any $\eta > 0$, there exists an equilibrium of the perturbed game that lies no more than η from the set E. A *stable component* is then defined as a minimal connected stable set of equilibria. Kohlberg and Mertens have shown that every game has at least one stable component, and that, for almost every signalling game, all equilibria within a given connected component give rise to the same probability distribution on endpoints.

5.5. *Perturbed games and robust equilibria*

Our earlier discussion of the Saloner/Matthews–Mirman contribution emphasized the robustness of the solution to the introduction of noise. More generally, robustness to "reasonable" structural changes in the game seem desirable. This leads us to the discussion of the reputation-effects model of Kreps, Wilson, Milgrom and Roberts (1982), which is one of the most important applications of the theory of dynamic games of incomplete information.

This work actually started with a robustness issue: in the finite horizon repeated prisoner's dilemma the only equilibrium is "fink, fink" at each period. As we observed in Section 3, this conclusion seems extreme for long, finite games; in response, the four authors decided to perturb the prisoner's dilemma game slightly by introducing a small probability that each party is willing to play the suboptimal strategy tit-for-tat. Similarly, in the context of Example 1, one could introduce a probability that firm 1 enjoys preying (is crazy). Then, if the horizon is sufficiently long and the discount rate sufficiently small, it may be worthwhile for a sane type (one whose payoff is as originally specified) to pretend at the start that it is a crazy type. By cooperating in the repeated prisoner's dilemma game or preying in the predation game, the sane type invests in reputation that will induce the other player to take actions that are favorable to the former (cooperate; stay out). Thus, in games that are repeated for a long time, a small difference in information can make a big difference in terms of outcome.

Fudenberg and Maskin (1986a) develop the reputation-effects model to its logical conclusion. They show that, for any ε, when the horizon goes to infinity and for discount factors close to 1, all individually rational payoffs of a finitely repeated, full-information game can arise as PBE of a slightly perturbed, incomplete-information game, in which the objective function of each player is the one of the original game with probability $(1 - \varepsilon)$ and can be any "crazy" objective function with probability ε. In the Friedman tradition, the result that one can obtain any payoff Pareto superior to a Nash payoff is easy to derive. Consider a Nash equilibrium of the original game ("fink, fink" in the repeated prisoner's dilemma) and an allocation that dominates this Nash equilibrium, and the corresponding prescribed strategies ("cooperate, cooperate"). Suppose that with probability ε, each player has the following objective function: "I like to play the strategy corresponding to the superior allocation as long as the others have followed their corresponding strategies; if somebody has deviated in the past, my taste commands me to play my Nash equilibrium strategy forever." Now suppose that the horizon is long. Then by cooperating, each player loses some payoff at most over one period if the other player deviates. When deviating, he automatically loses the gain of being able to cooperate with the crazy type until the end. So, as long as there remains enough time until the end of the horizon, ("enough" depends on ε) deviating is not optimal. The proof for points that do not dominate a Nash equilibrium is harder.

The reputation-effects literature shows that adding a small ε of incomplete information to a long but finitely repeated game could make virtually anything into a PBE. However, for a fixed finite horizon, a sufficiently small ε of incomplete information has a more limited effect. If the ε's concern only each player's information about his own payoffs, then as ε vanishes the set of PBE converges to the set of perfect equilibria of the *normal form* of the original game. (*Not* the agent normal form, so this set can include equilibria that are not subgame-perfect.) If we moreover admit the possibility that players have private information about their opponents' payoffs, then the sequential rationality requirements of PBE completely lose their force. More precisely, any Nash equilibrium of an extensive form is a PBE (indeed, a stable PBE) of a perturbed game in which payoffs differ from the original ones with vanishingly small probability. These points are developed in Fudenberg, Kreps and Levine (1988).

Consider the game in Figure 5.13. Player 1 has two possible types, t_1 and t_2, with $\text{Prob}(t = t_1) = 1 - \varepsilon$. When $t = t_1$, the game is just as in the game of Figure 5.5, where the backwards-induction equilibrium was (D, R). When $t = t_2$, though, player 2 prefers R to L. The strategies (U_1, D_2, R) are a PBE for this game; if player 2 sees D, he infers that $t = t_2$. Thus, a "small" perturbation of the game causes a large change in play – player 1 chooses U with probability $(1 - \varepsilon)$. Moreover, this equilibrium satisfies all the currently known refinements.

Most of these refinements proceed by asking what sort of beliefs are "reasonable" – what should players expect following unexpected events? If they have very small doubts about the structure of the game, the unexpected may signal, as here, that things are indeed other than had previously seemed likely.

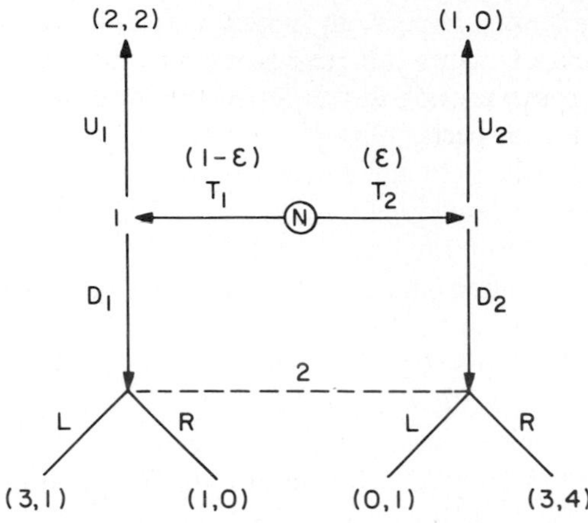

Figure 5.13

Thus, small changes in the information structure can always extend the set of predictions to include all of the Nash equilibria, and in long repeated games the "robustness" problem is even more severe. What then is the predictive content of game theory? In real-world situations, it may be the case that only some types are unlikely (most types of "craziness" are not plausible). The players may then have a fairly good idea of what game is played. However, the economist, who is an outsider, may have a hard time knowing which information structure is the relevant one. Because the equilibrium of the game is very sensitive to the information structure, making predictions can be even more difficult than usual when reputation effects are important. If this is true, the economist should collect information about the way real-world players play their games and which information structure they believe they face, and then try to explain why particular sorts of "craziness" prevail.

The above implies a fairly pessimistic view of the likelihood that game theory can hope to provide a purely formal way of choosing between PBEs. It would be rash for us to assert this position too strongly, for research on equilibrium refinements is proceeding quite rapidly, and our discussion here may well be outdated by the time it appears in print. However, at present we would not want to base important predictions solely on formal grounds. In evaluating antitrust policy, for example, practitioners will need to combine a knowledge of the technical niceties with a sound understanding of the workings of actual markets.

6. Concluding remark

Our already incomplete discussion of equilibrium concepts for dynamic games of incomplete information is likely to be out of date very shortly, as the pace of activity in this field is very intense, and current refinements have not yet been tested for a wide class of models. Our purpose was only to provide an introduction, a survey and some cookbook recipes for readers who currently want to apply these techniques to specific games.

References

Abreu, D. (1986) 'Extremal equilibria of oligopolistic supergames', *Journal of Economic Theory*, 39:191–225.

Abreu, D. (1988) 'On the theory of infinitely repeated games with discounting', *Econometrica*, 56:383–396.

Abreu, D., Pearce, D. and Stacchetti, E. (1986) 'Optimal cartel equilibria with imperfect monitoring', *Journal of Economic Theory*, 39:251–269.

Akerlof, G. (1970) 'The market for 'lemons'', *Quarterly Journal of Economics*, 90:629–650.

Anderson, R. (1985) 'Quick-response equilibria', mimeo.

Aumann, R. (1959) 'Acceptable points in general cooperative *n*-person games', in: *Contributions to the theory of games IV*. Princeton, N.J.: Princeton University Press.

Aumann, R. (1964) 'Mixed vs. behavior strategies in infinite extensive games', *Annals of Mathematics Studies*, 52:627–630.

Aumann, R. (1974) 'Subjectivity and correlation in randomized strategies', *Journal of Mathematical Economics*, 1:67–96.

Aumann, R. (1976) 'Agreeing to disagree', *Annals of Statistics*, 4:1236–1239.

Aumann, R. (1986) 'Correlated equilibria as an expression of rationality', *Econometrica*, forthcoming.

Aumann, R. and Machler, M. (1967) 'Game theoretic aspects of gradual disarmament', Hebrew University, Jerusalem, mimeo.

Aumann, R. and Shapley, L. (1976) 'Long term competition: A game theoretic analysis', mimeo.

Aumann, R., Katznelson, Y., Radner, R., Rosenthal, R.W. and Weiss, B. (1981) 'Approximate purification of mixed strategies', Bell Laboratories, mimeo.

Banks, J. and Sobel, J. (1987) 'Equilibrium selection in signaling games', *Econometrica*, 55:890–904.

Baron, D. and Besanko, D. (1984) 'Regulation, asymmetric information, and auditing', *Rand Journal*, 15:447–470.

Benoit, J.P. and Krishna, V. (1985) 'Finitely repeated games', *Econometrica*, 53:890–904.

Bernheim, D. (1984) 'Rationalizable strategic behavior', *Econometrica*, 52:1007–1028.

Bernheim, D. and Whinston, M. (1985) 'Coalition-proof Nash equilibria, II: Applications', Stanford University.

Bernheim, D., Peleg, B. and Whinston, M. (1985) 'Coalition-proof Nash equilibria, I: Concepts', Stanford University, mimeo.

Brandenburger, A. and Dekel, E. (1985a) 'Hierarchies of beliefs and common knowledge', mimeo.

Brandenburger, A. and Dekel, E. (1985b) 'Rationalizability and correlated equilibria', *Econometrica*, forthcoming.

Bulow, J. (1982) 'Durable-goods monopolists', *Journal of Political Economy*, 90:314–332.

Chamberlin, E. (1956) *The theory of monopolistic competition*. Cambridge, Massachusetts: Harvard University Press.

Cho, I.-K. (1986) 'Equilibrium analysis of entry deterrence: Reexamination', Princeton University, mimeo.

Cho, I.-K. and Kreps, D. (1987) 'More signalling games and stable equilibrium', *Quarterly Journal of Economics*, 102:179–221.

Coase, R.H. (1972) 'Durability and monopoly', *Journal of Law and Economics*, 15:143–149.

Crawford, V. and Sobel, J. (1982) 'Strategic information transmission', *Econometrica*, 50:1431–1452.

Cremer, J. (1986) 'Cooperation in ongoing organizations', *Quarterly Journal of Economics*, 101:33–50.

Dasgupta, P. and Maskin, E. (1986) 'The existence of equilibrium in discontinuous economic games, I: Theory', *Review of Economic Studies*, 53:1–26.

Davidson, C. and Deneckere, R. (1986) 'Long-run competition in capacities, short-run competition in price and the Cournot model', *Rand Journal of Economics*, 17:404–415.

Debreu, G. (1952) 'A social equilibrium existence theorem', *Proceedings of the National Academy of Sciences*, 38:886–893.

Fan, K. (1952) 'Fixed point and minimax theorems in locally convex topological linear spaces', *Proceedings of the National Academy of Sciences*, 38:121–126.

Farquharson, R. (1969) *Theory of voting*. New Haven: Yale University Press.

Farrell, J. (1983) 'Renegotiation-proof equilibrium in repeated games', MIT, mimeo.

Farrell, J. (1984). 'Credible neologisms in games of communication', MIT, mimeo.

Fraysse, J. and Moreaux, M. (1985) 'Collusive equilibria in oligopolies with finite lives', *European Economic Review*, 27:45–55.

Friedman, J. (1971) 'A noncooperative equilibrium for supergames', *Review of Economic Studies*, 38:1–12.

Friedman, J. (1977) *Oligopoly and the theory of games*. Amsterdam: North-Holland.

Friedman, J. (1984) 'Trigger strategy equilibria in finite horizon supergames', mimeo.

Fudenberg, D. and Kreps, D. (1987) 'Reputation with simultaneous opponents', *Review of Economic Studies*, 54:541–568.

Fudenberg, D. and Levine, D. (1983) 'Subgame-perfect equilibria of finite and infinite horizon games', *Journal of Economic Theory*, 31:227–256.

Fudenberg, D. and Levine, D. (1986) 'Limit games and limit equilibria', *Journal of Economic Theory*, 38:261–279.

Fudenberg, D. and Levine, D. (1988) 'Open-loop and closed-loop equilibria in games with many players', *Journal of Economic Theory*, 44:1–18.

Fudenberg, D. and Maskin, E. (1986a) 'Folk theorems for repeated games with discounting or with incomplete information', *Econometrica*, 54:553–554.

Fudenberg, D. and Maskin, E. (1986b) 'Discounted repeated games with unobservable actions', mimeo.

Fudenberg, D. and Maskin, E. (1987) 'Nash and perfect equilibria of discounted repeated games', mimeo.

Fudenberg, D. and Tirole, J. (1983a) 'Capital as a commitment: Strategic investment to deter mobility', *Journal of Economic Theory*, 31:227–250.

Fudenberg, D. and Tirole, J. (1983b) 'Sequential bargaining with incomplete information', *Review of Economic Studies*, 50:221–247.

Fudenberg, D. and Tirole, J. (1985) 'Preemption and rent equalization in the adoption of new technology', *Review of Economic Studies*, 52:383–401.

Fudenberg, D. and Tirole, J. (1986) 'A theory of exit in oligopoly', *Econometrica*, 54:943–960.

Fudenberg, D. and Tirole, J. (1987) 'Perfect Bayesian equilibrium: An expository note', MIT, mimeo.

Fudenberg, D., Levine, D. and Tirole, J. (1985) 'Infinite horizon models of bargaining with one-sided incomplete information', in: Alvin Roth, ed., *Bargaining with incomplete information*. Cambridge: Cambridge University Press.

Fudenberg, D., Kreps, D. and Levine, D. (1988) 'On the robustness of equilibrium refinements', *Journal of Economic Theory*, 44:354–380.

Geanakoplos, J. and Polemarchakis, H. (1978) 'We can't disagree forever', IMSSS discussion paper no. 277, Stanford University.

Gertner, R. (1985a) 'Simultaneous move price-quantity games and non-market clearing equilibrium', MIT, mimeo.

Gertner, R. (1985b) 'Dynamic duopoly with price inertia', MIT, mimeo.

Ghemawat, P. and Nalebuff, B. (1985) 'Exit', *Rand Journal of Economics*, 16:84–94.

Glicksberg, I.L. (1952) 'A further generalization of the Kakutani fixed point theorem with application to Nash equilibrium points', *Proceedings of the National Academy of Sciences*, 38:170–174.

Green, E. (1984) 'Continuum and finite-players, non-cooperative models of competition', *Econometrica*, 52:975–994.

Green, E. and Porter, R. (1984) 'Noncooperative collusion under imperfect price information', *Econometrica*, 32:87–100.

Green, J. and Heller, W. (1981) 'Mathematical analysis and convexity with applications to economics', in: K. Arrow and M. Intriligator, eds., *Handbook of Mathematical Economics*. Amsterdam: North-Holland Publishing Co., 15–52.

Grossman, S. and Hart, O. (1983) 'An analysis of the principal–agent problem', *Econometrica*, 51:7–46.

Grossman, S. and Perry, M. (1986) 'Perfect sequential equilibrium', *Journal of Economic Theory*, 39:97–119.

Gul, F., Sonnenschein, H. and Wilson, R. (1986) 'Foundations of dynamic monopoly and the Coase conjecture', *Journal of Economic Theory*, 39:155–190.

Hanig, M. (1985) 'A differentiable game model of duopoly with reversible investment', MIT, mimeo.

Harris, C. (1985a) 'A characterization of the perfect equilibria of infinite-horizon games', *Journal of Economic Theory*, 37:99–125.

Harris, C. (1985b) 'Existence and characterisation of perfect equilibrium in games of perfect information', *Econometrica*, 53:613–628.

Harris, C. (1986) 'A note on the existence of optimal simple penal codes', Nuffield College, mimeo.

Hart, S. (1979) 'Lecture notes: Special topics in game theory', IMSSS technical report.

Hart, S. and Schmeidler, D. (1986) 'Correlated equilibria: An elementary proof of existence', Tel Aviv University, mimeo.

Harsanyi, J. (1964) 'A general solution for finite non-cooperative games, based on risk dominance', in M. Dresher et al., eds., *Advances in game theory. Annals of Mathematics*, 52:627–650.

Harsanyi, J. (1967–1968) 'Games with incomplete information played by Bayesian players', *Management Science*, 14:159–182, 320–334, 486–502.

Harsanyi, J. (1973) 'Games with randomly disturbed payoffs: A new rationale for mixed-strategy equilibrium points', *International Journal of Game Theory*, 2:1–23.

Hendricks, K. and Wilson, C. (1985a) 'Discrete versus continuous time in games of timing', mimeo.

Hendricks, K. and Wilson, C. (1985b) 'The war of attrition in discrete time', C.V. Starr Center working paper no. 85-32, New York University.

Holmström, B. (1982) 'Moral hazard in teams', *Bell Journal of Economics*, 13:324–340.

Judd, K. (1985) 'Closed-loop equilibrium in a multi-stage innovation race', discussion paper no. 647, Kellogg Graduate School of Management, Northwestern University.

Katz, M. and Shapiro, C. (1984) 'Perfect equilibrium in a development game with licensing or imitation', discussion paper no. 85, Woodrow Wilson School, Princeton.

Kohlberg, E. (1981) 'Some problems with the concept of perfect equilibrium', NBER Conference, University of California, Berkeley.

Kohlberg, E. and Mertens, J.F. (1986) 'On the strategic stability of equilibria', *Econometrica*, 54:1003–1038.

Kreps, D. (1984) 'Signalling games and stable equilibrium', mimeo.

Kreps, D. and Scheinkman, J. (1983) 'Quantity precommitment and Bertrand competition yield Cournot outcomes', *Bell Journal of Economics*, 14:326–337.

Kreps, D. and Wilson, R. (1982a) 'Sequential equilibrium', *Econometrica*, 50:863–894.

Kreps, D. and Wilson, R. (1982b) 'Reputation and imperfect information', *Journal of Economic Theory*, 27:253–279.

Kreps, D., Wilson, R., Milgrom, P. and Roberts, J. (1982) 'Rational cooperation in the finitely-repeated prisoner's dilemma', *Journal of Economic Theory*, 27:245–252.

Kuhn, H. (1953) 'Extensive games and the problem of information', *Annals of Mathematics Studies*, 28:193–216.

Lockwood, B. (1983) 'Perfect equilibria in repeated games with discounting,' mimeo.

Luce, R. and Raiffa, H. (1957), *Games and decisions*, Chapters 1, 3–5. New york: Wiley.

Maskin, E. and Tirole, J. (1988) 'A theory of dynamic oligopoly, II: Price Competition', *Econometrica*, 56:571–600.

Matthews, S. and Mirman, L. (1983) 'Equilibrium limit pricing: The effects of private information and stochastic demand', *Econometrica*, 51:981–996.

Maynard Smith, J. (1974) 'The theory of games and the evolution of animal conflicts', *Journal of Theoretical Biology*, 47:209, 274.

McLennan, A. (1985) 'Justifiable beliefs in sequential equilibrium', *Econometrica*, 53:889–904.

McManus, M. (1962) 'Numbers and size in Cournot oligopoly,' *Yorkshire Bulletin of Social and Economic Research*, 14:14–22.

Mertens, J.F. and Zamir, S. (1985) 'Formulation of Bayesian analysis for games with incomplete information', *International Journal of Game Theory*, 14:1–29.

Milgrom, P. (1981) 'An axiomatic characterization of common knowledge', *Econometrica*, 49(2):219–222.

Milgrom, P. and Roberts, J. (1982a) 'Limit pricing and entry under incomplete information', *Econometrica*, 50:443–460.

Milgrom, P. and Roberts, J. (1982b) 'Predation, reputation, and entry deterrence', *Journal of Economic Theory*, 27:280–312.

Milgrom, P. and Weber, R. (1982) 'A theory of auctions and competitive bidding', *Econometrica*, 50:1089–1122.

Milgrom, P. and Weber, R. (1986a) 'Topologies on information and strategies in games with incomplete information', discussion paper no. 463, Northwestern MEDS.

Milgrom, P. and Weber, R. (1986b) 'Distributional strategies for games with incomplete information', *Mathematics of Operations Research*, 10:619–631.

Moulin, H. (1979) 'Dominance solvable voting schemes', *Econometrica*, 47:1337–1353.

Myerson, R. (1978) 'Refinements of the Nash equilibrium concept', *International Journal of Game Theory*, 7:73–80.

Myerson, R. (1979) 'Optimal auction design', *Mathematics of Operations Research*, 6:58–73.

Myerson, R. (1983) 'Bayesian equilibrium and incentive compatibility: An introduction', discussion paper no. 548, Northwestern MEDS.

Myerson, R. and Satterthwaite, M. (1983) 'Efficient mechanisms for bilateral trading', *Journal of Economic Theory*, 29:265–281.

Nalebuff, B. (1982) 'Brinkmanship', Harvard University, mimeo.

Nash, J.F. (1950) 'Equilibrium points in *N*-person games', *Proceedings of the National Academy of Sciences, U.S.A.*, 36:48–49.

Novshek, W. (1985) 'On the existence of Cournot equilibrium', *Review of Economic Studies*, 52:85–98.

Ortega-Reichert, A. (1967) 'Models for competitive bidding under uncertainty', Ph.D. thesis, Stanford University.

Pearce, D. (1984) 'Rationalizable strategic behavior and the problem of perfection', *Econometrica*, 52:1029–1050.

Pitchik, C. (1982) 'Equilibria of a two-person non-zerosum noisy game of timing', *International Journal of Game Theory*, 10:207–221.

Porter, R. (1983) 'Optimal cartel trigger price strategies', *Journal of Economic Theory*, 30:313–338.

Radner, R. (1980) 'Collusive behavior in non-cooperative epsilon-equilibria of oligopolies with long but finite lives', *Journal of Economic Theory*, 22:136–154.

Radner, R. Myerson, R. and Maskin, E. (1986) 'An example of a repeated partnership game with discounting and with uniformly inefficient equilibria', *Review of Economic Studies*, 53:59–70.

Reynolds, S. (1985) 'Capacity investment, preemption and commitment in an infinite horizon model', mimeo.

Riley, J. (1980) 'Strong evolutionary equilibrium and the war of attrition', *Journal of Theoretical Biology*, 82:383–400.

Roberts, J. and Sonnenschein, H. (1976) 'On the existence of Cournot equilibrium without concave profit functions', *Journal of Economic Theory*, 13:112–117.

Roberts, J. and Sonnenschein, H. (1977) 'On the foundations of the theory of monopolistic competition', *Econometrica*, 45:101–113.

Rotemberg, J. and Saloner, G. (1985) 'Price leadership,' mimeo.

Rotemberg, J. and Saloner, G. (1986) 'A supergame-theoretic model of business cycles and price wars during booms', *American Economic Review*, 76:390–407.

Rubinstein, A. (1977) 'Equilibrium in supergames', Center for Mathematical Economics and Game Theory, Hebrew University of Jerusalem.

Rubinstein, A. (1979) 'Equilibrium in supergames with the overtaking criterion', *Journal of Economic Theory*, 21:1–9.

Rubinstein, A. (1982) 'Perfect equilibrium in a bargaining model', *Econometrica*, 50:97–110.

Saloner, G. (1981) 'Dynamic equilibrium limit pricing in an uncertain environment', Graduate School of Business, Stanford University, mimeo.

Schelling, T. (1960) *The strategy of conflict*. Cambridge, Mass.: Harvard University Press.

Scherer, F.M. (1980) *Industrial market structure and economic performance*, 2nd edn. Boston: Houghton-Mifflin.

Selten, R. (1965) 'Spieltheoretische Behandlung eines Oligopolmodells mit Nachfrageträgheit', *Zeitschrift für die gesamte Staatswissenschaft*, 12:301–324.

Selten, R. (1975) 'Reexamination of the perfectness concept for equilibrium points in extensive games', *International Journal of Game Theory*, 4:25–55.

Simon, L. (1985) 'Games with discontinuous payoffs I: Theory', mimeo.

Simon, L. and Stinchcombe, M. (1986) 'Extensive form games in continuous time. Part I: Pure strategies', mimeo.

Sobel, J. and Takahashi, I. (1983) 'A multi-stage model of bargaining', *Review of Economic Studies*, 50:411–426.

Spence, A.M. (1974) *Market signalling*. Cambridge: Harvard University Press.

Spence, A.M. (1979) 'Investment strategy and growth in a new market', *Bell Journal of Economics*, 10:1–19.

Starr, R. and Ho, Y.C. (1967) 'Further properties of nonzero-sum differential games', *Journal of Optimization Theory and Applications*, 3:207–219.

Stokey, N. (1981) 'Rational expectations durable goods pricing', *Bell Journal of Economics*, 12:112–128.

Tarski, A. (1955) 'A lattice-theoretical fixpoint theorem and its applications', *Pacific Journal of Mathematics*, 5:285–308.

Topkis, D. (1970) 'Equilibrium points in nonzero-sum N-person subadditive games', technical report ORC 70-38, Operations Research Center, University of California, Berkeley.

Vives, X. (1985) 'Nash equilibrium in oligopoly games with monotone best responses', CARESS working paper no. 85-10, University of Pennsylvania.

Weiss, A. and Wilson, C.A. (1984) 'An analysis of games of timing with complete information: An application to oil exploration', mimeo.

Chapter 6

THEORIES OF OLIGOPOLY BEHAVIOR*

CARL SHAPIRO**

Princeton University

Contents

*This chapter is dedicated to the 150th anniversary of the publication of Cournot's (1838) theory of oligopoly.

**I thank the Institute for International Economic Studies at the University of Stockholm which provided an excellent environment while I was beginning to write this chapter, and the National Science Foundation, which provided financial support under Grant SES 86-06336. I also thank Hal Varian for his help in implementing this chapter on his VERTEX system, and Blaise Allaz for translating Bertrand's (1883) Book Review from French into English. Avinash Dixit provided extremely useful comments on a rough draft. Richard Gilbert, Gene Grossman, Barry Nalebuff, Rob Porter, Steve Salant, Jean Tirole, Hal Varian, and Robert Willig read a preliminary version and made numerous helpful suggestions.

Handbook of Industrial Organization, Volume I, Edited by R. Schmalensee and R.D. Willig

1. Introduction

The study of oligopolistic industries lies at the heart of the field of industrial organization. One's beliefs about the behavior of large firms in concentrated markets colors one's views on a broad range of antitrust and regulatory policies. And these beliefs derive in turn from theory and evidence of oligopolists' behavior. In this chapter, I present and evaluate the primary competing theories of oligopolistic behavior.

Oligopoly theory has a long history, as befits such a central topic in microeconomics. Sir Thomas Moore coined the term oligopoly in his *Utopia* (1516), and noted that prices need not fall to competitive levels simply due to the presence of more than a single supplier.[1] And we are about to mark the 150th anniversary of the publication of Cournot's (1838) pathbreaking book, wherein he provided the first formal theory of oligopoly. In an influential review of Cournot's book (it took economists some fifty years to become aware of Cournot's work) Bertrand (1883) criticized the theory developed by Cournot. Indeed, to read Edgeworth (1925), one would think that Cournot's theory had long since been discredited.[2] Despite this rather negative reception given to Cournot's theory,[3] it remains today the benchmark model of oligopoly. In fact, a glance at virtually any microeconomics textbook reveals that few if any subsequent developments in oligopoly theory are generally regarded as important enough for inclusion.[4] Part of the goal of this chapter is to clarify just how oligopoly theory has, and has not, progressed in the 150 years since Cournot developed his theory. Although oligopoly fits conceptually between the extremes of monopoly and perfect competition, its study requires a rather different set of tools, namely those of game theory.[5] The hallmark of oligopoly is the presence of strategic interactions among rival firms, a subject well suited for game-theoretic analysis. This chapter presumes a working knowledge of such concepts as Nash equilibrium and subgame

[1] I rely here on Schumpeter (1954, p. 305) for the reference to More.

[2] Writing in 1897, Edgeworth stated (1925, pp. 117–118) "Cournot's conclusion has been shown to be erroneous by Bertrand for the case in which there is no cost of production; by Professor Marshall for the case in which the cost follows the law of increasing returns; and by the present writer for the case in which the cost follows the law of diminishing returns."

[3] But see also Fisher (1898), who stated: "Cournot's treatment of this difficult problem [duopoly] is brilliant and suggestive, but not free from serious objections."

[4] The theories from the past century that most often are cited seem to be Stackelberg's (1934) modification of Cournot's theory and Sweezy's (1939) kinked demand curve theory.

[5] Actually, Cournot's plan was to smoothly fill in the cases between pure monopoly and perfect competition. Schumpeter notes, however (1954, p. 981), that "as we leave the case of pure monopoly, factors assert themselves that are absent in this case and vanish again as we approach pure competition," so that "the unbroken line from monopoly to competition is a treacherous guide".

perfect equilibrium, although the latter is developed somewhat in Sections 3 and 4.[6]

The material in this chapter is closely related to that in the chapters on collusion and cartels, entry deterrence, and product differentiation. In applications, these neighboring topics are inevitably intertwined with the analysis of noncooperative output, pricing, and investment policies that constitutes the bulk of the current chapter. For the purposes of this chapter, I define the boundaries of oligopoly theory by excluding explicitly cooperative behavior, by assuming a fixed number of active oligopolists,[7] and by avoiding any analysis of spatial competition.

Within these boundaries, we would like oligopoly theory to provide predictions regarding the relationship between market structure and performance, as measured, say, by price–cost margins. For a given set of active firms, and cost and demand conditions, what outputs and prices do we expect to prevail? Are two to three firms sufficient to ensure a relatively competitive outcome, or does this require many rivals? What institutional arrangements are conducive to (i.e. facilitate) relatively collusive behavior?

We also rely on oligopoly theory to provide a way of thinking about strategic behavior more generally, and its antitrust implications. By strategic behavior I mean not just production and pricing policies, but also decisions regarding investments, inventories, product choice, marketing, and distribution. Although there is no general theory encompassing this entire range of behavior, oligopoly theory can help us to understand many dimensions of strategic rivalry and to identify particular strategies that have anticompetitive effects.

Oligopoly theory has of course been the subject of numerous previous surveys. Stigler, in his influential 1964 paper, wrote (p. 44): "No one has the right, and few the ability, to lure economists into reading another article on oligopoly theory without some advance indication of its alleged contribution." Following this principle, it seems appropriate for me to explain the relationship between this chapter and previous surveys of oligopoly theory. Scherer (1980, chs. 5–7) is a standard reference at the undergraduate level. Dixit (1982) gives a short summary of three of the main strands of modern oligopoly theory. Friedman (1983) provides a fairly recent general coverage of the topic. Fudenberg and Tirole (1986a) is a selected survey of advanced topics in dynamic oligopoly, and

[6] I also assume that the reader is familiar with the concepts of pure and mixed strategies. See Chapter 5 by Fudenberg and Tirole in this Handbook for an introduction to the game-theoretic tools most often utilized in industrial organization.

[7] Here a firm is "active" if it has borne any sunk entry costs necessary to operate in the industry; thus I am steering clear of issues relating to entry deterrence. Throughout this chapter I also leave in the background the fundamental forces, such as economies of scale, that limit the number of firms in the industry. Of course, oligopoly theory is most interesting when the number of firms so determined is rather small. See Chapter 1 by John Panzar in this Handbook for a discussion of technology and market structure.

Kreps and Spence (1985) discuss many of the intriguing issues that arise in dynamic rivalry. But none of these authors makes an effort to report on and critique the vast number of articles on oligopoly in the past decade. The current chapter aims to be both systematic and comprehensive at a more advanced level than, say, Friedman (1983), but with an emphasis on the *economics* of oligopoly, rather than the game theory itself.

The various modern theories of oligopoly behavior are essentially a set of different games that have been analyzed; these games do not represent competing theories, but rather models relevant in different industries or circumstances. Accordingly, this chapter is organized on the basis of the structure of these games. Some readers may find that I give short shrift to such classic topics as price leadership or monopolistic competition. But this is a conscious choice in order to emphasize the more recent, game-theoretic contributions.

I begin in the next section with static models of oligopoly, distinguished according to the strategies available to the competing firms (quantities and prices being the two leading candidates). I then move on in Section 3 to games that are simple repetitions of the static games – finitely or infinitely repeated quantity or price games. Section 4 begins the study of strategic behavior by looking at two-period games. I discuss there many of the dimensions of competition that are absent in supergames. These include investments in physical capital, the establishment of a customer base, and R&D investments. These ideas are continued in Section 5, where I look at dynamic games in which the firms can make lasting commitments so that history matters – games that are *not* simple repetitions of the static competition. A summary and conclusion follow.

Before embarking on my analysis, it is best to provide the reader with a word of warning. Unlike perfect competition or pure monopoly, there is no single "theory of oligopoly". The rival theories presented below would seem each to have its appropriate application, and none can be considered *the* prevailing theory. Indeed, there has long been doubt about the wisdom of seeking a single, universal theory of oligopoly, and I share this doubt.[8] Only by making special assumptions about the oligopolistic environment – each of which will be appropriate in only a limited set of industries – can we expect to wind up with a specific prediction regarding oligopoly behavior. I view the development of oligopoly theory as providing us with an understanding of which environments lead to various types of equilibrium behavior, and with some sense of the methods by which large firms both compete and seek to avoid competition. But I do not expect oligopoly theory – at least at this stage of its development – to give tight inter-industry predictions regarding the extent of competition or collusion.

[8]Schumpeter (1954, p. 983), for example, appears to concur with Pigou's conclusion regarding the indeterminateness of duopoly equilibrium in his *Wealth and Welfare* (1912).

2. Static oligopoly theory

The natural starting place in a study of oligopoly theory, both logically and historically, is a static model of strategic interactions. Although a timeless model of oligopoly cannot, by definition, treat the essential issue of how rivals *react* to each other's actions, it does serve to elucidate the basic tension between competition and cooperation and provide an essential ingredient for the richer, dynamic analysis below. Of course, static oligopoly theory can only provide predictions about short-run behavior, taking the firms' capital stocks, and hence their variable cost functions, as given. I shall consider strategic investment plans in Sections 4 and 5 below.

Any theory of oligopoly must confront the essential tension in small-numbers rivalry: each firm is tempted to compete aggressively to increase its own market share, but if all firms do so, they all suffer. Another way of putting this is that oligopolistic interactions necessarily have the underlying structure of a prisoner's dilemma game.[9] What we can seek in a static theory of oligopoly is a prediction about the particular resolution of this tension between competition and cooperation, based upon such fundamentals as demand conditions, cost conditions, and the number of competing firms. As we shall see, even within the class of static models, the precise way in which rivalry is modeled has a profound impact on equilibrium behavior.

2.1. *Cournot oligopoly: Competition in outputs*

I present here a modern version of Cournot's (1838) theory of oligopoly. Consider n firms competing to supply a homogeneous good, the demand for which is given by $p(X)$, where p is the price, and $X \equiv x_1 + \cdots + x_n$ is industry output, x_i being firm i's output. Firm i produces according to the cost function $C_i(x_i)$. I shall at times denote firm i's marginal cost, $C_i'(x_i)$, by simply c_i; this is exactly accurate in the convenient case of constant marginal costs, but is otherwise a notational short-cut. Firm i's profits are

$$\pi_i = p(X)x_i - C_i(x_i)$$

if it produces x_i and total output is X.

[9] As discussed above, I restrict attention to noncooperative behavior; for a treatment of cartels, mergers, and explicit collusion, see Chapter 7 by Jacquemin and Slade in this Handbook.

2.1.1. The Cournot equilibrium

In a timeless model, each firm makes but a single decision, which in some way captures how "aggressive" is its attempt to make sales. In the Cournot model, all firms choose their outputs simultaneously. In other words, the Cournot equilibrium is a Nash equilibrium in quantities. Given a set of choices, $\{x_i\}$, price adjusts to clear the market, i.e. $p = p(X)$. Formally, the Cournot equilibrium output vector, $(x_1, \ldots, x_n)$, is determined by the n equations, $\partial \pi_i / \partial x_i = 0$, $i = 1, \ldots, n$. The ith equation typically is called firm i's *reaction curve*, since it represents firm i's optimal choice of x_i as a function of its rivals' choices.[10] Like any Nash equilibrium, the Cournot equilibrium is the set of self-enforcing actions from which no firm would unilaterally wish to deviate.

Maximizing π_i with respect to x_i, firm i's reaction curve is given by the first-order condition[11] $p(X) + x_i p'(X) = c_i$, which we can re-write as $p(X) - c_i = -x_i p'(X)$, or

$$\frac{p(X) - c_i}{p(X)} = \frac{s_i}{\varepsilon}, \quad i = 1, \ldots, n, \tag{1}$$

where $s_i \equiv x_i / X$ is firm i's market share, and $\varepsilon > 0$ is the market elasticity of demand at X, $\varepsilon \equiv -p(X)/Xp'(X)$. Equation (1) is the basic *Cournot oligopoly pricing formula*.

A Cournot equilibrium exists under quite general conditions, even for differentiated products. Basically, we need each firm's profits to be quasi-concave in its output. See Friedman (1971) for details. An overly strong condition that is sufficient for existence is that π_i actually be concave in x_i, i.e. $\partial^2 \pi_i / \partial x_i^2 < 0$ at all x_i, X. This condition is of course just firm i's second-order condition when evaluated at the equilibrium point. In the case of homogeneous products, it becomes:

$$a_i \equiv 2p'(X) + x_i p''(X) - C_i''(x_i) < 0, \quad i = 1, \ldots, n. \tag{2}$$

If the demand function is concave, $p''(X) \leq 0$, and if the cost function exhibits nondecreasing marginal cost, $C_i'' \geq 0$, then equation (2) is satisfied.

More recently, Novshek (1985) has provided us with a somewhat weaker condition that nonetheless guarantees the existence of a Cournot equilibrium in

[10]For homogeneous goods, firm i's optimal quantity depends only upon its rivals' aggregate output, $X_{-i} \equiv X - x_i$.

[11]The second-order condition, $2p'(X) + x_i p''(X) - C_i''(x_i) < 0$, requires that the firm's marginal revenue curve intersect its marginal cost curve from above. I assume this condition is met for each firm. I also assume that the n firms each earn non-negative profits when their outputs are given by (1). In other words, I am avoiding issues of entry and exit, taking n as exogenous.

the case of homogeneous products. Assuming that the demand and cost functions are differentiable and monotonic, he shows that an equilibrium exists so long as $Xp'(X)$ declines with X, i.e. so long as

$$p'(X) + Xp''(X) \leq 0 \tag{3}$$

at all X. This condition is equivalent to

$$b_i \equiv \partial^2\pi_i/\partial x_i\,\partial x_j = p'(X) + x_i p''(X) \leq 0, \tag{4}$$

for all $x_i \leq X$.[12] Condition (4) states that firm i's marginal revenue must not rise with its rivals' outputs. Comparing equations (2) and (4) reveals that Novshek's generalization consists of greatly reducing the requirements on the cost functions that are needed to ensure existence.

Uniqueness of equilibrium is not nearly so general, as the reaction curves may easily intersect more than once. But Friedman (1977, p. 71 and p. 171) provides conditions under which equilibrium is unique. An overly strong sufficient condition for uniqueness is

$$\frac{\partial^2\pi_i}{\partial x_i^2} + \sum_{j\neq i}\left|\frac{\partial^2\pi_i}{\partial x_i\,\partial x_j}\right| < 0 \quad, i = 1,\ldots,n.$$

In the case of homogeneous goods, this uniqueness condition becomes $a_i + (n-1)|b_i| < 0$, $i = 1,\ldots,n$. Since a_i must be negative in equilibrium, this inequality can be rewritten as

$$|a_i| > (n-1)|b_i|, \quad i = 1,\ldots,n. \tag{5}$$

We shall see below that inequality (5) is useful when performing comparative statics exercises. Unfortunately, inequality (5), while sufficient for uniqueness, is far too strong: it usually is not met. In fact, direct substitutions demonstrate that (5) *must* be violated whenever (a) $p'' \leq 0$ and $n \geq 3$, or (b) inequality (3) holds and $n \geq 4$.

In the case of constant marginal costs, inequality (3) is sufficient for uniqueness. If this condition holds strictly, there can be at most one Cournot equilibrium in which all firms produce positive quantities. The proof of this fact is as follows. Suppose that two equilibria existed, with corresponding output vectors $(x_1^A,\ldots,x_n^A)$ and $(x_1^B,\ldots,x_n^B)$. Let $x^A \equiv \sum_{i=1}^n x_i^A$, and define x^B similarly. Label the equilibria so that $x^A \geq x^B$. This implies that the corresponding prices

[12] Clearly, (4) implies (3) by setting $x_i = X$. But (3) implies (4) as well: if $p''(X) \leq 0$, (4) is surely satisfied, and if $p''(X) > 0$, then (3) implies (4) since $Xp''(X) \geq x_i p''(X)$ for all $x_i \leq X$.

obey $p^A \leq p^B$. Comparing the first-order conditions for x_i, $p(X) + x_i p'(X) = c_i$, in each of the two equilibria, and using the fact that $p^A \leq p^B$, we have $x_i^A p'(X^A) > x_i^B p'(X^B)$ for all i. Adding up these inequalities across firms gives $x^A p'(X^A) > x^B p'(X^B)$. This last inequality is inconsistent with inequality (3) and the labeling convention $x^A \geq x^B$. Inequality (3) is therefore sufficient to rule out multiple interior equilibria.

2.1.2. *Characterization of the Cournot equilibrium*

The Cournot oligopoly pricing formula, equation (1), captures a number of features of oligopoly behavior that we might hope for from a theory of oligopoly. (a) Each firm recognizes that it possesses (limited) market power. There is a divergence between its price and marginal revenue: $MR_i = p(X) + x_i p'(X)$, so $p - MR_i = -x_i p'(X) > 0$. (b) The Cournot equilibrium is somewhere "in between" the competitive equilibrium and the monopoly solution. (c) The greater is the market elasticity of demand, the smaller are the markups at each firm. (d) The markup at firm i is directly proportional to that firm's market share. (e) The market shares of the firms are directly related to their efficiencies.[13] But (f) less efficient firms are able to survive in the industry with positive market shares.

In the symmetric case, all firms have the same cost function, and (1) becomes:

$$\frac{p-c}{p} = \frac{1}{n\varepsilon}, \tag{6}$$

where c is the common level of marginal cost. Of course, for $n = 1$, this equation is simply the monopoly markup formula, $(p - c)/p = 1/\varepsilon$. Equation (6) captures the notion that markets with more (equally placed) rivals perform more competitively. Indeed, as the number of firms grows, (6) indicates that prices approach marginal costs. But with some range of decreasing average costs, it is not possible for each of n firms to earn non-negative profits in a Cournot equilibrium if n is sufficiently large. So one must exercise considerable care before one can conclude that the Cournot equilibria approach the perfectly competitive equilibrium as n approaches infinity.[14]

[13] Note also that by summing (1) across firms one obtains an equation relating the equilibrium price to the sum of the firms' marginal costs (as well as n and ε). Cournot (1838, p. 86) was aware of this aggregation property.

[14] As Novshek (1980) points out, simply adding more firms cannot give the traditional Marshallian outcome: with fixed demand, as n grows each firm's Cournot output must approach zero, whereas with U-shaped average cost curves the competitive limit calls for strictly positive production levels at each firm. Instead, Novshek takes the limit of free-entry Cournot equilibria as the minimum efficient scale of operation becomes small in comparison with demand. With this limiting procedure, he establishes both that Cournot equilibria with free entry exist as $n \to \infty$ and that they approach perfect competition in the limit.

Quite generally, the Cournot equilibrium is not Pareto optimal from the point of view of the firms.[15] With each firm maximizing its own profits, given its rivals' outputs, the result cannot be maximal overall profits, since increases in a single firm's output have a (negative) effect on its rivals' profits. This "negative externality" causes the Cournot equilibrium to entail a higher aggregate output and lower price than does the collusive outcome. The inability of the firms to achieve the collusive outcome as a noncooperative equilibrium reflects the underlying prisoner's dilemma structure of the problem: each firm has an incentive to defect from collusion by producing more output, and all the oligopolists end up with lower profits due to these defections.

With quantity competition, firm i's optimal output typically is a decreasing function of its rivals' aggregate output. This will be the case as long as a given firm's marginal revenue is reduced when a rival increases its output. Formally, this is so if and only if $\partial^2\pi_i/\partial x_i\,\partial x_j < 0$, which is exactly condition (4) above, namely $b_i < 0$. Hahn (1962) assumed this condition to hold for all firms.[16] When the Hahn condition is met, the firms' *reaction functions are downward sloping*, a fact of considerable significance when we explore multistage models below.

Another way to characterize the Cournot equilibrium is to ask the following question: "What does a Cournot equilibrium maximize?" We know that the answer to this question is neither industry profits (since the Cournot equilibrium does not replicate collusion) nor social welfare (since prices are not equated to marginal costs). In fact, Bergstrom and Varian (1985a) have shown that the Cournot equilibrium maximizes a *mixture* of social welfare and profits.

Define gross benefits by the total area under the demand curve,

$$B(X) \equiv \int_0^X p(z)\,\mathrm{d}z,$$

and define total welfare as the sum of producer and consumer surplus, or, equivalently, total benefits less total costs,[17]

$$W(X) \equiv B(X) - nC(X/n).$$

Then Bergstrom and Varian show that the first-order conditions for the Cournot equilibrium are the same as would arise if a social planner were aiming to

[15]Of course, collusion, while Pareto optimal for the firms, leaves consumers even worse off than in the Cournot equilibrium. Neither the Cournot equilibrium nor the collusive outcome is Pareto optimal when consumers and firms are considered together.

[16]A sufficient condition for $b_i < 0$ is that $p''(X) < 0$ at all X, i.e. that demand be concave.

[17]Here I assume that the n firms are equally efficient, and restrict attention to symmetric equilibria.

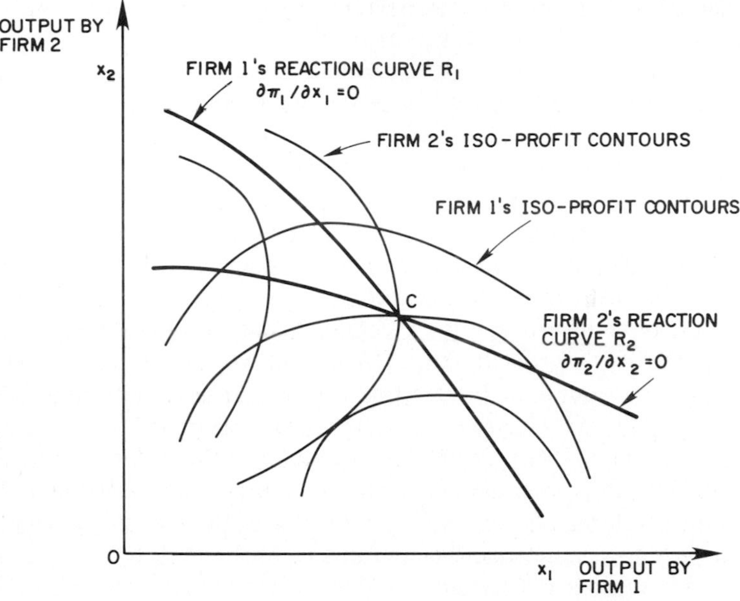

Figure 6.1. Cournot duopoly.

maximize the following function:

$$F(X) \equiv (n-1)W(X) + \pi(X),$$

where $\pi(X) \equiv p(X)X - nC(X/n)$ is industrywide profits. In other words, the Cournot equilibrium maximizes a weighted sum of welfare and profits. As the number of firms becomes large, the Cournot equilibrium becomes closer and closer to welfare maximization. Since welfare is the sum of consumer surplus, $S(X) \equiv B(X) - p(X)X$, and profits, $\pi(X)$, maximizing $F(X)$ is equivalent to maximizing $(n-1)S(X) + n\pi(X)$. In comparison with a social planner, extra weight is put on profits over consumer surplus, especially when n is small.

A diagrammatic treatment of Cournot duopoly is provided in Figure 6.1. Firm i's reaction curve is labeled R_i, $i = 1, 2$. The intersection of the two reaction curves at point C represents the Cournot equilibrium. Several of each firm's isoprofit contours, $\pi_i(x_1, x_2) = \bar{\pi}$, are included in the figure to show their relationship with the reaction curves. Tangencies between these isoprofit contours correspond to Pareto-optimal outcomes for the two firms. Observe that both firms' profits would increase if they could reduce their outputs in a coordinated fashion. Of course, by the definition of the Cournot equilibrium, neither firm *alone* could raise its profits with such a contraction. Typically, the joint-profit maximizing point lies to the southwest of the Cournot equilibrium point, as shown in Figure 6.1.

2.1.3. An historical note: The dual to Cournot equilibrium

Before leaving the topic of Cournot equilibrium, it is instructive to compare the standard Cournot oligopoly model, originally presented in Cournot's book in chapter 7, with his treatment of the "Mutual Relations of Producers" in chapter 9. In the latter chapter, he studies a situation in which two monopolists – one controlling copper, the other zinc – sell to the competitive brass industry. Brass is produced in fixed proportions from copper and zinc. Let the demand for brass be given by $D(p_b)$, where p_b is the price of brass. Scaling units so that one unit of brass is produced using one unit each of copper and zinc, we must have $p_b = p_c + p_z$, where the prices of copper and zinc are p_c and p_z, respectively.

Cournot studies the equilibrium in the game where the copper and zinc monopolists each set prices simultaneously. Letting their marginal costs be c_c and c_z, and solving for the reaction functions $\partial\pi_c/\partial p_c = 0$ and $\partial\pi_z/\partial p_z = 0$, we find the equations analogous to equation (1):

$$\frac{p_i - c_i}{p_i} = \frac{1}{\sigma_i \varepsilon}, \quad i = c, z, \tag{7}$$

where $\sigma_i \equiv p_i/p_b$ is firm i's factor share and ε is the elasticity of demand for brass.

Equation (7) gives the *dual* to the usual Cournot equation, (1). Notice especially that each firm sets a *higher* price than would a coordinated monopolist controlling both copper and zinc, whose behavior would be described by the single equation $(p - c)/p = 1/\varepsilon$, where $p \equiv p_c + p_z$ is a composite price and $c \equiv c_c + c_z$. Here, each monopolist ignores the fact that raising his own price *reduces* the demand and profits for the other monopolist. With these "negative externalities", prices are set too high from the point of view of joint-profit maximization. Another way to see this is to recognize that each monopolist would have an incentive to raise his price above the coordinated monopoly level if the other were pricing at the level that maximizes joint profits.[18]

[18]This example generalizes easily to n inputs in much the same way as does the usual Cournot equilibrium. The finding of super-monopolistic pricing is reminiscent of the double markup problem in the case of a chain of vertical monopolies. It is interesting also to note that Cournot adopted a pricing game for his copper and zinc example, in contrast to his better-known quantity game in the conventional oligopoly context. See Bergstrom (1979) for a generalization of Cournot's copper and zinc example to many factors of production and neoclassical production functions, and for an integration of Cournot's two theories of duopoly, stressing the duality relationship between them. An exercise for the reader is to work out the Nash equilibrium in quantities in the copper and zinc example.

Cournot's copper and zinc example illustrates a general principle in oligopoly theory: results which apply when discussing competition among suppliers of *substitutes*, the usual subject of oligopoly, are typically reversed when considering rivalry among suppliers of *complementary* goods. See Singh and Vives (1984) and Vives (1985) for more recent examples of this principle.

2.1.4. Comparative statics

Often one is interested in the properties of Cournot equilibria as underlying parameters shift. As we shall see below, many of the principles in *multiperiod models* rely formally on the comparative statics properties of the basic Cournot model: in two-period models (see Section 4 below), for example, first-period actions alter the parameters underlying the second-period competition. My discussion here relies on Dixit's (1986) excellent and quite complete analysis of comparative statics for oligopoly.

For the purposes of comparative statics questions, it is important to determine if the reaction functions intersect in the "right way", i.e. so that Cournot's naive adjustment process (each firm adjusting its output in response to the other's according to its reaction curve) is stable. In the duopoly case, this requires that R_1 intersect R_2 from above, as shown in Figure 6.1. More generally, Dixit provides us with a simple set of sufficient conditions ensuring "stability". Suppose that each firm's second-order condition is met, i.e. that inequality (2), $a_i < 0$, is satisfied for all i, and that the Hahn condition, $b_i < 0$, holds. Then inequality (5), the condition ensuring uniqueness of equilibrium, is sufficient for stability (although it remains a very strong condition that often is violated – see the discussion above regarding uniqueness of equilibrium). Basically, both uniqueness and "stability" are ensured if the reaction curves only can intersect in the "right way", as described above.[19] In what follows, I assume that the appropriate "stability" conditions are in fact met. But the reader should be aware that the comparative statics results reported here, and the findings in Section 4 below, are reversed if these conditions are not met.

Consider first the effect of changing a parameter that affects only firm i's "marginal profitability", $\partial \pi_i / \partial x_i$. Such a shift might arise, for example, from a change in that firm's capital stock, R&D findings, or tax treatment. Consider a change of this type that is favorable to firm i in the sense of raising that firm's marginal profitability; a reduction in marginal costs or in taxes would have this effect. Then the prima facie effect of the change is to induce x_i to increase, since $\partial \pi_i / \partial x_i > 0$ at the original equilibrium point. In fact, after tracing through the

[19] See Dixit (1986, p. 117) for further discussion of (weaker) stability conditions, and such conditions in models with differentiated products or conjectural variations. See also Seade (1980) for an earlier discussion of stability and instability.

full equilibrium effect of such a change, it is possible, using standard comparative statics techniques, to show the following: (i) x_i will rise, (ii) X will rise, (iii) π_i will rise, and (iv) x_j and π_j will fall for all $j \neq i$.[20]

This type of shift favorable to firm i occurs in two-period models when firm i undertakes first-period investments in physical capital or in R & D that lower its own second-period marginal costs or shift out its second-period demand. Another example of this type of shift would arise if firm i were to enter into a separate market, such as a foreign market. Sales in the foreign market would lower the firm's marginal costs in the home market if marginal costs decline with output, $C_i'' < 0$, and raise them if $C_i'' > 0$. The comparative statics properties of the Cournot equilibrium in the home market provide information about the incentives to enter the foreign market (see Section 4 below for further discussion of this point).

Next, consider the effect of a shift in an industrywide parameter, say one that enhances demand, reduces all firms' costs, or reduces their taxes. Such a shift will increase the marginal profitability at *all* firms. Seade (1985) treats this case in some detail, focusing on the effects of an industrywide cost or tax increase (affecting all firms equally). In the case of constant marginal costs, Seade shows that the key parameter for evaluating comparative statics effects is the *elasticity of the slope of the inverse demand function*, $E \equiv -Xp''(X)/p'(X)$.[21] He shows that each firm's output will fall in response to the cost increase. More surprisingly, he finds that price will rise by *more* than marginal cost (e.g. by more than the size of an excise tax – a greater than full passthrough of the tax) if and only if E exceeds unity, as it must if demand is isoelastic. He also shows in the case of symmetric oligopoly that profits will increase with the cost or tax increase if and only if E exceeds 2, which it does for any constant elasticity demand curve with elasticity less than unity.[22] The reason for this perverse result is that the output contraction (and thus the higher price) induced by higher costs more than offsets the direct effect of these higher costs.

Finally, consider a shift in the *distribution* of costs across firms. If such a shift leaves the sum of the firms' (constant) marginal costs unchanged, it is in some sense orthogonal to the industrywide cost or tax shift just discussed. Since the total output X depends only on the sum of the firms' marginal costs, as noted earlier, such a shift will not alter price or aggregate output. With X constant as the c_i's vary, we can use firm i's first-order condition for x_i directly to see that

$$\Delta x_i = \frac{\Delta c_i}{p'(X)},$$

[20] Again, see Dixit (1986, pp. 120–121) for details.

[21] For the case of iso-elastic demand, $E = 1 + 1/\varepsilon$, where $\varepsilon > 0$ is the elasticity of demand.

[22] But note that the requirement of "stability" puts an upper bound on the value of E; if $n = 5$, for example, stability requires that $E < 6$.

so long as all firms continue to produce positive quantities. Thus, as Bergstrom and Varian (1985b) point out, each firm's shift in output is proportional to its shift in costs, with the constant of proportionality, $1/p'(X)$, equal across firms.

2.1.5. *Performance measures*

Another attractive feature of the Cournot equilibrium is that it allows us to draw some direct relationships between market structure and performance, where structure is captured via n and ε and performance is measured by the sum of consumer and producer surplus. These relationships are derived by aggregating equation (1) across firms.

A natural way to gauge the performance of an oligopolistic industry is to see how large are the firms' markups; we know that large divergences between price and marginal cost are related to poor performance and substantial market power. Define the *industrywide average markup* as the average of the firms' markups, weighted by their market shares:

$$\frac{p-\bar{c}}{p} = \sum_{i=1}^{n} s_i \frac{p-c_i}{p}.$$

Substituting for firm i's markup from (1), we have in a Cournot equilibrium:

$$\frac{p-\bar{c}}{p} = \sum_{i=1}^{n} \frac{s_i^2}{\varepsilon}$$

or

$$\frac{p-\bar{c}}{p} = \frac{H}{\varepsilon}, \tag{8}$$

where $H \equiv \sum_{i=1}^{n} s_i^2$ is the Herfindahl index of concentration.

Equation (8) suggests that, in the Cournot equilibrium, there is a negative relationship between the Herfindahl index and industry performance. It is only suggestive, however, unless we provide a solid foundation for using the industry-wide average markup as a welfare measure. Dansby and Willig (1979) show how to provide a solid welfare basis for a formula much like (8). They develop the theory of *industry performance gradient indexes*. Basically, beginning with any industry configuration of prices and outputs, their index is defined as the answer to the following question: "By how much would welfare rise if we could perturb the industry a small amount in the optimal welfare-improving direction?"[23] High values of the index correspond to poor performance, at least in the local sense that welfare would rise sharply if the firms could be induced (by, say, antitrust or regulatory policies) to expand their outputs slightly. For many policy purposes, small changes in the industry output vector are all that we can hope to induce.

The general expression for the industry performance gradient index, ϕ, is

$$\phi = \left(\sum_{i=1}^{n} \left(\frac{p_i - c_i}{p_i} \right)^2 \right)^{1/2}, \tag{9}$$

where the formula allows for heterogeneous products since the firms' prices, the p_i's, need not be equal. For the case of Cournot oligopoly with homogeneous products, $p_i = p$ for each i, and we can use equation (1) in conjunction with (9) to derive the industry performance gradient index as

$$\phi = \sqrt{H}/\varepsilon,$$

a modified version of equation (8). Thus, Cournot's theory provides an intuitively reasonable prediction of the relationship between equilibrium market structure (as measured by market shares), and performance. More concentrated industries have a higher ϕ, capturing poorer (local) performance. Amazingly, this relationship can be summarized using a simple concentration index, the Herfindahl Index, in conjunction with the elasticity of industry demand, ε.

2.2. Bertrand oligopoly: Competition in prices

A natural objection to the Cournot quantity model is that in practice businesses choose prices rather than quantities as their strategic variables. Indeed, the actual process of price formation in Cournot's theory is somewhat mysterious. Bertrand (1883), in his review of Cournot's book, was the first to criticize Cournot on these grounds, and his name has since been attached to simple pricing games, just as Cournot's is with simple quantity games. Stigler's (1964) excellent discussion of oligopoly theory makes a quite convincing case (see especially pp. 45–48) that one must pay attention to the particulars of price-cutting strategies, including selective discounts, if one is to develop a genuine understanding of oligopoly (although Stigler's interest is in the policing of tacit collusion and his arguments are explicitly dynamic).

[23] A "small amount" is captured by constraining the output perturbation vector to have unit length, where the prices are used as scaling factors so that the units of distance are dollars. See Dansby and Willig (1979, pp. 250–251).

Bertrand pointed out that with prices as strategic variables, each of two rival firms would have a strong incentive to undercut the other's price in order to capture the entire market. With equally efficient firms, constant marginal costs and homogeneous products, the only Nash equilibrium in prices, i.e. *Bertrand equilibrium*, is for each firm to price at marginal cost.[24]

To verify that the Bertrand equilibrium involves marginal cost pricing, one must simply check that neither firm would benefit from charging a different price, given that its rival prices at marginal cost.[25] To see that no other pricing pattern is a Nash equilibrium, label the firms so that $p_1 \leq p_2$ and consider any candidate equilibrium in which firm 1 sets a price above marginal cost. The equilibrium cannot involve firm 2 pricing strictly higher than firm 1, since firm 2 would then earn no sales and could increase its profits by undercutting firm 1 (slightly). Nor can the equilibrium involve firm 2 matching 1's price, as each firm would then have an incentive to (slightly) lower its price in order to capture all, rather than half, of the market.

Bertrand equilibria are equally easy to derive in the case where the firms' costs are unequal, so long as the assumption of constant returns to scale is retained. With n firms, if firm i has constant marginal costs of c_i, and we label the firms so that $c_1 < c_2 \leq \cdots \leq c_n$, then the Bertrand equilibrium involves firm 1 serving the entire market at a price of $p = c_2$, so long as c_2 does not exceed the monopoly price for a firm with unit cost c_1.[26] Here we see dominance by the most efficient producer, firm 1, who is partially disciplined by the presence of firm 2. Unlike the Cournot equilibrium, industry output is produced at least cost. Like the Cournot equilibrium – and in contrast to the simpler Bertrand equilibrium – the equilibrium is *not* the first-best allocation, since prices faced by consumers are in excess of marginal cost.

Bertrand equilibria are not without their own problems, especially with homogeneous goods. The greatest difficulty is that, with homogeneous goods (or with close but not perfect substitutes), Bertrand equilibria in pure strategies typically fail to exist absent the special assumption of constant marginal cost. In the central case of *increasing* returns to scale, "destructive competition" drives prices down to marginal cost, but this cannot be an equilibrium as prices then fail to cover average costs. Adding even a small fixed cost to the basic Bertrand model

[24]As is usually done, I assume here that a firm stands ready to serve all customers at its quoted price. Although not restrictive in the case of constant marginal costs, this assumption does matter when there are increasing marginal costs.

[25]The addition of more firms does not alter the Bertrand equilibrium.

[26]One must be careful to avoid the open set problem that arises because firm 1 would like to set its price as close to c_2 as possible but not actually at c_2, as that would permit firm 2 to share the market at $p = c_2$. Technically, one can avoid this problem by assuming that firm 2 declines to match the price c_2, since it is indifferent to doing so. I prefer to think of firm 1 as pricing "just below" c_2, and each other firm as being unable to gain sales at its best "credible" price, i.e. the lowest price at which it would not lose money were it to make sales.

of constant marginal costs causes nonexistence of equilibrium. Since oligopoly theory is most relevant is markets with significant scale economies, this lack of existence (or reliance on mixed strategies) must be considered a serious drawback to the application of Bertrand equilibria.[27]

Edgeworth (1925, pp. 118–120) provides an example of the nonexistence of Bertrand equilibrium in the presence of *decreasing* returns to scale. Edgeworth's nonexistence argument runs as follows. He assumes that each of two firms has constant marginal cost up to some capacity level. Suppose that neither of the duopolists has sufficient capacity to serve the entire market if price is at marginal cost, but each can accommodate more than half of the market at that price. As in the case of unlimited capacities, there can be no equilibrium with the firms charging equal prices above marginal cost, for each firm would have excess capacity and an incentive to undercut the other (slightly). Nor can equilibrium have one firm undercutting the other, for then the lower-priced firm should raise its price (retaining some discount). But, due to the capacity constraints, it also cannot be an equilibrium for each firm to set price at marginal cost. In such a configuration, either firm would have an incentive to *raise* its price: doing so would allow it to make *some* sales, since its rival cannot meet the entire industry demand at marginal cost. These sales would generate some revenues in excess of variable costs, and the profits so earned must exceed those from selling to half of the market at marginal cost. Since each firm has an incentive to undercut its rival's price when that price is high, but raise price when the rival is pricing at marginal cost, Edgeworth suggested that the market would fail to settle down, and rather that prices would *cycle* between high and low values. This theoretical pricing pattern is known as an Edgeworth cycle, although Edgeworth did not formally analyze the dynamic pricing game (see Section 5 below).

Although Bertrand equilibria in pure strategies do not generally exist in the absence of the constant returns to scale assumption, *mixed* strategy equilibria do exist under quite general conditions.[28] General mixed-strategy existence theorems for Bertrand–Edgeworth competition are available in Dasgupta and Maskin (1986), and are summarized nicely in Maskin (1986). See also Levitan and Shubik (1972). Kreps and Scheinkman (1983) look at Edgeworth's case of constant marginal costs up to some capacity level, and show how the nature of equilibrium depends upon the firms' capacities in relation to demand. Essentially, equilibrium may be of three possible types. If capacities are large, we get the original

[27]But note that with a reinterpretation of the timing of production and pricing, the nonexistence problem is solved in the contestability literature. The key there is that a firm need not actually incur any of the fixed costs unless it actually succeeds in capturing the market.

[28]All models of Bertrand–Edgeworth rivalry must specify a rationing rule which determines how a limited quantity available at a lower price is allocated among consumers. Such a rule determines the remaining (residual) demand facing the higher-priced firm. The existence of a mixed strategy equilibrium is not sensitive to the choice of rationing rule, although the equilibrium strategies are.

Bertrand equilibrium with prices at marginal cost. If capacities are small, each firm simply sets the price consistent with each producing to capacity. And for intermediate levels of capacity, we have a mixed strategy equilibrium.[29] The necessity of resorting to mixed strategies must, however, be considered a drawback associated with pricing games in homogeneous goods markets. And this technical necessity is related to a fundamentally unrealistic feature of such games: a firm's sales (and payoff) are a discontinuous function of its strategy (i.e. its price).[30]

Even in the special case of constant costs in which the Bertrand equilibrium does exist, it entails marginal cost pricing, independent of the number of firms or the elasticity of aggregate demand. This extreme prediction about the relationship between market structure and markups is not in accord with the bulk of the empirical evidence on oligopoly (see Chapter 17 by Tim Bresnahan in this Handbook). Both because its predictions are unrealistic, and because of existence problems, the Bertrand equilibrium has not become the standard static oligopoly theory. For homogeneous goods, Cournot's model remains the workhorse oligopoly theory.

Many of the difficulties with Bertrand equilibria are mitigated when the competing products are not perfect substitutes. With product differentiation, sales and profits are no longer discontinuous functions of prices.[31] And the Bertrand equilibrium involves prices above marginal costs, since each firm retains some market power by virtue of product heterogeneity.

To discuss differentiated-product pricing equilibria, we must first specify the demand system. Begin with the general demand functions (written in their direct form), $x_i = D_i(p_1, \ldots, p_n)$. Writing $\boldsymbol{p} = (p_1, \ldots, p_n)$, firms i's profits are given by

$$\pi_i = p_i D_i(\boldsymbol{p}) - C_i(D_i(\boldsymbol{p})). \tag{10}$$

The n equations or reaction functions characterizing the Bertrand equilibrium are of course $\partial \pi_i / \partial p_i = 0$, $i = 1, \ldots, n$. Using equation (10), firm i's reaction func-

[29]For demand $p = A - X$, constant marginal costs of c, and n firms with capacity $\bar{x}$ each, prices fall to c iff $\bar{x} \geq (A - c)/(n - 1)$, whereas the firms sell at their capacities iff $\bar{x} \leq (A - c)/(n + 1)$. In between we get the mixed strategy equilibrium. See Brock and Scheinkman (1985, proposition 1), for a succinct summary of this symmetric case.

[30]Note also that in a mixed strategy equilibrium each firm would have an incentive to change its ex ante optimal but ex post suboptimal price.

[31]Although product differentiation is clearly an important element of many oligopolistic industries, space does not permit me to treat it more systematically or in any depth. For a much more complete discussion of product differentiation, with emphasis on spatial competition, see Chapter 12 by Eaton and Lipsey, in this Handbook.

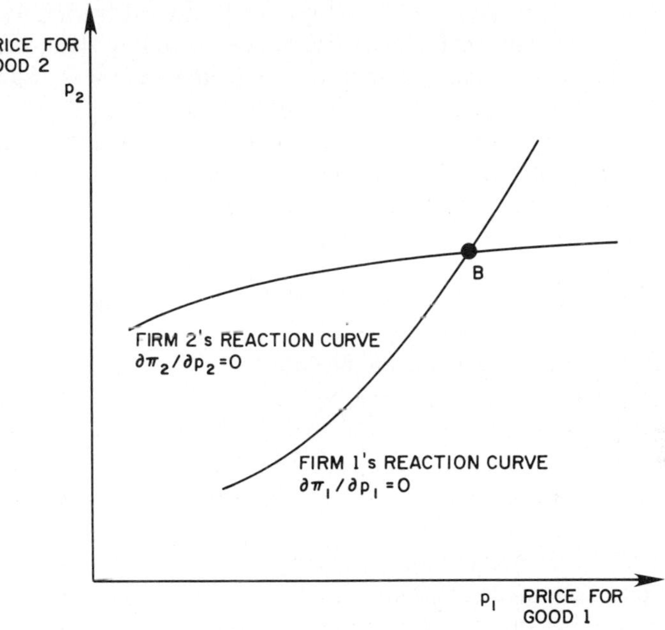

Figure 6.2. Bertrand duopoly with differentiated products.

tion can be written as

$$\frac{\partial \pi_i}{\partial p_i} = D_i(p) + (p_i - c_i)\frac{\partial D_i}{\partial p_i} = 0. \tag{11}$$

Of course, the existence of a Bertrand equilibrium is far from assured. We have already noted the nonexistence problem in the case of perfect substitutes, a problem that persists if the products are close substitutes. Here I characterize Bertrand equilibria with differentiated products without explicitly checking for existence.

The firms' reaction functions under pricing competition typically slope *upwards*, in contrast to those in Cournot equilibrium. This pattern is displayed in Figure 6.2. Firm i's optimal price is an increasing function of firm j's price if and only if $\partial^2\pi_i/\partial p_i\,\partial p_j > 0$. This condition is equivalent to

$$(p_i - c_i)\frac{\partial^2 D_i}{\partial p_i\,\partial p_j} + \frac{\partial D_i}{\partial p_j} - c_i''\left(\frac{\partial D_i}{\partial p_i}\right)\left(\frac{\partial D_i}{\partial p_j}\right) > 0. \tag{12}$$

Equation (12) is the dual of the Hahn condition, $\partial^2\pi_i/\partial x_i\,\partial x_j < 0$. Since $\partial D_i/\partial p_j > 0$ for substitutes, (12) is satisfied for a linear system, and in fact for any system with convex demand and cost functions, i.e. $\partial^2 D_i/\partial p_i\,\partial p_j > 0$ and $c_i'' > 0$.

With n firms, it is difficult to say much more about differentiated-product pricing equilibria without further assumptions about the demand system.[32] It is often helpful to assume a symmetric demand system. One convenient demand system[33] is derived from a benefit function:

$$B = G\left(\sum \varphi(x_i)\right), \tag{13}$$

which generates inverse demands of the form:

$$p_i = G'\left(\sum \varphi(x_i)\right)\varphi'(x_i). \tag{14}$$

By taking $G(S) \equiv S^\beta$ and $\varphi(x) \equiv x^\alpha$, one can study both the degree of substitutability between products and the demand for the entire product class by varying the parameters α and β. Another approach is to restrict attention to duopoly but preserve a more general demand system of the form $D_i(p_1, p_2)$, $i = 1,2$. For the purposes of working out an example, the simplest route is to explore duopoly with a special functional form. Perhaps the simplest demand system is the linear system described in inverse form by

$$p_i = \alpha_i - \beta_i x_i - \gamma x_j, \quad i, j = 1,2,\ i \neq j. \tag{15}$$

Here $\gamma > 0$ captures the notion of substitutes; $\gamma^2 = \beta_1\beta_2$ corresponds to perfect substitutes. With this linear demand system, the reaction curves also are linear, it is a simple matter to invert the system to write the demand function in their direct form, and both the Bertrand and Cournot equilibria can be directly computed.

2.3. Cournot vs. Bertrand

Which of these two competing static theories of oligopoly is "correct"? As a prelude to discussion of this question, it is instructive to see why the Nash equilibria in quantities and in prices are so different. The reason is that a single firm faces a very different *firm-specific demand* in the two cases. In duopoly, for

[32] Of course, one may derive the demand system directly from preferences over product characteristics. See Chapter 12 by Eaton and Lipsey in this Handbook for an analysis of such spatial competition.

[33] See Spence (1976) for further discussion of this demand system.

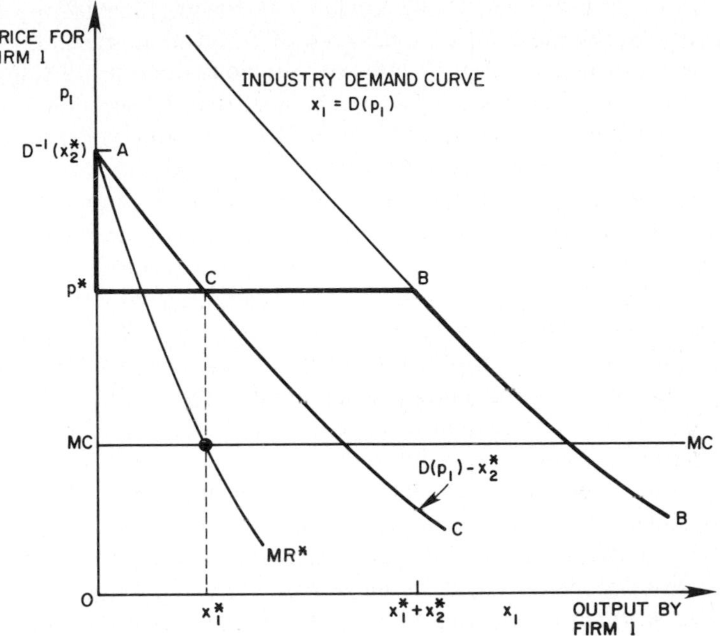

Figure 6.3. Quantity vs. price competition.

example, firm 1's demand as a Cournot duopolist is the locus ACC in Figure 6.3 (for $x_2 = x_2^*$). If, instead, the firms played a pricing game and firm 2 set a price $p^* = p(x_1^* + x_2^*)$, the Cournot price, then the demand facing firm 1 would be Ap^*BB. Firm 1 sees a *more elastic demand in the case of pricing competition*, and equilibrium prices are correspondingly lower. With quantity competition, each firm realizes that the other is committed to producing its announced quantity; with pricing competition, in contrast, each firm recognizes that it can take the entire market from its rival if it offers a lower price. This awareness leads to more aggressive behavior in the case of pricing competition.

Since the Bertrand equilibrium is so special, and in fact may not exist, in the case of homogeneous goods, it is instructive to extend our comparison of Cournot and Bertrand to the case of differentiated products. In fact, even in differentiated-product oligopoly models, Bertrand equilibria tend to be more competitive than are Cournot equilibria (although the sensitivity of equilibrium to the specification of the strategic variable is not quite so striking absent the homogeneity assumption). Under quite general conditions, pricing competition between duopolists leads to lower prices, higher outputs, and hence better performance than does quantity competition (for a given set of demand and cost functions). Singh and Vives (1984) provide a thorough comparison of Bertrand and Cournot equilibria for the special case of constant marginal costs and the linear demand system of equation (15). So long as the goods are substitutes, i.e. $\gamma > 0$, the Bertrand equilibrium is more competitive. Cheng (1985) provides a geometric proof of this same result that applies to a more general class of cost and demand functions. Vives (1985) gives fairly general conditions under which Cournot equilibria involve higher prices and profits (and lower welfare) than do Bertrand equilibria. The key to these comparisons is the difference in firm-specific demand depending upon the strategic variable being employed.

Apart from comparing price and quantity equilibria, we may wonder which one can be expected to arise, and in which industries. One approach to this question is to endogenize the choice of quantity vs. price strategies. Assuming that the technology of production and marketing makes either strategy feasible (pricing competition with unlimited capacities would *not* seem feasible if production is invariably subject to capacity constraints), it does seem fruitful to treat the choice of strategy as itself a variable. In their linear example, Singh and Vives (1984) consider a two-stage game in which each firm first selects "price" or "quantity" as its strategic mode, and then chooses a price or a quantity, according to its mode of operation. Singh and Vives show that it is a dominant strategy for each firm to select a quantity strategy, leading ultimately to the Cournot equilibrium. Each firm is better off if its rival faces a relatively inelastic demand, so that the rival will set a relatively high price or low quantity. This can be accomplished by adopting a quantity strategy.[34]

Klemperer and Meyer (1985) take a similar approach, but within a single-stage game where each firm may select a price or a quantity. They point out that, given its rival's choice, a firm can achieve any point on its residual demand curve equally well with a price or a quantity, so there are in general multiple equilibria. Both the Bertrand and the Cournot outcomes are equilibria in their model.[35] Klemperer and Meyer's main point, however, is that this multiplicity vanishes when uncertainty (about demand, say) is introduced. With uncertainty, a firm (monopolist or oligopolist) is in general *not* indifferent between a price and a quantity strategy. These authors go on to explore the factors – such as the slope of the marginal cost curves or the nature of the demand uncertainty – that determine whether the equilibrium entails price or quantity strategies.

An entirely different resolution of the "Cournot vs. Bertrand" debate is suggested by Kreps and Scheinkman (1983), although not within the context of a static model. They take the view, to which I adhere, that capital is a relatively

[34]But it is fairly unclear what it means for a firm to commit itself to a price or quantity strategy.
[35]This is an example of the multiplicity of equilibria when firms can select supply functions; see below for a discussion of more general supply-function equilibria.

sluggish variable, whereas prices can be adjusted rapidly. This leads to a model of capacity competition followed by pricing competition. In other words, firms first select capacities and then they play a pricing game subject to the endogenous capacity constraints inherited from the first period.[36] Kreps and Scheinkman show that the Cournot outcome is the equilibrium in this two-stage game, if one assumes a particular rationing rule for the second-period Bertrand-Edgeworth competition. They postulate the following rationing rule when firm 1 sets a lower price, $p_1 < p_2$, but can only serve demand $x_1 < D(p_1)$ at that price: the demand remaining for firm 2 is given by $D(p_2|p_1, x_1) \equiv D(p_2) - x_1$. This residual demand would arise if the consumers who place the *highest* value on having the product are the ones who purchase from firm 1.[37]

Kreps and Scheinkman's model is one way of dealing both with a major criticism of Cournot (it lacks a mechanism by which prices are set), and of Bertrand (with unlimited capacities it gives unrealistic predictions). But Davidson and Deneckere (1986) argue that Kreps and Scheinkman's finding is not robust with respect to the rationing specification. They point out that Kreps and Scheinkman's rationing rule is extreme in the sense that it leaves the *worst* possible residual demand for the higher-priced firm 2. Davidson and Deneckere explore the model of capacity choice followed by pricing competition using an alternative rationing rule that generates the *best* possible residual demand for the higher-priced firm. The alternative rule [which they attribute to Shubik (1959) and Beckmann (1965)] postulates that demand at the low price of p_1 is made up of a random sample of all consumers' demands at p_1. With this rationing rule, the residual demand is given by $D(p_2|p_1, x_1) \equiv D(p_2)[1 - x_1/D(p_1)]$, for all $p_2 > p_1$. Presenting numerical examples, Davidson and Deneckere show that, with this random rationing rule, equilibrium tends to be more competitive than under Cournot behavior. Their analysis further suggests that the static Cournot outcome cannot be supported as an equilibrium in the two-stage capacity and pricing game for most "intermediate" rationing rules.[38]

The choice between a pricing game and a quantity game cannot be made on a priori grounds. Rather, one must fashion theory in a particular industry to reflect the technology of production and exchange in that industry. For example, competition via sealed bids between firms without capacity constraints fits the Bertrand model quite nicely, whereas competition to install sunk productive capacity corresponds to Cournot.

[36]See Osborne and Pitchik (1984) for further analysis of this model, and Vives (1986) for a related model with a more general cost structure.

[37]Alternatively, it would arise if all consumers first have the opportunity to buy from firm 1 and are assumed to purchase according to their individual demands at that price, with each consumer retaining his individual residual demand for firm 2.

[38]See Dixon (1986) for further analysis of two-stage games as they relate to the Bertrand vs. Cournot debate.

After matching one's model of oligopolistic behavior to these features of production and distribution, one must test the theory's predictions against actual industry behavior. A common view is that pricing competition more accurately reflects actual behavior, but the predictions of Cournot's theory are closer to matching the evidence. Whichever static theory one prefers, it is clear that a serious theory of oligopoly behavior cannot be timeless.[39]

The Bertrand equilibrium concept suffers especially if one restricts attention to static models. The assumption implicit in the Bertrand model, that one firm can capture *all* of its rival's sales simply by offering a lower price, lacks realism. It is exactly in such a situation that the rival could be expected to respond most rapidly and vigorously, but reactions are ruled out entirely in this static theory. Within the context of static models, it seems less objectionable to assume, à la Cournot, that the rival is committed to a level of sales, such as would occur for a perishable good produced in advance or produced at low marginal cost subject to capacity constraints. Certainly, in most contexts prices can be changed quite rapidly; this need not be the case for quantities.

2.4. Can there be reactions in a static model?

In contrast to the entirely static view of Cournot equilibrium embodied in the statement that "the Cournot equilibrium is a Nash equilibrium in outputs", Cournot himself (1838, p. 81) thought of equilibrium being reached after an alternating sequence of quantity choices (reactions) by each of the duopolists, with each firm behaving according to its own reaction function.[40] This interpretation of the Cournot equilibrium is strained at best, however. Most simply, we are analyzing a static model, in which reactions are quite impossible. The alternating move game underlying Cournot's dynamics leads to a different outcome, since the Cournot reactions are myopic, not fully optimal, in that model (see Section 5 below). So, despite its widespread use, the term "reaction curve" is a misnomer.[41]

The unfortunate use of the term "reaction curve" in the study of Cournot oligopoly has contributed to a persistent confusion about the proper interpretation of the basic Cournot equilibrium. The correct interpretation is that the Cournot equilibrium point, like any Nash equilibrium point in a game, is a self-enforcing or self-confirming set of actions, from which no firm would want to

[39] This line of argument suggests that the most appropriate games to study are dynamic ones with price-setting. I report on the price-setting supergame literature below.

[40] As noted above, the convergence of this myopic adjustment process to the Cournot equilibrium point remains an essential "stability" condition when performing comparative statics or looking at multistage games.

[41] Dixit (1986, p. 110) observes that the phrase "firm i's equilibrium locus" would be superior to "reaction curve" but concedes that it is too late now to change our terminology.

deviate unilaterally. Instead of restricting their attention to the equilibrium point at which the reaction curves intersect, however, quite a few authors have attempted to interpret the reaction curves in a literal sense as responses to rival output choices. This effort has led to the study of the (pseudo) dynamics of the Cournot system, assuming that each firm responds to the other(s) according to its own reaction function. This line of research is a natural attempt to introduce responses into Cournot's model. And it is plain that rival responses are crucial in oligopoly. But one cannot properly analyze dynamic oligopoly using the simple Cournot reaction curves, as they are unlikely indeed to represent the firms' optimal dynamic responses.[42] A proper treatment of such dynamic games is reserved for Sections 3 and 5 below.

Another line of research attempts to retain a completely static structure but nonetheless generalize the Cournot model to include reactions. This approach represents an attempt to capture the concept of conscious parallelism – the recognition among oligopolists that price changes will likely be matched by rivals – in a static model. Despite the extreme conceptual problems of analyzing reactions within a static game, this approach has generated a considerable literature of its own. One reason for the hardiness of this questionable line of research is that proper dynamic models (see below) are much more difficult to work with, and lack the definitive results to be found in the static games.

An early example of the static approach to tacit collusion is the well-known *kinked demand curve* theory of oligopoly developed by Sweezy (1939) and Hall and Hitch (1939). Sweezy suggested that each firm would expect its rivals to match any price reductions, but not price increases. Given these expectations, price reductions provide no gain in market share, and are unprofitable. Similarly, a price increase causes a drastic loss of business. The conclusion is that the initial price – arbitrary though it was – is "stable", i.e. an equilibrium. Each firm perceives a demand curve with a *kink* at the initial price, demand is more elastic for price increases than for price decreases. The kink leads to a certain price rigidity, as modest shifts in demand or cost conditions will elicit no change in prices.[43] Plausible and popular as Sweezy's theory is, it strains the confines of the static model. Surely the speed of rival responses matters, and one should check that the postulated responses are in fact optimal.

The most common method of studying "reactions" in the static, homogeneous good model is to use the concept of *conjectural variations*, as developed by

[42] See Friedman (1977, p. 76) for references to the literature on Cournot pseudo-dynamics. As Friedman notes, "All the work is characterized by the assumption of single-period profit maximization, and it does not face up to the inconsistency stemming from the firm's incorrect assumptions about rivals' behavior. These shortcomings greatly reduce the potential value of the articles." I shall say a bit more about the literature on reaction functions in repeated oligopoly games in Section 3 below.

[43] But see Stigler (1947) for an empirical study undermining the kinked demand curve theory.

Bowley (1924). A firm's conjectural variation is defined as the response it *conjectures* about rival outputs if the initial firm alters its own output. Formally, firm i conjectures that $\partial X/\partial x_i = 1 + \nu_i$, where $\nu_i \equiv [\partial X_{-i}/\partial x_i]^e$ is firm i's *expectation*, or conjecture, about rivals' responses. With this conjecture, firm i perceives that an increase in its output will affect profits according to $\partial \pi_i/\partial x_i = p(X) - c_i + x_i(1 + \nu_i)p'(X)$, and is led via profit maximization to the modified reaction curve:

$$\frac{p(X) - c_i}{p(X)} = \frac{s_i(1 + \nu_i)}{\varepsilon}, \quad i = 1, \dots, n. \tag{16}$$

In the Cournot model, $\nu_i = 0$ for every firm i, and equation (16) reduces to the usual Cournot equation, (1). A large value of ν_i captures a belief that other firms will "respond" aggressively to any attempt by firm i to increase its output. Such beliefs lead firm i to *less* aggressive behavior, i.e. a smaller output and a higher price, than under Cournot, as can be seen from (16). The expectation of aggressively competitive rival responses actually leads to more collusive equilibrium behavior. This apparent paradox will appear repeatedly in the supergame literature below. In terms of Figure 6.1, a higher value of ν_i shifts firm i's reaction curve inward.

In the symmetric case, a value of $\nu_i = n - 1$ captures a belief by firm i that its rivals will increase output in lock step with its own expansion, so firm i believes that it cannot increase its market share by increasing output. With such conjectures, each firm finds it optimal to produce its share of the collusive industry output; equation (16) becomes simply the monopoly markup formula, $(p - c)/p = 1/\varepsilon$. The other extreme value of ν_i is -1. In this case, firm i believes that $\partial X/\partial x_i = 0$, so $\mathrm{d}p/\mathrm{d}x_i = 0$: the firm is a price-taker, and sets price at marginal cost.[44]

Conjectural variations are a convenient way of parameterizing oligopolistic behavior. As such, they can be quite useful for comparative statics purposes. By parametrically changing the ν_i's, one can study the equilibrium of an oligopoly model for various behavioral parameters, i.e. various conjectures. But the idea behind conjectural variations is logically flawed, and they cannot constitute a bona fide theory of oligopoly. This is a fortiori true of the so-called "consistent conjectures" [Bresnahan (1981), Perry (1982)] which impose the requirement that, in the neighborhood of the equilibrium, a firm's conjecture about a rival's response equal the slope of that rival's reaction curve. Conjectural variations in general are an attempt to capture a dynamic concept, response, in a static model.[45] They may be useful if they can be shown to correspond to the equilibria

[44] A common error is to equate this conjectural variation outcome with the Bertrand equilibrium. The two are indeed equal if the firms have constant and equal marginal costs, but not otherwise.

[45] See also Makowski (1983) and Daughety (1985) for rather different attacks on the logical foundations of consistent conjectures. At another level, conjectural variations suffer in that they are inherently difficult, if not impossible, to measure.

in some class of dynamic oligopoly games, but at this time remain an ad hoc shortcut to the study of oligopolistic interactions.

An alternative way to build "reactions" into a static model is to specify strategies that are by their nature contingent upon rival behavior. For example, a strategy that consists of a *supply function*, $x_i(p)$, has this quality: the actual amount brought to market will depend upon rivals' announcements of their own supply schedules, since the price itself is jointly determined by all of the $x_i(\cdot)$'s. In fact, both Cournot and Bertrand strategies are special cases of supply functions. Cournot requires that a firm announce a perfectly *inelastic* supply function, and Bertrand insists that the supply function be perfectly *elastic*. Grossman (1981) presents an analysis of supply function equilibria in a market with large fixed costs and more potential producers than can be accommodated in the market. Under these conditions, supply function equilibria are extremely competitive.[46] Unfortunately, when all of the (potential) firms can be profitably accommodated in the market, as is the standard working assumption in oligopoly theory (ignoring issues of entry deterrence), there is a great multiplicity of supply function equilibria. The difficulty is that each firm is, given its rivals' supply functions, indifferent between a whole class of supply functions that yield the same equilibrium price and output. This indifference means that the firm could select supply functions specifying very different out-of-equilibrium behavior, and hence support any outcome.[47] What is missing is a notion of a "credible" or "reasonable" supply function for a firm to announce. Absent some restriction on the set of supply functions that firms can specify, there is no way to narrow down the set of equilibria in a useful fashion so as to yield further insights or theoretical predictions.

Another way to incorporate contingent strategies is to study equilibria in "contracts", or contingent price and quantity offers. Salop (1986) presents several illuminating examples demonstrating how contracts that are apparently quite competitive can serve instead as *facilitating practices*, promoting collusive outcomes.[48] One natural and interesting class of contracts discussed by Salop is that

[46]To achieve this result, Grossman restricts the set of allowable supply functions to those that would not lose money at any price. This is essentially a way of imposing "credibility" on the strategies without actually developing a dynamic model.

[47]Indeed, any output vector that allows each firm to earn non-negative profits can be supported as a supply function equilibrium. All that is required is that each firm be optimizing against its rivals' supply functions. Formally, these supply functions serve the same role as do conjectures in the conjectural variations literature, where again any individually rational point can be supported as an equilibrium with the appropriately chosen conjectures [see Laitner (1980) for a proof of this claim]. But Klemperer and Meyer (1986) suggest a possible resolution to this problem by introducing uncertainty about demand.

[48]Of course, many contracts among competing oligopolists can facilitate collusion. A merger (or profit-sharing contract) is the most obvious example; having each oligopolist sell his interest to a common third party is another possibility [see Bernheim and Whinston (1985) for a formalization of this using a common marketing agent]. I leave these contracts for Jacquemin and Slade to discuss in Chapter 7 of this Handbook on mergers and cartels, focusing attention here on the role of simple pricing contracts in facilitating collusion.

of *meeting competition clauses*. These provisions are contingent strategies in which a firm announces that its price is the minimum of some posted price, p, and the lowest price posted by another firm. In general, it is a Nash equilibrium for each firm to announce that its price is the minimum of the monopoly price and the lowest rival price. With these strategies, the monopoly price prevails, since each firm realizes that it cannot gain market share with a price reduction. Meeting competition clauses automatically incorporate – without any explicit dynamic structure – the aggressive responses to price-cutting that are needed to support collusion.[49] Put differently, meeting competition clauses formalize a particular set of supply functions or reactions that yield collusive outcomes.

Salop also analyzes *most favored nation clauses*, whereby a firm promises a given buyer that no other buyer will receive a better price. Again, an apparently pro-competitive clause may actually stifle competition: each firm is unable to engage in discriminatory price-cutting, and any type of secret price-cutting is more difficult to accomplish. Although each buyer may accept – indeed, value – the most favored nation clause, in equilibrium all buyers may pay higher prices as a result. A more complete analysis of games with these types of contingent strategies remains to be undertaken.[50]

All of the efforts described in this subsection are aimed at introducing reactions into the standard, static models of oligopoly. While the goal of this research is laudable, and indeed essential if one is to come up with an acceptable theory of oligopoly, the methods – especially those employed in the conjectural variations literature – are generally inappropriate. To study reactions, retaliation, price wars, and tacit collusion we require explicitly dynamic models of oligopoly.

3. Repeated oligopoly games

The limitations of static oligopoly have been evident at least since Stigler's (1964) classic paper. Stigler identified and stressed the importance of such factors as the speed with which competitors learn of a rival's price cut, the probability that such a competitive move is in fact detected, and the scope of retaliation by the other oligopolists.[51] Stigler's view of oligopoly theory as a problem of policing a tacitly

[49] But note that other equilibria also can be supported with meeting competition clauses. For any price between marginal cost and the monopoly price, it is an equilibrium for each firm to adopt a strategy of offering goods at that price and meeting any lower prices. Again we face the problem of multiple equilibria in contingent pricing strategies.

[50] Doyle (1985) is one effort along these lines that incorporates advertising into the game. Cooper (1986) shows how retroactive most-favored customer clauses can dampen firms' incentives to compete for customers in the second period of a two-period model; Holt and Scheffman (1987) undertake a related analysis. See Section 4 below for a further discussion of the effects of contracts on competition.

[51] Stigler also emphasized that tacitly colluding oligopolists seek a price structure involving some price discrimination, and that loyalty on the part of buyers is a key factor in assessing the profitability of any secret price-cutting. But these latter ideas have not been developed in the subsequent literature.

collusive industry configuration is now the norm. In the years since Stigler's paper was published, a great deal of work has been done to develop the theory of tacit collusion, particularly the role of defections and the reactions to them.

Quite generally, the success of oligopolists in supporting a tacitly collusive scheme depends upon their ability to credibly punish any defector from the scheme. Stronger, swifter, or more certain punishments allow the firms to support a more collusive equilibrium outcome, just as a higher value of the conjectural variation parameter, v_i, led firm i to behave more collusively in Subsection 2.4 above. This relationship tends to create some peculiar results: anything (such as unlimited capacities) that makes more *competitive* behavior feasible or credible actually promotes *collusion*. I call this the *topsy-turvy* principle of tacit collusion. The very competitive behavior is reserved as a threat to punish those who undermine the tacit collusion; it is never actually invoked in equilibrium, at least in nonstochastic models, which involve no "mistakes" or price wars in equilibrium.

Perhaps the most natural – and seemingly simple – way to go beyond static oligopoly theory is to study *stationary environments* in which each firm repeatedly sets its price or output and can respond to such choices by its rivals. Such models are called *repeated games*, and those with infinite repetitions are denoted *supergames*. The game played at each date is called the *stage game*. Repeated games are a formal way of focusing attention on reactions, since they involve play over time but the underlying environment is unchanging and the firms are unable to make lasting investments or commitments.[52] The past has no tangible effect on the present or the future; any effect arises purely because the oligopolists *remember* what has happened and condition their actions on that history.

3.1. Finitely repeated oligopoly games

3.1.1. Perfect equilibria in finitely repeated oligopoly

The simplest possible repeated oligopoly game involves a two-fold repetition of, say, Cournot oligopoly. At least in principle, this game permits each firm to respond (in the second period) to its rivals' actions (in the first period). Indeed, looking at Nash equilibria (as opposed to subgame perfect equilibria) in the twice-repeated Cournot oligopoly game, there are equilibria very different from a simple two-fold repetition of the static Cournot outcome. For example, it may be an equilibrium for the firms to collude perfectly in the first period and then play the static Cournot equilibrium in the second period.

[52] Nor can the oligopolists' customers make commitments or investments, such as building up their inventories when prices are low. In fact, the specification of repeated games requires that demand be intertemporally separable.

To highlight the difference between Nash and subgame perfect equilibria, and to introduce the issues involved in repeated oligopoly, I now characterize the set of symmetric Nash equilibria in this twice-repeated quantity game and compare it with the set of subgame perfect equilibria. I shall show that there is a range of Nash equilibria, only one of which is a subgame perfect equilibrium. All of the rest of the Nash equilibria are supported by incredible threats.

I begin with the Nash equilibria. Each firm's strategy consists of two parts: its first-period output, and its second-period output conditional on its rivals' first-period outputs. Let demand be given by $p(X)$, and assume for simplicity that the firms have constant and equal marginal costs of c. Let firm i's overall payoff be $\pi_{i1} + \delta\pi_{i2}$, where π_{it} is its payoff during period t and δ captures the relative importance of the second period.

First, notice that *any* equilibrium must involve static Cournot behavior in the second period; otherwise some firm would have an incentive to alter its second-period behavior. Call π_i^{C} firm i's (unique) static Cournot payoff. The range of Nash equilibria arises because of different *first-period* behavior in different equilibria.

Let $\pi(x) \equiv xp(nx) - cx$ be a single firm's profits if each of the n oligopolists selects output x. Call $\pi^{\mathrm{d}}(x) \equiv \max_y p(y + (n-1)x)y - cy$, the maximal profits that firm i can earn in a single period while deviating, given that all other firms are producing x. Now consider what output levels x can be supported as equilibrium choices during the first period. The best chance of supporting a particular x is to specify that deviations from producing x will be met by as severe a punishment as possible. The most severe punishment is to flood the market in the subsequent period (for example, by producing enough to drive price down to cost), thereby giving the deviating firm a second-period payoff of zero. Facing this (incredible) threat, a firm will comply with the specified equilibrium strategy of producing x during the initial period if and only if its equilibrium payoff, $\pi(x) + \delta\pi^{\mathrm{C}}$, is at least as large as its payoff from deviating, $\pi^{\mathrm{d}}(x)$. Any x for which the inequality

$$\pi(x) + \delta\pi^{\mathrm{C}} \geq \pi^{\mathrm{d}}(x) \tag{17}$$

can be supported as the first-period output in a symmetric Nash equilibrium.

Equation (17) typically will be satisfied for a range of outputs both greater and less than the Cournot level, x^{C}. This range is increasing in the discount factor, δ, and will include the fully collusive outcome if δ is large enough. For example, if $c = 0$ and $p(X) = 1 - X$, then $x^{\mathrm{C}} = 1/(n+1)$, $\pi^{\mathrm{C}} = 1/(1+n)^2$, $\pi(x) = (1 - nx)x$, and $\pi^{\mathrm{d}}(x) = (1 - (n-1)x^2)/2$. In particular, when $n = 2$ and $\delta = 1$, the Cournot output is $1/3$, whereas inequality (17) requires that x fall between $1/9$ and $5/9$.

Observe how the Nash equilibrium solution concept permits the incredible threat of flooding the market to be brandished in an indiscriminate fashion. A firm deviating from x during the initial period will be punished quite independently of the direction of the actual deviation from equilibrium or of any costs associated with executing the threat. For example, it is an equilibrium for the firms to produce so much in the first period as to drive price below cost, with each firm fearing that if it were to reduce its first-period output (an action that actually helps its rivals), the rivals will retaliate by flooding the market in the second period, eliminating the Cournot profits that otherwise would have been earned. Likewise, collusion during the first period can be achieved only by using the incredible threat of a price war during the second period if a firm deviates from collusion.

In fact, all of these Nash equilibria but one are supported by incredible threats. For example, in the collusive equilibrium described above, it is not credible that one's rival will flood the market if one defects during the initial period. Once the first period is past, it will not be in any firm's interest to carry out such a threat. The equilibrium concept of subgame perfection requires that every out-of-equilibrium strategy (threat *or* promise) be credible in the following sense: future strategies out of equilibrium (in our case, second-period behavior in the event of defection from first-period collusion) must *themselves* constitute an equilibrium in the future (sub)game.

Since the only equilibrium outcome in the second-period subgame of the twice-repeated Cournot game is the static Cournot outcome, *whatever* happened during the first period, any threat to behave differently in the future is not credible. Therefore, once we restrict our attention to credible threats, i.e. once we refine our equilibrium concept from Nash equilibrium to subgame perfect equilibrium, we find a unique equilibrium in the twice-repeated Cournot game (so long as the one-shot game itself has a unique equilibrium). Using the standard method of solving such a game backwards (just as one solves a finite optimal control problem backwards), it becomes clear that the unique equilibrium (henceforth, the modifier "subgame perfect" is implicit) is simply a two-fold repetition of the static Cournot outcome. Since no *credible* punishment for defectors is possible, it is not possible to support any first-period outcome other than the standard Cournot equilibrium. There are in fact no linkages in behavior between the two periods.

The preceding analysis points out the importance of the distinction between Nash equilibrium and subgame perfect equilibrium in dynamic games of all sorts, and in particular in the study of dynamic oligopoly. Although the perfect equilibrium solution concept is not without its own problems, it is now quite clear that for applications to oligopoly it is an essential refinement of Nash equilibrium that the serious student of oligopoly theory must thoroughly understand.

I have just shown that adding a second period to the static Cournot model, and refining our solution concept to subgame perfect equilibrium, simply implies a two-fold repetition of Cournot behavior. This surprising and counterintuitive result carries over to any finite number of repetitions of the Cournot game. Indeed, it applies to finite repetitions of any static oligopoly game.[53] Quite generally, the unique subgame perfect equilibrium of a finitely repeated game with a unique Nash equilibrium in the stage game is a simple repetition of the stage-game equilibrium.[54]

3.1.2. Alternative approaches to finitely repeated oligopolistic rivalry

The lack of any dynamics in finitely repeated oligopoly games might be considered an indictment on the perfect equilibrium solution concept that generates this result, or, indeed, on the entire game-theoretic approach being adopted. I remark here on two types of attacks suggesting that it is misleading to focus on perfect equilibria in finitely repeated oligopoly games.

Within the game-theoretic paradigm, it is clear that the triviality of equilibria in finitely repeated games is not robust with respect to either the structure of the game or the equilibrium concept. If we permit the length of the game, T, to be infinite (or at least *possibly* infinite), we suddenly get many perfect equilibria, some of which are very collusive, rather than just repetitions of the static equilibrium (see Subsection 3.2 below). Technically, there is a discontinuity in the equilibrium structure as $T \to \infty$. We also introduce genuine dynamics into the equilibrium behavior of the firms if we admit for some incomplete information, e.g. regarding the firms' costs or demand conditions (although this modification need not support tacit collusion – see Sections 4 and 5 below). And if we look for *ε-perfect equilibria* – i.e. configurations in which no firm can gain more than $\varepsilon > 0$ by deviating – we again can support very different behavior, even for ε close to 0.[55]

Another way of circumventing the "paradox" of the triviality of perfect equilibria in finitely repeated games is to throw out the very strong assumption

[53] This fact undermines earlier efforts to improve on the one-shot Cournot game by introducing reactions into finitely repeated quantity games. Friedman's (1968) reaction function equilibria are not subgame perfect.

[54] The qualification that there be a unique equilibrium in the one-shot game is essential. With multiple equilibria in the one-shot game, it is credible to "threaten" to revert to a less favorable equilibrium for the remaining periods in the event of defection. I regard these threats as an artifact of the definition of subgame perfect equilibrium, especially if the multiple equilibria can be Pareto ranked. (Why would the players not return to a Pareto-preferred equilibrium?) See the material below on renegotiation for a further development of this theme. See Benoit and Krishna (1985) for a thorough analysis of finitely repeated games with multiple equilibria, and Friedman (1985) for a similar study focused more explicitly on oligopoly.

[55] In fact, as Radner (1980) shows, as the length of the game becomes large, it is an ε-perfect equilibrium for the firms to collude for an arbitrarily long time.

that all firms have perfect computational abilities, act with perfect rationality and foresight, and know with certainty that the same is true of all of their competitors. At one level, this alternative approach is simply a recognition that the world is complex, and one cannot simply rely on the backwards induction analysis to conclude that repetitions of the static equilibrium strategies are optimal. Rosenthal (1981), for example, suggests that each firm might have some subjective beliefs regarding its rivals' future actions, not being confident that they will perform the flawless calculations underlying the perfect equilibrium.[56] Surely any businessperson finds the competitive environment far too complex to rely on the chain of calculations necessary in our perfect equilibrium calculation above.

This objection to formal game theory is borne out in the experimental evidence regarding finitely repeated games. The experimental evidence is strongest and clearest in the case of the finitely repeated prisoner's dilemma. Of course, this simple game is a special case of a repeated oligopoly game. Axelrod (1984) gives some of the most compelling evidence that cooperation *does* emerge in this game, even among very sophisticated players. He suggests an evolutionary approach to the problem rather than a game-theoretic approach. In particular, the "tit-for-tat" strategy of beginning with cooperation and then matching one's rival's previous move has extremely attractive survival properties in environments consisting of a variety of alternative rules.[57] "Tit-for-tat" does not thrive by besting its rivals, something it can never do, or by virtue of being the optimal response to *any* rival rule, but rather by finding a mix of cooperation and punishment.

3.2. Infinitely repeated oligopoly games: Supergames

It would appear that our attempt to use the theory of repeated games in order to focus purely on strategic interactions over time has completely failed to bring any such reactions into our analysis. Either we restrict attention to credible threats, in which case only the trivial repetitions of static equilibria are equilibria in finitely repeated games, or we do not, in which case we can support a wide range of behavior as Nash equilibria.

But a closer look at the result cited above, and the arguments supporting it, reveal a peculiar strength to the backwards induction or unraveling argument which narrowed down the equilibria to one. Threats of all sorts were not credible

[56] This approach has been pursued *within* the formal confines of game theory by examining games of incomplete information, as in, for example, Kreps and Wilson (1982b). But other ways of approaching this problem may prove even more fruitful.

[57] Survival is defined in an evolutionary sense: the population of players adopting a given rule or strategy grows or shrinks over time according to the performance of those players adopting the rule. For a much richer study of evolutionary processes in oligopolistic competition, see Nelson and Winter (1982).

in the final period, and hence in the penultimate period, and so on. The inability of the firms to tacitly collude in a credible fashion rests very heavily on the exogenously given terminal date at which rivalry ends. In reality, of course, competition continues indefinitely, or at least the firms cannot be sure just when it will end. What happens if one developes a theory of repeated rivalry without the artificial device of a known, finite end date?

This question has spawned a large literature on *infinitely* repeated oligopoly games. In fact, these games have exactly the opposite problem to the finitely repeated games when it comes to developing a useful, predictive theory of oligopoly: there is generally a plethora of perfect equilibria. This is especially true when there is no discounting, but remains the case when there is discounting if the per-period discount factor used to convert a stream of profits into a firm's payoff, δ, $0 < \delta < 1$, is close to unity. A high discount factor corresponds to short periods in a game that is likely to continue for a long time.[58]

Infinitely repeated games are fundamentally different from finitely repeated ones in that there is always the possibility of retaliation and punishment in the future. With an infinite horizon, the requirement that threats be credible turns out to be much less restrictive than it was in finite horizon games. Formally, a supergame consists of an infinite number of repetitions of some stage game. The repetitions take place at dates $t = 0, 1, \ldots,$ with player i's action at date t denoted by x_{it}, $i = 1, \ldots, n$. Denote by $\pi_{it} \equiv \pi_i(\boldsymbol{x}_t)$ player i's period-t payoff if the vector of actions $\boldsymbol{x}_t \equiv (x_{1t}, x_{2t}, \ldots, x_{nt})$ is played at date t. Player i's overall payoff in the game is given by[59]

$$\pi_i = \sum_{t=0}^{\infty} \delta^t \pi_{it}.$$

Note that the history of the game up to date t has no direct impact on either the payoffs or the feasible strategies from date t onwards. The game beginning at date t looks the same for all t, in the sense that the feasible strategies and the prospective payoffs that they induce are always the same. This stationarity reflects the absence of any investments by the firms (or any changes in the underlying competitive environment). History matters only because the firms

[58]Formally, δ may be thought of as the product of two terms: $\delta = \mu e^{-iT}$, where μ is the hazard rate for the competition continuing (i.e. the probability that the game continues after a given period, given that it has not previously ended), and e^{-iT} is the pure interest component of the discount factor, with period length T and interest rate i. In most papers, it is assumed that the competition surely continues indefinitely, i.e. $\mu = 1$, so that $\delta = e^{-iT}$. But it is worth noting that (with risk-neutral firms) these models are equally able to handle the case of an uncertain terminal date, so long as the hazard rate is constant.

[59]Many of the supergame results below generalize quite easily to the case of discount factors that vary, both across firms and with time. Friedman (1971), for example, allows the payoffs to be of the form $\pi_i = \sum \alpha_{it} \pi_{it}$.

remember what has happened in the past and condition their current actions on previous behavior. In this sense, any tacit collusion in supergames is of a "pure bootstrapping" variety; history matters because the players decide that it matters.

Supergames are well suited for the exploration of the efficacy of tacit collusion. Indeed, one of the primary questions addressed in the oligopolistic supergame literature is the following: Can the oligopolists, without any explicit collusion, support the profit-maximizing outcome (or any given Pareto optimal outcome) purely with credible threats to punish any defector who failed to cooperate with the proposed collusive arrangement?

3.2.1. *Tacit collusion with reversion to noncooperative behavior*

Friedman's (1971) important paper demonstrated that tacit collusion can indeed support any Pareto optimal outcome in an oligopolistic supergame if δ is close to unity, as it will be if the market participants can respond rapidly to each other. Friedman's equilibrium involves the following strategies: each firm produces its share of the collusive output in each period, so long as all others continue to do so. If, however, any firm produces more than its "quota" under this arrangement, this defection signals a collapse of a tacitly collusive arrangement, and each firm plays its (static) noncooperative strategy thereafter. In the case of quantity-setting supergame, i.e. repeated Cournot, each firm plays its static Cournot output following any deviation.

If these strategies indeed form a subgame perfect equilibrium, then tacit collusion works perfectly. We need to check that no firm would want to defect from the collusive scheme, and that the punishment strategies are themselves credible. Credibility requires that the punishment itself form a perfect equilibrium. A punishment involving repetition of an equilibrium in the stage game is credible, since it is always a perfect equilibrium to simply repeat any equilibrium in the stage game indefinitely. In quantity-setting supergames, this type of punishment is known as *Cournot reversion*.

To check the "no defection" condition for firm i, denote that firm's flow of profits under a candidate tacitly collusive equilibrium by π_i^*,[60] and its profits during the period in which it deviates from this collusive scheme by π_i^{d}. Call firm i's (flow) profits during the infinitely long *punishment phase* π_i^{p}; π_i^{p} may simply be the Cournot profit level, but we will consider more complex and severe punishments below. Firm i earns $\pi_i^*/(1-\delta)$ by cooperating. We have an equilibrium so long as this is no less than the deviant's profits, $\pi_i^{\mathrm{d}} + \delta\pi_i^{\mathrm{p}}/(1-\delta)$,

[60]Of special interest will be the case in which $\pi_i^* = \pi_i^{\mathrm{c}}$, firm i's profits when the firms collude fully to maximize their joint profits (if side payments are feasible) or to achieve a point on their Pareto frontier. But the calculations below apply to *any* candidate supergame equilibrium with so-called "grim" strategies calling for perpetual punishment of any defector.

for every firm i. Simple algebra indicates that this condition is equivalent to

$$\delta \geq \frac{\pi_i^{\mathrm{d}} - \pi_i^*}{\pi_i^{\mathrm{d}} - \pi_i^{\mathrm{p}}}, \quad i = 1, \ldots, n. \tag{18}$$

Under quite general conditions, each firm earns more during periods of tacit collusion than during the punishment phase, $\pi_i^* > \pi_i^{\mathrm{p}}$ for all i, and the profits that a defector earns are bounded, $\pi_i^{\mathrm{d}} < \infty$ for all i. If these conditions are satisfied, then equation (18) must be met for every firm i if δ is close enough to unity. In particular, any Pareto optimal set of outputs, or any set of outputs that maximizes joint profits, is supportable as a subgame perfect equilibrium. Basically, any short-run gains from defection, $\pi_i^{\mathrm{d}} - \pi_i^*$, are necessarily outweighed by the loss forever after of $\pi_i^* - \pi_i^{\mathrm{p}}$, i.e. by the collapse of the tacitly collusive arrangement. Equation (18) tells us that we need only mild punishments ($\pi_i^{\mathrm{p}} < \pi_i^*$) and bounded profits from defection ($\pi_i^{\mathrm{d}} < \infty$) if δ is close enough to unity.

This leads us to one of the most important conclusions with genuine policy implications that comes out of oligopoly theory. Whatever one believes about the various π's, it is clear that lower values of δ inhibit tacit collusion. If industry behavior permits each oligopolist to rapidly and surely observe rival defections, the scope for tacit collusion is great. Policies designed to make secret price cuts possible are valuable in undermining tacit collusion, or "conscious parallelism". And industry practices that inhibit secret price-cutting should be subject to close antitrust scrutiny.[61]

The feasibility of tacit collusion when detection lags are short is rather sobering for those who would conclude on theoretical grounds that oligopolistic behavior tends to be quite competitive. After all, supergame theory tells us that the fully collusive outcome is an equilibrium, quite independently of demand conditions or the number of oligopolists, so long as firms can rapidly detect and respond to "cheating" on the tacitly collusive scheme. The lower prices threatened as a price war never actually are charged. Worse yet from the point of view of industry performance, structural remedies would appear to hold out little hope of undermining tacit collusion if swift reversion to a noncooperative equilibrium is possible.[62] Nor need the entry of more firms improve industry behavior.[63]

[61]Again I refer the reader to Stigler's (1964) article for a discussion of the problems of policing a tacitly collusive scheme. See also the subsection below on trigger price strategies.

[62]But note the peculiar character of these supergame equilibria: firms believe that swift and perpetual punishment will follow if they defect, but defection and punishment never occur in equilibrium. Clearly, one should check the robustness of the results presented here to the presence of some noise that may cause price wars to actually break out in equilibrium. The literature on trigger price strategies undertakes this task.

[63]On the contrary, the incumbent firms may dissipate their collusive profits in deterring entry. Alternatively, entry, or nonprice competition, may dissipate the profits by raising industrywide average costs.

Although (18) is always met for δ close to unity, it is of some interest to explore the factors that tend to make tacit collusion successful. The simplest way to measure "success" is by finding the highest level of profit for firm i, π_i^* that can be supported as an equilibrium.[64] In terms of the reduced-form π's, equation (18) indicates that a higher value of π_i^* can be maintained in equilibrium if defection is less profitable (π_i^{d} smaller), if punishment is more severe (π_i^{p} smaller), or if detection and punishment are swifter (δ larger).

All of these findings are intuitive at this reduced-form level, but some of their implications in terms of the underlying structural variables are not. Generally, any underlying market condition that makes *very* competitive behavior possible and credible can, by lowering π_i^{p}, actually promote collusion. This is the "topsy-turvy" principle of supergame theory to which I alluded above.[65]

Here are two applications of the topsy-turvy principle. On the cost side, we usually think of flat marginal cost curves as leading to relatively competitive behavior. But the ability to rapidly expand production allows firms to punish a defector more harshly, and can promote collusion. Or, as Rotemberg and Saloner (1986b) point out, a quota on imports may make it impossible for a foreign firm to punish a domestic defector, and hence the quota may enhance competition. One must exercise extreme caution is using counterintuitive results of this sort that are based on the topsy-turvy principle. In the quota case, for example, the quota would have to be nonbinding in equilibrium for it to serve as an effective threat; in practice, quotas are binding and appear not to play the suggested pro-competitive role.

What does supergame theory tell us about the relationship between market structure and tacit collusion? In particular, how does the success of tacit collusion depend upon the number of firms, n? In a symmetric, quantity-setting supergame, an increase in n lowers each firm's share of the collusive profits, π_i^*, lowers its profits following Cournot reversion, π_i^{p}, and lowers its profits during defection, π_i^{d} [since its rivals together produce a fraction $(n-1)/n$ of the collusive output]. For the example of linear demand, $p = A - X$, and constant marginal costs $c < A$, direct substitutions into equation (18) tell us that tacit collusion with Cournot reversion supports the monopoly output level if and only if

$$\delta \geq \frac{(n+1)^2 - 4n}{(n+1)^2 - 16n^2/(n+1)^2}.$$

If we take $\delta = 0.99$ to approximate monthly detection lags and an annual interest

[64]In fact, much of the literature focuses on a narrower question of when tacit collusion works perfectly: "When is joint profit maximization sustainable as an equilibrium?"

[65]Avinash Dixit has noted the "Orwellian" character of the topsy-turvy principle, suggesting the theme "competition is collusion".

rate of 12 percent, then tacit collusion works perfectly so long as there are no more than 400 firms! This calculation is again discouraging for those who would believe on the basis of economic theory that oligopolies perform competitively. If one believes that oligopolists can somehow coordinate on a Pareto optimal supergame equilibrium, if one takes realistic values of the key parameters, and if one assumes that a firm can accurately observe its rivals' defections, then no firm would find the short-run gains from defection large enough to justify the long-run breakdown of tacit collusion.

Friedman's result that the collusive outcome can be sustained as a noncooperative equilibrium if δ is close to unity is actually a special case of a general result in supergames. Under quite general conditions, repetition of *any* individually rational outcome in the stage game can be supported as a supergame equilibrium with sufficiently little discounting.[66] The supporting strategies specify that any defecting firm be punished (by having the other firms minmax that firm), that any firm failing to participate in the punishment of another be punished, etc. See Fudenberg and Maskin (1986) for an excellent treatment of such "Folk theorems". The great multiplicity of supergame equilibria when δ is close to unity is a drawback to the entire supergame literature which I shall discuss at greater length below.

The presence of so many supergame equilibria when δ is close to unity suggests two approaches if one is to develop further the theory of oligopolistic supergames. The first is to examine the equilibrium structure of such games when δ is *not* close to unity, i.e. in circumstances where there are significant lags in reacting to rivals or the game is likely to end at a relatively early date. The second approach is to abandon the assumption of rapid and flawless observability of defections. I discuss these approaches in turn. Under either approach, there remain many supergame equilibria, so the natural question continues to be that of how collusive an outcome can be supported. When this question is answered, we can examine how its answer varies with structural parameters.

3.2.2. Pareto optimal equilibria in quantity-setting supergames

Abreu (1986) has recently provided us with an important advance in our understanding of the structure of pure strategy equilibria for oligopolistic supergames with discounting. He seeks to identify (p. 192) "the *maximal* degree of collusion sustainable by credible threats for arbitrary values of the discount factor". As discussed above, to achieve maximal credible collusion, one must design the most severe credible punishments for defectors. To make a punish-

[66]An outcome is individually rational for firm i if it gives that firm a payoff no lower than the one that firm i could guarantee itself against any play by the other $n-1$ firms. In other words, firm i must earn at least its *minmax* level of profits.

ment regime credible, it is necessary to punish a player who fails to participate in the punishment of another player. Using this idea, Abreu has been able to characterize quite generally the optimal punishment strategies, which he calls optimal penal codes, and hence the most collusive perfect equilibria. As we shall see, the Cournot reversion discussed above is *not* in general an optimal punishment, and hence cannot support the most collusive equilibria.[67]

I begin by reporting Abreu's (1988) general results about supergames with discounting. He shows that the key to characterizing the Pareto optimal equilibrium points is to construct the perfect equilibrium yielding player i the lowest payoff, for $i = 1, \ldots, n$. Then one supports the most collusive outcomes using equilibrium strategies that call for a reversion to player i's least-preferred perfect equilibrium if that player defects from the strategies specified in the initial equilibrium. And, importantly, if player j does not participate in the punishment of player i (i may equal j here), the strategies specify that player j will then be punished via reversion to *his* least-preferred perfect equilibrium. Effectively, Abreu has shown that one may restrict attention to strategies in which history matters only through the identity of the most recent defector (where failure to properly punish a previous defector itself counts as defection).

In this way, Abreu manages to simplify the problem to one of identifying the n least-preferred perfect equilibria, for players $i = 1, \ldots, n$. When these equilibria are identified, call w_i the payoff to player i in his worst perfect equilibrium. Then an outcome in which player i earns $\pi_i{}^*$ each period, but could defect and earn $\pi_i{}^{\mathrm{d}}$ during a single period, is an equilibrium if and only if $\pi_i{}^*/(1 - \delta)$ is no less than $\pi^{\mathrm{d}} + \delta w_i$ for all $i = 1, \ldots, n$.

In symmetric games, the n punishment equilibria are simply permutations of one another, distinguished on the basis of which player is being punished. Punishment is supported by the threat to impose this single worst equilibrium path on any firm defecting from the prevailing punishment. So, in symmetric games, the key to identifying most-collusive outcomes is to find the single equilibrium path yielding player one, say, the lowest payoff.

In applying his general findings to symmetric oligopolistic games, Abreu's strongest results come when he restricts attention to symmetric punishments, i.e. punishments which specify that all firms act identically. As he points out, (1986, p. 198), "the restriction to symmetric paths is neither natural nor in principle innocuous". Despite the symmetry of the overall game, the presence of a defector destroys the symmetry when it is necessary to mete out punishments. Symmetric punishments are nonetheless a natural generalization of Cournot reversion, since Cournot reversion is itself symmetric.

[67]Of course, for δ close to unity, Cournot reversion is optimal. The point is that more sophisticated punishments expand the range of discount factors over which full collusion can be supported, and support more collusive outcomes when δ is smaller yet.

Within the class of symmetric punishments, Abreu proves that the optimal punishment has a simple, two-phase structure: immediately following the defection, each firm participates in a "price war" by producing a higher output than previously; but immediately thereafter all firms return to their optimal, tacitly-collusive output levels. It is striking that, when optimally punishing a defector, the industry returns after only a single period to the most collusive sustainable configuration. Abreu describes these types of punishments as offering a stick and a carrot; apparently, the carrot (returning to collusion) is necessary to make the stick (the one-period price war) both credible and as menacing as possible.

Abreu's intuitive argument establishing the optimality of two-phase symmetric punishments is simple and instructive. Consider any arbitrary (but credible) punishment path Y calling for per-firm outputs of y_t at dates $t = 1, \ldots$. Call the most collusive supportable per-firm output level x^*. Consider replacing Y by a two-stage path X having per-firm output x^{p} at $t = 1$, and x^* thereafter. The path X consists of a price war followed by a return to tacit collusion. Producing x^* forever yields each firm a payoff at least as high as does $\{y_2, y_3, \ldots\}$, so we can select $x^{\mathrm{p}} > y_1$ to make the overall per-firm payoffs under X equal to those under Y. Then X can be used as punishment path in place of Y so long as it too is a perfect equilibrium. Since playing x^* indefinitely is by definition supportable, the only thing to check is that no firm would want to defect during the price war. But, since $x^{\mathrm{p}} > y_1$, defecting from X during the first period is less attractive than defecting from Y, which itself was unprofitable (since Y forms a perfect equilibrium). And by construction the two paths yield the same payoff from compliance. Therefore, each firm finds it optimal to participate in the price war by producing x^{p}.

Note that each firm must earn lower profits during the price war than it would in the static Cournot equilibrium, since its overall payoff under the optimal punishment is lower than under Cournot reversion, despite its higher profits during the second phase of the punishment. In fact, each firm may easily lose money during the price war, especially if δ is moderately large. All that is required for individual rationality is that no firm lose money prospectively at any time, looking ahead to both the price war and the subsequent return to collusion.

Not only do the optimal symmetric punishments take on this simple two-stage form. They are about as easy to calculate as one could expect, given the complexity of the problem. Let $\pi(x) \equiv p(nx)x - cx$ be the per-firm profit when each firm produces x, and call $\pi^{\mathrm{d}}(x)$ the maximal profits that firm i can earn in a single period while deviating, given that all other firms are producing x.[68] Suppose that the monopoly output is not supportable as an equilibrium. Then the best collusive output, x^*, and the price-war output x^{p}, are defined by the two

[68] Formally, $\pi^{\mathrm{d}}(x) = \max_y p(y + (n-1)x)y - cy$.

equations:

$$\pi^{\mathrm{d}}(x^*) - \pi(x^*) = \delta(\pi(x^*) - \pi(x^{\mathrm{p}})) \tag{19}$$

and

$$\pi^{\mathrm{d}}(x^{p}) - \pi(x^{\mathrm{p}}) = \delta(\pi(x^*) - \pi(x^{\mathrm{p}})). \tag{20}$$

The first of these two equations is our familiar no-defection condition. In this case it requires that each firm just be indifferent between tacitly colluding and defecting.[69] The left-hand side of (19) gives the benefit of defection, and the right-hand side the cost, namely the lost profits due to the single-period price war. The second equation requires that each firm be willing to go along with the punishment, realizing that failure to do so would simply extend the price war for another period. The left-hand side of (20) is the gain from defection during the price war, and the right-hand side is the loss tomorrow from having a price war rather than collusion at that time. As Abreu emphasizes, one needs only to look ahead a single period in order to evaluate the attractiveness of any (possibly long and complicated) deviation.

One reason why Abreu's work is important to our understanding of tacit collusion is that he proves quite generally that the optimal punishment strategies are more severe than Cournot reversion. In fact, Abreu shows the following: so long as Cournot reversion supports an outcome that is more collusive than Cournot itself, Cournot reversion cannot be the most severe credible symmetric punishment. Quite generally, a firm can credibly be made worse off than it would be by simple repetition of the Cournot equilibrium. Therefore, unless Cournot reversion itself supports the monopoly outcome, a greater degree of collusion can be sustained using Abreu's stick and carrot strategies than simply through threats to revert to Cournot behavior.

Abreu also demonstrates conditions under which symmetric punishments (and, hence, two-phase punishments) are fully optimal. This occurs if and only if they can support continuation (punishment) equilibria in which the firms earn zero profits – clearly the lowest possible. For large enough values of δ, this is always the case. Otherwise, however, Abreu shows that asymmetric punishments do strictly better. An interesting feature of asymmetric punishments is that the firms meting out the punishment produce strictly higher output, during the initial period of punishment, than does the firm being punished. It also is generally true that the firm being punished "cooperates" with its punishment, in the sense that

[69]If the monopoly output *can* be supported, then we must set x^* in equation (19) equal to x^{c}, each firm's share of the fully collusive, monopoly output, and replace the equality in equation (19) by an inequality. With these changes, equation (19) reads $\pi^{\mathrm{d}}(x^{\mathrm{c}}) - \pi(x^{\mathrm{c}}) \leq \delta(\pi(x^{\mathrm{c}}) - \pi(x^{\mathrm{p}}))$. See Abreu (1986, p. 203).

it does not select an output along its static Cournot reaction schedule. Abreu concludes with some statements and some conjectures about the nonstationarity of optimal asymmetric punishments.

3.2.3. Price-setting supergames

Much of the literature on oligopolistic supergames follows the discussion above in looking at quantity-setting supergames. This is natural in view of the advantages of the Cournot model over the Bertrand model for homogeneous goods. Repeated Bertrand games, i.e. price-setting supergames, are however an obvious alternative approach. The general theorems cited above regarding supergame equilibria when $\delta \to 1$ tell us that collusion is equally well supportable in price games as in quantity games when responses are rapid.

Generally, the fact that the static Bertrand equilibrium is so competitive means that punishments in pricing games are severe. This can make it *easier* to support collusion in a price-setting supergame than in the related quantity-setting supergame.[70] Again we have an application of the topsy-turvy principle of supergames. Reversion to the static Bertrand equilibrium is a more severe punishment than is Cournot reversion, and may support more collusive behavior. In fact, the distinction between noncooperative reversion and optimal punishments is greatly muted in price-setting supergames.

In the central case of homogeneous goods and constant marginal costs, Bertrand reversion gives the firms zero profits, and therefore must be the optimal punishment. Setting $\pi^{\mathrm{p}} = 0$, our fundamental no-defection condition, equation (18) becomes:

$$\pi_i^{\mathrm{d}} \leq \frac{\pi_i^*}{1-\delta}, \tag{21}$$

where the left-hand side of (21) is the total payoff from defection and the right-hand side is the payoff from cooperation. In the symmetric case, we can say much more about the relationship between π_i^{d} and π_i^*. Optimal defection involes a slight reduction in price to capture the entire market. This strategy garners profits of $\pi_i^{\mathrm{d}} = n\pi_i^*$ for firm i, since it expands its sales by a factor of n. Making this substitution, we see that equation (21) simplifies to

$$n(1-\delta) \leq 1. \tag{22}$$

The efficacy of tacit collusion depends not at all on the price chosen, since π_i^*

[70] But this effect must be balanced against the fact that deviation is generally more profitable under Bertrand than under Cournot behavior.

has disappeared, but only on the number of firms and the speed of retaliation.[71] Therefore, the oligopolists will support the monopoly price if they can tacitly collude at all. Again, for plausible parameters, tacit collusion would appear to work well; for $\delta = 0.99$, equation (22) is satisfied for any $n < 100$.

Brock and Scheinkman (1985) analyze Bertrand reversion without the special assumption of constant marginal costs. Instead, they assume that the firms produce subject to capacity constraints. In this case, Bertrand reversion means playing the mixed strategies that constitute the static equilibrium (since we know from Subsection 2.2 above that there is generally no pure strategy Bertrand equilibrium with capacity constraints). Even in this case, however, Bertrand reversion is the worst that could happen to a given firm (i.e. each firm earns only its minmax payoff) since each firm's expected profits in the mixed strategy equilibrium equal those that it would earn if each rival were producing at capacity and the given firm were optimizing against the resulting residual demand.[72] In this context, Brock and Scheinkman ask how the degree of sustainable collusion relates to the number of firms. Without capacity constraints, we can see from equation (22) that an increase in n reduces the degree of sustainable collusion, because each firm finds defection more tempting when its own market share is low.[73] But this monotonicity result may fail in the presence of capacity constraints; with limited capacities, a larger number of firms lowers the punishment profits, π_i^{P}, and hence may support greater collusion. Again the topsy-turvy principle rears its head. And again one must be careful in applying the topsy-turvy result. In this case, an increase in the number of firms could promote tacit collusion only in an oligopolistic industry with perpetually unused capacity.

Rotemberg and Saloner (1986a) add an interesting wrinkle to these models of price-setting supergames. They study tacit collusion in the presence of observable but temporary shifts in industry demand. Their goal is to explain oligopoly behavior over the course of the business cycle. Each period the oligopolists observe the current state of demand, as summarized by a realization of the random variable $\tilde{\theta}$, where demand increases with θ. Crucially, the random shocks to demand exhibit no serial correlation. With this assumption, today's demand conditions convey no information about future demand, so the *future* always looks the same, although the current-period payoffs depend upon the current state of demand. Call $\bar{\pi}_i^*$ firm i's expected flow profits under tacit collusion, where the expectation is taken over $\tilde{\theta}$. Denote by $\pi_i^*(\theta)$ and $\pi_i^{\mathrm{d}}(\theta)$ firm i's current profits from cooperating and defecting, respectively, and when the state

[71] The reason for this strong result is that higher prices raise *both* the profits from defection and the profits from cooperation. In the special case of constant marginal costs and unlimited capacities, these effects just cancel out to give equation (22).

[72] See Brock and Scheinkman (1985, p. 373).

[73] At any price, an increase in n raises π_i^{d} but does not alter π_i^{P}, which is uniformly zero.

of demand is θ. These profits depend of course upon the price specified by the tacitly collusive scheme when the state of demand is θ.

With constant marginal costs, Bertrand reversion generates zero profits, $\pi_i^{\mathrm{p}} = 0$, and defecting when demand is in state θ gives firm i an overall payoff of $\pi_i^{\mathrm{d}}(\theta)$. In contrast, cooperating yields a payoff of $\pi_i^*(\theta) + \delta\bar{\pi}_i^*/(1-\delta)$. Comparing these two payoffs, the no-defection condition, equation (18), becomes:

$$\pi_i^{\mathrm{d}}(\theta) - \pi_i^*(\theta) \leq \frac{\delta}{1-\delta}\bar{\pi}_i^*. \tag{23}$$

As we saw above, the gains from defection on the left-hand side of equation (23) are $(n-1)\pi_i^*(\theta)$, since cooperation gives a $1/n$ share of the market and profits of $\pi_i^*(\theta)$, while defection allows a firm to capture the entire market, earning profits of $n\pi_i^*(\theta)$. Making this substitution, equation (23) becomes simply:

$$(n-1)\pi_i^*(\theta) \leq \frac{\delta}{1-\delta}\bar{\pi}_i^*. \tag{24}$$

Equation (24) can be rewritten as

$$n(1-\delta) \leq 1 - \delta\frac{\pi_i^*(\theta) - \bar{\pi}_i^*}{\pi_i^*(\theta)}$$

to highlight the comparison with equation (22). Unlike equation (22), the π_i^* terms do not cancel in equation (24).

Now Rotemberg and Saloner's main point is that, for a given price, the left-hand side of equation (24), i.e. the gain from defection, increases with θ. This implies that tacit collusion becomes more difficult in high-demand states, in the sense that prices must be lowered when θ is large in order to sustain collusion. They conclude that the oligopolists are able to support less collusion during high-demand states than low-demand ones in order to prevent defection.[74] Note that the title's reference to "price wars during booms" is somewhat misleading, since prices are generally higher during business cycle peaks than troughs, and since price wars never occur in equilibrium. During booms, the oligopolists collude somewhat less in order to prevent the collapse of the implicit cartel.

Rotemberg and Saloner go on to discuss the implications of this finding for the behavior of oligopolies over the course of the business cycle. To the extent that

[74] This result does not carry over in general to the case of nonconstant costs, since both the optimal strategy when defecting and Bertrand reversion are quite different in that case. Nor does the incentive to defect necessarily increase with the state of demand for quantity-setting supergames. Rotemberg and Saloner do show, however, that their main point remains valid for both price and quantity competition if demand and marginal costs are linear.

oligopolists engage in less collusion during periods of high demand than during slack periods, their behavior accentuates the exogenously given shocks to demand. I find these results suggestive, but they must be treated with caution for several reasons. First, their predictions are at odds with the bulk of the empirical evidence on business cycles and oligopoly behavior. For example, Domowitz, Hubbard and Petersen (1986) report a positive sensitivity of price–cost margins to demand conditions that is most pronounced in highly concentrated industries. Scherer (1980) also cites evidence that undermines the "price wars during booms" theory.[75] Second, as Rotemberg and Saloner point out, capacity constraints are likely to be binding during periods of high demand, in which case defection is well-nigh impossible, and price-cutting is hardly necessary at these times in order to prevent defection. Third, Rotemberg and Saloner's assumption that demand shocks display no serial correlation seems inappropriate in a discussion of business cycles. The more natural assumption of white noise innovations in demand would likely give very different results, as (expected) future variables would move along with current conditions. Finally, this paper is subject to the general criticisms of supergames that I enumerate below.

3.2.4. *Oligopolistic supergames with imperfect monitoring*

So far, I have assumed that any deviation from the tacitly collusive scheme by firm i is immediately and accurately observed by all of that firm's rivals (although there may be a lag before they can respond). This assumption is clearly both crucial to the models above and unlikely to be met in practice. Indeed, efforts by firms to facilitate the exchange of pricing information via trade associations indicate that such information is not inevitably or typically available and that oligopolists value such information. Quite appropriately, antitrust law casts a skeptical eye on the exchange of customer-specific pricing information among oligopolists.

The question thus arises: *What happens to tacit collusion if oligopolists cannot easily observe rivals' price-cutting or production levels*?[76] In order formally to study this question, one needs a model of repeated rivalry in which the firms cannot perfectly observe, or infer, their rivals' actions.[77] The literature on *trigger*

[75] But Rotemberg and Saloner present some evidence of their own that supports their theory.

[76] A related question, "What happens to tacit collusion if oligopolists cannot easily observe each other's costs?", becomes relevant when firms' costs vary over time and these variations are not perfectly correlated across firms. As with unobservable production levels, unobservable costs pose a barrier to effective tacit collusion, since the firms as a whole would like to shift production towards the lower-cost firms at any given date, but each firm has an incentive to claim that its costs are low in order to have its allowable output increased. For the effect of exchanging cost information in a static model, see Shapiro (1986).

[77] There is a close relationship between oligopolistic supergames with imperfect monitoring and repeated moral hazard situations where each agent can temporarily gain by reducing effort, but may be punished if this shirking is observed by the other agents.

price strategies explicitly introduces informational imperfections that make it difficult for a firm to determine with certainty just when, or by how much, a rival has exceeded its collusive output level. This approach is the most direct descendent of Stigler's (1964) work on oligopoly theory.

Within the context of a homogeneous-goods, quantity-setting model, a natural way to incorporate imperfect monitoring of rivals is to assume that a firm can observe the market price in period t, p_t (which it receives for its products), but not the production levels of its rivals, x_{jt}, $j \neq i$. But with known demand, the firm could use the market price to infer the aggregate production of its rivals, using the identity $X_{-i} \equiv D(p) - x_i$, where $D(\cdot)$ is the direct demand function. And perfect information about rivals' production is exactly the assumption that we are trying to relax. Therefore, a coherent theory of imperfect cartel monitoring must incorporate demand (or cost) uncertainty. Demand shocks are then confounded with rivals' defections. With this structure, we can restate the cartel monitoring problem as the following question: *What happens in supergames if each oligopolist cannot distinguish with certainty between downturns in demand and expansion by a rival*?

Consider a quantity-setting supergame with stochastic demand. The simplest way to introduce demand uncertainty is to assume that demand in period t is of the form $p_t = \theta_t p(X)$, where θ_t is the realization of the demand shock at period t. To keep matters simple, assume that the θ_t's are drawn independently according to the cumulative distribution function $F(\theta)$. Without loss of generality we can take the expectation of θ to be unity. When one of the oligopolists observes a low price during period t, it cannot in general tell whether the low price is a consequence of a low realization of θ or of extra output by a rival. Importantly, we must assume firm i cannot observe its rivals' outputs either contemporaneously or subsequently.[78]

Green and Porter (1984) and Porter (1983a) have explored a class of supergame strategies known as *trigger price strategies* using this model. A trigger price strategy is a particular way of coordinating tacit collusion. Each firm produces its tacitly collusive or "cooperative" output, x^* until price falls below the trigger price, $\tilde{p}$, during some period. Any price below $\tilde{p}$ initiates a punishment phase or price war consisting of Cournot reversion for $T - 1$ periods. After T periods, the firms return to their original strategies, again cooperating at x^* until price falls below the trigger. Although trigger price strategies are not in general the optimal way to police tacit collusion (see below), they are relatively simple and have an element of realism to them. A trigger price scheme is characterized by three parameters: $\tilde{p}$, x^*, and T.

[78]I have already discussed what happens when firms can observe defections with a lag; this corresponds to a low value of δ.

Consider now the problem of selecting the trigger price parameters in order to generate the highest possible profits per firm.[79] In equilibrium, no firm will choose to defect from the tacitly collusive output x^*, but occasionally an unfavorable demand shock will drive prices below the trigger level and cause the firms to initiate a price war (Cournot reversion). The basic tradeoff is therefore the following: a low trigger price reduces the per-period probability of initiating a price war, but requires longer punishments or lower collusive profits in order to deter firms from cheating on the arrangement.

Denote by $\pi^* \equiv p(nx^*)x^* - C(x^*)$ a firm's expected profits during a period in which all firms produce x^*, and denote each firm's expected profits during Cournot reversion by π^{P}, in accordance with my earlier notation. Instead of working directly with the trigger price, $\tilde{p}$, it is useful to work with the induced (per-period) probability, $\tilde{\psi}$, of reverting to Cournot behavior. Cournot reversion occurs if and only if $p_t < \tilde{p}$. Given that in equilibrium each firm follows the tacitly collusive strategy of producing x^*, $p_t < \tilde{p}$ if and only if $\theta_t p(nx^*) < \tilde{p}$, which occurs with probability

$$\tilde{\psi} \equiv F\left(\frac{\tilde{p}}{p(nx^*)}\right). \tag{25}$$

Given $\tilde{\psi}$, x^*, and T, the overall payoff to each firm is given implicitly by[80]

$$V = \pi^* + (1-\tilde{\psi})\delta V + \tilde{\psi}\left(\pi^{P}(\delta + \cdots + \delta^{T-1}) + \delta^T V\right). \tag{26}$$

The expected payoff V comprises the following terms: (i) the current expected payoff from cooperation, (ii) the payoff V beginning tomorrow, discounted by the probability, $1-\tilde{\psi}$, that a price war will *not* be initiated during the current period, and (iii) the payoff upon beginning a price war, multiplied by the probability of that event, $\tilde{\psi}$. This last term is in turn made up of a stream of Cournot (punishment) payoffs for $T-1$ periods followed by a return to tacit collusion. Solving equation (26) for V we have:

$$V = \frac{1}{1-\delta}\,\frac{\pi^*(1-\delta) + \pi^{\mathrm{P}}\tilde{\psi}(\delta - \delta^T)}{(1-\delta) + \tilde{\psi}(\delta-\delta^T)}. \tag{27}$$

Observe that $V(1-\delta)$, the expected per-period payoff, is a weighted average of

[79]As we did above in the case of supergames with perfect monitoring, we are presuming that the firms can somehow coordinate and communicate at time zero to select a Pareto optimal sugergame equilibrium.

[80]This formula applies at the beginning of the game and also at any point when the firms are not engaged in a price war.

π^* and π^{P}, where the weights depend upon δ, $\tilde{\psi}$, and T. Equation (27) can be manipulated to yield:

$$V = \frac{\pi^{\mathrm{P}}}{1-\delta} + \frac{\pi^* - \pi^{\mathrm{P}}}{(1-\delta) + \tilde{\psi}(\delta - \delta^T)}, \tag{28}$$

which decomposes V into the returns from static, noncooperative behavior, $\pi^{\mathrm{P}}/(1-\delta)$, plus the single-period gains from colluding, appropriately discounted.

In order for a triplet $\{x^*, \tilde{\psi}, T\}$ to constitute a trigger price equilibrium, it must not be possible for any firm to raise its expected profits by producing more than x^*. In other words, we must have:

$$\left.\frac{\partial \pi_i}{\partial x_i}\right|_{x^*} \leq \delta \frac{\mathrm{d}\psi}{\mathrm{d}x_i}\left(\frac{\pi^* - \pi^{\mathrm{P}}}{1-\delta+\psi\delta}\right), \tag{29}$$

where $\psi \equiv F(\tilde{p}/p(x_i + (n-1)x^*))$ is the probability of a price war breaking out, so the $\mathrm{d}\psi/\mathrm{d}x_i$ term on the right-hand side of (29) measures the increased probability of a price war as x_i increases. The final term on the right-hand side of (29) is the cost to firm i of initiating a price war.

The (tacit) cartel management problem can now be stated as maximizing V in equation (28) subject to the inequality constraint in (29).[81] Equation (29) can be used to determine the smallest sustainable output x^* as a function of ψ and T, and then V can be maximized with respect to these variables.

In some ways, the most significant contribution of the papers by Green and Porter is in formalizing the notion of tacit collusion with imperfect price information. Some of their main "results" are really built into their definition of a trigger price equilibrium: (a) there are no defections in equilibrium, but price wars occur during periods of weak demand; the firms recognize that low prices are in fact due to unfavorable demand shocks, but carry out the specified punishments because they realize that failing to do so would cause the tacitly collusive scheme to collapse; (b) there are alternating phases of relatively collusive behavior and Cournot behavior – the firms begin by cooperating but inevitably experience price wars; (c) the collusive phases have random lengths; and (d) there is a single punishment – Cournot reversion for $T-1$ periods – for all crimes.

Green and Porter also provide some results characterizing the optimal trigger price strategies. First, Porter (1983a) shows that it is optimal for the firms to

[81] Of course, (29) is only a local condition, so one must really check that global deviations in x_i also are unprofitable.

produce in excess of the monopoly output in order to ease the problem of cartel enforcement; $x^* > x^c$ so long as $\delta < 1$.[82] Essentially, a small reduction in output below the monopoly level has no first-order effect on π^*, but it does reduce the gains from defection. Second, Green and Porter show that the optimal length of the punishment phase may be infinite, i.e. grim strategies may be optimal even in an uncertain environment. In fact, the optimal length of Cournot reversion is generally infinite [see Abreu, Pearce and Stacchetti (1986)]. Finally, Porter (1983b) presents some empirical support for the use of trigger price strategies by looking at the railroad industry in the 1880s.

Abreu, Pearce and Stacchetti (1986) provide a significant generalization of the Green and Porter analysis. They look for the fully optimal tacitly collusive equilibria with imperfect monitoring. They do not restrict attention to trigger strategies. In particular, they permit the punishment to depend upon the crime (the actual price observed), they allow for the possibility that prices prior to $t-1$ affect the behavior at time t, and they do not assume Cournot reversion as the mode of behavior during the punishment phase.

Abreu, Pearce and Stacchetti are able to derive some very powerful results characterizing the equilibria that are optimal among all pure-strategy symmetric sequential equilibria.[83] They show that there are only two (per-firm) output levels ever produced under the optimal scheme. One is the first-period output in the *best* symmetric sequential equilibrium, and the other is the first-period output in the *worst* symmetric sequential equilibrium. Each firm chooses between these two output levels on the basis of two factors: the output that was specified in the previous period, and the price that prevailed at that time. So, the firms need not look back further than one period and need not tailor the punishment to the price observed, even when such strategies are permitted. These results imply that the sequence of production levels is a Markov chain with only two states. The state is either cooperative or punitive. There is a transition rule from one state (output level) to another, depending upon the price observed.

Most recently, Abreu, Milgrom and Pearce (1987) have explored equilibria in the repeated prisoner's dilemma game using with a rather different (imperfect) monitoring technology. Although this work is at an early stage, it seems likely to have implications for oligopolistic supergames more generally. Their specification is designed to separate two aspects of repeated games with imperfect monitoring that typically are intertwined: (1) the frequency with which moves are made, and

[82] When $\delta = 1$, tacit collusion always works perfectly. See Radner (1986). Each firm can check statistically for defections by its rivals, reverting to punishment only when it becomes virtually certain that defection has occurred. This cautious punishment behavior could not deter cheating in the discounted game, but in the undiscounted game the magnitude of the punishment is not reduced merely because it is delayed.

[83] The restriction to symmetric punishments is less objectionable here than in Abreu's earlier work since no firm can determine which rival has defected.

(2) the lag with which firms receive information about their rivals' actions. In supergames with perfect monitoring, frequent opportunities to move necessarily go hand in hand with rapid observations of rival actions. In these games, we know that increasing the frequency of moves and observations, i.e. reducing the lag between moves, which is equivalent to raising δ, helps support collusion.[84] In the papers on imperfect monitoring discussed above, frequent moves go along with rapid, if imperfect, observations of defections. Again, increasing the frequency of moves and observations, as modeled by an increase in δ, helps support collusion.

Abreu, Milgrom and Pearce disentangle the timing of moves and the arrival of information by abandoning the assumption that even noisy industry aggregates are immediately observable to the oligopolists. Under their monitoring technology, the players may receive a public signal that carries information about whether anyone is defecting. In one version of the model, the signal is bad news: it is more likely to arrive if at least one firm is currently defecting than if none is.[85] In another version of the model, the signal is good news.

With this monitoring technology, varying the frequency of moves, t, is quite different from varying the rate at which the players discount the future. In particular, the limit as $t \to 0$ does not correspond to the limit as $\delta \to 1$: quick is not the same as patient. Although collusion is always possible in the limit as $\delta \to 1$, Abreu, Milgrom and Pearce's main result is that the best symmetric equilibrium payoff may be *increasing* in t for t close to zero. In other words, reducing the frequency of moves may make collusion more effective. The reason appears to be the following: although quicker moves increase the possibilities for punishment, they also increase the scope for defection. In the "bad news" model, this unexpected result is likely to arise near $t = 0$ if the players are patient or if the signal is much more likely to arrive during defection than during cooperation. In the "good news" model, only the static equilibrium (defection for all players) can be supported in the limit as $t \to 0$.

Abreu, Milgrom and Pearce's work is useful in focusing attention on the distinction between the timing of moves and the timing of information flows. Rather different technological factors determine these two aspects of oligopolistic interactions. Although the speedy arrival of accurate information about rival activities does increase the efficacy of collusion, it is not in general true that collusion is supported by an increase in the frequency with which firms can move.[86]

[84]And both of these changes are equivalent to a change in the firms' preferences that increase their patience.

[85]I.e. the Poisson process generating the signal has a higher arrival rate when not all firms are cooperating than when they are.

[86]Moreover, additional work by Abreu, Milgrom and Pearce suggests that increasing the lag with which imperfect information is observed by the players may enhance rather than undermine collusion.

The literature on repeated oligopoly games with demand uncertainty is a valuable extension of the basic supergame theory, and one that is likely to grow along with the related literature on repeated moral hazard. The key contribution to date of these theories is that they actually predict the occurrence of price wars in equilibrium. In contrast, in the previous supergame theories, while the credibility and size of punishments was critical, price wars never actually occurred.

3.2.5. Critique of supergames as a basis for oligopoly theory

Although the literature on quantity-setting supergames represents an enormous step beyond simple, static Cournot oligopoly, this literature suffers from several theoretical problems that limit its applicability and predictive power, even in industries where the environment might reasonably be taken as stationary. There are two major problems associated with oligopolistic supergames, each relating to the proper interpretation of supergame equilibria.

First, there is the difficulty of selecting among the vast multiplicity of equilibria. The huge number of supergame equilibria must be considered a major liability of this whole theoretical development. Certainly, game theory does not *predict* the collusive outcome; it simply indicates that such an outcome is supportable as a noncooperative equilibrium. The literature, and my survey of it, focuses on the set of Pareto optimal points within the larger set of equilibria, but in general there are still many Pareto optimal equilibrium points. Friedman (1971) developed the concept of *balanced temptation equilibrium* to select a point within the set of Pareto optimal equilibria.[87] but the balanced temptation criterion is itself ad hoc, and any less-collusive outcome also can be sustained using the same punishment strategies, since the gains from defection are smaller if the outcome is less collusive. Nor has any simple restriction on the firms' strategies yet been proposed that narrows down the equilibrium set in an instructive way.[88] So we have done no more than identified a large set of perfect equilibrium payoff vectors, and observed that the fully collusive point often is in this set.

Is there any reason to believe that the participants can focus on one of the Pareto preferred points in this equilibrium set? At the least, we have a bargaining problem among the firms, as each fights for a point on the Pareto frontier most favorable to itself. And bargaining theory allows for the possibility of an inefficient outcome. More generally, we have no compelling reason to rule out

[87]In my notation, a balanced temptation equilibrium is a Pareto optimal equilibrium at which the right-hand side of equation (18) is independent of i.

[88]For example, Stanford (1986) looks at "reaction function" strategies in a duopolistic supergame. These strategies require a firm to condition its period-t action solely on its rival's action during period $t-1$. Stanford shows that with this restriction the only subgame perfect equilibrium is simple repetition of the stage-game equilibrium.

Pareto dominated equilibrium points in games with multiple equilibria. While doing so has the advantage of narrowing down the set of equilibria that one must consider, it smacks of a cooperative behavioral axiom. And the firms may have difficulty adhering to the strategies necessary to support the most-collusive equilibria, at least in the case of complex, asymmetric punishments.

A second objection to supergame equilibria is that the punishments specified are *not* credible, even though we have restricted our attention to subgame perfect equilibria. This criticism goes back to the underlying interpretation of Nash equilibrium that was used to restrict attention to the Pareto optimal equilibria themselves. According to this interpretation of Nash equilibrium (which applies especially in the presence of multiple supergame equilibria), the participants communicate fully at time zero, specifying their behavior for the rest of the game. Then they go their separate ways, and implement what they have discussed. If the bargaining process does not fail at time zero, they should select a point on the Pareto frontier to enact. And so long as the specified strategies form a perfect equilibrium, it will not be in the interest of any party to deviate. The Nash equilibrium is a self-enforcing agreement, possibly a complex one calling for severe punishments for defectors.

Under this view of a Nash equilibrium as a self-enforcing agreement, however, it is not clear why the firms *jointly* would actually implement the severe punishments specified by their initial agreement. In other words, is it credible never to *renegotiate* in order to prevent a reversion to a price war? If the firms have the opportunity to communicate fully at time zero, why do they not again have such an opportunity in the event of a defection? Certainly a casual study of cartel behavior suggests that renegotiation occurs. While it is in the interest of the firms to commit themselves *not* to renegotiate, such behavior may not be credible. Indeed, to the extent that a defector knows he will be forgiven in the renegotiation, defection becomes attractive and collusion difficult. We see here a corollary of the topsy-turvy principle. Topsy-turvy antitrust policies that permit oligopolists to renegotiate and re-establish a collusive outcome in the event of a defection may in fact undermine tacit collusion and promote competition.

In a very interesting paper, Farrell and Maskin (1987) have developed a concept of renegotiation in repeated duopoly games. I think of their renegotiation concept as a type of "collective perfection requirement". Farrell and Maskin define a *set* of equilibria (and the corresponding payoffs) in a supergame as *renegotiation proof* if it satisfies two conditions: (a) each equilibrium in the set is supported as an equilibrium using only other members of the set itself as equilibria in subgames, and (b) no point in the set Pareto dominates any other point. The idea here is that the firms have identified the points in the renegotiation proof set as achievable, and will again find them achievable in any subgame, but they realize that it never is credible for the players as a group to pick a Pareto dominated continuation equilibrium. Implicit in this definition is that there will be no breakdown in the renegotiation process (such a breakdown could itself be a punishment if it is credible). In general, there will exist many renegotiation-proof equilibrium sets.

Farrell and Maskin demonstrate two conditions that characterize renegotiation-proof equilibria for discount rates close enough to unity: first, the player doing the punishing must prefer the punishment regime to the original equilibrium; and second, the player being punished must rather behave as specified in his punishment than defect yet again while his rival attempts to punish him. Typically, punishment consists of switching to an equilibrium (in the renegotiation-proof set) that is unfavorable to the defecting firm.

In their application of the renegotiation-proof concept to repeated oligopoly, Farrell and Maskin show how the requirement that equilibrium be renegotiation proof restricts the set of equilibrium payoffs that can be supported as supergame equilibria for discount factors close to unity. Whereas all points on the Pareto frontier are supergame equilibria for δ close to 1, those points giving the firms very different payoffs are not renegotiation proof: a firm with a very low payoff would simply defect, knowing that its rival would rather return to the original equilibrium than engage in punishment.

For the example of Cournot duopoly with $p(X) = 1 - X$ and zero costs, the Pareto frontier is the set of (flow) payoffs $(\pi, 1/4 - \pi)$, for $0 \leq \pi \leq 1/4$. In contrast, only points at which each firm earns at least $1/36$ each period are renegotiation proof. The set of renegotiation-proof equilibrium payoffs can be narrowed somewhat further by requiring that the renegotiation-proof set contain no points Pareto dominated by any element of *any* renegotiation-proof equilibrium set. Farrell and Maskin call such sets *strongly renegotiation proof*. In the example above, a payoff on the Pareto frontier can be sustained in a strongly renegotiation-proof way if and only if each player earns at least $1/16$ on a flow basis.

In view of the obvious incentives of oligopolists to avoid having to engage in mutually destructive punishments, I consider the concept of renegotiation-proof equilibria a promising way of refining supergame theory.[89] Unfortunately, although the renegotiation-proof criterion is appealing and narrows down the set of equilibria, a great many equilibria survive this refinement.

4. Two-stage competition

Repeated games are limited in that history has no tangible effect on prospective competition. The subgame beginning at any date is identical to the original game.

[89] See also the independent development by Bernheim and Ray (1987). Pearce (1987) has developed a rather different concept of renegotiation proofness and applied it to oligopoly theory, and several authors are currently working on notions of renegotiation, e.g. in the context of contracting.

The remainder of this chapter moves away from this very strong assumption to look at the wide range of competitive behavior involving investments that materially alter the subsequent competitive environment. Extending our study to such models allows us to explore such concepts as pre-emption and strategic commitment.

The natural place to begin studying strategic behavior is in the context of two-period models of oligopoly. Two-period models have the advantage of being quite tractable while highlighting the importance of timing. They suffer, however, from their artificial timing structure: the second and final period is essentially one of static oligopoly, albeit one influenced by the first-period actions. For truly dynamic models of repeated interaction, see Section 5 below.

It is important to realize the essential role of sunk costs in a dynamic, strategic environment. All of the analysis to follow considers equilibria in games where the firms can make *commitments* at early dates that influence the competition to follow. But no action is a commitment if it is swiftly and costlessly reversible. It is the sunkness – at least the partial sunkness – of various investments that qualifies them as strategic decisions. Sunkness is implicit in all of the models I refer to in this section. For example, when I discuss the strategic aspects of investments in physical plant and equipment, it must be understood that such investments are strategic only to the extent that they would be costly to reverse, i.e. only to the extent that they are sunk investments. This proviso applies to virtually all of the recent literature on dynamic oligopoly theory, and should serve to emphasize one of the themes of the contestability literature, namely the importance of sunk costs.

An enormous number of two-period models of strategic interactions have been studied in the past several years. Each of these models employs the equilibrium concept of subgame perfection, requiring that the firms correctly anticipate the outcome of the second-period competition as a function of any first-period choices that they make. All of these two-period models conform to the following general structure: in the initial period, one or more of the firms has the opportunity to take some action that will have real economic consequences for the state of competition in the second period. Let us call these first-period actions the "strategic" ones. In the second period, some simple Nash equilibrium emerges, given the conditions inherited from the initial period. Subgame perfection requires that these second-period actions form a (static) Nash equilibrium in the game at that time. The second-period strategies might be called "tactical" responses to the earlier strategic choices.

The analysis invariably focuses on identifying the "strategic effects" that influence first-period behavior, and on attempting to characterize the resulting strategic rivalry. Isolating the strategic effects requires one to define some nonstrategic baseline for first-period behavior. In what follows, I take as the baseline the open-loop equilibrium in which each firm chooses its first-period actions taking as given its rivals' actions in *both* periods.[90] Any differences between the open-loop equilibrium and the subgame perfect equilibrium arise because a firm accounts for the influence of its first-period strategy on its rivals' later actions. Many of the basic ideas of strategy and tactics found in this growing literature can be traced back to Schelling's (1960) classic book, *The Strategy of Conflict*.

4.1. A simple model of two-stage competition

I begin my treatment of two-period models by outlining a very simple generic model of two-period duopolistic competition that shows the basic mathematics of strategic competition. Below, I shall show how a very large number of ideas in oligopoly theory can be interpreted as strategic and tactical behavior in two-period models.

The basic situation in which we are interested is as follows: a first-period decision by one firm has an effect on the environment in which rivalry is played out in the future, and hence on the subsequent choices made by that firm's rival or rivals. To isolate this strategic principle, and to show how it alters the original firm's first-period behavior, my generic model permits only one firm to make a strategic decision in period one.[91]

Let firm 1 have the opportunity to make a strategic investment during the first period. Measure the extent of firm 1's investment, or commitment, by its first-period outlay, K (measured in period-two dollars). For simplicity, assume that K alters the costs (or demand) faced by firm 1 during the second period, but does not affect firm 2's costs (or demand). The obvious example is investment in some type of capital (physical or human) that affects variable costs. After this investment is made, the firms play some noncooperative duopoly game in the second period. Writing firm 1's second-period profits as $\pi_1(x_1, x_2, K)$, where x_i is firm i's second-period action, firm 1's total profits (again, measuring in period-two dollars) are $\pi_1(x_1, x_2, K) - K$. The sunkness of the investment K is implicit in this specification, which does not permit any disinvestment during the second period. Firm 2's profits are $\pi_2(x_1, x_2)$.

To find the subgame perfect equilibrium in this game, one must first determine the equilibrium in the second period for *any* possible K (i.e. for any possible

[90] Formally, the open-loop equilibrium is a Nash equilibrium in strategy profiles, where a firm's strategy profile indicates what action it will take at each date that it moves. In an open-loop equilibrium, a firm cannot affect its rivals' future actions by its own current actions, since it takes as given both its rivals' current actions and their future actions.

[91] The principles emerging from my simplified structure are doubly present when each of several firms can act strategically. A natural class of games in which only a single firm can strategically invest are entry-deterrence games in which only one of the oligopolists, the initial incumbent, is active in the initial period. See Chapter 8 by Richard Gilbert in this Handbook.

first-period history), and then "fold back" to determine firm 1's optimal choice of K. Formally, we can think of K as a shift parameter in firm 1's profit function, and hence in its reaction function. At a cost, firm 1 can shift its own reaction function through its choice of K. Observe that the strategic aspect of the investment K in this model is *not* that it alters firm 2's incentives or opportunities, but rather that investment by firm 1 alters that firm's *own* incentives at a later date.[92]

For any given K, the equations determining x_1 and x_2 are simply $\partial\pi_i/\partial x_i = 0$, $i = 1, 2$. These two equations define the Nash equilibrium choices in the continuation game as a function of K, $x_i^*(K)$. The equilibrium second-period profits are therefore given by $\pi_i^*(K) \equiv \pi_i(x_1^*(K), x_2^*(K), K)$.

What governs firm 1's choice of K? Acting strategically, firm 1 sets K to maximize $\pi_1^*(K) - K$. Differentiating this with respect to K using the definition of $\pi_1^*(K)$ gives:

$$\frac{\partial\pi_1(x_1^*, x_2^*, K)}{\partial x_1}\frac{\mathrm{d}x_1^*}{\mathrm{d}K} + \frac{\partial\pi_1(x_1^*, x_2^*, K)}{\partial x_2}\frac{\mathrm{d}x_2^*}{\mathrm{d}K} + \frac{\partial\pi_1(x_1^*, x_2^*, K)}{\partial K} - 1 = 0.$$

The first term here is zero by the definition of x_1^*, so we have:[93]

$$\frac{\partial\pi_1(x_1^*, x_2^*, K)}{\partial x_2}\frac{\mathrm{d}x_2^*}{\mathrm{d}K} + \frac{\partial\pi_1(x_1^*, x_2^*, K)}{\partial K} = 1. \tag{30}$$

The two terms on the left-hand side of equation (30) measure firm 1's marginal benefits of increased investment. The second of these terms is the direct effect on firm 1's profits; more capital expenditures in the initial period lead to smaller (variable) costs during the second period. This effect of course has nothing to do with the presence of a competitor or the opportunity to act strategically. It is the first term in (30) that captures the strategic incentive to invest. In the case of Cournot competition, $\partial\pi_1/\partial x_2$ tells us how firm 1's profits vary with firm 2's output, and $\mathrm{d}x_2^*/\mathrm{d}K$ measures the effect of firm 1's investment on firm 2's output.

[92] Of course, if K appeared directly in π_2, then firm 1 *could* alter firm 2's incentives, but this channel is not necessary for firm 1 to act strategically.

[93] The fact that the first term drops out is an example of a general application of the envelope theorem to multistage games. Given that a firm is optimizing in the future, its actions today, while they may affect its own future choices, cannot (to the first order) thereby raise the firm's objective function. To alter the firm's subsequent payoff, today's actions must either have direct effects on its future payoffs or alter the actions taken by others in the future.

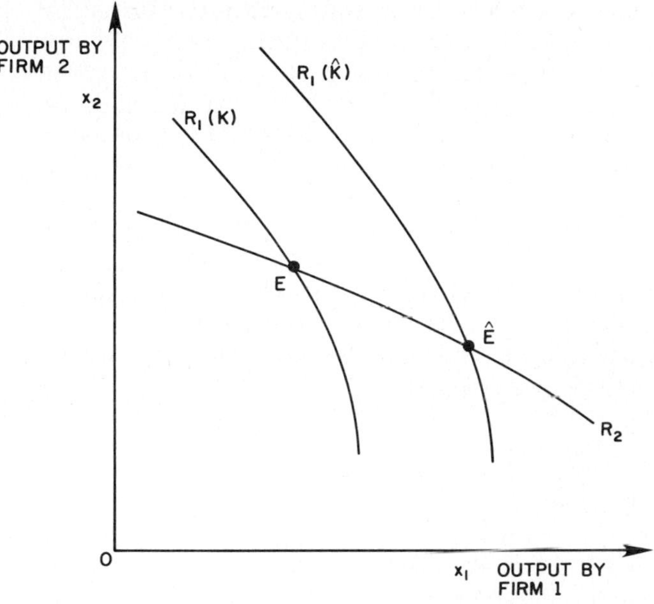

Figure 6.4. Strategic investment with quantity competition ($\hat{K} > K$).

How does K alter x_2? In the current simple model, where K does not directly enter into firm 2's profit function, K can only alter x_2 through its effect on x_1.[94] Again, the point is that firm 1 alters its *own* incentives in the second period, and thereby manipulates firm 2's behavior at that time. This "self-manipulation" is displayed in Figure 6.4 for the standard case of Cournot duopoly with homogeneous products. In that case, firm 1's reaction curve is shifted outwards by additional investment; this in turn causes firm 2 to contract, to firm 1's benefit. The conclusion is that, in a homogeneous-product Cournot oligopoly, a firm has a strategic incentive to invest in capital as a way of increasing its market share and profits.

More generally, but still within the context of our formal model, by working through the comparative statics effect of a change in K on x_1 and x_2, we have:

$$\frac{\mathrm{d}x_2^*}{\mathrm{d}K} = \frac{\partial^2 \pi_1}{\partial x_1\, \partial K} \frac{\partial^2 \pi_2}{\partial x_1\, \partial x_2} \Bigg/ |M| \,, \tag{31}$$

[94] If K shifts the demand for firm 2's products or firm 2's costs, then it would *directly* influence x_2, and the formulas to follow would have an additional term.

where $|M|$ is the determinant of the second-derivative matrix:

$$M = \begin{pmatrix} \dfrac{\partial^2 \pi_1}{\partial x_1^2} & \dfrac{\partial^2 \pi_1}{\partial x_1 \, \partial x_2} \\ \dfrac{\partial^2 \pi_2}{\partial x_2 \, \partial x_1} & \dfrac{\partial^2 \pi_2}{\partial x_2^2} \end{pmatrix}$$

associated with the system of equations $\partial \pi_i / \partial x_i = 0$, $i = 1, 2$. $|M|$ is positive if the system is stable [i.e. if inequality (5) is satisfied].

The preceding analysis shows that the sign of the strategic effect, the first term in (30), is the same as the sign of

$$\frac{\partial^2 \pi_1}{\partial x_1 \, \partial K} \frac{\partial^2 \pi_2}{\partial x_1 \, \partial x_2} \frac{\partial \pi_1}{\partial x_2}.$$

This expression is the product of (i) the effect of investment on 1's incentive to produce output, (ii) the effect of 1's output on 2's output, and (iii) the effect of 2's output on 1's profits. In the case of Cournot duopoly and physical capital investment discussed above and displayed in Figure 6.4, (i) is positive, while (ii) and (iii) are negative.[95] On net, firm 1 has a strategic incentive to invest because this causes it to produce more, and hence firm 2 to produce less, which is to firm 1's advantage.

It is a simple matter to apply the above model to differentiated product pricing competition instead of Cournot duopoly. Simply re-interpret the second-period strategies x_1 and x_2 as prices instead of outputs (with apologies for the notation). Now, added investment reduces 1's costs, and leads firm 1 to set a lower price, $\partial^2 \pi_1 / \partial x_1 \, \partial K < 0$, which induces firm 2 to lower its price, $\partial^2 \pi_2 / \partial x_1 \, \partial x_2 > 0$, harming firm 1, since $\partial \pi_1 / \partial x_2 > 0$. Consequently, firm 1 has a strategic incentive to *under*invest in capital, as a way of keeping prices high. This case of upward-sloping reaction curves is shown in Figure 6.5.

4.2. *Welfare effects of strategic behavior*

It is difficult to make general statements regarding the welfare consequences of the strategic behavior identified above. As usual in Industrial Organization, there are two wedges to consider: (1) the effect of the practice on consumers, and (2) the effect on rival firms. Since strategic investment by firm 1 is undertaken up to

[95]Strictly speaking, (ii) is negative only if b_2 from equation (4) is negative, as I assume.

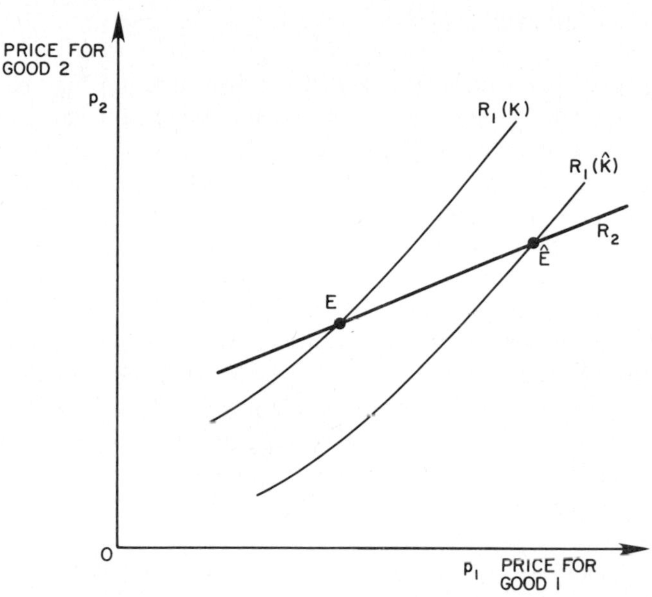

Figure 6.5. Strategic investment with pricing competition ($\hat{K} < K$).

the point where its marginal effect on firm 1's profits is zero, its marginal effect on welfare is the sum of its effects on consumers and on rivals.

In the case emphasized above – investment in physical capital followed by quantity competition – investments by firm 1 harm firm 2 (since firm 1 takes a more aggressive stance), but they typically *benefit* consumers since total output rises (here we are using comparative statics results from Subsection 2.1). The net effect cannot in general be signed: we cannot be sure whether the strategic incentive to invest actually raises or lowers welfare.[96]

The situation is quite similar in the case of strategic investment and pricing competition. Again the two wedges point in different directions: strategic under-investment by firm 1 leads to less fierce pricing competition, to the benefit of firm 2. But now consumers are made worse off on account of higher prices. As much as we have learned about strategic behavior, we unfortunately have little *general* guidance regarding the effect of this behavior on overall industry performance. In particular cases (see below) welfare results can be obtained, but the wide variety of strategic behavior precludes any general welfare theorems.

[96]Brander and Spencer (1983) is an example of this ambiguity in the context of R&D investment. Similar ambiguities arise when investments are used to deter entry.

4.3. Taxonomy of strategic behavior

There is a general point underlying the distinction between Figures 6.4 and 6.5. In the case of quantity competition, investment by firm 1 causes that firm to behave more aggressively (by selling more in response to any x_2), and this in turn induces firm 2 to behave *less* aggressively (actually sell less in equilibrium). Strategic overinvestment is the result. In the case of pricing competition, investment by firm 1 again leads it to be more aggressive, but in response to firm 1's lower price, firm two behaves *more* aggressively, not less, since it lowers its own price. This leads to strategic underinvestment.

This distinction between the downward-sloping reaction curves of Cournot rivalry and the upward-sloping reaction curves of Bertrand competition has been understood for some time. But recently, Fudenberg and Tirole (1984) and Bulow, Geanakoplos and Klemperer (1985) have supplied us with a taxonomy of such possibilities and some language to describe them. To establish a consistent notation, define the x_i's so that $\partial\pi_i/\partial x_j < 0$; a higher x_i represents more aggressive behavior by firm i.

Bulow, Geanakoplos and Klemperer have coined the terms "strategic substitutes" and "strategic complements" to capture the two cases just discussed (although this distinction was generally appreciated well before their paper was written). "Strategic substitutes" is defined by the inequality $\partial^2\pi_2/\partial x_1\,\partial x_2 < 0$, while "strategic complements" is the reverse inequality. In their terminology, I have just shown that quantity competition involves strategic substitutes, whereas price competition involves strategic complements [assuming that the appropriate conditions, equations (4) and (12), are satisfied]. With strategic substitutes, more aggressive behavior by firm 1 (an increase in x_1) induces less aggressive behavior by firm 2 (a reduction in x_2). As Bulow, Geanakoplos and Klemperer point out, the normal notion of substitutes captures the effect of x_1 on firm 2's profitability, i.e. $\partial\pi_2/\partial x_1 < 0$, whereas strategic substitutes captures the effect of x_1 on the *marginal* profitability of firm 2, $\partial^2\pi_2/\partial x_1\,\partial x_2 < 0$. They focus on the $\mathrm{d}x_2^*/\mathrm{d}K$ term from equation (31), calling this the core of their paper (see p. 494).

Fudenberg and Tirole (1984) provide a somewhat less formal but more general taxonomy of strategic behavior in two-period games. Certainly, their terminology is more graphic. When $\partial^2\pi_1/\partial x_1\,\partial K > 0$, they say that "investment makes the incumbent tough". With downward-sloping reaction curves, $\partial^2\pi_2/\partial x_1\,\partial x_2 < 0$, and we have our familiar overinvestment result, which Fudenberg and Tirole call the "top dog" strategy. With upward-sloping reaction curves, they call the underinvestment the "puppy dog" strategy: firm 1 underinvests in order to be a less threatening rival. The other possibility is that investment makes firm 1 "soft". This is defined by the condition $\partial^2\pi_1/\partial x_1\,\partial K < 0$. As we know from equation (31), this reverses the strategic effect. With downward-sloping reactions, we now get underinvestment by the incumbent in order to be more aggressive, which Fudenberg and Tirole call the "lean and hungry" strategy. If the reaction curves slope upwards, we have the "fat cat" strategy of overinvesting to be less aggressive, and hence inducing one's rival also to be less aggressive. Fudenberg and Tirole's four diet/animal strategies correspond to the four possible sign combinations of the two terms in the numerator of equation (31).[97]

4.4. Examples of two-period models

There are a remarkable number of applications of the basic strategic effects identified above. Although many of these examples involve strategic behavior by more than one firm, the general principles we have just seen continue to describe the essence of the strategic interactions. In all cases, it is essential not only that a firm make a strategic commitment, but also that this commitment be communicated to the rival. Absent credible communication, no strategic advantage can be obtained.[98]

(1) *Stackelberg leadership*. Stackelberg leadership is the granddaddy of two-stage models. It demonstrates the value of being the leader, now called a *first-mover advantage*. First, one firm selects its output; then the other firm follows with its own output choice. Formally, the leader's strategy is an output and the follower's strategy is a function specifying its output for each possible output by the leader. Stackelberg (1934) identified the leader's strategic advantage, anticipating as it does its rival's response. In terms of Figure 6.1, the leader (say, firm 1) selects its most-preferred point on the follower's (firm 2's) reaction schedule. Clearly, the leader must be at least as well off as he would be as a Cournot duopolist, since he has the option of setting his Cournot output (knowing that this will induce Cournot behavior by the follower). In general, the leader can earn higher profits than his Cournot profits.

The presence of a first-mover advantage carries over to Stackelberg pricing games with differentiated products. If two firms set their prices sequentially, again a firm can improve on its Bertrand payoff by strategically selecting its

[97]Fudenberg and Tirole's taxonomy also includes the distinction between entry-deterring and entry-accommodating behavior. Let firm 1 be the incumbent in the first period and firm 2 be the potential entrant. Now the *total* effect of K on π_2, $\mathrm{d}\pi_2^*/\mathrm{d}K$, and not just the marginal effect of K on x_2^*, comes into play. The reason is that firm 2 has an entry decision as well as a choice of x_2, i.e. firm 2's profit function is not concave in x_2, since it must bear some fixed entry costs if it selects $x_2 > 0$. In Dixit's (1980) model, overinvestment both deters entry and gives a strategic advantage if entry is not deterred. But in other models firm 1 may overinvest to deter entry, even though it would underinvest if entry were a foregone conclusion. The general principle is to cause one's rival to behave less aggressively given that entry cannot be deterred, but to reduce one's rival's profits as a way of deterring entry. See Gilbert, Chapter 8 in this Handbook, for further discussion of this point.

[98]Again, I refer the reader to Schelling (1960) for a pioneering discussion of the importance of communicating threats and commitments to one's opponent.

price, realizing that choosing a higher price will induce its rival to do the same. An exercise for the reader is to identify the Stackelberg point on Figure 6.2.

In today's terminology, Stackelberg and Cournot equilibria are each (subgame perfect) Nash equilibria, but to different games.[99] The difference is solely one of the timing of moves, but the importance of timing is one of the main lessons to be derived from the whole class of two-period games. The most durable criticism of Stackelberg's work, namely the exogenous specification of who is the leader and who is the follower, foreshadows a general criticism of simple timing models: the results depend upon the exact specification of the extensive form game being played, so one must be careful to justify this exogenous specification.

(2) *Strategic investment*. One or more firms has the opportunity in the first period to make capital investments that will influence its variable costs in the second period. I referred to this example most often in the development of the generic two-period model above. Investment is strategic, and pricing or output decisions are tactical. These models were originally developed by Spence (1977) and Dixit (1980) to study entry deterrence. With quantity competition, there is a strategic incentive to overinvest; this tendency is reversed with pricing competition. Investing in inventories can be studied in a similar fashion, although this analysis is complicated by the presence of storage costs. See Rotemberg and Saloner (1985) for a discussion of tacit collusion in the presence of inventories, and Arvan (1985) and Saloner (1986) for some examples of the strategic use of inventories as investments.

Strategic investment in capacity need not lead to overinvestment. Our generic two-period model tells us that with pricing competition (and, say, differentiated products) there will be a strategic incentive to underinvest. Gelman and Salop (1983) identified a similar strategy in the context of optimal entry strategies: a firm may succeed in entry by committing itself (if possible) to remaining small and thereby evoking a less aggressive response on the part of its rival. In this case Fudenberg and Tirole's (1984) term "puppy-dog ploy" seems especially appropriate.

(3) *Learning-by-doing*. When firms learn from experience, their first-period production levels affect their second-period costs, and hence competition at that time. The strategic incentives here are much like those above for investment in physical capital, except that investment consists of a larger first-period production level. With quantity competition, strategic concerns drive firms to produce more at early dates than they otherwise would. Of course, when examining the time path of output, this effect must be balanced against the natural incentive to

[99] Without the refinement to subgame perfection, any output by the leader giving him non-negative profits would be an equilibrium (much as any individually rational outcome is an equilibrium in the simultaneous-move output game if the firms' strategies are supply functions). All but one of these equilibria are supported by incredible threats on the part of the follower, however.

produce more in the second period when marginal costs are lower. See Fudenberg and Tirole (1983a) for the clearest two-period exposition.

(4) *Cost-reducing R&D*. Consider a model in which oligopolists first engage in a phase of R&D and later play an output or pricing game. The R&D investments affect second-period costs, possibly with spillovers; see, for example, Spence (1984). With quantity competition, a firm realizes that lower costs confer on it a strategic advantage. See Brander and Spencer (1983) for a clear exposition of this in a two-period model. The strategic effect stimulates the firms' R&D investments. Again, the reverse is true with pricing competition.

(5) *Network competition*. In the first period, competing firms build up customer bases, which have value in the second period because buyers benefit from being part of the crowd ("demand-side scale economies"). Katz and Shapiro (1986a, 1986b) study the intense first-period competition to attract customers when products are incompatible. They also examine the strategic effects of designing compatible products in order to reduce this intense early competition.

(6) *Patent licensing*. Initially, firms sign contracts to be licensees of new products or processes. Given the provisions of these contracts, the licensees then compete as oligopolists. Each firm recognizes that giving its rival access to a superior technology will put it at a strategic disadvantage (or eliminate a strategic advantage) in the subsequent oligopolistic rivalry.[100] But licensing may still occur if a mutually beneficial licensing contract can be constructed. See Katz and Shapiro (1985).

(7) *Advertising*. In the first period, advertising budgets are chosen. These expenditures influence second-period rivalry since advertising is durable. As Schmalensee (1983) has shown, a firm may enjoy a strategic advantage by underinvesting in advertising. Such a strategy may make that firm more aggressive in seeking new customers during the second period, since it has fewer loyal customers. In Fudenberg and Tirole's language, this is the lean and hungry look.

(8) *Information exchange*. In an uncertain environment with private information about demand or cost conditions, rival firms first have the opportunity to exchange (reveal) their information about industry conditions. Then they compete in the second period on the basis of that information. Again the incentive to reveal information is different for quantity than for pricing competition. And it depends upon whether the information regards demand or cost conditions. See Vives (1984) and Shapiro (1986).

(9) *Mergers*. First, firms have the opportunity to consolidate their operations by merging. Then the set of remaining entities plays an oligopoly game. The first-period merger decisions are strategic. Salant, Switzer and Reynolds (1983)

[100]This theme has been explored very nicely by Salop and Scheffman (1983) under the rubric "raising rivals' costs", They discuss various tactics by which a firm might reduce the efficiency of its rivals' operations. One such tactic is to withhold a superior technology or key input from one's rival.

show for the case of constant marginal costs that mergers are typically unprofitable under Cournot competition. Davidson and Deneckere (1985a) show that this result is reversed for pricing competition. The reason is that a merger causes the participants collectively to behave less aggressively; this is a benefit with pricing competition, but not with quantity competition. Perry and Porter (1985) and Farrell and Shapiro (1988) examine mergers in the presence of increasing marginal costs, i.e. when firms own some industry-specific capital.

(10) *Product selection*. A natural way of studying product selection is to treat it as a first-period choice, followed by second-period pricing competition. Oligopolists have an incentive to choose product varieties that are not too close as substitutes, in order to diminish second-period pricing or output competition. For analyses along these lines see Prescott and Visscher (1977), Shaked and Sutton (1982), Brander and Eaton (1984), and Judd (1985).

(11) *Financial structure*. Another way in which a firm might commit itself to more aggressive behavior is through its choice of a debt–equity ratio. This possibility is explored in Brander and Lewis (1986). They consider a model in which firms first decide how much debt to issue (total capital requirements are fixed), and then compete as duopolists. The key point is that a more leveraged firm will act more aggressively in the output market, so long as profits are uncertain and bankruptcy is a possibility.

Debt financing leads to more aggressive behavior because of the following two effects: (i) with more debt, the owners of a firm have an incentive to increase the variability of its profits, and (ii) an increase in output raises the variability of a firm's profits in the presence of uncertain demand. The second point requires an assumption that the marginal profitability of output is higher when conditions are more favorable, i.e. $\partial^2\pi_i/\partial x_i\,\partial\theta > 0$, $i = 1, 2$, where overall profitability increases with the random variable θ. Point (i) follows from the observation that the returns to the owners are given by the maximum of π_i and 0; since this maximum is a convex function of π_i, a mean-preserving spread in π_i raises the returns to the owners. Put differently, the owners prefer large to small (positive) profits, but are indifferent between small and large losses. In particular, an increase in debt financing by firm i raises the critical value of θ_i, $\hat{\theta}_i$, at which the owner's of firm i break even (for a given choice of x_1 and x_2). To see point (ii), note that an increase in output (in the relevant range) raises profits in favorable states and lowers them in unfavorable states, so long as $\partial^2\pi_i/\partial x_i\,\partial\theta > 0$. These observations led Brander and Lewis to conclude that firms have a strategic incentive to use debt financing as a way of committing themselves to be more aggressive. Of course, this result is limited to the case of "strategic substitutes", and is reversed for second-period pricing competition.[101]

[101] Brander and Lewis (1985) explore another aspect of the strategic role of financing – the effect of bankruptcy costs – in their companion piece.

(12) *Labor contracts and managerial incentives.* Just as investment in physical capital can lower marginal costs and serve a strategic role, so can labor contracts or managerial incentive schemes.

In arranging its labor contracts, the key (with, say, quantity competition) is for an oligopolist to turn variable costs into fixed costs, thereby committing itself to a more aggressive stance. This could be done by raising base wages in order to reduce overtime rates (so that during a boom in demand an expansion in production calling for overtime work would be less expensive on the margin). Or a firm could agree with its union that the firm could hire new or temporary workers at wages lower than those paid to current union members. Similarly, a contract specifying generous severance pay would lower the opportunity cost of keeping workers on the job and induce more aggressive behavior during downturns in demand.

In designing managerial incentive schemes, the owner of an oligopolistic firm will strive to give incentives to the firm's manager to act aggressively (again, in the case of quantity competition). It should be apparent to the reader by now that allowing the owner of just one firm to commit itself to a managerial incentive scheme (e.g. paying the manager on the basis of market share, revenues, etc.) allows that firm unlimited commitment power. Consider the effect of such a commitment prior to a Cournot duopoly game. By appropriately rewarding the manager on the basis of sales, say, the owner with commitment power could achieve the Stackelberg leadership point. The more interesting case arises when all firms have equal opportunities to commit themselves to managerial contracts. As we would expect, in the case of quantity competition, each owner causes his manager to act more aggressively than otherwise, with an end result of more competition and lower profits. The reverse results hold for pricing competition. In either case, although it may appear to an outside observer that the managers are not maximizing profits (in the second stage), this is only because owners, in the interest of profit maximization, have strategically instructed them not to do so. See Fershtman and Judd (1984) and Sklivas (1985) for analyses along these lines. But as Katz (1987) shows, the strategic scope for incentive contracts is completely eroded if it is impossible to verify the existence of such contracts to one's rivals.[102]

(13) *Long-term contracts with customers.* There are many contracts that a firm might sign with customers in the first period in order to give it a strategic edge in

[102] In particular, effective commitment by an owner–manager pair requires that the owner and the manager be able to convince others that they have not written a *new* contract superceding the one to which they claim to have committed. The problem arises because, given what others believe firm i's contract to specify, it is in the joint interests of the owner and the manager at firm i to sign a new contract instructing the manager to maximize profits (given the actions of rival firms as induced by the contract they believed to apply). Katz makes a strong case that it is difficult to verify the primacy of any contract that the owner and manager reveal.

later competition. With declining marginal costs, for example, a firm that has already contracted for a significant amount of business will have lower marginal costs for the remaining business and act more aggressively. Or a firm could offer first-period customers a discount if they are left stranded with an unpopular product, i.e. one with a small final market share (this would give the firm an incentive to achieve a high market share in the second period).[103]

Another example that I have discussed in Subsection 2.4 above is that of Retroactive Most-Favored-Customer Clauses. As Salop (1986) and especially Cooper (1986) note, a firm can alter its second-period incentive to cut prices by signing most-favored-customer agreements with first-period customers. Given these contracts, the firm can commit itself to less aggressive behavior, a benefit (and hence a facilitating practice) in a subsequent Bertrand game.

Holt and Scheffman (1986) show how most-favored-customer clauses and meet-or-release provisions of contracts can support the Cournot equilibrium (as well as more competitive equilibria) in a two-period pricing model. Each firm, realizing that second-period discounts from the first-period list price will be matched, takes other firms' outputs as given, just as in the Cournot model. A price reduction can increase a firm's sales by attracting unattached buyers, but since it cannot cut into rival sales, it acts exactly like an increase in quantity in the single-period Cournot model. Holt and Scheffman also consider *selective* discounts, whereby a firm offers a lower price only to a particular group of its rivals' buyers. They find that when firms can offer selective discounts, it is generally not possible to support supra-competitive list prices.

(14) *Investing in disinformation*. So far I have emphasized first-period actions that influence the state of second-period rivalry through tangible variables such as capacity or product selection. Another way in which first-period decisions can influence later behavior is through the *information* that they generate. Needless to say, these effects can only arise when the firms are uncertain about some aspect of the market environment, and when one firm's actions affect the information received by its rival(s) about the market.

Riordan's (1985) model is a nice example of strategic manipulation of information in a duopoly.[104] The two firms play a twice-repeated Cournot game, but are uncertain of the demand conditions in either period and cannot observe their rival's output level. Critically, the demand shock is positively serially correlated across the two periods. Each firm uses the first-period price as information in its effort to estimate the demand shock at that time. A lower price in the first period

[103]Contracts in which the price ultimately paid is contingent on the firm's market share are natural in the presence of network externalities, because customers then care directly about the market share of the brand that they buy.

[104]Strategies of this type have been explored more fully in the context of entry deterrence. See Chapter 8 by Richard Gilbert in this Handbook, the papers on limit pricing by Milgrom and Roberts (1982a) and by Harrington (1986), and that on predation by Kreps and Wilson (1982b).

leads a firm to estimate that demand was less favorable. This in turn – due to the serial correlation of demand shocks – convinces the firm that second-period demand is weaker, and the firm reduces output accordingly. So, a lower first-period price induces each firm to select a lower second-period output. But now note that each firm has an incentive to manipulate the other's information: by producing more at the beginning, a firm can cause its rival to take a more pessimistic view of market conditions and produce less later on (hence the title of the paper). Again we get overinvestment in the first period: the firms produce more at that time than they would under static Cournot competition. This result would be reversed if demand shocks were negatively correlated across periods, due, for example, to the presence of inventory holdings by buyers. An opposite result also would be found if the firms were Bertrand rather than Cournot competitors. As with so many of the results in this section, the strategic incentives to manipulate information are sensitive to the precise nature of the tactical competition.

An analogous overproduction result also arises in a model with cost uncertainty. Suppose that each duopolist is uncertain of its rival's cost, and they play a twice-repeated Cournot game. Now each firm has an incentive to expand its production during the first period in an effort to make its rival believe that its costs are lower than they in fact are. Such a message would cause the rival to scale back its second-period output. Mailath (1985) analyzes the corresponding duopolistic two-period pricing game with uncertain costs. He finds that cost uncertainty causes the firms to behave less competitively, as each firm would like its rival to believe its costs are high. See Roberts (1987) for an excellent and much more complete discussion of models of this sort, and Milgrom and Roberts (1987) for an insider's critique of the contribution of the literature on asymmetric information games to industrial organization.

(15) *Customer switching costs*. If consumers must bear a cost when switching from one supplier to another, the first-period sales have a lasting effect on competition. As with network competition and learning-by-doing, each firm benefits in the second period if it acted aggressively during the initial period. In many cases, however, having a base of locked-in, first-period consumers may make a firm less aggressive during the second period, because the firm's incentives to lower its prices are reduced (assuming that it cannot price discriminate). See Klemperer (1985) and Farrell and Shapiro (1987).

(16) *Multimarket oligopoly*. Commitments made in one market can affect subsequent competition in a second market, if there are linkages between markets on either the cost side or the demand side. Naturally, these ideas have application to international oligopolistic competition. Increased involvement by a given firm in market A, due to some commitment by the firm to that market, will cause that firm to behave more aggressively in market B if either (i) there are economies of scale or scope across the markets, so that the firm's marginal costs in market B are lowered by its increased presence in market A, or (ii) there are positive

demand interdependencies across markets, so that selling in market A enhances the demand for the firm's products in B. In general, if the two markets are linked in either way, the firm must account for the strategic effects in market B of its (prior) presence or scale of operations in market A. See Bulow, Geanakoplos and Klemperer (1985) for a further development of this theme.

(17) *International oligopoly*. In the case of international oligopoly, the first-period strategic behavior may not be undertaken by the oligopolists themselves, but rather by their home governments acting in their own interests. Take the case of a home firm and a foreign firm competing for business in a third country. One might think that there was no constructive role for the home government, since its interests coincide with those of the home firm (to maximize that firm's profits). This would indeed be the case in the absence of strategic effects (e.g. for a domestic firm selling as a monopolist in a foreign market). But the home government may be able to induce the home firm into more aggressive behavior, even when the firm could not so commit itself. For example, an export subsidy to the firm would have this effect. With quantity competition, therefore, the increase in profits can exceed the subsidy payments, generating a net domestic gain at the expense of the foreign competitor. See Brander and Spencer (1985) for a clear exposition of this case, and Krugman (1984) and Dixit and Kyle (1985) for related analyses.

While some policymakers cherish this result as a justification for their protectionism, it should be applied with extreme caution for at least three reasons. First, its application can easily lead to an "export subsidy war". If each country can subsidize its home firm, the ultimate beneficiaries will be consumers in the third country. Just as with strategic investment, we have a prisoner's dilemma structure: if each government acts strategically, both exporting countries are worse off. Second, the policy prescription is sensitive to the assumption of quantity competition, i.e. to the case of "strategic substitutes". If the firms play a pricing game, export taxes rather than subsidies are optimal (although the "export tax war" benefits both countries, in contrast to the subsidy war under quantity competition). See Eaton and Grossman (1986) for an explanation of when taxes are optimal and when subsidies are optimal. Third, Dixit and Grossman (1986) point out that a subsidy to one industry must ultimately come at the expense of some other industry, and there may be a decrease in its profits if it, too, is oligopolistic. In a symmetric model, subsidies are not optimal, even when firms play quantity games.

In this section I have explored a great many dimensions of strategic behavior. It should be clear that strategic considerations may encourage or discourage investments of various sorts, depending upon the specifics of the post-investment rivalry. But we do have a unified theory in the sense that the same strategic principles apply in so many economic environments, and we can generally relay on the comparative statics properties of our *static* oligopoly theory to provide information about strategic behavior. What we lack – and should not strive for, in my opinion – is a general theory of the effect of such strategic behavior on the firms' profits or on industry performance. In some cases, strategic investments heighten competition to the firms' disadvantage (a prisoner's dilemma structure at the investment stage) and consumers' advantage. In other cases, quite the opposite is true. Again, we must look in some detail at the characteristics of a particular industry if we are to determine into which group it falls.

5. Dynamic rivalry

I have yet to discuss truly dynamic models of oligopoly – models of many periods in which the economic environment changes with time. In other words, I have not combined the repeated rivalry aspects of supergames with the investment and commitment aspects of two-period models. That is the topic of the current section. Naturally, such games are the most complex of all those discussed in this chapter, and their tractability represents a genuine problem. But they hold out the most hope of advancing our understanding of oligopolistic rivalry, and currently represent the area of greatest research activity in oligopoly theory. For the reader planning to pursue independent research in this area, I recommend close study of Fudenberg and Tirole's (1986a) excellent monograph on dynamic oligopoly in addition to the material below.

5.1. What makes for dynamics?

If we are to study dynamic oligopoly games, we had best understand what the fundamental sources of these dynamics are. In other words, why does an oligopolistic market environment change over the course of time? It is useful to categorize the sources of dynamics for the purposes of developing different models and theories.

Some industries experience changing conditions quite independently of their own behavior. One obvious example is an emerging industry where, say, exogenous technological progress is rapidly lowering costs; such industries are the subject of the literature on adoption of new technology (see Chapter 14 by Reinganum in this Handbook). Another example would be a declining industry where, say, demand is falling over time [see, for example, Ghemawat and Nalebuff (1985)]. Or an industry may experience cyclical changes in demand or factor cost conditions, perhaps due to economy-wide business cycles. A thorough treatment of these *exogenous* sources of industry dynamics, while a rich topic in the study of oligopolistic behavior, is beyond the scope of this chapter.

Oligopolistic markets may also experience *endogenous* changes in the conditions of competition. These endogenous changes, being subject to strategic maneuvering by the oligopolists, are the subject of this section. I will distinguish two types of industry conditions that may evolve over time. The first are *tangible* industry conditions such as the firms' capital stocks, the firm's technological capabilities, or previous commitments made by buyers to particular sellers. See Section 4 for more examples of tangible capital variables that may change over time in response to firms' strategic choices. I shall emphasize these tangible industry conditions below. The second type of industry condition that may be strategically controlled is an intangible, i.e. the *beliefs* about market conditions that are held by the oligopolists or their customers. The point is that one firm may take actions designed to manipulate its rivals' information, and hence their future actions, in a way that is favorable to itself. The circumstances in which this signaling behavior can be expected to arise, and the mechanisms through which it operates, are quite different from strategic investments in tangible assets. For these reasons, the literature breaks quite naturally into these two categories.

5.2. The state–space approach to dynamic oligopoly models

In turning our attention to models of dynamic oligopoly, we need to refine our methods in order to focus our attention on the strategic aspects of commitment, just as we already have done in Section 4 for two-period models. The particular problem that we immediately face is the following: if we are to examine infinite horizon models, all of the intricacies that were present in the study of supergames remain with us in principle. For example, consider a dynamic game in which the oligopolists make investment decisions each period that affect their capital stocks, and then play a pricing or output game each period given the associated variable cost curves. In such a game, the whole supergame calculus of defection and retaliation remains present; indeed, it is made more complex by the fact that the gains from defection and the credibility of punishment are dependent on the firms' capital stocks.

In order to focus on the strategic aspects of competition, i.e. on the changing economic environment, it is extremely useful to fold the tactical decisions into the background and work with some *reduced-form profit functions* indicating the firms' flow profits as functions of the "state variables". The state variables measure the economic conditions at any point in time. Formally, a state variable is anything that affects the ensuing subgame. Typically, the state variables adjust slowly in response to the firms' current decisions. In the example of an investment and pricing game, the state variables are simply the firms' capital stocks, and we would assume that firm i's profits during period t are given by some function $\pi_i(\boldsymbol{K}_t)$, where $\boldsymbol{K}_t \equiv (K_{1t}, \ldots, K_{nt})$ and K_{it} is firm i's capital stock at date t.[105] Using the language of Section 4, the firms behave strategically by making medium- to long-run commitments that alter market conditions (the *state*) into the future; short run, tactical decisions are subsumed in the reduced-form profit functions.

Restricting attention to strategies that depend only on the state of the industry is exactly the *opposite* of the approach taken in the supergame literature. In supergames, there is *no* state variable, so the state–space restriction would require the firms' strategies to be constant over time. Simple repetitions of the static, stage-game equilibrium would be the only possibility. And in dynamic games, the most collusive equilibria (which were the focus of the analysis in supergames) generally rely on strategies that are *not* merely functions of the tangible state variables. These observations may make it appear that the state–space approach is very restrictive. But all it really does is rule out the type of bootstrapping that led to so many supergame equilibria. To see this, note that in a finite horizon game (with a unique equilibrium) the strategies necessarily are functions only of the state of the market.[106] All of the two-period models discussed above were state–space models in this sense. What the state–space approach allows us to do is focus on dynamic strategies involving commitment, i.e. those that alter future market conditions, without restricting our attention to finite-horizon games.[107] Another advantage of the state–space approach, in contrast to supergame theory, is that the equilibrium structure generally does *not* change suddenly as the number of periods becomes infinite.

In the case of tangible capital variables, the capital stocks themselves serve as the state variables. Anything that involves a commitment – either by one of the oligopolists or by one of their customers – can serve as a state variable, since commitments affect the prospective competition, i.e. the continuation game. I have already given many examples of state variables that apply in different markets. For these tangible variables, the equations of motion of the state variables are determined by the technologies of production and consumption, e.g. by the sunkness of investment made by each oligopolist. In the case of intangible variables, the state measures the firms' or consumers' beliefs about relevant but uncertain market conditions (such as cost or demand parameters). These models are quite different in structure, since the equations of motion for the state

[105] We could derive the $\pi_i(\boldsymbol{K})$ functions from the underlying cost and demand conditions by assuming, say, Cournot behavior at any date.

[106] This follows from our use of subgame perfection as an equilibrium concept. Previous behavior (cooperation vs. defection) is critical in determining firms' current behavior in the supergame literature, but past actions cannot affect current behavior in state–space games unless they alter current conditions.

[107] Finite horizon games often are awkward to analyze because the number of remaining periods is ever-changing. A finite horizon introduces an *exogenous* element of nonstationarity into the model; calender time is one of the state variables. Many of the lessons of finite-horizon state–space games can be gleaned from two-period models.

variables are determined by Bayesian updating, given some priors as initial conditions.

In adopting the state–space approach to dynamic oligopoly, we are implicitly putting a great deal of weight on the *payoff-relevant* features of the economic environment, i.e. those features that enter directly into the firms' prospective payoffs. In practice, there are a great many payoff-relevant capital variables in a given market; the art here is to identify the qualitatively important ones for the purpose of industry analysis. The multitude of possible strategic variables highlights both the importance of strategic commitments and the criticality of identifying the most significant strategic variables in any particular industry. As with two-period models, the literature is most naturally partitioned according to the particular state variables being studied. I follow this organizing principle for the remainder of this section.

5.3. Pricing and quantity games

It is natural to begin with our old friends, prices and quantities, as candidate strategic variables. Although prices are most often tactical choices folded into the reduced-form profit functions (as in the investment and pricing example outlined above), there are a number of settings in which they themselves can serve as the state variables. Previous pricing and production decisions *directly* influence current and future rivalry when these variables are sluggish or costly to adjust. In such circumstances, prices or quantities exhibit inertia, and hence have a direct effect on the continuation game.[108]

Cyert and DeGroot (1970) were the first to explore the commitment role of production decisions in an explicitly dynamic game. They examined an *alternating-move* duopolistic quantity game. With alternating moves, in contrast to the repeated but simultaneous move structure of supergames, there is a genuine state of the market when firm 2, say, is on the move. The state consists of firm 1's previous production choice, which by assumption must remain in force until firm 1 again has the opportunity to move. Cyert and DeGroot realized that by examining a finite-horizon, alternating-move quantity game, they could introduce genuine dynamics into the standard Cournot model without facing the problems associated with finitely or infinitely repeated games. Since the firms' commitments expire at different times, they actually are reacting to each other over time.

The alternating-move quantity game is a finite, perfect information game, so it (generically) has a unique perfect equilibrium. But the dynamics in this game's

[108]Of course, there are strategic aspects to pricing decisions whenever today's prices or outputs influence future competition through *other* state variables. For example, in the case of learning-by-doing, the state variable is cumulative sales, which is influenced by current prices. I return to these other state variables below.

perfect equilibrium are *not* trivial as they are in a finitely repeated Cournot game. Rather, we find a series of strategic commitments by the firms: each firm realizes when it comes to select a quantity that its choice will affect its rival's subsequent decision. Since these reaction functions are negatively sloped in the quantity game, each firm has an incentive to produce more than the Cournot duopoly output, much as we saw overinvestment in, say, Dixit (1980). Restricting their attention to quadratic payoff functions (such as would arise with linear demand and constant marginal costs), Cyert and DeGroot show that each firm's reaction function is linear. They use numerical methods to examine the limiting properties of the reaction functions as the finite horizon becomes long. In their example, the limiting behavior is indeed more competitive than Cournot behavior.

More recently, Maskin and Tirole (1987) have examined this same alternating-move game for more general profit functions and using an infinite horizon. They use the term *Markov perfect equilibrium* for the state–space approach, since the state space consists exactly of the rival's last quantity choice.[109] After displaying the general differential equations that the equilibrium reaction functions, $R_1(x_2)$ and $R_2(x_1)$, must satisfy, they too restrict attention to quadratic payoff functions. Looking for symmetric equilibria in linear reaction functions, they are able to prove that there exists a unique linear Markov perfect equilibrium, that this equilibrium is dynamically stable (i.e. from any starting point the output levels converge to the steady state), and that this equilibrium is the limit of Cyert and DeGroot's finite-horizon equilibrium.[110] They also establish that each firm's steady-state output is strictly greater than the Cournot output, unless the single-period discount factor, δ, equals zero (in which case the naive Cournot adjustment process is optimal, and steady-state behavior is simply Cournot). In fact, the steady-state output increases with δ. It is of some interest to note that the limit of the alternating-move game as the time between moves becomes small ($\delta \to 1$) does *not* approach the repeated Cournot outcome of the (finite-horizon) simultaneous-move game.

As we might expect, the more important is the future (large δ), the greater incentive each firm has to pre-empt its rival by expanding output; the equilibrium consequence is lower per-period prices and profits than under Cournot behavior. In this sense Maskin and Tirole's analysis provides support in an explicitly dynamic model for strategic principles we discovered in two-period models. But beware: what was technically a very simple problem in the two-period model – the

[109]See the first paper in their series, Maskin and Tirole (1988a), for further discussion of the Markov perfect equilibrium solution concept. They point out, for example, that a Markov perfect equilibrium is also a perfect equilibrium: given that other firms react only to the state variables, a single firm can also ignore the non payoff-relevant aspects of history.

[110]Here we have an example of why infinite horizon models can be easier to work with than their finite horizon counterparts: with the finite horizon, the reaction functions must be of the form $R_{it}(x_j)$; firm i's reaction depends not only on j's last move, x_j, but also on the number of periods remaining, hence t. With an infinite horizon, by contrast, we can write simply $R_i(x_j)$.

overinvestment result in the case of "strategic substitutes" – has become quite difficult in the infinite horizon model, and indeed has only been established in the very special case of linear demand and constant marginal costs. Note also that the assumption of alternating moves is somewhat artificial; this becomes all the more apparent if one considers more than two firms: oligopoly is not a board game.[111]

Just as we made the distinction between repeated quantity and repeated pricing games in Section 3, we can study alternating-move games in which the duopolists set prices rather than quantities. Maskin and Tirole (1986b) provides an excellent analysis of Markov perfect equilibria in the alternating-move pricing game with homogeneous products and constant marginal costs. Now each firm's strategy specifies a price that it will set in response to its rival's price: $R_1(p_2)$ and $R_2(p_1)$.

Unlike their unique symmetric equilibrium in the alternating-move quantity game, Maskin and Tirole identify multiple equilibria in the pricing game. They establish by means of examples that both Edgeworth cycles (see Subsection 2.2) or kinked demand curves (see Subsection 2.4) can be supported as Markov perfect equilibria. In the Edgeworth cycle equilibrium, each firm undercuts the other until prices are driven to marginal cost, at which point one of the firms (with positive probability) raises its price (to the monopoly price).[112] In the kinked demand curve equilibrium, each firm would more than match a price reduction (making such behavior unprofitable), but would not respond to a price increase. The equilibrium strategies here too involve mixing, but now mixing does not arise in equilibrium. Maskin and Tirole go on to characterize the class of kinked demand curve equilibria and to prove that for δ close to unity, an Edgeworth cycle equilibrium must exist. For δ close to unity, they also show that the monopoly pricing kinked demand curve is the only renegotiation-proof Markov perfect equilibrium (see Section 3 above for a discussion of the renegotiation-proof criterion).

We might expect on the basis of our two-period models that strategic pricing behavior would be quite different from strategic output choices, since each firm now recognizes that a higher price on its part will lead its rival to set a higher price in the subsequent period ("strategic complements"). Dynamic pricing reactions should lead to more collusive behavior than the static pricing game, although the reverse was true in the quantity game. Maskin and Tirole show that the intuition from two-period models does indeed extend – with some complications – to the infinite horizon model. In the quantity game, the cross partial derivatives of the profit function, $\partial^2\pi_i/\partial x_i\,\partial x_j$, are negative, leading to

[111]But Maskin and Tirole make significant progress in endogenizing the timing of the moves in their series of papers (1987, 1988a, 1988b).

[112]As Maskin and Tirole point out, these cycles do not rely on capacity constraints, as did Edgeworth's (1925) original example.

dynamic reaction functions that are negatively sloped and behavior that is more competitive than Cournot. In the pricing game, the comparable cross partials, $\partial^2\pi_i/\partial p_i\,\partial p_j$, vary in sign depending upon p_i and p_j, so the dynamic reaction functions are nonmonotonic; this is the source of the multiple equilibria. But in general, the Markov perfect equilibrium profits of the firms are positive, as opposed to the zero profits in the static Bertrand model with constant and equal marginal costs. And an increase in δ, i.e. more rapid responses, leads to more competitive behavior in the quantity game, but may well allow the monopoly price to be supported in a kinked demand curve equilibrium in the pricing game. This comparison of price and quantity games is encouraging insofar as it suggests that the findings in the two-period model are robust. By contrast, remember that there was virtually no distinction between pricing and quantity competition in supergames with δ near unity.

Another reason why prices or quantities might serve as commitments is that they may be costly to change. For the case of quantities, I defer this to the following subsection on capacities and investment games. Analyses of dynamic pricing games when there is a "menu cost" of changing prices have been developed by Marshak and Selten (1978) and Anderson (1985). both of these papers study games in which each firm can react very quickly to its rivals' price changes, but must incur a (small) cost every time it changes its own price. Anderson shows how collusion can be supported using simple strategies that match price cuts but not price increases (as in the kinked demand curve theory of oligopoly), even when the costs of changing prices are very small. More recently, Gertner (1985) has studied the Maskin and Tirole alternating-move model under the assumption that each firm bears a cost whenever it changes its price. This modification increases the number of state variables from one to two: even when firm 1 is on the move, its previous price (as well as firm 2's previous price) matters, because firm 1 would bear a cost if it were to set any other price. Gertner assumes that the firms can react quickly enough to each other's price changes so that no firm could benefit from a price change solely on the basis of its profits prior to its rival's reaction. He then establishes that the monopoly price can be supported as an equilibrium, although this is not the unique equilibrium. He also argues that the renegotiation-proof criterion can be used to select the monopoly price equilibrium.

5.4. Investment games

Much of my discussion of prices vs. quantities, the importance of dynamics, etc. suggests that we should study dynamic oligopoly when the firms make strategic investment decisions (with the state variables being physical capital stocks), and tactical pricing decisions. We did analyze two-period models of this sort in Section 4 above; it would be very useful to extend these models to many periods.

Much of the literature on dynamic investment games aims to understand the role of physical capital investments in deterring entry. The main references here are Spence (1979), Eaton and Lipsey (1980, 1981), and Fudenberg and Tirole (1983b). See Chapter 8 by Gilbert in this Handbook for further discussion of these games.

Rather few papers explore dynamic oligopolistic interactions among established firms who can make physical capital investments. One such model is Gilbert and Harris (1984), which investigates the time pattern of investments in a growing market. Gilbert and Harris assume that investments are "lumpy", i.e. come in discrete plant units. Given the state variable, k, the number of plants that have been built, each firm earns a flow of profits per plant of $p(k)$.[113] They look for the perfect equilibrium of investment dates. Since they assume that a plant is infinitely durable and allows production at constant marginal cost up to capacity, they effectively are looking at dynamic quantity choices, where quantities can only rise over time. Of course, infinitely durable capital permits firms to make significant, lasting commitments. Gilbert and Harris show that in a perfect equilibrium the race to install the next plant implies that it will be built as soon as market conditions are favorable enough so that it can earn non-negative profits. Of course, these profits must be computed over the entire, infinite lifetime of the plant, accounting for all future construction. This analysis shows how capacity competition can dissipate profits; but the paper does not give us much guidance on how investments affect tactical oligopoly pricing behavior, since the firms are assumed always to produce at capacity.

Benoit and Krishna (1987) and Davidson and Deneckere (1985b) examine the effect of investments on pricing strategies in a model where capacity choices are strategic and pricing competition is of the Bertrand–Edgeworth variety. Basically, they extend the two-period model of Kreps and Scheinkman (1983) to many periods.[114] In a duopoly model where the firms make once-and-for-all capacity choices and then compete via prices, we know from the Kreps and Scheinkman paper that it is an equilibrium for the firms to choose their Cournot quantities as capacities and then set the Cournot prices in each subsequent period; this is a trivial extension of the two-period model. But the point of extending the pricing game to many periods is to identify *other* symmetric equilibria.

[113] This reduced-form profit function would come about if, say, each plant had a unit capacity and involved no variable costs, and if the tactical oligopoly behavior involves production at capacity for all plants.

[114] Davidson and Deneckere use the same rationing rule (high value consumers buy at the lower price), and both papers use the same production technology (a firm with capacity x can produce up to x at no cost, but cannot produce more than x) as do Kreps and Scheinkman. Benoit and Krishna assume for some of their results that the demand function is concave, $p''(X) < 0$, whereas Davidson and Deneckere take demand to be linear.

Given initial investment levels $\{x_1, x_2\}$, we have a price-setting supergame with capacity constraints. So this analysis also extends Brock and Scheinkman's (1985) paper, which examined the pricing supergame under the assumption of exogenously given and equal capacities (see Section 3 above). Benoit and Krishna are able to establish the existence of equilibria involving higher prices than under Cournot behavior. By replacing the one-shot pricing game in the second period of Kreps and Scheinkman's two-period model with a pricing supergame, more collusive pricing equilibria are possible. This in turn has implications for the capacity decisions in the initial period. In particular, all equilibria other than the "Cournot" one involve the firms choosing capacities in excess of their subsequent production levels.[115] Both Benoit and Krishna, and Davidson and Deneckere, stress the result that the firms build excess capacity in order to better discipline their subsequent pricing behavior.[116] Firm 1 must build some excess capacity if it is to be in a position to punish firm 2 for expanding *its* capacity. In this sense, it is costly for the firms to sustain outcomes more collusive than Cournot.

It is also possible to wed capacity choices with the alternating move pricing games discussed in the previous subsection. Maskin and Tirole (1986b) find examples with small capacity costs and a discount factor near unity in which the firms build excess capacity that is never used. Gertner (1985) also identifies a strategic role for excess capacity in his model of price inertia.

5.5. *Intangible state variables*

In markets where the oligopolists face considerable uncertainty about underlying conditions, there is a potential role for strategic information manipulation or signaling. The state variables are the firms' or consumers' posteriors regarding such relevant variables as cost or demand parameters. Firms may invest, in the sense of sacrificing current profits, in order to manipulate their rivals' beliefs in a favorable way. In such games, it is important to specify the process by which beliefs are updated, both in and out of equilibrium (just as *behavior* in and out of equilibrium is essential in understanding perfect equilibria). The workhorse solution concept is thus *Bayesian perfect equilibrium*, which combines Harsanyi's (1967–68) solution concept for games of incomplete information with the credibility constraints of perfect equilibrium. See also Kreps and Wilson (1982a) for an articulation of the slightly more sophisticated sequential equilibrium solution concept, and Fudenberg and Tirole, Chapter 5 in this Handbook, for a further

[115] This result need not carry over to games in which the investment decisions can be modified quickly (the limiting case of this being the standard pricing supergame with constant marginal costs). Benoit and Krishna also study a model with this type of "flexible capacity".

[116] The topsy-turvy principle (large capacities allow firms to behave very competitively and hence support collusion) has now infected the investment game, since the continuation game following capacity choices is a supergame.

discussion of refinements of solution concepts in dynamic games with incomplete information.

What sort of uncertain variables are important for oligopolistic rivalry, and how might a firm be able to manipulate its rivals' expectations about these variables? The natural candidates are cost parameters and demand parameters. In quantity competition, for example, firm 1 benefits if firm 2 believes either (a) that firm 1's costs are low, (b) that firm 2's own costs are high, or (c) that demand is low.[117] Therefore, firm 1 will try to take actions to convince firm 2 that firm 1's costs are low. The theory of signaling tells us that for an action to signal low costs, it must be easier to undertake by a firm whose costs really are low. The obvious strategy is to expand output as a signal of lower costs. In equilibrium, today's output by firm 1 affects firm 2's beliefs about firm 1's costs. Of course, firm 2 understands firm 1's signaling incentives, and in a separating equilibrium it infers firm 1's costs perfectly. Therefore, firm 1's "disinformation" campaign is not successful; but the campaign nonetheless has an effect on firm 1's behavior. I refer the reader to Wilson (1983) and especially to Roberts (1987) for a more extensive discussion of these incomplete information models than is provided here.

Much of the literature on information manipulation has focused on the possibility of entry deterrence. This emphasis is natural, since it permits one to examine models with a single incumbent engaging in strategic signaling. The usual reference here is Milgrom and Roberts (1982a). Again, see Gilbert, Chapter 8 in this Handbook. Other papers study information manipulation, or "bluffing", as a predatory tactic; see Kreps and Wilson (1982b), Milgrom and Roberts (1982b), or Salop and Shapiro (1980). These applications of strategic signaling are covered in Chapter 9 on predation by Ordover and Saloner (1987) in this Handbook. Kreps, Milgrom, Roberts and Wilson (1982) come much closer to oligopoly theory in applying these same ideas to the repeated prisoner's dilemma game.

While little work has been done on information models in the context of dynamic oligopoly, many of the principles discovered in the entry deterrence and predation literatures have implications for oligopolistic behavior in markets where private information is significant. In repeated Cournot models with private demand information, for example, we expect more competitive behavior as firms try to send unfavorable demand information to their rivals [see Riordon (1985) again]. With uncertain information about firm-specific costs, we would again expect more competitive behavior than repeated Cournot, as firms attempt to signal their low costs to their competitors. But if a quantity-setting firm is signaling *industrywide* cost conditions via its outputs, we may have less competi-

[117]See the related discussion in Section 4 above. And note that (a) and (c) are reversed in the case of pricing competition. As usual, strategic incentives depend upon the slope of the reaction curves.

tive behavior.[118] And these results would probably be reversed if firms set prices rather than quantities. The incomplete information theories also can be applied to study a declining industry, as the firms engage in a war of attrition [although this situation has only been analyzed for the case of uncertain fixed costs – see Fudenberg and Tirole (1986b)], with each trying to send a signal to the other that will induce exit.

5.6. *Simple state–space games*

Clearly, there are many more dimensions of industry behavior that might serve as state variables and be subject to strategic control. I provided many such examples in Section 4 above. Here I indicate (without any claim of being comprehensive) a very few simple state variables that have been or might be examined in infinite horizon models. I see this as a promising area for future research, constrained mainly by the tractability of differential games.

(1) *Sunk investments*. A simple state variable is the extent of commitment to the market made by various sellers in the form of sunk investments. Models of this sort can become tractable if the state–space and the reduced-form profit functions are kept very simple. Gilbert and Harris (1984) did this by restricting attention to unit lumps of capital, so the state variable was a non-negative integer (as well as the date, since they studied a growing market). Likewise, Dixit and Shapiro (1986) consider the number of firms currently committed to the market (where each firm can either be "IN" or "OUT"). By assuming that flow profits are a simple reduced-form function of the number of firms (or plants), the game can be solved.

(2) *Learning-by-doing or network externalities*. With learning-by-doing or network externalities, previous sales affect the firms' current positions. With learning-by-doing, these sales affect current and future costs; with network externalities, it is demand that depends upon past sales. If the learning spills over across firms so that each firm learns equally from its own production and from production by rivals, the relevant state variable is cumulative industrywide sales; see Stokey (1986) for a fine analysis of this case. Cumulative industrywide sales also constitute the state variable in the case of network externalities where all products are fully compatible (so that a consumer only cares how many other consumers in total have bought, not which brands they purchased). Without perfect spillovers in the case of learning-by-doing, or without perfect product compatibility in the networks case, the state variables are cumulative sales by each of the firms. See Spence (1981) and Farrell and Saloner (1986), respectively.

[118]This is the oligopoly theory parallel to Harrington's (1986) point that a firm would lower its output to deter entry if it is signaling industrywide costs, the reverse of Milgrom and Roberts (1982a) finding in the case of firm-specific costs.

(3) *Consumer switching costs*. With consumer lock-in, previous choices by consumers affect current and future rivalry. Now the simple state variables are the market shares, say, of the rival firms. Farrell and Shapiro (1987) are able to solve a simple game of this sort by assuming identical tastes and identical switching costs across consumers, thereby greatly narrowing down the state space.

(4) *Shallow pockets*. In many markets, firms find it increasingly difficult or costly to attract financing as they attempt to borrow more money. Given these borrowing constraints, the firms' profits at a given date affect their investment opportunities at later dates. Then the firms' cash reserves constitute state variables, and aggressive pricing by one firm may serve a strategic purpose of undermining its rival's financial standing. Judd and Petersen (1986) have explored this type of effect in the context of entry deterrence.

(5) *R&D competition*. In dynamic R&D competition, the natural state variables are the firms' current progress on their R&D projects. See especially Fudenberg, Gilbert, Stiglitz and Tirole (1983), Harris and Vickers (1985), and Grossman and Shapiro (1987) for simple R&D state–space games in which a firm may have a lead or fall behind in the race.

This list of state variables in dynamic games is by no means exhaustive; I have omitted, for example, games with exogenously changing conditions in which the only state variable is time itself. But this brief list should indicate the range of possibilities for dynamic, state–space models. Further work in these and related areas may prove fruitful, as virtually all of the work on these topics is confined to two-period models. The main barrier to further progress at this point in time is simply tractability.

6. Conclusions

Having warned the reader at the outset that there are many theories of oligopoly, I am left with the task of identifying the lessons learned from the collection of models discussed above. I would emphasize my view that the variety of models of oligopolistic interactions is a virtue, not a defect. I would seek a single theory of oligopolistic behavior no more than I would a single set of behavioral rules for the survival of all species. Yes, some types of behavior, such as protecting one's young or developing the ability to survive on a varied diet, are beneficial to a wide variety of species, but the principle that tacit collusion works better when defections can be swiftly detected and punished has comparable generality. And just as the tactic of strategic investment works only in certain industries, survival based on being large and powerful and thereby having the ability to fend off predators is utilized by only a modest number of species.

What then are the lessons we can draw from the various models surveyed here? I regard these game-theoretic models as providing the industry analyst with a bag of tools. In other words, we have been able to identify quite a large number of strategic considerations that come into play when there are large firms and enough sunk costs so that threats of entry are not the primary determinate of industry behavior, at least for the short to medium run. One class of strategic behavior revolves around firms' efforts to tacitly collude, i.e. to favorably solve their basic prisoner's dilemma problem. Here we have learned about the factors that tend to facilitate collusion, e.g. careful monitoring of rival actions, the ability to write contracts with automatic price matching provisions, or the ability to change prices or production levels quickly in response to other firms' actions. The second class of behavior that we understand better on the basis of these models is that of strategic investment, where investment ranges from expenditures on sunk physical capital to strategic manipulation of a rival's information about market conditions. While there are no general results in the area of strategic investment, we have enough examples to understand quite well the strategic role of many business practices. What we are most in need of now are further tests of the empirical validity of these various theories of strategic behavior.[119]

Let me close with a sort of user's guide to the many oligopoly models I have discussed. By "user", I mean one who is attempting to use these models to better understand a given industry (not someone out to build yet another model). Here is where the "bag of tools" analogy applies. After learning the basic facts about an industry, the analyst with a working understanding of oligopoly theory should be able to use these tools to identify the main strategic aspects present in that industry.[120] One industry may be competitive because rapid expansions in capacity are possible in short order and consumers are willing to switch suppliers in response to small price differentials. In another industry, advertising may serve a key strategic role, since brand loyalty is significant. Yet another industry may succeed in achieving a tacitly collusive outcome because secret price-cutting is impossible. And so on. Hopefully, as further progress is made, we will learn about additional modes of strategic behavior and understand more fully the strategies already identified.

References

Abreu, D. (1986) 'Extremal equilibria of oligopolistic supergames', *Journal of Economic Theory*, 39:191–225.

Abreu, D. (1988) 'On the theory of infinitely repeated games with discounting', *Econometrica*, 56:383–396.

[119]See Chapter 17 by Bresnahan in this Handbook for a survey of the relevant empirical findings.

[120]Of course, entry conditions may be such that the interactions among active producers are of secondary importance. This depends very much on the magnitude of sunk costs in the industry. I refer the reader to the chapters on contestability and entry deterrence for a working understanding of these essential components of industry analysis.

Abreu, D., Milgrom, P. and Pearce, D. (1987) 'Information, timing, and repeated partnership', Harvard University, unpublished.

Abreu, D., Pearce, D. and Stacchetti, E. (1986) 'Optimal cartel equilibria with imperfect monitoring', *Journal of Economic Theory*, 39:251–269.

Anderson, R. (1985) 'Quick-response equilibrium', University of California, Berkeley, unpublished.

Arvan, L. (1985) 'Some examples of dynamic Cournot duopoly with inventory', *Rand Journal of Economics*, 16:569–578.

Axelrod, R. (1984) *The Evolution of Cooperation*. New York: Basic books.

Beckman, M. (1965) 'Edgeworth–Bertrand duopoly revisited', in: R. Henn, ed., *Operations Research Verfahren, III*. Verlag Anton Hain: Meisenhein.

Benoit, J.P. and Krishna, V. (1985) 'Finitely repeated games', *Econometrica*, 53:905–922.

Benoit, J.P. and Krishna, V. (1987) 'Dynamic duopoly: Prices and quantities', *Review of Economic Studies*, 54:23–35.

Bergstrom, T. (1979) 'Cournot equilibrium with factor markets', University of Michigan.

Bergstrom, T. and Varian, H. (1985a) 'Two remarks on Cournot equilibria', *Economics Letters*, 19:5–8.

Bergstrom, T. and Varian, H. (1985b) 'When are Nash equilibria independent of the distribution of agents' characteristics?' *Review of Economic Studies*, 52:715–718.

Bernheim, D. and Ray, D. (1987) 'Collective dynamic consistency in repeated games', Stanford University, unpublished.

Bernheim, B.D. and Whinston, M.D. (1985) 'Common marketing agency as a device for facilitating collusion', *Rand Journal of Economics*, 16:269–281.

Bertrand, J. (1883) 'Book review of *Theorie mathematique de la richesse sociale* and of *Recherches sur les principles mathematiques de la theorie des richesses*', *Journal des Savants*, 67:499–508.

Bowley, A. (1924) *Mathematical Foundations of Economics*. New York: Oxford University Press.

Brander, J.A. and Eaton, J. (1984) 'Product line rivalry', *American Economic Review*, 74:323–334.

Brander, J.A. and Lewis, T.R. (1985) 'Bankruptcy costs and the theory of oligopoly', University of British Columbia.

Brander, J.A. and Lewis, T.R. (1986) 'Oligopoly and financial structure: the limited liability effect', *American Economic Review*, 76:956–970.

Brander, J. and Spencer, B. (1983) 'Strategic commitment with R&D: The symmetric case', *Bell Journal of Economics*, 14:225–235.

Brander, J. and Spencer, B. (1985) 'Export subsidies and international market share rivalry', *Journal of International Economics*, 18:83–100.

Bresnahan, T.F. (1981) 'Duopoly models with consistent conjectures', *American Economic Review*, 71:934–94.

Brock, W.A. and Scheinkman, J.A. (1985) 'Price-setting supergames with capacity constraints', *Review of Economic Studies*, 52:371–382.

Bulow, J., Geanakopolos, J. and Klemperer, P. (1985) 'Multimarket oligopoly: Strategic substitutes and complements', *Journal of Political Economy*, 93:488–511.

Cheng, L. (1985) 'Comparing Bertrand and Cournot equilibria: A geometric approach', *Rand Journal of Economics*, 16:146–152.

Cooper, T.E. (1986) 'Most-favored-customer pricing and tacit collusion', *Rand Journal of Economics*, 17:377–388.

Cournot, A.A. (1838) *Researches into the mathematical principles of the theory of wealth*, English edition of *Researches sur les principles mathematiques de la theorie des richesses*. New York: Kelley.

Cyert, R.M. and Degroot, M. (1970) 'Multiperiod decision models with alternating choice as a solution to the duopoly problem', *Quarterly Journal of Economics*, 84:410–429.

Dansby, R.E. and Willig, R.D. (1979) 'Industry performance gradient indices', *American Economic Review*, 69:249–260.

Dasgupta, P. and Maskin, E. (1986) 'The existence of equilibria in discontinuous economic games II: Applications', *Review of Economic Studies*, 53:27–41.

Daughety, A.F. (1985) 'Reconsidering Cournot: The Cournot equilibrium is consistent', *Rand Journal of Economics*, 16:368–379.

Davidson, C. and Deneckere, R. (1985a) 'Incentives to form coalitions with Bertrand competition', *Rand Journal of Economics*, 16:473–486.

Davidson, C. and Deneckere, R. (1985b) 'Excess capacity and collusion', Michigan State University, unpublished.

Davidson, C. and Deneckere, R. (1986) 'Long-run competition in capacity, short-run competition in price, and the Cournot model', *Rand Journal of Economics*, 17:404–415.

Dixit, A.K. (1980) 'The role of investment in entry deterrence', *Economic Journal*, 90:95–106.

Dixit, A.K. (1982) 'Recent developments in oligopoly theory', *American Economic Review*, 72:12–17.

Dixit, A.K. (1986) 'Comparative statics for oligopoly', *International Economic Review*, 27:107–122.

Dixit, A.K. and Grossman, G. (1986) 'Targeted export promotion with several oligopolistic industries', *Journal of International Economics*, 20, forthcoming.

Dixit, A.K. and Kyle, A.S. (1985) 'The use of protection and subsidies for entry promotion and deterence', *American Economic Review*, 75:139–152.

Dixit, A.K. and Shapiro, C. (1986) 'Entry dynamics with mixed strategies', in: L.G. Thomas, ed., *Strategic planning*. Lexington, Mass.: Lexington Books, 63–79.

Dixon, H. (1986) 'The Cournot and Bertrand outcomes as equilibria in a strategic metagame', *Economic Journal*, 96:59–70.

Domowitz, I., Hubbard, R.G. and Petersen, B.C. (1986) 'Business cycles and the relationship between concentration and price–cost margins', *Rand Journal of Economics*, 17:1–17.

Doyle, C. (1985) 'Price matching strategies and oligopoly', Department of Applied Economics, University of Cambridge, unpublished.

Eaton, B.C. and Lipsey, R.G. (1980) 'Exit barriers are entry barriers: The durability of capital as a barrier to entry', *Bell Journal of Economics*, 11:721–729.

Eaton, B.C. and Lipsey, R.G. (1981) 'Capital, commitment, and entry equilibrium', *Bell Journal of Economics*, 12:593–604.

Eaton, J. and Grossman, G. (1986) 'Optimal trade and industrial policy under oligopoly', *Quarterly Journal of Economics*, 101:383–406.

Edgeworth, F. (1925) 'The pure theory of monopoly', *Papers Relating to Political Economy*, 1:111–142.

Farrell, J. and Maskin, E. (1987) 'Notes on renegotiation in repeated games', Harvard University, unpublished.

Farrell, J. and Saloner, G. (1986) 'Installed base and compatibility: Innovation, product preannouncements, and predation', *American Economic Review*, 76:940–955.

Farrell, J. and Shapiro, C. (1987) 'Dynamic competition with switching costs', *Rand Journal of Economics*, 19:123–137.

Farrell, J. and Shapiro, C. (1988) 'Horizontal mergers: An equilibrium analysis', John M. Olin Discussion Paper no. 17, Princeton University.

Fershtman, C. and Judd, K. (1984) 'Equilibrium incentives in oligopoly', *American Economic Review*, 77:927–940.

Fisher, I. (1898) 'Cournot and mathematical economics', *Quarterly Journal of Economics*, 12:119–138.

Friedman, J.W. (1968) 'Reaction functions and the theory of duopoly', *Review of Economic Studies*, 35:257–272.

Friedman, J.W. (1971) 'A noncooperative equilibrium for supergames', *Review of Economic Studies*, 38:1–12.

Friedman, J.W. (1977) *Oligopoly and the theory of games*. New York: North-Holland.

Friedman, J.W. (1983) *Oligopoly theory*. New York: Cambridge University Press.

Friedman, J.W. (1985) 'Cooperative equilibria in finite horizon noncooperative supergames', *Journal of Economic Theory*, 35:290–398.

Fudenberg, D. and Maskin, E. (1986) 'The folk theorem in repeated games with discounting and incomplete information', *Econometrica*, 54:533–554.

Fudenberg, D. and Tirole, J. (1983a) 'Learning by doing and market performance', *Bell Journal of Economics*, 14:522–530.

Fudenberg, D. and Tirole, J. (1983b) 'Capital as commitment: Strategic investment to deter mobility', *Journal of Economic Theory*, 31:227–250.

Fudenberg, D. and Tirole, J. (1984) 'The fat-cat effect, the puppy-dog ploy and the lean and hungry look', *American Economic Review Papers and Proceedings*, 74:361–366.

Fudenberg, D. and Tirole, J. (1986a) 'Dynamic models of oligopoly', in: A. Jacquemin, ed., *Fundamentals of pure and applied economics*, vol. 3. New York: Harwood.

Fudenberg, D. and Tirole, J. (1986b) 'A theory of exit in duopoly', *Econometrica*, 54:943–960.

Fudenberg, D., Gilbert, R., Stiglitz, J. and Tirole, J. (1983) 'Preemption, leapfrogging, and competition in patent races', *European Economic Review*, 22:3–31.

Gelman, J. and Salop, S. (1983) 'Capacity limitation and coupon competition', *Bell Journal of Economics*, 14:315–325.

Gertner, R. (1985) 'Dynamic duopoly with price inertia', Department of Economics, M.I.T., unpublished.

Ghemawat, P. and Nalebuff, B. (1985) 'Exit', *Rand Journal of Economics*, 16:184–193.

Gilbert, R. and Harris, R. (1984) 'Competition with lumpy investment', *Rand Journal of Economics*, 15:197–212.

Green, E. and Porter, R. (1984) 'Noncooperative collusion under imperfect price information', *Econometrica*, 52:87–100.

Grossman, G. and Shapiro, C. (1987) 'Dynamic R&D competition', *Economic Journal*, 97:372–387.

Grossman, S. (1981) 'Nash equilibrium and the industrial organization of markets with large fixed costs', *Econometrica*, 49:1149–1172.

Hahn, F. (1962) 'The stability of the Cournot oligopoly solution concept', *Review of Economic Studies*, 29:329–331.

Hall, R.L. and Hitch, C.J. (1939) 'Price theory and business behavior', *Oxford Economic Papers*, 2:12–45.

Harrington, J. (1986) 'Limit pricing when the potential entrant is uncertain of its cost function', *Econometrica*, 54:429–437.

Harris, C. and Vickers, J. (1985) 'Perfect equilibrium in a model of a race', *Review of Economic Studies*, 52:193–209.

Harsanyi, J.C. (1967–68) 'Games with incomplete information played by Bayesian players', Parts I, II, and III, *Management Science*, 14:159–182, 320–334, 486–502.

Holt, C. and Scheffman, D. (1986) 'Facilitating practices: The effects of advance notice and best-price policies', *Rand Journal of Economics*, 18:187–197.

Judd, K. (1985) 'Credible spatial preemption', *Rand Journal of Economics*, 16:153–166.

Judd, K. and Petersen, B. (1986) 'Dynamic limit pricing and internal finance', *Journal of Economic theory*, 39:368–399.

Katz, M. (1987) 'Game-playing agents: Contracts as precommitments', Department of Economics, Princeton University, unpublished.

Katz, M.L. and Shapiro, C. (1985) 'On the licensing of innovations', *Rand Journal of Economics*, 16:504–520.

Katz, M.L. and Shapiro, C. (1986a) 'Technology adoption in the presence of network externalities', *Journal of Political Economy*, 94:822–841.

Katz, M.L. and Shapiro, C. (1986b) 'Product compatibility choice in a market with technological progress', *Oxford Economic Papers*, 38:146–165.

Klemperer, P. (1985) 'Markets with consumer switching costs', *Quarterly Journal of Economics*, 102:375–394.

Klemperer, P. and Meyer, M. (1985) 'Price competition vs. quantity competition: The role of uncertainty', *Rand Journal of Economics*, 17:618–638.

Klemperer, P. and Meyer, M. (1986) 'Supply function equilibria under uncertainty', Graduate School of Business, Stanford University.

Kreps, D. and Scheinkman, J. (1983) 'Quantity pre-commitment and Bertrand competition yield Cournot outcomes', *Bell Journal of Economics*, 14:326–337.

Kreps, D. and Spence, A.M. (1985) 'Modelling the role of history in industrial organization and competition', in: G.R. Feiwel, ed., *Issues in contemporary microeconomics and welfare*. London: MacMillan, 340–378.

Kreps, D. and Wilson, R. (1982a) 'Sequential equilibrium', *Econometrica*, 50:863–894.

Kreps, D. and Wilson, R. (1982b) 'Reputation and imperfect information', *Journal of Economic Theory*, 27:253–279.

Kreps, D., Milgrom, P., Roberts, J. and Wilson, R. (1982) 'Rational cooperation in the finitely repeated prisoners' dilemma', *Journal of Economic Theory*, 27:245–252.

Krugman, P. (1984) 'Import protection as export promotion: International competition in the presence of oligopoly and economies of scale', in: H. Kierzkowski, *Monopolistic competition and international trade*. New York: Oxford University Press, 180–193.

Laitner, J. (1980) 'Rational duopoly equilibrium', *Quarterly Journal of Economics*, 95:641–662.

Levitan, R. and Shubik, M. (1972) 'Price duopoly and capacity constraints', *International Economic Review*, 14:326–337.

Mailath, G. (1985) 'Welfare in a simultaneous signaling duopoly model', Caress working paper no. 85-29, University of Pennsylvania.

Makowski, L. (1983) '"Rational conjectures" aren't rational, "reasonable conjectures" aren't reasonable', economic theory discussion paper no. 66, University of Cambridge.

Marshak, T. and Selten, R. (1978) 'Restabilizing responses, inertia supergames and oligopolistic equilibria', *Quarterly Journal of Economics*, 92:71–93.

Maskin, E. (1986) 'The existence of equilibrium with price-setting firms', *American Economic Review*, 76:382–386.

Maskin, E. and Tirole, J. (1987) 'A theory of dynamic oligopoly III: Cournot competition', *European Economic Review*, 31:947–968.

Maskin, E. and Tirole, J. (1988a) 'A theory of dynamic oligopoly I: Overview and quantity competition with large fixed costs', *Econometrica*, 56:549–569.

Maskin, E. and Tirole, J. (1988b) 'A theory of dynamic oligopoly II: Price competition, kinked demand curves, and Edgeworth cycles', *Econometrica*, 56:571–599.

Milgrom, P. and Roberts, J. (1982a) 'Limit pricing and entry under incomplete information: An equilibrium analysis', *Econometrica*, 50:443–459.

Milgrom, P. and Roberts, J. (1982b) 'Predation reputation and entry deterrence', *Journal of Economic Theory*, 27:280–312.

Milgrom, P. and Roberts, J. (1987) 'Information asymmetries, strategic behavior, and industrial organization', *American Economic Review Papers and Proceedings*, 77:184–193.

Nelson, R. and Winter, S. (1982) *An evolutionary theory of economic change*. Cambridge, Mass.: Harvard University Press.

Novshek, W. (1980) 'Cournot equilibrium with free entry', *Review of Economic Studies*, 47:473–486.

Novshek, W. (1985) 'On the existence of Cournot equilibrium', *Review of Economic Studies*, 52:85–98.

Osborne, M. and Pitchik, C. (1984) 'Price competition in a capacity-constrained duopoly', discussion paper no. 185, Department of Economics, Columbia University.

Pearce, D. (1987) 'Renegotiation-proof equilibria: Collective rationality and intertemporal cooperation', Yale University, unpublished.

Perry, M. (1982) 'Oligopoly and consistent conjectural variations', *Bell Journal of Economics*, 13:197–205.

Perry, M. and Porter, R. (1985) 'Oligopoly and the incentive for horizontal merger', *American Economic Review*, 75:219–227.

Porter, R. (1983a) 'Optimal cartel trigger-price strategies', *Journal of Economic Theory*, 29:313–338.

Porter, R. (1983b) 'A study of cartel stability: The joint executive committee, 1880–1886', *Rand Journal of Economics*, 14:301–314.

Prescott, E. and Visscher, M. (1977) 'Sequential location among firms with foresight', *Bell Journal of Economics*, 8:378–394.

Radner, R. (1980) 'Collusive behavior in noncooperative epsilon-equilibria of oligopolies with long but finite lives', *Journal of Economic Theory*, 22:136–154.

Radner, R. (1986) 'Repeated partnership games with imperfect monitoring and no discounting', *Review of Economic Studies*, 53:43–57.

Riordan, M. (1985) 'Imperfect information and dynamic conjectural variations', *Rand Journal of Economics*, 16:41–50.

Roberts, J. (1987) 'Battles for market share: Incomplete information, aggressive strategic pricing, and competitive dynamics', in: T. Bewley, ed., *Advances in economic theory, invited papers from the Vth World Congress*. New York: Cambridge University Press.

Rosenthal, R. (1981) 'Games of imperfect information predatory pricing and the chain-store paradox', *Journal of Economic Theory*, 25:92–100.

Rotemberg, J. and Saloner, G. (1985) 'Strategic inventories and the excess volatility of production', working paper no. 1650-85, Sloan School of Management, M.I.T.

Rotemberg, J. and Saloner, G. (1986a) 'A supergame-theoretic model of business cycles and price wars during booms', *American Economic Review*, 76:390–407.

Rotemberg, J. and Saloner, G. (1986b) 'Quotas and the stability of implicit collusion', N.B.E.R. working paper no. 1948.

Salant, S., Switzer, S. and Reynolds, R. (1983) 'Losses from horizontal merger: The effects of an exogenous change in industry structure on Cournot–Nash equilibrium', *Quarterly Journal of Economics*, 98:185–199.

Saloner, G. (1986) 'The role of obsolescence and inventory costs in providing commitment', Department of Economics, M.I.T.

Salop, S. (1986) 'Practices that credibly facilitate oligopoly co-ordination', in: J. Stiglitz and F. Mathewson, eds., *New developments in the analysis of market structure*. Cambridge: M.I.T. Press, 265–290.

Salop, S. and Scheffman, D. (1983) 'Raising rivals' costs', *American Economic Review Papers and Proceedings*, 73:267–271.

Salop, S. and Shapiro, C. (1980) 'Test market predation', Federal Trade Commission, unpublished.

Schelling, T. (1960) *The strategy of conflict*. New York: Oxford University Press.

Scherer, F.M. (1980) *Industrial market structure and economic performance*. Chicago: Rand McNally.

Schmalensee, R. (1983) 'Advertising and entry deterrence', *Journal of Political Economy*, 90:636–653.

Schumpeter, J. (1954) *History of economic analysis*. New York: Oxford University Press.

Seade, J. (1980) 'The stability of Cournot revisited', *Journal of Economic Theory*, 23;15–27.

Seade, J. (1985) 'Profitable cost increases and the shifting of taxation: Equilibrium responses of markets in oligopoly', Warwick University, unpublished.

Shaked, A. and Sutton, J. (1982) 'Relaxing price competition through product differentiation', *Review of Economic Studies*, 49:3–14.

Shapiro, C. (1986) 'Exchange of cost information in oligopoly', *Review of Economic Studies*, 53:433–446.

Shubik, M. (1959) *Strategy and market structure*. New York: Wiley.

Singh, N. and Vives, X. (1984) 'Price and quantity competition in a differentiated duopoly', *Rand Journal of Economics*, 15:546–554.

Sklivas, S. (1985) 'The strategic choice of managerial incentives', discussion paper no. 184, Center for the Study of Organizational Innovation, University of Pennsylvania.

Spence, A.M. (1976) 'Product selection, fixed costs, and monopolistic competition', *Review of Economic Studies*, 43:217–235.

Spence, A.M. (1977) 'Entry, capacity, investment and oligopolistic pricing', *Bell Journal of Economics*, 8:534–544.

Spence, A.M. (1979) 'Investment strategy and growth in a new market', *Bell Journal of Economics*, 10:1–19.

Spence, A.M. (1981) 'The learning curve and competition', *Bell Journal of Economics*, 12:49–70.

Spence, A.M. (1984) 'Cost-reduction, competition, and industry performance', *Econometrica*, 52:101–122.

Stanford, W. (1986) 'Subgame perfect reaction function equilibria in discounted duopoly supergames are trivial', *Journal of Economic theory*, 39:226–232.

Stigler, G. (1947) 'The kinky oligopoly demand curve and rigid prices', *Journal of Political Economy*, 55:432–449.

Stigler, G. (1964) 'A theory of oligopoly', *Journal of Political Economy*, 72:44–61.

Stokey, N. (1986) 'The dynamics of industrywide learning', in: W.P. Heller, R.M. Starr and D.A. Starrett, eds., *Equilibria analysis: Essays in honor of Kenneth J. Arrow, Volume II*. London: Cambridge University Press, 81–104.

Sweezy, P. (1939) 'Demand under conditions of oligopoly', *Journal of Political Economy*, 47:568–573.

Vives, X. (1984) 'Duopoly information equilibrium Cournot and Bertrand', *Journal of Economic Theory*, 34:71–94.

Vives, X. (1985) 'On the efficiency of Cournot and Bertrand competition with product differentiation', *Journal of Economic Theory*, 36(1):166–175.

Vives, X. (1986) 'Commitment, flexibility and market outcomes', *International Journal of Industrial Organization*, 4.

von Stackelberg, H. (1934) *Marktform und Gleichgewicht*. Vienna: Springer.

Wilson, R. (1983) 'Reputations in games and markets', Stanford University, unpublished.

Chapter 7

CARTELS, COLLUSION, AND HORIZONTAL MERGER

ALEXIS JACQUEMIN

Université Catholique de Louvain

MARGARET E. SLADE*

University of British Columbia

Contents

*We would like to thank James Friedman, Paul Geroski, Victor Ginsburgh, Jonathan Hamilton, and the editors of this volume for thoughtful comments on an earlier draft.

Handbook of Industrial Organization, Volume I, Edited by R. Schmalensee and R.D. Willig

1. Introduction

Problems of industrial structure and concentration have concerned economists and politicians for at least a century. During this period, attitudes towards cartels, mergers, and collusion have undergone many changes. Nevertheless, no consensus as to an appropriate policy for dealing with increasing concentration has emerged. Instead we see trends in antitrust policy and in academic thought which evolve in a desultory fashion.

In the last decade, these difficulties have grown. Economic thought concerning collusive practices and mergers has changed profoundly, mainly in the light of game-theoretic analysis. Unfortunately, this change has not led to more general and robust conclusions. On the contrary, it is the source of a more fragmented view. The diversity of models and results, which are very sensitive to the assumption selected, suggests a "case-by-case" approach where insight into the ways in which firms acquire and maintain positions of market power becomes essential. It is nevertheless important to bring to light a typology of situations and practices for which recent developments in economic analysis offer sounder theoretical characterizations than in the past.

In this chapter we attempt to highlight the principal theoretical and practical problems of the economics of cartels, collusion, and horizontal merger. Due to space limitations, not all issues can be covered in depth or given equal weight. Furthermore, because the new theoretical approaches are not easily modified to encompass welfare considerations, except in a very partial-equilibrium setting, the positive side of the analysis has received more weight than the normative. Where coverage is summary, the interested reader can make use of the references at the end of the chapter.

The organization of the paper is as follows. In Section 2 the principal factors that facilitate or hinder collusion are considered. This is an informal discussion of the circumstances under which one might expect cartels to be stable or collusive agreements to be long-lived.

Section 3 deals with types and extent of horizontal collusion. Under this heading, we cover both explicit agreement and tacit collusion. The principal forms of explicit agreement are cartels, joint ventures, and horizontal mergers. Even though in principle these are easily distinguishable legal or illegal arrangements, it is not always simple to separate the underlying economic theory into neat categories. For example, the same considerations that might lead to a merger being privately profitable might also lead to the formation of a successful cartel. The division of the subject-matter is therefore sometimes arbitrary. In each category – mergers, cartels, and joint ventures – we try to cover both theoretical models and empirical evidence. The subject of mergers is particularly broad and we limit outselves to horizontal mergers between firms in the same product market.

The subsection on tacit collusion is not a highly technical theoretical presentation, which can be found in Chapters 5 and 6 of this Handbook. Instead, we consider the tools that can be used as instruments for tacit collusion and the likelihood of such collusion being successful. Under empirical evidence, we limit ourselves to models that are dynamic and explicitly game theoretic.

Section 4 deals with collusion, public interest, and government policy. Under this heading, we first consider the problem of identifying collusive behavior; the emphasis here is empirical. Subjects covered include testing for deviations from price-taking behavior and the conclusions that can be drawn from firm bidding strategies. We next consider collusion and restriction of competition. In particular we discuss theoretical and empirical measurement problems encountered in defining the geographic and product market where restriction of competition occurred and in estimating the deadweight loss due to this restriction.

Section 4 also discusses efficiency tradeoffs. Because many of these issues are dealt with in other chapters, the coverage herc is very summary. The subjects that are discussed include static economies of scale, scope, and product variety and dynamic efficiencies of learning and innovative activity. Finally, industrial policy is considered. The discussion centers on market failures and when such failures might call for government intervention or some form of planning.

2. Factors that facilitate or hinder collusion

Whether firms collude tacitly or overtly, legally or illegally, they face many problems. First, an agreement must be reached. Second, as soon as price is raised above the noncooperative level, firms have an incentive to cheat on the collusive arrangement. If the agreement is to persist, therefore, there must be methods of detecting cheating. And finally, once cheating is detected it must be punished. Each stage in the process has its own peculiar problems. In spite of the difficulties faced by firms, however, we do observe successful collusion.

This section discusses the factors that facilitate or hinder collusion. Our presentation borrows heavily from Stigler (1964), Scherer (1980), Gravelle and Rees (1980), Hay (1982), Cooper (1986) and Salop (1986).

2.1. Reaching an agreement

Sellers who recognize their mutual interdependence will have an incentive to cooperate as long as the profit which each can obtain when acting jointly is higher than when they act independently. And in fact, in a static framework with costless collusion, firms can always do at least as well when colluding as when acting noncooperatively. This is true because the noncooperative solution is always a feasible collusive outcome.

Let us take the case of two quantity-setting sellers. Denote firm i's output by q^i, cost function by $C^i(q^i)$, and inverse-demand function by $h^i(q^1, q^2)$, $i = 1, 2$. Then each firm's profit, $\pi^i(q^1, q^2)$ is $h^i(q^1, q^2)q^i - C^i(q^i)$.

Successful collusion means locating on the profit-possibility frontier. This frontier is associated with the set of output pairs (q^{1*}, q^{2*}) which solve

$$\max_{q^1, q^2} \pi^1(q^1, q^2) + \lambda\left(\pi^2(q^1, q^2) - \bar{\pi}^2\right), \qquad \bar{\pi}^2 \in \left[0, \Pi^{\mathrm{M}}\right]. \tag{1}$$

Joint-profit maximization obtains when λ, which is endogenously determined, equals one.

When firms are symmetric, reaching an agreement is relatively easy. In this case the equilibrium will be symmetric with $q^{1*} = q^{2*} = q^{\mathrm{M}}$, $\pi^{1*} = \pi^{2*} = \pi^{\mathrm{M}}$, and the collusive profit $\pi^{1*} + \pi^{2*}$ will equal the monopoly profit Π^{M}. In other cases, however, unless side payments are possible, joint-profit maximization may not be a reasonable goal. Reaching an agreement is therefore more difficult when firm heterogeneities are introduced.

Let us first consider the asymmetries already incorporated into equation (1): product and cost differences. With product heterogeneity, each firm will charge a different price and quantities sold will be measured in diverse units. Instead of agreeing on a single price or industry output, therefore, it becomes necessary to agree on a whole schedule of prices or outputs, thus multiplying the possible points of disagreement. When each firm produces a range of products, negotiations can be simplified by tying all product prices to the price of a prespecified product.

With cost heterogeneity, difficulties with the division of profits arise. If industry profit is maximized, industry marginal revenue is equated to each firm's marginal cost. When firms have different marginal cost curves, therefore, joint-profit maximization requires that firms produce unequal output, earn unequal profit, and may even require that some firms close down altogether.

One way of obtaining the consent of participants is to divide the market by customer or by geographic region. Unfortunately, this will not usually lead to joint-profit maximization or location on the profit-possibility frontier. Many other non joint-profit-maximizing outcomes are also possible. Because they involve complex bargaining problems, however, it is difficult to characterize the solution a priori. Outcomes will often depend on the bargaining strengths of the parties involved.

Although often difficult to administer and sometimes illegal, side payments can be the most effective way of obtaining an agreement in a situation of product and cost heterogeneity. Side payments can be analyzed in the context of the model expressed by equation (1) and illustrated in Figure 7.1.

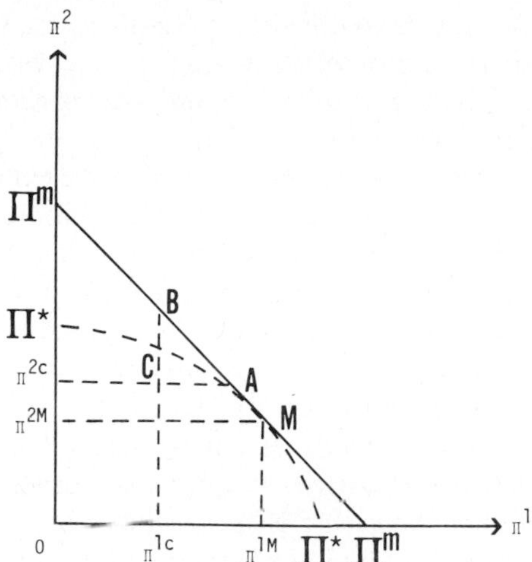

Figure 7.1. Possible collusive outcomes with and without side payments.

In the figure, firm 1's profit π^1 is on the horizontal axis and firm 2's profit π^2 is on the vertical axis. The dashed curve Π^*–Π^* is the profit-possibility frontier without side payments. The point M corresponds to the outputs that maximize joint profit Π^*. M dominates all points within the rectangle $0\pi^{2M}M\pi^{1M}$, but not all feasible alternatives.

Indeed, suppose that the firms do not collude but adopt Cournot–Nash behavior. Let point C represent the Cournot–Nash equilibrium with $\pi^{1C} + \pi^{2C} < \pi^{1M} + \pi^{2M}$. Without side payments, firm 2 will not accept the outcome M, given that it would lose $\pi^{2C} - \pi^{2M} > 0$. It is possible, however, for both firms to increase their profits simultaneously by agreeing to produce q^{1M} and q^{2M} and to divide the fruits of their joint action in such a way that firm 2, as well as firm 1, gains relative to its noncooperative prospect. This requires a side payment $S > 0$ from 1 to 2.

Let $\hat{\pi}^i$, $i = 1, 2$, denote the profit received by firm i, inclusive of side payments. The set of possible side payments S from 1 to 2 defines a linear relationship:

$$\hat{\pi}^2 = \Pi^{\mathrm{M}} - \hat{\pi}^1, \tag{2}$$

which is represented in Figure 7.1 by the straight line Π^{M}–Π^{M}, the profit-possibility frontier with side payments. On this line, only the set of points on the segment AB is acceptable to both firms. The exact point on the segment AB that is chosen will depend on the relative bargaining strengths of the two firms.

The problem of reaching an agreement is still more delicate when one considers other types of asymmetry such as differences in preferences. For example, in a dynamic context firms may have different discount rates. In this case, they will disagree about the weights to be given to current and future profits. One firm may want to charge a high price, for example, even though entry is thereby encouraged, whereas the other may take a longer run view. Preferences can also differ about means of coordinating. For example, one seller may be willing to resort to illegal devices while the other may be only willing to collude tacitly.

Thus far, we have discussed situations where all information is known to all parties. If conditions in a market are stable and known with certainty, negotiations can be infrequent. Once uncertainty is introduced, however, agreements must be reached more often, thereby increasing negotiation costs. In addition, divergence of opinion about future conditions becomes likely. Firms can disagree about costs, demand, entry of rivals, and many other factors. Most important, these factors can make it impossible for firms to locate the profit-possibility frontier, a prerequisite for choosing a point on the curve.

Industries that are subject to rapid technical change find it particularly difficult to reach agreements. Technical change can introduce differences in product lines, production costs, and demand conditions. In addition, the pace and direction of innovation is difficult to predict.

Additional uncertainties are introduced when agreements cannot be overt, due to legal restrictions for example. In this case, firms must devise ways of signaling the need to change price or output. In the case of price-setting firms, a recognized price leader can be agreed upon or the price of a major input can be used as a focal point. These schemes may not lead firms to the profit-possibility frontier but may enable prices to remain above noncooperative levels.

Whenever a price must be raised, the firm to initiate the increase runs the risk of not being followed and therefore losing sales. One way to avoid this difficulty is to agree to give advance notice of price changes. In this way, by responding to one another's price announcements, firms can negotiate a new price through a series of iterations that involve no actual sales.

Our discussion thus far has centered around firms that collude on price or output. Firms, however, can choose from a rich set of nonprice instruments of rivalry, such as advertising, product quality, productive capacity, and R&D expenditure. Analysis of these alternate forms of collusion can be found in other chapters in this Handbook.

2.2. *Incentives to cheat*

Reaching an agreement is only the beginning of the process. When a collusive arrangement has been consummated, the mere fact that price is above the noncooperative level and that marginal revenue for a firm is greater than its marginal cost gives the firm an incentive to cheat. Unfortunately from the point of view of cartel stability, the more successful firms are at raising price, the greater is the incentive to chisel. A cartel therefore contains the seeds of its own undoing.

The incentive to increase output, or to cut price in the case of a price-setting cartel, will not be the same for all firms in an industry or for all industries. The elasticity of the individual-firm demand curve is an important factor affecting incentives: the greater this elasticity the greater the temptation to cut price and to increase sales. The firm-specific elasticities are affected by both the industry-wide elasticity and by the number and size distribution of firms. Very small firms are most apt to take price as parametric and therefore to expect large profits as a result of defection.

Both marginal and fixed costs can affect the profitability of cheating. When marginal costs rise steeply in the neighborhood of the collusive output, price cutting is less profitable. And when fixed costs are a high fraction of total costs, restricting output may result in excess capacity and therefore a temptation to cut price and increase market share.

Finally, if sales are large and infrequent or if detection lags are long, cheating is encouraged. Each of these factors implies that substantial increases in sales can be obtained from a single price cut and that cutting is therefore more profitable.

2.3. Detection

Because incentives to cheat are pervasive, firms that enter into a collusive agreement must be able to detect secret price cuts or output increases initiated by rivals. In the following discussion we assume that price is the choice variable.

When price is not observable, firms may have to rely on the behavior of their own sales for detection purposes. If there are not many firms in a market, a secret cut by one firm causes a large fall in rival sales and will thus be noticeable. We therefore expect collusion to be more successful when sellers are few (but see Subsection 3.2.2 below).

Collusion should also be more successful when buyers are many. If the probability of detecting a single price cut, ρ, is independent of the number of cuts given, and if n price cuts are given, the probability that cheating will be detected is $1 - (1 - \rho)^n$, which rapidly approaches one as n increases.

Detection is also facilitated when sellers have more information about rival behavior. Information can be increased by individual firms getting together to pool sales information. This practice, however, may be frowned on by antitrust authorities. For this reason, firms may resort to trade associations for gathering and disseminating information.

Buyers can also be used to reveal price information. When price bids are open, prices are public knowledge. Under other circumstances, however, sellers may have to provide buyers with an incentive to reveal their offers. One method of doing this is to promise to match secret price cuts initiated by others.

Finally, an event that could happen by chance once is much less likely to be random if repeated. For this reason, temporal patterns of sales are more revealing than single-period information. When sales are frequent, therefore, detection is facilitated.

2.4. Prevention

Detection by itself is not sufficient to deter cheating. It still remains necessary to punish the offender. Various forms of complex punishment strategies are discussed in the later sections on cartels and tacit collusion. Here we consider only practices facilitating prevention through self commitment and involving contractural arrangements or sales strategies.

In an attempt to deter cheating, virtually any punishment can be threatened. For example, a firm can announce that if cheating is detected it will cut price below average cost until the cheater is driven out of the market. Such a threat, however, may not be credible. If called upon to carry out the punishment, it might not be in the firm's best interest to do so. Announced punishments must therefore be credible if they are to deter.

It has long been recognized that threats can be made credible through precommitment. If a firm has no choice but to carry through with its threatened action, a punishment is believable. In the present context, precommitments can be achieved through the use of long-term contracts with buyers. We discuss contractual arrangements that have binding effects.

Some contractual clauses make defection more costly to sellers and are thus forms of self punishment. And others commit rival sellers to punishing defectors. One form of clause that is frequently found in contracts, the "most favored customer" clause, assures a buyer that if the seller ever gives a lower price to another buyer he will (retroactively) give the same cut to the buyer with the clause. The seller thus ties his own hands and makes it virtually impossible to cut price.

Another form of clause, the "meet or release" clause, assures a buyer that if a rival seller offers him a lower price, the seller with the contract will either match the price or release the buyer from the contract. The buyer is thus given an incentive to reveal lower offers. Many contracts do not include the release part of the clause. When this is true, the seller has again tied his own hands and committed himself to punishing his rivals by matching their price cuts.

It might be asked why buyers are willing to accept such clauses in their contracts if the end result is to raise their own costs. The answer is that each buyer individually values the clause but when all buyers accept such clauses, all are made worse off.

Similar precommitment can be achieved even when there are no long-term contracts. For example, many department stores offer to "meet competition". They guarantee that if a buyer can find a better price for the same item elsewhere, the lower price will be matched. The effect of this practice is very similar to a "meet or release" contractual arrangement.

An illustration of the effect of a "meet" clause (excluding the release option) is based on the simplest 2×2 structure for the prisoner's dilemma. Let us assume a duopoly, where each player can choose to charge the monopoly price p^{H} or a lower price p^{L}. When both charge p^{H}, each earns half the monopoly profit or 10, and when both charge p^{L} a lower profit of 5 is earned. However, when one charges p^{H} while the other charges p^{L}, the low-priced producer captures most of the market and earns 12 whereas the high-priced producer earns only 3. This game is summarized by the following payoff matrix:

	Player II	
Player I	H	L
H	(10, 10)	(3, 12)
L	(12, 3)	(5, 5)

where $(\cdot, \cdot)$ denotes payoffs to players 1 and 2, respectively.

This game has a single noncooperative or Nash equilibrium, the dominant strategy $(p^{\mathrm{L}}, p^{\mathrm{L}})$. In this case, the Nash outcome is not Pareto optimal; both players would be better off if they could commit themselves to playing p^{H}. Without commitment, however, each has an incentive to undercut.

The use of a meeting competition clause restructures the payoffs of the duopolists so as to facilitate the achievement and maintenance of the cooperative outcome. If each rival must meet the other's offer, the off-diagonal price pairs are unattainable. Given the remaining alternative, neither duopolist wishes to deviate from the Pareto optimal price pair $(p^{\mathrm{H}}, p^{\mathrm{H}})$.

2.5. *Evidence*

Empirical tests of factors that facilitate or hinder collusion are of two sorts: econometric and experimental. In a series of experiments, Grether and Plott (1981) compare the pricing performance of an industry with and without certain types of contractual clauses, advance notice of price changes, and public price posting. They find that the combination of these practices is sufficient to raise price significantly above the level observed when the practices are removed.

Other experimental results suggest that the predictive power of the joint-profit-maximization assumption tends to vanish with a reduction of information about other agents' actions and with an increase in the number of firms [Friedman and Hoggatt (1980) and Plott (1982)].

Econometric tests have been undertaken by Hay and Kelley (1974) and by Jacquemin, Nambu and Dewez (1981). Hay and Kelley examine price-fixing cases handled by the U.S. Department of Justice in an attempt to determine what factors affect the likelihood of conspiring. They find that most cases involve ten or fewer firms and that when large numbers conspire, a trade association is almost always implicated. In addition, product homogeneity is found to significantly increase the probability of forming a conspiracy.

Finally, Jacquemin, Nambu and Dewez construct a dynamic model of the optimal lifetime of a cartel and test it using data on Japanese export cartels. Again, product homogeneity is found to be a factor that leads to longevity. In addition, cartels that involve the domestic as well as the export market are seen to be more successful. Overall, therefore, the empirical evidence is in substantial agreement with our a priori intuition.

3. Types and extent of horizontal collusion

3.1. Explicit agreement

Horizontal collusion can be explicit or it can be tacit. In this subsection we examine the principal forms of explicit agreement whereas Subsection 3.2 deals with tacit collusion.

There exists an entire spectrum of cooperative arrangements that fall between the poles of arm's-length interaction in a market and complete merger of assets. Public and private gains associated with these arrangements have to be measured relative to the alternatives available. These include colluding in the same fashion with a different firm and not forming a coalition at all but performing the functions internally or relying on the market. In addition, it is possible to enter into a different type of coalition, for example a joint venture instead of a licensing agreement or a merger instead of a joint venture.

We limit our analysis to three modes of formal cooperation, starting with the most flexible, a cartel, to the most complete, a merger, with, in between, the case of joint venture. To avoid confusion, we assume that a cartel is formed when a group of independent firms join forces to make price or output decisions.[1] This arrangement can be legal or illegal. In contrast, a joint venture occurs when two

[1]A cartel is distinguished from pure tacit agreement by the fact that participants meet to communicate and to select strategies.

or more independent firms join together to form a third firm – the joint venture – which one or several of the parents manage. The parent firms cooperate only through the venture. Finally, a merger between two or more firms occurs when their assets are combined. In this case, the constituent firms lose their independent identities and act as a unit.

3.1.1. *Cartel arrangements*

The principal problems facing a cartel are choosing a point on the contract surface, detecting deviations from the agreed-upon point, deterring such deviations, and limiting entry by outsiders. The problems involved in reaching agreement and in detecting cheating were discussed in the previous section. Here we deal with punishment strategies in greater detail and consider the conditions under which there exist stable cartels. The problem of entry is touched upon very briefly; those wishing more details are referred to Chapter 8 in this Handbook.

As we saw in Subsection 2.2, when a cartel is formed each participant may have an incentive to break away. By becoming a member of a price-taking fringe, for example, the defecting firm can free ride and increase its profit [Patinkin (1947), Bain (1948), and Stigler (1950)]. Strategies that deter defection must therefore be devised.

One of the first rigorous treatments of the issue of punishment is by Orr and MacAvoy (1965). They consider the problem faced by symmetric firms that choose price to maximize profit subject to linear demand and cost conditions. Lags in the dissemination of price information imply that individual firms have an incentive to undercut the agreed-upon price. To deter cheating, loyal firms must adopt punishment strategies.

Orr and MacAvoy consider two classes of strategies: exact matching of price cuts and choosing price to maximize the profit of loyal-member firms in the presence of cheating. Let us examine the first strategy.

In deciding whether to cheat, given that others will follow, the potential cheater must compare the present value of his profit stream when collusion is sustained at the collusive price p^* to the present value when he defects. Let his single-period collusive profit be π^*. The present value of this stream is then

$$PV^* = \pi^*/r, \tag{3}$$

where r is the discount rate.

Suppose that the detection lag is τ. When the defector chooses a price $p^{\mathrm{d}} < p^*$, he receives a single-period profit $\hat{\pi}(p^{\mathrm{d}})$ for τ periods (corresponding to his own price of p^{d} and rival prices of p^*) and a profit of $\pi^{\mathrm{d}}(p^{\mathrm{d}})$ thereafter (corresponding to everyone charging p^{d}). The present value of this stream is therefore

$$PV^{\mathrm{d}}(p^{\mathrm{d}}) = \{(1 - \mathrm{e}^{-r\tau})\hat{\pi}(p^{\mathrm{d}}) + \mathrm{e}^{-r\tau}\pi^{\mathrm{d}}(p^{\mathrm{d}})\}/r. \tag{4}$$

The cheater will choose p^{d} to maximize (4). Let $p^{\mathrm{d}*}$ be this maximized value.

To determine if cheating is profitable, we calculate the detection lag $\bar{\tau}$ that causes the cheater to just break even. This means that (4) with p^{d} replaced by $p^{\mathrm{d}*}$ is equated to (3) and solved for $\bar{\tau}$. Then, for all lags greater than $\bar{\tau}$, cheating pays. Orr and MacAvoy show that the potential defector is indifferent to remaining loyal only when $\tau = 0$. That is, when detection is instantaneous, $p^{\mathrm{d}*}$ equals p^*; in all other cases, however, price matching does not deter and defection pays.

In contrast, if the cartel adopts the second strategy and sets its price to yield the maximum profit for the loyal cartel members, given that a cheater is maximizing its own profit in the face of the cartel policy, cheating is deterred. In this case, both loyal members and the cheater have linear reaction functions which intersect at positive prices, and both equilibrium prices are lower than p^*.

Another approach to punishment is taken by Osborne (1976), who looks at possible strategies that a quantity-setting cartel of n firms can use to deter cheating. Osborne's model is illustrated in Figure 7.2 for n equal two. Firm outputs are shown on the axes and the line C–C is the contract curve – the best that any one firm can do, given its rival's profit. The curves marked π_j^i are isoprofit contours for firm i, where $j < j'$ implies that $\pi_j^i > \pi_{j'}^i$.

Suppose that the point $q^* = (q^{1*}, q^{2*})$ of joint-profit maximization has been chosen. If seller 1 considers his rival's output to be fixed at q^{2*}, he will increase his own output to q^{1D} (point D). Firm 2, therefore, must devise a punishment

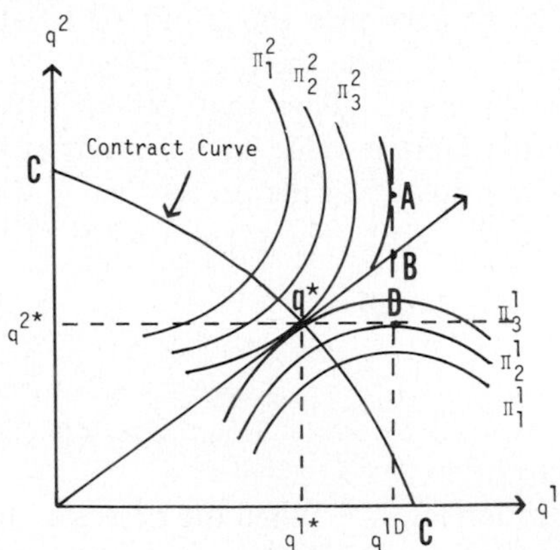

Figure 7.2. Maintaining market share can inhibit cheating.

to deter such cheating. Osborne shows that when one member cheats and increases output, if the other reacts so as to maintain market shares (moving to the point B) cheating is deterred. This is true because the line joining the origin and q^* (the line corresponding to maintaining the market shares implied by q^*) is orthogonal to the gradient of each firm's profit function. As long as both firms know that they will always move along this line, they also know that cheating cannot increase profit.

A problem with the Osborne paper is that retaliation is assumed to be instantaneous. As Orr and MacAvoy demonstrated, however, detection lags make a difference. We saw that cheating is deterred in the Orr and MacAvoy paper as long as retaliation is instantaneous, but not when lags are introduced.

An additional problem is that Osborne's strategy is in general not credible or subgame perfect in the sense of Selten (1975).[2] Given that firm 1 is producing q^{1D}, firm 2 would be better off choosing the larger output associated with point A, where its isoprofit curve is tangent to the line $q^1 = q^{1D}$. And if the model were dynamic, this process would continue until Cournot–Nash outputs were reached.

In a comment on Osborne, Rothschild (1981) identifies precise conditions under which the quota rule will work in a static model. He shows that the successful application of Osborne's rule depends crucially on the number of firms in the cartel, its initial output level, and the size of the increase of the cheater's output.

From our discussion it should be obvious that without binding contracts cartel problems are very similar to those encountered by tacitly colluding firms. That is, collusion must be supported by noncooperative equilibrium strategies. Credible noncooperative strategies are discussed at greater length in Subsection 3.2 where repeated games are introduced.

Here we suppose instead that firms in a cartel give up trying to punish and simply let defectors form part of a price-taking fringe. Will any members remain in the cartel or will the industry become competitive? This is the problem addressed by d'Aspremont, Jacquemin, Jaskold-Gabszewicz and Weymark (1983) (hereafter DJGW) in the context of n identical firms, $k \leq n$ of which participate in a price-setting cartel. When the cartel is formed, both cartel, and fringe members benefit. The problem is that fringe members benefit more. Firms in the cartel may thus be tempted to drop out and free ride.

DJGW define alternative notions of stability. Let $\pi^{\mathrm{c}}(k)$ and $\pi^{\mathrm{f}}(k)$ be the single-period profits that cartel and fringe members receive, respectively, when there are k firms in the cartel. A cartel is said to be internally stable if, when a member leaves, its departure depresses price sufficiently so as to make defection

[2]A strategy is subgame perfect if at each decision point the induced strategy is Nash for the remaining game or subgame. The concept of subgame perfection was introduced in order to exclude the possibility that disequilibrium behavior is prescribed on unreached subgames.

unprofitable. Formally, a cartel is internally stable if

$$\pi^{\mathrm{f}}(k-1) \leq \pi^{\mathrm{c}}(k). \tag{5}$$

A cartel is said to be externally stable if, when a fringe firm joins, the resulting price increase is insufficient to compensate for the higher profit that could be earned by free riding. Formally, a cartel is externally stable if

$$\pi^{\mathrm{c}}(k+1) \leq \pi^{\mathrm{f}}(k). \tag{6}$$

A cartel is said to be stable if it possesses both internal and external stability. DJGW then show that with a finite number of firms, there always exists a stable cartel. With a continuum of firms, in contrast, a stable cartel does not exist.

The intuition behind their result is as follows. With a continuum of firms, each one has a negligible impact on price and profit and can thus ignore the effect of its entry and exit. Under these conditions, everyone free rides. With a finite number of firms, in contrast, profits change discretely with entry and exit and it never pays the last firm to drop out.

Building on DJGW, Donsimoni (1985) examines the impacts of variations in cost and demand conditions on the structure of the stable cartel. In the Donsimoni model, demand and cost functions are linear and costs vary across firms. As before, with a finite number of firms there always exists a stable cartel. In addition, the members of the stable cartel are the efficient firms (those with low costs). Finally, the size of the cartel is a decreasing function of the industry elasticity of demand.

The DJGW and Donsimoni papers assume that the cartel's objective is joint-profit maximization. Schmalensee (1985), however, points out that with cost asymmetries and in the absence of side payments, maximization of industry profit may not be a reasonable objective. Using the tools of cooperative bargaining theory to determine possible outcomes, he shows that a leading firm with a significant cost advantage is unlikely to join a cartel. His result obtains because noncooperative behavior yields the low-cost firm approximately its monopoly profit.[3]

In all the papers considered thus far, the number of firms in or outside the cartel is fixed at n. Selten (1984) considers the consequences of free entry. In general, joint-profit maximization permits a greater number of competitors in a market than noncollusive behavior. There are thus two forces at work. Collusive behavior leads to higher industry profit, which induces entry. And entry in turn depresses profit. Selten shows that under reasonable assumptions on demand and

[3]Other cartel-stability papers include Kobayashi (1982), d'Aspremont and Jaskold-Gabszewicz (1985), Donsimoni, Economides and Polemarchakis (1986), Ayres (1986), and Economides (1986).

cost, industry-wide profit can be increased when collusion is forbidden. Collusive behavior thus leads to both lower concentration and to lower profitability, violating our usual notions about structure–conduct–performance.

If, as in the Selten model, cartels are bad for business, we must ask ourselves why they exist. One possible answer is that firms are myopic and do not bind their own hands by, for example, lobbying for anticartel laws. Another possible explanation is that a large fraction of successful cartels are in industries where entry is difficult. This situation is typified by firms extracting an exhaustible resource. In order to extract, firms must possess reserves. Not only is the stock of reserves finite, in addition, many minerals occur in discrete deposits. When this is true, the number of potential firms is automatically limited.[4]

Most natural-resource cartels are legal organizations whose members are exporting countries. Many other forms of cartels have also been temporarily successful, ranging from firms that participate in criminal price-fixing agreements to groups of firms that adopt practices that are not illegal per se, but have the effect of keeping price above noncooperative levels. Three illustrative cases are discussed here.

The classic case of a price-fixing agreement is the electrical-equipment conspiracy of the 1950s. It involved at least 29 U.S. companies selling heavy electrical equipment. The conspiracy consisted of meetings to fix prices on standardized items as well as pricing formulas for custom products. In addition, shares of all sealed bids were assigned to each company. Some of these arrangements were very complicated. For example, a "phases of the moon" system was used to allocate low-bidding privileges. In spite of these arrangements, agreeing parties chiseled repeatedly and even touched off price wars, illustrating the difficulties of making a collusive agreement stick [Smith (1961)].

A somewhat intermediate situation is illustrated by the U.S. tobacco case of 1946. Tobacco producers were convicted of illegally conspiring to fix prices, even though the evidence was purely circumstantial. Evidence such as patterns of strikingly parallel pricing and purchasing behavior was used to sustain criminal charges. No formal agreement was ever detected [Nichols (1949)].

At the opposite extreme from the electrical-equipment conspiracy is the case brought by the U.S. Federal Trade Commission against the manufacturers of lead-based gasoline additives. Not only were no criminal charges brought, intent to conspire was not even claimed. The companies were charged with using practices such as advance notice of price changes and public announcements of prices that had the effect of raising price. This was thus a case of pure tacit collusion and signaling [F.T.C. (1981)].

[4]The literature on exhaustible-resource cartels is large. Many new dynamic issues are introduced by the intertemporal nature of the maximization problem. These include complex forms of strategic behavior, dynamic inconsistency, and open versus closed-loop solution concepts. These issues are discussed in Jacquemin and Slade (1986) and the references therein.

Whether a cartel is legal or illegal, there are natural forces that tend to reduce profitability. For example, high profits invite entry and defection by members causes instability which can eventually lead to breakdown. It is natural to ask, therefore, if cartelized industries are in fact more profitable than average.

The results from investigations into this question are mixed. For example, Asch and Seneca (1976) using U.S. data on firms that were convicted of conspiracy, find that collusive firms are considerably less profitable than noncolluders, whereas Phillips (1977), using U.K. data on trade associations, finds that effective price fixing has a weak positive effect on price–cost margins. If the Asch and Seneca results are believed, it could mean that Selten (1984) is correct – cartels are bad for business. However, it could merely mean that attempts at price fixing are more apt to be undertaken or detection is facilitated in industries where profits are falling.

3.1.2. Corporate merger

The corporate merger is the ultimate form of collusion; when two firms merge, they cease to have separate identities and act thereafter as a single unit. Many motives have been advanced for the prevalence of merger activity and they differ according to its horizontal, vertical, or conglomerate nature.

In this chapter we are principally interested in the horizontal merger, the most troubling form from a policy point of view (due to its effect on concentration) and the one that is subject to the closest scrutiny from antitrust authorities. The reason for economists' concern with horizontal combinations can best be seen by exploring the relationship between industry concentration and pricing policy.

Contrary to what has sometimes been argued, it is possible to derive a relationship between an index of monopoly power such as the Lerner (1933–34) index and an index of concentration such as the k-firm concentration ratio, the Hirschman (1945, 1964)–Herfindahl (1950) (hereafter HH) index, or the entropy index. Derivations of this sort can be found in Saving (1970) and Cowling and Waterson (1976).

Consider an industry with n firms producing a homogeneous product. Let $p = h(\sum_i q^i) = h(Q)$ be the inverse demand function, where p is price, q^i is the output of the ith firm, and Q is industry output, and let $C^i(q^i)$ be total-cost functions. Each firm chooses q^i to maximize profit

$$\max_{q^i} h(Q)q^i - C^i(q^i). \tag{7}$$

The first-order conditions for this maximization are

$$q^i\left(\partial h/\partial q^i + \sum_{j \neq i} \partial h/\partial q^j \, \partial q^j/\partial q^i\right) + p - MC^i = 0, \quad i = 1,\ldots,n, \tag{8}$$

where MC^i is firm i's marginal cost. Let ε be the industry price elasticity of demand, $-(\partial Q/\partial p)(p/Q)$; s^i be firm i's market share, q^i/Q; and r^{ji} be firm i's conjecture about firm j's response to a unit output change initiated by i, $\partial q^j/\partial q^i$. Algebraic manipulation of equation (8) yields:

$$L^i = (p - MC^i)/p = (s^i/\varepsilon)\left(1 + \sum_{j \neq i} r^{ji}\right)$$

$$= (s^i/\varepsilon)(1 + R^i), \tag{9}$$

where L^i is the Lerner index for firm i and $R^i = \sum_{j \neq i} r^{ji}$ is i's conjecture about the response of industry output to a unit output change on i's part.

Equation (9) shows the familiar relationship between firm i's price–cost margin, its market share, its conjecture, and the industry price elasticity of demand. To obtain a comparable relationship for the industry as a whole, (9) must be aggregated. Encaoua and Jacquemin (1980) show that when different firm-specific weights w^i are used in the aggregation of (9), different indices of concentration emerge. Suppose, for simplicity, that $R^i = R$ for all i. Then if

$$w^i = \begin{cases} 1, & \text{for } i = 1, \dots, k \text{ and } 0 \text{ for } i = k+1, \dots, n, \\ s^i, & \\ \log_a s^i, & a > 1, \end{cases} \tag{10}$$

where firms are arranged in order of decreasing size, the corresponding aggregate price–cost margins $\bar{L}$ are

$$\bar{L} = \sum_i w^i L^i = \begin{cases} C_k(1 + R)/\varepsilon, \\ C_{\mathrm{H}}(1 + R)/\varepsilon, \\ C_{\mathrm{E}}(1 + R)/\varepsilon, \end{cases} \tag{11}$$

respectively, where C_k is the k-firm concentration index, $\sum_{i=1}^{k} s_i$; C_{H} is the HH index, $\sum_{i=1}^{n}(s^i)^2$; and C_{E} is the entropy index, $\sum_{i=1}^{n} s^i \log_a s^i$.

Equation (11) shows how aggregate price–cost margins are related to standard indices of concentration, where the indices are determined by the aggregation scheme. It is obvious from (11) that $\bar{L}$, which is a measure of the output-market distortion, is directly related to industry concentration and to firm i's conjecture and is inversely related to the industry price elasticity of demand.

A horizontal merger can thus affect industry price–cost margins in two ways: through the concentration index and through the conjectured response. It is often assumed that with fewer firms, behavior becomes more collusive (R increases).[5] When this is the case, the two effects of a horizontal merger work in the same direction to increase the output-market distortion.[6]

The analysis thus far has been static. Pindyck (1985) defines an instantaneous Lerner index for dynamic markets and shows how it can be aggregated over time. A dynamic market is one in which price and output are determined intertemporally. Examples include markets for exhaustible resources and markets where learning effects, adjustment costs, or lags in demand are important.

The underlying feature of these markets is that full marginal cost, FMC, includes marginal user cost as well as marginal production cost, where marginal user cost is the present value to price-taking firms of future profit forgone due to an increase in output today. Marginal user cost is thus positive in exhaustible-resource markets and negative when learning occurs. FMC is evaluated at the oligopoloy output level.

Pindyck defines the instantaneous Lerner index L^* as

$$L_t^* = (p_t - FMC_t)/p_t = 1 - FMC_t/p_t. \tag{12}$$

The conventional Lerner index thus overstates the extent of monopoly power in exhaustible-resource markets, whereas it understates power in markets with learning.

To obtain a time-aggregate index, I_{m}, (12) is weighted by expenditure and integrated to yield:

$$I_{\mathrm{m}} = 1 - \left(\int_0^{\infty} \mathrm{e}^{-rt} FMC_t Q_t \,\mathrm{d}t \Big/ \int_0^{\infty} \mathrm{e}^{-rt} p_t Q_t \,\mathrm{d}t \right). \tag{13}$$

This index describes the monopoly power of a firm looking into the future from a particular point in time. It will of course change with different choices of $t = 0$. I_{m} equals zero when the industry is competitive and increases as price deviates from full marginal cost.

Equation (13) gives the index of monopoly power for a single firm. It can be aggregated in one of several ways to obtain an industry-wide index and in general will be positively related to industry concentration.

[5]A recently proposed measure of aggregate power in organization is directly based on the ability of agents to induce a change of regime through coalition formation. The formula is the sum, taken over all possible coalitions, of the product of two probabilities for each coalition: its probability to form and its probability to become winning [d'Aspremont et al. (1987)]. In the framework of oligopoly theory, this index is viewed as the probability that a given coalition of firms will be able to induce a shift from a competitive to a noncompetitive regime [s'Aspremont and Jacquemin (1985)].

[6]When firms produce multiple products, some of which are substitutes and others complements, the calculation of an index of market power is more complex. With these complications in mind, Encaoua, Jacquemin and Moreaux (1986) derive an index of global market power for diversified firms.

So far we have assumed that the equilibrium relationship involves concentration and price. Nothing has been said about the effect of concentration on cost. There are two schools of thought on this subject. The first claims that high concentration, at least when monopoly power is protected, leads to higher costs and to what Leibenstein (1966) calls X-inefficiency. And the second maintains that the causality runs the other way. Low-cost firms increase their market shares at the expense of less efficient firms. As a result, low-cost firms have large market shares and high concentration is a mark of efficiency [Demsetz (1973) and Peltzman (1977), for example].[7]

Unless X-inefficiency is the predominant effect, however, increased concentration through merger tends to increase total industry profit and profit per firm. Nevertheless, it is not at all clear that the acquiring firm benefits from its efforts. This problem was recognized long ago by Stigler (1950) who noted that the promoter of a merger might expect to receive every form of encouragement from other firms, short of participation.

Recently, there has been a resurgence of interest in the subject of the private profitability of participating in a merger. We therefore conclude our theoretical analysis of horizontal merger with a discussion of these articles.

There are many reasons why mergers need not be privately profitable. For example, Dowell (1984) notes that when there are industry-specific nonsalvageable assets, it is possible for pre- and post-merger industry price and output to be the same. In this case, a merger does not result in increased profits, either for the industry as a whole or for the firms in the industry.

The intuition behind Dowell's result is illustrated in Figure 7.3. When there are nonsalvageable assets, the marginal cost of output expansion ($LRMC$) is greater than the cost reduction due to output contraction ($SRMC$). The firm's marginal-cost curve therefore has a discontinuity at the pre-merger (competitive) output level, Q^c. At this point, pre-merger price is determined by the intersection of demand and long-run marginal cost. After the merger, price is determined by the intersection of marginal revenue, MR, and short-run marginal cost. Even though the marginal-revenue schedule lies below the demand schedule D, it may cut the marginal-cost curve at its point of discontinuity and thus result in the same price/output combination. The result is a sort of "kinked supply curve" that leads to rigid prices for many demand schedules. Under these circumstances, firms have little incentive to merge. And even when the outcome of a merger is an increased price, nonsalvageable assets are a restraining factor.

[7]A complementary argument in favor of concentration through mergers is based on the idea of a market for corporate control [Manne (1965)]. According to this theory, failure to maximize profit reduces stock prices below their potential value, inducing takeovers and the replacement of old with new, more efficient managers. Empirical studies, however [see for example, Singh (1971)], suggest that it is unlikely that the reorganization that occurs after takeover leads to more profitable utilization of assets.

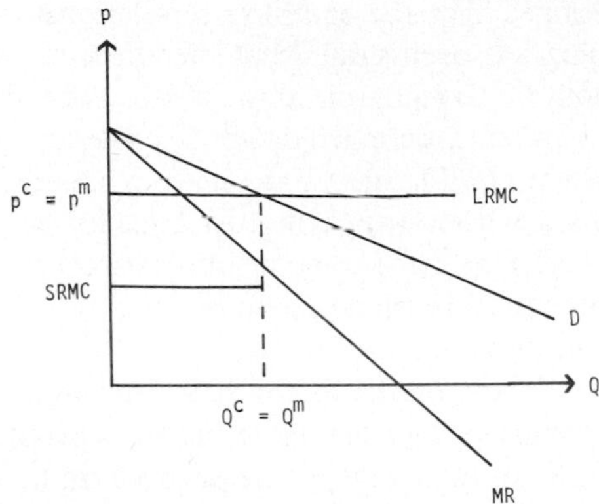

Figure 7.3. The effect of nonsalvageable assets on the post-merger outcome.

Using a completely different approach, Salant, Switzer and Reynolds (1983) (hereafter SSR) notice the curious fact that the effect of horizontal merger on a Cournot–Nash industry equilibrium can be to increase industry profit while at the same time reducing the profitability of the merged firms below the sum of their premerger profits. They consider the case of symmetric oligopolists facing linear demand and cost conditions (constant marginal costs). Under these assumptions, industry equilibrium is symmetric with each firm producing the same output and earning the same profit.

Suppose that there are initially n firms and that each earns $\pi(n)$. When two firms merge, it will surely be the case that

$$\pi(n) < \pi(n-1) \tag{14}$$

and

$$n\pi(n) < (n-1)\pi(n-1). \tag{15}$$

These are standard conditions stating that the profit of each firm as well as total industry profit increases as the number of firms is reduced.

Under reasonable conditions on demand and cost, however, it can also be the case that

$$\pi(n-1) < 2\pi(n). \tag{16}$$

What equation (16) says is that the profit to the single merged firm can be less than the sum of the pre-merger profits of its constituent firms.

Notice that this is not a dominant-firm/competitive-fringe model. There are no price takers. In the new equilibrium, each firm shares the output restriction equally. The peculiar result obtains because there is nothing to distinguish the merged firm from the $n - 2$ nonmerged firms. In the new symmetric equilibrium, therefore, all firms produce $1/(n - 1)$ of the industry output.

This model, however, violates our intuitive notions of what a merger is all about. If we start with n identical firms and two merge, we expect the result to be $n - 2$ small old firms and one large new firm. Deneckere and Davidson (1985), and Perry and Porter (1985), by introducing different notions of size, reverse the SSR results.

Deneckere and Davidson consider the case of price-setting firms producing differentiated products. In their model, when firms merge the merged firm can continue to manufacture the entire product line of each constituent firm. For example, if we start with n firms each producing a single product, after a merger between two firms the new firm produces twice as many products as the remaining firms in the industry. Under these assumptions, the SSR results can be reversed.

Perry and Porter choose a different route. In their model, each firm has some fraction of a tangible asset K, whose total supply is fixed at one. When two firms merge, the newly created firm controls the assets belonging to each of its constituents. It is assumed that the long-run technology is subject to constant returns but that, due to the presence of the fixed factor K, each firm's short-run marginal-cost curve is upward sloping. A large firm (one with more K) can therefore produce the same output at lower cost than a small firm.

Two cases are considered, a dominant-firm/competitive-fringe model and an oligopoly with large and small firms. The results from the first model are very similar to those obtained by d'Aspremont, Jacquemin, Jaskold-Gabszewicz and Weymark (1983). For example, Perry and Porter find that there is always an incentive for a dominant firm to form. Whether or not additional firms merge depends on the precise demand and cost parameters. In general, however, there will be an equilibrium number of merged firms – a stable cartel.

The second model is closer to SSR. With increasing marginal costs, however, the incentive to merge usually remains. In fact, the SSR model is essentially the limiting case of the Perry and Porter model which obtains as the marginal-cost curve flattens.

There are thus many theories that can explain the stylized facts. Mergers can be unprofitable because they do not increase monopoly power, because they do not improve efficiency, or because, although they enhance monopoly power, this effect is more than compensated for by various forms of internal inefficiency, including managerial and financial aspects. With this perspective in mind, it is useful to turn to empirical studies for further insights. They are numerous and concern two main issues.

The first is the effect of mergers on aggregate and industrial concentration. In the United States, until the Celler–Kefauver antimerger act of 1950, horizontal mergers were dominant and are often viewed as having led to substantial increases in both overall and industrial concentration [Stigler (1950), Markham (1955), Weiss (1965)]. According to a study by McGowan (1965), concentration would not have risen at all in the 1950s if no mergers had been undertaken. The merger movement of the 1960s, however, was very different as it was conglomerate in nature. Although this new wave did not cause important increases in industrial concentration, it did contribute to maintaining a high level of aggregate concentration. It can indeed be argued that although overall concentration held more or less steady during much of the 1960s [White (1981)], the fact that acquiring firms were on average much larger than other companies implies that internal growth rates of the largest companies were less than the growth in assets for the manufacturing sector as a whole. According to Mueller (1972), the latter is what one expects if the largest companies are in the mature phase of their life cycle. In the 1970s and 1980s, merger activity has continued and it seems that aggregate concentration is again rising.

In Europe, the post World War II period was characterized by merger waves of impressive proportions. In the absence of significant antimerger laws, horizontal mergers remained dominant and transformed the corporate economy of Europe in the 1960s. With the exception of petroleum, the largest European firms are now of comparable size to the largest in the United States, and both are significantly larger than their Japanese counterparts. As a consequence, overall concentration has increased markedly. Between 1953 and 1970, the share of net U.K. manufacturing output supplied by the hundred largest firms rose from 27 to 40 percent [Hannah and Kay (1976)]; similar results occurred in France, Germany, Sweden, and in the Netherlands. For the EEC as a whole, sales of the 50 largest firms relative to gross industrial output increased from 15 percent in 1965 to 25 percent in 1976 [Jacquemin and Cardon (1973), Locksley and Ward (1979)]. Finally, although mergers were not the sole cause of increased concentration in European industries, they were a crucial factor. Estimations of industrial-concentration-ratio changes attributable to mergers in U.K. industrial sectors [Utton (1972), Aaronovitch and Sawyer (1975), Hannah and Kay (1976), Hart (1979), Prais (1981), Cowling et al. (1980)], and in West Germany [Müller (1976)] show a predominant role played by these mergers.[8]

A second issue is the effect of mergers on profitability. As discussed previously, increased profitability can derive from increased efficiency as well as from an increase in market power. The role of a purely arithmetic effect must also be taken into account. Indeed, when a firm below average profitability acquires

[8]According to Hart (1979) and Prais (1981), however, internal growth of firms was primarily responsible for increased concentration in the United Kingdom prior to 1950.

another firm having a higher profit rate, unless the merger causes a sufficient decline in the acquired firm's profitability, the combined profit rate of the two merged firms will automatically be higher than the acquiring firm's initial rate.

When measuring the effect of mergers on profitability, a timing problem is also present in the sense that it is necessary to observe the effects of a merger, not simply at the time it is announced and finalized, but over a sufficient period after the consummation. Most of the existing studies of the effects of horizontal merger show that on average they either had no effect or led to slight decreases in profitability, even if an extended period of time is considered [for the United Kingdom, see Singh (1971), Utton (1974), Meeks (1977), Cowling et al. (1980), and for Continental Europe, see studies in Mueller (1980)].

Studies have also been undertaken for the United States [for an early one, see Reid (1968) and the critical discussion in the *Journal of Finance* (June 1974)] and have led to the same type of conclusion. Recently, Mueller (1985) conducted an analysis for a sample of 280 U.S. mergers of the 1962–72 period. He found evidence of a significant averaging effect due to mergers, but once he controlled for this effect, no residual consequence on profits was found. Given that it is unlikely that mergers reduce market power generally, such results suggest, on average, that efficiency could have declined enough to offset benefits induced by possible increases in market power.[9]

After examining both theoretical and empirical studies, we conclude that the benefits of merger are not evident, either from the point of view of the shareholder or of society as a whole. A general presumption in favor of mergers, therefore, does not appear to be justified.

3.1.3. Joint ventures

A joint venture occurs when two or more firms join together to form a third, often with a particular project in mind. For example, the parents might incorporate to produce an input or to enter a geographic region where neither operates. The first is an example of a vertical and the second of a horizontal joint venture. We focus our attention on horizontal ventures.

The joint venture is thus a rather peculiar hybrid form of organization somewhere between interacting in a market and merging assets. It is a fairly common business arrangement but one that has received little attention from economists, at least at the theoretical level. The legal and antitrust implications of joint venture are analyzed by Mead (1967), Pitofsky (1969), and Brodley (1976, 1982) and the economic motives for participating in joint ventures are examined by Mariti and Smiley (1983).

[9]Another type of analysis concerns a merger's effect on shareholder returns. For a positive view, see the survey of Jensen and Ruback (1983) and for a criticism of the methodology see Mueller (1985).

As with most financial and economic arrangements, there are both efficient and inefficient aspects to joint ventures. We begin our discussion with an analysis of the inefficiencies.

The most obvious objection to a joint venture is that it has much in common with a cartel or horizontal merger. Through participation in the venture, the financial interests of the parents are linked. Parents will certainly not want to compete vigorously with the venture and may also compete less forcefully with each other. Joint ventures are particularly suspect when they take over existing operations of firms. Even when a new geographic region is entered, however, the venture may foreclose entry by an independent firm.

Joint ventures can assume many financial forms. To focus on the similarities between joint ventures and mergers, we analyze a particular financial arrangement, the partial-equity interest. Our discussion follows Reynolds and Snapp (1986). Other financial arrangements are considered by Bresnahan and Salop (1986).

Under a partial-equity interest, the output of a venture is selected by one partner, the controller, and profits are divided according to each partner's share of equity. Suppose that there are n firms in the market for a homogeneous product. Let $h(Q)$ be the inverse-demand function, $C^i(q^i)$ be the ith firm's cost function, and V^{ik} be the ith firm's ownership interest in the kth firm. Under these assumptions, the ith firm's profit can be written as

$$\pi^i = \left(1 - \sum_{k \neq i} V^{ki}\right)\left[h(Q)q^i - C^i(q^i)\right] + \sum_{k \neq i} V^{ik}\left[h(Q)q^k - C^k(q^k)\right]. \tag{17}$$

Assuming Cournot–Nash behavior and using the notation of Subsection 3.1.2, the first-order condition for the maximization of (17) can be manipulated to yield:

$$\begin{aligned} L^i &= (p - MC^i)/p \\ &= \frac{1}{\varepsilon}\left[s^i + \frac{\sum_{k \neq i} V^{ik} s^k}{1 - \sum_{k \neq i} V^{ki}} \right]. \end{aligned} \tag{18}$$

The comparable condition when there are no joint ventures is

$$L^i = s^i/\varepsilon, \tag{9'}$$

which is equation (9) with $R^i = 0$ (Cournot–Nash behavior).

We see that even when behavior is noncooperative, price–cost margins can be increased by joint ventures. For example, if there are ten identical firms and no joint ventures, the price–cost margin will be $1/10\varepsilon$, one-tenth the monopoly markup. If each firm has a 10 percent financial interest in every other, in contrast, the price–cost margin increases to its monopoly level of $1/\varepsilon$.

In addition, if the likelihood of collusion is increased by the venture, effects can be synergistic. Joint ventures, particularly those that are jointly managed, can be used as vehicles of coordination, both tacit and overt. For example, it is difficult to draw the line between discussions on pricing policy for the output of the venture and more general pricing strategies for the parents. Similarly, through the venture the parents can share cost information. The exchange of information can facilitate both agreement on a common policy and detection of defection from the agreement.

A common subsidiary can also enable firms to make the side payments that may be necessary to redistribute rents from collusion. Whereas it is difficult for completely independent firms to effect monetary transfers, when operations are linked side payments can be disguised in the form of cheaper supplies for, or unequal division of profits from the common project.

Finally, the venture can be used to exclude certain competitors in a market, thereby putting them in a disadvantageous position. This problem is particularly acute with vertical joint ventures, where competitors may not have access to a scarce input. With horizontal arrangements, the venture may be used to deny outside firms the use of a new technology or marketing facility.

Just as there are disadvantages to this particular form of organization, there are also advantages. Through the venture, firms can benefit from economies of scale in their production processes while remaining separate entities. Joint ventures are therefore very prevalent in industries where scale economies are important, such as automobile production.

Investment rationalization can also be a motive for participating in a venture. Such arrangements are therefore frequently observed in declining industries with high fixed costs, such as many metal industries.

When capital markets are imperfect, joint ventures can enable small firms to participate in projects that are otherwise beyond their means. This is an often advocated reason for allowing joint ventures in bidding for, and production of, offshore oil and gas. These arrangements can also enable small firms to diversify and share risks.

Joint ventures can be used to enter markets that are artificially restricted. In the presence of high tariffs and quotas, for example, foreign companies often enter into joint ventures with domestic firms, thus reducing costs to both producers and consumers.

Perhaps the most important economy associated with joint ventures is the production and exchange of information. Ordover and Willig (1985) and Grossman and Shapiro (1984), in discussions of cooperative arrangements in high-technology industries, advocate special treatment for research joint ventures. There are three reasons why this might be a good policy. First, scientific knowledge has many aspects of a public good. When firms cannot capture the rents from research, they tend to underinvest in the activity. Second, in high-technology industries monopoly rents are quickly dissipated as new products and processes are introduced. The problems associated with cooperation are therefore substantially lessened. And finally, when there is too much competition in R&D markets firms tend to introduce innovations too quickly, thereby dissipating the rents from the new product or process [Barzel (1968)]. Cooperative efforts can thus eliminate wasteful haste as well as duplication of effort.

R&D joint ventures are not completely benign, however. Vickers (1985) demonstrates that research joint ventures, insofar as they pool incumbents' incentives to deter entry, can be effective entry-deterring devices. He also shows that the formation of joint ventures for large innovations can weaken the incumbents' incentive to innovate by removing the competitive stimulus.

Because joint ventures are so prevalent in offshore oil and gas production, much of the empirical literature examines these arrangements. Rockwood (1983) tests whether joint ventures in bidding for U.S. offshore oil and gas leases increases the bidding-market power of firms. To do this, he examines cash bonuses bid for offshore tracts. He finds that joint ventures have had a significant positive impact on the level of cash bonuses and concludes that through joint ventures firms are able to offset the problems implied by imperfect capital markets.

Like Rockwood, DeBrock and Smith (1983) examine joint bidding in offshore petroleum-lease auctions and find that this practice leads to significant economies. They conclude that joint bidding increases the total social value of lease offerings without significantly decreasing the percentage of the social value captured by the government. They attribute their result to the pooling of information. Prior to bidding, participants engage in exploratory tests. The pooling of this information results in more accurate estimates of lease values. And better informed participants bid more aggressively.

Much of the evidence from offshore oil and gas bidding therefore seems to be positive. This evidence should be interpreted with caution, however, because there has been no effort to assess whether joint bidding facilitates coordination of output-market decisions. It is entirely possible that the government is made better off (because it receives more money for leases) while at the same time consumers are made worse off (because they pay higher prices for the product).

Although enhanced product-market power through joint ventures is not very likely in the crude-petroleum market (a world market) it is quite possible in others. Empirical research based on cross-industry analysis of a large sample of U.S. joint ventures [Berg and Friedman (1981) and Duncan (1982)] suggests that, when parents are horizontally related, a potential for market-power augmentation often exists.

A joint venture that has drawn much attention recently is that between General Motors and Toyota. These two giant companies have formed a subsidiary to produce subcompact cars at GM's previously closed plant in Fremont, California. In conjunction with this case, Bresnahan and Salop (1986) develop a method of modifying the Hirshman–Herfindahl concentration index to accommodate the peculiar financial arrangements of joint ventures. When they apply their index to the GM/Toyota data, they find substantial increases in the index due to the formation of the venture. The market for automobiles is highly concentrated internationally and becoming more so. A joint project between two of the largest firms in the industry, therefore, poses difficult problems from a policy point of view and deserves close scrutiny.

It is difficult to make sweeping judgements concerning the efficiency of joint ventures. As with other forms of cooperative arrangements, much depends on the particular circumstances and on the alternatives available. Just as with mergers, however, there is no a priori presumption in their favor. Firms wishing to undertake large horizontal joint projects should be prepared to argue convincingly in their defense.

3.2. Tacit collusion

Not all collusion involves explicit agreement. Collusive behavior can also be tacit. To explain how this can occur, we introduce a game-theoretic setting. We begin with an examination of the prisoner's dilemma introduced earlier. This simple game is analyzed in a one-shot and repeated-game framework. The general result is that even though there may be only one noncooperative solution to a one-shot or stage game, when the game is repeated it can have a very large number of noncooperative equilibria. Some of these outcomes involve higher payoffs for all players than the single-period solution and are thus said to be tacitly collusive.

The multiplicity of equilibria is one of the problems associated with the repeated-game approach. Instead of providing us with a theory of oligopoly, it can explain all possible behaviors. Moreover, it even suggests that almost all industries will be collusive almost all of the time. For this reason, many recent studies of tacit collusion are attempts to narrow down or restrict the set of outcomes. We will examine how this narrowing down is accomplished.

Another problem is that the story works too well, in the sense that strategies are devised so that no one ever has an incentive to cheat. In the models, therefore, only stationary equilibrium price/quantity combinations are observed. We know, however, that the real world is characterized by seemingly disequilibrium phenomena such as price wars. Other recent studies that we discuss attempt to explain this apparent contradiction between theoretical and observed behavior.

A final issue that we wish to pursue is whether the insights gained from the repeated-game approach are compatible with out intuitive notions about factors that facilitate and hinder collusion. We therefore examine such issues as whether collusion is easier when there are fewer firms in an industry and whether the sharing of information facilitates collusion.

3.2.1. Simple stories of tacit collusion

Our presentation in this subsection is very informal. Those wishing a more rigorous treatment are referred to Friedman (1986).

Consider again the prisoner's dilemma introduced in Section 2. Without commitment, each player has an incentive to undercut his rival. The net result is that both are worse off than they would be if they could cooperate. When the game is played more than once, however, players can condition their behavior at any stage on observed past behavior of others. In this way, by threatening to punish undesirable actions and reward cooperation, it is at least possible for collusion to be enforced.

Consider, however, what happens when the game is repeated a finite number of times and there is no discounting. In the last period, because there is no future, everyone plays p^{L}. And in the second-to-last period, because each knows that the other will play p^{L} in the last period no matter what happens in the current period, each player again plays p^{L}. By backwards induction, the entire game unravels and we observe the noncooperative solution in every period. This is similar to the famous "chain-store paradox".

The situation is very different, however, when the game is repeated infinitely often or when there is uncertainty about the end of the game. Suppose that each player wishes to maximize his discounted stream of profits Γ^i,

$$\Gamma^i = \sum_{t=1}^{\infty} \delta^{t-1} \pi_t^i, \quad i = 1,2, \tag{19}$$

where π_t^i is the ith player's profit in period t and $\delta = 1/(1+r)$ is the discount factor (r is the discount rate). It is well known that if δ is sufficiently close to one, any individually rational outcome can be sustained as a credible Nash equilibrium of the repeated game. This is the content of the so-called "Folk Theorem" of repeated games.

To see why this works in the prisoner's dilemma case, consider a strategy introduced by Friedman (1971) that supports p^{H}: each player cooperates initially and plays p^{H} in the first period and in every subsequent period until defection is observed. If either player defects, however, p^{L} is played by both in the next period and forever afterwards. It is straightforward to derive the conditions on δ for which this is a credible Nash equilibrium for the repeated game.

A similar result holds if there is uncertainty about the end of the game. In this case, δ in equation (19) must be interpreted as the probability that the game will continue into the next period. When this probability is sufficently high, any individually rational outcome can be sustained.

The one-period prisoner's dilemma has a single Nash equilibrium $(p^{\mathrm{L}}, p^{\mathrm{L}})$. In a game with multiple equilibria, however, even when the game is repeated a finite number of times and there is no discounting, there can be a very large number of noncooperative outcomes. In the last period, each player will play Nash. Because there are multiple solutions, however, it is not clear which Nash outcome will prevail and there is therefore room for manipulative behavior. The game does not unravel and many tacitly collusive outcomes are possible. This issue is discussed by Benoit and Krishna (1985) and Friedman (1985).

The theoretical possibilities for tacit collusion are therefore large. If the game is repeated infinitely often, if there is uncertainty about the end of the game, or if the one-shot game has multiple equilibria, virtually any outcome can be sustained. It is hard to conceive of a real-world situation that is not characterized by one of these conditions. The question thus changes from "can tacit collusion occur?" to "what form is it likely to take?" This is the question that we explore in more detail in the next subsection.

Casual inspection also leads us to believe that tacit collusion is possible. The number of industries that have been accused of "conscious parallelism" is large and includes cement, drugs, dyes, lumber, theaters, and tobacco.

3.2.2. Models of tacit collusion

We have seen that the number of tacitly collusive strategies and outcomes is very large. If our object is to restrict this set, an obvious question to ask is: Is there an optimal strategy that is independent of the strategies chosen by the other players? Axelrod (1984) examines this issue in the context of the repeated prisoner's dilemma game and shows that the answer is no.

This is not the end of the question, however. For a practical test of strategy effectiveness, Axelrod designed a tournament. Game theorists were asked to submit their favorite strategies, which were played against each other in a series of computer simulations. The result was that the highest average score was obtained by the simplest strategy, tit for tat. Tit for tat consists of playing p^{H} on the first move and in each subsequent move playing what the opponent played in the previous period.

As a further test, a second tournament was run. Each strategy from the first round was submitted to the second in proportion to its success in the first. This process was repeated many times. In the long run, tit for tat displaced all other rules and went to what biologists call fixation.

Tit for tat has three properties that are desirable: it is a "nice" strategy, that is, it does not defect first; it is provoked by the first defection of the other player; and it is forgiving – it does not punish forever. Strategies with these properties have also been analyzed for more complex games.

Kalai and Stanford (1985) study an infinitely repeated symmetric Cournot duopoly game with discounting. They limit their attention to strategies that are similar to tit for tat – linear reaction functions – and show that any pair of these functions gives rise to a unique pair of quantities in stationary equilibrium. These strategies are Nash for the infinitely repeated game.

Suppose that each player has the same reaction function:

$$q_t^i = \bar{q} + R\left(q_{t-1}^j - \bar{q}\right), \quad i = 1,2, \ j = 2,1, \ -1 \leq R \leq 1. \tag{20}$$

In equation (20), R is the slope of the reaction function; a slope of one thus corresponds to tit for tat.

Each R gives rise to a unique equilibrium output pair, $q^{1*} = q^{2*} = q(R)$. Nash strategies for the infinitely repeated game consist of playing $q(R)$ in the first period and thereafter following the reaction functions (20), with $\bar{q}$ replaced by $q(R)$.

Unfortunately, as Kalai and Stanford show, these strategies are not credible. The problem is that when one player defects, by reacting to one another as the functions (20) prescribe, the players stay off the equilibrium path for too long. This problem can be remedied, however, if the reaction time Δt is shortened. The effect of shortening the time to response is twofold: punishment comes sooner and it is less costly for the punisher. Kalai and Stanford show that with short reaction times, strategies of the form of (20) have strong credibility properties. Similar results were derived independently by Anderson (1983).

The problem of a multiplicity of outcomes, however, has not been solved. Any quantity between the competitive and the monopoly can be sustained by varying R between minus and plus one. To make the solution determinate, we must select a particular R.

MacLeod (1985) adopts an axiomatic-bargaining approach to reduce the number of equilibrium outcomes. He considers a class of reaction functions that depend only on previous-period prices and the opponent's price change. By introducing three axioms that these functions must satisfy, he reduces the solution to tit for tat.

Another reaction-function model is due to Brander and Spencer (1985). They consider the case of n identical quantity-setting oligopolists and focus on the notion of entry to narrow down the set of equilibria.[10] In their model, a unique

[10] Brander and Spencer's model is not dynamic but it could be made so. Instead of R, they use a conjectural-variation parameter, λ.

price/quantity combination is associated with any R, given the number of firms n; and larger R's correspond to higher profits. Profits, however, invite entry, which occurs until profitability is driven to zero. There is therefore a locus of n/R combinations that are consistent with zero profits. The problem is to select among them.

Brander and Spencer determine a unique equilibrium by introducing a schedule reflecting how the ease of collusion R depends on the number of firms n. With this additional assumption, we have two equations:

$$\Pi(n, R) = 0 \quad \text{and} \quad R = f(n), \tag{21}$$

which can be solved to yield a unique equilibrium n^*, and R^*.

It may seem that there are many ways to obtain unique outcomes. Those that we have considered, however, are slightly ad hoc. By invoking a set of axioms or by producing a function that relates R to n, one merely pushes the indeterminacy back one stage. It still remains to explain where the axioms or the functions come from, and this is not a simple problem.

A very different approach to reducing outcomes is taken by Spence (1978), who explores the effect of imperfect information on reaction-function equilibria. In Spence's model, imperfect information consists of an inability of firms to monitor their rivals' actions. He shows that when imperfect monitoring is combined with randomness in the payoff functions, the set of reaction-function equilibria shrinks towards the set of Nash equilibria of the one-shot game. With perfect monitoring, the incentive to cheat must be weighed against the probability of detection. The probability of detection therefore works very much like the discount rate in previous models in that it causes future punishment to be weighed less heavily. As either departs from one, the set of sustainable outcomes shrinks.

With the models discussed thus far, strategies are credible or subgame perfect. They therefore deter cheating. A consequence is that only stationary equilibrium behavior is observed; that is, the same price–quantity combination is played in every period. We know, however, that seemingly disequilibrium behavior such as price wars is endemic to many markets. Models are therefore required that are credible but nevertheless exhibit price–quantity dynamics. We therefore turn our attention to such models.

Perhaps the best-known model of price wars is due to Green and Porter (1984) who, like Spence, explore the effects of imperfect information. In their model, price is determined by industry output and a random variable θ. Each firm observes this price and its own output but cannot observe the output of its rivals. When an unusually low price is realized, there are two possibilities. Either demand is very low or a rival has cheated and increased production. It is therefore always possible for cheating to go undetected. Green and Porter show that cheating can be deterred by threatening to produce at Cournot–Nash levels for a period of fixed duration whenever the market price drops below some trigger price, $\tilde{p}$.[11]

The idea is to select a collusive output $q^i = q^*$, a trigger price $\tilde{p}$, and a punishment period T. An equilibrium trigger-price strategy $(q^*, \tilde{p}, T)$ always exists because q^* can be taken to equal the Cournot level. There will in general, however, be many equilibria.

Porter (1983a) goes on to study the problem of selecting an optimal trigger-price strategy from the firm's point of view. He calculates values of $(q^*, \tilde{p}, T)$ that maximize expected industry discounted value, subject to the constraint that no firm wants to deviate from q^*. He finds that, in general, q^* is greater than $1/n$ times the monopoly output. In addition, optimal industry output is a nondecreasing function of both n and the variance of θ.

This model not only limits the number of outcomes, it also reconciles seemingly disequilibrium phenomena such as price wars with equilibrium behavior on the part of implicitly colluding firms. With a trigger-price strategy, no firm ever cheats. Nevertheless, if the support of θ is large, price will periodically drop below $\tilde{p}$ and a period of Cournot–Nash reversion will ensue.

In the Green and Porter model, price wars occur only during downturns. Rotemberg and Saloner (1986) claim, however, that wars are at least as common during booms and build a model to explain this phenomenon. As with all such models, a firm's decision to defect involves weighing the single-period profit from cheating versus future losses due to induced noncooperative behavior. If demand is high, the benefit from undercutting is large. On the other hand, because punishments are meted out in the future when demand tends to return to its normal level, the punishment from deviating is less affected by the current state of demand. Price decreases therefore occur in good times.

Inability to detect cheating, as in Green and Porter, is not the only reason why price wars occur. In many markets, especially at the retail level, price is the firm's choice variable and it can be observed by all players. Slade (1985) constructs a model that produces price wars when there is little scope for cheating and secret price cutting.

Like the previous models, the Slade model relies on demand uncertainty, but uncertainty is of a very different sort. Instead of demand being stationary, it is subject to periodic but infrequent discontinuous shifts. When a demand shift occurs, in order to determine the new demand conditions and to calculate the new equilibrium prices, players must change prices. Price wars are therefore information-seeking devices. The dynamics inherent in the model are such that

[11] It has been shown [Abreu, Pearce and Stracchetti (1986)] that in this model a one-period reversion to an output greater than the Cournot–Nash output is the most effective way of policing the cartel.

considerable cutting and undercutting occurs before the new equilibrium is established.

In all of these models, price wars are equilibrium strategies of supergames; no one ever cheats. This is perhaps a shortcoming of the models from a practical if not from a game-theoretic point of view. Our intuitive feeling is that firms do intentionally cheat on collusive agreements (recall the electrical-equipment conspiracy) and that there are many reasons why price wars occur in addition to demand shocks. Nevertheless, economists have devised few theories to explain cheating in collusive agreements.[12]

In many models, the stochastic nature of demand and costs leads to firms having incomplete information. Stigler (1964), Spence (1978), and Green and Porter (1984) all show that when actions are not observable, detection of cheating is impeded and output restriction is less severe as a consequence. It is natural therefore to ask if oligopolists have private incentives to share information. If firms are going to collude explicitly then the answer is yes – sharing information facilitates reaching and enforcing an agreement. But what about tacit situations?

This question has been studied by many. Novshek and Sonnenschein (1982), Clarke (1983), Vives (1984), Li (1985), and Gal-Or (1985) analyze the effects of information exchange among oligopolists each of which has a private signal about the intercept of a linear demand function, and Fried (1984), Li (1985), Katz (1985), and Shapiro (1986) examine the effects of sharing information about firm-specific costs. These studies suggest that in many situations firms that do not plan to collude, while having an interest in acquiring information, do not find it to be in their private interest to share this information. To clarify the flavor of these results, we discuss Clark's model.

In this model, firms receive information about a, the random demand intercept net of unit cost, and must decide whether to share this information. Pooling of information has two consequences: it reduces the variance of the errors in the estimates of a and it correlates the strategies that the firms choose. The first effect increases expected profits but, in Cournot competition, the second effect is detrimental. Clarke shows that the second effect dominates so that there is never a mutual incentive for firms to share private information unless they plan to collude. Reciprocally, information-sharing agreements and pooling schemes can be expected to signal collusion.

Other papers such as those by Vives (1984) and Li (1985) show that Clarke's result is not general but depends on specific assumptions. Vives demonstrates that the result depends on the assumptions of Cournot competition and of

[12] Our list of supergame price-war models is not exhaustive. For example, Maskin and Tirole (1988) construct a model that leads to Edgeworth cycles. The notion of cheating on collusive agreements was introduced by Stigler (1964). It has recently been developed in a repeated-game context by Rees (1985) among others.

homogeneous products, whereas Li shows that it depends on the assumption of uncertainty about a common (and not a firm-specific) parameter. When these assumptions are changed, other outcomes are possible. In particular, firms may wish to share.

Through these studies, therefore, we gain new insights into the effects of information acquisition and transition on oligopolistic behavior. Contrary to simplistic views, sharing can be compatible with the search for a noncooperative, noncollusive equilibrium. More important, circumstances under which sharing facilitates collusion can be identified.

Imperfect information can lead to other counterintuitive results. It is generally believed that collusion is more likely when there are fewer firms in an industry. Horizontal mergers are therefore viewed with suspicion. Davidson and Deneckere (1984), however, show that when a tacitly collusive agreement is enforced by a trigger-price strategy that is not sustainable, a merger reduces the chance that collusion becomes sustainable in the future.

The reason for their result is as follows. Enforcement of tacit collusion is easier when the threat point (the noncooperative outcome) is less desirable; that is to say, it is easier to threaten when the punishment is severe. A merger, however, increases the profitability of outside firms and, in particular, the threat point becomes more profitable. As losses due to retaliation decline, collusion becomes more difficult to sustain.

Other very different models can produce the same result – that collusion is easier to sustain when there are more firms in the industry. For example, Fraysse and Moreaux (1985) consider a market where there are n symmetric potential Cournot competitors. The game is repeated a finite number of times and there is no discounting.

Because there are fixed costs, it is possible that in equilibrium not all firms will produce. It is not clear, however, which firms will be active. For this reason, there may be multiple noncooperative equilibria of the one-shot game and collusive behavior can arise even though the game is repeated only finitely often. The threat of excluding a deviant firm from the market is credible and therefore gives rise to manipulative behavior.

Fraysse and Moreaux show that tacit collusion can occur when there is an intermediate number of firms. There must be enough potential competitors so that multiple equilibria exist. But there must not be so many firms that profit is negative when all produce.

At this stage some broad conclusions can be suggested. The most striking result is the multiplicity of theoretical possibilities for tacit collusion, many of which can be enforced by simple strategies such as tit for tat or Nash reversion. In addition, seemingly disequilibrium dynamics such as price wars may not be evidence of cartel breakdown. Instead, they may be phases of equilibrium tacitly collusive strategies. We return to the (too) broad result that almost all industries can be tacitly collusive almost all of the time.[13] To go beyond this, it is necessary to analyze the particular circumstances of an industry in an attempt to determine the feasibility of collusion. In many cases, this will lead us back to the old notions of factors that facilitate or hinder collusion that were discussed in Section 2.

In addition, many theories seem to be in conflict with intuitive notions about structure–conduct–performance. For example, under many circumstances firms will share too little information from a social point of view. Also, the ease and strength of collusion may not be a monotonic function of the number of firms in the industry. These findings, if robust, add greatly to the complexity of competition policy. It seems necessary to examine empirical research such as the cross-industry studies covered in Chapter 17 of this Handbook to determine just how important these results actually are. Here we turn to some recent attempts to test for tacit collusion in a game-theoretic setting.[14]

3.2.3. Testing for tacit collusion

In this subsection we examine empirical models that are explicitly dynamic. Static models are discussed later under the heading of "testing deviations from price-taking behavior". Two questions are important in the dynamic literature. The first is whether it is possible to detect punishment phases or periods of price wars using data on prices and quantities, and the second is whether we can use price-war data to determine what strategies firms use to support tacitly collusive outcomes. In contrast, the principal question that the static literature explores (see Subsection 4.1.1) is just how collusive tacitly collusive outcomes really are. That is, they ask how far price deviates from marginal cost in a particular industry equilibrium.

Porter (1983b) tests the Green and Porter (1984) model of tacit collusion under uncertain demand. His principal object is to distinguish tacitly collusive from punishment phases. He uses weekly aggregate time-series data on the Joint Executive Committee railroad cartel from 1880 to 1886. This price-setting cartel controlled eastbound rail transportation from Chicago to the eastern seaboard for many years.

The econometric test exploits the fact that, if collusion is being supported by a trigger-price strategy, there will be periodic switches between collusive and

[13]When optimal (most severe) punishments such as those studied by Abreu (1986) are introduced, this result becomes even stronger.

[14]Our theoretical treatment of tacit collusion has been far from comprehensive. Many other tools for tacit collusion have been analyzed in the literature. For example, Rotemberg and Saloner (1985) study the role of inventories in supporting collusion, Bernheim and Whinston (1985) show how a common-marketing agency can generate a collusive outcome, and Brock and Scheinkman (1985) explore the effects of capacity constraints on the ability to punish defectors. Finally, Roberts (1985) shows how adverse selection can complicate detection and punishment. For a comparison of the supergame and state–space analysis of tacit collusion, see Fudenberg and Tirole (1986).

noncollusive output levels. The model thus lends itself to simultaneous-equation switching-regression estimation. The regression probabilities are unknown but endogenously predicted.

Porter finds that in reversionary periods behavior is Bertrand, as predicted by the model. And in collusive periods, Cournot outputs are produced. Firms therefore are able to improve their situation through repeated play but profit falls far short of the monopoly level. Finally, the hypothesis that no switches in firm behavior occurred is easily rejected by the data, lending support to the model of two regimes.

Slade (1987a) also tests for tacit collusion and finds support for profits higher than those implied by Nash behavior in the one-shot game. She uses daily time-series data on retail gasoline prices, sales, and unit costs that were collected in Vancouver, British Columbia, during a price-war period. The data pertain to individual service stations. As a consequence, demand, reaction, and cost functions can be estimated at a very disaggregate level. The empirical test discriminates between the continuous reaction-function and discontinuous punishment strategies developed in Slade (1985).

In a second test, Slade (1987b) develops Bayesian models where firms use price wars to learn about new demand conditions and about rival strategies. The technique of Kalman filtering is employed to model the learning process. She finds that the empirical evidence points to the use of very simple supergame strategies over more complex alternatives. This conclusion is not surprising, given that collusion in this market is purely tacit and that no overt communication takes place.

These studies conclude that repeated play enables firms to enhance their profit position vis-à-vis the noncooperative outcome of the one-shot game. Nevertheless, industry profit is far short of the monopoly level. In both industries, pricing decisions are made at frequent intervals. It therefore seems unlikely that high discount rates are the cause of failure to achieve near-monopoly profit. Instead, coordination and communication difficulties are probably greater than assumed in most theoretical analyses.

An interesting variant of the empirical-supergame approach can be found in Roberts and Samuelson (1985) who test for nonprice competition and collusion in the U.S. cigarette industry. They find that in some instances equilibria are not subgame perfect. If this were to become an empirical regularity, we might have to conclude that theoretical notions of perfection are too stringent.

4. Collusion, public interest, and government policy

Having completed our survey of models of collusive behavior, it is time to turn to issues of public interest and government policy. First, we look at empirical techniques that can be used to identify collusion. Next, we discuss methods of and problems associated with measuring the welfare losses due to restriction of competition. We then turn to possible efficiencies associated with concentration and the tradeoffs that must be made as a consequence. Finally, we consider whether market failures call for government intervention or some form of planning.

4.1. *Identifying collusion*

We have already seen how the structure of markets might affect the ease of colluding. Factors that play a role include the number and size distribution of firms, the information structure of the market, firm technology and costs, and consumer tastes. Here we discuss empirical tests that can be used to identify collusion, both tacit and explicit. Under this heading, we cover econometric tests of deviations from price-taking behavior and patterns of firm bidding.

4.1.1. *Testing deviations from price-taking behavior*

There is a large literature on the subject of testing for the absence of price-taking behavior. These studies assess equilibrium deviations of price from marginal cost in specific industries. Rather than discuss each article, we set up a general method and then discuss possible modifications.

Consider an industry comprised of n firms that produce a homogeneous product. We reproduce a typical firm's first-order condition for profit maximization, equation (9) from Subsection 3.1.2,

$$(p - MC^i)/p = (s^i/\varepsilon)(1 + R^i). \tag{9''}$$

Given data on prices, quantities, and the determinants of costs, equation (9″) can be estimated econometrically to obtain parameter values for the vector R^i.[15] This often involves estimating a demand equation, n cost functions, and n first-order conditions as a simultaneous system. Although the studies differ in many respects, this is essentially the approach taken by Iwata (1974), Cubbin (1975), Gollop and Roberts (1979), Geroski (1982), and Roberts (1984a).

When estimates of R^i have been obtained, tests of various oligopoly models can be performed. For example, $R^i = -1$ is the relevant hypothesis for price-taking behavior and $R^i = 0$ tests the Cournot assumption. In addition, if certain firms are found to be price takers or Cournot–Nash players, while others have positive conjectures, dominant-firm and Stackelberg models can be evaluated.

There are many possible modifications to this procedure. For example, Bresnahan (1987) and Slade (1986c) consider differentiated products and Appel-

[15] If there are many firms in the industry, some structure must be placed on R^i and MC^i.

baum (1979, 1982) analyzes the use of aggregate data. In addition, estimated R's can be related to exogenous factors that can contribute to the likelihood of collusion [Anderson (1984)], to the characteristics of the firms [Slade (1986c)], to the ease of entry [Spiller and Favaro (1984)] or to the role of import competition [Ilmakunnas (1985)]. Finally, Gelfand and Spiller (1987) assess oligopolistic interaction in multiple-product markets and Roberts (1984b) tests for the presence or absence of nonprice competition among firms.

Estimated conjectures can best be interpreted as providing a convenient summary description of market behavior, which will often involve a mix of cooperative and noncooperative elements. With this in mind, Schmalensee (1987) suggests a natural measure of the extent to which industry behavior is collusive. This measure is $1/\phi$, where ϕ is defined by

$$\phi = \sum_{i=1}^{n} 1/(1 + R^i). \tag{22}$$

The measure is generally confined to the unit interval, with $1/\phi = 1$ implying perfect collusion.

Another approach to testing price-taking behavior relies on discrete shifts in exogenous variables to identify modes of pricing conduct. Just and Chern (1980), Sumner (1981), Bresnahan (1982), and Sullivan (1985) are examples of this second class. It is clear that responses to either demand or supply shocks can differ according to industry conduct. Just and Chern examine a radical change in production technology in a market where buyers have market power and Sumner and Sullivan look at changes in tax treatment in a market where sellers have market power.

The methods that rely on shifts in exogenous variables require both pre and post-change data. Baker and Bresnahan (1985), however, develop a technique for assessing a change in market power (due to a merger in their case) from pre-change data alone. When potential and not actual gains or losses are to be assessed, this method should prove useful.

As is expected, the findings of these studies differ, depending on the industry examined. Some industries are best characterized by price-taking, others by Cournot, and still others by dominant-firm behavior modes. Most, however, do not fit neatly into a particular category. Nevertheless, price taking seems to be the exception rather than the rule. This may just mean, however, that industries that are obvious oligopolies were selected for the tests.

Finally, a problem with all of these approaches is that it is impossible to distinguish pure tacit collusion from illegal price-fixing or other explicit cartel agreements. What matters for the empirical estimates is the outcome and not the cause of noncompetitive pricing. This problem seems difficult and perhaps impossible to overcome.

The normative implications of noncompetitive pricing are discussed in Subsection 4.2.

4.1.2. *Bidding strategies*

Two questions emerge when examining bidding strategies. The first is whether particular patterns of bidding are associated with collusion and the second is whether competition in bidding is desirable.

The conventional wisdom holds that identical bids suggest collusion. For example, federal agencies in the United States are required to report cases of identical bids. However, it is not clear why members of a cartel would decide to bid identically. When they do, the problem of output allocation is not solved. Much more conducive to allocating the rents from collusion in a prespecified manner is a system of rotating low bids (the system practiced by the electrical-equipment conspiracy).

In an empirical analysis of U.S. firms that were successfully prosecuted for collusive bidding, Comanor and Schankerman (1976) find that a system of rotating bids is more likely when participants are few. When large numbers of firms are involved, however, identical bids are found more frequently. Because firms can be very ingenious in devising rotating systems, and because identical bids can be the result of identical firms operating in competitive markets, it seems difficult to draw general conclusions about collusion from bidding patterns. Nevertheless, Hendricks and Porter (1987), using data on offshore oil and gas leases, find evidence that neighbor firms coordinate their bidding decisions.

The second question deals with the optimality of competitive-bidding systems. Wilson (1977) shows that under reasonable assumptions, when the number of bidders increases, the value of a winning bid converges to the true value of the item being auctioned. Competition in bidding therefore seems desirable.

Many markets where bidding is important, however, are characterized by few participants and uncertainty about the value of the item being auctioned. This is particularly true of markets for mineral leases and offshore oil. Reece (1978) shows that under these circumstances, firms capture a large share of the rent and advocates government-sponsored exploration programs as a consequence. This is a type of collusion in the form of information sharing. DeBrock and Smith (1983) conclude that under the same circumstances, joint bidding by firms (which results in private information sharing) is more efficient than a noncooperative system.

Our assessment is therefore that noncooperative bidding is not always optimal. In markets where firms are few and information is scarce, some form of cooperation may be preferable.

4.2. *Collusion and restriction of competition*

In this subsection we deal with the detrimental effects of collusion. The discussion centers on the measurement of welfare loss in both partial and general-equilibrium settings. It is well known that distortions in an economy lead to losses in productive efficiency. Whether it is possible to measure these losses and whether efficiency should be the sole welfare criterion are the issues addressed here.

4.2.1. Market definition

In the discussion of the effects of concentration on pricing, it was implicitly assumed that a market was well defined. For example, equation (9) shows that deviations from marginal-cost pricing are directly proportional to market share, q^i/Q. But what is Q? Before a market distortion can be measured, it is necessary to agree upon a market.

It is generally recognized that a market has two principal dimensions, product characteristics and geographic extent. Because most products have close substitutes and because many geographic markets overlap, however, it is rarely easy to delineate either dimension exactly.

To facilitate discussion, suppose that we focus on a market as the ideal product line and geographic region from the point of view of firms wishing to collude. That is to say, a market should be large enough so that price can be raised above marginal cost without generating repercussions from outside that bring it back down, and it should be small enough so that it can be coordinated efficiently. Within this framework, we can ask about the principal determinants of the market.

When delineating a product market, one must consider close substitutes. If two commodities are substitutes in use, it is not profitable to restrict the output of only one because consumers will easily switch. Similarly, if two commodities are substitutes in production, it is not profitable to restrict the output of only one because plants that produce the second will quickly convert. Second-hand markets must also be considered. Many recycled products are virtually identical to new and therefore severely limit the market power of primary producers.

When delineating a geographic market, one must consider transport costs, artificial barriers such as tariffs and quotas, and the other costs of transaction across regions. If, transaction costs are low relative to price, two regions should be in the same geographic market for a given product. Considerations of geographic-market extent are extremely important for open economies. For example, it is meaningless to say that Belgian industry is highly concentrated if Belgium is not the appropriate market.

In addition to product and spatial characteristics, markets also have a time dimension. It is in general true that markets are larger in the long than in the short run. With the passage of time, consumer tastes and production technologies change, transport costs are lowered, and artificial barriers can disappear.

Most empirical market-definition studies concentrate on the spatial aspects of markets. However, similar techniques can be used to delineate product markets. There are two standard approaches; one can look at trade flows or at the behavior of product prices over time.

Elzinga and Hogarty (1973) set up a test based on trade flows. They consider a region to be a market if imports and exports are not important. A problem with trade statistics, however, is that they do not detect overlapping markets where, for example, A trades with B, B trades with C and so forth. Nevertheless, in the case of differentiated products, trade statistics may be the only reliable information.

In the case of international markets, it is not clear whether import figures (trade flows) or the entire productive capacity of foreigners should be used in calculating market shares. Landes and Posner (1981) suggest that if foreign products can penetrate a market, barriers are sufficiently low so that all foreign production could be diverted.

Leitzinger and Tamor (1983) examine this issue by testing whether U.S. industry profitability is more highly correlated with U.S. or with world concentration ratios and find that world concentration is a significantly better predictor. If this is true for the United States, it is apt to be even more so for smaller more open economies. Neverthelesss, there are many markets such as sand and gravel that are distinctly local and one should not jump to the conclusion that all markets are worldwide. A careful analysis is required in each case.

When products are relatively homogeneous, the time-series behavior of prices can be used to identify markets. Stigler and Sherwin (1985) provide a static analysis of the use of prices in market delineation. Because there may be lags in price responses across regions, however, a static analysis is insufficient.

Dynamic models are developed by Horowitz (1981), Spiller and Huang (1986), and Slade (1986a). Horowitz tests for the dynamic stability of price differences across regions after a shock has disturbed them from their equilibrium values. Slade uses time-series tests for causality and exogeneity to see if price determination in one region is statistically exogenous to the process that determines prices in another. Finally, Spiller and Huang use switching-regression techniques to distinguish periods of arbitrage from periods of autarky as supply, demand, and transport conditions change.

Special market-definition issues pertaining to unique markets are discussed by Ordover and Willig (1985) for R&D and by Slade (1986b) for natural resources.

4.2.2. Measuring welfare loss

Suppose that we can divide an economy into sectors that represent valid markets. It is then possible to estimate the deadweight loss due to oligopoly pricing in each sector and to sum over the sectors to obtain an economy-wide loss measure. This is the procedure used by Harberger (1954), criticized by many, and followed by an even greater number.

First, one should note that this procedure captures only the efficiency aspects of the loss due to monopoly pricing. We put this aside for the moment.

Assume that an economy consists of N sectors. Let p, q, MC, and ε be vectors of prices, quantities, marginal costs, and price elasticities of demand for the different sectors. Harberger used the formula for deadweight loss D,

$$D \simeq 1/2\, \Delta q^{\mathrm{T}} \Delta p, \tag{23}$$

due to Hotelling (1938) to approximate the economy-wide loss. In (23), the symbol Δ represents a change due to oligopoly pricing.

Expression (23) can be written as

$$D \simeq -1/2(p - MC)^{\mathrm{T}} M (p - MC), \tag{24}$$

where M is a diagonal matrix with each diagonal element M_{ii} equal to

$$M_{ii} = -\varepsilon^i q^i / p^i = \partial q^i / \partial p^i. \tag{25}$$

M_{ii} is evaluated at the distorted prices. Using the fact that, when marginal costs are constant, $(p^i - MC^i)/q^i$ equals the rate of return on sales, D can be expressed in terms of observable variables alone.[16]

Hotelling derived his formula by disregarding higher-order terms in a Taylor-series expansion of a utility function. (23) therefore yields an approximate measure when deviations from competitive pricing are small. Neverthelesss, Harberger applied the formula to an economy where distortions were sizable. Substantial error can therefore be expected. His conclusion is that D is less than one-tenth of 1 percent of national income. Similar studies by Schwartzman (1960) and others yield similar conclusions.

Bergson (1973) gives a systematic analysis of the problems inherent in this sort of calculation. He criticizes the model on two counts, both of which are familiar to welfare theorists. First, demand in Harberger's analysis is Marshallian demand. In order for it to be possible to calculate what Bergson calls net compensating variations from Marshallian demand curves, it must be true that income effects are zero.

Second, equation (23) neglects all general-equilibrium effects in that it is assumed that price changes have no repercussions in other sectors. In order for (23) to yield correct answers, therefore, it must additionally be true that all cross elasticities of demand are zero. These are very severe restrictions.

To remedy these problems, Kay (1983) proposes a general-equilibrium formula for estimating deadweight loss based on an expenditure function, a tool that is borrowed from the optimal-taxation literature. Let $E(p, u)$ be the minimum expenditure needed to achieve utility u at a vector of prices p.[17] Then D is

$$D = E(p, \bar{u}) - E(MC, \bar{u}) - (p - MC)^{\mathrm{T}} q, \tag{26}$$

[16] Harberger assumed that ε^i equals one for all i.

[17] We assume a representative consumer in order to abstract from distributional effects.

where $\bar{u}$ is the utility at distorted prices. Using a Taylor-series expansion, this expression can be approximated by

$$D \simeq -1/2(p - MC)^{\mathrm{T}}((\partial q^i/\partial p^j)_{\bar{u}})(p - MC), \tag{27}$$

where $(\partial q^i/\partial p^j)_{\bar{u}}$ is a full matrix of cross partials evaluated at $\bar{u}$.[18]

The informational requirements for computing D from (27) are large indeed. Instead, Kay derives upper and lower bounds on D corresponding to the assumptions that all firms play Nash and collusively, respectively. Because the spread in these bounds is wide, Kay concludes that at least potentially, substantial monopoly losses are possible.

Even though the informational requirements for calculating actual losses using general-equilibrium methods are large, the successful construction of applied general-equilibrium models which incorporate noncompetitive sectors [see, for example, Harris (1984)] means that such exercises are not beyond reach.

Another attack on the Harberger approach emerges from the rent-seeking literature [Tullock (1967) and Posner (1975)]. The basic idea is that the existence of an opportunity to obtain profits will attract resources into efforts to obtain monopolies up to the point where all monopoly profits are dissipated. The last term in equation (26), therefore, which represents monopoly profit, should not be subtracted when losses are estimated. If we call this term Π, then the true social cost of monopoly is $D + \Pi$. Using Harberger's numbers, Posner calculates the social cost of monopoly at 3.4 percent of national income, a considerably larger number than 0.1 percent. Cowling and Mueller (1978), in an independent study, calculate $D + \Pi$ to be 13 percent of gross corporate product.

Finally, let us recall the role of what Liebenstein (1966) calls X-inefficiency. Once external pressures are reduced so that cost minimization and profit maximization are not required for survival, technical inefficiency and organizational slack can emerge within the firm. The effect can be to increase MC and therefore to reduce measured D as well as measured Π, with a resulting understatement of deadweight loss.

Others claim that social costs are less than $D + \Pi$. For example, Littlechild (1983) argues that not all profit is due to monopoly. When one takes into account windfall gains and managerial creativity as sources of profit, losses are very much reduced. Finally, Rogerson (1982) constructs a game-theoretic model to show that the Posner claim is true only at the margin. Firms may be inframarginal because they are incumbents or because they have lower costs of gaining the information required to participate. As a consequence, not all rent is transformed

[18]Equations (24) and (27) look very similar. It should be noted, however, that in (24) $\partial q/\partial p$ is evaluated for movements along the Marshallian demand curve, whereas in (27) movements are along the Hicksian demand curve.

into costs. In both models, the social cost of monopoly lies somewhere between D and $D + \Pi$.

So far we have discussed only economy-wide measures of deadweight loss. One rarely has the opportunity, however, of moving from a distorted to a totally undistorted economy. More relevant is the question of calculating efficiency gains due to moving a single sector towards undistorted prices. Here, the prospects for even approximate measurement are much poorer.[19] The theory of second best tells us that we cannot even predict the sign of the change, no less the magnitude. Neverthelesss, this is the important policy issue faced in all antitrust cases.

Attempts at measuring welfare changes in a partial-equilibrium setting usually finesse the issue. For example, Dansby and Willig (1979) assume that welfare is a function solely of the outputs of the firms in the industry, thus bypassing all general-equilibrium considerations.

Dixit and Stern (1982) suggest the use of shadow prices to circumvent issues of second best. For example, they advocate using shadow wage rates when there is unemployment and shadow prices for imports when currencies are overvalued. Issues of second best, however, arise in closed, fully employed economies. Neverthelesss, this is a step in the right direction in that it deals with issues of less than full employment ignored by others.

The difficulties associated with calculating efficiency gains in a partial-equilibrium setting do not lead us to conclude that governments should abandon all policies towards monopolization and merger. Instead, we believe first that there is no general a priori argument or evidence suggesting that monopoly distortions in an economy are negligible; and second, that economic policy should not be based on issues of productive efficiency alone but should take into account the many consequences of monopolization including distributional and employment effects [for an early view, see Adams and Dirlam (1976)]. This prescription of course only complicates the problem. Nevertheless, the profession has in general gone very far in one direction and has tended to neglect the others.

Efficiency gains or losses may not even be the largest source of welfare change. For example, consider the effect of OPEC. Prior to OPEC it could be argued that world oil prices were too low. Multinational producers did not have property rights in the Middle East and were thus most likely neglecting user costs in making pricing decisions. In contrast, after OPEC, prices may have been too high due to monopoly power. It is difficult to deduce anything about efficiency under these circumstances, even when the conditions for neglecting general-equilibrium effects are met. In contrast, few would feel that the massive transfer of wealth from consumers to the owners of oil-producing properties was negligible from a welfare point of view.

[19] One can, of course, use GE formulas to calculate these losses, but often only single-sector data are available.

For a more concrete example, Comanor and Smiley (1975) estimate the impact of monopoly profit on the distribution of household wealth in the United States. Unlike the Harberger results for efficiency, they find that the presence of monopoly has had a major impact on the degree of inequality. In fact, they estimate that the relative wealth position of over 93 percent of households would be improved in the absence of monopoly pricing.

Employment effects could also be important. General-equilibrium formulas for deadweight loss are based on the assumption that when workers are released from the monopolized sector, they find jobs in the competitive sector. This assumption, however, is often not realistic. For example, if INCO closes its mines in Sudbury, Ontario, workers have few alternatives, at least in the short run. If the opportunity wage rate elsewhere is zero, losses due to monopolization will be large indeed. This assumption is very extreme and not likely to be met in practice. Nevertheless, it also seems unrealistic to assume full employment when calculating losses.

These considerations suggest that perhaps too much time is being spent in estimating the area of triangles and not enough effort is being expended on assessing other consequences of monopoly.

4.3. Efficiency tradeoffs

In the previous subsection we considered the detrimental effects of concentration and collusion. Here we examine possible efficiencies. Much has been written on this subject, which is very broad.[20] We limit ourselves to a brief treatment of specific issues most of which are covered at length elsewhere in this Handbook. In particular, we consider the static economies of scale, scope, and product variety and the dynamic efficiencies of learning and technical change.

4.3.1. Static efficiencies

Economies of scale have long been proposed as an antitrust defense [see, for example, Williamson (1968, 1977) and the references therein]. The formal analysis of economies of scope, in contrast, is somewhat more recent [see, for example, Willig (1979), Panzar and Willig (1981) and Waterson (1983)]. The two sorts of economies, however, can be analyzed in a similar framework.

Economies of scale are said to exist whenever long-run average cost declines with output. This can occur either because there are set-up costs or because marginal costs decline as production expands. Economies of scope arise when joint production of two or more products is cheaper than the cost of producing

[20] For example, see Dewey (1959), McGee (1971), and Bork (1978).

the products separately. Again, the economy can work either through fixed or through marginal cost. We assume that the products produced are substitutes so that under monopoly there is a tendency to restrict the output of both.

When either economy occurs, there is a tradeoff between cost reduction and output restriction as the number of firms varies. The net effect will in general depend on many factors including the own and cross-price elasticities of demand, the own and cross-output elasticities of total cost, the degree of collusion in the market, and whether the nature of collusion changes with the number of firms.

By making sufficient assumptions about demand, cost, and collusion, one can obtain partial-equilibrium formulas for the sizes of cost savings and surplus reductions. This is not our intention here. Rather, we simply wish to emphasize that, when scale and scope economies exist over a broad range of outputs, under a fairly wide range of assumptions few firms may be preferred to many. In addition, the optimal market structure will almost never be perfectly competitive.

Whether or not mergers are beneficial under these circumstances, however, is a very different issue. Mergers occur between existing firms whose cost structures are not completely flexible. When two firms merge, it is not clear if cost reductions can be realized ex post. For example, if the economy is due to fixed costs, it may be impossible to realize a cost saving without closing one firm's production facilities. As with most complex issues, detailed analysis is required for each special case.

A further question is: When there are economies of scale or scope, does a free-entry equilibrium result in an optimal number of firms? This problem is analyzed by von Weizsacker (1980), Perry (1984), and Mankiw and Whinston (1986) who conclude that the answer is no. In particular, the circumstances under which there will be too many firms so that entry restrictions are desirable are not pathological.

The analysis when there is a variety of products is not very different from the analysis of scale and scope. Suppose that each firm produces a single product but that products differ across firms. Suppose, in addition, that average costs decline with output. Variety is valued by consumers who have heterogeneous tastes. In this case, the tradeoffs are between product variety (which equals the number of firms), market power (which may be inversely related to the number of firms), and cost savings (which are inversely related to the number of firms). Again, the precise directions and magnitudes of these effects depend on tastes, technology, and other market parameters. In formal analyses of this situation Spence (1976) and Dixit and Stiglitz (1977) show that it is possible for a free-entry equilibrium to result in too many firms (too much variety). When this is true, entry restrictions could again improve welfare.

The same caveat, however, about ex ante and ex post applies here. When a merger between two existing firms occurs, there may be little change in either the number of products produced or the cost of producing these products. Nevertheless, the presumption is that mergers reduce variety.

In the previous analysis of variety, differentiation is horizontal. That is to say, if all products are offered at the same price, consumers differ in their preferences (some prefer red and some prefer blue cars, for example). If differentiation is vertical, when prices are equal everyone prefers the highest quality (everyone wants a high-speed car). Shaked and Sutton (1983) show that with vertical differentiation and price competition, if variable costs do not increase too rapidly with quality, there exists a limit to the number of firms that can profitably coexist in the market. Under these circumstances, a structural policy designed to increase the number of firms in a market would result in reduced welfare.

Economies of scope, scale, and product variety, therefore result in complex tradeoffs that must be weighed in forming competition policy. Determining the optimal number of firms is never a simple problem. One can say, however, that when these economies are prevalent, approximating the competitive outcome is not a reasonable goal.

4.3.2. Dynamic efficiencies

Dynamic economies occur over time and, as with most intertemporal problems, the issues are even more complex than with static economies. We examine two dynamic effects: learning and technical change.

Learning is said to occur when unit cost declines with cumulative output. In assessing competition policy, it is important whether learning occurs within an industry or within a firm. When the benefits of learning cannot be captured by firms, there is no incentive to have fewer firms in an industry. Under these circumstances, however, another set of problems arises due to the public-good nature of learning. Ghemawat and Spence (1985) discuss this distinction. In the standard economic analysis of learning [Spence (1981) and Fudenberg and Tirole (1983)] learning is firm specific.

The special dynamic issues that arise as a consequence of learning, such as the possibility of strategic behavior, are beyond the scope of this chapter. The interested reader is referred to the references above. From the point of view of competition policy, however, learning bears a resemblance to scale economies. For example, there exists a tradeoff between cost reduction and output restriction as the number of firms varies. The calculation of the sizes of these effects is even more complex than with static economies but the same qualitative conclusions hold. In particular, it is not generally the case that more firms are preferred to less or that unregulated markets lead to optimal outcomes.

Technical change, which expands the production possibilities available to society, is perhaps the most important dynamic economy. Few economists would disagree with the claim that the dynamic-efficiency gains from continuing innovation far outweigh the static gains from marginal-cost pricing. In addition, in markets where innovation is frequent, competition policy can be less vigilant. Monopoly rents will be constantly eroded as new products and processes are introduced. The real question is what role market structure plays in the innovative process.

The debate about the relationship between market structure and innovation has been going on at least since the time of Schumpeter (1934) and yet economists still hold diametrically opposed views on the subject [see Nelson and Winter (1982) for a discussion of the issues]. It is, however, possible to make a case for the position that perfectly competitive markets can be inimical to technical change.

First, it is not always easy to capture the rents from innovation. When knowledge takes the form of a public good and there are few firms in an industry, however, private and social costs of innovation differ less than under competition. As a consequence, underinvestment in research is less dramatic. Second, if capital markets are imperfect and internal funds are needed to finance R&D, oligopoly rents can provide these funds.

However, if empirical evidence were to suggest a positive correlation between market concentration and innovation, such a correlation would not reveal the direction of causation.[21] In the previous examples, it was claimed that a concentrated market could be conducive to innovation. The reverse pattern could also be true. A firm that innovates successfully may grow and capture a larger share of the market, causing concentration to increase.

We have seen how competitive markets may not be conducive to research. At the opposite extreme a monopolized market may also be inimical to innovation. Without the pressure of rivals, a monopolist may have few incentives to invest in R&D. In addition, the monopolist has a vested interest in protecting current product lines.

Dasgupta and Stiglitz (1980) build a theoretical model that confirms many of these intuitive notions concerning the relationship between market structure and innovation. In their model, at least for low levels of concentration, there is a positive correlation between concentration and R&D effort. In addition, they find that there may be excessive duplication of effort in an unregulated economy, in the sense that too much is spent relative to the cost reduction produced. Finally, they find that a pure monopolist underinvests in R&D.

We thus see that with dynamic economies, similar conclusions hold as with static. Conditions of perfect competition as well as of monopoly may not be optimal. In addition, unregulated markets may not result in efficient outcomes.

[21]The reader is referred to Chaper 19 in this Handbook for an in-depth discussion of the empirical evidence.

With dynamic efficiencies, however, we must add to these shared complexities. The problems of weighing tradeoffs are even more difficult because it is insufficient to merely determine magnitudes of effects. The time pattern of costs and benefits must also be considered.

To conclude, an analysis of the multiple aspects of efficiency and of the second-best problems characterizing many situations suggests that it would be presumptuous to identify precisely the efficiency consequences of most business conduct and to advocate fine-tuned optimal antitrust rules. Nevertheless, these difficulties do not lead us to conclude that governments should abandon all policy towards monopolization and merger.

We know that there is no theorem proving the optimality of non-neoclassical, Schumpeterian forms of competition [see, for example, Marris and Mueller (1980)]. The inability of firms to appropriate a sufficient proportion of consumers' surplus can lead to a composition of product types and a rate of technical advance which can vary widely from what would be socially desirable. In our opinion, the general presumption must be that an antitrust policy augmenting competitive forces is needed to enhance economic efficiency. The burden of proof that specific practices which appear to represent a restriction of competition actually represent an increase in competition in a second-best sense or in the relevant dynamic and uncertain framework must be supported by those wishing to adopt these practices.

4.4. Industrial policy

Most countries seem to accept the need for some form of antitrust policy. It is believed that many monopolies and cartels are detrimental to the public interest and that therefore public authorities should be wary. Anticombines laws and the vigor of enforcement of these laws vary from country to country. Nevertheless, there seems to be a consensus that this is a legitimate government activity.

Behind the acceptance of the need for antitrust policy lies the notion that competitive markets are socially optimal and that therefore industries should be made workably competitive. It is of course also accepted that some industries such as communications are natural monopolies. These industries are therefore either nationalized or regulated.

We have just seen, however, that in many instances competitive-market structures are not optimal and that the workings of an unregulated market mechanism, even in the absence of scale economies, can result in inefficient outcomes. A question that naturally comes to mind, therefore, is whether antitrust policy is enough or whether there is a need for an overall industrial policy. This is the final question that we wish to address.

The term industrial policy is very broad and ranges anywhere from a plan concerning the desired number and size distribution of firms in every industry to a vague intent to subsidize certain types of activity while discouraging others.

More specifically, there are two extreme views of industrial policy.[22] For many, the best industrial policy is no policy at all. Where a policy aims at slowing down the process of structural change and keeping alive declining sectors, it damages the rest of the economy. And when it tries to influence growth through the redeployment of human and physical capital, it often lacks valid criteria. In both cases, allowing the government to replace markets as the allocator of resources raises the familiar issues of political failures and rent-seeking behavior [see, for example, Curzon-Price (1981)].

At the other end of the spectrum, some argue that free-market forces do not establish appropriate outcomes and that market failures are significant. A voluntary policy based on a national consensus and a close relationship between government and enterprises could then represent a substantial improvement in social welfare [see, for example, Magaziner and Reich (1982)].

More recent approaches adopt less sanguine views and try to establish connections between the vague concept of industrial policy and recent theoretical works in industrial organization [Geroski and Jacquemin (1985), Yarrow (1985), and Dixit (1986)]. A central issue is the strategic behavior of governments; governments as well as firms appear to be players. By committing themselves to suitable policies, they are able to change the outcome of the oligopoly game.

In this sense, every country has an industrial policy. The problem with existing policies, however, is that they are not written down, openly debated, and agreed upon. Instead, they come in through the back door in the form of investment-tax credits, depletion allowances, tariff protection, tax-free status, and other forms of subsidies and special tax treatment. These policies have unacknowledged effects. For example, capital-intensive industries may be encouraged at the expense of those that are more labor intensive.

An advantage to an articulated industrial policy is that special treatment of certain industries has to be justified and reconciled with an overall pattern. Instead, what we see today is privileges going to industries with outstanding lobbying skills. The results surely cannot be efficient.

In this subsection we examine cooperative behavior that governments can usefully encourage. There are many areas where noncooperative solutions are suboptimal. Some of these situations take the form of a prisoner's dilemma. Excessive expenditures on advertising or wasteful duplication of R&D effort are just two examples. In these instances, even firms might welcome the opportunity to have their hands tied – to precommit themselves to less effort. It is therefore not only the consumer that might benefit from government intervention.

[22] For various approaches to industrial policy, see the papers published in Jacquemin (1985).

We would like to single out two areas where we feel that special policy might be beneficial. These areas, which lie at opposite extremes, are R&D intensive industries and declining industries.

The public-good nature of knowledge has already been stressed. When this is an important consideration, firms underinvest in basic research. Patents are a partial remedy to the problem but do not eliminate it entirely. In addition, duplication of R&D effort can be wasteful and can lead to less cost reduction than if firms shared information. In line with the U.S. and EEC Regulations on cooperative research,[23] a lenient antitrust policy towards research joint ventures or cooperative laboratories could aid the dissemination of information and therefore increase efficiency.

Research activities can also be very risky. When risk is coupled with the need for large up-front outlays, private firms may be hesitant to undertake potentially profitable activities. Some forms of basic research require long periods from initial undertaking to final payoff. If firms have shorter planning horizons or higher discount rates than society, again, socially beneficial projects may not be undertaken.

Finally, "first mover" advantages coupled with effective barriers based on sunk costs such as R&D expenditures characterize many high-technology industries, and small historical accidents (such as which firm was the first to innovate) can have a large cumulative role in the temporal unfolding of an industry. This opens the door to a number of strategic issues including the role of government in R&D subsidies and in encouraging concerted actions to overcome existing barriers or to favor one equilibrium outcome over another. Government support may lead to equilibria in which favored firms choose to enter the international market while rivals have to decide otherwise. These situations are typified by industries such as aerospace, semicondutors and computers.

All of these factors point toward the need for cooperative research programs where governments play an active role. We do not mean to imply that all countries should subsidize high-technology industries. This would be particularly inappropriate in regions where labor is in excess supply and technological improvements move firms in the direction of capital intensity.[24] We do feel, however, that special cooperative policies might be warranted.

At the other extreme we have declining industries. Economic theories of firm exit rarely point to the optimality of a market solution [Ghemawat and Nalebuff (1985), for example]. We do not mean to suggest that governments should subsidize dying industries and prolong their lives artificially. It is often easier,

[23]For the United States, see the National Cooperative Research Act of 1984, Pub.L. 98-462, 98 Stat. 1815, and for the EEC, the block exemption Regulation R&D Agreements, *Journal of the European Communities*.

[24]It is often true, however, that high-technology industries are labor intensive. This accounts for the fact that many electronics firms are located in countries of moderate development in the Far East.

however, for a program of rationalization to proceed in an orderly fashion if it has the participation of an uninvolved party such as the government.

Indeed, in exit games the question of who goes first is at the heart of strategic competition. In various circumstances, it can be shown that even when it is clear to all that a market is in decline, each firm may decide to remain and, in such circumstances, there may be persistently low returns and little innovation in the industry over long periods of time. Outside intervention might then be needed to implement a program of rationalization to ensure exit in an orderly fashion.

Here again, there is little need for antitrust vigilance but for a different reason. With an industry that is dying, deviations from marginal-cost pricing have only a transitory impact on welfare. Government intervention in declining industries should therefore lean towards cooperative solutions rather than being concerned with the losses due to concentration.

By singling out particular industries that could benefit from cooperation, we do not wish to propose specific solutions to special problems. Rather, we wish to emphasize that there are many areas where cooperation at the national and international level can be beneficial.[25] The most important point, however, is that there is a need for countries to articulate, debate, and reach a consensus on industrial policy. Leaving this important area to special-interest lobbyists as is current practice does not seem likely to lead to efficient outcomes.

References

Aaronovitch, S. and Sawyer, M. (1975) 'Mergers, growth, and concentration', *Oxford Economic Papers*, 20:136–155.

Abreu, D. (1986) 'Extreme equilibrium of oligopolistic supergames', *Journal of Economic Theory*, 39:191–225.

Abreu, D., Pearce, D. and Stracchetti, E. (1986) 'Optimal cartel equilbira in supergames', *Journal of Economic Theory*, 39:251–269.

Adams, W. and Dirlam, J. (1976) 'Private planning and social efficiency', in: A. Jacquemin and H. de Jong, eds., *Theory of the firm and industrial organization, fundamentals of pure and applied economics*. New York: Harwood.

Anderson, J.E. (1984) 'Identification of interactive behavior in air service markets 1973–1976', *Journal of Industrial Economics*, 32:489–507.

Anderson, R.A. (1983) 'Quick response equilibrium', Department of Economics and Mathematics, University of California, Berkeley, mimeo.

Appelbaum, E. (1979) 'Testing price taking behavior', *Journal of Econometrics*, 9:283–294.

Appelbaum, E. (1982) 'The estimation of the degree of oligopoly power', *Journal of Econometrics*, 19:287–299.

[25]Because of arguments similar to those discussed in the case of private agents, countries have strong incentives to engage in noncooperative behavior even though the outcome is worse for all. In order to overcome these difficulties, it is necessary to design institutions that will enforce cooperative behavior and that do not ignore the strategic aspect of group decision-making. As shown by the Gibbard–Satterthwaite theorem [see, for example, the discussion in Green and Laffont (1979)], however, it is impossible to solve all the incentive problems involved in such a design.

Asch, P. and Seneca, J.J. (1976) 'Is collusion profitable?', *Review of Economics and Statistics*, 58:1–12.
Axelrod, R. (1984) *The evolution of cooperation*. New York: Basic Books.
Ayres, I. (1986) 'Deriving cartel behavior in a model with fringe competition', M.I.T., mimeo.
Bain, J.S. (1948) 'Output quotas in imperfect cartels', *Quarterly Journal of Economics*, 62:617–622.
Baker, J.B. and Bresnahan, T.F. (1985) 'The gains from merger and collusion in product-differentiated industries', *Journal of Industrial Economics*, 33:427–444.
Barzel, Y. (1968) 'Optimal timing of innovations', *Review of Economics and Statistics*, 50:348–355.
Benoit, J.P. and Krishna, V. (1985) 'Finitely repeated games', *Econometrica*, 53:905–922.
Berg, S. and Friedman, P. (1981) 'Impacts of domestic joint ventures on industrial rates of return', *Review of Economics and Statistics* 63:293–298.
Bergson, A. (1973) 'On monopoly welfare losses', *American Economic Review*, 63:853–870.
Bernheim, B.D. and Whinston, M.D. (1985) 'Common marketing agency as a device for facilitating collusion', *Rand Journal of Economics*, 16:269–281.
Bork, R. (1978) *The antitrust paradox*. New York: Basic Books.
Brander, J.A. and Spencer, B.J. (1985) 'Tacit collusion, free entry, and welfare', *Journal of Industrial Economics*, 38:277–294.
Bresnahan, T.F. (1982) 'The oligopoly solution concept is identified', *Economics Letters*, 10:87–92.
Bresnahan, T.F. (1987) 'Competition and collusion in the American automobile industry: The 1955 price war', *Journal of Industrial Economics*, 35:457–482.
Bresnahan, T.F. and Salop, S.C. (1986) 'Quantifying the competitive effects of horizontal joint ventures among competitors', *International Journal of Industrial Organization*, 4:155–176.
Brock, W.A. and Scheinkman, J.A. (1985) 'Price setting supergames with capacity constraints', *Review of Economic Studies*, 52:371–382.
Brodley, J.F. (1976) 'The legal status of joint ventures under the antitrust laws: A summary assessment', *Antitrust Bulletin*, 21:453–483.
Brodley, J.F. (1982) 'Joint ventures and antitrust policy', *Harvard Law Review*, 95:1523–1590.
Clarke, R.N. (1983) 'Collusion and the incentives for information sharing', *Bell Journal of Economics*, 14:383–394.
Comanor, W.S. and Schankerman, M.A. (1976) 'Identical bids and cartel behavior', *Bell Journal of Economics*, 7:281–286.
Comanor, W.S. and Smiley, R.H. (1975) 'Monopoly and the distribution of wealth', *Quarterly Journal of Economics*, 89:177–194.
Cooper, T.E. (1986) 'Most favored customer pricing and tacit collusion', *Rand Journal of Economics*, 17:377–388.
Cowling, K. and Mueller, D. (1978) 'The social costs of monopoly power', *Economic Journal*, 88:727–748.
Cowling, K. and Waterson, M. (1976) 'Price-cost margins and market structure', *Economica*, 43:247–274.
Cowling, K. et al. (1980) *Mergers and economic performance*. Cambridge: Cambridge University Press.
Cubbin, J. (1975) 'Quality change and pricing behavior in the U.K. car industry, 1956–1968', *Economica*, 42:43–58.
Curzon-Price, V. (1981) *Industrial policies in the European economic community*. London: MacMillan.
Dansby, R.E. and Willig, R.D. (1979) 'Industry performance gradient indices', *American Economic Review*, 69:249–260.
Dasgupta, P. and Stiglitz, J. (1980) 'Industrial structure and innovative activity', *Economic Journal*, 90:266–293.
d'Aspremont, C. and Jacquemin, A. (1985) 'Measuring the power to monopolize', *European Economic Review* 27:57–74.
d'Aspremont, C. and Jaskold-Gabszewicz, J. (1985) 'Quasi monopolies', *Economica*, 52:141–151.
d'Aspremont, C., Jacquemin, A. and Mertens, J.F. (1987) 'A measure of aggregate power in organizations', *Journal of Economic Theory*, 43:184–191.
d'Aspremont, C., Jacquemin, A., Jaskold-Gabszewicz, J. and Weymark, J. (1983) 'On the stability of collusive price leadership', *Canadian Journal of Economics*, 16:17–25.
Davidson, C. and Deneckere, R. (1984) 'Horizontal mergers and collusive behavior', *International Journal of Industrial Organization*, 2:117–132.

DeBrock, L.M. and Smith, J.L. (1983) 'Joint bidding, information pooling, and the performance of petroleum lease auctions', *Bell Journal of Economics*, 14:395–404.

Demsetz, H. (1973) 'Industry structure, market rivalry, and price policy', *Journal of Law and Economics*, 16:1–10.

Deneckere, R. and Davidson, C. (1985) 'Incentives to form coalitions with Bertrand competition', *Rand Journal of Economics*, 16:473–486.

Dewey, (1959), *Monopoly in economics and law*. Chicago: Rand McNally.

Dixit, A.K. (1986) 'Optimal trade and industrial policies in the U.S. automobile industry', N.B.E.R. working paper, Boston.

Dixit, A. and Stern, N. (1982) 'Oligopoly and welfare: A unified presentation with applications to trade and development', *European Economic Review*, 19:122–143.

Dixit, A.K. and Stiglitz, J. (1977) 'Monopolistic competition and optimum product differentiation', *American Economic Review*, 67:297–308.

Donsimoni, M.P. (1985) 'Stable heterogeneous cartels', *International Journal of Industrial Organization*, 3:451–467.

Donsimoni, M.P., Economides, N.S. and Polemarchakis, H.M. (1986) 'Stable cartels', *International Economic Review*, 27:317–328.

Dowell, R. (1984) 'Asset salvageability and the potential for trade restraint through merger', *Rand Journal of Economics*, 15:537–545.

Duncan, J. (1982) 'Impacts of new entry and horizontal joint ventures on industrial rates of return', *Review of Economics and Statistics*, 64:339–342.

Economides, N.S. (1986) 'Non-cooperative equilibrium coalition structures', Department of Economics, Columbia University, New York, mimeo.

Elzinga, K.G. and Hogarty, T.F. (1973) 'The problem of geographic–market delineation in anti-mergers suits', *Antitrust Bulletin*, 18:45–81.

Encaoua, D. and Jacquemin, A. (1980) 'Degree of monopoly, indices of concentration, and threat of entry', *International Economic Review*, 21:87–105.

Encaoua, D., Jacquemin, A. and Moreaux, M. (1986) 'Global market power and diversification', *Economic Journal*, 96:525–533.

Fellner, W. (1949) *Competition among the few*. New York: Knopf.

Fraysse, J. and Moreaux, M. (1985) 'Collusive equilibria and oligopolies with finite lines, *European Economic Review*, 27:45–55.

Fried, D. (1984) 'Incentives for information production and disclosure in a duopolistic environment', *Quarterly Journal of Economics*, 99:367–384.

Friedman, J.W. (1971) 'A noncooperative equilibrium for supergames', *Review of Economic Studies*, 38:1–12.

Friedman, J.W. (1985) 'Cooperative equilibria in finite horizon noncooperative supergames', *Journal of Economic Theory*, 35:390–398.

Friedman, J.W. (1986) *Game theory with applications to economics*. Oxford: Oxford University Press.

Friedman, J.W. and Hoggat, A.C. (1980) *Experiment in noncooperative oligopoly*. Greenwich: J.A.I. Press.

F.T.C. (1981) 'Initial Decision', in re Ethyl Corp. et al., docket no. 9128.

Fudenberg, D. and Tirole, J. (1983) 'Learning by doing and market performance', *Bell Journal of Economics*, 14:522–530.

Fudenberg, D. and Tirole, J. (1986) 'Dynamic models of oligopoly', in A. Jacquemin, ed., *Theory of the firm and industrial organization, fundamentals of pure and applied economics*. New York: Harwood.

Gal-Or, E. (1985) 'Information sharing in oligopoly', *Econometrica*, 53:329–343.

Gelfand, M.D. and Spiller, P.T. (1987) 'Entry barriers and multiproduct oligopolies', *International Journal of Industrial Organization*, 5:101–114.

Geroski, P.A. (1982) 'The empirical analysis of conjectural variations in oligopoly', University of Southampton, mimeo.

Geroski, P.A. and Jacquemin, A. (1985) 'Industrial change, barriers to mobility, and European industrial policy', *Economic Policy*, 1:169–205.

Ghemawat, P. and Nalebuff, B. (1985) 'Exit', *Rand Journal of Economics*, 16:184–193.

Ghemawat, P. and Spence, M. (1985) 'Learning curve spillovers and market performance', *Quarterly Journal of Economics*, 100:839–852.

Gollop, F.M. and Roberts, M.J. (1979) 'Firm interdependence in oligopolistic markets', *Journal of Econometrics*, 10:313–331.

Gravelle, H. and Rees, R. (1980) *Microeconomics*. London: Longman.

Green, E.J. and Porter, R.H. (1984) 'Noncooperative collusion under imperfect price information', *Econometrica*, 52:87–100.

Green, J.R. and Laffont, J.J. (1979) *Incentives in public decision making*. Amsterdam: North-Holland.

Grether, D.M. and Plott, C.R. (1981) 'The effects of market practices in oligopolistic markets: An experimental examination of the ethyl case', California Institute of Technology, mimeo.

Grossman, G.M. and Shapiro, C. (1984) 'Research joint ventures: An antitrust analysis', discussion paper in economics no. 68, Woodrow Wilson School, Princeton University.

Hannah, L. and Kay, J.A. (1976) *Concentration in modern industry: Theory, measurement, and the U.K. experience*. London: Macmillan.

Harberger, A.C. (1954) 'Monopoly and resource allocation', *American Economic Review*, 44:77–92.

Harris, R. (1984) 'Applied general equilibrium analysis of small open economies with scale economies and imperfect competition', *American Economic Review*, 74:1016–1032.

Hart, P.E. (1979) 'On bias and concentration', *Journal of Industrial Economics*, 27:211–226.

Hart, P.E. and Prais, S.J. (1956) 'The analysis of business concentration: A statistical approach', *Journal of the Royal Statistical Society, Series A*, 119:150–181.

Hay, G.A. (1982) 'Oligopoly, shared monopoly, and antitrust law', *Cornell Law Review*, 67:439–481.

Hay, G.A. and Kelley, D. (1974) 'An empirical survey of price fixing conspiracies', *Journal of Law and Economics*, 17:13–38.

Hendricks, K. and Porter, R.H. (1987) 'An empirical study of an auction with asymmetric information', University of British Columbia and Northwestern University, mimeo.

Herfindahl, O.C. (1950) 'Concentration in the U.S. steel industry', Ph.D. dissertation, Columbia University.

Hirschman, A.O. (1945) *National power and the structure of foreign trade*. University of California, Berkeley.

Hirschman, A.O. (1964) 'The paternity of an index', *American Economic Review*, 54:761–762.

Horowitz, I. (1981) 'Market definition in antitrust analysis: A regression-based approach', *Southern Economic Journal*, 48:1–16.

Hotelling, H. (1938) 'The general welfare in relation to problems of taxation and of railway and utility rates', *Econometrica*, 6:242–269.

Ilmakunnas, P. (1985) 'Identification and estimation of the degree of oligopoly power in industries facing import competition', in: J. Swalbach, ed., *Industry structure and performance*. Berlin: Sigma.

Iwata, G. (1974) 'Measurement of conjectural variations in oligopoly', *Econometrica*, 42:947–966.

Jacquemin, A., ed. (1985) *European industry: Public policy and corporate strategy*. Oxford: Oxford University Press.

Jacquemin, A. and Cardon, M. (1973) 'Size structure, stability, and performance of the largest British and EEC firms', *European Economic Review*, 4:393–408.

Jacquemin, A. and Slade, M.E. (1986) 'Cartels, collusion, and horizontal merger', working paper no. 86-05, Department of Economics, University of British Columbia.

Jacquemin, A., Nambu, T. and Dewez, I. (1981) 'A dynamic analysis of export cartels', *Economic Journal*, 91:685–696.

Jensen, M. and Ruback, R. (1983) 'The market for corporate control', *Journal of Financial Economics*, 11:5–50.

Just, R.E. and Chern, W.S. (1980) 'Tomatoes, technology and oligopsony', *Bell Journal of Economics*, 11:584–402.

Kalai, E. and Stanford, W. (1985) 'Conjectural variations strategies in accelerated Cournot games', *International Journal of Industrial Organization*, 3:133–154.

Katz, M.L. (1985) 'A welfare analysis of cost information sharing among oligopolists: Signalling versus direct exchange', discussion paper no. 98, Princeton University.

Kay, J.A. (1983) 'A general equilibrium approach to the measurement of monopoly welfare loss', *International Journal of Industrial Organization*, 1:317–331.

Kobayashi, T. (1982) 'Stable cartels in symmetric Cournot oligopoly', discussion paper no. 180, Kyoto Institute of Economic Research, Kyoto University, Japan.

Landes, W.M. and Posner, R.A. (1981) 'Market power in antitrust cases', *Harvard Law Review*, 94:937–996.

Leibenstein, H. (1966) 'Allocative efficiency vs. *X*-efficiency', *American Economic Review*, 56:392–415.
Leitzinger, J.J. and Tamor, K.L. (1983) 'Foreign competition in antitrust law', *Journal of Law and Economics*, 26:87–102.
Lerner, A.P. (1933–1934) 'The concept of monopoly and the measurement of monopoly power', *Review of Economic Studies*, 1:157–175.
Li, L. (1985) 'Cournot oligopoly with information sharing', *Rand Journal of Economics*, 16:521–537.
Littlechild, S.C. (1983) 'Misleading calculations of the social costs of monopoly power', *Economic Journal*, 91:348–363.
Locksley, G. and Ward, T. (1979) 'Concentration in manufacturing in the EEC', *Cambridge Journal of Economics*, 3:91–97.
MacLeod, W.B. (1985) 'A theory of conscious parallelism', *European Economic Review*, 27:25–44.
Magaziner, T. and Reich, R. (1982) *Minding America's business*. New York:Harcourt Brace Jovanovitch.
Mankiw, N.G. and Whinston, H.D. (1986) 'Free entry and social inefficiency', *Rand Journal of Economics*, 17:48–58.
Manne, H.G. (1965) 'Mergers and the market for corporate control', *Journal of Political Economy*, 73:110–120.
Mariti, P. and Smiley, R.H. (1983) 'Cooperative agreements and the organization of industry', *Journal of Industrial Economics*, 31:437–451.
Markham, J.W. (1955) 'Survey of the evidence and finding on mergers', in: *Business concentration and price policy*. Princeton: Princeton University Press.
Marris, R. and Mueller, D.C. (1980) 'The corporation, competition, and the invisible hand', *Journal of Economic Literature*, 18:32–63.
Maskin, E. and Tirole, J. (1988) 'A theory of dynamic oligopoly, II: Price competition', *Econometrica*, 56:571–600.
McGee, J.S. (1971) *In defense of industrial concentration*. New York: Praeger.
McGowan, J. (1965) 'The effect of alternative antimerger policies on the size distribution of firms', *Yale Economic Essays*, 5:465–471.
Mead, W. (1967) 'The competitive significance of joint ventures', *Antitrust Bulletin*, 12:819–849.
Meeks, G. (1977) *Disappointing marriage: A study of the gains from merger*. Cambridge: Cambridge University Press.
Mueller, D.C. (1972) 'A life cycle theory of the firm', *Journal of Industrial Economics*, 20:199–219.
Mueller, D.C., ed. (1980) *The determinants and effects of mergers: An international comparison*. Cambridge: Oelgeschlayer, Gunn, and Main.
Mueller, D.C. (1985) *Profit in the long run*. Cambridge: Cambridge Univerisity Press.
Müller, J. (1976) 'The impact of mergers on concentration: A study of eleven West German industries', *Journal of Industrial Economics*, 25:113–132.
Nelson, R.R. and Winter, S.G. (1982) 'The Schumpeterian tradeoff revisited', *American Economic Review*, 72:114–132.
Nichols, W.H. (1949) 'The tobacco case of 1946', *American Economic Review*, 39:284–296.
Norton, R.D. (1986) 'Industrial policy and American renewal', *Journal of Economic Literature*, 24:1–40.
Novshek, W. and Sonnenschein, H. (1982) 'Fulfilled expectations Cournot duopoly with information acquisition and release', *Bell Journal of Economics*, 13:214–218.
Ordover, J.A. and Willig, R.D. (1985) 'Antitrust for high technology industries: Assessing research joint ventures and mergers', *Journal of Law and Economics*, 28:311–334.
Orr, D. and MacAvoy, P. (1965) 'Strategies to promote cartel stability', *Economica*, 32:186–197.
Osborne, D.K. (1976) 'Cartel problems', *American Economic Review*, 66:835–844.
Panzar, D.C. and Willig, R.D. (1981) 'Economies of scope', *American Economic Review*, 71:268–272.
Patinkin, D. (1947) 'Multiple-plant firms, cartels, and imperfect competition', *Quarterly Journal of Economics*, 61:173–205.
Peltzman, S. (1977) 'The gains and losses from industrial cconcentration', *Journal of Law and Economics*, 20:229–264.
Perry, M.K. (1984) 'Scale economies, imperfect competition, and public policy', *Journal of industrial Economics*, 32:313–333.

Perry, M.K. and Porter, R.H. (1985) 'Oligopoly and the incentives for horizontal merger', *American Economic Review*, 75:219–227.

Phillips, A. (1977) 'An econometric study of price-fixing, market structure, and performance in British industry in the early 1950's', in: K. Cowling, ed., *Market structure and corporate behavior*. London: Gray-Mills, 177–192.

Pindyck, R.S. (1985) 'The measurement of monopoly power in dynamic markets', *Journal of Law and Economics*, 28:193–222.

Pitofsky, R. (1969) 'Joint ventures under antitrust law: Some reflections on Penn–Olin, *Harvard Law Review*, 82:1007–1063.

Plott, C.R. (1982) 'Industrial organization theory and experimental economics', *Journal of Economic Literature*, 10:1485–1527.

Porter, R.H. (1983a) 'Optimal cartel trigger-price strategies', *Journal of Economic Theory*, 29:313–338.

Porter, R.H. (1983b) 'A study of cartel stability: The joint executive committee: 1880–1886', *Bell Journal of Economics*, 14:301–314.

Posner, R.A. (1975) 'The social costs of monopoly and regulation', *Journal of Political Economy*, 83:807–827.

Prais, S.J. (1981) 'The contribution of mergers to industrial concentration: What do we know?', *Journal of Industrial Economics*, 24:321–329.

Reece, D.K. (1978) 'Competitive bidding for offshore petroleum leases', *Bell Journal of Economics*, 9:369–384.

Rees, R. (1985) 'Cheating in a duopoly game', in: P.A. Geroski, L. Philips and A. Ulph, eds., *Oligopoly, competition, and welfare*. Oxford: Basil Blackwell.

Reid, S. (1968) *Mergers, managers, and the economy*. New York: McGraw-Hill.

Reynolds, R. and Snapp, B.R. (1986) 'The economic effects of partial equity interests and joint ventures', *International Journal of Industrial Organization*, 4:141–154.

Roberts, K. (1985) 'Cartel behavior and adverse selection', *Journal of Industrial Economics*, 33:401–414.

Roberts, M.J. (1984a) 'Testing oligopolistic behavior: An application of the variable profit function', *International Journal of Industrial Organization*, 2:367–383.

Roberts, M.J. (1984b) 'Testing for non-price competition in oligopolistic industries', Pennsylvania State University, mimeo.

Roberts, M.J. and Samuelson, L. (1985) 'Non-price competition and dynamic equilibria in oligopolistic industries', Department of Economics, Pennsylvania State University, mimeo.

Rockwood, A. (1983) 'The impact of joint ventures on the market for OCS oil and gas leases', *Journal of Industrial Economics*, 31:453–468.

Rogerson, W.P. (1982) 'The social cost of monopoly and regulation: A game-theoretic analysis', *Bell Journal of Economics*, 13:391–401.

Rotemberg, J.J. and Saloner, G. (1985) 'Strategic inventories and the excess volatility of production', working paper no. 1650-85, Sloan School, M.I.T., Cambridge, Massachusetts.

Rotemberg, J.J. and Saloner, G. (1986) 'A supergame-theoretic model of business cycles and price wars during booms', *American Economic Review*, 76:390–407.

Rothschild, R. (1981) 'Cartel problems: Note', *American Economic Review*, 71:179–181.

Salant, S.W., Switzer, S. and Reynolds, R.J. (1983) 'Losses from horizontal merger: The effects of an exogenous change in industry structure on Cournot–Nash equilibrium', *Quarterly Journal of Economics*, 48:185–199.

Salop, S. (1986) 'Practices that credibly facilitate oligopoly coordination', in: J. Stiglitz and F. Mathewson, eds., *New developments in the analysis of market structure*. Cambridge, Mass.: M.I.T. Press.

Saving, T.R. (1970) 'Concentration ratios and the degree of monopoly', *International Economic Review*, 11:139–146.

Scherer, F.M. (1980) *Industrial market structure and economic performance*. Chicago: Rand McNally.

Schmalensee, R. (1987) 'Competitive advantage and collusive optima', *International Journal of Industrial Organization*, 5:351–368.

Schumpeter, J.A. (1934) *The theory of economic development: An inquiry into profits, capital, credit, interest, and the business cycle*. Translated from the German (1926) edition. Cambridge: Harvard University Press.

Schwartzman, D. (1960) 'The burden of monopoly', *Journal of Political Economy*, 68:627–630.

Selten, R. (1975) 'Reexamination of the perfectness concept for equilibrium points in extensive Games', *International Journal of Game Theory*, 4:25–55.

Selten, R. (1984) 'Are cartel laws bad for business?', in: H. Hauptmann, W. Krelle and K.C. Mosler, eds., *Operations research and economic theory*. Berlin: Springer-Verlag.

Shaked, A. and Sutton, J. (1983) 'Natural oligopolies', *Econometrica*, 51:1469–1483.

Shapiro, C. (1986) 'Exchange of cost information in oligopoly', *Review of Economic Studies*, 53:433–446.

Singh, A. (1971) *Takeovers, their relevance to the stock market and the theory of the firm*. Cambridge: Cambridge University Press.

Slade, M.E. (1985) 'Price wars in price-setting supergames', working paper no. 85-35, Department of Economics, University of British Columbia, forthcoming in *Economica*.

Slade, M.E. (1986a) 'Exogeneity tests of market boundaries applied to petroleum products', *Journal of Industrial Economics*, 34:291–304.

Slade, M.E. (1986b) 'Measures of market power in extractive industries: The legacy of *U.S. vs. General Dynamics*', *The Antitrust Bulletin*, 31:91–111.

Slade, M.E. (1986c) 'Conjectures, firm characteristics and market structure: An empirical assessment', *International Journal of Industrial Organization*, 4:347–370.

Slade, M.E. (1987a) 'Interfirm rivalry in a repeated game: An empirical test of tacit collusion', *The Journal of Industrial Economics*, 35:499–516.

Slade, M.E. (1987b) 'Learning through price wars: An exercise in uncovering supergame strategies', working paper no. 87-08, Department of Economics, University of British Columbia, Vancouver.

Smith, R.A. (1961) 'The incredible electrical conspiracy', *Fortune*, May: 224.

Spence, A.M. (1976) 'Product selection, fixed costs, and monopolistic competition', *Review of Economic Studies*, 43:217–235.

Spence, A.M. (1978) 'Tacit coordination and imperfect information', *Canadian Journal of Economics*, 11:490–505.

Spence, A.M. (1981) 'The learning curve and competition', *Bell Journal of Economics*, 12:49–70.

Spiller, P.T. and Favaro, E. (1984) 'The effects of entry regulation on oligopolistic interaction: The Uruguayan banking sector', *Rand Journal of Economics*, 15:244–254.

Spiller, P.T. and Huang, C.J. (1986) 'On the extent of the market: Wholesale gasoline in the northeastern United States', *Journal of Industrial Economics*, 35:131–146.

Stigler, G.J. (1950) 'Monopoly and oligopoly by merger', *American Economic Review*, 40:23–34.

Stigler, G.J. (1964) 'A theory of oligopoly', *Journal of Political Economy*, 72:44–61.

Stigler, G.J. and Sherwin, R.A. (1985) 'The extent of the market', *Journal of Law and Economics*, 28:555–585.

Sullivan, D. (1985) 'Testing hypotheses about firm behavior in the cigarette industry', *Journal of Political Economy*, 93:586–598.

Sumner, D.A. (1981) 'Measurement of monopoly behavior: An application to the cigarette industry', *Journal of Political Economy*, 89:1010–1019.

Tullock, G. (1967) 'The welfare costs of tariffs, monopolies, and theft', *Western Economic Journal*, 5:224–232.

Utton, J. (1972) 'Mergers and the growth of large firms', *Bulletin of the Oxford University Institute of Economics and Statistics*, 34:194–196.

Utton, J. (1974) 'On measuring the effect of industrial mergers', *Scottish Journal of Political Economy*, 21:13–28.

Vickers, J. (1985) 'Pre-emptive patenting, joint ventures, and the persistence of oligopoly', *International Journal of Industrial Organization*, 3:261–273.

Vives, X. (1984) 'Duopoly information equilibrium: Cournot or Bertrand', *Journal of Economic Theory*, 34:71–94.

von Weizsacker, C.C. (1980) 'A welfare analysis of barriers to entry', *The Bell Journal of Economics*, 11:399–420.

Waterson, M. (1983) 'Economies of scope within market frameworks', *International Journal of Industrial Organization*, 1:223–237.

Weiss, L. (1965) 'An evaluation of mergers in six industries', *Review of Economics and Statistics*, 47:172–181.

White, L.J. (1981) 'What has been happening to aggregate cconcentration in the United States?', *Journal of Industrial Economics*, 29:223–230.

Williamson, O.E. (1968), 'Economies as an antitrust defense: The welfare tradeoffs', *American Economic Review*, 58:18–36.

Williamson, O.E. (1977) 'Economies as an antitrust defense revisited' in: A.P. Jacquemin and H.W. de Jong, eds., *Welfare aspects of industrial markets*. Leiden: Martinus Nijhoff.

Willig, R.D. (1979) 'Multiproduct technology and market structure', *American Economic Review*, 69:346–351.

Wilson, R. (1977) 'A bidding model of perfect competition', *Review of Economic Studies*, 44:511–518.

Yarrow, G. (1985) 'Strategic issues in industrial policy', *Oxford Review of Economic Policy*, 1:95–109.

Chapter 8

MOBILITY BARRIERS AND THE VALUE OF INCUMBENCY

RICHARD J. GILBERT*

University of California, Berkeley

Contents

*I am grateful to Patrick Bolton, Joe Farrell, Drew Fudenberg, Alexis Jacquemin, John Panzar, Pierre Regibeau, Bobby Willig and Xavier Vives for helpful conversations. This chapter owes a particular debt to Joe Bain.

Handbook of Industrial Organization, Volume I, Edited by R. Schmalensee and R.D. Willig

1. Introduction

The literature on the organization of markets is replete with definitions of barriers to entry. Bain defined the conditions of entry as "the extent to which, in the long run, established firms can elevate their selling prices above the minimal average costs of production and distribution (those costs associated with operation at optimal scales) without inducing potential entrants to enter the industry".[1] Bain's definition concentrates on the ability of established firms to earn excess profits. Stigler proposed a definition of barriers to entry that emphasizes the existence of relative cost advantages of established firms vis-à-vis new entrants. According to Stigler, "A barrier to entry may be defined as a cost of producing (at some or every rate of output) which must be borne by a firm which seeks to enter an industry but is not borne by firms already in the industry".[2,3] Baumol and Willig define an entry barrier as "anything that requires an expenditure by a new entrant into an industry, but that imposes no equivalent cost upon an incumbent".[4]

Others have proposed definitions of entry barriers that directly address considerations of economic efficiency. Ferguson identifies barriers to entry as "factors that make entry unprofitable while permitting established firms to set prices above marginal cost, and to persistently earn monopoly return".[5] Ferguson's definition recognizes the divergence between price and marginal cost as an impairment to economic efficiency. Von Weizsacker also makes a direct connection between entry and economic welfare. Building on Stigler's definition, von Wiezsacker defines a barrier to entry as: "A cost of producing which must be borne by a firm which seeks to enter an industry but is not borne by firms already in the industry and which implies a distortion in the allocation of resources from the social point of view".[6]

None of these definitions addresses the reasons why entry may be excluded. Consider a market large enough for a single firm to earn a profit, but not large enough for two or more firms to operate and both be profitable. The market is a natural monopoly, but that does not mean that entry is impossible. A new firm

[1] Bain (1968, p. 252).
[2] Stigler (1968, p. 67).
[3] Demand considerations are not excluded from Stigler's measure of barriers to entry. For example, consumer loyalties affect the costs that a new firm must incur in order to reach a particular level of sales. To the extent that the new firm has to overcome more consumer resistance than did the established firm, the entrant would experience a Stiglerian barrier to entry.
[4] Baumol and Willig (1981, p. 408).
[5] Ferguson (1974, p. 10).
[6] Von Weizsacker (1980a, p. 400).

may be able to undercut the monopoly price of the established firm and force the firm to exit the market. If this could be accomplished with relative ease, barriers to entry in this market are low. If not, the established firm may be able to earn monopoly profits, in which case there would be a barrier to entry according to Bain and Ferguson. Stigler would assign an entry barrier to the industry only if potential entrants suffer a cost disadvantage relative to the existing firm, while von Weizsacker would impose the additional requirement that entry should increase social surplus. But none of these definitions explains why an established firm might, or might not, enjoy an advantage over other firms that may occupy the market.

The height of entry barriers in this market depends on the factors that determine the ability of the incumbent firm to maintain its output in the face of entry, about which more will be said in the remainder of this chapter. This example also illustrates that the mobility of capital into an industry may well depend on the mobility of capital out of an industry. Concerns about limitations on entry should not be divorced from concerns about barriers to exit. Market efficiency depends on the conditions that restrict the mobility of capital in all directions.

Bain's treatise on barriers to new competition [Bain (1949, 1956)] distinguished the conditions of entry from the determinants of barriers to entry. His definition can be defended as a means to measure the height of entry barriers, rather than as a means to identify the reasons why entry is easy or hard. Toward the latter end, he proposed economies of scale, product differentiation, and cost asymmetries as the main determinants of entry barriers. Bain's proposed determinants are discussed in Section 2, which argues that they only approximate the reasons for limits to the mobility of capital.

The definitions proposed by Stigler, von Weizsacker, and Baumol and Willig strike at the heart of asymmetries that might favor an incumbent firm over a potential entrant. The central question in entry deterrence is the value that is attached to incumbency: Why is it that an established firm may lay claim to a profitable market while other (equally efficient) firms are excluded? However, these defintions concentrate on the relative costs of an incumbent and a new entrant, which is unnecessarily confining. Suppose the established firm could commit itself to producing the monopoly output, and this being the case, no other firm can enter at a profit. (Several ways in which this might be accomplished are discussed in this chapter.) Entry would be excluded in this market, but it is difficult to see why the incumbent has a cost advantage over a new firm. One might argue that a new firm could enter and if it could not undermine the incumbent's commitment (e.g. through bribing customers to change their allegiance), it is at a cost disadvantage. This type of argument would resurrect Stigler's cost asymmetry as the determinant of entry barriers, but at the risk of constructing a tautology.

Von Weizsacker considers a cost asymmetry a barrier to entry only if it implies "... a distortion from the social point of view". Consider a Chamberlin (1933) model of an industry with differentiated products and free entry. There are no monopoly profits in this industry, so according to Bain (and Ferguson) there are no barriers to entry. Firms are symmetrical in the Chamberlin model, so there are no Stiglerian barriers either. But Chamberlinian competition could result in an excessive number of products as measured by total economic surplus,[7] in which case von Weizsacker's approach would conclude that there are "negative" entry barriers in this industry. Welfare would be improved by making entry more difficult.

This chapter distinguishes between determinants of barriers to the mobility of capital and the welfare implications of entry and exit. The first task is confined to identifying situations in which a firm that is established in an industry benefits by reason of its incumbency. An incumbency advantage does not necessarily imply that welfare would be improved by encouraging entry. In many of the examples discussed in this chapter, quite the opposite is true. Consumers may be disadvantaged if forced to switch to another supplier. Industry costs would increase if entry eroded the benefits of economies of scale or learning. Entry prevention may result in both lower prices and lower costs than would occur if entry were allowed.

What is a barrier to entry? This chapter takes the view that *a barrier to entry is a rent that is derived from incumbency*. It is the additional profit that a firm can earn as a sole consequence of being established in an industry. No attempt is made to collect an exhaustive list of the determinants of entry. This chapter identifies factors that may limit capital mobility and support an incumbency advantage, but no factor stands alone as either necessary or sufficient. Crucial to the consequences for capital mobility is the combined incidence of structural factors that may impede entry or exit and industry behavior. For illustration, suppose all firms have the cost function $C(x) = mx + F$. If industry behavior is such that two or more established firms would act as perfect competitors, then entry would result in price equal to marginal cost and no firm would earn a profit. The only sustainable market structure would be a monopoly. Contrast this with a situation where incumbent firms always choose to keep their prices unchanged in response to entry. In the latter case, entry may be feasible even in an industry that is a natural monopoly.

A theory of barriers to entry cannot be constructed in isolation from a theory of oligopoly behavior. As Chapter 6 by Carl Shapiro in this Handbook shows, the scope for oligopolistic interactions is so wide that a predictive model of how firms behave may be no easier to construct than a model of the weather based on the formation of water droplets.

[7]See Dixit and Stiglitz (1977).

The plan of this chapter is as follows. Section 2 describes Bain's determinant's of barriers to entry and shows how they may be interpreted in the light of more recent contributions to the theory of strategic entry deterrence. This section introduces the role of behavior in the determination of the conditions of entry, which is discussed further in Section 3. An objective of this study of capital mobility is the development of a theory of endogenous industry structure. Progress that has been made in this direction is discussed in Section 4. Section 5 calls attention to the importance of exit barriers and specific assets in the theory of capital mobility.

Strategic entry deterrence is designed to influence the behavior of potential rivals. It is effective only to the extent that potential competitors look to current behavior as indicative of future market conditions. The role of information and its consequences for entry-deterring behavior is the subject of Section 6.

If it is not possible to provide an exhaustive list of the determinants of barriers to entry, it is at least possible to describe a market in which barriers to capital mobility do not exist. This is the world of perfectly contestable markets, discussed in Section 7. Firms are equally efficient and each firm can imitate the products and services of any other firm. Cost functions need not be convex, but all expenditures are potentially reversible. The result is a market that performs as close as possible to the competitive ideal. Price equals marginal cost unless the industry is a natural monopoly, in which case price equals average cost. A key characteristic of a perfectly contestable market is that each firm acts as if it faces a perfectly horizontal demand function for any increase in price. This condition can serve as a definition for the absence of barriers to entry.

Section 8 is a brief discussion of the connections between barriers to entry and market performance. It is emphasized that the existence of barriers to the movement of capital does not imply a reduction in economic welfare. Mobility constraints are welfare decreasing relative to a first-best allocation of economic resources. But we do not live in a first-best world. Mobility barriers arise for reasons of technology and consumer tastes and need not impair efficiency in an imperfectly competitive economy. Indeed, there are many circumstances where welfare is strictly improved by impeding entry into an industry.

This chapter overlaps with others in this Handbook. It is impossible to divorce strategic entry deterrence from considerations of oligopoly behavior discussed by Carl Shapiro. Chapter 9 by Janusz Ordover and Garth Saloner on predation is closely related to issues discussed here. A distinction is that predation deals with strategies whose rationality depends on inducing exit and preventing future entry, whereas entry deterrence is concerned with the conditions that impede capital mobility. The connections are nevertheless quite close and I encourage readers interested in this subject to consult these other sources.

With the large number of papers that have appeared in recent years dealing with strategic behavior and barriers to entry, there is not enough room to do complete justice even to this limited subject. In an attempt to confine my inquiry, I have arbitrarily limited the scope of this chapter to the theory of mobility barriers, excluding all of the empirical work on the subject. This is a regrettable omission, but see Geroski, Gilbert and Jacquemin (forthcoming) for a survey of this topic.

2. Determinants of the conditions of entry

As determinants of the conditions of entry, Bain (1949) identified economies of large scale, product differentiation, and absolute cost advantages of established firms. This list is neither a complete nor accurate enumeration of the factors that may limit capital mobility in an industry. Nonetheless, Bain's determinants of entry provide a convenient jumping-off point to discuss the structural determinants of mobility barriers. The sections that follow briefly describe Bain's arguments and show how they have been interpreted and extended in light of more recent developments.

2.1. Scale economies, sunk costs, and limit pricing

According to Bain, "The condition that there should be no significant economies to the large scale firm means of course that an entrant firm, even if it enters at an optimal or lowest-cost scale, will add so little to industry output that its entry will have no perceptible effect on going prices in the industry."[8] In the absence of scale economies, entry is not limited by the size of the market. Bain and several of his contemporaries, notably Sylos-Labini (1962) and Modigliani (1958), investigated the consequences of market size for the conditions of entry when the production technology exhibits economies of scale. Their work led to the classic "limit-pricing" model of behavior by a dominant firm or cartel.

2.1.1. The Bain–Sylos-Labini–Modigliani limit pricing model

The essential assumptions of the Bain–Sylos-Labini–Modigliani (BSM) limit pricing model are:

(1) There are two periods: pre-entry ($t = 0$) and post-entry ($t = 1$). Entry may occur only in period 1.

(2) There is a single established firm or a coordinated cartel, "the incumbent" (labelled i), and a single potential entrant (e).

(3) Consumers are indifferent between purchases from the incumbent or the entrant and have no costs of switching suppliers.

[8] Bain (1968, p. 13).

(4) Demand does not change over time.

(5) In period $t = 0$, the incumbent can commit to an output level x_i which it must maintain at all future periods.

The last assumption implies that the incumbent can act as a Stackelberg leader in output. The entrant acts as a Cournot follower, believing that the established firm will continue to produce at its pre-entry output level regardless of the entrant's actions or the final price that prevails in the market.

The market price is $P(x_i)$ in the first period and $P(x_i + x_e)$ in the second period, where x_e is the entrant's production. Suppressing factor prices, the entrant's profit is

$$\pi_e(x, x_i) = P(x_i + x)x - C_e(x), \tag{1}$$

where $C_e(x)$ is the entrant's cost function. Let x_e be the entrant's profit-maximizing output taking x_i as given. The firm should enter if its maximum profits are positive and should stay out otherwise. The *limit output*, Y, is the smallest x_i for which x_e is zero (no entry). The associated *limit price* is P_L.

The elements of the limit pricing model come together in Figure 8.1. The incumbent and the potential entrant have the same average cost curve, AC. The potential entrant takes the incumbent's output as a given and maximizes its profit given the residual demand curve $D(P) - x_i$. This is shown by using x_i rather

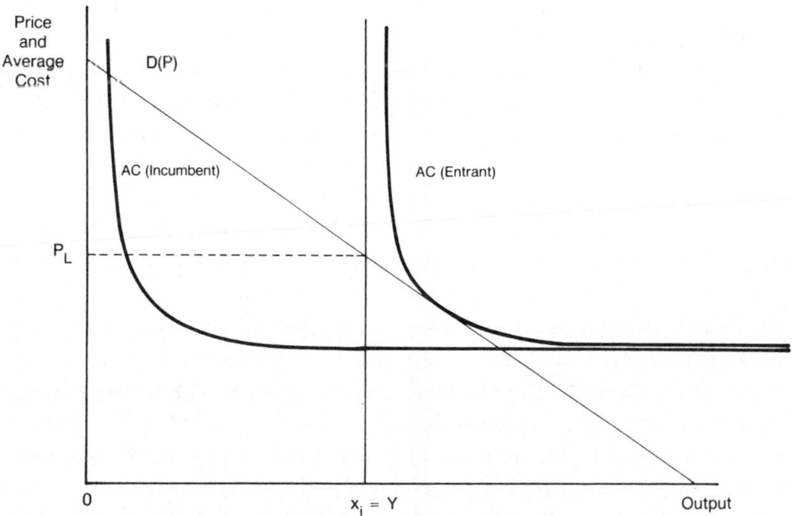

Figure 8.1. Limit pricing.

than the original axis as the ordinate for the entrant's demand and cost curves. As shown in Figure 8.1, given x_i, there is no output at which the entrant can earn a positive profit. This is the smallest output that yields everywhere negative profits for the entrant, hence $x_i = Y$. The associated price is the limit price, P_L.

All else equal, the limit price is lower the flatter is the residual demand curve. Also, entry is easier if the entrant's minimum efficient scale is small and if the average cost falls quickly to its lowest level.

In the BSM model the entrant behaves as a Cournot competitor. For the special (but simple) case of linear demand,

$$P = a - bX, \tag{2}$$

and the cost function,

$$C(x) = mx + F, \tag{3}$$

the entrant's reaction function is

$$x_e = \begin{cases} (a - m - bx_i)/2b, & \text{if } x_i \leq Y, \\ 0, & \text{otherwise,} \end{cases} \tag{4}$$

where

$$Y = (a - m)/b - 2(F/b)^{1/2}. \tag{5}$$

Bain used the term *blockaded entry* to refer to a situation where the output of established firm(s) exceeds the limit output when the possibility of entry is ignored. For example, a monopolist blockades entry if the monopoly output is larger than the limit output. If entry is not blockaded, established firm(s) have to compare the benefit of entry prevention against the cost. If the conditions of entry are such that the established firm(s) can prevent entry with a limit output that is not too large, the benefits from preventing entry exceed the cost. This is the condition Bain refered to as *effectively impeded entry*. When entry is very easy, the limit price may be so low that incumbent firm(s) are better off allowing entry to occur. Bain called this *ineffectively impeded entry*.

Figure 8.2(a) shows the entrant's reaction function for the case where Y is relatively small (entry is difficult). Also shown are two isoprofit curves. The curve labelled π^L goes through the point $(x_i = Y, x_e = 0)$, and corresponds to the profit earned when entry is prevented. The curve labelled π^A corresponds to the maximum profit that the incumbent could earn if entry is allowed. This is the Stackelberg optimum for the incumbent when entry is allowed and corresponds to the profit earned at the point (S, E). Incumbent profits are a maximum at the

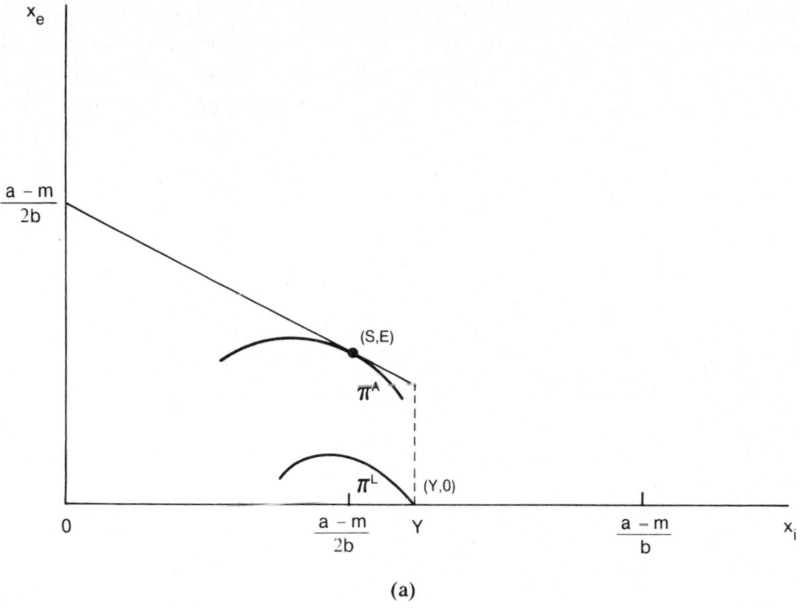

(a)

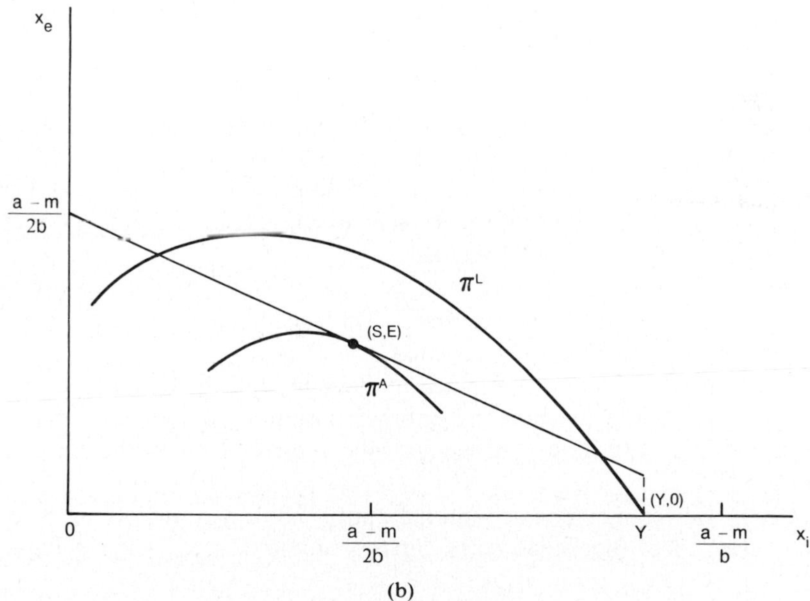

(b)

Figure 8.2. (a) Effective impeded entry; (b) ineffectively impeded entry.

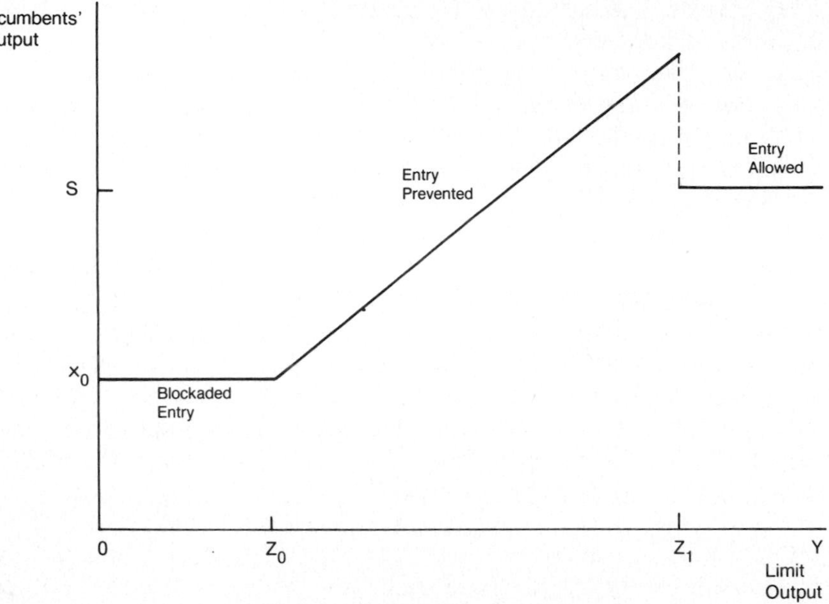

Figure 8.3. Zones of strategic behavior.

monopoly point ($x_i = (a - m)/2b$, $x_e = 0$) and higher isoprofit curves correspond to lower profits. Because isoprofit curves do not cross and π^A is above π^L in Figure 8.2(a), the incumbent is better off when entry is prevented. Entry is "effectively impeded". Note that if Y were to the left of the monopoly output, $(a - m)/2b$, entry would be blockaded.

Figure 8.2(b) shows a situation with easy entry. Now the positions of the π^L and π^A isoprofit contours are reversed. The incumbent is better off allowing entry and entry is "ineffectively impeded".

The BSM limit output is determined by demand and the entrant's technology. Figure 8.3 shows the incumbents' optimal output as a function of the limit output, Y.[9] The following conclusions follow directly from the limit pricing model:

(i) Let x_0 be the incumbents' optimal output ignoring entry. If x_0 exceeds Y, entry is blockaded. Blockaded entry corresponds to $Y \leq x_0 = Z_0$ in Figure 8.3.

[9] The limit output is treated as a parameter in Figure 8.3, but it need not be outside the influence of the incumbent firm(s). Williamson (1963) describes the use of marketing expenditures to influence limit prices. Expenditures that affect factor prices [see Williamson (1968) and Salop and Scheffman (1983)] may affect limit prices as well. This is discussed below under "raising rivals' costs".

(ii) The smallest limit output for which incumbents maximize profits by allowing entry strictly exceeds x_0.

(iii) At the limit output for which the incumbent is indifferent between preventing and allowing entry, total output is strictly lower and price is strictly higher when entry is allowed.

These results are illustrated in Figure 8.3 and follow from the discontinuity of the entrant's reaction function. If the firm enters the market, it produces an output bounded away from zero. Consider the incumbents' incentive to prevent entry when Y is near x_0. If $Y = x_0$, the incumbents' total profit when entry is ignored is the same as when entry is prevented. If Y is slightly larger than x_0, the incumbents can earn almost the same amount by preventing entry. But if entry is allowed, the new firm produces a strictly positive amount and therefore the total profits of the incumbent firms must fall by a discrete amount. Thus the incumbents are better off preventing entry when Y is only slightly larger than x_0.

In Figure 8.3, Z_1 is the limit output at which incumbents are indifferent between allowing and preventing entry. Incumbents produce Z_1 if entry is prevented, but if entry is allowed, incumbents produce a total output $S < Z_1$. [See the Stackelberg solutions in Figure 8.2(a, b).] To be indifferent, given their lower output with entry, the post-entry price must be higher than the limit price.

2.1.2. *Behavior in the theory of limit pricing*

The BSM model assumes that the incumbent firms can convince potential entrants that they will continue to produce at the pre-entry output level regardless of whether or not entry occurs. This assumption was recognized as crucial early in the development of the theory of limit pricing. One can easily see how alternative theories of firm behavior would upset the limit pricing result.

Suppose the potential entrant conjectures that if it were to enter the market, it would compete with established firms as a Cournot oligopolist. For the case of a single established firm, the resulting post-entry equilibrium would appear as in Figure 8.4. The entrant cares only about profits in the post-entry game. It will choose to enter if the Cournot equilibrium output is to left of the limit output, Y, and will stay out of the market otherwise. The established firm's pre-entry price and output have no bearing on the equilibrium of the post-entry game and will properly be disregarded by the potential entrant. There is no scope for limit pricing in this model. The incumbent might as well set the monopoly price in the pre-entry period. Any other choice would sacrifice profits in the pre-entry period with no consequences for the likelihood of entry.

Cournot competition is not the only plausible conjecture for the nature of competition in the post-entry game. Spence (1977) examined a model of entry deterrence in which he assumed that the post-entry game would be perfectly competitive, which implies that the post-entry price equals marginal cost. Again,

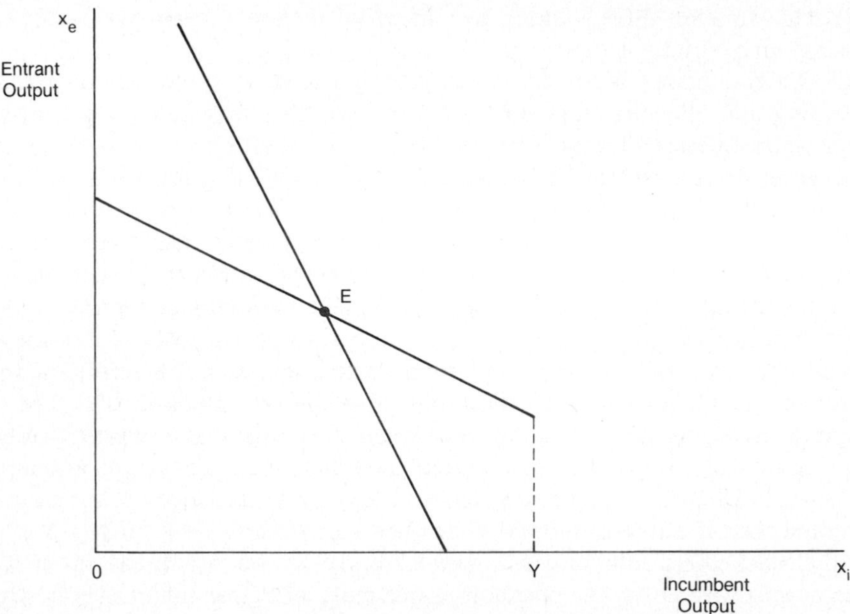

Figure 8.4. Equilibrium with entry.

pre-entry output is no longer an indication of post-entry profitability and the BSM limit pricing model breaks down. Spence argued that the incumbent firms may invest in additional production capacity in order to lower their post-entry marginal cost and therefore lower the post-entry price and profitability for the entrant. Because the pre-entry price is no longer a signal of post-entry profitability, the incumbents can choose the monopoly price in the pre-entry stage, given their production costs.

The BSM, Cournot, and perfectly competitive models differ only in their assumptions about the *behavior* of the firms in the industry. Structural factors play an important role in the profitability of entry and in its effect on market performance, but behavior is crucial. For example, suppose incumbents could deliver a message to all potential entrants that says "if you enter, we will produce enough to force the price down to zero". Call this the "tough" strategy. It contrasts with a "soft" strategy, in which incumbents play their Cournot–Nash best responses. The payoff matrix corresponding to these strategies is shown in Table 8.1. The payoffs are listed for the incumbents first and the entrant second. The potential entrant receives zero if it does not enter. Its preferred outcome is to enter and have the incumbents play soft. Entry against tough opponents is a disaster. The incumbents prefer no entry, in which case whether they are "tough" or "soft" is irrelevant. They earn a return of "1" in either case.

Table 1
Payoff matrix

		Incumbent firms	
		Tough	Soft
Potential entrant	Entry	[−1, −1]	[0, 1]
	No entry	[1, 0]	[1, 0]

There are two Nash equilibria of this game: [tough, no entry] and [soft, entry]. Taking the incumbent's threat as a serious proposition, the entrant's best response is to remain out of the industry. Given the entrant's strategy, the incumbent's best choice is to threaten an aggressive response if entry should occur. But the problem with the incumbent's threat (specifically, the equilibrium [tough, no entry]) is why would a potential entrant take it seriously? If the firm actually entered, the incumbent's best response is to play "soft". The entry game in Table 8.1 has two Nash equilibria, but only one of them is an equilibrium of a sequential game in which the entrant could forecast how an incumbent firm would respond if it tested the market by entering. In the language of Selten (1975), [soft, enter] is a "subgame perfect Nash equilibrium" of the sequential game. The equilibrium [tough, no entry] is not perfect: it is not robust to the experiment in which the firm tests the market by entering. (See Chapter 5 by Drew Fudenberg and Jean Tirole and Chapter 6 by Carl Shapiro in this Handbook for definitions of subgame perfect Nash equilibrium.)

The concept of perfection eliminates threats that are not "credible". But what is "credible" depends on the micro-structure of the game and perhaps on expectations of the entrant about the behavior that can be expected from incumbent firms.[10]

Dixit (1981) posed the problem of an entrant's rational conjecture about post-entry competition in the following way. Suppose there is one incumbent, one potential competitor, and two periods: "before" and "after" entry. Entry can occur only in the second period. If entry occurs, Dixit supposes that the two firms behave as Cournot competitors. Agents have perfect foresight about the consequences of actions taken in the first period for equilibrium outcomes in the second period. The incumbent uses this "look-ahead" to determine its best first-period actions.

[10]The importance of behavioral expectations is evident in the work of Kreps and Wilson (1982) and Milgrom and Roberts (1982b), in the context of Selten's (1978) and Rosenthal's (1981) chain store paradox. While these considerations are clearly relevant to entry deterrence, they have been examined primarily in the context of "predatory" behavior, and are discussed by Ordover and Saloner in Chapter 9 of this Handbook.

Let the vector z_t summarize the incumbent's actions in period $t = 1, 2$. The entrant's optimal output is $r(z_1, z_2)$. By solving for the entrant's optimal response conditional on the incumbent's choice of z_1, Dixit ensures that all equibria of the entry game have the property of being perfect Nash equilibria, as defined by Selten (1975) and Kreps and Wilson (1982b). The incumbent's total profit is

$$\pi_i(z_1) + \beta\pi_i(z_1, z_2, r(z_1, z_2)). \tag{6}$$

The incumbent has an incentive to act strategically in the first period only if the entry decision depends on z_1. If not, the incumbent should maximize first-period profits without regard to entry. *Strategic entry deterrence requires an intertemporal linkage between actions that the incumbent may take prior to entry and the probability or extent of subsequent entry.*

This intertemporal linkage can arise in many ways. An incumbent may attempt to influence rivals' future demand through advertising or building a reputation for quality and service. An incumbent may locate retail branches in preferred locations or acquire key resources in an attempt to disadvantage future potential entrants. None of these strategies guarantees successful entry deterrence, but they establish the feasibility of strategic behavior by providing a connection between pre-entry behavior and post-entry outcomes.

Dixit achieves an intertemporal linkage by allowing for capital expenditures that, once made, become irreversible or "sunk" in the next period. This allows an established firm to *commit* to an output that it could not sustain as an equilibrium if its first-period expenditure were reversible. The incumbent is able to turn a liability (irreversibility of capital investment) into a key asset that makes entry deterrence feasible. This is a striking feature in Dixit's model, but one that follows directly from the logic of game theory [see, for example, Schelling (1960)].

Consider the case of linear demand, $P = a - bX$, and identical firms with constant marginal costs. If investment is perfectly reversible, the cost structure is simply

$$C(x) = mx + F, \tag{7}$$

where F is a fixed cost that can be recovered upon exit from the industry.

The reaction functions of the incumbent and the potential are shown in Figure 8.4. There is a single Nash equilibrium with both firms operating. Entry is profitable in the second period if (as shown) the Cournot equilibrium output is less than Y. Dixit introduces a simple, yet very important extra dimension to this example. He allows production cost to depend on installed capacity, K, in addition to output. Both are measured in the same units (e.g. tons/yr of output and tons/yr of capacity). Capacity has a cost of s per unit and, once installed,

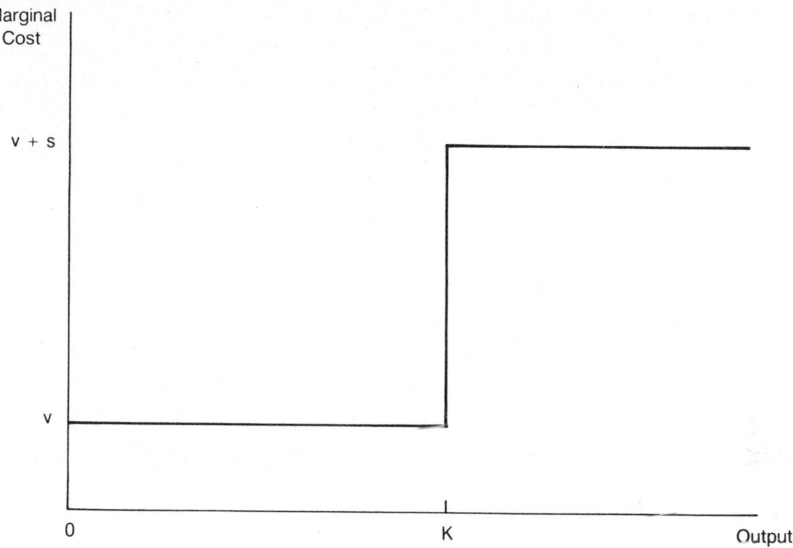

Figure 8.5. Marginal cost function with sunk costs.

has no alternative use. The cost function is

$$C_i(x, K) = vx + sK + F, \quad \text{for } x < K,$$
$$= (v + s)x + F, \quad \text{for } x = K. \tag{8}$$

The marginal cost function is shown in Figure 8.5. The marginal cost is v whenever there is excess capacity and $v + s$ when capacity and output are equal. F remains as a reversible fixed cost.

The incumbent has sunk costs in the amount of sK, where K is the incumbent's installed capacity. A potential entrant has no sunk costs, because it has not yet invested in capacity. The entrant's cost function is simply

$$C_e(x) = (v + s)x + F. \tag{9}$$

The reaction functions corresponding to the cost functions in (8) for the incumbent and (9) for the potential entrant are shown in Figure 8.6. The reaction function labelled $R^i(x_e \mid m)$ is the incumbent's reaction function when the firm has no excess capacity (that is, when $K = x_i$), so that its marginal cost is $v + s = m$. If $K > x_i$, the incumbent's marginal cost is only v and its reaction curve is $R^i(x_e \mid v)$, which is to the right of the reaction function with no excess capacity. The reaction function that the incumbent is "on" depends upon the

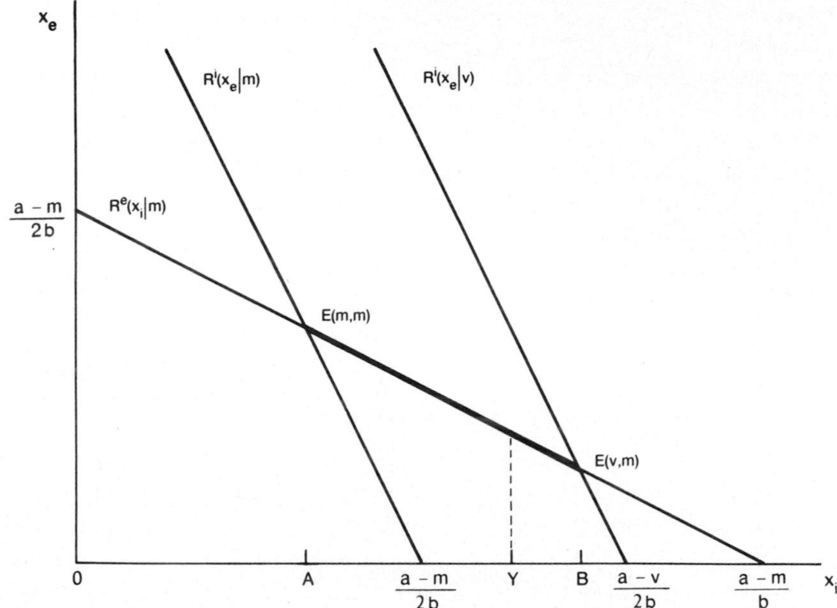

Figure 8.6. Reaction functions and equilibria with capacity investment.

installed capacity and its output x_i. The entrant has no installed capacity. Therefore, with respect to the entry decision, the entrant faces a marginal cost of $v + s$, which includes the cost of capacity. The entrant's reaction function is shown as $R^e(x_i \mid m)$ in Figure 8.6.

If the incumbent has no installed capacity, its reaction function is $R^i(x_e \mid m)$ and the Cournot equilibrium occurs at the point $E(m, m)$. If the incumbent holds excess capacity, its reaction function is $R^i(x_e \mid \mathrm{v})$ and the Cournot equilibrium occurs at $E(v, m)$. Depending on the incumbent's choice of capacity, K, the post-entry equilibrium can be at any point between A and B on the entrant's reaction function. The point A corresponds to the incumbent's equilibrium output at $E(m, m)$. This is the incumbent's smallest output that can be sustained as a Cournot equilibrium. The point B corresponds to the incumbent's output at $E(v, m)$ and is the incumbent's largest output that can be sustained as a Cournot equilibrium. Outputs intermediate between A and B are equilibria for corresponding capacity investments, K. If, given an investment in capacity, K, the equilibrium output that results if a firm entered the market is such that the entrant would not break even, a rational firm would choose to stay out of the market. Thus the incumbent's capacity investment is a way to make a BSM limit output "credible".

Although sunk costs in the Dixit model allow an established firm to prevent entry, sunk costs are actually a barrier to *exit*, not *entry*. The fact that some of the incumbent's costs are sunk means that the incumbent cannot leave the market and recover its costs. If it could costlessly exit, the incumbent would have the same reaction function as the entrant and strategic entry deterrence would be impossible. The possibility that the entrant may incur sunk costs is irrelevant because the entrant never makes a mistake in the Dixit model. The entrant has perfect foresight and there is no "third period" in which new information may arise. Sunk costs are an exit barrier for the incumbent that permits the firm to act strategically and capitalize on the entrant's needs to operate at a large scale in order to make a profit. Sunk costs are not themselves an entry barrier. Sunk costs allow an established firm to commit to a preferred output, much as a Stackelberg leader. If the entrant's cost function is non-convex, this output commitment can succeed in preventing entry.

Capital investment in the Dixit model can be an effective entry deterrent even if the potential entrant has the same cost function as the incumbent (or even if it has lower costs). This seems to be in contrast with Stigler's definition of a barrier to entry, which relies on asymmetric costs of established and new firms. In the Dixit example there is room in the industry for more than one firm, both the entrant and the incumbent have the same ex ante cost function, and entry can be deterred. Yet there is no Stiglerian barrier to entry based on ex ante costs. One can interpret Stigler's definition to exclude costs that are sunk, but this is not the apparent intention of his definition. Also, in the Dixit model, the amount of costs that are sunk do not correspond to the height of the barrier to entry as measured by the cost advantage the entrant must have to successfully enter the industry [see Schmalensee (1981a)].

The result in Dixit's model is incumbent behavior that is similar to the limit pricing behavior in the BSM model. The incumbent invests in (sunk) capacity which allows the firm to commit to a fixed output in excess of A in Figure 8.6. This commitment is larger than the incumbent's post-entry equilibrium output that would result if its capital costs were not sunk. The output commitment reduces the demand available to the entrant and allows the incumbent firm to exploit economies of scale in the entrant's production technology.

Entry deterrence in the Dixit model is the result of both scale economies for the entrant and behavior by the incumbent that enforces a limit output. The limit output is made credible by the sunk cost technology of the incumbent firm. Although sunk costs imply economies of scale in the short run (when capital is sunk), the incumbent's production technology need not display economies of scale in new investment for successful entry deterrence.

Dixit's example yields predictions that are consistent with the BSM model of limit pricing in that the entrant can correctly forecast that the incumbent will not change its output in response to entry. But the comparative statics of the models can be very different. For example, in the BSM model, a ceterius paribus decrease in the elasticity of demand makes entry more difficult. Not so in the Dixit model. Entry prevention requires the ability to commit to an entry-deterring output. If demand is less elastic, the incumbent may not have an incentive to produce the quantity required for entry prevention. The incumbent may be better off preventing entry, but the incumbent may not be able to commit to the necessary limit output [see Gilbert (1986)].

The logical lesson from the Dixit model is that strategic incentives for entry deterrence depend on the correlation between actions which the incumbent can take prior to entry and competition in the post-entry game. By investing in sunk capital, the incumbent can lower its marginal cost and increase its post-entry equilibrim output. Actions which make the post-entry game more (less) competitive for the incumbent would increase (decrease) the scope for feasible entry deterrence. Figure 8.7 illustrates how an action that lowers the incumbent's marginal cost by a greater amount would affect the post-entry game. With a marginal cost v_1, the incumbent's maximum equilibrium output is B_1. With a marginal cost $v_2 < v_1$, the incumbent's maximum output increases to B_2. If the

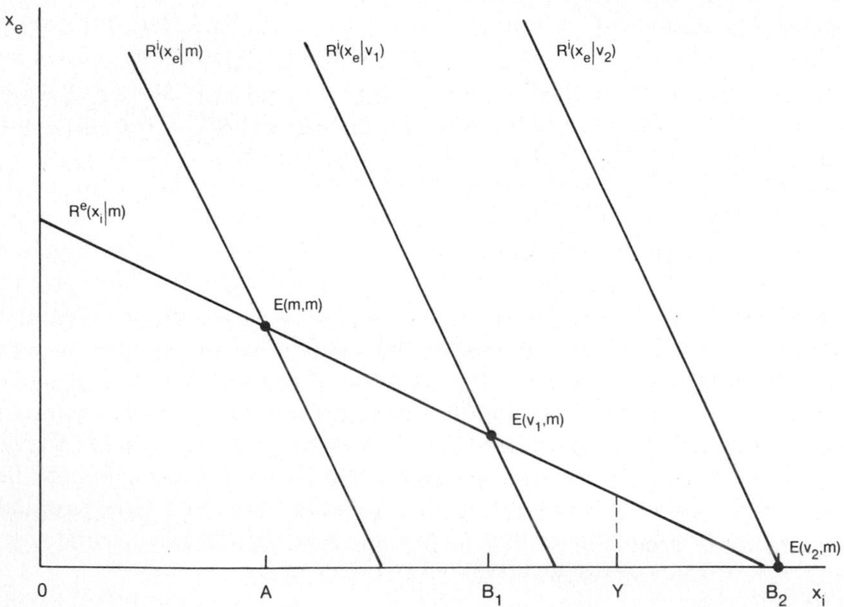

Figure 8.7. Equilibria with different marginal costs.

limit output were between B_1 and B_2 (as shown), entry could be prevented with marginal cost v_2, but not with v_1.

The incumbent never holds excess capacity in the Dixit model because the post-entry equilibrium output never exceeds the incumbent's pre-entry output. Any pre-entry excess capacity would remain unused after entry and therefore could not serve as an entry deterrent. Bulow et al. (1985b) argue that this result depends on the slopes of the firms' reaction functions. Dixit assumed that firms' reaction functions are everywhere downward sloping. Therefore, post-entry equilibria are always to the left of the incumbent's pre-entry output and pre-entry excess capacity would never be used post-entry. If reaction functions slope up, this result could be reversed and excess capacity may be desirable. The incentive for strategic entry deterrence and its relation to the slopes of reaction functions is discussed in more detail in Section 3 below.

2.2. Absolute cost advantages

Bain defined the absence of absolute cost advantages of an established firm by the following conditions.

> ...For a given product, potential entrant firms should be able to secure just as low a minimal average cost of production after entry as established firms had prior to this entry. This in turn implies (a) that established firms should have no price or other advantages over entrants in purchasing or securing any productive factor (including investible funds); (b) that the entry of an added firm should have no perceptible effect on the going level of any factor price; and (c) that established firms have no preferred access to productive techniques.[11]

2.2.1. Opportunity costs, profits, and rents

Absolute cost advantages appear to be the simplest of Bain's determinants of the condition of entry. If a potential entrant has a cost disadvantage with respect to an established firm, this is a factor that can allow the established firm to maintain price above cost. But one does not have to go far to uncover problems with the notion of absolute cost advantages as a barrier to entry. A cost disadvantage arising from inefficient production techniques should not be considered a barrier to entry. At a minimum, absolute cost disadvantages should be qualified to refer to some factor of production that is denied the potential entrant, and but for this omitted factor, the firm would be as efficient as established firms.

[11] Bain (1956, p. 12).

An ambiguity in Bain's discussion of absolute cost advantages is the role of opportunity costs. A scarce factor of production, be it a retail outlet on the best street in town, managerial expertise, or a superior ore deposit, has an opportunity cost of use. This opportunity cost must be considered in any decision to continue operations or to transfer ownership of a scarce factor to a competitor. When this opportunity cost is considered, an apparent absolute cost advantage may disappear.

Demsetz (1982) poses as a conundrum for definitions of barriers to entry the example of taxi medallions issued by a municipality and traded at market-determined prices. The medallions are limited in supply and are required to operate a taxi. The medallion requirement is an impediment to the total entry of taxi services in this market. Yet because medallions trade at market-determined prices, they are not an absolute cost advantage for any established taxi and they do not allow established taxis to elevate price above cost (given the opportunity cost of medallions). Even if established taxis obtained their medallions for free, the market price remains the opportunity cost of their use.

Consider a more extreme example, that of a key patent such as the xerography process. Although there is no public, market-determined price for the patent, it has a market value which is the present value of the profits it can earn in its next best use. This is the opportunity cost of the patent for its owner. Unless the patent is worth more to its owner than its opportunity cost, it should be sold and thus would not be a barrier to entry for any firm willing to pay the price.

There is no distinction between the taxi medallion and the patent as a barrier to entry. In either case, the medallion or the patent may give its owner some power to set price, depending of course on the circumstances of competition in the markets where they are used. But neither the patent nor the medallion allow their owners to earn an economic profit when the value to each owner equals the value in its next best use and this opportunity cost of ownership is taken into account.

In the context of mobility barriers, the question is whether absolute cost advantages confer a rent to incumbency. The test for the existence of a mobility barrier is whether access to the scarce resource allows a firm to earn positive profits *after accounting for the opportunity cost of the resource*, when there is potential entry from equally efficient firms. If the value of the resource in its next best use is the same as its value to the incumbent, its opportunity cost includes the profits that can be earned with the resource, and hence there can be no rent to incumbency.

An absolute cost advantage can confer an incumbency advantage if the value of the resource in its next best use is less than its value to the incumbent firm, for reasons other than inefficiency on the part of potential entrants. One possibility, discussed in Section 5 below, is that resources may be specific to particular firms. For example, it may be the case that the value of the xerography patent (prior to expiration and mandatory licensing), to the owners and managers of the physical assets called the Xerox Corporation, exceeded its value to any other firm.

Although absolute cost advantages need not be mobility barriers, they may nonetheless impede the total entry of productive resources into an industry and interfere with economic efficiency. The supply of taxi medallions reduces the supply of taxi services. Patent rights intentionally impede total entry into an industry. But neither the patent nor the medallions necessarily confer an incumbency advantage.

As Demsetz (1982) maintains, the real entry barrier in the taxi service industry is at the level of the municipality that has the power to issue medallions. Similarly, in the patent example the entry barrier is at the level of the legal authority in the Patent Office to issue patents. Moreover, at these stages, incumbency rents can be identified. The incumbent in this case is the legal authority that governs the supply of the scarce resource. Regulatory barriers to the supply of patent rights, or the supply of alternative (legally recognized) taxi medallions, confer rents on the established authorities. The barriers to the mobility of resources are not typically present in the "downstream" industries that use the scarce resources, but rather exist "upstream" in the structure of regulatory authority.

2.2.2. *Endogenous cost advantages*

Strategic behavior intended to impede the mobility of capital may take place on the demand side of the market, for example through advertising designed to exploit brand preferences, or on the supply side by attempting to increase cost asymmetries. This subsection considers strategic behavior targeted to exploiting experience-related cost advantages (or "learning-by-doing") and network economies that arise in demand. As these cost asymmetries either result from or are intensified by firm behavior, they are grouped under the category of "endogenous" cost advantages. This subsection concludes with a brief review of the more general topic of strategic attempts by incumbent firms to raise rivals' costs.

2.2.2.1. Experience-related cost asymmetries. "Practice makes perfect" is the underlying presumption of theoretical and empirical studies of economies related to on-the-job experience. There are many engineering and econometric studies in support of the conclusion that, at least in several important industries, more time on the job is associated, ceterus paribus, with lower production costs [see, for example, Lieberman (1984)]. Experience may be measured by time, cumulative output or some other variable related to job tenure. From the perspective of mobility deterrence, the interesting characteristic of experience-related economies is that an established firm enjoys a cost asymmetry relative to new entrants, and this asymmetry can be preserved by merely imitating the actions of competing firms. This presumes that the benefits of experience are a private good and do not spread to other industry participants. If so, the cost asymmetry may be lost or at least severely reduced and any strategic advantages that may follow from experience would be correspondingly limited. Lieberman (1984) has found that the diffusion of learning is common, but it will be ignored in what follows in order to concentrate on the value of experience economies in entry deterrence.

The learning-by-doing phenomenon can be illustrated with a simple two-period model. In the first period, there is an established firm with constant marginal cost c_1. In the second (and final) period, the firm's constant marginal cost depends on its first period output x_1 with

$$c_2(0) = c_1 \quad \text{and} \quad c_2'(x_1) < 0.$$

In the second period one or more firms may enter the industry. Each of the potential entrants has a constant marginal cost c_1, the same as the incumbent's first-period marginal cost.

The conditions of entry, and in particular whether entry will be prevented, depend not only on the cost advantage of the established firm, but also on the nature of competition in the second period. For example, with Bertrand–Nash competition and any cost advantage for the established firm, the second-period price will be just below the entrant's cost. Hence, any cost advantage for the incumbent would be sufficient to prevent entry.

Depending on the nature of competition in the industry and the rate at which learning-by-doing lowers costs, learning economies need not have the effect of making entry more difficult. Indeed, it is possible that learning economies can make the established firm more willing to allow entry into the industry. Consider an example where the established firm has one of two choices. It can either prevent entry by committing to a price less than c_1 in the second period, or it can choose to allow entry, in which case all firms in the industry act as Cournot competitors. The assumption that the incumbent can commit to a second-period price is analogous to the quantity commitment in the BSM limit pricing model. It also shares with that model the problem of maintaining a credible commitment.

Assume that there is a single potential entrant, although the analysis is easily extended to more than one. The established firm can prevent entry and earn arbitrarily close to

$$\pi^{\mathrm{L}} = (c_1 - c_2) X(c_1), \tag{10}$$

where c_2 is the firm's cost in the second period ($c_2 = c_2(x_1) \le c_1$) and $X(c_1)$ is total demand at the entry-preventing price c_1.

If c_2 is very close to c_1, the established firm cannot earn much by preventing entry and is better off allowing entry to occur. In addition, if c_2 is much less than

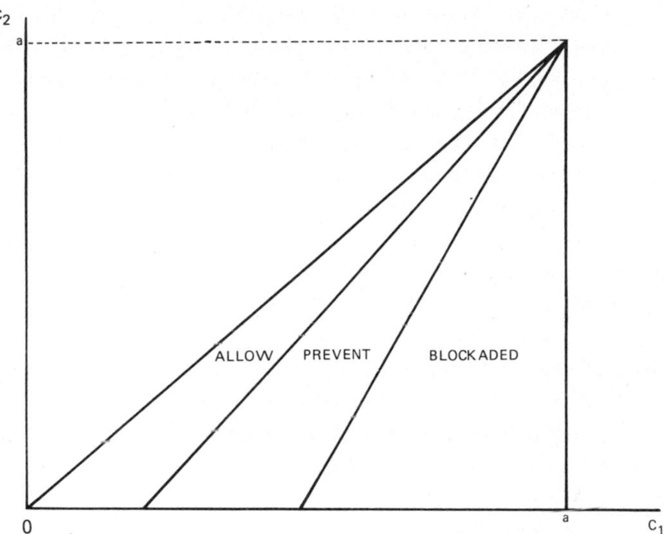

Figure 8.8. Zones of strategic behavior with learning ($c_2 \leq c_1 \leq a$).

c_1, the established firm may be better off with entry because the resulting price could be higher than the entry-preventing price, c_1. This means that learning economies need not make entry more difficult into an industry.

The circumstances for which the established firm would allow entry are summarized in Figure 8.8 for the case of linear demand. Entry would be allowed if c_2 is close to (or larger than) c_1. If c_1 is close to the demand intercept, a, or if c_1 is very small, entry is allowed for any value of $c_2 < c_1$. Entry is blockaded by the monopoly output when c_2 is much less than c_1. For intermediate values of c_1, the established firm would allow entry if learning is either very slow or very rapid. Entry prevention occurs only for intermediate cost advantages. For a small cost advantage, entry is allowed because preventing entry by pricing at c_1 squeezes the established firm's profits more than competition does. This is all the more important a consideration when c_1 is small. If the established firm's cost advantage is large, entry is allowed (or blockaded) because the entrant will not produce much anyway, and this is less costly than pricing at a level sufficient to deter all entry.[12]

Experience-related economies do not necessarily constitute a barrier to entry and their existence may facilitate entry in some situations. Experience-related economies do imply increasing returns to scale, as the concentration of produc-

[12]Mookherjee and Ray (1986) find similar strategic incentives for entry deterrence in a repeated-game model with learning.

tion allows a greater cost reduction. This assumes, of course, that there are no other factors at work that inhibit the value of learning, and it also assumes that learning is firm specific and does not spill over to competitors. These restrictions are severe. [See Spence (1984) and Kreps and Spence (1984) for a discussion of the consequences of spill-overs in a model with learning.]

The consequences of experience-related advantages for strategic behavior are likely to depend on the specific competitive situation in which they may occur. Fudenberg et al. (1983) and Harris and Vickers (1985) consider models of innovation in which experience lowers the expected cost of winning a patent. One can imagine the process of research and development toward a patentable product as an Easter egg hunt, and a firm that has spent longer at the hunt and turned over more stones is at an advantage in securing the ultimate prize. In the Fudenberg et al. model, a firm that is ahead in the race for a patent can be "leapfrogged" by a particularly aggressive (and lucky) rival. Nonetheless, they show that if a firm has a large enough lead, rival firms will exclude themselves from the race and the leader will enjoy a monopoly. If the firms are close in experience, they compete vigorously until one of the firms pulls ahead and becomes the clear leader, at which point the other firms drop out of the race.

2.2.2.2. Network economies. Network economies refer to complementarities that may exist in consumption or production. The telecommunications industry is an often-cited example of network economies. The value of telephone service to any one subscriber depends on the number of subscribers to the system with whom the customer might wish to speak. Learning economies are a special case of network economies where experience replaces the effects of market size.

A simple way in which to model network economies that arise on the demand side of the market is through an inverse demand specification, $P(Q, N)$, where Q is total demand and N is the number of subscribers, with $P_N(Q, N) > 0$. This captures the positive externality of market size for willingness-to-pay for the service. Network economies imply an economy of scale: either willingness-to-pay increases or production cost decreases with the size of the market. The implications for entry deterrence parallel the results for markets with experience-related economies. Their consequences are explored in Katz and Shapiro (1985, 1986) and Farrell and Saloner (1986).

Product standardization is a means to appropriate economies that arise as a result of complementarities in production or demand and hence is closely related to network economies. Adams and Brock (1982) suggest that compatibility standards can be used by an established firm to maintain monopoly power. Matutes and Regibeau (1986a, 1986b) explore this proposition further and find that the opportunity to produce compatible (or incompatible) products can have diverse effects. The opportunity to produce compatible products can lead to higher profits and increased total surplus, although consumers can be worse off with product standardization. Product standardization can lessen a firm's ability to price discriminate among different customers. This can be particularly disadvantageous for a large firm, but it can also enable a firm to forestall entry by making a credible commitment to charge uniform prices across markets that may serve as entry points into the industry.

2.2.2.3. Raising rivals' costs.[13] Production decisions that exploit experience-related economies are one example of strategic behavior that has consequences for cost asymmetries. Salop and Scheffman (1983, 1986) explore a general market environment in which unilateral behavior by established firms has the effect of raising industry costs of operations. The gist of their model follows closely Bain's second condition for the absence of absolute cost advantages: "...(b) that the entry of an added firm should have no perceptible effect on the going level of any factor price". Salop and Scheffman argue that behavior intended to increase industry costs can benefit established firms (despite increasing their own cost) because it causes rival firms to reduce their output (perhaps to zero). Salop and Scheffman's arguments are related to an observation by Williamson (1968), who noted that efforts to increase union wages in coal mining could benefit a firm by making entry of rival firms into the industry more difficult. A classic allegation of strategic behavior designed to raise costs for potential competitors is the Alcoa Corporation's acquisition of bauxite ore deposits which, it was argued, was designed to foreclose entry.[14]

Patent activity can be directed to increasing the cost of entry as well as improving productivity. An extreme example is a "sleeping patent" whose value derives from denying access to the technology by competing firms [see Gilbert (1981) and Gilbert and Newbery (1982)]. But patents are rarely of sufficient scope to block competing technologies and hence their value in entry prevention is limited.

The "raising rival cost" argument can be illustrated with a simple model. Suppose there is an established firm and a single potential entrant. The entrant's costs depend on its own output, x_e, and the vector of factor costs, $\boldsymbol{w}$. The latter depend on the competitive environment, which I will summarize by a vector $\boldsymbol{a} = (\boldsymbol{a}_i, \boldsymbol{a}_e)$ describing the actions of the incumbent firm ($\boldsymbol{a}_i$) and the entrant ($\boldsymbol{a}_e$). The entrant's profit conditional on entry is

$$\begin{aligned}\pi_e &= \max_x P(x)x - C_e(x, \boldsymbol{w}(\boldsymbol{a}_i, \boldsymbol{a}_e)) \\ &= \pi_e(\boldsymbol{a}_i, \boldsymbol{a}_e). \qquad (11)\end{aligned}$$

Similarly, the incumbent's profit is $\pi_i(\boldsymbol{a}_i, \boldsymbol{a}_e)$.

[13]This subject is discussed in more detail by Ordover and Saloner in Chapter 9 of this Handbook.
[14]*U.S. v. Aluminium Company of America*, 148 F.2d 416 (2d Cir. 1945).

Now consider the example in which the incumbent and a potential entrant compete for a scarce resource. This could be a superior ore deposit, a favorable retail location, or a key patent. Let $\boldsymbol{a} = (1, 0)$ correspond to the case where the incumbent wins the bidding race and $\boldsymbol{a} = (0, 1)$ correspond to the case where the entrant wins. Furthermore, suppose $\pi_e(0,1) > 0$ and $\pi_e(1,0) < 0$, so that if the incumbent wins, entry is prevented.

Following Gilbert and Newbery (1982) and Geroski and Jacquemin (1985), the incumbent can outbid the entrant at a cost $V = \pi_e(0,1)$. Its net return would be $\pi_i(1,0) - V$, and pre-emption would be preferred to entry if

$$\pi_i(1,0) - V > \pi_i(0,1) \tag{12}$$

or if

$$\pi_i(1,0) > \pi_i(0,1) + \pi_e(0,1). \tag{13}$$

The profit on the left is the monopoly profit when entry is prevented and the right-hand side is the total duopoly profit with entry. In circumstances where the incumbent can choose a monopoly price when pre-emption of the scarce resource excludes entry, this inequality will be satisfied and "raising rivals' costs" through pre-emption of the scarce resource would be a preferred strategy for the incumbent.

This simple example illustrates the exclusionary power of a strategy designed to raise rivals' costs. Williamson (1968) provides another example in which union wage rates are exploited by an incumbent in order to raise an entrant's average cost and make entry unprofitable.

Despite the apparent advantages to incumbent firms of strategies that raise rivals' costs, there are reasons to doubt whether such strategies can be supported as equilibrium outcomes of market competition. Although pre-emptive behavior may increase incumbent profits with potential entry, an incumbent may be unable to commit to a pre-emption strategy [in the patenting case see Reinganum (1983) and Gilbert and Newbery (1984)]. Entry prevention may require an incumbent to lower prices instead of, or in addition to, acquiring scarce assets (as in the BSM model), which could reverse the inequality in (13) and make the incumbent prefer to accommodate entry.

Even in situations where pre-emptive acquisition is sufficient to deter entry and the incumbent can commit to an entry-preventing strategy, accommodation may be preferable. Lewis (1983) considers the case in which a dominant firm and a competitive fringe bid for indivisible units of a scarce resource (e.g. ore deposits). He shows that the profitability of the resource to the dominant firm (and therefore the winner of the bid) depends on the size of the acquisition. While a dominant firm would outbid an entrant for a single, once-and-for-all acquisition [as in Gilbert and Newbery (1982)], this typically will not be the case when there are many sources of supply. Each successful bid by the dominant firm results in a higher price. The higher price makes a subsequent acquisition by an entrant more profitable and increases the cost of pre-emption by the dominant firm. Thus, in Lewis's example, the profitability of raising rivals' costs through pre-emptive acquisitions is mixed. Lewis also notes that it can be optimal for a dominant firm to divest some of its assets before it acquires new capacity. By doing so, the firm lowers the value of the new capacity to the fringe and hence reduces the price of pre-emption.

Related to strategies that raise rivals' costs are agreements amongst established firms and/or customers that limit access by actual or potential competitors to particular markets.[15] Aghion and Bolton (1987) provide an interesting and potentially far-reaching example of self-enforcing contracts that facilitate entry prevention. They consider the simple case of a single established firm, a single potential entrant, and a single customer who is willing to pay a maximum of $1 for one unit from either firm. The incumbent has a known cost $c_i = 1/2$. The entrant's cost, c_e, is uncertain, but it is common knowledge that c_e is distributed uniformly in the interval $[0, 1]$. The potential entrant observes the realized cost c_e before it has to make the entry decision. If it enters the market, the two firms act as Bertrand competitors, so that the resulting price is $P_e = \max[c_i, c_e] = \max[1/2, c_e]$.

In the absence of agreements between the agents in this market, entry will occur with probability $q = \text{prob}[c_e < 1/2] = 1/2$. The incumbent earns an expected profit:

$$\pi_i = q \cdot 0 + (1 - q) \cdot (p^m - c_i). \tag{14}$$

Entry occurs only if the entrant has a lower cost, in which case the incumbent earns nothing with Bertrand competition. If entry does not occur, the incumbent is a monopolist and chooses $p^m = 1$. Thus, $\pi_i = 1/4$.

Similarly, the buyer's expected consumer surplus is

$$S = q \cdot 1/2 + (1 - q) \cdot 0 = 1/4. \tag{15}$$

The entrant has an expected profit of 1/8, so that total surplus in this market is 5/8.

Now suppose the incumbent offers the customer a contract which specifies a price of P if the customer buys from the incumbent and a payment of P_0 if the customer buys from the entrant. The contract is of the "take or pay" variety. If

[15]Strategies that limit the size of a rival's market increase average costs if the rival's production technology exhibits increasing returns to scale. Hence demand-reducing strategies can be similar in effect to cost-increasing strategies.

accepted, the customer can buy from the incumbent at a price P or from the entrant at a price $P_e + P_0$, where P_e is the entrant's price. If the rival enters, its optimal price is $P_e = P - P_0$, and the condition $c_e < P_e$ is necessary and sufficient for the entrant to make a profit.

Consider $P = 3/4$ and $P_0 = 1/2$. Entry occurs only if c_e is less than $P - P_0 = 1/4$, which is also the probability of this event. The buyer is indifferent between this contract and potential competition with no contract. The contract yields the same expected consumer surplus (the subscript "c" denotes the contract):

$$S_c = (3/4) \cdot (1 - 3/4) + (1/4) \cdot (1 - (1/4 + 1/2)) = 1/4. \tag{16}$$

But the incumbent earns an expected profit of

$$\pi_c = (3/4) \cdot (3/4 - 1/2) + (1/4) \cdot (1/2) = 5/16, \tag{17}$$

which is better than the 1/4 it earned with no contract. The entrant has an expected profit of 1/32.

Although the incumbent is better off and the buyer is no worse off, total surplus is reduced with the take or pay contract: 19/32 versus 5/8. The loss is in the potential entrant's expected profit, which is reduced from 1/4 to 1/32.

Although the take or pay contract reduces the probability of entry and total surplus, the customer is no worse off. This is possible because with Bertrand competition, no contract, and entry, the customer's surplus depends only on the incumbent's cost and not on the entrant's. The customer benefits from competition, but not from the entrant's lower cost (the price equals 1/2 with entry). As As a result, the incumbent is able to strike a deal with the customer that leaves the customer no worse off.

The key to entry prevention in the Aghion and Bolton model is the entrant's inability to negotiate with the customer. Suppose the entrant could sign a contract that would give the customer 51 percent of the profits it would earn from entry. This would increase the consumer's reservation surplus level from 1/4 to more than 5/16. This reservation level would be high enough to make the take or pay contract unprofitable for the incumbent.

Aghion and Bolton provide a stimulating analysis of the scope for entry preventing contracts with important implications for issues in competition and public policy (for example, antitrust issues associated with complex leasing agreements).[16] Their work is also closely related to the economics of "switching

[16]For examples of contracts and entry prevention in U.S. antitrust law, see *Telex v. IBM* and *Brown Shoe v. U.S.*

costs" discussed in Subsection 2.3.1 below, as the take or pay contract has the characteristic of generating an endogenous cost for switching to another supplier.

2.3. Product differentiation

Product differentiation exists whenever consumers do not view goods as perfect substitutes. This may arise as a consequence of differences in product quality and performance, or for reasons that have to do with the reputation of the seller or a perception on the part of the buyer of "status" associated with a particular brand name. Switching from one brand to another may incur costs, in which case products that are identical ex ante may be viewed as imperfect substitutes once the consumer has chosen a particular brand.

Product differentiation allows producers some flexibility to raise price without losing all of their customers. This is the sine qua non of monopoly power; but as Chamberlin (1933) observed, monopoly power does not imply that firms earn monopoly profits. Entry, in the Chamberlain model, results in normal profits despite the local monopoly enjoyed by producers of differentiated products.

Although product differentiation need not imply monopoly profits, Bain (1956) nonetheless concluded that product differentiation was the single most important determinant of the ability of firms to earn supranormal profits. Using survey techniques, Bain identified the following factors contributing to product differentiation barriers in twenty industries studied: customer inertia; habit and loyalty; advertising-induced brand allegiance; product reputation; established dealer systems; customer dependence on services from established firms; patents; and prestige from conspicuous consumption of known brands.[17] Not surprisingly, the highest product differentiation entry barriers were associated with consumer-goods industries. This agrees with Comanor and Wilson's (1979) review of the advertising–profits relationship, which supports the conclusion that product differentiation advantages associated with advertising occur disproportionally in the consumer-goods sector.

Product differentiation necessarily implies a barrier to entry in the sense that the producer of one brand cannot replicate another brand without incurring a disadvantage in either cost or sales. In this sense, product differentiation is similar to an absolute cost advantage (but note that, unlike a pure cost advantage, each brand can have a product differentiation advantage over other brands).

Although product differentiation precludes perfect imitation and therefore limits the effectiveness of entry, it does not mean that established firms are

[17] Bain (1956, p. 123).

advantaged relative to latecomers. The producer of a new product or service has to prove its worth to skeptical consumers. Subsequent producers must contend with the reputation of an established firm, but may have the advantage of a better-informed customer base.[18] It is not obvious whether the first firm or subsequent entrants have the tougher job.

This is the essence of the conclusions in Schmalensee (1974), who argues that any firm-specific advantages resulting from advertising expenditures must depend on the existence of an asymmetry in the way that firms' advertising expenditures affect their demands. An established firm benefits from a stock of advertising "goodwill", but this goodwill arises from previous expenditures and does not influence post-entry advertising decisions.

Advertising and marketing expenditures may serve to impede the mobility of capital into (and out of) an industry by increasing product differentiation and by exacerbating the effects of scale economies on the profitability of entry. As Demsetz (1982) maintains, these effects should not be categorically interpreted as entry barriers in the sense of reducing economic performance and leading to prices above minimum average cost. Product differentiation is a reflection of consumer preferences which must be respected in any welfare calculation. Brand preferences may be based on a product's reputation for quality or a firm's reputation for service. They may reflect a belief that an established brand will provide better value in the long run. Any analysis of product differentiation as a barrier to capital mobility must contend with the private and social value of these beliefs.

Advertising and marketing expenditures may have implications for strategic entry deterrence when these activities complement scale-related barriers. Suppose we begin with the proposition that product differentiation per se has no normative implications for capital mobility. However, when combined with a scale-related barrier to entry, firms might find it profitable to enhance product differentiation in order to exploit the benefits of scale. Spence (1980) shows how advertising expenditures can influence the optimal scale of production by affecting both the cost of operations and the revenues that can be collected at a particular level of output. Bresnahan (1986) investigates the extent to which advertising expenditures actually contribute to economies of scale.

Although advertising and marketing can clearly affect the optimal scale of operations, the direction is by no means obvious. Advertising provides an important information function for a new entrant. Advertising is a means by which new firms can inform customers of an alternative, and perhaps more

[18]Farrell (1986a) notes that new entrants may have a tougher time convincing customers that they will deliver comparable quality. In Farrell's model, competition lowers the future benefits from investments in quality. If consumers believe that new entrants do not have sufficient incentives to invest in high quality, they may be reluctant to experiment with their products. This result depends on the value of future profits to the entrant and on the firm's ability to warrant the quality of its goods.

attractive, source of supply. The classic example is Benham's (1972) study of the effects of advertising restrictions on the market prices of eyeglasses. Benham found that prices of eyeglasses in states that imposed advertising restrictions were significantly higher than the prices in states with more permissive advertising regulations.[19]

Using a variant of the BSM model that allows for differentiated products, Dixit (1979) traces the interactions between economies of scale, the extent of product differentiation, and the scope for entry deterrence.[20] There is an established firm (firm 1) and a potential entrant (firm 2), with demands of the form:

$$p_1 = \alpha_1 - \beta_1 x_1 - \gamma x_2,$$
$$p_2 = \alpha_2 - \beta_2 x_2 - \gamma x_1, \tag{18}$$

with $\alpha_i, \beta_i > 0$ and $\gamma^{1/2} \leq \beta_1 \beta_2$. The products are substitutes if $\gamma > 0$.

Each firm has costs $C_i = mx + F$. As in the BSM model, the established firm can commit to an output and act as a Stackelberg leader. The limit output in this model is

$$Y = \left[\alpha_2 - m - 2(\beta_2 F)^{1/2}\right] / \gamma. \tag{19}$$

The extent of product differention affects all of the parameters of demand for the two brands. Dixit calls particular attention to the effects on the intercepts of the inverse demand functions (α_i) and the cross-product term (γ).[21] An increase in advertising and marketing expenditures that enhances brand 1 at the expense of brand 2 may increase α_1 relative to α_2 and decrease γ. The α effect measures an increased willingness to pay for brand 1 relative to brand 2 at every level of output. A decrease in γ lowers the cross-elasticity of demand for the two brands (they become poorer substitutes).

Ignoring the cost of product differentiation, the incentive for product enhancing activities can be examined by comparing the Stackelberg profits with entry in the BSM model to the profits earned at the limit output. A decrease in α_2 lowers the limit output, while a decrease in γ has the opposite effect. The α effect

[19] Benham's conclusions have been verified by Haas-Wilson (1986) in a follow-up study of the eyeglass market. But note Peters' (1984) theoretical result that, in some circumstances, advertising restrictions can lead to lower prices.

[20] Note that Dixit's model assumes perfect information and therefore ignores the role of advertising as an information source. The implications of advertising for consumer search and consequent market performance are discussed in Grossman and Shapiro (1984).

[21] Note that product differentiation can be expected to affect the β terms as well.

increases the profit when entry is prevented and the γ effect goes the other way. Entry prevention is more difficult when products are poorer substitutes. This result seems to contradict much of the literature that associates product differentiation with entry deterrence. It is, however, intuitive. Products must be substitutes in order for the output of one product to adversely affect the profits earned by the other products. If the products are independent, limit pricing is useless.

The effect on the limit output is not sufficient to determine the consequences of product differentiation for entry deterrence because it is necessary to compare the incumbent's profit when entry is prevented to the profit the firm would earn if entry occurred. Dixit does this and concludes that an increase in α_1 relative to α_2 makes entry deterrence more likely (meaning that the set of parameters for which firm 1 will successfully impede entry is larger). The γ effect goes the opposite way. Product differentiation, corresponding to a lower γ, makes entry deterrence less likely. A lower cross-elasticity lowers the profit when entry is deterred and raises the profit when entry occurs, making entry easier on both counts.

Dixit's results are an important lesson for the role of product differentiation in strategic entry deterrence. He concludes that

> a greater absolute advantage in demand (or cost) for established firms makes entry harder, but lower cross-price effects with potential entrants make entry easier. This suggests that industrial organization economists should keep these two aspects distinct, instead of lumping them together into one vague concept of product differentiation as they usually do.

He adds a caveat warning the reader of added complications that may emerge from the dynamics inherent in the problem and the assumption of Stackelberg commitment behavior in the BSM model. In view of more recent developments, these warnings are particularly apt.

2.3.1. Switching costs

Switching costs represent a consumer disutility from changing brands. A change from one brand to another may incur direct costs, such as investment in training required to change from one brand of word processing software to another. A switch need not consume economic resources to be perceived as costly. Those loyal to a particular brand of beer may have a distaste for sampling other brands.

Switching costs are a source of economies of scale in consumption. With switching costs, a customer is better off continuing to purchase from his original supplier even though another supplier offers the same product at a slightly lower price. A firm that sells Q units to customers each of whom has a switching cost,

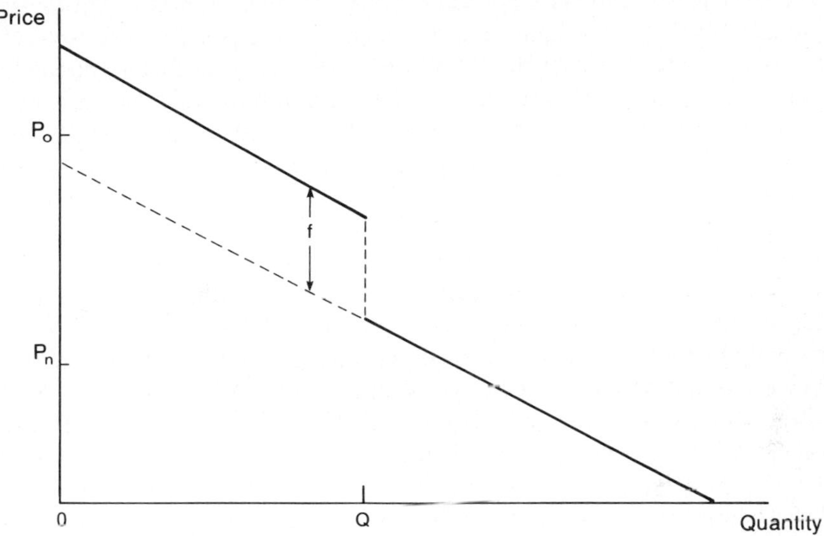

Figure 8.9. Demand with switching costs.

f, has a demand curve as in Figure 8.9. Ignoring possibilities for price discrimination, the firm has a choice of pricing high to exploit existing customers (e.g. selling to its old customers at a price P_o), or pricing low to attract new customers (e.g. selling to both old and new at a price P_n).[22]

The cost of switching is an obvious source of monopoly power to established suppliers [see Schmalensee (1981b) and Klemperer (1986)]. It also suggests that there may be many equilibrium configurations of supply for a market with switching costs, which may depend on the historical circumstances that lead to a particular pattern of trade.

Switching costs favor an established supplier, but their implications for industry structure are far from obvious. Customer expectations of how firms will react to price competition is crucial to the effects of switching costs. For example, suppose that customers of established firms believe that equilibrium prices will be the same for all firms. Given any cost of switching suppliers, however small, they will choose to remain with their original supplier. This gives established firms a

[22] The existence of "locked-in" customers is a powerful incentive for firms to develop strategies that permit discriminating between old and new customers. An example is the alleged price discrimination by IBM in the pricing of disk drives to new and old computer purchasers (see *Telex v. IBM*).

sure hold over their customer base. Alternatively, customers may act in the spirit of Nash and evaluate competitive price offers assuming other prices will not change. In this case an established firm's grip on its old customers may be less secure. But the presence of fixed costs makes reaction functions non-convex and equilibria in pure strategies need not exist. There is nothing inherently wrong with this result. It merely underscores the critical importance of competitive behavior in deducing equilibrium outcomes from the structural characteristics of markets.

Farrell and Shapiro (1986) investigate an overlapping-generations model of competition with switching costs in which either a new supplier or the established supplier acts as a Stackelberg price leader and there is no opportunity for price discrimination. Both firms have identical and constant marginal costs. When the entrant moves first and sets a price, p, the incumbent can either (a) sell to only its old customers at a price $p + f$ (or slightly below) or (b) compete for all customers by setting a price slightly below p. They show that there is a unique equilibrium in which the entrant serves only new customers at a price p and the established supplier serves only old customers at a price $p + f$. The incumbent never competes for the new customers. The reason is that the new customers are equally valuable to the incumbent and the rival, but the incumbent has an incentive to price higher and keep its old customers.

In the presence of economies of scale, Farrell and Shapiro show that a customer base with switching costs can lead an established firm to allow entry when entry prevention would be more efficient. This result parallels the example with learning. In the learning case, it would be efficient for the firm with lower costs to price low and exploit experience economies. But the firm may choose to exploit its low cost by pricing high and allowing entry. Similarly, the firm with a customer base could price low and prevent entry or price high, keep its old customers, and allow entry to occur. If economies of scale are not too great, the latter course of action is the best strategy.

These results follow under the assumption that the entrant acts as a Stackelberg price leader. If the incumbent is the price leader, there is a unique equilibrium with a single price charged by both firms (the same for both new and old customers). Old customers strictly prefer to buy from their old firm, while new customers are indifferent. Profits for both firms are higher when the incumbent is the price leader, but curiously the entrant benefits even more in this instance. There is a "second-mover advantage" in the game with the incumbent as the price leader.

The presence of switching costs need not lead to entry deterrence in the Farrell/Shapiro models. Switching costs do allow firms to profit from locked-in customers and they affect the structure of the market. These models are further examples of the distinction between the effects of structural factors on entry and their effects on market structure and performance.

3. Fat cats and puppy dogs

The models discussed so far indicate a wide range of strategic behavior by established firms faced with the threat of entry. In the Dixit model, a firm may invest aggressively in order to tip the scale of the post-entry game in its favor, and in doing so may prevent entry. But in Farrell and Shapiro's switching cost model, the established firm may choose to mine its installed base of customers and allow entrants to serve new customers. A similar result occurs in a model of advertising by Schmalensee (1983). An established firm's goodwill leads a firm to price high and allow entry. Is there any rhyme and reason to these examples? Is there a prescription to follow that will tell when an established firm will choose to accommodate or actively prevent entry?

Fudenberg and Tirole (1984) and Bulow et al. (1985b) provide a taxonomy of behavior in response to entry. Their approach does not permit an instant answer to how established firms will behave in a particular competitive situation, but they succeed in identifying key factors. I will follow the approach in Fudenberg and Tirole (1984), who employ an unconventional, but descriptive notation in their characterization of firm behavior.

The incumbent can respond to the threat of entry with a strategic investment, K. This could take many forms, including capacity, advertising, R&D, or a combination of these activities. The incumbent's profit with entry, conditional on K, is a function of its own output, x_i, and the entrant's output, x_e: $\pi(x_i, x_e \mid K)$. The consequence of an increase in K for the incumbent's profit is

$$(\partial\pi/\partial x_i)\mathrm{d}x_i/\mathrm{d}K + (\partial\pi/\partial x_e)(\partial x_e/\partial x_i)\mathrm{d}x_i/\mathrm{d}K + \partial\pi/\partial K. \tag{20}$$

The key factors in Fudenberg and Tirole's taxonomy are the slope of entrant's reaction curve and the effect of incumbent investment on the firm's equilibrium output.[23] The slope of the entrant's reaction curve is $\partial x_e/\partial x_i$ and the effect of incumbent investment on its equilibrium output is $\mathrm{d}x_i/\mathrm{d}K$. If $\mathrm{d}x_i/\mathrm{d}K > 0$, investment makes the incumbent "tough" and in the opposite case, investment makes the incumbent "soft". As an example, in the Dixit entry deterrence problem, reaction curves slope down and investment makes the incumbent tough.

The optimal behavior for the incumbent depends as well on the other factors in (20) and on whether the incumbent chooses to deter or accommodate entry. Fudenberg and Tirole describe four types of behavioral strategies that an incumbent may use: the "top dog", the "puppy-dog ploy", the "fat cat", and the "lean and hungry look".

[23] In the terminology of Bulow et al. (1985b), these factors determine whether the firms' products are "strategic complements" or "strategic substitutes".

(i) *The "top dog"*. The top dog overinvests to deter entry. This is the optimal deterrence strategy in models such as Spence (1977) and Dixit (1981). Investment makes the incumbent tough and, in response, the entrant would cower and produce less (the reaction curve is downward sloping). Top-dog behavior is optimal in this case whether or not entry is actually prevented. Even if entry is allowed in the Dixit model, the incumbent will play the top-dog role to increase its post-entry profits.

(ii) *The "fat cat"*. Suppose reaction curves are upward sloping as in the case of Bertrand competition with differentiated products. In addition, suppose that more investment makes the incumbent soft. Fudenberg and Tirole provide an example where the incumbent's optimal price is an increasing function of investment in advertising because the ads lower the elasticity of demand for the product, so that more advertising makes the incumbent soft. By being soft, the fat cat encourages its rival to be less aggressive. This strategy involves overinvestment (relative to the case where the strategic interactions are ignored) in order to optimally accommodate entry.

(iii) *"The lean and hungry look"*. If reaction curves are upward sloping and investment makes the incumbent soft, entry prevention calls for a lean and hungry look. In the advertising example, the incumbent may underinvest (relative to no entry) in order to commit itself to aggressive pricing if entry occurs.

(iv) *"The puppy-dog ploy"*. The "puppy-dog" ploy is underinvestment in order to make the incumbent firm appear more friendly to a new entrant. This can be an optimal strategy if reaction functions are upward sloping, less investment makes the incumbent soft, and the incumbent expects entry to occur. Gelman and Salop (1983) provide an example where the entrant is the puppy dog. By committing itself to an low investment strategy, the entrant projects a friendly image that is intended to evoke a more accommodating strategy by the incumbent.

4. Entry, dynamics, and industry structure

The BSM model of limit pricing inspired early criticism directed in particular to the assumptions about the entry of a rival firm. Stigler (1968) argued that it may be more desirable to retard the rate of entry rather than impede entry altogether. Harrod (1952) and Hicks (1954) pointed to the tradeoff between short-run profits and long-run losses from entry. Caves and Porter (1977) criticized the theory of entry deterrence for confining itself to the either/or question of whether a dominant firm will exclude an entrant, and ignoring the more subtle and important issues of the movement of capital into, out of, and among segments of an industry.

These criticisms are still relevant: there is as yet no coherent theory that can describe the evolution of market structure and it may be presumptuous to expect that such a theory can be constructed. Many attempts have been made to refine models of entry deterrence, adding elements of realism in the dynamics of the entry and exit and in competition among established and new firms. What follows is a sampling from a large and growing literature.

4.1. Dynamic limit pricing

Gaskins' (1971) influential paper was one of the first attempts to characterize optimal pricing over time for an industry faced with a continuous threat of entry. Gaskins specified entry as a flow rate of change of rival output $x(t)$ that depends on the price set by established firms, $p(t)$, and the rivals' long-run marginal cost, c_e:

$$dx/dt = f(p(t), c_e). \tag{21}$$

At any time t, the total amount of rival output is

$$x(t) = \int_0^t f(p(t), c_e)\,dt, \tag{22}$$

which depends only on the time path of the prices set by the established firms. Established firms choose a price path $p(t)$ to maximize present value profits:

$$\pi = \int_0^t (p(t) - c_i)q(p(t), t)e^{-rt}dt, \tag{23}$$

where $q(p(t), t)$ is the difference between demand at price $p(t)$ and rival output $x(t)$.

With entry characterized by equation (21), the established firms' optimal price policy can be determined by the solution to a classical one control variable (p) and one state variable (x) optimal control problem. The optimal policy is a tradeoff between the gains from monopoly pricing and the cost of entry induced by a high price. Entry erodes the established firms' market share and pushes price down at a rate that depends on industry growth. For a stationary market, price approaches the competitive level.

A main criticism of Gaskins' model is that entry is not an equilibrium process. The entry equation (21) is not the result of optimizing decisions by a pool of potential entrants, but is specified exogenously in the model. The incumbent firm (or cartel) is presumed to act rationally, choosing a price policy to maximize present value profits. But there is no corresponding maximization problem for the firms that make up the flow of entry into the industry. Firms are not symmetric in the Gaskins model in their degree of rationality. Indeed, even if entry continues to the point where the incumbent firm(s) make up a very small share of the industry, they continue to act strategically, taking into account the reactions of their competitors, while the behavior of the new entrants is given exogenously. Only incumbent firm(s) can boast an identity in the Gaskins model. Entrants are relegated to a nameless component of an output flow.

The entry rate depends only on the current industry price. This need not be a deficiency of the model if there is no other information available which firms can use to condition their entry decisions. Of course actual entrants should be concerned not with current prices, but with the prices that will prevail after they enter the industry. The Gaskins model implies entry behavior that is too myopic. If nothing else, potential entrants should make use of the entry equation (21) to forecast future profitability. After all, if this is known to the incumbent firm(s), it should be common knowledge for the potential entrants as well. The one case in which this information has no value would be for potential entrants that have no investment at risk, e.g. if the investment required for entry is completely reversible.

Some of the theoretical shortcomings of the Gaskins model have been addressed by others. Kamien and Schwartz (1971) extend the Gaskins model to the case of stochastic entry. The probability that entry occurs by time t is $F(t)$. If entry occurs at time t, the incumbent firms (which act as a monolithic cartel) earn a profit flow $e^{gt}\pi_2$, where g is a market growth rate. This is less than the maximum monopoly profit, $e^{gt}\pi_1$. Unlike the monopoly profit, the profit with entry is given exogenously and does not depend on the market price. The rate of change in the probability of entry, conditional on no entry by date t, is the hazard rate $F'(t)/(1-F(t))$. The entry hazard rate in the Kamien and Schwartz model evolves according to the function $h(p(t), g)$, where $p(t)$ is the market price and g is the market growth rate. The hazard rate is an increasing function of the market price and the growth rate.

Established firms choose a price function $p(t)$ to maximize

$$\int_0^{\infty} e^{-(r-g)t}[\pi_1(p(t))(1-F(t)) + \pi_2 F(t)]\,dt \tag{24}$$

subject to

$$F'(t) = h(p(t), g)(1-F(t)) \quad \text{and} \quad F(0) = 0.$$

Kamien and Schwartz show that the solution to this optimal control problem is a constant p^*. Given p^*, the cartel's total discounted profit is

$$V(p^*) = (\pi_1(p^*) - \pi_2)/(r - g + h(p^*)) + \pi_2/(r - g). \tag{25}$$

The optimal price balances the gain from entry prevention (a lower probability, h, of entry) against the effects of a lower price on the transient profits earned before entry occurs. If π^{m} is the unconstrained monopoly profit, they show that, given some smoothness assumptions about the effect of price on the entry probability,

$$\pi^{\mathrm{m}} > \pi_1(p^*) > \pi_2.$$

The Kamien and Schwartz formulation is quite elegant in that it represents entry as a fully dynamic and stochastic processs. Its major shortcoming, however, is that the entry processs is still an exogenous specification of the model. Entry is not determined as the result of optimizing decisions on the part of potential rivals.

Flaherty (1980) introduces a model of rational entry, but assumes that firms commit to output paths for all future time. This assumption is similar to the output commitment in the BSM model [and to the price path commitment in Gaskins (1971) and Kamien and Schwartz (1971)]. The output commitment allows an incumbent firm to prevent entry by specifying an output path that it may not choose to produce if it did not have the commitment option. Encaoua and Jacquemin (1980) extend the limit pricing model to include non-price-strategic variables.

Gilbert and Harris (1984) model an oligopolistic market with free entry and increasing returns to scale in new capital investment. Not surprisingly, the implications for equilibrium market structure depend on the behavioral strategies of the firms. The extension of Nash–Cournot behavior to this market implies that each firm takes the planned investment sequence of its competitors as given and responds with the sequence that maximizes its present value profits. If firms compete as Nash–Cournot oligopolists, the evolution of the market is similar to that assumed in the Gaskins limit pricing formulation. The market converges gradually over time to a long-run equilibrium and firms earn profits that are proportional to their initial market shares. However, entrants account for all new investment, so that a dominant firm's profits are limited to its earnings on its installed base. Furthermore, firms earn a positive profit in the long run, even with free entry.

In contrast to the Nash–Cournot case, if firms act to pre-empt rival investment in the expectation that early investment will force rivals to alter their investment plans, each new investment earns zero profits and the scope for entry deterrence depends critically on the post-entry pricing game. If post-entry price competition is such that all capacity owned by incumbents pre-entry would be used post-entry, incumbents cannot prevent entry and earn positive profits when there are no entry costs other than the cost of a new plant [see Mills (1988) for the consequences of entry costs]. If however, incumbent firms can hold excess capacity pre-entry which they would (credibly) use after entry occurs, entry can be prevented. The ability of incumbents to prevent entry is constrained by the amount of capacity that they can maintain as excess before entry, and use after entry occurs.

In a recent addition to the dynamic limit pricing literature, Judd and Petersen (1986) introduce financing into the entry processs. They assume that the rate of entry is governed by the need for firms to finance their expansions with internally-generated funds. The extent to which this is possible depends of course on the rate of profit, which the established firm(s) can control through its pricing decision. The connection between the pricing decision and the entrant's flow of funds to finance entry is a convenient way to make entry an endogenous feature of the model. Their results retain many of the features of Gaskins' model, but differ in some predictions. For example, with slow growth the optimal price drops to the fringe long-run marginal cost in finite time. If the market has a high initial growth rate and then slows, the optimal price path may rise to a peak as the growth rate declines. While the market is growing it pays the established firms to keep the price low and retard the growth of the fringe. When the growth rate slows, the established firms take their profits and then price gradually falls to a competitive level as the fringe continues to expand. The Judd and Petersen model is a useful extension of the limit pricing theory, but one can question its relevance to a world with venture capitalists, junk bonds, and innovative corporate finance.

Despite its theoretical limitations, the Gaskins model of dynamic limit pricing (along with its refinements) is an appealing description of pricing behavior for industries that are characterized by dominant firms. The exogenous specification of the entry flow is not theoretically justified, but it may capture an important element of dynamic competition. The Gaskins model identifies entry as a *disequilibrium* process. The exogenous specification of the entry flow is not inconsistent with an environment in which potential entrants have imperfect formation about the existence of entry opportunities and where searching out entry opportunities is costly and time-consuming.[24] If it were possible to model these aspects of the entry processs, the result could be an entry flow rate that appears similar to equation (21) in the Gaskins model. Indeed, perhaps models of entry deterrence that assume potential entrants are rational and fully informed

[24]These considerations suggest the applicability of the literature on bounded rationality, disequilibrium economics and innovation to the dynamics of entry [see, for example, Williamson (1975) and Nelson and Winter (1982)].

are missing a critical aspect of entry dynamics. For these reasons, it is not surprising that the Gaskins model has been used successfully in empirical models of dominant firm pricing, such as Blackstone (1972) and Brock (1975).

A major criticism of the dynamic limit pricing literature is the assumption of Stackelberg behavior by the dominant firm. Spence (1979) describes a model in which firms are strategically similar, yet a form of limit pricing behavior emerges. In Spence's model firms are constrained in their maximum rates of growth. Either as a result of a head start of a larger maximum growth rate, one firm may win the race for market share. At any point in the race, either firm may stop or continue to invest, thereby altering the future structure of the market. These simple alternatives lead to some interesting, and complex, outcomes. For example, suppose that there are two firms, 1 and 2, and firm 1 is ahead. If both firms continue to invest, firm 2 will lose money. Through rapid growth it is feasible for firm 1 to prevent the entry of firm 2. But firm 2 may threaten to remain in the market and, if its threat is taken seriously, firm 1 may choose to stop investing and accommodate its rival. The position in the race for market share gives each firm a menu of threats and counterthreats that may influence the eventual structure of their market. Fudenberg and Tirole (1983) identify those threats which are credible in the Spence model and show how they effect equilibrium industry structure.

The Spence model and its refinement by Fudenberg and Tirole illustrate the endogeneity of industry structure. The scope for entry deterrence and the emergence of dominant firms derive from strategic advantages related to technology, demand, behavior, and initial structural conditions. Firms may begin on a common footing, but over time their relative positions in the market confer different strategic opportunities. The outcomes in these models reflect a comment by Caves and Porter: "The incumbent's actions affect both the entrant's conjectures about industry conditions following his entry and the 'structural' barriers to entry. Thus, the entry barriers we observe are partly structural but at least partly endogenous."[25]

4.2. Multiple incumbents and entrants

The classic description of entry-deterring behavior is posed in the context of a single dominant firm or a perfectly coordinated cartel. The BSM model and its extensions yield sharp conclusions about the behavior of firms in the face of entry and about consequent market performance. But these conclusions are not tempered by the forces of competition within an established industry. According to

[25]Caves and Porter (1977, p. 250).

Stigler (1968), the BSM approach to limit pricing solves the theory of oligopoly "by murder".[26]

Few industries are represented by a single firm that acts to impede entry over a sustained period. Tight as well as loose oligopolies face problems of coordination among their own activities. These problems are compounded if they must also coordinate activities aimed at deterring entry.

Moving from the monolithic case of the dominant firm/perfect cartel to more realistic situations of oligopolistic competition raises new questions about the scope for entry prevention. For example, can meaningful distinctions be drawn with respect to competition between incumbent firms versus competition between incumbents and new entrants? What role does potential entry play with respect to the evolution of industry structure? Does oligopolistic competition facilitate entry prevention or do the problems of coordination in oligopoloy make entry prevention more difficult?[27]

Most of these questions remain as unresolved topics for further research. Despite the great progress that has been made in oligopoly theory and entry deterrence, relatively little is known about the interactions between strategic entry deterrence and market structure. One exception to this general trend is the extensive literature on contestibility theory, which is discussed separately in Section 7.

Gilbert and Vives (1986) extend the BSM model of entry prevention to the case of more than one incumbent firm. There are $i = 1, \ldots, M$ incumbents and a single entrant [the results generalize to more than one potential entrant if entry occurs sequentially – see Vives (1982)]. Incumbents act non-cooperatively and each chooses an output x_i, taking other firms' outputs as given. Entry is prevented if $\sum x_i = X_i \geq Y$, where Y is the limit output. Demand is linear and the technology is as in equation (7): constant marginal costs with a fixed cost associated with entry.

Gilbert and Vives show that as a result of non-cooperative behavior entry prevention is excessive in the sense that the industry prevents entry at least as much as would a perfectly coordinated cartel. Moreover, there are multiple equilibria involving entry prevention and these can co-exist with an equilibrium in which entry is allowed. When equilibria involving entry prevention and accommodation occur simultaneously, the accommodation equilibrium dominates

[26]Stigler (1968, p. 21).

[27]For example, Caves and Porter (1977, pp. 247–248) write: "... an investment in entry deterrence generally protects not just the investor but his oligopolistic rivals as well, and thus raises special problems for the form and extent of collusion... the industry's level of investment in deterrence, in the absence of collusion among going firms, could be either greater or less than its level in the case of full collusion on the design of these investments and distribution of the rents. The negative effect of nonappropriable benefits from the collective good cuts against the positive effect of styling the investment to divert the benefits toward the firm making it."

the equilibrium in which entry is prevented. Each incumbent firm and the entrant is better off with entry.

Entry prevention is a public good for the incumbents, much as national defense is for a country's citizens. Yet there is no tendency to provide too little entry deterrence in the Gilbert and Vives model. Each incumbent benefits from entry prevention by an amount proportional to its output. When entry is prevented and the aggregate incumbent output is Y, each incumbent earns

$$\pi_{\mathrm{i}}^{\mathrm{L}} = (P(Y) - m)x_{\mathrm{i}} - F. \tag{26}$$

The limit price exceeds m and (26) is strictly increasing in x_{i} for $x_{\mathrm{i}} \leq Y$. Furthermore, given the output of all other incumbents, X_{-i}, any decrease in firm i's output below $Y - X_{-i}$ would lead to entry and a discontinuous fall in firm i's profit. Thus, if entry is prevented, each incumbent would like the task of entry prevention. This incentive, coupled with non-cooperative behavior in which incumbent firms choose investments simultaneously, results in equilibria with "excessive" entry prevention.

Elements of a theory of strategic entry deterrence and market structure can be gleaned from a simple extension of the BSM model to allow for sequential entry by more than one firm. Suppose we assume that there is a single incumbent firm, $i = 0$, and a sequence of entrants, $j = 1,\ldots, N$. Each entrant is identified with a (timeless) period in which it may choose to enter the industry. In period 0 the incumbent may choose any output x_0, which it must produce in period 0 and in all future periods. Firm j may choose to enter only in period $t = j$ and each firm that enters takes as given the output of the incumbent firm and all prior entrants, but is strategic about the effect of its output on possible future entrants.

These assumptions describe a simple market in which new firms may enter sequentially, as in Prescott and Visscher (1978). The behavioral assumptions imply that each new firm acts Cournot with respect to the incumbent and all previous entrants, and acts as a Stackelberg leader with respect to future entrants.

Let X_j be the total output of the first j firms in the market and let $R_i(X_j)$ be firm i's optimal output taking X_j as given, but taking into account the reactions of all future entrants $k = i + 1,\ldots, n$. Firm i's output is the solution to

$$\max_{x_{\mathrm{i}}} \pi(x_{\mathrm{i}}, X_{i-1}, R_{i+1}(X_i),\ldots, R_n(X_{n-1})). \tag{27}$$

Each firm's optimal output (if it exists) can be determined through backward induction beginning with the last firm, n, but this computation can be very difficult for general cost and demand conditions. As a simple example, consider again the case of a homogeneous industry with linear demand, $P = a - bX$, constant marginal cost, m, and a fixed cost of entry, F, which becomes sunk once entry occurs. Vives (1982) and Gilbert (1986) show that the optimal response for firm i is

$$R_i(X_j) = ((a - m)/b - X_j)/2. \tag{28}$$

That is, it is optimal for each firm to act as a monopolist with respect to the residual demand function formed by subtracting from total demand the total output of the incumbent and all previous entrants.[28]

The incumbent firm has to chose whether to exclude all entrants by setting the limit output or allowing entry to occur. In this model, there is no point in allowing one or more firms to enter and then excluding others. Also, if the incumbent allows entry, it is in the interest of all future entrants to allow entry. Limit pricing earns the incumbent a profit equal to

$$\pi^{\mathrm{L}} = (P(Y) - m)Y - F, \tag{29}$$

while if entry is allowed, the incumbent's profit is

$$\pi^{\mathrm{E}} = (P(X_j) -)x_0. \tag{30}$$

Here X_j is the total output given that j firms enter and x_0 is the incumbent's optimal output.

The free entry number of firms is the largest number, J, for which $X_j < Y$. If the number of potential entrants, N, is strictly smaller than J, the incumbent maximizes profits by allowing entry to occur. If N is equal to J (or larger), the incumbent should limit price [see Omari and Yarrow (1982) and Gilbert (1986)]. If entry is deterred, the market structure is, of course, a monopoly. Even if entry is allowed, this market would be very concentrated, with the first four firms accounting for at least 93 percent of the industry output.

This simple model is clearly unsatisfactory as a predictive model of industry structure. Some of its limitations are quite obvious. It is essentially a static model. Entry is instantaneous and perfectly predictable. In addition, the incumbent and successful entrants are able to commit to outputs which are sustained in the face of subsequent entry. This behavior is consistent with the BSM model, but it is patently unrealistic as a model of actual behavior in a dynamic market.

The model can be extended to constrain the behavior of firms to outputs that can be sustained as post-entry equilibria given the production technology and

[28] Firm j's optimal output, conditional on entry, is (coincidentally) the same as the Cournot output ignoring all future entry [see equation (4)]. In this special case, strategic and myopic behavior on the part of the new entrants yield the same outputs.

behavioral strategies by applying the principles discussed in Dixit's formulation of the limit pricing model to the case of many potential and actual entrants. Eaton and Ware (1987) investigate the consequences of credible commitment in a model with sequential entry. The structure of their model parallels the assumptions above, with the number of potential entrants arbitrarily large (free entry) and with the added restriction that all outputs must be credible (i.e. all outputs must be Cournot equilibria of the post-entry game). They assume a technology with irreversible capital investment and a demand function with everywhere decreasing marginal revenue. A main conclusion of their analysis is that the equilibrium number of firms in the industry is the smallest number which can deter the entry of an additional firm. With free entry, incumbent firms in their model would maximize profits by deterring entry if they could. If Y is the limit output, the first incumbent firm i that could produce $Y - X_{i-1}$ as an equilibrium output would do so and entry would be deterred. If firm i and the firms that precede it cannot produce enough in equilibrium to equal or exceed the limit output, entry will occur. Entry will continue to occur until the limit output can be sustained as a perfect equilibrium by the incumbent firms.

Bernheim (1984) offers a description of industry dynamics employing sequential entry. As in Eaton and Ware (1987), incumbent firms choose whether to prevent or accommodate entry. If they accommodate, the new entrant joins the incumbents in choosing whether to prevent or accommodate further entry. By characterizing the industry in terms of general functional forms for profits and the cost of entry deterrence, Bernheim achieves an apparent increase in generality, but the analysis necessarily employs assumptions that may limit the applicability of the results. Bernheim argues that there is, in general, more than one stable size for industry, defined as a number of established firms which will prevent further entry. If the number of actual established firms is not stable, additional firms will enter unopposed until the smallest stable size exceeding the initial industry size is reached. It is reassuring that these conclusions do not contradict the results in Eaton and Ware (1987).

Potential entrants have to evaluate not only the response of incumbent firms to entry, but also the likelihood that future entry will undermine profits. The threat of excessive entry is particularly severe when entrants act with incomplete information about the decisions of potential competitors. Incomplete information about rival decisions will exist if the time between the decision to enter and actual entry is long and the entry decision is irreversible. Then an entrant cannot know if, and how many, other firms will choose to enter. Sherman and Willett (1967) considered the consequence of simultaneous entry and concluded that the possibility of mistakes can discourage entry and (in the context of the BSM model), lead to a higher limit price. Dixit and Shapiro (1985) considered how the possibility to rectify entry mistakes, through exit or additional entry, may affect entry incentives.

With incomplete information about the actions of other competitors the entry decision is an investment under conditions of uncertainty. This gives rise to what Richardson (1960) called "the nomination problem". There is an optimal number of entrants (most likely greater than one) but no mechanism to determine which of many potential entrants should be "nominated" to enter. Farrell (1986b) investigates how non-binding communications (in the absence of side payments) among potential entrants might avoid the waste from too much or too little entry. He shows that communication, which he calls "cheap talk", can mitigate, but not in general eliminate, the nomination problem. His results provide some substance for the type of industry displays, pronouncements, and jawboning that often precede a significant entry decision. As in the mating rites of birds, such behavior may have important efficiency consequences and need not be a mere flaunting of intent.

5. Exit barriers and asset specificity

Exit barriers are costs or forgone profits that a firm must bear if it leaves an industry. For example, a firm might have to pay workers severance fees if it abandons a market. A regulated firm might be forbidden to abandon a market, or have to guarantee service in certain markets in exchange for the right to leave another market. Exit barriers exist if a firm cannot move its capital into another activity and earn at least as large a return. In this respect sunk costs are likely to contribute to exit barriers. Sunk capital expenditures generate earnings that would be lost if a firm exits the market.

Barriers to exit affect entry in two ways. They have a direct impact on an entrant by adding to the costs that an unsuccessful entrant must bear to exit an industry. They also have an indirect effect on entry by influencing the incentives of established firms. If exit barriers are large, established firms can be counted upon to remain as competitors if entry occurs (and may act as if their backs are to the wall).

The Dixit model of credible entry deterrence is an example of the indirect effect of a barrier to exit. Sunk costs affect the behavior of established firms. With Cournot competition, sunk costs make an incumbent firm more aggressive. If capital investments were recoverable, the opportunity cost of capital would be an additional component of the firm's marginal cost function and the firm's reaction function would shift to the left. The firm would produce less at every level of rival output and perhaps exit the market, making entry more profitable.

Capital is sunk only to the extent that it is embodied in a durable investment. Eaton and Lipsey (1980, 1981) make the point that the durability of capital is a constraint on a firm's ability to exploit a sunk cost barrier to entry. When capital wears out, an established firm and an entrant are on a level playing field (provided all of the firm's capital wears out at the same time, which seems rather unlikely). The durability constraint also would favor, for reasons of entry deterrence, investments in long-lived capital and would discourage leasing.

Exit costs depend on a firm's opportunities to move capital into alternative markets. Many firms operate in several markets that have similar production technologies and that share the benefits of the firm's marketing experience and goodwill. A firm in such a multiproduct environment has relatively low barriers to the movement of capital from one market to another. Judd (1985) argues that entry should be relatively easy in such markets. Head-on competition with a new entrant reduces an incumbent firm's profit both in the market where entry occurred and in markets for substitute goods where the incumbent may operate. By leaving the market where the incumbent competes head-on with the new firm, it can raise profits both in the entry market and in the markets for substitute goods. Anticipating this incentive for exit by the incumbent, a potential rival would be encouraged to enter the incumbent's market. Judd's model is a good example of the general proposition in Fudenberg and Tirole (1984) and Bulow et al. (1985b) that strategic behavior in a particular market is shaped by competitive effects in related markets.[29]

Exit costs increase the cost of entry into an industry that proves unprofitable. The direct cost of exit is irrelevant if, as assumed so far, potential entrants correctly forecast post-entry profits and avoid markets where earnings would fall below the opportunity cost of their capital. Perfect foresight is rare and the cost of potential mistakes is likely to be a major factor in the decision to enter markets and in the availability of external financing. Caves and Porter (1976) investigate the significance of exit costs and how they correlate with industry behavior. Ghemawat and Nalebuff (1985) and Fudenberg and Tirole (1986a) show how barriers to exit can lead to wars of attrition which make entry mistakes costly.

Caves and Porter (1976) argue that exit costs are attributable to *specific assets* that impede capital mobility. An asset is specific to a particular economic activity if the value of its services strictly exceeds its value in an alternative use. The difference in value relative to the next best use is a measure of the cost of exit. Williamson (1975, 1985) uses the concept of asset specificity to develop a theory of market and institutional structure and it is tempting to extend this approach to the determination of entry and exit barriers.

Asset specificity is at the heart of Bain's absolute cost advantage and product differentiation barriers to entry. I have argued that absolute entry advantages need not be a barrier to entry. The owner of a unique asset should value the asset at its opportunity cost, which is determined by the market. If the asset is specific,

[29]For an interesting application of the importance of multimarket interactions to the case of product standardization choice, see Matutes and Regibeau (1986a, 1986b).

its opportunity cost is less than its value and there is an absolute (opportunity) cost advantage. Consider the example of the xerography patent. If the patent were not specific to the Xerox Corporation, it would have a market value exactly equal to its value to Xerox and it would not represent a barrier to entry. But if Xerox has physical and human capital that is complementary to the xerography patent and that enhance its value relative to other uses, the xerography patent becomes a specific asset and represents a true absolute cost advantage. Other firms cannot pay Xerox enough to make the company part with the patent. The complementary capital can take varied and subtle forms. The company may have technological skills, other patents, marketing experience, or a reputation for service that complement the basic xerography patent and increase its value. The management of the company may have human capital that depends on the xerography patent and that causes them to value the patent more than its opportunity cost. Caves and Porter (1976) suggest that managers' specific human capital is one reason why firms appear to cling to apparently unprofitable activities. Managerial asset specificity impedes the mobility of capital out of struggling industries.

Investments in advertising and marketing are asset specific. Goodwill is a measure of the success of product differentiation. Economic profits would not exist if any firm could replicate the product of another firm at the same cost. Thus, asset specificity is also fundamental to product differentiation as an apparent barrier to entry.

The concept of asset specificity is central to the mobility of financial capital in the structuring of markets. Although the entry deterrence literature has focused on movements of physical capital, industry structure can change as a result of merger, divestiture, and takeovers. Strategies that discourage the movement of physical capital need not impede the movement of financial capital. But asset specificity can be a barrier to financial capital movements. The performance of physical assets may be specific to the reputation of a particular firm or to the executive style of a particular management team. As a result, the value of these assets may be strictly greater when they exist under the logo of a particular firm or when they operate under a particular management team. The value of the assets to an entrant would be less than in its present use and a takeover would be unsuccessful.

The concept of asset specificity is also central to the BSM and Spence/Dixit models of entry deterrence. In the Dixit model, sunk costs allow an established firm to commit to an output large enough to deter entry. Sunk costs are asset specific, and this example of entry deterrence appears to be another case where asset specificity is at the heart of barriers to entry and exit. More generally, entry deterrence is feasible because the incumbent firm has a mechanism which enables it to commit to an output level that makes entry unprofitable. In the Dixit model, this mechanism is sunk costs (specific assets). But any mechanism that allows the incumbent firm to commit to an output at least as large as the limit output will do, provided that the incumbent is also able to signal this capability to potential entrants. The incumbent might have a magic button that it could push and shift its reaction function to the right by an amount large enough to deter entry. One might argue that the entrant would want to push this button too, and would be willing to buy the button from the incumbent. The incumbent would be willing to sell the button at a price equal to its value. If the value to the entrant is the same as the value to the incumbent, the magic button becomes no different from a taxi medallion and does not confer an incumbency advantage. However, if the magic button is an asset whose value is specific to the established firm, its value will exceed the price an entrant would be willing to pay and it could provide an incumbency advantage.

6. The role of information in entry deterrence

Limit pricing sacrifices current profits in order to discourage entry. It has value only to the extent that potential entrants interpret pre-entry prices as indicative of post-entry market conditions. The signalling aspect of limit pricing suggests analyzing strategic entry deterrence as a problem in the economics of information. This observation was made by Salop (1979) and posed in game-theoretic form by Milgrom and Roberts (1982a).

Fudenberg and Tirole (1986b) provide a simplified description of the Milgrom–Roberts model, which I follow here. There is a single incumbent and a single potential entrant. All aspects of the market are known with certainty, with the exception that the entrant does not know the incumbent's cost. The incumbent's marginal cost is a constant equal to either C_1 or C_2, with $C_1 < C_2$. There are two periods: "pre-entry" and "post-entry". Post-entry profits are discounted by a factor δ. The entrant's profits, conditional on the incumbent's cost, are

$$\pi^{e}(C_2) > 0 > \pi^{e}(C_1). \tag{31}$$

The entrant can guarantee a return of 0 if it stays out. With complete information about the incumbent's cost, entry would occur only if the incumbent is high cost. With incomplete information, the firm will choose to enter only if the prior probability that the incumbent has cost C_2 is sufficiently high, which I assume to be the case.

The incumbent wants to avoid competition and it can accomplish this if it could convince the entrant that it is low cost (C_1). Suppose that in order to deter entry the incumbent can choose either a low price P_1 or a high price, P_2, which it must charge in both periods if entry does not occur. As there are only two "types" of incumbents, two pre-entry prices are sufficient to distinguish the incumbent's cost if the pricing decision is a function of cost. An equilibrium that accomplishes this distinction is called a "separating" equilibrium. If the entrant believes that the pricing decision is not correlated with the incumbent's cost, price does not convey information about the incumbent's type and the equilibrium is called "pooling."

Fudenberg and Tirole argue that a pooling equilibrium does not exist in this model. For if a pooling equilibrium did exist, the incumbent's pricing decision would not convey any information about its cost and would have no effect on the entry decision. In that case, the incumbent's best pre-entry price would be its monopoly price. But the monopoly price depends on its cost, so an entrant would know the incumbent's cost by observing its price. This cannot be in a pooling equilibrium, so a pooling equilibrium cannot exist.

Let us turn next to a separating equilibrium. It is reasonable (although not absolutely necessary) to assume that the high price will be associated with a high cost incumbent. If the firm is known to be high cost, it might as well choose the monopoly price. Therefore, $P_2 = P_2^{\mathrm{m}}$. Our task, then, reduces to showing the existence of a separating equilibrium with $P_1 < P_2^{\mathrm{m}}$.

For a separating equilibrium to exist, it must be *incentive compatible* for both a low cost and high cost incumbent. A high cost firm should not want to imitate a low cost firm. If the high cost firm can imitate a low cost firm by charging a price P_1, entry would be deterred and it would earn $\pi^{\mathrm{i}}(P_1 \mid C_2)$ in both periods. This must be less than the profit it would earn by being honest. Since honesty would lead to entry, an honest high cost firm would charge a monopoly price in the first period. Entry would occur in the second period and the firm would earn $\pi^{\mathrm{d}}(C_2)$, where "d" represents the profit earned in a duopoly. The incentive compatibility condition for a high cost firm reduces to

$$\pi^{\mathrm{m}}(C_2) - \pi^{\mathrm{i}}(P_1 \mid C_2) > \delta\left[\pi^{\mathrm{i}}(P_1 \mid C_2) - \pi^{\mathrm{d}}(C_2)\right]. \tag{32}$$

Similarly, a low cost incumbent should not want to deviate from a limit pricing strategy. If it did, it could do no better than charge a monopoly price in the first period. If a low cost incumbent deviates from P_1, it is reasonable to assume that a high cost incumbent would also deviate. This could risk entry if the first period price no longer signalled low cost. Thus, the low cost incumbent has to compare $\pi^{\mathrm{i}}(P_1 \mid C_1)(1 + \delta)$ with $\pi^{\mathrm{m}}(C_1) + \delta\pi^{\mathrm{d}}(C_1)$, which reduces to

$$\pi^{\mathrm{m}}(C_1) - \pi^{\mathrm{i}}(P_1 \mid C_1) < \delta\left[\pi^{\mathrm{i}}(P_1 \mid C_1) - \pi^{\mathrm{d}}(C_1)\right]. \tag{33}$$

Figure 8.10 shows the comparison. The first incentive compatibility condition, inequality (32), is satisfied for any P_1 less than P_{a}. Inequality (33) is satisfied for any P_1 greater than P_{b}. Thus, any $P_1 \in (P_{\mathrm{b}}, P_{\mathrm{a}})$ can be part of a separating

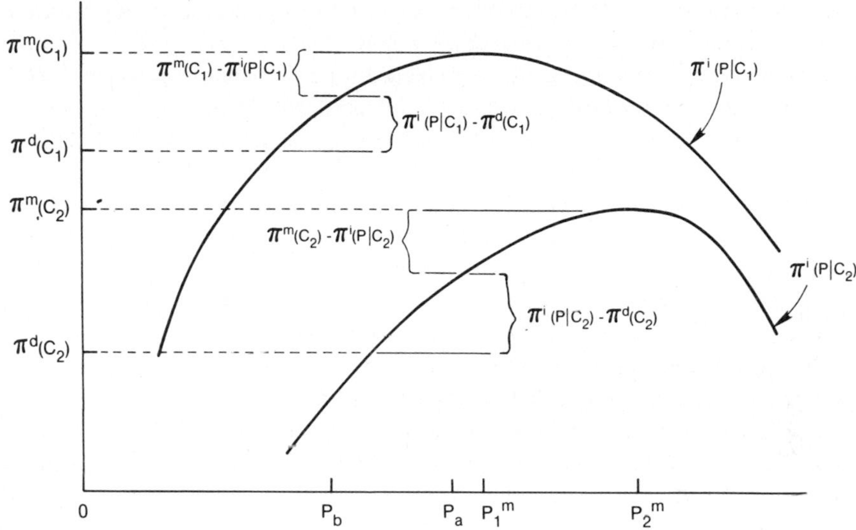

Figure 8.10. Incentive-compatibility conditions.

equilibrium in which an incumbent charges P_1 in the first period only if it is low cost, and charges P_2^m if it is high cost. Entry is deterred at P_1, but occurs if the first period price is P_2^m.

The uncertainty of the incumbent's cost is crucial to the existence of limit pricing in this model. If the incumbent's cost were known to the entrant, the entry decision would be independent of the incumbent's price in the pre-entry period. Entry would occur if, and only if, the incumbent is high cost.

Limit pricing in the Milgrom and Roberts model is a means by which the incumbent can send a signal to the potential entrant about post-entry market profitability. Note that in a separating equilibrium the incumbent's true cost is revealed to the potential entrant. This leads Milgrom and Roberts to conclude that limit pricing need not "limit" entry. The probability that entry will occur is just the probability that the incumbent is high cost. This is the same probability of entry for a perfect-information model, in which nature moves first to determine whether the incumbent is high or low cost and the potential entrant is informed of the result. Yet the important distinction is that incumbent pricing is a strategic decision in the imperfect information model.

The consequences of imperfect information for entry deterrence depend on the information structure. Matthews and Mirman (1983), Saloner (1981), and Harrington (1984) describe signalling models in which prices are noisy signals of market conditions. As a result of exogenous disturbances, a potential entrant is not able to determine post-entry market conditions with certainty given an incumbent's pricing decision. They show that in a noisy information structure, the probability of entry can be an increasing function of an incumbent's price, which provides a theoretical foundation for models of limit pricing such as Kamien and Schwartz (1971) and Gaskins (1971). Moreover, the probability of entry depends on the information structure and may differ from the entry probability with perfect information about market conditions.

An extension of the Milgrom and Roberts model by Harrington (1986) illustrates the importance of the information structure. Harrington allows the entrant's cost function to be uncertain and positively correlated with the incumbent's cost (not unreasonable if they use similar production technologies). If the potential entrant believes its cost is high, it will stay out of the industry. With the extra twist of positively correlated costs, the incumbent has an incentive to price high in order to signal a high cost and thereby convince the entrant that its cost is high too. In order to discourage entry, the incumbent prices high, not low.

7. Contestable markets

The theory of contestable markets targets potential entry as a primary determinant of market structure and performance. Baumol, Panzar and Willig (1982) (henceforth BPW) define a "perfectly contestable market" with reference to the notion of *sustainable* industry configurations. Let $\boldsymbol{y}$ be a vector of industry outputs, $C(\boldsymbol{y})$ the cost of producing $\boldsymbol{y}$, which is assumed to be the same for all firms, $\boldsymbol{p}$ the industry price vector and $\boldsymbol{Q}(\boldsymbol{p})$ the vector of demands at price $\boldsymbol{p}$. Suppose a potential entrant offers to sell $\boldsymbol{y}^{\mathrm{e}}$ at a price $\boldsymbol{p}^{\mathrm{e}}$. An industry price vector is sustainable if

$$\boldsymbol{p}^{\mathrm{e}}\boldsymbol{y}^{\mathrm{e}} \leq C(\boldsymbol{y}^{\mathrm{e}}), \quad \text{for all } \boldsymbol{p}^{\mathrm{e}} \leq \boldsymbol{p} \text{ and } \boldsymbol{y}^{\mathrm{e}} \leq \boldsymbol{Q}(\boldsymbol{p}^{\mathrm{e}}). \tag{34}$$

Note that implicit in the definition of sustainability is the presumption that capital movements take place instantaneously, while prices are fixed. An entrant can test the market and bring capital into production while prices charged by established firms remain fixed. This contrasts with the behavioral assumptions in models such as Bertrand–Nash, in which prices can change instantaneously and quantities adjust to clear markets.

The definition of a perfectly contestable market is a market in which a necessary condition for an industry configuration to be in equilibrium is that it be sustainable. Contestability is not the outcome of a particular dynamic game, but rather is defined as a property of equilibrium outcomes [but see BPW (1986) for a dynamic treatment of contestable markets]. Sustainability from entry is the essential element. A market is perfectly contestable if an equally efficient entrant is unable to find a combination of price and outputs that enable it to enter and earn a profit.

A perfectly contestable market is an illustration of a market without barriers to entry or exit. There is no product differentiation and no cost advantages. There is no uncertainty. Switching costs and learning economies are non-existent. Production may exhibit increasing returns to scale, but firms do not incur any costs that are not perfectly reversible in the event of exit from the market (there are no sunk costs).

The realism of the contestability assumptions can be questioned [see, for example, Schwartz and Reynolds (1983) and Weitzman (1983)], but that is not my purpose. The absence of barriers to entry and exit in the contestability theory provide a convenient benchmark to ascertain the consequences of barriers to competition. BPW show that if a market is perfectly contestable and if an equilibrium exists, then price will equal marginal cost for any product produced in positive amounts by two or more firms. If only one firm exists in a perfectly contestable market equilbrium, total revenues will exactly equal total production costs.[30]

The contestability result is about as good as anyone can hope for. Contestable markets either mimic perfectly competitive markets, or they act as perfectly regulated monopolies with (average) price equal to average cost.[31] Central to the contestability result is the assumption that no costs are sunk. The absence of sunk costs is important in two respects. First, with no sunk costs, a potential rival can consider hit-and-run entry without concern about irreversible investments. A potential rival would enter the market if he anticipated any possible situation in which profits would be positive. In a contestable market, entry is an option which can be exercised at no cost. If there is any possibility of profit, however small, it pays to enter. Second, with no sunk costs and with identical technologies, the incumbent firm and a potential entrant bear the same cost at each level of output. There is no strategic asymmetry between an entrant and an established firm because each faces exactly the same cost and revenue function.

The theory of perfectly contestable markets illustrates how market structure and performance may be determined in a world free of barriers to the mobility of capital. As a theoretical description of strategic behavior, it is a special case whose assumptions can be criticized, but the acid test of any theoretical model is its predictive performance. Contestability theory has support in the observation of competitive conditions in markets for commuter air service [see Bailey and Panzar (1981) and Bailey, Graham and Kaplan (1984)]. What remains uncertain,

[30] But note that a perfectly contestable market equilbrium need not exist.

[31] With vector-valued outputs, the relevant consideration is whether total revenue equals total cost. The correspondence to price and average cost is exact for the case of a scalar output.

however, is the extent to which markets that have weak barriers to capital mobility conform to the theory of contestable markets, and at what point are mobility barriers large enough that markets are not contestable. [See Farrell (1986b) for a discussion of the robustness of contestability.]

8. Mobility barriers and economic performance

Economic analysis of entry barriers is motivated by the search for structural factors that undermine market performance, and the discussion of various determinants of mobility barriers in this chapter may suggest a causality that runs from a barrier to an impediment to market efficiency. But this would be a mistaken conclusion. Although product differentiation can be associated with high profit rates and economies of scale can allow a firm to elevate price above minimum average cost (or at least above marginal cost), this does not mean that market performance is compromised. Product differentiation exists because consumers value one brand more than another and there are likely to be good reasons for this to be the case. As Demsetz (1982) argues, firms that enjoy the benefits of product differentiation do so as the result of investments in reputation and quality and the "barrier" that may exist to imitation is a flow of quasi-rents that are the earnings from these investment activities [see Shapiro (1983)].

Entry in actual markets can fall short of the amount that would be desired by an enlightened and perfectly informed social planner whose objective is to maximize economic surplus. This is demonstrated by the results in, for example, Spence (1976), Dixit and Stiglitz (1977), and Perry (1984). Mankiw and Whinston (1986) describe market externalities that lead to too much or too little entry.

The economies-of-scale/sunk cost entry barrier provides an illustration of the welfare effects of a barrier to competition. The existence of scale economies itself implies that an efficient market structure would be concentrated. If costs are everywhere subadditive, the efficient market structure is a single firm. Entry prevention is consistent with an efficient market structure.

Welfare judgements as to the effects of mobility barriers in actual markets are difficult to make because actual markets inevitably operate in a region of the second best and any attempt to improve market performance must recognize the imperfections of market intervention. We can say that a single firm is the optimal market structure with increasing returns to scale, but optimality is rarely a feasible alternative in markets characterized by imperfect competition.

As an illustration of competitive alternatives, consider the BSM model with a single established firm and a single entrant. The cost functions are as in equation (7): constant marginal costs and a fixed cost of entry. Figure 8.3 shows the range of alternative market structures as a function of the limit price. The established firm prevents entry whenever Y is less than Z_1 (entry is blockaded when Y is less than Z_0) and allows entry otherwise.

Suppose a central planner can tax either output or factor prices in this simple economy and can exclude entry, but firms cannot operate at a loss. What is the (constrained) optimum for this economy? Contestability theory provides the answer – a single firm operating at the point where price equals average cost. This market structure minimizes cost and pricing at average cost yields the maximum consumer surplus subject to the break-even constraint. The contestability outcome can be sustained by means of a non-linear tax that is arbitrarily large for any output less than x^*, where x^* is the output at which the demand price is equal to the firm's average cost, and zero otherwise. The non-linear tax supports the constrained optimum and allows the operation of only one firm – the rival is deterred.

What if the planner is limited to controlling only the conditions of entry? In the BSM model, this amounts to controlling only the cost of entry, or effectively, the limit output Y. Making entry easier has the effect of increasing Y, while making entry more difficult lowers Y. Assuming transferable utility, U, and linear costs, total surplus is

$$U(X) - mX - nF, \tag{35}$$

where X is total output, m the marginal cost of production, F the fixed cost, and n the number of firms. If entry of a second firm is allowed, total surplus is $U(X^{\mathrm{E}}) - mX^{\mathrm{E}} - 2F$, while if entry is prevented, surplus is $U(X^{\mathrm{P}}) - mX^{\mathrm{P}} - F$.

Provided X^{P} is no greater than the perfectly competitive level where price equals marginal cost, a sufficient condition for entry prevention to be welfare increasing is $X^{\mathrm{P}} > X^{\mathrm{E}}$. This condition is also necessary only in the limit of zero entry costs.

Suppose that $Z_1 > X^{\mathrm{E}}$. If the incumbent prevents entry by producing Z_1, welfare is strictly higher than if entry occurred for any value of $F \geq 0$. But for $Y > Z_1$, the incumbent will not prevent entry. Now suppose that the central planner taxes entry. The tax makes entry more difficult and therefore lowers the limit output. Suppose the tax is chosen so that $Y' = Z_1$. The incumbent will prevent entry and because $Z_1 > X^{\mathrm{E}}$ welfare will be increased relative to the case where there is no tax and entry occurs.

It is not difficult to show that $Z_1 > X^{\mathrm{E}}$ for the case of linear demand.[32] This leads to the following result for the case of linear demand. If the incumbent firm

[32]A similar result holds for the (possibly) more realistic scenario in which the firms compete on equal footing as Cournot competitors if entry occurs.

does not prevent entry, *there exists a tax on entry which leads to entry prevention and results in a strict improvement in economic welfare.*[33]

9. Concluding remarks

I have chosen to focus in this chapter on the factors that interfere with the mobility of capital into and out of an industry and that specifically confer an advantage to incumbency. In the process, many of the historically advanced determinants of barriers to entry were found to be irrelevant to the gains from incumbency. Economies of scale, per se, are not sufficient to protect a firm from potential competition. Absolute cost advantages do not imply incumbency rents, unless the scarce factors are also specific to the incumbent firm. The concept of asset specificity surfaced frequently as an underlying determinant of the gains to incumbency.

The emphasis in this chapter on mobility barriers and incumbency should be distinguished from classical concerns with barriers to entry. The latter can be interpreted to include policies that affect the aggregate supply of productive resources in an industry. This is the focus of von Weizsacker, who defines a barrier to entry in terms of cost differentials between established firms and new entrants that imply a distortion in the allocation of resources from a social point of view. In contrast, I define a barrier to entry as a rent that is derived from incumbency. A limitation on the number of available taxi medallions is a barrier to entry of productive resources because it reduces the supply of taxi services. But it does not confer an advantage to early entrants in the taxi market, because the opportunity cost of the medallion is an (equal) cost of service for incumbent firms and new entrants alike.

Strategic behavior can exploit mobility barriers to the advantage of an established firm. Sunk costs and economies of scale allow a firm to commit to a level of output that prevents entry. Learning and network economies confer a first-mover advantage that can be manipulated to enhance profits. Investments in advertising and product differentiation can be used to exploit scale-related barriers to capital mobility and limit competition by potential rivals.

There is no doubt that structural market characteristics which impede the mobility of capital can be used to the benefit of an established firm. The welfare implications of this advantage are another matter. Barriers to capital mobility are the result of technological conditions and consumer preferences that must be considered in any welfare analysis. Strategic behavior that exploits capital bar-

[33] For an interesting discussion of the welfare effects of entry subsidies and protectionist policies in an international context, see Dixit and Kyle (1985).

riers can improve economic performance relative to a more accommodating stance toward potential entrants.

Structural barriers to capital mobility can be used to impede entry of rival firms, but they may also support strategies that welcome competition. An established firm might open the door to a new competitor, betting that the two firms will reach a mutually beneficial arrangement, while relying on entry barriers to discourage further competition. A firm with a large base of "locked-in" customers may choose to price high and thereby encourage new competitors to enter and lock-in other customers, instead of pricing low and keeping the market for itself. In some situations, as in Farrell and Gallini (1986) and Shepard (1986), an established firm may go out of its way to encourage competition. In these models, a monopolist is disadvantaged by its (unavoidable) temptation to exploit locked-in customers. Customers know they will be exploited and, as a result, are reluctant to trade. By encouraging competition, the monopolist can guarantee that customers will be treated fairly in the future, and this can increase the value they place on trading with the monopolist in the present.

Contestability theory illustrates how markets that are free of barriers to capital mobility might perform and the results are admirable. Production costs are minimized and price is equal to marginal cost, except in markets that are natural monopolies. The equilibria in the examples discussed in this chapter are rarely as appealing. Although many of the market equilibrium outcomes described in this chapter could, in principle, benefit from the visible hand of an omniscient intervenor, they may be as good as can be expected given imperfect competition, imperfect information,and the limited policy instruments available for the regulation of market performance.

References

Adams, W. and Brock, J. (1982) 'Integrated monopoly and market power: System selling, compatibility standards, and market control', *Quarterly Review of Economics and Business*, 22:29–42.

Aghion, P. and Bolton, P. (1987) 'Contracts as a barrier to entry', *American Economic Review*, 77:388–401.

Bailey, E. and Panzar, J. (1981) 'The contestability of airline markets during the transition to deregulation', *Law and Contemporary Problems*, 44:125–145.

Bailey, E., Graham, D. and Kaplan, D. (1984) *Deregulating the airlines: An economic analysis*. M.I.T. Press.

Bain, J. (1949) 'A note on pricing in monopoly and oligopoly', *American Economic Review*, 39:448–464.

Bain, J. (1956) *Barriers to new competition*. Cambridge: Harvard University Press.

Bain, J. (1968) *Industrial organization*. New York: Wiley.

Baumol, W. and Willig, R. (1981) 'Fixed cost, sunk cost, entry barriers and sustainability of monopoly', *Quarterly Journal of Economics*, 95:405–431.

Baumol, W., Panzar, J. and Willig, R. (1982) *Contestable markets and the theory of industry structure*. Harcourt Brace Jovanovitch.

Baumol, W., Panzar, J. and Willig, R. (1986) 'On the theory of perfectly contestable markets', in: J. Stiglitz and F. Mathewson, eds., *New developments in the analysis of market structure*. Cambridge: MIT Press.

Benham, L. (1972) 'The effect of advertising on the price of eyeglasses', *Journal of Law and Economics*, 15:337–352.

Bernheim, D. (1984) 'Strategic deterrence of sequential entry into an industy', *Rand Journal of Economics*, 15:1–12.

Blackstone, E.A. (1972) 'Limit pricing and entry in the copying machine industry', *Quarterly Review of Economics and Business*, 12:57–65.

Bresnahan, T. (1986) 'Advertising and economies of scale', working paper, Stanford University.

Brock, G. (1975) *The U.S. computer industry*. Cambridge: Ballinger.

Brown Shoe Co., Inc. v. United States, 370 U.S. 294 (1962); *Telex Corp. v. International Business Machines Corp.*, 510 F.2d 894 (1975).

Bulow, J., Geanakopolos, J. and Klemperer, P. (1985a) 'Holding excess capacity to deter entry', *The Economic Journal*, 95:178–182.

Bulow, J., Geanakopolos, J. and Klemperer, P. (1985b) 'Multimarket oligopoly: Strategic substitutes and complements', *Journal of Political Economy*, 93:488–511.

Caves, R. and Porter, M. (1976) 'Barriers to exit', in: R. Masson and P. Qualls, eds., *Essays in industrial organization in honor of Joe S. Bain*. Cambridge: Ballinger.

Caves, R. and Porter, M. (1977) 'From entry barriers to mobility barriers', *Quarterly Journal of Economics*, 91:241–267.

Chamberlin, E. (1933) *The theory of monopolistic competition*. Cambridge: Harvard University Press.

Comanor, W. and Wilson, T. (1979) 'Advertising and competition: A survey', *Journal of Economic Literature*, 17:453–476.

Cubbin, J. (1981) 'Advertising and the theory of entry barriers', *Economica*, 48:289–298.

Demsetz, H. (1982) 'Barriers to entry', *American Economic Review*, 72:47–57.

Dixit, A. (1979) 'A model of oligopoly suggesting a theory of barriers to entry', *Bell Journal of Economics*, 10:20–32.

Dixit, A. (1981) 'The role of investment in entry deterrence', *Economic Journal*, 90:95–106.

Dixit, A. (1982) 'Recent developments in oligopoly theory', *American Economic Review*, 72:12–17.

Dixit, A. and Kyle, A. (1985) 'The use of protection and subsidies for entry promotion and deterrence', *American Economic Review*, 75:139–152.

Dixit, A. and Shapiro, C. (1985) 'Entry dynamics with mixed strategies', in: L.G. Thomas, ed., *Strategic planning*. Lexington, Mass.: Lexington Books, 63–79.

Dixit, A. and Stiglitz, J. (1977) 'Monopolistic competition and optimal product diversity', *Review of Economic Studies*, 43:217–235.

Eaton, B. and Lipsey, R. (1980) 'Exit barriers are entry barriers: The durability of capital as a barrier to entry', *Bell Journal of Economics*, 11:721–729.

Eaton, B. and Lipsey, R. (1981) 'Capital, commitment and entry equilibrium', *Bell Journal of Economics*, 12:593–604.

Eaton, B. and Ware, R. (1987) 'A theory of market structure with sequential entry', *Rand Journal of Economics*, 18:1–16.

Encaoua, D. and Jacquemin, A. (1980) 'Degree of monopoly, indices of concentration and threat of entry', *International Economic Review*, 31:87–105.

Encaoua, D., Geroski, P. and Jacquemin, A. (1986) 'Strategic competition and the persistence of dominant firms', in: J. Stiglitz and F. Mathewson, eds., *New developments in the analysis of market structure*. Cambridge, Mass., 55–89.

Farrell, J. (1986a) 'Moral hazard as an entry barrier', *Rand Journal of Economics*, 17:440–449.

Farrell, J. (1986b) 'How effective is potential competition?', *Economics Letters*, 20:67–70.

Farrell, J. (1987) 'Cheap talk, coordination and entry', *Rand Journal of Economics*, 18:34–39.

Farrell, J. and Gallini, N. (1986) 'Monopoly incentives to attract competition', working paper, University of California, Berkeley.

Farrell, J. and Saloner, G. (1986) 'Installed base and compatibility: Innovation, product preannouncements, and predation', *American Economic Review*, 76:940–955.

Farrell, J. and Shapiro, C. (1986) 'Dynamic competition with lock-in', working paper, University of California, Berkeley.

Ferguson, J. (1974) *Advertising and competition: Theory, measurement, fact*. Cambridge: Ballinger.

Flaherty, M. (1980) 'Dynamic limit pricing, barriers to entry, and rational firms', *Journal of Economic Theory*, 23:160–182.

Fudenberg, D. and Tirole, J. (1983) 'Capital as a commitment: Strategic investment to deter mobility', *Journal of Economic Theory*, 31:227–250.

Fudenberg, D. and Tirole, J. (1984) 'The fat-cat effect, the puppy-dog ploy, and the lean and hungry look', *American Economic Review Papers and Proceedings*, 74:361–366.

Fudenberg, D. and Tirole, J. (1986a) 'A theory of exit in duopoly', *Econometrica*, 54:943–960.

Fudenberg, D. and Tirole, J. (1986b) *Dynamic models of oligopoly*. New York: Harwood.

Fudenberg, D., Gilbert, R., Stiglitz, J. and Tirole, J. (1983) 'Preemption, leapfrogging and competition in patent races', *European Economic Review*, 22:3–31.

Gaskins, D. (1971) 'Dynamic limit pricing: Optimal pricing under threat of entry', *Journal of Economic Theory*, 2:306–322.

Gelman, J. and Salop, S. (1983) 'Capacity limitation and coupon competition', *Bell Journal of Economics*, 14:315–325.

Geroski, P. and Jacquemin, A. (1985) 'Industrial change, barriers to mobility, and European industrial policy', *Oxford Review of Exonomic Policy*, 1:170–218.

Geroski, P., Gilbert, R. and Jacquemin, A. (forthcoming) 'Barriers to entry and strategic competition', in: J. Lesourne and H. Sonnenschein, eds., *Fundamentals of pure and applied economics*. New York: Harwood.

Ghemawat, P. and Nalebuff, B. (1985) 'Exit', *Rand Journal of Economics*, 15:184–193.

Gilbert, R. (1981) 'Patents, sleeping patents, and entry deterrence', in: S. Salop et al., *Strategy, predation and antitrust analysis*, Federal Trade Commision report, 205–270.

Gilbert, R. (1986) 'Preemptive competition', in: J. Stiglitz and F. Mathewson, eds., *New developments in the analysis of market structure*. Cambridge, Mass.: MIT Press, 90–125.

Gilbert, R. and Harris, R. (1984) 'Competition with lumpy investment', *Rand Journal of Economics*, 15:197–212.

Gilbert, R. and Newbery, D. (1982) 'Preemptive patenting and the persistence of monopoly', *American Economic Review*, 72:514–526.

Gilbert, R. and Newbery, D. (1984) 'Preemptive patenting and the persistence of monopoly: Comment', *American Economic Review*, 74:238–242.

Gilbert, R. and Vives, X. (1986) 'Entry deterrence and the free rider problem', *Review of Economic Studies*, 53:71–83.

Grossman, G. and Shapiro, C. (1984) 'Informative advertising with differentiated products', *Review of Economic Studies*, 51:63–82.

Haas-Wilson, D. (1986) 'The effect of commercial practice restrictions: The case of optometry', *Journal of Law and Economics*, 29:165–186.

Harrington, J. (1984) 'Noncooperative behavior by a cartel as an entry-deterring signal', *Rand Journal of Economics*, 15:426–434.

Harrington, J. (1986) 'Limit pricing when the potential entrant is uncertain of its cost function', *Econometrica*, 54:429–437.

Harris, C. and Vickers, J. (1985) 'Perfect equilibrium in a model of a race', *Review of Economic Studies*, 52:193–209.

Harrod, R. (1952) 'Theory of imperfect competition revised', in: *Economic essays*. New York: Harcourt Brace.

Hicks, J. (1954) 'The processs of imperfect competition', *Oxford Economic Papers*, 6:41–54.

Judd, K. (1985) 'Credible spatial preemption', *Rand Journal of Economics*, 16:153–166.

Judd, K. and Petersen, B. (1986) 'Dynamic limit pricing and internal finance', *Journal of Economic Theory*, 39:368–399.

Kamien, M. and Schwartz, N. (1971) 'Limit pricing and uncertain entry', *Econometrica*, 39:441–454.

Katz, M. and Shapiro, C. (1985) 'Network externalities, competition and compatibility', *American Economic Review*, 75:424–440.

Katz, M. and Shapiro, C. (1986) 'Technology adoption in the presence of network externalities', *Journal of Political Economy*, 94:822–841.

Klemperer, P. (1986) 'Markets with consumer switching costs', Ph.D. dissertation, Stanford University.

Kreps, D, and Spence, A.M. (1984) 'Modelling the role of history in industrial organization and competition', in: G. Feiwel, ed., *Contemporary issues in modern microeconomics*. London: Macmillan.

Kreps, D. and Wilson, R. (1982a) 'Reputation and imperfect information', *Journal of Economic Theory*, 27:253–279.

Kreps, D. and Wilson, R. (1982) 'Sequential equilibrium', *Econometrica*, 50:863–894.

Lewis, T. (1983) 'Preemption, diverstiture, and forward contracting in a market dominated by a single firm', *American Economic Review*, 73:1092–1101.

Lieberman, M. (1984) 'The learning curve and pricing in the chemical processsing industries', *Rand Journal of Economics*, 15:213–228.

Mankiw, G. and Whinston, M. (1986) 'Free entry and social inefficiency', *Rand Journal of Economics*, 17:48–58.

Matthews, S. and Mirman, L. (1983) 'Equilibrium limit pricing: The effects of private information and stochastic demand', *Econometrica*, 51:981–995.

Matutes, C. and Regibeau, P. (1986a) 'Mix and match: Product compatibility without network externalities', working paper, University of California, Berkeley.

Matutes, C. and Regibeau, P. (1986b) 'Product compatibility as a credible commitment', working paper, University of California, Berkeley.

Milgrom, P. and Roberts, J. (1982a) 'Limit pricing and entry under incomplete information: An equilibrium analysis', *Econometrica*, 50:443–459.

Milgrom, P. and Roberts, J. (1982b) 'Predation, reputation and entry deterrence', *Journal of Economic Theory*, 27:280–312.

Mills, D. (1988) 'Preemptive investment timing', *Rand Journal of Economics*, 19:114–122.

Modigliani, F. (1958) 'New developments on the oligopoly front', *Journal of Political Economy*, 66:215–232.

Mookherjee, D. and Ray, D. (1986) 'Dynamic price games with learning-by-doing', working paper no. 884, Stanford Graduate School of Business.

Mueller, D. (1985) 'Persistent performance among large corporations', in: L.G. Thomas, ed., *Strategic planning*. Lexington, Mass.: Lexington Books.

Nelson, R. and Winter, S. (1982) *An evolutionary theory of economic change*. Cambridge, Mass.: Harvard University Press.

Omari, T. and Yarrow, G. (1982) 'Product diversification, entry prevention and limit pricing', *Bell Journal of Economics*, 13:242–248.

Perry, M. (1984) 'Scale economies, imperfect competition, and public policy', *Journal of Industrial Economics*, 32:313–330.

Peters, M. (1984) 'Restrictions on price advertising', *Journal of Political Economy*, 92:472–485.

Prescott, E. and Visscher, M. (1978) 'Sequential location among firms with perfect foresight', *Bell Journal of Economics*, 8:378–393.

Reinganum, J. (1983) 'Uncertain innovation and the persistence of monopoly', *American Economic Review*, 73:741–747.

Richardson, G. (1960) *Information and investment*. New York: Oxford University Press.

Rosenthal, R. (1981) 'Games of perfect information, predatory pricing and the chain store paradox', *Journal of Economic Theory*, 25:92–100.

Saloner, G. (1981) 'Dynamic limit pricing in an uncertain environment', working paper, Stanford University.

Salop, S. (1979) 'Strategic entry deterrence', *American Economic Review*, 69:335–338.

Salop, S. and Scheffman, D. (1983) 'Raising rivals' costs', *American Economic Review*, 73:267–271.

Salop, S. and Scheffman, D. (1986) 'Cost-raising strategies', working paper no. 146, Federal Trade Commission, Bureau of Economics.

Schelling, T. (1960) *The strategy of conflict*. Cambridge, Mass.: Harvard University Press.

Schmalensee, R. (1974) 'Brand loyalty and barriers to entry', *Southern Economic Journal*, 40:579–591.

Schmalensee, R. (1978) 'Entry deterrence in the ready-to-eat breakfast cereal industry', *Bell Journal of Economics*, 9:305–327.

Schmalensee, R. (1981a) 'Economics of scale and barriers to entry', *Journal of Political Economy*, 89:1228–1232.

Schmalensee, R. (1981b) 'Product differentiation advantages of pioneering brands', *American Economic Review*, 72:349–365.

Schmalensee, R. (1983) 'Advertising and entry deterrence', *Journal of Political Economy*, 90:636–653.
Schmalensee, R. (1986) 'Advertising and market structure', in: F. Mathewson and J. Stiglitz, eds., *New developments in the analysis of market structure*. Cambridge, Mass.: MIT Press, 373–396.
Schwartz, M. and Reynolds, R. (1983) 'Contestable markets: An uprising in the theory of industrial structure: Comment', *American Economic Review*, 73:488–490.
Selten, R. (1975) 'Reexamination of the perfectness concept for equilibrium points in extensive games', *International Journal of Game Theory*, 4:25–55.
Selten, R. (1978) 'The chain store paradox', *Theory and Decision*, 9:127–159.
Shapiro, C. (1983) 'Premiums for high quality products as returns to reputation', *Quarterly Journal of Economics*, 98:659–680.
Shepard, A. (1986) 'Licensing to enhance demand for new technologies', working paper, Yale University.
Sherman, R. and Willett, T. (1967) 'Potential entrants discourage entry', *Journal of Political Economy*, 75:400–403.
Spence, A.M. (1976) 'Product selection, fixed costs, and monopolistic competition', *Review of Economic Studies*, 43:217–236.
Spence, A.M. (1977) 'Entry, capacity, investment and oligopolistic pricing', *Bell Journal of Economics*, 8:534–544.
Spence, A.M. (1979) 'Investment, strategy and growth in a new market', *Bell Journal of Economics*, 10:1–19.
Spence, A.M. (1980) 'Notes on advertising, economies of scale and entry barriers', *Quarterly Journal of Economics*, 95:493–508.
Spence, A.M. (1981) 'The learning curve and competition', *Bell Journal of Economics*, 12:49–70.
Spence, A.M. (1984) 'Cost reduction, competition and industry performance', *Econometrica*, 52:101–122.
Spulber, D. (1981) 'Capacity, output and sequential entry', *American Economic Review*, 75:897–899.
Stigler, G.J. (1968) *The organization of industry*. Homewood, Ill.: Richard D. Irwin, Inc.
Sylos-Labini, P. (1962) *Oligopoly and technical progress*. Cambridge, Mass.: Harvard University Press.
Telex Corp. v. International Business Machines Corp., 510 F.2d 894 (1975).
U.S. v. Aluminum Company of America, 148 F.2d 416 (1945).
Vives, X. (1982) 'A note on sequential entry', working paper, University of California.
Von Weizsacker, C. (1980b) 'A welfare analysis of barriers to entry', *Bell Journal of Economics*, 11:399–420.
Von Weizsacker, C. (1980b) 'Barriers to entry: A theoretical treatment', in: M. Beckmann and H.P. Kunzi, eds., *Lecture notes in economics and mathematical systems*. New York: Springer-Verlag.
Waagsten, T. (1982) 'Fixed costs, limit pricing and investments as barriers to entry', *European Economic Review*, 17:75–86.
Ware, R. (1984) 'Sunk cost and strategic commitment: A proposed three-stage equilibrium', *Economic Journal*, 94:370–378.
Waterson, M. (1984) *Economic theory of the industry*. New York: Cambridge University Press.
Weitzman, M. (1983) 'Contestable markets: An uprising in the theory of industry structure: Comment', *American Economic Review*, 73:486–487.
Williamson, O. (1963) 'Selling expense as a barrier to entry', *Quarterly Journal of Economics*, 77:112–128.
Williamson, O. (1968) 'Wage rates as barriers to entry: The Pennington case in perspective', *Quarterly Journal of Economics*, 85:85–116.
Williamson, O. (1975) *Markets and hierarchies: Analysis and antitrust implications*. New York: The Free Press.
Williamson, O. (1985) *The economic institutions of capitalism*. New York: The Free Press.

Chapter 9

PREDATION, MONOPOLIZATION, AND ANTITRUST

JANUSZ A. ORDOVER

New York University

GARTH SALONER*

Massachusetts Institute of Technology and Hoover Institution

Contents

*We should like to thank the National Science Foundation for financial support. The C.V. Starr Center for Applied Economics at New York University provided the typing services. Ken Rogoza served as a most able editorial assistant. We should like to thank Steven Salop and Richard Schmalensee for most helpful comments.

Handbook of Industrial Organization, Volume I, Edited by R. Schmalensee and R.D. Willig

1. Introduction

In this chapter, we shall study a wide range of strategies that can be employed by incumbent firms to either protect or to extend their market shares against competitive attacks by actual and potential entrants. The hallmark of these strategies is that, invariably, they reduce the expected level of profits that incumbent's rivals – present and future – can hope to earn. As such, they differ from those types of conduct whose aim is to implement and enforce collusive arrangements among market participants. Unlike many collusive strategies, these hostile and exclusionary strategies which are the focus here, and which include low prices, output expansions, introductions of new products, redesigns of the existing products, promotions, and so on, are difficult to distinguish from and, in fact, are a part and parcel of market rivalry that economists find salutary for economic welfare, that policy-makers wish to promote, and that business leaders often deplore (but find unavoidable).

We spend most of this chapter surveying descriptive models in which an incumbent firm engages in "battles for market share". With the help of those models, we inquire under what conditions an incumbent can profitably extend its share or protect it against encroachments by actual and potential rivals. The focus is, thus, on those hostile and exclusionary strategies that actually emerge in equilibria of (reasonably) well-specified models of market rivalry. Finally, whenever possible, we explore the welfare properties of these equilibria and inquire whether some restrictions on incumbent firm behavior could have improved the equilibrium outcome, from the social standpoint.

The interest in those questions is not solely academic. In the United States, in the European Community, and in some of the EC member states, diverse laws and public policies restrain market behavior of firms. It is, therefore, important to examine the underpinnings of those policies, study their soundness, and provide suggestions for reforms.

Theoretical models studied here provide a guarded support for the proposition that strategic choices made by dominant firms are not invariably consistent with the objective of welfare-maximization and that some constraints on firm behavior may, in fact, increase welfare. That is, in some reasonably realistic models, constraining the dominant incumbent firm actually improves welfare. These theoretical findings and prescriptions are difficult to translate into workable and enforceable standards that in *actual market settings* would, without fail, promote conduct that enhances social welfare and would discourage conduct that harms welfare. The source of the problem is the strategic setting itself. In the context of strategic interactions, it is difficult to distinguish between those actions which are intended to harm actual (and potential) rivals that stifle competition, and thereby reduce economic welfare, and those actions which harm present rivals and discourage future entry but which, nevertheless, promote economic welfare. Or, as legal scholars are often fond of saying, actions which are consistent with "competition on the merits".

Here, then, the challenge for industrial organization theory is twofold. The first is to identify circumstances in which single-firm strategies have adverse effects on welfare. The second is to provide workable rules – if such are needed – that could be used as a basis for setting policies that restrain the conduct of dominant incumbent firms. Although some progress has been made on both fronts, it is fair to say that much work is still needed.

The main advance offered by the strategic approach to the analysis of single-firm conduct over the traditional methodology is that it tries to embed the concepts of purpose and intent into sound economic models in which strategy sets and information available to present and future market participants are made explicit. This new "new learning" about dominant firm behavior, which builds on strategic considerations, suggests that welfare-reducing, aggressive and exclusionary conduct is more likely than would be indicated by the old "new learning", which applied static models of competition and monopoly to the analysis of profitability of these types of strategies. At the same time, by pointing out the irrelevance of noncredible threats for market outcomes, the strategic approach more precisely characterizes the set of scenarios in which aggressive and exclusionary conduct can plausibly occur in equilibrium.

In what follows, we review these practices which can be used by an incumbent firm to extend or to protect its market share. In Section 2 we present a fairly general model of strategic conduct. In Section 3 we discuss economic models in which pricing and nonpricing actions may induce the exit of rivals. Section 4 looks at actions that do not necessarily lead to rivals' exit but, instead, place rivals at a competitive disadvantage, in particular by raising their costs. Section 5 considers scenarios in which anticompetitive conduct is facilitated by governmental policies and actions. In Section 6 we review various tests that have been devised to sort out "procompetitive" from "anticompetitive" conduct. Brief conclusions are offered in Section 7.

Note on terminology. In the next four sections, we shall term *anticompetitive* or *predatory* those aggressive and exclusionary business strategies that, when deployed, have the effect of lowering a properly evaluated measure of social welfare. This usage is not entirely consistent with the standard usage in antitrust case law and literature, as is made clear in Section 6.

Note on legal setting. In the United States, single firm conduct is scrutinized primarily under Section 2 of the Sherman Act, which deems it illegal to "monopolize, or attempt to monopolize... any part of the trade or commerce...". In Europe, unilateral conduct is scrutinized under Article 86 of the Treaty of Rome, the treaty for the European Economic Community. The Article prohibits "any abuse...of a dominant position". Such abuse may consist of, for example, imposing unfair selling prices, limiting production or technical development to the prejudice of consumers, and imposing tie-ins.

In the United States, an important development in the area of Section 2 enforcement has been a growing importance of economic analysis in the process of assessment of firm conduct. This trend is best evidenced in the recent Supreme Court decision in *Japanese Electronics*, a fifteen-year-old predation case. Reasonably sound analyses of various manifestations of foreclosure strategies have been offered by the Supreme Court in *Hyde*, *Northwest Stationers*, and *Aspen Ski*.[1] There is less evidence, on the other hand, that the European Community Court of Justice has been greatly impressed by economic analyses of anticompetitive conduct. At the same time, a recently settled EEC action against IBM implicitly focused on the potential for strategic abuses of technological leadership: a possibility which has not been warmly received in the U.S. courts but which, nevertheless, is quite consistent with the strategic view of dominant firm conduct.

Note on the legal literature. In this chapter we generally refrain from discussion of antitrust cases in the United States or elsewhere. For the analysis of U.S. law, the reader is referred to Sullivan (1977), Areeda and Turner (1978, vol. III), and Areeda (1982). Areeda and Hovenkamp (1986) and Hovenkamp (1985) provide an up-to-date discussion of the cases and legal doctrines from a legal-economic perspective. A more selective discussion can be found in Bork (1978), which contains an influential critique of Section 2 enforcement, in Posner (1976), and in the Posner and Easterbrook (1981) casebook. For the European Community, Fox (1984, 1986) and Hawk (1986) are excellent sources which offer a comparative vantage point. A reader who wishes to stay current with the developments in the law must read court decisions and articles in the law reviews.

2. Framework for economic analysis of dominant firm conduct

Economic and legal assessment of the welfare consequences of strategies that firms use to preserve or enhance market share is difficult for at least the following reasons. First, these business practices and strategies are generally part and parcel of competitive interactions in the marketplace. Thus, price-cutting, introduction of new products, promotional campaigns, etc. all constitute reasonable responses by incumbents to increased actual or potential competition [Porter (1980, 1985)].

[1] *Hyde v. Jefferson Parish Hosp. Dist. No.* 2, 104 S. Ct. 1551 (1984); *Northwest Wholesale Stationers v. Pacific Stationery & Printing Co.*, 105 U.S. 2613 (1985); *Aspen Skiing Co. v. Aspen Highlands Skiing Corp.*, 105 S. Ct. 2847 (1985).

Second, many practices, while not fully consistent with firm behavior in the idealized textbook model of perfect competition, can, nevertheless, often be explained on efficiency grounds. Thus, for example, "technological tie-ins" [Sidak (1983)] which entail bundling of various complementary components of a system, or even refusals to deal with a rival firm, may be justified on the ground that they enable the firm to earn a reasonable rate of return on its investment in R&D or in the creation of new information.

Third, some of these practices, while potentially harmful to consumers, do not harm present or future competition. That is, they do not elevate entry barriers, induce exit of an existing rival, or deter socially desirable entrants from coming into the market. For example, a tie-in designed to facilitate price discrimination can lower consumers' welfare but need not be harmful to competition as it might when it is imposed by a monopolist unthreatened by potential entrants. At the same time, exit-inducing and entry-deterring behavior can improve welfare if it keeps the market from becoming overcrowded.

Fourth, many of these practices that are scrutinized for their effects on competition and welfare are sufficiently unusual to be unfamiliar to jurors, judges, or economists. Consequently, a reasonably reliable assessment of their effects is difficult [see Williamson (1985) for a more complete discussion].

Economic analysis of firm conduct proceeds on the plausible assumption that a firm's decision-makers are motivated in the choice of their actions by the goal of long-run profit maximization[2] and that they have reasonable estimates of how their actions affect their firm's profitability and the profitability of their rivals. As part of profit maximization, a firm's management can engage in potentially *anticompetitive* conduct on three interrelated fronts. First, they can engage in practices designed to deter potential entrants. Such pure deterrence strategies need not harm existing rivals of the dominant firm.[3] Second, they can engage in practices that disadvantage actual rivals, without necessarily causing their exit, but which relax the competitive constraint exercised by them over the dominant firm. Third, they can engage in actions that actually cause the exit of an existing rival or rivals. These types of actions can have a substantial deterrence effect on potential rivals and, in fact, may only be rational if they have this demonstration effect. Similarly, precommitments made purely for deterrence purposes, such as investment in capacity, may harm existing rivals and facilitate aggressive strategies towards actual competitors. Furthermore, actions that disadvantage actual rivals can, in principle, disadvantage potential rivals as well.

[2]This is a significant simplification because it is well established that managers may pursue objectives other than profit maximization. See Chapter 3 by Bengt Holmstrom in this Handbook. Nevertheless, we shall assume that a firm's owners provide incentives for the managers to advance that goal.

[3]These practices, and others, are analyzed by Richard Gilbert in Chapter 8 of this Handbook.

We consider a dominant firm that is facing a rival or a well-defined group of rivals. The subject of the analysis is the response of the dominant incumbent firm to the act of entry and to the strategies adopted by the new rival. We do not focus explicitly here on purely entry-deterring strategies.

We can model strategic interaction between the incumbent and the rival entrant in a variety of ways. Consider the incumbent's profit function:

$$\pi^{\mathrm{I}}(\cdot) = \pi^{0}\left(a_0^{\mathrm{I}}, a_0^{\mathrm{E}}\right) + \pi^{\mathrm{f}}\left(a_1^{\mathrm{I}}\left(a_0^{\mathrm{I}}, a_0^{\mathrm{E}}\right), a_1^{\mathrm{E}}\left(a_0^{\mathrm{I}}, a_0^{\mathrm{E}}\right); a_0^{\mathrm{I}}; a_0^{\mathrm{E}}\right). \tag{2.1}$$

In expression (2.1), superscript I stands for the "incumbent" and E stands for the "entrant". In (2.1), we disaggregate I's profits into current profits, $\pi^0(\cdot)$, and into (appropriately discounted expected) future profits, $\pi^{\mathrm{f}}(\cdot)$. The pair $(a_0^{\mathrm{I}}, a_0^{\mathrm{E}})$ denote the current period actions of I and E. It is important to emphasize here that the a's can represent vectors of complex actions, as will be discussed later. The level of future profits depends on future actions of I and E, namely $a_1^{\mathrm{I}}(\cdot)$ and $a_1^{\mathrm{E}}(\cdot)$, respectively, which are in turn related to the current period actions of the two players. We also posit that $\pi^{\mathrm{f}}(\cdot)$ depends directly on $(a_0^{\mathrm{I}}, a_0^{\mathrm{E}})$.[4]

For the purpose of the analysis, we assume that a_0^{E} is given and focus on the optimal choice of the incumbent's current action, a_0^{I}. We assume that the incumbent dominant firm optimizes against the rival's current action, i.e. acts in response to entry or some market-share-enhancing aggressive action by an existing rival. [Formulation (2.1) also allows for simultaneous moves by the incumbent and the rival, however.] The incumbent also takes into account the future consequences of its current action, with the understanding that the future will evolve optimally. (Here we can point out that in any litigation in which monopolization is alleged, the plaintiff must identify that set of the incumbent's actions which it considers to be anticompetitive. Hence, a_0^{I} is that action which has triggered the antitrust complaint.)

In formulation (2.1), a_0^{I} is not restricted to pricing conduct: it can stand for any form of business strategy including R&D investment, capital expansion, raising rivals' costs by foreclosing access to essential inputs, advertising, rent-seeking in political and legal arenas, or even a choice of managers to run the firm [Fershtman and Judd (1984)]. It is important to recognize that predation can take forms other than price-cutting.[5] The reason for this lies in McGee's (1958) observation that price predation is rarely, if ever, profitable for a dominant firm

[4] We have given (2.1) an intertemporal interpretation. An alternative interpretation treats $\pi^0(\cdot)$ as profits in one market and $\pi^{\mathrm{f}}(\cdot)$ as profits in some other, strategically interrelated, market [see, for example, Bulow, Geanakoplos and Klemperer (1985)]. This interpretation is exploited in various models of reputation-building, as discussed in Subsection 3.1.2 below [see, for example, Easley, Masson and Reynolds (1985)].

[5] Areeda (1982) advances the position that many varieties of nonpricing conduct of dominant firms should be free of scrutiny for their potential anticompetitive effects.

because the costs of a predatory price-cutting strategy tend to increase with the size of the market share of the predator whereas the rival's losses are smaller the smaller is its market share. McGee's assessment of rationality of price predation can be criticized for at least three reasons: first, if the predator can effectively price discriminate across markets or customers then the costs of price predation need not be related to market share; second, price predation in one market can have spill-over effects in other markets – a fact that McGee does not fully appreciate in his cost–benefit calculus; and third, the predator may have no other option but to rely on price as a signal of market conditions that are relevant to rivals' decision whether or not to remain in the market.

Nevertheless, it is correct to conclude that the firm contemplating aggressive market strategy will seek the cheapest strategy that will enable it to accomplish the desired goal of inducing exit and/or discouraging entry. In particular, it may select a strategy whose cost does not increase with market share. For example, per-unit costs of an R&D program decline with the size of the innovator's market. The same may hold for advertising and for raising rivals' costs through manipulation of regulatory policies [Bartel and Thomas (1986) discuss economies of scale in regulatory compliance].

Differentiating expression (2.1) with respect to a_0^{I}, we obtain the first-order necessary condition for the choice of a_0^{I}:

$$\frac{\mathrm{d}\pi^{\mathrm{I}}}{\mathrm{d}a_0^{\mathrm{I}}} = \frac{\mathrm{d}\pi^0}{\mathrm{d}a_0^{\mathrm{I}}} + \frac{\partial\pi^{\mathrm{f}}}{\partial a_1^{\mathrm{I}}} \cdot \frac{\mathrm{d}a_1^{\mathrm{I}}}{\mathrm{d}a_0^{\mathrm{I}}} + \frac{\partial\pi^{\mathrm{f}}}{\partial a_1^{\mathrm{E}}} \cdot \frac{\mathrm{d}a_1^{\mathrm{E}}}{\mathrm{d}a_0^{\mathrm{I}}} + \frac{\partial\pi^{\mathrm{f}}}{\partial a_0^{\mathrm{I}}} = 0. \tag{2.2}$$

Consider initially the first and fourth terms in (2.2). The first term captures "innocent" short-term effects of an action on I's profits. In the absence of strategic interactions and direct intertemporal linkages in the profit function, the optimal choice of a_0^{I} would be governed by the direct derivate $\mathrm{d}\pi^0/\mathrm{d}a_0^{\mathrm{I}}$. In the presence of direct intertemporal links, the incumbent must also consider the direct consequences of the current action on future profits via the partial derivative $\partial\pi^{\mathrm{f}}/\partial a_0^{\mathrm{I}}$.

Turning now to the second and third terms in (2.2), we note that potentially anticompetitive strategic interactions enter through these components of the expression. For example, the second term can capture the fact that the level of the current action may make future aggressive behavior more profitable. The third term can capture the fact that the choice of the current action can make the entrant less aggressive in the future (in the extreme case, the current choice of a_0^{I} can cause the entrant to exit, i.e. to select $a_1^{\mathrm{E}} = 0$).

Plainly it would be wrong to conclude that a dominant firm behaves anticompetitively when it considers the indirect profit effects of an action in the choice of that action, as displayed in the second and third terms of equation (2.2). Such a definition of anticompetitive behavior would be most unfortunate: it would frequently condemn as illegal actions those that (a) elevate consumers' welfare and (b) are part of innocent competitive interactions. For example, let a_0^{I} be the incumbent's investment in R&D. Such an investment will have an impact on I's next-period optimal actions. Thus, successful process R&D may enable I to significantly lower its next period's product price. Similarly, successful R&D effort may cause E to withdraw its product offerings, which, in turn, further elevates I's future profits. Furthermore, it would be unreasonable to expect I to disregard the impact of its R&D program, for example, on the viability of E.

In fact, it is important that whatever legal restrictions are imposed on single-firm conduct, that they do not prevent the incumbent from exploiting the available intertemporal complementarities on both the demand and cost sides. This admonition is especially relevant for the proper public policy treatment of nonprice strategies such as capacity expansion, advertising, introduction of new products, or even various exclusionary contracts, all of which have intertemporal profit implications. Even current pricing decisions have intertemporal profit implications, as when current prices are used as signaling devices (see Subsection 3.1.3). All this implies that if the dominant firm accounts for the effect $\{(\partial \pi^{\mathrm{f}}/\partial a_1^{\mathrm{I}})(\mathrm{d}a_1^{\mathrm{I}}/\mathrm{d}a_0^{\mathrm{I}})\}$ in its optimal choice of a_0^{I}, it is not necessarily behaving in an anticompetitive manner.

Consider next the term $\{(\partial \pi^{\mathrm{f}}/\partial a_1^{\mathrm{E}})(\mathrm{d}a_1^{\mathrm{E}}/\mathrm{d}a_0^{\mathrm{I}})\}$. As we have already indicated, in a strategic context firms factor in the effects of their actions on their rivals' reactions. For example, any firm is likely to assess the effects of its R&D expenditures on the viability of rival offerings. In particular, a firm's investment program (including capacity expansion, R&D, and advertising) may only be profitable if it actually causes the exit of its rivals and enables the innovator to garner the whole market, or retard entry into an already overcrowded market. Thus, while causing its rivals' exit or retarding entry may be viewed as monopolization par excellence, such actions may, in fact, be conducive to social welfare maximization.

The preceding discussion suggests that it would unduly restrict firms' conduct, and most likely harm social welfare, if incumbent firms were to be forced to select only those actions that are short-run profit maximizing. On the other hand, it does not advance matters to say that incumbent firms should be allowed to maximize long-run profits. Such a posture would allow firms to select a_0^{I} according to condition (2.2) above. Consequently, it would rule out the possibility of ever finding any firm engaging in anticompetitive behavior precisely because rational anticompetitive behavior maximizes long-run profits, hence is consistent with (2.2). To escape the difficulties inherent in defining anticompetitive behavior in a strategic context, one can take refuge – as we shall in the next sections – in a social welfare criterion and use this criterion to scrutinize firm conduct. From that vantage point, single-firm conduct is anticompetitive if it affects competition (i.e. actual and potential rivals) and lowers social welfare. However, the welfare criterion cannot be easily implemented in the context of antitrust litigation.[6] Various efforts, discussed in Section 6, have been made to devise tests of anticompetitive conduct which do not rely explicitly on the welfare criterion. As such, these tests cannot always be consistent with the welfare criterion. How well they perform is a matter of debate which will be briefly reviewed in Section 6.

3. Pricing and nonpricing models of anticompetitive behavior

In this section we look at various models of pricing and nonpricing strategies that involve the use of the predator's competitive strengths to muscle, or drive, its rival out of the industry and deter future entry. Subsection 3.1 examines the use of pricing to achieve this end, while Subsection 3.2 examines nonpricing actions.

3.1. Predatory pricing

The prevalence of predatory pricing has been the subject of heated debate that is difficult to resolve on empirical grounds. Various commentators have argued, however, that in several markets pricing has been used to create or maintain high seller concentration. The best-known example is that of the Standard Oil Company which, under the leadership of John D. Rockefeller, attained a 90 percent market share of the U.S. petroleum refining industry between 1870 and 1899. Among the many practices[7] used to attain this position was price warfare practiced openly both by Standard Oil and by "independent" distributors actually under its control. Whether or not this was a shrewd strategy is subject to debate. There is little doubt, however, that Standard Oil at least attempted to use pricing as a weapon to drive its rivals out. In a letter to H.A. Hutchins, an associate, Rockefeller wrote in 1881:

> We want to watch, and when our volume of business is to be cut down by the increase of competition to fifty percent, or less, it may be a very serious question whether we had not better make an important reduction [in price], with a view of taking substantially all the business there is [Scherer (1980, p. 336)].

[6]Scherer (1976) and Comanor and Frech (1984) disagree with this view. Scherer's position is criticized in Areeda and Turner (1975) and Easterbrook (1981a).

[7]Other strategies included securing discriminatory rail freight rates and foreclosing supplies of crude oil. See Scherer (1980, pp. 336–337) for a more detailed discussion and for other references.

The activities of a conference of shipowners in the China–England trade provides a second example. Yamey (1972) reports that, as in the Standard Oil case, the conference used a variety of strategies to keep out new entry. One of these strategies was the undercutting of freight rates when rival vessels were present. In particular, the conference decided that:

> if any non-conference steamer should proceed to Hankow to load, independently any necessary number of conference steamers should be sent at the same time to Hankow, *in order to underbid the freight which the independent shipowners might offer, without any regard to whether the freight they should bid would be remunerative or not* [Yamey (1972, p. 139), emphasis added].

As a result of this decision, when three independent ships were sent to Hankow, the conference responded by sending in their own ships and freight rates fell dramatically. The House of Lords concluded that the rates were "so low that if they [the conference] continued it they themselves could not carry on trade".[8]

The theoretical literature on predatory pricing analyzes three major sets of models: those based on asymmetric financial constraints (the long purse predatory scenarios); those based on reputation; and those based on signaling.[9] Roberts (1985) provides a briefer but more technical review of these models. Virtually all models focus on the case of duopoly in which case, since new entry or re-entry is assumed away or does not occur in equilibrium, the reward to inducing exit is the difference in the present value of the flow of profits from monopoly and duopoly.

The basic idea behind the long purse models is that a firm with greater financial resources can outlast its rival in a "fight to the death" and is, therefore, in a position to drive its rival out. In the signaling models there is some asymmetry of information (usually about the firms' costs or industry demand conditions) and the predator prices low in order to convince its rival that conditions are such that the rival is better off exiting (because the incumbent's costs are low or industry demand is low). The reputation models, by contrast, simply assume that it is feasible to drive the rival out and instead focus on a particular aspect of the profitability of doing so, namely the effect that this might have on future entry.

Although the feasibility and profitability of predatory pricing are necessary conditions for predation to be rational, they are not sufficient. Even if the increase in post-exit profitability is sufficient to compensate the predator for the costs incurred during its predatory episode, the predation will only have been

[8]Other examples of alleged predatory pricing include Borden's price warfare against firms selling reconstituted lemon juice (in competition with its ReaLemon brand) and General Food's response to the entry of Folger's coffee in competition with Maxwell House. For an extensive discussion of this case see Schmalensee (1979) who also offers a plausible rule for testing for predatory conduct. See also Scherer (1980, pp. 335–340) for additional references.

[9]There is also an emerging strand of inquiry which analyzes markets in which there are increasing returns. We make some remarks on this work in our concluding comments to this section.

rational if there were no more profitable strategy at the predator's disposal for achieving the same result. Although this may seem obvious, it was not until the appearance of McGee's (1958) article that the implications of this notion were clearly articulated.

McGee argued that merger is always a preferred alternative to predation. The argument is straightforward. Consider two firms that operate in a single market and suppose that there is no possibility of new entry or of re-entry by a firm that exits. Furthermore, suppose that it is feasible for one of the firms to drive its rival out and that the monopoly profits that would accrue post-exit are sufficient to compensate the predator for its reduction in profits during the predatory episode. Compare that predatory strategy with the alternative strategy of a merger prior to the predatory episode. Clearly the profits of the merged firm would exceed the sum of the profits of the predator and the rival under the predatory scenario. Even if the predator can perform as well as the merged entity post-exit, the merged firm would have earned monopoly profits before the exit instead of the low profits (or losses) that would result from the cut-throat predatory pricing. Absent any asymmetries of information, the firms will both recognize that the outcome from the merger dominates that from predation and thus negotiate merger terms that will make them both better off. Thus, McGee argues, even if it is feasible, predation is irrational.

McGee's argument has been criticized on several grounds. First, the point of the reputation models (which we discuss in greater detail below) is that much of the benefit from an episode of predation is the impact that it has on *future* entry or on entry in other industries. Indeed, if the monopolizing firm shows a willingness to merge with any rival, it may face a stream of entrants who enter just for the possibility of being bought out [see Rasmusen (1985) for a model along these lines]. Thus, the simple single-market calculus above is inappropriate in a multi-market or multi-entrant context. Second, the same externality arises in models of predation based on signaling. A firm that is successful in convincing its current rival that exit is the most profitable strategy, also thereby has an effect on later entry. Third, there are legal constraints on mergers. The elimination of the rival is most advantageous when it results in a large increase in market concentration. However, it is precisely in these circumstances that a proposed merger is likely to violate antimerger legislation. In choosing between two unlawful methods of increasing its market power, Posner (1976) argues that a firm may choose predation since it may be more difficult to detect.[10]

[10]In a more recent article, McGee (1980) counters that these same antimerger laws render predation unattractive as well. Once the predator has successfully driven its rival from the market it may be prevented by anitmerger legislation from buying its rival's assets. Therefore, "physical capital remains, and will be brought back into play by some opportunist once the monopolizer raises prices..." [McGee (1958, pp. 140–141)]. McGee's counterargument assumes that the rival's assets are industry specific. If this is the case, however, his argument is correct only if the "opportunist" who buys up the rival's assets has reason to believe that it will enjoy a more fortunate fate at the hands of the predator. In this regard, see the discussion on reputation for predation below.

Furthermore, in those cases in which a merger is possible, the terms of the merger may themselves depend on the actions the firm can credibly threaten should the merger negotiations fail. Whether or not predatory pricing is a credible threat under those circumstances depends on the rationality and feasibility of such behavior. Thus, even where mergers are possible, an understanding of predatory pricing is required. We therefore turn to an examination of theories of predatory pricing.

3.1.1. The long purse

Many students of predation have suggested that the primary means of inducing exit consists of waging a price war that inflicts losses on the rival until its resources are exhausted. Clearly for this to be a feasible strategy for the predator, unless it has a cost advantage, it must have greater resources to draw on to outlast its foe.[11]

This "deep pocket" or "long purse" predatory scenario was first modeled by Telser (1966). Telser simply assumed that the rival's ability to raise equity and debt financing was limited and that limit was known by the potential predator who was also assumed to have greater resources. Furthermore, the rival was assumed to have to incur some fixed costs to remain in operation. Thus, by driving the market price below the rival's variable costs resulting in a loss at least as large as the fixed costs, the predator exhausts the rival's reserves and drives it out of the market. Provided the monopoly rents the predator receives once exit has occurred are sufficient to compensate it for the reduction in profits during the predatory episode, predation is both feasible and rational.

Notice, however, that in this model predation would never occur in equilibrium. Since all of the relevant parameters (including the firm's resources) are assumed to be common knowledge, the rival would leave at its first opportunity (or the first hint of predation) rather than waste resources on a pointless price war. Indeed, had it envisioned this showdown, it would not have entered in the first place. Thus, Telser's model cannot provide a complete theory of predation. It does, however, demonstrate that having a long purse may provide a *credible threat* of post-entry predation and thus could deter entry.

This point is made more forcefully by Benoit (1984) in the first full game-theoretic treatment of "deep pockets". As in Telser's model, Benoit assumes that the firms have limited financial backing and that the incumbent can survive a greater length of time before it would be forced into bankruptcy. Furthermore, if the incumbent chooses to fight entry, each firm makes a loss. Benoit's result is that

[11] For example, Edwards writes: "An enterprise that is big in this sense obtains from its bigness a special kind of power, based upon the fact that it can spend money in large amounts. If such a concern finds itself matching expenditures or losses, dollar for dollar, with a substantially smaller firm, the length of its purse assures it of a victory" [Edwards (1955, pp. 334–335)].

even if the incumbent firm would only find it profitable to engage in a successful fight for just *one period*, then, no matter how long the entrant could actually withstand a price war, the only perfect equilibrium involves the entrant not entering and the existing firm threatening to fight in every period.

Benoit's argument uses a backward-induction proof. Consider what happens when the entrant has exhausted its resources and cannot fight for one more period without going bankrupt. If the rivalry has reached that stage, it is optimal for the incumbent to fight for one more period and drive the entrant out of the industry (since it prefers a period of fighting followed by monopoly forever to cooperating with the entrant forever). However, then it is optimal for the entrant to leave at the beginning of the period and save itself what is left of its resources. Now consider the period before the last. The incumbent knows that if it fights the entrant will then, at the end of the period, have sufficient resources for no more than one period. But then, by the argument above, the entrant will leave at the end of this second-to-last period if the incumbent fights, and so the incumbent will fight. This argument proceeds all the way back to the first period in the usual way.

While this result is somewhat striking, the assumptions of the model are extremely strong: it is highly unlikely that how long each firm could survive a price war is common knowledge. Even more troubling, perhaps, is the postulated degree of rationality assumed by the players. Not only must both the incumbent and the entrant be able to carry out the above calculations, but it must be common knowledge that they can. When Benoit relaxes this common knowledge assumption, he finds that indeed entry may occur in equilibrium.[12]

A major gap in the theory is the lack of a convincing explanation for the disparity in the stringencies of the financial constraints facing the incumbent and its rival. In Benoit's complete information model, for example, if the entrant could secure a line of credit from a bank that assured it of greater resources than the incumbent, the unique perfect equilibrium would have the entrant driving the incumbent out, and without ever having to suffer a single period of price war. Moreover, the bank should be perfectly willing to participate in this venture. Thus, for any long purse story to be plausible, it is essential that the inability of the target firm to borrow be explained.

Recognizing this, Fudenberg and Tirole (1985, 1986b) have suggested that such an explanation may be provided by recent advances in the theory of financing under asymmetric information. Suppose that a firm's ability to borrow depends on its own net asset value. Then, in a two-period model, a firm that is relatively well endowed may have an incentive to prey on a less financially solid rival in the

[12]Benoit uses the kind of incomplete information repeated game used by Kreps and Wilson (1982) and Milgrom and Roberts (1982b) which we discuss below. Accordingly, we omit a discussion of Benoit's incomplete information model here.

first period. In so doing, the predator may reduce the rival's asset value below the amount it needs in order to be able to borrow in the second period. In that case the rival will be forced out of the market.

What is required for this argument to go through is a theory that shows that a firm may be unable to borrow if its net asset value falls below some critical level. According to Fudenberg and Tirole, the asymmetric information model of Gale and Hellwig (1986) provides this link. Gale and Hellwig consider a one-period model in which a debtor has a potential project with a random payoff whose expectation exceeds the required capital investment. The debtor is assumed to have insufficient funds to finance the project himself. A bank that finances the remainder only observes the actual return on the project if it incurs some auditing cost. They show that the optimal debt contract has the debtor reimburse the bank some predetermined amount if he chooses not to default. If the debtor defaults, the bank audits and confiscates the entire net return.

If the net asset value of the firm is low, however, so that the bank must finance most of the project, then the probability of audit will be quite high (since the firm will choose to default for more moderate realizations of the return on the project). But then if the audit cost is high, the bank may be unwilling to finance the project at an interest rate that is worthwhile to the firm. Thus, a low net asset value for the firm may deprive it of access to financial markets.

The Fudenberg–Tirole insight is a crucial one for the long purse argument: the very handicap that makes the target firm vulnerable to attack may also foreclose it from access to the financial markets. Given the potential importance of their result, additional work is required to relax their assumptions. In particular, their argument rests on the inability of the target firm to borrow in the second period after its resources have been depleted by the first-period predatory episode. However, if the target firm signed a long-term contract at the beginning of the first period that covered the second period as well as the first, and if this long-term access to financing was observable by others, then the incentive for predation may disappear. This important issue awaits further investigation.

3.1.2. *Predation for reputation*

Critics were quick to point out that McGee's (1958) argument that predation is generally unprofitable assumed that the predator faces only a single rival. If, however, the predator faces rivals in other markets as well, it may be concerned about the effect of its pricing in one market on its rivals in another market. Yamey (1972, p. 131), for example, points out that "the aggressor will, moreover, be looking beyond the immediate problem of dealing with its current rival. Alternative strategies for dealing with that rival may have different effects on the flow of future rivals."

Table 9.1

		Payoffs	
		Incumbent	Entrant
Incumbent's actions	Predatory prices	P^{I}	P^{E}
	Accommodated entry	A^{I}	A^{E}

When a predator faces a finite number of potential entrants, Selten's (1978) "chain-store paradox" demonstrates, however, that rational strategies in one market cannot be affected by behavior in another market. There is thus no role for a reputation effect.

The "chain-store paradox" considers an incumbent monopolist in N geographically separated markets. The incumbent faces N potential entrants, one in each market. The potential entrants must make their entry decisions sequentially, one potential entrant making its decision each "period". If entry occurs, the incumbent can engage in predatory pricing against the entrant that will be sure to lead to a loss for the latter. Alternatively, the incumbent can behave in a more accommodating manner. For example, the firms could play Cournot or cooperate (implicitly or explicitly) in setting prices. We can summarize the post-entry payoffs in any particular market as shown in Table 9.1. If an entrant chooses not to enter we can normalize its payoffs to 0 and set those for the incumbent to M, the monopoly payoff.

For this model to have the desired interpretation, we need $M > A^{\mathrm{I}} > 0 > P^{\mathrm{I}}$ (so that the incumbent prefers monopoly to accommodating entry which in turn it prefers to predation) and $A^{\mathrm{E}} > 0 > P^{\mathrm{E}}$ (so that an entrant desires to enter if and only if it will not be preyed upon).

To begin with suppose that $N = 1$. In this setting, if the incumbent is faced with actual entry, it will accommodate it (since $P^{\mathrm{I}} < A^{\mathrm{I}}$). Knowing this, the entrant will enter. Thus, the unique perfect equilibrium is accommodated entry.

Now consider what happens if $N = 2$. Might the incumbent now have an incentive to prey on the first entrant in the hope of scaring the second off? If $P^{\mathrm{I}} + \delta M > (1 + \delta)A^{\mathrm{I}}$, where δ is the discount factor, the incumbent prefers to prey on the first entrant and receive monopoly profits in the second period to accommodating entry in both periods. It seems that in this case the incumbent has an incentive to prey on the first entrant.

The flaw in this logic is what gives rise to the chain-store paradox. When the second period is reached the game looks identical to the incumbent and the (then) single potential entrant, as in the game with $N = 1$. Recall that the unique equilibrium there entailed accommodation and entry. Thus, the same must be true here. Whether the incumbent practiced predatory pricing in the first period or not is irrelevant to the game that the second potential entrant faces. It is "water under the bridge", and displays of aggressive behavior at that stage will not impress the second potential entrant if it expects rational behavior from the incumbent for the remainder of the game. However, if this is the case, then there is no incentive for predation in the first period. The incumbent realizes that its first-period behavior will not influence the outcome in the second period. Thus, the first-period payoffs are all that are relevant for its first-period decision, and accordingly it will accommodate entry. The unique subgame perfect equilibrium to the game with two potential entrants (or by the same argument, N potential entrants) entails accommodated entry into every market.

This result is counterintuitive. The belief that behavior across markets is related is widespread. For example, Scherer (1980) suggests: "If rivals come to fear from a multimarket seller's actions in Market A that entry or expansion in Markets B and C will be met by sharp price cuts or other rapacious responses, they may be deterred from taking aggressive actions there."

The argument underlying the chain-store paradox relies strongly on backward induction. Indeed, it is readily shown [Milgrom and Roberts (1982b)] that if the incumbent faces an infinite flow of potential entrants (and maximizes the present discounted value of profits) it can use a credible threat of predation to keep out entry.

To see this set $N = \infty$ in the above model. Then the following are equilibrium strategies: the incumbent preys (i.e. prices aggressively and attempts to induce exit) if entry occurs and if it has never accommodated entry; otherwise the incumbent accommodates entry. If entry is ever met by accommodation, every subsequent potential entrant enters; otherwise (if there has been no entry or if all previous entry was met with predation) all potential entrants stay out.

There is no entry along the equilibrium path. The first potential entrant expects to be preyed upon if it enters, and so stays out. The same is then true for all subsequent potential entrants. But why are the first potential entrant's expectations reasonable? If it enters and is preyed upon, the equilibrium strategies of the remaining entrants imply that no further entry will take place. The net present value of the incumbent's profits if it preys is therefore $P^{\mathrm{I}} + \delta M/(1 - \delta)$. If it fails to prey on the first entrant, however, it will face entry from all subsequent entrants, irrespective of its future actions. In this situation the incumbent will find it optimal to continue to accommodate all later entry – thus validating the entrants' beliefs – since one period of accommodation rules out any gains from future exit-inducing behavior. Hence, if accommodation occurs in the first period, the net present value of incumbent's profits is $A^{\mathrm{I}}/(1 - \delta)$. Thus, predation is worthwhile if $P^{\mathrm{I}} + \delta M/(1 - \delta) > A^{\mathrm{I}}/(1 - \delta)$ or $A^{\mathrm{I}} - P^{\mathrm{I}} < \delta(M - A^{\mathrm{I}})/(1 - \delta)$

(the one-period cost of predation is less than the future benefits from preying this period). This expression holds for δ sufficiently close to 1 since $M > A^{\mathrm{I}}$.

This equilibrium embodies extremely simple reputation maintenance. The beliefs of potential entrants that support such an equilibrium are that the incumbent will induce the exit of every entrant. However, if the incumbent ever fails to prey, it loses its predatory reputation (which, notice, at the beginning of the game it has done nothing to earn). Moreover, once it has lost this reputation, it can do nothing to regain it. No matter how many times it later preys on an entrant, if it ever fails to prey it loses its reputation for all time.

Extending the model to an infinite horizon is, for several reasons, an unsatisfactory resolution of the chain-store paradox. First, as is common in infinite-horizon games, this game has many perfect equilibria, one of which is that accommodated entry occurs in every period. Second, the beliefs that sustain the predatory equilibrium are highly implausible. Finally, and most importantly, in many practical situations, such as rivalrous entry into distinct *geographic* markets, the number of potential entrants is finite.

Also, the backward-induction argument of the chain-store paradox is also unsettling, aside from its reliance on the finite horizon, because it attributes an extreme degree of rationality to the players. The pathbreaking work of Kreps and Wilson (1982), Milgrom and Roberts (1982b), and Kreps, Milgrom, Roberts and Wilson (1982), illustrates how important the assumption of rationality is in this setting. Suppose, for example, that instead of the parameter values above, we have $P^{\mathrm{I}} > A^{\mathrm{I}}$ so that the incumbent actually prefers predation to accommodating entry. In that case, the unique subgame perfect equilibrium is for the entrant to stay out. This is not surprising, of course. If predation is profitable, it will occur. What is surprising is that if there is only a small probability (in a sense about to be made precise) that predation is profitable, it may still occur.

Suppose that it is conceivable that for a particular incumbent it might be the case that $P^{\mathrm{I}} > A^{\mathrm{I}}$. We will call such an incumbent "tough". There are two possible interpretations of "toughness": either predation is more profitable than accommodation in a single market, or the profitability is lower but the incumbent is "irrational" and prefers to prey even when it is unprofitable to do so. If it is the case for the incumbent that $A^{\mathrm{I}} > P^{\mathrm{I}}$, we call the incumbent "weak". Finally, suppose that the potential entrant assesses with probability p that the incumbent is tough. One would not want a model of predation to be based on a great deal of irrationality. However, even a small value of p can have dramatic consequences for the willingness of *rational* firms to prey.

To see the effect of the possible presence of a "tough" predator, consider the chain-store model described above, with $N = 2$. Suppose that $(1 - p)A^{\mathrm{E}} + pP^{\mathrm{E}} > 0$ so that the entrant would enter in a one-period game. There is no pure strategy equilibrium to the game with these parameter values. To see this, suppose first that there is a pure strategy equilibrium in which the weak incumbent fights entry in the first period. Then the second entrant learns nothing from first-period behavior and enters. But if fighting in the first period does not deter second-period entry, then the weak incumbent has no incentive to fight in the first period. Thus, this cannot be an equilibrium. Now, suppose instead that the weak incumbent does not fight entry in the first-period equilibrium. Then, if the second entrant observes that first-period entry was fought, it will be certain that the incumbent is tough and will stay out. But then even the weak incumbent would want to fight in the first period since it would earn $P^{\mathrm{I}} + \delta M^{\mathrm{I}} > (1-\delta)A^{\mathrm{I}}$. So there does not exist a pure strategy equilibrium.

The mixed strategies are described by Kreps and Wilson (1982). Here they can be characterized as follows: (i) the first potential entrant enters, (iia) the second potential entrant enters if entry by the first entrant was not fought, and (iib) it randomizes over entering and staying out if entry was fought (the probabilities with which it takes each action are derived below); (iii) the tough incumbent fights entry in both periods; (iv) the weak incumbent randomizes over fighting and accommodating entry in the first period (again, the probabilities with which it takes each action are derived below); (v) if entry occurs in the second period, the weak incumbent accommodates it.

In this equilibrium, the weak incumbent acts as if it is tough in the first period (with some probability) to create a reputation for toughness, i.e. to attempt to persuade future entrants that it is "tough". Obviously, a reputation is more valuable the larger is N.

For these strategies to constitute a perfect Bayesian equilibrium, each action must be optimal at the time it is taken, given the strategies of the other player. Actions (iii) and (v) are clearly optimal. By definition, the tough incumbent prefers to fight entry than to accommodate it. Furthermore, the weak incumbent prefers to accommodate entry in the second period since that is also the last period. Condition (iia) is also satisfied since [from (iii)] only the weak incumbent ever accommodates entry.

We can now turn to condition (iib). Let $\Pr\{f \mid w\}(\Pr\{f \mid t\})$ denote the probability that the weak (tough) incumbent fights in the first period. Then, if the second entrant observes that entry was fought in the first period, it uses Bayes' rule to calculate the probability that the incumbent is tough:

$$\begin{aligned}\Pr\{t \mid f\} &= \Pr\{f \mid t\}\Pr\{t\}/(\Pr\{f \mid t\}\Pr\{t\} + \Pr\{f \mid w\}\Pr\{w\}) \\ &= p/(p + \Pr\{f \mid w\}(1-p)),\end{aligned}$$

where we have used the fact that $\Pr\{f \mid t\} = 1$. If the second potential entrant is to be prepared to randomize [as required in (iib)], it must be indifferent between entering and staying out. This requires that $\Pr\{t \mid f\}P^{\mathrm{E}} + (1 - \Pr\{t \mid f\})A^{\mathrm{E}} = 0$

or $\Pr\{t \mid f\} = A^{E}/(A^{E} - P^{E})$. Combining this with the expression for $\Pr\{t \mid f\}$ a few lines above (and rearranging), we require that $\Pr\{f \mid w\} = -pP^{E}/(1-p)A^{E}$ (which is positive since $P^{E} < 0$). Thus, if the weak incumbent fights entry in the first period with this probability, the second entrant's posterior estimate that it is facing a tough opponent will be raised by just enough to make it indifferent between entering and staying out. In that case it will be prepared to randomize and condition (iib) will be satisfied.

For the weak incumbent to be prepared to randomize in the first period, i.e. for it to be indifferent between fighting and not, the following must hold:

$$P^{I} + \delta\big(\Pr\{\text{entry} \mid \text{fights}\}A^{I} + (1 - \Pr\{\text{entry} \mid \text{fights}\})M\big) = A^{I}(1+\delta).$$

Rearrangement of this expression shows that the probability with which the second entrant enters, if the first entry was fought, must, therefore, be given by $1 - (A^{I} - P^{I})/\delta(M^{I} - A^{I})$. If the second entrant enters with this probability after the first-period entry was fought, the weak incumbent will be indifferent between fighting and accommodating in the first period and so will be prepared to randomize, satisfying condition (iv).

The remaining condition to be satisfied is (i), that the first potential entrant will enter. This will be true as long as $pP^{E} + (1-p)(\Pr\{f \mid w\}P^{E} + (1 - \Pr\{f \mid w\})A^{E}) \geq 0$.

The above example illustrates the nature of the Kreps–Wilson equilibrium in an extremely simple two-period example. The key point is the following: if the players' prior that the incumbent is tough is only p, in equilibrium entry will actually be fought in the first period with a probability greater than p since, not only does the tough incumbent fight, but also the weak incumbent fights with positive probability. If it fails to fight, it reveals its weakness and faces certain entry in the second period. By fighting, on the other hand, it keeps the entrants in doubt as to its true type, and this may deter second-period entry.

In models with more periods this effect is even more pronounced. Indeed, when there are many periods remaining, the weak incumbent will fight with certainty even if p is very low [see Kreps and Wilson (1982) for the details]. Thus, the firms need only assess a very small probability that the incumbent is of the type that would certainly fight (i.e. that the incumbent is "tough" or "irrational") in order for predation to be rational for "weak" or "rational" incumbents as well.

This example seems somewhat fragile for at least the following reasons: there is incomplete information only about the incumbent's costs, there are only two possible types of incumbent, and the incumbent faces a different potential entrant each period. However, Kreps and Wilson (1982) and Milgrom and Roberts (1982b) show that the reputation effect survives the relaxation of these assumptions.

These models with incomplete information are most powerful when there is long-term, but finite, competition. When the time horizon is infinite, we have seen that equilibrium predation strategies are easy (perhaps too easy) to find without appealing to incomplete information.[13] When the time horizon is short, on the other hand, and if predation is to be a rational strategy, the probability that the incumbent is "tough" can no longer be arbitrarily small.

The focus of the models discussed thus far is on the effect of predation on later entry. In practice, the incumbent may face entry from a number of different potential entrants in each of its geographical markets. Easley, Masson and Reynolds (1985) extend the analysis to this case and Lipman (1985) considers a continuous time version in which the incumbent faces a different potential entrant in each market and where any entrant can enter at any time. A novel feature of these models is that each entrant may decide to delay entry in the hope of learning something about the incumbent from the latter's response to entry by another potential entrant. If that is the case, even if predation does not succeed in deterring entry, it may nonetheless involve a welfare loss by delaying competition. It is not clear how important this effect is likely to be in practice, however, since there is a plethora of other pressures that drive the entrants towards early entry which may well be stronger than the incentive to delay.

3.1.3. Signaling predation

Recently, several models have been proposed that also rely on incomplete information but where, in contrast to the previous subsection, the incumbent's motive is to induce exit rather than to deter entry.

Suppose, for example, that firm 1 (which will emerge as the "predator") has constant marginal costs of production which are either high ($\bar{c}_1$) or low ($\underline{c}_1$). Let the probability that firm 2 assesses that $c_1 = \underline{c}_1$ be given by p. (As usual, p is common knowledge.) Now suppose that firm 2 has constant marginal costs of c_2. Finally, suppose that there are only two periods and that the firms use quantities as their strategic variable.

To make this setting interesting, assume that firm 2 can exit at the end of the first period if it wishes. Furthermore, suppose that it prefers to exit (stay) if it is common knowledge that it is facing the low-cost (high-cost) type of firm 1, i.e. $\pi_2^c(\underline{c}_1, c_2) < 0 < \pi_2^c(\bar{c}_1, c_2)$, where $\pi_2^c(\cdot)$ is firm 2's Cournot profits.

In this setting, firm 1 has an obvious incentive in the first period to convince firm 2 that its costs are low. In that case, firm 2 will leave the market to firm 1 which will then enjoy a monopoly in the final period. This is formally very similar

[13] One should not overstress the importance of the uniqueness of the equilibrium in these models. As Fudenberg and Maskin (1986) have shown, if one varies p (while still keeping it arbitrarily small), one can generate any pair of payoffs for the players that can arise in an infinitely repeated game.

to the limit-pricing model of Milgrom and Roberts (1982a). The only essential difference between the two models is that here firm 2 is already in the market whereas in the limit-pricing model, firm 2 is a potential entrant. In the analogous separating equilibrium, the low-cost firm 1 produces a sufficiently large output that the high-cost type is unwilling to replicate its behavior even if doing so means the difference between monopoly and duopoly in the second period.

In distinguishing itself from the high-cost firm, the low-cost firm produces more than it normally would and causes the first-period price to fall temporarily and results in the exit of firm 2.

Although the model and the equilibrium are closely related to the limit-pricing model, the analysis is somewhat more complicated. Here the amount that each firm of type 1 must produce in a separating equilibrium depends on what firm 2 produces. (When firm 2 is only a potential entrant this complication does not arise.) However, what firm 2 finds optimal to produce in turn depends on what each type of firm 1 produces. To see this, consider a simple example with linear demand, $P = a - bq$, where q is industry output. Let $\underline{q}_1$ and $\bar{q}_1$ denote the output choice of the low and high-cost types of firm 1, respectively.

Firm 2 chooses q_2 to maximize

$$p\{(a - b(\underline{q}_1 + q_2))q_2 - c_2 q_2\} + (1 - p)\{(a - b(\bar{q}_1 + q_2))q_2 - c_2 q_2\}. \tag{3.1}$$

Maximizing with respect to q_2 and rearranging gives the best-response function $q_2 = (a - c_2 - b(p\underline{q}_1 + (1 - p)\bar{q}_1))/2b$. Thus, q_2 depends on both $\underline{q}_1$and $\bar{q}_1$. Now, in a separating equilibrium, $\underline{q}_1$ must be sufficiently large so that the high-cost firm prefers to reveal its type rather than to mimic the low-cost type, i.e.

$$\begin{aligned}(a - b(\bar{q}_1 + q_2) - \bar{c}_1)\bar{q}_1 + \delta\pi_1^{c}(\bar{c}_1, c_2)\\ > (a - b(\underline{q}_1 + q_2) - \bar{c}_1)\underline{q}_1 + \delta\pi_1^{m}(\bar{c}_1),\end{aligned} \tag{3.2}$$

where $\pi_1^{m}(\bar{c}_1)$ is firm 1's monopoly profits in the second period when it is the high-cost type, and $\bar{q}_1$ is the high-cost type's "regular output". That is simply the output that maximizes $\bar{q}_1(a - b(\bar{q}_1 + q_2) - \bar{c}_1)$, i.e.

$$\bar{q}_1 = (a - bq_2 - \bar{c}_1)/2b. \tag{3.3}$$

In a separating equilibrium, therefore, the low-cost type chooses $\underline{q}_1$ to maximize $(a - b(\underline{q}_1 + q_2) - \underline{c}_1)\underline{q}_1$ subject to (3.2).

In the interesting case where (3.2) is a binding constraint, the equilibrium levels of $\bar{q}_1$, $\underline{q}_1$, and q_2 are obtained by solving (3.1), (3.2), and (3.3) simultaneously. In equilibrium, q_1 is often higher than it would be in a simple one-period game since the low-cost type is prepared to produce more than it otherwise would in order to credibly signal its type. But since q_2 is decreasing in q_1 from (3.1), this means that holding $\bar{q}_1$ constant, firm 2 will produce less. But this in turn means that the high-cost firm will produce more than it otherwise would since $\bar{q}_1$ is increasing in q_2 from (3.3).

The first-period separating equilibrium is therefore richer than in the Milgrom–Roberts limit-pricing model. There, the high-cost firm produces its usual one-period output and only the low-cost firm limits prices. Here, both types of firm 1 produce more than their one-period outputs (even though the high-cost firm is not signaling) and firm 2 produces less. The possibility that it is facing a low-cost firm and that such a firm would engage in a predatory expansion of output for signaling purposes intimidates firm 2 into reducing its output. This in turn provides an incentive to the nonsignaling high-cost firm to increase its output.

This formulation of the problem is adapted from Saloner (1987). However, several other papers demonstrate the same idea in different settings. The earliest model is probably due to Salop and Shapiro (1980).[14] They suppose that an entrant can enter a "test market" before committing itself to a national market. This provides the incumbent with an opportunity to demonstrate that it is the kind (low-cost) of firm that is not worth entering against in the national market. Their focus is on the pooling equilibrium. As discussed below, their formulation of "test-market predation" is used by Scharfstein (1984) to develop policy guidelines to prevent test-market predation. Finally, Roberts (1986) formulates an analogous model to the one analyzed above but where the incomplete information is about demand rather than costs. In that model, firm 2 observes only the industry price and not the output of firm 1. Firm 2 is unsure whether demand is high or low and attempts to infer this from the price it observes. For simplicity, Roberts assumes that the level of demand is the same in both periods. In equilibrium, a low price signals that demand is low and firm 2 chooses to exit.

In these models, even if exit is never optimal for firm 2, firm 1 may nonetheless have an incentive for output expansion. The reason is this: even if firm 2 does not leave, firm 1 would prefer firm 2 to believe that it is the low-cost rather than the high-cost firm. This is immediate from (3.1), which shows that q_2 is strictly decreasing in the probability that firm 2 assigns to firm 1 being low cost. If, ceteris paribus, the low-cost firm produces more than the high-cost firm, firm 2 in turn produces less if it believes it is facing a low-cost firm. This idea is originally

[14] In an early paper, Masson and Eisenstat (1975) suggest that asymmetric information may provide an incentive for predation in order to signal that costs are low. They do not present, however, an equilibrium model.

due to Mailath (1984) who derives the separating equilibrium for a continuum of types and also provides conditions for uniqueness of the equilibrium.

The above models typically use a two-period discrete time formulation. Also, one of the firms is typically assumed to be the "natural" predator. The symmetric case in which both firms may be unsure as to whether they can survive against their rival in the long run is examined by Fudenberg and Tirole (1986a). In their formulation, each firm knows its own costs but not those of the rival. In their model, pricing and output decisions are suppressed. Rather, the value of remaining in the industry if the rival has not exited is a general function of time. Thus, the only strategic decision is the exit decision.[15] The model is therefore a game of timing, with each firm deciding when to quit. In equilibrium, exit times are decreasing in the firm's true cost so that each firm becomes increasingly pessimistic about the prospects for driving its rival out as time progresses. An attractive feature of the model is that there is no artificial designation of the predator firm. Unfortunately, since pricing is suppressed, predatory pricing issues cannot be analyzed.

In the signaling models, the presence of incomplete information provides firm 1 with two incentives to increase output. The first is to induce exit, and the second is to induce the rival to curtail its production if it does not leave. These dual incentives have in common that they reduce the firm's perception of the profitability of remaining in the industry. This suggests a third incentive for predation in the first period and one that calls into question McGee's critique of predation: predation *in anticipation of merger* to "soften up" the rival and improve the takeover terms.

This incentive is explored by Saloner (1987). Formally, the above two-stage model is expanded to three. In the first period firms 1 and 2 choose outputs. At the end of the first period, firm 1 makes a take-it-or-leave-it takeover offer to firm 2. If firm 2 accepts the offer, firm 1 has a monopoly for the final period. If firm 2 rejects the offer, the firms again choose outputs in the final period (after firm 2 updates its assessment of the costs of firm 1 using the inferences it makes from firm 1's first-period output choice and its takeover offer price). Here, firm 1 has two incentives to convince firm 2 that its costs are low. If firm 2 believes it is facing a low-cost firm its expected profits in the second period are low and hence it will accept a low takeover price. Furthermore, if firm 2 rejects firm 1's offer (which it would never do in this equilibrium model but which it might do in a richer model with two-sided uncertainty), then firm 2 will produce less in the second period thereby increasing firm 1's profits. Thus, in this model, contrary to

[15] Exit decisions by firms have not been rigorously analyzed in a strategic context until recently. See for example, Ghemawat and Nalebuff (1985, 1987), Londregan (1986), and Whinston (1987).

McGee's claim, even if a merger is possible, strategic pricing is nonetheless likely to occur in order to improve the terms of an acquisition.

In this version of the model a merger is inevitable. Thus, the strategic pricing does not affect the ultimate industry structure, merely the terms at which the monopolization is achieved. Therefore, strategic pricing would not be considered "predatory" under most definitions,[16] since the acquirer's pricing strategy is not responsible for the elimination of the target. However, if there is the possibility of entry in the final period, then the merger is not necessarily inevitable. For example, suppose that the entrant will enter only if the existing firms merge and the entrant believes that firm 1 is the high-cost firm. In that case, the merger will not occur unless the potential entrant has been convinced that firm 1 has low costs. Then, an expansion of output by firm 1 in the first period can achieve several objectives: it can convince the potential entrant to stay out if a merger occurs, it can thereby convince firm 2 to merge, and, finally, it can convince firm 2 to sell out on favorable terms. In this model, the output expansion serves both a limit-pricing function [à la Milgrom and Roberts (1982a)] and a predation function.

A recent study of the activities of American Tobacco from 1891 to 1906 by Burns (1986) lends considerable support to the contention that predatory pricing can improve the terms of a takeover. During that period, American Tobacco acquired some 43 rival firms. Burns estimates that the alleged predation is associated with up to a 60 percent reduction in the acquisition costs of American Tobacco. The benefits of the predation are estimated to have more than offset the reduction of profits during the predatory episodes.

The above signaling models have in common that firm 1 is better informed about some payoff-relevant variable (costs or demand) than is firm 2, and increases its output to signal to firm 2 that conditions are, in fact, not amenable to its continued presence. Much of the same behavior can, however, be derived even when there is no incomplete information but rather uncertainty and imperfect observability. Models of this type have been developed by Riordan (1985) and Fudenberg and Tirole (1986b).

The focus of Riordan's paper is the relationship between a firm's output choice and its rival's past actions, rather than on predation. However, his model is easily adapted to consider predatory pricing. He studies a two-period model like those considered above. In his model, however, demand is uncertain each period and, in contrast to Roberts' model, neither firm has superior information about the level of demand. In addition, neither firm observes the other's output (even ex post). Furthermore, exit is assumed not to be possible. The key assumption is that demand is intertemporally positively correlated. Thus, in the first period, each firm would like to convince its rival that demand is low since the latter will

[16]See the discussion in Section 6 below on formal definitions of predation.

then produce a low output the following period. Since only price is observable, the firm accomplishes this by producing more in the first period than it otherwise would. The observed price is then low leading to the inference that demand is low. Even though the rival firm is not fooled in equilibrium, the firm must still expand output since, otherwise, a high price will result which will lead the rival to make an inference that demand is higher than it actually is. If, in addition, exit were possible, however, a firm that could convince its rival that demand was sufficiently weak might be able to induce the latter to leave the market.

The Fudenberg and Tirole model is similar except that they assume that the uncertainty is about firm 2's fixed costs rather than about demand and the firms have price as the choice variable. Thus, firm 2 observes its profits net of fixed costs but not the fixed costs themselves nor firm 1's price. Firm 1 now has an incentive to engage in secret price-cutting since in so doing it lowers firm 2's net profits. Firm 2 then infers that its fixed costs are relatively high and may exit. The purpose of firm 1's action is to make it harder for firm 2 to infer what its true fixed costs are. Fudenberg and Tirole refer to this attempted tampering with the signal that firm 2 receives from the market about its fixed costs as "signal jamming". This is a good label for the behavior but not for the outcome since, in equilibrium, firm 2 is not fooled and makes the appropriate inferences despite firm 1's attempt to mislead it.

As suggested by the work of Fudenberg and Tirole (1984) and Bulow, Geanakoplos and Klemperer (1985), the conclusions of many of the above models are reversed if the decision variable is changed from outputs to prices with differentiated products or vice versa. For example, in the Roberts or Riordan models, if price were the strategic variable, then firm 1 would want to convince firm 2 that (current) demand is high which would entail charging a higher-than-usual price. The Fudenberg and Tirole model is immune to this criticism since firm 1 wants to convince firm 2 that its profits are low. To do this, it must "attack" firm 2's first-period profits, which it can do either by lowering its price secretly or by expanding output. Similarly, in the Saloner model, firm 1 needs to convince its rival that its profits would be low if it stayed. Since it is signaling that it has low costs, it could do this either by expanding output or by lowering price in a differentiated products model.

3.1.4. Concluding remarks on theories of predatory pricing

The image that populist stories of predatory pricing conjure up are of weak rivals being driven into bankruptcy by the industry giant. Yet the strand of work that has received the most attention, namely the signaling models, is of the gentle persuasion variety. The "predator", with a moderate show of strength, persuades the rival that its resources would be better spent elsewhere. And the reputation models are silent on the question of how the exit is achieved. While there is nothing to say that the populist view is the correct one, it is nonetheless probably true that the most fruitful avenue for further work is in developing models in which the financial constraints are carefully modeled.

While the long purse story may be able to claim an older ancestry, the signaling models have the edge in their handling of entry. Whereas the long purse story must appeal to the reputations models for its explanation of why the incumbent is not faced with new entry when it attempts to raise its price post-exit, the signaling models have no such problems. The very signaling that induces the entrant to leave the market also persuades others not to enter.

As a final comment, it is worth noting that with the exception of the infinite horizon reputations model, every formal model we have discussed relies on some form of asymmetric information.[17] It is, however, possible to develop other models in which predation is feasible and rational but where all firms are perfectly informed. In industries which are subject to increasing returns, perhaps because of the benefits from compatibility, entrants may only have a small "window of opportunity" for successful entry. If the entry is sufficiently delayed, then the incumbent may be able to close the window of opportunity by pricing aggressively until its secure position has been achieved. Models in which strategic/predatory pricing emerges as a result of the presence of compatibility benefits have been analyzed by Farrell and Saloner (1986a), Hanson (1985), and Katz and Shapiro (1986).

3.2. *Nonprice conduct aimed at eliminating competitors*

In the previous subsection we examined how a firm could use price as a weapon to drive a rival out of the market and discourage future entry. In this subsection we describe some nonprice mechanisms for achieving the same ends. Unfortunately, the scenarios reviewed below have not attracted the same amount of rigorous analysis as the pricing games.

3.2.1. *Predatory product innovation*

Recall that we have identified two conditions that are necessary for predatory pricing to be effective, namely that the predator must be capable of driving the rival out of the market, and that it must be able to enjoy a higher level of profitability once that has been achieved. The first condition may be substantially easier to achieve through new product innovation than through a price reduction. Consider the simplest case examined by Ordover and Willig (1981). Suppose that

[17]See Milgrom and Roberts (1987) for a critique of asymmetric information games.

the predator and the rival are producing identical products at marginal costs of c per unit and are competing in prices. Suppose, furthermore, that the predator introduces a new product which it can produce at constant marginal cost of $c + d$ per unit and which consumers value some amount, $e > d$, more than the old product. The equilibrium when the two firms remain active in the market is for the predator to price the new product at a little less than $c + e$. In that case it earns profits while the rival makes no sales. If the rival has even small fixed costs, it will then choose to exit. If there are re-entry barriers, defined as the cost that a firm that has exited a market must incur to resume production, the predator will then be able to raise its price.

Notice that so long as the rival remains viable (so that the price cannot exceed $c + e$), the innovation increases welfare. Yet, if the innovator can raise the price to the monopoly level, there may well be a welfare loss even though the quality of the product has been increased. Schwartz (1985) has demonstrated, however, that the Ordover–Willig characterization of anticompetitive, exit-inducing innovations is unsatisfactory. He shows in a simple model of pre-innovation duopoly that there exist socially valuable innovations which are profitable only due to the monopolist profits forthcoming from the induced exit of the competing duopolist. Schwartz's results are not surprising, given the well-known disparities between social and private incentives to innovate. Consequently, the rationality of anticompetitive product introductions remains unexplored despite its obvious policy relevance. This is unfortunate because, intuitively, such strategies are not subject to the McGee–Easterbrook objection that they impose a higher cost on a predator than on the prey. This point is elaborated in a recent paper by Campbell (1986) that shows in the context of location models that product *redesign*, which makes the incumbent's product more like the entrant's product, can impose greater costs on an entrant than on the incumbent.[18] However, Campbell does not show that the incumbent would so redesign its product in a perfect equilibrium. Indeed, Judd's (1985) analysis shows that the incumbent may have an incentive to redesign its product to accommodate an entrant's new offering.

3.2.2. *Predatory compatibility changes*

A special case of predatory product innovation, and one which has been the subject of a great deal of antitrust litigation in the United States, occurs when the dominant manufacturer of a system redesigns the system so as to render the components incompatible with those of its rival's components. Even if the old system can still be offered, if the new system is superior, as we discussed above, it

[18] In his attempt to define anticompetitive product innovations, Campbell (1986) makes a distinction between product changes that are designed to increase the firm's own area of consumer interest and those that are designed to diminish the consumer area of a firm's rival. Such a distinction seems spurious since most desirable (and welfare-reducing) design changes have both effects.

can be priced in such a way as to eliminate the sales of the old system. If entry to the new system is foreclosed to the rival and re-entry with the old system is difficult, the predator will be able to raise prices to the monopoly level. Even if the rival is able to compete in the market for the new system, if redesigning its components is time-consuming, the predator will at least be able to enjoy a temporary price increase. [See Ordover and Willig (1981, 1982) for a more detailed discussion of this phenomenon, Farrell and Saloner (1986b) for a general discussion of competitive compatibility issues, and Besen and Saloner (1987) for an exhaustive review of the theoretical literature and its application to policy in the market for telecommunications services.]

3.2.3. Predatory vertical restraints

Ordover, Sykes and Willig (1985) have argued that a firm which has a dominant market position may have an incentive to extend that dominance by integrating forward into its downstream market. This, of course, does not occur if the other firm has an uncontested monopoly position upstream and sells to identical downstream buyers who use the input in fixed proportions and employ a CRS production technology. In that case, the firm is able to appropriate all the potential gains to monopoly power by means of a "perfect price squeeze". If either of the "ifs" fails to hold, however, it may be possible for the firm to extend its monopoly power. The possibility for anticompetitive conduct arises when such leveraging requires that the dominant firm induces the exit of an efficient (or even more efficient) downstream supplier.

Suppose, for example, that there are two groups of final consumers. One group has a higher willingness to pay for either the good produced by the upstream firm alone, or for the system consisting of one unit of the good produced by the upstream firm and one unit of the good produced by the downstream firm. In such situations, the profit-maximizing pricing scheme may involve a low price for the upstream good (which is then purchased only by the low valuation consumers) and a relatively high price for the bundled system (which is purchased by the high valuation consumers). In the presence of competing downstream firms, however, this price discrimination scheme cannot be effectively carried out since the high valuation users will be able to put together a low-priced good from the upstream firm with a low-priced good from the rival downstream manufacturers.

A variety of strategies may enable the upstream firm to extend its market power in these circumstances. For example, where the downstream good must be used with the upstream good as part of a system, the upstream firm can attempt to condition the sale of the upstream good on the purchase of its brand of downstream good; or it can make the warranty of the upstream good conditional on the use of its brand of downstream good. Alternatively, where the upstream and downstream goods must be physically interconnected, the upstream firm can offer its component to rival sellers at a disadvantageous price. All of these strategies which disadvantage downstream rivals may raise welfare, if price discrimination is desirable, for example. And they frequently have a sound business rationale as when informational imperfections require tying of components in the market. In limited circumstances, the exclusionary strategies mentioned above result in undue restrictions on the scope of choices open to consumers and may harm welfare.

3.2.4. Predatory product preannouncements

Farrell and Saloner (1986a) show that an action as seemingly benign as a firm (truthfully) announcing in advance that it will introduce a new product at some future date can eliminate competition and reduce welfare. In markets characterized by demand-side economies of scale, consumers may become "locked-in" to a technology that achieves a sufficiently large "installed base" of users (once the installed base is large enough, the benefits of "going along with the crowd" may outweigh the benefits from the new technology). In such a setting, a firm that has new technology may be able to prevent the lock-in by announcing its product in advance and giving consumers that have not yet purchased the old technology the opportunity of waiting for the new technology. In this way the new technology may be adopted, whereas it would not have been adopted before. If the new technology is proprietary, the rivals may be eliminated by this strategy. Moreover, even though the new technology is preferred by new consumers, the consumers who have already purchased the old technology are "stranded". Overall, welfare may be reduced.

4. Putting rivals at a disadvantage

Most of the attention in the literature has been devoted to attempts by incumbents to reduce competition by eliminating their competitors. In contrast to attempts by incumbents to "muscle out" their rival, in this section we turn to actions which involve the use of "sabotage" by the incumbent to put the *rival* at a competitive disadvantage.

This goal can be accomplished by raising the rival's costs or by impairing its ability to generate demand for its product.[19] The line of work addressing these

[19] In a way, a low price (a predatory price) impairs a rival's ability to generate demand for its product as will redesign of needed components, as in Subsection 3.2.2 above. From this perspective many anticompetitive strategies put a rival at a disadvantage in the sense in this section [see also Campbell (1986)].

issues was initiated by Salop and his co-authors Krattenmaker, Scheffman, and Schwartz under the general rubric of "raising rivals' costs".[20]

An example of a cost-raising tactic is the signing of an exclusive dealing contract in which the supplier of an input agrees not to supply the rival firms. Another example, which falls short of outright exclusion, is taking actions that raise the price at which the rival can obtain the resources. Notice that it may be worthwhile for the firm to raise its own costs in order to raise those of the rival. This is important since the firm engaging in this exclusionary tactic may, for instance, have to pay a premium for an exclusive dealing arrangement. An example of a demand-impairing action is signing customers up to long-term contracts or refusing to participate in a joint-marketing arrangement with the rival (as occurred, for example, in the *Aspen* case). The rationale for categorizing both types of actions as "raising rivals' costs" is that in the case of a demand-impairing action the rival must incur additional promotional costs if it wants to restore its competitive position. However, since the rival need not necessarily respond by increasing its promotional effort, we prefer to use the broader (but less catchy) phrase "putting the rival at a disadvantage". In what follows we concentrate on cost-raising activities.

In any model, a firm's competitive position is improved if its rival is placed at a cost disadvantage. For example, consider two firms competing in Cournot fashion. Suppose they face constant marginal costs c_1 and c_2 and that the inverse demand function is linear, $P = a - b(q_1 + q_2)$. At the Cournot equilibrium, firm i's output is $q_i^c = (a - 2c_i + c_j)/3b$ and its profit is $\pi^i = (a - 2c_i + c_j)^2/9b$. Not surprisingly, in equilibrium firm i's profits are increasing in c_j so that firm i is always better off the higher its rival's costs.

Simply asserting that a firm would prefer its rival to be at a cost disadvantage does not, however, mean that it is feasible and profitable for the firm to place its rival at such a disadvantage. In particular, there are three issues that need to be addressed. First, when the firm raises the rival's costs by excluding its rival from access to some scarce resource, the current owner of the resource, understanding the value of its resource to the rival, ought not to give up its right to supply the rival for less than that value. Thus, the value of the exclusion to the firm engineering the exclusion must be greater than the value to the rival. Second, when its current suppliers are removed from the market or raise their prices, the rival must not be able to enter into a mutually profitable arrangement with substitute suppliers which would restore its competitiveness.[21] Third, the excluding firm must have some market power if it is to exploit the rival's disadvantage.

To see how the first of these conditions can be satisfied, consider the above Cournot example and examine the effect of an increase of c_j on the

[20] See Salop and Scheffman (1983, 1984, 1987), Krattenmaker and Salop (1986a, 1986b) and Salop, Scheffman and Schwartz (1984).

[21] That is, the rival cannot have available to it credible counterstrategies in the sense of Easterbrook (1981a).

profits of firm i and on those of the rival, firm j, itself. Differentiating we have $\partial\pi^i/\partial c_j = 2(a - 2c_i + c_j)/9b = 2q_i^c/3$ and $\partial\pi^j/\partial c_j = 2(a - 2c_j + c_i)(-2)/9b = -4q_j^c/3$. Therefore, the gain to firm i from an increase in c_j is (locally) greater than the loss to firm j from that increase provided $q_i^c > 2q_j^c$. Thus, in a Cournot model, provided firm i is more than twice the size of its rival, it would be willing to expend greater resources to raise its rival's costs than the rival would be willing to expend in an attempt to keep them down. This result follows from the fact that the large firm benefits more from a price increase than does its smaller rival.[22]

The second condition might be trivially satisfied. For example, the exclusive dealing contract may remove the low-cost suppliers of the input from the market leaving only the high-cost suppliers. However, the situation is not always as clear cut. For purposes of illustration, consider the case where all suppliers of an input have access to the same technology but where after some of them are removed from the market by an exclusive dealing arrangement, the remaining suppliers are able to increase the price they charge because of the more concentrated market structure that they now enjoy.

This case is less straightforward. The reason is that the pricing arrangement between the rival and the remaining firms is inefficient. Thus, the rival may be able to reach an agreement with the suppliers whereby suppliers reduce their prices to what they were before, in return for an appropriate side payment. In other words, the rival may have an effective *counterstrategy* to the firm that masterminded the foreclosure.

To see how this works, consider the following simple example. Suppose that two Cournot competitors use an input in fixed proportions that is supplied by either of two Bertrand suppliers. Suppose that demand for the finished good is given by $P = a - Q$ and that all costs are marginal costs which we set equal to zero for simplicity.[23] In that case, the Bertrand input suppliers charge zero for the input and the equilibrium in the finished goods market has $P = a/3$, $q_1 = q_2 = a/3$. The downstream firms' profits are $\pi^1 = \pi^2 = a^2/9$.

Now suppose that one of the downstream firms, say firm 1, purchases one of the input suppliers. The remaining input supplier becomes a monopolistic supplier to the rival. It sets its price, taking into account the effect on the demand of the rival. If the rival faces costs of $\underline{c}$ per unit, its equilibrium output is $q_2 = (a - 2\underline{c})/3$. The supplier therefore chooses $\underline{c}$ to maximize $\underline{c}(a - 2\underline{c})/3$, so it sets $\underline{c} = a/4$. The firms' profits are then $\pi^1 = (5a/4)^2/9$ and $\pi^2 = (a/2)^2/9 = a^2/36$.

[22]See Salop and Scheffman (1983) for the comparable analysis of a dominant firm facing a competitive fringe which we present in Section 6, below.

[23]This is a particularly simple form of the vertical structure. Greenhut and Ohta (1979) analyze the richer case where both tiers of the market are characterized by oligopoly.

It therefore seems as though this method of raising its rival's costs is profitable for firm 1.[24] But notice that firm 2 has an effective counterstrategy. Its input supplier is earning $((a - 2\underline{c})/3)(9/4) = a^2/24$. The combined profit of firm 2 and its supplier is therefore $a^2/36 + a^2/24 = 5a^2/72$. If these two firms were to enter into an agreement reducing $\underline{c}$ to zero, the situation would be restored to what it was before firm 1 had purchased its supplier. Then the combined profits of firm 2 and its supplier would be $a^2/9 > 5a^2/72$. There are thus gains to such an agreement. There are two main ways to obtain these gains: the firms could merge, or firm 2 could be charged a two-part tariff for the input (for example, it could be charged marginal cost plus a fixed fee to compensate its supplier for its lost profits).

It thus appears that firm 2 has an effective counterstrategy to firm 1's purchase of a supplier. This result depends, however, on the assumed quantity competition in the downstream market. In particular, it may not hold in the more realistic case where the firms produce differentiated products and use prices as the strategic variable.[25]

This can be seen from Figure 9.1. The firms' best-response functions prior to firm 1's merger with one of the input suppliers are given by BR_1 and BR_2. Firm 2's equilibrium level of profitability is illustrated by the isoprofit curve P. After the merger, however, firm 2's costs increase and its best-response function moves outwards since for any price of firm 1, firm 2 wants to charge a higher price than it did when it faced the lower pre-merger prices. We label the new best-response function BR_2' and the resulting equilibrium N'.[26] A particularly illustrative case is where N' is on P, as drawn.

The key question is what can be said about the firms' profitability at N' compared to that at N. Clearly, firm 1 is better off since its costs have not changed and both firms are charging higher prices. More importantly, the sum of the profits of firm 2 and its supplier are the same as at N. To see this notice that P represents firm 2's profits when it faces input prices of zero, which is equal to the input supplier's costs. Therefore, P also represents the sum of the profits of firm 2 and its input supplier for any price charged by the input supplier (and, in particular, for the price charged by the input supplier after the merger has taken

[24] In this simple example firm 2's loss exceeds firm 1's gain so that it would be surprising to see firm 1 outbid firm 2 for the input supplier. However, as we saw above, this would not be the case if firm 1 was significantly larger than firm 2. In any case, this is tangental to the point we are making here.

[25] The details of this analysis are being pursued by us in collaboration with Steven Salop.

[26] Notice that total output decreases in equilibrium. This is in contrast to the successive oligopoly models of Greenhut and Ohta (1979) and Salinger (1984). The outcome differs from those models because here the input suppliers are originally perfectly competitive. The merger does not produce any efficiency gains since there is no "double marginalization" to be avoided. If, in our example, there had been three input suppliers and the two remaining suppliers continue to compete in Bertrand style after the merger of the third supplier, then there would be no effect on output or price. If, on the other hand, the two remaining suppliers were now able to achieve some degree of implicit collusion and raise their prices, the conclusions derived above would go through as before.

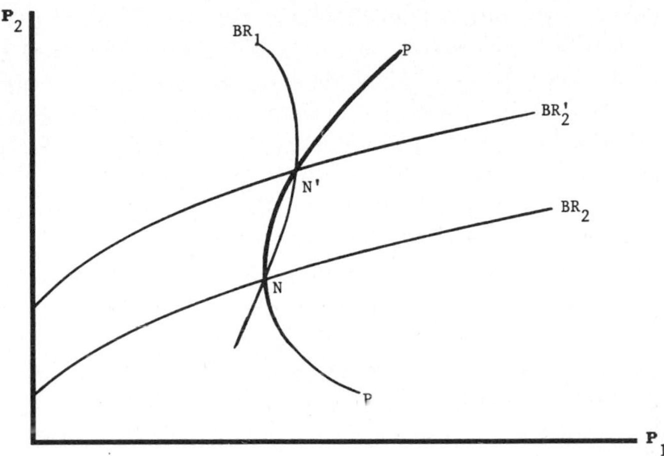

Figure 9.1

place). Thus, firm 2 and its supplier taken as a unit are indifferent between the new and the old equilibria (N vs. N'). Of course, firm 2's supplier is better off since it is now receiving a positive price. Therefore, firm 2 must be worse off.

The upshot of this is that firm 2 does not have an effective counterstrategy here: by merging with its supplier and restoring the equilibrium to N, the increase in firm 2's profits would be insufficient to compensate its supplier for the latter's loss in profits.

The net effect of firm 1's action is that it is better off, firm 2 is worse off, and firm 2's supplier is better off. The prices of both firms have increased and since they were too high to start with (from a social welfare point of view), social welfare has decreased.[27] This result holds not just for increases at N' but also in a neighborhood of that point.

Thus, raising rivals' costs may be achieved through excluding the rival from the low-cost suppliers of an input or by removing some of the potential suppliers from the market place. In the *Alcoa* case, for example, Judge Learned Hand reported that at one time Alcoa purchased from power companies the promise that they would not sell electricity to other aluminum producers and that Alcoa did not itself purchase electricity from them.

[27] In the case presented here, the firm is able to achieve an increase in the rival's costs by merging with just one upstream supplier. In general, it may have to merge with several. In that case, suppliers purchasing later will generally have more leverage and will demand a higher price. Of course, farsighted early firms will realize the benefits they confer on later target firms and will attempt to appropriate some of these gains. These issues are discussed by Mackay (1984).

Raising rivals' costs through exclusionary practices comes in a variety of guises. For example, an extreme case is where the firm forecloses access to *all* suppliers of an essential input: as in the essential facilities problem. Another example is where a purchase contract between the firm and a supplier contains a restrictive covenant in which the latter agrees to sell to the rival only at unfavorable terms. This kind of restriction, litigated in the *Klor's* case, for example, is much more common than the naked restraint exemplified by the exclusionary rights in the *Alcoa* case.

In these cases, the effect of the increase in the rival's cost is to reduce its market share. A more extreme case is where the increase in costs renders future participation unprofitable for the rival so that it leaves the market. Clearly, if this is the case, the incentives for a firm to raise its rival's costs are even greater than otherwise. Williamson (1968) discusses how this strategy might have been employed in the *Pennington* case, where the defendant was accused of attempting to drive rival companies out of coal mining by securing an increase in industry-wide wages through negotiations with the union. [See also Maloney, McCormick and Tollison (1979) on the effects of unionization on industry profits.]

A great virtue of this general approach is that it encompasses a wide range of potentially anticompetitive practices. Unfortunately, the development of the theory lags somewhat behind the potential applications. The ability of a firm to outbid its rival for access to the resource as well as the rival's ability to respond to the increase in its costs depends on the exact nature of the foreclosure. As we saw above, it is also sensitive to the model formulation. Additional theoretical work seems warranted. Furthermore, virtually all the work in this area has focused on cost-raising techniques. Demand-impairing actions have not received much attention.

5. Government facilitation of anticompetitive behavior

In the preceding sections we surveyed the conduct of dominant firms in laissez-faire markets. In this section we focus on incentives for anticompetitive behavior in scenarios in which "government" plays an explicit role. These scenarios are of interest for at least the following three reasons. First, novel incentives for anticompetitive behavior may arise in such situations (Subsection 5.1). Second, the misuse of governmental powers may provide an extremely effective anticompetitive tool, as when it leads to the exclusion from the market of new firms which may be more efficient than the incumbent. In particular, manipulation of the political process may be an effective method of raising rivals' costs (Subsection 5.2). Third, in the international context, predatory activity can be undertaken by governments on behalf of home firms or facilitated by various industrial policies of the home government (Subsection 5.3).[28]

5.1. Anticompetitive practices and a regulated firm

Rate of return (ROR) regulation can provide a dominant firm with novel incentives for engaging in behavior that excludes from the market an equally (or more) efficient rival. To see how this occurs, assume that the allowed rate of return, s, exceeds the true cost of capital to a firm, r. This implies that the potential flow of profits to the ROR regulated firm reflects the margin, $s - r$, applied to the firm's total capital stock, K. Consequently, the firm has an incentive to take actions to increase its capital stock even if such actions are not otherwise profitable or efficient. Thus, we are dealing here with yet another perverse effect of ROR regulation, some of which have been noted by Averch and Johnson (1962) and Wellisz (1963) [Ordover, Sykes and Willig (1985)]. Here, it is important to realize that a ROR regulated firm that engages in an Averch–Johnson (A–J) type of anticompetitive activity does not require a period of recoupment during which the profits dissipated by the anticompetitive activity are made up and more. In fact, the regulated firm may maintain its inefficient (exclusionary) activity forever, or until it is sued by its rivals, and finance the losses with inefficiently high prices in other markets in which it does not face competition. Consequently, predatory activity by an inefficiently regulated firm is not subject to the usual criticism that it will never be undertaken by a rational firm because recoupment may be impossible [Brennan (1986a)].

To see how A–J predation works, consider the following scenario which is explored by Ordover, Sykes and Willig (1985, section 3). The regulated firm, firm A, offers two complementary or vertically integrated services, 1 and 2. There are Q identical consumers who are willing to pay b for a system comprising one unit of each service. The regulated firm has a protected monopoly in the provision of service 1. Service 2 is, however, open to competition. Production costs for the regulated firm are as follows:[29]

$$\text{Service 1:}\quad C_{A1} = V_1 Q + rK_1,$$

$$\text{Service 2:}\quad C_{A2} = V_{A2} Q + rk_{A2} Q,$$

[28] Strategic trade policies are reviewed more extensively in Dixit (1985). See also Chapter 20 by Paul Krugman in this Handbook.

[29] We assume that capital is used in fixed proportions here so that the usual A–J input distortion does not arise.

where, V_1 and V_{A2} are unit variable costs, K_1 is capital used in service 1, and k_{A2} is the capital–output ratio in service 2. For the rival firm, firm B, the unit cost is c_{B2}.

We now analyze the incentives for firm A to gain control over service 2 in a variety of scenarios. Assume first that firm B supplies service 2. Then, A's prices are

$$P_1^* = b - c_{B2}, \qquad \text{if ROR constraint is not binding}$$

and

$$P_1^* = V_1 + sK_1/Q, \quad \text{if ROR constraint is binding.}$$

Here, as before, s is the allowed rate of return. Thus, by producing service 1 alone, firm A can earn a profit equal to

$$\min\{(s-r)\cdot K_1, Q[b - c_{B2} - V_1] - rK_1\}.$$

Next, assume that A has a monopoly over the provision of services 1 and 2. Firm A's prices are now

$$P_{12}^* = b, \qquad \text{if ROR is not binding,}$$

and

$$P_{12}^* = V_1 + V_{A2} + sk_{A2} + sK_1/Q, \quad \text{if ROR is binding.}$$

Thus, the firm can earn profits equal to

$$\min\{(s-r)\cdot(K_1 + k_{A2}Q), Q[b - V_{A2} - V_1 - rk_{A2}] - rK_1\}.$$

To ascertain A's incentives to exclude firm B from the provision of service 2, we must consider the maximum profits A can earn in various possible scenarios. These scenarios differ according to how efficient A is in the provision of the service in question and whether the rate of return constraint is binding or not. Plainly, iff the constraint is never binding (because b is low, for example) then A will monopolize 2 iff $V_{A2} + rk_{A2} < c_{B2}$. However, if the constraint binds even when A provides only service 1, then it can earn $(s-r)Qk_{A2}$ in additional profits regardless of which firm is the lowest cost supplier. If $c_{A2} = V_{A2} + rk_{A2} > c_{B2}$, then A can monopolize service 2 only if it engages in anticompetitive activities such as tying the sale of service 2 to the sale of service 1, redesigning service 1 to make it incompatible with the variants of service 2 produced by rivals and so on. (Note that if $c_{A2} < c_{B2}$, all the standard tests would detect predatory pricing of service 2 by firm A.)[30]

Brock (1983) doubts whether rate-of-return regulation provides strong incentives to engage in predatory cross-subsidy. He points out that "because a rate-of-return regulated firm uses an inefficient input mix, it has a higher actual cost.... As a result [it] tends to produce at least one product at a lower level than any reasonable social benchmark." For example, one such benchmark could be the vector of output produced by the firm in the partially regulated second-best (or Ramsey) optimum. Brock shows that in a two-product case, the welfare effects of a dominant firm aggressively displacing the fringe's output are ambiguous. Brock agrees, however, that even though cross-subsidy may be a "poor investment" for the regulated firm, the "gain to predation... through the indirect effect of rate base augmentation" cannot be entirely disregarded, as we have shown in the beginning of this section. Brock also points out that if regulation is likely to be looser in the future, then the likelihood of price predation as compared to the no-regulation case is increased, ceteris paribus. As Brock also observes, the regulation also opens up the possibility of anticompetitive activity through investment in *barrier-to-entry capital of a political form*. Such an investment makes sense if the regulated firm wants to protect its rate base or if it must raise entry barriers in order to ensure sustainability. We take up these and related matters in the next subsection.

5.2. Anticompetitive uses of the political and legal process

Perhaps one of the most efficient methods for disadvantaging existing and prospective competitors that is available to an incumbent firm is through the strategic use (or abuse) of the political and legal process. Disadvantages inflicted upon the existing rival and the entry barriers created by means of such strategies are frequently more permanent than those that could be generated through more standard means. In addition, because they often constitute an exercise of other important rights, such as the First Amendment and due process rights in the United States, these strategies are generally more difficult to detect or control [Bork (1978), Brock (1983), Baumol and Ordover (1985)].[31] Indeed, in the United States, the courts have formulated an exception to the Sherman Act, the *Noerr–Pennington* doctrine, according to which concerted action consisting solely of activities aimed at influencing public officials does not violate the Sherman Act. Thus, the Noerr–Pennington doctrine leaves a great deal of room for an

[30] For the analysis of other possible cases, see Ordover, Sykes and Willig (1985).

[31] Brock (1981) provides an extensive, if somewhat tendentious, history of AT&T's uses and abuses of the regulatory process to control competitive entry into the provision of long-distance telephone services and terminal equipment.

active use of the governmental process with the purpose of disadvantaging established rivals and deterring future entry.

The courts also constitute an arena in which anticompetitive strategies can be implemented. [See Baumol and Ordover (1985) for some examples.] There, however, unlike in the political arena, it is frequently the weaker or smaller firms rather than the dominant firms that are more likely to take an activist role. Indeed, the data base developed by the Georgetown Project on Private Antitrust Litigation[32] indicates that plaintiffs tended to be much smaller than the defendants, that many of the allegedly anticompetitive practices are not likely to have anticompetitive effects [Salop and White (1985, table 5)], and that many of the plaintiffs were dealers of the defendant's products [Salop and White (1985, table 6)] who most likely employed the antitrust law opportunistically.

Despite the importance of these issues, their analytic treatment in the economic literature is not entirely satisfactory probably because of the difficulty in modeling the political process itself. Brock (1983) argues that the dominant firm's activity in the regulatory arena can be modeled as an investment in barrier-to-entry capital of a political form.

The fringe firm solves the standard static profit maximization problem:

$$\max_{\{q\}} pq - q^2/2L(k),$$

where, $L(0)$ and $L(\infty) > 0$, $L' < 0$. As modeled, the fringe firm's unit production cost depends on the stock of barrier-to-entry capital accumulated by the dominant firm. Fringe firms are assumed not to have any direct regulatory costs, although $L(k)$ can be interpreted as reflecting the optimal level of regulatory expenditures by a representative fringe firm.

The dominant firm maximizes the discounted present value of profits by selecting the path of investments in regulatory activity:

$$\max_{\{I(t)\}} \int_0^{\infty} \mathrm{e}^{-rt}(p - c) \cdot \{(\bar{y} - q) - p_{\mathrm{I}} I\} \mathrm{d}t$$

$$\text{s.t.} \quad \dot{k} = I - \delta k,$$

$$k(0) = k_0, \quad 0 \leq I \leq \overline{M},$$

where $\bar{y}$ is the fixed market demand, q is the fringe's supply, p_{I} is the price of the unit of investment in political barrier-to-entry capital whose stock is denoted by k, and whose flow is I.

[32] Salop and White (1985, 1986) describe the data base and the key findings.

Now assume that $L'' < 0$ if $k < \tilde{k}$ and $L'' > 0$ if $k \geq \tilde{k}$. These conditions ensure that near $\tilde{k}$, a small investment in political/regulatory activity significantly deters entry. However, at small values of k_0, the efficacy of such investment is low. Brock shows that if a dominant firm starts with a low level of the relevant capital (say a small legal staff and a small stable of economists), it may choose not to invest in political/regulatory entry-deterring activities. If, however, k_0 exceeds some critical level the dominant firm will make such an investment. From this exercise, Brock concludes that "the formation of k should be discouraged with as much vigor as possible". Whether such a policy prescription is sound and whether it can be implemented is more problematic. First, much of the predatory activity of this type can be performed using variable inputs such as outside counsel and economists. Consequently, discouragement of the accumulation of k need not yield desirable results. More efficacious may be disadvantageous tax treatment of legal and related expenses. Second, Brock's suggestion seems to imply that firms should be discouraged from developing the capability to react skillfully to their regulators. This may have highly undesirable welfare consequences, if the regulatory process is not perfect.[33]

Salop, Scheffman and Schwartz (1984) also treat investment in political activity as a method of raising rivals' costs. They construct a model which enables the analyst to sort out market failure rationales for a particular regulation from rent-seeking, special interest rationales. Indeed, the Salop–Scheffman–Schwartz model does not admit market failure. Instead, it identifies the industry characteristics and those aspects of the regulatory process that are conducive to rent-seeking, special interest, or competition-disadvantaging regulatory activities by firms.

The set-up is a standard extension of the raising rivals' cost approach [see Salop and Scheffman (1983, 1984)]. The dominant firm's costs, $A(x, r)$, and rivals' costs, $B(x, r)$, depend on output, x, and on the value of the regulatory parameter, r. If B_r and $B_{rx} > 0$, then the dominant firm will profit from an increase in r, as long as the impact of an increase on its own cost is moderate, in a sense that can be made rigorous within the model. When both A and B do not collude after the regulation is imposed, then firm A benefits from more stringent regulation if

$$\partial p^{s}/\partial r \geq (\partial A/\partial r)/x,$$

where Q is total output and $p^{s}(Q, r)$ is the supply price function. Hence, the impact on profits is $\partial \pi^{A}/\partial r \geq 0$, if and only if the market supply curve shifts up by more than the dominant firm's average cost. A sufficient condition is that the common increase in marginal cost, ΔMC, exceeds $\partial(A/x)/\partial r$. Most interestingly, the authors demonstrate that whereas $\partial Q/\partial r < 0$, we cannot deduce from

[33]This has been pointed out to us by Richard Schmalensee.

changes in the individual firm's output whether this firm has benefited or not from a more stringent regulation [Salop, Scheffman and Schwartz (1984, result 4)]. This is an important finding because antitrust analysts often look to output effects of a practice as indicators of underlying incentives and overall welfare effects. In any case, the analysis shows that, ceteris paribus, the larger are the partial derivatives, $\partial A/\partial r$, $\partial B/\partial r$, $\partial(A/x)/\partial r$, $\partial(B/x)/\partial r$, and the demand and supply elasticities, ε^{D}, ε^{S}, the stronger are the incentives for pursuing anticompetitive strategies in the political/regulatory marketplace.

As stated, the model is not closed because the supply side of regulatory actions has been left unspecified. The supply side must reflect the reality of the political process. What that reality consists of depends on the specifics of the situation. For example, the political process may be willing to "supply" the regulation only if both A and B gain, or A gains more than B loses, or A gains [Salop, Scheffman and Schwartz (1984), Ordover and Schotter (1981)]. Of course, A is more likely to abuse the political/regulatory process under the third of these regimes. The second regime is interesting because it suggests a possibility of competition for the regulators' favors. How costly it will be for A to obtain them depends again on details of political process.

The Salop–Scheffman–Schwartz analysis greatly clarifies the linkages between the individual incentives of firms to engage in rent-seeking activities that disadvantage rivals and the actual mechanics of the supply of regulation. It is thus a significant advance over much of the rent-seeking literature.

There is some, albeit scant, empirical evidence on the strategic abuses of the regulatory process. For example, Bartel and Thomas (1986) demonstrate that U.S. work safety regulations (OSHA) and environmental protection regulations (EPA) have differentially disadvantaged small and large firms and firms located in diverse geographic regions of the United States. Thus, Bartel and Thomas show that OSHA and EPA regulations might have increased profits of large firms by as much as 3 percent and those located in the northern states by as much as 9 percent. They also show that unionized workers have been able to capture a significant portion of the rents generated by predatory regulatory activity. Similar findings of strategic abuses of the regulatory process can be found in Marvel (1977) and Oster (1982) [see also, Pashigian (1984, 1986) and Evans (1986)].

An important extension of the rent-seeking, responsive-protectionism literature would be to examine the incentives of management-operated firms to influence the political process. The extensive protectionist lobbying by major U.S. corporations indicates that senior management of these firms expect to benefit from protectionist regulations which hobble and restrain competitors. But what about the owners of these firms? The issue does not arise when owners are also managers or when owners have all the relevant information so that they can induce the first-best supply of effort and optimal choice of investments from the managers. When information is asymmetric, moral hazard problems intrude. In the presence of moral hazard, a reduction in market competition can exacerbate the principal–agent conflict, leading to inefficiencies in firms' operations.

This can be demonstrated in a simple model [Willig (1985)] of a managerial firm in which the owner's payoff is some function $V(c, b)$, $V_c > 0$, where c is an observable measure of cost and b is a statistic that reflects the intensity of market competition; $c = \theta/e$, where θ is a random variable $\theta \in [\theta_0, \theta_1]$; and e is the manager's effort. Manager's utility is $U(R, e) = R - \alpha e$, where $R(\cdot)$ is the compensation schedule. The manager reports θ which elicits $R(\theta)$, his payment, $c(\theta)$, the cost target, and $\phi(\theta)$, the probability that the firm will be operated. Then, unless $\theta = \theta_0$, the firm's costs are higher than they would be if the owner knew the realization of θ. Changes in market conditions, operating through the parameter b, affect managerial utility and profits. For example, if an increase in b implies an increase in the elasticity of demand at the initial equilibrium level of output, then this form of increased competitive pressure benefits management while maintaining profits at the original level [Willig (1985)]. Other forms of increased competition may, however, lower managerial utility.

These findings are important because they suggest that the economic consequences of increased protectionist activity may depend on how the activity affects the product market interactions among rival firms. Furthermore, in the principal–agent context, the owners must simultaneously choose compensation schedules that provide managers with the correct incentives to invest in cost-reduction and rent-seeking (protection-generating) activities. Given the maintained assumption of asymmetric information, the key analytic question is whether managers will overinvest resources in protectionist activities as compared to the amount that would have been expended by the owners. Briefly, then, modeling rent-seeking activities must reflect the potential conflict of interest between managers and owners.

5.3. Anticompetitive practices in an open economy

In many domestic industries, import competition substantially reduces the sales of domestic producers. In principle, such competition is highly desirable from the social welfare standpoint. Occasionally, however, import competition may reduce nationalistic social welfare or may have otherwise unfair economic and social consequences. In this subsection we briefly survey some novel policy considerations that arise when assessing anticompetitive conduct in international trade. In particular, these special considerations relate directly or indirectly to the policies of foreign governments [Ordover, Sykes and Willig (1983)]. In fact, were it not for the potential role that a foreign government can play in determining the outcome of competitive interactions in the international market place, the analyses of various anticompetitive practices presented earlier in this chapter would carry over without any significant modifications.[34]

When a foreign government precommits to a strategic subsidy or tariff, it can move the equilibrium of a game played by its firms against firms which are domiciled elsewhere. We refer to the latter as domestic firms. When the nonintervention equilibrium entails rents, by acting as a Stackelberg leader, the foreign government can redistribute the potentially available rents in favor of *its* home firms. This is, perhaps, the key insight yielded by the application of strategic industrial organization models to international trade.[35] From the standpoint of domestic welfare, the consequences can be mixed: domestic consumers are likely to benefit from the strategic actions of the foreign government while domestic firms lose. The losses to firms, in terms of diverted profits, can, in principle, outweigh gains in consumers' surplus causing domestic social welfare to fall. This would render the actions of the foreign government anticompetitive, if anticompetitive practices were to be defined as any practice which lowers domestic social welfare. Yet, there is no persuasive reason why the foreign government should be kept to the same standards of conduct as that which applies to domestic and foreign *firms*. In particular, the notion that the foreign government should pursue (innocent) profit-maximizing strategies is not compelling. On the other hand, foreign firms which can be presumed to be profit maximizing and which are direct beneficiaries of their home government's actions need not have themselves engaged in actions that would violate the test for anticompetitive conduct offered in Section 2 of this chapter.[36]

One way out of this policy conundrum is to confine antitrust scrutiny of behavior to conduct of firms and leave the scrutiny of governmental policies to international trade authorities. A difficult middle ground arises when the foreign government merely acts to facilitate anticompetitive behavior by coordinating export policy. The *Japanese Electronics* case presents a market scenario which has not been fully explored in the economics literature. In that case, the plaintiffs alleged that Japanese exporters of television sets engaged in predatory cartel behavior designed to eliminate American manufacturers of television sets. They also alleged that predatory conduct was facilitated by the Japanese government's export policies, which required each Japanese exporter to sell only to assigned U.S. accounts, as well as by maintained and condoned collusion among Japanese

[34] It may be more difficult, however, to actually carry out the tests of anticompetitive conduct. For example, cost calculations relevant for cost-based tests of predatory pricing are made even more complicated than they usually are because of fluctuations in the exchange rates. Some additional difficulties are discussed in Ordover, Sykes and Willig (1983a) and Ordover (1987).

[35] The relevant literature is surveyed by Paul Krugman in Chapter 20 of this Handbook and Dixit (1985). See also the volume edited by Krugman (1986b).

[36] In the famous *Polish Golfcart* case, the District Court noted that passing on the benefits of a subsidy to consumers in terms of lower prices constitutes a normal response to market opportunities, *Outboard Marine Co. v. Pezetel*, 461 F. Supp. 384 (D. Del. 1978).

firms in their home market, which had the effect of increasing incentives to export into the lucrative U.S. market. The analytically interesting problem raised by the *Japanese Electronics* case is whether or not collusive predation is ever possible and how the incentives to predate are related to the home market structure of the foreign firms.[37]

6. Tests of anticompetitive behavior

In the preceding sections we surveyed many different aspects of strategic marketplace competition. We have shown that in some instances such strategic business conduct not only harms competitors but also augments the ability of the dominant firm to maintain, or even increase, a supracompetitive rate of return on its investments. In other words, by its tactics, a dominant incumbent can harm the competitive process and lower long-run social welfare. This observation suggests a deceptively simple test, or definition, of anticompetitive conduct in the context of strategic interactions surveyed in this chapter. According to this definition, *business conduct would be deemed anticompetitive if it were to injure competitors and reduce the level of long-run social welfare relative to the level that would be attained in the absence of the complained-of conduct or business tactic.*

There are many problems with this definition-cum-test of anticompetitive behavior. Perhaps the most severe is its implementability in the adversarial setting of antitrust litigation. Such an open-ended inquiry into the welfare effects of business conduct would not only consume significant resources but, more importantly, because of its complexity, would frequently lead to erroneous results. Furthermore, by its very nature, such an open-ended test of anticompetitive conduct would complicate business planning and might increase incentives for anticompetitive abuse of antitrust laws [Baumol and Ordover (1985)].

Recognition of the difficulty in formulating legal rules for determining anticompetitive conduct in strategic environments has provoked at least three different responses. The first response has been to urge removal of virtually all constraints on single firm behavior, including the behavior of dominant firms. The rationale for this position is that firms reach a dominant position by virtue of

[37] The key issue here is whether predatory firms can effectively free-ride on each others' investments in anticompetitive activities. Plainly, to the extent that anticompetitive conduct entails sacrifice of current profits for future increments in market power, each firm would prefer others to make that sacrifice. Hence, predatory firms must evolve some mechanism for effecting collusion and for punishing those who deviate from the collusive strategy. What this punishment amounts to is not obvious: predation already involves pricing low which clearly rules out low prices as the appropriate punishment. Hence, in the predatory context, punishments must involve reverting to high prices (or low levels of output). A related problem of collusive entry-deterrence has been explored by Harrington (1984). Parenthetically, we may add that the Supreme Court found the plaintiffs' contentions factually absurd.

business acumen, or luck, and to restrain their behavior penalizes bigness and creates discincentives to aggressive competition. Furthermore, proponents of this view perceive markets to be quickly self-correcting so that any marketplace advantages which are not related to superior skill and efficiency are quickly eroded. Consequently, anticompetitive conduct is, in general, unprofitable.[38]

The second response has been to propose a narrowing down of possible scenarios in which a firm's conduct could be scrutinized for its possible anticompetitive effects. This would be accomplished by postulating a set of "filters" designed to screen out potentially meritorious claims of anticompetitive conduct from those that are most likely without merit [Joskow and Klevorick (1979), Easterbrook (1984)]. Claims which have passed through these filters could then be assessed by means of simple, well-defined standards, such as the Areeda–Turner (1975) standard for predatory pricing which compares price to the appropriate marginal cost. The rationale for this public policy response is that anticompetitive behavior is rare, but it cannot be ruled out completely. The two-stage procedure of filtering out claims and then applying simple rules to assess conduct effectively reduces the risk of labeling vigorous procompetitive conduct as anticompetitive. Avoiding this type of error is conceivably more important, from a public policy standpoint, than committing the converse error of labeling conduct as procompetitive which, in fact, is anticompetitive.

The third response posed by the conundrum of analyzing competitive behavior in strategic settings calls for open-ended rules. This position is expounded by Scherer (1976), for example. According to Comanor and Frech (1984), who also adopt this view, a strategic perspective demands "a detailed investigation of the purpose and effects of specific acts under the Rule of Reason". As such, this approach harks back to the more traditional antitrust methodology which focused on purpose and intent and eschewed simple rules.[39]

In our view, simpler, more explicit tests of anticompetitive behavior are likely to be preferable, even if in some circumstances these tests would produce type I and type II errors. In the rest of this section, we review some of these tests, examine their welfare properties, and conclude that additional research is needed

[38]This position is well articulated by McGee (1958, 1980). See also Easterbrook (1984). The recent U.S. Supreme Court decision in the *Japanese Electronics* case [*Zenith Radio Corp. v. Matsushita Elec. Indus. Co.*, 494 F. Supp. 1190 (E.D. Pa. 1980); *Matsushita Elec. Indus. Co. v. Zenith Radio Corp.*, 106 S. Ct. 1348 (1986)], has fully accepted the view that rational anticompetitive behavior is likely only if the firm can expect to recoup the upfront costs of its anticompetitive campaign. Schmalensee (1987) reviews the literature on the causes and persistence of dominant market positions and develops the point that workable, welfare-enhancing rules for single-firm conduct are difficult to devise when competition is imperfect. See also Mueller (1986) and Encaoua, Geroski and Jacquemin (1986).

[39]Sullivan (1977) provides an excellent exposition of the "traditional" approach to the analysis of anticompetitive conduct.

to determine how well these tests perform in a wide variety of realistic market scenarios.

Much of the extensive relevant literature has concerned itself with deriving tests of predatory pricing. This is so for two reasons. First, the classic form of predation allegedly entails a dominant firm selectively cutting its prices, driving a smaller rival out of the market, and then raising its price, being no longer constrained by the forced-out rival. The second reason is that much of the modern legal-economic scholarship on predation grew out of the response to the article by Areeda and Turner (1975), which developed a cost-based test of predatory pricing.

(1) *The Areeda and Turner rule* (1975, 1978). Areeda and Turner (A–T) have proposed that any price above reasonably anticipated short-run marginal cost should be lawful. Conversely, a price below short-run marginal cost should be deemed unlawful. Turning to the actual application of their standard, they note that calculations of marginal costs may be difficult. Consequently, A–T propose that the average variable cost be used as a workable surrogate for marginal cost. Thus, under a modified A–T test, a price below a reasonably anticipated average variable cost is presumptively unlawful. The rationale for the A–T cost-based test is obvious: a perfectly competitive firm sets its profit-maximizing output at the level at which $p = MC$. Any price lower is not short-run profit-maximizing, hence must involve sacrifice of profits, which is the first prerequisite for predatory conduct.

The A–T test has been embraced by U.S. Courts in many antitrust cases. Some courts have, however, opted for different, and potentially more stringent, cost-based price tests entailing, for example, average total cost floors. Areeda (1982), Hurwitz and Kovacic (1982), Hovenkamp (1985), and Areeda and Hovenkamp (1986) provide summaries of the pertinent case law and the emerging trends in judicial analysis of predation. The test itself has been scrutinized by Scherer (1976), Brodley and Hay (1981), Hay (1981), Zerbe and Cooper (undated), as well as others.

Two main criticisms have been levied against the A–T test for predatory pricing. The first is technical and pertains to the use of AVC as a surrogate for MC. Here the basic point is that in some instances MC can be significantly above the AVC, which makes it easier for a dominant firm to engage in predatory price-cutting without violating the standard. In other instances, when there is substantial excess capacity, AVC can be significantly below MC. To suggest, as A–T have done, that AVC can be used as a surrogate only when it does not significantly differ from MC, defeats the whole purpose of using this surrogate cost measure in the first place. Indeed, A–T's analysis of the appropriate measures of AVC is rather inadequate. It does not derive the correct cost concepts from the analysis of the predatory conduct itself and, consequently, does not provide clear guidance of how to treat such important components of total cost as capital and advertising expenses. Ordover and Willig (1981) provide an extensive discussion of the cost concepts pertinent for the analysis of predatory conduct using cost-based price floors.[40]

The second, most important criticism of the A–T test goes to the core of the test itself. It questions whether *MC* is the correct price floor: whether some potentially higher price floor would not be more appropriate from the welfare standpoint given the strategic nature of predatory conduct. Inasmuch as the welfare properties of marginal cost pricing are based on static considerations, these are not necessarily the relevant ones for the analysis of inherently strategic interactions between the dominant incumbent firm and its actual and prospective rivals. As we have shown in equations (2.1) and (2.2) in Section 2, in a strategic context the firm must account for the effects of its actions on rivals and for rivals' reactions to its actions. Consequently, the selection of a behavioral rule that is totally divorced from strategic interactions seems to beg the question of how anticompetitive conduct is to be handled in a strategic context.[41] The essence of these strategic interactions is in the consequences of the alleged predator's conduct on the viability and profitability of its rivals, actual and potential. From that vantage point, the relationship between the predator's marginal cost and price loses much of its probative value. For example, in fully specified models of reputational and signaling predation, such as those reviewed in Subsections 3.1.2 and 3.1.3, successful predation does not necessarily require prices below *MC* or *AVC*. It requires, however, prices that convey to the rival the signal that it should not enter or remain in the market. Such prices bear no systematic relation to the incumbent's *AVC*. Similarly, in models in which an entrant has only a small "window of opportunity", as when there are significant externalities related to the size of the installed base of the product, a temporary price reduction can deny the entrant the only chance to introduce its product. In this scenario, the level of price is chosen with an eye towards attracting the newly arriving customers to the installed base and away from the entrant's product. Such a level of price is obviously related to the relative benefits of the two competing products (plus whatever externalities flow from the installed base). Production costs themselves are less pertinent.

Yet, the rationale for using *MC* as the appropriate price floor is quite appealing. It stems from the fact that uninhibited competitive interactions, say à la Bertrand, can drive the price down to the level of marginal cost. Hence, an imposition of a cost-floor test more stringent than the *MC* will constrict the scope of competitive interactions in the marketplace. At the same time, restrain-

[40]See also Areeda (1982).

[41]Ordover and Willig (1981) show that the Areeda–Turner test can be derived from a fully strategic analysis but only under very restrictive assumptions.

ing an incumbent's responses to competitive entry may facilitate socially desirable entry. This is emphasized by Williamson (1977) in his critique of the Areeda–Turner test. This point can be made more rigorous by means of a simple example [Dasgupta and Stiglitz (1985)]. Assume a market for a homogeneous product with $D'(p) < 0$. Every potential firm has constant production costs of $\underline{c}$. Bertrand competition leads to $p^* = c$ and zero profits for all participating firms. Assume that there are two potential competitors, I and E. Firm I is already in the market. Firm E can either enter or stay out. To enter it must incur K in sunk costs. If entry occurs, I and E select prices simultaneously. Finally, let $\bar{\pi}$ denote monopoly profits exclusive of entry costs. Then Dasgupta and Stiglitz (1985) show that if $0 < K < \bar{\pi}$, there is a unique (subgame) perfect equilibrium in which firm E does not enter and I earns $\bar{\pi} - K$.

Now assume that the predation rule prohibits prices at or below average long-run cost. In the example at hand, $p_{\min} = c + K/\bar{q}(p_{\min})$, where $\bar{q}(p_{\min})$ is the volume of sales per firm if both firms are in the market and both charge $p_{\min}$. Hence, $\bar{q}(p_{\min}) = 1/2D(p_{\min})$. Let $p_{\min} + \delta$, δ arbitrarily small, be the minimum nonpredatory price, then there is a unique subgame perfect equilibrium in which both firms enter and charge the minimum nonpredatory price [Dasgupta and Stiglitz (1985)]. If K is small, $p_{\min} + \delta \approx c$, hence the average cost rule induces an approximately welfare optimal outcome. However, as K gets higher, the inefficiency from having two firms in the market begins to weigh heavier and may even exceed the inefficiency from monopolistic pricing in the presence of scale economies which would be sustained by the A–T rule.

(2) *The Joskow and Klevoric rule* (1979). The test developed by J–K to test for predation attempts to capture the strategic aspects of conduct alluded to above. J–K advocate a two-tier approach to testing for predatory pricing. The first tier examines the *structural* preconditions for the likelihood of successful and rational predation. These structural preconditions include (a) the dominant firm's market share; (b) the size of other firms in the market; (c) the stability of market shares over time; (d) the dominant firm's profit history; (e) residual elasticities of demand; and (f) the conditions of entry. The first-tier tests are designed to filter out allegations of predatory conduct which are likely to be proved baseless.

In those markets in which preconditions for rational successful price predation are satisfied, J–K impose a stricter cost-based price floor than proposed by A–T. J–K first argue that MC is not the appropriate floor. Instead, they note that prices below AVC are presumptively illegal because at such prices the predator is not even covering avoidable costs. More importantly, they argue that any price below the average *total* cost should be presumptively illegal. This is because in a competitive market, the equilibrium price will equal ATC and, furthermore, it is highly unlikely that a post-entry price in a market predisposed to predation would be so low as to impose losses on the incumbent dominant firm. The J–K test does allow for this latter possibility, however, by permitting an affirmative defense demonstrating that the price below *ATC* is short-run profit-maximizing.[42]

J–K also consider the possibility that temporary price cuts to a level above *ATC* could be predatory. According to J–K, a price cut to a level above *ATC* would be predatory if it were reversed within a reasonable period of time, say two years. In this, they follow Baumol (1979) whose predation rule is discussed below.

(3) *The Posner rule* (1976). Posner's test substitutes long-run *MC* for the cost floors in the A–T test. Posner recognizes that predation is a strategic, long-term phenomenon and hence must be assessed using long-run cost standards. According to Posner, a price below *LRMC* is presumptively predatory when coupled with the intent to exclude an equally or more efficient competitor. How to determine intent is not fully explained by Posner.

(4) *The Williamson rule* (1977). Williamson develops a rule for predation which aims to capture the strategic aspects of anticompetitive conduct. The novelty of Williamson's approach is that it does not focus directly on cost–price comparisons in testing for predation against a new entrant. Instead, Williamson's rule would deem as predatory any "demand adjusted" output expansion in response to new entry. Conversely, if the incumbent maintains or constricts its output following entry, it behaves in a nonpredatory manner, according to Williamson's rule. However, the incumbent's output level, whether higher or lower than the pre-entry level, would be deemed predatory if following entry the market price for its product were to fall below *AVC*.

Whereas the theoretical underpinnings for the A–T test were provided by the standard model of short-term profit maximization in a competitive market, Williamson's rule builds on a model of limit pricing and entry deterrence. Williamson's scenario is that of an incumbent firm prepositioning itself to combat a potential entrant, in the event that the potential entrant actually comes in. To that extent, the Williamson scenario appears more relevant to the problem of designing rules that would curb socially undesirable entry-deterring strategies.

Regarding welfare properties of his rule, Williamson argues that the incumbent subject to the no-expansion rule chooses a pre-entry level of output which is higher than the level that it would select if it were constrained by A–T's *MC* [or *AVC* rule]. Insofar as higher output implies a higher level of welfare, Williamson's rule is superior to the A–T rule. However, other considerations intrude. If the incumbent is more constrained under the Williamson rule than it would be under the A–T rule, it may find it more difficult to deter entry. Consequently, an incumbent constrained by the nonexpansion rule may choose accommodation, while the incumbent constrained by the *MC* price floor may select deterrence. To the extent that in some circumstances entry deterrence leads to higher social

[42] Williamson (1977) adopts both *SRAC* and *LRAC* floors for predatory prices against established rivals; his "loose oligopoly" case.

welfare than does accommodation, Williamson's rule is welfare-inferior to the A–T rule. Thus, Williamson's demonstration that the output restriction rule is welfare-superior to the marginal cost rule is not uniformly valid. This issue is extensively discussed by Reynolds and Lewis (undated). [See also Easley, Masson and Reynolds (1985).]

(5) *The Baumol rule* (1979). Contestability theory provides the theoretical underpinnings for the predation rule developed by Baumol. Baumol's rule would prohibit a dominant firm from cutting its price(s) in response to entry and then reversing the price cut once the entrant has left the market. That is, Baumol would permit the incumbent firm to react aggressively to entry provided that it then maintains the level of price for a prespecified period of time. In essence, Baumol's rule is concerned less with price cuts than with reversals of price reductions, although Baumol introduces a side constraint that the price cannot fall below the average incremental cost (AIC).[43]

In support of the rule, Baumol reasons that an incumbent firm subjected to his rule would select the pre-entry price which yields it the maximum available rate of return, consistent with the existing entry barriers. In particular, if these entry barriers are minimal or nonexistent, the incumbent's pre-entry price would generate approximately a normal (competitive) rate of return. There is no reason, however, for this claim. As long as entry is not instantaneous, an incumbent may initially maintain a supracompetitive price and then, following entry, lower it to a level determined by the post-entry game between itself and the entrant. Indeed, the incumbent may find it optimal to set the pre-entry price at the unconstrained monopoly level. Furthermore, if the incumbent can credibly threaten with an output expansion and a low price following entry, as it can under the Baumol rule, it may thereby deter an equally efficient entrant [Dasgupta and Stiglitz (1985)]. This means that the Baumol rule does not invariably lead to a socially optimal outcome. The difference between the contestability result and the outcome in the predatory setting considered by Baumol lies precisely in the fact that contestability analysis assumes that the incumbent cannot respond to the lower price offered by the entrant.

The preceding tests or rules for defining predatory behavior focused on pricing. In particular, they have focused on price responses by a single-product firm to entry or a threat thereof.[44] Surely, potentially anticompetitive conduct encompasses a richer class of business strategies than product pricing. And within the

[43]AIC of product i is defined as

$$AIC_i(y) = [C(y_1,\dots,y_i,\dots,y_n) - C(y_1,\dots,y_{i-1},0,y_{i+1},\dots,y_n)]/y_i,$$

where $C(\cdot)$ is the total cost function. AIC is, therefore, a generalization of an average cost for multi-product cost functions.

[44]Ordover and Willig (1981) discuss the modifications in the cost-based price floors for multi-product firms. Areeda (1982) argues that no modifications are necessary. Baumol (1986) provides an interesting critique of Areeda's position.

category of predatory pricing itself, various forms of anticompetitive conduct can also be distinguished, as we have demonstrated in Section 3 [see also Salop and Shapiro (1980)]. Rules for defining predatory conduct that apply to a wide range of business practices have been developed by Ordover and Willig (1981) and by Salop et al. [Salop and Scheffman (1983), Salop, Scheffman and Schwartz (1984), and Krattenmaker and Salop (1986b)].[45] Whereas Ordover and Willig attempt to provide a general standard for judging predation, Salop et al. focus explicitly on business strategies that raise rivals' costs.

(6) *The Ordover and Willig rule* (1981). The approach adopted by O–W is to begin with a general definition of predatory conduct and to then derive specific tests of predation from the rule itself. They define predation as "... a response to a rival that sacrifices part of the profit that could be earned, under competitive circumstances, were the rival to remain viable, in order to induce exit and gain consequent additional monopoly profits". In other words, a particular response to entry violates the O–W standard if (i) the incumbent had available another response to entry that would have been less harmful to the rival; (ii) when viewed ex ante, the incumbent's chosen action must have been more profitable, given the rival's exit, than the less harmful alternative action; and (iii) assuming that the rival remains a viable potential competitor in the market, the incumbent's chosen response, when viewed ex ante, is less profitable than the alternative less harmful action.

The O–W definition, and the tests derived from it, can be best interpreted as an attempt to reinterpret expression (2.2) in Section 2, which we repeat here:

$$\frac{\mathrm{d}\pi^{\mathrm{I}}}{\mathrm{d}a_0^{\mathrm{I}}} = \frac{\mathrm{d}\pi_0^{\mathrm{I}}}{\mathrm{d}a_0^{\mathrm{I}}} + \frac{\partial \pi^{\mathrm{f}}}{\partial a_1^{\mathrm{I}}} \cdot \frac{\mathrm{d}a_1^{\mathrm{I}}}{\mathrm{d}a_0^{\mathrm{I}}} + \frac{\partial \pi^{\mathrm{f}}}{\partial a_1^{\mathrm{E}}} \cdot \frac{\mathrm{d}a_1^{\mathrm{E}}}{\mathrm{d}a_0^{\mathrm{I}}} + \frac{\partial \pi^{\mathrm{f}}}{\partial a_0^{\mathrm{I}}} .$$

According to O–W, the choice of a_0^{I} is not anticompetitive as long as the derivative $\mathrm{d}a_1^{\mathrm{E}}/\mathrm{d}a_0^{\mathrm{I}}$ is reinterpreted as reflecting a counterfactual state-of-the-world in which an entrant remains viable despite the incumbent's chosen action. Viability simply means that an entrant who has been induced to exit can costlessly reenter the market. A viable entrant exercises a competitive constraint equal in its effectiveness to that of a dormant firm that has merely shut down its operation without dispersing productive assets while waiting out the predatory campaign.

This can be restated more precisely. Let $\underline{a}_0^{\mathrm{I}}$ and $\underline{a}_0'$ be two alternative current actions that the incumbent can take in response to entry. Action $\underline{a}_0^{\mathrm{I}}$ induces exit, hence is potentially anticompetitive, but $\underline{a}_0'$ need not. Let a_1^{E} take one of three "values", depending on whether the entrant is "in", whether it is "out", and whether it is "viable". Again, being "viable" is a counterfactual action or state of

[45]Areeda (1982) provides some arguments why nonpricing conduct should be excluded from the purview of predatory analysis.

the entrant. Then action $\underline{a}_0^{\mathrm{I}}$ is predatory if:

$$\text{(i)}\quad \pi_0^{\mathrm{I}}(\underline{a}_0^{\mathrm{I}}) + \pi^{\mathrm{f}}(a_1^{\mathrm{I}}|\underline{a}_0^{\mathrm{I}}, \text{entrant "out"})$$

$$> \pi_0^{\mathrm{I}}(\underline{a}_0') + \pi^{\mathrm{f}}(a_1^{\mathrm{I}}|\underline{a}_0', \text{entrant "in"}),$$

$$\text{(ii)}\quad \pi_0^{\mathrm{I}}(\underline{a}_0^{\mathrm{I}}) + \pi^{\mathrm{f}}(a_1^{\mathrm{I}}|\underline{a}_0^{\mathrm{I}}, \text{entrant "viable"})$$

$$< \pi_0^{\mathrm{I}}(\underline{a}_0') + \pi^{\mathrm{f}}(a_1^{\mathrm{I}}|\underline{a}_0', \text{entrant "in"}).$$

Condition (i) says that action $\underline{a}_0^{\mathrm{I}}$ is more profitable than the alternative action $\underline{a}_0'$ if $\underline{a}_0^{\mathrm{I}}$ induces exit and $\underline{a}_0'$ does not. Condition (ii) says that assuming counterfactually that under $\underline{a}_0^{\mathrm{I}}$ the entrant remains viable, then $\underline{a}_0'$ is more profitable with the entrant remaining in the market. In the nonstochastic setting, an entrant's viability is coextensive with being in the market, albeit not necessarily producing.

Both conditions are needed for a test of predation. If (ii) were not present, (i) would require, for example, that the incumbent has a duty to ensure the rival's survival in the market. Condition (ii) alone would mandate that the incumbent selects that action that maximizes its discounted present value of profits on the condition that the entrant is in the market. This is undesirable: an entrant could claim predation if the incumbent refused to play a Cournot strategy instead of engaging in Bertrand competition, for example. Viewed another way, condition (ii) captures the profit sacrifice entailed by the choice of action $\underline{a}_0^{\mathrm{I}}$, were the entrant to remain viable. Condition (i) shows the profit motive behind the actual choice; the choice of $\underline{a}_0^{\mathrm{I}}$ yields higher *actual* discounted profits. The expression also shows that predation is not a rational strategy if the rival's exit does not yield any additional profit relative to the situation in which it remains a viable competitor.

For each category of conduct, a different test of predation is needed precisely because in every case the alternative less harmful response will be different. For example, when the alleged predatory action involves a price cut that induces a rival's exit, a less harmful response would entail the incumbent charging a higher price and selling less of its product. In fact, the application of the O–W standard to price cuts yields the familiar cost-based tests of predatory pricing in some market scenarios. The standard also yields tests for predatory product innovations, as we have discussed in Subsection 3.2. The application of the standard to product innovations suggests that (i) raising the price of some system components needed by a rival supplier may be a useful predatory strategy; (ii) market acceptance is not conclusive evidence of the economic superiority of a new product;[46] and (iii) predation may be a successful strategy when a vertical price squeeze cannot be effectively implemented [Ordover, Sykes and Willig (1985)].

The O–W standard has been criticized for being difficult to implement, for being opaque, for being divorced from standards of economic efficiency, and for being potentially harmful to dynamic efficiency by virtue of discouraging product innovations. These criticisms can be found in Easterbrook (1981b, 1984), Scheffman (1981), Sidak (1983) and Schmalensee (1985). A more positive assessment can be found in Fudenberg and Tirole (1986b) and Williamson (1982) [see also, Ordover, Sykes and Willig (1983b) for a partial response to the critics].

(7) *The Salop et al. rule* [Krattenmaker and Salop (1986b)].[47] Salop et al. have analyzed business strategies designed to elevate rivals' costs. In Section 4 we have discussed these strategies at some length. According to the S–S–K standard, a practice, such as an acquisition of an exclusionary right, is anticompetitive if (i) it significantly raises rivals' marginal costs; and (ii) the firm that has implemented the cost-increasing strategy can increase its price after its rivals' costs have been increased, i.e. the strategy incremented the firm's control over price, hence its market power. According to S–S–K, the firm engaged in allegedly anticompetitive cost-raising conduct would have two affirmative defenses against the allegation of exclusionary conduct. First, it could demonstrate that its rivals have available to them effective counterstrategies which would shield them from the adverse effects of the initial strategy and which could actually render the initial strategy unprofitable. Second, the firm could demonstrate that the practice, while harmful to consumers, nevertheless yields such efficiencies that, on balance, aggregate social welfare is increased.

The appeal of the S–S–K approach is that it focuses on those types of business conduct which, while potentially anticompetitive, do not necessarily require the incumbent to sacrifice current profits for the sake of future gain. In the S–S–K model, anticompetitive behavior need not entail intertemporal profit sacrifice, it does not require the rival's exit, and it does not require any pre-entry positioning moves. Anticompetitive behavior consists of strategic conduct that raises rivals' costs. Once this conduct is adopted, harmed rivals instantaneously cut back on output. The dominant firm can then immediately increase its market share or raise price or both. Hence, the risks associated with standard predatory strategies are reduced because higher profits accrue instantaneously. Consequently, this type of anticompetitive conduct is feasible even if the dominant firm does not have a deeper pocket or superior access to financial resources.

The classic scenario for the Salop–Scheffman type of anticompetitive conduct involves a dominant firm facing a price-taking fringe. The dominant firm selects

[46] For a judicial discussion of the issue, see *Berkey Photo. Inc. v. Eastman Kodak Co.*, 603 F. 2d 263 (2d Cir. 1979).

[47] Theoretical underpinnings of the rule are presented in Salop and Scheffman (1983, 1986) and Salop, Scheffman and Schwartz (1984).

action a which elevates costs. The dominant firm's problem is to select market price, p, and the level of the action variable, a, which maximizes its short-run profit, namely

$$\max_{\{p,\,a\}} p \cdot x - C(x, a)$$

$$\text{s.t. } x = D(p) - S(p, a): \quad a \geq 0.$$

To make the problem interesting, we assume that $C_a > 0$ and $S_a < 0$. A sufficient condition for the optimal value of a to be positive is[48]

$$1/\left[1 + s \cdot \varepsilon^{\mathrm{D}}/(1-s)\varepsilon_{\mathrm{s}}^{\mathrm{F}}\right] > \Delta AC_{\mathrm{D}}/\Delta MC_{\mathrm{F}}, \tag{6.1}$$

where ε^{D} and $\varepsilon_{\mathrm{s}}^{\mathrm{F}}$ are the elasticities of market demand and fringe supply, respectively; $s = x/D(p)$; ΔAC_{D} and ΔMC_{F} represent, respectively, the strategy-induced *changes* in the dominant firm's average cost (C_a/x) and the representative fringe firm's marginal cost (which equals $-S_a/S_p$). The policy question is whether *any* choice of a that satisfies (6.1) is to be regarded as anticompetitive.

Thus, from the policy standpoint, the S–S–K approach invites inquiry into the likelihood that a particular exclusionary strategy (such as boycott, refusal-to-deal, tie-in, or vertical merger) will have anticompetitive effects. The inquiry proceeds in two stages. First, it must be determined whether the strategy will significantly elevate rivals' costs, as captured in expression (6.1) above. To this end, S–S–K suggest an approach related to the methodology in the U.S. Department of Justice Merger Guidelines where the likelihood of the anticompetitive effects of a merger is gauged, at the preliminary level, by calculating the Herfindhal–Hirschman Index (HHI) of concentration for the relevant market and then comparing it to the appropriate benchmark [Krattenmaker and Salop (1986b)]. Krattenmaker and Salop then develop additional "objective" criteria, such as "cost share" and "net foreclosure rate", which are needed to evaluate the likelihood of anticompetitive effects from an exclusionary strategy in various strategic contexts.

The second stage of the appropriate inquiry involves determining whether the cost-raising strategy increased the firm's ability to raise price. Here, again, S–S–K would rely on structural characteristics of the relevant market. However, they caution that standards for horizontal mergers should not be adopted without modifications which are appropriate to the "vertical" nature of many of the exclusionary strategies.

[48]This is a correct version of equation (2) in Salop and Scheffman (1983).

The S–S–K approach is subject to at least two criticisms.[49] First, it leaves open the question under what conditions rivals cannot render unprofitable the exclusionary strategy pursued by a firm which is determined to harm them. If any exclusionary strategy can be met with an effective counterstrategy, then rivals have little to fear from cost-raising tactics. We have demonstrated that whether a rival has access to an effective counterstrategy depends on the details of the analyzed situation. Second, the S–S–K rule may potentially stymie competitive interactions among rival firms. This is because in some instances such interactions do raise rivals' costs and enable one firm to subsequently increase market price. For example, rendering a complementary component incompatible with a rival's components may be an inevitable outcome of R&D rivalry among firms. Yet, such redesigns could raise a rival's costs and increase the innovator's market power. Nevertheless, the methodology developed by S–S–K puts some coherence and rigor into the analysis of exclusionary strategies.

7. Conclusions

The discussion in the preceding section suggests that none of the rules, standards, and tests of predatory conduct invariably leads to higher social welfare in the long run when applied to realistic market situations. This is not surprising. Anticompetitive behavior can manifest itself in many different ways. It is unreasonable to expect, therefore, that one rule will be equally applicable to all types of conduct in all possible market situations. However, the problem is even worse than that. When perfect competition is not attainable, and the market is not fully contestable, there is no presumption that more firms in the market is preferable to fewer firms. Consequently, rules which restrict the ability of firms to deter entry in the first place may stimulate undesirable entry.[50] And, conversely, this means that rules regulating the strategic conduct by dominant firms must carefully weigh the considerations of salutary effects of entry and of unrestricted competition among incumbent firms. This is not an easy balance to strike. On this score, as of this writing, theoretical industrial organization economics provides only limited guidance for policy-makers.

Nevertheless, some important policy lessons have been generated by the strategic models of single-firm conduct. First and foremost, the strategic approach has been effective in debunking the comfortable proposition that predatory conduct is more costly to the predator than to the prey and, hence, is irrational and not likely to occur. It has been demonstrated in Section 3, that in a

[49] Brennan (1986b) provides an extensive critique of the S–S–K approach.

[50] The social desirability of entry is analyzed in a number of papers. For more recent contributions, see Bernheim (1984) and Mankiw and Whinston (1986).

variety of realistic market settings, anticompetitive conduct is feasible and profitable. The old "new learning" derived its key proposition about the profitability of anticompetitive conduct by focusing on price predation rather than on the richer set of business strategies. Furthermore, the implicit models which underpinned the key conclusions of the old "new learning" did not fully reflect the nature of strategic market interactions. The "new learning" does not lend a credence to the populist view that dominant incumbent firms have almost unbridled power to control the behavior of rivals and to deter entry.

Second, this insight has also brought the recognition that no single "bright-line" standard for defining predation can be expected to correctly proscribe any behavior which reduces welfare and to promote procompetitive conduct. This is because the market settings in which predation is rational deviate along many dimensions from the perfectly competitive ideal. Markets in which predatory conduct is rational are characterized by imperfect and asymmetric information, scale economies, intertemporal and intermarket cost and revenue linkages, barriers to entry and reentry, etc. As Ordover and Willig noted, "...it is unreasonable to expect workable tests for predatory conduct to accomplish more than the cure of the social ills from predation" [Ordover and Willig (1981)]. Yet in markets in which predatory conduct is likely and profitable, more far-reaching competition policy may be desirable.

Third, much of the policy debate over standards for predatory pricing has not been properly grounded in sound economic models in which price predation is rational. As the models of Subsection 3.1 indicate, price predation is most likely to be effective in markets in which entrants are significantly less informed than are the incumbent firms. This means that the analysis of informational asymmetries characterizing a particular market may be of significant importance for testing the claim that rational predation has occurred. We do not know of a single antitrust case in which this issue has been explicitly raised.

Fourth, the focus on price predation seems misplaced given the richness of strategies employed by firms in their battles for market share [Porter (1980, 1985)]. In fact, many of these strategies are more likely to be successful than would be price predation, given the reversibility of price commitments. Regarding nonprice and cost-raising predation, simple cost-based rules are often inadequate for discerning predatory from nonpredatory conduct. However, standards for nonprice and cost-raising predation are not as fully developed and their welfare properties less fully scrutinized than one would wish for final policy recommendations.

Even though great strides have been made, the strategic approach to antitrust is not yet fully developed. There has been little work testing the empirical content of various strategic models of firm behavior. In this regard, the work of Burns (1986) and West and von Hohenbalken (1986) is especially valuable. Experimental work by Harrison (1985), Isaac and Smith (1985a, 1985b), not reviewed here, is also valuable for testing the predictive power of various models of anticompetitive conduct. On the theoretical side of the enterprise, additional work on nonprice and cost-raising, rival-disadvantaging predation is clearly warranted. Finally, a better understanding of how the sophisticated strategic analyses can be translated into workable standards, which can be applied in the context of antitrust litigation and business counselling, is needed.

References

Areeda, P.E. (1982) *Antitrust law: An analysis of antitrust principles and their application (Supplement).* Boston: Little, Brown and Company.

Areeda, P.E and Hovenkamp, H. (1986) *Antitrust law: 1986 Supplement.* Boston: Little, Brown and Company.

Areeda, P.E. and Turner, D.F. (1975) 'Predatory pricing and related practices under section 2 of the Sherman Act', *Harvard Law Review*, 88:697–733.

Areeda, P.E. and Turner, D.F. (1976) 'Scherer on predatory pricing: A reply', *Harvard Law Review*, 89:891–900.

Areeda, P.E. and Turner, D.F. (1978) *Antitrust law.* Boston: Little, Brown and Company.

Averch, H. and Johnson, L.L. (1962) 'Behavior of the firm under regulatory constraint', *American Economic Review*, 52:1053–1069.

Bartel, A.P. and Thomas, L.G. (1986) 'Predation through regulation: The wage and profit impacts of OSHA and EPA', working paper, School of Business, Columbia University.

Baumol, W.J. (1979) 'Quasi-permanence of price reductions: A policy for prevention of predatory pricing', *Yale Law Journal*, 89:1–26.

Baumol, W.J. (1986) *Superfairness.* Cambridge: M.I.T. Press, ch. 6.

Baumol, W.J. and Ordover, J.A. (1985) 'Use of antitrust to subvert competition', *Journal of Law and Economics*, 28:247–266.

Benoit, J.P. (1984) 'Financially constrained entry into a game with incomplete information', *Rand Journal of Economics*, 15:490–499.

Bernheim, B.D. (1984) 'Strategic deterrence of sequential entry into an industry', *Rand Journal of Economics*, 15:1–11.

Besen, S.M. and Saloner, G. (1987) 'Compatibility standards and the market for telecommunications services', working paper, The RAND Corp., Washington, D.C.

Bork, R. (1978) *Antitrust paradox.* New York: Basic Books.

Brennan, T.J. (1986a) 'Regulated firms in unregulated markets: Understanding the divestiture in U.S. v. AT & T', working paper no. 86-5, Economic Analysis Group, Antitrust Division, U.S. Department of Justice, Washington, D.C.

Brennan, T.J. (1986b) 'Understanding 'raising rivals' costs',' working paper no. 86-16, Economic Analysis Group, Antitrust Division, U.S. Department of Justice, Washington, D.C.

Brock, G.E. (1981) *The telecommunications industry.* Cambridge: Harvard University Press.

Brock, W.A. (1983) 'Pricing, predation, and entry barriers in regulated industries', in: D.S. Evans, ed., *Breaking up Bell.* New York: North-Holland, 191–229.

Brodley, J.F. and Hay, G. (1981) 'Predatory pricing: Competing economic theories and the evolution of legal standards', *Cornell Law Review*, 66:738–803.

Bulow, J.I., Geanakoplos, J.D. and Klemperer, P.D. (1985) 'Multimarket oligopoly: Strategic substitutes and complements', *Journal of Political Economy*, 93:488–511.

Burns, M.R. (1986) 'Predatory pricing and the acquisition costs of competitors', *Journal of Political Economy*, 94:266–296.

Campbell, T.J. (1986) 'Spatial predation and competition in antitrust', working paper no. 27, Stanford Law School, Stanford University.

Comanor, W.S. and Frech III, H.E. (1984) 'Strategic behavior and antitrust analysis', *American Economic Review*, 74:372–376.

Dasgupta, P. and Stiglitz, J.E. (1985) 'Sunk costs, competition and welfare', working paper 85-12, Department of Economics, Princeton University.

Dixit, A. (1985) 'Strategic aspects of trade policy', mimeo, Department of Economics, Princeton University.

Easley, D., Masson, R.T. and Reynolds, R.J. (1985) 'Preying for time', *Journal of Industrial Organization*, 33:445–460.

Easterbrook, F.H. (1981a) 'Predatory strategies and counterstrategies', *University of Chicago Law Review*, 48:263–337.

Easterbrook, F.H (1981b) 'Comments on Ordover and Willig', in: S.C. Salop, ed., *Strategy, predation, and antitrust analysis*. Washington, D.C.: Federal Trade Commission, 415–446.

Easterbrook, F.H. (1984) 'The limits of antitrust', *Texas Law Review*, 63:1–40.

Edwards, C.D. (1955) 'Conglomerate bigness as a source of power', in: National Bureau of Economic Research conference report, *Business concentration and price policy*. Princeton: Princeton University Press, 331–359.

Encaoua, D., Geroski, P. and Jacquemin, A. (1986) 'Strategic competition and the persistence of dominant firms: A survey', in: J.E. Stiglitz and G.F. Mathewson, eds., *New developments in the analysis of market structure*. Cambridge: M.I.T. Press, 55–86.

Evans, D.S. (1986) 'The differential effect of regulation on plant size: Comment on Pashigian', *Journal of Law and Economics*, 29:187–200.

Farrell, J. and Saloner, G. (1986a) 'Installed base and compatibility: Innovation, product preannouncements and predation', *American Economic Review*, 76:940–955.

Farrell, J. and Saloner, G. (1986b) 'Economic issues in standardization', in: James Miller, ed., *Telecommunications and equity: Policy research issues*. New York: North-Holland, 165–178.

Fershtman, C. and Judd, K. (1984) 'Equilibrium incentives in oligopoly', working paper no. 642, Center for Mathematical Studies in Economics and Management Science, Northwestern University.

Fox, E. (1984) 'Abuse of a dominant position under the Treaty of Rome – A comparison with U.S. law; in: B. Hawk, ed., *The annual proceedings of the 1983 Fordham Corporate Law Institute*. New York: Mathew Bender, 367–421.

Fox, E. (1986) 'Monopolization and dominance in the United States and the European Community: Efficiency, opportunity, and fairness', *Notre Dame Law Review*, 61:981–1020.

Fudenberg, D. and Maskin, E. (1986) 'The folk theorem in repeated games with discounting and incomplete information', *Econometrica*, 54:533–554.

Fudenberg, D. and Tirole, J. (1984) 'The fat-cat effect, the puppy-dog ploy and the lean and hungry look', *American Economic Review*, 74:361–366.

Fudenberg, D. and Tirole, J. (1985) 'Predation without reputation', working paper no. 377, M.I.T.

Fudenberg, D. and Tirole, J. (1986a) 'A theory of exit in duopoly', *Econometrica*, 54:943–960.

Fudenberg, D. and Tirole, J. (1986b) 'A 'signal-jamming' theory of predation', *Rand Journal of Economics*, 17:366–376.

Gale, D. and Hellwig, M. (1986) 'Incentive-compatible debt contracts: The one-period problem', *Review of Economic Studies*, 52:647–664.

Gelfand, M.D. and Spiller, P.T. (1984) 'Entry barriers and multiproduct oliogopolistic strategies', working paper no. E-84-19, Hoover Institution, Stanford University.

Ghemawat, P. and Nalebuff, B. (1985) 'Exit', *Rand Journal of Economics*, 16:184–194.

Ghemawat, P. and Nalebuff, B. (1987) 'The devolution of declining industries', mimeo.

Greenhut, M.L. and Ohta, H. (1979) 'Vertical integration of successive oligopolists', *American Economic Review*, 69:137–147.

Hanson, W. (1985) 'Bandwagons and orphans: Dynamic pricing of competing technological systems subject to decreasing costs', working paper, Department of Economics, University of Chicago.

Harrington, Jr., J.E. (1984) 'Noncooperative behavior by a cartel as an entry-deterring signal', *Rand Journal of Economics*, 15:416–433.

Harrison, G.W. (1985) 'Predatory pricing in experiments', discussion paper no. 85-10, College of Business and Public Administration, University of Arizona.

Hawk, B. (1986) *United States, Common Market and International antitrust*, 2nd ed. New York: Law and Business Inc.

Hay, G. (1981) 'A confused lawyer's guide to predatory pricing', in S.C. Salop, ed., *Strategy, predation, and antitrust analysis*. Washington, D.C.: Federal Trade Commission, 155–202.

Hovenkamp, H. (1985) *Economics and antitrust law*. St. Paul, Minn.: West Publishing.

Hurwitz, J.D. and Kovacic, W.E (1982) 'Judicial analysis of predation: The emerging trends', *Vanderbilt Law Review*, 35:63–157.

Isaac, R.M. and Smith, V.L. (1985a) 'Experiments concerning antitrust issues: Sunk costs and entry, and predatory behavior', a consultants' report, Federal Trade Commission, Washington D.C.

Isaac, R.M. and Smith, V.L. (1985b) 'In search of predatory pricing', *Journal of Political Economy*, 93:320–345.

Joskow, P.L. and Klevorick, A.K. (1979) 'A framework for analyzing predatory pricing policy', *Yale Law Journal*, 89:213–270.

Judd, K.L. (1985) 'Credible spatial preemption', *Rand Journal of Economics*, 16:153–166.

Katz, M. and Shapiro, C. (1986) 'Technology adoption in the presence of network externalities', *Journal of Political Economy*, 94:822–841.

Krattenmaker, T.G. and Salop, S.C. (1986a) 'Competition and cooperation in the market for exclusionary rights', *American Economic Review*, 76:109–113.

Krattenmaker, T.G. and Salop, S.C. (1986b) 'Anticompetitive exclusion: Raising rivals' costs to achieve power over price', *Yale Law Journal*, 96:209–295.

Kreps, D. and Wilson, R. (1982) 'Reputation and imperfect information', *Journal of Economic Theory*, 27:253–279.

Kreps, D., Milgrom, P., Roberts, J. and Wilson, R. (1982) 'Rational cooperation in the finitely-repeated prisoners' dilemma', *Journal of Economic Theory*, 27:245–252.

Krugman, P. (1986a) 'Industrial organization and international trade', working paper no. 1957, NBER, Cambridge.

Krugman, P., ed. (1986b) Strategic trade policy and the new international economics. Cambridge, Mass.: M.I.T. Press.

Lipman, B.L. (1985) 'Delaying or deterring entry: A game-theoretic analysis', working paper, GSIA, Carnegie Mellon University.

Londregan, J. (1986) 'Entry and exit over the industry life cycle', mimeo.

Mackay, R.J. (1984) 'Mergers for monopoly: Problems of expectations and commitments', working paper 112, Federal Trade Commission, Washington, D.C.

Mailath, G.J. (1984) 'The welfare implications of differential information in a dynamic duopoly model', Princeton University, mimeo.

Maloney, M., McCormick, R. and Tollison, R. (1979) 'Achieving cartel profits through unionization', *Southern Economic Journal*, 42:628–634.

Mankiw, N.G. and Whinston, M.D. (1986) 'Free entry and social inefficiency', *Rand Journal of Economics*, 17:48–58.

Marvel, H.P. (1977) 'Factory regulation: A reinterpretation of early English experiences', *Journal of Law and Economics*, 20:379–402.

Masson, R.T. and Eisenstat, P. (1975) 'A stochastic rationale for predatory pricing', working paper, Department of Justice, Antitrust Division.

McGee, J. (1958) 'Predatory price cutting: The Standard Oil (N.J.) case', *Journal of Law and Economics*, 1:137–169.

McGee, J. (1980) 'Predatory pricing revisited', *Journal of Law and Economics*, 23:289–330.

Milgrom, P. and Roberts, J. (1982a) 'Limit pricing and entry under incomplete information: An equilibrium analysis', *Econometrica*, 50:443–460.

Milgrom, P. and Roberts, J. (1982b) 'Predation, reputation and entry deterrence', *Journal of Economic Theory*, 27:280–312.

Milgrom, P. and Roberts, J. (1987) 'Informational asymmetries, strategic behavior and industrial organization', *American Economic Review, Papers and Proceedings*, 77:184–193.

Mueller, D.C. (1986) *Profits in the long run*. New York: Cambridge University Press.

Ordover, J.A. (1987) 'Conflicts of jurisdiction: Antitrust and industrial policy', *Law and Contemporary Problems*, 50:165–177.

Ordover, J.A. and Schotter, A. (1981) 'On the political sustainability of taxes', *American Economic Review*, 71:278–282.

Ordover, J.A. and Willig, R.D. (1981) 'An economic definition of predation: Pricing and product innovation', *Yale Law Journal*, 91:8–53.

Ordover, J.A. and Willig, R.D. (1982) 'An economic definition of predation: Pricing and product innovation', final report to the Federal Trade Commission, September 1982.

Ordover, J.A., Sykes, A.D. and Willig, R.D. (1983a) 'Unfair international trade practices', *New York University Journal of International Law and Politics*, 15:323–337.

Ordover, J.A., Sykes, A.D. and Willig, R.D. (1983b) 'Predatory systems rivalry: A reply', *Columbia Law Review*, 83:1150–1166.

Ordover, J.A., Sykes, A.D. and Willig, R.D. (1985) 'Non-price anticompetitive behavior by dominant firms toward the producers of complementary products', in: F. Fisher, ed., *Antitrust and regulation: Essays in memory of John McGowan*. Cambridge, Mass.: M.I.T. Press, 315–330.

Oster, S. (1982) 'The strategic use of regulatory investment by industry subgroups', *Economic Inquiry*, 20:604–618.

Pashigian, B.P. (1984) 'The effect of environmental regulation on optimal plant size and factor shares', *Journal of Law and Economics*, 27:1–28.

Pashigian, B.P. (1986) 'Reply to Evans', *Journal of Law and Economics*, 29:201–209.

Pittman, R.W. (1982) 'Predatory investment: U.S. v. IBM', discussion paper no. 82-5, Economic Policy Office, U.S. Department of Justice, Antitrust Division, Washington, D.C.

Pittman, R.W. (1984) 'Tying without exclusive dealing', discussion paper no. 84-13, Economic Policy Office, U.S. Department of Justice, Antitrust Division, Washington, D.C.

Porter, M.E. (1980) *Competitive strategy: Techniques for analyzing industries and competition*. New York: Free Press.

Porter, M.E. (1985) *Competitive advantage: Creating and sustaining superior performance*. New York: Free Press.

Posner, R. (1976) 'Predatory pricing', in: R. Posner, ed., *Antitrust law: An economic perspective*. Chicago: University of Chicago Press, 184–196.

Posner, R. and Easterbrook, F. (1981) *Antitrust*, 2nd. ed. St. Paul, Minn.: West Publishing.

Rasmusen, E. (1985) 'Entry for buyout', working paper, Graduate School of Management, UCLA, Los Angeles.

Reynolds, R.J. and Lewis, L.M. (undated) 'Predatory pricing rules and entry deterrence', U.S. Department of Justice, mimeo.

Reynolds, R.J. and Masson, R.T. (undated) 'Predation: The 'noisy' pricing strategy', mimeo.

Riordan, M.H. (1985) 'Imperfect information and dynamic conjectural variations', *Rand Journal of Economics*, 16:41–50.

Roberts, J. (1985) 'Battles for market share: Incomplete information, aggressive strategic pricing, and competitive dynamics', working paper, Graduate School of Business, Stanford University.

Roberts, J. (1986) 'A signaling model of predatory pricing', *Oxford Economic Papers* (*Supplement*), (*N.S.*), 38:75–93.

Rotemberg, J.J. and Saloner, G. (1987) 'The cyclical behavior of strategic inventories', working paper no. E-87-22, Hoover Institution, Stanford University.

Salinger, M.A. (1984) 'A welfare analysis of market foreclosure due to vertical mergers by oligopolists', Columbia Business School, mimeo.

Saloner, G. (1987) 'Predation, merger and incomplete information', *Rand Journal of Economics*, 18:165–186.

Salop, S.C., ed. (1981) *Strategy, predation, and antitrust analysis*. Washington, D.C.: Federal Trade Commission.

Salop, S.C. and Scheffman, D.T. (1983) 'Raising rivals' costs', *American Economic Review*, 73:267–271.

Salop, S.C. and Scheffman, D.T. (1984) 'Multi-market strategies in a dominant firm industry', working paper no. 100, Federal Trade Commission, Bureau of Economics, Washington, D.C.

Salop, S.C. and Scheffman, D.T. (1987) 'Cost-raising strategies', working paper no. 146, Federal Trade Commission, Bureau of Economics, Washington, D.C., *Journal of Industrial Economics*, 36:19–34.

Salop, S.C. and Shapiro, C. (1980) 'A guide to test market predation', mimeo.

Salop, S.C. and White, L.J. (1985) 'Private antitrust litigation: An introduction and framework', mimeo.

Salop, S.C. and White, L.J. (1986) 'Economic analysis of private antitrust litigation', *Georgetown Law Review*, 74:1001–1064.

Salop, S.C., Scheffman, D.T. and Schwartz, W. (1984) 'A bidding analysis of special interest regulation: Raising rivals' costs in a rent seeking society', in: R. Rogowsky and B. Yandle, eds., *The political economy of regulation*: *Private interests in the regulatory process*. Washington, D.C.: Federal Trade Commission, 102–127.

Scharfstein, O. (1984) 'A policy to prevent rational test-market predation', *Rand Journal of Economics*, 2:229–243.

Scheffman, D.T. (1981) 'Comment on Ordover and Willig', in: S.C. Salop, ed., *Strategy, predation, and antitrust analysis*. Washington, D.C.: Federal Trade Commission, 397–414.

Scherer, F.M. (1976) 'Predatory pricing and the Sherman Act: A comment', *Harvard Law Review*, 89:869–890.

Scherer, F.M. (1980) *Industrial market structure and economic performance*, 2nd ed. Boston: Houghton Mifflin.

Schmalensee, R. (1979) 'On the use of economic models in antitrust: The ReaLemon case', *University of Pennsylvania Law Review*, 127:994–1050.

Schmalensee, R. (1985) 'Standards for dominant firm conduct: What can economics contribute?', working paper no. 1723-85, M.I.T., Cambridge.

Schmalensee, R. (1987) 'Standards for dominant firm conduct: What can economics contribute?', in: D. Hay and J. Vickers, eds., *The economics of market dominance*. Oxford: Basil Blackwell, 61–88.

Schwartz, M. (1985a) 'Anticompetitive effects of exclusive dealing? What Comanor and Frech really show', discussion paper no. 85-9, Economic Policy Office, U.S. Department of Justice, Antitrust Division, Washington, D.C.

Schwartz, M. (1985b) 'Welfare effects of exit-inducing innovations', mimeo.

Selten, R. (1978) 'The chain-store paradox', *Theory and Decision*, 9:127–159.

Sidak, J.G. (1983) 'Debunking predatory innovation', *Columbia Law Review*, 93:1121–1149.

Sullivan, L.A. (1977) *Handbook of the law of antitrust*. St. Paul, Minn.: West Publishing.

Telser, L.G. (1966) 'Cutthroat competition and the long purse', *Journal of Law and Economics*, 9:259–277.

Wellisz, S.H. (1963) 'Regulation of natural gas pipeline companies: An economic analysis', *Journal of Political Economy*, 71:30–43.

West, D.S. and von Hohenbalken, B. (1986) 'Empirical tests for predatory reputation', *Canadian Journal of Economics*, 19:160–178.

Whinston, M.D. (1987) 'Exit with multiplant firms', working paper 1299, Harvard Institute for Economic Research.

Williamson, O.E. (1968) 'Wage rates as barriers to entry: The Pennington case in perspective', *Quarterly Journal of Economics*, 85:85–116.

Williamson, O.E. (1977) 'Predatory pricing: A strategic and welfare analysis', *Yale Law Journal*, 87:284–340.

Williamson, O.E. (1982) 'Antitrust enforcement: Where it has been; where it is going', in: J. Craven, ed., *Industrial organization, antitrust, and public policy*. Boston: Kluwer–Nijhoff Publishing, 41–68.

Williamson, O.E. (1985) *The economic institutions of capitalism*. New York: Free Press.

Willig, R.D. (1985) 'Corporate governance and product market structure', Princeton University, mimeo.

Yamey, B. (1972) 'Predatory price cutting: Notes and comments', *Journal of Law and Economics*, 15:129–142.

Zerbe, Jr., R.O. and Cooper, D.S. (undated) 'Economic welfare and the empirical content of predatory pricing', mimeo.

Chapter 10

PRICE DISCRIMINATION

HAL R. VARIAN*

University of Michigan

Contents

*Thanks to Robert Willig, Robert Wilson, Jean Tirole, and Michael Bradley for providing materials for this survey. Severin Borenstein, Eduardo Ley, Jeff MacKie-Mason, Steve Salant, Richard Schmalensee and Kyuho Whang provided generous comments, suggestions and corrections for which I am very grateful.

Handbook of Industrial Organization, Volume I, Edited by R. Schmalensee and R.D. Willig

1. Introduction

Price discrimination is one of the most prevalent forms of marketing practices. One may occasionally doubt whether firms really engage in some of the kinds of sophisticated strategic reasoning economists are fond of examining, but there can be no doubt that firms are well aware of the benefits of price discrimination.

Consider, for example, the following passage taken from a brochure published by the Boston Consulting Group:

> A key step is to avoid average pricing. Pricing to specific customer groups should reflect the true competitive value of what is being provided. When this is achieved, no money is left on the table unnecessarily on the one hand, while no opportunities are opened for competitors though inadvertent overpricing on the other. Pricing is an accurate and confident action that takes full advantage of the combination of customers' price sensitivity and alternative suppliers they have or could have [Miles (1986)].

Although an economist might have used somewhat more technical terminology, the central ideas of price discrimination are quite apparent in this passage.

Every undergraduate microeconomics textbook contains a list of examples of price discrimination; the most popular illustrations seem to be those of student discounts, Senior Citizen's discounts, and the like. Given the prevalence of price discrimination as an economic phenomenon, it is surprisingly difficult to come up with an entirely satisfactory definition.

The conventional definition is that price discrimination is present when the same commodity is sold at different prices to different consumers. However, this definition fails on two counts: different prices charged to different consumers could simply reflect transportation costs, or similar costs of selling the good; and price discrimination could be present even when all consumers are charged the same price – consider the case of a uniform delivered price.[1]

We prefer Stigler's (1987) definition: price discrimination is present when two or more similar goods are sold at prices that are in different ratios to marginal costs. As an illustration, Stigler uses the example of a book that sells in hard cover for \$15 and in paperback for \$5. Here, he argues, there is a presumption of

[1]For further discussion, see Phlips (1983, pp. 5–7).

discrimination, since the binding costs are not sufficient to explain the difference in price. Of course, this definition still leaves open the precise meaning of "similar", but the definition will be useful for our purposes.

Three conditions are necessary in order for price discrimination to be a viable solution to a firm's pricing problem. First, the firm must have some market power. Second, the firm must have the ability to sort customers. And third, the firm must be able to prevent resale. We will briefly discuss each of these points, and develop them in much greater detail in the course of the chapter.

We turn first to the issue of market power. Price discrimination arises naturally in the theory of monopoly and oligopoly. Whenever a good is sold at a price in excess of its marginal cost, there is an incentive to engage in price discrimination. For to say that price is in excess of marginal cost is to say that there is someone who is willing to pay more than the cost of production for an extra unit of the good. Lowering the price to all consumers may well be unprofitable, but lowering the price to the marginal consumer alone will likely be profitable.

In order to lower the price only to the marginal consumer, or more generally to some specific class of consumers, the firm must have a way to sort consumers. The easiest case is where the firm can explicitly sort consumers with respect to some exogenous category such as age. A more complex analysis is necessary when the firm must price discriminate on the basis of some *endogenous* category such as time of purchase. In this case the monopolist faces the problem of structuring his pricing so that consumers "self-select" into appropriate categories.

Finally, if the firm is to sell at different prices to different consumers, the firm must have a way to prevent consumers who purchase at a discount price from reselling to other consumers. Carlton and Perloff (forthcoming) discuss several mechanisms that can be used to prevent resale:

- Some goods such as services, electric power, etc. are difficult to resell because of the nature of the good.
- Tariffs, taxes and transportation costs can impose barriers to resale. For example, it is common for publishers to sell books at different prices in different countries and rely on transportation costs or tariffs to restrict resale.
- A firm may legally restrict resale. For example, computer manufacturers often offer educational discounts along with a contractual provision that restricts resale.
- A firm can modify its product. For example, some firms sell student editions of software that has more limited capabilities than the standard versions.

The economic analyst is, of course, interested in having a detailed and accurate model of the firm's behavior. But in addition, the economist wants to be able to pass judgment on that behavior. To what degree does price discrimination of various types promote economic welfare? What types of discrimination should be encouraged and what types discouraged? Price discrimination is illegal only insofar as it "substantially lessens competition". How are we to interpret this phrase? These are some of the issues we will examine in this survey.

2. Theory

2.1. Types of price discrimination

The traditional classification of the forms of price discrimination is due to Pigou (1920).

First-degree, or *perfect* price discrimination involves the seller charging a different price for each unit of the good in such a way that the price charged for each unit is equal to the maximum willingness to pay for that unit.

Second-degree price discrimination, or *nonlinear* pricing, occurs when prices differ depending on the number of units of the good bought, but not across consumers. That is, each consumer faces the same price schedule, but the schedule involves different prices for different amounts of the good purchased. Quantity discounts or premia are the obvious examples.

Third-degree price discrimination means that different purchasers are charged different prices, but each purchaser pays a constant amount for each unit of the good bought. This is perhaps the most common form of price discrimination; examples are student discounts, or charging different prices on different days of the week.

We will follow Pigou's classification in this survey, discussing the forms of price discrimination in the order in which he suggested them. Subsequently, we will take up some more specialized topics that do not seem to fit conveniently in this classification scheme.

We have had the benefit of a number of other surveys of the topic of price discrimination and have not hesitated to draw heavily from those works. Some of these works are published and some are not, and it seems appropriate to briefly survey the surveys before launching in to our own.

First, we must mention Phlips' (1983) extensive book, *The Economics of Price Discrimination*, which contains a broad survey of the area and many intriguing examples. Next, we have found Tirole's (1988) chapter on price discrimination to be very useful, especially in its description of issues involving nonlinear pricing. Robert Wilson's class notes (1985) provided us with an extensive bibliography and discussion of many aspects of product marketing, of which price discrimination is only a part. Finally, Carlton and Perloff (forthcoming) give a very nice overview of the issues and a detailed treatment of several interesting sub-topics. We are especially grateful to these authors for providing us with their unpublished work.

2.2. First-degree price discrimination

First-degree price discrimination, or perfect price discrimination, means that the seller sells each unit of the good at the maximum price that anyone is willing to pay for that unit of the good. Alternatively, perfect price discrimination is sometimes defined as occurring when the seller makes a single take-it-or-leave-it offer to each consumer that extracts the maximum amount possible from the market.

Although the equivalence of these two definitions has been long asserted – Pigou mentions it in his discussion of first-degree price discrimination – it is not entirely clear just how generally the two definitions coincide. Is the equivalence true only in the case of quasilinear utility, or does it hold true more generally? As it turns out, the proposition is valid in quite general circumstances.

To see this, consider a simple model with two goods, x and y and a single consumer. We choose y as the numeraire good, and normalize its price to one. (Think of the y-good as being money.) The consumer is initially consuming 0 units of the x-good, and the monopolist wishes to sell x^* units for the largest possible amount of the y-good. Let y^* be the amount of the y-good that the consumer has after making this payment; then y^* is the solution to the equation

$$u(x^*, y^*) = u(0, y), \tag{1}$$

and the payment is simply $y - y^*$. This is clearly the largest possible amount of the y-good that the consumer would pay on a take-it-or-leave-it basis to consume x^* units of the x-good.

Suppose instead that the monopolist breaks up x^* into n pieces of size Δx and sells each piece to the consumer at the maximum price the consumer would be willing to pay for that piece. Let (x_i, y_i) be the amount the consumer has at the ith stage of this process, so that thus $y_{i-1} - y_i$ is the amount paid for the ith unit of the x-good. Since utility remains constant during this process we have

$$\begin{aligned} u(x_1, y_1) - u(0, y) &= 0, \\ u(x_2, y_2) - u(x_1, y_1) &= 0, \\ &\vdots \\ u(x^*, y_n) - u(x_{n-1}, y_{n-1}) &= 0. \end{aligned} \tag{2}$$

We want to show that y_n, the total amount held of the y-good after this process is completed, is equal to y^*, the amount paid by the take-it-or-leave-it offer described above.

But this is easy; just add up the equations in (2) to find

$$u(x^*, y_n) - u(0, y) = 0.$$

Examining (1) we see that $y_n = y^*$, as was to be shown.

2.2.1. Welfare and output effects

It is well known that a perfectly discriminating monopolist produces a Pareto efficient amount of output, but a formal proof of this proposition may be instructive. Let $u(x, y)$ be the utility function of the consumer, as before, and for simplicity suppose that the monopolist cares only about his consumption of the y-good. (Again, it is convenient to think of the y-good as being money.) The monopolist is endowed with a technology that allows him to produce x units of the x-good by using $c(x)$ units of the y-good. The initial endowment of the consumer is denoted by (x_c, y_c), and by assumption the monopolist has an initial endowment of zero of each good.

The monopolist wants to choose a (positive) production level x and a (negative) payment y of the y-good that maximizes his utility subject to the constraint that the consumer actually purchases the x-good from the monopolist. Thus, the maximization problem becomes:

$$\max_{x, y} y - c(x)$$

$$\text{s.t. } u(x_c + x, y_c - y) \geq u(x_c, y_c).$$

But this problem simply asks us to find a feasible allocation that maximizes the utility of one party, the monopolist, subject to the constraint that the other party, the consumer, has some given level of utility. This is the definition of a Pareto efficient allocation. Hence, a perfectly discriminating monopolist will choose a Pareto efficient level of output.

By the Second Welfare Theorem, and the appropriate convexity conditions, this Pareto efficient level of output is a competitive equilibrium for some endowments. In order to see this directly, denote the solution to the monopolist's maximization problem by (x^*, y^*). This solution must satisfy the first-order conditions:

$$1 - \lambda \frac{\partial u(x_c + x^*, y_c - y^*)}{\partial y} = 0,$$

$$- c'(x^*) + \lambda \frac{\partial u(x_c + x^*, y_c - y^*)}{\partial x} = 0. \tag{3}$$

Dividing the second equation by the first and rearranging gives us:

$$\frac{\partial u(x_c + x^*, y_c - y^*)/\partial x}{\partial u(x_c + x^*, y_c - y^*)/\partial y} = c'(x^*).$$

If the consumer has an endowment of $(x_c + x^*, y_c + y^*)$ and the firm faces a parametric price set at

$$p^* = \frac{\partial u(x_c + x^*, y_c - y^*)/\partial x}{\partial u(x_c + x^*, y_c - y^*)/\partial y},$$

the firm's profit maximization problem will take the form:

$$\max_x p^*x - c(x).$$

In this case it is clear that the firm will optimally choose to produce x^* units of output, as required.

Of course, the proof that the output level of a perfectly discriminating monopolist is the same as that of a competitive firm only holds if the appropriate reassignment of initial endowments is made. However, if we are willing to rule out income effects, this caveat can be eliminated.

To see this, let us now assume that the utility function for the consumer takes the quasilinear form $u(x) + y$. In this case $\partial u/\partial y \equiv 1$ so the first-order conditions given in (3) reduce to

$$\frac{\partial u(x_c + x^*)}{\partial x} = c'(x^*).$$

This shows that the Pareto efficient level of output produced by the perfectly discriminating monopolist is independent of the endowment of y, which is what we require. Clearly the amount of the x-good produced is the same as that of a competitive firm that faces a parametric price given by $p^* = \partial u(x_c + x^*)/\partial x$.

2.2.2. *Prevalence of first-degree price discrimination*

Take-it-or-leave-it offers are not terribly common forms of negotiation for two reasons. First, the "leave-it" threat lacks credibility: typically a seller has no way to commit to breaking off negotiations if an offer is rejected. And once an initial offer has been rejected, it is generally rational for the seller to continue to bargain.

Second, even if the seller had a way to commit to ending negotiations, he typically lacks full information about the buyers' preferences. Thus, the seller cannot determine for certain whether his offer will actually be accepted, and must trade off the costs of rejection with the benefits of additional profits.

If the seller was able to precommit to take-it-or-leave-it, and he had perfect information about buyers' preferences, one would expect to see transactions made according to this mechanism. After all, it does afford the seller the most possible profits.

However, vestiges of the attempt to first-degree price discrimination can still be detected in some marketing arrangements. Some kinds of goods – ranging from aircraft on the one hand to refrigerators and stereos on the other – are still sold by haggling. Certainly this must be due to an attempt to price discriminate among prospective customers.

To the extent that such haggling is successful in extracting the full surplus from consumers, it tends to encourage the production of an efficient amount of output. But of course the haggling itself incurs costs. A full welfare analysis of attempts to engage in this kind of price discrimination cannot neglect the transactions costs involved in the negotiation itself.

2.2.3. Two-part tariffs

Two-part tariffs are pricing schemes that involve a fixed fee which must be paid to consume any amount of good, and then a variable fee based on usage. The classic example is pricing an amusement park: one price must be paid to enter the park, and then further fees must be paid for each of the rides. Other examples include products such as cameras and film, or telephone service which requires a fixed monthly fee plus an additional charge based on usage.

The classic exposition of two-part tariffs in a profit maximization setting is Oi (1971). A more extended treatment may be found in Ng and Weisser (1974) and Schmalensee (1981a). Two-part tariffs have also been applied to problems of social welfare maximization by Feldstein (1972), Littlechild (1975), Leland and Meyer (1976), and Auerbach and Pellechio (1978). In this survey we will focus on the profit maximization problem.

Let the indirect utility function of a consumer of type t facing a price p and having income y be denoted by $v(p, t) + y$. If the price of the good is so high that the consumer does not choose to consume it, let $v(p, t) = 0$. The prices of all other goods are assumed to be constant. Note that we have built in the assumption that preferences are quasilinear; i.e. that there are no income effects. This allows for the cleanest analysis of the problem.[2]

Let $x(p, t)$ be the demand for the good by a consumer of type t when the price is p. By Roy's Identity, $x(p, t) = -\partial v(p, t)/\partial p$. Suppose that the good can be produced at a constant marginal cost of c per unit.

[2] The literature on two-part tariffs seems a bit confused about this point; some authors explicitly examine cases involving income effects, but then use consumer's surplus as a welfare measure. Since consumers' surplus is an exact measure of welfare only in the case where income effects are absent, this procedure is a dubious practice at best.

Initially, we consider the situation where all consumers are the same type. If the firm charges an entrance fee e, the consumer will choose to enter if

$$v(p,t) + y - e \geq y,$$

so that the *maximum* entrance fee the park can charge is

$$e = v(p,t).$$

The profit maximization problem is then

$$\max_{e,p}\; e + (p-c)x(p,t)$$

$$\text{s.t. } e = v(p,t).$$

Incorporating the constraint into the objective function and differentiating with respect to p yields:

$$\frac{\partial v(p,t)}{\partial p} + (p-c)\frac{\partial x(p,t)}{\partial p} + x(p,t) = 0.$$

Substituting from Roy's Identity yields:

$$-x(p,t) + (p-c)\frac{\partial x(p,t)}{\partial p} + x(p,t) = 0,$$

which in turn simplifies to

$$(p-c)\frac{\partial x(p,t)}{\partial p} = 0.$$

It follows that if all the consumers are the same type, the profit maximizing policy is to set price equal to marginal cost and set an entrance fee that extracts all of the consumers' surplus. That is, the optimal policy is to engage in first-degree price discrimination. This is, of course, a Pareto efficient pricing scheme.

Things become more interesting when there is a distribution of types. Let $F(t)$ denote the cumulative distribution function and $f(t)$ the density of types. Suppose that $\partial v(p,t)/\partial t < 0$, so that the value of the good is decreasing in t. Then if the firm charges an entrance fee e and a price p, a consumer of type t will choose to enter if

$$v(p,t) + y - e \geq y.$$

Thus, for each p there will be a marginal consumer T such that

$$e = v(p, T).$$

Given p, the monopolist's choice of an entrance fee is equivalent to the choice of the marginal consumer T. For any T we can denote the aggregate demand of the admitted consumers as

$$X(p, T) = \int_0^T x(p, t) f(t)\, \mathrm{d}t.$$

Note carefully the notational distinction between the demand of the admitted consumers, $X(p, T)$, and the demand of the marginal consumer, $x(p, T)$.

The profit maximization problem of the monopolist is

$$\max_{T, p}\ v(p, T) F(T) + (p - c) X(p, T),$$

which has first-order conditions:

$$\frac{\partial v}{\partial p} F(T) + (p - c)\frac{\partial X}{\partial p} + X(p, T) = 0,$$

$$\frac{\partial v}{\partial T} F(T) + v(p, T) F'(T) + (p - c)\frac{\partial X}{\partial T} = 0.$$

Using Roy's Identity and the fact that $F'(T) = f(T)$, these conditions become:

$$-x(p, T) F(T) + (p - c)\frac{\partial X}{\partial p} + X(p, T) = 0, \tag{4}$$

$$\frac{\partial v}{\partial T} F(T) + v(p, T) f(T) + (p - c)\frac{\partial X}{\partial T} = 0. \tag{5}$$

Multiply and divide the middle term of the first equation by X/p to find:

$$-x(p, T) F(T) + X(p, T)\frac{p - c}{p}\frac{\partial X}{\partial p}\frac{p}{X} + X(p, T) = 0. \tag{6}$$

Let ε denote the elasticity of aggregate demand of the admitted consumers so that

$$\varepsilon = \frac{\partial X(p, T)}{\partial p}\frac{p}{X(p, T)}.$$

Using this notation, we can manipulate (6) to find:

$$\frac{p-c}{p}|\varepsilon| = 1 - \frac{x(p,T)}{X(p,T)/F(T)}. \tag{7}$$

Expression (7) tells us quite a bit about two-part tariffs. First, note that the expression is a simple transformation of the ordinary monopoly pricing rule:

$$\frac{p-c}{p}|\varepsilon| = 1.$$

When a two-part tariff is possible, the right-hand side is adjusted down by a term which can be interpreted as a ratio of the demand of the marginal consumer to the demand of the average admitted consumer. When the marginal consumer has the same demand as the average consumer – as in the case where all consumers are identical – the optimal two-part tariff involves setting price equal to marginal cost, as we established earlier.

We would normally expect that the marginal consumer would demand less than the average consumer; in this case, the price charged in the two-part tariff would be greater than marginal cost. However, it is possible that the marginal consumer would demand more than the average consumer. Imagine a situation where the marginal consumer does not value the good very highly, but wants to consume a larger than average amount, i.e. $v(p,T)$ is small, but $|\partial v(p,T)/\partial p|$ is large. In this case, the optimal price in the two-part tariff would be less than marginal cost, but the monopolist makes up for it through the entrance fees. (This is an example of the famous auto salesman claim – where the firm loses money on every sale but makes up for it in volume – due to the entrance fee!)

For more on the analytics of two-part tariffs, see the definitive treatment by Schmalensee (1981a). Schmalensee points out that two-part tariffs are essentially a pricing problem involving two especially complementary goods – entrance to the amusement park and the rides themselves. Viewed from this perspective it is easy to see why one of the goods may be sold below marginal cost, or why p is typically less than the monopoly price. Schmalensee also considers much more general technologies and analyzes several important subcases such as the case where the customers are downstream firms.

2.2.4. *Welfare effects of the two-part tariff*

We have already indicated that a two-part tariff with identical consumers leads to a full welfare optimum. What happens with nonidentical consumers?

Welfare is given by consumers' surplus plus profits:

$$W(p,T) = \int_0^T v(p,t)f(t)\mathrm{d}t + (p-c)X(p,T).$$

Differentiating with respect to p and T and using Roy's Identity, yields:

$$\frac{\partial W(p,T)}{\partial p} = -\int_0^T x(p,t)f(t)\mathrm{d}t + (p-c)\frac{\partial X}{\partial p} + X(p,T),$$

$$\frac{\partial W(p,T)}{\partial T} = [v(p,T) + (p-c)x(p,T)]f(T).$$

Evaluating these derivatives at the profit maximizing two-part tariff (p^*, T^*) given in (4) and (5) we have

$$\frac{\partial W(p^*,T^*)}{\partial p} = (p^*-c)\frac{\partial X}{\partial p} = x(p^*,T^*)F(T^*) - X(p^*,T^*),$$

$$\frac{\partial W(p^*,T^*)}{\partial T} = -\frac{\partial v(p^*,T^*)}{\partial T}F(T^*) > 0.$$

The first equation will be positive or negative as the demand of the marginal consumer is greater or less than the demand of the average consumer. If all consumers have the same tastes, the marginal consumer and the average consumer coincide so that price will be equal to marginal cost and therefore optimal from a social viewpoint. Normally, we would expect the marginal consumer to have a lower demand than the average consumer, which implies that price is greater than marginal cost. Hence, it is too high from a social viewpoint, and welfare would increase by lowering it. However, as we have seen above, if the marginal consumer has a higher demand than the average consumer, price will be set below marginal cost, which implies that the monopolist *under*prices his output.

The second equation shows that the monopolist always serves too small a market, since $\partial v/\partial T < 0$ and $F(T) > 0$ by assumption. This holds regardless of whether price is greater or less than marginal cost.

Although the primary focus of this essay is on the profit maximizing case, we can briefly explore the welfare maximization problem. Setting the derivatives of welfare equal to zero and rearranging, we have

$$\frac{\partial W(p,T)}{\partial p} = (p-c)\frac{\partial X}{\partial p} = 0,$$

$$\frac{\partial W(p,T)}{\partial T} = [v(p,T) + (p-c)x(p,T)]f(T) = 0.$$

The first equation requires that price be equal to marginal cost; using this fact the second equation can be rewritten as

$$\frac{\partial W(p,T)}{\partial T} = v(p,T)f(T) = 0.$$

This equation implies that consumers be admitted until the marginal valuation is reduced to zero (or as low as it can go and remain non-negative.) This simply says that anyone who is willing to purchase the good at marginal cost should be allowed to do so, hardly a surprising result.

A more interesting expression results if we require that the firm must cover some fixed costs of providing the good. This adds a constraint to the problem of the form:

$$v(p,T)F(T) + (p-c)X(p,T) = K,$$

where K is the fixed cost that must be covered. The first term on the left-hand side is the total entrance fees collected, and the second term is the profit earned on the sales of the good.

Here it is natural to take the objective function as being the consumers' welfare alone, rather than the consumers' plus the producer's surplus. This leads to a maximization problem of the form:

$$\max_{p,T} \int_0^T v(p,t)f(t)\mathrm{d}t - v(p,T)F(T)$$

$$\text{s.t. } v(p,T)F(T) + (p-c)X(p,T) = K.$$

The first-order conditions for this problem are

$$-X(p,T) + x(p,T)F(T) - \lambda\Big[-x(p,T)F(T) + (p-c)\frac{\partial X}{\partial p} + X(p,T)\Big] = 0,$$

$$-\frac{\partial v}{\partial T}F(T) - \lambda\Big[\frac{\partial v}{\partial T}F(T) + v(p,T)f(T) + (p-c)x(p,T)f(T)\Big] = 0.$$

It is of interest to ask when the constrained maximization problem involves setting price equal to marginal cost. Rearranging the first equation, we have

$$(1+\lambda)[x(p,T)F(T) - X(p,T)] = \lambda(p-c)\frac{\partial X}{\partial p}.$$

From this expression it is easy to see that if price equals marginal cost we must have either

$$x(p,T) = \frac{X(p,T)}{F(T)},$$

which means that the average demand equals the marginal demand, or

$$\lambda = -1.$$

We have encountered the first condition several times already, and it needs no further discussion. Turning to the second condition, we note that if $\lambda = -1$, the second first-order condition implies that $v(p,T) = 0$, i.e. that the entrance fee is zero. This can only happen when the fixed costs are zero, so we conclude that essentially the only case in which price will be equal to marginal cost is when the average demand and the marginal demand coincide.

2.2.5. *Pareto improving two-part tariffs*

Willig (1978) has observed that there will typically exist pricing schemes involving two-part tariffs that Pareto dominate nondiscriminatory monopoly pricing. This is a much stronger result than the welfare domination discussed above: Willig shows that all consumers *and* the producer are at least as well off with a particular pricing scheme than with flat rate pricing.

To illustrate the Willig result in its simplest case, suppose that there are two consumers with demand functions $D_1(p)$ and $D_2(p)$ with $D_2(p) > D_1(p)$ for all p. For simplicity we take fixed costs to be zero. Let p_f be any price in excess of marginal cost, c. In order to construct the Pareto dominating two-part tariff, choose p_t to be any price between p_f and c and choose the lump-sum entry fee e to satisfy:

$$e = (p_f - p_t)D_2(p_f).$$

Now consider a pricing scheme where all consumers are offered the choice between purchasing at the flat rate p_f or choosing the two-part tariff. If neither consumer chooses the two-part tariff, the situation is unchanged and uninteresting. If consumer 2 chooses the two-part tariff, then it must make him better off.

The revenue received by the firm from consumer 2 will be

$$\begin{aligned}(p_\mathrm{f} - p_\mathrm{t})D_2(p_\mathrm{f}) + p_\mathrm{t}D_2(p_\mathrm{t}) &= p_\mathrm{f}D_2(p_\mathrm{f}) + p_\mathrm{t}(D_2(p_\mathrm{t}) - D_2(p_\mathrm{f}))\\ &> p_\mathrm{f}D_2(p_\mathrm{f}).\end{aligned}$$

The inequality follows from the fact that demand curves slope down and $p_\mathrm{t} < p_\mathrm{f}$. Hence, revenue from consumer 2 has increased, so the firm is better off. We only have to examine the case of consumer 1. If consumer 1 stays with the flat rate, we are done. Otherwise, consumer 1 chooses the two-part tariff and the revenue received from him will be

$$\begin{aligned}(p_\mathrm{f} - p_\mathrm{t})D_2(p_\mathrm{f}) + p_\mathrm{t}D_1(p_\mathrm{t}) &\geq (p_\mathrm{f} - p_\mathrm{t})D_1(p_\mathrm{f}) + p_\mathrm{t}D_1(p_\mathrm{t})\\ &= p_\mathrm{f}D_1(p_\mathrm{f}) + p_\mathrm{t}(D_1(p_\mathrm{t}) - D_1(p_\mathrm{f}))\\ &\geq p_\mathrm{f}D_1(p_\mathrm{f}).\end{aligned}$$

The first inequality follows from the assumption that $D_2(p_\mathrm{f}) > D_1(p_\mathrm{f})$ and the second from the fact that demand curves slope down. The conclusion is that the firm makes at least as much from consumer 1 under the two-part tariff as under the flat rate. Hence, offering the choice between the two pricing systems yields a Pareto improvement. As long as consumer 2 strictly prefers the two-part tariff – the likely case – this will be a strict Pareto improvement.

Of course this argument only shows that it is *possible* for a flat rate plus a two-part tariff to Pareto dominate a pure flat rate scheme. It does not imply that moving from flat rates to such a scheme will necessarily result in a Pareto improvement, since a profit maximizing firm will not necessarily choose the correct two-part tariff. Thus the result is more appropriate in the context of public utility pricing rather than profit maximization. See Srinagesh (1985) for a detailed study of the profit maximization case and Ordover and Panzar (1980) for an examination of the Willig model when demands are interdependent.

2.3. *Second-degree price discrimination*

Second-degree price discrimination, or nonlinear price discrimination, occurs when individuals face nonlinear price schedules, i.e. the price paid depends on the quantity bought. The standard example of this form of price discrimination is quantity discounts.

Curiously, the determination of optimal nonlinear prices was not carefully examined until Spence (1976). Since then there have been a number of contributions in this area; see the literature survey in Brown and Sibley (1986). Much of his work uses techniques originally developed by Mirrlees (1971, 1976), Roberts

(1979) and others for the purpose of analyzing problems in optimal taxation. Much of the work described by Brown and Sibley is motivated by public utility pricing. Here the appropriate objective is welfare maximization rather than profit maximization. Since this literature is already discussed in another contribution to this Handbook, we will focus only on the profit maximization problem.

Our treatment follows the excellent discussion in Tirole (1988) which in turn is based on Maskin and Riley (1984). However, we conduct the main derivation using a general utility structure and resort to the special case considered by these authors only when needed.

2.3.1. Two types of consumers

It is useful to begin by considering a situation where there are only two types of consumers, a fraction f_1 of type t_1 and a fraction f_2 of type t_2. The monopolist wants to sell x_1 to the type 1 consumers and amount x_2 to the type 2 consumers, collecting total payments of r_1 and r_2 from each type.

The utility functions of the consumers are of the quasilinear form $u(x_i, t_i) + y_i$, where y_i is the consumption of the numeraire good. For convenience, we take the endowment of the numeraire good to be zero. We also assume that $u(x, t_2) > u(x, t_1)$ and that $\partial u(x, t_2)/\partial x > \partial u(x, t_1)/\partial x$. These assumptions imply that not only is consumer 2 willing to pay more than consumer 1 for a given amount of the good, but also that consumer 2's *marginal* willingness-to-pay exceeds consumer 1's. We will refer to consumer 2 as the *high-demand* consumer and consumer 1 as the *low-demand* consumer. The assumptions imply that the demand function for the high-demand consumer is always greater than the demand function for the low-demand consumer, a property sometimes known as the *noncrossing condition*.

The demand constraints facing the monopolist are as follows. First, each consumer must want to consume the amount x_i and be willing to pay the price r_i:

$$u(x_1, t_1) - r_1 \geq 0,$$

$$u(x_2, t_2) - r_2 \geq 0.$$

This is simply defining the domain of the problem we will analyze. Second, each consumer must prefer this consumption to the consumption of the other consumer:

$$u(x_1, t_1) - r_1 \geq u(x_2, t_1) - r_2,$$

$$u(x_2, t_2) - r_2 \geq u(x_1, t_2) - r_1.$$

These are the so-called *self-selection constraints*. If the plan (x_1, x_2) is to be feasible in the sense that it will be voluntarily chosen by the consumers, then each consumer must prefer consuming the bundle intended for him as compared to consuming the other person's bundle.

Our assumptions about the utility functions and the fact that the monopolist wants the prices to be as high as possible imply that two of the above four inequalities will be binding constraints. Specificially the low-demand consumer will be charged his maximum willingness-to-pay, and the high-demand consumer will be charged the highest price that will just induce him to consume x_2 rather than x_1. Solving for r_1 and r_2 gives:

$$r_1 = u(x_1, t_1)$$

and

$$r_2 = u(x_2, t_2) - u(x_1, t_2) + u(x_1, t_1).$$

The profit function of the monopolist is

$$\pi = [r_1 - cx_1]f_1 + [r_2 - cx_2]f_2,$$

which, upon substitution for r_1 and r_2 becomes:

$$\pi = [u(x_1, t_1) - cx_1]f_1 + [u(x_2, t_2) - u(x_1, t_2) + u(x_1, t_1) - cx_2]f_2.$$

This expression is to be maximized with respect to x_1 and x_2. Differentiating, we have

$$\left[\frac{\partial u(x_1, t_1)}{\partial x_1} - c\right]f_1 + \left[\frac{\partial u(x_1, t_1)}{\partial x_1} - \frac{\partial u(x_1, t_2)}{\partial x_1}\right]f_2 = 0, \tag{8}$$

$$\frac{\partial u(x_2, t_2)}{\partial x_2} - c = 0. \tag{9}$$

Equation (8) can be rearranged to give:

$$\frac{\partial u(x_1, t_1)}{\partial x_1} = c + \left[\frac{\partial u(x_1, t_2)}{\partial x_1} - \frac{\partial u(x_1, t_1)}{\partial x_1}\right]\frac{f_2}{f_1}, \tag{10}$$

which means that the low-demand consumer has a (marginal) value for the good that exceeds marginal cost. Hence, he consumes an inefficiently small amount of the good. Equation (9) says that at the optimal nonlinear prices, the high-demand consumer has a marginal willingness-to-pay which is equal to marginal cost. Thus, he consumes the socially correct amount.

The result that the consumer with the highest demand faces a marginal price equal to marginal cost is very general. If the consumer with the highest demand faced a marginal price in excess of marginal cost, the monopolist could lower the marginal price charged to the largest consumer by a small amount, inducing him to buy more. Since marginal price still exceeds marginal cost, the monopolist would make a profit on these sales. Furthermore, such a policy would not affect the monopolist's profits from any other consumers, since they are all optimized at lower values of consumption.

In order to get more explicit results about the optimal pricing scheme, it is necessary to make more explicit assumptions about tastes. For example, it is common to observe price discounts in certain types of goods – high-demand consumers pay a lower per-unit cost than low-demand consumers. Maskin and Riley (1984) show that if preferences take the specific form $u(x, t) + y = tv(x) + y$, then the optimal pricing policy will exhibit quantity discounts in this sense.

2.3.2. *A continuum of types*

Suppose now that there are a continuum of types, and let $f(t)$ be the density of consumers of type t. For convenience, let the types range from 0 to T. Let the utility function of a consumer of type t be given by $u(x, t) + y$, and let $r(x)$ be the revenue collected from a consumer who chooses to consume x units of the good. Again, we assume that increasing t increases both the total and the marginal willingness-to-pay, which in this context means that

$$\frac{\partial u(x, t)}{\partial t} > 0$$

and

$$\frac{\partial^2 u(x(t), t)}{\partial t \partial x} > 0.$$

Let $x(t)$ be the optimal consumption of a consumer of type t when facing a revenue function $r(\cdot)$. The self-selection constraints imply that a consumer of type t prefers his consumption to a consumer of type s, which means

$$u(x(t), t) - r(x(t)) \geq u(x(s), t) - r(x(s)).$$

Consider the function $g(s)$ defined by

$$g(s) = [u(x(t), t) - r(x(t))] - [u(x(s), t) - r(x(s))].$$

We have just seen that $g(s) \geq 0$ and of course $g(t) = 0$. It follows that $g(s)$ reaches its minimum value when $s = t$. Hence, the derivative of g with respect to

s must vanish at $s = t$, which implies:

$$\left(\frac{\partial u(x(t), t)}{\partial x} - \frac{\partial r(x(t))}{\partial x}\right)\frac{\mathrm{d}x(t)}{\mathrm{d}s} = 0,$$

which in turn implies that

$$\frac{\partial u(x(t), t)}{\partial x} - \frac{\partial r(x(t))}{\partial x} = 0. \tag{11}$$

This is the analog of the self-selection constraint given above.[3]

Let $V(t)$ be the maximized utility of an agent of type t when facing a pricing schedule $r(\cdot)$. That is,

$$V(t) \equiv u(x(t), t) - r(x(t)). \tag{12}$$

We will have occasion to use the derivative of $V(t)$. Using (11) we calculate

$$\begin{aligned} V'(t) &= \left(\frac{\partial u(x(t), t)}{\partial x} - \frac{\partial r(x(t))}{\partial x}\right)\frac{\mathrm{d}x}{\mathrm{d}t} + \frac{\partial u(x(t), t)}{\partial t} \\ &= \frac{\partial u(x(t), t)}{\partial t}. \end{aligned}$$

This is simply the envelope theorem – the total derivative of utility reduces to the partial derivative after substituting in the first-order conditions for maximization.

The monopolist wants to choose $x(t)$ so as to maximize profits subject to the self-selection constraints. Profits are given by

$$\pi = \int_0^T [r(x(t)) - cx(t)]f(t)\mathrm{d}t.$$

The trick is to build the self-selection constraints into the objective function in a useful way. Using (12) we can rewrite profits as

$$\pi = \int_0^T [u(x(t), t) - cx(t)]f(t)\mathrm{d}t - \int_0^T V(t)f(t)\mathrm{d}t. \tag{13}$$

Integrating the last term by parts, we have

$$\int_0^T V(t)f(t)\mathrm{d}t = V(t)(F(t) - 1)\Big]_0^T - \int_0^T V'(t)[F(t) - 1]\mathrm{d}t.$$

[3] The self-selection constraint can also be thought of as no-envy constraint. The calculation given here was used in examining envy-free allocations in Varian (1976).

[Here we have used $F(t) - 1$ as the integral of $f(t)$.] The utility of type 0 is normalized to be 0, and $F(T) = 1$; hence, the first term on the right-hand side of this expression vanishes. Substituting from (12) leaves us with

$$\int_0^T V(t)f(t)\mathrm{d}t = -\int_0^T \frac{\partial u(x(t),t)}{\partial t}[F(t) - 1]\mathrm{d}t.$$

Substituting this back into the objective function, equation (13), gives us the final form of the profit function:

$$\pi = \int_0^T \left\{ [u(x(t),t) - cx(t)] f(t) - \frac{\partial u(x(t),t)}{\partial t}[1 - F(t)] \right\} \mathrm{d}t.$$

Along the optimal path, the derivative of the integrand with respect to each $x(t)$ should vanish. This gives us the first-order condition:

$$\left[\frac{\partial u(x(t),t)}{\partial x} - c \right] f(t) - \frac{\partial^2 u(x(t),t)}{\partial t \partial x}[1 - F(t)] = 0.$$

Solving for $\partial u/\partial x$ yields:

$$\frac{\partial u(x(t),t)}{\partial x} = c + \frac{\partial^2 u(x(t),t)}{\partial t \partial x}\left[\frac{1 - F(t)}{f(t)} \right]. \tag{14}$$

It is instructive to compare this expression to the formula for the optimal marginal price in the case of two consumers given in (10). Note the close analogy. As in the case with two consumers, all consumers pay a price in excess of marginal cost except for the consumer with the highest willingness-to-pay, consumer T.

In order to derive further results about the shape of the optimal policy, it is necessary to make more detailed assumptions about preferences and the distribution of tastes. For example, suppose that we adopt the form of preferences used by Maskin and Riley (1984), $tv(x) + y$. Let $p(x) = r'(x)$ be the marginal price when purchases are x. Equation (11) then implies that $r'(x(t)) = tv'(x(t))$ is the optimal solution. Substituting this into (14) and rearranging yields:

$$\frac{p(x(t)) - c}{p(x(t))} = \frac{1 - F(t)}{tf(t)}.$$

The expression $(1 - F(t))/f(t)$ is known as the *hazard rate*. For a wide variety of distributions, including the uniform, the normal, and the exponential, the hazard rate increases with t. Assuming this, and using the concavity of $v(x)$, it is not hard to show that $x(t)$ increases with t and the marginal price $p(x(t))$ decreases with $x(t)$. Thus, this form of preference leads to quantity discounts, a result first proved by Maskin and Riley (1984).

The reader should be warned that our derivation of the profit maximizing nonlinear price was rather cavalier. We assumed differentiability as needed as well as assuming that various second-order conditions would be satisfied. Unfortunately, these assumptions are not innocuous. Optimal pricing policies can easily exhibit kinks so that consumers of different types end up bunching at common quantities, or gaps, so that some consumer types end up not being served. For a detailed and lucid taxonomy of what can go wrong, as well as some illustrative examples, see the discussion in Brown and Sibley (1986, pp. 208–215). See Ordover and Panzar (1982) for a treatment of the nonlinear pricing of inputs.

2.3.3. *Welfare and output effects*

Katz (1983) has examined the welfare and output effects of nonlinear pricing. He shows that in general the monopolist may produce too little or too much output as compared with the social optimum, but when the noncrossing condition is satisfied, the monopolist will typically restrict total output. In general, total welfare will be positively associated with total output so that changes in output may serve as appropriate indicators for changes in welfare.

2.4. *Third-degree price discrimination*

Third-degree price discrimination occurs when consumers are charged different prices but each consumer faces a constant price for all units of output purchased. This is probably the most common form of price discrimination.

The textbook case is where there are two separate markets, where the firm can easily enforce the division. An example would be discrimination by age, such as youth discounts at the movies. If we let $p_i(x_i)$ be the inverse demand function for group i, and suppose that there are two groups, then the monopolist's profit maximization problem is

$$\max_{x_1, x_2} p_1(x_1)x_1 + p_2(x_2)x_2 - cx_1 - cx_2.$$

The first-order conditions for this problem are

$$p_1(x_1) + p_1'(x_1)x_1 = c,$$

$$p_2(x_2) + p_2'(x_2)x_2 = c.$$

Let ε_i be the elasticity of demand in market i, we can write these expressions as

$$p_1(x_1)\left[1 - \frac{1}{|\varepsilon_1|}\right] = c,$$

$$p_2(x_2)\left[1 - \frac{1}{|\varepsilon_2|}\right] = c.$$

It follows that $p_1(x_1) > p_2(x_2)$ if and only if $|\varepsilon_1| < |\varepsilon_2|$. Hence, the market with the more elastic demand – the market that is more price sensitive – is charged the lower price.

Suppose now that the monopolist is unable to separate the markets as cleanly as assumed, so that the price charged in one market influences the demand in another market. For example, consider a theater that has a bargain night on Monday; the lower price on Monday would presumably influence demand on Tuesday to some degree.

In this case the profit maximization problem of the firm is

$$\max_{x_1, x_2} p_1(x_1, x_2)x_1 + p_2(x_1, x_2)x_2 - cx_1 - cx_2,$$

and the first-order conditions become:

$$p_1 + \frac{\partial p_1}{\partial x_1}x_1 + \frac{\partial p_2}{\partial x_1}x_2 = c,$$

$$p_2 + \frac{\partial p_2}{\partial x_2}x_2 + \frac{\partial p_1}{\partial x_2}x_1 = c.$$

We can rearrange these conditions to give:

$$p_1[1 - 1/|\varepsilon_1|] + \frac{\partial p_2}{\partial x_1}x_2 = c,$$

$$p_2[1 - 1/|\varepsilon_2|] + \frac{\partial p_1}{\partial x_2}x_1 = c.$$

It is not easy to say anything very interesting about these equations, but we will try.

One simplification we can make is to assume there are no income effects so that $\partial p_1/\partial x_2 = \partial p_2/\partial x_1$, i.e. the cross price effects are symmetric.[4] Subtracting the second equation from the first and rearranging, we have

$$p_1\left[1 - \frac{1}{|\varepsilon_1|}\right] - p_2\left[1 - \frac{1}{|\varepsilon_2|}\right] = [x_1 - x_2]\frac{\partial p_2}{\partial x_1}.$$

It is natural to suppose that the two goods are substitutes – after all, they are the same good being sold to different groups – so that $\partial p_2/\partial x_1 > 0$. Without loss of generality, assume that $x_1 > x_2$, which, by the equation immediately above, implies that

$$p_1\left[1 - \frac{1}{|\varepsilon_1|}\right] - p_2\left[1 - \frac{1}{|\varepsilon_2|}\right] > 0.$$

Rearranging, we have

$$\frac{p_1}{p_2} > \frac{1 - 1/|\varepsilon_2|}{1 - 1/|\varepsilon_1|}.$$

It follows from this expression that if $|\varepsilon_2| > |\varepsilon_1|$, we must have $p_1 > p_2$. That is, if the *smaller* market has the more elastic demand, it must have the lower price. Thus, the intuition of the separate markets carries over to the more general case under these additional assumptions.

2.4.1. *Welfare effects*

Much of the discussion about third-degree price discrimination has to do with the welfare effects of allowing this form of price discrimination. Would we generally expect consumer plus producer surplus to be higher or lower when third-degree price discrimination is present than when it is not?

Since Robinson (1933) first raised this question, it has been the subject of a number of investigations, including Battalio and Ekelund (1972), Holahan (1975), Hsu (1983), Ippolito (1980), Kwoka (1984), Yamey (1974), Hausman and MacKie-Mason (1986), Schmalensee (1981b), and Varian (1985). Varian's results are the most general and serve as the focus of our discussion.

We begin with formulating a general test for welfare improvement. Suppose for simplicity that there are only two groups and start with an aggregate utility

[4]Actually assuming no income effects is a stronger assumption than we need. Willig (1976) and Varian (1978) have shown that all that is necessary is that the income elasticities of goods 1 and 2 are locally constant over some region in price–income space.

function of the form $u(x_1, x_2) + y$. Here x_1 and x_2 are the consumptions of the two groups and y is money to be spent on other consumption goods. The inverse demand functions for the two goods are given by

$$p_1(x_1, x_2) = \frac{\partial u(x_1, x_2)}{\partial x_1},$$

$$p_2(x_1, x_2) = \frac{\partial u(x_1, x_2)}{\partial x_2}.$$

We assume that $u(x_1, x_2)$ is concave and differentiable, though this is slightly stronger than needed.

Let $c(x_1, x_2)$ be the cost of providing x_1 and x_2, so that social welfare is measured by

$$W(x_1, x_2) = u(x_1, x_2) - c(x_1, x_2).$$

Now consider two configurations of output, (x_1^0, x_2^0) and (x_1', x_2'), with associated prices (p_1^0, p_2^0) and (p_1', p_2'). By the concavity of $u(x_1, x_2)$, we have

$$u(x_1', x_2') \leq u(x_1^0, x_2^0) + \frac{\partial u(x_1^0, x_2^0)}{\partial x_1}(x_1' - x_1^0) + \frac{\partial u(x_1^0, x_2^0)}{\partial x_2}(x_2' - x_2^0).$$

Rearranging and using the definition of the inverse demand functions we have

$$\Delta u \leq p_1^0 \Delta x_1 + p_2^0 \Delta x_2.$$

By an analogous argument we have

$$\Delta u \geq p_1' \Delta x_1 + p_2' \Delta x_2.$$

Since $\Delta W = \Delta u - \Delta c$, we have our final result:

$$p_1^0 \Delta x_1 + p_2^0 \Delta x_2 - \Delta c \geq \Delta W \geq p_1' \Delta x_1 + p_2' \Delta x_2 - \Delta c. \tag{15}$$

In the special case of constant marginal cost, $\Delta c = c\Delta x_1 + c\Delta x_2$, so the inequality becomes:

$$(p_1^0 - c)\Delta x_1 + (p_2^0 - c)\Delta x_2 \geq \Delta W \geq (p_1' - c)\Delta x_1 + (p_2' - c)\Delta x_2. \tag{16}$$

Note that these welfare bounds are perfectly general, based only on the concavity of the utility function, which is, in turn, basically the requirement that demand curves slope down. Varian (1985) derived the inequalities using the indirect utility function, which is slightly more general.

In order to apply these inequalities to the question of price discrimination, let the initial set of prices be the constant monopoly prices so that $p_1^0 = p_2^0 = p^0$, and let (p_1', p_2') be the discriminatory prices. Then the bounds in (16) become:

$$(p^0 - c)(\Delta x_1 + \Delta x_2) \geq \Delta W \geq (p_1' - c)\Delta x_1 + (p_2' - c)\Delta x_2. \tag{17}$$

The upper bound implies that *a necessary condition for welfare to increase is that total output increase*. Suppose to the contrary that total output decreased so that $\Delta x_1 + \Delta x_2 < 0$. Since $p^0 - c > 0$, (17) implies that $\Delta W < 0$. The lower bound gives a sufficient condition for welfare to increase under price discrimination, namely that the sum of the *weighted output* changes is positive, with the weights being given by price minus marginal cost.

The simple geometry of the bounds is shown in Figure 10.1. The welfare gain ΔW is the indicated trapezoid. The area of this trapezoid is clearly bounded above and below by the area of the two rectangles.

As a simple application of the welfare bounds, let us consider the case of two markets with linear demand curves:

$$x_1 = a_1 - b_1 p_1; \qquad x_2 = a_2 - b_2 p_2.$$

For simplicity set marginal costs equal to zero. Then if the monopolist engages in price discrimination, he will maximize revenue by selling halfway down each demand curve, so that $x_1 = a_1/2$ and $x_2 = a_2/2$.

Now suppose that the monopolist sells at a single price to both markets. The total demand curve will be

$$x_1 + x_2 = a_1 + a_2 - (b_1 + b_2)p.$$

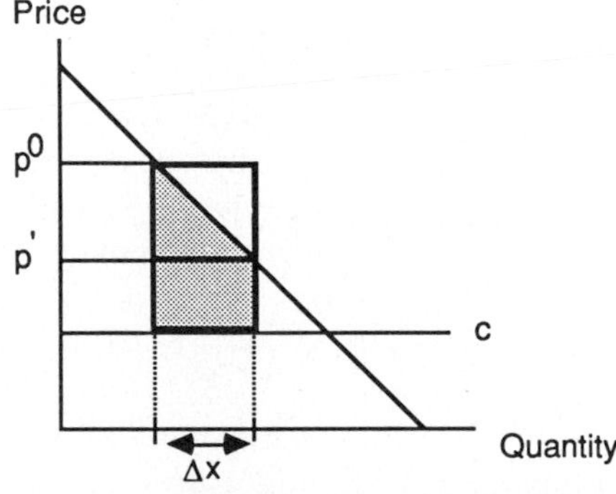

Figure 10.1. Illustration of the welfare bounds.

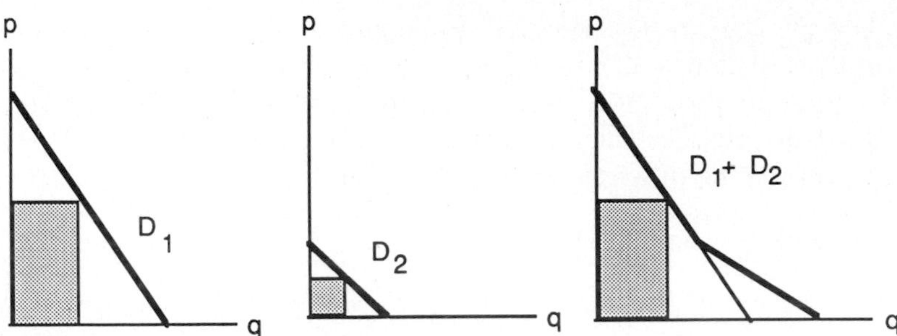

Figure 10.2. An example where the monopolist chooses not to serve one of the markets.

To maximize revenue the monopolist will operate halfway down the demand curve which means that

$$x_1 + x_2 = \frac{a_1 + a_2}{2}.$$

Hence, with linear demand curves the total output is the same under price discrimination as under ordinary monopoly. The bound given in (17) then implies that welfare must decrease under price discrimination.

However, this result relies on the assumption that both markets are served under the ordinary monopoly. Suppose that market 2 is very small, so that the profit maximizing firm sells zero to this market if price discrimination is not allowed, as illustrated in Figure 10.2.

In the case allowing price discrimination results in $\Delta x_1 = 0$ and $\Delta x_2 > 0$, providing an unambiguous welfare gain by (17). Of course, this is not only a welfare gain, but is in fact a Pareto improvement.

This example is quite robust. If a new market is opened up because of price discrimination – a market that was not previously being served under the ordinary monopoly – then we will typically have a Pareto improving welfare enhancement. This case is emphasized by Hausman and MacKie-Mason (1986) with respect to new patents. On the other hand, if linearity of demand is not a bad first approximation, and output does not change too drastically in response to price discrimination, we might well expect that the net impact on welfare is negative.

2.4.2. *Output effect of price discrimination*

Since the change in output provides some clue as to the welfare change, it is worthwhile considering conditions under which it has a determinate sign. Robinson (1933), Battalio and Ekelund (1972), Edwards (1950), Smith and

Formby (1981), Finn (1974), Greenhut and Ohta (1976), Löfgren (1971), Silberberg (1970), Schmalensee (1981b) and others have contributed to this question. For some general results and a good summary of the literature, see Shih and Mai (1986), whose treatment we follow here.

Let x_i' be the output in the ith market under discrimination and x_i^0 be the output under uniform pricing. By manipulating the first-order conditions for profit maximization and using the mean-value theorem, it can be shown that the difference between the total output under uniform and discriminatory pricing is given by

$$X^0 - X' = \frac{1}{2} \sum_{i=1}^{n} (x_i^0 - x'_i)[p_i(\hat{x}_i) - c] \frac{p_i''(\hat{x}_i)}{p_i'(\hat{x}_i)^2}. \tag{18}$$

In this expression, $\hat{x}_i$ is an output level between x_i' and x_i^0 (this is where the mean value theorem is used). Following Robinson, we call a market *strong* if $x_i' < x_i^0$ and *weak* if $x_i' > x_i^0$. It follows from equation (18) that if all weak markets have strictly convex demands and all strong markets have concave or linear demands, then total output will be greater under discrimination than under uniform pricing and vice versa.[5] Of course if all markets have linear demands, total output is constant, as we have observed earlier.

2.4.3. Intermediate goods markets

Katz (1987) has examined the welfare effect of price discrimination in intermediate goods markets. This phenomenon is of some interest since the Robinson–Patman Act (discussed below) was explicitly concerned with this form of price discrimination. There are two important differences in the analysis of intermediate goods markets as compared to final goods markets. The first is that the buyers' demands for the product are interdependent: the profits and factor demands by a downstream firm depend on the factor demands of its competitors. The second is that the buyers in intermediate goods markets often have the possibility of integrating upstream and produce the intermediate good themselves.

The first effect means that the welfare analysis must take into account the induced changes in the degree of competition engendered by different policies. The second effect means that the welfare analysis must take into account

[5]Note that Robinson, and several other subsequent authors, reverse the sense of concave and convex when discussing these results.

inefficiencies in production decisions caused by the different policies. Accordingly, there are two components to the change in welfare when price discrimination is allowed in intermediate goods markets. The first is the standard effect on the output of the final good which we have discussed above. The second is the decision of whether or not to integrate and the resulting impact on the costs of production.

These two components interact in complex ways. Katz shows that if there is no integration under either regime, total output and total welfare are both lower when price discrimination is allowed than when it is forbidden. In fact, under reasonable conditions price discrimination in intermediate goods markets can lead to higher prices being charged to *all* buyers of the good, a result that cannot arise in final goods markets.

Katz shows that integration can only occur when price discrimination is banned, not when it is allowed. If there is increasing returns in the intermediate good production, this means that price discrimination may serve to prevent socially inefficient integration.

2.5. *Defining the market*

In most of the literature on third-degree price discrimination, the determination of the different groups of consumers is taken as exogenous to the model. The monopolist has already decided to charge one price to people over 18 and another price to people under 18, or one price to customers who purchase drinks between 5 and 7 p.m. and another price to those who purchase drinks at other hours. The only issue is what the prices should be.

However, it is clear that the choice of how to divide the market is a very important consideration for the monopolist. In this subsection we will briefly examine this decision in a highly specialized framework.

We will conduct our discussion in terms of pricing beverages by time of day, but a variety of other interpretations are possible. We assume that the demand for drinks at an arbitrary time t depends only on the time and the price charged at that time, so we write $x(p_t, t)$. The assumption that demands are independent across the times of day is admittedly a drastic simplification. We assume that $0 \leq t \leq 1$.

Then if the monopolist charges p_1 before time T and p_2 after time T, the total amount that he sells in each time period will be given by

$$X_1(p_1, T) = \int_0^T x(p_1, t)\mathrm{d}t,$$

$$X_2(p_2, T) = \int_T^1 x(p_2, t)\mathrm{d}t.$$

The profit maximization problem of the monopolist can then be written as

$$\max_{p_1, p_2, T} (p_1 - c)X_1(p_1, T) + (p_2 - c)X_2(p_2, T).$$

The first-order conditions for this problem are

$$(p_1 - c)\frac{\partial X_1}{\partial p_1} + X_1(p_1, T) = 0,$$

$$(p_2 - c)\frac{\partial X_2}{\partial p_2} + X_2(p_2, T) = 0,$$

$$(p_1 - c)x_1(p_1, T) - (p_2 - c)x_2(p_2, T) = 0.$$

The first two equations are the standard marginal revenue equals marginal cost conditions. They can be transformed into the standard elasticity form and can be interpreted in exactly the same way. Thus, if the elasticity of demand increases with the time of day, consumers after the breakpoint will pay a price lower than those before the breakpoint.

The third equation is new; it indicates how the monopolist determines the optimal breakpoint. The interpretation of this condition is straightforward: when the monopolist chooses the optimal breakpoint T, the profits earned from charging marginal consumer the higher price must equal the profits earned from charging the lower price.

What about the welfare effects of the choice of breakpoint? Is the monopolist choosing the correct breakpoint given his pricing decision? Or will there be a systematic distortion?

As it turns out there is a very general result available here: social welfare will *always* increase by shifting the breakpoint in the direction of the lower prices. In our context of pricing beverages by time of day we can refer to this as the *Happy Hours Theorem*: Happy Hours are always too short.

The proof is easy. Consider moving the breakpoint a small amount in the direction of lower prices. This certainly makes the consumers better off. But since the breakpoint was the profit maximizing choice by the monopolist, changing the breakpoint slightly must have a zero first-order effect on profits. Hence, consumer plus producer surplus must necessarily increase.

In the context of our independent demand example, if the elasticity of demand is increasing with the time of day, then the monopolist always sets the breakpoint too early in the day, while the reverse is true if the elasticity of demand decreases with the time of day.

Note that the Happy Hours Theorem itself does not rely on the assumption of independent demands; it is true in complete generality. In other contexts it can be interpreted as saying that airlines always have too severe requirements for the special fares, and that the definition of Senior Citizens used by price discrimination is always too stringent.

2.6. Bundling

Bundling refers to the practice of selling two or more goods in a package. *Pure bundling* means that the goods are only available in the package, while *mixed bundling* means that the goods are available either individually or bundled together in a package. Examples of bundling include *prix fixe* menus, mandatory service contracts, season tickets, and so on. Mixed bundling includes such practices as roundtrip air fares, all inclusive vacation plans, and different sizes of packaged goods.

The earliest reference to the phenomenon of bundling appears to be that of Burnstein (1960), followed by Stigler (1963). Adams and Yellen (1976) provide a clear discussion with numerous examples.

Despite the prevalence of bundling as a marketing phenomenon, there is only a small theoretical literature concerning this topic, probably due to the difficulty of getting analytic results. Schmalensee (1984) conducts extensive numerical simulations to address some of the questions surrounding the bundling literature. We will begin by summarizing the framework of Adams and Yellen (1976).

The simplest case of bundling is that involving quantity bundling. Formally, this is a case of second-degree price discrimination, i.e. nonlinear pricing. The simplest example occurs when there are two types of consumers, a high-demand and a low-demand type, but the firm cannot explicitly discriminate between the two types.

Suppose that the high-demand consumer is willing to pay $10 for one unit of the good or $11 for two units, while the low-demand consumer is willing to pay $1 for one unit or $2 for two units. Suppose for simplicity that marginal costs are zero. Then in this case an effective strategy for the firm is to sell the good only in pairs, allowing the monopolist to price discriminate between the high-demand and low-demand consumers. Here quantity bundling serves as a way to satisfy the self-selection constraints and allows the monopolist to engage in price discrimination.

Another example of bundling is discussed in Stigler (1963), who describes the common practice of "block booking" movies. This practice required that theaters bought films in packages, or bundles, rather than buying the individual films separately.

Suppose that there are two theaters, A and B. A is willing to pay $9000 for film 1, $3000 for film 2, and $12 000 for the package. B is willing to pay $10 000 for film 1, $2000 for film 2, and $12 000 for the package. Notice that the value of the bundle to each theater is simply the sum of the values of the two films; there are no "interaction effects" in the consumption of the two goods.

Suppose that costs are zero, so that the movie rental company is only interested in maximizing revenue. If the rental company rents each film individually, profit maximization requires that it rents film 1 for \$9000 and film 2 for \$2000 making a total of \$11 000 from each theater. But if it rents only the bundled package it makes \$12 000 from each theater. Effectively the rental company has managed to price discriminate between the two theaters; it is renting film 1 to theater A for \$9000 and to firm B for \$10 000, and similarly for film 2.

This example illustrates an important point: bundling is most effective when there is a negative correlation between the consumers' valuations of the goods. In the case illustrated, theater A's value for film 1 is less than theater B's, but theater A's value for film 2 is higher than theater B's.

Adams and Yellen (1976) present a series of useful diagrams to analyze the effects of bundling. Consider a model in which each consumer wants at most one unit of each of two goods, which are produced costlessly by a monopolist. The reservation prices of the two goods will be denoted by r_1 and r_2. For simplicity, we suppose that each consumer's value of the bundle is simply the sum of his or her reservation prices r_1 and r_2. Let $f(r_1, r_2)$ denote the density function for consumers who have reservation prices (r_1, r_2).

Figure 10.3(a) depicts the outcome under separate, nonbundled sales. The firm picks prices (p_1, p_2), and sells to all consumers in the shaded area, N. Figure 10.3(b) shows the outcome of pure bundling. The monopolist sells only the package at some price p_b and all consumers in the shaded area B are purchasers.

Finally, Figure 10.4 illustrates the effect of mixed bundling. Here we suppose that the monopolist will sell the items separately at prices p_1 and p_2, or together

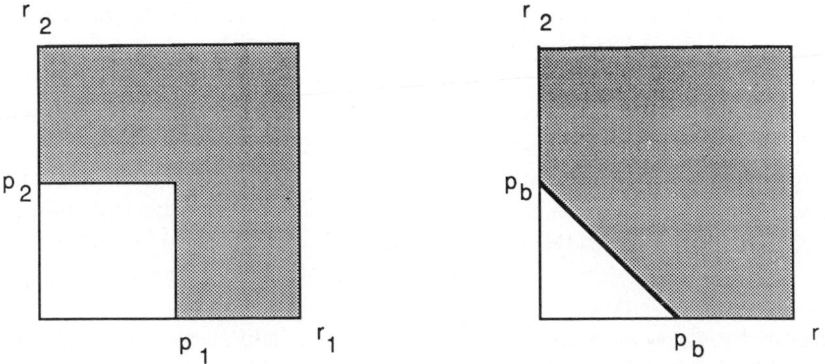

Figure 10.3. Illustration of nonbundled and bundled strategies.

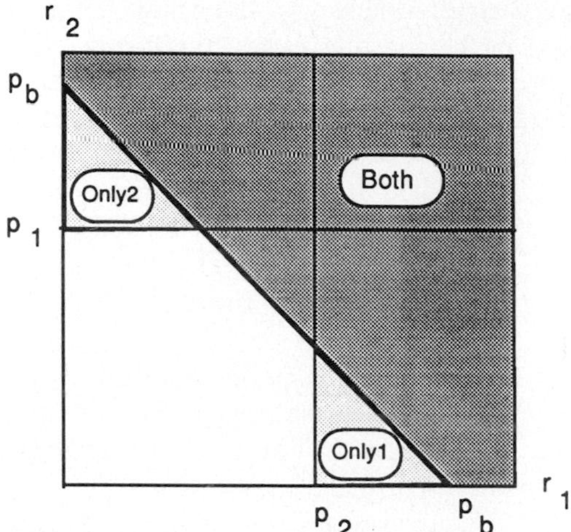

Figure 10.4. Illustration of mixed bundling strategy.

in a bundle at price p_b. The areas Only 1, Only 2, and Both indicate the goods purchased by the consumers with various combinations of reservation prices.

Adams and Yellen (1976) show using examples in this diagrammatic framework that nearly anything can happen with bundling: bundling may be more or less profitable than nonbundling, and consumers' surplus and total welfare may be higher or lower.

Since analytic results in the general model are so sparse, it is sensible to look for plausible restrictions that yield results. For example, Schmalensee (1982) shows that if the monopolist can only bundle its product with another good that is competitively produced, it is never better off bundling than simply selling its product separately. However, if there is a negative correlation among buyers' reservation prices, it may pay the monopolist to engage in mixed bundling.

Adams and Yellen (1976) show that mixed bundling always dominates pure bundling. McAfee, McMillan and Winston (1987) have derived a condition on the distribution of reservation price which guarantees that mixed bundling will dominate unbundled sales. In particular, they show that if the buyers' reservation prices are independently distributed, then mixed bundling will *always* dominate unbundled sales. Furthermore, when purchases can be monitored, then bundling is preferred to unbundled sales for virtually all distributions of reservations prices.

Schmalensee (1984) describes a detailed set of simulations using Gaussian distributions for the reservation prices of consumers. One of the most interesting results of Schmalensee's simulations is the role played by the distribution of buyers' valuations of the two goods. Intuition suggests that bundling is most effective when buyers' valuations are negatively correlated – buyers who value good 1 highly place a small value on good 2 and vice versa. However, Schmalensee suggests that the real role of bundling is to reduce the heterogeneity of buyers' valuations. He demonstrates that, in the Gaussian case, the standard deviation of the valuation of the bundles is always less than the sum of the standard deviations for the individual components. By reducing the dispersion of buyers' valuations, the monopolist is better able to extract the surplus from the population.

Although Schmalensee's simulations provide significant insight into bundling, it would still be helpful to have some analytic results. One plausible research strategy is to examine restrictions on preferences under which analytic results might be feasible. Suppose, for example, that we consider the case of the representative consumer – where the aggregate demand behavior of the population behaves like that of a single representative consumer.

Let $u(x_1, x_2) + y$ be the utility function of this representative consumer for goods x_1 and x_2, which may be bundled, and y, which represents all other goods. The inverse demand functions for the two goods purchased separately are given by

$$p_1(x_1, x_2) = \frac{\partial u(x_1, x_2)}{\partial x_1},$$

$$p_2(x_1, x_2) = \frac{\partial u(x_1, x_2)}{\partial x_2}.$$

Suppose that the bundle consists of 1 unit of good 1 and k units of good 2 and that it sells for a price of p_b. If we let x_b be the number of units of the bundle purchased, the utility maximization problem of the representative consumer can be written as

$$\max_{x_b} u(x_b, kx_b) + y$$

$$\text{s.t. } p_b x_b + y = m.$$

Substituting from the constraint and differentiating, we see that the inverse demand function for the bundle is given by

$$p_b(x_b, kx_b) = \frac{\partial u(x_b, kx_b)}{\partial x_1} + k\frac{\partial u(x_b, kx_b)}{\partial x_2}. \tag{19}$$

This equation says that the marginal willingness-to-pay for the bundle is simply sum of the willingnesses-to-pay for the individual components, which is quite plausible.

Let the constant marginal costs of the two goods be c_1 and c_2. The profit maximization problem for the monopolist who sells the unbundled goods is

$$\max_{x_1, x_2} \left(p_1(x_1, x_2) - c_1 \right) x_1 + \left(p_2(x_1, x_2) - c_2 \right) x_2, \tag{20}$$

while the profit maximization problem for the bundled monopolist is

$$\max_{x_b, k} \left(p_b(x_b, kx_b) - c_1 - kc_2 \right) x_b. \tag{21}$$

We can now state our main result: in the context of the above model, the monopolist can achieve exactly the same profits whether he bundles or not – there is no inherent advantage to either strategy.

In order to prove this, simply substitute the expression for the inverse demand function given in (19) into (21) and rearrange to get:

$$\max_{x_b, k} \left[p_1(x_b, kx_b) - c_1 \right] x_b + \left[p_2(x_b, kx_b) - c_2 \right] kx_b. \tag{22}$$

Comparing (20) and (22) we see that they describe exactly the same maximization problem: for any pair (x_1^*, x_2^*) that yields a given profit level in (20) we can set $x_b^* = x_1^*$ and $k = x_2^*/x_1^*$ to achieve exactly the same profit level in (22), and vice versa. Hence, in the context of a representative consumer model, bundling does no better than not bundling.

Upon reflection this is not terribly surprising. Bundling is inherently a strategy that exploits differences in willingness-to-pay across people, and bundling with a single consumer – or an economy that acts like a single consumer – cannot be expected to be of much interest. However, the representative consumer model can be used to generate some other interesting questions. For example, for what distributions of willingness-to-pay does the reservation price model of Adams and Yellen reduce to the representative consumer model? The answer to this question would give us more of handle on determining for what distributions bundling is profitable. Will mixed bundling generally dominate separate sales in the reservation price model? Since mixed bundling dominates pure bundling, one being a special case of the other, we expect that the answer to this question is yes.

3. Applications

As we saw in the introductory remarks, price discrimination is a very commonly used marketing tactic. In the following subsections, we will discuss a number of ways that firms can use to price discriminate among their customers.

3.1. Spatial price discrimination

Firms often use delivery charges – or the absence of delivery charges – to price discriminate among customers. For example, cement in Belgium is sold at a uniform delivered price throughout the country; while plasterboard is sold at a uniform delivered price in the United Kingdom. See Phlips (1983, pp. 23–30) for a detailed discussion of such pricing policies in Europe.

Even though delivery costs of these goods can be a significant fraction of their value, firms may find it profitable to charge one price for all areas. In many cases, FOB pricing – in which the customers provide the transportation and pays one price for "freight on board" at a central warehouse – is explicitly excluded by the providers of the good. Instead, the producers offer only a price which includes delivery charges.

In order to model the effect of transportation costs on the monopolist's pricing policy, let x be the quantity sold at a particular location, let the inverse demand function for the delivered good be denoted by $p(x)$ and let the total transportation costs to the given location be denoted by tx. The net demand function facing the firm is then $p(x) - t$. Assuming constant marginal costs, the profit maximization problem for the firm becomes:

$$\max_x \,[p(x) - t - c]x,$$

which has the standard first-order conditions:

$$p(x) + p'(x)x = c + t. \tag{23}$$

How will the net price to the consumer change as the transportation costs change? The above formulation makes it clear that this is the same as asking how the price to consumers changes as we change an excise tax on a monopolist.

Implicitly differentiating (23) with respect to t and solving for $\mathrm{d}x/\mathrm{d}t$, we have

$$\frac{\mathrm{d}x}{\mathrm{d}t} = \frac{1}{2p'(x) + p''(x)x}.$$

Hence,

$$\frac{\mathrm{d}p}{\mathrm{d}t} = \frac{\mathrm{d}p}{\mathrm{d}x}\frac{\mathrm{d}x}{\mathrm{d}t} = \frac{1}{2 + p''(x)x/p'(x)}.$$

Thus, the amount of the transportation costs that are passed along depends on the second derivative of the inverse demand function, $p''(x)$. We can examine a few special cases. If the inverse demand curve is linear, $p''(x) = 0$ and therefore half of the transportation costs will be paid by the consumers. In this case the monopolist practices freight absorption and discriminates against customers with lower transport costs. This is similar to the examples of cement and plasterboard described above: the firm effectively absorbs part or all of the transportation costs.

If the inverse demand curve has a constant elasticity of ε, then the monopolist charges a constant markup on marginal cost, so that the customers at each distance will effectively pay more for delivery than the actual delivery costs. However, this form of price discrimination is especially sensitive to consumer arbitrage – consumers with lower transportation costs can transship to those with higher transportation costs, essentially undermining the monopolist's position.

Delivered pricing systems have sometimes been attacked as anticompetitive under the Robinson–Patman Act; for a discussion of some of the issues involved and citations to a number of relevant cases, see Neale and Goyder (1980, pp. 245–248).

3.2. Intertemporal discrimination

Often new products are introduced at a high price which later declines. For example, books are typically introduced in expensive hardcover editions and only later published as less expensive paperbacks. Such a policy appears to be a form of intertemporal price discrimination: the monopolist attempts to first extract the surplus from the high-demand consumers and only later sells to the low-demand consumers.

This kind of intertemporal price discrimination was first analyzed in detail by Stokey (1979). She considered a model with a continuum of consumers and times in which the consumers and the firm have the same discount rate. In the context of this model, Stokey proved a very surprising result: the profit maximizing policy of the firm is to charge a uniform price, *not* to engage in price discrimination.

We will investigate Stokey's result in the context of a much simpler model based on the discussion in Subsection 2.5 concerning self-selection constraints. Suppose that there are two consumers with reservation prices r_1 and r_2 and a common discount factor of $0 < \alpha < 1$. Without loss of generality, suppose that $r_1 > r_2$. The monopolist, who also has a discount rate of α, can costlessly supply up to two units of the good.

We now consider whether it is optimal to price discriminate in this model. Suppose that the monopolist sets prices p_1 and p_2 that succeed in inducing consumer 1 to consume in the first period and consumer 2 to consume in the second period. Then each consumer must prefer the discounted net value of his purchase to that of the other consumer; this gives us the self-selection constraints:

$$r_1 - p_1 \geq \alpha(r_1 - p_2), \tag{24}$$

$$\alpha(r_2 - p_2) \geq r_2 - p_1. \tag{25}$$

The first inequality says that the period 1 purchaser prefers his choice to buying in period 2, while the second inequality states the analogous condition for consumer 2. If we multiply these two inequalities together and cancel the α from each side, we have

$$(r_1 - p_1)(r_2 - p_2) \geq (r_1 - p_2)(r_2 - p_1).$$

After some manipulation, this inequality becomes:

$$(p_2 - p_1)(r_2 - r_1) \geq 0.$$

Since $r_1 > r_2$ by assumption, we must have $p_1 \geq p_2$, which simply means that the price in the first period must be higher than the price in the second, hardly a surprising result.

The problem faced by the price discriminating monopolist can now be written as

$$\max_{p_1, p_2} p_1 + \alpha p_2$$

$$\text{s.t. } r_1 - p_1 \geq \alpha(r_1 - p_2), \tag{26}$$

$$\alpha(r_2 - p_2) \geq r_2 - p_1, \tag{27}$$

$$r_1 \geq p_1, \tag{28}$$

$$r_2 \geq p_2. \tag{29}$$

Although there are four constraints in this linear program, they are not all independent. Rearranging (26) we have

$$r_1 \geq \frac{1}{1-\alpha}(p_1 - \alpha p_2).$$

Subtracting p_1 from each side gives:

$$r_1 - p_1 \geq \frac{1}{1-\alpha}(p_1 - \alpha p_2) - p_1$$

$$= \frac{\alpha}{1-\alpha}(p_1 - p_2) \geq 0.$$

It follows that (26) implies (28), so we drop (28) from the set of constraints.

At the solution to this linear programming problem, at least two of the constraints will be binding. Eliminating the trivial cases, this leaves us with three possibilities.

Case 1. $r_1 - p_1 = \alpha(r_1 - p_2)$ and $\alpha(r_2 - p_2) = r_2 - p_1$. Manipulating these inequalities gives us $(1-\alpha)r_1 = p_1 - \alpha p_2 = (1-\alpha)r_2$, a contradiction.

Case 2. $r_2 = p_2$ and $\alpha(r_2 - p_2) = r_2 - p_1$. These two equations imply that $p_1 = p_2$, so uniform pricing is optimal.

Case 3. $r_2 = p_2$ and $r_1 - p_1 = \alpha(r_1 - p_2)$. Solving for p_1 and substituting into the profit function shows that the profits of the firm are

$$\pi = r_1 + \alpha(2r_2 - r_1). \tag{30}$$

If these are the maximum profits the firm can make, they must dominate the policy of selling only in period 1 at a price of either r_1 and only satisfying the high-demand customers or selling at r_2 and satisfying both customers. Hence we must satisfy the following two inequalities:

$$r_1 + \alpha(2r_2 - r_1) \geq r_1,$$

$$r_1 + \alpha(2r_2 - r_1) \geq 2r_2.$$

However, it is easily checked that these inequalities imply $r_1 = 2r_2$. Substituting back into the profit function (30) we find that $\pi = r_1 = 2r_2$, so that the profits from price discrimination are equal to those from uniform pricing.

In summary, the optimal policy of the firm either involves charging a constant price in each period or selling at a price of r_1 or r_2 in the first period, and not selling at all in the second period. Neither alternative involves intertemporal price discrimination.

Salant (1987) asks why this extreme solution arises in the case of intertemporal price discrimination, but not in the general case of nonlinear pricing. He points out that the general analysis of nonlinear pricing typically *assumes* appropriately curved objective functions and constraints and limits itself to examining only interior solutions. In the intertemporal case, linearity of the objective function and constraints is a very natural assumption, and we should not be surprised that boundary solutions may be optimal.

However, the result that intertemporal price discrimination is not profit maximizing is a disturbing one, since firms seem to engage in such behavior. There are several ways to relax the assumptions of the model to allow for intertemporal price discrimination. For example, if the discount rates differ across consumers, price discrimination can easily be optimal. Similarly, if the discount rates of the consumers differ from that of the monopolist, price discrimination may be optimal.

It is easy to see when this may occur in our model. The only case involving the profit function of the firm is Case 3. Letting β be the discount factor of the monopolist, a sufficient condition for price discrimination to be optimal is that the discounted profits from price discrimination dominate selling only in the first period:

$$(1-\alpha)r_1 + (\alpha+\beta)r_2 \geq \max\{r_1, 2r_2\}.$$

It follows that intertemporal price discrimination can be optimal only when $\beta > \alpha$, i.e. when the monopolist is less impatient than the consumers. Landsberger and Meilijson (1985) examine the profitability of price discrimination when discount rates differ and derive a similar condition using Stokey's original continuous-time formulation.

We have also assumed that the good was costlessly produced. It is trivial to generalize our argument to the case of constant marginal costs, but if marginal costs are increasing the argument may fail. In the case of increasing marginal costs, it may be profitable to spread out the sales over time so as to keep production costs down.

One assumption implicit in our analysis is that the firm can *credibly precommit* to charging a constant price every period. To see that this can be a problem, let us consider the case where it is profitable to serve only the first-period consumers. In this case the prices are set at $p_1 = p_2 = r_1$, but no consumers purchase in the second period.

However, once the monopolist has satisfied the needs of the high-demand, first-period consumers, he is left with only the low-demand consumers. In this subgame, the optimal policy of the monopolist is to charge the low-demand consumers their reservation price r_2 in the second period. But the first-period consumers should be able to realize that the monopolist will charge this lower price second period – and therefore refuse to purchase in the first period!

The problem is that the solution of charging a constant price each period is not *subgame perfect* – the behavior of the monopolist is not optimal for each subgame in which he may find himself. Without the ability to precommit to the constant price schedule, the monopolist may be unable to enforce the constant-price, no-discrimination solution.

In our model, the only subgame perfect equilibrium is to charge $p_1 = r_2$ and sell to both groups of consumers in the first period, *regardless* of the size of the two groups of consumers. Any policy in which firm sells only to the high-demand consumers is not credible in that the firm will always be tempted to sell at a lower price later on. Note that this result follows no matter how small r_2 is, or no matter how many period or groups of consumers are involved. The inability to precommit has essentially eroded the monopoly power of the firm!

This possibility was first pointed out by Coase (1972). He argued that as long as there were no constraints on the rate of sales, all units of the good would be sold in the first period at marginal cost. (Coase implicitly assumed that there were consumers with arbitrarily low reservation prices, so that the price would be pushed as low as possible. In our model, the price is pushed down to the lowest reservation price.)

This "Coase conjecture" has been analyzed formally by Stokey (1981), Bulow (1982), Kahn (1986), Gul, Sonnenschein and Wilson (1986), and Bagnoli, Salant and Swierzbinski (1987). The analysis is somewhat delicate, as it depends on a sensitive limiting argument about how often the monopolist is allowed to adjust prices. Stokey (1981) shows that if the monopolist can only adjust prices at discrete points in time, then the further apart these points are, the higher are the monopoly profits. Essentially the requirement that prices can only be adjusted at discrete times makes it credible that the monopolist will charge a particular price at least until the next opportunity to adjust it. This tends to make the precommitment constraint on the monopolist less binding, and therefore leads to higher profits.

3.3. *Vertical integration and price discrimination*

To understand how vertical integration can help enforce price discrimination, let us consider a model where a producer of a primary product, such as aluminum, sells to two competitive industries that product distinct final goods. To take an extreme case, suppose that each of the final goods producers uses one unit of the input to produce one unit of their output. Let $p_1(x_1)$ and $p_2(x_2)$ be the inverse demand functions for the outputs of the two industries; for simplicity suppose that these demand functions have constant elasticities of ε_1 and ε_2, respectively.

In this case, it is easy to see that it will typically pay the producer of the primary product to price discriminate in its provision to the two industries. Effectively the primary producer controls the output in each industry and will set the price of the primary product to maximize its profits. This leads to the conventional solution:

$$p_1^* \left[1 - \frac{1}{|\varepsilon_1|} \right] = c,$$

$$p_2^* \left[1 - \frac{1}{|\varepsilon_2|} \right] = c.$$

The solution is only viable if the monopolist is able to prevent arbitrage. If the industry that receives the lower price can resell to the high price industry, the monopolist's price discrimination policy cannot be implemented. However, there is a strategy that can accomplish much the same thing. Suppose that industry 2 has the larger elasticity of demand and therefore the lower price. Then the monopolist can integrate forward by operating a firm in industry 2, selling its output at price p_2^* and sell the rest of the primary product at a uniform higher price of p_1^*.

In this case the firms in industry 1 will still be willing to pay the higher price, but the firms in industry 2 will be squeezed by the monopolist's transfer pricing to its subsidiary. If nothing is done, the firms in industry 2 will be driven out of business, and the monopolist will be able to enforce the price discrimination outcome through the vertical integration mechanism.

There have been a number of attempts to address the problem of how to detect subsidized transfer pricing of this sort. See Perry (1978, 1980, and Chapter 4 in this Handbook) and Joskow (1985) for a more detailed discussion of price discrimination as a motive for vertical integration.

3.4. *Imperfect information*

There are conflicting intuitions about the effect of imperfect information in monopolized markets. One the one hand, search activities by consumers represent a price paid by consumers that is not captured by the firm, so it is in the interest of the firm to "internalize" that cost by eliminating price dispersion. On the other hand, if consumers *differ* in their costs of search, price dispersion may be an effective means of sorting consumers and dividing the market, thereby allow for price discrimination in equilibrium.

Sorting consumers based on the basis of their cost of search is especially convenient since it is natural to suppose that consumers who are well informed about prices being offered elsewhere have more elastic demands than consumers who are poorly informed. Or, more generally, consumers with low costs of search will have more elastic demands than consumers with high costs of search. This observation suggests that it may be profitable for stores to use "noisy prices" as a selection device to discriminate among consumers.

This phenomenon was first examined by Salop (1977) and later extended by Berninghaus and Ramser (1980) and Wiesmeth (1982). In Salop's model there is a single monopolist with several outlets; the consumers know the distribution of prices charged at the various outlets, but do not know precisely which stores charge which prices. Hence, they engage in costly search before purchasing the good. Consumers have different search costs and different reservation prices for the good. Salop (1977) and Wiesmeth (1982) show that, under certain assumptions about the joint distribution of search costs and reservation prices, the monopolist can use price dispersion to sort consumers in a way that increases his profits.

Sorting by information costs in an important idea, but the particular case examined by Salop does not seem terribly plausible. Causal empiricism suggests that chain stores, such as McDonald's, typically try to charge uniform prices across their outlets rather than randomizing their prices. It seems that the first intuition – that of minimizing consumer search costs – is a more important consideration for chain stores and franchises than price discrimination.

However, instead of price dispersion across space, we can consider price discrimination across time. Suppose we consider a model where there are several imperfectly competitive firms, each with one outlet, that randomly charges different prices in different weeks. By randomizing their prices, the stores are able to compete for the price-sensitive consumers when their prices are low, but still charge high prices to price-insensitive consumers on the average. One can interpret this behavior as stores engaging in random sales. Varian (1981) has constructed a formal model of this behavior to determine the equilibrium pattern of sales. Here we briefly consider Varian's model.

Suppose that there are n stores selling an identical product which have identical, strictly decreasing average cost curves. Each store chooses the frequency $f(p)$ with which it advertises each price. Some fraction of the consumers read the ads and learn the entire distribution of prices; they therefore only shop at the lowest price store. The rest of the consumers shop at random. Each consumer purchases at most one unit of the good.

We seek to characterize a symmetric Nash equilibrium in this model. The first observation is that since average costs are always declining, there can be no pure strategy equilibrium in which all firms charge a single price. The only possible equilibrium therefore involves a mixed strategy.

It turns out that one can show that the equilibrium frequency distribution must be *atomless* – that is, there can be no prices that are charged with strictly positive probability. The intuition is not difficult: suppose that there were such an atom – some price that all stores charged with positive probability. Then there would be a positive probability of a tie at such a price, so some number of stores would split the informed consumers. By choosing a frequency distribution that charged a slightly lower price with positive probability, a store would capture the entire market of informed consumers in the event that the other stores tied, and only make slightly smaller profits in the other events. Hence, charging one price with positive probability cannot be a profit maximizing symmetric Nash equilibrium.

Given this observation, it is not difficult to calculate the expected profits of a firm. If $F(p)$ is the equilibrium price distribution function, then exactly two events are relevant. Either the firm in question is charging the lowest price, an event which happens with probability $(1 - F(p))^{n-1}$, or it does not have the lowest price, an event which has the complementary probability. If it has the lowest price, it gets $I + U$ customers, where I is the total number of informed customers and U is the number of uninformed customers per store.

Suppose for simplicity that the firm has constant marginal costs of zero and fixed costs of k. Then the expected profits of a representative firm are

$$\pi = \int_0^\infty \{(1 - F(p))^{n-1}[pI + pU - k] + [1 - (1 - F(p))^{n-1}][pU - k]\} f(p) \mathrm{d}p.$$

If the store is choosing the optimal density function $f(\cdot)$, then the integrand must be constant – if expected profits were higher at some price than at some other price, it would pay the store to charge the more profitable price more frequently. Assuming free entry, this constant level of profits must be zero. This gives us the equilibrium condition:

$$(1 - F(p))^{n-1}[pI + pU - k] + [1 - (1 - F(p))^{n-1}][pU - k] = 0.$$

Solving for $F(p)$ gives us

$$F(p) = 1 - \left(\frac{k - pU}{pI}\right)^{1/(n-1)}$$

This distribution function is the unique symmetric Nash equilibrium pricing pattern in this model. The associated density function, $f(p)$, is simply the derivative of this distribution function.

Rather than having the normal bell shape that we expect from a probability distribution, the equilibrium density $f(p)$ has a U-shape – that is, each store charges high and low prices more often than intermediate prices. This seems quite intuitive: a store wants to charge high prices to exploit the uninformed and low prices to compete for the informed. Intermediate prices serve neither goal and so are charged less frequently. However, they are still charged sometimes, since if no one ever charged an intermediate price, it would pay some store to do so.

For more on sales and related marketing techniques, see Conlisk, Gerstner and Sobel (1984), Sobel (1984), Gerstner (1985), Png and Hirschleifer (1986), and Raju (1986).

3.5. Quality differences

It has long been recognized that a monopolist may use quality differences to discriminate among consumers. Witness, for example, Dupuit's insightful remarks:

> It is not because of the few thousand francs which would have to be spent to put a roof over the third-class carriages or to upholser the third-class seats that some company or other has open carriages with wooden benches... What the company is trying to do is prevent the passengers who can pay the second class fare from traveling third-class; it hits the poor, not because it wants to hurt them, but to frighten the rich... And it is again for the same reason that the companies, having proved almost cruel to third-class passengers and mean to second-class ones, become lavish in dealing with first-class passengers. Having refused the poor what is necessary, they give the rich what is superfluous. [Quoted by Ekelund (1970).]

This passage clearly states the considerations facing the monopolist: by exaggerating the quality difference in the classes of service, he can effectively price discriminate between customers with different willingnesses-to-pay for the basic transportation service.

This phenomenon has been modeled by Mussa and Rosen (1978), Maskin and Riley (1984) and several others. At a formal level quality difference can be analyzed using techniques of nonlinear pricing. For example, consider the model of nonlinear pricing described in Subsection 2.3. In this model we used $u(x, t)$ to represent the utility of a consumer of type t who consumed a quantity x of the good in question, and used $c(x)$ to denote the cost of producing the quantity x. The pricing function, $r(\cdot)$, measured the cost of purchasing a quantity x.

But suppose instead we let x be the *quality* of a good, $c(x)$ the cost of producing it, and $r(x)$ the price of purchasing one unit of quality level x. Given these substitutions, the quantity–pricing problem considered in Subsection 2.5 is isomorphic to the quality–pricing problem of a monopolist. All of the analysis and results go through virtually unchanged.

The fundamental constraint in the quality–pricing problem is the same as that in the quantity–pricing, namely the self-selection constraint: choosing a pricing scheme that induces consumers of each quality level to prefer their own quality to any other quality. This is the emphasis of the Dupuit passage quoted above: the nature of the quality choices made are exaggerated so as to satisfy the self-selection constraints. We would generally expect that the monopolist would widen the quality choice spectrum in order to more effectively discriminate among the consumers it faces.

The major result of the nonlinear pricing model is that the largest consumer faces a price equal to marginal cost; here the analogous result is that the monopolist sells the highest quality item at its marginal cost of production. Purchasers of lower quality items in general pay more than the marginal cost of the quality they choose. For more on quality choice see Mussa and Rosen (1978), Maskin and Riley (1984), Milgrom (1987), Gabszewicz, Shaked, Sutton and Thisse (1986), and Oren, Smith and Wilson (1982).

3.6. Monopolistic competition

Although we generally describe price discrimination in terms of pure monopoly behavior, many of the most common real life examples of price discrimination occur in markets with free entry. For example, magazine subscriptions and movies are sold at student discounts; drug stores provide Senior Citizen discounts; and airlines sell trips for different durations at different prices. Certainly none of these industries could be thought of as pure monopolies. Instead, they would probably be characterized by the presence of significant product differentiation and by the availability of relatively free entry and zero long-run profits. In short, most economists would think of these industries as monopolistically competitive.

Of course, the effects we have described in the pure monopoly context are still relevant in a monopolistically competitive environment. We have taken the demand curve facing the monopolist as exogenously given. In equilibrium the demand facing a particular firm depends on the other firms' behavior, but under the common Nash–Cournot assumption, each firm will take those other firms actions as given. Insofar as we only wish to describe a *single* firm's behavior, the previous discussion has been adequate.

However, when we turn our attention to a model with multiple firms, several new effects can arise. In particular, we can ask how price discrimination tends to affect the number of firms in equilibrium and the variety of products they offer. Does price discrimination tend to increase or decrease welfare in a monopolistically competitive environment? What is the most effective form of discrimination when there are heterogeneous products?

There have been a few attempts to address these questions in a monopolistically competitive framework. In general the authors have taken one of the standard models of monopolistic competition, allowed the firms to price discriminate, and then investigated the effect of this price discrimination on the equilibrium behavior of the firms.

Katz (1984b) applied such a research strategy using the Salop and Stiglitz (1977) "bargains and ripoffs" model. In this model, there are two types of consumers, the informed and uninformed. The informed consumers know the prices charged by all stores and the uninformed know none of the prices being charged. Each type of consumer has a reservation price, L-shaped demand, but the informed consumers wish to purchase a larger amount than the uninformed.

In the Salop and Stiglitz model, in which stores could only charge a uniform price, there could exist equilibria involving price dispersion. They showed that for some parameter configurations, there would be exactly two prices charged in equilibrium: low-price stores competed for the informed consumers and high-price stores exploited the uninformed consumers.

Katz (1984b) asked what would happen if the stores were allowed to price discriminate. He showed that in this case there would exist a unique, symmetric equilibrium where all stores charged the same price schedule. The price schedule exhibits quantity discounting and thereby allows the stores to discriminate between the high-demand, informed consumers and the low-demand uninformed consumers.

In the equilibrium involving price discrimination, the price paid by the informed consumers is lower and the price paid by the uninformed consumers is higher than in the uniform pricing equilibrium. There are more firms in the price discrimination equilibrium than the uniform pricing equilibrium. If uninformed consumers are a small part of the market, then uniform pricing is better in terms of total surplus, but this result is reversed if the uninformed consumers dominate the market.

Borenstein (1985) and Holmes (1986) have investigated a different set of issues in the context of the location model of Lerner and Singer (1937) and Salop (1979). Here the emphasis is much more on the product heterogeneity aspect of price discrimination and on the form that price discrimination can take in such an environment.

In the classic monopolistically competitive location model described by Lerner and Singer (1937), consumers are located around a circle. Each consumer's location indicates his most preferred brand preference, and each consumer faces some travel cost if he consumes a more distant brand. In most treatments of this model, consumers have identical reservation prices and travel costs; Borenstein (1985) relaxes this assumption and allows consumers to differ in both characteristics. Differences in reservation price are interpreted as the usual differences in tastes; differences in travel costs are interpreted as the strength of brand preference.

Borenstein assumes that firms observe some characteristic of consumers that allows them to sort on one or the other of these two dimensions, and charge different prices accordingly. He uses numerical simulation to determine the effectiveness of the two forms of price discrimination. Borenstein finds that the effectiveness of the two forms of price discrimination depends on the type of equilibrium exhibited by the model.

If the monopolistically competitive equilibrium is highly competitive, with firms packed close together in the product space, then sorting by reservation price does not have much effect on the total size of the market – consumers simply switch form one brand to another. In this case, price discrimination on the basis of reservation price simply redistributes consumers from one brand to another and does little in the way of enhancing total sales or overall welfare. In this sort of equilibrium sorting on the base of strength of brand preference is the more effective form of price discrimination yielding larger price differentials, larger profits in the short run, and more firms in the long-run equilibrium.

On the other hand, if the monopolistically competitive equilibrium is more "monopolized" than "competitive", the strength of preference criterion is not as effective a means of sorting consumers as is the standard reservation price method. This equilibrium is much like the standard story of monopoly price discrimination: output and welfare can either increase or decrease under discrimination as compared with uniform pricing. However, Borenstein shows that in this case welfare is more likely to increase when price discrimination is allowed than in the standard monopoly case. This follows from free entry: allowing price discrimination will increase the profits of the existing firms and thereby induce entry. But with more firms in the market, the market will be more competitive which will be better for the consumers.

The Katz model and the Borenstein model emphasize different aspects of price discrimination under monopolistic competition: Katz is really concerned with the equilibrium form of the optimal second-degree price discrimination rule, while Borenstein is concerned with the sorting criterion involved with using third-degree price discrimination. The questions they investigate are similar, however: How does this new dimension affect the industry performance in a monopolistically competitive environment? It appears that there are a variety of other models of monopolistic competition that could benefit from similar analyses.

3.7. Legal aspects of price discrimination

Price discrimination has long been regarded as a dubious practice from the legal viewpoint, though the complaints about the practice voiced by legislators are typically not those voiced by economists. In this subsection we will briefly review the history and current legal thought on price discrimination. The major source for this material, and an excellent guide to antitrust law in general, is Neale and Goyder (1980).

The Clayton Act of 1914 was the first attempt to make price discrimination illegal. The intent of Congress appeared to have been to restrict the practice of "predatory pricing" rather than to restrict price discrimination per se. The focus of the law involved situations where a supplier provided a good to retailers in one region at a price below cost in order to drive out the competition; the law was intended to protect small businesses from such competition, not to protect the end customers.

The law recognized that not every difference in pricing should be construed as price discrimination, but the attempts to define exactly what was and was not legal were not very successful. The original section 2 of the Clayton Act read:

> That it shall be unlawful for any person engaged in commerce... to discriminate in price between different purchasers of commodities... where the effect of such discrimination may be to substantially lessen competition or tend to create monopoly in any line of commerce; *Provided*, that nothing herein contained shall prevent discrimination in price between purchasers of commodities on account of differences in the grade, quality, or quantity of the commodity sold, or that makes only due allowance for differences in the cost of selling or transportation, or discrimination in price in the same or different commodities made in good faith to meet competition....

The astute reader of this survey will note that the proviso allows for many of the forms of price discrimination we have discussed. The ambiguity of the definition of price discrimination resulted in very few cases being successfully brought to trial under this section.

In the early 1930s the spread of chain stores, in particular groceries, brought pressure to bear for strengthening the law against price discrimination, and in 1936 Congress passed the Robinson–Patman Act. As with the Clayton Act, the Robinson–Patman Act was primarily designed to protect the small independent from the large chain, rather than to protect the end users. However, the Robinson–Patman Act had a different focus. Rather than focusing on the powerful supplier who used local price cutting to drive out competitors, the Act was designed to control the large, powerful *buyers* who could use their size to negotiate more favorable terms than their competition.

Section 2 of the Robinson–Patman Act goes as follows:

> That it shall be unlawful for any person engaged in commerce, in the course of such commerce, either directly or indirectly, to discriminate in price between different purchasers of commodities of like grade and quality ... where the effect of such discrimination may be substantially to lessen competition or tend to create a monopoly in any line of commerce, or to injure, destroy, or prevent competition with any person who either grants or knowingly receives the benefit of such discrimination, or with customers of either of them.

As Neale and Goyder (1980, p. 215) put it:

> The Robinson–Patman revision of section 2 of the Clayton Act, whatever its other failing, has at least given rise to plenty of cases; but since many of these have been disposed of by consent order and other informal processes, the legal principles now regarded as applicable have been established in relatively few litigated cases.

Given the focus of the law on protecting small businesses from large chains, it is not surprising that many of the first cases brought to trial under the Robinson–Patman Act were cases of *second-degree* price discrimination – i.e. nonlinear pricing. A notable example was the *Federal Trade Commission v. Morton Salt* (Supreme Court, 1948). Morton Salt charged different prices for different quantities of table salt; the discounts ranged up to 15 percent, but only five large chain stores had ever qualified for this magnitude of discount. It was claimed that this form of price discrimination injured competition at the retail store level. Much of the judicial debate centered on the issue of whether the magnitude of the discounts was substantial enough to create serious injury to competition.

In other cases, such as *American Can Company v. Bruce's Juices*, the debate was centered on the issue of whether the cost reductions associated with larger customers justified the price differences charged. In this case, it was found that discounted schedule was "tainted with the inherent vice of too broad averaging" since 98 percent of the customers involved failed to qualify for the discounts offered. However, in *American Can Company v. Russelville Canning* (1951) the Eight Circuit Court of Appeals decided that a pricing schedule did not have to be precisely related to costs at each level of sales, but only needed to have been adopted in good faith after some reasonable study of costs.

The other main line of defense against the Robinson–Patman Act is that the low prices were charged only to meet "in good faith" the prices charged by the competition. *Standard Oil Company (Indiana) v. Federal Trade Commission* (Supreme Court, 1951) is an important case in point. Standard Oil sold gasoline to larger jobbers who supplied their own stations at prices of 1.5 cents per gallon less than the prices at which Standard directly supplied individual retailers. The Federal Trade Commission argued that this differential resulted in "injuring, destroying and preventing competition between said favored dealers and retailer dealers".

Standard first attempted to show that the difference in price could be accounted for by differences in costs of supply, but this defense was not successful. The second line of defense was to show that other refiners were attempting to get the business of the four large jobbers by offering them equally low prices. Although rejected by the FTC, this defense was accepted by the Supreme Court. Subsequently, the Supreme Court has attempted to clarify exactly what evidence should be brought to bear in adopting a defense of meeting the competitors' prices. [See Neale and Goyder (1980, pp. 224–228).]

Essentially, the burden of proof should be on the alleged price discriminator to show that it was meeting lawful prices of its competition, rather than simply copying the pricing strategy of other discriminators. However, subsequent cases have weakened the nature of the proof required in these cases: typically the defense of meeting the competition is only required to "embody the standard of the prudent businessman responding fairly to what he reasonably believes is a situation of competitive necessity". *Continental Banking Company* (1963).

Economic aspects of the Robinson–Patman Act

In reading the legal discussion of the Robinson–Patman Act, one is struck by the difference between the legal concerns and the concerns of economists. The legal issues surrounding the issue of price discrimination and the Robinson–Patman Act are those of unfair competition, predatory pricing, and the like. The issues of concern to ecomomists are those of efficient pricing.

As we saw in the discussion of the welfare effects of third-degree price discrimination, we can expect that allowing price discrimination will typically enhance welfare if it provides a means of serving markets that the monopolist would otherwise not serve. Conversely, if the size of the market does not increase under price discrimination, there can be no net increase in consumers' plus producers' surplus. Thus, it would seem that an economically sound discussion of whether price discrimination is in the social interest should focus on the output effects. However, as we have seen above, this consideration has not played much of a role in the legal discussion of price discrimination.

4. Summary

As we indicated at the beginning of this chapter, price discrimination is a ubiquitous phenomenon. Nearly all firms with market power attempt to engage in some type of price discrimination. Thus, the analysis of the forms that price discrimination can take and the effects of price discrimination on economic welfare are a very important aspect of the study of industrial organization.

In this survey we have seen some of the insights offered by the economic theory of price discrimination. However, much work remains to be done. For example, the study of marketing behavior at the retail level is still in its infancy. Retail firms use a variety of marketing devices – sales, coupons, matching offers, price promotions, and so on – that apparently enhance sales. The marketing literature has examined individual firm choices of such promotional tools. But what is the ultimate effect of such promotions on the structure and performance of market equilibrium? What kinds of marketing devices serve to enhance economic welfare and what kinds represent deadweight loss?

One particularly interesting set of questions in this area that has received little attention concerns the computational costs involved in using complex forms of price discrimination. In the post-deregulation airline industry of the United States, airlines have taken to using very involved pricing schemes. Finding the most inexpensive feasible fight may involve a considerable expenditure of time and effort. What are the welfare consequences of this sort of price discrimination? Do firms appropriately take into account the computational externality imposed on their customers?

Even in more prosaic case of public utilities, pricing schedules have become so complex that households often make the "wrong" choice of telephone service or electricity use. Questions of simplicity and ease-of-use have not hitherto played a role in the positive and normative analysis of price discrimination. Perhaps this will serve as a fruitful area of investigation in future studies of price discrimination.

Bibliography

Note: In addition to the items cited in the text, the bibliography contains all of the articles appearing in the *Journal of Economic Literature* during the period 1967–1985 which mentioned 'price discrimination' in their titles or abstracts.

Adams, W. and Yellen, J. (1976) 'Commodity bundling and the burden of monopoly', *Quarterly Journal of Economics*, 90:475–498.

Auerbach, A. and Pellechio, A. (1978) 'The two-part tariff and voluntary market participation', *Quarterly Journal of Economics*, 92:571–587.

Axel, B. (1977) 'Search market equilibrium', *Scandanavian Journal of Economics*, 79:20–40.

Bagnoli, M., S. Salant and J. Swierzbinski (1987) 'Pacman refutes the Coase conjecture: durable goods monopoly with discrete demand', University of Michigan working paper.

Baldwin, T.F., Wirth, M.O. and Zenaty, J.W. (1978) 'Economics of per-program pay cable-television', *Journal of Broadcasting*, 22:143–154.

Banks, F.E. (1975) 'Peak loads and price discrimination: A comment', *Kyklos*, 28:649–653.

Baron, D.P. and Debondt, R.R. (1981) 'On the design of regulatory price adjustment mechanisms', *Journal of Economic Theory*, 24:70–94.

Battalio, R. and Ekelund, R. (1972) 'Output change under third degree price discrimination', *Southern Economic Journal*, 39:285–290.

Beilock, R. (1985) 'Is regulation necessary for value-of-service pricing?', *Rand Journal of Economics*, 16:93–102.

Berninghaus, S. and Ramser, H (1980) 'Preisdiskriminierung durch Desinformation', *Zeitschrift für Sozialpolitik*, 99.

Bilas, R.A. (1969) 'Third degree price discrimination and the mulitiple plant monopolist: A note on the allocation of output', *Southern Economic Journal*, 36:82–86.

Bilas, R.A. and Miller, J.C. (1971) 'Pigou's three degrees of price discrimination', *Rivista Internazionale di Scienze Economiche e Commerciali*, 18:837–850.

Bittane, E. (1984) 'Price discrimination and economic integration: Some theoretical considerations', *Giornale degli Economisti e Annali di Economia*, 43:699–712.

Blackstone, E.A. (1975) 'Restrictive practices in the marketing of electrofax copying machines and supplies: The SCM Corporation case', *Journal of Industrial Economics*, 23:189–202.

Blair, R.D. and Cheng, L. (1984) 'On dumping', *Southern Economic Journal*, 3:857–865.

Borenstein, S. (1985) 'Price discrimination in free-entry markets', *Rand Journal of Economics*, 16:380–397.

Bosch-Font, F. (1974) 'Option value ownership and price discrimination', *Kyklos*, 27:255–269.

Bosch-Font, F. (1975) 'The Paretian concept of ownership and price discrimination in public utilities: A generalization (A response to F.E. Banks' critique)', *Kyklos*, 28:654–655.

Bowman, W.S. (1957) 'Tying arrangements and the leverage problem', *Yale Law Journal*, 67:19–36.

Boyle, S.E. and Hogarty, T.F. (1975) 'Pricing behavior in American automobile industry, 1957–1971', *Journal of Industrial Economics*, 24:81–95.

Brown, D. and Heal, G. (1980) 'Two-part tariffs, marginal cost pricing and increasing returns in a general equilibrium framework', *Journal of Public Economics*, 13:25–49.

Brown, S. and Sibley, D. (1986) *The theory of public utility pricing*. Cambridge: Cambridge University Press.

Bruggink, T. (1982) 'Third-degree price discrimination and regulation in the municipal water industry', *Land Economics*, 58:86–95.

Bulow, J. (1982) 'Durable-goods monopolists', *Journal of Political Economy*, 90:314–332.

Burnstein, M.L. (1960) 'The economics of tie-in sales', *Review of Economics and Statistics*, 42:68–73.

Canenbley, C. (1972) 'Price discrimination and EEC cartel law: A review of the Kodak decision of the Commission of the European Communities', *Antitrust Bulletin*, 17:269–281.

Carlton, D. and Perloff, J. (1981) 'Price discrimination, vertical integration, and divestiture in natural resource markets', *Resources and Energy*, 3:1–11.

Carlton, D. and Perloff, J. *Modern industrial organization*. Glenview, Ill.: Scott, Foresman and Co.

Caves, R.E. (1985) 'International trade and industrial organization: Problems, solved and unsolved', *European Economic Review*, 28:377–395.

Cebula, R.J. (1980) 'Market interdependence and third-degree price discrimination: Comment', *Quarterly Review of Economics and Business*, 2:106–109.

Chamberlin, J. (1977) 'Price discrimination and product demand in the electric utility industry', *Review of Business and Economic Research*, 13:68–88.

Chernick, H.A. (1981) 'Price discrimination and Federal project grants', *Public Finance Quarterly*, 9:371–394.

Chiang, R. and Spatt, C. (1982) 'Imperfect price discrimination and welfare', *Review of Economic Studies*, 49:155–181.

Clarke, R. and Else, P.K. (1979) 'A note on price discrimination and the labour managed firm', *Bulletin of Economic Research*, 31:87–92.

Coase, R.H. (1972) 'Durability and monopoly', *Journal of Law and Economics*, 15:143–149.

Conlisk, J., Gerstner, E. and Sobel, J. (1984) 'Cyclic pricing by a durable goods monopolist', *Quarterly Journal of Economics*, 99:489–505.

Cooper, E.H. (1977) 'Price discrimination law and economic efficiency', *Michigan Law Review*, 75:962–982.

Cooper, R. (1984) 'On allocative distortions in problems of self-selection', *Rand Journal of Economics*, 15:568–577.

Cremer, J. (1984) 'On the economics of repeat buying', *Rand Journal of Economics*, 15:396–403.

Cross, M.L. and Hershbarger, R.A. (1979) 'Price discrimination in the homeowners program', *Journal of Risk and Insurance*, 46:147–157.

Culler, S.D. and Ohsfeldt, R.L. (1986) 'The determinants of the provision of charity medical care by physicians', *Journal of Human Resources*, 21:138–156.

Davidson, R.K. (1955) *Price discrimination in selling gas and electricity*. Baltimore: Johns Hopkins Press.

Demsetz, H. (1973) 'Joint supply and price discrimination', *Journal of Law and Economics*, 16:389–405.

Donaldson, D. and Eaton, B.C. (1981) 'Patience, more than its own reward: A note on price discrimination', *Canadian Journal of Economics*, 14:93–105.

Dorsel, L. (1983) 'Nonprice competition – equilibrium and optimum', *Revue Economique*, 34:1057–1088.

Edwards, E.O. (1950) 'The analysis of output under discrimination', *Econometrica*, 18:168–172.

Ekelund, R.B. (1970) 'Price discrimination and product differentiation in economic theory: An early analysis', *Quarterly Journal of Economics*, 84:268–278.

Endres, A. (1984) 'Optimal product variation', *Jahrbücher für Nationalökonomie und Statistik*. 199:557–574.

Endres, A. (1985) 'Tie-in financing and pragmatic price discrimination', *Metroeconomica*, 37:119–133.

Etgar, M. (1975) 'Unfair price discrimination in P-L insurance and the reliance on loss ratios', *Journal of Risk and Insurance*, 42:615–624.

Feldman, D. and Tower, E. (1985) 'Errata: Profitable destabilizing speculation as intertemporal price discrimination', *American Economist*, 29:84.

Feldman, D.H. and Tower, E. (1984) 'Profitable destabilizing speculation as intertemporal price discrimination', *American Economist*, 28:60–63.

Feldstein, M. (1972) 'Equity and efficiency in public sector pricing: The optimal two part tariff', *Quarterly Journal of Economics*, 86:175–187.

Fenton, M. (1976) 'Price discrimination under nonmonopolistic conditions', *Applied Economics*, 8:135–144.

Finn, T.J. (1974) 'The quantity of output in simple monopoly and discriminating monopoly', *Southern Economic Journal*, 41:239–243.

Formby, J.P., Layson, S.K. and Smith, W.J. (1983) 'Price discrimination, 'adjusted concavity,' and output changes under conditions of constant elasticity', *Economic Journal*, 93:892–899.

Frantzen, D.J. (1985) 'The pricing of manufactures in an open economy: A study of Belgium', *Cambridge Journal of Economics*, 9:371–382.

Gabor, A. (1955) 'A note on block tariffs', *Review of Economic Studies*, 23:32–41.

Gabszewicz, J-J., Shaked, A., Sutton, A. and Thisse, J. (1986) 'Segmenting the market – the monopolist's optimal product mix', *Journal of Economic Theory*, 39:273–389

Galor, E. (1985) 'Differentiated industries without entry barriers', *Journal of Economic Theory*, 37:310–339.

Gately, D. (1976) 'The one-day sale: An example of intertemporal price discrimination', *Scandinavian Journal of Economics*, 78:496–500.

Gerber, D.J. (1982) 'The German approach to price discrimination and other forms of business discrimination', *Antitrust Bulletin*, 27:241–273.

Gerstner, E. (1985) 'Sales: Demand–supply variation or price discrimination?', *Journal of Economics and Business*, 37:171–182.

Goldberg, V.P. (1971) 'Price discrimination and product variation in cellophane', *Antitrust Bulletin*, 16:531–542.

Goldman, M., Leland, H. and Sibley, D. (1984) 'Optimal nonuniform pricing', *Review of Economic Studies*, 51:305–320.

Gould, J.P. (1984) 'Firm-specific differentiation and competition among multiproduct firms – Comments', *Journal of Business*, 57:173.

Gould, J.R. (1977) 'Price discrimination and vertical control: A note', *Journal of Political Economy*, 85:1063–1071.

Grant, R.M. (1981) 'Recent developments in the control of price discrimination in countries outside North America', *Antitrust Bulletin*, 26:593–632.

Greenhut, J.G. and Greenhut, M.L. (1975) 'Spatial price discrimination, competition and locational effects', *Economia*, 42:401–419.

Greenhut, M.L. and Ohta, H. (1976) 'Joan Robinson's criterion for deciding whether market discrimination reduces output', *Economic Journal*, 86:96–97.

Greenhut, M.L. and Ohta, H. (1979) 'Output effects of spatial price discrimination under conditions of monopoly and competition', *Southern Economic Journal*, 46:71–84.

Greenhut, M., Hwang, M.J. and Ohta, H. (1974) 'Price discrimination by regulated motor carriers: Comment', *American Economic Review*, 64:780–784.

Greenhut, M.L., Ohta, H. and Sailors, J. (1985) 'Reverse dumping: A form of spatial price discrimination', *Journal of Industrial Economics*, 34:167–181.

Gul, F., Sonnenschein, H. and Wilson, R. (1986) 'Foundations of dynamic monopoly and the Coase conjecture', *Journal of Economic Theory*, 39:155–190.

Hansen, R.S. and Roberts, R.B. (1980) 'Metered tying arrangements, allocative efficiency, and price discrimination', *Southern Economic Journal*, 47:73–83.

Hartwick, J.M. (1978) 'Optimal price discrimination', *Journal of Public Economics*, 9:83–89.

Hausman, J. and MacKie-Mason, J. (1986) 'Price discrimination and patent policy', working paper, University of Michigan.

Herander, M. (1982) 'The impact of government price discrimination and its equivalence with the tariff', *Weltwirtschaftliches Archiv*, 118:525–545.

Hilton, G.W. (1958) 'Tying sales and full-line forcing', *Weltwirtschaftliches Archiv*, 8:265–276.

Holahan, W.L. (1975) 'The welfare effects of spatial price discrimination', *American Economic Review*, 65:498–503.

Hollas, D.R. and Friedland, T.S. (1980) 'Competition, regulation, and second-degree price discrimination in the municipal electric industry', *Quarterly Review of Economics and Business*, 3:41–59.

Holmes, T. (1986) 'The effects of third degree price discrimination oligopoly', University of Wisconsin working paper. Forthcoming *American Economic Review*.

Hooks, D.L. (1971) 'Monopoly price discrimination in 1850: Dionysius Lardner', *History of Political Economy*, 3:208–223.

Hoover, E.M. (1936–1937) 'Spatial price discrimination', *Review of Economic Studies*, 4:182–191.

Horsky, D. and Sen, S.K. (1980) 'Interfaces between marketing and economics – An overview', *Journal of Business*, 53:5.

Horvitz, P.M. and Shull, B. (1969) 'Branch banking, independent banks and geographic price discrimination', *Antitrust Bulletin*, 14:827–844.

Hoskins, W.L. and Whitesell, W.E. (1970) 'Geographic price discrimination and banking competition', *Antitrust Bulletin*, 15:675–678.

Hoy, M. (1984) 'The impact of imperfectly categorizing risks on income inequality and social welfare', *Canadian Journal of Economics*, 17:557–568.

Hsu, S-K. (1983) 'Monopoly output and economic welfare under third-degree price discrimination', *Southern Economic Journal*, 1:234–239.

Hupen, R. and Seitz, T. (1981) 'Neues zu einem alten Problem – Preisdifferenzierung bei willkurlicher Marktteilung (An old problem reconsidered – Price discrimination with arbitrary market segmentation)', *Jahrbücher für Nationalökonomie und Statistik*, 196:333–340.

Hwang, M.-J. (1979) 'A model of spatial price discrimination for the pricing schedule of coal', *Journal of Regional Science*, 19:231–243.

Ippolito, R.A. (1980) 'Welfare effects of price discrimination when demand curves are constant elasticity', *Atlantic Economic Journal*, 8:89–93.

Itoh, M. (1983) 'Monopoly, product differentiation and economic welfare', *Journal of Economic Theory*, 31:88–104.

Joskow, P. (1985) 'Mixing regulatory and antitrust policies in the electric power industry: The price squeeze and retail market competition', in: F. Fisher, ed., *Antitrust and regulation: Essays in memory of John J. McGowan*. Cambridge, Mass.: M.I.T. Press.

Kahn, C. (1986) 'The durable goods monopolist and consistency with increasing costs', *Econometrica*, 54:275–294.

Kangun, N. (1970) 'Race and price discrimination in the marketplace: A further study', *Mississippi Valey Journal of Business and Economics*, 5:66–75.

Katz, E. and Berrebi, Z.M. (1980) 'On the price discriminating labour cooperative', *Economics Letters*, 6:99–102.

Katz, M. (1987) 'The welfare effects of third-degree price discrimination in intermediate goods markets', *American Economic Review*, forthcoming.

Katz, M.L. (1983) 'Nonuniform pricing, output and welfare under monopoly', *Review of Economic Studies*, 50 N.1:37–56.

Katz, M.L. (1984a) 'Firm-specific differentiation and competition among multiproduct firms', *Journal of Business*, 57:149.

Katz, M.L. (1984b) 'Price discrimination and monopolistic competition', *Econometrica*, 52:1453–1471.

Kessel, R.A. (1958) 'Price discrimination in medicine', *Journal of Law and Economics*, 1:20–53.

Keyes, L.S. (1984) 'Armentano's antitrust and monopoly: A review article', *Journal of Post Keynesian Economics*, 6:354–359.

Klein, B. and Saft, L. (1984) 'Tie-in contracts and franchising quality control mechanisms', working paper, UCLA, Los Angeles.

Koch, J.V. (1970) 'A closer look at price discrimination in an imperfect world', *Mississippi Valley Journal of Business and Economics*, 5:11–23.

Koller, R.H. (1973) 'Why regulate utilities? To control price discrimination', *Journal of Law and Economics*, 16:191–192.

Kubo, Y. (1986) 'Quality uncertainty and guarantee – A case of strategic market-segmentation by a monopolist', *European Economic Review*, 30:1063–1079.

Kushner, J. and Masse, I.J. (1976) 'Patents as a basis for international price discrimination', *Antitrust Bulletin*, 21:639–656.

Kwoka, J.E. (1984) 'Output and allocative efficiency under second-degree price discrimination', *Economic Inquiry*, 22:282–286.

La Croix, S.J. (1983) 'Marketing, price discrimination, and welfare', *Southern Economic Journal*, 49:847–852.

La Croix, S.J. (1984) 'Marketing, price discrimination, and welfare: Reply', *Southern Economic Journal*, 3:900–901.

Laffont, J.-J., Maskin, E. and Rochet, J.-C. (1982) 'Optimal nonlinear pricing with two-dimensional characteristics', working paper.

Landsberger, M. and Meilijson, I. (1985) 'Intertemporal price discrimination and sales strategy under incomplete information', *Rand Journal of Economics*, 16:424–430.

Latham, R.J. and Schechter, M.C. (1979) 'The price structure of the legal services industry: Minimum fee schedules and price discrimination', *Antitrust Bulletin*, 24:43–62.

Lee, C.H. and Warren, E.H. (1976) 'Rationing by seller's preference and racial price discrimination', *Economic Inquiry*, 14:36–44.

Lee, C.H. and Warren, E.H (1978) 'Racial price discrimination', *Economic Inquiry*, 16:453–456.

LeGrand, J. (1975) 'Public price discrimination and aid to low income groups', *Economica*, 42:32–42.

Leland, H.E. and Meyer, R.A. (1976) 'Monopoly pricing structures with imperfect discrimination', *Bell Journal of Economics*, 7:449–462.

Lerner, A. and Singer, H. (1937) 'Some notes on duopoly and spatial competition', *Journal of Political Economy*, 45:145–186.

Levedahl, J.W. (1984) 'Marketing, price discrimination, and welfare: Comment', *Southern Economic Journal*, 3:886–891.

Littlechild, S.C. (1975) 'Two-part tariffs and consumption externalities', *Bell Journal of Economics and Management Science*, 6:661–670.

Löfgren, K.G. (1971) 'The theory of intertemporal price discrimination. An outline', *Swedish Journal of Economics*, 73:333–343.

Lovell, C.A. (1978) 'Two-stage model of discriminatory pricing', *Canadian Journal of Economics*, 11:56–68.

Lovell, C.A. and Wertz, K. (1981) 'Price discrimination in related markets', *Economic Inquiry*, 19:488–494.

Lovell, C.A. and Wertz, K. (1985) 'Third degree price discrimination in imperfectly sealed markets', *Atlantic Economic Journal*, 13:1–11.

Mai, C.-C. and Shih, J.-J. (1984) 'Output effect of the labour-managed firm under price discrimination', *Economic Journal*, 94:931–935.

Maskin, E. and Riley, J. (1984) 'Monopoly with incomplete information', *Rand Journal of Economics*, 15:171–196.

Masson, R.T. (1974) 'Costs of search and racial price discrimination: Reply', *Economic Inquiry*, 12:428–430.

Masson, R.T. and Wu, S.Y. (1974) 'Price discrimination for physicians' services', *Journal of Human Resources*, 9:63–79.

Mathewson, G.F. and Winter, R.A. (1984) 'An economic theory of vertical restraints', *Rand Journal of Economics*, 15:27–38.

Matthews, S.A. (1983) 'Selling to risk averse buyers with unobservable tastes', *Journal of Economic Theory*, 30:370–400.

McAfee, R.P., McMillan, J. and Whinston, M. (1987) 'Multiproduct monopoly, commodity bundling, and correlation of values', working paper no. 1296, Harvard University.

McNicol, D.L. (1979) 'Price discrimination and peak-load pricing subject to rate of return constraint', in: R.O. Zerbe, ed., *Research in law and economics*, *Vol. 1*. Greenwich, CT: JAI Press, 213–238.

Mertens, Y. and Ginsburgh, V. (1985) 'Product differentiation and price discrimination in the European community: The case of automobiles', *Journal of Industrial Economics*, 34:151–66.

Miles, A. (1986) *Pricing*. Perspectives on marketing series. Boston: Boston Consulting Group.

Milgrom, P. (1987) 'An essay on price discrimination', UC Berkeley Working Paper.

Mirman, L. and Sibley, D. (1980) 'Optimal nonlinear prices for multiproduct monopolies', *Bell Journal of Economics*, 11:659–670.

Mirrlees, J.M. (1971) 'An exploration in the theory of optimal taxation', *Review of Economic Studies*, 38:175–208.

Mirrlees, J.M. (1976) 'Optimal tax theory: A synthesis', *Journal of Public Economics*, 6:327–358.
Moorthy, K.S. (1984) 'Firm specific differentiation and competition among multiproduct firms – Comment', *Journal of Business*, 57:167.
Moran, R.A. (1973) 'Cooperative advertising: An alternative interpretation of price discrimination', *California Management Review*, 15:61–63.
Murphy, M.M. (1977) 'Price discrimination, market separation, and the multi-part tariff', *Economic Inquiry*, 15:587–599.
Murphy, M. and Ott, M. (1977) 'Retail credit, credit cards and price discrimination', *Southern Economic Journal*, 43:1303–1312.
Mussa, M. and Rosen, S. (1978) 'Monopoly and product quality', *Journal of Economic Theory*, 18:301–317.
Nagle, T. (1984) 'Economic foundations for pricing', *Journal of Business*, 57:3.
Neale, A. and Goyder, D. (1980) *The Antitrust Laws of the U.S.A.* Cambridge: Cambridge University Press.
Ng, Y. and Weisser, M. (1974) 'Optimal pricing with a budget constraint – The case of the two part tariff', *Review of Economic Studies*, 41:337–345.
Norman, G. (1981) 'Spatial competition and spatial price discrimination', *Review of Economic Studies*, 48:97–111.
Norman, G. (1983) 'Spatial competition and spatial price discrimination: A correction', *Review of Economic Studies*, 50:755–756.
Oi, W. (1971) 'A Disneyland dilemma: Two-part tariffs for a Mickey Mouse monopoly', *Quarterly Journal of Economics*, 85:77–96.
Okuguchi, K. (1983) 'Price discrimination in related markets: Comment', *Economic Inquiry*, 21:439–440.
Olson, J.E. (1972) 'Price discrimination by regulated motor carriers', *American Economic Review*, 62:395–402.
Olson, J.E. (1974) 'Price discrimination by regulated motor carriers: Reply', *American Economic Review*, 64:785–786.
Ordover, J. and J. Panzar (1980) 'On the nonexistence of Pareto superior outlay schedules', *Bell Journal of Economics*, 11:351–354.
Ordover, J. and J. Panzar (1982) 'On the nonlinear pricing of inputs', *International Economic Review*, 23:659–675.
Oren, S., Smith, S. and Wilson, R. (1982) 'Linear tariffs with quality discrimination', *Bell Journal of Economics*, 13:455–471.
Oren, S., Smith, S. and Wilson, R. (1984) 'Pricing a product line', *Journal of Business*, 57:73–100.
Ozawa, T. (1971) 'Intermarket price discrimination under pure monopoly: A supplementary note', *Nebraska Journal of Economics and Business*, 1:55–59.
Papps, I. (1980) 'Price discrimination under non-monopolistic conditions?', *Applied Economics*, 12:363–366.
Pattison, J.C. (1973) 'Some aspects of price discrimination in the airline industry', *Journal of Economic Issues*, 7:136–147.
Perry, M. (1978) 'Price discrimination and forward integration', *Bell Journal of Economics*, 9:209–217.
Perry, M. (1980) 'Forward integration: Alcoa 1888–1930', *Journal of Industrial Economics*, 29:37–53.
Peterman, J.L. and Carney, M. (1978) 'A comment on television network price discrimination', *Journal of Business*, 51:343–352.
Phillips, O.R. and Battalio, R.C. (1983) 'Two-part tariffs and monopoly profits when visits are variable', *Bell Journal of Economics*, 14:601–604.
Phlips, L. (1980) 'Intertemporal price discrimination and sticky prices', *Quarterly Journal of Economics*, 94:525–542.
Phlips, L. (1983) *The economics of price discrimination*. Cambridge: Cambridge University Press.
Pigou, A.C. (1920) *The economics of welfare*. London: Macmillan.
Png, I. and Hirschleifer, D. (1986) 'Price discrimination through offers to match price', working paper, UCLA Management School, Los Angeles.
Posner, R. (1976) 'The Robinson–Patman Act: Federal regulation of price differences'. Washington, D.C.: American Enterprise Institute for Public Policy Research.
Primeaux, W.J. (1973) 'Price variability and price discrimination: A case study', *Marquette Business*

Review, 17:25–29.
Primeaux, W.J. and Nelson, R.A. (1980) 'An examination of price discrimination and internal subsidization by electric utilities', *Southern Economic Journal*, 47:84–99.
Pursell, G. and Snape, R.H. (1973) 'Economies of scale, price discrimination and exporting', *Journal of International Economics*, 3:85–91.
Raju, J. (1986) 'A theory of price-promotions', thesis, Graduate School of Business, Stanford University.
Reinganum, J. (1979) 'A simple model of equilibrium price dispersion', *Journal of Political Economy*, 87:851–858.
Riordan, M.H. (1984) 'On delegating price authority to a regulated firm', *Rand Journal of Economics*, 15:108–115.
Roberts, K. (1979) 'Welfare considerations of non-linear pricing', *Economic Journal*, 89:66–83.
Robinson, J. (1933) *Economics of imperfect competition*. London: Macmillan.
Rust, J. (1986) 'When is it optimal to kill off the market for used durable goods?', *Econometrica*, 54:65–86.
Saidi, N. and Srinagesh, P. (1981) 'On non-linear tariff schedules', *Journal of International Economics*, 11:173–195.
Salant, S. (1987) 'When is inducing self-selection suboptimal for a monopolist', working paper, University of Michigan.
Salop, S. (1977) 'The noisy monopolist: Imperfect information, price dispersion and price discrimination', *Review of Economic Studies*, 44:393–406.
Salop, S. (1979) 'Monopolistic competition with outside goods', *Bell Journal of Economics*, 10:141–156.
Salop, S. and Stiglitz, J. (1977) 'Bargains and ripoffs: A model of monopolistically competitive price dispersion', *Review of Economic Studies*, 44:493–510.
Sandler, T. and Tschirhart, J.T. (1980) 'The economic theory of clubs – An evaluative survey', *Journal of Economic Literature*, 18:1481–1521.
Schmalensee, R. (1981a) 'Monopolistic two-part pricing arrangements', *Bell Journal of Economics*, 12:445–466.
Schmalensee, R. (1981b) 'Output and welfare implications of monopolistic third-degree price discrimination', *American Economic Review*, 71:242–247.
Schmalensee, R. (1982) 'Commodity bundling by single-product monopolies', *Journal of Law and Economics*, 25:67–71.
Schmalensee, R. (1984) 'Gaussian demand and commodity bundling', *Journal of Business*, 57:S211–S230.
Schneidau, R.E. and Knutson, R.D. (1969) 'Price discrimination in the food industry: A competitive stimulant or tranquilizer?', *American Journal of Agricultural Economics*, 51:1143–1148.
Scotchmer, S. (1985) 'Two tier pricing of shared facilities in a free-entry equilibrium', *Rand Journal of Economics*, 16:456–456.
Scott, F.A. and Morrell, S.O. (1985) 'Two-part pricing for a multi-product monopolist', *Economic Inquiry*, 24:295–307.
Shapiro, D.L. (1974) 'Costs of search and racial price discrimination', *Economic Inquiry*, 12:423–427.
Sherman, R. and Visscher, M. (1982) 'Rate-of-return regulation and two-part tariffs', *Quarterly Journal of Economics*, 97:27–42.
Shih, J.-J. and Mai, C.-C. (1986) 'A generalized analysis of output effect under third-degree price discrimination', working paper, Academia Sinica, Taipei, Taiwan.
Silberberg, E. (1970) 'Output under discriminating monopoly: A revisit', *Southern Economic Journal*, 37:84–87.
Smith, W.J. and Formby, J.P. (1981) 'Output changes under third degree price discrimination: A reexamination', *Southern Economic Journal*, 48:164–171.
Sobel, J. (1984) 'The timing of sales', *Review of Economic Studies*, 51:353–368.
Sorenson, J., Tschirhart, J. and Whinston, A. (1978) 'Theory of pricing under decreasing costs', *American Economic Review*, 68:614–624.
Spatt, C.S. (1983) 'Imperfect price discrimination and variety', *Journal of Business*, 56:203–216.
Spence, M. (1976) 'Nonlinear prices and welfare', *Journal of Public Economics*, 8:1–18.
Spratlen, T.H. (1970) 'A note on immobility as a factor in racial price discrimination', *Mississippi Valley Journal of Business and Economics*, 6:85–88.

Spremen, K. (1978) 'Welfare implications and efficiency of entrance fee pricing', *Zeitschrift für Nationalökonomie*, 38:231–252.

Spulber, D.F. (1981) 'Spatial non-linear pricing', *American Economic Review*, 71:923–933.

Spulber, D.F (1984) 'Competition and multiplant monopoly with spatial nonlinear pricing', *International Economic Review*, 25:425–439.

Srinagesh, P. (1985) 'Nonlinear prices with heterogeneous consumers and uncertain demand', *Indian Economic Review*, 20:299–315.

Srinagesh, P. (1986) 'Nonlinear prices and the regulated firm', *Quarterly Journal of Economics*, 101:51–68.

Steel, W.F. (1974) 'Making economics relevant: A project for measuring price discrimination in supermarkets', *Journal of Economic Education*, 5:112–115.

Stigler, G. (1963) 'United States v. Loew's Inc.: A note on block booking', *Supreme Court Review*, 152:152–157.

Stigler, G. (1987) *Theory of price*. New York: Macmillan.

Stiglitz, J. (1977) 'Monopoly, nonlinear pricing, and imperfect information: The insurance market', *Review of Economic Studies*, 44:407–430.

Stokey, N. (1979) 'Intertemporal price discrimination', *Quarterly Journal of Economics*, 93:355–371.

Stokey, N. (1981) 'Rational expectations and durable goods pricing', *Bell Journal of Economics*, 12:112–128.

Sutton, J. (1986) 'Vertical product differentiation – Some basic themes', *American Economic Review*, 76:393–398.

Sweeney, G. (1984) 'Marketing, price discrimination, and welfare: Comment', *Southern Economic Journal*, 3:892–899.

Timonen, J. and Hamalainen, R.P. (1978) 'A dynamic example of the intertemporal price discrimination problem', *Scandinavian Journal of Economics*, 4:449–453.

Tirole, J. (1988) *Theory of industrial organization*. Cambridge, Mass.: M.I.T. Press.

Trotter, S.D. (1985) 'The price-discriminating public enterprise, with special reference to British rail', *Journal of Transport Economics and Policy*, 19:41–64.

Varian, H. (1976) 'Two problems in the theory of fairness', *Journal of Public Economics*, 5:249–260.

Varian, H. (1978) 'A note on locally constant income elasticities', *Economics Letters*, 1:9–13.

Varian, H. (1981) 'A model of sales', *American Economic Review*, 70:651–659; erratum, March, 1981.

Varian, H. (1983) *Microeconomic analysis*. New York: Norton.

Varian, H. (1985) 'Price discrimination and social welfare', *American Economic Review*, 75:870–875.

Watts, P.E. (1955) 'Block tariffs: A comment', *Review of Economic Studies*, 53:941–973.

Weinblatt, J. and Zilberfarb, B. (1981) 'Price discrimination in the exports of a small economy: Empirical evidence', *Weltwirtschaftliches Archiv*, 117:368–379.

Weymark, J.A. (1986) 'Bunching properties of optimal nonlinear income taxes', *Social Choice and Welfare*, 3:213–232.

White, D.L. and Walker, M.C. (1973) 'First degree price discrimination and profit maximization', *Southern Economic Journal*, 2:313–318.

Wiesmeth, H. (1982) 'Price discrimination based on imperfect information: Necessary and sufficient conditions', *Review of Economic Studies*, 49:391–402.

Williams, W.E. (1977) 'Racial price discrimination: A note', *Economic Inquiry*, 15:147–150.

Williams, W.E. (1978) 'Racial price discrimination: Another note', *Economic Inquiry*, 16:457.

Willig, R. (1976) 'Integrability implications for locally constant demand elasticities', *Journal of Economic Theory*, 12:391–401.

Willig, R. (1978) 'Pareto-superior nonlinear outlay schedules', *Bell Journal of Economics* 9:56–69.

Wilson, R. (1985) 'Economic theories of price discrimination and product differentiation: A survey', Graduate School of Business, Stanford University.

Woo, W.T. (1984) 'Exchange rates and the prices of nonfood, nonfuel products', *Brookings Papers on Economic Activity*, 2:511–530.

Yamey, B. (1974) 'Monopolistic price discrimination and economic welfare', *Journal of Law and Economics*, 17:377–380.

Yandle, B. (1971) 'Monopoly-induced third-degree price discrimination', *Quarterly Review of Economics and Business*, 11:71–75.

Zanon, L. (1981) 'Price discrimination and Hoffman–LaRoche', *Journal of World Trade Law*, 15:305–322.

Chapter 11

VERTICAL CONTRACTUAL RELATIONS

MICHAEL L. KATZ*

University of California at Berkeley

Contents

*This chapter is dedicated to one of my graduate advisors, J.F., who in 1979 told me to stop working on vertical restraints because all of the interesting theoretical questions had been definitely answered and the public policy debate was over. I am grateful to Mark Gersovitz for extensive comments on an earlier draft of this chapter.

Handbook of Industrial Organization, Volume I, Edited by R. Schmalensee and R.D. Willig

1. Introduction

This chapter is a study of the contractual relationship between two parties at successive stages in the vertical chain of production and marketing for a good. In other words, this chapter surveys the theory of the sale of intermediate goods.

There are several important respects in which intermediate good markets differ from final good markets and thus merit independent study.[1] First, intermediate good markets often involve large transactions made by sophisticated buyers. Second, the products being sold may possess very complex bundles of attributes, making problems of moral hazard more severe, or at least more complicated. Third, the buyers' demands for an intermediate good are interdependent when the buyers are product-market competitors with one another. Fourth, the buyers of an intermediate good typically are involved in a game in the downstream product market, and the sales contract for the upstream product may affect the equilibrium of this downstream game. Lastly, buyers of intermediate goods often can credibly threaten to integrate backward into supply of the intermediate good.[2]

A simple uniform posted price often is held up as the typical contract form in final good markets. Given the sophistication of buyers and the large scale of individual transactions, more complex selling schemes may be practicable intermediate good markets. Sellers may utilize sophisticated pricing mechanisms or nonprice contractual provisions. This chapter explores the private and social incentives to utilize such contracts.

In looking at contracts that go beyond a simple uniform price, attention is focused on several contractual provisions that often are seen in practice.

Quantity-dependent pricing

The price that the buyer pays per unit of the intermediate good may depend on the total amount of the good that the buyer purchases. A two-part tariff is a particularly simple form of quantity-dependent pricing. Under a two-part tariff,

[1] In that portion of Chapter 14 of this Handbook devoted to patent licensing, Jennifer Reinganum examines the terms of sale for one particular type of input: knowledge. As is evident after having read her chapter and the present one, the work on patent licensing has evolved along rather different lines than has the traditional literature on vertical contracts.

[2] Of course, these effects sometimes arise in final goods markets. For example, demands are interdependent in the cases of snob goods, bandwagon goods, and goods subject to network externalities. The threat of integration may arise in the provision of services (e.g. house cleaning and gardening).

the buyer pays a fixed fee plus a constant per-unit charge to purchase the input. Thus, the average per-unit price falls with the purchase volume. In the vertical relations literature, the fixed fee in a two-part tariff often is called a *franchise fee*. Another well-known form of quantity-dependent pricing is termed *forcing* in the vertical relations literature. Under a forcing contract, the dealer is required to purchase a given amount of the input. Such a requirement can be thought of as a quantity-dependent pricing scheme under which the buyer's total payment to the input supplier is fixed for any quantity of input below some set level. The practice of *bundling* two units of a good into a single package also is an example of quantity-dependent pricing.

Quantity-dependent pricing need not be confined to a single good. A multi-product seller may make the price paid by the buyer for any one input a function of the quantities of all of the inputs that he purchases from that seller. For example, if one firm sells both inputs A and B, the amount charged for a unit of input A may depend on the size of the buyer's purchase of input B.

At times, the term "vertical restraint" has been used to refer to any contractual provision between two levels in the supply chain that goes beyond the use of a simple uniform price. Thus, some authors consider quantity-dependent pricing of the sort just described to be a vertical restraint. In this chapter, I reserve the term "vertical restraint" for those provisions of an intermediate good contract that make the buyer's payment to a given seller depend on variables other than the quantities of the inputs purchased from that seller.

Three such provisions can be thought of as multiproduct quantity-dependent pricing scheme under which the price charged by a given seller depends, in part, on the quantities purchased from *other* input suppliers.

Ties

A *tie* occurs when a manufacturer agrees to sell input A to a buyer only if the buyer also purchases input B from that manufacturer (and no other). A tie can be thought of as a type of multi-product (across firms) quantity-dependent pricing; the seller's price for A is infinite if the quantity of B purchased from another firm is positive. In general, the price at which the tied goods are sold also may vary with the quantities purchased from the seller who imposes the tie. As a rule, however, the vertical restraints literature has focused almost exclusively on ties for which the prices are independent of these quantities. One exception to this rule is the consideration of *multi-product bundling* under which units of several inputs are sold in fixed proportions at a package price.

It is worth noting that while a tie may be enforced through a contract, it need not be. When several inputs must be used together (i.e. form a system), it may be possible for the manufacturer to create a technological tie by designing his products so that they can work only with each other (i.e. are incompatible with components produced by other manufacturers).

Royalties

The amount paid by the buyer to the seller need not be based solely on the unit sales of the intermediate good. Under a royalty scheme, the input buyer's payment is a function of his sales in the final goods market, measured in terms of either dollar revenues or physical units. Because these sales depend on the quantities of other inputs employed, royalties are equivalent to a certain form of multiproduct quantity-dependent pricing that cuts across input suppliers.

Requirements contracts and exclusive dealing

Under a *requirements contract*, a purchaser of input A agrees to make all of his purchase of input A from the same manufacturer. A requirements contract also can be thought of as a tying arrangement under which input A is tied to itself. In those cases in which the input being sold is a branded final product for which the buyer serves as a retailer, a requirements contract is also known as an *exclusive dealing* arrangement. Under an exclusive dealing arrangement, the dealer agrees not to sell any of the brands of rival manufacturers. The exclusive dealing arrangement may limit the retailer to selling the goods of only one producer (e.g. a McDonald's franchise only sells McDonald's brand products). Alternatively, the dealer may be allowed to carry the products of several manufacturers who are not direct competitors with one another (e.g. a grocery store might be restricted to selling only one brand of light bulb but still be allowed to sell thousands of other products).

In addition to specifying pricing practices, the intermediate good sales contract may govern the terms under which the buyer can sell the final output produced using the manufacturer's input. These provisions, known as resale restraints, are most prevalent in intermediate good markets in which the buyer serves as a retailer for the manufacturer's product. Two types of resale restraint are both the empirically most important and theoretically most analyzed.

Resale customer restraints

The input sales contract may contain provisions that restrict the set of consumers to whom the purchaser may sell the final output produced with the input. These restrictions may be framed in terms of geographic location, or in terms of some other customer attribute.

Exclusive territories, or territorial restrictions involve the manufacturer's giving each dealer the sole right to serve consumers in a specific geographic region. This geographical exclusivity may be enforced by limiting the geographic location of authorized dealers while allowing a dealer to serve any customer who comes into the store. Alternatively, the manufacturer may explicitly forbid a retailer from serving consumers who are located in the territory assigned to another dealer. This type of restriction is necessary when consumers could otherwise be induced to cross sales territories.

The second type of resale restraint is a *customer restriction*. Under customer restrictions, certain classes of consumer are reserved for the manufacturer's own sales force. A personal computer manufacturer, for example, might reserve sales to Fortune 200 companies for the manufacturer's national sales force.

Resale price restraints

In addition to limiting the customers that a dealer may serve, the contract may restrict the price at which the dealer can sell his output. This restriction, known as *resale price maintenance*, may take the form of a price floor, a price ceiling, or both simultaneously.

The bulk of this chapter concerns itself with the private incentives to utilize the six contractual provisions just identified. In Sections 2 through 4, I use increasingly complex models to examine the private motivations for intermarket contracts that go beyond a simple uniform-pricing scheme. Within each section, I first identify conditions motivating the use of simple quantity-dependent pricing. I then show that under these conditions, there exist private incentives to implement vertical restraints as well.

In many instances, a given practice may be a potential response to several different contracting problems. No attempt is made in these sections to assess which motivation or the use of a particular type of vertical restraint is the leading or most important one. This point is taken up briefly in the discussion of public policy presented in Section 5, where I compare the social and private incentives to implement different vertical contractual provisions.

Before proceeding with the analysis of the private and social incentives to use sophisticated pricing and direct vertical restraints, there are two points worth noting. The first concerns the nature of benchmarks to which to compare vertical restraints. Much of the existing literature on vertical restraints views their use as an intermediate case falling between the two extremes of uniform pricing and vertical integration. In comparing vertical restraints with vertical integration, this literature typically views integration as giving one party unified interests and complete control of all aspects of the combined operations.[3] A better term for what is examined might be an "unnatural union" of both interest and incentives across levels.

Sophisticated pricing and vertical restraints are responses to problems of moral hazard, adverse selection, and the need to share risk. How does vertical integration solve these problems? It is far from self-evident that these problems should disappear simply because the two parties are labelled as being in a single firm. Grossman and Hart (1986) adopt the extreme view that vertical integration does nothing to alter either the set of feasible contracts between the stages of production or the goals of the self-interested decision-makers at the two stages. While extreme, it seems to me to be a more defensible view than the opposite extreme that has been taken by much of the literature on vertical restraints and vertical integration.

To date, we have no fully articulated and convincing theory of what vertical integration *is*. Accordingly, I view the subject of this chapter to be a theory of contractual arrangements between different stages in the production chain, either within a single firm or across unrelated firms. There is little in the analysis below that lets one distinguish between a vertical restraint used by two divisions within a single firm and a vertical restraint used as part of an arm's length transaction between two separate firms.

The other point to note before getting on with the analysis concerns the relationship between the vertical restraints literature and the principal–agent literature. The study of vertical contractual relationships is just a special case of the general analysis of the principal–agent problem. The fully general analysis of the principal–agent problem remains to be conducted, however. In the interim, vertical restraints constitute an interesting and important class of special cases in which the additional structure allows one to develop a more complete characterization of the equilibrium contract than might otherwise be possible. For example, in the vertical restraints literature, attention is concentrated on a relatively narrow set of contractual provisions. While artificially limiting the set of feasible contracts often leads to incorrect conclusions, at least there is an extensive body of data showing that these practices are of empirical importance. This pattern suggests that more sophisticated provisions may be unnecessary, infeasible, or too costly to implement.

By drawing attention to characteristics of actual markets, the study of vertical restraints also points out two rather large holes in the standard principal–agent

[3]For examples of this approach, see Chapter 4 by Martin Perry in this Handbook.

literature. First, vertical restraints typically involve a principal with multiple agents, a problem that only recently has been given serious attention in the principal–agent literature. Second, vertical restraints usually are imposed in markets in which the agents of several different principals compete with one another. Such game-playing agents have been almost entirely neglected in the principal–agent literature. Unfortunately, while the existence of game-playing agents has been obvious to those studying vertical restraints, these authors have, for the most part, chosen to ignore formal analysis of such problems, relying instead on unwarranted extrapolation from models in which there is a single principal with one or more agents.

2. Private incentives: A single manufacturer with a single dealer

This section and the next two examine the private incentives to utilize vertical restraints. These incentives are illustrated through the use of a simple model which is presented in stages of increasing complexity in order to show the various roles that specific contractual provisions may play. As a starting point, this section considers an upstream monopolist who sells his output to a downstream monopolist. The downstream firm's output may be a final good or may itself be an input into yet another stage of production. With only a single party at each vertical stage, there is no role for the assignment of exclusive territories or the requirement of exclusive dealing. But all of the other practices discussed in the introduction may be feasible and, as will be shown, there may be private incentives to implement each of them.

2.1. The basic model

There is a single producer of an intermediate good, x, which is used by a single downstream firm in the production of output. I will refer to the upstream firm as the "manufacturer" and the downstream firm as the "dealer", but the downstream firm need not be merely retailer for the upstream firm. For example, the "manufacturer" might be a coal mine and the "dealer" an electric utility. Moreover, although I will refer to them as separate firms, for most of the analysis the buyer and seller could equally well be two business units within a single firm.

The manufacturer's output is combined with another input, y (competitively supplied by firms in another upstream industry at price m) and with retailer effort, e, to produce downstream revenues, $R(x, y, e; \theta)$.[4] Depending on the

[4]Strictly speaking, since there are other input suppliers, this is a multi-manufacturer setting. I will use the term "single manufacturer" to refer to markets in which there is only one strategic supplier. Markets in which y is oligopolistically supplied will be treated in Section 4.

case under consideration, θ may represent a parameter of market demand or a characteristic of the dealer that is not subject to dealer choice. Initially, the realization of θ is taken to be common knowledge between the dealer and the manufacturer. Later this assumption will be dropped to allow for uncertainty and for asymmetric information.

The variable e may be a measure of promotional effort, such as how hard the salesman works at convincing potential customers of the product's worth, that negatively affects the dealer's level of utility. Or e may be some decision variable, such as the color of the box in which the good is sold, that does not directly enter the retailer's utility function. In most of the analysis, I will treat x, y, e, and θ as scalars. In general, they may all be vectors, and most of the analysis extends trivially.

The dealer's utility, $U(I, e; \theta)$, depends on his income, I, his level of effort, e, and any retailer characteristics captured by θ. Let $W(x, y, e, \theta)$ denote the payment made by the dealer to the manufacturer. Under contract W, a type $= \theta$ dealer earns a net income of $R(x, y, e; \theta) - W(x, y, e, \theta)$ when he chooses input levels of x, y, and e.

Conditional on his accepting the contract, the dealer makes input choices to maximize his expected utility. Let $x^*(W, \theta)$, $y^*(W, \theta)$, and $e^*(W, \theta)$ denote the solution to

$$\underset{x,\, y,\, e}{\text{maximize}}\ U[R(x, y, e, \theta) - W(x, y, e, \theta) - my, e; \theta].$$

Given the agent's choices, the manufacturer earns:

$$W[x^*(W, \theta), y^*(W, \theta), e^*(W, \theta), \theta] - C[x^*(W, \theta)],$$

where $C(x)$ is the total cost of producing output x. For expositional simplicity, suppose that $C(x) = K + cx$, K and c constants.

To close the model, one must specify the contract bargaining game between the manufacturer and the dealer. In the principal–agent literature, the convention (which I will follow) is to assume that the *bargaining* is efficient and generates a (constrained) Pareto-efficient contract.[5] For convenience, rather than trace out the entire Pareto set, I will give all the power to the principal (i.e. the manufacturer) by letting him make take-it-or-leave-it contract offers. As long as the principal has some bargaining power and the principal and agent are symmetri-

[5]This assumption does not imply that the private first-best outcome is attained. Rather, it implies that given the set of feasible contracts and the information constraints faced by the two parties, there is no implementable contract that is Pareto superior to the equilibrium one.

cally informed, this assumption does not affect the qualitative nature of the equilibrium contract.[6]

The manufacturer would like to implement a contract that both induces the dealer to maximize the total expected profits of the two levels and gives all of these profits to the manufacturer. Let $x^{\pi}(\theta)$, $y^{\pi}(\theta)$, and $e^{\pi}(\theta)$ denote the solution to

$$\underset{F,x,y,e}{\text{maximize}}\ F - cx$$

$$\text{subject to}\quad U[R[x, y, e; \theta] - F - my, e; \theta] \geq 0,$$

where F is a scalar. The constraint in the problem above is the agent's individual rationality constraint; the agent accepts the contract offer only if the contract generates a higher utility level than the agent's next-best alternative, where the agent's opportunity utility is normalized to 0.[7]

One type of contract that induces the dealer to choose $x^{\pi}(\theta)$, $y^{\pi}(\theta)$, and $e^{\pi}(\theta)$ while transferring all rents to the manufacturer is the following:

$$W[x, y, e, \theta] = \begin{cases} G(\theta) & \text{if } \langle x, y, e\rangle = \langle x^{\pi}(\theta), y^{\pi}(\theta), e^{\pi}(\theta)\rangle, \\ G_0, & \text{otherwise,} \end{cases}$$

where $G(\theta)$ satisfies $U[R[x^{\pi}(\theta), y^{\pi}(\theta), e^{\pi}(\theta), \theta] - G(\theta) - my^{\pi}(\theta), e^{\pi}(\theta); \theta] = 0$ and G_0 is some constant that yields the agent less than his reservation utility level. Under this contract, the manufacturer orders the dealer to choose $x^{\pi}(\theta)$, $y^{\pi}(\theta)$, and $e^{\pi}(\theta)$, pays the agent his reservation wage in the event of compliance, and charges the agent a penalty otherwise.[8]

Except in special cases, such a contract would require a great deal of information on the manufacturer's part. In order to enforce the contract, the manufacturer would have to calculate the actions that the dealer should have taken and then verify that the dealer took them. To obtain this information, the manufacturer typically would have to engage in extensive and expensive monitoring of the dealer. Moreover, the need to provide complete instructions to the dealer could lead to tremendous contractual complexity and administrative cost. Hence, whether the two parties are independent corporations or are divisions within a single firm, such a contract is unlikely to be feasible or optimal.

[6]Alternative bargaining institutions are considered in the later discussion of an asymmetrically informed manufacturer–dealer pair.

[7]Cases in which the uncertainty is over the dealer's opportunity utility level can be represented by a parameterization of U with respect to θ.

[8]As noted in the introduction, many authors (in my opinion, mistakenly) implicitly attribute the ability to implement such a contract to a vertically integrated firm.

2.2. The use of the price system

2.2.1. Single-product pricing

The essence of the contract design problem is to overcome the externalities between the two stages. The actions of one party affect the profits of both, but the party at each stage makes his decisions based solely on the effects on his own profits or utility. In the version of the model introduced thus far, this problem takes the form of dealer moral hazard.

There is a very simple contract that can overcome dealer moral hazard. Under this contract, the dealer pays a fixed fee to the manufacturer and then buys the intermediate good at cost. Formally, $W[x] = F(\theta) + cx$, where $F(\theta)$ solves:

$$U[R(x^{\pi}(\theta), y^{\pi}(\theta), e^{\pi}(\theta); \theta) - cx^{\pi}(\theta) - my^{\pi}(\theta) - F(\theta), e^{\pi}(\theta); \theta] = 0.$$

As noted earlier, $F(\theta)$ often is called a franchise fee in the vertical restraints literature.

At the margin, the dealer appropriates any increase in the combined profits of the dealer and manufacturer brought about by the dealer's actions. Since he is the residual claimant to them, the dealer acts to maximize those profits (including the cost of effort in these calculations). This contract yields the manufacturer the maximal feasible level of profits given the agent's opportunity utility level.[9] Under this contract, there are no incentive problems, and there is no need for the manufacturer to monitor the dealer once the contract has been signed and the franchise fee paid.

If (a) the manufacturer can implement a two-part tariff, and (b) the manufacturer and the dealer have complete information about the state of the world, then the manufacturer can fully maximize profits without relying on either multi-product pricing or direct vertical restraints even though dealer effort may be unobservable to the manufacturer.[10] Given the extent to which a two-part tariff economizes on contractual complexity and the need to monitor the agent, one would not expect to see the other forms of pricing or resale restraints in the setting analyzed above.

Both (a) and (b) may fail to be satisfied in practice. When there are multiple dealers, antitrust authorities might declare the use of fixed fees or other forms of

[9] This result is well known in both the principal–agent [e.g. Harris and Raviv (1979)] and price discrimination [e.g. Oi (1971)] literatures.

[10] The one role for a direct vertical restraint in this simple model is to keep the manufacturer from stealing customers from the dealer (i.e. competing in the downstream market) after having signed the contract.

nonuniform pricing to be illegal price discrimination. Arbitrage among dealers might also limit the use of quantity-dependent pricing. Of course, neither of these restrictions arises in the simple single-dealer setting under examination in this section, and it is hard to see why a manufacturer could not use a two-part tariff here. It is useful to consider the uniform-pricing case in this section, however, as a foundation for the multi-dealer analysis of the next one.

When the manufacturer is restricted to selling his output at a constant wholesale price [i.e. $W(x) \equiv wx$, w a constant], he must set the wholesale price greater than marginal cost in order to profit from the sale of his output. But faced with $w > c$, the dealer no longer acts to maximize joint profits.

In the presence of market power, the contract between the manufacturer and the dealer must both transfer income and make use of decentralized information (i.e. give the dealer incentives). When a two-part tariff is feasible, the manufacturer has two objectives and two instruments – the wholesale price can be set to induce the paper incentives and the franchise fee can be set to transfer rents. When the manufacturer is restricted to chosing $W(x) \equiv wx$, he has only one instrument – the wholesale price. In a sense, the two roles overload a single-parameter contract. If the wholesale price is either set above marginal cost to transfer income to the manufacturer or set below marginal cost to transfer income to the dealer, the dealer's incentives are distorted. Consequently, the possibility arises that utilizing other forms of pricing and vertical restraints would raise profits.

Even when two-part tariffs are feasible, the manufacturer may be unable to set a price schedule with the marginal price equal to marginal cost and the fixed fee chosen to extract all of the dealer's surplus. The manufacturer's setting such a schedule typically requires the manufacturer to make the value of the fixed fee contingent on the value of θ. In many situations, the manufacturer, the dealer, or the courts do have the information needed to write and/or enforce such contracts. In these instances, there are roles for other contractual provisions.

2.2.2. *Incomplete information and pricing above cost*

I will proceed by discussing several cases of informational incompleteness under which the manufacturer would find it privately optimal to set the marginal price above marginal cost, inducing distortions in the dealer's behavior. Having done this, I will explore the roles of vertical restraints in ameliorating these distortions.

To keep the exposition as simple as possible, I will assume that the wholesale pricing scheme can be no more complicated than a two-part tariff. The restriction to two-part tariffs is not essential to the qualitative results. If one were to allow a more general single-product, quantity-dependent pricing scheme, one still would find points on the schedule at which the marginal price did not equal marginal cost and distortions would be induced.[11]

2.2.2.1. Risk sharing. In the presence of uncertainty and dealer risk aversion, the agency contract must play a third role: share risk (i.e. provide insurance for the dealer). Three roles turn out to be one too many for a single-product pricing scheme, such as two-part tariff.

Suppose that *neither* the manufacturer nor the dealer knows the value of θ at the *time of contracting*, although they have the same prior beliefs about its value. Moreover, suppose that, if the dealer accepts the contract, the dealer learns the value of θ before making any production decisions. The manufacturer and/or the courts never learn the value of θ, and thus neither F nor w can be made contingent on θ.[12]

If the manufacturer and dealer both are risk neutral, then the restriction that F not vary with the value of θ presents no problem. A simple two-part tariff with the wholesale price equal to marginal cost still can be used to decentralize the decision-making while fully transferring income. The only difference is that now the franchise fee must be set so that it yields the dealer an *expected* utility level (EU) equal to his opportunity level. When the dealer is risk averse, however, marginal cost pricing is not the manufacturer's optimal strategy. While a tariff with $w = c$ does a good job of generating dealer incentives, the retailer bears all of the risk – the manufacturer's profits are equal to F no matter what the value of θ. This pattern of risk sharing is not an efficient one.

Given his risk neutrality, if the manufacturer could observe the value of θ, he would set F contingent on that value so that the agent would bear no risk. This form of insurance completely protects the agent from bad realizations of θ while fully overcoming dealer moral hazard. When the manufacturer cannot base the vertical contract directly on the realization of θ, he has to rely on a signal of θ's value. Holmstrom (1979) and Shavell (1979) showed that the manufacturer may be able to take the dealer's choice of x as a signal on which to base insurance payments. This intuition comes most clearly when x is the sole input in the production of dealer revenues. In this case, express final market revenues as

[11] Rey and Tirole (1986) pointed out that two-part tariffs may be one form of quantity discounting that is particularly resistant to arbitrage across dealers. To assess a fixed fee, a manufacturer need monitor only whether any given dealer is using the input, not how much the dealer is *using* (which may differ from the quantity *purchased* directly from the manufacturer). Given that all dealers face the same wholesale price, there is no role for arbitrage among fee-paying dealers. Again, this is a multidealer argument that is made here in anticipation of the later analysis.

[12] In some cases, the principal could allow the agent's *report* of θ to influence the levels of w and F (i.e. the dealer would be offered a menu of contracts). I will not consider that possibility here. The analysis is similar to that of the informed manufacturer case below. In any event, if the manufacturer does use a menu of contracts to sort dealer types, equilibrium will entail $w(\theta) > c$ for some values of θ.

$R = R(x; \theta)$. Suppose that $R_\theta > 0$ for all θ and all $x > 0$, while $R_{x\theta} > 0$ for all θ and $x \geq 0$. Given any wholesale price, a low value of θ induces the dealer to choose a low level of x.

The manufacturer would like to compensate the dealer for low realizations of θ. Since θ and the dealer's choice of x are positively related, the manufacturer can do this by simultaneously lowering F and raising w in a way that raises the dealer's income for low unit-sales levels but lowers the dealer's income for high unit-sales levels. The adverse effects on the dealer's incentives limits the usefulness of this insurance, but some insurance is optimal.

To see this point formally, suppose that $w = c$. Consider the effects of the manufacturer's simultaneously raising w by $\mathrm{d}w$ and lowering F by $\mathrm{d}F$, where

$$\mathrm{d}EU = -\int_{\underline{\theta}}^{\bar{\theta}} U_I[I^*(\theta); \theta][x^*(W, \theta)\,\mathrm{d}w + \mathrm{d}F]h(\theta)\,\mathrm{d}\theta = 0,$$

$h(\cdot)$ is the density function for the distribution of θ over the support $[\underline{\theta}, \bar{\theta}]$, and $I^*(\theta) = R[x^*(W, \theta); \theta] - wx^*(W, \theta) - F$. The change in manufacturer's profits is

$$\mathrm{d}\pi = \int_{\underline{\theta}}^{\bar{\theta}} \{x^*(W, \theta)\,\mathrm{d}w + \mathrm{d}F\}h(\theta)\,\mathrm{d}\theta > 0,$$

by the concavity of $U(\cdot)$ and the monotonicity of $x^*(\cdot, \cdot)$ with respect to θ. Since $w = c$ by hypothesis, there is no first-order effect on manufacturer profits from the cutback in x induced by the rise in the wholesale price. If $w < c$, the cutback in x would raise manufacturer profits by even more.

2.2.2.2. An informed dealer. In many instances, the manufacturer and dealer are asymmetrically informed at the time of contracting. Suppose that it is common knowledge that the dealer is better informed about the value of θ than is the manufacturer. Consider the extreme case in which the dealer knows the realization of θ at the time of contracting, but the manufacturer never observes the value of θ.

The manufacturer may be concerned with the value of θ for two reasons. First, the level of compensation necessary to induce the agent not to seek alternative employment may depend on the value of θ. Second, when θ represents a dealer-specific characteristic, some types of dealer may be more valuable to the manufacturer than others.

Begin with the case of dealer-specific θ. For example, θ may be a measure of the dealer's ability or his disutility of effort (i.e. some types really hate to work, but others do not mind it much). Suppose that one is blessed with a market in which for any value of w both $x^*(W, \theta)$ and the maximal value of F such that

$$U[R(x^*, y^*, e^*; \theta) - wx^* - my^* - F, e^*; \theta] \geq 0$$

are increasing in θ. In this situation, if the manufacturer could choose the dealer's type, he would choose one with the maximal value of θ.

In situations of asymmetric information, the structure of the bargaining institutions utilized by the manufacturer and dealer can affect the nature of the equilibrium contract. Hence, I will examine the contracting process somewhat more fully here than in the rest of this chapter. Begin by considering a market in which there is a competitive supply of would-be dealers. Caves and Murphy (1976) have suggested that the manufacturer can use the franchise fee as a screening device. Since dealer surplus is increasing in θ, only those potential dealers with θ above some cut-off level would find it profitable to accept the franchise agreement. This scheme does not, however, use all of the information that is available to the manufacturer when there is more than one potential dealer.

In a different context, Demsetz (1968) has argued that an auction could serve to induce the parties (here, the potential dealers) to reveal their private information. For example, suppose that the manufacturer set up an auction of the following form. The ith would-be dealer submits a bid F_i. The manufacturer agrees to sell the input to the highest bidder at a wholesale price equal to marginal cost and a franchise fee equal to the *second*-highest bid received. Ties are broken at random.

Under this second-price auction, it is a dominant strategy for a type-$\tilde{\theta}$ dealer to bid $\tilde{F}$, where $\tilde{F}$ satisfies

$$\max_{x,\, y,\, e} U\left[R\left(x, y, e; \tilde{\theta}\right) - cx - my - F, e; \tilde{\theta}\right] = 0.$$

The unique Nash equilibrium in bids entails the manufacturer's getting all of the surplus that would be available from the agent with the second-highest value of θ in the population of potential dealers even though the manufacturer does not know the value of the franchise. Since $w = c$, the equilibrium contract overcomes any problems of dealer moral hazard. Moreover, the potential dealer with the highest realization of θ always is selected. Loosely speaking, if the number of bidders is large relative to the variance of θ, then this process tends to appropriate most of the downstream profits. If θ is a market-specific parameter, rather than a dealer-specific one, the scheme appropriates dealer profits completely.[13]

With a single potential dealer, the manufacturer's dealer selection problem is simply whether to have a dealer or not. The manufacturer could decide that it would rather shut down than have a bad dealer, but as long as F and $w - c$ are

[13] When the value of θ need not be constant across dealers, the second-price auction presented in the text may not be privately optimal form of auction to run. There is now a large literature on optimal auction design. See, for example, Milgrom and Weber (1982).

non-negative, there is no reason to do so.[14] The reason the manufacturer cares about the dealer's type is that it determines the compensation necessary to attract the dealer. One approach is to set $w = c$ and set F sufficiently low that even the worst type of dealer would receive at least his opportunity utility level. Such a scheme would, however, overcompensate high-θ dealers. On the other hand, higher values of F would risk turning away the dealer for low realizations of θ.

When there is only a single potential bidder, competitive pressure cannot be used to induce the dealer to reveal his private information about θ. This information must be elicited through either the bargaining process or the contract itself. If multiple rounds of bargaining are possible, the manufacturer might offer a contract and see whether it was rejected. In the event of a rejection, one side would make a counteroffer. When the dealer's costs of bargaining vary systematically with the value of θ, the manufacturer may be able to take the dealer's bargaining behavior as a signal of the underlying value of θ. For example, if both the value of being a dealer and the costs of bargaining are increasing functions of θ [as in Rubinstein (1985)], then the manufacturer may be able to infer that a dealer has a high value of θ from the fact that he gives in during an early round of bargaining. When the costs of bargaining do not arise from delay, however, there may be little reason to expect the needed correlation to hold.

The contract itself may provide a mechanism by which to elicit the dealer's private information. Suppose that the manufacturer makes a single take-it-or-leave-it contract offer. As in the case of symmetric uncertainty, the dealer may signal his value of θ through his choice of x. To see how such signalling might work, again suppose that x is the sole input and that for any given contract a high-θ dealer would purchase more of the input than would a low-θ dealer. It is optimal for the manufacturer to set $w > c$ to use the relationship between x^* and θ to extract rents from high-θ dealers without driving low-θ dealers from the market.

Suppose, counterfactually, that the profit-maximizing two-part tariff entails $w = c$ and $F = F_0$. There must exist some θ_0 such that $h(\theta_0) > 0$ and

$$\underset{x}{\text{maximum}}\ U[R(x;\theta_0) - F_0 - cx;\theta_0] = 0,$$

since otherwise the manufacturer could increase profits by raising F.

Now raise w and lower F such that $x^*(W_0, \theta_0)\,\mathrm{d}w = -\mathrm{d}F > 0$. For infinitesimal changes, there is no change in the set of dealer types who accept the contract. The change in the manufacturer's profits is

$$\mathrm{d}\pi = \int_{\underline{\theta}}^{\bar{\theta}} \{x^*(W_0, \theta)\,\mathrm{d}w + \mathrm{d}F\}h(\theta)\,\mathrm{d}\theta > 0.$$

[14] When there are multiple dealers and reputation effects arise, this conclusion will need to be modified. See Section 3 below.

The inequality follows from the fact that $x^*(W_0, \theta) > x^*(W_0, \theta_0)$ for all $\theta > \theta_0$. Therefore, the privately optimal contract entails a wholesale price that is greater than the input's marginal cost of production.

2.2.2.3. An informed manufacturer. Suppose that θ is a parameterization of a market characteristic (e.g. the demand for the downstream output or the unpleasantness of dealer's job) that is better known by the manufacturer than by the dealer at the time of contracting. If it is common knowledge that the manufacturer knows the value of the intermediate good better than does the dealer, then for a range of θ's the privately optimal wholesale price may be greater than the marginal cost.

Consider the following illustrative example. Both R and R_x are increasing in θ. θ takes one of two values, $\underline{\theta}$ or $\bar{\theta}$, where $\underline{\theta} < \bar{\theta}$. The manufacturer observes the realization of θ at the outset but θ never is observable to the courts, so a contract contingent upon θ is unenforceable. The dealer learns θ after signing the contract but before making production decisions. x is the sole input in the production of downstream revenues. Finally, θ does not enter the dealer's utility function directly.[15]

Consider the following outcome. A manufacturer with a low-value franchise offers $\underline{W}(x) = \underline{F} + cx$, where $\underline{F}$ satisfies

$$U\left[R^*(\underline{W}, \underline{\theta}) - \underline{F} - cx^*(\underline{W}, \underline{\theta})\right] = 0.$$

A manufacturer with a high-value franchise offers $\overline{W}(x) = \bar{F} + \bar{w}x$, where $\bar{F}$ and $\bar{w}$ are the solution to the following problem:

$$\underset{w,\,F}{\text{maximize}}\ F + (w - c)x^*(W, \bar{\theta})$$

$$\text{subject to}\quad U\left[R^*(W, \bar{\theta}) - F - wx^*(W, \bar{\theta})\right] \geq 0 \tag{1}$$

and

$$F + (w - c)x^*(W, \underline{\theta}) \leq \underline{F}. \tag{2}$$

Given that R and R_x are increasing in θ, x^* is increasing in θ and $\underline{W}$ satisfies constraint (2) with equality while (1) does not bind. Moreover, $\underline{W}$ is more profitable than any other contract with $w \leq c$. Starting at $\underline{W}$, consider the effects of raising the wholesale price by $\mathrm{d}w$ and changing the franchise fee by $\mathrm{d}F =$

[15] Equilibria with $w > c$ also could arise if θ affected the dealer's utility function rather than his revenue function. For example, they would arise if dealer effort were an input to production of downstream revenues, $U_\theta \geq 0$, $U_{\theta e} > 0$, $R_{xe} > 0$, and R were independent of θ.

$-x^*(c, \underline{\theta})\,\mathrm{d}w$. The constraints still would be satisfied and manufacturer profits would rise. Therefore, the solution to this problem entails wholesale pricing above marginal cost.

The manufacturer's private information is fully revealed to the dealer under this outcome. A manufacturer with a high-value franchise signals this fact by accepting a combination of wholesale price and license fee that he would find unattractive if he actually had a low-value franchise – by setting $w > c$, the manufacturer gives himself a stake in the dealer's volume and makes credible his claim that his dealer will have a high-volume, high-revenue operation. A manufacturer with a low-value franchise "admits" this fact and offers an efficient contract (i.e. $\underline{w} = c$).

This separating outcome is an equilibrium if dealer's beliefs are as follows. If $w = c$ and $F = \underline{F}$, or if $F + (w - c)x^*(W, \underline{\theta}) > \underline{F}$, then the dealer believes that the offer has been made by a low-θ manufacturer. Otherwise, the dealer infers that the manufacturer has a high value of θ. These beliefs are confirmed along the equilibrium path.[16]

To see that this outcome is an equilibrium, consider a deviation by the manufacturer. Clearly, any deviation by a low-θ manufacturer would be unprofitable unless it "fooled" the dealer. And, by construction, a low-θ manufacturer would not find it profitable to mimic a high-θ manufacturer. Also by construction, the strategy played under the candidate equilibrium by a high-θ manufacturer maximizes his profits subject to the constraint that the dealer believes him to have a high-value franchise. Suppose, then, that the deviation induces the dealer to believe that the high-θ manufacturer actually is a low-θ manufacturer. The greatest profits that such a deviation could generate are given by the solution to

$$\begin{aligned} &\underset{w,\,F}{\text{maximize}}\ F + (w - c)x^*(W, \bar{\theta}) \\ &\text{subject to}\quad U[R^*(W, \underline{\theta}) - F - wx^*(W, \underline{\theta})] \geq 0. \end{aligned} \tag{3}$$

Constraint (3) can be written as

$$U\{R^*(W, \underline{\theta}) - cx^*(W, \underline{\theta}) - [F + (w - c)x^*(W, \underline{\theta})]\} \geq 0.$$

Recall that $\underline{F}$ satisfies:

$$U[R^*(\underline{W}, \underline{\theta}) - cx^*(\underline{W}, \underline{\theta}) - \underline{F}] = 0,$$

[16] I am not pretending to offer a complete analysis of the equilibria of this game. For a general discussion of the type of equilibrium selection arguments that support the primacy of this equilibrium see Banks and Sobel (1987).

and hence constraint (3) implies that

$$R^*(W,\underline{\theta}) - cx^*(W,\underline{\theta}) - [F + (w-c)x^*(W,\underline{\theta})] \geq R^*(\underline{W},\underline{\theta}) - cx^*(\underline{W},\underline{\theta}) - \underline{F}.$$

It follows that $F + (w-c)x^*(W,\underline{\theta}) \leq \underline{F}$, with strict inequality for any $w \neq c$. That is, constraint (3) is stronger than (2). Moreover, it is evident that constraint (3) is stricter than (1) as well. Therefore, there is no profitable deviation from the candidate strategy given the dealer's beliefs.

2.2.3. *Manufacturer moral hazard*

Up to this point, the dealer has been the only party to make decisions after the contract has been signed. The manufacturer's sole action has been to provide as much of the intermediate good the dealer demands. Typically, there are other dimensions to manufacturer behavior. For example, the manufacturer may be able to affect the quality of his output. Or, the manufacturer may provide promotional support of sales of the *downstream* product. These activities may be such that explicit contracting is infeasible either due to problems of measurement and observability, or due to the need to vary the levels of these activities in response to market conditions that are themselves unobservable to the courts.

If the manufacturer's post-contracting effort affects downstream market revenues and explicit contracting over this effort is infeasible, then the privately optimal wholesale price may again be greater than marginal cost. If $w \leq c$, the manufacturer has no incentive to encourage final sales. Hence, setting $w > c$ is the only way to get the manufacturer to provide effort. If the level of manufacturer support is sufficiently important to downstream sales, the benefits from the increase in manufacturer incentives will outweigh the negative effects from the distortion in dealer incentives that raising the wholesale price above marginal cost induces.

2.3. *The need for more sophisticated contracts*

For a variety of reasons, the privately optimal wholesale price may differ from marginal cost. A divergence between the wholesale price and marginal cost levels distorts the dealer's incentives. In such cases, other forms of pricing and direct vertical restraints may be useful means of ameliorating these distortions.

2.3.1. *Multi-product pricing: Ties and royalties*

As Burstein (1960b) observed, the manufacturer faces a taxation problem: he would like to collect as much revenue as possible from the dealer. His ability to do so is limited by the dealer's individual rationality constraint. By tying inputs, the manufacturer can face the dealer with the following decision. Either the dealer accepts the manufacturer's set of prices (i.e. his set of commodity taxes) on the set of tied inputs, or the dealer faces the market price vector for the inputs produced by other firms and an infinite price for the manufacturer's input. As Burstein put it, the dealer is confronted with an "all-or-nothing choice" of prices. The dealer makes this choice by comparing the two resulting levels of utility.

Given the form of the dealer's individual rationality constraint, when there is no uncertainty about θ and no problem of manufacturer moral hazard, it is in the interest of the manufacturer to raise revenues through an efficient set of taxes. Hence, the earlier result that the firm would like to set $w = c$ and collect the revenue through the use of a nondistorting fixed fee. If franchise fees are illegal and the manufacturer relies on single-product pricing, he must set the wholesale price greater than marginal cost in order to extract downstream surplus. Such pricing distorts dealer behavior and limits the extent to which the manufacturer can extract downstream profits. As a general rule, the greater the number of commodities that the manufacturer can subject to taxation, the more efficiently revenues can be raised and the greater are manufacturer profits.[17] As Burstein pointed out, this relationship can hold even when the demands for the tied goods are *completely unrelated*.

It is useful to think of the distortions induced by $w > c$ in terms of derived demand. Wholesale pricing above cost induces the dealer to purchase too little of the manufacturer's output for two reasons. First, the dealer engages in input substitution away from x. Second, in response to higher costs, the dealer may contract his output and thus reduce the quantity of all inputs simultaneously. In those cases in which final output is unambiguously defined (i.e. the dealer cannot affect the final product quality), the second problem can be viewed in terms of pricing the final output – the dealer takes w as the marginal cost in computing the final price, and thus sets the final price too high when $w > c$. This practice is known in the literature as "double marginalization".[18]

To prevent distortions in relative input levels, the manufacturer would like to mandate the use of inputs in efficient proportions. Barring this power, the manufacturer may be able to induce the dealer to choose an efficient input mix through the use of a tying arrangement. If all inputs can be subject to taxation (i.e. tied), the manufacturer can mark up the prices of all inputs proportionally. Let n denote the price of input y when it is tied with x. By settiing prices such that $w/n = c/m$, the manufacturer can induce the dealer to choose an efficient

[17] This principle is stated, and its implications for business behavior are more fully drawn out, in Burstein (1960a).

[18] Spengler (1950) appears to have first identified the double marginalization effect in the context of vertical control. He pointed out that if one takes the unnatural union view of vertical integration, then the elimination of the double mark-up is a benefit of vertical integration when only single-product, uniform pricing is allowed.

mix of x and y (recall that m is the competitive supply price of input y). A tying arrangement works perfectly to overcome input mix distortions when it can be applied to all inputs. When some or all of the other input levels (e.g. dealer effort) are unobservable to either the manufacturer or the courts, it is impossible to implement a comprehensive tie-in, and input distortions may be induced. Loosely speaking, these distortions can be minimized by increasing the prices of those tied inputs that are the least substitutable for untied inputs.[19]

Turn now to the distortion in level of final output, and suppose that no input substitution is possible. Given this assumption, for any input, i, there is a function $f_i(\cdot)$ such that the firm cannot produce z units of output unless $f_i(z)$ units of input i are utilized. If all inputs must be used in proportions that vary only with the level of final output, then any multi-product pricing scheme is equivalent to some (possibly nonuniform) single-product price schedule.

Ties need not be equivalent to single-product price schedules when input substitution is feasible. Suppose, for example, that the manufacturer supplies two inputs, one fixed and the other variable. Moreover, suppose that the manufacturer has a monopoly on the variable factor but faces competition in the supply of the fixed factor. In this setting, a tie may serve as an implicit two-part tariff. The manufacturer prices the variable input at marginal cost and uses a mark-up on the fixed input as a franchise fee. As with a two-part tariff, the manufacturer is able to transfer rents in a way that does not distort the dealer's marginal cost function. Hence, the final output level is unaffected. Of course, when there is no perfectly fixed input, the manufacturer may find it optional to implement a multi-product tie.

When the incompleteness of information is the reason that $w > c$ in the first place, the manufacturer's intermediate good pricing problem is an extremely complex one. For example, suppose that the manufacturer cannot observe the dealer's value of θ and that one factor is fixed and the other variable. For incentive reasons (i.e. to minimize the input distortion) the manufacturer should raise the price of the fixed input to collect revenue. But in order to obtain a signal of θ, it may be necessary to mark up the price of the variable input.[20] In general, the manufacturer will find it profitable to tie the purchase of y to the purchase of x and sell both inputs at prices that deviate from their production cost.[21]

[19] For a more complete discussion of these issues, the reader is referred to the literature on optimal commodity taxation. See, for example, Atkinson and Stiglitz (1980).

[20] In the vertical restraints literature, this practice is known as metering. Bowman (1957) and Telser (1965) credit Aaron Director with first having suggested that businesses use tying to facilitate metering. For a brief mention of this theory, see Director and Levi (1956).

[21] If input y is not competitively supplied, there may be another role for ties. Suppose that inputs x and y are complementary in the sense that lowering the price of x raises the demand for y, and thus may raise the profits of the firms producing y. The producer of x does not count the increase in other firms' sales as a benefit when calculating its optimal price for x. When the two inputs are tied, the single seller internalizes the externality across inputs. See Bowman (1957) for an early discussion of this point.

Royalties are another form of multi-product pricing that may be available to the manufacturer. Under a revenue royalty scheme, the manufacturer receives some fraction of the dealer's final market revenues. A royalty can be thought of as a form of multi-product pricing because it is equivalent to a proportional mark-up on all inputs. Hence, royalties can be used like ties to alleviate input distortions. Formally, let the dealer's revenues net of payments to the manufacturer be denoted by $T[R]$. Suppressing θ for notational convenience, the dealer

$$\underset{x,\,y,\,e}{\text{maximizes}}\; U\{T[R(x, y, e)] - cx - my, e\},$$

which leads to an efficient input mix. Likewise, in cases in which dealer output is well defined and observable, a royalty scheme has the advantage over a tie that the manufacturer does not have to monitor the levels of other downstream inputs (e.g. dealer effort) in order to limit input distortions. Of course, the imposition of a royalty scheme still distorts the dealer's overall incentives to produce revenues.

The use of royalties also can increase the manufacturer's profits when the manufacturer and dealer are asymmetrically informed about some parameter, θ, and the final price is more sensitive to the value of θ than is the level of the dealer's input use. Suppose, for example, that the demand for final output is given by

$$D(p;\theta) = \begin{cases} D^0 & \text{if } p \le \theta, \\ 0, & \text{if } p > \theta, \end{cases}$$

and that only the dealer observes the realization of θ. Then x alone is of no value as a signal of θ, but clearly observing R (or the final price) is. Thus, a revenue-based royalty can be one way of extracting the rents that might otherwise accrue to a dealer with a high realization of θ.

There can be important benefits from using both ties and royalties simultaneously. A contract under which all inputs are priced below cost by the same percentage as the revenue royalty rate is equivalent to a pure profits tax. In this case, there is no distortion in the dealer's behavior. Unfortunately (from the manufacturer's viewpoint), it often is impossible to subsidize dealer effort.

2.3.2. Resale restraints

As noted above, there are two reasons for which the dealer's derived demand curve for x is downward sloping: (a) he responds to an increase in his marginal costs by reducing the total amount of output sold; and (b) he responds to an increase in the cost of a single input by substituting other inputs for x in the production of final output. A resale price ceiling appears to be the obvious solution to the problem posed by (a) since the dealer restricts his output by raising the final price of the good. If the manufacturer places the ceiling on the final price, this output restriction is constrained (as long as the ceiling does not lead to the dealer's shutting down).

Suppose that, for any fixed two-part tariff, dealer profit and output both are increasing in θ. Then, if the optimal two-part tariff involves a wholesale price that is greater than marginal cost and the dealer cannot affect the final product quality, a two-part tariff coupled with a resale price ceiling is privately superior to a two-part tariff alone. If the dealer type charging the highest final price is not one for whom the individual rationality constraint is binding, then imposing a ceiling on the final price raises unit sales (and manufacturer profit) without inducing any dealer to drop out of the market. If the dealer type charging the highest price is one for whom the individual rationality constraint is binding, then the manufacturer should set the ceiling price equal to the highest current price, raise w by $\mathrm{d}w$, and lower F by $\mathrm{d}F = -x^*(w, \underline{\theta})\,\mathrm{d}w$, where $\underline{\theta}$ denotes the lowest dealer type. This shift has no effect on either the type-$\underline{\theta}$ dealer's profit or the profit that the manufacturer derives from this type of dealer. It can be shown, however, that the manufacturer's profit derived from all other types of dealer increase.

While the use of a price ceiling can attenuate the dealer's restriction of final output, resale price maintenance does not work perfectly in cases in which there is uncertainty or asymmetric information. If θ is uncontractable, then it is impossible to set $p = p^{\pi}(\theta)$ for all θ.[22] In the single-dealer case, this failing of resale price maintenance is an important one because uncertainty or asymmetric information are the motivations for resale price maintenance when two-part tariffs are feasible.

Resale price maintenance also fails to solve the input substitution problem; if input substitution is feasible, the dealer tends to use too little of x relative to the other inputs whether or not a price ceiling is imposed. A related problem concerns the definition of a resale price ceiling. For what good is the ceiling price set? In order to establish the profitability of a price ceiling, it was assumed above that the dealer could not affect the quality of the final product. Typically, the dealer can affect product quality (e.g. the dealer can provide varying levels of service to final consumers). The dealer may respond to a price ceiling by reducing the quality of his output.[23] Essentially, this is another form of input mix

[22] This analysis is a special case of Rey and Tirole's (1986) examination of the resale price maintenance in a multi-dealer setting.

[23] Let $D(p,q)$ denote the final demand function, and let $C[D(p,q),q]$ denote the dealer's total cost function. The dealer's profit-maximizing choice of product quality is an increasing function of the price he charges under the following conditions: $D_1 < 0$, $D_2 > 0$, $D_{12} \geq 0$, $C_1 > 0$, $C_2 > 0$, $C_{11} \geq 0$, and $C_{12} \geq 0$.

distortion. To complicate matters, this effect occurs on top of the input mix distortion induced by the nonmarginal-cost pricing of the manufacturer's output.

Turning to nonprice restrictions, customer restraints may be utilized to extract rents from the dealer when the manufacturer and dealer are imperfectly informed at the time of contracting. Suppose that θ effects only the market revenue function $R(x, y, e; \theta)$. If the variation in R is due to uncertainty with respect to a particular class of customers, the manufacturer may reserve that class for his own sales force. Of course, some form of contract is needed between the manufacturer and his own sales force, and contracting problems may arise in this relationship as well. It makes sense to implement this division of customers only if there is some reason that the manufacturer is better able to monitor his own sales force (perhaps that is what is meant by the sales force being "his own"), or if his own sales force need be given less discretion, so that problems of moral hazard are less severe. This type of customer restraint is an example of what is known more generally in the literature as *tapered* vertical integration , where one firm is present at a vertical stage as both a buyer and a seller. Like all theories of vertical integration, this one needs further development.

3. Private incentives: A single manufacturer with many dealers

Most manufacturers sell their output to more than one dealer. In the case of a manufacturer with a single dealer, correcting the externalities between the manufacturer and the dealer is the essence of the contracting problem. These externalities, and the need to correct for them, remain present when the manufacturer has multiple dealers. There is a new type of externality as well – externalities across the dealers. In making his decisions, each dealer ignores the effects that his actions have on the profits of the other dealers. Dealers thus may fail to maximize joint profits, opening up a potential role for vertical restraints even in those situations in which the manufacturer is otherwise able to extract all of the existing surplus from the dealers.[24]

While the presence of multiple dealers opens up new control problems for the manufacturer, it also opens up a new control instrument. With multiple dealers, the manufacturer can implement a relative performance scheme under which a dealer's compensation depends not just on his performance, but also on the performance of other dealers. And, of course, when there are multiple dealers, the

[24] There is another new effect that can arise in the multiple dealer case. Public policy may force the manufacturer to offer the same contract to all dealers. In such cases, the manufacturer must essentially act as if he does not know the type of any given dealer. The distortions induced by two-part pricing and the possible remedies are similar to those discussed in the case of a single dealer. In fact, if the dealers serve isolated markets, the two problems are isomorphic to one another.

assignment of exclusive territories by the manufacturer no longer is a trivial policy.

3.1. Externalities across dealers

It sometimes is argued that the manufacturer's profits are greatest when his dealers are perfect competitors with one another. If no input substitution is possible and the dealers simply choose their output levels for a good of fixed quality, then this argument is correct. Under perfect competition, the difference between the final product price, p, and the wholesale price, w, is as low as is compatible with non-negative dealer profits. Hence, under downstream perfect competition, for any given level of w, manufacturer profits, $X(p)\{w - c\}$, are as large as possible [here, $X(p)$ denotes the dealers' aggregate demand for the manufacturer's output]. By competing with one another, the dealers drive down their margins and allow the manufacturer to appropriate all of the profits from production and sale of the good.

When dealers can do more than simply choose a single uniform price for their output, the manufacturer need not favor strong intrabrand competition. Intrabrand competition may inhibit certain aspects of dealer behavior that would increase manufacturer profits. In particular, dealer competition may constrain certain forms of final good pricing and limit promotional activities. In these situations, resale restraints may be imposed to obtain outcomes that are not supportable as competitive equilibria in the final market.

3.1.1. Price competition as a negative externality

Consider first the effects of dealer competition on downstream pricing. In the presence of strong intrabrand competition, dealers are forced to charge each consumer a price based on the cost of supplying that consumer. Both high price–cost margins and price discrimination against final consumers are incompatible with vigorous intrabrand competition. Yet, these may be profit-maximizing forms of pricing.

3.1.1.1. The erosion of the price–cost margin.[25] The manufacturer would like to induce the monopoly price, $p^{\pi}(c; \theta)$. Faced with wholesale price w, competitive retailers set price $p^{c}(w; \theta) < p^{\pi}(w; \theta)$. Relying solely on the price mechanism,

[25]As shown by the analysis in Section 2, if dealers are imperfect competitors and either franchise fees are infeasible or informational incompleteness leads to wholesale pricing above marginal cost, then the manufacturer may find that the dealers' price–cost margin is too high. In the present section, I focus solely on the new problem of an unprofitably low margin that arises when there are competing dealers.

the only way for the manufacturer to induce $p^{\pi}(c; \theta)$ is to raise the wholesale price above marginal cost. As long as x is a variable input and is essential to downstream production [i.e. $R(0, y, e; \theta) = 0$ for all y, e, and θ], there exists some $w > c$ such that $p^c(w; \theta) = p^{\pi}(c; \theta)$. In the absence of any input substitution possibilities, this wholesale price induces the joint-profit-maximizing downstream equilibrium, and the manufacturer can extract any dealer surplus (or cover any dealer losses) through the appropriate choice of the franchise fee.[26] When input substitution is possible, setting $w > c$ distorts the dealer's behavior. Hence, there may be private gains from the use of multi-product pricing or resale restraints.

As many authors have noted [e.g. Dixit (1983) and Mathewson and Winter (1984)], if all parties know θ at the time of contracting, the manufacturer can impose a resale price *floor* equal to $p^{\pi}(c; \theta)$ while setting $w = c$ and using F to appropriate any dealer surplus.[27] Note, however, that if the manufacturer does not know the value of θ at the time of contracting, he may be unable to set the price floor equal to $p^{\pi}(c; \theta)$ for all realizations of θ.

Another way to prevent the erosion of the dealer margin is to eliminate intrabrand competition through the assignment of exclusive territories. The analysis presented in Section 2 can be interpreted as showing that if the manufacturer and dealers all have complete information and the manufacturer assigns exclusive territories, then the manufacturer's profits are maximized by setting $w = c$ and raising F until each dealer just earns his opportunity utility level. Of course, as was discussed in Section 2, the assignment of exclusive territories alone need not be sufficient to attain the perfect extraction of dealer rents when the parties have incomplete information.

3.1.1.2. Price discrimination. Intrabrand competition may reduce overall industry profits (and thus the amount of rents that the manufacturer can extract) by blocking price discrimination in the final market. A simple example illustrates this point. Suppose that consumers are located in two identical cities, A and B. There are N_1 consumers in each city who demand either one or no unit of the good with reservation price $\bar{p}_1$. There are N_2 consumers in each city who demand either one or no unit of the good with reservation price $\bar{p}_2$, where $\bar{p}_1 < \bar{p}_2$. There are two dealers, each of whom is able to identify the type of any given customer. One dealer is located in city A, and one is located in city B. There are no transportation costs between the two cities. The dealers are Bertrand competitors; each dealer chooses his final good prices under the assumption that the prices of his rival are fixed.

[26] Recall that negative franchise fees are allowed.

[27] If lump-sum payments to dealers are infeasible, then in some instances the manufacturer may use a resale price floor to preserve the downstream margin as a means of transferring income to the dealers.

The manufacturer provides the sole input into downstream production and must choose a contract for his dealers. The manufacturer would like to have his dealers charge $\bar{p}_i$ to type-i consumers, $i = 1, 2$, and use the fixed fee charged to the dealers to appropriate all of the profits. But when the contract is simply a two-part tariff, the dealers drive the final pricc down to the wholesale price level for *all* consumers, and there is no price discrimination. The manufacturer must choose between setting $w = \bar{p}_1$ and earning profits of $2(\bar{p}_1 - c)(N_1 + N_2)$, or setting $w = \bar{p}_2$ and earning profits of $2(\bar{p}_2 - c)N_2$.

The manufacturer can facilitate price discrimination by placing territorial customer resale restraints on his dealers. If the manufacturer assigns exclusive territories to the two dealers, then each dealer is a downstream monopolist within his home city. Given any $w \leq \bar{p}_1$, each dealer charges $\bar{p}_1$ to the N_1 consumers with low reservation prices and $\bar{p}_2$ to the N_2 consumers with high reservation prices, yielding profits of $(\bar{p}_1 - w)N_1 + (\bar{p}_2 - w)N_2 - F$. The manufacturer can set F to drive dealer profits to zero. The resulting manufacturer profits are $(2\bar{p}_1 - c)N_1 + 2(\bar{p}_2 - c)N_2$, which are greater than the profits under nonexclusive territories.

Somewhat more generally, if two-part tariffs are available to the manufacturer, dealers are risk netural, the manufacturer and dealers are symmetrically informed ex ante, and there is no problem of manufacturer moral hazard, then the assignment of exclusive territories yields weakly greater profits than does dealer competition.[28] The reason for this result is as follows. Under either downstream monopoly or competition, the manufacturer appropriates all of the profits through his choice of the fixed fee. Under competition, the manufacturer can induce any nondiscriminatory pricing scheme, although $w > c$ results in an inefficient input mix. Under exclusive territories, the manufacturer can set $w = c$ to induce profit-maximizing discriminatory scheme without inducing an inefficient dealer input mix. The assignment of exclusive territories yields strictly higher profits than does competition whenever a final good monopolist would find it profitable to discriminate.

Other resale restraints also may serve to facilitate downstream price discrimination. Suppose that, in the example above, the customers with low reservation prices correspond to national accounts. By imposing a resale restraint based on customer class, the manufacturer can set $w = \bar{p}_2$ to induce a price of $\bar{p}_2$ for sales made to local accounts through his dealers, while selling at $\bar{p}_1$ to the

[28]This result does not generalize to markets in which franchise fees are infeasible. If the manufacturer is restricted to choosing a uniform wholesale price, then he weakly prefers perfect competition downstream to a set of local monopolists who act as third-degree price discriminators. The reason is as follows. The manufacturer's profits are $w - c$ times the quantity sold and, for any given uniform price, demand is greater when the dealers are perfect competitors than when they are local monopolists.

national accounts that he has reserved for himself. Of course, in the simple example considered here, the price charged by the manufacturer is lower than w, so that explicit restrictions on dealer sales to national accounts are unneeded. In the presence of input substitution possibilities or imperfect competition among the dealers serving high-value consumers, however, the manufacturer might have incentives to set $w < p_1$, and explicit customer restraints would be needed.

Bowman (1955) noted that a common argument of his day was that resale price maintenance could be used to facilitate price discrimination by preventing the dealers from making sales to low-price customers. The manufacturer's relative ability to monitor his dealers' prices versus their customer lists would be an important consideration in choosing between the two types of resale restraint to support price discrimination.

The discussion so far has not addressed the question: How do the manufacturer and his dealers identify the different customer types in order to price discriminate? In some cases, the manufacturer and his dealers may discriminate among final consumers through the use of a sorting mechanism. Bolton and Bonnano (1987) analyzed a market in which consumers differ in their tastes for some service that can be viewed as product quality. By offering different variants of the good, the firms can induce consumers to reveal their types through their purchase decisions, facilitating a greater extraction of consumer surplus. Suppose, for example, that the costs of quality and distribution of consumer tastes are such that industry profits are maximized when two variants of the final good are offered, one with high quality and one with low.

Can the manufacturer induce this outcome given that each dealer is free to choose the single quality that he offers? For simplicity, assume that there are two dealers. Bolton and Bonnano found that, for sufficiently low values of the wholesale price, the dealers do choose to produce different variants of the good. The dealers differentiate themselves vertically in order to relax price competition.[29] For these low values of the wholesale price, dealer competition leads to downstream prices that are below their joint-profit-maximizing levels. If the manufacturer raises the wholesale price, however, dealer differentiation and the resultant consumer sorting are eliminated. Intuitively, if the wholesale price is set too high, a low-quality dealer finds himself undercut by the high-quality dealer. Two-part pricing alone cannot induce the joint-profit-maximizing outcome.

One way to preserve the dealer's price–cost margins is to impose a resale price floor (which is independent of dealer quality). But when price competition is limited, the dealers turn to quality competition. Again, both dealers offer high-

[29]As Bolton and Bonanno (1987) note, this type of result is a well-known one in the literature on vertically differentiated oligopoly [see, for example, Shaked and Sutton (1982)].

quality variants and the dealer variety is eliminated. While the imposition of a resale price restraint can raise profits in this setting, it does not work perfectly.

Bolton and Bonnano went on to show that a more sophisticated contract in which any given dealer's franchise fee is a function of all of the prices charged in the downstream market can work perfectly in their simple setting. As they noted, however, such a contract might be very costly to enforce when the number of dealers is large.[30]

In some instances, the cost of selling to a given customer may depend upon characteristics of that customer. In such a market, price discrimination may take the form of charging equal prices to two consumers even though the firm incurs different costs to serve them. As Caves (1986) discussed, resale price maintenance may facilitate this form of price discrimination by forcing dealers to charge uniform prices. Hence, resale price maintenance may provide a means of discriminating against consumers who desire low levels of promotional activities or service and thus are cheaper to serve.

So far, I have discussed cases in which the manufacturer would like to induce prices that discriminate against final consumers within a single geographic region. The manufacturer also might want to practice price discrimination across geographic regions. As White (1981) observed, even if dealers are located in different regions, varying the wholesale price to dealers in each region may be insufficient to achieve price discrimination. When the dealers are perfect competitors who can costlessly arbitrage across regions, the price in all regions is driven to "just under" the second lowest value of w_i.[31] Similar effects arise even when arbitrage across regions is costly (i.e. dealers are spatially differentiated), although clearly the arbitrage problem is less severe.

The imposition of (enforceable) territorial restrictions can be used to prevent arbitrage and allow geographic price discrimination. Note that if each dealer has an exclusive territory, then in the absence of other incentive or informational problems, the manufacturer can induce optimal discrimination by setting all of the wholesale prices equal to marginal cost. Obviously, the use of a system of resale price maintenance under which the maintained price varied across regions also would achieve the desired downstream geographic discrimination.

3.1.2. Dealer free riding

3.1.2.1. Tangible presale services. As just shown, the manufacturer may implement vertical restraints when intrabrand competition limits certain forms of pricing. Similarly, vertical restraints may be profitable when the competitive

[30] In order to enforce the contract, each dealer would have to observe the prices charged by all other dealers.

[31] In the event that two or more firms tie for having the lowest price, these firms price at the common value of w.

equilibrium fails to support promotional activities at the level that would maximize joint profits.

Suppose that there are two Ford dealers in some city. If one of the dealers runs a series of television commercials promoting Ford automobiles, these ads benefit both the dealer paying for the ads and the other dealer, who is going along for a free ride. The advertising dealer's incentives to run the commercials are smaller than the joint-profit-maximizing incentives for two reasons: (1) in choosing his level of advertising, a dealer ignores any increase in profits that his rival enjoys as a result of advertising spillovers; and (2) given the rivalry between the two dealers, the spillovers may reduce the profits of the advertising firm, further diminishing incentives. This sort of argument can be applied to other types of promotional and service activities, such as operating showrooms and having salesmen provide pre-sale information to consumers.

The manufacturer could rely on the price system to restore some of the lost incentives. One way, using single-product pricing, is to set the wholesale price below marginal cost in order to make the additional sales generated by promotional activities more valuable to the dealers. But such a two-part tariff would lead to other incentive problems, and in any case, intrabrand competition might erode the dealers' margins. The manufacturer might be able to implement a multi-product pricing scheme to subsidize the inputs to promotional activities. But, again, the erosion of the dealers' margins may reduce the profitability of this strategy. Moreover, the use of such schemes may be limited by the manufacturer's inability to observe the input levels. This problem is particularly acute when unobservable dealer effort is one of the inputs to the production of promotional activities.

Turning to resale restraints, Telser (1960) and Yamey (1954) noted that resale price maintenance can be used to preserve a large dealer margin that generates downstream incentives to engage in promotional activities.[32,33] The imposition of resale price maintenance does not, however, correct the distortion that nonmarginal cost pricing of the input might cause. Telser and Yamey also identified a second, and somewhat indirect, way in which a resale price floor encourages the provision of promotional effort. A restriction on price competition makes it difficult for a low-service dealer to free ride on a high-service dealer because it limits the ways in which the low-service dealer can attract consumers away from the other dealer. In this way, resale price maintenance both protects a high-service

[32] Silcock (1938) presented an informal version of this argument.

[33] Bowman (1952, 1955) and Comment (1951) also argued that resale price maintenance was necessary to compensate dealers for providing services subject to externalities. In these articles, the problem is treated as one of adverse selection with two types of dealer (i.e. low-cost, low-service dealers and high-cost, high-service dealers) rather than one of moral hazard. These informal models correspond closely to Marvel and McCafferty's (1984) model of quality certification discussed in Subsection 3.1.2.3 below.

dealer and gives a low-service dealer an incentive to raise his service level. This type of effect is likely to be strongest when the promotional activity is something like a showroom or expert advice, where the customer has to come into the store to receive the service. Of course, if a dealer can offer particular services that are enjoyed by his customers only, then he may use these services to attract customers from other dealers and free ride on their provision of those promotional activities with a public good nature.

Recently, Mathewson and Winter (1984) and Perry and Porter (1986) examined the use of resale price maintenance to correct for service externalities in fully-specified algebraic models. Telser and Yamey, in contrast, relied solely on verbal arguments. Mathewson and Winter considered a market in which the dealers are spatially-differentiated monopolistic competitors. Mathewson and Winter found that manufacturer would indeed use a resale price floor if he could couple it with a franchise fee (or equivalent form of nonuniform pricing), Perry and Porter considered a modified version of Dixit's (1979) model of monopolistic competition with quality (service) competition. They extended Dixit's model, which is itself an extension of the well-known Dixit–Stiglitz (1976) model, to allow for service externalities. Surprisingly, under this specification of demand and market equilibrium, if the manufacturer's only two instruments are a uniform wholesale price and the ability to fix the resale price, the resulting retail margin is independent of the degree of service externality. Rather than a floor to preserve dealers' promotional incentives, the limit on resale pricing takes the form of a *ceiling* to control the double marginalization problem. This result is a provocative one, and it will be interesting to see to what extent this finding carries over to other model specifications.[34]

In addition to using resale price restraints to limit dealers' free riding indirectly, the manufacturer can use customer resale restraints to block free riding directly. One way is to impose a system of exclusive territories under which the final market is divided into nonoverlapping geographic segments with one dealer in each segment. While exclusive territories may limit dealer free riding, there are costs associated with them. The efficient size of market region in terms of transportation and production costs may differ from the efficient market size based on media coverage or other promotional considerations. And, as discussed below, intrabrand competition may serve as a valuable control instrument to the manufacturer, an instrument that is lost when exclusive territories are assigned.

Nongeographic customer restraints can work much like exclusive territories to prevent free riding. Faced with customer restrictions, a dealer is prevented from

[34]Asymmetric equilibria (i.e. full-service dealers co-existing with discounters) also deserve attention. Perry and Porter (1986) restricted their attention to symmetric equilibria.

stealing the business of a consumer in whom another dealer has invested time and money in making a sales pitch or providing other customer-specific promotional services for the manufacturer's brand. This may be one reason why large customers, who have offices in many sales regions, often are reserved for national-account sales forces.

3.1.2.2. Product reputation. Reputational externalities can arise when product quality is unobservable to consumers prior to purchase and they form expectations about the quality of one dealer's product based in part of the quality of other dealers' products. Reputational effects are likely to be particularly important in the case of a franchise, where the dealer presents himself to final consumers under the manufacturer's trade name. A consumer's prediction of the quality of a Burger King hamburger served in Berkeley, for example, is likely to be heavily influenced by the quality of hamburgers consumed in the past at other Burger Kings.

Two conditions must be satisfied in order for dealer reputations to give rise to externalities. One, customers must believe that the product quality observed by sampling (i.e. buying a unit of the good) at one dealer is a good predictor of the product quality offered by another dealer. Consumers may believe such a link exists either because the dealers all use the same input provided by the manufacturer that is a key determinant of product quality, or merely because the consumers know that all dealers face the same optimization problem in choosing their actions.[35] The second necessary condition for the existence of reputational externalities is that either individual consumers are mobile across dealers, or a consumer bases his or her expectations on the experience of other consumers who are spread across dealers.

If product quality is not influenced by dealer choices (i.e. quality is determined entirely at attributes of the manufacturer's input), then the existence of reputational externalities poses no additional problems of dealer moral hazard. Often, however, the dealer can affect consumers' valuation of the good. Suppose that there are multiple inputs to downstream production and that consumers care about the input mix. The relative input levels can be thought of as the "quality" of the service provided by the output. Moreover, suppose that consumers are unable to judge the quality prior to purchase and do rely on past experience with the good. Any one dealer's choice of quality affects the future demand (i.e. repeat purchases) both for his output and for the output of all of the other retailers. As

[35]In fact, consumers probably believe that all dealers offer the same quality of product simply because that is what consumers typically observe in product markets. The reasons given in the text really are explanations of why these beliefs tend to be correct in equilibrium.

in the case of promotional externalities, dealers fail to internalize the reputational externality in choosing their input mixes and hence tend to undersupply costly quality.

The manufacturer's potential responses to reputational externalities are similar to those in the case of promotional externalities. For example, the manufacturer could lower the wholesale price and impose a resale price floor to make repeat purchases more valuable and thus increase the incentives to provide high-quality output. But again, such pricing could induce other distortions.

Some authors argued that resale price maintenance is profitable when the price itself affects a product's reputation and consumers' perceptions of its value. Taussig (1916) suggested that a resale price floor could be used to keep prices high in a market in which final consumers are sensitive to price as an indicator of the snob value of a "prestige good" (a rose by any other price might not smell as sweet). He asserted that such effects are particularly likely in markets in which the dealer is simply a retailer for the manufacturer's branded product. Absent a resale price floor, any one dealer might have incentive to lower his price in order to attract more sales, even though the overall effect of this move would be to lower the total unit sales of the good by eroding its image. Proponents of resale price maintenance argued that this effect would be particularly strong in markets in which multi-product dealers would otherwise use the manufacturer's product as a loss leader to attract consumers.[36]

Silcock (1938) argued that resale price maintenance could increase unit sales of a good by providing uniform pricing. He asserted that in the absence of price dispersion, consumers would tend to buy out of habit. He then argued that price dispersion across dealers would encourage consumer search, which would, in turn, induce consumers to think about product quality and whether they really wanted the good. As the final leg of his argument, Silcock posited that an introspective consumer would tend to purchase less of the good than would a buyer who acts out of habit.

Returning to more narrowly conceived economic models, the manufacturer may have incentive to implement a multi-product pricing scheme in response to problems of reputational externalities. By tying the other inputs to downstream production to his product, the manufacturer may be able to choose the relative prices in such a way as to induce the collectively optimal input mix for each dealer. In fact, manufacturer-imposed standards on the quality of dealer output can be thought of as a particular tie entailing multi-product quantity-dependent pricing. As always, when unobservable dealer effort is one of the inputs, complete tying is infeasible, and it may be impossible to induce the joint-profit-maximizing quality level.

[36]Bowman (1955) discussed, and rejected, the loss leader argument.

3.1.2.3. Quality certification. Marvel and McCafferty (1984) also considered a market in which consumers value product quality or stylishness, but are unable to observe these attributes prior to purchase. Unlike the cases just considered, the dealers in their model cannot influence the product's quality (i.e. there is no input substitution). Despite this fact, dealers can affect consumers' *prepurchase* beliefs about these attributes.

Each dealer carries a variety of products and establishes a *dealer-specific* reputation for not carrying products of quality below some threshold level. For example, a stereo store might stock the products of several different manufacturers and establish a reputation for carrying only that equipment that is of the highest quality. Or, a certain overpriced New York department store might carry only those designer denims that it knew to be stylish. In either case, as long as the quality or stylishness of a given product is known to be constant across dealers, consumers can use the fact that a high-threshold dealer carries a good as a means of product certification.

Consumers raise their expectations of the manufacturer's product quality when they observe the good being sold by a store that has a reputation for carrying only high-quality products even if they do not purchase that good from the store. Consumers do not care about the cutoff level or reputation of the particular dealer from whom they purchase the good, and they purchase the product from the store with the lowest price. Thus, by stocking the good, a dealer with a high quality threshold raises consumer expectations, expands demand, and creates a positive externality for all dealers and, ultimately, for the manufacturer.

Quality certification is costly. These costs can arise from the extra testing or market research that dealers with high thresholds must conduct to ensure that their more stringent standards are met. Marvel and McCafferty took the distribution of quality thresholds among potential dealers to be exogenous.[37] In other words, a potential dealer is unwilling to alter his reputation for the sake of a single product. This assumption may be a reasonable one for a dealer who sells a large number of different products (e.g. a department store).

A key feature of the Marvel–McCafferty model is that market demand is increasing in the number of dealers selling the product. This effect arises when dealers are differentiated and consumers value dealer variety.[38] In a market in which the downstream firms are spatially-differentiated retailers, the greater the number of dealers, the lower the average distance that a consumer must travel to reach a dealer carrying the manufacturer's product. Or, consumers may value

[37]Hence, in contrast to the case of tangible presale services considered in Subsection 3.1.2.1 above, the manufacturer faces a problem of dealer adverse selection rather than dealer moral hazard.

[38]Marvel and McCafferty's assumption that retailers are differentiated appears to be somewhat unnatural in the light of their assumption that all dealers are price takers in the final good market. Their analysis could, however, be generalized to allow for some downstream market power.

dealer variety because the downstream firms use the manufacturer's output to produce differentiated goods.

Given that certification is costly and there is a benefit from increased dealer density, the manufacturer may desire a mix of dealers. The manufacturer would like to have some dealers with high thresholds in order to certify the product's quality, while having other dealers with low thresholds in order to minimize distribution costs.[39] The manufacturer's problem is to induce this pattern of dealers.

If the manufacturer can select his retailers and can set dealer-specific two-part tariffs, then he can implement the desired distribution of dealers exactly. The quality certification mechanism does not introduce any new reasons to use contractual provisions beyond single-product pricing as long as the manufacturer is allowed to charge different prices to different dealers. In effect, the manufacturer can purchase certification services by setting a low (or even negative) franchise fee for dealers with high quality thresholds. Such a pricing scheme may, however, run afoul of the Robinson–Patman Act.[40]

Suppose, as did Marvel and McCafferty, that the manufacturer can set only a uniform wholesale price (i.e. franchise fees or lump-sum payments are infeasible), and that the manufacturer's right to refuse dealers is limited to setting a marketwide standard. That is, the manufacturer can choose a single quality level such that any store with a quality threshold below that level is prohibited from carrying the product, but any store with a higher threshold must be allowed to serve as a dealer if it so desires.

The manufacturer faces an adverse selection problem. For any given wholesale price, low-threshold, low-cost dealers tend to drive high-threshold, high-cost dealers out of the market, lowering the product's image. Hence, the manufacturer may find it desirable to set a binding standard in order to facilitate the survival of stores with high quality thresholds. The problem with this approach is that by throwing out low-cost dealers, the manufacturer limits his coverage of the market.

The manufacturer may be able to increase his profits by implementing a resale price floor. By setting a final price floor, the manufacturer can increase the equilibrium price–cost margin and the profits of existing dealers. New dealers will be attracted. Given the order in which firms find it profitable to enter the market, these new dealers will have higher quality thresholds than any of the existing dealers. Hence, the product's image will be improved and sales will rise.

[39] Formally, consumers in Marvel and McCafferty's model base their expectations of product attributes by taking the highest quality cutoff level of any store that stocks the manufacturer's product. Under this extreme assumption, the manufacturer's optimal portfolio of dealer types comprises a single dealer with a threshold just equal to the true product quality and all other dealers with the lowest possible thresholds.

[40] For a further discussion of this point, see Bowman (1952) and Comment (1951).

The manufacturer's profits will rise as well. Put another way, through a resale price floor, the manufacturer can insure the survival of a high-threshold dealer, while continuing to have low-cost, low-threshold dealers serve customers.[41]

Although not considered by Marvel and McCafferty, the assignment of exclusive territories might also be used to protect high-cost, high-threshold firms. But note that, for this strategy to be profitable, the certification effects would have to carry across the boundaries of the exclusive territories, a condition that might be unlikely to hold.

3.2. *A new control instrument*

3.2.1. *Relative performance schemes*

When there is uncertainty about some parameter of the dealer's profit function and the dealer is risk averse, the agency contract must both provide the dealer with incentives and provide the dealer with insurance. In the single-dealer case, there is a conflict between these two roles for the contract. When there are multiple dealers, the manufacturer may be able to separate these two roles and offer a contract that provides both full incentives and full insurance.

These points are best seen within the context of a simple example. The upstream firm owns a patent that he can license to (for now) a single, risk averse, downstream firm. The downstream firm earns revenues of

$$R(x, e; \theta) = \begin{cases} 0, & \text{if } x = 0, \\ r(e + \theta), & \text{if } x = 1, \end{cases}$$

where $r(\cdot)$ is some increasing function. At the time of contracting, the dealer does not know the realization of θ, although he learns it before choosing his level of effort.[42] The dealer cares about θ solely through its influence on r; θ does not enter the dealer's utility function directly. Ex post, the manufacturer can observe the value of r (and hence the sum of e and θ), but he cannot observe the individual values of e and θ.

Define $e^{\mathrm{m}}(\cdot)$ and $F^{\mathrm{m}}(\cdot)$ as the solution to

$$\underset{e(\cdot),\, F(\cdot)}{\text{maximize}} \; \underset{\theta}{E}\, F(\theta)$$

$$\text{subject to} \quad \underset{\theta}{E}\, U[r(e(\theta) + \theta) - F(\theta), e(\theta)] \geq 0.$$

[41] If there is an unlimited number of dealers of each type, then in equilibrium all stores are of the lowest threshold allowed, and there is nothing that the manufacturer can do indirectly.

[42] As was shown in Section 2, when the value of θ is known to would-be dealers at the time of contracting, an auction among would-be dealers can serve as a relative (prospective) performance scheme.

$e^{\mathrm{m}}(\cdot)$ and $F^{\mathrm{m}}(\cdot)$ are the solution to the manufacturer's problem when contractual provisions based on the realization of θ are enforceable. This solution satisfies the first-order conditions $U_1 = \mu$ for all θ, μ some constant, and $U_1 r' + U_2 = 0$. The dealer has a constant marginal utility of income across realizations of θ, and the level of effort always is the efficient one.

This contract is not incentive compatible when θ is unobservable to the manufacturer. If the license fee were to depend on the report of θ, the dealer always would report that value that minimized the license fee. Under this outcome, the dealer would not be insured against poor realizations of θ, but he would supply effort at the efficient level.

Suppose that contracts based on r are enforceable. That is, all parties, including the courts, can observe $\theta + e$, although only the dealer can observe the components of this sum individually. When the license fee depends only on the value of r, it is a royalty scheme: $F(r)$. The dealer's payoff is $U[r - F(r), e]$. The manufacturer would like to set the royalty rate to insure the dealer against low realizations of θ while at the same time inducing the downstream firm to supply the optimal amount of effort.

To provide full incentives to supply effort, the dealer's compensation must be a sharply increasing function of his gross profit (i.e. $\mathrm{d}F/\mathrm{d}r = 0$). But, under this contract, the dealer bears all of the risk. A full insurance contract (i.e. $\mathrm{d}F/\mathrm{d}r = -1$), on the other hand, would eliminate any incentive to provide effort. Given his incomplete and imperfect information, the manufacturer is unable to separate dealer shirking from bad luck. The profit-maximizing contract represents a compromise between the provision of insurance and incentives.

Now, suppose that the manufacturer has two dealers, 1 and 2, who serve markets that are independent of one another in the sense that the actions of one dealer have no effect on the sales or profits of the other dealer; there is no direct competition between the dealers. Moreover, suppose that each market is identical to the one just considered for the case of a single dealer. It might appear that the optimal contract for the single-dealer problem is the optimal contract for each dealer in this case as well. It need not be. When the values of the unobservable parameters that affect dealer profits are correlated across markets, the manufacturer may be able to increase his profits by implementing a relative performance scheme under which a given dealer's compensation depends not just on his performance, but also on the performance of the other dealer.

To keep matters as simple as possible, suppose that the realization of θ is the same for all dealers. θ may be thought of as a measure of the quality of the innovation that is being licensed. The following contract attains the full private optimum. Define $F^{\mathrm{n}}(r)$ such that

$$F^{\mathrm{n}}[r(e^{\mathrm{m}}(\theta) + \theta)] = F^{\mathrm{m}}(\theta).$$

The royalty paid by dealer i is equal to $F^{\mathrm{n}}(r_j)$, $j \neq i$, where r_j is the revenue earned by dealer j.

Faced with this contract, firm i chooses $e_i(\theta)$ to

$$\underset{e(\theta)}{\text{maximize}}\ U\left[r(e(\theta)+\theta)-F^{\mathrm{n}}(r_j), e(\theta)\right].$$

There exists a symmetric equilibrium in which, for all i and θ, $e_i(\theta) = e^{\mathrm{m}}(\theta)$, and thus $F^{\mathrm{n}}[r(e_i(\theta)+\theta)] = F^{\mathrm{m}}(\theta)$.[43]

The essential benefit of the relative performance mechanism is that it allows the manufacturer to separate insurance and incentives in the contract. Dealer incentives are realized by making each dealer the residual claimant to the revenues that he generates. The dealer is simultaneously insured by making the fixed fee depend upon the performance of the *other* dealer. If the other dealer does poorly, then the original dealer pays a lower "royalty" than he otherwise would.

When θ is not constant across dealers and the realizations are not perfectly correlated, this type of contract does not fully solve the incentive and insurance problems. It is clear, however, that relative performance schemes often can increase manufacturer profits in more general environments.

3.2.2. *The market mechanism as an incentive and insurance scheme*

The sort of scheme sketched above does not resemble any of the contract types typically considered in the vertical restraints literature. Rey and Tirole (1986) applied this type of analysis to more traditional contract forms. They showed, inter alia, that direct competition between the dealers can serve as one form of relative performance scheme.

The following example illustrates their analysis. Output is produced according to a constant proportions downstream production technology where one unit of the input provided by the monopolistic manufacturer must be combined with one unit of a competitively supplied unit, with cost θ_2, to produce one unit of output. There are two dealers, one located in city A and the other in city B, where each city has a demand curve $P = \theta_1 - X$. There are no transportation costs between the two cities. The dealers are Bertrand competitors and face the same values of θ_1 and θ_2 as one another.

At the time of contracting, all parties know the underlying parameters of the dealer's profit function except for θ_1 and θ_2. After the contracts have been signed, but before any price or output decisions are made, the dealers learn the realizations of θ_1 and θ_2.

[43]Shleifer (1985) considers a similar sort of relative performance scheme in the context of a regulated industry.

The joint-profit-maximizing price is $p^m(c; \theta_1, \theta_2) = (\theta_1 + \theta_2 + c)/2$. The manufacturer would like to induce the dealers to set this price. Since θ_1 and θ_2 are unobservable to the manufacturer, the contract cannot be contingent upon their realizations. Suppose that the manufacturer relies solely on single-product pricing and allows unfettered competition between the dealers. If the manufacturer set $W(x) = F + wx$ and imposed no other restrictions on dealer behavior, the dealers would drive the final price down to $w + \theta_2$. Dealer competition is relative performance scheme in the following sense: the residual demand curve that a dealer faces depends on the cost level of his downstream rival.

Unlike the monopoly price, the competitive price shows no response to shifts in demand as measured by θ_1. The equilibrium price fully adjusts to changes in cost θ_2, however. In fact, the competitive price overadjusts. The use of a two-part tariff fails to solve the problem of dealer moral hazard in price setting. Note, though, that the two-part tariff does provide the dealers with full insurance; each dealer earns $-F$ no matter what the values of θ_1 and θ_2.

Now, suppose that the manufacturer imposes exclusive territories and restricts each dealer to selling in his home city only. Each dealer is a final good monopolist in his home city and sets price equal to $p^m(w; \theta_1, \theta_2)$. The manufacturer's setting $w = c$ fully solves the dealer moral hazard problem, but the dealers bear all of the risk – the manufacturer's profits are equal to $2F$, independent of the realizations of θ_1 and θ_2. Exclusive dealing ameliorates one problem and exacerbates another.

Lastly, consider resale price maintenance in the form on a fixed price (i.e. a simultaneous floor and ceiling). Clearly, this price does not adjust to either changes in costs or demand.

Which contractual provisions will the manufacturer find privately optimal to implement? In the absence of uncertainty, the policies of unfettered dealer competition, resale price maintaince, and exclusive territories coupled with a franchise fee all lead to the same outcome in the final good market and to the same levels of manufacturer and dealer profits. A major finding of Rey and Tirole's work is that these policies are not equivalent in the presence of uncertainty about the optimal final good price. In the presence of uncertainty, the manufacturer has a real choice to make.

The manufacturer–dealer contract has three potential roles to play in this setting: incentive provision, income transfer, and insurance. If the dealers are risk neutral, then there is no need for insurance provision. The privately optimal two-part tariff coupled with exclusive territories yields the maximal level of manufacturer profits; the wholesale price gives dealers the correct incentives and the franchise fee transfers income. Both dealer competition and resale price maintenance do relatively poorly in terms of incentive provision. Under dealer competition prices fail to respond to changes in demand,[44] although they do

[44] This result does not carry over to more general cost structure or to non-Bertrand firms.

(suboptimally) respond to changes in cost under competition. And, of course, prices do not respond at all under resale price maintenance. Therefore, with risk neutral dealers and either cost or demand uncertainty, the manufacturer strictly prefers the assignment of exclusive territories to either unfettered intrabrand competition or resale price maintenance. Rey and Tirole showed that resale price maintenance and competition do equally well from the point of view of expected manufacturer profits.[45]

Rey and Tirole assumed that the dealers' downstream prices were the only dimension of dealer moral hazard or adverse selection. More generally, there are several types of incentive problem that can arise as a result of asymmetric information. As discussed in Section 2 above, the manufacturer may have incentives to set $w > c$ in response to these problems when his dealers are assigned exclusive territories. Pricing the intermediate good above cost leads to overly-high final good prices when the dealers have exclusive territories and there are no resale price restraints. Hence, in a general setting, the manufacturer may find it optimal to impose resale price maintenance or to allow dealer competition. A similar result obtains when fixed fees are infeasible.

What if the dealers are risk averse? Following Rey and Tirole, take the case of infinitely risk averse dealers. That is, consider dealers who care only about the minimal level of profits that they might receive. Under competition, the dealers are fully insured against both cost and demand shocks. If there are no cost shocks, full insurance with respect to demand shocks is feasible under resale price maintenance (by imposing a downstream price–cost margin equal to 0). When dealers face solely demand uncertainty, resale price maintenance and competition are equally profitable for the manufacturer.[46] Because of their superior insurance properties, both policies are preferred to the assignment of exclusive territories.[47] Turning to cost shocks, resale price maintenance does poorly in providing insurance, and it is the least profitable of the three policies. Competition is the most profitable, while the assignment of exclusive territories falls in between the two. In summary, dealer competition can sometimes serve as an effective relative performance scheme.

3.3. The number of dealers

The manufacturer's profits typically vary with the number of dealers. As shown above, an increase in the number of dealers may have negative effects due to the

[45]Rey and Tirole noted that this equivalence is a general one when the dealers face solely demand uncertainty. In the presence of cost uncertainty, however, this result is dependent on the linearity of demand.

[46]Rey and Tirole also showed that when dealers are slightly differentiated, resale price maintenance is superior to dealer competition because it avoids the problems associated with double marginalization.

[47]Recall from Section 2 that the manufacturer insures a dealer with an exclusive territory by setting $w > c$, which distorts dealer incentives.

increased dealer pricing and promotional externalities. In his study of the tuna industry, Gallick (1984) identified another reason that having more than one dealer may lower the manufacturer's profits. Suppose that the quality of the manufacturer's output varies across units in a way that cannot be controlled by the manufacturer, but can be observed by him. If the manufacturer can sell his output to a variety of dealers, then each dealer must be concerned about getting an adverse selection of output. In response, each dealer may have to examine the quality of the input that he purchases. This inspection is costly and is of no collective value if all dealers value any given quality of output equally. Having the manufacturer sell all of his output to a single dealer avoides this adverse selection problem and economizes on inspection costs.

Of course, having multiple dealers can give rise to several types of benefits. First, having multiple dealers may be a valuable element of the vertical control scheme. The resulting increase in intrabrand competition serves to limit the markup of the final price over marginal cost, which in some cases is beneficial to the manufacturer. Moreover, his having multiple dealers allows the manufacturer to develop a benchmark against which to measure any one dealer's performance. A second benefit of multiple dealers arises when dealer variety is valuable to consumers: the derived demand for the manufacturer's output is an increasing function of the number of dealers, ceteris paribus. Finally, increased dealer variety may allow greater discrimination against final consumers by increasing the fineness of the partition of consumer types that is created by consumers' self-selecting across dealers.

There are several different ways in which the manufacturer may influence the number of dealers. The number of dealers may be chosen directly by the manufacturer (he simply refuses to deal with more than a set number of downstream firms). Alternatively, the manufacturer may indirectly control the number of dealers through his pricing policy or the nonterritorial resale restraint provisions of his contract offer. Suppose, for instance, that there is free entry into the downstream industry and the manufacturer affects the number of dealers indirectly through his single-product price schedule. Changes in either the franchise fee or the wholesale price change the equilibrium number of dealers. In the case of the fixed fee, the effect of pricing on the number of dealers is straightforward. The higher the fixed fee, the lower the number of retailers in a zero-profit equilibrium.[48]

Katz and Rosen (1985) and Seade (1985) showed that raising the wholesale price may *raise* or lower the number of retailers. The initially surprising result that a higher input price can increase the number of firms has the following intuition. Raising the price to any one firm, lowers that firm's equilibrium output

[48] To get the desired number of retailers, the manufacturer might have to set a negative franchise fee.

and profit levels. This decrease in output increases the profits of rival firms. The gain to rivals may dominate the loss to the higher-cost firm, so that an industry-wide price shift may increase industry profits and make new entry profitable. In effect, the increase in dealer marginal cost induces a cartel-like cutback in downstream output whose benefits may dominate the increased costs.

Turning to resale restraints, Gould and Preston (1965) examined the manufacturer's incentives to impose a resale price floor in a downstream market with a symmetric, perfectly competitive equilibrium.[49] Gould and Preston argued that, when final consumers value dealer variety, a manufacturer would have incentives to implement a resale price floor in order to increase the number of dealers by preserving their price–cost margin.[50] Early proponents of resale price maintenance claimed that resale price floors would be even more strongly needed in markets with asymmetric equilibria in which some (multi-product) dealers would use a product as a loss leader, discouraging other dealers from carrying the good.[51]

Bittlingmayer (1983), Mathewson and Winter (1983b), and Perry and Porter (1986) examined the use of resale price maintenance by a manufacturer with monopolistically competitive dealers.[52] Contrary to Gould and Preston, these authors all found that a manufacturer who cannot set a nonzero franchise fee will use a resale price *ceiling* to keep down both the dealers' price–cost margin and, hence, the number of dealers. In these models, resale price restraints are used to ameliorate the double marginalization problem rather than to increase the number of dealers. Since the dealers in Gould and Preston's model are perfect competitors, there is no problem of double marginalization, and the manufacturer imposes a resale price floor. Perry and Porter did, however, find that a manufacturer who can set positive franchise fees will impose a resale price floor which either increases or leaves unchanged the number of dealers in comparison with the equilibrium absent resale price maintenance.

One reason for the manufacturer in the Perry and Porter model to impose a resale price floor is to give dealers incentives to provide promotional activities that are subject to externalities. Gould and Preston pointed out that when the manufacturer sets a resale price floor for this reason, he may find it desirable to limit the number of dealers directly. One way to restrict the number of dealers is to assign a limited number of exclusive territories.

[49] Gould and Preston themselves noted that the assumption of perfect competition among dealers appears to be inconsistent with consumers' valuing dealer variety. Gould and Preston hypothesized that their analysis would carry over to markets with monopolistically competitive dealers.

[50] This point also was made informally by Bowman (1955) and Silcock (1938).

[51] See Bowman (1955) for a discussion of, and attack on, the loss leader argument. See Yamey (1952) for an interesting history of the use of this argument by supporters of resale price maintenance.

[52] Bittlingmayer (1983) and Mathewson and Winter (1983b) considered spatially-differentiated dealers facing either linear or exponential point demand functions in a market with linear transportation costs and no promotional spillovers. Perry and Porter (1986) is described in Subsection 3.1.2.2 above.

As Preston (1965) observed, the imposition of exclusive territories also can be used to raise profits per dealer and increase the number of dealers that the downstream market can support. The reason is that, for any given wholesale price and set of dealers, the assignment of exclusive territories leads to higher final prices than does competition among dealers. In the face of dealer moral hazard or adverse selection, the manufacturer may find it preferable to assign exclusive territories rather than to rely on negative franchise fees.

4. Private incentives: Multiple manufacturers

The situation most often encountered in actual markets, but least seen in economics journals, is that of multiple manufacturers, each of whom has many dealers. As in the cases examined in earlier sections, there may be externalities across these dealers. There also is a new type of externality that may arise when there is more than one upstream firm: externalities across manufacturers.

In this section I will focus on the new issues that these externalities raise, including: (1) the possibility of service externalities across *brands*; (2) the effects of vertical contracts on interbrand competition; and (3) the effects of vertical contracts on the conditions of entry into the manufacturing stage. I will discuss each of these areas in turn. In this discussion, I will consider, inter alia, the use of the final type of vertical restraint identified in the introduction: when there is more than one upstream producer, a manufacturer may require his dealers to agree not to carry the products of rival suppliers.

4.1. Free riding across manufacturers

Consider the following variant of the free riding story that was told for the case of a single manufacturer with multiple dealers. There is a stereo dealer who carries several brands of hi-fi equipment. Suppose that the manufacturers rely solely on uniform pricing and that one manufacturer engages in heavy advertising that attracts consumers to the dealer. Once consumers have come into the store, the dealer has incentives to persuade the consumers to purchase whichever brand offers the largest profit margin. That brand need not be the one that conducted the advertising responsible for attracting the consumers to the store. As with free riding across dealers, free riding across manufacturers may lead to levels of promotional activity below the profit-maximizing ones.[53]

[53] In those cases in which competition among manufacturers would otherwise lead to equilibrium advertising intensities above their collusive levels, the manufacturers may benefit from the reduction in advertising incentives due to free riding.

There are several means by which to deal with the problem of free riding across brands. One is to adjust the single-product pricing policy. The advertising manufacturer could lower his wholesale price and compensate for this price reduction by increasing the franchise fee. If each manufacturer set his wholesale price equal to his marginal cost, then there would be no distortions in the dealer's marginal incentives. As was seen in Sections 2 and 3, however, a two-part tariff with a low wholesale price may suffer several disadvantages. It may exacerbate problems of manufacturer moral hazard and adverse selection. And a low wholesale price may lead to unprofitably low prices for downstream output due to inter-dealer competition.

The imposition of a resale price floor could eliminate this second problem. But the price floor would do nothing to mitigate the problems of manufacturer moral hazard and adverse selection. Resale price maintenance also would fail to mitigate the problems of wholesale price cutting by rival manufacturers and inefficient risk-bearing by the dealers.

In principle, multiproduct pricing could be used in response to free riding across brands. The advertising manufacturer could demand a royalty payment based on the dealer's total revenues or unit sales across all brands. Under such a scheme, the advertising manufacturer would appropriate some of the promotional benefits that spill over to rival brands.[54] In many respects, this form of multiproduct pricing is like a cooperative advertising agreement.

Marvel (1982) identified the imposition of exclusive dealerships as another way for a manufacturer to respond to the problem of within-store brand switching. Of course, any gains from exclusive dealing due to greater appropriation of promotional efforts must be balanced against the increase in distribution costs due to lost economies of scope in downstream selling. Exclusive dealing also might reduce manufacturer profits through its effects on the pattern of consumer sampling. Consumers engaged in sequential search may have incentives to sample multi-brand retailers first in order to minimize search costs. Consequently, single-brand retailers might suffer diminished sales.

4.2. *Lock-in*

A complete contract typically is unprofitable (due to the tremendous costs of calculation and administration) or entirely infeasible (due to the incompleteness of information). Hence, the agreement between the two parties rarely, if ever, fully specifies what should happen in all possible contingencies. This incompleteness of contracts gives rise to possible opportunistic behavior by one or both of

[54]Antitrust authorities probably would object to this type of arrangement on the grounds that it is an illegal attempt to monopolize the final good market.

the parties to the contract. Opportunistic behavior presents a particular problem when one side of the manufacturer–dealer relationship makes expenditures on assets that have value only in that relationship. Once the relationship-specific costs have been sunk by one party, the other party may reopen bargaining over the terms of the contract.

For concreteness, assume that the manufacturer is the one who must make significant relationship-specific investments. Once the manufacturer has made the sunk investments, he is locked-in to the relationship to some extent. The dealer may be able to take advantage of this fact to renegotiate the contract in a way that is more favorable to him. The dealer may induce renegotiation by threatening to break off the relationship or to engage in behavior that takes advantage of uncontracted contingencies that have arisen since the initial signing of the contract.

Both parties may suffer from the possibility of opportunistic behavior by the dealer. Faced with the prospect of the dealer's renegotiating the contract, the manufacturer may choose an inefficiently low level of investment in order to limit the extent to which he is locked-in to the relationship. This reduction in the investment level may reduce the value of the relationship to both parties. Hence, both parties may have ex ante incentives to limit the dealer's ability and incentive to engage in opportunistic behavior.

There are two types of force that can limit the dealer's opportunistic behavior and, thus, can help restore efficiency in investment and production choices. One force arises from the fact that the relationship is an ongoing one. If the dealer takes advantage of the manufacturer today, he may be forgoing future profits that could be enjoyed from the relationship.[55] As recognized by Schelling (1956, 1960) and developed more fully by Williamson (1983) and others, the parties may take actions designed to increase the value of maintaining the relationship to both sides. One way is to have the dealer offer a hostage. That is, to have the dealer invest in a relationship-specific asset of his own. This hostage serves two roles. First, it attenuates the dealer's threat to terminate the relationship. Second, the existence of a hostage makes the *manufacturer's* terminating the relationship a stronger punishment that can be imposed on the dealer in response to his behaving opportunistically.

In some instances, the pricing and resale restraint provisions of the manufacturer–dealer contract can serve to create hostages. One means of creating a hostage, for example, is to have a low wholesale price coupled with a large franchise fee; the right to the low wholesale price becomes a relationship-specific asset owned by the dealer. In this case, an artificial asset is created. Alternatively,

[55]See Williamson (1983) and the references cited therein for a more complete discussion of self-enforcing long-term contracts.

the contract may be used to create a relationship-specific asset out of an asset that would exist in any event but would not otherwise be a relationship-specific one. Dealer reputation may be a candidate for such an asset. A multi-brand dealer may be able to develop a reputation as a good dealer per se. When the dealer carries only one brand, his reputation may become inextricably linked with that product. Hence, an exclusive dealing arrangement may lead to the dealer's reputation becoming a relationship-specific asset.

Another way to deal with opportunistic recontracting is to limit the threats that the dealer can make.[56] A requirements contract, for instance, eliminates the buyer's ability to threaten to take his business to another manufacturer. Suppose that the manufacturer offers the dealer insurance in the form of a long-term contract that specifies a constant wholesale price in a market in which the spot prices charged by other manufacturers vary over time. If two-part tariffs are feasible, the manufacturer can sell the option to buy the input at a given price for a lump-sum payment made in advance (or spread over time according to a path that is independent of the dealer's purchase levels). If franchise fees are infeasible, however, the manufacturer must rely on the dealer's "paying" for this insurance by making purchases when the price set in the contract is greater than the current spot market price. But the dealer has incentives to make purchases from other manufacturers during such periods. As Blair and Kaserman (1984) noted, tying in the form of a requirements contract can prevent the dealer from diverting purchases to other manufacturers in periods of low spot prices.

While the emphasis here has been on opportunistic behavior by the dealer, the manufacturer could engage in such actions as well. In the case just considered, if the dealer pays for insurance in advance, then the contract has to set the long-term price and terms of delivery to ensure that manufacturer will, in fact, deliver the product in times of high market prices. This example brings up the important, if obvious, point that the parties need to make sure that their attempts to correct for dealer misincentives do not themselves generate manufacturer misincentives. The parties must seek a balance in creating a bilateral hostage exchange to facilitate efficient trade of the intermediate good.

4.3. *Effects on interbrand competition*

The nature of manufacturer–dealer contracts may affect competition among manufacturers or among the dealers of the different manufacturers. The manu-

[56]As Farrell and Shapiro (1987) showed, it is not always the case that efficiency is improved by limiting the one party's ability to take inefficient actions. Such a prohibition may drive the opportunistic party to take even more inefficient actions to achieve the same end.

facturers would like to use the pricing and restraint provisions of these contracts as means of diminishing interbrand competition. There are several mechanisms through which the manufacturers' contracts with their dealers may at least partially attain this goal.

4.3.1. *Lower cross-price elasticities*

In many models of oligopoly, the lower are the cross-price elasticities of demand, the weaker is interbrand competition and the higher are producer profits. There are two ways in which provisions of the manufacturer–dealer contract may be used to lower the cross-price elasticities of demand. First, as discussed earlier in this section and in Subsection 3.1.2, the imposition of vertical restraints may increase the levels of promotional activities and other forms of nonprice competition, which may in turn strengthen product differentiation and lower cross-brand elasticities. Thus, as Comanor (1968) argued, restraints such as resale price maintenance or exclusive territories may weaken *interbrand* competition.

The second way in which vertical restraints may lower cross-price elasticities is through their effects on consumer search costs. When all manufacturers demand that their dealers agree to exclusive arrangements and dealers are spatially differentiated, consumer search costs are higher than they would be if a single dealer were to carry several different brands of the product. Under exclusive dealing arrangements, consumers who want to comparison shop are forced to visit several stores. The higher costs of comparison shopping tend to discourage consumers from undertaking this search activity, limiting the extent of interbrand competition and raising industry profits.

Will manufacturers all demand exclusive dealing arrangements? The answer depends in part on the contracting institutions. Suppose that each manufacturer independently chooses the price of his output and whether to demand an exclusive arrangement. If all other manufacturers demand exclusive dealing, then a manufacturer has no real choice to make and may as well require an exclusive arrangement himself; industrywide exclusive dealing always is one equilibrium. What if manufacturers are allowed to coordinate their contract offers? In this case, industrywide exclusive dealing is an equilibrium outcome if and only if the value that consumers place on comparison shopping is sufficiently low that it does not pay any subset of manufacturers to allow their dealers to carry each other's products.

4.3.2. *Facilitate collusion among manufacturers*

The manufacturers would collectively gain from successful collusion. Typically, individual firms have incentives to cheat on any collusive agreement, and the firms must be able to monitor one another in order to collude successfully.

Contract provisions that improve monitoring may thus facilitate collusion.[57] Telser (1960) examined the role of resale price maintenance in facilitating collusion. Absent resale price maintenance, it may be difficult to tell if the retail price has dropped because the manufacturer has cheated on the collusive agreement or because one of the dealers has chosen to lower his final price on his own initiative. Under resale price maintenance, each brand has a single final price which is set by its manufacturer. Thus, it is relatively simple for the upstream firms to monitor whether their rivals are adhering to the cartel agreement.[58] Collusion also may be easier to sustain because the number of participants in any given agreement is reduced.

Similarly, territorial restraints can facilitate collusions by limiting the number of parties to the agreement. Here, the collusion across brands takes place among the dealers. If each brand assigns exclusive territories to his dealers and territories across brands largely match one another, then only those dealers in any given territory need to reach a collusive agreement.

Telser also noted that exclusive dealing arrangements might be used to limit manufacturers' incentive to make secret wholesale price cuts. If a dealer carries several different brands, any given manufacturer may lower his wholesale price in an attempt to get the dealer to promote that brand at the expense of its rivals. If each dealer carries a single brand, then obviously no such effect arises. Of course, there still would be incentives to lower the wholesale price in order to encourage increased promotional competition among dealers carrying different brands.[59] This type of promotional activity may, however, be easier to monitor than would be in-store promotional activity aimed at inducing consumers to switch brands.

4.3.3. Common agency: Exclusive dealing in reverse

Interbrand competition can be viewed as a negative externality across manufacturers. An obvious way to internalize this externality is to vest all of the decision-making power in a single economic actor who has been made the residual claimant to industry profits. If he is risk neutral, this residual claimant will maximize industry profits. Brennan and Kimmel (1983) and Bernheim and Whinston (1985) identified a common dealer as a natural party to serve as the

[57] As shown by Abreu, Milgrom and Pearce (1987), improvements in monitoring may have the opposite effect in some cases.

[58] If a manufacturer cannot discriminate among his dealers, then the need for resale price maintenance to improve monitoring may be limited. Cheating by the manufacturer would be comparatively easy to detect – rival manufacturers would look for instances in which several dealers for a given brand lowered their retail prices simultaneously.

[59] In his examination of the use of resale price maintenance to facilitate collusion by improving the manufacturers' monitoring of each other, Bowman (1955) concluded that this wholesale price cutting and the resulting promotional competition would undermine the use of resale price maintenance to sustain collusion.

internalizing agent. If all manufacturers sold their output to a single downstream firm and each manufacturer set his wholesale price equal to his marginal cost, the common dealer would act to maximize the collective profits of the two stages.[60]

A big question is: Will the manufacturers all in fact choose to sell to a single dealer? In effect, Brennan and Kimmel examined an industry in which there is a single potential downstream dealer.[61] But more generally, one must consider the possibility that some manufacturer could hire an independent dealer who could free ride on the output restrictions of the other, cartelized brands. As yet, economic theory does not offer compelling answers to questions concerning coalition formation. It is, however, useful to consider a simple and rather artificial coalition formation process.[62]

There are two manufacturers playing the following five-stage game. In stage one, the firms simultaneously announce the contracts that each one is willing to offer a common dealer. In stage two, each firm announces whether it is willing to go with the common dealer under these terms. If they agree to do so, then at stage three the manufacturers simultaneously offer these two-part tariffs to a common dealer. If either manufacturer refuses to seek a common dealer, then in stage three the manufacturers simultaneously offer two-part tariffs (which need not be equal to the contracts proposed in stage one) to different dealers. In the penultimate stage, any dealer to whom an offer has been made decides whether to accept it. The fifth stage consists of some product-market game played among those dealers who accept contracts.

It is convenient to summarize the fifth-stage outcome with a reduced form profit function. Let $\pi^{\mathrm{m}}(w_1, w_2)$ denote downstream industry profits when there is a multi-product monopolist with input costs w_1 and w_2. Let $\pi_1^{\mathrm{d}}(w_1, w_2)$ denote the profits of dealer i when there is a duopoly in the final good market and dealers 1 and 2 face input prices w_1 and w_2, respectively. A natural assumption is that

$$\pi^{\mathrm{m}}(w_1, w_2) \geq \pi_1^{\mathrm{d}}(w_1, w_2) + \pi_2^{\mathrm{d}}(w_1, w_2),$$

for all w_1 and w_2, with strict inequality whenever the duopolists are not able to achieve the cartel outcome.

[60]Alternatively, one could consider a market in which there are many risk neutral, common dealers, but each one is assinged an exclusive territory.

[61]Brennan and Kimmel (1983) examined a setting in which upstream firms produce joint products, A and B. There is a single potential dealer for product A, while there is a perfectly competitive industry willing to distribute product B. Brennan and Kimmel showed that the sole potential dealer for good A might want to refuse to distribute a manufacturer's output of A unless that firm also distributed his output of B through that distributor. In this way, the distributor could serve as a common agent for all upstream firms for both goods.

[62]This is not the process studied by Bernheim and Whinston (1985). They used a model with a more natural contracting process to reach conclusions similar to those presented here.

In the fourth stage, any dealer who has been offered a contract yielding non-negative profits accepts that contract.

If the manufacturers have chosen to make bids to a common dealer in the second stage, then in the third stage the first-stage offers are put forth. If the manufacturers have chosen to make bids to separate dealers, then in the third stage manufacturer i chooses w_1 and F_i to

$$\begin{aligned}&\text{maximize} \quad F_i + \{w_i - c\}x_i(w_1, w_2)\\&\text{subject to} \quad \pi_i^{\mathrm{d}}(w_1, w_2) - F_i \geq 0.\end{aligned}$$

Let w_i^{n} (for Nash) denote the equilibrium value of w_i given that the manufacturers choose separate agents. For convenience, assume that the values of w_1^{n} and w_2^{n} are unique.

In the second stage, the manufacturer i decides whether to have a common dealer by comparing $\pi_i^{\mathrm{d}}(w_1^{\mathrm{n}}, w_2^{\mathrm{n}})$ with the profits that he would earn under the proposals made in the first stage.

Now, consider the first stage. Since he later can veto the use of a common agent, manufacturer i chooses his bid to maximize his profits under common agency conditional on inducing the other parties to accept the agreement. Hence, if manufacturer j $(j \neq i)$ has bid (F_j, w_j), manufacturer i's best reply is the solution to

$$\begin{aligned}&\text{maximize} \quad F_i + \{w_i - c\}x_i(w_1, w_2)\\&\text{subject to} \quad \pi^{\mathrm{m}}(w_1, w_2) - F_1 - F_2 \geq 0\\&\qquad\qquad\quad \text{and}\\&\qquad\qquad\quad F_j + \{w_j - c\}x_j(w_1, w_2) \geq \pi_i^{\mathrm{d}}(w_1^{\mathrm{n}}, w_2^{\mathrm{n}}).\end{aligned}$$

The form of the agent's individual rationality constraint, the first constraint, reflects the institutional structure that he must either accept both offers or reject both offers. As noted several times previously, the optimal wholesale price is $w_i = c$. The fixed fee is set to drive the dealer's net profits to 0.

It is trivial to verify that there is a continuum of subgame perfect equilibria under each of which the manfacturers hire a common agent, $F_1 + F_2 = \pi^{\mathrm{m}}(c, c)$, $F_i \geq \pi_i^{\mathrm{d}}(w_1^{\mathrm{n}}, w_2^{\mathrm{n}})$, and $w_i = c$, for $= 1, 2$. Under all of these equilibria, the externality across manufacturers is fully internalized by the common agent and industry profits are maximized. The equilibria differ only in the division of profits between the two manufacturers.

Given the (theoretical) benefits of common agency, why would manufacturers ever choose to have exclusive dealers? One possible explanation is that the result above is sensitive to the institutional structure. Another reason for choosing separate dealers may follow from the fact that, when $w_i > c$, a common agent does not maximize industry profits. As shown throughout this chapter, there are forces limiting the profitability of marginal cost (wholesale) pricing even when there is a common dealer. An important area for further exploration is whether independent dealers can be more profitable than a common one in such settings. For example, it would be interesting to see whether the use of separate dealers might be more profitable than a common agent because downstream competition better overcomes the double marginalization problem.

4.3.4. *Observable contracts as precommitments*

The provisions of the contracts between manufacturers and their dealers may influence the nature of competition among dealers of different brands. Suppose that each dealer carries a single brand and that the dealers carrying brand A can observe the sales contracts or franchise agreements under which the dealers of brand B operate. Brand-A dealers will condition their product-market behavior on the contracts of their rivals. As several authors [i.e. Fershtman and Judd (1986, 1987), Rey and Stiglitz (1986), and Ross (1987)] have pointed out, a profit-maximizing manufacturer takes these effects into account in choosing the contract to offer his dealers.[63]

The following two-stage game illustrates how the presence of observable agency contracts can affect the product-market equilibrium. In the first stage, each manufacturer offers a contract to his dealer, which the dealer then accepts or rejects. The manufacturers in this example are restricted to offering two-part tariffs. After the first stage is complete, the dealers' contracts become common knowledge among all parties. Then, in the second stage, each dealer chooses a level of final output. x is the only input needed to produce final output, and one unit of x is required per unit of final output.

In any pure strategy equilibrium, manufacturer i must set the franchise fee charged to his dealer equal to $\pi_1^{\mathrm{d}}(w_1, w_2)$. Thus, given w_j, manufacturer i's profits when it chooses w_i (and adjusts the fixed fee appropriately) are

$$\pi_i^{\mathrm{d}}(w_1, w_2) + \{w_i - c\}x_i(w_1, w_2).$$

Suppose that firm i sets $w_i = c$. Differentiating manufacturer i's profits with respect to w_i, one obtains:

$$\partial\pi_i^{\mathrm{d}}/\partial w_i + x_i = x_i P' \partial x_j/\partial w_i.$$

For a Cournot dealer, $x_i P' \partial x_j/\partial w_i$ is negative. Thus, the manufacturer has

[63] Schelling (1960) first suggested the strategic use of contracts as precommitments. Spencer and Brander (1983) and Brander and Spencer (1985) presented a formal model of this type of effect in the context of international trade policy.

incentives to set w_i below c. Under the condition that an increase in x_j shifts down the residual marginal revenue curve for dealer i, the two-stage perfect Nash equilibrium entails each manufacturer's setting his wholesale price below marginal cost.[64]

The intuition behind this result is clear. By setting his wholesale price below marginal cost, the manufacturer makes his dealer a more aggressive competitor in the product market. Faced with a more aggressive rival, the other dealer reduces his output, raising the profits of the first dealer. That dealer's manufacturer then appropriates the profits through the fixed fee.

The set of feasible contracts is greatly restricted in the example just considered. Fershtman, Judd and Kalai (1987) and Katz (1988b) demonstrated that the form of the contract restriction is central to the character of the equilibrium. In fact, once one allows for a relatively general set of contracts, essentially any individually rational outcome in the product market can be attained as the perfect equilibrium in the two-stage game. Thus, if this line of analysis is to be developed further, effort must be concentrated on finding natural restrictions to place upon the nature of contracts.

4.3.5. *The effects of unobservable contracts*

What if the contract between a manufacturer and his dealer is not observable to the other manufacturers and their dealers? Can unobservable contracts affect the behavior of rival firms? The answer is: "Yes, but not for strategic reasons." Because the contract is unobservable to his rivals, in choosing his contract, the manufacturer ignores any effects that his choice might have on the behavior of other manufacturer's or their dealers. As shown in Katz (1988a), however, this is not to say the vertical contracts have no effect on the product–market outcome.

The effects of unobservable manufacturer–dealer contracts are most easily seen under the extreme assumption that the vertical contracts must take the form of a single uniform price. Again, suppose that there are two manufacturers, each with one dealer. In equilibrium, a manufacturer must set $w > c$ in order to earn positive profits. Even though dealer 1 cannot observe dealer 2's contract, dealer 1 knows that dealer 2 must face a wholesale price that is greater than marginal cost. In fact, under the extreme assumption that he knows all of the parameters of manufacturer 2's contracting problem, dealer 1 can deduce the equilibrium value of w_2 and act accordingly. Dealer 2 can engage in similar reasoning, as can the two manufacturers. Hence, equilibrium entails a lower level of final output and higher final price than would equilibrium if each manufacturer–dealer pair were

[64]This type of two-stage game arises in many other contexts and is discussed more generally in Chapter 6 by Carl Shapiro in this Handbook. He shows, inter alia, that equilibrium may entail $w > c$ for other types of product–market competition.

a single decision-maker with a complete unity of incentives. Similar effects may arise with more general contracts in settings where a manufacturer–dealer contract serves to share risk or governs a situation characterized by asymmetric information.

4.3.6. Raise rivals' costs

A manufacturer's profits typically are an increasing function of his rivals' costs. Thus, a manufacturer is willing to take costly actions that serve to raise his rivals' costs.[65] As discussed in Section 3, Katz and Rosen (1985) and Seade (1985) showed that when marginal costs are increased by some action, even a *symmetric* (across all firms) cost increase may raise a manufacturer's profits. And, if there are asymmetries among manufacturers, some of the manufacturers may be able to exploit them.[66] A standard argument in the vertical restraints literature points to the role of foreclosure through exclusive dealing arrangements as a means of raising rivals' costs. Suppose that there are economies of scale and scope in distribution. In this case, a system of exclusive dealers raises the distribution costs of smaller firms by more than it raises the distribution costs borne by larger firms. Thus, smaller firms are put at a disadvantage by this industry configuration. The net effect may be to raise the profits of larger firms, even though their costs of distribution are raised as well.

In a similar vein, intuition supports the idea that by demanding an exclusive dealing arrangement, a manufacturer with a large market share may be able to tie up the good dealers (e.g. retailers with locational advantages or who enjoy the greatest economies of scope) – if a dealer has to go with a single brand, he will tend to choose the market leader ceteris paribus.

Mathewson and Winter (1987) examined a model constructed to capture this intuition formally.[67] In their model, two manufacturers of substitute goods compete for the sales services of a single potential dealer.[68] There is a two-stage

[65]Raising the costs of both actual and potential rivals is discussed more generally in Chapter 8 by Richard Gilbert in this Handbook.

[66]In addition to coining the term, "raising rivals' costs", Salop and Scheffman (1983) provide a general analysis of a dominant firm's incentives to increase asymmetrically the costs of firms in a competitive fringe.

[67]Comanor and Frech (1985) also developed a model that attempted to embody this intuition. In their model, there is one firm that has a product differentiation advantage (in terms of the desirability of its brand to final consumers) over a competitive fringe of rival manufacturers. There are two types of retailer, one with low costs, one with high. Comanor and Frech claimed to show that the manufacturer with a differentiation advantage would impose exclusive dealing on the low-cost dealers. Schwartz (1987) argued convincingly that Comanor and Frech failed to incorporate fully the constraints on this manufacturer imposed by dealer rationality. Given the nature of their assumptions (in particular the claim that dealer margin should be taken as fixed), it is difficult to assess what the results of their model are.

[68]In terms of the intuition above, there is a second dealer with arbitrarily high costs.

game. In the first stage, each manufacturer states whether he will demand exclusive dealing. In the second stage, each manufacturer submits a bid to the dealer in the form of a uniform wholesale price (i.e. franchise fees are not allowed). If neither manufacturer has demanded an exclusive relationship, then the dealer purchases both intermediate products. If either manufacturer does demand an exclusive arrangement, then the dealer must choose from which of the two manufacturers to buy. Mathewson and Winter showed by example that if the demand for one of the intermediate goods is larger than for the other, then the manufacturer of the preferred product may demand an exclusive arrangement.

4.4. *Entry deterrence*

Raising *potential* rivals' costs also can be profitable. Incumbent manufacturers typically will see their profits depressed by entry and, thus, will seek to minimize the threat of entry by maximizing its cost and difficulty. In many ways, raising the costs of actual and potential rivals are similar. The main reason for treating entry deterrence separately is that there is a temporal asymmetry among the rival firms – the incumbents are in the market and the potential entrants are not. Thus, the incumbents may possess first-mover advantages. There also may be systematic differences in the sizes of entrants and incumbents. One typically would expect an entrant initially to have a lower market share than the incumbents.

Consider a single incumbent facing a single potential entrant in a market in which a dealer must have units of two inputs in order to produce final output. If the incumbent ties the sales of the two products, then the potential entrant will find it to be unprofitable to come into the market and sell only one of the two intermediate goods. The entrant will be forced to enter both markets. If there are substantial fixed and sunk costs of entering the two markets simultaneously, then the risk of entry is increased. Bork (1954) argued that the need to raise capital for entry into two markets simultaneously would not make entry more difficult since the potential reward from entry would be commensurately increased. Williamson (1979) argued that, when the profitability of entry depends upon specialized knowledge or skills that are not readily observable, a potential entrant's lack of experience in a given market may increase the firm's cost of raising capital. The threat of entry would thus be reduced if, in order to come into the target market, the entrant also had to come into a market with which he was unfamiliar.

Similar effects may arise when the "tying" occurs over time. Suppose that a firm has a monopoly or near monopoly today, but that it fears entry in the future. The firm may have incentives to reach long-term requirements contracts with consumers in order to foreclose the market to potential entrants. If all of the contracts came up for renewal on the same date, entry might be delayed, but not prevented. The potential entrant could come in on the common contract expiration date without being at a disadvantage due to the contracts. Of course, the entrant would have to wait for the contracts to expire. When the dates are staggered and there are large fixed costs of entry, requirements contracts may block entry forever. In the presence of the staggered contracts, the entrant is able to compete for only a small portion of the total business at any one time. Given the large fixed costs of entry, it may not be profitable to go after demand in bits and pieces.

There also may be a foreclosure motivation behind exclusive dealing. The incumbent manufacturer may be able to take advantage of the temporal asymmetry by tying-up all of the top-notch retailers. Or, as discussed above, when there are economies of scale and scope in distribution, a system of exclusive dealers will raise the distribution costs of smaller firms (e.g. recent entrants) by more than it will raise the distribution costs borne by larger firms. By making small scale entry unprofitable, the incumbent (1) raises the financial risk (i.e. sunk costs) of entry; (2) makes it more credible that the incumbent will not accommodate an entrant (the entrant has to get a large market share in order to survive and thus is a greater threat to the incumbent); and (3) makes it costlier to enter since growth typically takes time.

A key objection raised by many analysts [e.g. Bork (1978) and Posner (1976)] is this: Why would a dealer sign a contract that lowers the probability of entry and lessens competition among suppliers? If there are many dealers, the answer is clear: each one may think that his individual signing decision has no effect on the likelihood of entry, and that actions by other dealers will block entry completely. Aghion and Bolton (1987) showed that a rational dealer may sign an entry-limiting contract even when the number of dealers is small. The contract that they examined has the following features. It is a long-term requirements contract that specifies the penalty to be levied on the dealer for breach of contract. This penalty is set so that an efficient entrant would find it profitable to offer the dealer such a low price that the dealer would find it profitable to breach the contract. In effect, the manufacturer–dealer contract forces the entrant to pay an entry fee that is then split between the manufacturer and dealer, giving the dealer incentives to sign the entry-limiting contract.[69]

In addition to blocking entry into a market that it already monopolizes, a firm may use its market power in one input market to block entry into another one. There is a long tradition in the vertical restraints literature of asking whether a manufacturer would use a tying contract to "leverage" a monopoly position in one input market into a second monopoly position in another input market. The prevailing view, due in large part to the efforts of members of the "Chicago

[69]This is another example of the use of the manufacturer–dealer contract as a form of precommitment.

school" of antitrust, is that a monopolist would not find it profitable to engage in leveraging.[70]

In a recent paper, Whinston (1987) showed that an incumbent could, in fact, find it profitable to use bundling to engage in what Whinston calls "strategic foreclosure". The basic idea can be seen in the following example. There are two inputs to downstream production, x and y. Initially, both are supplied by an upstream multi-product monopolist. Entry into production of x is completely blocked, say by patent protection. There is a single potential entrant into production of y, however. If the potential entrant choose to come in, the two firms play a differentiated products pricing game. Absent a bundling arrangement, there may be no way for the incumbent to deter entry into this market; the entrant may rationally predict that the incumbent would accommodate entry into the production of y. Suppose, however, that the incumbent can engage in bundling and set a package price for one unit of x and one unit of y that is lower than the sum of the price of x and the price of y. Given the proper demand conditions, this bundling has the effect of shifting downward the incumbent's (price–space) reaction curve in the y market to the point that entry becomes unprofitable. Intuitively, bundling can make the incumbent more aggressive in the y market because every additional unit of y sold as part of a bundle leads to greater profits from the sale of x as well. The ability to bundle may thus give the incumbent a credible threat to use against a potential entrant. Hence, a manufacturer may, in fact, use bundling to "leverage" his monopoly in one market into a monopoly in another one when the second market would otherwise have had a less-than-perfectly-competitive structure.

In closing this section, it should be noted that while incumbents would like to use vertical restraints to restrict entry, vertical restraints also may have indirect effects that encourage it. In particular, as noted several times earlier, some contract provisions may serve to increase product differentiation. This increased differentiation may make it easier for the entrant to find a market niche. This type of incentive is an example of what Fudenberg and Tirole (1984) amusingly have labelled the "fat-cat effect".

5. Welfare analysis

5.1. The two wedges

Heretofore, the analysis has focused on the profitability of vertical restraints. What about the welfare effects? An approach to welfare analysis taken by much of the literature is to focus on a specific practice and construct a list of reasons

[70]See Bowman (1957) for an early expression of this opinion. Whinston (1987) provides a discussion of the recent dominance of the no-leverage view.

why it may raise or lower welfare. I will take a different tack to frame the survey. Rather than looking directly at the welfare effects of a given practice, I will compare the private incentives to implement a vertical contract provision with the social ones.

Taking total surplus as the social maximand, there are two sources of divergence, or wedges, between a manufacturer's contract design incentives and the social incentives.[71,72] First, a manufacturer ignores any effects that his actions have on the level of consumer surplus. Viewed another way, activities that transfer surplus from consumers to the firm generate a private benefit for which there is no corresponding social benefit.

The second wedge is the difference between firm and industry profits. A manufacturer ignores the effects that his contract choice has on the profits of other firms, including his dealers and rival manufacturers and their dealers. The presence of these wedges may distort the manufacturer's incentives with respect to both the price and nonprice (e.g. promotional effort and product quality) decisions that he induces his dealers to make.

5.2. *Price distortions*

Consider a market in which all of the customers of any given manufacturer must be served at the same uniform price (i.e. no price discrimination is feasible). Since lower prices raise consumer surplus, there is a tendency for the manufacturers to do too little to keep downstream prices low. The standard monopolistic output restriction is one consequence of this fact. Turning to the issues at hand, the consumer surplus wedge also affects the use of vertical restraints. Suppose, for example, that the manufacturer must incur administrative costs to impose a resale price ceiling (e.g. the cost of monitoring the dealers' prices). To the extent that the price ceiling benefits consumers, the manufacturer's private incentives to impose the ceiling are lower than the social incentives.[73] Consequently, the manufacturer may fail to implement such a scheme even when imposition of the profit-maximizing price ceiling would raise welfare. When a given vertical restraint leads to higher final prices and lower consumer surplus, the bias runs in the opposite direction. For example, when input substitution is possible, the

[71] The welfare analysis of vertical restraints is, like all welfare analysis in the field of industrial organization, merely an application of the Fundamental Theorem of Industrial Organization. For a more general treatment of the Fundamental Theorem, see Katz and Shapiro (1987).

[72] Although the discussion is framed in terms of the manufacaturer's contract design incentives, it is clear that analogous effects arise in cases in which the dealer proposes the contract.

[73] Interestingly, Mathewson and Winter (1983a) showed that a resale price *floor* also could lower the prices charged by some dealers. This effect arises when the equilibrium absent the price floor would entail price dispersion and the price floor causes this asymmetric equilibrium to collapse. In this case, there would be a similar bias against a price floor.

assignment of exclusive territories may allow the manufacturer profitably to raise the price charged to final consumers.

This line of argument can be applied to the analysis of price discrimination as well.[74] To the extent that price discrimination lowers consumer surplus, there tends to be too much of it. Moreover, the manufacturer's incentives to impose vertical restraints (such as exclusive territories) that facilitate discrimination are socially excessive. There are other cases, however, in which profit-maximizing price discrimination raises consumer surplus in comparison with profit-maximizing uniform pricing. In these cases, the bias runs in the opposite direction.[75]

5.3. Nonprice distortions

In many instances, the effect of vertical restraints is to stimulate promotional activities and other forms of nonprice competition. Changes in the level of nonprice activities may affect welfare both directly and indirectly: directly because consumers may value the activities, and indirectly because changes in nonprice activities may affect the nature of price competition.

5.3.1. Promotional efforts

The effects of promotional activities have been viewed in several different lights by the literature. Much of the traditional debate centers on the question of whether promotional activities should be viewed as the provision of information (assumed to be good), or as a way to create false image differentiation (assumed to be bad). Given the unsettled nature of this field, the reader will not be surprised to find that the welfare analysis of the effects of vertical restraints on the provision of promotional activities is itself something of a mess. Rather than debate the merits of various labels, here I will try to catalogue (at least some of) the effects of promotional activities.

First, suppose that the advertising conveys false information that has the effect of shifting out the demand curve faced by the advertising firm. This case was examined by Dixit and Norman (1978) for a final good market in which all inputs are supplied at constant prices by perfectly competitive firms. For the reason already discussed, Dixit and Norman found that to the extent that advertising leads to increased prices, manufacturers tend to have overly high incentives to induce advertising. It does not, however, follow that all false

[74] Romer (1986) applied this reasoning to the case of a final good monopoly under the presumption that discrimination lowers consumer surplus.

[75] As Hal Varian makes clear in Chapter 10 of this Handbook, models of discrimination under oligopoly and monopolistic competition still are in their infancy, and more analysis is needed before reaching even tentative conclusions.

advertising lowers welfare. The increased demand due to the false advertising may counteract the usual monopolistic or oligopolistic output restriction, leading to an increase in allocative efficiency.

Comanor (1968) examined markets in which there are multiple brands and promotional efforts are aimed at convincing consumers that different brands are not good substitutes for one another, even though they in fact are. This "image differentiation" lowers between-brand cross-elasticities and reduces price competition. The net effect is to lower consumer surplus. Thus, the firms' private benefits may exceed the social benefits, and firms may devote excessive resources to advertising. Moreover, the price increases may lead to reductions in the quantities sold, further lowering total surplus.

Promotions need not be misleading to have adverse effects on the degree of interbrand price competition. Dixit and Norman's results carry over to advertising that provides truthful information. Similarly, promotional activities that reveal true product differences to consumers may have some of the same adverse effects as activities that create false image differentiation. As Salop and Stiglitz (1978) pointed out, the provision of product information need not benefit consumers. To the extent that this information reveals true product differentiation, it may reduce interbrand price competition and lower consumer surplus. Of course, the information may allow consumers to make better matches, or product choices. The net effect of information provision may be to raise or lower consumer surplus.

Information provision by one firm also has ambiguous effects on the profits of rival firms. These firms may benefit from the increased product differentiation, even if the differentiation is vertical (i.e. the promoting firm reveals that his product is of higher quality). It follows that information may be over- or under-supplied by the market. Hence, vertical restraints that lead to greater promotional activities may ameliorate or exacerbate the problem.

Fisher and McGowan (1979) argued that some promotional efforts do more than inform consumers about existence – they actually make consumers better able to derive benefits from consumption. For example, the dealer may provide information as to how to use the product. When the promotional activities are of direct value to consumers, one can then think of the degree of promotion as an aspect of product quality, to which the discussion now turns.

5.3.2. The input mix: Product quality and productive efficiency

The dealer's choice of input mix may affect consumers in two ways. First, the input mix affects costs. Consumers care about this effect only to the extent that it influences product pricing. Second, when the input mix is a dimension of product quality, consumers care about the input mix directly.

Spence (1975) showed that a monopolist may over- or underprovide quality. The reason is a simple one. When the marginal consumer values quality by more than the average inframarginal consumer, the monopolist can raise price and quality (holding unit sales constant) in a way that lowers consumer surplus. Hence, in this case the monopolist tends to oversupply quality given his output level. The direction of the bias is reversed when the marginal consumer values quality by less than does the average inframarginal consumer. Not surprisingly, given that the direction of distortion in quality is ambiguous, it is difficult to say whether vertical restraints that promote the provision of product quality are socially beneficial.

In cases in which consumers are indifferent between a family of input mixes (i.e. there are many ways to produce output of a given quality level) sophisticated pricing such as quantity-dependent pricing, ties, and royalties tend to have beneficial welfare effects by correcting inefficient input choices by dealers for a given quality level.

5.3.3. The number of dealers and product variety

The number of dealers affects welfare both as a component of service itself and through its indirect effects on the provision of other dimensions of service. Unfortunately, there are two reasons why it is difficult to assess the welfare effects that vertical contracts have through their effects on the number of dealers.

First, in some instances, a given vertical restraint may be used by a manufacturer to either increase or decrease the number of dealers in comparison with the outcome under which that provision is proscribed.[76] The second problem is that even if one knows the effect of a given vertical practice on the equilibrium number of dealers, the sign of the welfare change is not immediate. There is a well-developed literature analyzing the product selection problem in a final good industry with competitively supplied inputs. This literature demonstrates that, in general, there may be excessive or insufficient variety under either monopoly [e.g. Katz (1980)] or monopolistic competition [e.g. Spence (1976), Dixit and Stiglitz (1977), and Salop (1979)]. In the light of the fact that vertical restraints can raise or lower variety, there is a strong need for research as to whether the biases tend to move together systematically.

5.4. What does all of this have to do with public policy?

Much of the literature on vertical restraints has been conducted with the express aim of deriving policy conclusions. But in many, if not most, instances there is no

[76] Recall the discussion of exclusive territories and franchise fees in Subsection 3.3.

widespread agreement on whether a particular practice is socially beneficial or harmful. This unhappy state of affairs is due, in part, to the fact that all of the practices can be beneficial in some instances and harmful in others, and it may be extremely difficult to distinguish between the two cases.

To date, much of the policy debate has been conducted in terms of asking whether a given practice is pro- or anticompetitive, and thus whether a given practice should be banned or not. I believe that this approach is misguided on at least two counts. First, welfare effects may have nothing to do with "competition", per se. Some vertical restraints (e.g. tying) can arise, and have welfare consequences, even when both levels of the supply chain are monopolized. Second, the type of answer sought is the wrong one. On theoretical grounds, at least, any given restraint may be good or bad. Theory alone (or theory coupled with a handful of examples) is not going to answer a question of the form: Should resale price maintenance be per se illegal?

Confronted with ambiguous welfare effects, the courts and many economists have called for a rule of reason approach. But a fully general rule of reason is likely to be more than the courts can handle.[77] The key to policy design is to develop workable rules by which to identify observable market conditions under which given practices are socially desirable. In attempting to accomplish this goal, the courts and many economists [e.g. Posner (1977) and Williamson (1979)] typically have focused on the degree of market concentration as the critical condition. This aspect of market structure is concentrated on in the belief that a vertical agreement is unlikely to have "anticompetitive" effects when it is among parties having a low combined market share either upstream or down.

While this work is a beginning, it is essential that the analysis be expanded to include factors such as the market's information structure, risk characteristics (e.g. size of sunk investments), and the degree to which parties become locked-in to one another (e.g. the amount of transactions-specific capital). It also is essential that this work identify means of isolating the effects of vertical restraints in comparison with alternative institutional and contractual arrangements.

5.4.1. *The proper benchmark*

The measurement of both the social benefits and the social costs of a vertical practice depend critically on the choice of benchmark, as can be illustrated by the analysis of resale price maintenance. Consider, first, the social benefits of resale price maintenance. As discussed in Subsection 3.1.2.1 earlier, it has been argued that resale price maintenance is socially beneficial because it leads to increased equilibrium levels of service and promotional activities. One problem with this

[77]See Posner (1981) for a discussion of some of the problems with the rule of reason approach, both as developed by the courts and more generally.

argument is that it takes as given the fact that increased promotion is socially beneficial. Abstracting from that problem, there is another difficulty. As Comanor (1968) and Yamey (1966) argued, before concluding that vertical restraints are essential to ensure the provision of promotional activities, one must examine whether there are alternative institutional arrangements by which the manufacturer could ensure the supply of activities subject to externalities across dealers.

One approach is to have the manufacturer supply the services himself. But asymmetric information about downstream market conditions (e.g. the dealer may be better informed about the downstream market than is the manufacturer) may limit the profitability of this approach. Moreover, even if the manufacturer can observe downstream conditions, so-called antidiscrimination policy [e.g. Sections 2(d) and 2(e) of the Robinson–Patman Act] limits the manufacturer's ability to vary the level of promotional support across dealers in response to differing local market conditions.[78] Finally, when effort is one of the inputs to downstream promotion, the upstream decision-maker may not have the time to conduct downstream promotional activities in addition to carrying out his other tasks (i.e. the manufacturer may have a higher opportunity cost of his time than does the dealer).

The manufacturer could finance downstream promotional activities directly, while letting the dealers choose the direction and intensity of these efforts. For example, the manufacturer could pay dealers for maintaining showrooms. There may be problems with this sort of payment, however. First, if the dealer does not bear the costs, he may engage in excessive levels of these activities. Second, the dealer may defraud the manufacturer when the level of promotional activities is unobservable to the manufacturer. I know of one case in which a radio station sold false advertising receipts to dealers who in turn submitted the bills to the manufacturers for reimbursement. Another reason we do not observe such schemes more often in the United States may again be the Robinson–Patman Act, which prevents differential payments to retailers based on the promotional services (such as having good reputations) that the retailers provide the dealers.[79]

Comanor and other economists have suggested another form of financing at least some promotional activities – charge consumers for the services (such as technical advice from salespeople) that they receive. In this way, consumers who do not want the services do not have to pay for them, and those that want them do pay. Of course, this approach does not work when the promotional activities have a nonexcludable public good nature such as in the case of media advertising.

Where antitrust authorities allow it, the dealers themselves might attempt to internalize the externalities by forming cooperative ventures. For example, the

[78]Schwartz (1986) discusses the inefficiencies in distribution induced by Robinson–Patman Act more fully.

[79]This defect of the Robinson–Patman Act was noted by Bowman (1952, 1955) in his discussion of the private incentives to implement resale price maintenance. See also, Comment (1951).

Ford dealers in a single region might jointly advertise on television. An important issue is whether some dealers will choose to stay out of the cooperative venture and free ride. In response to such problems, one could imagine the manufacturer *requiring* his dealers to form cooperative ventures as one of the terms of the contract.

Lastly, the manufacturer might be able to implement a contract that made any one dealer's compensation a function of the collective performance of the manufacturer and all of his dealers. But to give each dealer full incentives, the manufacturer would have to give *each* dealer 100 percent of the *collective* increase in joint profits (of the manufacturer and all of his dealers) at the margin.[80]

This laundry list of alternatives demonstrates that it is not at all clear that resale price maintenance is essential to the provision of promotional services and other activities subject to free riding. There are many possible substitutes, although each has limitations. Theory alone does not tell us whether policy-makers' allowing resale price maintenance would lead to a great increase in service and promotional activities.

Comparative analysis also can be used to assess the potential social harm from a given practice. A standard argument put forth by proponents of resale price maintenance [e.g. Bork (1978)], for example, is the following one: resale price maintenance cannot have adverse welfare effects because the manufacturer could achieve the same effect by raising the wholesale price of the good. The usefulness of this approach is limited by that fact that this claim is correct only if: (a) downstream input substitution is infeasible; (b) the costs for all retailers to serve all customers are the same; and (c) all final consumers are equally sensitive to a dealer's price. When condition (a) is not satisfied, raising the wholesale price induces distortions in the downstream input mix. When conditions (b) and (c) are not satisfied, absent resale price maintenance different consumers would face different prices. There is no way that the manufacturer can force retailers to charge all customers the same price solely through raising the wholesale price.

5.4.2. *Consistency of public policy*

As the analysis of Sections 2 through 4 makes clear, various vertical restraints often are (partial) substitutes for one another. For example, in some settings, resale price maintenance and territorial restrictions are both ways to maintain high dealer margins. The fact that two practices may have many of the same

[80] Many of the issues that arise in the design and implementation of such schemes are discussed in the principal–agent literature. See, for example, Holmstrom (1982).

effects as one another suggests that the public policy treatment of them should be similar in many cases.[81]

There also is a need for consistency between the treatment of vertical restraints and refusals to deal. A refusal to deal occurs when a manufacturer refuses to allow a retailer to act as a dealer for the manufacturer's product on the same terms as are granted other retailers. There may be cases in which a refusal to deal is merely the result of the manufacturer's recognizing that a particular dealer is unscrupulous or is unlikely to meet his responsibilities to the manufacturer. But a refusal to deal also can serve as a means of enforcing an implicit vertical restraint. For example, de facto resale price maintenance could be imposed by refusing to deal with any discounters. Public policy towards refusal to deal should follow from the treatment of the other vertical restraints. Unfortunately, it may be very difficult to distinguish between a refusal to deal where the manufacturer is keeping out a dealer who would otherwise behave in inefficient ways and one where the manufacturer is keeping out a dealer who would act in economically efficient ways but contrary to the private interests of the manufacturer.

In addition to being internally consistent, public policy toward vertical restraints also should be consistent with other antitrust policy. For example, to the extent that resale price maintenance is an attempt to make the monitoring of prices easier, resale price maintenance and price information sharing should be subject to the same treatment.

At present, there is one particularly striking incongruity in U.S. antitrust policy. Integrated firms are allowed to implement almost any contract internally. Thus, antitrust laws that restrict independent firms' writing of arm's length contracts may have the effect of encouraging vertical integration even in cases in which this form of business organization is not the most efficient one.[82] For this reason, a public policy that prevents pernicious vertical practices by unintegrated firms may actually be worse than a policy that allows these practices – to the extent that vertical integration is possible, these practices (or their equivalent) may take place in any event, and the costs of production and distribution under vertical integration may be higher due to the use of an inefficient organizational form.

The need for consistency also arises in the case of price discrimination. A principle of consistency would argue for vertical restraints that are motivated solely by discrimination to be treated similarly to an act of price discrimination itself. One way to ensure consistency is to treat all instances of price discrimina-

[81]One does not want to make too much of the similarity of effects of different practices. As shown in earlier sections, the identity between two practices never is exact, and theory does not support the view that two different practices should be treated identically in all markets.

[82]Although they subscribed to the "unnatural union" view of vertical integration, Blair and Kaserman (1978) made a similar point for the particular case of a tying contract.

tion under price discrimination laws, rather than relying on proscriptions against certain vertical practices.

This last point brings up another important one. In addition to recognizing the need for consistency in public policy, policy makers should recognize that in some instances, other antitrust laws may be substitutes for strictures against vertical restraints. Laws covering price discrimination, for instance, may be sufficient to deal with that problem directly, so there is no need to prohibit exclusive territories for fear that they facilitate price discrimination.

Finally, it should be noted that antitrust laws may themselves motivate the use of vertical restraints. For example, as discussed in the previous subsection, resale price maintenance may be a response to the fact that a manufacturer cannot make differential payments to dealers even though some dealers provide valuable (and costly) services to the manufacturer that others do not. These effects should be taken into account when setting antitrust policy.

References

Abreu, D., Milgrom, P. and Pearce, D. (1987) 'Information and timing in repeated partnerships', unpublished draft, Harvard University.

Aghion, P. and Bolton, P. (1987) 'Contracts as a barrier to entry', *American Economic Review*, 77:388–401.

Atkinson, A.B. and Stiglitz, J.E. (1980) *Lectures in public economics*. New York: McGraw-Hill.

Banks, J.S. and Sobel, J. (1987) 'Equilibrium selection in signaling games', *Econometrica*, 55:647–661.

Bernheim, B.D. and Whinston, M.D. (1985) 'Common marketing agency as a device for facilitating collusion', *Rand Journal of Economics*, 16:269–281.

Bittlingmayer, G.A. (1983) 'A model of vertical restriction and equilibrium in retailing', *Journal of Business*, 50:477–496.

Blair, R.D. and Kaserman, D.L. (1978) 'Vertical intergration, tying, and antitrust policy', *American Economic Review*, 68:397–402.

Blair, R.D. and Kaserman, D.L. (1984) 'Tying arrangements and uncertainty', *Research in finance*, Supplement I, *Management under government intervention: A view from Mount Scopus*.

Bolton, P. and Bonanno, G. (1987) 'Vertical restraints in a model of vertical differentiation', unpublished manuscript, Harvard University.

Bork, R.H. (1954) 'Vertical integration and the Sherman Act: The legal history of an economic misconception', *University of Chicago Law Review*, 22:157–201.

Bork, R.H. (1978) *The antitrust paradox: A policy at war with itself*. New York: Basic Books.

Bowman, Jr., W.S. (1952) 'Resale price maintenance – A monopoly problem', *Journal of Business*, 25:141–155.

Bowman, Jr., W.S. (1955) 'Prerequisites and effects of resale price maintenance', *University of Chicago Law Review*, 22:825–873.

Bowman, Jr., W.S. (1957) 'Tying arrangements and the leverage problem', *Yale Law Journal*, 67:19–36.

Brander, J.A. and Spencer, B.J. (1985) 'Export subsidies and international market share rivalry', *Journal of International Economics*, 18:83–100.

Brennan, T.J. and Sheldon, K. (1983) 'Joint production and monopoly extension through tying', discussion paper 84-1, Economic Policy Office, U.S. Department of Justice.

Burstein, M.L. (1960a) 'A theory of full-line forcing', *Northwestern University Law Review*, 55:62–95.

Burstein, M.L. (1960b) 'The economics of tie-in sales', *Review of Economics and Statistics*, 42:68–73.
Caves, R.E. (1986) 'Vertical restraints in manufacaturer–distributor relations: Incidence and economic effects', in : R.E. Grieson, ed., *Antitrust and regulation*. Lexington: Lexington Books.
Caves, R.E. and Murphy, W.F. (1976) 'Franchising: Firms, markets and intangible assets', *Southern Economic Journal*, 42:572–586.
Comanor, Jr., W.S. (1968) 'Vertical territoriality and customer restrictions: White Motor and its aftermath', *Harvard Law Review*, 81:1419–1438.
Comanor, Jr. W.S. and Frech, III, H.E. (1985) 'The competitive effects of vertical agreements?', *American Economic Review*, 75:539–546.
Comment (1951) 'Resale price maintenance and the antitrust laws', *University of Chicago Law Review*, 18:369–380.
Demsetz, H. (1968) 'Why regulate utilities?', *Journal of Law and Economics*, 11:55–65.
Director, A. and Levi, E.H. (1956) 'Law and the future: Trade regulation', *Northwestern University Law Review*, 61:281–296.
Dixit, A.K. (1979) 'Quality and quantity competition', *Review of Economic Studies*, 46:587–599.
Dixit, A.K. (1983) 'Vertical integration in a monopolistically competitive industry', *International Journal of Industrial Organization*, 1:63–78.
Dixit, A.K. and Norman, V. (1978) 'Advertising and welfare', *Bell Journal of Economics*, 9:1–17.
Dixit, A.K. and Stiglitz, J.E. (1977) 'Monopolistic competition and optimal product diversity', *American Economic Review*, 67:297–308.
Farrell, J. and Shapiro, C. (1987) 'Optimal contracts with lock-in', Department of Economics, University of California, Berkeley, working paper 87-58.
Fershtman, C. and Judd, K.L. (1986) 'Strategic incentive manipulation and the principal–agent problem', unpublished manuscript, Northwestern University.
Fershtman, C. and Judd, K.L. (1987) 'Equilibrium incentives in oligopoly', *American Economic Review*, 77:927–940.
Fershtman, C., Judd, K.L. and Kalai, E. (1987) 'Cooperation through delegation', research report no. 163, Hebrew University of Jerusalem.
Fisher, F.M. and McGowan, J.J. (1979) 'Advertising and welfare: Comment', *Bell Journal of Economics*, 10:726–727.
Fudenberg, D. and Tirole, J. (1984) 'The fat-cat effect, the puppy-dog ploy, and the lean and hungry look', *American Economic Review*, 74:361–366.
Gallick, E.C. (1984) 'Exclusive dealing and vertical integration: The efficiency of contracts in the tuna industry', Bureau of Economics staff report to the Federal Trade Commission.
Gould, J.R. and Preston, L.E. (1965) 'Resale price maintenance and retail outlets', *Economica*, 32:302–312.
Grossman, S. and Hart, O.D. (1986) 'The costs and benefits of ownership: A theory of vertical and lateral integration', *Journal of Political Economy*, 94:691–719.
Harris, M. and Raviv, A. (1979) 'Optimal incentive contracts with imperfect information', *Journal of Economic Theory*, 20:231–259.
Holmstrom, B. (1979) 'Moral hazard and observability', *Bell Journal of Economics*, 10:74–91.
Holmstrom, B. (1982) 'Moral hazard in teams', *Bell Journal of Economics*, 13:324–340.
Katz, M.L. (1980) 'Multiplant monopoly in a spatial market', *Bell Journal of Economics*, 11:519–535.
Katz, M.L. (1988a) 'Game-playing agents: Unobservable contracts as precommitments', unpublished draft, Berkeley, University of California.
Katz, M.L. and Rosen, H.S. (1985) 'Tax Analysis in a oligopoly model', *Public Finance Quarterly*, 13:3–20.
Katz, M.L. and Shapiro, C. (1987) 'The two wedges: The fundamental theorem of industrial organization', unpublished manuscript, Princeton University.
Marvel, H.P. (1982) 'Exclusive dealing', *Journal of Law and Economics*, 25:1–25.
Marvel, H.P. and McCafferty, S. (1984) 'Resale price maintenance and quality certification', *Rand Journal of Economics*, 15:346–359.
Mathewson, G.F. and Winter, R.A. (1983a) 'The incentives for resale price maintenance under imperfect information', *Economic Inquiry*, 21:337–348.

Mathewson, G.F. and Winter, R.A. (1983b) 'Vertical intergration by contractual restraints in spatial markets', *Journal of Business*, 50:497–517.

Mathewson, G.F. and Winter, R.A. (1984) 'An economic theory of vertical restraints', *Rand Journal of Economics*, 15:27–38.

Mathewson, G.F. and Winter, R.A. (1987) 'The competitive effects of vertical agreements: Comment', *American Economic Review*, 77:1057–1068.

Milgrom, P.R. and Weber, R.J. (1982) 'A theory of auctions and competitive bidding', *Econometrica*, 50:1089–1122.

Myerson, R.B. (1983) 'Mechanism design by an informed principal', *Econometrica*, 51:1767–1797.

Oi, Walter, (1971) 'A Disneyland dilemma: Two-part tariffs for a Mickey Mouse monopoly', *Quarterly Journal of Economics*, 85:77–96.

Perry, M.K. and Porter, R.H. (1986) 'Resale price maintenance and exclusive territories in the presence of retail service externalities', unpublished manuscript, Bell Communications Research, Inc.

Posner, R.A. (1976) *Antitrust law: An economic perspective*. Chicago: University of Chicago Press.

Posner, R.A. (1977) 'The rule of reason and the economic approach: Reflections on the *Sylvania* decision', *University of Chicago Law Review*, 45:1–20.

Posner, R.A. (1981) 'The next step in antitrust treatment of restricted distribution: Per se legality', *University of Chicago Law Review*, 48:6–26.

Preston, L.E. (1965) 'Restrictive distribution arrangements: Economic analysis and public policy standards', *Law and Contemporary Problems*, 30:506–529.

Rey, P. and Stiglitz, J.E. (1986) 'The role of exclusive territories in producers' competition', unpublished draft, Princeton University.

Rey, P. and Tirole, J. (1986) 'The logic of vertical restraints', *American Economic Review*, 76:921–939.

Romer, D. (1986) 'Costly price discrimination', unpublished draft, Princeton University.

Ross, T.W. (1987) 'When sales maximization is profit-maximizing: A two-stage game', working paper CIORU 87-01, Carleton University.

Rubinstein, A. (1985) 'A bargaining model with incomplete information about time preferences', *Econometrica*, 53:1151–1172.

Salop, S.C. (1979) 'Monopolistic competition with outside goods', *Bell Journal of Economics*, 10:141–156.

Salop, S.C. and Scheffman, D.T. (1983) 'Raising rivals' costs', *American Economic Review*, 73:267–271.

Salop, S.C. and Stiglitz, J.E. (1978) 'Information, welfare, and product diversity', unpublished manuscript, Princeton University.

Schelling, T.C. (1956) 'An essay on bargaining', *American Economic Review*, 46:281–306.

Schelling, T.C. (1960) *The strategy of conflict*. New York: Oxford University Press.

Schwartz, M. (1986) 'The perverse effects of the Robinson–Patman Act', *The Antitrust Bulletin*, 31:733–757.

Schwartz, M. (1987) 'The competitive effects of vertical agreements: Comment', *American Economic Review*, 77:1063–1068.

Seade, J. (1985) 'Profitable cost increases and the shifting of taxation: Equilibrium responses of markets in oligopoly', unpublished manuscript, Warwick University.

Shaked, A. and Sutton, J. (1982) 'Relaxing price competition through product differentiation', *Review of Economic Studies*, 40:3–14.

Shavell, S. (1979) 'Risk sharing and incentives in the principal and agent relationship', *Bell Journal of Economics*, 10:55–73.

Shleifer, A. (1985) 'A theory of yardstick competition', *Rand Journal of Economics*, 16:319–327.

Silcock, T.H. (1938) 'Some problems of price maintenance', *Economic Journal*, 48:42–51.

Spence, A.M. (1975) 'Monopoly, quality, and regulation', *Bell Journal of Economics*, 6:417–429.

Spence, A.M. (1976) 'Product selection, fixed costs, and monopolistic competition', *Review of Economic Studies*, 43:217–235.

Spencer, B.J. and Brander, J.A. (1983) 'International R & D rivalry and industrial strategy, *Review of Economic Studies*, 50:707–722.

Spengler, J.J. (1950) 'Vertical integration and antitrust policy', *Journal of Political Economy*, 58:347–352.

Taussig (1916) 'Price maintenance', *American Economic Review Papers and Proceedings*, 6:170–184.
Telser, L.G. (1960) 'Why should manufacturers want fair trade?', *Journal of Law and Economics*, 3:86–105.
Telser, L.G. (1965) 'Abusive trade practices: An economic analysis', *Law and Contemporary Problems*, 30:488–505.
Whinston, M.D. (1987) 'Tying, foreclosure, and exclusion', discussion paper number 1343, Harvard Institute of Economic Research.
White, L.J. (1981) 'Vertical restraints in antitrust law: A coherent model', *The Antitrust Bulletin*, 26:327–345.
Williamson, O.E. (1979) 'Assessing vertical market restrictions: Antitrust ramifications of the transactions cost approach', *University of Pennsylvania Law Review*, 127:953–993.
Williamson, O.E. (1983) 'Credible commitments: Using hostages to support exchange', *American Economic Review*, 73:519–540.
Yamey, B.S. (1952) 'The origins of resale price maintenance: A study of three branches of retail trade', *The Economic Journal*, 62:522–545.
Yamey, B.S. (1954) *The economics of resale price maintenance*. London: Sir Isaac Pitman.
Yamey, B.S., ed. (1966) *Resale price maintenance*. Chicago: Aldine Publishing Company.

Chapter 12

PRODUCT DIFFERENTIATION

B. CURTIS EATON

Simon Fraser University

RICHARD G. LIPSEY

Queen's University and C.D. Howe Institute

Contents

Handbook of Industrial Organization, Volume I, Edited by R. Schmalensee and R.D. Willig

1. Introduction

In a loose sense, any set of commodities closely related in consumption and/or in production may be regarded as differentiated products. Close relation in consumption depends on consumers' tastes. Do consumers perceive two products to be close substitutes for each other? Close relation in production concerns economies of scope. Is there any cost economy in having two products produced by one firm rather than two? The same set of products may be closely related in both production and consumption, as with yellow and orange tennis balls, in the former but not the latter, as with size 12 and size 8 shoes, or in the latter but not the former, as with coffee and tea.

We follow most of the existing literature in dealing with industries producing a large number of products that are closely related in consumption, while ignoring the interesting issues that arise from the presence of scope economies. We also ignore issues arising out of consumption complimentarities, e.g. should IBM produce software as well as hardware?

1.1. The awkward facts

Elementary scientific methodology tells us that theories aspiring to empirical relevance must be consistent with the observed facts. For this reason, awkward facts are to be welcomed; indeed, the more awkward they are, the greater are the constraints that they place on our theorizing.

Seven of the most important awkward facts that are available to constrain theorizing about product differentiation are listed below.

(1) Many industries, including most that produce consumers' goods, produce a large number of similar but differentiated products. Observe, for example, the variety of cars and bicycles on the streets of any moderately sized city.

(2) The consumers' goods produced by different firms in the same industry are differentiated from each other so that two products produced by two different firms are rarely, if ever, identical. Consider, for example, the differences between the competing middle-priced cars produced by GM, Ford and Chrysler.

(3) The set of products made by the firms in any one industry is a small subset of the set of possible products. Consider, for example, all of the different cars that could be produced by marginally varying the characteristics of existing cars one way or the other – e.g. a bit more or less acceleration, or braking power, or fuel consumption.

(4) In most industries each firm produces a range of differentiated products; indeed, a typical pattern in consumers' goods industries is for a large number of differentiated products to be produced by quite a small number of firms. For example, most of the many soaps, cleansers and detergents on sale in the United States today are produced by two firms.

(5) Any one consumer purchases only a small subset of the products that are available from any one industry. For example, how many brands of toothpaste has the reader purchased in the recent past?

(6) Consumers perceive the differences among differentiated products to be real and there is often approximate agreement on which ones are, and are not, close substitutes. Consider how many loyal supporters there are for different brands of cigarettes, cars and cameras. Also consider how much agreement there is that different brands of low-tar cigarettes are closer substitutes for each other than for any high-tar cigarette, and that different types of subcompact cars are closer substitutes for each other than for any full-sized car.

(7) Tastes are revealed to vary among consumers because different consumers purchase different bundles of differentiated commodities and these differences cannot be fully accounted for by differences in their incomes. For example, look into different houses inhabited by people of roughly similar incomes and observe that while each has a car, a refrigerator, a TV, a hi-fi, a tape deck, a video recorder, a camera, a stove, and so on, each has a different mix of brands, styles and types of these generic products.

The literature on product differentiation can be seen as a search for answers to three basic questions that arise out of the above awkward facts. What are the processes that give rise to these facts? What are their positive implications? What can be said about their normative implications?

The models used to study these problems are standard in their broad outline, although not in many substantial details. Most employ equilibrium techniques and use comparative statics to derive their predictions. From among the possibilities open to them, firms are assumed to choose the alternatives that will maximize profits.

A complete model of product differentiation would specify (i) the set of possible products, (ii) the technology associated with each product, (iii) the tastes of consumers over the set of possible products, and (iv) an equilibrium concept. At any significant level of generality such a model seems intractable. Hence, most of the literature involves strong simplifying assumptions of one sort or another.

1.2. Technology

There is little debate over the cost aspects of relevant models. Of the assumptions that are typically made, some are needed to accommodate one or another of the awkward facts, while others are employed merely for analytical convenience. Awkward fact (3), that the number of produced products is a small subset of the number of possible products, would seem to have two main lines of possible explanation.

(i) *Demand side explanations*. Given linearly homogeneous production functions, the explanation must come from the demand side. The explanation would be that consumers wish to consume only the subset of products currently being produced. This could be understood in terms of a representative consumer, or in terms of consumers with tastes that differ but are concentrated on the subset of produced goods.

(ii) *Supply side explanations*. Now let there be a diversity of tastes such that every differentiated product would be demanded by some consumers if all were priced at minimum average cost. Given linearly homogeneous production functions, all possible products would then be produced. For example, if there were a continuum of consumers' preferences over some set of product characteristics, there would be a continuum of products produced to satisfy these tastes. In these circumstances the limitation on the number of produced products must come from the supply side. The explanation of awkward fact (3) is then provided by production non-convexities, which result from such things as product development costs, and indivisibilities of fixed capital, and which imply decreasing average costs over an initial range of output. This explanation is the one that we accept, along with most of the writers in the field.

These non-convexities are commonly captured by the assumption of a simple cost function with a fixed cost of entry and (for convenience) a constant marginal cost of production that may or may not be subject to a capacity constraint. (Of course the cost function may be product specific.)

1.3. Two approaches to consumers' preferences

A basic requirement on the demand side of the problem is to have a model that accommodates awkward fact (1) – many differentiated products are produced and consumed in the typical consumer good industry.

1.3.1. The address branch

One branch of the literature captures awkward fact (1) by positing a distribution of consumers' tastes over some continuous space of parameters describing the nature of products. Different consumers have different most preferred locations in this space and thus can be thought of as having different *addresses* in that space. Products are also defined by their addresses in the space, and this makes the set of all possible products infinite.

This approach follows Hotelling's (1929) seminal paper and we refer to it as the *address branch*. Tractability demands a relatively simple parameterization of tastes. A major issue here is whether the parameterization of preferences is sufficiently rich to approximate the real diversity of consumers' tastes.

1.3.2. The non-address branch

The other branch follows traditional value theory in assuming that consumers' preferences for differentiated goods are defined over a predetermined set of all possible goods, which set may be finite or countably infinite. For obvious reasons we call this the *goods-are-goods* or the *non-address* branch. Chamberlin's original vision of monopolistic competition lies in this branch of the literature. Once again, tractability requires parameterization of tastes.

Within this branch, there are two possible ways of accounting for the purchase of many differentiated commodities. The first assumes that the aggregated preferences for differentiated goods can be captured by the fiction of a representative consumer. Since the problem of aggregating tastes over diverse consumers is ignored, the approach is more flexible in some important respects than the address approach.

It should be clear, however, that this approach does not directly incorporate awkward facts (5), (6) and (7), which relate to differences among consumers. This raises the question: Can the representative consumer's utility function be derived from a model which does allow for these awkward facts?

The second approach is to assume differences in individual tastes and deduce aggregate behavior from individual motivations. All models that have taken this approach so far have used some variant of Chamberlin's symmetry assumption which, loosely interpreted, means that all products are in equal competition with all other products. (This is discussed in more detail below.)

In the next section we consider the non-address branch and in subsequent sections the address branch.

2. Non-address branch

2.1. The representative consumer approach

The seminal papers are Spence (1976a, 1976b) and Dixit and Stiglitz (1977). In these models there is a large number of possible products in the sector or industry of interest. Product demands arise from the utility maximizing decisions of a representative consumer with a strictly quasi-concave utility function:

$$u = U(y, x_1, \dots, x_n),$$

where y is quantity of a composite commodity, which is produced under conditions of constant returns to scale, and x_i is quantity of the ith sectoral good. Cost functions, $C_i(x_i)$, are potentially product specific, and ordinarily take the following convenient form:

$$C_i(x_i) = K_i + c_i x_i,$$

where K_i is a fixed cost, associated with product development or indivisible capital, and c_i is a constant marginal cost. Prices are normalized so that the price of the composite commodity is \$1, and costs are denominated in dollars or units of the composite commodity.

In the basic models, each product is produced by at most one firm, and, when the number of possible products is sufficiently large, not all products will be produced. Given any set of produced products, the equilibrium is (ordinarily) a Cournot equilibrium – firms choose quantities to maximize profit. [Koenker and Perry (1981) use conjectural variations to generalize this aspect of the basic model.] In free-entry equilibrium all products which are produced earn non-negative profit, and entry of any additional product is not profitable. That is, there exists no non-produced product which could cover its costs in the Cournot equilibrium which would result if the product were produced.

This sort of model is obviously quite flexible and well adapted to welfare analysis. One can create a variety of tractable models by choosing appropriate functional forms for the utility function. Since profit can be measured in units of the composite commodity, welfare analysis is relatively easy. Supposing that profits accrue to the representative consumer, welfare comparisons merely involve comparisons of the representative consumer's utility in alternative situations. If utility is linear in the composite commodity [as in Spence (1976a)] an equivalent welfare criterion is maximization of total surplus.

Two sorts of normative questions have been addressed in these models. The first concerns possible biases in the set of produced products, and is discussed in the following section. The second concerns possible biases in the number of products produced, and is best discussed in the context of Chamberlin's vision of monopolistic competition.

Product selection bias

Given the number of products produced in equilibrium, are some products produced which should not be, and others not produced which should be? We can convey the basic insights regarding possible biases in product selection by adapting the model used in Spence (1976b). Let the utility function take the following form:

$$u = y + a_1x_1 + a_2x_2 - 1/2\left(b_1x_1^2 + 2dx_1x_2 + b_2x_2^2\right),$$

where the parameters a_i, b_i and d are positive and $d < b_i$, $i = 1, 2$. To focus on product selection bias, we suppose that both products cannot profitably be produced in a Cournot equilibrium, and ask which one will be produced and which one should be produced. Since utility is linear in y we use the total surplus optimality criterion.

In the monopoly equilibrium the gross profit of firm i (total profit plus K_i) is

$$\Pi_i = \theta_i^2/4b_i,$$

and the gross surplus generated by product i (total surplus plus K_i) is

$$S_i = 3\theta_i^2/8b_i,$$

where $\theta_i = a_i - c_i$. Thus, firm i captures two-thirds of the gross surplus generated by its product. There is a selection bias if the product which produces the larger total surplus is not produced in equilibrium.

To illustrate the possibility of a selection bias, suppose that $K_1 > K_2$ and that $\Pi_2 - K_2 > 0$, or equivalently, that $S_2 > 3K_2/2$ (the second product is profitable). In this case there is inevitably a selection bias if product 1 generates the larger total surplus ($S_1 - K_1 > S_2 - K_2$) but does not generate positive profit ($S_1 < 3K_1/2$), and hence will not be produced. Note also that if $K_i > 3S_i/2$ for $i = 1, 2$, either product is viable by itself, but, by hypothesis, both are not. Hence, multiple equilibria are possible.

To see the forces which tend to generate a selection bias, suppose initially that $S_i = 3K_i/2$, $i = 1, 2$, so that either product would earn zero profit, and that $K_1 > K_2$. Either product is then viable, but the first generates a discretely larger surplus. Then a small increase in K_1 or b_1 or a small decrease in θ_1 (equal to $a_1 - c_1$) renders product 1 unprofitable, even though it still generates the larger surplus. Thus, among other things, large product development costs and price inelastic demand functions tend to produce a selection bias. This point is developed more fully in Spence (1976a, 1976b).

A standard result in welfare economics is that price discrimination may be welfare improving if there are significant product development costs or economies of scale. This is because a non-discriminating monopolist cannot capture all the surplus it creates. In the model developed here it is easy to show that if firms can perfectly discriminate (that is, capture all the surplus they create), there is no selection bias and the first best optimum is achieved. Spence (1976a) develops this result in a more general context.

It is also worth noting that when $d < 0$, making the products complements, it is possible that neither product by itself is profitable, but that, as a package, they are profitable. In this case, one expects *one* firm to produce both products.

2.2. Monopolistic competition and the representative consumer

A major contribution of the non-address branch is the formalization of Chamberlin's model of monopolistic competition. Hart (1985) is especially interesting in this regard. The representative consumer approach can be used to construct a Chamberlinian model of monopolistic competition as follows. Write the utility function as:

$$u = U(y, V(x_1, \dots, x_n)),$$

and assume that $V(\cdot)$ is a symmetric function. [Dixit and Stiglitz (1977), for example, use a symmetric CES specification.] Similarly, assume that the cost functions are identical, so that $c_i = c$ and $K_i = K$ for all i. This generates a Chamberlin model because the demand functions inherit the symmetry of $V(x_1, \dots, x_n)$.

The major issue in this case is whether there are too few or too many products in equilibrium. Dixit and Stiglitz (1977) provide an interesting analysis of this problem. In the unconstrained optimum, prices of all produced goods must equal c, an impossibility in the Chamberlin equilibrium. A constrained optimality criterion is therefore appropriate – the constraint being that all firms must cover their costs of production. They discover cases in which the equilibrium is a constrained optimum and cases in which there are too few and too many products in equilibrium, relative to the constrained optimum. Hence, there is no presumption that the number of products is optimal in Chamberlin's model of monopolistic competition.

An important question that arises with the model of the representative consumer is what lies behind the assumed utility function. Of course, one answer is that all individual's preferences are identical. This answer is, however, inconsistent with awkward facts (5), that each consumer buys only a small subset of the available commodities, and (7), that tastes are revealed to differ among individuals. Hence, a number of authors have investigated the micro foundations of the Chamberlin model.

2.3. Chamberlin's model and diversity of tastes

A number of papers derive the symmetric demand functions of Chamberlin's models from diverse consumer tastes. See, especially, Anderson et al. (1988), Ferguson (1983), Hart (1985), Perloff and Salop (1985) and Sattinger (1984). We will develop the Perloff and Salop model as a way of illustrating the type of preferences that are required for symmetry. Although we will not develop the point, these models are interesting for another reason as well: implicit in them is a way to develop models that are hybrids of the address and non-address approaches. See, especially, Deneckere and Rothschild (1986).

There is a large number, N, of consumers and an infinite number of possible products. Any consumer buys at most one product, and if he buys a product he buys exactly one unit of it. Given n produced goods, a consumer's preferences over the n goods are described by $(B\theta_1, \ldots, B\theta_n)$. $B\theta_i$ is the value (in units of a composite commodity) that the consumer attaches to one unit of good i. For all consumers, θ_i is a random drawing from a differentiable density function, $f(\theta)$, with finite support, and B is a parameter that captures preference intensity.[1]

Consider two products with prices p_i and p_j. Product i is preferred to product j if $B\theta_i - p_i > B\theta_j - p_j$ or if $\theta_j < \theta_i + p_j/B - p_i/B$. Since θ_i and θ_j are independent drawings from $f(\theta)$, we can compute the probability that any consumer prefers product i to product j. Given p_i, p_j and (for the moment) θ_i, the probability that i is preferred to j is $F(\theta_i + p_j/B - p_i/B)$, where $F(\cdot)$ is the cumulative density function associated with $f(\cdot)$. But θ_i is also a random variable and hence the probability that any consumer prefers i to j is

$$\int F(\theta_i + p_j/B - p_i/B) f(\theta_i)\, \mathrm{d}\theta_i.$$

Given n produced goods, the probability that any consumer prefers i to all other produced products is

$$H_i(p_i, \bar{p}, n) = \prod_{j \neq i} \int F(\theta_i + p_j/B - p_i/B) f(\theta_i)\, \mathrm{d}\theta_i,$$

where $\bar{p}$ is the vector of prices, p_j, $j \neq i$. Assuming that there is at least one good for which $B\theta > p$ for each consumer, the (expected) demand function for good i is

$$Q_i(p_i, \bar{p}, n) = NH_i(p_i, \bar{p}, n).$$

These demand functions exhibit some obvious symmetry properties. First, $Q_i(p_i, \bar{p}, n)$ is symmetric in the prices p_j, $j \neq i$. For example, if $n = 3$, then

$$Q_1(p_1, p_2, p_3, 3) = Q_1(p_1, p_3, p_2, 3).$$

Furthermore, if all prices are identical, as they are in equilibrium, quantities demanded from each firm are identical and equal to N/n.

[1]It is not necessary for symmetry that different consumers' θ's are drawn from the *same* density function. What is necessary is that any consumer's θ's be *independent* drawings from some density function. The way to construct hybrid models is to fix the number of possible products and let any consumer's $(\theta_1, \ldots, \theta_n)$ be a drawing from some *joint* density function.

Now let us characterize the symmetric equilibrium of this model. For concreteness, it is useful to consider the case in which $f(\theta)$ has uniform density on $[u, v]$. To characterize the equilibrium price given n, $p(n)$, set all prices but the ith price equal to a common value, p. Then the ith firm's profit is a function of p_i, p and n. Setting the partial derivative of its profit function with respect to p_i equal to zero, and all prices equal to $p(n)$, we obtain:

$$p(n) = c + B(v - u)/n.$$

As n increases without bound, $p(n)$ approaches c. As preference intensity, B, goes to zero, all goods become perfect substitutes and $p(n)$ approaches c. This reflects the fact that this model is just the Bertrand model in the limit where $B = 0$.

To characterize the free-entry equilibrium, we use the zero-profit condition. In free-entry equilibrium the equilibrium number of firms, $\bar{n}$, is such that each firm earns zero profit. The zero-profit condition implies that

$$\bar{n} = [BN(v - u)/K]^{1/2}.$$

It is also easy to determine the optimal number of firms in free-entry equilibrium. Given n, the expected maximum value of $B\theta_i$, $M(n)$, is

$$M(n) = B(nv + u)/(n + 1).$$

The expected value of total surplus, when all goods are sold at a common price, is then $N[M(n) - c] - nK$.

The optimal number of products, n^*, maximizes total surplus:

$$n^* = [BN(v - u)/K]^{1/2} - 1.$$

Observe that n^* is $\bar{n} - 1$: in free-entry equilibrium, the number of firms is approximately the optimal number.

Because, by assumption, each firm produces at most one product, the Chamberlinian equilibrium is inconsistent with awkward fact (4). This raises an interesting question: If firms were allowed to produce more than one product in a Chamberlin model, would they choose to do so? That is to say, is the equilibrium of such a model consistent with awkward fact (4), when the one-firm, one-product assumption is relaxed?

Two key characteristics of this model are now apparent. First, the zero-profit condition that we used above is appropriate only because of symmetry. There is an integer problem (see Section 5 below) in that n firms might make small profits while $n + 1$ firms would make losses. But within the limits of this integer problem (which is trivial when n is at all large) zero profit is appropriate because a new entrant takes customers equally from all existing products. We shall see below that because symmetry is not a property of address models, the zero-profit condition for entry equilibrium does not apply to them.

Second, symmetry arises because the θ's for each consumer are independent random drawings from some density function. It follows that if one good i were removed from the choice set of n differentiated goods, all those consumers who were purchasing i would redistribute themselves uniformly over the other $n - 1$ goods. This property is an appealing one where differentiation is spurious. If all soaps were identical so that perceived differences were solely a product of brand-image advertising, the removal of one soap might lead to this symmetric redistribution of purchases.

This property would not be found, however, where consumers agree on what differentiated products are, and are not, close substitutes for each other, and, in such cases, it conflicts with awkward fact (6). For example, the removal of one low-tar brand of cigarette would lead mainly to increases in the demands for other low-tar products, and not to symmetric increases in the demands for low-tar, medium-tar and high-tar cigarettes. Since the properties of equilibrium in models which do allow for such agreement among consumers are significantly different for those that do not, the propositions that follow from the Chamberlin model must be suspect in those cases where agreement exists. [For further discussion, see Archibald, Eaton and Lipsey (1986).]

3. The address approach

A key aspect of the address approach is that it allows for diversity of consumers' tastes while making the closeness of substitutability among goods at least partially an objective phenomenon. In all consumers' minds, two low-tar cigarettes will be closer substitutes than a low- and a high-tar cigarette; two subcompact cars will be closer substitutes than a subcompact and a stretch limousine; two adjacent drugstores will be closer substitutes than two drugstores at the opposite ends of town.

3.1. Describing a good

In the address branch, a good is described by (θ, p), where p is its price and θ is its "address", some relevant physical description of the good. The address can either be a scalar or a vector and the descriptor, θ, can have many different interpretations. Here are the most common:

- θ may be the location of a firm in some physical space. On a line, it is one number; on a plane, two.

- θ may be the description of the good in some other "spectrum"; for example, the spectrum of color, or a "quality" spectrum.
- θ may be the time at which a service is delivered as, for example, with airline or TV scheduling.
- In Lancaster's characteristics model, a specific good embodies characteristics, z, in fixed proportions. Thus, in the two-characteristics case, we can describe goods by one number, for example, $\theta = z_1/z_2$, where z_1/z_2 is the fixed proportion of the quantity of characteristic one to the quantity of characteristic two.

3.2. Consumers' preferences

Consider first the usual model of spatial competition where firms and consumers are distributed over some geographic space. Any consumer's preferences can be described by a standard utility function, $U(x, y)$, where x is quantity of the good sold by spatially differentiated firms and y is quantity of a composite commodity. Let $\bar{\theta}$ be the consumer's address in the physical space, θ_i the address of firm i, and $T(\theta_i, \bar{\theta})$ the cost of transporting a unit of x from θ_i to $\bar{\theta}$, and assume that consumers bear transport costs. The consumer will, of course, buy x from the firm with the lowest delivered price, $p_i + T(\theta_i, \bar{\theta})$. Thus, awkward fact (5), that each consumer buys only a small number of the goods available, is a theorem in this address model. (As we will see it is also a theorem in Lancaster's characteristics model.)

To emphasize the common features of all address models, it is useful to represent the consumer's preferences in the model of spatial competition indirectly:

$$W(\theta, p, \bar{\theta}) = \max_{x,\, y} \left\{ U(x, y) \text{ s.t. } \left[p + T(\theta, \bar{\theta}) \right] x + y = 1 \right\}.$$

The level surfaces of the indirect utility function $W(\theta, p, \bar{\theta})$ in a one-dimensional physical space when transport costs are a linear function of distance are illustrated in Figure 12.1. They are linear tents centered on the consumers location, $\bar{\theta}$.

In Lancaster's characteristics model any good embodies characteristics in fixed proportions, and quantities of the characteristics are arguments of consumer's utility functions. In the primal space with two characteristics the utility function is $U(g(z_1, z_2), y)$, where $g(z_1, z_2)$ is a utility aggregator, z_1 and z_2 are the quantities of characteristics embodied in group goods, and y is the quantity of a composite commodity. If goods are combinable, so that aggregate quantities of z_1 and z_2 obtained by a consumer are simply the sums of the quantities of characteristics embodied in the bundle of goods he purchases, the utility-maximizing consumer needs to purchase no more goods than there are character-

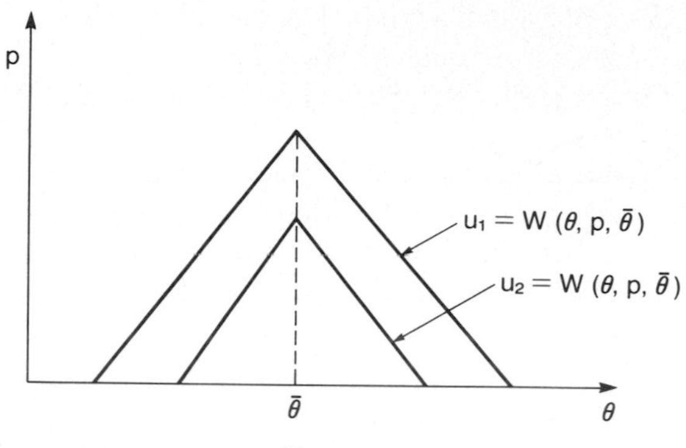

Figure 12.1

istics. Hence, when the number of characteristics embodied in a group of goods is small relative to the number of goods embodying them, awkward fact (5) is again a theorem. See Lancaster (1966).

The recent literature on Lancaster's characteristics model has assumed that each consumer purchases at most one out of a group of differentiated goods, arguing that for technological or other reasons, goods are not combinable. [See Lancaster (1979) and Archibald and Eaton (1987) for a consideration of the very thorny issues concerning combinability.] In this case it is again convenient to derive an indirect representation of the consumer's preferences. A good may be described by the quantities of characteristics, z_1 and z_2, embodied in a unit of that good. The unit in which we measure quantity of the good is, of course, arbitrary. If the good is some brand of cigarettes and the initial unit is a pack of cigarettes, then $(10z_1, 10z_2)$ describes the good when the unit is a carton containing 10 packs. Of course, in any description of the good, z_1/z_2 is fixed.

Thus, we have a degree of freedom that we can use to simplify the way in which goods are described. We illustrate by considering one convenient *units convention*. The good is described by the angle, θ, whose tangent is the (fixed) ratio of z_1 to z_2. The units convention is a quarter circle in the (z_1, z_2) space – the line $z_1^2 + z_2^2 = 1$. The parametric (on θ) representation of this convention is

$$z_1 = \cos\theta, \qquad z_2 = \sin\theta.$$

The indirect utility function is then defined as

$$W(\theta, p) = \max_{x,\, y} \{U(g(x\cos\theta, x\sin\theta), y) \text{ s.t. } px + y = 1\}.$$

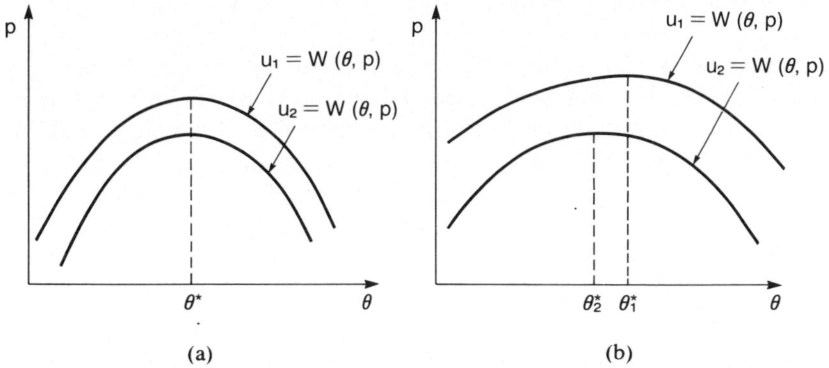

Figure 12.2

The level surfaces of the associated indirect utility function, when z_1 and z_2 are goods, are illustrated in Figure 12.2. When $g(z_1, z_2)$ is homothetic, as it is in Figure 12.2(a), the consumer has a well-defined address, θ^*: for all p, θ^* is the most preferred good. When this is not so, the consumer's address depends on his or her utility level, as illustrated in Figure 12.2(b).

With three characteristics, any units convention involves two θ's. For example, θ_1 might be the ratio z_1/z_2, and θ_2 the ratio z_1/z_3. In general, the choice of a units convention in an n characteristic model requires $n - 1$ θ's.

At a more general level, a consumer's preferences in an address model are described by an indirect utility function, $W(\theta, p)$, where θ is the description of a good in θ space. If θ is interpreted as quality – anything of which more is better – level surfaces will be upward-sloping. In the color-spectrum example shown in Figure 12.3, there are no apparent constraints on the shape of the level surfaces. A consumer could, for example, have strong preferences for the three primary colors and not be attracted to intermediate shades.

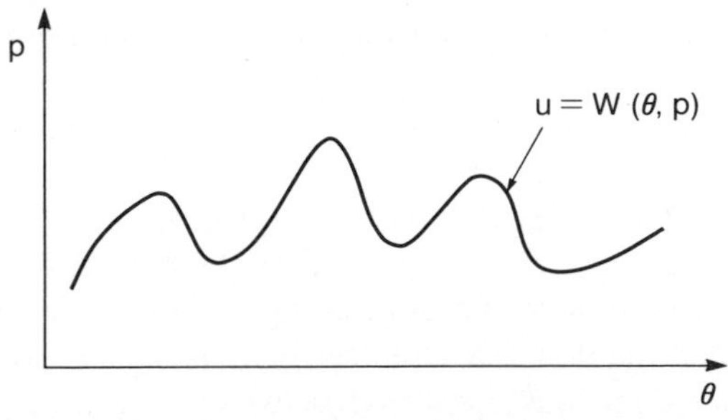

Figure 12.3

3.3. Aspects of an address model

The purpose of address models of product differentiation is to explain observed product diversity by reference to technology and diversity of tastes. Any such model requires the specification of diverse preferences, technology and an equilibrium concept.

Diversity of tastes is ordinarily captured by specifying a continuum of preferences in some appropriate space. In the one-dimensional model of spatial competition diversity is captured by specifying a density of consumers' addresses. Lane (1980) analyzes a two-characteristic model. He uses a Cobb–Douglas specification for $g(z_1, z_2)$, and captures diversity by assuming that the parameter of the Cobb–Douglas function is uniformly distributed on $[0,1]$.

Technology is ordinarily described by a cost function, $C(\theta, q)$, which specifies the cost of producing q units of a good with description θ. In most models the cost function takes the familiar form:

$$C(\theta, q) = K(\theta) + C(\theta)q.$$

The fixed cost, $K(\theta)$, is often associated with product development or with some other product-specific capital input, and is, therefore, a sunk cost.

Recent address models use subgame perfection in some form as the equilibrium concept. In the simplest case, to characterize free-entry equilibrium potential entrants are treated as players in a game of perfect information. In more complex models, the entire industry structure is generated by an extensive form game of sequential entry. Where sunk costs are an important aspect of the technology, any rational theory of product diversity would seem to require subgame perfection. Sunk costs imply that firms have something to lose if their profit expectations are incorrect. Subgame perfection forces these expectations to be correct.

Two important questions now arise. First (for all consumers) is $W(\theta, p)$ continuous in θ and p? We believe that for the vast majority of cases, the answer is "yes". Second, are the level surfaces of $W(\theta, p)$ single peaked? In many cases the answer is clearly "yes" – e.g. where goods are differentiated by location, by quality, or by the fixed ratio of one Lancastrian characteristic to another. In other cases it is clearly possible that the answer is "no" – e.g. when goods are differentiated by color.

If the answer to both questions is "yes", we are in a world that is quite different from the "goods-are-goods" world of the non-address branch. Given a large set of available products, n, suppose we identify all consumers who buy product A. Now eliminate A from the set of available products. The fact that level surfaces are single peaked implies that the second choices of the consumers who bought A will be distributed over a small subset of the remaining products.

Now suppose that we perturb the price of A slightly. Then quantities demanded of a small subset of products will change. That is, the price of A will be an argument of a small subset of the product demand functions. Hence, the Chamberlin symmetry assumptions are violated. Moreover, aggregate choice behavior cannot be captured by the fiction of a representative consumer with a strictly quasi-concave utility function. For any strictly quasi-concave utility function, there is a non-empty set of prices $(p_1, \ldots, p_n)$ such that all n prices enter all n demand functions in a non-trivial way.

If level surfaces of $W(\theta, p)$ have many peaks (and tastes differ among consumers), then it is conceivable that second choices will be (uniformly) distributed over the remaining products and that the price of A is an argument of all demand functions. In this case there is no necessary conflict between the representative consumer and the address approaches to product differentiation.

4. An illustrative address model

We begin by developing an extremely simple model in which addresses are the only endogenous variables. That is, the model focuses exclusively on competition in addresses. It illustrates a number of important and robust propositions that arise in a wide range of address models. Having developed the simple model, we consider the robustness of the results in Section 5.

4.1. Competition in addresses

The space in which goods are differentiated is a segment of the real line of unit length. We refer to the good with address θ_i as good i. In general, the space may be interpreted as a geographic space – a main street, for example – or as some more general charactistics space. Lancaster (1979) and Salop (1979) carefully develop the characteristic interpretation in this type of model.

The cost function, which is independent of the good's address, is

$$C(q) = K + cq,$$

where q is output, c is a constant marginal cost – which, without loss of generality, we take to be zero – and K is a sunk cost associated with an address-specific, and infinitely durable investment, I. Thus, $K = rI$, where r is the rate of interest reflecting the opportunity cost of investing in this industry. The cost I may be thought of either as a product development cost or as the cost of some type of physical capital of which only one indivisible unit is needed. To focus exclusively on competition in addresses, we assume that prices of all goods are exogenous and equal to one. To focus on non-collusive free-entry equilibrium, we assume that each good is produced by a separate firm and that there is an arbitrarily large number of potential entrants.

Let $\bar{\theta}$ be the address of some consumer in the characteristics space. Let good i, with address θ_i, be the good nearest to $\bar{\theta}$. The consumer's utility function is

$$U(x, y, \bar{\theta}, \theta_i) = \begin{cases} y, & \text{if } x < 1, \\ y + R - T(D), & \text{if } x \geq 1, \end{cases}$$

where D is the distance from $\bar{\theta}$ to θ_i (that is, $D = |\bar{\theta} - \theta_i|$), y is the quantity of a composite commodity, and x is the quantity of good i. We assume that $R - T(D)$, the consumer's reservation price for good i, exceeds 1 (the exogenous price of good i) for all θ_i and $\bar{\theta}$ in the unit interval, which implies that the consumer demands one unit of good i. We assume that $T'(D) > 0$, which allows us to interpret $\bar{\theta}$ as this consumer's most preferred good since the consumer's utility is maximal when $\theta_i = \bar{\theta}$. We capture diversity of consumers' tastes by assuming that $\bar{\theta}$ is uniformly distributed on the unit interval with unit density. Notice that consumers differ only with respect to their most preferred good.

In a model of spatial competition $T(D)$ is the cost of transporting one unit of the good a distance D. In a more general characteristics framework, $T(D)$ is a utility cost (measured in units of the composite commodity) associated with the distance from θ_i to $\bar{\theta}$, the consumer's most preferred good. For concreteness and clarity we will use the spatial competition interpretation of the model.

4.2. Free-entry equilibrium

It is a simple matter to characterize the free-entry equilibrium of this model. Let w denote the length of any interval between any two adjacent goods. We call any such interval an *interior interval*. We assume that potential entrants play a game of perfect information. Given our assumption that I is an address-specific, infinitely durable investment, the potential entrant knows that the addresses of the two goods at either end of the interval of length w are fixed, which, given our other assumptions, allows the entrant to calculate its post-entry profit. For any address in this interval, the entrant would attract the custom of half of the customers in the interval. Its gross profit, total profit plus K, would then be $w/2$, and it would *not* enter if and only if

$$w \leq 2K,$$

which is the no-entry condition for any interior interval. (We assume for convenience that zero profit does not induce entry.)

Let v denote the length of the interval between either boundary of the space and the good nearest that boundary, the peripheral good. The entrant's best address in either peripheral segment is adjacent to the peripheral good, where it obtains the purchases of all of the customers in the peripheral segment. So, the no-entry condition for either peripheral segment is

$$v \leq K.$$

These two conditions completely determine the free-entry equilibrium of this simple model. Interior segments can be no larger than $2K$, and the peripheral segments can be no larger than K. Some important, and we stress *robust*, features of free-entry equilibrium in this model deserve attention.

4.3. *Pure profit in free-entry equilibrium*

The profit any existing good earns is obviously directly proportional to its market. To maximize the profit of an interior good in free-entry equilibrium, denoted by Π^i, we simply maximize the size of the interior segments on either side of the good. Setting each of these segments equal to $2K$, we see that the good's market is $2K$ since it attracts half of the custom from each of these two segments. Maximal pure profit in free-entry equilibrium is then K, which implies that the maximum rate of return an interior good can earn on its specific investment, I, is $2r$. The maximal pure profit of a peripheral good in free-entry equilibrium is also K.

4.4. *Non-uniqueness of free-entry equilibrium*

Another obvious consequence of the no-entry conditions is that free-entry equilibrium is not unique. Any configuration of addresses satisfying these conditions is a free-entry equilibrium.

4.5. *No invisible hand*

Any configuration of addresses is Pareto optimal in this model because any relocation of any firm must make some people worse off. Hence, Pareto optimality is not a useful welfare criterion for the model. To consider optimality, some form of aggregation of gains and losses is essential in address models. In the spatial interpretation of the model, the obvious criterion is the minimization of the total resource cost of serving the market, which is equivalent to maximizing the sum of producers' and consumers' surplus. Since consumers' demands are perfectly price inelastic in this model, the only welfare issue concerns the optimal amount of diversity. That is to say, the failure of price to be equal to marginal cost is not indicative of market failure since demand is not responsive to price.

There are two resource costs in this model: costs associated with goods, K per good, and transport costs. If $T''(D) \geq 0$, it is intuitive and easily proven that the configuration of addresses which minimizes transport costs, given n goods, is $(1/2n, 3/2n, \ldots, 1 - 1/2n)$. In this configuration, the total resource cost, $R(n)$, is

$$R(n) = n\left[K + 2\int_0^{n/2} T(D)\,\mathrm{d}D\right].$$

The second term in the brackets is transport costs borne by a representative good's customers, and K is, of course, the cost associated with the good. Ignoring the obvious integer problem, the optimal number of goods, n^*, is characterized by $R'(n^*) = 0$.

It is now easy to see that there is no invisible hand at work in this model. To characterize free-entry equilibrium we needed to know nothing about $T(D)$, whereas we do need to know $T(D)$ to determine n^*. It follows that there may be too much, too little, or just the right amount of diversity in free-entry equilibrium.

There are two intuitive ways to see this. First, suppose that the optimal configuration, $(1/2n^*, 3/2n^*, \ldots, 1 - 1/2n^*)$, is a free-entry equilibrium. Since free-entry equilibrium is not unique, there are any number of non-optimal free-entry equilibria. But the optimal configuration is not necessarily a free-entry equilibrium. Suppose, for concreteness, that $T(D) = tD$. In this case n^* is an increasing function of t. Then if t is sufficiently small, n^* will be so small that the no-entry conditions will not be satisfied in the optimal configuration. In this case, there is too much diversity in any free-entry equilibrium. Furthermore, if t is sufficiently large, n^* will be so large that each good in the optimal configuration could not cover its costs. In this case, although the optimal configuration is a free-entry equilibrium, it is difficult to imagine an entry process that would give rise to it. That is to say, if we insist that goods cover their costs, there will be too little diversity in free-entry equilibrium when t is large.

4.6. *Foresighted entry*

Is any one of the many free-entry equilibria which are possible in this model a salient equilibrium – one we would expect to see? Prescott and Visscher (1977) ask this question in this model when entry is sequential. [Hay (1976) examines sequential entry in a model with endogenous prices. See Baumol (1967, n. 4. p. 679) for an extremely insightful early discussion of the issue of entry in an address model.] Each firm is constrained to own at most one good, the market is initially unserved, and the order in which firms confront the entry decision is predetermined. The sequential entry process is modelled as a game of perfect information and hence the equilibrium they derive is subgame perfect.

We know from our earlier discussion that $\underline{w} = K$ is the size of market which produces zero pure profit for one good. Let $\underline{n}$ be the smallest integer, n, such that $n \geq 1/2\underline{w}$, and consider the following configuration of $\underline{n}$ firms: $[1/2\underline{n}, 3/2\underline{n}, \ldots, 1 - (1/2\underline{n})]$. As you can easily verify, this configuration deters entry, and any configuration with fewer than $\underline{n}$ firms does not. Thus, this configuration is a free-entry equilibrium that maximizes the pure profit that can be extracted from the market. As you can also verify, if $1/2\underline{w}$ is not an integer, there are other configurations of $\underline{n}$ firms that satisfy the no-entry conditions.

To see the nature of the Prescott–Visscher equilibrium, suppose that $1/2\underline{w}$ is an integer. In this case

$$[1/2\underline{n}, 3/2\underline{n}, \ldots, 1 - (1/2\underline{n})]$$

is the only configuration of $\underline{n}$ firms which deters further entry, and in this configuration each firm earns pure profit K, the maximum possible profit in free-entry equilibrium. This configuration is the unique perfect equilibrium configuration of the sequential entry game, although any firm in the sequence can be located at any of the $\underline{n}$ locations in the configuration. To see that it is a perfect equilibrium, consider the sequence in which firm 1 locates at $1/2\underline{n}$, firm 2 at $3/2n$, firm three at $5/2\underline{n}$, and so on. It is clear that the $\underline{n}$th firm would choose to locate at $1 - (1/2\underline{n})$ if the first $\underline{n} - 1$ chose to locate at $(1/2\underline{n}, \ldots, 1 - 3/2\underline{n})$ since by choosing $1 - (1/2\underline{n})$, it gets the maximum possible profit in free-entry equilibrium, K, and since any other location would induce entry of an additional firm which would leave firm $\underline{n}$ with a profit less than K. Knowing this, firm $\underline{n} - 1$ will choose to locate at $1 - 3/2\underline{n}$ if firms 1 through $\underline{n} - 2$ locate at $(1/2\underline{n}, \ldots, 1 - 5/2\underline{n})$, because only this location offers $\underline{n} - 1$ the maximum possible profit in free-entry equilibrium. Replicating this argument for firms $\underline{n} - 2, \ldots,$ and 1, we see that this sequence is subgame perfect because it offers each firm the maximum possible profit in free-entry equilibrium.

Notice that awkward fact (2), that firms rarely produce identical products, is a theorem in this model with foresighted entry. Each firm in the sequence (except the first) has the option of producing a product identical to its predecessor's, but it chooses to maximally differentiate its product from its predecessor's, subject to entry being unprofitable in the interval between the two products.

When $1/2\underline{w}$ is not an integer, the problem is more complex. Prescott and Visscher argue that the following sequence is subgame perfect: firm 1 enters at $\underline{w}$,

2 at $1 - \underline{w}$, 3 at $3\underline{w}$, 4 at $1 - 3\underline{w}, \dots$, and firm $\underline{n}$ anywhere in the segment between firms $\underline{n} - 1$ and $\underline{n} - 2$ that does not leave a market larger than $2\underline{w}$ on either side of it. In this sequence, the first $n - 3$ firms earn pure profit equal to K and the last 3 firms pure profit greater than zero and less than K.

Suppose now that we drop the restriction that each firm owns at most one address. Then the perfect equilibrium exhibits *monopoly preemption*: the first firm preempts the entire market by locating $\underline{n}$ plants in such a way that no interior segment exceeds $2\underline{w}$ and neither peripheral segment exceeds $\underline{w}$. Observe that from a resource cost, or total surplus, perspective the two solutions are essentially the same (they are necessarily identical when $1/2\underline{w}$ is an integer), despite the fact that the first industry structure is unconcentrated and the second exhibits maximal concentration.[2] The only significant difference between the two is distributional – all of the profit is captured by one firm in the monopoly preemption case. Thus, in this model, awkward fact (4), that a few firms produce many products, is a theorem where entry of firms is sequential. (As we will see in Section 7, when prices and/or quantities are endogenous, *monopoly* preemption is not an implication of sequential entry.)

4.7. *History matters*

The non-uniqueness of equilibrium implies that the present characteristics of markets may not depend solely on their current demand and cost conditions. Their past histories can matter in important ways. This can easily be illustrated using the Prescott–Visscher model when $1/2\underline{w}$ is an integer.

Consider two markets, A and B. Market A displays all of the features described in the previous section, so that in sequential equilibrium there are $\underline{n}$ firms in the market and each firm is earning a pure profit of K. Market B, however, has a past history that differs from A in one key respect. When the sequence of entry occurred in B, the density of customers was two instead of one. The result was $2\underline{n}$ plants, each earning pure profits of K. After entry, however, there was an unanticipated fall in consumer density to one. The two markets are now identical in terms of demand and cost conditions. Market B will, however, continue to have twice the number of firms as market A and the firms in B will earn zero pure profits while those in A will earn pure profits of K.

If we looked only at the present conditions in these markets, we would be unable to explain their differences. Only a knowledge of their past histories provides the correct explanation – as must generally be the case whenever equilibrium is not unique.

[2]They are not identical when $1/2\underline{w}$ is not an integer. The monopolist need not locate the first and last plants at $1/2\underline{w}$ and $1 - 1/2\underline{w}$, but when each firm chooses one location, the first and last plants will be so located.

5. Pure profit reconsidered

The possibility of pure profit in free-entry equilibrium is clearly a crucial aspect of this and other address models. It is crucial to the non-uniqueness of equilibrium and to the strategic behavior in the context of foresighted entry. Because it is so important and so often misunderstood, we consider the genesis of pure profit at length.

5.1. The importance of sunk costs

In spatial models a continuum of firms would allow all production to occur at the point of consumption so reducing transport costs to zero. In characteristics models a continuum of products would allow everyone to consume their own most preferred good.

The geographic concentration of production in firms located at discrete addresses is an obvious characteristic of the real world. To explain this along with awkward fact (3), that the number of products produced is much less than the number of possible products, some source of increasing returns to scale, or its cost equivalent, is necessary. In our simple model the cost I is the source of decreasing average total costs.

The address-specificity of I is at the heart of the pure-profit result since it is the sunk nature of this cost at any address which forces the entrant to regard addresses as fixed. It is, of course, entirely possible that this cost is not completely address specific. To the extent that it is not, the magnitude of pure profit possible in free-entry equilibrium is altered.

We can briefly consider this possibility by using a simplified version of the analysis in Eaton and Lipsey (1978) supposing that a portion s of I is address specific and therefore that $(1 - s)$ is not. Consider a symmetric configuration of many addresses in which the interior segments are of length w and peripheral segments are of length $w/2$, and each firm occupies only one address. Now ask under what circumstances one existing firm would change its address in response to entry. Suppose that the entrant locates just next to an existing firm and so takes one-half of that firm's market. Any rational relocation decision is obviously quite complex since the existing firm must itself ask whether or not it must take the addresses of other firms, including the entrant's, as given and, if not, it must solve their relocation problems. To avoid solving this problem and to maximize the existing firm's perceived incentive to relocate, suppose that the existing firm believes (or more properly that the entrant believes that the existing firm believes) that by relocating it will touch off a series of instantaneous relocations that would leave it and the entrant with a market identical to its pre-entry market – a market of length w. Given this belief, the existing firm will relocate if and only if

$w - sK > w/2$, since its anticipated market, if it relocates, is w and only $w/2$ if it does not. This inequality implies that the existing firm will not relocate if $w \leq 2sK$.

If the entrant foresees this result (notice that it could not be more optimistic about the possibility of relocation), it will not enter if $w \leq 2sK$ since its post-entry market would be $w/2$, which is not large enough to cover its costs. That is, $w/2 - K < 0$ when $w < 2sK$. This result in turn implies that the maximum pure profit in free-entry equilibrium is sK. Thus, if s is greater than 0, the magnitude, but not the existence of profit, is an issue.

5.2. The durability of sunk capital, predatory entry and profit dissipation

To focus on the influence of durability, we return to the case in which sunk capital is completely address specific. Infinitely durable, address-specific, sunk capital commits any plant to remain at its present address forever – it creates in essence a property right to the flow of pure profits available in free-entry equilibrium. As a result, the only sort of entry which is possible is *augmenting entry* – entry that increases the number of addresses.

When sunk capital is not infinitely durable, a second type of entry becomes a possibility. This is *predatory entry* – entry that causes an existing address to be abandoned when its associated capital expires. In these circumstances, a property right to some, but not all, of the pure profit that would be available if augmenting entry were the only possibility can be created by premature replacement of sunk capital in the market. As we show, this behavior tends to dissipate profit.

To see what is involved, we use a simplified version of the analysis in Eaton and Lipsey (1980). We suppose that sunk capital, which again costs I, has a durability of H periods. When unconcerned about predatory entry, a sitting firm replaces its plant every H periods. But a new entrant could establish its plant at the same location just as the sitting firm was about to replace its own capital. The market would then "belong" to the new entrant. But foreseeing that strategy, the sitting firm could renew its capital at some earlier date. We want to find the optimal premature replacement strategy.

To set the stage for a consideration of predatory entry, and its preemption by the early renewal of address-specific capital, we first derive a constraint on the size of intervals between plants which is implied by the possibility of augmenting entry. The constraint is analogous to the no-entry conditions derived in Subsection 4.2. Consider entry into an interior segment of length w. (For simplicity we ignore peripheral segments.) The present value of augmenting entry, discounted over an infinite time horizon and evaluated at the instant of entry, is

$$w/2r - I/[1 - E(rH)],$$

where $E(x) \equiv e^{-x}$. The first term is the present value of the entrant's revenues and the second the present value of its costs. The condition for augmenting entry to be unprofitable is

$$w \leq 2rI/[1 - E(rH)] \equiv M.$$

For simplicity we suppose that $w = M$ so that firms are separated by the maximum distance consistent with no augmenting entry. We once again assume that each existing firm owns only one address. We wish to find a premature replacement strategy that deters predatory entry. The strategy we consider is for each firm to replace its address-specific capital δ periods prematurely. Thus, each firm incurs the cost I every $H - \delta$ periods and hence never has a commitment to the market less than δ periods.

At the instant in time when capital is replaced, the present value of any existing firm, if the strategy deters predatory entry, is

$$V(\delta) = M/r - I/[1 - E(r(H - \delta))],$$

which is obviously decreasing in δ. Thus, the problem is to find the minimum value of δ, which we denote by δ^*, that deters predatory entry. Think of δ^* as the optimal entry deterring strategy.

The point in time at which predatory entry is most attractive is the instant before an existing firm replaces its capital. At this point, the present value of a predatory entrant which adopts the address of an existing firm, and itself uses the optimal entry deterring strategy, δ^*, is

$$U(\delta, \delta^*) = -I + [M/2][1 - E(r\delta)] + M[E(r\delta) - E(r(H - \delta^*))] + V(\delta^*)E(r(H - \delta^*)).$$

The second term reflects the power of premature replacement as an entry deterrent – the successful predatory entrant must contend with the existing firm for δ periods, and its sales over this interval of time are only $M/2$ per period.

The existing firm's strategy, δ, will deter entry if $U(\delta, \delta^*) \leq 0$. Since $V(\delta)$ is decreasing in δ, δ^* is the value of δ such that $U(\delta, \delta^*) = 0$. That is, δ^* is defined by $U(\delta^*, \delta^*) = 0$. As the reader can verify, $\delta^* = H/2$.

If augmenting entry were the only issue, δ would be zero, and any existing firm's present value at time of replacement would be $V(0) = I/(1 - E(rH))$, which is identical to the present value of the firm's address-specific capital cost. But predatory entry is an issue, and the maximum present value of the firm is only $V(\delta^*) = I/[1 - E(rH/2)]$. As H gets large, $V(\delta^*)$ approaches $V(0)$ and as H gets small, $V(\delta^*)$ goes to zero. In the latter limit all of the potential profit is dissipated by premature replacement.

Profit dissipation also arises in the context of *foreseen* market growth. [See Eaton and Lipsey (1979).] In a growing market, entry itself is premature since only by prematurely entering can a firm create the necessary property right to appropriate the profit available in free-entry equilibrium. Indeed, with many potential entrants and parametric prices, all of the profit is dissipated by premature entry – that is, entry occurs when the present value of entry is zero.

These dissipation results are, of course, in no way inconsistent with the existence of flows of pure profit in static free-entry equilibrium. Indeed, it is this possibility that drives the premature entry and/or capital replacement which itself is partially or totally profit dissipating. And, of course, these results are not (necessarily) welfare improving. For example, the premature replacement of capital to deter predatory entry is associated with a pure deadweight welfare loss.

5.3. *Endogenous prices*

To articulate in the simplest possible way what we think are the essential issues peculiar to address models, we have assumed that prices are exogenous. In this subsection we discuss some thorny problems that arise when prices are endogenous, and we ask if the basic properties of free-entry equilibrium found in our simple model are robust with respect to endogenous prices. We continue to assume that any firm occupies at most one address. We add the assumption that the configuration of addresses is symmetric on a circular market (which avoids boundary problems) as in Salop (1979). Let $p(n)$ be the symmetric Nash equilibrium price in this circular model with n firms.

If we suppose that entrants are price takers – that entrants believe that the post-entry prices of existing firms will be $p(n)$ – then pure profit is impossible in free-entry equilibrium. For example, an entrant that adopted some existing firm's address and charged a price just lower than $p(n)$ would anticipate positive profit as long as the existing firm was earning positive profit. Hence, zero profit is not a property of free-entry equilibrium if entrants assume that they are price takers.

But in a model where existing firms have sunk costs which commit them to the market, foresighted entrants will not take price as given. The existing firm, which would be wiped out by the price-cutting entrant, will not maintain price. Rather, it will respond by reducing price, and the entrant can foresee that it will. For this reason, Eaton and Lipsey (1978) and Novshek (1980) impose a no-mill-price-undercutting restriction. They do not allow any entrant (or any existing firm) to believe that it can adopt a price which would reduce an existing firm's sales to zero without any reaction. The resulting free-entry equilibrium – where the prices of existing firms are Nash equilibrium prices subject to this restriction, and where entrants take established firms' prices as given but do not consider undercutting – exhibits pure profits.

The no-mill-price-undercutting restriction can be seen as an attempt to rule out an entrant's profit expectations which are wildly inconsistent with its post-entry profit realization. Consider again the price-cutting entrant which expects to appropriate virtually all of an existing firm's profits by replicating its address and undercutting its price. If, given addresses, the price equilibrium is a Nash price equilibrium, then the post-entry prices of the entrant and its intended victim will be equal to marginal cost, and the entrant's profit expectations will not be fulfilled. The entrant is a victim of its own myopic profit expectation. If the entrant must incur address-specific sunk costs, then it will not take the prices of existing firms as given. Instead, it will attempt to anticipate the post-entry price equilibrium. This, of course, suggests that the appropriate equilibrium concept for the subgame in which a potential entrant makes its entry decision is subgame perfection.

Eaton and Wooders (1985) use this approach to characterize the symmetric free-entry equilibria of a model similar to our basic model, in which the price equilibrium in both the pre- and post-entry games is a Nash equilibrium in pure price strategies, and in which each firm owns one address. Their free-entry equilibria exhibit the two fundamental features of our basic model: the maximum rate of return on sunk capital is $3.33r$, and there may be too much, too little, or the optimal degree of product diversity in equilibrium. (Relative to our basic model, the maximum profit in equilibrium is larger because existing firms respond to entry by reducing price, a result which entrants foresee.) This establishes that parametric prices are not a necessary condition for the basic characteristics of the model discussed in Section 3.

There is, in addition, a potential problem of non-existence of price equilibrium associated with price undercutting. The problem is articulated by d'Aspremont, Gabszewicz and Thisse (1979). If, for example, transportation costs in our basic model are linear in distance, then the Nash price equilibrium (for given addresses) does not always exist. If, on the other hand, transportation costs are quadratic in distance (as in the model proposed by d'Aspremont, Gabszewicz and Thisse and employed by Eaton and Wooders), then the price equilibrium does exist.

5.4. The integer problem, balkanization and localized competition

The pure-profit result in address models is sometimes *wrongly* attributed to what we call the integer problem. The integer problem, which we brushed aside in our discussion of the Chamberlin model, occurs in non-address models when n firms can make a profit and $n + 1$ firms cannot, and its source is increasing returns to scale or its cost equivalent. As a result, n firms can earn profit in a non-address model that is in equilibrium with respect to foresightful entry. The same problem arises in an address model in which we *arbitrarily assume* that the number of firms is maximized, subject to the constraint that no firm incurs losses.

In either case – and assuming for convenience that sunk costs per period are K, marginal cost is constant, and price parametric – the maximum pure profit consistent with entry equilibrium is K/n. So, for example, one firm can earn up to twice the normal rate of return on its sunk capital ($2r$), two up to $1.5r$, and 10 up to $1.1r$. The integer problem can thus account for substantial long-run profits in industries where demand is sufficient to sustain only a few firms – natural monopolies and natural oligopolies – but as more and more firms can be supported by the market, the excess profit attributable to the integer problem rapidly diminishes.

But in address models, the location of existing goods or products balkanizes the market into a number of overlapping submarkets. As a result, competition is localized – each good has only a few neighboring goods with which it competes directly, regardless of the number of goods serving the entire market. This localized competition imparts a natural oligopoly characteristic to address models – indeed, this is what Kaldor (1935) intended by the phrase "overlapping oligopolies". It also allows the maximum profit consistent with free-entry equilibrium to remain constant as the number of firms in the market is increased. For example, let the density of customers grow in the model considered above. The minimum number of goods consistent with free-entry equilibrium will now grow, and the distance between goods will diminish but each good will continue to have only two neighbors and the maximum profit consistent with free-entry equilibrium will remain at $2r$. [See Eaton and Wooders (1985) for an illustration of this result when price is endogenous.]

The driving feature of these results is that the expected size of the market for a new entrant, R^{e}, is significantly smaller than the market enjoyed before entry by the firms which will be the entrant's neighbors, R^{a} (given identical prices). In our simple model R^{e}/R^{a} is one-half, and, hence, existing firms can earn up to twice the normal return on capital without attracting entry.

5.5. *How robust is balkanization?*

What happens to balkanization and its implication of localized competition when our restrictive assumptions are relaxed? We discuss models of spatial competition first.

A key assumption concerns transportation costs. If these are identical for all consumers and convex in distance, then competition is clearly local in nature. Thus, in one-dimensional models, each firm is in direct competition with at most two others.

Suppose, however, that transport costs are a concave function of distance and identical for all consumers. It is now possible that a low-price firm may be in competition with several high-priced ones, diminishing the extent to which competition is localized.

Another way in which this result can occur is if "transportation costs" are subjective and differ among consumers. Again, a low-price firm could be in direct competition with a number of high-price firms selling identical products from different addresses. In both of the above cases a firm's market area is no longer a connected subset of the entire market, and competition is not localized to the same extent. Analogous possibilities arise in characteristics models – a phenomenon referred to as "cross-over" by Lancaster (1979).

Notice that in both of the above cases there is still some balkanization of the market in that the entry of either one low-priced or one high-priced firm at a specific address will not take sales in one set of *equal* increments from all existing low-priced firms and another set of equal increments from all existing high-priced firms.

Another issue relevant to balkanization concerns the dimensionality of the space itself. Models of spatial competition in a two-dimensional space exhibit the key properties of equilibrium in our simple one-dimensional model. In particular, competition is localized and plants can earn substantial pure profit in entry equilibrium. For example, in a two-dimensional model analogous to the one-dimensional model developed here, Eaton and Lipsey (1976) show that the pure profit of all plants in free-entry equilibrium can be as large as $0.96K$.

In the characteristics model, the number of characteristics embodied in goods, and hence the dimensionality of the space, may be an important determinant of the extent to which competition is localized. Archibald and Rosenbluth (1975) consider the number of neighbors a firm can have in the case where goods are combinable. With two characteristics, each good can be in direct competition with at most two neighboring goods and in the case of three characteristics, the average number of neighbors cannot exceed 6. However, with four characteristics, the average number of neighbors can be as large as $n/2$, where n is the number of goods. Apart from the Archibald–Rosenbluth results for the combining case, we know virtually nothing about how the number of characteristics affects the number of neighbors.

Archibald and Rosenbluth focus on the average number of neighbors a firm can have. This does not seem to us to be the important question. Instead, what matters is whether or not R^{e} is bounded away from R^{a}. We suspect this is a characteristic that will be robust to increasing the number of dimensions.

Schmalansee (1983) observes quite rightly that the extent to which competition is localized cannot be resolved by the theorists' paper and pencil. It is at root an empirical question. He develops some empirical tests for localization. The payoff to careful empirical work in this area is, we think, immense.

6. Vertical differentiation and natural oligopoly

In a model of vertical differentiation goods are differentiated in a one-dimensional space but, in contrast to the illustrative model discussed above, the characteristic θ that describes a vertically differentiated good is something of which more is better from every consumer's perspective. In contrast, the earlier model in which consumer's had different preferred θ's can be called one of horizontal differentiation.

There are at least two ways in which vertical differentiation can arise. First, the technology might be such that the product only contained one variable characteristic. Say it is quality, which we assume can vary over the range $0 < \theta < 1$. Second, consumers might live at points θ on a one-dimensional housing estate occupying the range $1 < \theta < 2$, while retail stores were constrained by zoning laws to locate at points $\theta < 1$. The first case is driven solely by technology and the second by institutional arrangements. [Notice in the second case, which is due to Gabszewicz and Thisse (1986), the estate must be one-dimensional and the stores must be constrained to locate on only one side of it.]

Vertical differentiation is an address model but the fact that everyone agrees on the most preferred address for the good or store gives it some special characteristics. One issue that has attracted attention in recent years concerns the circumstances under which the model produces a *natural oligopoly*. In this section we outline the results obtained in a simple model which is designed to illustrate some of the arguments developed by Gabszewicz and Thisse (1979, 1980, 1986) and Shaked and Sutton (1982, 1983).

In this model θ is interpreted as a measure of quality and we assume that the feasible quality range is $0 \leq \theta \leq 1$. Each consumer buys one unit of his or her most preferred good, given the prices and θ's of the available goods. The indirect indifference curves for each consumer have the following form:

$$\bar{u} = m\theta - p,$$

where θ and p are quality and price, and m is the willingness of consumers to trade off quality against price. We capture diversity by assuming that m is uniformly distributed on $[a, b]$ with density D, where $b > a > 0$.

Now consider a consumer's choice between two goods, (θ_1, p_1) and (θ_2, p_2), with $\theta_1 > \theta_2$. If $p_2 > p_1$, all consumers prefer good one, so suppose that $p_2 < p_1$. The "market boundary" in θ space, $\overline{m}$, satisfies:

$$\overline{m}\theta_1 - p_1 = \overline{m}\theta_2 - p_2$$

or

$$\overline{m} = (p_1 - p_2)/(\theta_1 - \theta_2).$$

For $m > \overline{m}$, (θ_1, p_1) is preferred to (θ_2, p_2), and for $m < \overline{m}$, the opposite is true. From this, we see that the demand functions are:

$$D_1(\theta, p) = D(b - \overline{m}),$$

$$D_2(\theta, p) = D(\overline{m} - a).$$

We assume that the only cost of production is K, a sunk cost which is independent of θ. Hence, the marginal cost of producing a higher quality good is zero. The property that is necessary and sufficient for the natural oligopoly result is that the marginal cost of producing higher quality be less than a.

Firms choose price non-cooperatively. If one firm enters it will choose $\theta = 1$, since it will be profitable to produce all the quality possible when people are more than willing to pay its marginal cost. Now let a second firm enter. If it also chooses $\theta = 1$, competition will drive price to zero so that sunk costs will not be covered.

This parallels the natural monopoly result in the undifferentiated Bertrand model. With foresighted entry and constant marginal costs, a second firm will never enter no matter how large the market. But unlike the spaceless model with a homogeneous good, the second firm has the option of building a worse mouse trap (or purposely polluting its mineral spring!). This allows it to differentiate itself from the first firm and so avoid ruinous price competition. It will pay a second firm to enter with a poorer product, if consumers' tastes are diverse enough. Specifically, for $\theta_2 < 1$ the second firm commands a positive market share in the non-cooperative price equilibrium if and only if $b > 2a$. Hence, if $b > 2a$, and K is not too large, there will be at least two firms in this market. Will there be three? It again depends on diversity of consumers' tastes. If they are not too diverse (if $b < 4a$), and if there are three firms, then the one with the smallest θ does not command a positive market share in the non-cooperative price equilibrium. Hence, if $4a > b > 2a$, and if K is not too large, we will have natural duopoly. Notice that the market share conditions for natural duopoly do not depend on the density of consumers, D. With more diversity of tastes we can have more firms, but there is always a maximum number of firms that can coexist in a non-cooperative price equilibrium, and the maximum is independent of D.

Let us now consider sequential entry in the natural duopoly case. What may not be immediately obvious is that, if the second firm does not fear entry from a third firm, it will go all the way to shoddy quality and choose $\theta_2 = 0$. If, however, firm 2 foresees the possibility of entry by a third firm, it will choose a θ_2^* sufficiently close to 1 so that a third firm does not anticipate positive profits at any θ_3.

Now let the density of customers, D, or the size of the fixed costs, K, vary. As D goes to infinity or K goes to zero, θ_2^* goes to 1, while prices go to zero. These results reflect asymptotic optimality. The common sense of the result is that, as the size of the sales to be obtained from a third firm locating between $\theta_1 = 1$ and θ_2 rises, or as the sunk cost K declines, firm 2 must choose its θ closer and closer to θ_1 in order to keep a third firm out. In the limit the two firms select $\theta = 1$ and price is equal to zero. But since fixed cost per unit of output approaches zero in either limit, the two firms will remain profitable.

These results reflect the more general result in this type of model. As long as every consumer would choose maximal quality if asked to pay the marginal cost of producing it, the number of firms is bounded above, and is independent of customer density.

Given the assumptions about tastes for and costs of added quality, the results are driven by the destructiveness of price competition. As in the spaceless model, a second firm would never enter if it had to produce an identical product but, if consumers' tastes are sufficiently diverse, entry with a worse mouse trap is profitable.

In the spaceless model, the natural monopoly result does not hold when competition is in quantities instead of prices. The number of firms in a subgame perfect sequential entry exercise then varies positively with the size of the market. An analogous result occurs in the model of quality competition outlined here. Because individual demand is price inelastic – total quantity demanded is $(b - a)D$ regardless of the prices and θ's of firms – there are many non-cooperative quantity equilibria in the model. To make the quantity setting equilibrium more interesting, assume that each consumer's demand function for the consumer's most preferred good is $1 - p$.

Some tedious manipulation then shows that in the sequential entry game with two firms, the first firm chooses $\theta_1 = 1$ and the second chooses $\theta_2 = 1$. That is to say, although firm 2 could choose to differentiate its product, it will not choose to do so when competition is in quantities instead of prices. Just as the natural monopoly feature of the Bertrand model vanishes when we suppose that competition is in quantities instead of prices, so does the natural oligopoly feature of this model vanish when we switch to quantity competition. No firm will ever choose θ less than one when competition is in quantities, and hence the model is, in essence, now an undifferentiated Cournot model. [Bonanno (1986) derives the same result in a slightly different model.]

We conclude that the natural oligopoly result in an address model with vertical differentiation is driven by the assumption that price is the strategic variable, as well as certain necessary taste and cost assumptions. It is also worth noting that cases in which commodities can be differentiated by only a single characteristic are few in number.

7. Price versus quantity competition

Most address models in which prices are endogenous are based on the presumption that competition is in prices. One reason for this modelling choice is analytical convenience – when one aggregates demand in an address model the natural way to proceed is to derive demand functions. The resulting functions are frequently quite difficult to invert – with n firms one must invert an n-equation system. Thus, it is more convenient to assume that competition is in prices.

Obviously, analytical convenience is not a sufficient reason for assuming that competition is in prices since, as the following examples illustrate, there are significant differences between address models in which competition is in prices and those in which competition is in quantities. (The circumstances in which oligopolists may play either a pricing or a quantity game are discussed by Carl Shapiro in Chapter 6 of this Handbook, so we make only a few points of special relevance to address models.)

We saw in the discussion of natural oligopoly that the very nature of the equilibrium is different: with price competition, products are differentiated; with quantity competition, they are not.

Deneckere and Davidson (1985) show that in a model of differentiated products and many firms, when entry is not a concern, any sort of merger is profitable if competition is in prices, whereas mergers are only rarely profitable if competition is in quantities.

d'Aspremont, Gabszewicz and Thisse (1979) have shown that the very existence of price equilibrium is in question in address models that do not invoke the no-mill-price-undercutting assumption. One source of non-existence in these models is the temptation to undercut, which requires that price be the strategic variable. Salant (1986) shows that the undercutting temptation is removed when competition is in quantities and goes on to prove the existence of quantity equilibrium in one-dimensional address models in a fairly general setting.

One argument for the appropriateness of price competition is that firms must announce price in an address model. Given cost and demand conditions, impersonal market forces cannot give rise to market-clearing prices in differentiated products as they can with undifferentiated products. But this fact does not necessarily mean that prices are the strategic variable.

Salant (1986), for example, argues that in many industries there are long lags in production – the next period's output is committed by this period's production decisions. In this case firms' quantity decisions precede their price decisions. Such firms are forced to ask at what price tomorrow can today's production be marketed? That is, they are forced to make conjectures concerning market-clearing prices for their quantities. In these circumstances, it seems appropriate to model competition in quantities.

In an analysis of undifferentiated products that is clearly also applicable to differentiated ones, Kreps and Scheinkman (1983) consider a two-stage model in which duopolists simultaneously choose quantities in stage 1 and prices in stage 2. The subgame perfect equilibrium in their model is identical to a Cournot equilibrium in spite of competition being in prices in stage 2. The intuition is that firms recognize the destructiveness of Bertrand competition and commit themselves in advance to curbing their non-cooperative pricing behavior by choosing a limited quantity. Where this model applies, we would expect Cournot results when demand is correctly predicted, but Bertrand-style price wars whenever unexpectedly low demand occurs.

Singh and Vives (1984) consider a two-stage game in which each firm first selects price or quantity as its strategic variable and then competes according to its selected variable in the second stage. In their model the dominant strategy is to select quantity, and this leads to the Cournot equilibrium.

These studies convince us that there is likely to be a range of real circumstances in which quantity, rather than price, will be chosen as the strategic variable. This in turn suggests a research agenda: rework address models using quantity competition. Here is one obvious example. In response to non-existence of price equilibrium in Hotelling's model, d'Aspremont, Gabszewicz and Thisse (1979) present a modified version of Hotelling's model in which the sequential equilibrium exhibits *maximum* differentiation. Is this result robust to competition in quantities? Will differentiation be less than optimal if competition is in quantities? We suspect the answers are "no" to the first question and "yes" to the second.

8. Multi-address firms

The great bulk of the literature on product differentiation in both large- and small-group situations has used the simplifying assumption of one-address firms. On a research agenda of tackling the easiest problems first, this is understandable. But awkward fact (4) states that the vast majority of real-world firms are multi-address, both in characteristic and geographic space. This is obvious in the consumers' goods sector – toiletries, tobacco products, refrigerators, automobiles, etc. The growth of retail chains has spread the same effect to the retail sector. For example, many single-outlet restaurants, which were the dominant form within living memory, have given way in the lower price range to such chains as

Macdonald's, Kentucky Fried Chicken, and the Dutch Oven. To come to grips with reality, the model needs to be extended to analyze multi-address firms.

One valuable step in this direction, using the non-address approach, has recently been taken by Brander and Eaton (1984). They deal with a model of four products. The pairs (1, 2) and (3,4) are close substitutes, while the pairs (1, 3), (1, 4), (2, 3), and (2, 4) are more distant substitutes as defined by cross-elasticities of demand. Because they use the goods-are-goods approach, they are able to use competition in quantities without difficulty.

The results are driven by the property that when two single-product firms compete, profits in equilibrium are lower the more substitutable are the two goods. As a result, a *segmented market structure*, with one firm producing products 1 and 2 and the other firm producing products 3 and 4, yields higher profits than an *interlaced market structure*, where each firm produces one good from the pair (1, 2) and one good from the pair (3, 4).

It follows immediately that when two firms enter the market sequentially choosing (by assumption) two products each, and knowing that no other firms will enter, the segmented structure will result. One firm will choose the pair (1, 2) while the other chooses (3, 4), thus minimizing the profit-reducing competition between them.

If firms are also allowed to choose the number of products they produce, the above result holds only for some intermediate levels of demand. At one extreme, demand may be so low that, if one firm chooses any one of the four products, the other would choose not to enter. This is a natural monopoly. At the other extreme, demand may be so great that, even if one firm chooses all four products, the other firm would still choose to enter. This will lead to an overlapping market structure. Only for intermediate levels of demand is segmentation the unique subgame perfect equilibrium.

Finally, if the two firms fear further entry, they may be led to select an interlaced, rather than a segmented, market structure. Since the interlaced market structure is more competitive and therefore discourages entry, it may result in higher duopoly profits than would result from the oligopoly that would evolve if the two firms encouraged entry by selecting a segmented structure. The general insight is that creating a more competitive n-firm situation may deter entry and result in higher profits for the n firms than the profit they would earn in any $n + 1$-firm free-entry equilibrium. Brander and Eaton's analysis leads to the conjecture that in a growing market, the natural evolution may be from monopoly, to a segmented duopoly, to an interlaced oligopoly.

Two earlier studies of multi-unit firms in address models are Schmalensee (1978) and Eaton and Lipsey (1979). Schmalensee studied a situation where a firm could deter entry by proliferating differentiated products so as to avoid presenting a new entrant with a market niche large enough to be profitable. The monopoly preemption result in our basic model of horizontal differentiation is a simple illustration of Schmalensee's argument.

Eaton and Lipsey analyzed a growing market initially large enough to support production at just one address. If the incumbent firm does not preempt the market, and if there are many potential entrants, then entry at a new address will occur at the point in time, T, when the present value of entry is zero. But the incumbent firm can deter entry by itself choosing a new address an instant before T. If the incumbent chooses the new address, the profit generated by the whole market will be larger (than if an entrant chooses the new address) for the simple reason that the incumbent will choose the new address, and the two prices, to maximize total profit. This implies that the incumbent will choose to deter entry. (The argument is similar to the one we used above in discussing the deterrence of predatory entry by premature replacement of sunk capital.)

Judd (1985) has pointed out that these preemption arguments neglect to consider the possibility that a new entrant, who would find entry unprofitable *given* the existing occupied addresses, might still be able to enter by inducing the incumbent to vacate one or more addresses – a strategy of predatory entry.

To see what is involved, consider a market of unit length with uniform customer density. Suppose that if firm 1 were to locate at two addresses, 1/4 and 3/4, an entrant which took these locations as given could not cover its costs, which are composed of a constant marginal cost and a cost of entry. Suppose also that two firms could cover their costs if one of them was located at 1/4 and the other at 3/4.

Now suppose that a first firm considering entering at locations 1/4 and 3/4 anticipates the possibility of predatory entry. We consider three cases in which the original firm is at 1/4 and 3/4 and the new firm at 1/4.

Case 1: Competition in prices. Competition in prices would drive price down to marginal cost at 1/4, and the incumbent would earn zero gross profit from his address at 1/4. Price would, of course, exceed marginal cost at 3/4 and the market boundary would be at some point to the right of 1/2. If firm 1 were to abandon its address at 1/4, the prices at 1/4 and 3/4 would both rise and the market boundary would be at 1/2. Hence, firm 1's profit would increase. Foreseeing this result, one would not attempt the (1/4, 3/4) preemption strategy.

Case 2: Cooperative pricing. Now suppose that post-entry pricing is cooperative. (Firm 1 could induce cooperative pricing if it could credibly announce a price-following strategy – "we will not knowingly be undersold" is, for example, a stated policy of some well-known retailers.) The prices at 1/4 and 3/4 are now identical regardless of whether there are two or one plants at address 1/4. In this case, firm 1 would not abandon address 1/4. Knowing this, there would be no predatory entry and the (1/4, 3/4) preemption strategy works.

Case 3: Competition in quantities. In this case, the predatory entry strategy might or might not induce firm 1 to abandon address 1/4. If the cross-elasticities between the goods at the two addresses are high enough, it would. If they are low enough, it would not. The $(1/4, 3/4)$ preemption strategy may or may not be profitable to firm 1.

Thus, the possibility raised by Judd of predatory entry in these preemptive models means that the obvious preemption strategy of locating plants at $1/4$ and $3/4$ may or may not be subgame perfect, depending on how fierce is post-entry competition. Of course, there may be other preemption strategies which are subgame perfect, even when competition is in prices. Consider, for example, the preemptive strategy of locating two plants at 0 and at 1. If competition is in prices, an entrant could induce firm 1 to abandon one of these addresses, but there may be no address for the entrant which both induces firm 1 to abandon an address and also offers the entrant positive profit in the ensuing duopoly equilibrium.[3]

9. Product diversity and economic policy

Rational economic policy requires an understanding of the welfare issues which arise in the context of differentiated products. The model using the representative consumer has the advantage of being tractable. Welfare results are easily derived from it. However, tractability in deriving incorrect results is no advantage, and we do know that in address models, whenever preferences are single peaked in (θ, p) space, aggregate consumer behavior cannot be caught by a representative consumer. Thus, it seems to us that while there may be cases for which the representative-consumer approach is appropriate, there are many problems for which an address model seems appropriate. Nothing can be learned about these problems from representative-consumer, or Chamberlinian models, since they do not capture all of the awkward facts.

Similar remarks apply to Chamberlin-style models that employ the symmetry assumption, even when they are rooted in individual taste differences, since these models appear to be inconsistent with awkward (6). So if the address model characterization of consumers' behavior captures important aspects of reality, there is no reason to believe welfare propositions derived from either of these approaches. For people interested in giving policy advice relevant to the bulk of manufacturing industries that sell differentiated goods this is a serious matter.

[3]In contrast to the rich set of possibilities considered in the text, Judd appears to claim that multi-address preemption is never subgame perfect. In his model, where curiously there are no addresses, just two goods, the claim is driven by his assumption that firm 1's revenue from plants at $1/4$ and $3/4$ when firm 2 also has a plant at $1/4$ is less than its revenue from one plant at $3/4$ while 2's single plant is at $1/4$. This amounts to solving the preemption issue by assumption: since predatory entry is assumed always to work, preemption is never subgame perfect.

Notice that the standard market failure associated with the divergence of price from marginal cost necessarily arises in markets for differentiated products whenever demand is not perfectly price inelastic. Market failure is a ubiquitous problem in address models with balkanization and localized competition since in free-entry equilibrium the position of each product is very much like the standard stylization of a natural monopoly. If the standard natural monopoly problem is difficult to solve in practice, the natural monopoly problem in address models is much more so since it is a pervasive problem.

In addition, the problem of optimal product diversity arises. This is, we believe, an even more difficult problem – one that, from a policy perspective, we know very little about. Our basic address model is a useful device for conveying the awkward nature of this problem since the only optimality issue is diversity. We showed in our discussion of that model that there is no general relationship between product diversity in free-entry equilibrium and optimal product diversity. However, it is clear that the diversity observed in free-entry equilibrium is unlikely to be the optimum amount. Even if the optimum diversity is a free-entry equilibrium, there are many other free-entry equilibria and no market force which pushes the equilibrium to the optimum. The awkward problem is that we do not even know the nature of the bias – whether there is likely to be too much or too little diversity in equilibrium.

If we interpret the basic model as a model of spatial competition, it is conceivable that one could discover at a modest cost all of the data necessary to determine optimal diversity. The principal difficulty concerns transport costs, the function $T(D)$ in the model. Where transport costs are out-of-pocket costs, it is not an overwhelming task to estimate the transport cost function. Where, however, $T(D)$ reflects the opportunity cost of shoppers' time, as in the retail sector, and especially where there is diversity over shoppers' opportunity costs, the task is far from trivial. There are also additional difficult issues concerning multi-purpose shopping. The point is that, even in this relatively simple environment, it is not obvious that we would recognize an optimum if we saw one. Even assuming that we could recognize one (that we could compute the optimum), the presence in any real situation of sunk capital implies that the optimal policy program which takes the market from an initial situation to the optimum is quite complex.

When we interpret the basic model as a model of differentiation in some characteristics space, we believe that we would be quite unable to recognize an optimum if we saw one. In this case $T(D)$ refers to a utility cost associated with the divergence of the characteristics of the best available good from the individual consumer's most preferred bundle of characteristics. Now we face the problem of recovering preferences from observed market behavior. In our basic model this is not an impossibly difficult task – we could, for example, imagine an experiment in which we systematically varied the price of one or more products. Provided that consumers did not play strategic games, the experiment would generate sufficient data for us to discover $T(D)$. There is, of course, no reason to believe that consumers' preferences are diverse in only one dimension, the most preferred good. In the basic model, the function $T(D)$ might very well be consumer specific. In this case, any experiment that would allow us to discover preferences would be far from trivial. It seems clear, however, that experimentation would be necessary in either case – we could not discover preferences from the data revealed in free-entry equilibrium.

The phenomenon of preemption via product proliferation has been raised as a real policy issue in an action by the U.S. Federal Trade Commission [see Schmalensee (1978]. From our perspective, the issue is whether or not this sort of preemptive activity is or is not anti-social. We can use the insights generated by Brander and Eaton (1983) to articulate, but not to answer, the question. Where prices are endogenous, the fewer the number of firms that engage in preemptive product proliferation, the higher will be the welfare losses associated with the divergence of price from marginal cost, but the greater will be actual product diversity. For example, the number of products necessary for a monopolist to preempt entry exceeds the number necessary for duopolists to preempt entry. Whether monopoly preemption is more socially desirable than some other free-entry equilibrium then depends on whether or not the added diversity associated with monopoly preemption outweighs the conventional welfare loss associated with non-competitive pricing. And so on. Thus, the question is well defined. The difficult problem concerns the discovery of consumers' preferences.

There is one exception to these disturbing results. In "large economies" equilibrium is (at least approximately) optimal when all goods are substitutes. See Hart (1979) and Jones (1987) for general results and Eaton and Wooders (1985) for results in an address model. We can illustrate what we mean by a "large economy" in the context of the simple address model we have used throughout the chapter. In that model we can create a large economy by letting the density of customers go to infinity, or by letting the product development cost, I, go to zero. With endogenous prices, prices of all firms approach marginal cost and the number of goods gets arbitrarily large in either asymptotic experiment. Hence, in the limit, every consumer is able to purchase his or her most preferred good at marginal cost. These results raise an important question: How large is large enough, and is this much "largeness" commonly – or ever – encountered empirically?

10. An historical postscript

A brief outline of some of the key points in the historical development of models of product differentiation may help to put the material discussed in this paper into perspective. Before discussing Figure 12.4, which systematizes the main points, we stress that we do not have space to give credit to all of the main

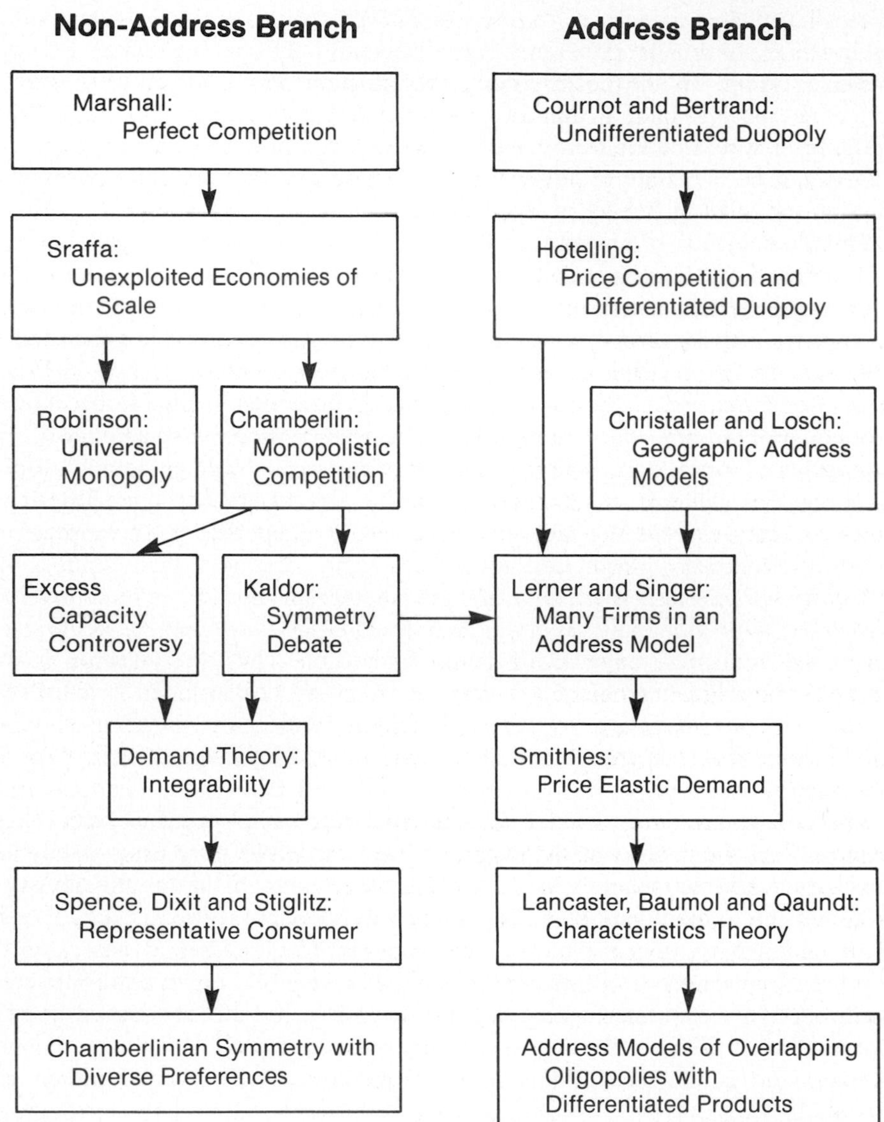

Figure 12.4. Historical perspective.

contributors. Our concern is with the flow of ideas, and we mention names only as illustrative benchmarks.

The left-hand side of the chart shows the development of the large group case of product differentiation. Shortly after the death of Alfred Marshall, Sraffa (1926) pointed out the inconsistency between the observed facts of unexploited scale economies in many manufacturing industries and the Marshallian theory of perfect competition, where all scale economies must be exhausted in long-run equilibrium.

Chamberlin (1933) and Robinson (1934) responded to Sraffa's challenge. Robinson assumed a single monopolist in each industry. Although her work greatly clarified the theory of monopoly, it proved to be a dead end as a response to Sraffa's point. Instead, the way was pointed by Chamberlin. In his theory, a large group of competitive firms, each producing one differentiated product and operating under conditions of free entry, produced an equilibrium where each firm's output was less than minimum efficient scale. The theory was a triumph in making a small amendment – differentiated products – to Marshall's theory of perfect competition, which then reconciled competitive theory with the empirical observation of unexploited economies of scale.

Ironically, the reason for its triumph soon became the greatest cause of concern about the theory. It resolved Sraffa's problem by showing that something very close to perfect competition could be consistent with the observation of unexploited scale economies. However, the presence of unexploited economies of scale, which became known as the excess capacity theorem, gave rise to innumerable controversies in response to its apparent implication of free-market inefficiency.

The controversy over the alleged adverse welfare implications of the excess capacity theorem finally faded away when it became understood that, in a society that values diversity, there is a trade-off between economizing on resources, by reducing the costs of producing existing products, and satisfying the desire for diversity, by increasing the number of products. The optimum diversity occurs when existing products are produced at points to the left of the minimum-efficient scale – therefore, "excess capacity" is *not* necessarily socially inefficient.[4]

A second, and quite different, strand of criticism of monopolistic competition was developed largely by Kaldor (1934, 1935). He attacked Chamberlin's symmetry assumption which made competition *generalized* in that, within one industry no firm had "near neighbors" who bore the main effects of any change in its behavior, and "distant" neighbors who bore smaller effects. Given symmetry, free entry would drive profits to zero (or at least to the small positive amount allowed by the integer problem). Kaldor argued that, although products at one end of the

[4]Bishop (1967) analyzed this issue in a Chamberlinian model. Lancaster (1979) does so in a characteristics model.

product spectrum in a given industry would be close substitutes for each other, they would be poor substitutes for those at the other end of the spectrum. He was intuitively working with an address model where goods are located in some appropriate space of characteristics. He saw competition as *localized*, even within an industry, and argued for a model of overlapping oligopolies rather than for a model of generalized intra-industry competition.[5]

Chamberlin, himself, did make a brief excursion into the area of small numbers competition and the short section on "mutual interdependence recognized" was at the time an original contribution to that theory. Furthermore, Chamberlin (1951) accepted Kaldor's arguments against the symmetry assumption. Nonetheless, his theory of large group competition had by then taken on a life of its own due to the extended and heated nature of the debates mentioned above.

By the 1960s, decreasing attention was being paid to the Chamberlinian model of monopolistic competition. Two reasons are worth mentioning. First, the realization slowly took hold that virtually all industries containing a multitude of differentiated products contained only a few firms [awkward fact (4)]. [See, for example, Markham (1964).] Thus, although the typical, real-world set of differentiated products was a large group, the typical set of competing firms was a small group. Second, growth of interest in location theory showed that localized, rather than generalized, competition was also common in many industries where firms are differentiated by their geographic location. Although, for example, there are many drugstores in a city, each has a few nearby, and many more-distant, neighbors. Here again a model of overlapping oligopolies, rather than one of symmetrically situated monopolistic competitors, seemed more appropriate.

The 1970s saw a revival of interest in all aspects of product differentiation. This was no doubt partly due to the experience of both the EEC countries after the signing of the treaty of Rome and of the GAAT participants during the Kennedy round of tariff reductions. Specialization following on these major tariff cuts among countries of roughly similar per capita incomes did not cause whole industries to close down in some countries and to expand greatly in others. Instead, in each existing industry in each country firms found product niches in which they could compete. So specialization took the form of a reduction of product lines in each country with great expansion of intra-industry, international trade. The increased production runs in each differentiated product afforded substantial reductions in unit costs. As a result the gains from specialization turned out to be substantially more than had been estimated from older constant-cost models of inter-industry specialization.

The outburst of theorizing in demand theory in the 1960s assisted the revival of interest in Chamberlin's model. Ever since the event of the "new welfare

[5]For a survey of all of the aspects of the debate up to 1960 – which is close to the time when the debate subsided – see Archibald (1961).

economics" in the 1940s, economists had worried about the construction of a community welfare function that could be derived from individual utility functions. In the 1960s the integrability literature showed, with standards of rigor not demanded in the 1940s, that under certain specific conditions, the community's demand behavior, and the welfare of its individuals, could be captured in a single community utility function.

In the 1970s Spence (1976a, b), and Dixit and Stiglitz (1977), developed models of monopolistic competition that used the concept of the representative consumer. A further development came with the models of Ferguson (1983), Sattinger (1984), Hart (1985) and Perloff and Salop (1985) who assumed different consumers with different tastes and then generated models of monopolistic competition that displayed the symmetry property.

To understand the development of small group competition with differentiated products we need to begin with Cournot's model of quantity competition between oligopolists producing identical products. Then came Bertrand's formulation of the alternative of price competition showing that non-cooperative behavior would drive price to marginal cost. Bertrand's critique of Cournot opened an important issue that still faces us: What conditions will favor the use of price or quantity as the strategic variable for oligopolistic competition?

The seminal article for the development of theories of competition among oligopolists producing differentiated products was Hotelling's (1929) address branch model. Address models of geographic location trace their lineage to the fundamental work of Christaller (1933) and Losch (1938). Hotelling's starting point was Bertrand's critique of Cournot. He made a crucial change of assumption by letting his duopolists compete to sell a differentiated rather than a homogeneous product.

Hotelling showed that when two competing firms were differentiated from each other, either by having different geographic locations or by producing products differentiated in some one-dimensional characteristics space, price competition could leave price high enough to cover capital costs, thus yielding a stable, long-run equilibrium. Lerner and Singer (1941) expanded Hotelling's model by increasing the number of firms beyond two. Smithies (1941) considered the consequence of altering Hotelling's restrictive demand assumption. Thirty years after its publication, however, only a modest amount of work could trace its lineage back to Hotelling's approach.

As with the other strand, a renewed interest in the address models of product differentiation was aided by developments in demand theory. The model developed by Lancaster (1966) and Quandt and Baumol (1966), in which consumers' preferences are defined over characteristics which themselves are embodied in goods, provided a structure in which the firm's decisions concerning product differentiation could be meaningfully analyzed. The following year Baumol (1967) studied a producer's optimal product design and observed that the new characteristic models provided "a promising approach to a problem that seems previously to have appeared to be intractable". Address models of competition among firms selling differentiated goods first concentrated on a proposition that had been developed from a variant of Hotelling's model, a proposition which Boulding (1966) christened the principle of minimum differentiation. [See Eaton and Lipsey (1975).] In response to that paper, Prescott and Visscher (1977) and Hay (1976) took up the issue of foresightful entry and interest quickly spread to many other issues as well.

References

Anderson, S.P., de Palma, A. and Thisse, J.F. (1988) 'A representative consumer theory of the logit model', *International Economic Review*, 29, forthcoming.

Archibald, G.C. (1961) 'Chamberlin *versus* Chicago', *Review of Economic Studies*, 29:1–28.

Archibald, G.C. and Eaton, B.C. (1988) 'Two applications of characteristics theory', in: G. Fiewel, ed., *Essays in memory of Joan Robinson*. London: MacMillan.

Archibald, G.C. and Rosenbluth, G. (1975) 'The 'new' theory of consumer demand and monopolistic competition', *Quarterly Journal of Economics*, 80:569–590.

Archibald, G.C., Eaton, B.C. and Lipsey, R.G. (1986) 'Address models of value theory', in: J.E. Stiglitz and G.F. Mathewson, eds., *New developments in the analysis of market structure*. Cambridge: MIT Press, 3–47.

Baumol, W.J. (1967) 'Calculation of optimal product and retailer characteristics: The abstract product approach', *Journal of Political Economy*, 75:674–685.

Bishop, R.L. (1967) 'Monopolistic competition and welfare economics', in: R. Kuenne, ed., *Monopolistic competitive theory: Studies in impact*. New York: Wiley, 251–263.

Bonnano, G. (1986) 'Vertical differentiation with Cournot competition', *Economic Notes*, 2:68–91.

Boulding, K. (1966) *Economic analysis*. New York: Harper.

Brander, J.A. and Eaton, J. (1984) 'Product line rivalry', *American Economic Review*, 74:323–326.

Chamberlin, E.H. (1933) *The theory of monopolistic competition*. Cambridge: Harvard University Press.

Chamberlin, E.H. (1951) 'Monopolistic competition revisited', *Economica*, 18:343–355.

Christaller, W. (1933) *Die zentralen Orte in Suddeutschland: Eine okonomisch-geographische Untersuchung uber die Gesetzmassigkeit der Verbrietung und Entwicklung der Siedlungen mit stadtischen Funktionen*. Jena: Fischer.

d'Aspremont, C., Gabszewicz, J.J. and Thisse, J.F. (1979) 'On 'Hotelling's stability in competition'', *Econometrica*, 47:1145–1150.

Deneckere, R. and Davidson, C. (1985) 'Incentives to form coalitions with Bertrand competition', *Rand Journal of Economics*, 16:473–486.

Deneckere, R. and Rothschild, M. (1986) 'Monopolistic competition and optimum preference diversity', discussion paper no. 684, Northwestern University.

Dixit, A.K. and Stiglitz, J.E. (1977) 'Monopolistic competition and optimum product diversity', *American Economic Review*, 67:297–308.

Eaton, B.C. and Lipsey, R.G. (1975) 'The principle of minimum differentiation reconsidered: Some new developments in the theory of spatial competition', *Review of Economic Studies*, 42:27–49.

Eaton, B.C. and Lipsey, R.G. (1976) 'The non-uniqueness of equilibrium in the Loschian location model', *American Economic Review*, 66:77–93.

Eaton, B.C. and Lipsey, R.G. (1978) 'Freedom of entry and the existence of pure profit', *Economic Journal*, 88:455–469.

Eaton, B.C. and Lipsey, R.G. (1979) 'The theory of market preemption: The persistence of excess capacity and monopoly in growing spatial markets', *Economica*, 46:149–158.

Eaton, B.C. and Lipsey, R.G. (1980) 'Exit barriers are entry barriers: The durability of capital as a barrier to entry', *Bell Journal of Economics*, 11:721–729.

Eaton, B.C. and Wooders, M.H. (1985) 'Sophisticated entry in a model of spatial competition', *Rand Journal of Economics*, 16:282–297.
Ferguson (1983) 'On the theory of demand for differentiated goods', University of Victoria, mimeo.
Gabszewicz, J.J. and Thisse, J.F. (1979) 'Price competition, quality and income disparities', *Journal of Economic Theory*, 20:340–359.
Gabszewicz, J.J. and Thisse, J.F. (1980) 'Entry (and exit) in a differentiated industry', *Journal of Economic Theory*, 22:327–338.
Gabszewicz, J.J. and Thisse, J. (1986) 'On the nature of competition with differentiated products', *Economic Journal*, 96:160–172.
Hart, O.D. (1979) 'Monopolistic competition in a large economy with differentiated commodities', *Review of Economic Studies*, 46:1–30.
Hart, O.D. (1985) 'Monopolistic competition in the spirit of Chamberlin: Special results', *Economic Journal*, 95:889–908.
Hay, D.A. (1976) 'Sequential entry and entry-deterring strategies in spatial competition', *Oxford Economic Papers*, 28:240–257.
Hotelling, H. (1929) 'Stability in competition', *Economic Journal*, 39:41–57.
Jones, L.E. (1987) 'The efficiency of monopolistically competition equilibria in large economies: Commodity differentiation with gross substitutes', *Journal of Economic Theory*, 41:356–391.
Judd, K.L. (1985) 'Credible spatial preemption', *Rand Journal of Economics*, 16:153–166.
Kaldor, N. (1934) 'Mrs. Robinson's 'economics of imperfect competition'', *Economica*, 1:335–341.
Kaldor, N. (1935) 'Market imperfections and excess capacity', *Economica*, 2:33–50.
Koenker, R.W. and Perry, M.K. (1981) 'Product differentiation, monopolistic competition, and public policy', *Bell Journal of Economics*, 12:217–231.
Kreps, D.M. and Scheinkman, J.A. (1983) 'Quantity precommitment and Bertrand competition yield Cournot outcomes', *Bell Journal of Economics*, 14:326–337.
Lancaster, K.J. (1966) 'A new approach to consumer theory', *Journal of Political Economy*, 74:132–157.
Lancaster, K.J. (1979) *Variety, equity, and efficiency*'. New York: Columbia University Press.
Lane, W. (1980) 'Product differentiation in a market with endogenous sequential entry', *Bell Journal of Economics*, 11:237–260.
Lerner, A. and Singer, H. (1941) 'Some notes on duopoly and spatial competition', *Journal of Political Economy*, 45:423–439.
Losch, A. (1938) 'The nature of economic regions', *Southern Economic Journal*, 5:71–78.
Markham, J.W. (1964) 'The theory of monopolistic competition after thirty years', *American Economic Review*, 54:53–55.
Novshek, W. (1980) 'Equilibrium in simple spatial (or differentiated product) models', *Journal of Economic Theory*, 22:313–326.
Perloff, J.M. and Salop, S.C. (1985) 'Equilibrium with product differentiation', *Review of Economic Studies*, 52:107–120.
Prescott, E.C. and Visscher, M. (1977) 'Sequential location among firms with foresight', *Bell Journal of Economics*, 8:378–393.
Quandt, R.E. and Baumol, W.J. (1966) 'The demand for abstract transport modes: Theory and measurement', *Journal Regional Science*, 6:13–26.
Robinson, J. (1934) *The economics of imperfect competition*. London: Macmillan.
Salant, D.J. (1986) 'Equilibrium in a spatial model of imperfect competition with sequential choice of locations and quantities', *Canadian Journal of Economics*, 19:685–715.
Salop, S. (1979) 'Monopolistic competition with outside goods', *Bell Journal of Economics*, 10:141–156.
Sattinger, M. (1984) 'Value of an additional firm in monopolistic competition', *Review of Economic Studies*, 51:321–3332.
Schmalensee, R. (1978) 'Entry deterrence in the ready-to-eat breakfast cereal industry', *Bell Journal of Economics*, 9:305–327.
Schmalensee, R. (1983) 'Econometric diagnosis of competitive localization', working paper no. 1390-83, MIT.
Shaked, A. and Sutton, J. (1982) 'Relaxing price competition through product differentiation', *Review of Economic Studies*, 49:3–13.
Shaked, A. and Sutton, J. (1983) 'Natural oligopolies', *Econometrica*, 51(5):1469–1483.

Singh, N. and Vives, X. (1984) 'Price and quantity competition in a differentiated duopoly', *Rand Journal of Economics*, 15:546–554.

Smithies, A. (1941) 'Optimum location in spatial competition', *Journal of Political Economy*, 49:423–439.

Spence, A.M. (1976a) 'Product selection, fixed costs, and monopolistic competition', *Review of Economic Studies*, 43:217–235.

Spence, A.M. (1976b) 'Product differentiation and welfare', *American Economic Review*, 66:407–414.

Sraffa, P. (1926) 'The laws of returns under competitive conditions', *Economic Journal*, 34:535–550.

Chapter 13

IMPERFECT INFORMATION IN THE PRODUCT MARKET

JOSEPH E. STIGLITZ*

Princeton University and NBER

Contents

*Financial support from the National Science Foundation, The John M. Olin Foundation, and the Hoover Institution is gratefully acknowledged. This chapter is not intended as a comprehensive survey of what has become a voluminous literature. Rather, it is my objective to present a simple exposition of some of the major underlying themes. For a survey of the search literature, see, for instance, Lippman and McCall (1976). Several of the specific models presented here have not been published elsewhere, while the presentation of other models, in particular, the Salop–Stiglitz "Bargains and Ripoffs" (1977) model differs substantially from the published version. I am deeply indebted to Steve Salop with whom I have worked closely on the questions under discussion here. His influence should be apparent.

Handbook of Industrial Organization, Volume I, Edited by R. Schmalensee and R.D. Willig

PART I

1. Introduction and overview

In traditional competitive theory, each firm is a price taker. Each firm (and its customers) has perfect information concerning prices: if it attempts to charge more than the market price, it will lose all of its customers. Similarly, its customers have precise information concerning the nature of the commodities which it sells: if it attempts to cheat them by lowering the quality by even a little bit, it is immediately caught.

The theory describing the processes by which market prices are reached is much less well developed than the theory describing what the equilibrium prices are. Most commonly, reference is made to the Walrasian auctioneer, who calls off prices, with customers and producers passively responding with their demands and supplies.

In most markets, there is no Walrasian auctioneer, nor anyone who even vaguely resembles him. Firms set their prices. Yet this fact is not, in itself, necessarily a telling criticism: markets may act as if firms were price takers, and adjustments to disturbances might well occur as they would if there were a Walrasian auctioneer. Indeed, the Walrasian auctioneer has long been thought of as a convenient fiction.

It is our contention that in many instances, this traditional view is fundamentally incomplete, incorrect and misleading. It is incomplete, in the sense that there are many aspects of the market which it simply fails to explain; it is incorrect, in that its predictions concerning the behavior of the market are often wrong; and it is misleading, in that it often leads to policy prescriptions of dubious validity.

Among the predictions of the traditional theory are that a given commodity is sold at the same price by all stores (the Law of the Single Price); that price differences for "similar" commodities simply reflect differences in qualities (including difficult to measure differences in service qualities); and that cost increases (such as those associated with a specific tax) are passed along to consumers.[1] These, as well as the underlying assumption that firms face horizontal demand curves for their products are empirically testable propositions. Do firms believe that they face a horizontal demand schedule? Do consumers believe that price differences simply reflect differences in qualities, that there are no bargains to be had? Do prices respond quickly to cost changes in the way predicted by the theory? This chapter is not concerned with the literature attempting to test these propositions; rather, it begins with the presumption that

[1]Assuming a constant returns to scale technology (horizontal supply curve). In other cases, they are partially passed along.

these empirical predictions of the theory are not true.[2] We trace the disparity between the traditional paradigm's predictions and what is observed to that paradigm's failure to recognize that information is imperfect and costly. Though all would recognize that there are some costs of information, believers in the traditional paradigm argue that the market works in the manner described by that paradigm, provided only that there are enough individuals who are well informed. These well-informed individuals engage in arbitrage activities, ensuring that all stores charge the same prices for the same commodities, and that the price they charge is the competitive price (the marginal cost of production).[3]

We show here that the above view is not well founded. We show that the presence of imperfect and costly information gives firms market power; that well-informed individuals (individuals who have low costs of information acquisition) may indeed confer some externality on others, by ensuring that there are some low price stores, but that there will remain high price stores attempting to take advantage of the ill-informed consumer. In such situations, the theory of perfect competition is no longer relevant; some variant of a theory of monopolistic competition is required.

On the other hand, one simply cannot borrow the traditional theories of imperfect competition to analyze markets where the cause of the limitations on competition is costly information. For instance, changes in the number of firms (what might be thought of as an increase in the degree of competition) may have markedly different effects than those predicted by traditional theories of imperfect competition. If there are many firms, if any single firm lowers its price, it will not induce much search, and thus it may have limited incentives for lowering its price. On the other hand, if there are very few firms, if any one of them lowers its price, it may induce a considerable amount of search. This suggests that markets with duopolies or with a limited number of firms may be more competitive than markets with a large number of firms. The validity of this intuition turns out to be somewhat sensitive to the precise specification of the information or search structure of the model; although at least in some simple models this intuitive argument is not quite correct, it should at least serve to remind us that the relationship between the number of firms and the degree of competition is far more subtle and complicated than suggested, for instance, by Cournot's earlier analysis.

Not only does imperfect information result in firms having market power, with the degree of market power related to the number of firms in a possibly quite complicated way: we show further that under a variety of circumstances, the market will be characterized by a price distribution. The Law of the Single Price is repealed.

[2]See Pratt, Weiss and Zeckhauser (1979) and Scitovsky (1976) for a discussion of some of the evidence on price distributions.

[3]Thus, these "arbitrageurs" ensure that the market acts *as if* everyone were perfectly informed.

Furthermore, we argue that the Walrasian auctioneer provides an inappropriate model of adjustment.[4] We show that imperfect information gives rise to price rigidities, so that under certain circumstances markets simply fail to respond to certain kinds of disturbances (which would, under the conventional theory, lead to marked price changes). This aspect of the theory may play a role in explaining the price rigidities which are central to understanding certain macro-economic phenomena.

Imperfect information in product markets has further consequences on the qualities and varieties of commodities produced. Firms must have an incentive for producting high quality products, for not cheating their customers; in many (most) cases, individuals do not observe the quality of what they purchase until after they have purchased it. An examination of the consequences of this – including the mechanisms by which quality is assured – is one of the subjects surveyed in this chapter, as are the consequences for the variety of commodities produced.

Consumers obtain information in a variety of ways. Most of this chapter is concerned with information that individuals obtain through deliberate activities to become more informed, through search. Some of the information is obtained as a by-product of other activities – the dissemination of information through social contact – and we discuss this too. Finally, some of the information they obtain is the result of deliberate activities on the part of firms to inform consumers, through advertising. Advertising is an important economic activity, with over 2 percent of GNP being spent on it in recent years. Yet, I would argue that most of this expenditure does not fit neatly within the economists' model, neither that which assumes fully informed individuals with well defined tastes, nor the one (with which we shall be concerned here) which assumes uninformed consumers (with well-defined tastes.) Advertising may have more to say about economists' approach to the theory of consumers' behavior than economists have to say about advertising! These are issues to which we turn in Part II.

1.1. Methodological remarks

As is so often the case in economics, our analysis is partly an enquiry into how economic models work, and partly an enquiry into how the economy functions. In the preceding paragraph, we have suggested that the traditional competitive paradigm, with fully informed consumers, should be rejected because it generates empirical predictions of dubious validity. Another criterion by which a theory is to be judged is its robustness. Thus, one of our objectives is to explore how robust the standard competitive paradigm is to the introduction of imperfect information: we show that it is in fact not very robust; slight modifications of the

[4] This is perhaps an unfair criticism: no one probably took the tantamount process seriously.

standard model result in the non-existence of the market equilibrium; alternative modifications result in the market equilibrium price being the monopoly price or in market equilibrium being characterized by a price dispersion.

Though we may not fully believe some of these conclusions – is the market equilibrium price the monopoly price, even with arbitrarily small search costs? – they convey an important message: market prices may well be significantly above marginal costs, even when there are a large number of firms; and an examination of the assumptions underlying these results may provide us with considerable insights, not only into the workings of the model, but also into the workings of the economy.

Skeptics may ask: Are not the issues we are raising here second order refinements of the basic theory? Is it not still true that if demand increases, price will increase? If costs increase, price will increase? Are not the basic lessons of economics, of, say, the law of supply and demand still valid? I hope to persuade the reader that the concerns raised here are not in fact second order refinements but first order effects. Not only is the traditional theory unable to explain certain important phenomena (such as the central role of price discrimination – which in the standard perfectly competitive paradigm can play no role at all – or the persistence of price distributions); but changes in parameters (e.g. costs of production) may have markedly different effects than those predicted by the perfectly competitive paradigm. Moreover, the welfare consequences may differ markedly. Markets with imperfect information are, in general, not even constrained Pareto efficient, that is they are not efficient even when we take into account the costs of information.[5] Unfortunately, we cannot pursue these welfare questions (and the associated questions of the appropriate policy interventions) in this chapter. The theory developed here does, however, provide the basis of a Theory of Consumer Protection.

1.2. On the use of derived demand curves

Information is exchanged between consumers and firms in a variety of ways. Individual consumers find out about prices, qualities, and locations where products can be obtained both through systematic search activities (by visiting stores and shopping centers, by reading newspapers, etc.) and as a by-product of other activities (talking to their friends). Stores try to convey information to potential customers by a variety of advertising media. For most of this chapter, we focus on models in which information is obtained as a result of customers' activities, not through firm advertising.

[5]See Greenwald and Stiglitz (1986).

Even within this more narrowly defined range of information acquisition processes, a large number of alternatives remain – with often different consequences. We begin by reviewing several simple models and then attempt to synthesize from these models the general lessons to be learned. In each case, we ask how the presence of imperfect information affects the demand curves facing the firm. Thus, while the traditional model may not be appropriate for analyzing most markets for consumer goods, it provides us with an indispensable tool for interpreting what is going on in the market.

When imperfect information results in the demand curve becoming less than infinitely elastic, it implies that imperfect information confers a degree of monopoly power on the stores [Figure 13.1(a)].. When a store raises its price a little, it does not lose all of its customers; when it lowers it a little, it does not get the entire market. When, by lowering the price a little, the store recruits no additional customers, then the equilibrium price will be the monopoly price [Figure 13.11(b)]. When, under the hypothesis that all firms charge the same price, there is a kink in the demand curve, as depicted in Figure 13.1(c) (where the elasticity with respect to price decreases exceeds that with respect to price increases), then there cannot exist an equilibrium in which all firms charge the same price. For assume there were a zero profit (Nash) equilibrium. As should be apparent, firm profits would then be increased either by lowering or raising prices. Such kinks should not come as a surprise: there is a natural asymmetry of information – the consumer knows the price of the store that he is at; he does not know the prices of stores that he is not at. Contrast the effects of a single store deviating from an equilibrium in which all stores charge the same price, either by raising or by lowering its price. When a single store raises its price, the costs of finding one of the multitude of low price stores for an individual who has the bad fortune of arriving at the high price store is relatively low, and hence it is plausible that the firm faces a relatively elastic response to price increases. On the other hand, if a firm lowers its price, the cost of finding that one low price firm – the needle in the haystack – may be relatively high. But while relatively few individuals at each of the rival stores may be induced to search, there are many stores from which the firm which has lowered its price can recruit customers. Thus, it is possible that the increase in demand to a price decrease be either greater or less than the decrease in demand to a price increase. Figure 13.1(c) illustrates the case where the elasticity of demand with respect to price decreases exceeds that with respect to price increases.

By contrast, Figure 13.1(d) illustrates the case where, under the hypothesis that all firms charge the same price, there is a kink in the demand curve, with the elasticity with respect to price decreases being less than that with respect to price increases. It is under these circumstances that the market will exhibit the kind of price rigidity, with its important macro-economic implications, to which I alluded earlier. Since there is a discontinuity in the marginal revenue schedule, small

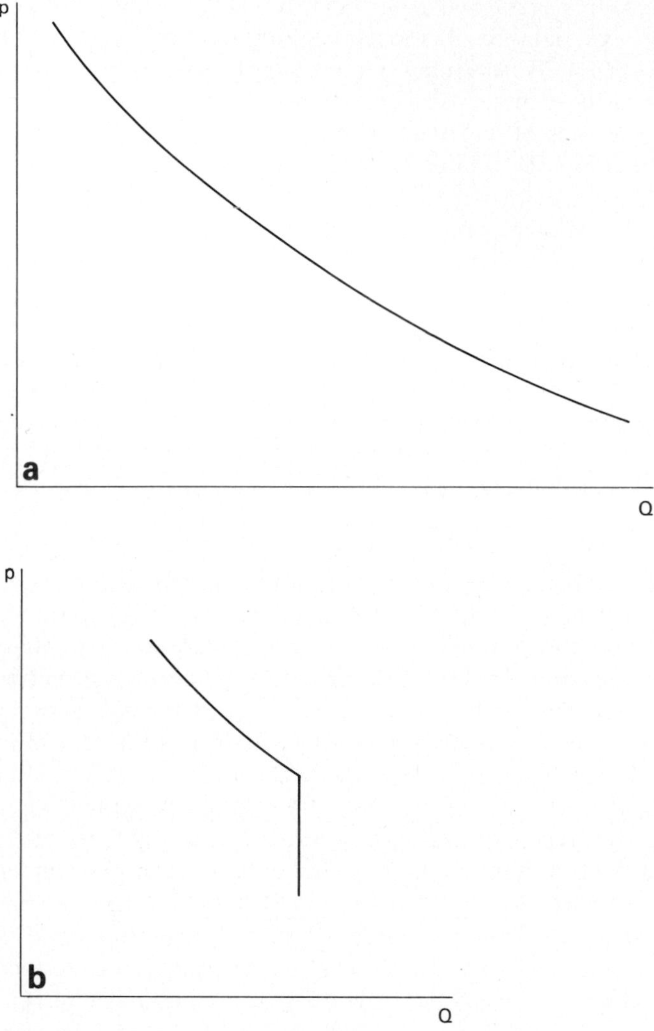

Figure 13.1. (a) Imperfect information may reduce the demand elasticity facing a firm. It no longer perceives itself as facing a horizontal demand curve, as in the standard competitive paradigm. (b) In some limiting cases, the firm recruits no new customers when it lowers its price. (c) In some cases, when all firms charge the same price, the demand curve facing any firm has a kink, with the elasticity of demand for price decreases exceeding that for price increases. It is clear that, under these circumstances, there cannot exist a zero profit single price equilibrium. Profits would be increased if any firm either increased or decreased its price. (d) In some cases, when all firms charge the same price, the demand curve facing any firm may have a kink, with the elasticity of demand for price increases exceeding that for price decreases. (e) In some cases, when all firms charge the same price, the demand curve facing any firm may have a discontinuity. Again, under these circumstances, there cannot exist a zero profit single price (Nash) equilibrium, except at a price equal to minimum average cost.

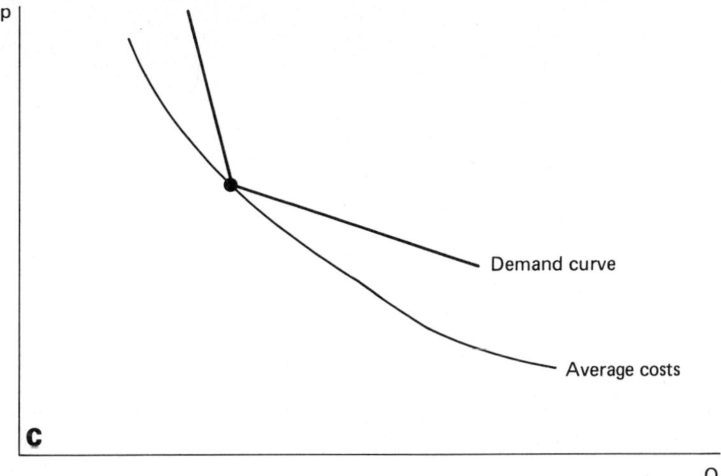

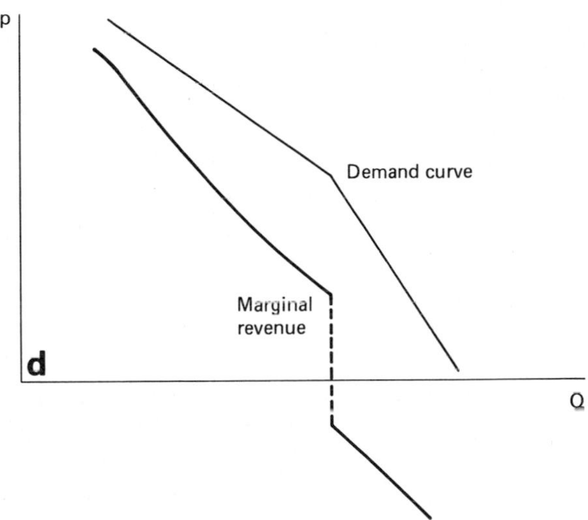

Figure 13.1. *Continued.*

changes in the marginal cost of production will give rise to no changes in output or price.

If there is a discontinuity in the demand curve [Figure 13.1(e)] – if all other firms charge the same price and it lowers its price, its demand increases discretely – then the only single price equilibrium must be at a price equal to the minimum average cost.

One of our objectives then is to ascertain the conditions under which demand curves of each of these forms is generated. Most of the analysis of this chapter

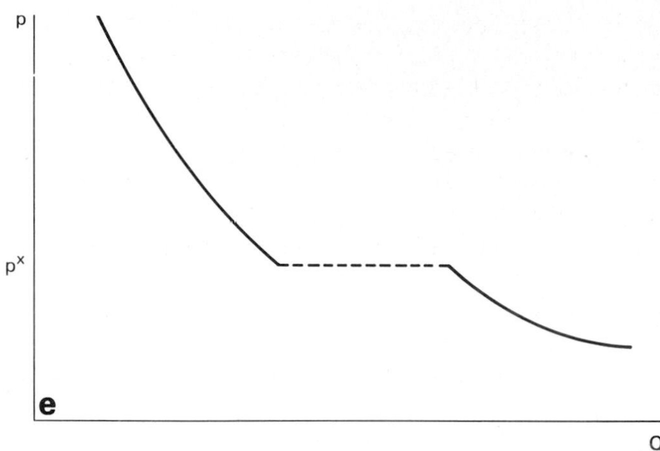

Figure 13.1. *Continued.*

can be thought of as applying to consumer manufactured goods, goods which individuals purchase with sufficient infrequency that they are often uninformed concerning the prices, qualities, and locations of the available goods. These goods are often marked by considerable heterogeneity. Nonetheless, I begin the analysis by analyzing a market for homogeneous goods, in order to focus attention on one information problem – the absence of price information. In Part II, I turn to the more general problem where there is uncertainty about both prices and qualities. Since the demand curve facing manufacturers is a derived demand curve – derived from the underlying demand curves of the stores which purchase goods from it – many of the results obtained here apply equally to manufacturers. Thus, in those cases in which we argue that there are price rigidities, this may be true both at the retail and manufacturing level. On the other hand, I am not sure how important these considerations are for the inputs into manufacturing. One might be tempted to argue that for such enterprises, search costs are small relative to their expenditures. But many of the results of our analysis remain valid even if search costs are very small indeed. (It is precisely in this sense that the standard paradigm is not robust.)

The existence of imperfect information gives rise to a demand for information. There are important economies of scale in the production of information. Thus, imperfect information may give rise to firms which specialize in the production and dissemination of information. But this does not resolve our problem: consumers have to make judgments about the quality of the information provided; and they have to become informed concerning the prices charged by these information gathering services. Furthermore, in heterogeneous markets, it is often difficult for any information gathering service to convey fully the requisite information about product characteristics, especially in the presence of rapidly changing technologies – as most readers of Consumers' Report will testify. These information intermediaries face further problems: because of the public good nature of information,[6] they may have difficulty appropriating the returns to the information that they produce. A good report on a product will be quickly disseminated by the producer. Individuals can obtain the information from neighbors or from the public library. In spite of the problems facing information intermediaries, they exist. Indeed, one can view wholesalers, or even retailers as being largely information intermediaries. I do not develop here a theory of information intermediaries, but it should be apparent from the previous discussion that the central issues with which we are concerned here would be unaffected by their presence.

2. Three paradoxes

We begin our analysis with a discussion of three paradoxes which serve to illustrate how sensitive the conclusions of the traditional paradigm are to its assumptions concerning information. We show that under a seemingly plausible modification of the standard competitive paradigm,

(i) if all individuals have strictly positive search costs, no matter how small, at least for all searches after the first, if an equilibrium exists, the equilibrium cannot be characterized by a price distribution;

(ii) the unique price is the monopoly price, but

(iii) if all individuals face strictly positive search costs for all searches, including the first, then no equilibrium exists.[7]

Thus, the presence of even small costs of information dramatically changes the standard results: equilibrium may fail to exist, and when it does, it looks very different; even with free entry, prices rise from the competitive level to the monopoly level; all that free entry does is dissipate the resulting profits by excessive expenditures on fixed costs.

We establish these results in a simple model; the arguments can easily be extended to more general cases. We postulate a market for a homogeneous commodity, in which consumers can only obtain information about the price being charged by a store by actually going to the store. We wish to capture the conventional notion of competitive markets. Accordingly, we assume that there is an arbitrarily large number of identical firms, and that each of the large number

[6] For a fuller discussion of these issues, see Stiglitz (1989).

[7] The first two results are generally attributed to Diamond (1971) and the last result to Salop and Stiglitz (1977a, 1982).

of individuals is equally likely to go to each of these stores. Furthermore, we assume that each firm assumes that it has no effect on consumers' search behavior, and each consumer believes that he has no effect on producer pricing strategies. The tth search costs the jth individual s_t^j. We assume that $s_t^j > 0$ for $t > 1$. The results are most easily seen in the case where[8] demand curves are of the form:

$$q = 1, \quad \text{if } p < u, \tag{1a}$$

$$0 \leq q \leq 1, \quad \text{if } p = u$$

$$q = 0, \quad \text{if } p > u. \tag{1b}$$

The individual demands 1 unit of the commodity, provided the price is less than the reservation price u. In this case, u is the monopoly price; the monopolist would charge a price of u, regardless of the costs of production (provided they are less than u). If he decreases the price, he does not gain any sales, but if he increases the price beyond u, he loses all of his customers (see Figure 13.2).[9]

We assume the individual is risk neutral. We first establish the impossibility of a price distribution by contradiction: assume there were a price distribution. Consider the firm with the lowest price, $p_{\min} < u$. Let $s_{\min}$ denote the minimum value of s_j^t, for $t > 1$ and all j; by assumption $s_{\min} > 0$. If the firm with the lowest price were to raise its price by any amount less than $s_{\min}$ (keeping $p \leq u$), it would obviously not pay any of its current customers to leave to search for a better deal. But that means that that firm could not have been maximizing its profits.

Indeed, the same argument shows that the unique single price equilibrium is u, the monopoly price. For the lowest price store will always increase its profits by raising its price slightly, so long as its price is less than u. Since no firm will charge more than u, the only possible equilibrium is one in which all stores charge u.

But now, it is easy to show that if $s_1^j > 0$ for all j, there cannot exist any equilibrium. For the individual has to decide whether to enter the market or not.

[8] We drop the superscript j when there is no confusion.

[9] This demand function can be derived from the utility function:

$$U = uq + Q_0, \quad \text{for } 0 < q < 1,$$

$$U = u + Q_0, \quad \text{for } q \geq 1,$$

where q is the quantity of the good being sold by the store consumed, and Q_0 is the quantity of other goods consumed:

$$Q_0 = I_0 - pq,$$

where I_0 is the individual's income, and p is the price.

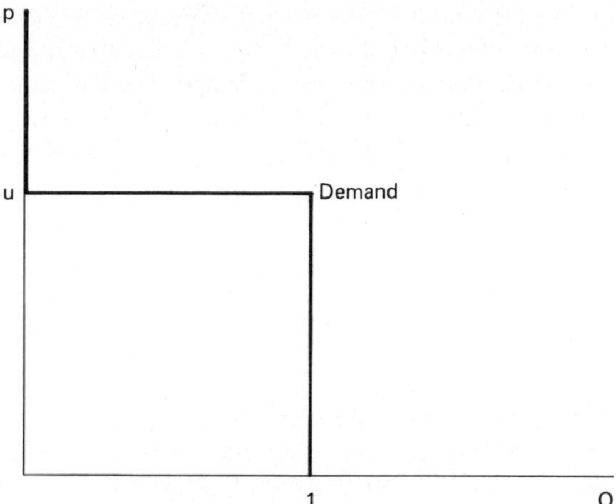

Figure 13.2. Simplified demand structure: individuals demand 1 unit provided price is less than or equal to u; zero if price exceeds u.

If he enters the market, his utility is

$$U = u - p + I_0 - s_1^j = I_0 - s_1^j;$$

while if he does not, his utility is

$$U = I_0.$$

It is clear he will not enter the market. But if no one enters the market, it is clear that there cannot exist any firm (let alone a large number of firms). But if there were no firms in the market, it would pay a single firm to enter, charging a price somewhat less than u (the optimal price would be somewhere between u minus the maximum value of s_1^j and u minus the minimum value of s_1^j.) Thus, there cannot exist any (Nash) equilibrium to the market.

In effect, the excessive greed of the store owners destroys the market. Each store ignores the effect of its actions on the number of shoppers. Each store thus tries to extract the last ounce of surplus out of the marginal shopper; but if it does this (and any store can do this under the conditions stipulated), then the marginal shopper drops out of the market; and as soon as he drops out of the market, the greedy stores raise their prices to try to extract the last bit of surplus out of the shopper who is now marginal. The process continues until there are no shoppers: the market has been destroyed.

It is clear that this argument holds even if different individuals have different reservation prices (u). Indeed, it holds even if individuals have general utility functions, so long as the stores can use non-linear price schedules[10] to extract surplus from their customers.[11]

2.1. The resolution of the paradoxes

Markets do exist. Something must, therefore, be missing from the simple analysis presented above. That analysis does show how sensitive the conventional model is to a slight perturbation in information assumptions: even a slight cost of search leads either to a monopoly price or to the non-existence of a competitive equilibrium. There are several possible resolutions to the paradox – each entailing dropping one of the assumptions of the previous analysis. One approach is to drop the assumption of competitive markets, so that each firm believes that its actions affect whether individuals enter the market. If there are a few firms (as there are in many markets) then this is a plausible hypothesis.[12]

[10] The main reason that stores cannot use non-linear price schedules, the possibility of arbitrage, may not be relevant, precisely because of the costs of shopping and marketing which are of concern here.

[11] We can easily show that there cannot exist an equilibrium with a single non-linear price function. In that case, everyone will purchase at the first store at which they arrive. The price function must be such that at least some individual enjoys zero surplus, given that he has arrived at the store; for assume that all individuals enjoy some strictly positive surplus (given that they have already spent s_1^j to enter the market). Then, if the store increases the fixed charge for shopping at the store by an amount which is less than or equal to $\min[s_2^j, V^j]$, where V^j is the surplus enjoyed by the jth individual, then no individual will leave the store, and the store's profits will be increased. But, by exactly the same reasoning as given above, any individual who enjoys zero surplus, given that he has arrived at a store, will not enter the market, if it is costly to do so. Hence, no one enters the market. Thus, if an equilibrium is to exist, it must entail different stores employing different price functions. But this is not possible, if all individuals are identical, or if they are "similar" enough. Assume, in particular, that we can order individuals, so that $i > j$ implies that if $V^j(R, q) > V^j(0,0)$, where $V^j(R, q)$ is the utility of the jth individual when he pays R dollars for q units of output, then $V^i(R, q) > V^i(0,0)$, while if $V^i(R, q) < V^i(0,0)$, $V^j(R, q) < V^j(0,0)$ – that is, i gets some consumer surplus out of the transaction if j does; and if i does not, neither does j; i unambiguously has a stronger preference for the good than j. Then, each store will set its price function so that the marginal individual buying at its store will enjoy no surplus. Given that, the individual with the lowest preference for the commodity (which by our assumption is well defined) will either not buy at any store at which he arrives or will enjoy a zero surplus if he does buy. Thus, he does not enter the market.

[12] Our earlier analysis showed that there could not exist a Nash equilibrium. This argument holds whether there are a finite or infinite number of firms. But with a finite number of firms, it becomes less convincing that Nash is the appropriate equilibrium concept. An equilibrium, in which firms take as given consumers' search *strategies*, but in which each firm takes the prices of other firms as given, may be more convincing. It is easy to show that there can exist such equilibria, with or without price distributions. In the analysis below we show that with a finite number of firms there can exist Nash equilibria with price distributions.

Alternatively, there may exist equilibria in which different firms charge different prices or sell commodities with different qualities. There is, in other words, noise in the market:[13] There must be some chance that the marginal individual who enters the market does not have all of his surplus extracted. This may be because there is a price distribution, with the lowest price in the price distribution being below $u - s_1^j$, so the individual gets some surplus; or it may be because the individual who is marginal at one store is not marginal at another, because more than one commodity is sold on the same market, with firms unable to distinguish who likes which commodity. Individuals who happen to arrive at the store which sells their most favored commodity will then enjoy some surplus.

In the sections below, we construct several simple models with price dispersion and commodity heterogeneity. These models differ from the simple example just presented in one of two ways:[14]

(a) *The specification of the information technology*. The model just presented assumed that there was a cost associated with acquiring each additional piece of information, and that in the absence of search, individuals had no information. A more general information acquisition technology may be written:

$$S^j = S^j(T), \tag{2}$$

where T is the number of stores sampled (about which price information is obtained). Thus, in the previous model,

$$S^j(1) > 0, \quad \text{for all } j.$$

The standard sequential search a model postulates that each search costs the same amount, so that S takes on the form:

$$S^j(T) = s^jT. \tag{2a}$$

In the model presented in the next section, the information acquisition technology takes on the simple form:

$$S^j(T) = S^j, \quad \text{for all } T \geq 1, \tag{2b}$$

[13] There is one other possibility to which we do not attach much importance: If there are enough individuals with zero search costs, competition for these individuals may be sufficiently keen to keep prices low enough so that the marginal individual is not deterred from entering the market. Even then, however, we normally expect that equilibrium will be characterized by price dispersion. We consider this possibility below.

[14] Most of the models differ from those presented above in a third way: there are only a finite number of firms. But while focusing on the case where there are a fixed number of firms helps to clarify what is going on, the assumption is not critical for most of the results, as we shall see.

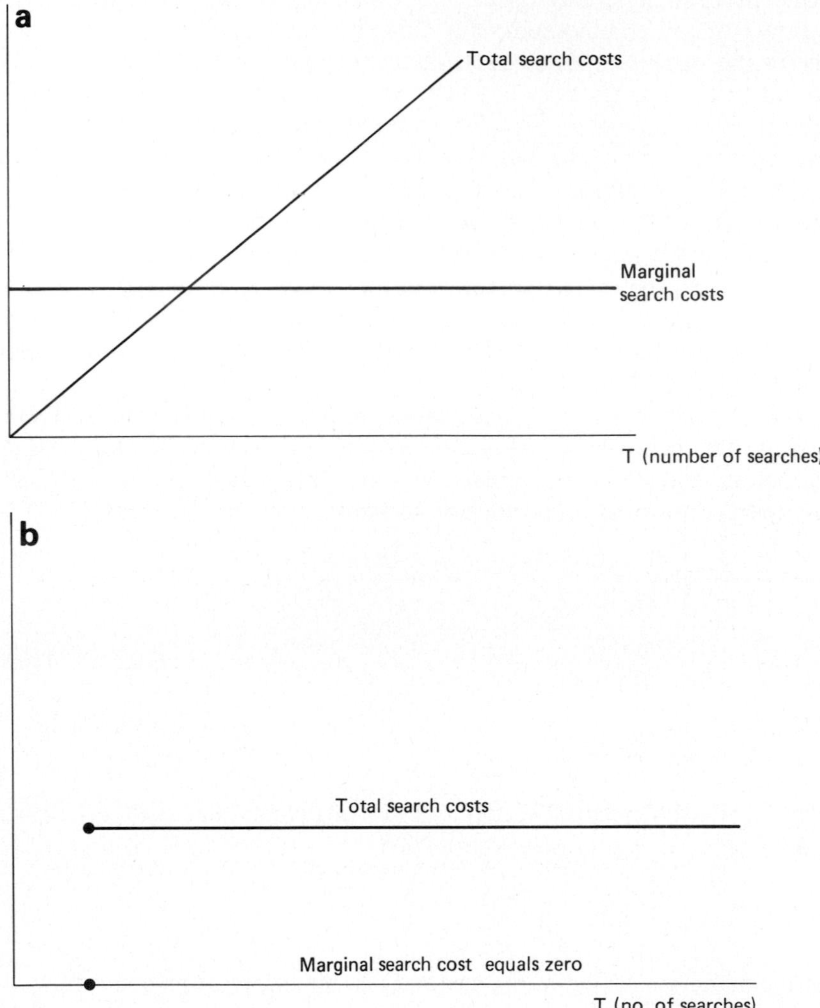

Figure 13.3. (a) Standard sequential search technology: each search costs the same amount. (b) "Newspaper technology": individual acquires complete information by paying a fixed cost. (c) More general convex search technology. (d) Concave search technology: successive searches cost an increasing amount. (e) Limiting case: more than two searches are prohibitively expensive.

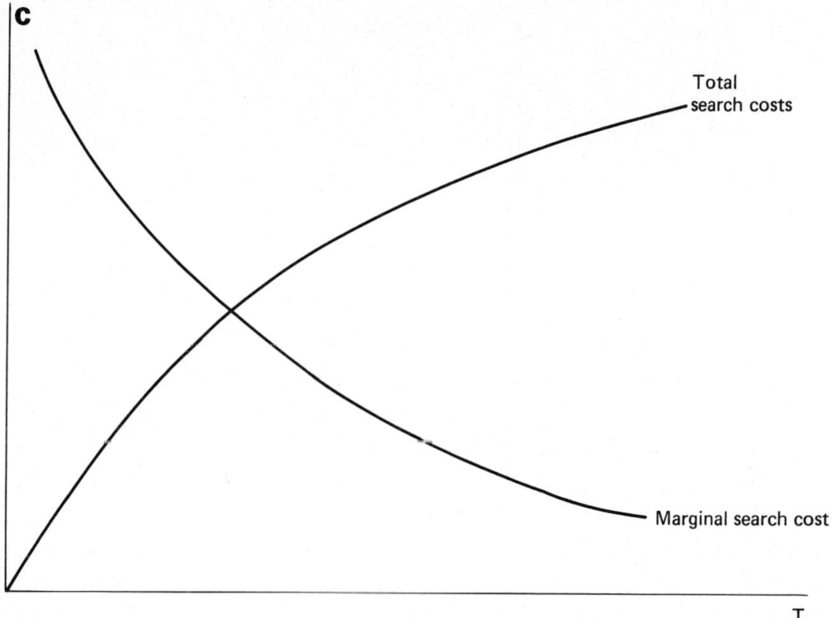

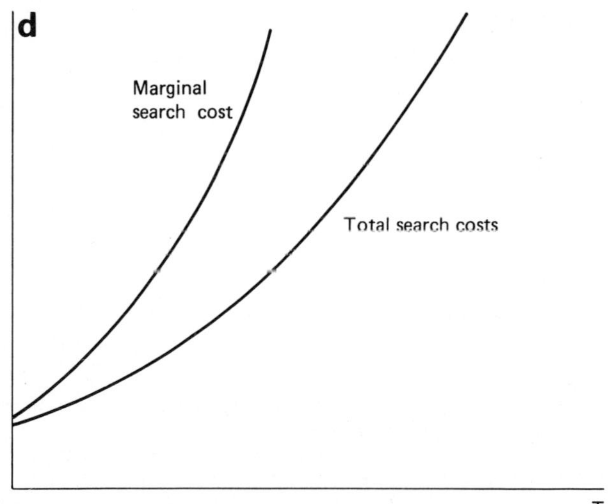

Figure 13.3. *Continued.*

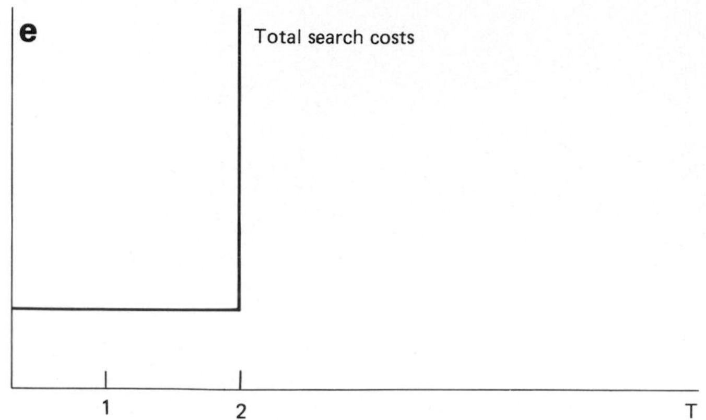

Figure 13.3. *Continued.*

that is, there is a fixed cost associated with obtaining complete information about all stores. That is the case where an individual can buy a newspaper which describes the prices charged by all stores (and the costs of reading the newspaper are essentially zero). Still another interesting technology is that which arises when stores are clustered in shopping areas. Then there is a fixed cost of going to the shopping area, but a very low cost of going from one store to the next within the shopping area. As a limiting case, we could assume that

$$S^j(T) = S^j\,, \quad \text{for } 1 \leq T \leq k, \tag{2c}$$

$$S^j(T) = 2S^j, \quad \text{for } k+1 \leq T \leq 2k, \tag{2d}$$

etc. (In this case, there are k stores in each shopping area, and there is a fixed cost of S^j of going to a shopping area.) The various information acquisition technologies are illustrated in Figure 13.3.

Another variant of the "shopping-information acquisition technology" which we will discuss below is one in which the individual can store commodities when he finds a good deal. (Implicitly, the example given earlier involved a market for a non-storable commodity, like strawberries.) Still another information acquisition technology which will be modeled is that where individuals acquire information through social contacts.[15]

(b) *Market heterogeneity*. The model presented in the previous section assumed, as we have already noted, that only a single homogeneous commodity was sold on the market. It is not obvious how modern retailing should be interpreted in terms of "markets". What is clear is that if one goes shopping for a sweater, the set of items one finds in different stores may differ markedly. The market for

[15]Advertising represents a quite different kind of information acquisition/dissemination technology, which we will discuss below.

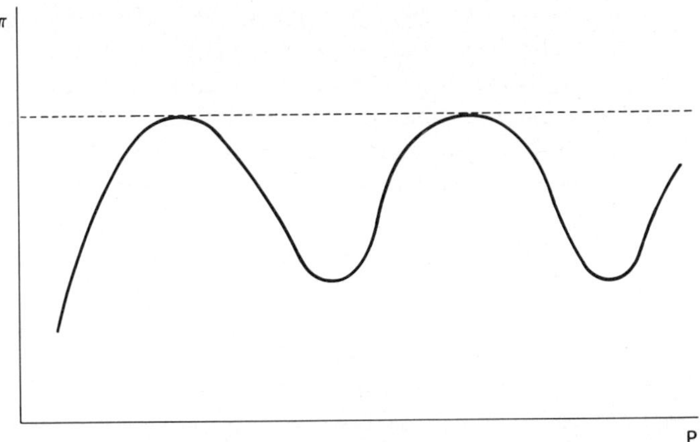

Figure 13.4. Profits as a function of price. For there to be an equilibrium price distribution, the profit function must not only have multiple peaks, but the value of profits at each observed peak must be the same.

sweaters involves selling heterogeneous commodities. This has important implications for the nature of the market equilibrium, which we spell out later.

PART II. Equilibrium price distributions, monopoly power, and price rigidities: Homogeneous goods

3. Constructing models with price distributions

In the following sections we present several alternative models which may generate price distributions. At first blush, it might appear difficult to construct such models. In Figure 13.4 we have plotted the profits of the firm as a function of the price charged. For there to be a price distribution not only must this profit function have multiple peaks, but also the peaks must be at precisely the same level of profits. This seems like an implausible condition to be satisfied, for an arbitrarily specified production and information acquisition technology. But in fact, it turns out easier to construct examples of equilibrium price distributions than at first might seem to be the case.[16]

The earliest investigations of price distributions [see, for example, Stigler (1961)] turned out to be inconsistent: though he considered the consequences of

[16]Had we not been able to construct equilibrium price distributions, we would have faced a dilemma: in Part I we suggested that it was easy to construct models in which, under the hypothesis that all firms charge the same price, the demand curve facing any firm has a kink because of information asymmetries; if this kink is such that the elasticity of demand with respect to price decreases exceeds that for price increases, as well may be the case, then there cannot exist a single price equilibrium.

price distributions for consumer behavior, given the derived demand curves all firms with the same technology would have charged the same price.

With different firms facing different marginal costs, it is easy to construct equilibrium price distributions. Indeed, even when they face the same demand curve (which, because of imperfect information, is downward sloping), the price at which marginal revenue equals marginal costs is different if marginal costs differ.[17]

But there may exist price distributions even when all firms have the same technology.[18] The profit function facing any firm depends critically on the prices charged by other firms; and that dependence takes on a form which easily allows construction of profit functions of the shape depicted in Figure 13.4.

Firms that charge high prices make high profits per sale, but have a low level of sales; firms that charge low prices make low profits per sale, but have a high level of sales. The level of sales at, for instance, low price stores depends on the number of high price stores (and the prices which they charge). There is a set of proportions (of high and low price stores) such that profits at the high and low price stores are exactly the same. There are several ways of modelling the trade-offs between price and quantity sold (the demand curve facing the firm), some of which we describe briefly in the following sections.[19]

The general structure of these price distribution models can be represented simply. Consider first a two-price distribution. The quantity sold by a high price store is a function of the number of low price stores, the number of high price stores, and the price at the low and high price stores; similarly for the low price store. Thus we write:

$$Q^{\mathrm{H}} = D^{\mathrm{H}}(p^{\mathrm{H}}, p^{\mathrm{L}}, N^{\mathrm{H}}, N^{\mathrm{L}}),$$
$$Q^{\mathrm{L}} = D^{\mathrm{L}}(p^{\mathrm{H}}, p^{\mathrm{L}}, N^{\mathrm{H}}, N^{\mathrm{L}}).$$

From this, we can immediately derive the revenue functions (pQ), the profit functions, π, and the marginal revenue functions (MR). Equilibrium is the

[17]There is still a problem in constructing a price distribution: because the demand curve facing a firm will depend on the price distribution, the prices charged (where marginal revenue equals marginal cost) will depend on the price distribution. We need to find a "fixed point" where the hypothesized price distribution, given the distribution of costs, generates the hypothesized price distribution. See Reinganum (1979) and Stiglitz (1974). [Stiglitz' paper is set in the context of the labor market, but the trade-offs are precisely the same. Although in the simpler version of Stiglitz' model, firms with high training costs paid higher wages to minimize total labor costs (raising wages lowers turnover costs), in other versions all firms had the same technological opportunity set; in equilibrium, some firms chose to pay high wages and to employ a technology involving high training costs; while others chose to pay low wages and to employ a technology involving low training costs. The observed differences in technology were thus endogenous. Stiglitz shows that there are in fact multiple equilibrium price distributions.]

[18]This is not the only problem associated with constructing models with equilibrium price distributions. One needs to explain why price information does not eventually get disseminated. See below.

[19]Similarly, if firms "recruit" customers by advertising, some stores will have a high profit per sale, offset by a high recruitment cost per customer.

solution to the four equations:

$$\pi_i = \pi_i(p^{\mathrm{H}}, p^{\mathrm{L}}, N^{\mathrm{H}}, N^{\mathrm{L}}) = 0, \quad i = \mathrm{H}, \mathrm{L}, \tag{3}$$

$$MR^i = MR^i(p^{\mathrm{H}}, p^{\mathrm{L}}, N^{\mathrm{H}}, N^{\mathrm{L}}) = MC, \quad i = \mathrm{H}, \mathrm{L}, \tag{4}$$

where MC is the marginal cost of production. The first set of equations are the zero profit equations, the second the profit maximizing equations. Graphically, the solution is represented by the tangency of two demand curves to the average cost curves; one is the demand curve given the prices charged by the low price stores and all other high price stores; the other is the demand curve given the prices charged by the high price stores and all other low price stores (see Figure 13.5).

It is straightforward to extend this structure to the case of a multi-price distribution; for each additional price, we add two extra equations (the zero profit and the profit maximizing equation), and two additional unknowns, the price, and the number of stores charging that price. It is not enough, of course, simply to write down these equations, and to assert that there is a solution. In each case, one must be able to show that there exist meaningful solutions to the relevant equations (e.g. involving positive prices and quantities). In the models below, we do this. In some cases, the only possible equilibria involve only two possible prices while in other cases, the price distribution may take on a more general form.

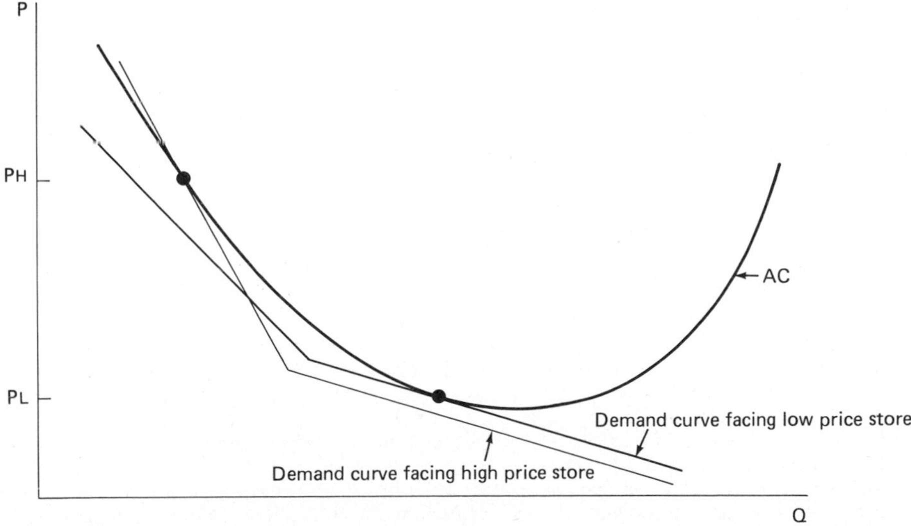

Figure 13.5. With a two-price equilibrium, the low price store has just enough more customers to compensate it for its lower price.

3.1. Alternative interpretations

There are two ways of interpreting the price distributions in the models we present below. One is that the same store always charges the same price, some charging low prices, others charging high prices; the other is that each store has a random price, charging a high price a fraction of the time, a low price the remainder of the time. (In terms of game theoretic language, each firm pursues a mixed strategy.)

The difficulty with models in which the same store always charges a low price is that, under most situations, customers will come to learn of the low price store. The one exception is when new individuals are continually entering the market, e.g. in tourist industries. (Of course, in markets for new commodities, price dispersions may persist for an extended period of time.)

Nonetheless, for most (but not all)[20] of the models we present below, our analysis applies precisely only to the case where some stores always charge a high price, others only a low price. This greatly simplifies the calculations, but it should be clear that the models can easily be extended to the "random price" interpretation.[21] The difference between the two interpretations arises from the fact that when each store randomly charges a low price, the fraction of stores charging a low price will be a random variable. This has two consequences. The average value of the average cost will not be the same as the value of the average cost at the average output, and the equilibrium price distribution must take this into account. Furthermore, we show that in the case we focus on, equilibrium is characterized by a price distribution with only two prices. This is true even if a strictly positive fraction of consumers have zero search costs. But this cannot be the case when firms use mixed strategies. For there is some probability that all stores will charge the high price. In that case, any store consistently charging just epsilon less than the high price will have strictly greater profits than the firms charging the high price, for it will garner, for itself, all of the zero search cost individuals. More generally, there cannot be a mass point in the distribution at the highest price. (We omit the details of the proof, as well as the calculation of the price distribution.)

4. Bargains and ripoffs

When individuals differ in their costs of acquiring information, those who can easily obtain information can find the low price stores; thus high price stores sell only to those facing high costs of information acquisition. Low price stores sell to

[20]The model presented in Section 6 is couched explicitly in the vocabulary of "sales", i.e. stores randomly lowering their prices.

[21]Varian (1980) does this for the "bargains and ripoffs" model presented below.

those with low costs of information acquisition and to those with high costs who are lucky enough to arrive on their doorsteps. The market equilibrium prices thus serve to discriminate (imperfectly) among individuals with different search costs. Low search cost individuals confer an externality on high search cost individuals. But there are enough high search cost individuals that small stores charging high prices, exploiting the hapless consumers with high search costs who do arrive at their doorstep and who cannot afford to continue looking for a bargain, survive. [This section represents an extension of work done jointly with Steve Salop (1977b). We consider here the case where there is a continuum of types of individuals. The earlier paper considered the case with two types only.]

To see this, assume that individuals can, at a cost s, obtain complete information concerning the price distribution. Individuals differ though in the magnitude of s; the fraction of the population with search costs less than s is given by $F(s)$. We continue with our assumption concerning individuals' utility function, so that the individual purchases one unit of the commodity, provided the price is less than u.

An equilibrium price distribution must satisfy the following properties:

(1) *Profit maximization*: Each small firm chooses a price p to maximize profits given the prices of the other firms.

(2) *Firm entry equilibrium*: Each firm earns zero profits.

(3) *Search equilibrium*: Each consumer searches optimally given his search costs and the price distribution.

(4) *Consumer entry equilibrium*: Each consumer enters the market if and only if expected consumer's surplus is non-negative.

We shall derive conditions under which a non-degenerate equilibrium price distribution exists. To do this, we shall first characterize such an equilibrium (if it exists).

There will, in equilibrium, be two types of individuals, those who purchase information (with $s \leq s^*$), and those who do not, with $s > s^*$. We refer to the former as the informed, the latter as the uninformed. The informed only purchase at the lowest available price, which we denote by $p_{\min}$. The uninformed simply purchase at the first store at which they arrive. (Implicitly, we assume that sequential search is prohibitively expensive.) Thus, the expected price which they pay is $\bar{p}$, the average price on the market.[22]

The demand curve facing any firm is depicted in Figure 13.6: At any price above $p_{\min}$ (but below u) the store only sells to the uninformed who happen to arrive; for prices above u, the store sells nothing. For prices at $p_{\min}$ the store gets its pro-rata share of the informed, plus the uninformed who happen to arrive

[22] Uninformed individuals are assumed to have no information concerning the price charged at any store. Hence, they are equally likely to go to any store.

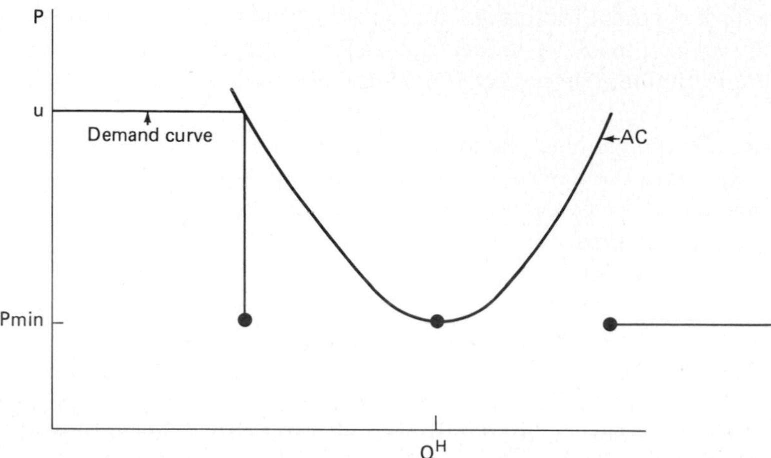

Figure 13.6. "Bargains and Ripoffs". At any price below $p_{\min}$, the firm acquires all informed individuals as customers. Accordingly, the only possible equilibrium "low price" must be at minimum average cost. (At $p = p_{\min}$, the firm acquires a pro-rata share of the informed.)

there. At prices below $p_{\min}$, the store gets all customers. It should be immediately clear that:

(1) the high price store (catering only to the uninformed) must charge a price of u, the monopoly price; while

(2) the low price store must charge a price of a, the minimum average cost (see Figure 13.6):

$$a = \min\{A(X)\}, \tag{5}$$

where $A(X)$ is the average cost associated with producing a quantity X. For if $p_{\min}$ were at any price above a, it would pay any store to reduce its price by epsilon, garnering for itself the entire market of informed consumers.[23]

Clearly, the low price store makes zero profit. For the high price store to make zero profits, it must have sufficient sales that its average costs equal u. Thus, denoting the sales of the high price store by Q^{H}, and that of the low price store by Q^{L}, we have:

$$u = A(Q^{\mathrm{H}}) \tag{6a}$$

[23] This assumes that the firm has the option of turning down excess demand.

or

$$Q^{H*} = A^{-1}(u). \tag{6b}$$

Since

$$a = p_{\min} = A(Q^{L}), \tag{7a}$$

by inverting we have:

$$Q^{L*} = A^{-1}(a). \tag{7b}$$

Finally, we can solve for the equilibrium number of stores and the fraction, λ, charging the low price, given s^*, and the search cost of the individual with the highest s who searches (so that the fraction of the population searching is $F(s^*)$):

$$Q^{L*} = \frac{L[1 - F(s^*)]}{M} + \frac{LF(s^*)}{\lambda M} = Q^{H*} + \frac{LF(s^*)}{\lambda M}, \tag{8a}$$

$$Q^{H*} = \frac{L[1 - F(s^*)]}{M^*}, \tag{8b}$$

where M = number of stores and L = number of individuals.

We can also easily solve for the fraction of the population that decides to become informed. For the marginal individual who becomes informed, the cost of becoming informed, s^*, is just equal to his expected gain,

$$\bar{p} - p_{\min}.$$

But the average price is calculated as

$$\bar{p} = \lambda a + (1 - \lambda)u.$$

Thus, s^* is the solution to the equation:

$$s^* = \lambda a + (1 - \lambda)u - a = (1 - \lambda)(u - a). \tag{9}$$

Thus, (8a) and (9) provide two equations in the two unknowns, s^* and λ. The solution may be more easily seen if we rewrite (8a) as [using (8b)]:

$$\lambda = \frac{F(s^*)}{(1 - F(s^*))} \frac{Q^{H*}}{Q^{L*} - Q^{H*}} \equiv \phi(s^*). \tag{10}$$

It is clear that ϕ is a monotonically increasing function of s^*, from which it immediately follows that there is a unique equilibrium. It can take one of three forms:

(a) If $s_{\min}$, the minimum cost of acquiring information, exceeds $u - a$, then the unique equilibrium entails $\lambda = 0$, i.e. there is a single price equilibrium at the monopoly level: it does not pay anyone to acquire information;

(b) If

$$\frac{F(0)}{(1 - F(0))} \frac{Q^{\mathrm{H}*}}{(Q^{\mathrm{L}*} - Q^{\mathrm{H}*})} > 1,$$

then there are so many individuals with zero search costs that the unique equilibrium is at the competitive level, $p = a$.

(c) Otherwise, there is a price distribution, with $0 < \lambda < 1$.

It is easy to use Figure 13.7 to see how changes in the critical parameters affect the nature of the price distribution.

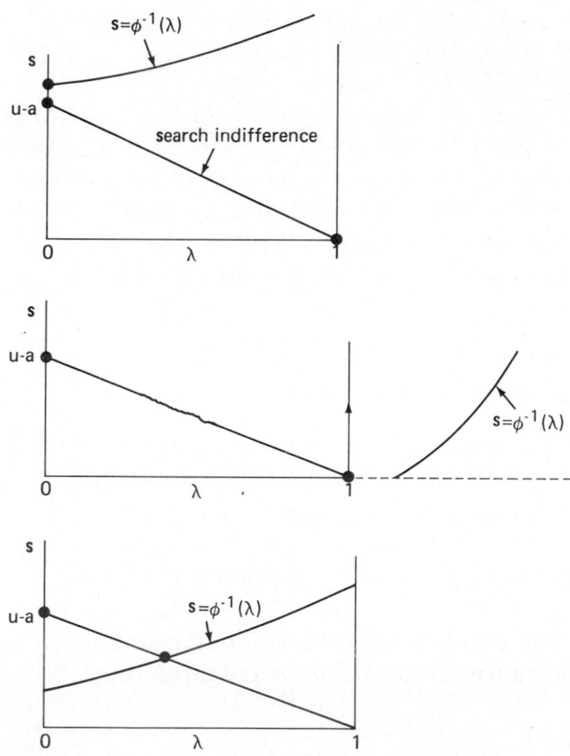

Figure 13.7. "Bargains and ripoffs". (a) With high search costs, the unique equilibrium is the monopoly price. (b) With many low search cost individuals, the unique equilibrium is the competitive price. (c) More generally, the unique equilibrium entails a price distribution.

5. A general theory of equilibrium pricing with search

The essential argument for why market equilibrium may be characterized by a price distribution should now be clear. The information technology of bargains and ripoffs has the property that when the price at any store is lowered enough, the store becomes the low price store, and thus garners for itself all of the informed individuals. Its demand curve, at low prices, is extremely elastic, as typified by Figure 13.1(c). On the other hand, because of the presence of uninformed individuals, when it raises its price, it loses relatively few sales. Thus, the demand elasticity at high prices is relatively low. The shape of the demand curve facing any firm is thus (for a wide range of parameter values) inconsistent with there being a single price equilibrium.

We can ask: Are there other conditions, circumstances, or assumptions under which the demand curves have the property that at low prices, demand elasticities are high, relative to their values at high prices? In this and the next section, we explore two such situations. In this section, we consider more general search technologies. In the next, we introduce storage.

The essential property of the search-information technology that we employed was that the marginal cost of search was decreasing. Assume, for instance, that the search cost technology is convex, as in Figure 13.3(c), and that all firms charge the same price, p^*. Assume some store raises its price by 1 percent, but customers believe that all other stores have kept their prices constant. Then all those with low search costs will leave; in particular, since all individuals know that it will take precisely one search, all those for whom[24]

$$S(1) \leq \Delta p,$$

where now

$$\Delta p = p \quad p^*,$$

the difference between the price charged by the store and the price charged by all other stores, p^*, will leave. In the symmetric equilibrium, if there are L consumers, each consumer consumes 1 unit, and there are M stores, then sales in equilibrium are L/M; while if the store increases its price, sales are $[(1 - F^*)L]/M$, where $F(S(1))$ is the distribution of individuals by search costs, and $F^* = F(\Delta p)$, i.e. the store loses all of its low search cost individuals. If $f(S^*(1))$ is the density function ($f = \partial F/\partial S(1)$), and we denote by ε^+ the elasticity of demand with respect to price increases, then

$$\varepsilon^+ = f(0)p^*. \tag{11}$$

[24] Where it will be recalled that $S(T)$ is the total search costs associated with T searches. We assume that the first sample costs zero. T refers to the number of *additional* searches.

On the other hand, if any store were to lower its price (and it was known that some store had lowered its price, but not which one), all those with low search costs who were at other stores would leave. If S^e is the expected search cost, then the firm would recruit, from each store, all those for whom expected search costs were less than or equal to Δp.[25] Total sales would be:

$$\hat{F}(\Delta p)L + \frac{(1-\hat{F}(\Delta p))L}{M}, \tag{12}$$

where $\hat{F}(S^e)$ is the fraction of individuals with expected search costs (to find the one low price store) less than or equal to S^e. Accordingly, the elasticity of demand is:

$$\varepsilon^- = \hat{f}(0)p^*(M-1), \tag{13}$$

where $\hat{f} = \partial\hat{F}/\partial S^e$. Thus, the elasticity of demand with respect to price decreases exceeds that with respect to price increases – there cannot be a single price equilibrium – if

$$\hat{f}(M-1) > f. \tag{14}$$

If each search costs the same amount, and search is conducted without replacement (that is, when an individual samples a store, he remembers where it is, and does not return), then the expected number of searches (for a consumer who initially arrived at a high price store) is $M/2$. (If there are three stores, there is a 50 percent chance he will find the low price store on the first search, and a 50 percent chance he will find it on the second.) Thus, expected search costs are $sM/2$. Thus,

$$\hat{F}(x) = F(2x/M),$$

and accordingly,

$$\hat{f}(0) = \frac{2f(0)}{M}.$$

Thus, condition (14) is satisfied if

$$2(M-1) > M$$

[25] We continue to assume risk neutrality. With risk aversion, ε^- will be decreased.

or

$$M > 2.$$

If there are more than two stores, then with constant search costs and search without replacement, there cannot exist a single price equilibrium. The reason for this is that with search without replacement, the effective search costs are convex: it becomes increasingly less expensive to find the low price store.

5.1. Search with replacement[26]

When there is search with replacement, when a store raises its price, there is a probability of $(M-1)/M$ of finding the low price store on each sample. Hence, the expected number of searches is $M/(M-1)$, and with constant search costs, expected search costs are $s[M/(M-1)]$. It then follows that

$$\varepsilon^{+}=f(0)p\frac{M-1}{M}. \tag{15}$$

Conversely, if one store lowers its price, the probability of finding that low price store, on any search, is $1/M$. Thus, the expected number of searches is M and

$$\varepsilon^{-}=f(0)p\frac{M-1}{M}=\varepsilon^{+}. \tag{16}$$

There is no kink in the demand curve. Equations (15) and (16) generate the standard result that *as the number of firms increases, the elasticity of demand facing any firm increases, and hence the equilibrium price will fall*. Notice how this result contrasts with our earlier result that with fixed search costs, no matter how small, the equilibrium prices will be the monopoly price.

The earlier analysis, while recognizing that as the number of firms increases it becomes increasingly difficult to locate a low price store, ignored the fact that there were a correspondingly larger number of stores from which to draw customers. In the central case of constant search costs, these two effects exactly cancel each other.

Even in this case, equilibrium may be characterized by a price distribution, when there is a continuum of firms. Lower price stores sell to more individuals.

[26]Search with replacement means that individuals do not remember where they previously sampled; the probability of sampling any store is $1/M$. If stores are pursuing mixed strategies with respect to pricing (with no serial correlation), it is clear that the appropriate model is one of search with replacement. In other cases, it is not obvious which provides a better description of individual behavior.

There is a distribution of stores by prices (given the distribution of individuals by search costs) such that at each price, expected sales at each store are such that price equals (expected) average cost.[27]

Furthermore, if we now postulate that search costs are a convex function of the number of searches, since the probability distribution for the number of searches to find the (one) low price store is (first order) stochastically dominated by the probability distribution for the number of searches to find one of the $M - 1$ stores who have not raised their prices, there is always a kink in the demand curve: market equilibrium is always characterized by a price distribution.

5.2. Price rigidities

By precisely the same argument, we can show that when there is search with replacement, and search costs are concave, then there is a kink in the demand curve: the elasticity of demand for price decreases is always less than for price increases. Accordingly, there is a discontinuity in the marginal revenue schedules: prices will not adjust to small changes in marginal costs.

In this case, we can show that as the number of stores increases, the maximum mark-up increases – to the monopoly price; while the minimum price decreases. That is, *it is possible that as the number of firms increases, prices actually rise*. The reason for this, as we have suggested, is that as the number of stores increases, it is increasingly difficult to recruit customers – it is difficult for them to find the store that has lowered its price. This intuition is even more compelling in the case of markets with heterogeneous commodities, particularly when different individuals have different preferences for different commodities. It then becomes increasingly difficult for individuals to find out about other relevant vendors, even from "neighborly communication". To put the matter somewhat heuristically, in atomistic markets, firms may believe that by lowering their prices, they recruit no customers, and hence they act as monopolists; in markets with fewer firms, they believe that lowering prices will be more effective in increasing sales. Moreover, if individuals communicate with their neighbors (as in Subsection 7.2 below), if there are relatively few stores, it is more likely that any individual will have a neighbor who shops at the low price store. Information that a store has lowered its price may spread more rapidly. Again, increasing the number of stores may have an anti-competitive effect. Pauly and Satterthwaite (1981) have constructed

[27]Note the difference here between the interpretations of the model when there is a continuum of firms, and when there are, say two firms, each pursuing a mixed strategy. With mixed strategies, there can only be a mass point at a price equal to minimum average cost; for if one firm had a mass point at, say, $\hat{p}$, it would never pay the other firm to have a mass point at the same price, for by undercutting by ε it discretely increases the probability that it will recruit more customers, at an arbitrarily small cost.

a model (designed to explore the market for doctors) showing that increasing the number of firms need not lead to lower prices under these circumstances.[28]

6. Theory of sales

In the previous section[29] we showed how there could exist an equilibrium price distribution, in a competitive (or should I say, monopolistically competitive) situation, where the only source of market power was that resulting from imperfect information. Firms were able to price discriminate, to take advantage of differences in search costs, by charging, on average, a higher price to those with high search costs than to those with low search costs.[30]

Now we consider a case where individuals are, ex ante, identical. Like the previous models, there is no exogenous source of noise, no external disturbances to the market which have to be equilibrated. Instead, noise is introduced solely by the internal functioning of the market. Thus, the information imperfection is created by the market itself.

In our model, although all individuals have identical preferences and incomes and all firms have identical technologies,[31] some firms charge high prices and others charge low prices. Those customers who (unluckily) arrive at a high-price firm purchase only for their immediate needs and re-enter the market later. Those who (luckily) arrive at a low price store "economize" by purchasing more than is required for immediate consumption and storing the excess for future consumption. High price stores earn a larger profit per sale, but make fewer sales. Equilibrium entails equal profits for the two kinds of stores, that is, the lower volume of the high price stores exactly compensates for the higher profit per sale.

As in the earlier model, there are two interpretations of this price dispersion: we can think of there being dispersion across stores, or as stores engaged in random pricing. The latter interpretation seems particularly congenial with this particular model, especially as it provides an explanation of unadvertised spe-

[28] It should be noted, however, that product heterogeneity is essential to their argument. With a larger number of firms it becomes increasingly unlikely that you and your neighbor prefer the same subset of firms, so that the information conveyed to you by your neighbor becomes increasingly irrelevant.

[29] This section is based on joint work with Steve Salop. For a more extended version, see Salop and Stiglitz (1982). A still more extensive treatment is provided in the working paper of the same title, Princeton University mimeo, 1981.

[30] The idea of using price distributions as discriminating devices was first developed by Salop (1977) in the context of markets dominated by a single monopolist.

[31] The assumptions of identical firms and customers and no exogenous noise are made to show clearly that the kind of price dispersion analyzed here is distinctly different from that analyzed in other models of price dispersion [for example, Salop (1977), and Salop and Stiglitz (1977b)] where price dispersion serves to differentiate among different groups of customers; where it is generated by costly arbitrage; or where it arises from differences in technology [Reinganum (1979), Stiglitz (1974)].

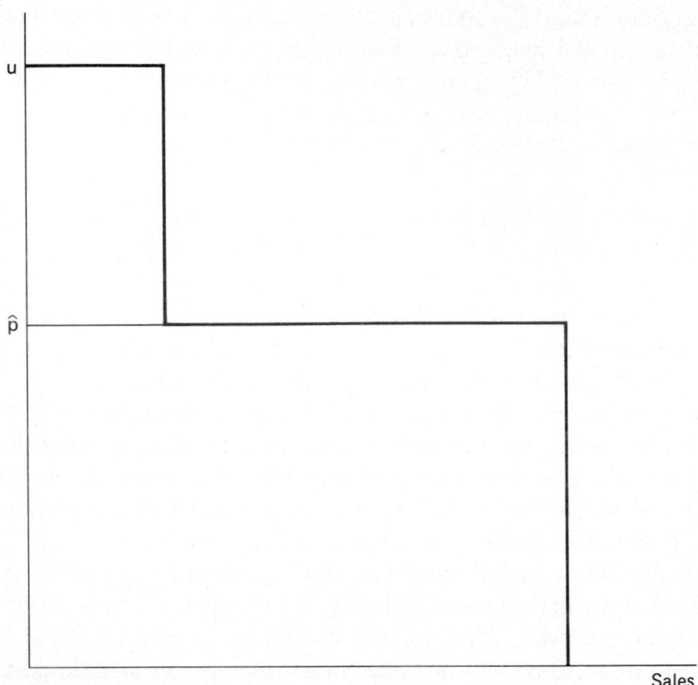

Figure 13.8. Theory of Sales: demand curves with single price equilibrium. If all firms charged the same price, say the monopoly price, then any store lowering its price below $\hat{p}$ would discretely increase its sales. For the monopoly price to be an equilibrium, the increase in sales must not be enough to compensate for the decrease in price.

cials. Here, not only does the expectation of such unadvertised specials serve to draw customers to the store, but they also led to increased sales to those who do arrive: once the individual is in the store, he is more likely to buy several units of the good, more than he needs for his current consumption. He purchases, in other words, for future consumption.[32]

The reason that this model gives rise to price dispersion can easily be seen. If all stores charged the same price, then any store that lowered its price enough would find (under certain conditions to be derived below) that it faced a much higher demand, as some individuals who arrived at it would purchase for future consumption. Thus, the demand curve appears as in Figure 13.8.

Interest in this model is motivated not only by its ability to provide an explanation for sales. It has been conjectured that with storage, markets might behave more competitively. Even if individuals can only engage in limited search

[32]See Steiner (1978).

each period, the relevant market embraces many periods, and thus search costs become relatively less significant. Though there are some limiting cases in which this is true [see Dow (1987)], our analysis below shows that as long as there is storage as well as search costs, the market equilibrium may deviate significantly from that of the conventional competitive paradigm.

6.1. The model

We assume every consumer lives two periods. Each consumer demands one unit of the commodity each period at any price no greater than some reservation price u. Thus, a monopolistic producer would choose $p = p^{\mathrm{m}} = u$. We refer to this as the "monopoly price". In the presence of price dispersion, a consumer who enters the market may either purchase one unit each period, or purchase two units in period 1, consume one unit and store the rest for consumption in period 2. If the consumer purchases for storage, the additional transaction cost c of re-entering the market is saved. However, a storage cost δ must be incurred.[33] The decision to buy-and-store or shop again balances these two considerations.

Suppose consumers know a priori the distribution of prices charged in the market. In the absence of more detailed information, the consumer randomly selects a store in period 1. Suppose that store quotes a price p. Let $\hat{p}$ denote that "reservation price" which leaves the consumer indifferent between purchasing for storage and purchasing only for present consumption with the intention of re-entering the market next period. In order to focus on these interperiod transactions costs, we assume the consumer is not permitted to reject the price p and select a new store in period 1. We assume, in other words, that the cost of a second search in any period is so great that the individual will never undertake it.[34]

Noting that the consumer will obtain the average price $\bar{p}$ next period and must also pay transactions cost c, $\hat{p}$ is given by:[35]

$$\hat{p} + \delta = \bar{p} + c. \tag{17}$$

In addition, we require:

$$\hat{p} \leq u - \delta.$$

[33]Here, we assume storage costs are proportional to the number of units purchased, but do not depend on the price paid. If the "storage costs" consist of interest and spoilage, then they will be proportional to the price. Assuming this does not alter the analysis in any substantial way.

[34]Our assumption simplifies the analysis, but is not essential. It represents the extreme assumption concerning concavity of the search cost function, an assumption which normally serves to make price dispersion less likely. As is conventional in the search literature, we assume consumers know the probability distribution of price. Their prior distribution of price for each store is the same, and hence each store has exactly the same number of customers ready to arrive at its doorstep.

[35]This assumes risk neutrality on the part of the consumer. This is not a critical assumption.

(Otherwise it does not pay the individual to purchase the commodity for storage.) More generally, we write:

$$\hat{p} = \min[\bar{p} + c - \delta, u - \delta]. \tag{18}$$

6.2. Characterization of equilibrium

As in our earlier model of bargains and ripoffs, an equilibrium price distribution must satisfy the properties of Firm Equilibrium (Profit Maximization, Firm Entry Equilibrium) and Consumer Equilibrium (Search Equilibrium, Consumer Entry Equilibrium).

We shall derive conditions under which a non-degenerate equilibrium price distribution exists. To do this, we shall first characterize such an equilibrium (if it exists).

As in our previous model, there are at most two prices. The reason for this is simple: stores that cater to those who do not store will simply charge the monopoly price. Lowering the price a little gains them no new sales. If the store lowers the price enough, to the reservation level, at which individuals purchase for future consumption, sales increase discretely. Further reductions in price do not (in this model) increase sales any further. The demand curve thus appears as in Figure 13.9. Thus, we have not only established that there can be at most two prices, but we have also shown that:

$$p^{\mathrm{H}} = u, \tag{19a}$$

$$p^{\mathrm{L}} = \hat{p}. \tag{19b}$$

As before, we denote the fraction of the firms charging the high price by $1 - \lambda$ and the fraction charging the low price by λ. Then the mean price is:

$$\bar{p} = (1 - \lambda)p^{\mathrm{H}} + \lambda p^{\mathrm{L}}. \tag{20}$$

Substituting (20) into the reservation price equation (17), we obtain:

$$\hat{p} = p^{\mathrm{L}} = (1 - \lambda)p^{\mathrm{H}} + \lambda p^{\mathrm{L}} - (\delta - c), \tag{21}$$

or, upon using (19), we have:

$$p^{\mathrm{L}} = u - \frac{\delta - c}{1 - \lambda}. \tag{22}$$

If $\delta > c$, p^{L} is a declining function of λ, as depicted in Figure 13.10. Equilibrium also requires that profits at the high price and low price stores be the same. The equal profit condition allows calculation of the fraction of low price firms, λ, as follows.

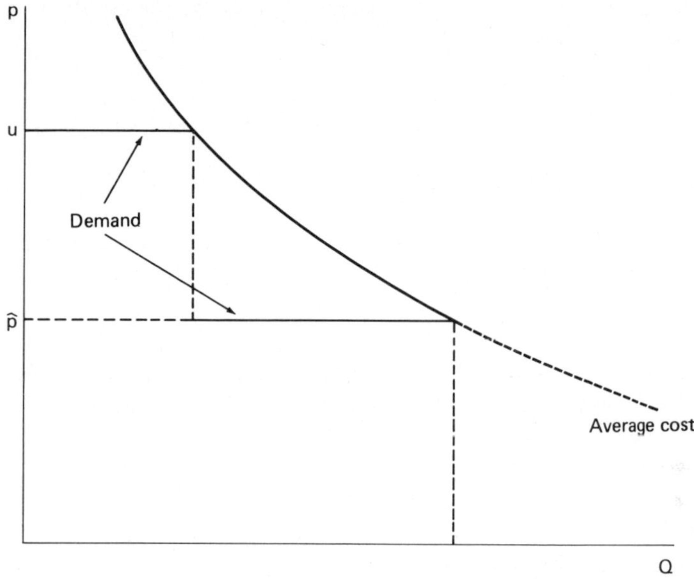

Figure 13.9. Theory of sales: demand curves with price dispersion. If some firms charge the monopoly price u and others the price $\hat{p}$, then the increased sales from lowering price to $\hat{p}$ must exactly compensate for the decreased price.

There are L consumers of each generation and M firms. Each firm attracts L/M young customers and $[(1-\lambda)L]/M$ old customers who were unlucky and selected a high price store when they were young.[36] Since both unlucky young and old customers purchase one unit each, sales Q^{H} of each p^{H} firm are given by:

$$Q^{\mathrm{H}} = \frac{(1+1-\lambda)L}{M}.$$

The sales of the low price firms are higher. Each sells two units to their young customers and one unit to their old customers, or

$$Q^{\mathrm{L}} = \frac{(2+1-\lambda)L}{M}.$$

For simplicity, we assume that the marginal costs of production are zero. Thus,

[36] We assume all of them re-enter the market the second period.

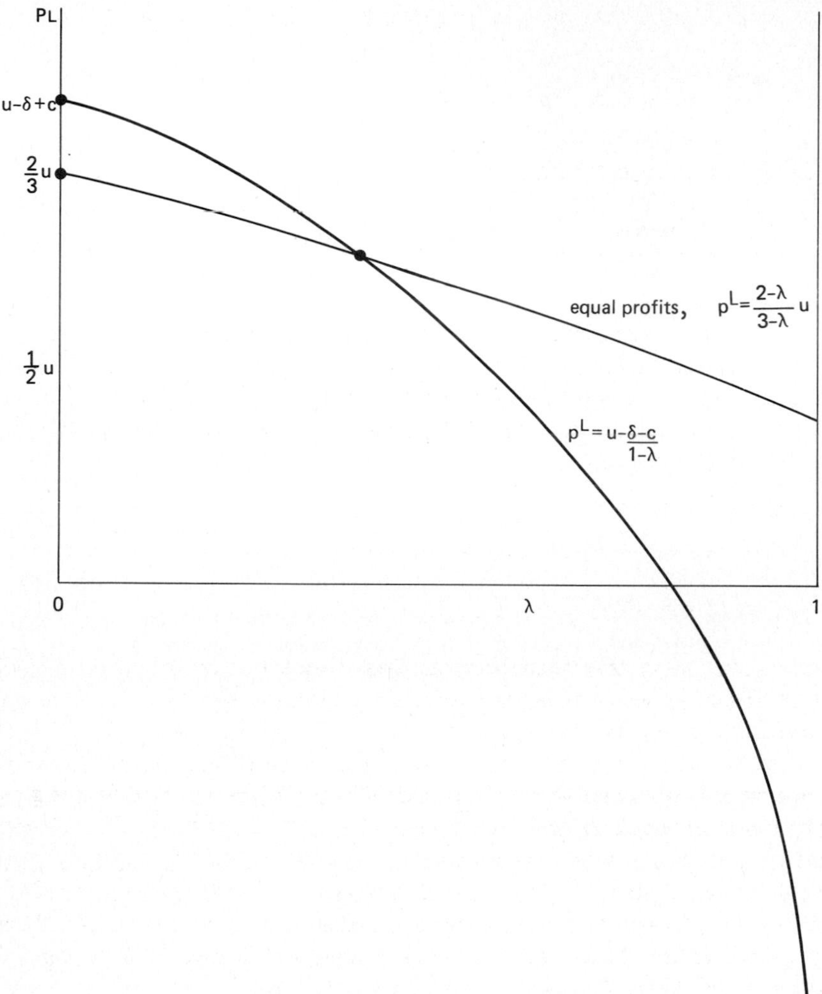

Figure 13.10. Theory of sales: the equilibrium values of p^{L} and λ which satisfy the equal profit and profit maximizing conditions.

equal profits implies:

$$p^{\mathrm{H}}Q^{\mathrm{H}} = p^{\mathrm{L}}Q^{\mathrm{L}}.$$

Using the three preceding equations, we obtain:

$$(2-\lambda)u = p^{\mathrm{L}}(3-\lambda).$$

The relationship between p^{L} and λ, entailing equal profits, is plotted in Figure

13.10. It is easy to see that there is a unique intersection, characterized by:

$$p^{\mathrm{L}} = \frac{u + (\delta - c)}{2}, \qquad p^{\mathrm{H}} = u,$$

and the fraction of firms charging the high price:

$$1 - \lambda = \frac{2(\delta - c)}{u - (\delta - c)}.$$

In order to ignore the question of whether the individual enters the market, we focus our attention on the case where $c = 0$. (The more general case is discussed below.) For a two-price equilibrium to exist, clearly $0 < \lambda < 1$. We can thus show that if $c = 0$, *a necessary and sufficient condition for the existence of a two-price equilibrium (TPE) is that*

$$\delta < u/3.$$

6.3. Single price equilibria

We established earlier that there were at most two prices in equilibrium. In the previous subsection we considered two-price equilibria. We now consider single price equilibria (SPE). We can show:

$p = u$ *is a single price equilibrium if and only if* $\delta > u/3$ *and* $c = 0$. *If* c *is greater than* 0, *there is no single price equilibrium.*

If c is greater than 0, and $p = u$, it will not pay individuals to enter the market. If $c = 0$, $p = u$ is an equilibrium if and only if it does not pay a firm to lower its price to the "reservation level (for storage)" and sell for storage. The reservation price when all firms charge $p = u$ is $u - \delta$.

If this is an equilibrium, profits must fall if the firm lowers its price, even though sales are increased; that is, since half of its customers are young and half old,[37] sales are increased by 50 percent and we require $3(u - \delta)/2 < u$ or $\delta > u/3$.[38]

[37]Recall that the individual purchased at a low price store for storage for two reasons: it reduced his total transactions cost and he was uncertain about whether the store he sampled next period would have a low price. In the case of $c = 0$, only the latter effect is relevant, but this, by itself, is sufficient to give rise to an equilibrium price distribution.

[38]If $c_1 = 0$ (search costs for the first period are zero) but $c_2 > 0$, no one will shop the second period. Hence sales are increased by 100 percent if prices are lowered to $u - \delta$ (since there are only young customers, at a price $u - \delta$, they all buy for storage). Then a single price equilibrium at $p = u$ requires $2(u - \delta) < u$, or $\delta > u/2$.

This result, together with our earlier results, implies that if $c = 0$, there is a SPE with $p = u$ if $\delta > u/3$, and a TPE if $\delta < u/3$. Whether there exists a price dispersion or a single price equilibrium depends simply on the magnitude of storage costs. If they are low (relative to the reservation price u), the only market equilibrium entails price dispersion.

If it pays firms to have "sales" to induce individuals to purchase for future consumption, storage costs cannot be too great. And if the storage costs are not too great, it always pays to have sales.

To see that if $c > 0$, there cannot exist a SPE, recall that we have already established that if $c > 0$, we cannot have a SPE with $p = u$. For $p < u$ to be a SPE, there must be storage. It is easy to show, using the reservation price equation, that if individuals store in a SPE, $c > \delta$; moreover, profit maximization requires $p = u - \delta$ (individuals are just indifferent to storing).[39] Hence, the consumer surplus obtained by an individual is $2u - 2p - \delta - c = \delta - c < 0$. No one will enter the market, a contradiction.[40]

Hence, if $c > 0$, whenever there does not exist an equilibrium with price dispersion, no equilibrium exists. *Ruthless competition with a small degree of monopoly power destroys the market equilibrium.*

The problem may be alleviated by the existence of a price distribution, a form of noise created by the market itself.[41] Noise ensures that there is some chance that the individual will get a good buy; it is this hope which induces him to enter the market.

Thus,

Necessary and sufficient conditions for the existence of an equilibrium when $c > 0$ are that $u > 3(\delta - c)$ and $\delta > c$. When an equilibrium exists, it is characterized by the two-price equilibrium described earlier.[42]

[39]If $p < (u - \delta)$, any firm could increase its price by δ and lose no sales.

[40]If $c_1 = 0$, $c_2 > 0$, there is a SPE at $u - \delta$, provided $\delta < \min[u/2, c_2]$. The condition $\delta < c_2$ ensures that individuals do not search second period. The condition $\delta < u/2$ ensures that firms do not raise their prices to u (i.e. $u/2 < u - \delta$).

[41]This result parallels those of Grossman and Stiglitz (1980); in their analysis of the capital market, noise was essential in ensuring the existence of equilibrium when information was costly. In contrast to the model presented here, however, the noise was completely exogenous.

[42]The analysis has been couched in terms of different firms charging different prices, rather than each firm having a random price policy. The analysis is completely unaffected, however, if firms choose a low price p^L a fraction λ of the time, and a high price p^H the remainder of the time, provided firms do not know the actual proportion of firms which have charged a low price in the previous period (and provided firms are risk neutral.) Individual's decisions concerning whether to buy for storage or not are based on the expected price which they must pay next period; and accordingly, firm's sales at any price are based on the expected number of young versus old customers, and on the firm's beliefs about the reservation price (for storage) of the young.

6.4. *Non-existence of equilibrium with discriminating firms*

The assumption that the firm could not tell who was a young purchaser, or who an old, was essential to our earlier analysis. If the firm could perfectly discriminate, then it would charge each enough to eliminate all consumers' surplus, given that the individual had already arrived at the store. (For old individuals, this would entail $p = u$, for young, this would entail selling two units, for a total amount of $2u - \delta$.) But then, if $c_1 > 0$ (where c_1 is the cost of entering the market the first period), it would not pay any individual to enter the market: there exists no equilibrium.[43]

If firms can employ a non-linear pricing schedule, they will always be able to identify who is young.[44] Only the young will be willing to purchase two units; all that the firms need to do is to allow a sufficiently large quantity discount that the individual prefers to store rather than to enter the market the next period. As a result, it can be shown that if search is costly, no equilibrium exists. The welfare consequences of allowing price discrimination may indeed be far worse than envisioned in traditional price theory.

7. Alternative theories of price distributions

The simple models we have constructed may be extended in a number of directions; these extensions suggest that our model is reasonably robust to alterations in the assumptions. The one result that is not robust[45] is that concerning the high price: the high price will not, in general, be the monopoly price. The reason for this is that, in general, there is an *extensive* margin of sales: as the firm raises its price, it loses some customers; as it lowers its price it gains some customers. Different models may differ in the reasons for which this

[43] To establish this result, we first show that individuals never enter the market the second period. Assume an individual re-entered the market the second period. He would have had to have purchased only one unit the first period. Assume $\hat{p}$ is the reservation price for purchasing a second unit. Clearly, provided $\hat{p} > 0$, it would have paid the store to have offered to sell the individuals a second unit at a price $\hat{p}$. Thus, the first store could not have been maximizing profits. Thus, the only possible equilibrium entails individuals purchasing two units the first period. But if all individuals purchase two units the first period, the only possible equilibrium entails firms charging $2u - \delta$ for the two units, and consumers' surplus is again negative. (This follows immediately from the fact that any firm selling to the old would charge a price equal to u.)

[44] The use of non-linear price schedules as devices by which a monopolist can partially discriminate among various customers is discussed in Salop (1977), Stiglitz (1977), and Katz (1981).

[45] The other result that is not robust is that equilibrium will be characterized by a two-price price distribution. It is easy to construct examples with many prices, and in many of the examples, there are price distributions involving a continuum of prices, rather than a finite number of prices.

happens, and the extent to which it happens, but it is only in certain limiting cases that there is no extensive margin.

In the following subsections, we briefly sketch three of these generalizations. In the first, we assume that the individual, when he acquires information, finds out about a subset of the stores, rather than all of the stores, as in "Bargains and Ripoffs", or rather than only one store, as in the conventional sequential search model.

In the second, we assume that individuals find out about the prices charged at other stores by talking to their neighbors. These two extensions are important, because to the extent that the individual can make simultaneous price comparisons across stores, competition will be more effective. The stores can be thought of as engaging in a bidding war for the customers who happen to have found out about them. Again, although in certain limiting cases, competitive outcomes obtain [see, in particular, Dow (1987) and Perloff and Salop (1985)] in the general case, equilibrium is characterized by a price distribution, with high prices possibly considerably in excess of the competitive price.

In our third example, we replace information costs by transportation costs. Even in those cases where information costs are not significant, transportation costs may be, and these alone are enough to generate price distributions.

These examples illustrate two of the important reasons for the existence of an extensive margin. When some individuals have some information about prices at some stores, an increase in price may induce some of those individuals to switch to a less expensive store. Similarly, when there are differences in stores (here represented by differences in locations) there are likely to be individuals who are essentially indifferent between buying at one store and another; again an increase in price will induce a switch. In all of these models, individuals have rational expectations about the distribution of prices charged by different stores; but the existence of an extensive margin does not depend on that; so long as there are some individuals whose beliefs are such that, when the store at which they are at increases its price, they are induced to search, there will be an extensive margin. Indeed, since, particularly in changing environments, different individuals are likely to have different information about the prices charged at different stores (simply from the randomness associated with search), there are likely to be differences in beliefs about the value of further search. Thus, models in which individuals do not know the probability distribution of prices, but come to have views concerning that probability distribution from observations,[46] while they may easily generate equilibrium price distributions, are likely to have price distributions in which the maximum price is less than the monopoly price.

[46] It makes little difference here whether those probability judgments are formed in accordance with Bayesian procedures.

7.1. Search with limited information

An unrealistic aspect of the "Bargains and Ripoffs" analysis is that when individuals obtain information, they obtain perfect information about all stores. Now we assume, somewhat more realistically, that each individual finds out the prices at a subset of all the stores, but that they each find out about different stores. Assume, in particular, that they find out only about n stores, where n is less than M, the total number of stores. For n small enough, there is some possibility that the individual who has purchased information only finds out about the high price stores; this means that if any high price store were to lower its price, it would gain a few customers, those who purchased information, but were unlucky enough simply to obtain information about high price stores. This gives some elasticity to the demand curve. Indeed, if there are some individuals who have only obtained information about high price stores, if one of these stores lowers his price by an epsilon, he gains all such individuals as customers; this discontinuity in his demand curve means that there cannot be a two-price equilibrium, or indeed any price distribution with a mass point other than at the lowest price (the minimum average cost a). The calculation of the equilibrium price distribution may be done most easily for the case where the individual obtains information about only two stores. We simplify further by assuming a constant marginal cost of production m and a fixed cost C. Let $P(p)$ be the distribution of stores by prices; for convenience, define

$$G(p) = 1 - P(p).$$

When all individuals find out about precisely two firms, the profits (gross of fixed costs) at a firm which charges a price p equal

$$(p - m)[(1 - F^*) + F^*G(p)]\frac{L}{M}, \tag{23}$$

where $F^* = F(s^*)$ is the fraction of individuals who purchase information (the remainder are uninformed and purchase at the first store at which they arrive). Then the zero profit condition becomes:

$$(p - m)[(1 - F^*) + F^*G(p)]\frac{L}{M} = C. \tag{24}$$

Equation (24) can be solved for $G(p)$ as a function of F^*:

$$G(p) = \frac{\dfrac{CM}{L(p - m)} - (1 - F^*)}{F^*}. \tag{25}$$

To complete the analysis, we need to specify the boundary conditions: clearly u is the maximum price, and there can be no mass points at u, so

$$G(u) = 0. \tag{26}$$

This means that we can solve (25) for M/L, given F^*:

$$\frac{M}{L} = \frac{(u - m)(1 - F^*)}{C}. \tag{27}$$

Substituting (27) into (25) we obtain:

$$G(p) = \frac{u - p}{p - m}\frac{1 - F^*}{F^*}. \tag{28}$$

Figure 13.11 shows the solution for different values of F^*.

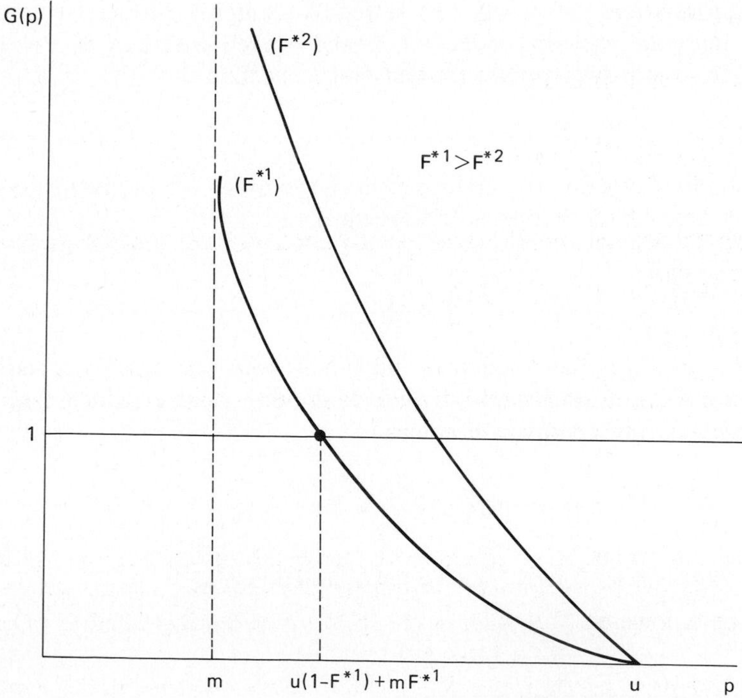

Figure 13.11. As F^*, the fraction of informed individuals increases, more stores charge lower prices.

Equation (28) reveals two important properties of the equilibrium price distribution: the more informed individuals there are, the lower prices will be; but while the minimum price [where $G(p)$ equals 1] exceeds marginal costs so long as there are some uninformed individuals,[47] the maximum price remains at u, the monopoly price.

The fraction becoming informed, F^*, now needs to be determined. The marginal individual is indifferent between acquiring information and not. If he does not, his expected price is:

$$\bar{p} = \int_{\underline{p}}^{u} p \, \mathrm{d}P(p), \tag{29}$$

where $\underline{p} = p_{\min}$, the price at which $G(p) = 1$, i.e.

$$p_{\min} = F^*m + (1 - F^*)u. \tag{30}$$

If he does, the probability that he pays a price in excess of $\hat{p}$ is equal to the probability that both pieces of information yield prices in excess of $\hat{p}$, i.e.[48]

$$H(\hat{p}) = G^2(\hat{p}). \tag{31}$$

Thus, his expected price is:

$$p^* = \int_{\underline{p}}^{u} p \, \mathrm{d}[1 - H(p)]. \tag{32}$$

An individual for whom the costs of acquiring the information is s^* will be indifferent, where

$$s^* = \bar{p} - p^*. \tag{33}$$

If, as before, $F(s)$ is the fraction of individuals with search costs less than s, then the fraction acquiring information is just

$$F(s^*) = F^*. \tag{34}$$

We are now in a position to characterize the equilibrium. Note that in (28) if F^* increases, the price distribution unambiguously moves to lower prices so the mean price is lowered. But what is crucial for determining whether to purchase

[47]Our analysis requires that $F^* < 1$, for otherwise at $p = u$, $G(p) = CM/L(u - m) > 0$. But there cannot be a masspoint at $p = u$; for it would then pay any firm to shave its price by ε.

[48]Assuming independent draws.

information is the difference in mean price one obtains if one searches once (that is, does not acquire information) or twice (acquires information). Denoting this difference by Δ, we have:

$$\Delta = \int_{\underline{p}}^{u} p[\mathrm{d}H - \mathrm{d}G]. \tag{35}$$

Integrating by parts, we obtain [using the facts that $H(p_{\min}) = G(p_{\min}) = 1$ and $G(u) = H(u) = 0$]:

$$\Delta = \int_{\underline{p}}^{u} [G - H]\,\mathrm{d}p$$

$$= \int_{\underline{p}}^{u} G(1 - G)\,\mathrm{d}p. \tag{36}$$

Clearly, Δ is simply a function of F^*, which is a function of Δ. Equilibrium is the solution to

$$F(\Delta(F^*)) = F^*. \tag{37}$$

The solution is depicted diagrammatically in Figure 13.12. For low values of F^*, Δ is negative.[49]

Up to some point the return to searching increases the larger the number of informed individuals (since this increases the number of low price stores). And, of course, the larger the return to searching, the larger the number of individuals searching. Hence, there may be multiple equilibria.

[49]Actually, of course, Δ cannot be negative; what is negative is the right-hand side of (36), where we have substituted (28) into (36). Upon rewriting, we obtain:

$$\Delta = \frac{1 - F^*}{F^{*2}} \int_{\underline{p}}^{u} \frac{u - p}{[p - m]^2} [(u - m)F - (u - p)]\,\mathrm{d}p.$$

Differentiating with respect to F^*, we obtain:

$$-\frac{2 - F}{F(1 - F)}\Delta + \frac{1 - F^*}{F^{*2}} \int_{\underline{p}}^{u} \frac{u - p}{(p - m)}(u - m)\,\mathrm{d}p. \tag{38}$$

Note that at $\Delta = 0$ and $F < 1$, this is positive, but after a critical value, it becomes negative, so that Δ reaches zero again when $F^* = 1$. Thus, the Δ function has the shape depicted.

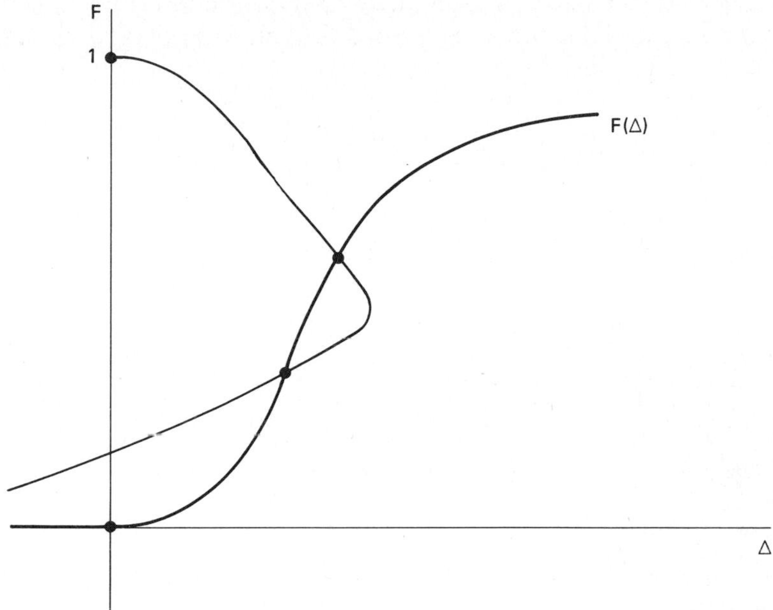

Figure 13.12. Equilibrium price distributions with limited information: individuals find out about two stores.

7.2. Equilibrium with a limited number of stores

In the preceding models we have assumed that the number of stores was endogenously determined, and that the fixed costs of entry were sufficiently low that there were a large number of stores. We now ask: What happens either if entry is limited, or costs of entry are increased, so that the equilibrium number of firms is reduced? We show that in these models, reducing the number of firms may actually lower the average price paid by consumers.

Assume in particular that the number of stores is very limited, but each store pursues a mixed strategy, that is a random pricing policy. Again, there will be some price elasticity: by lowering one's price, one obtains (probabilistically) more customers. We can characterize the symmetric equilibrium. For simplicity, we assume the fraction of informed individuals, F^*, is fixed. We assume, as in "Bargains and Ripoffs", that informed individuals become fully informed about the price distribution, so that they all purchase at the lowest price store; while uninformed individuals purchase randomly. Thus, if all M stores pursue a mixed strategy characterized by $G(p)$, the probability that a store that charges $\hat{p}$ will be the lowest price store, and thus recruit all of the informed, is just the probability that all other $M-1$ stores choose a price in excess of $\hat{p}$, i.e. $G(\hat{p})^{M-1}$. Thus, assuming for simplicity that $m=0$, the firm's profits from charging a price $\hat{p}$ is:

$$\frac{\hat{p}(1-F^*)L}{M}+\hat{p}G(\hat{p})^{M-1}F^*L=K,$$

for all $\hat{p}$ in the distribution, i.e.

$$G(p;K)=\left[\frac{K-\dfrac{p(1-F^*)L}{M}}{pF^*L}\right]^{[1/(M-1)]}$$

First, note that there are multiple equilibria. We simply require that

$$K\leq\frac{u(1-F^*)L}{M},$$

so that $G(p;K)=0$ at some $p\leq u$. This in turn implies that, as before, F^* must be less than unity, that is, there must be some uninformed individuals.

Secondly, even when K is set to equal the fixed costs of entry, C, there are multiple equilibrium: any value of M for which

$$M\leq\frac{u(1-F^*)L}{C},$$

generates an equilibrium.

Thirdly, the expected price paid, both by the informed and the uninformed, increases with the number of firms. The expected price paid by the uninformed is just $\int p\,\mathrm{d}G(p)$. But since

$$\frac{\partial\ln G(p)}{\partial M}=-\frac{1}{(M-1)}\ln G+\frac{1-F}{F(M-1)G^{M-1}M^2}>0,$$

it is clear that the probability distribution of the prices they pay unambiguously worsens as M increases.

Similarly, the probability that an informed individual pays a price equal to or greater than p is just the probability that all M stores charge an amount equal to or greater than p, that is, it is just equal to $G(p)^M$. Straightforward differentiation establishes that

$$\frac{\partial \ln G(p)^M}{\partial M} = -\frac{1}{(M-1)}\ln G + \frac{M(1-F)}{F(M-1)G^{M-1}M^2} > 0,$$

so that the informed are unambiguously worse off as well.

The results of this[50] and preceding sections should be contrasted with the limiting case where individuals obtain information about only one store when they search. As long as the process of search yields information about more than one store, there is some price elasticity, some effective competition. It is only in the limiting case that the paradoxes described earlier arise. The information which results in price distributions may, of course, be obtained in other ways, as the following subsection illustrates.

7.3. *Price distributions with friendly neighbors*

Neighborly communication gives rise to price distributions of very much the same form as described in the previous subsection. Assume, for instance, that each individual goes to one store, and a fraction F^* talk to one neighbor. Thus, a fraction F^* of individuals have information about two, and only two, stores. The model is precisely the one described above, which gives rise to a price distribution.

7.4. *Price distributions in models with transportation costs*

One can easily construct models with price distributions, with known price differences, where individuals differ in their transportation costs per unit distance, s.[51] Consider, for instance, the standard model in which individuals are uniformly arrayed along a line of infinite length (with total density of one per unit length). The fraction of those at any location with transportation costs less

[50]See also Perloff and Salop (1985) for a model where individuals simultaneously find out about several stores before making their purchasing decisions.

[51]Thus, this section differs from the remainder of the chapter in assuming perfect information. Information, like transportation costs, can be viewed as a form of transactions costs. The point of this section is to show some of the formal similarities between the two, in particular for their consequences for the nature of market equilibrium. In Section 11, we consider product variety. One standard way of representing product variety is by a locational model of the form presented in this section. Papers combining spatial location models, representing product diversity, and imperfect information, include Wolinsky (1986) and Salop and Stiglitz (1987).

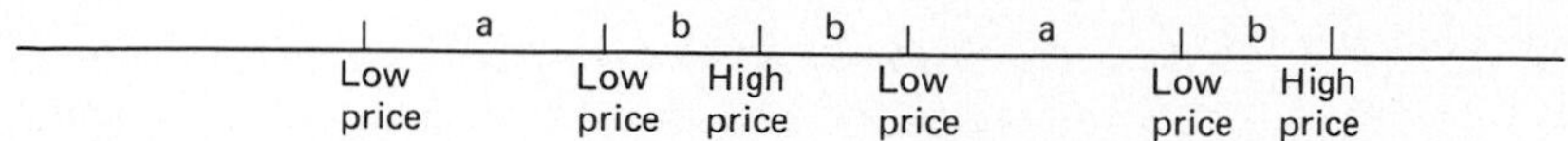

Figure 13.13. Equilibrium price distribution with transport costs: store configuration.

than or equal to s is given by $F(s)$.[52] There is a fixed cost C of establishing a new store, and a marginal cost of production of m. Figure 13.13 illustrates a possible configuration of stores, with every high price store surrounded by two low price stores, and every low price store with one high price and one low price store as neighbors. The distance between adjacent low price stores is a, between a low price and a high price store, b, with $a > b$. Low price stores have larger market areas. Indeed, an individual located near a high price store might actually travel some distance to the low price store, if his transportation costs are small enough. An individual located a distance v from the high price store will be indifferent to going to the low price store if

$$p^{\mathrm{H}} + sv = p^{\mathrm{L}} + s(b - v). \tag{39}$$

Denote this marginal individual by $\hat{s}^{\mathrm{H}}(v;\, p^{\mathrm{H}}, p^{\mathrm{L}})$. It is clear that:

$$\frac{\partial \hat{s}^{\mathrm{H}}}{\partial p^{\mathrm{H}}} = \frac{1}{b - 2v}. \tag{40}$$

As the high price store raises its price, more individuals at any location decide to travel to the low price store. Conversely, as the low price store raises its price.

Similarly, an individual located a distance v from one low price store, in the direction of another low price store, will be indifferent to going to the first store if the first store charges a price p and his transportation costs are such that

$$p + sv = p^{\mathrm{L}} + s(a - v). \tag{41}$$

We denote this marginal individual by $\hat{s}^{\mathrm{L}}(v;\, p, p^{\mathrm{L}})$. From this, we can calculate the demand at the high price and low price store:

$$Q^{\mathrm{H}} = 2\int_0^b \left[1 - F\left(\hat{s}^{\mathrm{H}}(v;\, p^{\mathrm{L}}, p^{\mathrm{H}})\right)\right] \mathrm{d}v = Q^{\mathrm{H}}(p^{\mathrm{H}}, p^{\mathrm{L}}, b), \tag{42a}$$

$$\begin{aligned} Q^{\mathrm{L}} &= \int_0^b F\left(\hat{s}^{\mathrm{H}}(v;\, p^{\mathrm{L}}, p^{\mathrm{H}})\right) \mathrm{d}v + \int_0^a F\left(\hat{s}^{\mathrm{L}}(v;\, p, p^{\mathrm{L}})\right) \mathrm{d}v \\ &= Q^{\mathrm{L}}(p, p^{\mathrm{L}}, p^{\mathrm{H}}, a, b). \end{aligned} \tag{42b}$$

[52] In the discussion below, we ignore the standard problems of existence of equilibrium, which arise for instance if all individuals have the same transportation costs. In that case, a store, by lowering its price enough, can capture all of its neighbor's store market, so demand curves are discontinuous. There are other ways of addressing this problem besides that undertaken here (for instance, assume non-linear transport costs), with similar results.

Of course, in equilibrium, the second term of (42b) is just $a/2$, and the first term is just $b - (Q^{\mathrm{H}}/2)$. (That is, the two low price stores charge the same price, and hence split the area between them; and all those who do not purchase at the high price store must go to the low price store.) From this, we can easily calculate the marginal revenue schedules, and the total revenue schedules. Equilibrium is characterized by p^{H}, p^{L}, a, b such that marginal revenue MR equals marginal cost, m (profit maximization):

$$MR^i = m, \quad i = \mathrm{H}, \mathrm{L},$$

and entry occurs until profits are driven down to zero:

$$(p^i - m)Q^i = C, \quad i = \mathrm{H}, \mathrm{L}.$$

These equations are precisely of the form of equations (3) and (4) introduced earlier: market equilibrium may well be characterized by a price distribution.[53]

8. Concluding remarks

This part of the chapter has considered models exploring four properties of markets *for homogeneous commodities* in which it is costly to obtain information:

(1) Equilibrium may not exist.

(2) When equilibrium exists, prices in such markets may be considerably in excess of the competitive level (marginal costs); and an increase in the number of firms may not result in a lowering of prices.

(3) Alternatively, equilibrium may be characterized by a price distribution.

(4) Demand curves may be kinked.

One general result emerges from the analysis: *the results of the standard competitive model, in which it is assumed that there is perfect information, are not robust. Slight modifications in the assumptions – even assuming ε search costs – affect both the existence and nature of equilibrium.* Though this result seriously calls into question the credence that should be given to the standard Walrasian model, it also raises questions concerning the robustness of our results, particularly to alterations in the specific nature of the informational assumptions. That is precisely why we have explored so many variants of the basic model. The results we have obtained do appear to be robust.

In the end, the question that we need to ask is: To what extent do these models help us to understand the functioning of product markets?

[53]Note that much of the literature on monopolistic competition has focused on the case of symmetric equilibria, where all firms charge the same price.

Any attempt to understand the functioning of product markets must take into account two aspects of these markets which we have, until now, ignored; the rich variety of goods produced and the difficulties of ascertaining quality. In Part III of this chapter we address those issues. Still, bearing in mind this limitation, it is useful to summarize what may be learned from the analysis of markets with homogeneous commodities. The essential lesson is simple: markets (for homogeneous commodities) are likely to be characterized by price distributions and to be *imperfectly* competitive.[54]

8.1. Monopoly power

Costly information gives rise to monopoly power; firms are able to charge more than the competitive price, even when there are some individuals for whom search is costless. Even with relatively small search costs, prices may be well in excess of the marginal cost of production. Free entry simply results in the dissipation of the rents conferred on firms by their monopoly power in excessive entry costs. The result that prices will equal the monopoly price is clearly a polar case: it assumes that there is no extensive margin (that is, that the firm assumes that by lowering its price, it gains no additional customers, or that by raising its price slightly, it loses no customers). If individuals obtain information about several stores simultaneously (say from talking with their neighbors, or because they purchase newspapers, or because they visit shopping centers, where they can glean information about the prices at several stores at almost zero marginal cost, or because they follow what might appear to be non-optimal non-sequential search strategies, obtaining information about several stores before they make any purchase), if individuals have different beliefs concerning the prices to be found in different stores, or if there are some individuals with very low search costs, or if there is product heterogeneity and individuals have different tastes, then there will be some extensive margin. Markets are more aptly described by a model of *monopolistic* competition than either by a model of perfect competition or monopoly.

A natural question to raise at this juncture is: Are there not means by which the inefficiencies arising from the fact that price exceeds marginal cost could be eliminated? Surely, the large discrepancy between price and marginal costs should induce *some* action on the part of some firm to capture these potential profits!

[54] The analysis of the first issue, that of existence, provides more a commentary on economic theory than on economics: the assumption that firms are able to extract all of the consumer surplus of the marginal consumer is clearly not true, for reasons that we discuss below.

The most obvious mechanism is advertising: firms expend resources to recruit customers. Advertising is not costless, but it does put a bound on the size of the discrepancy between price and marginal cost. Still, advertising raises problems not unlike those posed by search costs [Butters (1977b)]. Assume the cost of reaching a customer is fixed at a. If the marginal cost of production is m, a store which advertised that its price was $m + a + \varepsilon$ would find itself undercut by a firm advertising a price of $m + a + \varepsilon'$, with $\varepsilon' < \varepsilon$. Hence the only possible uniform price is $m + a$. Moreover, in the absence of coordination among firms sending out messages to recruit customers, there can be only one firm sending out messages. (Otherwise, there would be some unproductive messages, one individual receiving two messages that the price is $m + a$. But then one firm would lose money.) But if there is only one firm sending out messages, the market clearly is not perfectly competitive. The resolution of this problem provided by Butters is that equilibrium is described by a price distribution; firms that advertise a high price only recruit customers who are badly informed – who have received no messages advertising a lower price. Thus, the lower sales offset their higher prices. There is a particular distribution of prices where these two effects are just offsetting. Thus, market equilibrium may be described by price equaling marginal costs plus recruiting costs, but because there are many firms attempting to recruit, the total recruiting costs may be considerably in excess of the cost of sending one message. Indeed, the greater the number of stores, the more duplicative messages there are likely to be, and hence the higher prices are likely to be. Now, in effect, excess profits are dissipated in advertising costs rather than entry costs; but prices remain above marginal costs.

Again, the natural question is: Are there not still more efficient methods of conveying information? One possibility, which we discuss briefly in Part III of the chapter, is a reputation mechanism. Some stores establish a reputation for being low priced sellers. As we show there, to maintain any reputation requires price in excess of marginal costs, but the price–marginal cost margin may be far smaller than would be suggested by models without reputation. We suspect that this mechanism has been particularly effective in keeping retail prices of mass produced consumer goods low. For such goods, Sears and K Mart have established a reputation for low price/effective quality ratio. But these stores do not sell many more "specialized" goods, and the markets for these goods may well be described by the models of this chapter. (Though some economists might claim that the observed differences between the prices of these goods and the mass produced goods can be accounted for by quality differences, we suspect that most of the difference is not accounted for by differences in production costs, but in differences in marketing costs; and these differences in marketing costs are, at least partly, attributable to the information theoretic concerns of this chapter.)

The fact that firms have monopoly power has, in turn, several important consequences. With costly search, competition may take the form of attempting to find better ways of exploiting the small but finite degree of monopoly power associated with costly search and information. More successful firms may not be the more efficient firms, but rather those which are more effective in discrimination.[55] Although a perfectly discriminating monopolist without transaction costs is known to be Pareto efficient, perfect discrimination with transactions costs in a competitive environment will result in the non-existence of competitive equilibrium markets; no one will have the desire to enter the market; and imperfect discrimination results in a wide variety of distortions.

Although in our simpler models we showed that there were circumstances in which firms exercise their monopoly power so ruthlessly that they destroy the market, we suspect that the informational assumptions required to do so (to identify the characteristics of the marginal consumer), and the competitive assumptions (that there are so many firms that any given firm is unconcerned with the effect of what it does on whether individuals enter the market) are sufficiently rarely satisfied that this is not a problem.

On the other hand, the result that monopoly power may increase with the number of firms – as consumers find it increasingly difficult to find low price firms, and as firms, knowing this, find attempts to recruit customers by lowering prices, increasingly ineffective – may be relevant, particularly for markets with heterogeneous individuals and products, a subject to which we shall turn in Part III.

8.2. Price dispersion

The Law of the Single Price has long been enshrined as one of the central tenets of classical economic theory. Our interest in price dispersion, though, is motivated by more than simply dethroning such a long standing tenet; it is motivated more by the result that without some price dispersion, under a variety of circumstances, no equilibrium will exist: it is only the chance of obtaining a bargain that induces individuals to enter the market. As we suggested above, price dispersions (sales, unadvertised specials) are phenomena that need to be explained.

Though differences in locations, qualities, and dates make it difficult to ascertain precisely the magnitude of the price dispersion, there is little doubt about its presence. Moreover, to the extent that these aspects of product quality are viewed to be important, they call further into question the standard model's assumption of "thick" markets with homogeneous commodities. If the commod-

[55] There are some who claim that the success of several of the more profitable insurance companies in recent years has not been a result of inventing a better insurance policy, but rather of devising a set of insurance policies that more effectively exploited consumer ignorance concerning the actuarial probabilities of various events.

ity sold by each store is treated as a different commodity, what sense can we make of the competitive model's assumption of a large number of sellers of identical commodities?

Our models show not only that there may exist equilibria with price dispersion, but also that under some circumstances, the only possible equilibria are characterized by price dispersion. And this price dispersion is a reflection not only of the costs of arbitraging among firms charging different prices. The market creates the very noise which enables stores to take advantage of the monopoly power resulting from search costs. In some cases (such as "Bargains and Ripoffs"), the noise enables the market to discriminate between high and low search cost individuals; in other cases ("Theory of Sales") the market simply creates lucky and unlucky individuals.

There are two other reasons besides those upon which we have focused here that, with imperfect and costly information, market equilibrium may be characterized by price distributions. First, when different submarkets face different demand or supply shocks with costly information, the resulting price differences will not be fully arbitraged away. There will exist an "equilibrium amount of disequilibrium". With costly arbitrage, some price differences must persist, or else arbitragers will have no incentive to obtain the information required for them to detect price differences. By contrast, in the models we have focused on here, there is no exogenous source of noise; the market creates the noise.

Salop (1977) has discussed a second reason for price distributions: monopolists may use differences in search costs as a screening device, enabling the monopolist to price discriminate. High search cost individuals are forced to pay the average price, low search cost individuals are able to pay the minimum price that the monopolist charges. The models we have discussed here are, by contrast, competitive – at least in the sense that we allow free entry and that we assume there are many firms. In fully competitive models, of course, firms cannot discriminate (except to the extent that there are differences in costs of serving different customers). What we have shown is that competitive models with costly information are very much like monopolist models: though no single firm discriminates, the market as a whole effectively does.

8.3. Price rigidities

We also noted that the market demand curves facing firms may exhibit a downward kink, that is, that the elasticity of demand with respect to price decreases may be lower than with respect to price increases. These kinks give rise to a discontinuity in the marginal revenue schedules. This is important for its macro-economic consequences.

Changes in wages may not result in any alteration either in output or price. The location of the kink depends on individuals' beliefs about what different stores are doing (or, more accurately, since what is relevant is the store's perceptions of the demand curve it faces, the location of the kink depends on the store's beliefs about individual's beliefs about the price distribution). Thus, if all (stores believe all) individuals believe that all (other) stores have raised their prices by 5 percent, then the price at the kinked output will move up by 5 percent. The model is thus consistent with nominal or real price rigidities. There are multiple equilibria.

We have not, of course, provided a theory of how (stores' expectations of) individuals' expectations get formed, of how, in other words, certain conventions get established. If, for instance, the costs of inputs of different firms are highly correlated, and all firms in the past have passed on cost differences, then in fact the price at the kink will rise with a rise in the cost of inputs. But if, in the past, prices have not fallen when the cost of inputs has fallen, then one would observe a market equilibrium in which there is an asymmetric response to price increases and price decreases. In any case, the model is consistent with the establishment of a variety of conventions concerning the circumstances under which the industry changes its equilibrium price, and how prices get changed when they do change.

PART III

9. Quality and reputations

Until now, we have focused on the consequences of only two kinds of imperfection of information: concerning price and location of stores. Equally important are the consequences of imperfect information concerning the characteristics of products at the time of purchase.[56] Informational imperfections of this type have an impact both on the *quality* of goods produced and on the *variety*. This section discusses the consequences for product quality, the next for product variety.

There would seem to be an incentive for firms to take advantage of imperfect information concerning product characteristics by selling shoddy commodities which cost less to produce than high quality commodities. What prevents this?

This is, of course, only one of a number of similar situations where one individual is in a position to cheat or otherwise take advantage of another. A

[56] We are thus concerned here with markets in which *pre-purchase* inspection is limited; the characteristics of the commodity cannot be fully verified before purchase. We follow most of the literature in focusing on commodities in which there are repeat purchases. The individual forms his beliefs concerning the qualities of the commodity supplied by the given firm from his own experience. The spread of information from one individual to others is a rather different matter, which may be studied, for instance, by use of contagion models.

worker can shirk on his job, thus in effect cheating his employer of the promised labor services. A borrower can abscond with the lender's money. A Chinese restaurant can reduce the amount of pork contained in a dish called Moo Shi Pork to a barely perceptible level, or, in the absence of government health regulations, substitute dog meat for pork. In all of these situations, there is either no explicit contract (perhaps because to specify completely the nature of the economic transaction in a contract would be prohibitively costly: all menus would need to specify all the actions to be taken by the chef in preparing each dish, as well as detailed descriptions of all the ingredients; since these may vary from day to day, the menu would have to be reprinted every day) or, if there is a contract, it is sufficiently costly to resort to legal processes[57] that that is not viewed to be a viable recourse.[58]

In spite of widespread complaints about the prevalence of cheating, it is perhaps more of a surprise that it does not occur more frequently than it does. Why do "rational" individuals not take advantage of others, when they have the opportunity to do so? Do we need to rely on vague notions of "morality" or "social pressure"?

Economists at this juncture are wont to introduce the notion of *reputations*: firms produce high quality commodities because they fear the loss of reputation will do greater harm than the slight temporary advantage of cheating.[59]

[57]Possibly, because of the costs of verifying whether the terms of the contract were compiled with. Alternatively, there is a contract, but it is sufficiently incomplete that the outcome of a legal process is sufficiently indeterminate to make it not worth while to resort to legal processes.

[58]Note that guarantees do not resolve this problem: the firm may refuse to honor its guarantee, and guarantees seldom cover all possible contingencies. Moreover, there is, again, often sufficient ambiguity in the interpretation of guarantees to make the outcome of a legal process uncertain. Guarantees often call for certain actions on the part of a purchaser. Verifying whether these have or have not occurred is often a difficult and contentious matter. A guarantee can be viewed simply as a contract to deliver a commodity which is more fully specified than one without the guarantee.

[59]Models of reputation focus on goods which the individual purchases repeatedly, on what Nelson (1974) has called "experience goods". There is a vast literature on the economics of reputation. Similar models have been used to analyze reputations in a variety of settings. The basic result that reputation equilibria require price to exceed marginal costs is perhaps due to Klein and Leffler (1981), Allen (1984) and Shapiro (1982, 1983), though similar results can be found elsewhere in the literature [e.g. Becker and Stigler (1974)]. Reputation as a perfect equilibrium was perhaps first analyzed by Eaton and Gersovitz (1981a, 1981b) in the context of credit markets and Dybrig and Spatt (1983), in the context of production markets. More formal developments can be found in Kreps and Wilson (1982) and Kreps, Milgrom, Roberts and Wilson (1982). The problems of reputation equilibrium in firms with finite lives have been analyzed by Eaton (1986) in the context of banking. As we discuss further below, the game theoretic approach to reputations, in which individuals, in effect by introspection, come to figure out what they might reasonably expect as rational behavior from the firms with which they deal, is markedly different from the approaches taken by, for instance, Shapiro (1982, 1983) and von Weizacker (1980), who assume that individuals extrapolate past behavior to make inferences about likely future behavior. In the game theoretic literature, the fact that an individual has behaved badly in the past does not necessarily mean that he will (be believed to) behave badly in the future. To the extent that there are characteristics of the individual which are relevant for determining their future behavior, information about which is gleaned from examining past behavior, the two views may not be inconsistent. A model of this form is presented later.

Constructing an equilibrium theory of reputations in the context of competitive markets is, however, somewhat more difficult than it might seem at first glance. First, one needs to specify what the losses to be had from the loss of reputation are, or conversely what the gains to be had from maintaining it are. Again, this seems obvious: a firm which has lost its reputation will lose future sales. Customers retaliate against the cheater by refusing to deal with him.

It is immediate that if the reputation mechanism is to be effective, firms must make a profit *at the margin* on each sale. Otherwise, they would be indifferent to losing a sale. *Price must exceed marginal cost*. Thus, markets in which the reputation mechanism is used to ensure quality differ fundamentally from conventional markets with perfect information.

Three problems remain: first, to develop a consistent theory, retaliation – refusal to purchase from the firm that has cheated – must be a rational response. If a Chinese restaurant that cheats me by providing an inferior meal (relative to what I had come to expect) has a locational advantage for me, is there any reason I should refuse to go there simply because he has cheated me once? Only if I thought that he was likely to cheat me again. Although collectively, as consumers, we might be interested in "boycotting" firms which cheat, the provision of this kind of incentive for good behavior is a "public good"; any small consumer would wish to be a free rider. He would only join the boycott if he believed that there was persistence in cheating; but the rational consumer might well reason that if others are boycotting the firm, it will be making a special effort to retain what customers are left, and to attract new customers. Hence, the period immediately following being cheated is a particularly good one. A worker who has shirked and been fired may be as likely to work hard on the next job, to re-establish his credential as a good worker, as to shirk again. On a priori grounds, then, it is not obvious that it is in the interest of customers who have been cheated by firms selling shoddy products (employers who have been cheated by shirking workers, etc.) to punish the cheaters. But if they do not punish cheaters, individuals will have no incentive not to cheat, and reputation becomes an ineffective mechanism for enforcing honesty.[60]

There is a second problem in formulating a consistent and economically meaningful theory of reputation. If one constructs a model in which no one ever

[60]Shapiro and Stiglitz (1984) present one resolution to this punishment quandary in the context of labor markets; workers who shirk are fired; the punishment is provided by the period which the worker must subsequently spend in the unemployment pool. Stiglitz and Weiss (1983) present a similar resolution of the punishment quandary in credit markets: a firm which was observed to have an unsuccessful project (even though it might have been, and in equilibrium was, the bad outcome of the correctly chosen project) has his credit terminated; and in equilibrium, no other firm will, under the circumstances, extend credit to him. In both of these situations, there was a cost to the shirker (or potential shirker) associated with the termination of the relationship, but no cost to the firm (bank); there are social costs to these punishments, but they are not borne by the agent directly imposing them.

cheats and sells lousy commodities, then how are individuals to form expectations concerning the relationship between low quality at one date and low quality at subsequent dates? Clearly, if customers assume that cheating is persistent, they will refuse to buy from the firm which cheated them the previous periods, or they will only purchase if the price is low enough relative to prices offered in other stores. But there is no rational justification for this assumption, as we argued earlier. They could as well assume that cheating was an aberration, in which case there would be no punishment. Moreover, firms in deciding whether to cheat must form expectations concerning the consequences of their cheating. To do this, they must guess how consumers will respond. Again, if in equilibrium, no shoddy commodities or no cheating ever occur, they have no basis for forming those expectations.

There is a third problem: since for firms to have an incentive to maintain reputations, price must exceed marginal costs, profits are generated. How can these profits be "reconciled" with standard results on competitive markets, which argue that competition should drive profits to zero?

In this section we present simple models showing how these problems can be resolved. Before turning to these models, we note some important consequences of the analysis.

The fact that prices, in the context of reputations, are performing a function quite different from their usual roles (in supply and demand analysis) has fundamental consequences; *these markets may exhibit price rigidities*. See Allen (1988) and Stiglitz (1987b).

These price rigidities have two very important consequences.[61] First, decreases in demand may not be reflected in decreases in prices; prices fail to perform their conventional role in signalling changes in market conditions. Indeed, it is even possible for prices (relative to marginal costs) to rise in a recession.

Secondly, they serve as a barrier to entry. The standard argument for how a firm that has built a cheaper mousetrap makes a profit is that he lowers prices, inducing others to switch to his mousetrap. The rent he receives, the difference between the new price and the (lower) marginal cost of producing the mousetrap, is the return to his innovative activity. But if customers believe, when he attempts to recruit them by lowering his price a little, that he is really selling a lousier mousetrap, then he will fail to recruit customers: he will be unable to obtain a return to his innovation.[62]

[61] For a more extensive discussion of these issues, see Schmalansee (1982b), Stiglitz (1987a), and Farrell (1986).

[62] He may be able to recruit customers by lowering his price enough. But it pays to do this only if his invention is a sufficiently important one, that is, it has reduced the cost of production by enough. Reputation thus serves as a barrier to *small* innovations. But if it is costly to make innovations, it reduces the incentive to innovate more generally.

9.1. The simplest reputation model

Losing one's reputation entails being thought of as a "bad" firm (individual, etc.). In an economy in which all firms are identical, it thus would seem impossible to lose one's reputation. In the following simple model, even though individuals ex ante are identical, ex post they may differ; those who have been bad in the past may, simply because of that, be believed to be different from those who have not been bad in the past; and these beliefs are consistent: because of these beliefs, they behave differently.

Although we show that there exists a perfect equilibrium in which there are consistent expectations which enforce "good behavior", that is, it is rational in some sense for consumers to sever relationships with those who have cheated, it should be clear that since, in equilibrium, no firm ever cheats, the individual cannot confirm the "rationality" of these beliefs through experience. (The precise sense in which the beliefs which enforce the "good behavior" are rational will be specified below.)

Assume it costs c_g to make a good commodity, c_b to make a shoddy one. Assume that the shoddy commodity can be detected, but only after purchase. Assume that the individual will continue repurchasing, so long as the commodity is good. The firm has to decide, at any date, whether it should cheat. If it does not, it gets $p - c_g$ profits every period from the customer; if r is the discount rate, the present discounted value of its profits is $[(p - c_g)(1 + r)]/r$.

Assume that it believes that if it cheats, it will lose the customer forever. Its profits this period are $p - c_b$. Thus, for it not to cheat, given these beliefs, p must be sufficiently high:

$$\frac{(p - c_g)(1 + r)}{r} > p - c_b$$

or

$$p > c_g + r(c_g - c_b).$$

At very high discount rates, the price must exceed marginal cost by a considerable amount; at low discount rates, price can be very near marginal costs.

9.1.1. Consistency of beliefs

We now confirm that the beliefs that a firm will lose all of its customers if it cheats are consistent. Assume the firm believes that once it has cheated, it will never be able to regain its reputation. It believes that no one will offer any price in excess of the value of a shoddy product, which for simplicity, we shall assume is just c_b, for the commodities which it produces. The only commodities which it therefore pays for the firm to produce are the shoddy commodities.

Similarly, assume that consumers believe that the firm has those beliefs concerning their (i.e. the consumers') beliefs; then clearly, since the firm is going to produce shoddy products, the most that they will pay for the products is c_b. There is a perfect equilibrium in which, given that the firm has cheated, the firm only produces shoddy commodities, and individuals are only willing to pay c_b for its products.

9.1.2. Market equilibrium

The nature of the market equilibrium depends on how reputations are established (and destroyed). In our model, these are established upon an individual-by-individual basis. That is, individuals do not communicate with each other, and do not know whether the firm is selling commodities to other individuals. In a more realistic model individuals would take into account the information which could be gleaned from other individuals (both directly, and indirectly, from their actions).

Market equilibrium is characterized by price exceeding marginal cost. In conventional theory, these profits would give rise to entry, but here, it must be recalled, consumers are naturally skeptical of new entrants: anyone is willing to come along to produce, at low cost, a shoddy commodity and attempt to sell it for a price of p.

The problem is, how to convince potential new customers to buy one's product, to "switch". One way is to offer the commodity at a price below marginal costs. So long as the price exceeds the marginal cost of producing the low quality product, this conveys no information: if we assume there is an infinite supply of producers of shoddy commodities, all stand willing to sell their commodity at any price exceeding their marginal cost of production. However, for a firm to sell its commodities at any price below c_b does convey information: for a bad firm would lose money, not being able to gain anything in a repeat purchase; while a good firm might rationally be willing to sell at below the cost of production, if by doing so, it recruited a loyal customer, who would thereafter be willing to pay a price in excess of marginal cost.

The problem is that there are no contracts between firms and their customers; loyalty is superficial. If some new entrants sell their goods at a price below c_b, all customers, believing that it could only be high quality commodities which are being sold, stand willing to switch.

Thus, assume that a fraction ν of each firm's customers quit each period, to buy at a new entrant who is recruiting new customers by offering prices below c_b. Then, for it to pay a firm to maintain its reputation:

$$p \geq c_g + m(c_g - c_b),$$

where now

$$m = \frac{r + \nu}{1 - \nu}.$$

Notice that the less loyalty there is among customers (i.e. the higher is ν), the higher the price must be to induce firms not to cheat. The present discounted value of profits are $(1 + m)(c_g - c_b)$, or

$$\frac{1 + r}{1 - \nu}(c_g - c_b).$$

Thus, provided ν is not too large, a new entrant can offer to sell its product at a price below c_b, and entry will still be profitable. Of course, all individuals would prefer to switch.[63]

There is an "introductory offer" price, p_o, such that, if all firms take the quit rate among customers as given, expected profits are just zero. Of course, all individuals would prefer to pay p_o for the high quality good than p, the price that a high price store with a reputation is charging. Thus, there must be rationing. But if there is rationing, any firm that entered with an introductory offer between p_o and c_b would attract customers and make a positive profit. Hence, entry would occur until all customers had "switched". But if there is no customer loyalty, a reputation mechanism simply cannot work.

It is thus apparent that the only possible equilibrium offer entails p_o being just less than c_b. An equilibrium with excess demand can persist, since a firm that raises its introductory offer price will get no customers (since any lousy firm is willing to sell at the price c_b). We can then calculate the value of ν for which, at this price, profits are just zero:

$$(p_o - c_g) + (1 + m)(c_g - c_b)\frac{1 - \nu}{1 + r} = 0$$

or

$$(1 + m)\frac{1 - \nu}{1 + r} = 1.$$

But direct substitution of the value of m shows that this equation is satisfied for all values of ν: higher turnover rates necessitate higher prices, but they generate,

[63]Throughout, we are assuming that at p, the price charged by the high quality firm, the consumer surplus of the individual exceeds that which he could obtain from a low quality commodity sold at a price of c_b.

at any set of prices, lower profits. The two effects are exactly offsetting. Thus, there is a continuum of dynamic equilibria, each associated with a different rate of entry of new firms and different market prices.[64]

Some of these equilibria are unambiguously better (in expected utility terms) than others. (Since expected profits are zero, an equilibrium with higher expected utility is unambiguously Pareto superior.) If individuals have diminishing marginal utility of income, then they prefer the equilibrium in which prices vary the least, that is, the equilibrium with the highest loyalty ($\nu = 0$).

The model we have constructed thus has solved several of the problems we posed in the introduction to this part: profits are zero, prices convey information, firms have an incentive to maintain quality, and individuals have an incentive to quit firms that have cheated by selling low quality goods.

Several papers have attempted to "solve" the problem of positive profits by means other than introductory offers. One set of studies has firms expending resources on advertising [Kihlstrom and Riordan (1984), Milgrom and Roberts (1986)]. Firms would not advertise if they were suppliers of lousy commodities; for once the customer has tried the low quality commodity, he will not return, and the advertising would prove unprofitable. In most such models, advertising does not convey any information to the customer other than about product quality. In that context, firms who tried to recruit customers by offering introductory offers would succeed in recruiting all the customers; an equilibrium with advertising could not be sustained.

9.2. Reputations with heterogeneous firms

There is still one unsatisfactory aspect of these models: all firms are ex ante identical, and firms never, in fact, lose their reputations. In reality, individuals differ and firms differ. A loss of reputation entails an individual being "grouped" with those of "low reputation" (loose morals, shirkers, unproductive sloths). Customers cannot perfectly screen among firms. They make judgments about the

[64]There are some constraints on the equilibrium value of ν. Assume the utility associated with purchasing the good quality commodity is U_g, and that associated with the bad quality is U_b, and assume that there is, for simplicity, constant marginal utility of income; then $U_b - c_b$ must be less than $U_g - p$, or

$$U_g - U_b > (1 + m)(c_g - c_b)$$

or

$$\frac{1 - \nu}{1 + r} > \frac{c_g - c_b}{U_g - U_b}.$$

quality of the firm on the basis of past performance. Past performance tells them something about the "capabilities" and capacities of the firm. A firm that has produced shoddy products may have a comparative advantage in producing shoddy products. That is why it is more likely to produce shoddy commodities in the future.

Thus, assume that there are two types of firms. The high quality firms, denoted by a superscript 1, have a comparative advantage in producing high quality commodities, relative to the low quality firms, denoted by a superscript 2:

$$c_g^1 - c_b^1 < c_g^2 - c_b^2.$$

More precisely, we assume that at the price at which it pays a type 1 firm to maintain its reputation, it does not pay a type 2 firm, so that

$$c_g^1 + m\left(c_g^1 - c_b^1\right) < c_g^2 + m\left(c_g^2 - c_b^2\right).$$

In the extreme, we could assume that the type 2 firms simply could not produce the high quality commodities.

Assume, moreover, that there is a given probability, ν (the reason for this notation will be apparent in a moment) that a high quality firm loses its hold on quality, that is, it switches from being a high quality firm to being a low quality firm. We assume that ν is less than one-half, so that a firm that is good this period is more than likely to be good next period.

In this model, then, there are firms that find it profitable to "lose" their reputation. Any such firm, were it to continue to produce, would continue to produce the low quality commodities. Past performance has correctly identified the low quality firms. Given our assumption that all individuals prefer the high quality products (at the relevant prices), such firms would exit the market, and there would be a flow of new entrants, offering goods with introductory price offers low enough to dissipate the later profits. Notice, however, that if there are some individuals who prefer low quality firms,[65] the low quality firms could continue to produce in equilibrium.

The model presented in this section provides a resolution to what have, until now, appeared to be two competing approaches to the analysis of reputation. Some models, such as those of Shapiro (1982) and von Weizacker (1980), have provided what may be thought of as descriptive theories, in which individuals form their expectations of future behavior on the basis of past performance (von Weizacker refers to this as the "extrapolation principle"). By contrast, game theorists have formulated "forward looking" theories, where, at each moment,

[65] That is, individuals for whom the difference in utility between the high and low quality firms is insufficient to justify the price differences.

the consumers try to analyze what is reasonable behavior on the part of the firm. They ask: How would it "rationally" behave? In the simplest version (given earlier) past behavior conveys no information about the firm's characteristics: indeed, it is assumed that they are identical. Because firms never cheat, individuals never have an opportunity to test their out-of-equilibrium conjectures.[66]

In the model presented in this subsection, past behavior does convey information; individuals do form rational expectations based on past behavior; and the predictions that they would have made, from examining past behavior, are the same that they would make on the basis of a forward looking analysis of the firms' rational behavior. Differences in behavior are related to real differences in the characteristics of different firms, inferences about which are rationally made on the basis of the firm's previous behavior.[67]

In this model, as in those presented earlier, price conveys information. Price is an unusual signal. The reason that higher levels of education distinguish the more able from the less able is that it is more costly for the less able to obtain more education. If higher prices indicated that the product was a higher quality, or higher wages indicated that individuals were more productive workers, then would not firms simply announce a higher price, workers a higher wage? To be an effective signal, there must be a cost to charging a high price or a high wage, and the cost must differ between high quality and low quality firms.

In reputation models, it is not the high price which is the signal – a new firm entering the market at a high price would not be successful: it is the low introductory price which is the signal. And the net cost to offering a low price is obviously less for the high quality stores than for the low quality stores; for the high quality stores know that they will get repeat customers, to whom they can charge a price higher than their marginal costs.

9.2.1. Cyclical variations in mark-ups

Costs of production and discount factors change over the business cycle. For instance, if marginal costs of producing high and low quality goods remains the same, but the discount factor increases in recessions [as Greenwald and Stiglitz

[66]Indeed, much of the recent work in this area has a certain metaphysical character to it. Results depend upon assumptions concerning behavior in circumstances which the theory predicts will never occur. Since we would have no way of testing which of the alternative assumptions provides the best description of behavior, if the theory were correct, it is obviously hard to choose among these alternative theories. Indeed, the only inference that we should logically make when an out of equilibrium move is observed is that the theory is not correct. Several recent studies by Reny (1988) and Binmore and Brandenburger (1989) have provided more penetrating criticisms of the logical foundations of much of modern game theory.

[67]The model presented here does not completely resolve the difficulties associated with specifying out of equilibrium behavior. Since in equilibrium only two levels of prices are observed, inferences have to be made about quality levels associated with other price levels.

(1988) have argued to be the case], then to induce firms to maintain quality in a recession requires an increase in the mark-up. The ratio of price to marginal cost actually increases in a recession. Thus, these models exhibit a kind of price rigidity.

To see this, we assume that there are two states to the economy, denoted by superscripts 1 (the good state) and 2 (the bad state). Let π^i denote profits in state i. The probability of a change of state is assumed to be $1 - \alpha < 0.5$. The value of the firm, the present discounted value of profits, in state i, is:

$$V^i = \pi^i + \delta^i\big(\alpha V^i + (1 - \alpha)V^j\big),$$

where δ is the discount factor. After considerable manipulation, we can solve for

$$V^2 = \frac{\pi^2(1 - \alpha\delta^1) + \pi^1(1 - \alpha)\delta^2}{1 - \delta^1\delta^2 - \alpha(\delta^1 + \delta^2 - 2\delta^1\delta^2)},$$

with a symmetric expression for V^1. For a firm to maintain quality, in say state 2, the present discounted value of future (expected) profits must exceed the profits it could obtain this period by cheating, i.e.

$$V^2 \geq p^2 - c_b^2,$$

where p^i is the price in state i, and $c_b^i(c_g^i)$ is the cost of producing a bad (good) product in state i. Recalling the definition of

$$\pi^i = p^i - c_g^i,$$

and letting

$$\Delta^i = c_g^i - c_b^i,$$

the difference in costs of production in state i, we obtain, after some rearrangement:

$$\frac{1}{D}\big[\pi^2(\delta^1 + \alpha - 2\alpha\delta^1) + \pi^1(1 - \alpha)\big] \geq \frac{\Delta^2}{\delta^2},$$

where D is the denominator of the expression for V^2 above, with a symmetric expression for state 1. Assuming the prices are the lowest consistent with maintaining incentives (that is, $V^i = p^i - c_b^i$) and subtracting the two, we obtain, in equilibrium:

$$-\delta^2(\pi^2 - \pi^1)(-1 + \delta^1)(2\alpha - 1)$$
$$+ (\delta^2 - \delta^1)(\pi^1\alpha + \pi^2(1 - \alpha)) = \Delta^2 - \Delta^1.$$

Thus, if differences in costs of production do not vary significantly over the cycle, while discount factors do, if we think of state 2 as the recession and $\delta^2 < \delta^1$, then

$$\pi^2 > \pi^1.$$

Profits (per unit sale) must be higher in the recession than in the boom, in order to maintain an incentive for quality.

9.2.2. Alternative theories of price rigidities

In the preceding section, as well as in Part II, we have presented two alternative theories of price rigidities, reasons why the real product wage may not rise in recessions, as Keynes, and most competitive equilibrium theories, predict.

There are alternative explanations, some based on capital market imperfections [Greenwald, Stiglitz and Weiss (1984)] and some based on imperfect competition [see, for example, Hall (1987) and Stiglitz (1984)]. These alternative views are not necessarily inconsistent.[68] There is one view, however, which we should note briefly, that of Carleton (1979), who sees the price contracts among firms much as the implicit contract literature has viewed the wage contract between workers and their employers, as providing an insurance and risk-sharing mechanism. Some of the criticisms which have been leveled against the implicit contract literature seem equally applicable in the product market. Insurance contracts, appropriately specified, represent redistributions; they do not (necessarily) have the kinds of allocative effects that are associated with "true" price or wage rigidities. Thus, so long as there is a spot market for the commodity, and so long as transactions costs are not too high, the fact that some firm has contracted to buy oil on a long-term contract at a high price is of little relevance for the short-run supply or demand for oil. That should be driven by the spot price. The consequences would be little different from those which would arise if the firm had insured itself through a futures contract. Indeed, the transfers associated with the insurance should serve to stabilize the market, not exacerbate its fluctuations. These contractual arrangements do have implications for how we should use statistics

[68] Indeed, the Greenwald, Stiglitz and Weiss analysis is based on some of the same considerations that we have employed in the previous subsection.

concerning the prices at which goods are sold; for purposes of testing, for instance, the Keynesian hypothesis concerning short-term movements in the real product wage, what is relevant is the spot price, not any long-term contractual price.

10. Product variety

We have all had the experience of arriving at a restaurant, and being overwhelmed with a huge menu or wine list that goes on for pages and pages. The restaurant has seemingly provided us with an excessive array of choices. In a world where it is costless to obtain and process information, an increase in product variety would always have a positive benefit. With costly information, this is no longer true. It is apparent that the value of product variety may be significantly affected by costly information. While there is the possibility that one can find a product that is better matched to one's preferences, the costs of finding any particular product are obviously increased.

The interactions between product variety, information costs, and welfare in market economies are complicated.

First, the presence of costly information affects the demand elasticities for different commodities. When it increases the demand elasticities, it leads to lower prices, and less product diversity, When it decreases the demand elasticity, just the opposite occurs. Examples can be constructed where an increase in the cost of information increases the demand elasticity, while there are other instances where it decreases the demand elasticity. We have not yet ascertained general conditions under which each of these occurs.

Consider, for instance, two soft drinks. In the absence of information concerning their distinguishing qualities, they are viewed as perfect substitutes. If now drinkers are informed that one is Coke and one is 7-Up, they become imperfect substitutes: the demand elasticity has decreased.

On the other hand, when search is costly, and there are many commodities on the market, there will be many commodities in any individual's acceptance set. The fraction of customers, therefore, that are just indifferent to buying or continuing searching is smaller than it would be if information were costless. This, in turn, means that if the firm were to raise its price a little, it would lose relatively few customers: costly information leads to a relatively low demand elasticity. Salop and Stiglitz (1987) have constructed a simple model capturing this intuition. See also Wolinsky (1986).

Secondly, the presence of many commodities – and differences in individuals' preferences for different commodities – results in firms being unable to discriminate perfectly. This "noise" in the market enables the existence of an equilibrium, even in the absence of a price dispersion; but it may also result in a price dispersion, with the high price being the monopoly price, the low price the reservation price of the individual who arrives at a store, is ill-matched, and is just indifferent to going on to search for his more favored commodity. The following subsection presents a simple model illustrating this.

10.1. Product variety, imperfect discrimination, and price dispersions

We construct the simplest model illustrating how, in a market in which there is more than one commodity, stores will be unable to discriminate perfectly. This limited ability to discriminate is, as we emphasized earlier, necessary if a (competitive, Nash) market equilibrium is to exist. We assume, in particular, that there are two types of widgets, blue widgets and green widgets. Each store can only sell one kind of widget.[69] Then, if the store charges too high a price, it will induce a badly matched shopper (a blue widget lover arriving at a green widget store, or conversely) to continue shopping: it faces, at a critical reservation price level (to be calculated below) a significant price elasticity. Thus, one possible form of equilibrium is a single price equilibrium, where the price is set at the reservation price of the badly matched individual; but this means that the well matched individual enjoys some surplus, and it is the chance of getting this surplus which induces individuals to enter the market, and which accordingly enables equilibrium to exist.

On the other hand, it is possible that there may exist a price distribution, with some stores charging a high price, and only selling to those who are well-matched, and some stores charging a low price, selling to those who are ill-matched as well.

To ascertain the conditions under which each of these equilibria can arise, we assume that there is an equal number of blue and green widget lovers, and that the reservation price for a blue widget lover for a blue widget is u_1 and for a green widget is u_2 (and conversely for the green widget lover). The costs of search of all individuals are assumed identical, and equal to s. In equilibrium, half the stores sell green widgets, half blue widgets; the individual knows this, but does not know which sells which. As in our earlier search models, the individual knows (or has beliefs about) the probability distribution of prices; in particular, we consider first the possibility of a single price equilibrium.

Single-price equilibrium. The ill-matched individuals' reservation price is the lesser of u_2 and that price, $\tilde{p}$, such that the individual is indifferent between

[69]This assumption is more plausible where the differences in commodities are service characteristics – the store either has many salesmen, so that it takes but a few minutes to be waited on, or it has few salesmen, so that it may take an extended period to be served – with individuals differing in the extent to which they value these service characteristics (e.g. correlated with the value of their time). Clearly, it would be possible for any store to stock both blue and green widgets. On the other hand, inventory costs may be lower if the firm specializes in one of the two types of widgets.

paying $\tilde{p}$, thereby enjoying the surplus $u_2 - \tilde{p}$, and continuing to search, paying the price p^*. We assume the individual is risk neutral. Since, on average it will take him two searches, his expected utility will be $u_1 - p^* - 2s$.

Thus, if the firm's price is set so as to deter further search, p is set such that

$$u_2 - p = u_1 - p^* - 2s.$$

But this immediately implies that unless

$$u_1 - u_2 = 2s,$$

there cannot exist a single price equilibrium. If, conversely, the price is set so as to capture all of the surplus from the mismatched individual, it must be that

$$u_1 - p^* - 2s = u_1 - u_2 - 2s < 0$$

as the firm does not fear losing these individuals. But then the expected surplus of a shopper is:

$$\frac{u_1 - u_2}{2} - s < 0.$$

Hence, in this case, there cannot exist a single price equilibrium. But a slight modification of the model allows for a single price equilibrium: all we require is that the second search costs more than the first. Then the no search inequality becomes:

$$u_1 - u_2 < \text{expected search costs, } s^*$$

while the positive expected surplus inequality becomes:

$$\frac{u_1 - u_2}{2} - s_1 > 0,$$

where s_1 is the cost of the first search. Since

$$s_1 < s^*/2,$$

the first search is less than the average cost of finding a good match, the two inequalities may be simultaneously satisfied.

Two-price equilibrium. In the two-price equilibrium, some stores charge the price u_1, and some charge either u_2, or the price which just induces search among the ill-matched. Assume that the fraction charging a low price is λ. Then, by the same argument as earlier, if each search costs the same amount, the only possible equilibria must have the low price below u_2.

For simplicity, let us continue with the assumption that each search costs s. Now, the reservation price equation needs to be modified. If one continues to search for the widget of the preferred color, there is a probability $(1 - \lambda)/2$ that on a search one will find a high price well-matched store, and a probability $\lambda/2$ that one will find a low price well-matched store. Thus, the expected price one has to pay is:

$$\bar{p} = \lambda p^{\mathrm{L}} + (1 - \lambda) p^{\mathrm{H}}.$$

Since the low price will equal the reservation price, and the high price will equal u_1, the reservation price equation thus becomes:

$$\begin{aligned} u_2 - p^{\mathrm{L}} &= u_1 - \bar{p} - 2s, \\ &= \lambda\left(u_1 - p^{\mathrm{L}}\right) - 2s \end{aligned}$$

or

$$p^{\mathrm{L}} = u_1 - \frac{u_1 - u_2 - 2s}{1 - \lambda}.$$

The analysis proceeds just as in our analysis of the Theory of Sales; in equilibrium, the two kinds of stores must make equal profits. For simplicity, we assume a zero cost of production and a fixed cost of creating a firm. Thus, equal profits is equivalent to equal revenues. The low price stores sell to everyone who arrives at their doorstep; the high price stores only to the well matched. Since sales at the low price store must be twice those at the high price, prices must be half, i.e.

$$p^{\mathrm{L}} = u_1/2,$$

or, substituting into the reservation price equation, we obtain:

$$\lambda = \frac{2u_2 - u_1 + 4s}{u_1}$$

It is easy to verify that, provided

$$2u_2 - u_1 + 4s > 0$$

and

$$u_1 - u_2 - 2s > 0,$$

there exists a value of λ, $0 < \lambda < 1$, for which profits at all stores are equal, and all stores are maximizing profits. Equilibrium is characterized by a price distribution.[70]

11. Other mechanisms for conveying information about quality

Reputation is only one of several mechanisms by which the potential problems arising from consumers' inability to observe perfectly product quality prior to purchase become ameliorated. In this section we make note of several other mechanisms.

Disclosures. Firms could disclose their product quality. High quality firms have an incentive to disclose that they are in fact high quality. If they do not, they will be grouped with lower quality firms, and the price which consumers will be willing to pay will be accordingly lower. One might ask: Is it not in the interests of all firms that are lower than average not to disclose their quality? If disclosure were costless and there were severe penalties for fraud, then it pays every firm to disclose its quality. For assume that only the best firms disclosed their quality. The remaining firms would be grouped together, classified as low quality. It would then pay the best of these to disclose its quality. The process would continue until only the worst firm had not disclosed that it was, in fact, the worst firm. But, by what has been called the Walras' law of screening, if all but one firm has disclosed its quality, then, in effect, the worst firm has had itself disclosed as such [see Stiglitz (1975) and Grossman (1981)]. The assumptions underlying the analysis, that disclosure – and the verification and enforcement of truth-telling – are costless are sufficiently far from the mark that, at least in many markets, consumers continue to face considerable uncertainty about product quality.

Certification. In many markets, consumers may rely on information specialists, experts, to screen various products, to certify their qualities. Retail stores and middlemen can be thought of as performing this function. *Consumer Reports* provide some information concern product quality. The economics of certification, including who bears the cost, and the circumstances under which it does and does not pay to become certified, are discussed at greater length in Stiglitz (1989).

Guarantees. Guarantees provide one important way, not only to transfer risk [Heal (1977)], but also to convey information, in those situations where the critical quality variable concerns the likelihood that the product fails to perform. The fact that a firm is willing to insure its product against breakage may mean

[70] We still need to check the positive surplus condition, ensuring that individuals actually enter the market, and we have to confirm that an individual arriving at the high price store does not search for a low price store.

that it is confident that its product breaks down with only a low probability. If firms were risk neutral, then the guarantee serves effectively as a disclosure statement concerning quality. If firms are risk averse, then the magnitude of the guarantee (the amount of risk which the firm is willing to absorb) may serve as a self-selection device,[71] with higher quality firms being willing to provide better guarantees. Problems of moral hazard – the possibility of the product's breakage being due to misuse by the purchaser – put limits on the use of guarantees. In many cases, too, there may be ambiguities concerning whether the product is performing in the manner promised or expected, and enforcement of guarantees is often costly.

Prices. Prices often convey information. Elsewhere [Stiglitz (1987a)] I have provided a more extended discussion of the circumstances and mechanisms by which prices convey information. Here, I want only to mention a few aspects of this which are particularly relevant to the problem of product quality. (We have already noted one instance in which prices convey information: buyers know that if the firm charges too low a price, it will have no incentive to maintain its reputation, and hence maintain quality.)

Akerlof (1970), in his classic discussion of lemons in the automobile market, showed how prices affected the quality of cars being sold: when the price was low, only those with lemons were willing to sell their cars, and this was reflected in the prices buyers were willing to pay. He argued that imperfect (asymmetric) information concerning product quality lead to thin markets for used cars.

In most product markets, however, sellers do not passively take the market price as given (as Akerlof assumed). They can announce, for instance, a high price, higher than the price being charged by other firms. The question is: Why should consumers believe that the firm in question is offering a higher quality commodity, rather than just trying to fool them into paying more for the same quality as other stores are offering?

In monopolistic markets there are circumstances in which prices can convey information. Assume there are two types of consumers. Some value quality more than others. For simplicity we assume that a fraction α derive u_1 from the high quality commodity and u_2 from the low quality commodity. The other group gets the same utility, u_2 from the two qualities. Both groups have utility functions which are linear in the consumption of other goods, and purchase at most one unit of the commodity in question. Thus, an individual in the first group (which we will refer to as the quality lover) has a utility of $u_i - p$ if he buys a commodity of quality i. Assume the monopolist cannot discriminate among the two groups. Assume further that each firm has no choice concerning its quality, that is, a firm is endowed either with a low quality technology where it costs c_b to produce a unit, or a high quality technology, where it costs c_g to produce a unit.

[71]See Rothschild and Stiglitz (1976) for an analysis of competitive self-selection equilibria.

It is possible to show that there may be a revealing equilibrium, where the high quality firms charge a high price, sell to only a fraction of the consumers, and the low quality firms charge a low price. The highest price which the high quality lovers would be willing to pay is u_1 and the highest price which the low quality lovers would be willing to pay is u_2. These will be equilibrium prices provided

$$u_2 - c_b \geq (u_1 - c_b)\alpha$$

and

$$(u_1 - c_g)\alpha \geq u_2 - c_g .$$

In this particular example, the equilibrium is exactly the same as it would be in a standard monopoly-with-perfect-information equilibrium. But assume that the quantity demanded by the high quality lovers depended on the price. It is possible that at the price the monopolist would have charged, with perfect information, it pays the low quality producer to imitate, that is, the increased profits from higher prices more than offsets the lower sales. Then, there may exist a self-selection (signalling) equilibrium, in which the monopolist increases his price above the perfect-information monopoly price; at this higher price and correspondingly lower sales, profits are lower for the lower quality firm than if he simply announced that he was lower quality and sold his product at the low price.

In more competitive situations, however, price is not likely to be an effective signal of quality (apart from its role in reputation mechanisms discussed in the previous section). Assume there were a large group of high quality stores and a large group of low quality stores. Each consumer enters the market only once, and knows nothing about any particular firm other than the price being charged (but he has some understanding of how markets work). The high price firms claim to be high quality. Assume that there is a U-shaped cost curve. Free entry ensures that each in equilibrium is making zero profits and operating at the bottom of the U-shaped cost curve. There are two possibilities. Figure 13.14(a) illustrates the case where if a low priced, low quality firm switched, by increasing its price, and the market misinterpreted this to mean that he had also switched the quality of his product, his profits would be increased; there cannot exist a competitive signalling equilibrium. Figure 13.14(b) illustrates the other possibility where, even in competitive markets, prices may convey information concerning product quality.[72]

[72] The essential property is that the minimum point on the high quality average cost curve lie above the low quality average cost curve.

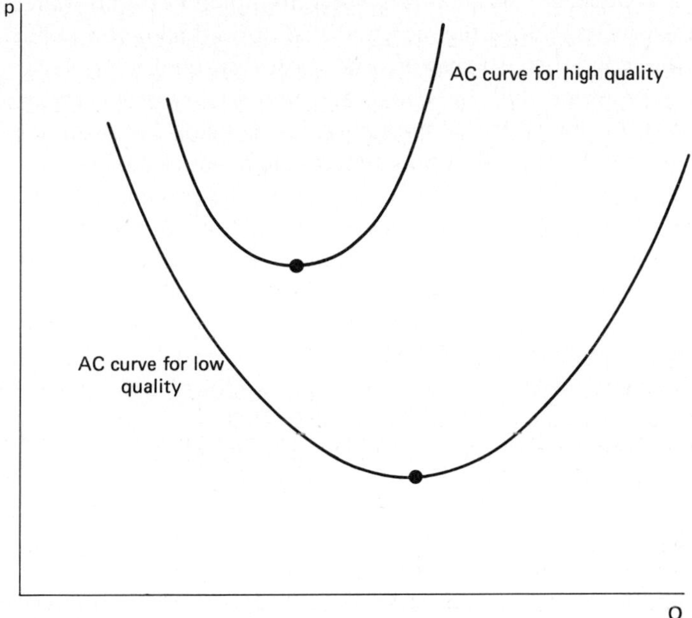

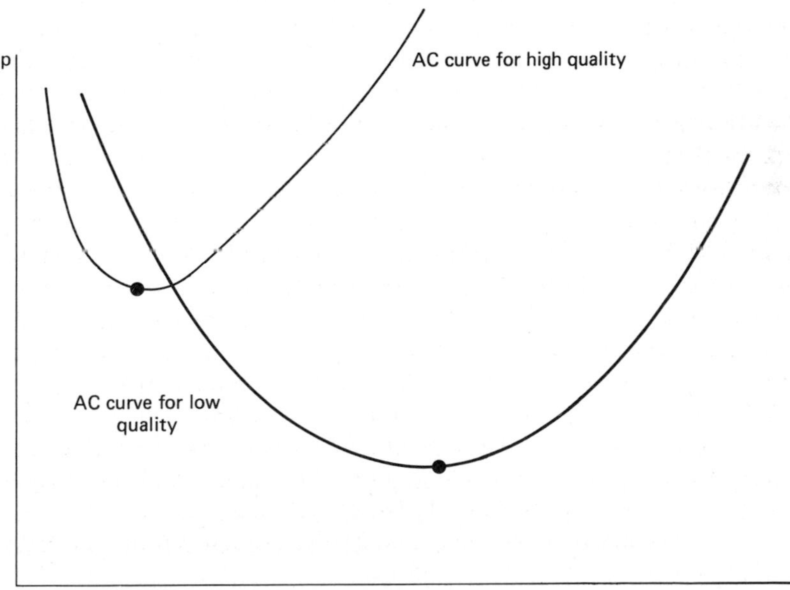

Figure 13.14. There may or may not exist competitive equilibria in which price conveys information about quality.

The reason that price may be an effective signal of quality is that there is a cost to raising price-reduced sales. If the marginal cost of producing low quality goods is lower, then the reduced sales is more costly to the low quality producer than to the high quality producer. Still, both high and low quality producers gain from higher prices, and it is therefore not surprising that in many circumstances, prices are ineffective in conveying information concerning product quality.

On the other hand, in the situations described in the preceding section where there are repeat customers, prices do convey information. But note that it is the low introductory offer which conveys information – it only pays a firm to sell at a price below marginal costs if it believes that the individual will return. Though the reputation models we constructed in the previous section work most effectively when the individual is a repeat customer, similar models can be constructed for items, such as consumer durables, which are purchased only periodically, so long as individuals communicate with each other, that is, the sense of consumer satisfaction is communicated from one individual to another.

12. Advertising

This chapter has focused on markets in which consumers are imperfectly informed, and gather information by search. Consumers also obtain information as a result of *advertising* by stores.

Most advertising is not informative. The typical Marlboro ad, with a cowboy smoking a cigarette, or a Virginia Slims ad, or a Budweiser Beer ad conveys no credible information concerning the nature of the product being sold, the price at which the product is sold, or where the product may be obtained. Firms spend money on ads such as these because they believe it increases their profits, because such ads have an effect on demand curves. But the effects on the demand curves are not those resulting from conveying information. The prevalence of these ads serves to remind us of the limitations of the theory of consumer behavior, which assumes rational individuals having well formed preferences. Such ads often seek to convince individuals of the existence of important differences, when there are none. To the extent that they are successful, they shift (at least part of) the demand curve upwards, leading to higher prices; with costly entry, the extra profits may be dissipated in excess entry. To the extent that there is no "real" product differentiation, welfare would seem to be unambiguously lowered: but how are we to judge welfare in a world in which individuals gain greater pleasure out of smoking a Marlboro cigarette, because they have pleasant sensations when they do that, stimulated by the images left in their mind by the ad?[73]

[73]For an argument that it is still possible to make welfare judgments, see Dixit and Norman (1978).

There are some forms of advertising which actually do convey information, and which affect demand curves because of the information which they convey.[74] Advertising a new product provides valuable information to the consumer that may stimulate him to try it out. Some newspaper ads do convey information about price and product availability. Price advertising can be modeled as reducing consumers' search costs, and in the models with homogeneous commodities ("Bargains and Ripoffs"), this not surprisingly leads to a decrease in average price. But the effect of advertising product variety may be ambiguous. As consumers become more aware of product differences, prices rise, leading to more entry. Though consumers may be better matched, if there is excess product differentiation in the initial equilibrium, it is possible that these losses exceed the gains from better matching [Salop (1978b), Salop and Stiglitz (1987)].

Advertising it not well modeled simply as another input into a production process. While economists have little to say about that large fraction of advertising which has little if any information value (either why it has the effects it has, or how to make welfare statements concerning its value), to the extent that advertising conveys information,[75] it presents the full range of difficulties that we encountered earlier in our analysis of market equilibrium where information is acquired via a process of search (including market equilibrium being characterized by price distributions).

13. Concluding remarks

Consumers are imperfectly informed. They do not know the characteristics of all the products in the market, or the prices at which they are available at all sellers. There is no Walrasian auction ensuring that a particular commodity is sold at the same price by all stores. There is no Government Inspector ensuring that what appear to be two identical commodities are in fact identical. And given the myriad of variations in product characteristics, the consumer is constantly having to make decisions concerning whether the differences in qualities are worth the differences in prices. We have argued that these informational imperfections have fundamental implications for how product markets function, at least for many (most) of the commodities which consumers purchase. These considerations may be relatively unimportant in the market for wheat, so favored by Principles textbooks, or perhaps even in the market for steel. But elsewhere, they are

[74] The models of Butters (1977a, 1977b) and Grossman and Shapiro (1984) provide examples of an attempt to analyze market equilibrium with informative advertising.

[75] I have deliberately had little to say about those models in which advertising is used to signal firm quality; as I argued earlier, there are better ways of signalling than providing uninformative advertising (what is sometimes called burning money) and thus it seems unlikely that that can be the only, or even primary, reason for advertising.

potentially of considerable importance. They help explain why such markets are inherently imperfectly competitive, why prices may be considerably in excess of marginal costs, why entry may be difficult. They help explain not only why equilibrium may be characterized by price dispersions, but also why, in some circumstances, equilibrium *must* be characterized by price dispersions. Finally, they help explain price rigidities, thus contributing to our understanding of why the economy fails to respond well to certain types of disturbances.

Appendix: Notation

M = number of stores
L = number of individuals
S_t^j = cost of the tth search for jth individual
$S^i(t)$ = total cost of finding out about t stores (for jth individual)
u = reservation price
p = price
I_0 = individual's income
Q_1^j = quantity of good consumed by jth individual
$F(s)$ = fraction of individuals with search costs less than or equal to s
Q^{H} = quantity sold by high price store
Q^{L} = quantity sold by low price store
λ = fraction of stores sharing the low price
a = minimum average cost (U-shaped cost curve)
m = marginal cost of production
C = fixed costs
$G(p)$ = proportion of stores charging price greater than p

References

Akerlof, G.A. (1970) 'The market for "lemons": qualitative uncertainty and the market mechanism', *Quarterly Journal of Economics*, 84:488–500.

Allen, F. (1984) 'Reputation and product quality', *Rand Journal of Economics*, 15:211–217.

Allen, F. (1988) 'A theory of price rigidities when quality is unobservable', *Review of Economic Studies*, 55:139–151.

Arrow, K.J. (1958) 'Toward a theory of price adjustment', in: P.A. Baran, T. Scitovsky and E.S. Shaw, eds., *The allocation of economic resources*. Stanford, California: Stanford University Press.

Arrow, K.J. and Rothschild, M. (1973) IMSSS 'Preliminary notes on equilibrium price distributions with limited information', working paper no. 34.

Axwell, B. (1977) 'Search market equilibrium', *Scandinavian Journal of Economics*, 79:20–40.

Bagwell, K. (1985) 'Information product differentiation as a barrier to entry', Discussion paper no. 129, Workshop on applied microeconomics, industrial organization, and regulation, Stanford University, October 1985.

Bagwell, K. (1987) 'Introductory price as a signal of cost in a model of repeat business', *Review of Economic Studies*, 54:365–384.

Bagwell, K. and Riordan, M.H. (1986) 'Equilibrium price dynamics for an experience good', working paper E-86-66, Stanford University.

Becker, G.S. and Stigler, G.J. (1974) 'Law enforcement, malfeasance, and compensation of enforcers', *Journal of Legal Studies*, 3:1–18.

Binmore, K. and Brandenburger, A. (1989) 'Common knowledge and game theory', *Journal of Economic Perspectives*, forthcoming.

Braverman, A. (1980) 'Consumer search and alternative market equilibria', *Review of Economic Studies*, 47:487–502.

Butters, G. (1977a) 'Equilibrium advertising and search for a heterogeneous good', presented at the Bell Laboratories Conference on information and market structure.

Butters, G. (1977b) 'Equilibrium distributions of sales and advertising prices', *Review of Economic Studies*, 44:465–492.

Carlton, D.W. (1979) 'Contracts, price rigidity, and market equilibrium', *Journal of Political Economy*, 87:1034–1062.

Conlisk, J., Gerstner, E. and Sobel, J. (1984) 'Cyclic pricing by a durable goods monopolist', *Quarterly Journal of Economics*, 99:489–506.

Cooper, R. and Ross, T.W. (1985) 'Product warranties and double moral hazard', *Rand Journal of Economics*, 16:103–113.

Diamond, P.A. (1971) 'A model of price adjustment', *Journal of Economic Theory*, 3:156–168.

Dixit, A. and Norman, V. (1978) 'Advertising and welfare', *Bell Journal of Economics*, 9:1–18.

Dow, J. (1987) 'Three essays on search and information', Ph.D. dissertation, Princeton University, unpublished.

Dybrig, P.H. and Spatt, C.S. (1983) 'Does it pay to maintain a reputation? Consumer information and product quality', working paper.

Eaton, J. (1988) 'Lending with costly enforcement of repayment and potential fraud', *Journal of Banking and Finance*, 10:291–293.

Eaton, J. and Gersovitz, M. (1981a) 'Debt with potential repudiation: Theoretical and empirical analysis', *Review of Economic Studies*, 48:289–309.

Eaton, J. and Gersovitz, M. (1981b) 'Poor country borrowing and the repudiation issue', Princeton studies in international finance no. 47, Princeton, New Jersey.

Farrell, J. (1980) 'Prices as signal of quality', Ph.D. dissertation, Brasenose College, Oxford.

Farrell, J. (1984) 'Moral hazard in quality, entry barriers, and introductory offers', MIT Department of Economics, working paper 344.

Farrell, J. (1986) 'Moral hazard as an entry barrier', *Rand Journal of Economics*, 17:440–449.

Greenwald, B. and Stiglitz, J. (1986) 'Externalities in economies with imperfect information and incomplete markets', *Quarterly Journal of Economics*, 101:229–264.

Greenwald, B. and Stiglitz, J.E. (1988) 'Financial market imperfections and business cycles', NBER working paper 2494.

Greenwald, B., Stiglitz, J.E. and Weiss, A. (1984) 'Informational imperfections in the capital markets and macro-economic fluctuations', *American Economic Review*, 74:194–199.

Grossman, G. and Shapiro, C. (1984) 'Informative advertising with differentiated products', *Review of Economic Studies*, 51:33–52.

Grossman, S. (1981) 'The informational role of warranties and private disclosure about product quality', *Journal of Law and Economics*, 24:461–484.

Grossman, S. and Stiglitz, J.E. (1980) 'On the impossibility of informationally efficient markets', *American Economic Review*, 70:393–408.

Hall, R.E. (1987) 'Market structure and macroeconomic fluctuations', *Brookings Papers*, 2:285–338.

Heal, G. (1977) 'Guarantees and risk sharing', *Review of Economic Studies*, 44:549–560.

Katz, M. (1981) 'Imperfect competition and heterogeneous consumers: The theory of screening in product markets', Ph.D dissertation, Oxford University, unpublished.

Kihlstrom, R.E. and Riordon, M.H. (1984) 'Advertising as a signal', *Journal of Political Economy*, 92:427–450.

Klein, B. and Leffler, K.B. (1981) 'The role of market forces in assuring contractual performance', *Journal of Political Economy*, 89:615–641.

Kreps, D.M. and Wilson, R. (1982) 'Reputation and imperfect information', *Journal of Economic Theory*, 27:253–279.

Kreps, D.M., Milgrom, P., Roberts, J. and Wilson, R. (1982) 'Rational cooperation in the finitely repeated prisoners dilemma', *Journal of Economic Theory*, 27:245–252.

Milgrom, P. and Roberts, J. (1986) 'Price and advertising signals of product quality', *Journal of Political Economy*, 94:796–821.

Mortensen, D.T. (1973) 'Search equilibrium in a simple multi-market economy', discussion paper no. 54, Center for Mathematical Studies, Northwestern University.

Nelson, P. (1970) 'Information and consumer behavior', *Journal of Political Economy*, 78:311–329.

Nelson, P. (1974) 'Advertising as information', *Journal of Political Economy*, 81:729–754.

Nelson, P. (1978) 'Advertising as information once more', in: D.G. Tuerck, ed., *Issues in advertising: The economics of persuasion*. Washington, D.C.: American Enterprise Institute.

Pauly, M.V. and Satterthwaite, M.A. (1981) 'The pricing of primary care physicians' services: A test of the role of consumer information', *Bell Journal of Economics*, 12:488–506.

Perloff, J. and Salop, S. (1985) 'Equilibrium with imperfect information and product differentiation', *Review of Economic Studies*, 52:107–120.

Pratt, J., Weiss, D. and Zeckhauser, R. (1979) 'Price differences in almost competitive markets', *Quarterly Journal of Economics*, 93:189–211.

Ramey, G. (1986) 'Information transfer and investment in product quality', IMSS technical report no. 499, Stanford University.

Reinganum, J.F. (1979) 'A simple model of equilibrium price dispersion', *Journal of Political Economy*, 87:851–858.

Reny, P.J. (1988) 'Common knowledge and extensive form games', *Journal of Economic Perspectives*, forthcoming.

Riordan, M.H. (1986) 'Monopolistic competition with experience goods', *Quarterly Journal of Economics*, 265–279.

Rogerson, W.P. (1983) 'Reputation and product quality', *Bell Journal of Economics*, 14:508–516.

Rogerson, W.P. (1986) 'The dissipation of profits by brand name investment and entry when pricing guarantees product quality', *Journal of Political Economy*, forthcoming.

Rosenthal, R.W. (1982) 'A dynamic oligopoly game with lags in demand: More on the monotonicity of price in the number of sellers', *International Economic Review*, 23:353–360.

Rosenthal, R.W. (1980) 'A model in which an increase in the number of sellers leads to a higher price', *Econometrica*, 48:1575–1579.

Rothschild, M. (1973) 'Models of market organization with imperfect information: A survey', *Journal of Political Economy*, 81:1283–1308.

Rothschild, M. and Stiglitz, J.E. (1976) 'Equilibrium in competitive insurance markets: An essay on the economic markets with imperfect information', *Quarterly Journal of Economics*, 90:629–649.

Salop, S. (1977) 'The noisy monopolist: imperfect information, price dispersion, and price discrimination', *Review of Economic Studies*, 44:393–406.

Salop, S. (1978a) 'Parables of information transmission', in: A. Mitchell, ed., *The effect of information on consumer and market behavior*, Chicago.

Salop, S. (1978b) 'Second best policies in imperfect competition', University of Pennsylvania, unpublished.

Salop, S. and Stiglitz, J.E. (1976) 'Search costs, monopoly power, and price distributions', Stanford University, mimeo.

Salop, S. and Stiglitz, J.E. (1977a) 'The theory of sales, or luck of the draw: A simple model of equilibrium price dispersion with identical agents', mimeo.

Salop, S. and Stiglitz, J.E. (1977b) 'Bargains and ripoffs: A model of monopolistically competitive price dispersion', *Review of Economic Studies*, 44:493–510.

Salop, S. and Stiglitz, J.E. (1982) 'The theory of sales: A simple model of equilibrium price dispersion with identical agents', *American Economic Review*, 72:1211–1230.

Salop, S. and Stiglitz, J.E. (1987) 'Information, welfare and product diversity', in: G. Feiwel, ed., *Arrow and the foundations of the theory of economic policy*, 328–340. London: Macmillan.

Schmalensee, R. (1978) 'A model of advertising and product quality', *Journal of Political Economy*, 86:485–503.

Schmalansee, R. (1982a) 'Advertising and market structure', in: G.F. Mathewson and J.E. Stiglitz, eds., *New developments in the analysis of market structure*, 373–396. Cambridge, Massachusetts; MIT Press.

Schmalansee, R. (1982b) 'Product differentiation advantages of pioneering brands', *American Economic Review*, 72:349–365.
Scitovsky, T. (1950) 'Ignorance as a source of oligopoly power', *American Economic Review*, 40:48–53.
Scitovsky, T. (1976) *The joyless economy*. Oxford: Oxford University Press.
Shapiro, C. (1982) 'Consumer information, product quality, and seller reputation', *Bell Journal of Economics*, 13:20–35.
Shapiro, C. (1983) 'Premiums for high quality products as returns to reputation', *Quarterly Journal of Economics*, 98:615–641.
Shapiro, C. and Stiglitz, J.E. (1984) 'Equilibrium unemployment as a worker discipline device', *American Economic Review*, 74:433–444.
Shilony, Y. (1976) 'Mixed pricing in locational oligopoly', *Journal of Economic Theory*, 14:373–388.
Spence, A.M. (1977) 'Consumer misperceptions, product failure and producer liability', *Review of Economic Studies*, 44:561–572.
Steiner, R. (1978) 'Marketing productivity in consumer-goods industries—Vertical perspective', *Journal of Marketing*, 42:60–70.
Stigler, G. (1961) 'The economics of information', *Journal of Political Economics*, 69:213–225.
Stiglitz, J.E. (1974) 'Equilibrium wage distributions', IMSSS technical report no. 154, Stanford University.
Stiglitz, J.E. (1975) 'Theory of screening, education and the distribution of income', *American Economic Review*, 65:283–300.
Stiglitz, J.E. (1977) 'Monopoly, non-linear pricing and imperfect information: The insurance market', *Review of Economics Studies*, 44:40–43.
Stiglitz, J.E. (1984) 'Price rigidities and market structure', *American Economic Review*, 74:350–356.
Stiglitz, J.E. (1986) 'Equilibrium wage distributions', *Economic Journal*, 95:595–618.
Stiglitz, J.E. (1987a) 'The causes and consequences of the dependence of quality on price', *Journal of Economic Literature*, 25:1–48.
Stiglitz, J.E. (1987b) 'Competition and the number of firms in a market: Are duopolies more competitive than atomistic markets?', *Journal of Political Economy*, 95:1041–1061.
Stiglitz, J.E. (1989) *Information and economic analysis*. New York: Oxford University Press, forthcoming.
Stiglitz, J.E. and Weiss, A. (1981) 'Credit rationing in markets with imperfect information', *American Economic Review*, 71:393–410.
Stiglitz, J.E. and Weiss, A. (1983) 'Incentive effects of terminations: Applications to the credit and labor markets', *American Economic Review*, 73:912–927.
Varian, H. (1980) 'A theory of sales', *American Economic Review*, 70:651–659.
Von Weizacker, C.C. (1980) *Barriers to entry: A theoretical treatment*. New York: Springer.
Wolinsky, A. (1986) 'True monopolistic competition as a result of imperfect information', *Quarterly Journal of Economics*, 101:493–512.

Chapter 14

THE TIMING OF INNOVATION: RESEARCH, DEVELOPMENT, AND DIFFUSION

JENNIFER F. REINGANUM*

The University of Iowa

Contents

*The financial support of the National Science Foundation (Grant No. SES-8216407), the Alfred P. Sloan Foundation and the Center for the Study of the Economy and the State is gratefully acknowledged.

Handbook of Industrial Organization, Volume I, Edited by R. Schmalensee and R.D. Willig

1. Introduction

The analysis of the timing of innovation posits a particular innovation (or sequence of innovations) and examines how the expected benefits, the cost of R & D and interactions among competing firms combine to determine the pattern of expenditure across firms and over time, the date of introduction, and the identity of the innovating firm. In the case of a sequence of innovations, the expected lifetime of a given innovation and the pattern of technological leadership are also determined endogenously. Given that an innovation has been perfected, the extent and timing of its dissemination into use may be examined. Again this may depend upon a number of factors, including the existence of rival firms and institutions which may facilitate or retard the dissemination of innovations.

Section 2 addresses issues of innovation production in the context of symmetric noncooperative models. The important questions which have been examined in this context include: What is the aggregate noncooperative investment in research and development and how is it distributed across firms and across time? How many firms enter the race, and what is the resulting equilibrium date of innovation? The answers to these questions can then be compared with various benchmarks, such as their cooperative or surplus-maximizing counterparts. The typical outcome of these comparisons is that aggregate expenditure on R & D is too high relative to the cooperative optimum; there are too many firms and each invests too much. These problems can be attributed to two types of market failure. At each date, each firm considers only its own marginal benefit from investment and does not take into account the reduction it imposes on the expected value of the other firms' investments; consequently, each firm invests too much. Moreover, since entry into the race is unrestricted, it will continue until all expected profits are dissipated; entering firms do not take into account the loss of intertemporal efficiencies by rival firms when they decide to enter. Thus, the firms (collectively) forego intertemporal efficiencies which could be realized by investing at a lower rate over a longer planning horizon. By analogy to the problem of the commons, there is "over-grazing" in the industry. Comparison with the surplus-maximizing investment is more difficult, since the innovator is typically unable to appropriate the full surplus. This will tend to depress investment in research and development, making the comparison ambiguous. See Hirshleifer and Riley (1979) for a more complete discussion of this issue.

Section 3 considers asymmetric models, in which the issues of primary interest have been the effects on investment incentives provided by current market power, anticipated future innovation, and the possession of a technological advantage (e.g. being closer to completion). Results in this area seem particularly sensitive to the presence or absence of technological uncertainty in the production of the innovation. When innovation is uncertain, a firm which currently enjoys a large market share will invest at a lower rate than a potential entrant, for an innovation which promises the winner a large share of the market. When innovation is deterministic, the opposite is true. Moreover, this same dichotomy extends to the case of a sequence of drastic innovations. When innovation is stochastic, the role of technological leader tends to circulate around the industry, while deterministic innovation results in a single, persistent technological leader. The effect of anticipated future innovation will also differ in these two cases; in the former, it reduces the value of winning the current race, since today's winner is likely to lose the next race; in the latter case, winning today is all-important, since today's winner also wins all future races. In a multi-stage game, the impact of having a technological lead is, as one might expect, to increase that firm's likelihood of winning the overall race, all else equal. Indeed, with all else equal and deterministic innovation, a very small head start is sufficient to ensure that the leading firm will win. However, if all else is not equal – that is, one firm anticipates greater benefits or faces lower costs – then an absolute disadvantage in terms of distance from completion will be overcome by the increased investment occasioned by the lagging firm's greater desire or effectiveness. When invention is stochastic, although firms with a technological lead invest at a higher rate than their lagging rivals, a lucky laggard may still win the race.

Section 4 investigates the extent of dissemination of the innovation, where this dissemination is achieved through licensing. Several recent papers have examined optimal fixed-fee licensing for a patentholder selling to an oligopolistic industry. This patentholder may be an independent researcher or a joint venture of a subset of the industry's firms. One robust finding is that, in the absence of involuntary spillovers, firms who are not members of the research joint venture are left worse off as a result of innovation. In the case of an independent research lab, all members of the downstream industry are worse off; the patentholder reaps more than the total cost savings attributable to the innovation. Research joint ventures tend to restrict the dissemination of an innovation relative to an independent researcher; moreover, incentives to develop an innovation are weaker the larger is the joint venture. Thus, joint ventures would tend to restrict both the development and dissemination of an innovation. Of course, in evaluating the desirability of a joint venture, one would have to weigh against these restrictive tendencies any benefits (such as a reduction in the duplication of effort, or scale efficiencies) which might be generated. The motivation for licensing in these models is the cost savings which are generated by the use of the innovation, which can be at least partially appropriated by the patentholder, even under a less than optimal licensing agreement. When future technical advance is possible, another incentive for licensing arises; a firm with a superior technology can license it to a rival firm in order to make further investment in R&D an unattractive strategy for the rival. Thus, the dissemination of the current technology (or the output of the current product) is enhanced at the expense of slower development of the next innovation.

Section 5 examines the timing of the adoption of an innovation, and summarizes recent work which provides alternative theoretical explanations for the observed diffusion of innovations into use. One explanation involves firms with differing initial priors about the profitability of the innovation. Information which accumulates over time is used to update these priors, and firms with more optimistic prior beliefs become "convinced" of an innovation's profitability sooner than those with less optimistic beliefs. The combination of adjustment costs which decline with the period of adjustment and benefits of adoption which decline with the number of other adopters (such as arise when firms enjoy some degree of market power) results in firms planning to adopt an innovation in sequence. Since each firm ignores the fact that its adoption decreases the value of adoption for all subsequent adopters, each firm adopts too early from the perspective of the industry as a whole; that is, industry profits would be higher if firms coordinated their adoption plans, resulting in a slower diffusion of the innovation. Similar results obtain for standard specifications of the social good. Finally, if a firm perceives network externalities (its own benefits from adoption increase with the number of other adopters), it may find it optimal to wait until its more eager colleagues have adopted it. In this case, it may be that "excess inertia" exists, so that despite the fact that all firms prefer life with the innovation to life without it, no one is sufficiently eager to initiate the adoption process. If the process is begun, however, the existence of network externalities generates a "bandwagon effect", since the value of adoption increases with the number of previous adopters.

Throughout this chapter I will focus on recent theoretical work, which is primarily game theoretic in nature. Recent empirical work in this area is surveyed in Chapter 19 of this Handbook. For more comprehensive surveys, see the monographs by Kamien and Schwartz (1980) and Stoneman (1983). In brackets, I note the source of each proposition. However, since I have made some modifications and re-interpretations, do not take these references too literally. To find out what the authors *really* claimed (and how they proved it) see the original papers.

An equally important – though less thoroughly investigated – aspect of technological change is the extent of innovation. This is typically examined in the context of cost reduction [e.g. Dasgupta and Stiglitz (1980a), Flaherty (1980), Telser (1982), Reinganum (1982b, 1983a), Spence (1984), Tandon (1984) and Katz (1986)], although an alternative measure for product innovation is the extent of product diversity [e.g. Spence (1976), Dixit and Stiglitz (1977) and Judd (1985b)]. The issue of the extent of innovation will not be dealt with here, primarily due to space constraints. Another relevant strand of the literature which will not be discussed here is the work on learning by doing [e.g. Arrow (1962b), Spence (1981) and Fudenberg and Tirole (1983)], in which cost reduction is achieved as a result of production experience.

The timing of innovation has been examined in two basic paradigms: (1) a deterministic "auction" model, which can be traced to Barzel (1968) and Scherer (1967) and appears subsequently in Dasgupta and Stiglitz (1980b), Gilbert and Newbery (1982) and Katz and Shapiro (1985b); and (2) a stochastic "racing" model, which was analyzed for the single-firm case by Lucas (1971), and Kamien and Schwartz (1971), and subsequently was generalized by Fethke and Birch (1982) and Grossman and Shapiro (1986). Kamien and Schwartz (1972) generalized the single-firm model to include a partial account of the effects of rivalry, and the stochastic racing model appears as a full equilibrium model in Loury (1979), Dasgupta and Stiglitz (1980b), Lee and Wilde (1980) and Reinganum (1981a, 1982a). Since both these paradigms have been used repeatedly to address problems of innovation timing and related issues, both will be described in some detail for the case of symmetric games of research and development. This will make it easier to address related issues such as pre-emptive innovation and the persistence of monopoly, and licensing and the diffusion of innovations, which rely to a considerable extent upon variations of these two basic paradigms. We will begin with the most restrictive environment, and relax assumptions as we go along.

A third paradigm for examining investment in R&D is that used by Futia (1980), Hartwick (1982) and Rogerson (1982). This model assumes that there is one innovation per period and the innovator is determined as a random function of the firms' investments. For example, if firm i invests x_i, it wins with probability $p_i = x_i/\sum x_j$. Thus, the game is not one of timing; it is rather a "contest" model. However, it does predict that firms overinvest in R&D and that each invests more the better is the patent protection. This sort of model has been examined in a laboratory experiment by Isaac and Reynolds (1985) who find that the experimental data are consistent with predicted Nash equilibrium play, and that the aforementioned predictions are indeed borne out in an experimental market.

2. Symmetric models

The first environment we wish to consider is one in which a particular invention is sought simultaneously by a number of identical potential inventors, which we will refer to as firms. The firm which produces the invention first is awarded a patent, which completely protects it from imitation or duplication. Invention is a costly activity, with the cost of invention by any given date being a decreasing convex function of the time prior to invention. One justification for this cost function would be that the firm is optimally allocating its efforts on the invention throughout this period but suffers from classical diseconomies of scale; hence postponing the date of invention allows the firm to reduce its invention costs, but at a decreasing rate. For a computational example, see Kamien and Schwartz (1974); for additional arguments in favor of costs having this form, see Scherer (1967).

An alternative but essentially equivalent formulation assumes that a commitment of funds today determines the eventual date of invention according to a decreasing and convex function. Since invention is completely deterministic, the firm which commits the greatest expenditure (today) will obtain the invention first. A simple formal model which summarizes this situation is the following "auction" model. Let P denote the value of winning to the inventor; by assumption, all others receive 0. Assume that P is constant, and that all firms use the same discount rate r. If firm i were to spend x_i on research and development, it would complete the invention at date $T_i = T(x_i)$, where $T(\cdot)$ is decreasing and convex. A *strategy* for firm i is a bid x_i, and a *Nash equilibrium* is a vector of bids with the property that no firm wishes to unilaterally change its bid. The firm with the largest bid wins; if more than one firm wins, then the patent is awarded randomly among the winning firms. The key assumption about this model is that *no real resources are expended until the winner is determined.* That is, the firms "bid" what they would spend, a winner is determined, and only the winning firm actually develops the invention (spends the amount of its bid). If real resources were committed, no Nash equilibrium exists in pure strategies; however, the result of Proposition 1 below can be sustained as a Stackelberg equilibrium in which the firm with the highest bid moves first.

Under these assumptions, firm i's payoff when the strategy (bid) vector is x is

$$V^i(x) = \begin{cases} P\mathrm{e}^{-rT(x_i)} - x_i, & \text{if } x_i > x_j, \text{ for all } j \neq i, \\ \dfrac{1}{n(x)}\left[P\mathrm{e}^{-rT(x_i)} - x_i\right], & \text{if } x_i = x_j > x_k, \\ & \quad \text{for } n(x) - 1\ j\text{'s and remaining } k\text{'s}, \\ 0, & \text{if } x_i < x_j, \text{ for some } j \neq i. \end{cases}$$

Proposition 1 [Dasgupta and Stiglitz (1980b)]

A Nash equilibrium for this game involves two or more firms bidding x^*, where x^* is the largest value of x such that $P\mathrm{e}^{-rT(x)} - x = 0$. Only one firm will actually invest x^*, and all firms make zero profits in equilibrium.

The intuition behind this result is clear; if any losing firm could pre-empt the winner and make positive profits, it would do so by bidding more. Hence, the winning firm must make zero profits given that it must spend its winning bid. The losing firms invest nothing and receive nothing.

A joint venture involving all firms in the industry would involve a single firm investing an amount x^{**} which maximizes $P\mathrm{e}^{-rT(x)} - x$. To see that this involves less investment than under noncooperative play, it suffices to note that for $x > x^*$, $P\mathrm{e}^{-rT(x)} - x < 0$. Thus, $x^{**} \leq x^*$, with a strict inequality so long as there is any investment level which yields strictly positive profits.

It was remarked earlier that a similar equilibrium configuration results if we specify one firm as a dominant firm, or first mover (Stackelberg leader). In this case, the dominant firm commits its expenditure at x^*, knowing that only this will keep rival firms from out-investing it and succeeding earlier. The lesson of this model is that one need not actually observe a "race" in progress; *potential* competition may make one run equally hard.

Alongside the auction model of invention is the second paradigm, in which the stochastic nature of invention is incorporated. In this framework, an investment of x_i still buys firm i a date of success, say $\tau_i = \tau(x_i)$, but now this date is regarded as random, indicating that success by any given date is only stochastically related to expenditure. A *strategy* in this framework is an investment level x_i. In earlier work on the management of research and development, Lucas (1971) and Kamien and Schwartz (1971) employed relatively general distribution functions. However, the addition of strategic rivals required some simplifications of other aspects of the problem, leading authors of recent game theoretic models [e.g. Loury (1979), Dasgupta and Stiglitz (1980b) and Lee and Wilde (1980)] to adopt the exponential distribution. That is, the probability that firm i is successful by date t is $\Pr\{\tau(x_i) \leq t\} = 1 - \exp\{-h(x_i)t\}$, where $h(x_i)$ is twice differentiable, strictly increasing, and satisfies:

$$\text{(i)}\quad h(0) = 0 = \lim_{x\to\infty} h'(x),$$

$$\text{(ii)}\quad h''(x) \geq (\leq) 0 \quad \text{as} \quad x \leq (\geq) \bar{x},$$

$$\text{(iii)}\quad h(x)/x \geq (\leq) h'(x) \quad \text{as} \quad x \geq (\leq) \tilde{x},$$

for some $(\bar{x}, \tilde{x})$ such that $0 \leq \bar{x} \leq \tilde{x} < \infty$.

Again let P denote the value of winning (assumed stationary) and r the common discount rate. Since success is not equivalent to winning, we need to compute the probability that firm i wins at any date t. Here the virtue of the exponential assumption becomes evident. Assuming that there are n firms whose processes are stochastically independent, the probability density that firm i wins at t is

$$\Pr\{\tau(x_i) \in [t, t+\mathrm{d}t] \text{ and } \tau(x_k) > t \text{ for all } k \neq i\}$$
$$= h(x_i)\exp\{-\textstyle\sum h(x_j)t\}\,\mathrm{d}t,$$

where the summation is taken over $j = 1, 2, \ldots, n$. For the exponential distribution, the expected date of invention is simply $1/\sum h(x_j)$. Let $a_i = \sum_{j \neq i} h(x_j)$ denote the aggregate rival hazard rate. Since the game is completely symmetric, we can write the payoff to any one firm as a function of its own investment x and the aggregate rival hazard rate a:

$$V(x, a) = \int_0^\infty P\mathrm{e}^{-rt}h(x)\exp\{-(a + h(x))t\}\mathrm{d}t - x$$
$$= \frac{Ph(x)}{a + h(x) + r} - x. \tag{1}$$

A *best response function* for firm i to the aggregate rival hazard rate a is a function $\hat{x}(\cdot)$ such that for all a, $V(\hat{x}(a), a) \geq V(x, a)$ for all x. A *symmetric Nash equilibrium* for a given number of firms n will be denoted $x^*(n)$ and satisfies the relation $x^* = \hat{x}(a^*)$, where $a^* = (n-1)h(x^*)$.

Proposition 2 [Loury (1979)]

As the number of firms in the industry increases, the equilibrium level of firm investment declines: $\mathrm{d}x^*/\mathrm{d}n < 0$.

This also implies that the expected success time for each firm rises, since $\mathrm{E}\tau_i = 1/h(x^*(n))$. However, the time of invention, denoted $\tau(n)$, is the time of the *first* success: $\tau(n) = \min_i\{\tau_i\}$. With more firms there are more chances for early success, even though each one is less likely to yield early success. Under the following stability condition, Loury shows that the expected time to invention, $\mathrm{E}\tau(n) = 1/nh(x^*(n))$, falls with an increase in n.

Assumption 1

Assume that $-h'(x^*)\hat{x}'(a^*) < 1$.

That is, in equilibrium a marginal increase in investment by any single rival firm causes the investment of a given firm to fall by a smaller amount. To understand this interpretation, suppose that one rival firm increases its investment by $\mathrm{d}x$; then $\mathrm{d}a = h'(x^*)\,\mathrm{d}x$, and the condition above says that $-h'(x^*)\,\mathrm{d}\hat{x} < h'(x^*)\,\mathrm{d}x$, or $-\mathrm{d}\hat{x} < \mathrm{d}x$.

Proposition 3 [Loury (1979)]

Under Assumption 1, increasing the number of firms reduces the expected date of invention.

Once equilibrium is characterized for an arbitrary number of firms, one can permit this number to be determined endogenously through entry (i.e. via a zero profit condition). It is easy to show that equilibrium expected profits decrease with increasing n; thus entry continues unless $V(x^*, a^*) = 0$.

Consider the alternative problem of firms investing cooperatively and sharing equally in the reward. There are several reasons why the solution to this problem does not coincide with the noncooperative equilibrium. First, the joint venture may not value the innovation at P; for example, antitrust regulation may prevent the venture from extracting the innovation's full value; on the other hand, perhaps the members of the joint venture can do better than P by a creative use of market segmentation. Second, noncooperative firms may not operate at the jointly optimal scale, and finally, the noncooperative equilibrium with entry may not result in the jointly optimal number of firms. If we assume that each firm values the innovation at P (whether investment is done noncooperatively or cooperatively), and that the research joint venture can also restrict entry, then it can be shown that for a given number of noncooperative firms, each invests too much. Moreover, in a noncooperative equilibrium with unrestricted entry, there will be too many firms relative to the joint optimum. Combining these two results with the fact that $\mathrm{d}x^*/\mathrm{d}n < 0$, while $\mathrm{d}(nx^*)/\mathrm{d}n > 0$ implies that in a free-entry noncooperative equilibrium there is too much investment in aggregate terms (relative to the joint optimum). This aggregate investment is produced by too many firms operating at less than efficient scale. Cooperation would involve fewer firms operating at efficient scale, but investing less in aggregate terms.

Proposition 4 [Loury (1979)]

Suppose that the function $V(x, (n-1)h(x))$ is a single-peaked (that is, increasing, then decreasing) function of x. Given a fixed number of firms, in industry equilibrium each firm invests more in R&D than is jointly optimal.

Each firm ignores its impact on its rivals' payoffs; consequently there is an excessive duplication of effort in the noncooperative equilibrium.

Proposition 5 [Loury (1979)]

If $\bar{x} > 0$, then unrestricted entry results in too many firms, each of which invests too little (relative to the cooperative optimum).

Lee and Wilde (1980) argued that the formalism which assumed that research and development expenditures were committed up front was inappropriate; since expenditure actually occurs over time, firms can stop investing once someone has succeeded. Instead, they permitted firms to choose a research intensity; once this intensity is fixed, the firm must either sustain this level of investment or cease investment altogether. Thus, the probability of success by any date t is still exponential, but the parameter now depends upon the *intensity* of research, rather than the *scale* of the lab. The new formula for firm i's payoff is:

$$V^i(x) = \int_0^{\infty} \exp\{-\sum h(x_j)\}[P\mathrm{e}^{-rt}h(x_i) - x_i]\mathrm{d}t - F$$

$$= \frac{Ph(x) - x}{a + h(x) + r} - F, \tag{2}$$

where F denotes some possible fixed cost which is involved in entering the industry.

Lee and Wilde showed that this modification can substantially alter some of the model's implications. In particular, in equilibrium an increase in the number of rivals is associated with an increase in the intensity of research and development investment.

The fact that in Nash equilibrium $x^*(n) = \hat{x}(a^*(n))$, where $a^*(n) = (n-1)h(x^*(n))$, can be used to determine $\mathrm{d}x^*/\mathrm{d}n$. Under the following stability condition, Lee and Wilde show that a firm's noncooperative equilibrium research intensity is an increasing function of the number of firms.

Assumption 2

Assume that $1 - (n-1)h'(x^*)\hat{x}'(a^*) > 0$.

This requires that if a firm's competitors all increase their investments just enough to generate a unit increase in rivalry, then the remaining firm must respond with less than a full unit increase in investment. If all other firms increase their investment rates by the amount $\mathrm{d}x$, the remaining firm must increase its investment rate by less than $\mathrm{d}x$. To see this, note that an increase of $\mathrm{d}x$ by all others implies $\mathrm{d}a = (n-1)h'(x)\mathrm{d}x$. The requirement that $\hat{x}'(a) < 1/(n-1)h'(x)$ is then equivalent to $\mathrm{d}\hat{x} < \mathrm{d}a/(n-1)h'(x)$ or $\mathrm{d}\hat{x} < \mathrm{d}x$.

Proposition 6 [Lee and Wilde (1980)]

Under Assumption 2, as the number of firms in the industry increases, the equilibrium rate of investment per firm increases; a fortiori the aggregate rate of investment increases.

Since the expected invention date is $1/nh(x^*(n))$, an increase in the number of competing firms is associated with an earlier invention date on average; there are more firms, and each firm invests at a higher rate. Again it is easy to show that $V(x^*, a^*)$ decreases with increasing n. Free entry then occurs until equilibrium expected profits are zero.

Proposition 7 [Lee and Wilde (1980)]

Suppose that the function $V(x,(n-1)h(x))$ is a single-peaked (that is, increasing, then decreasing) function of x. Given a fixed number of firms, in industry equilibrium each firm invests at a higher rate than is jointly optimal.

Proposition 8 [Lee and Wilde (1980)]

If $\bar{x} > 0$, then unrestricted entry results in too many firms, each of which invests at too high a rate (relative to the cooperative solution).

Although Lee and Wilde have shown that the noncooperative firm's research intensity is an increasing function of n, this does not directly contradict the Loury result. Instead, one would like to compare total expected investment in the Lee and Wilde model with total lump-sum investment in the Loury model. It turns out that no general ranking emerges, but plausible examples can be devised in which expected total investment declines with an increase in the number of competing firms. Thus, it is quite possible that these results are consistent. The remaining inconsistency is the effect of n on each noncooperative firm's expected success date; in Loury (1979), success by any one firm is delayed (on average) by an increase in n, while in Lee and Wilde (1980) it is hastened. However, the *first* success date is hastened by an increase in n in both models. Since this is the only *observable* indicator of success, from a positive perspective it is immaterial which of these two models is the more empirically representative. Similarly, if one were to interpret P as both the private and the social value of the innovation, then normative prescriptions are essentially the same for both models; restrict entry to the optimal number of firms, then adjust the patent value to eliminate over-investment.

Mortensen (1982) has shown that one aspect of the externality which competing firms impose on one another can be internalized by the following institution:

the winning firm receives the value P less a compensation paid to each losing firm which is equal to the foregone value of continued play. This institution induces noncooperative firms to select the optimal cooperative investment level *given the number of firms n*. Since this institution raises individual firm profits relative to the noncooperative equilibrium without this institution, more firms would prefer to enter the industry when this institution is in place. Thus, the cooperating firms must also be able to limit entry in order to fully internalize the externality. Since the foregone value of continued play is stationary in this model, equilibrium under this institution is relatively easy to characterize. Although this argument works equally well for asymmetric firms, the case of symmetric firms is simpler to describe and has been independently and more extensively analyzed by Stewart (1983).

Suppose that the winning firm receives the value P but must compensate the remaining $n-1$ firms in the amount $P(1-\sigma)/(n-1)$ each; thus the winning firm retains the amount σP. In this case, one can write the expected profit to firm i if it invests at rate x while the aggregate rival hazard rate is a, as

$$V(x, a) = \frac{P[\sigma h(x) + a(1-\sigma)/(n-1)] - x}{a + h(x) + r} - F. \tag{3}$$

At a symmetric Nash equilibrium for this game, which we will denote by $x^*(n, \sigma)$, it must be that

$$\frac{\partial V(x^*, a^*)}{\partial x} = \frac{(nh(x^*) + r)(P\sigma h'(x^*) - 1) - (Ph(x^*) - x^*)h'(x^*)}{(nh(x^*) + r)^2} = 0. \tag{4}$$

For comparison, joint profits $nV(x,(n-1)h(x))$ are maximized for $x^{**}(n)$ such that

$$\frac{(r + nh(x^{**}))(Ph'(x^{**}) - 1) - (Ph(x^{**}) - x^{**})nh'(x^{**})}{(nh(x^{**}) + r)^2} = 0. \tag{5}$$

Thus, $x^*(n, \sigma) = x^{**}(n)$ if

$$\sigma = \sigma^*(n) \equiv \frac{Ph'(x^{**}(n)) + n - 1}{nPh'(x^{**}(n))}.$$

That is, there is a winner's share $\sigma^*(n)$ which induces noncooperative firms to invest at the cooperative level.

If members of an industry can credibly set up such an institution for sharing the reward for innovation, then each member has incentives for (noncooperatively) choosing the cooperative investment level. Stewart (1983) interprets this as a model of imperfect patent protection (as opposed to cooperative innovation), but in this case the reward is unlikely to be P; it is likely that because of nonappropriability, some of the value of the innovation will be dissipated.

If one is willing to assume that the social value of the innovation is also P, then all of the above comparisons of noncooperative equilibrium and joint optimality are also applicable to the comparison between noncooperative equilibrium and social optimality.

The excessive investment in research which is implied by these models arises out of two sources. First, each firm wants to win the race, while society typically has no particular preferences regarding the identity of the winner, so long as there is one; this results in too much investment for a given number of firms. Second, because there is unrestricted access to the common pool of undiscovered innovations, too many firms will compete.

Reinganum (1981a, 1982a) undertook to generalize the earlier decision-theoretic work of Kamien and Schwartz (1972) to include explicit game-theoretic interactions among rivals. To this end, she posited that firms are free to react instantaneously to a number of features of the economic environment, including time, whether or not rival firms have already succeeded, their own and rival firms' accumulated investment. As in Lee and Wilde (1980), firms are assumed to be able to respond to a rival's success by ceasing investment; that is, we focus on the effects of flow expenditures upon the likelihood of success. However, unlike the Lee and Wilde formulation, the rate of expenditure is not restricted to be constant through time. Instead, firms may adjust the rate of expenditure in response to elapsed time and state variables which summarize rival progress. Reinganum (1982a) also considers the case of imperfect patent protection, which previous work eschewed.

Assume that a given number of firms n are competing to perfect a particular invention. Firm i succeeds if it perfects the invention, but firm i wins only if it succeeds before any other firm. If firm i wins, then firm i is designated the *innovator* and receives the "leader's" payoff P_L. However, assume that immediate reverse engineering may be possible and thus rival firms may also receive some benefit when firm i wins; the rival firms receive the *imitator's* or "follower's" payoff $P_F \leq P_L$. Use of the terms "leader" and "follower" does not connote any behavioral differences.

Each firm accumulates knowledge relevant to the innovation by investing resources on knowledge acquisition. This knowledge accumulates according to the differential equation $\dot{z}_i(t) = u_i(t, z(t))$, where $z_i(t)$ denotes firm i's knowledge stock at t, $z(t) = (z_1(t), \dots, z_n(t))$ and $u_i(t, z)$ denotes firm i's rate of knowledge acquisition at (t, z). We assume that $z_i(0) = 0$. The date of successful innovation is a random function of the amount of accumulated knowledge. Specifically, we assume that the probability of success given a knowledge stock of z or less is $F(z) = 1 - \exp\{-\lambda z\}$.

Thus, the amount of knowledge needed to succeed is exponentially distributed with mean $1/\lambda$. Since knowledge is accumulated over time, the distribution of firm i's random success time t_i is

$$\Pr\{t_i \leq t\} = F(z_i(t)) = 1 - \exp\{-\lambda z_i(t)\},$$

and the conditional probability density of success, given no success to date is

$$\Pr\{t_i \in (t, t + \mathrm{d}t] \mid t_i > t\} = \lambda u_i(t, z(t))\,\mathrm{d}t.$$

Thus, the conditional density of success depends only upon current investment. In the stochastic racing papers discussed above the date of invention was assumed to be exponentially distributed. In the current model, the amount of time needed for success need not be exponentially distributed. It will be so, of course, in the case of a constant rate of investment.

To complete the model, let $c(u) = (1/2)(\mathrm{u})^2$ represent the cost of acquiring new knowledge at the rate u. Let $[0, T]$ represent the planning horizon, and let r denote the discount rate. The assumption of a finite planning horizon is used primarily in order to allow us to use dynamic programming "backward". It may also be representative of many research situations in which funding will be terminated if concrete results are not forthcoming by a given date.

Previous studies have assumed that the patent value was constant independent of the date of success; more generally, one could argue that this patent value might grow over time as additional uses are discovered. Alternatively, some sort of exogenous obsolescence may be applicable, so that the patent value might decline over time. Thus, let g denote the rate of growth or decline of the patent value so that the values of winning and losing, respectively, at date t are (in present value terms) $P_{\mathrm{L}}\mathrm{e}^{gt}$ and $P_{\mathrm{F}}\mathrm{e}^{gt}$.

There are several possible formulations of strategies for differential games. The most commonly used are open-loop and feedback strategies. Open-loop strategies depend only upon the current date and the initial conditions of the problem. They may be obtained by applying standard optimal control arguments to the problem for each firm, and then solving the resulting linked systems of ordinary differential equations which characterize the equilibrium. Logically, open-loop strategies have the characteristic of precommitment; that is, one solves the problem from the initial conditions taking the time path of others' strategies as given. Feedback strategies are decision rules which are permitted to depend upon the current date and state variables, but not on the initial conditions. They are obtained by solving the problem from arbitrary (date, state) pairs; that is, by dynamic programming. Thus, feedback equilibria (Nash equilibria in feedback strategies) will embody the no-commitment assumption associated with subgame perfection [Selten (1975)]; noncredible threats about what a firm will do off the equilibrium path are ruled out. In situations in which firms have the information and the flexibility envisioned here, feedback equilibrium is the preferred solution concept. Although we will show below that our assumption that the conditional density of success depends only on current investment renders this distinction moot in this particular case, the method described below applies more generally.

A *strategy* for firm i will be a function $u_i(t, z)$, where z denotes the vector of state variables $z = (z_1, \dots, z_n)$. Given the strategy vector $u(t, z) = (u_1(t, z), \dots, u_n(t, z))$, one can solve for the trajectories of the state variables by solving the system of ordinary differential equations:

$$\dot{z}_i = u_i(t, z), \qquad z_i(0) = 0, \quad i = 1, 2, \dots, n.$$

Expected profits for firm i consist of three terms: costs are paid so long as no firm has yet succeeded. The probability that no firm has succeeded by t is

$$\Pr\{t_i > t \text{ for all } i\} = \exp\{-\lambda \textstyle\sum z_i(t)\}.$$

If firm i wins at t, then it receives $P_L e^{gt}$, while if firm i loses at t, it receives $P_F e^{gt}$. The probability that firm i wins at t is

$$\Pr\{t_i \in (t, t + dt], t_j > t \text{ for all } j\} = \lambda u_i(t, z) \exp\{-\lambda \textstyle\sum z_j(t)\}.$$

If $a_i(t, z) \equiv \sum_{j \neq i} \lambda u_j(t, z)$ denotes the aggregate rival hazard rate at t, then the probability that firm i loses at t (i.e. the probability that any rival firm wins at t) is

$$\begin{aligned}&\Pr\{t_k \in (t, t + dt] \text{ for any } k \neq i, t_j > t \text{ for all } j\} \\ &\quad = a_i(t, z) \exp\{-\lambda \textstyle\sum z_j(t)\}.\end{aligned}$$

Combining these terms and discounting to the present implies that firm i's payoff for any given strategy u_i and aggregate rival hazard rate a_i is

$$J^i(u_i, a_i) = \int_0^T e^{-rt} 3 \exp\{-\lambda \textstyle\sum z_j\}\left[P_L e^{gt} \lambda u_i + P_F e^{gt} a_i - (1/2)(u_i)^2\right] dt.$$

A *Nash equilibrium* is a vector of strategies $u^*(\cdot, \cdot)$ such that, for $i = 1, 2, \dots, n$, $J^i(u_i^*, a_i^*) \geq J^i(u_i, a_i^*)$ for all u_i.

Ideally we would like to solve this problem for arbitrary rates g of growth or decline in the patent value; failing this, we should at least select an interesting value for g. One interesting and computationally convenient value for g is $g = r$;

that is, the patent value grows at the rate of discount. The assumption of growth in the patent value seems plausible and, although this is an extremely high growth rate, it gives us an idea of the qualitative impact of patent value growth upon equilibrium investment and does so in a tractable manner. Qualitative features of the equilibrium should be the same for lower rates of growth in the patent value. One can conjecture on the basis of these results about the impact of declining patent values as well. Thus, from here on we assume $g = r$.

To characterize the Nash equilibrium for this game by using standard dynamic programming techniques, we must be concerned about two things: first, there should be a unique solution to the system $\dot{z} = u(t, z)$ through the boundary condition $z(t) = z$ for each $(t, z) \in [0, T] \times [0, \infty)^n$. Second, in order to assert the necessity of the partial differential equation of dynamic programming, we need the value functions to be continuously differentiable in (t, z). Both these requirements place restrictions upon the admissible set of strategies. It is relatively straightforward to find sufficient restrictions upon the strategies to guarantee that a unique solution exists for the system $\dot{z} = u(t, z)$. However, weak sufficient conditions for the continuous differentiability of the equilibrium value functions are unknown at this time. Our method of dealing with this problem is to forge ahead assuming sufficient smoothness and to argue subsequently that the solution we obtain is in fact a Nash equilibrium for the specified game.

Proposition 9 [Reinganum (1982a)]

A feedback Nash equilibrium strategy for each firm is

$$u_i^*(t, z; P_L, P_F) = \frac{2\lambda P_L(P_L - P_F)(n-1)e^{rt}}{(2n-1)P_L - [P_L + 2(n-1)P_F]\exp\{m(t)\}}.$$

The feedback Nash equilibrium payoff to each firm is

$$J^i(u_i^*, a_i^*) = P_L - \frac{2(P_L - P_F)P_L(n-1)}{(2n-1)P_L - [P_L + 2(n-1)P_F]\exp\{m(0)\}},$$

where $m(t) = (P_L - P_F)(n-1)\lambda^2(e^{rt} - e^{rT})/r$.

Notice that due to the "memorylessness" property of the exponential distribution of required knowledge – that is, the expected amount of additional knowledge given no success is independent of accumulated knowledge – the equilibrium strategies are independent of the state variables z. Since this is due to a special feature of the exponential distribution, it is not likely to carry over to games which involve alternative distribution functions. It is in some ways undesirable, since no firm can gain a convincing lead on its rivals, but it also likely accounts for the relative tractability of this model.

Proposition 10 [Reinganum (1982a)]

For $P_L > P_F$, an increase in P_L stimulates each firm to acquire knowledge at a higher rate, while an increase in P_F causes each firm to reduce its equilibrium rate of knowledge acquisition.

For the case of perfect patent protection, the equilibrium strategies are

$$u_i^*(t, z; P, 0) = \frac{2\lambda(n-1)P\,\mathrm{e}^{rt}}{2n-1-\exp\{P\lambda^2(n-1)(\mathrm{e}^{rt}-\mathrm{e}^{rT})/r\}}.$$

Proposition 11 [Reinganum (1982a)]

For the case of perfect patent protection, an increase in n increases the equilibrium rate of investment for each firm. Therefore an increase in n unambiguously decreases the expected time till innovation.

Next consider the limiting case $P_L = P_F$. In this case,

$$u_i^*(t, z; P_F, P_F) = \frac{2P_F\lambda\,\mathrm{e}^{rt}}{2-(2n-1)P_F\lambda^2(\mathrm{e}^{rt}-\mathrm{e}^{rT})/r}.$$

When patent protection is imperfect, the impact of an increase in the number of rival firms is much more complicated. In this case, it seems plausible that the payoffs P_L and P_F should both depend upon n. The determination of $P_L(n)$ and $P_F(n)$ might be regarded as the outcome of a subsequent licensing or oligopoly game. In order to determine the effect of increasing rivalry upon the equilibrium rate of investment, we now need to know the sign of

$$\frac{\mathrm{d}u_i^*}{\mathrm{d}n} = \frac{\partial u_i^*}{\partial n} + \frac{\partial u_i^*}{\partial P_L}P_L'(n) + \frac{\partial u_i^*}{\partial P_F}P_F'(n).$$

Under the most plausible circumstances, the sign of this expression is ambiguous, and will depend upon the specific nature of the institution or process which determines the relative payoffs to innovator and imitators (or licensor and licensees). For illustrative purposes, we could consider the case in which rewards are completely nonappropriable and are generated by a symmetric Cournot oligopoly. If P is the value of a monopoly on the innovation, then $P_L(n) =$

$P_F(n) = 4P/(n+1)^2$. In this case, it is straightforward to show that increasing n results in a uniform decrease in the rate of investment; that is, $du_i^*/dn < 0$ for all t.

A final comparison highlights the importance of the extent of appropriability in the determination of equilibrium investment. In the model developed above, there are no fixed costs associated with entering the industry. Thus, if entry is unrestricted, the equilibrium number of firms will be infinite. When patent protection is perfect:

$$\lim_{n\to\infty} u_i^*(t, z; P, 0) = P\lambda\, e^{rt}.$$

On the other hand, when patent protection is completely ineffective, then both $P_L(n)$ and $P_F(n)$ approach 0 as n gets large. In this case,

$$\lim_{n\to\infty} u_i^*(t, z; P_L(n), P_F(n)) = 0.$$

When patent protection is ineffective, no firm finds research and development a worthwhile undertaking.

In a companion piece, Reinganum (1981a) compares noncooperative and cooperative investment, and considers another form of nonappropriability which is characterized by spillovers in knowledge. To focus on these issues, assume that $n = 2$ and that patent protection is perfect.

Cooperation among firms involves coordinating research strategies, but it may also involve the cooperative exchange of knowledge. Thus, firms are able to operate on the lower portions of their cost curves while still generating the same aggregate amount of new knowledge. For cooperative firms, $\dot{z}_i = u_i(t, z) + \gamma u_j(t, z)$, where γ represents the fraction of new knowledge which can be shared with rival firms; γ may be less than unity because some knowledge may not be transferable or there may be some duplication in the knowledge acquired. Since the problem is symmetric, we can ignore subscripts: $z_i = z$, $u_i(t, z) = u(t, z)$, and $\dot{z}_i = \dot{z} = (1+\gamma)u(t, z)$. The payoff to the joint venture is the sum of the individual firms' payoffs (with the understanding that $\dot{z} = (1+\gamma)u(t, z)$; knowledge as well as profits are shared). Thus, joint profits are

$$J(u) = \int_0^T e^{-2\lambda z}\left[2P\lambda u(t, z) - e^{-rt}(u(t, z))^2\right]dt.$$

Proposition 12 [Reinganum (1981a)]

The cooperative rate of knowledge acquisition is

$$u^{**}(t, z) = \frac{(1+\gamma)P\lambda\, e^{rt}}{1 - P\lambda^2(1+\gamma)^2(e^{rt} - e^{rT})/r}.$$

The joint payoff is

$$J(u^{**}) = P - \frac{P}{1 - P\lambda^2(1+\gamma)^2(1-e^{rT})/r}.$$

In order to compare the timing of innovation under cooperative and noncooperative behavior, we need to compare the individual rates of knowledge acquisition. For noncooperative and cooperative rivals these are, respectively,

$$u^*(t, z) = \frac{2P\lambda e^{rt}}{3 - \exp\{m(t)\}}$$

and

$$\dot{z}^{**}(t;\gamma) = (1+\gamma)u^{**}(t, z) = \frac{(1+\gamma)^2 P\lambda e^{rt}}{1-(1+\gamma)^2 m(t)},$$

where $m(t) \equiv P\lambda^2(e^{rt} - e^{rT})/r$.

Proposition 13 [Reinganum (1981a)]

For $\gamma = 0$, $u^*(t, z) \geq \dot{z}(t; 0) = u^{**}(t, z)$ with equality only at $t = T$. That is, noncooperative rivals will (on average) succeed sooner than cooperative firms who are unable to share knowledge.

The cooperative rate of knowledge acquisition $\dot{z}^{**}(t;\gamma)$ is an increasing function of γ, so for $\gamma > 0$, it is typically the case that the rate of knowledge acquisition is higher for noncooperative rivals over the first portion, but higher for cooperative rivals over the latter portion of the planning horizon.

There are at least two ways in which a rival firm can benefit from a particular firm's investment in research and development. By imitating (or licensing) the innovation, the rival may be able to capture some of the benefits. However, even with perfect patent protection, the rival may benefit if some of the knowledge which is generated spills over to the rival firm. In this case, $\dot{z}_i = u_i(t, z) + \rho u_j(t, z)$, where $\rho \in [0, 1]$ denotes the extent of knowledge spillovers. For simplicity, we will suppose that spillovers in knowledge are complete; anything learned by firm i is also learned by firm j. Moreover, suppose that there is effectively no duplication. Then $\rho = 1$ and firm i's payoff is

$$J^i(u) = \int_0^T e^{-\lambda(z_1+z_2)}\left[P\lambda(u_1+u_2) - e^{-rt}(1/2)(u_1)^2\right]dt.$$

Analysis of this case proceeds as before, yielding the following results.

Proposition 14 [Reinganum (1981a)]

Let $u_i^*(t, z; \rho)$ denote the feedback Nash equilibrium strategies. For $\rho = 1$,

$$u_i^*(t, z; 1) = \frac{P\lambda \mathrm{e}^{rt}}{1 - 3P\lambda^2(\mathrm{e}^{rt} - \mathrm{e}^{rT})/r}.$$

The feedback Nash equilibrium payoffs are

$$J^i(u^*(t, z; 1)) = P/2 - \frac{P/2}{1 - 3P\lambda^2(1 - \mathrm{e}^{rT})/r}.$$

Several comparisons are possible. The problem for a central planner is equivalent to that of a joint venture with the substitution of the social value Q for the private value P. Thus, the socially optimal path is as in Proposition 12 with Q substituted for P.

Proposition 15 [Reinganum (1981a)]

Suppose that the social value of the innovation Q exceeds $P/2$, all knowledge is transferable ($\gamma = 1$) and spillovers are complete ($\rho = 1$). Then the noncooperative rate of knowledge acquisition is less than is socially optimal. Consequently, innovation will be delayed on average relative to the socially optimal date. Innovation by Nash rivals will occur later on average than the cooperative date.

Recall that for the opposite extreme case ($\gamma = 0$, $\rho = 0$), Nash rivals could be expected to innovate at an *earlier* date than cooperative firms. Thus, again we see the crucial effect of appropriability; that market structure which most promotes innovation depends critically upon the extent of spillovers.

It is also interesting to note that the existence of spillovers need not adversely affect the timing of innovation under noncooperative play. While it is true that each firm invests at a lower rate in the presence of spillovers, each also benefits from the investment of the other. For some parameter values, the existence of spillovers results in stochastically earlier innovation.

3. Asymmetric models

A topic of long-standing interest in industrial organization is the effect of current monopoly power upon a firm's incentives to engage in innovative activity [e.g. Schumpeter (1942)]. Arrow (1962a) argued that for a drastic innovation (one which leaves the inventor a monopolist), an incumbent monopolist would have less incentive to invent than would an inventor who currently has no share in the market. Gilbert and Newbery (1982) use the auction model to examine this question when an incumbent firm is faced with potential entrants who also compete for the innovation. They assume that each competing firm enters a bid which represents the maximum amount that firm will spend on research and development. The firm which bids the most is conceded to be the winner, and is required to invest the amount of its bid. For simplicity, assume that if the current monopolist, or incumbent, ties with one or more potential entrants, then the patent is awarded to the incumbent. If the incumbent wins with a bid of x_i, it receives $P^{\mathrm{m}}\mathrm{e}^{-rT(x_i)} - x_i$ in present value terms, where $T(x_i)$ is the date of completion and P^{m} is the capitalized value of the innovation if the relevant product market is monopolized. If a potential entrant wins with a bid of x_{e}, then the firms must share the market somehow. It is assumed that the entrant receives $P^{\mathrm{e}}\mathrm{e}^{-rT(x_{\mathrm{e}})} - x_{\mathrm{e}}$, while the incumbent receives $P^{\mathrm{i}}\mathrm{e}^{-rT(x_{\mathrm{e}})}$. In this case P^{e} and P^{i} represent the entrant's and incumbent's portions of the value of the innovation. Under most plausible specifications, $P^{\mathrm{m}} \geq P^{\mathrm{e}} + P^{\mathrm{i}}$; that is, there is some dissipation of rents when the market is noncooperatively shared rather than monopolized.

Proposition 16 [Gilbert and Newbery (1982)]

If $P^{\mathrm{m}} \geq P^{\mathrm{e}} + P^{\mathrm{i}}$, then the current incumbent will win the bidding game with a bid of x^*, where x^* is the largest solution of

$$P^{\mathrm{e}}\mathrm{e}^{-rT(x)} - x = 0. \tag{6}$$

Thus, a firm which currently enjoys monopoly power will pre-emptively patent the innovation and persist as a monopolist.

Following the same line of argument as in Proposition 1, competing potential entrants will bid up to x^* as described above. If the incumbent is willing to bid at least x^*, then it will win. By bidding less, the incumbent would receive $P^{\mathrm{i}}\mathrm{e}^{-rT(x^*)}$; by matching the potential entrants' bid, the incumbent would receive $P^{\mathrm{m}}\mathrm{e}^{-rT(x^*)} - x^*$. The latter option is preferred to the former if and only if $P^{\mathrm{m}}\mathrm{e}^{-rT(x^*)} - x^* \geq P^{\mathrm{i}}\mathrm{e}^{-rT(x^*)}$. Substituting from equation (6) for x^*, this reduces to $[P^{\mathrm{m}} - P^{\mathrm{i}} - P^{\mathrm{e}}]\mathrm{e}^{-rT(x^*)} \geq 0$.

Thus, the incentive for pre-emptive patenting and persistent monopoly arises from the dissipation of industry profits which one anticipates will accompany a less concentrated market structure. Notice that the incumbent firm need not *use* the innovation (e.g. implement the new technology or produce the new product); even a product or technology which is inferior to the incumbent's current one will elicit pre-emptive investment from the incumbent. In this case, one may find "sleeping patents", which are used solely to preserve the incumbent's monopoly position. While the use of inferior technologies is inefficient, so is monopoly; the industry composed of two competing firms, one of which employs an inefficient technology, may be welfare-preferred to the more concentrated but cost-efficient industry.

Gilbert and Newbery remarked that in the event that the above inequality is strict, an incumbent with a relative cost disadvantage in innovation would still pre-empt the potential entrant. Salant (1984) argued that this result is based on the assumption that there is no possibility of ex post licensing. If licensing is permitted, Salant shows that the firm which is most efficient at innovation will always win the patent, but may sell it to the other firm if the other firm is a more efficient producer. In any event, optimal licensing will still result in a monopolized market.

Katz and Shapiro (1987) examine pre-emption in a somewhat more general version of the auction model. They permit two active firms from the outset, and allow for the possibility of licensing or imitation following innovation. In addition, they envision an exogenous decline in the costs of developing an innovation due to ongoing and freely available basic research. Their analysis involves lengthy arguments, and we briefly summarize their model and results here.

Let π_0^i denote firm i's flow profits prior to development of the innovation. If firm i develops the innovation, its profits become π_i^i and its rival's profits become π_i^j. Let $\pi_i = \pi_i^i + \pi_i^j$ denote industry profits when firm i wins, and suppose without loss of generality that $\pi_1 \geq \pi_2$.

Each firm has two incentives to innovate. First, firm i has an incentive to win because its profits (are assumed to) rise if it develops the innovation; that is, $\pi_i^i \geq \pi_0^i$. Second, firm i has an incentive to win (to avoid losing) because its profits are (assumed to be) higher when it wins than when the rival wins; that is, $\pi_i^i \geq \pi_j^i$. The former incentive, $\pi_i^i - \pi_0^i$, is the "stand-alone" incentive, while the latter incentive, $\pi_i^i - \pi_j^i$, is a measure of the "incentive to pre-empt". Katz and Shapiro show that if firm 1 has both a larger stand-alone incentive and a larger incentive to pre-empt, then firm 1 will win the race. If firm 2 has the larger stand-alone incentive, but firm 1 has the larger incentive to pre-empt, then either firm may win.

Reinganum (1983b) addresses the question of the effect of current monopoly profit upon an incumbent firm's incentives to invest in research and development in the context of the stochastic racing model. This is done to compare the results with those of Gilbert and Newbery for the auction model and to provide a theoretical explanation of some stylized facts about the sources of innovation.

According to Scherer (1980, pp. 437–438):

> There is abundant evidence from case studies to support the view that actual and potential new entrants play a crucial role in stimulating technical progress, both as direct sources of innovation and as spurs to existing industry

members . . . new entrants contribute a disproportionately high share of all really revolutionary new industrial products and processes.

Gilbert and Newbery's analysis captures some of this in the sense that potential entrants do act as a spur to the current incumbent; on the other hand, potential entrants do not contribute directly. In the context of the Lee and Wilde (1980) stochastic racing model, Reinganum (1983b) shows that when the first successful innovator captures a sufficiently high share of the post-innovation market, then in a Nash equilibrium the incumbent firm invests less on a given project than does the potential entrant, or challenger. Thus, the incumbent is less likely to be the innovator than is the challenger.

The intuition for this result is straightforward, at least for the case in which the innovation is drastic; that is, when the innovator captures the entire post-innovation market. When innovation is uncertain, the incumbent firm receives flow profits before successful innovation. This period is of random length, but is stochastically shorter the more the incumbent (or the challenger) invests. The incumbent has relatively less incentive than the challenger to shorten the period of its incumbency.

This model provides a framework in which equilibrium play generates the stylized facts mentioned above: potential entrants stimulate progress both through their own investment and by provoking incumbents to invest more. In equilibrium, potential entrants contribute a disproportionate share of large innovations.

To illustrate this model and its results, consider a cost-reducing innovation in an industry with constant returns to scale. Let $\bar{c}$ denote the incumbent firm's current unit costs, and let c be the unit cost associated with the new technology. Let R be the current flow rate of profit; let $\Pi(c)$ denote the present value of monopoly profits under the new technology, which is also the value of the reward to the incumbent if it invents the new technology; finally, let $\pi_{\mathrm{I}}(c)$ and $\pi_{\mathrm{C}}(c)$ denote the present value of Cournot–Nash profits to the incumbent and challenger, respectively, if the challenger invents the new technology and the incumbent retains use of the current technology.

We will assume that the functions $\Pi(\cdot)$, $\pi_{\mathrm{I}}(\cdot)$ and $\pi_{\mathrm{C}}(\cdot)$ are continuous and piecewise continuously differentiable; $\Pi(\cdot)$ and $\pi_{\mathrm{C}}(\cdot)$ are nonincreasing, while $\pi_{\mathrm{I}}(\cdot)$ is nondecreasing. The innovation will be termed *drastic* if $c \leq c^0$, where c^0 is the largest value of c such that $\pi_{\mathrm{I}}(c) = 0$. That is, c^0 is the largest unit cost for the challenger which induces the incumbent to leave the post-innovation product market.

The assumption of constant returns to scale is important because it ensures that output is zero when profits are zero. Thus, for drastic innovations, the challenger becomes a monopolist and $\Pi(c) = \pi_{\mathrm{C}}(c)$. Note that $\Pi(c) \geq \pi_{\mathrm{I}}(c) + \pi_{\mathrm{C}}(c)$ with a strict inequality whenever the innovation is not drastic. The assumption that $c < \bar{c}$ ensures that $\Pi(c) > R/r$; that is, the present value of post-innovation monopoly profits exceeds the present value of pre-innovation monopoly profits. Moreover, $R/r > \pi_I(c)$ for all $c < \bar{c}$; this follows from the fact that $R/r = \Pi(\bar{c}) > \pi_I(\bar{c}) \geq \pi_I(c)$ for $c < \bar{c}$.

Let x_i, $i = \mathrm{I, C}$ denote the rate of investment for the incumbent and the challenger, respectively. This generates the hazard rate $h(x_i)$ for firm i. Let a_i, $i = \mathrm{I, C}$ denote the rival hazard rate for firm i; for instance, $a_I = h(x_C)$. For simplicity we will assume that the hazard function $h(\cdot)$ is twice continuously differentiable with $h'(\cdot) > 0$, $h''(\cdot) < 0$, $h(0) = 0$, and satisfies the conditions $\lim_{x \to 0} h'(x) = \infty$ and $\lim_{X \to \infty} h'(x) = 0$.

Assuming that patent protection is perfect, the race terminates with the first success. The expected profit to the incumbent as a function of its own investment rate and its rival's hazard rate is

$$V^I(x_I, a_I) = \int_0^\infty \mathrm{e}^{-rt} \mathrm{e}^{-(h(x_I)+a_I)t} [h(x_I)\Pi(c) + a_I \pi_I(c) + R - x_I] \mathrm{d}t$$

$$= \frac{h(x_I)\Pi(c) + a_I \pi_I(c) + R - x_I}{r + h(x_I) + a_I}.$$

The challenger's payoff is analogous:

$$V^C(x_C, a_C) = \int_0^\infty \mathrm{e}^{-rt} \mathrm{e}^{-(h(x_C)+a_C)t} [h(x_C)\pi_C(c) - x_C] \mathrm{d}t$$

$$= \frac{h(x_C)\pi_C(c) - x_C}{r + h(x_C) + a_C}.$$

The differences between these payoffs are due to the fact that the incumbent receives a flow payoff of R so long as no one has succeeded, and the incumbent receives a (possibly positive) payoff $\pi_I(c)$ if the challenger wins.

As usual, a *strategy* for firm i is an investment rate x_i; a *best response function* for firm i is a function $\hat{x}_i(a)$ such that for all a, $V^i(\hat{x}_i(a), a) \geq V^i(x_i, a)$ for all x_i. A *Nash equilibrium* is a pair (x_I^*, x_C^*) such that $x_I^* = \hat{x}_I(a_I^*)$, where $a_I^* = h(x_C^*)$, and $x_C^* = \hat{x}_C(a_C^*)$, where $a_C^* = h(x_I^*)$. That is, each firm plays a best response against the other's strategy.

Proposition 17 [Reinganum (1983b)]

There exists a Nash equilibrium pair $(x_I^*(c, R), x_C^*(c, R))$; $x_i^*(c, R)$ *is continuous in* (c, R) *for* $i = C, I$.

Proposition 18 [Reinganum (1983b)]

The incumbent's best response function is upward-sloping; thus the existence of the challenger provokes the incumbent to invest more than it otherwise would. If the innovation is drastic and $R > 0$, then in a Nash equilibrium the incumbent invests less than the challenger. That is, $x_I^*(c, R) < x_C^*(c, R)$.

An immediate corollary of Proposition 18 and the continuity of the Nash equilibrium strategies in the parameters (c, R) is that if $R > 0$, then there exists an open neighborhood of c^0 (which may depend on R), denoted $N(c^0; R)$, such that if the technology is not drastic, but $c \in N(c^0; R)$, then $x_I^*(c, R) < x_C^*(c, R)$. That is, there is a set of nondrastic innovations for which the incumbent firm will still invest less than the challenger. Since the incumbent invests less than the challenger, the challenger is more likely to win the asymmetric patent race. Thus, one would empirically observe that challengers contribute disproportionately more large innovations.

This model has been extended to an arbitrary number of firms and a sequence of innovations in Reinganum (1985), in order to generate a model of the Schumpeterian "process of creative destruction". For simplicity, we assume that each innovation is drastic. Then the model remains symmetric among all challengers.

Consider a market in which an incumbent monopolist competes with $n - 1$ identical challengers for a new innovation. The firms are assumed to be symmetric in all other respects; that is, they face the same innovation production possibilities. Each innovative success initiates a new stage; within each stage firms compete for the next generation. The game with t stages to go is constructed recursively from shorter horizon games under the assumption of subgame perfect Nash equilibrium play.

Nash equilibria are found to be symmetric among the challengers, with each challenger investing more than the incumbent. Thus, the incumbent firm enjoys temporary monopoly power, but is soon overthrown by a more inventive challenger.

The basic model is now familiar. It is essentially that of Lee and Wilde, except that we now specify the values of winning and losing the current race as v^W and v^L, respectively. These represent the values of continuing on in a Nash equilibrium fashion when one fewer innovations remain. The values are ultimately endogenous to the model, but at each stage they may be treated parametrically because they are independent of actions taken in the current stage.

Thus, for any given stage, the game is summarized by n, the number of competing firms; x_i, the investment rate of firm i; F, a fixed cost of entry; $h(\cdot)$, the hazard function; R, the current profit flow to the incumbent; r, the common discount rate; and v^W and v^L, the continuation values.

Let $a_i = \sum_{j \neq i} h(x_j)$ be the aggregate rival hazard rate. Again the payoff to firm i can be written as a function of its own research intensity x_i and its aggregate rival hazard rate a_i. Suppose, without loss of generality, that firm 1 is the incumbent. Then

$$V^1(x_1, a_1) = \int_0^{\infty} \mathrm{e}^{-rt} \mathrm{e}^{-(h(x_1)+a_1)t} \left[h(x_1) v^{\mathrm{W}} + a_1 v^{\mathrm{L}} + R - x_1 \right] \mathrm{d}t - F$$

$$= \frac{h(x_1) v^{\mathrm{W}} + a_1 v^{\mathrm{L}} + R - x_1}{r + h(x_1) + a_1} - F.$$

The payoffs to the challengers are analogous except that they accrue no flow profits. For $i = 2, 3, \ldots, n$,

$$V^i(x_i, a_i) = \int_0^{\infty} \mathrm{e}^{-rt} \mathrm{e}^{-(h(x_i)+a_i)t} \left[h(x_i) v^{\mathrm{W}} + a_i v^{\mathrm{L}} - x_i \right] \mathrm{d}t - F$$

$$= \frac{h(x_i) v^{\mathrm{W}} + a_i v^{\mathrm{L}} - x_i}{r + h(x_i) + a_i} - F.$$

Our induction hypothesis is that $v^{\mathrm{W}} > v^{\mathrm{L}}$. We shall show that if this hypothesis is true for some stage, then it is also true for the previous stage. In the last stage, only one innovation remains, so $v^{\mathrm{W}} = R_0/r$, where R_0 is the flow rate of profit on the last innovation, and $v^{\mathrm{L}} = 0$. Thus, the hypothesis is true for the last stage.

Assumption 3

There exists x^0 such that for each challenger i, $V^i(x^0, a) + F \geq v^{\mathrm{L}}$ for all a. This reduces to: there exists x^0 such that $h(x^0)(v^{\mathrm{W}} - v^{\mathrm{L}}) - x^0 \geq rv^{\mathrm{L}}$.

Assumption 3 says that there always exists an investment level for a challenger for which gross profits exceed the value of losing immediately. Note that Assumption 3 holds trivially at the last stage, in which $v^{\mathrm{L}} = 0$. Since v^{W} and v^{L} are parameters for the current stage, the assumed existence of such an x^0 is a restriction on the function $h(\cdot)$.

Proposition 19 [Reinganum (1985)]

The Nash equilibrium in the current stage is symmetric among the challengers; that is, $x_i^* \equiv x_{\mathrm{C}}$ for all $i \neq 1$. The incumbent invests less than each challenger in the current stage. That is, $x_1^* \equiv x_{\mathrm{I}} < x_{\mathrm{C}}$.

This proposition highlights the dynamic evolution of the market. The current incumbent, since it invests at a lower rate, is least likely to win the current race.

Thus, the industry is characterized by a turnover of the technological leadership rather than a single continuing leader. It is in this sense that the equilibrium process resembles Schumpeter's "process of creative destruction".

Proposition 20 [Reinganum (1985)]

Let V^{I} and V^{C} denote the equilibrium expected profit for the incumbent and each challenger, respectively. Then each firm would prefer to be the incumbent in the current stage than a challenger. That is $V^{\mathrm{I}} > V^{\mathrm{C}}$.

Under the hypothesis that $v^{\mathrm{W}} > v^{\mathrm{L}}$, we have deduced that $V^{\mathrm{I}} > V^{\mathrm{C}}$. But these are simply the continuation values for the previous stage. This completes the induction argument.

In this model the length of the current stage – and hence the reward to the incumbent over the current stage – is affected by each firm's investment. Since the challenger firms do not forfeit any current stream of profit by inventing, they have a greater marginal incentive to invest in research and development. We accorded the incumbent no advantage which was due to incumbency per se. If the incumbent were to enjoy (for example) a marginal cost advantage in the conduct of research, the conjecture is that the incumbent might then invest more. Thus, a sufficiently large incumbent advantage may reverse the main result of this model. However, by focusing on the no-advantage case, we are able to isolate this inertial tendency of the incumbent to invest less than each challenger.

Vickers (1984) has addressed similar questions with a sequence of process innovations in the context of the auction model. In particular, he wants to discover how the product market structure evolves over time; does one firm become increasingly dominant by winning most or all of the races, or is there a process of "action–reaction", in which market leadership is constantly changing hands? Using a two-firm model, he finds that when the product market is very competitive (e.g. Bertrand) then there is increasing dominance; but when it is not very competitive (e.g. Cournot) then there is action–reaction.

Vickers assumes a sequence of not-so-drastic innovations, so that the profit flows of the two firms typically depend upon the levels of technology represented by each firm's most recent patent. There are T periods in the game and we label them backwards; at t, there are t periods (and hence t innovations) to go. Each innovation is associated with a cost level c_t, with $c_1 < c_2 < \cdots < c_T$. At the beginning of period t there is a race for the innovation with cost level c_t, which takes the form of a simple auction in which the winner pays its bid (or alternatively, the maximum bid the loser would have been willing to make) and the loser does not forego its bid. Let $\pi(s, t)$ denote the flow profit (gross of research and development expenses) of a firm with cost level c_s when its rival has cost level c_t. This function is assumed to be non-negataive for s and t, decreasing in s and increasing in t. Let $\Pi(s, t) = \pi(s, t) + \pi(t, s)$ be joint profits. For simplicity, firms are assumed not to discount the future.

Proposition 21 [Vickers (1984)]

If $\Pi(t, t+1) > \Pi(t, t+k)$ for all t, k, then the evolution of the market has an "action–reaction" character; that is, firms alternate being the technological leader.

The reverse of the hypothesis of Proposition 21 is not sufficient to cause increasing dominance (that is, for the same firm to win all races). However, the following proposition gives a sufficient condition for increasing dominance.

Proposition 22 [Vickers (1984)]

If $\pi(s+k, s) = 0$ for all s and $k \geq 1$, then the evolution has an increasing dominance character; that is, the same firm wins every race.

Note that this result is for drastic innovations; thus this result and that of Reinganum (1985) parallel the results of Gilbert and Newbery (1982) and Reinganum (1983b) for a sequence of innovations. The use of the auction model again gives opposite results from the stochastic racing model. To understand why we obtain these disparate results, it is useful to recall the incentives for investment described by Katz and Shapiro (1987); the stand-alone incentive represents the difference between the firm's profits after versus before it innovates, while the incentive to pre-empt represents the difference between the firm's profits if it innovates instead of its rival. In the deterministic model, so long as the stand-alone incentive is non-negative, the incentive to pre-empt dominates the firm's decision (and an incumbent monopolist has a greater incentive to pre-empt than does a challenger). But when the date of rival success is drawn from a continuous distribution as in the stochastic racing model, concern about pre-emption is much less acute. Moreover, for drastic innovations, the pre-emption incentive is the same for both firms (both get monopoly profits if successful and nothing if unsuccessful), while the stand-alone incentive is greater for the challenger. Even for less drastic innovations, in which the pre-emption incentive is greater for the incumbent, the fact that pre-emption is only probabilistic means that both incentives come into play, with the result that for some less than drastic innovations, it is the greater stand-alone incentive for the challenger which carries the day.

The papers discussed so far in this section involved asymmetrically placed firms. However, the differences among firms did not confer an ex ante advantage upon any particular firm. That is, for a given level of investment in research and development, all firms were equally likely to become the winner. Differences in incentives generated ex post advantages, since in equilibrium firms chose to invest different amounts on innovative activity. The papers to be discussed in the remainder of this section describe models in which the nature of the asymmetry confers a *strategic* advantage upon one firm. These are essentially multi-stage models which culminate in a single innovation; however, a firm's position at an intermediate stage affects the effectiveness of its investment in research and development. Thus, at any intermediate stage (in which firms' positions differ) firms are not equally likely to become the winner even if they (from now on) invest the same amount.

Fudenberg et al. (1983) and Harris and Vickers (1985) have devised very similar models of such a multi-stage race. In Fudenberg et al. (1983), firms are envisioned as suffering from information and/or response lags regarding the research activities of their rivals. Lack of information or the inability to respond quickly allows firms that are only slightly behind to catch up before the leading firm can act to prevent it. The existence of these lags effectively makes time discrete for this model. In period t, firms are informed about their rivals' research activities up through period $t-1$. Invention is assumed to occur as soon as one firm has accumulated enough knowledge, as measured by total research and development spending. Firms may elect to learn at a high or a low rate in each period, and the costs of learning are strictly convex. Within the current period, each firm must choose its rate of knowledge acquisition without knowing its rival's choice.

They find that firms will choose the high rate only if they are sufficiently close together in terms of accumulated experience. If a firm lags by a sufficiently large amount, then it drops out of the race, allowing the remaining firm to proceed at the low rate. As the information lag becomes arbitrarily short, the lagging firm drops out immediately; only if the firms remain tied is there any competition. Thus, if firms begin with equal experience there is a short intense battle followed by the emergence of a single firm. If firms begin with unequal experience, the firm which is at an initial disadvantage simply never enters the race. They go on to show that as the length of the period of information lag decreases, the lag in experience for which the follower still competes also decreases. In the limit as the period length approaches zero, an arbitrarily small headstart in terms of knowledge is sufficient to cause the lagging firm to drop out immediately.

A somewhat more general version of this model appears in Harris and Vickers (1985). In Fudenberg et al. (1983), both players valued the patent equally, and both faced the same cost conditions. Thus, distance from completion could be measured as the difference between accumulated knowledge and required knowledge. Harris and Vickers allow firms to place different values on the reward and to face different cost functions. They too find that if one player is far enough ahead, then the other gives up. However, being "far enough ahead" in this case is not measured in terms of literal distance; it depends upon the value placed on winning and the costs of achieving a win. The Harris and Vickers (1985) model is also cast in discrete time, but players are assumed to move in alternate periods. In the limit as the length of the period approaches zero, the firm which has the opportunity to move first pre-empts the other completely. The equilibrium is somewhat easier to characterize due to the alternating moves assumption (there will be no mixed strategies).

Four significant factors combine to determine which player has a strategic advantage. First, firms may differ in their valuations of the patent. Second, they may discount the future to different degrees. Third, firms may differ in the efficiency (i.e. the cost) of performing research and development. Finally, firms may differ in the amount of knowledge and experience they have already acquired.

Formally, two players, denoted A and B, are competing for a single prize. They value the prize at P_{A} and P_{B}, respectively, with $P_i > 0$ for $i = \mathrm{A, B}$. At the beginning of the game, A and B are distances x_0 and y_0 from the finish line (i.e. A requires x_0 more units of knowledge, B requires y_0 more units of knowledge). Firm A is assumed to move first, then firm B, and so on. The first firm to reach 0 wins the prize. Progress toward the goal depends upon the amount a firm invests in each period. In particular, if firm i invests z he moves a distance of $w_i(z)$ toward the goal, where $w_i(0) = 0$ and $w_i(\cdot)$ is continuous and strictly increasing. Thus, after firm A has made his kth investment a_k, the positions are $x_{2k-1} = x_{2k-2} - w_{\mathrm{A}}(a_k)$ and $y_{2k-1} = y_{2k-2}$. After firm B has made his kth investment b_k, the positions are $x_{2k} = x_{2k-1}$ and $y_{2k} = y_{2k-1} - w_{\mathrm{B}}(b_k)$. Let N denote the smallest integer such that either $x_N \leq 0$ or $y_N \leq 0$; thus N is endogenously determined. The prize is awarded to the firm which first reaches 0; since firms move alternately, they will not reach 0 simultaneously. If no firm ever reaches 0, then no firm wins the prize. Let ρ_{B} and ρ_{A} denote the firms' discount rates. If A wins the prize with his kth investment, he receives $\rho_{\mathrm{A}}^{k-1}P_{\mathrm{A}} - \sum_{i=1}^{\infty} \rho_{\mathrm{A}}^{i-1}a_i$, where a_i is understood to drop to zero after one firm wins. If A does not win the prize, its payoff is $-\sum_{i=1}^{\infty}\rho_{\mathrm{A}}^{i-1}a_i$. Firm B's payoff is analogously defined.

A *strategy* for firm i is an infinite sequence of investment levels which may be chosen contingent upon the sequence of previous bids. The notion of equilibrium to be employed is subgame perfect Nash equilibrium [Selten (1975)]. A strategy pair is a *subgame perfect equilibrium* if its restriction to any subgame is a Nash equilibrium. The following convention will be maintained: if a player is indifferent between winning the prize with an overall payoff of zero and not winning the prize, then he will choose to win the prize.

Harris and Vickers define a sequence of critical distances from the finish line for A and B, denoted by $\{C_n\}_{n=0}^{\infty}$ and $\{D_n\}_{n=0}^{\infty}$. Heuristically, C_1 is the maximum distance that A can cover with one bid and obtain a non-negative payoff overall. C_2 is the maximum distance that A can cover subject to covering at least $C_2 - C_1$ with his first bid, and obtain a non-negative payoff overall. C_n is the maximum distance that A can cover with a sequence of non-negative investments, subject to moving within C_{n-1} with the first investment, and without spending more than the present value of the prize.

The sequence $\{C_n\}$ has the following properties: (1) the sequence $\{C_n\}$ is nondecreasing; (2) if $\{C_n\}$ ever fails to be strictly increasing it remains constant thereafter; and (3) it is possible for A to cover distance h and obtain a non-negative payoff overall if and only if $h \leq C_n$ for some n. For the formal definition of these sequences and the proof that they have these properties, the reader is referred to Harris and Vickers.

Proposition 23 [Harris and Vickers (1985)]

Suppose that A and B are respectively at distances x and y from the finish line. Then in perfect equilibrium, there are four mutually exclusive and exhaustive possibilities.

(i) For some $n \geq 1$, $x \leq C_n$ and $y > D_n$. Then firm A wins; his investments are those he would make in the absence of rivalry from firm B; firm B always invests 0. The point (x, y) belongs to A's "safety zone".

(ii) For some $n \geq 1$, $x > C_n$ and $y \leq D_n$. Then firm B wins; his investments are those he would make absent any rivalry from firm A; firm A always invests 0. The point (x, y) belongs to B's "safety zone".

(iii) For some $n \geq 0$, $C_n < x \leq C_{n+1}$ and $D_n < y \leq D_{n+1}$. Then if it is firm A's turn to move, firm A wins; his investments are those he would make if (absent rivalry) he were required to move to within C_n of the finish line with his first investment; B always invests 0. Conversely, if it is firm B's turn to move, then firm B wins; his investments are those which he would make if (absent rivalry) he were required to move to within D_n of the finish line with his first investment; A always invests 0. The point (x, y) belongs to a "trigger zone".

(iv) For all $n \geq 0$, $x > C_n$ and $y > D_n$; then neither firm wins and both always invest 0.

It is apparent that the equilibrium outcome depends upon the initial point (x_0, y_0). To show that it also depends upon the other parameters of the model, Harris and Vickers show that C_n is strictly increasing in P_A for $n \geq 1$ and that C_n is increasing in ρ_A for $n \geq 2$.

Again it is possible to determine what happens to this equilibrium as the reaction times shrink. In the limit, the trigger zone collapses to a curve; the safety zones for A and B lie on opposite sides of this curve. The fact that the curve depends upon more than just the distance to the finish line (e.g. the valuations, discount factors and cost functions) implies that this curve need not be the 45° line. Harris and Vickers give a specific example in which it is linear, but does not have unitary slope.

In either the discrete game or the limiting case, the equilibrium has similar features. If the game begins in one firm's safety zone, then the winner is already determined and that firm proceeds as though no rival existed; the rival invests nothing. If the game begins in a trigger zone, then the firm which is accorded the first move jumps immediately to its safety zone, after which it proceeds as though no rival existed and again the rival invests nothing.

Park (1984) and Grossman and Shapiro (1987) have analyzed a two-stage version of Lee and Wilde (1980) in order to investigate the impact of position (leading or lagging) upon equilibrium investment. They assume two stages with identical (stochastic) technologies for producing success. Completion of the intermediate stage does not result in a prize, but brings one closer to it; the first firm to complete both stages wins a prize worth P. The stationarity of the problem implies that one need only characterize four investment levels: the symmetric equilibrium investment level when both firms have completed 0 stages, denoted x_{00}; the investment levels for the case where (say) firm 1 has completed the first stage and firm 2 has not, denoted x_{10} and x_{01}, respectively; and the symmetric equilibrium investment level when both firms have completed the first stage, denoted x_{11}. Let V_{00}, V_{10}, V_{01} and V_{11} denote the corresponding Nash equilibrium profits.

By dynamic programming backward, one can characterize the subgame perfect Nash equilibrium rates of investment. Consider first the case where both firms have completed the first stage, but neither has completed the second stage. This is identical to the original Lee and Wilde (1980) case; the payoff to each firm can be written:

$$V^{11}(x, a) = \frac{h(x)P - x}{r + h(x) + a},$$

where a represents the rival firm's hazard rate.

Consider next the case in which firm 1 has succeeded with the first stage, but firm 2 has not. Since the same hazard function $h(\cdot)$ applies, we can write profits to firm 1 and 2, respectively, as

$$V^{10}(x, a) = \frac{h(x)P + aV_{11} - x}{r + h(x) + a}$$

and

$$V^{01}(x, a) = \frac{h(x)V_{11} - x}{r + h(x) + a}.$$

Finally, consider the case in which no firm has yet succeeded with the first stage. Each firm's expected payoff can be written:

$$V^{00}(x, a) = \frac{h(x)V_{10} + aV_{01} - x}{r + h(x) + a}$$

Proposition 24 [Grossman and Shapiro (1987)]

The rate of investment when both have succeeded in the first stage exceeds that of the leading firm which exceeds that of the lagging firm when only one firm has succeeded in the first stage; that is, $x_{11} > x_{10} > x_{01}$. Moreover, the rate of investment when both firms have succeeded with the first stage exceeds that when neither has succeeded; that is, $x_{11} > x_{00}$. The relationships between x_{10} and x_{00} and that between x_{01} and x_{00} are ambiguous.

The reason for the residual ambiguity is that success by one firm in the first stage has two effects. The lagging firm may reduce its rate of expenditure; this diminished rivalry induces the leading firm to reduce its expenditures as well. On the other hand, the fact that it is now closer to the prize causes the leading firm to increase its rate of expenditure. Success by its rival in the first stage would tend to cause the (now) lagging firm to reduce its investment rate, but an increase in the (now) leading firm's expenditure (due to its being closer to the prize) would tend to spur investment by the lagging firm. Simulations reported by Grossman and Shapiro indicated that the likely response to success by one firm in the first stage is for the leading firm to increase, and the lagging firm to decrease, its rate of expenditure.

Judd (1984) has formulated a more general version of the stochastic racing game of Lee and Wilde (1980) and Reinganum (1981a, 1982a) to include elements of feedback (recall that while Reinganum's method permitted feedback, the particular specification of the research and development process rendered the value of the state variable unimportant). The basic framework is that of Reinganum (1981a) with the exception that knowledge accumulates and depreciates according to the equation $\dot{z}_i = \gamma u_i - \delta z_i$ and the hazard rate is $\alpha u_i + \beta z_i$. If $\beta > 0$, firms' investment in R&D today increases their own current and future probabilities of success, and builds a stock of experience which may cause the rival firm to decrease its rate of investment tomorrow. Judd solves this problem for small values of the prize P by using perturbation methods and finds that indeed each firm's rate of investment does depend negatively upon its rival's accumulated experience.

The model in Judd (1985a) has the characteristic that firms have no exogenous strategic advantages (such as first moves or initial experience), but strategic advantages are acquired endogenously over time through acquired knowledge and intermediate successes. This model incorporates uncertainty of two types, one of which can be characterized as "more risky" than the other. Thus, it allows one to examine whether rivalry in research and development causes firms to invest in projects which are insufficiently or excessively risky.

Assuming that the prize and social benefits are small or that the rate of time preference is large (enough to make approximations valid), Judd finds that if the prize equals the social benefit, then firms invest relatively too much in the riskier discovery process. Despite this, it is optimal to allow competition to proceed until one firm has completely finished rather than to award the prize to the leader at some earlier juncture; moreover, the prize ought to be nearly equal to the social benefit. He also characterizes the dependence of investment on the current positions. It turns out that if one player advances, the other reduces its effort on the riskier project, but may increase its effort on the less risky project. The description and manipulation of the formal model is somewhat tedious, and the reader is referred to Judd (1985a) for proofs.

Suppose two firms compete for a particular innovation. The position of firm 1 is denoted by a nonpositive scalar x (firm 2's position is denoted y), the absolute value of which could be regarded as the extent of additional knowledge required for success. There are two parallel projects in which the firm can invest in attempting to complete the innovation. The first is characterized by *gradual jumps* which have a probability of $F(a)$ of hitting zero (if a is the firm's current position) and otherwise have a probability $f(s, a)\,\mathrm{d}s$ of landing in the interval $(s, s + \mathrm{d}s)$. There is also a more risky process which never lands at an intermediate value, but hits 0 with probability $G(a)$ if a is the current position. This process is characterized by *leaps*, and is a more risky process than the one that involves gradual jumps. The firms choose intensities at which to operate these processes; these intensities affect the likelihood, but not the magnitude of the resulting jumps. The symbols x and y denote the state variable for firms 1 and 2, respectively; $u\,\mathrm{d}t$ denotes the probability that the gradual jump process results in a jump of x if firm 1 chooses u; $v\,\mathrm{d}t$ is the probability of a jump of y if firm 2 chooses v. Let $f(s, a)\,\mathrm{d}s$ denote the probability of a jump from a to $(s, s + \mathrm{d}s)$ if a gradual jump occurs; $f(s, a) = 0$ if $s < a$ (firms only improve their positions). If $a' > a$, then $f(s, a')$ first-order stochastically dominates $f(s, a)$. $F(a)$ denotes the probability that the gradual jump process hits 0 from a given that a gradual jump occurs; $F(a)$ is increasing in a and is positive everywhere:

$$F(a) \equiv 1 - \lim_{\xi \to 0} \int_a^{\xi} f(s, a)\,\mathrm{d}s.$$

Let $wG(x)\,\mathrm{d}t$ symbolize the probability that firm 1 leaps to 0, where firm 1 chooses w; $zG(y)\,\mathrm{d}t$ is the probability that firm 2 leaps to 0, where firm 2 chooses z. $G(\cdot)$ is positive everywhere. Firm 1's costs are $\alpha u^2/2 + \beta w^2/2$, where α and β are positive scalars. Similarly, firm 2's costs are $\alpha v^2/2 + \beta z^2/2$. $P \geq 0$ represents the prize to the winner, and $\rho > 0$ is the common discount rate. Throughout Judd (1985a) uses infinitesimal notation; we will follow his convention here.

Consider first the research intensities of a joint venture between the two firms. In this case, the joint value function $W(x, y)$ satisfies the following dynamic programming equation:

$$\begin{aligned} W(x, y) = \max_{u, v, w, z} \Big\{ & -(\alpha u^2/2 + \alpha v^2/2 + \beta w^2/2 + \beta z^2/2)\,\mathrm{d}t \\ & + u\,\mathrm{d}t(1 - \rho\,\mathrm{d}t)\left[\int_x^0 W(s, y) f(s, x)\,\mathrm{d}s + PF(x)\right] \\ & + v\,\mathrm{d}t(1 - \rho\,\mathrm{d}t)\left[\int_y^0 W(x, s) f(s, y)\,\mathrm{d}s + PF(y)\right] \\ & + P(1 - \rho\,\mathrm{d}t)[wG(x) + zG(y)]\,\mathrm{d}t \\ & + (1 - \rho\,\mathrm{d}t)[1 - (u + v + wG(x) + zG(y))\,\mathrm{d}t]\,W(x, y)\Big\}. \end{aligned} \tag{7}$$

To interpret this, the value of being at state (x, y) is the value of choosing (u, v, w, z) optimally for the next $\mathrm{d}t$, and then continuing optimally. The choice of (u, v, w, z) incurs the costs on the first line; with probability $u\,\mathrm{d}t$ firm 1 experiences a gradual jump, which has an associated expected present value (this term appears on the second line above); similarly, with probability $v\,\mathrm{d}t$, firm 2 experiences a gradual jump, which has an associated expected present value (third line); there is also a probability $wG(x) + zG(y)$ that one of the firms will leap to success and an associated present value (fourth line); finally, there is a probability that neither firm experiences any advance at all, which event has expected present value $(1 - \rho\,\mathrm{d}t)W(x, y)$. The probability that both firms experience gradual jumps and/or leaps is of order $(\mathrm{d}t)^2$ and can safely be ignored.

Proposition 25 [Judd (1985a)]

There exists a unique solution $W(x, y)$ to the joint research problem, and $W(x, y)$ is C^∞ in P and ρ^{-1}.

Consider now a noncooperative version of this game. Assume that the position vector (x, y) is common knowledge. Then firms choose their research intensities contingent upon their current positions. Thus, the equilibrium concept used here is that of feedback equilibrium. Only symmetric equilibrium is considered. Let $V(x, y)$ represent firm 1's value function and $V(y, x)$ represent firm 2's value function. The equation of dynamic programming for firm 1 is

$$\begin{aligned} V(x, y) = \max_{u, w} \Big\{ & -[\alpha u^2/2 + \beta w^2/2]\,\mathrm{d}t \\ & + u\,\mathrm{d}t(1 - \rho\,\mathrm{d}t)\left[\int_x^{\infty} V(s, y) f(s, x)\,\mathrm{d}s + PF(x)\right] \\ & + v\,\mathrm{d}t(1 - \rho\,\mathrm{d}t)\int_y^0 V(x, s) f(s, y)\,\mathrm{d}s \\ & + P(1 - \rho\,\mathrm{d}t) w G(x)\,\mathrm{d}t \\ & + (1 - \rho\,\mathrm{d}t)[1 - (u + v + wG(x) + zG(y))\,\mathrm{d}t]\, V(x, y) \Big\}. \end{aligned} \tag{8}$$

Proposition 26 [Judd (1985a)]

There exists a $\bar{P} > 0$ such that for $P \in [0, \bar{P}]$, there is a symmetric feedback equilibrium value function $V(x, y)$ which is C^{∞} in P and ρ^{-1}.

Proposition 27 [Judd (1985a)]

Noncooperative equilibrium play results in overinvestment relative to the joint optimum. Moreover, this excess is greater the closer is either firm to success. If P is small, joint profits would be increased if resources were shifted from the risky "leap" process to the less risky "jump" process. Thus, noncooperative firms undertake more risk than is jointly optimal.

If one can legitimately interpret P as the social value of the innovation, then the same proposition describes the relationship between the noncooperative equilibrium and the social optimum.

4. Licensing

In the work discussed above, the value of a patent was taken as given. But how is this value determined? Arrow (1962a) described the value of a patent on a cost-reducing innovation as the revenue which an innovator could acquire by licensing the innovation to producing firms. He compared the value of licensing the innovation to a single producer versus members of a competitive industry, and found that the competitive environment yielded more revenue (even absent problems of bilateral monopoly, which might be expected to further reduce the value of licensing to a single producer). Thus, a competitive product market offered greater incentives for suppliers of innovations.

Kamien and Tauman (1984, 1986) performed a similar analysis when the downstream product market is oligopolistic, and members make their decisions to license in a strategic manner. By the term "firm" we refer only to producing firms; the patent holder is understood to be an independent researcher, not a current member of the industry. Assuming that firms are initially identical, with constant marginal costs c and a linear industry demand curve $p = 1 - bq$, Kamien and Tauman determined the maximum value to the patent holder from licensing a cost-reducing innovation to the industry. Given a license contract, which consists of a fixed fee and a linear royalty rate, the firms play a simultaneous-move game, where their strategies are either to license the innovation, or to forego licensing. The patent holder offers a licensing contract to maximize his profits, taking into account how the contract affects the subsequent Nash equilibrium among the firms.

The general game, which involves both a fixed fee and a linear royalty rate, is denoted game G. They examine two restrictions of the general game: G_1, in which the royalty rate is constrained to be zero, while the fixed fee is subject to choice; and G_2, in which the fixed fee is constrained to be zero, and the royalty rate is subject to choice. Their results are summarized in the three propositions below [Kamien, Tauman and Zang (1985) extend this analysis of licensing to the context of product innovation].

Proposition 28 [Kamien and Tauman (1984)]

(a) For any finite number n of firms, G_1 yields a higher payoff to the patent holder than G_2, and consumers benefit more under G_1 than under G_2. Firms make no more profit under G_1, and no less profit under G_2, than they did prior to the innovation. (b) The equilibrium of G_1 results in a monopoly if and only if the innovation is drastic. (A drastic innovation is here defined as one in which the monopoly price with the new technology does not exceed the competitive price under the old technology.) (c) If the innovation is not drastic, then in the limit (as the number of firms increases without bound), the patent holder makes the same profit in both G_1 and G_2; this profit is equal to the magnitude of the cost reduction times the original competitive output.

Since the game G permits the use of both a fixed fee and a royalty rate, the innovator must do at least weakly better under G than under either G_1 or G_2.

Proposition 29 [Kamien and Tauman (1984)]

(a) The equilibrium of G results in a monopoly if and only if the innovation is drastic. In this case, the profit is the difference between monopoly profit under the new technology and the licensee's oligopoly profit under the old technology. (b) If the innovation is not drastic, then the number of licensees is never below $(n + 2)/2$. (c) In the limit (as the number of firms increases without bound), the profit of the patent holder in G coincides with his profits in G_1 and G_2.

Finally, it is possible to compare the output levels, market prices and firms' profits before and after the innovation.

Proposition 30 [Kamien and Tauman (1984)]

In the (subgame) perfect Nash equilibrium of G: (a) total output increases and the market price falls as a result of the innovation; and (b) each firm is worse off relative to its profit prior to the innovation unless the patent is drastic and then only the monopoly breaks even.

Two key features of the Kamien and Tauman analysis are modified in Katz and Shapiro (1986). First, in Kamien and Tauman's model, the patent holder effectively *posts a contract*, which firms can either accept or reject. That is, it offers a pair consisting of a fixed fee and a royalty rate, and any firm which is willing to accept those terms may acquire a license. Of course, the optimal contract takes into account the subsequent equilibrium behavior of the potential buyers; that is, the patent holder computes its (equilibrium) demand function for licenses, and chooses its preferred point on that schedule. Second, in Kamien and Tauman (1984, 1986), the patent holder is understood to be an independent researcher.

Restricting attention to fixed fee contracts, Katz and Shapiro (1986) argue that when firms' demands for licenses are interdependent a superior selling strategy for an independent researcher involves offering a restricted number of licenses for auction with a minimum required bid. They also consider the optimal distribution strategy (within this class of auction-type strategies) for research joint ventures of arbitrary size. They find that dissemination of the technology is greater the smaller is the joint venture. Subsequently they examine the seller's incentives to develop the innovation given the feasibility of licensing. Again all downstream firms who are not members of the joint venture are worse off as a result of innovation.

Consider the case of a research lab which has developed an innovation which is potentially useful to the n member firms of a particular industry. Assume that each firm has need for a single license, and all n firms are identical.

Given this symmetry, firms' identities are irrelevant; the information which is relevant to the payoffs of the patent holder and the firms is the number of firms which will obtain a license. Let k denote the number of firms which obtain a license. Let $W(k)$ represent the profits of a firm that obtains a license when a total of k firms have done so, and let $L(k)$ denote the profits of a firm that does not obtain a license when a total of k firms have obtained licenses. These profits are gross of any licensing fees, which are assumed to be lump sums independent of subsequent output levels.

Assumption 4

(a) $L(k) \leq L(k-1)$ and (b) $L(k) < W(k)$, for $k = 1, 2, \ldots, n-1$.

That is, a firm that has not obtained a license is worse off the greater is the number of firms which have obtained licenses and, given that k firms obtain licenses, profits are greater for those who have than for those who have not obtained a license.

The set of selling strategies open to the patent holder is the set of multiple-object sealed-bid first-price auctions with a minimum bid. That is, the patent holder makes available k licenses, but requires a minimum bid of $\underline{b}$. Each firm may submit a single bid b_i (to prevent anti-competitive hoarding, which might be individually profitable); the licenses go to the firms with the k highest bids (provided the bid is at least $\underline{b}$) at the bid values, and any ties are broken at random. Thus, a sales policy can be summarized by a pair $(k, \underline{b})$. Katz and Shapiro refer to a policy of the form $(k, 0)$ as a *quantity* strategy and one of the form $(n, \underline{b})$ as a *price* strategy.

For a given policy $(k, \underline{b})$, we need to characterize the Nash equilibrium of the bidding game for the n firms. Firm i's willingness to pay clearly depends upon what it expects other firms to do. However, since there is complete and perfect information in this game, it is clear that in any bidding equilibrium all licensees pay the same price; if two licensees paid different prices, the one paying more could have lowered its bid and still received a license.

Consider first the case in which the patent holder is an independent research lab. If $k < n$ licenses are sold under the quantity strategy $(k, 0)$, then each firm knows that k licenses will be distributed, independent of his own actions. Then bidding for the licenses will drive the winning bid to $W(k) - L(k)$. The use of a price mechanism $(n, \underline{b})$ implies that each firm knows that one fewer licenses will be distributed if that firm refrains from buying one. In this case, the highest price obtainable for k licenses is $W(k) - L(k-1) \leq W(k) - L(k)$. Thus, a pure price strategy is strictly inferior to a pure quantity strategy when fewer than n licenses are sold and $L(\cdot)$ is strictly decreasing.

When n licenses are offered, a positive minimum bid is necessary since each firm will bid at most $\underline{b}$. To further characterize the outcome in this case, define the value of obtaining a license, given that $k-1$ other firms also obtain licenses, to be $V(k) = W(k) - L(k-1)$. Suppose that $V(k)$ decreases with k; in this case, each firm finds a license less valuable the greater the number of other firms which are licensed. This would be typical of a cost-reducing innovation in a simple Cournot model with linear demand and constant marginal costs. If the patent holder licenses all firms, each firm compares $W(n)$ to $L(n-1)$. The highest minimum bid which will still sell n licenses is $\underline{b} = V(n)$.

Proposition 31 [Katz and Shapiro (1986)]

If $V(\cdot)$ is strictly decreasing, then the optimal selling strategy (within the specified class) has one of two forms: (a) $(k, 0)$, where $k < n$ and the winning bid is $W(k) - L(k)$; or (b) $(n, \underline{b})$, where $\underline{b} = V(n)$.

An alternative form of market organization would involve a number of firms maintaining a research lab as a joint venture. Call members of the joint venture *insiders* and nonmembers *outsiders*. Insiders now face a tradeoff between profits they receive from licensing the innovation to competitors and the profits they receive from production. Thus, a research joint venture is likely to have reduced incentives to license the innovation. Assume that the research joint venture has available the same class of licensing policies $(k, \underline{b})$ but is also free to distribute licenses at no cost to some or all of its members. Suppose that m firms participate and share equally in the profits of the research joint venture. In this case, all members share the same objective function and are thus unanimous regarding the preferred licensing policy.

If k licenses are issued, and $\tilde{k}$ go to insiders, then profits to the insiders are $\tilde{k}W(k) + (m - \tilde{k})L(k) + R$, where R is revenue raised by licensing to outsiders. For given values of k and $\tilde{k}$, the joint venture will try to maximize R. From Proposition 31 we know that if $k < n$ licenses are distributed, the venture can extract a maximum of $W(k) - L(k)$ per license sold to outsiders, so $R = (k - \tilde{k})[W(k) - L(k)]$. Thus, insider profit is $k[W(k) - L(k)] + mL(k)$. This is independent of $\tilde{k}$, since (in equilibrium) the marginal revenue from a license equals the venture's opportunity cost.

Let $R^0(k)$ denote the licensing revenues that an independent researcher earns when it sells k licenses. When $k < n$ licenses are issued, $R^0(k) = k[W(k) - L(k)]$. For the joint venture of size m, $R^m(k) = k[W(k) - L(k)] + mL(k)$, or $R^m(k) = R^0(k) + mL(k)$. If the joint venture were to issue licenses to all firms, and $V(\cdot)$ is strictly decreasing, then total insider profit is $R^m(n) = mW(n) + (n - m)[W(n) - L(n-1)]$, since the minimum bid which induces all outsiders to buy is $[W(n) - L(n-1)]$.

Proposition 32 [Katz and Shapiro (1986)]

Suppose that $V(\cdot)$ is strictly decreasing. The m-firm joint venture's optimal selling strategy (within the specified class) has one of two forms: (a) $(k, 0)$, where $k < n$ and the winning bid is $W(k) - L(k)$; or (b) $(n, \underline{b})$, where the winning bid is $\underline{b} = W(n) - L(n-1)$.

Let k^m denote the number of licenses issued by the m-firm venture, where $m = 0, 1, 2, \ldots, n$; that is, k^m maximizes $R^m(k)$. To determine whether or not to issue an additional license, the m-firm venture examines:

$$\begin{aligned} \Delta R^m(k) &\equiv R^m(k) - R^m(k-1) \\ &= \left[R^0(k) - R^0(k-1)\right] + m\left[L(k) - L(k-1)\right]. \end{aligned}$$

For two ventures of sizes m and $m-1$, respectively, $\Delta R^m(k) - \Delta R^{m-1}(k) = L(k) - L(k-1) \leq 0$, so the m-firm venture has less incentive to sell the kth license than does the $(m-1)$-firm venture. If the m-firm venture issues n licenses, the comparison is between $\Delta R^m(n)$ and $\Delta R^{m-1}(n)$. If $V(\cdot)$ is strictly decreasing, then Proposition 32 may be applied to obtain $R^m(n) = R^0(n) + mL(n-1)$, and $\Delta R^m(n) = \Delta R^0(n)$, which is independent of m. Thus, the incentives of the independent researcher and the m-firm joint venture coincide for the nth license.

Proposition 33 [Katz and Shapiro (1986)]

Suppose that $V(\cdot)$ is strictly decreasing. Then an $(m-1)$-firm venture issues at least as many licenses as does an m-firm venture, for $m = 1, 2, \ldots, n$.

Thus, research joint ventures tend to restrict the distribution of licenses relative to an independent researcher, and the extent of the restriction increases with the size of the venture. Moreover, an outsider cannot be better off (and is strictly worse off whenever $m > 0$ and $L(\cdot)$ is strictly decreasing) as a result of the innovation. To see why, suppose $k^m < n$. In equilibrium, an outsider is indifferent about buying a license, and thus has profits of $L(k^m) \leq L(0)$. If $k^m = n$, then $\underline{b} \geq W(n) - L(m)$ since this would induce all outsiders to obtain a license. Thus, an outsider has net profits that are no greater than $W(n) - [W(n) - L(m)] \leq L(0)$.

Now consider a research lab (either independent or a joint venture) deciding whether or not to develop the innovation. If we identify a researcher's incentive to develop the innovation with its profits from licensing and production net of its previous profits from production, then for an m-firm venture this incentive is

$R^m(k^m) - R^m(0) = R^m(k^m) - mL(0)$ (note that this formula is equally valid for $m = 0$).

Proposition 34 [Katz and Shapiro (1986)]

Suppose that $V(\cdot)$ is strictly decreasing. Then an m-firm venture has greater incentives to develop the innovation than has an $(m - 1)$-firm venture.

In another paper, Katz and Shapiro (1985b) examine Nash equilibrium licensing and development behavior in a two-firm industry. One goal of this paper is to determine how the pattern of licensing depends upon the magnitude of the innovation. Assuming fixed fee licensing, they find that major innovations will not be licensed, but minor innovations will be licensed if firms are approximately equally efficient prior to innovation. If at least one firm would exclude the other (by refusing to license the innovation), then licensing will not occur because, in equilibrium, an excluding firm will be the innovator.

The aforementioned papers deal with a case in which no further innovation is anticipated; if another technology with equal or lower costs is possible, then an additional incentive to license the current innovation arises. Gallini (1984) has shown that an incumbent firm may choose to license a potential entrant to use its technology in order to forestall innovation by the entrant. That is, it will offer to share its market in order to make further innovation less attractive to the potential entrant.

Consider a homogeneous good market which consists of a single incumbent firm and a single potential entrant. These firms (and only these firms) may compete in the research and development of new production technologies. For simplicity, suppose that the incumbent currently has constant unit cost of c_3 and that two other cost levels exist: c_2 and c_1 with $c_1 < c_2 < c_3$. However, there may be a large number of technologies associated with each of these cost levels; thus discovery and patenting of a c_2 technology does not preclude the rival from discovering another route to the same cost. Research and development is therefore represented as sampling with replacement from a known discrete distribution over the cost levels $\{c_1, c_2, c_3\}$, with p_i denoting the probability that a technology with unit cost c_i is observed on any one draw. The results of each draw are revealed to both firms, but a patent prevents firms from immediately imitating the rival's technology. Each technology is assumed to be drastic in relation to the one with next highest cost; thus if one firm has c_3 and the other c_2, the low-cost firm is the current incumbent and is free to price its output at the monopoly price. Finally, production takes place once research and development has ceased.

The analysis begins with one incumbent firm, which possesses a technology with unit costs of c_2 and one potential entrant, which currently has unit costs of

c_3; thus the entrant must discover a c_2 or c_1 technology to enter. The incumbent must decide whether to license its c_2 technology to the potential entrant, thus granting it a permanent share of the market. It is assumed that when firms have the same costs, they share cooperative profits equally (an equivalent analysis applies if they are noncooperative in the product market). Let Π_i denote industry profits if both firms have cost c_i, $i = 1, 2$. If a license is agreed upon, research is terminated; if not, the firms decide noncooperatively and simultaneously whether or not to engage in further research. Their actions are to continue (C) or to terminate (T) research.

Under the following assumption, the discovery of a c_1 technology makes further research unprofitable for the rival firm. Thus, one only needs to determine when the *current* (i.e. c_2) technology will be licensed to induce a rival to terminate research. The c_1 technology would never be licensed; because the innovation is drastic and firms have constant unit costs, there are no efficiency gains to having more than one firm producing at the same time with the same technology. Thus, all research terminates with the discovery of a c_1 technology.

Assumption 5

Assume that $p_1\Pi_1/2 - D < 0$, where D represents the cost per observation.

Suppose that if the entrant discovers a c_2 technology, then it would prefer to produce in this market and share the cooperative profits rather than to continue researching alone until a c_1 technology is discovered.

Assumption 6

Assume that $\Pi_2/2 > \Pi_1 - D/p_1$.

In this case, the entrant expects more from continuing research alone than does the incumbent (since the incumbent only benefits from discovering a c_1 technology, while the entrant benefits from discovering either a c_1 or a c_2 technology). Moreover, the entrant has less incentive to stop research when its rival continues than does the incumbent.

For licensing to be an equilibrium, each firm's profit must be as great as it could achieve in a game without licensing. This is because by not offering or by rejecting a license, either firm can bring about this outcome. Refer to the equilibrium in the game with no licensing as the *alternative equilibrium*. Let R^{I}_{ij} and R^{E}_{ij} denote the payoffs to the incumbent and entrant, respectively, when the pair of actions ij with $i, j \in \{C, T\}$ are taken, assuming that the firms continue on in a Nash equilibrium fashion. If a c_1 technology has been discovered, both firms terminate research by Assumption 5. Thus, for cost pairs of the form

(c_1, c_j), $j = 1, 2, 3$ or (c_2, c_1), the equilibrium action pair is TT. At (c_2, c_2), TT is always a Nash equilibrium because Assumption 6 implies that if the incumbent terminates, the entrant would prefer to terminate rather than to continue researching alone; because the incumbent's incentives to continue researching alone are always weaker than the entrant's, if the entrant terminates at (c_2, c_2), then the incumbent will do so as well. However, if a firm continues to search at this cost pair, then its rival can stop and receive 0 or compete for a c_1 technology and receive (in expected value) $R' = \Pi_1/2 - D/p_1(2 - p_1)$. If $R' > 0$, then CC will also be a Nash equilibrium at (c_2, c_2). TT is Pareto superior to CC and is selected as the relevant equilibrium at this point, but the alternative selection would yield the same results.

Now it is possible to describe the payoffs from various strategy pairs at (c_2, c_3). If both firms terminate, $R^{\mathrm{I}}_{TT} = \Pi_2$ and $R^{\mathrm{E}}_{TT} = 0$. If both continue,

$$R^{\mathrm{I}}_{CC} = R^{\mathrm{E}}_{CC} = \frac{p_1(2 - p_1)\Pi_1/2 + p_2(1 - p_1)\Pi_2/2 - D}{1 - (1 - p_1)p_3}.$$

If the incumbent continues but the entrant terminates,

$$R^{\mathrm{I}}_{TC} = \frac{p_2\Pi_2}{2(1 - p_3)} \quad \text{and} \quad R^{\mathrm{E}}_{TC} = \frac{p_1\Pi_1 + p_2\Pi_2/2 - D}{1 - p_3}.$$

Finally, if the incumbent terminates and the entrant continues, $R^{\mathrm{I}}_{CT} = \Pi_1 - D/p_1$ and $R^{\mathrm{E}}_{CT} = 0$. Note that CT cannot be an equilibrium because this requires $R^{\mathrm{I}}_{CT} \geq \Pi_2$, which contradicts Assumption 6. The remaining three pairs of actions can be alternative equilibria for some parameter values.

A licensing equilibrium requires that there must exist a share of profits using the current technology such that both firms earn at least as much as they would in the alternative equilibrium. Moreover, each firm must receive as much under the licensing agreement as it would receive from continuing research alone (otherwise it will subsequently deviate from the agreement not to continue research). These two conditions will be met if the cooperative profits from the c_2 technology are at least as large as the sum of the firms' maximum profits from the alternative equilibrium or from continuing research alone. Let R^i_a denote the alternative equilibrium payoff to agent i, $i = \mathrm{I}, \mathrm{E}$. Then a licensing equilibrium requires that

$$\Pi_2 \geq \max\{R^{\mathrm{I}}_a, R^{\mathrm{I}}_{CT}\} + \max\{R^{\mathrm{E}}_a, R^{\mathrm{E}}_{TC}\}. \tag{9}$$

When the alternative equilibrium is TT, then no license will be offered. When the alternative equilibrium is CC, equation (9) reduces to $\Pi_2 \geq R^{\mathrm{I}}_{CT} + R^{\mathrm{E}}_{TC}$ or

$\Pi_2 \geq 2[\Pi_1 - D/p_1]$, which is always true under Assumption 6. When the alternative equilibrium is TC, there are two possibilities. If $R^{\mathrm{I}}_{TC} \geq R^{\mathrm{I}}_{CT}$, then equation (9) becomes $\Pi_2 \geq R^{\mathrm{I}}_{TC} + R^{\mathrm{E}}_{TC} = \Pi_1 - D/p_1$, which always holds. If $R^{\mathrm{I}}_{TC} < R^{\mathrm{I}}_{CT}$, then licensing requires $\Pi_2 > 2[\Pi_1 - D/p_1]$ as above. Assume that licensing always occurs when firms are indifferent.

Thus under Assumption 6, a licensing contract will always be struck to terminate research that would take place absent licensing. From the incumbent's perspective, licensing protects against the risk of discovery of a lower cost technology by the entrant. Moreover, resources which would have been devoted to research (by the entrant and possibly also by the incumbent) are saved.

One can relax Assumption 6 so that both firms have an incentive to continue research until a c_1 technology is obtained.

Assumption 7

Assume that $\Pi_2/2 \leq \Pi_1 - D/\rho_1$.

Under this complementary assumption, both firms face the same incentives to continue and terminate research. In this case, in order for a licensing equilibrium to exist, it must be that $\Pi_2 \geq 2[\Pi_1 - D/p_1]$; but this contradicts Assumption 7. Thus, in this case there will be no equilibrium with licensing.

Gallini and Winter (1985) extend the analysis of this strategic incentive for licensing to more general environments including nondrastic innovations. They find that licensing encourages additional research when the firms' current production costs are close and discourages further research when current production costs are relatively far apart. This is because there are two effects of licensing. First, having developed a superior technology, a firm can license it to its rival; this is the incentive which was pointed out by Salant (1984) in the context of Gilbert and Newbery's preemption model, and it is greatest when current costs are close together. Second, when costs are far apart the low cost firm has an incentive to offer a license to the high cost firm in order to make further research by the high-cost firm unattractive; this minimizes the erosion of the low-cost firm's market share while economizing on development expenditures.

5. Adoption and diffusion of innovations

In the previous section the extent of licensing was examined, but in a timeless framework; all licensing was assumed to be completed at once. However, an important empirical observation regarding the adoption of innovations is that adoption is typically delayed and that firms do not adopt an innovation simultanously. Instead, innovations "diffuse" into use over time.

The general pattern for economic models of diffusion is concisely described by David (1969, ch. II, p. 10):

> whenever or wherever some stimulus variate takes on a value exceeding a critical level, the subject of the stimulation responds by instantly determining to adopt the innovation in question. The reasons such decisions are not arrived at simultaneously by the entire population of potential adopters lies in the fact that at any given point of time either the "stimulus variate" or the "critical level" required to elicit an adoption is described by a distribution of values, and not a unique value appropriate to all members of the population. Hence, at any point in time following the advent of an innovation, the critical response level has been surpassed only in the cases of some among the whole population of potential adopters. Through some exogenous or endogenous process, however, the relative positions of stimulus variate and critical response level are altered as time passes, bringing a growing proportion of the population across the "threshold" into the group of actual users of the innovation.

The heterogeneity posited here may involve any firm characteristic which is relevant to the adoption decision. For instance, David (1969) offers both theoretical and empirical arguments in favor of the use of firm size. Other explanations, such as differential access to information regarding the innovation's profitability and/or managerial willingness to take risk, are also common. A combination of these two latter features generates the diffusion of innovation described in Jensen (1982), which provides a formal model of the type described by David.

When an innovation is first announced, a firm may be uncertain regarding its profitability should it adopt the innovation. However, this uncertainty may be reduced over time as information regarding the innovation accumulates. Jensen's formal model assumes that at any decision point in time, the firm has two options: it can adopt the innovation, which involves a fixed cost and is irreversible; or it can wait. If the firm waits, then it receives additional information regarding the innovation's profitability, but of course it foregoes for one period any profit it might have made by adopting the innovation. The firm begins with a prior estimate of the likelihood that the innovation will be profitable, and "learns" over time, updating its estimate in a Bayesian fashion. Thus, the firm's decision problem can be modelled as an optimal stopping problem. An optimal adoption rule has the following form: if the posterior estimate of the likelihood that the innovation would be profitable is sufficiently high, adopt; otherwise, wait. If an industry consists of firms who differ in their initial assessments of the innovation, then they will typically reach this critical level of estimated profitability at different times. Thus, the innovation will be observed to diffuse into use.

Suppose that a firm is currently at equilibrium in its industry; normalize its current profits to zero for simplicity. Suppose that an alternative production process (an innovation) is exogenously developed and may be acquired at a cost of C. This process has some stochastic features in the sense that with probability θ the firm earns (in present value terms) $R_1 = r_1/(1-\beta)$, where r_1 is the rate of flow profit and β is the discount factor; with probability $1-\theta$ the firm earns $R_0 = r_0/(1-\beta)$. It is assumed that $R_0 < R_1$. Thus, $1-\theta$ might be interpreted as the fraction of "down time" associated with the process. The parameter θ is unknown to the firm, but it is known to be one of two possible values, θ_1 or θ_2, with $1 > \theta_1 > \theta_2 > 0$. Assume that

$$\theta_1 R_1 + (1-\theta_1) R_0 - C > 0 > \theta_2 R_1 + (1-\theta_2) R_0 - C, \tag{10}$$

so that if $\theta = \theta_1$, the innovation can be classified as "profitable", while if $\theta = \theta_2$, the innovation can be termed "unprofitable". If the firm does not adopt the innovation in period i, it is assumed to receive a costless signal, representable as a Bernoulli random variable Z_i, which takes on the value 1 if the information is favorable and 0 if it is unfavorable. The probability that $Z_i = 1$ is the unknown parameter θ.

Given a sequence $Z_1, \ldots, Z_n$, the firm can construct an estimate of the parameter θ as follows. If p is the firm's prior probability that $\theta = \theta_1$, then its estimate of θ is

$$q(p) \equiv p\theta_1 + (1-p)\theta_2. \tag{11}$$

Its posterior probability that $\theta = \theta_1$ is $h_1(p) \equiv p\theta_1/q(p)$ if the observation is favorable and $h_0(p) \equiv p(1-\theta_1)/(1-q(p))$ if the observation is unfavorable. Assuming that the firm's initial prior probability that $\theta = \theta_1$ is g, then after n observations, k of which were favorable, the firm's posterior probability that $\theta = \theta_1$ is

$$p(n,k,g) \equiv \left[1 + (\theta_2/\theta_1)^k ((1-\theta_2)/(1-\theta_1))^{n-k} (1-g)/g\right]^{-1}. \tag{12}$$

Beginning from the initial prior g, the state variable for the decision process is $p(n, k, g)$, the firm's current probabilistic belief that the innovation is profitable. Assuming that an infinite number of decision periods exists, then $V(p)$, the maximum expected return when the current state is p, is defined as the solution to the following functional equation of dynamic programming:

$$V(p) = \max\{V^{a}(p), V^{w}(p)\}, \tag{13}$$

where the expected value of adoption is

$$V^{a}(p) \equiv q(p) R_1 + (1-q(p)) R_0 - C, \tag{14}$$

and the expected value of waiting one period and continuing optimally is

$$V^{w}(p) \equiv \beta[q(p)V(h_1(p)) + (1 - q(p))V(h_0(p))]. \tag{15}$$

Proposition 35 [Jensen (1982)]

There exists a unique $p^* \in (0,1)$ such that $V^{a}(p) \gtreqless V^{w}(p)$ if and only if $p \gtreqless p^*$.

Thus, the optimal adoption rule is to adopt the innovation at the first date n for which $p(n, k, g) \geq p^*$. Moreover, the probability of adoption at or before a given stage N is an increasing function of g, k, r_1, r_0 and β and is a decreasing function of C.

It is also easy to see that immediate adoption may not be optimal, but a profitable innovation will eventually be adopted with probability 1 if $g \neq 0$. If $g < p^*$, then the firm will wait at least one period to gather additional information about the innovation's profitability. However, by the law of large numbers, the Bayesian estimate of θ will eventually converge to its true value. If this is θ_1, then the firm will eventually adopt the innovation.

A firm is more likely to adopt by a given date the more favorable is its initial assessment of the innovation; thus a firm which begins by being sufficiently skeptical will delay adoption; if it is willing to learn, however, it will not forego a profitable innovation indefinitely. Clearly, the analogous result for unprofitable innovations is not true; some unprofitable innovations will be adopted due to optimistic initial beliefs or the receipt of favorable information. The length of the delay prior to adoption will be shorter (on average) the more optimistic the initial belief, the more favorable the information received, the higher the discount factor, and the higher the rate of flow profits; the length of delay will be greater (on average) the higher are the adoption costs.

Suppose now that there is an industry composed of a continuum of these firms; each receives the same information about the innovation, but they may begin with different prior beliefs about it. In this case, firms with different prior beliefs will adopt the innovation at different times. The traditional S-shaped diffusion curve can be obtained by means of appropriate assumptions regarding the distribution of prior beliefs within the industry.

McCardle (1985) has generalized this model to include explicit costs of information gathering. When information is costly, a firm may elect to reject the innovation (i.e. terminate sampling without adopting). In this case, the optimal decision function is "cone-shaped". That is, for sufficiently high posterior beliefs, the firm stops sampling and adopts the innovation; for sufficiently low posterior beliefs, it stops sampling and rejects the innovation; finally, for intermediate beliefs, it continues sampling. Jensen (1984a, 1984b) has also considered alternative specifications of sampling costs, as well as asymmetry in information processing capacity [Jensen (1984c)]. Mamer and McCardle (1985) extend the results of McCardle (1985) to a two-firm game in which the firms receive private signals at a fixed cost per signal. Roberts and Weitzman (1981) present a single-agent sequential decision model which is applicable to the innovation adoption problem and which uses a more general specification of uncertainty.

One difficulty with this formulation is that no firm anticipates any future technological improvements. Balcer and Lippman (1984) develop a one-firm model of the timing of adoption assuming that the firm has perfect information regarding the current best available technology, but is uncertain about the rate and magnitude of future improvements. They find that there is a critical technological lag beyond which the firm immediately adopts the best available technology; otherwise, it postpones adoption. The critical lag length increases with the anticipated rate of future innovation.

Another difficulty is that no firm perceives the impact of other firms' adoption decisions upon its own profits. Reinganum (1981b, 1981c) has argued that no ex ante heterogeneity among firms, nor any imperfect information regarding the innovation's profitability, is necessary to obtain diffusion of an innovation; under some circumstances, a certain amount of rationality and foresight on the part of firms is sufficient. In particular, suppose that an industry of n identical firms produces and markets a homogeneous good in a Cournot–Nash manner. When a cost-reducing, capital-embodied process innovation is announced, each firm must decide when to adopt it, accounting for the costs and benefits of the innovation itself, and for the effects of rival firms' adoption decisions. It is assumed that each firm must commit itself to an adoption date at once and without knowledge of its rival's decisions. The justification for this assumption is that adoption of a process innovation is a time-consuming activitity, with installation and adjustment costs a function of the planned adjustment path. Thus, the choice of an "adoption date" really represents a time at which adoption will be completed (assuming it begins immediately); it may be very costly to alter the planned path of adjustment once it has been selected. That is, the whole *path* of adjustment, not just a delivery date, would have to be changed. We assume that such alterations of plans are prohibitively costly.

Let $\pi_0(m)$ be the rate of profit flow to firm i when m firms have adopted the innovation, but firm i has not. Next let $\pi_1(m)$ be the flow of profit to firm i when m firms have adopted and i is among them. We assume that $\pi_0(m)$ and $\pi_1(m)$ are known with certainty.

Assumption 8

Profit rates are non-negative, and the increase in profit rates due to adopting $(m-1)$th is greater than due to adopting mth. That is, $\pi_0(m-1) \geq 0$

and $\pi_1(m) \geq 0$ with $\pi_1(m-1) - \pi_0(m-2) > \pi_1(m) - \pi_0(m-1) > 0$ for all $m \leq n$.

Let τ_i denote firm i's adoption date and let $p(\tau_i)$ represent the combined purchase price plus adjustment costs (in present value terms) required to bring the new technology on line by date τ_i. The function $p(\cdot)$ is assumed to be twice differentiable and convex.

Assumption 9

(a) $\lim_{t\to 0} p(t) = -\lim_{t\to 0} p'(t) = \infty$; (b) $\lim_{t\to\infty} p'(t) > 0$; (c) $p''(t) > re^{-rt}[\pi_1(1) - \pi_0(0)]$ for all t.

In keeping with the adjustment costs story, Assumption 9(a) implies that instantaneous adjustment is prohibitively costly, but costs drop off sharply as the adjustment period is lengthened. Assumption 9(b) states that there is an "efficient scale" or cost-minimizing period of adjustment; finally, Assumption 9(c) states that adjustment costs increase at a sufficiently fast rate as the adjustment period is compressed. This assumption ensures that firm i's objective function will be (locally) strictly concave in its choice variable.

Let $\tau = (\tau_1, \ldots, \tau_n)$ denote the vector of adoption times in increasing order of adoption and let τ_{-i} denote this vector without the ith element τ_i. Thus, $\tau = (\tau_i, \tau_{-i})$. Let $V^i(\tau)$ be the ith adopter's profit (in present value terms) when the vector of adoption dates is τ. Then

$$V^i(\tau) = \sum_{m=0}^{i-1} \int_{\tau_m}^{\tau_{m+1}} \pi_0(m) e^{-rt} dt + \sum_{m=i}^{n} \int_{\tau_m}^{\tau_{m+1}} \pi_1(m) e^{-rt} dt - p(\tau_i),$$

where $\tau_0 \equiv 0$ and $\tau_{n+1} \equiv \infty$.

Proposition 36 [Reinganum (1981c)]

The n-tuple of adoption dates τ^* defined by system (16) is a Nash equilibrium and $\tau_{i-1}^* < \tau_i^* < \tau_{i+1}^*$, $i = 1, 2, \ldots, n$:

$$\partial V^i / \partial \tau_i = [\pi_0(i-1) - \pi_1(i)] e^{-r\tau_i^*} - p'(\tau_i^*) = 0. \tag{16}$$

Thus, an equilibrium for this game is asymmetric, implying a "diffusion" of innovation over time, despite the facts that information is perfect and the firms are identical.

Reinganum's work focused on situations in which a firm was committed to its adoption date, regardless of any subsequent information it might receive regarding the adoption decisions of rival firms. This seems plausible under the adjustment costs interpretation given above. However, in many instances firms will be able to respond to the actions of rival firms without significant lags or associated costs of changing plans. Judd (1983) and Fudenberg and Tirole (1985) have examined this situation, and find that the pattern of adoption will still be characterized by diffusion, but that firms will be forced to adopt the innovation faster due to the threat of pre-emption by rival firms. In some cases, there may also exist a continuum of simultaneous adoption equilibria.

Fudenberg and Tirole (1985) show that, for the model described above, a firm's equilibrium payoff declines monotonically with its rank in the order of adoption. Judd (1983) argues that if firms are able to respond to the choices and/or actions of rival firms, such a situation cannot occur in equilibrium. Instead, firms would compete to be the first firm, knowing that rival firms would adjust their adoption plans in response. In order to characterize equilibrium when firms are able to respond quickly to rivals' behavior it is necessary to give an explicitly dynamic description of strategies. Following Judd (1983), let $d_i(t, k)$ be the decision rule for firm i; it specifies whether or not firm i adopts the innovation at t if k other firms have already done so; thus $d_i(t, k) = 1$ if firm i decides to adopt the innovation, and $d_i(t, k) = 0$ if firm i decides not to adopt the innovation at t. A decision rule $\{d_i\}_{i=1}^n$ is a (subgame perfect) equilibrium if and only if at each t, d_i maximizes the profits of firm i given the decision rules of the other firms and the value of k at t.

For simplicity, Judd makes the following assumptions [these turn out to involve some loss of generality, as shown by Fudenberg and Tirole (1985)]. He assumes that time is discrete, and that firms move in alternate periods (since periods are of very short duration, approximately simultaneous adoption is possible). Let us denote the subgame perfect equilibrium by $\{T_i^*\}_{i=1}^n$, and let $V^i(T_i^*, T_{-i}^*)$ denote firm i's payoff, where T_i^* denotes the equilibrium adoption time for firm i assuming that equilibrium adoption decision rules are used. Suppose without loss of generality that the ith firm is also the ith adopter. Assuming that optimal continuation play is independent of the identities of those firms who have already adopted, it can be shown that all firms must make the same profit in equilibrium; that is, $V^i(T^*) = V^j(T^*)$ for all i and j. To see this, suppose otherwise; suppose that $V^i(T^*) > V^j(T^*)$ for some $i \neq j$. If $i < j$ (that is, i adopts before j), then j cannot be using an optimal decision rule, because j could essentially "become" i by adopting slightly before i, causing firms $i, i + 1, \dots, n$ to respond optimally, and leaving j with profits arbitrarily close to $V^i(T^*)$. If $i > j$ (that is, j adopts before i), firm j could postpone adoption and again receive almost $V^i(T^*)$ by just pre-empting firm i. The adoption dates can be computed by backwards induction.

Proposition 37 [Judd (1983)]

There is a unique set of (subgame perfect) equilibrium innovation times $\{T_i^*\}_{i=1}^n$, and $T_i^* \leq \tau_i^*$ for all i.

Thus, the innovation still diffuses into use, but its diffusion is more rapid when firms are able to respond quickly to rivals' actions than when they are unable to respond.

Fudenberg and Tirole (1985) show that the assumption of discrete time is not without loss of generality. In their continuous time model (the analysis of which necessitates the use of some quite technical arguments), there may also exist a continuum of equilibria involving simultaneous adoption. These equilibria can be Pareto ranked, with later adoption being preferred. Finally, if one is free to assign different continuation values (that is, different subgame equilibria) to different adoption histories, then profits need not be equalized across all firms when $n > 2$.

Quirmbach (1986) has analyzed the case of coordinated adoption behavior in the framework of Reinganum (1981b, 1981c), and finds that diffusion is characteristic of optimal adoption under a variety of alternative objective functions. The key elements which combine to generate diffusion are (1) declining incremental benefits for later adopters, and (2) declining adoption costs. Thus, although there is no ex ante heterogeneity among firms, these characteristics of the market (along with firms' abilities to perceive them) generate ex post heterogeneity in the form of diffusion. For example, consider the case of coordinated adoption by all n members of the industry. Assuming noncooperative production, joint industry profits can be written:

$$W(\tau) = \sum_{m=0}^{n} \int_{\tau_m}^{\tau_{m+1}} [m\pi_1(m) + (n-m)\pi_0(m)] \mathrm{e}^{-rt} \mathrm{d}t - \sum_{m=1}^{n} p(\tau_m),$$

where again $\tau_0 \equiv 0$ and $\tau_{n+1} \equiv \infty$. Recall Assumption 8; defining $\Delta\pi(m) \equiv \pi_1(m) - \pi_0(m-1)$, Assumption 8 says that $\Delta\pi(m-1) > \Delta\pi(m) > 0$; that is, the incremental benefit of adoption declines with the number of previous adopters. For the cooperative firms, the analogs to Assumptions 8 and 9 are as follows.

Assumption 10

$\Delta B(m-1) > \Delta B(m) > 0$, where

$$\Delta B(m) \equiv [m\pi_1(m) + (n-m)\pi_0(m)] - [(m-1)\pi_1(m-1) + (n-m+1)\pi_0(m-1)].$$

Assumption 11

(a) $\lim_{t \to 0} p(t) = -\lim_{t \to 0} p'(t) = \infty$; (b) $\lim_{t \to \infty} p'(t) > 0$; (c) $p''(t) > re^{-rt}[\Delta B(1)]$ for all t.

Given these assumptions, we can characterize the jointly optimal adoption dates $\{\tau_i^0\}_{i=1}^n$ by differentiating $W(\tau)$ to obtain, for $i = 1, 2, \ldots, n$:

$$\partial W(\tau^0)/\partial \tau_i = -\Delta B(i) e^{-r\tau_i^0} - p'(\tau_i^0) = 0. \tag{17}$$

Proposition 38 [Quirmbach (1986)]

The cooperative optimum is characterized by a diffusion of innovation which is uniformly slower than the noncooperative diffusion; that is, $\tau_i^0 > \tau_{i-1}^0$ and $\tau_i^0 > \tau_i^*$, for $i = 1, 2, \ldots, n$.

The innovations envisioned above were those which exerted negative externalities upon the remaining members of the industry. However, in some cases the adoption of an innovation confers positive externalities upon all users. Examples include communications systems which allow agents to converse with one another, provided both employ compatible systems, and products such as video cassette players (or personal computers) where more movies (or software) will be available if more units are in operation. Unlike innovations which exert negative externalities on rival firms, these innovations suffer from an individual's unwillingness to adopt unilaterally; expectations about whether others will follow are crucial to the behavior of initial adopters. An interesting recent contribution to the literature on this subject is Farrell and Saloner (1985); for related work, see Dybvig and Spatt (1983) and Katz and Shapiro (1985a).

Consider an industry composed of two firms. When an innovation, consisting of a new standard, is announced, firms noncooperatively decide whether to adopt it. Adoption is considered to be an irreversible decision. For firm j, define $B_j(1, Y)$ to be the net benefit to firm j of unilaterally switching from the old standard X to the new standard Y. $B_j(2, Y)$ is the net benefit to j if both firms switch to Y. Status quo profits are normalized to zero so that firm j will be in favor of a change by the entire industry if and only if $B_j(2, Y) > 0$. Let $B_j(1, X)$ denote j's payoff if j unilaterally remains with the old standard X, while the other firm switches to the new standard Y. By the normalization assumption $B_j(2, X) = 0$. The assumption that adoption of the new standard confers positive externalities upon other adopters is formalized below.

Assumption 12

For $k = X$ or Y, $B_j(1, k) \leq B_j(2, k)$. That is, whatever choice j makes, he prefers to have the other firm make the same choice.

Proposition 39 [Farrell and Saloner (1985)]

Suppose that $B_i(2, Y) > B_i(2, X)$ and $B_j(2, Y) > B_j(1, X)$ for some i and $j \neq i$. Then the unique perfect equilibrium involves all firms switching.

To see why, assume that there are two decision periods. Since the firms have complete information, each firm can foresee whether or not the other firm will follow; thus if $B_i(2, Y) > B_i(2, X)$ and $B_j(2, Y) > B_j(1, X)$ for $j \neq i$ and $i = 1$ *or* 2, then the unique (subgame perfect) equilibrium involves all firms switching. This is because the firm which satisfies the hypotheses can ensure adoption by adopting unilaterally in the first period, knowing that the other firm will follow.

Since the assumption that $B_j(2, Y) > B_j(1, X)$ is weaker than the assumption that $B_j(2, Y) > B_j(2, X)$, an immediate corollary of Proposition 39 is that if $B_j(2, Y) > B_j(2, X)$ for $j = 1, 2$, then the unique perfect equilibrium involves all firms switching. Thus, firms need not be unanimous in their desire for the entire industry to adopt the new standard; it suffices for firm j to prefer company at the new standard than to maintain the old one alone.

Suppose now that each firm is uncertain about the other firm's evaluation of the new standard. This evaluation is simply indexed by a superscript i denoting the other firm's "type", with higher values of i indicating stronger preferences for the new standard Y. Let $B^i(1, k)$ denote the net benefits to the firm of type i from maintaining the standard k alone, and $B^i(2, k)$ the net benefits to the firm of type i from having the industry standardized at k, for $k = X$ or Y. The distribution of types is assumed to be uniform on the interval $[0, 1]$.

There are again two decision periods, and each firm can switch (irreversibly) either in period 1 or in period 2. In the first period, each firm must decide whether or not to switch based on its own type; in the second period, each firm must decide whether or not to switch based on its own type and the actions taken in period 1.

Assumption 13

$B^i(2, k) > B^i(1, k)$, $k = X, Y$. That is, networks are beneficial.

Assumption 14

$B^i(2, Y)$ and $B^i(1, Y)$ are continuous and strictly increasing in i; that is, higher types are uniformly more eager to switch to Y.

Assumption 15

$B^1(1, Y) > 0$ and $B^0(2, Y) < B^0(1, Y)$. At least one type is willing to switch unilaterally, and at least one type is willing to remain alone at the old standard.

Given Assumption 15 and incomplete information regarding the other firm's type, a firm which switches early cannot be assured that the other firm will follow. For intermediate values of i, the firm's decision will depend nontrivially upon the decision of its predecessor.

Assumption 16

$B^i(2, Y) - B^i(1, X)$ is monotone increasing in i. Thus, if a type i firm would prefer an industry switch to Y to remaining alone at X, so would any type $i' > i$.

Definition

A *bandwagon strategy* for a firm is defined by a pair $(i^*, \bar{i})$ with $i^* > \bar{i}$ such that
(a) if $i \geq i^*$, the firm switches in period 1;
(b) if $i^* > i \geq \bar{i}$, the firm does not switch in period 1, and switches in period 2 if and only if the other firm switched in period 1;
(c) if $i < \bar{i}$, the firm never switches.

A *bandwagon equilibrium* is defined to be a subgame perfect Bayesian Nash equilibrium in which each firm plays a bandwagon strategy. Farrell and Saloner characterize symmetric bandwagon equilibria; that is, those for which the pair $(i^*, \bar{i})$ is the same for both firms. They show that there is a unique such equilibrium, and that there are no equilibria which are not bandwagon equilibria.

Proposition 40 [Farrell and Saloner (1985)]

A unique symmetric bandwagon equilibrium exists.

The equilibrium in this game has two essential features: one is that it exhibits "bandwagon effects"; that is, some firm types would move early in hopes of inducing the other firm to follow (even though they would not prefer to switch unilaterally; that is, $B^i(1, Y) < 0$). Conversely, some firms who prefer the combined switch ($B^i(2, Y) > 0$) but are of types $i < i^*$ will wait until the other firm has switched before switching themselves. If both firms fall into this set, then the industry remains at the old standard, even though both firms prefer the combined switch to the new one, and even though such a switch would occur if information were complete. As Farrell and Saloner (p. 16) picturesquely put it, "both firms are fence-sitters, happy to jump on the bandwagon if it gets rolling but insufficiently keen to set it rolling themselves". There will be some combinations of firm types such that the sum of benefits is positive, yet the switch will not be made, and other combinations for which the sum of benefits is negative and the switch *will* be made (because one firm favors the switch enough to adopt unilaterally, and the other prefers company at the new standard to maintaining the old one alone).

6. Conclusions

From the collection of symmetric models discussed in Section 2, we come away with an appreciation of the extent to which rivalry and appropriability interact to determine the incentives for individual firm investment in research and development. For instance, we have seen that whether or not entry results in increased or decreased investment by a given firm can depend critically upon the extent to which the rewards to innovation are appropriable. Similarly, when rewards are sufficiently appropriable, firms will overinvest relative to the cooperative optimum; on the other hand, when rewards are sufficiently inappropriable, firms will underinvest relative to that benchmark.

The models in Section 3 focused upon situations in which firms are asymmetrically placed. This asymmetry might be inherited, as in the incumbent/challenger models, or it might have developed over time as a consequence of intermediate successes. In comparing the auction and stochastic racing paradigms, we found that the associated equilibria were sometimes qualitatively different. In view of the possible differences in results, it seems important to choose the appropriate paradigm. The stochastic racing model seems to more accurately capture what we think of as research or "invention"; an activity that might or might not yield a worthwhile end-product, and one that may take more or less time and money than expected. The auction model may well be preferred for the case of development or new product introduction, in which any substantial technological uncertainties have already been resolved. Both research and development are significant aspects of innovative activity, and although the dividing line between them is by no means clear, some attempt should be made to match the appropriate paradigm to the specific application.

The models described in Section 4 examined restricted forms of licensing (primarily fixed-fee contracts) in the context of oligopolistic production. Under this assumption, it is generally concluded that firms who are not members of the venture which holds the patent are worse off as a consequence of the innovation, whether or not they obtain a license to use it. Thus, one incentive for licensing is this redistribution of wealth away from nonmembers to members. When additional research may yield an equivalent or better innovation, another incentive to license arises. In this situation, it may be optimal to license a drastic innovation to a potential entrant so as to decrease incentives for future research.

In Section 5 we described models of the diffusion of innovation over time. Although an information-based model of diffusion has definite appeal in terms of realism, imperfect information is by no means necessary to explain why an innovation might diffuse relatively slowly into use. In the case of an innovation which is known to be profitable, the trick is to discover why firms might delay adoption. The key determinants prove to be declining adoption costs and the perception that the benefits of adoption decline with the number of previous adopters. This latter perception stems from strategic interactions in the product market; for example, oligopoly or multi-plant monopoly. It is interesting that a similar diffusion curve can be derived for the case of an innovation with positive external effects. When the value of adoption increases with the number of previous adopters, early adopters stimulate the subsequent diffusion of the innovation.

Most of this work has treated the process of research and development and the dissemination of its outcome as two separate issues. Invoking subgame perfection and dynamic programming suggests that this separation is legitimate and that one may fruitfully combine the results of these separate analyses. If various sorts of long-term commitments are possible, however, this approach will rule out some potentially interesting strategic features of the problem. For instance, a firm which could make credible a policy of never licensing to R&D rivals might be able to restrict the competition it faces in R&D. In this case, a model which simultaneously addresses both aspects of innovative activity would be required.

One important goal of future research should be to develop testable models of industry equilibrium behavior. The papers summarized here have used stark models in order to identify the significant characteristics of firms, markets and innovations which are likely to affect incentives to invest and/or adopt. But since it is largely restricted to these special cases (e.g. deterministic innovations, drastic innovations, two firms, symmetric firms), this work has not yet had a significant impact on the applied literature in industrial organization; its usefulness for policy purposes should also be considered limited. For these purposes, one needs a predictive model which encompasses the full range of firm, industry and innovation characteristics.

References

Arrow, K.J. (1962a) 'Economic welfare and the allocation of resources for invention', in: NBER conference no. 13, *The rate and direction of inventive activity: Economic and social factors*. Princeton: Princeton University Press.

Arrow, K.J. (1962b) 'The economic implications of learning by doing', *Review of Economic Studies*, 29:155–173.

Balcer, Y. and Lippman, S.A. (1984) 'Technological expectations and adoption of improved technology', *Journal of Economic Theory*, 34:292–318.

Barzel, Y. (1968) 'Optimal timing of innovations', *Review of Economics and Statistics*, 50:348–355.

Dasgupta, P. and Stiglitz, J. (1980a) 'Industrial structure and the nature of innovative activity', *Economic Journal*, 90:266–293.

Dasgupta, P. and Stiglitz, J. (1980b) 'Uncertainty, industrial structure and the speed of R&D', *Bell Journal*, 11:1–28.

David, P.A. (1969) 'A contribution to the theory of distribution', Research Memorandum no. 71, Research Center in Economic Growth, Stanford University.

Dixit, A.K. and Stiglitz, J.E. (1977) 'Monopolistic competition and optimum product diversity', *American Economic Review*, 67:297–308.

Dybvig, P.H. and Spatt, C.S. (1983) 'Adoption externalities as public goods', *Journal of Public Economics*, 20:231–247.

Farrell, J. and Saloner, G. (1985) 'Standardization, compatibility and innovation', *Rand Journal of Economics*, 16:70–83.

Fethke, G.C. and Birch, J.J. (1982) 'Rivalry and the timing of innovation', *Bell Journal*, 13:272–279.

Flaherty, M.T. (1980) 'Industry structure and cost-reducing investment', *Econometrica*, 48:1187–1209.

Fudenberg, D. and Tirole, J. (1983) 'Learning-by-doing and market performance', *Bell Journal*, 14:522–530.

Fudenberg, D. and Tirole, J. (1985) 'Preemption and rent equalization in the adoption of new technology', *Review of Economic Studies*, 52:383–401.

Fudenberg, D., Gilbert, R.J., Stiglitz, J. and Tirole, J. (1983) 'Preemption, leapfrogging and competition in patent races', *European Economic Review*, 22:3–31.

Futia, C.A. (1980) 'Schumpeterian competition', *Quarterly Journal of Economics*, 93:675–695.

Gallini, N.T. (1984) 'Deterrence by market sharing: A strategic incentive for licensing', *American Economic Review*, 74:931–941.

Gallini, N.T. and Winter, R.A. (1985) 'Licensing in the theory of innovation', *Bell Journal*, 16:237–252.

Gilbert, R.J. and Newbery, D.M.G. (1982) 'Preemptive patenting and the persistence of monopoly', *American Economic Review*, 72:514–526.

Grossman, G.M. and Shapiro, C. (1986) 'Optimal dynamic R&D programs', *Rand Journal of Economics*, 17:581–593.

Grossman, G.M. and Shapiro, C. (1987) 'Dynamic R&D competition', *Economic Journal*, 97:372–387.

Harris, C. and Vickers, J. (1985) 'Perfect equilibrium in a model of a race', *Review of Economic Studies*, 52:193–209.

Hartwick, J.M. (1982) 'Efficient prizes in prototype development contests', *Economics Letters*, 10:375–379.

Hirshleifer, J. and Riley, J.G. (1979) 'The analytics of uncertainty and information – An expository survey', *Journal of Economic Literature*, 17:1375–1421.

Isaac, R.M. and Reynolds, S.S. (1985) 'Innovation and property rights in information: An experimental approach to testing hypotheses about private R&D behavior', discussion paper no. 85-30, University of Arizona.

Jensen, R. (1982) 'Adoption and diffusion of an innovation of uncertain profitability', *Journal of Economic Theory*, 27:182–193.

Jensen, R. (1984a) 'Adoption of an innovation of uncertain profitability with costly information', working paper no. 84-8, Ohio State University.

Jensen, R. (1984b) 'Innovation adoption with both costless and costly information', working paper no. 84-22, Ohio State University.

Jensen, R. (1984c) 'Information capacity and innovation adoption', working paper no. 84-33, Ohio State University.

Judd, K.L. (1983) 'Equilibrium diffusion of innovation with no pre-commitment', mimeo.

Judd, K.L. (1984) 'Closed-loop equilibrium in an innovation race with experience', mimeo.

Judd, K.L. (1985a) 'Closed-loop equilibrium in a multi-stage innovation race', discussion paper no. 647, Center for Mathematical Studies in Economics and Management Science, Northwestern University.

Judd, K.L. (1985b) 'On the performance of patents', *Econometrica*, 53:567–585.

Kamien, M.I. and Schwartz, N.L. (1971) 'Expenditure patterns for risky R&D projects', *Journal of Applied Probability*, 8:60–73.

Kamien, M.I. and Schwartz, N.L. (1972) 'Timing of innovations under rivalry', *Econometrica*, 40:43–60.

Kamien, M.I. and Schwartz, N.L. (1974) 'Patent life and R&D rivalry', *American Economic Review*, 64:183–187.

Kamien, M.I. and Schwartz, N.L. (1980) *Market structure and innovation*. Cambridge: Cambridge University Press.

Kamien, M.I. and Tauman, Y. (1984) 'The private value of a patent: A game theoretic analysis', *Zeitschrift für Nationalokonomie/Journal of Economics* (Supplement), 4:93–118.

Kamien, M.I. and Tauman, Y. (1986) 'Fees versus royalties and the private value of a patent', *Quarterly Journal of Economics*, 101:471–492.

Kamien, M.I., Tauman, Y. and Zang, I. (1985) 'Optimal license fees for a new product', mimeo.

Katz, M.L. (1986) 'An analysis of cooperative research and development', *Rand Journal of Economics*, 17:527–543.

Katz, M.L. and Shapiro, C. (1985a) 'Network externalities, competition and compatibility', *American Economic Review*, 75:424–440.

Katz, M.L. and Shapiro, C. (1985b) 'On the licensing of innovations', *Rand Journal of Economics*, 16:504–520.

Katz, M.L. and Shapiro, C. (1986) 'How to license intangible property', *Quarterly Journal of Economics*, 101:567–590.

Katz, M.L. and Shapiro, C. (1987) 'R&D rivalry with licensing or imitation', *American Economic Review*, 77:402–420.

Lee, T. and Wilde, L.L. (1980) 'Market structure and innovation: A reformulation', *Quarterly Journal of Economics*, 94:429–436.

Loury, G.C. (1979) 'Market structure and innovation', *Quarterly Journal of Economics*, 93:395–410.

Lucas, Jr., R.E. (1971) 'Optimal management of a research and development project', *Management Science*, 17:679–697.

Mamer, J.W. and McCardle, K.F. (1985) 'Uncertainty, competition and the adoption of new technology', mimeo.

McCardle, K.F. (1985) 'Information acquisition and the adoption of new technology', *Management Science*, 31:1372–1389.

Mortensen, D.T. (1982) 'Property rights and efficiency in mating, racing and related games', *American Economic Review*, 72:968–979.

Park, J. (1984) 'Innovation competition under certainty', Ph.D. dissertation, Northwestern University.

Quirmbach, H.C. (1986) 'The diffusion of new technology and the market for an innovation', *Rand Journal of Economics*, 17:33–47.

Reinganum, J.F. (1981a) 'Dynamic games of innovation', *Journal of Economic Theory*, 25:21–41; (1985) 'Corrigendum', 35:196–197.

Reinganum, J.F. (1981b) 'On the diffusion of new technology: A game theoretic approach', *Review of Economic Studies*, 48:395–405.

Reinganum, J.F. (1981c) 'Market structure and the diffusion of new technology', *Bell Journal*, 12:618–624.

Reinganum, J.F. (1982a) 'A dynamic game of R and D: Patent protection and competitive behavior', *Econometrica*, 50:671–688.

Reinganum, J.F. (1982b) 'Strategic search theory', *International Economic Review*, 23:1–15.

Reinganum, J.F. (1983a) 'Nash equilibrium search for the best alternative', *Journal of Economic Theory*, 30:139–152.

Reinganum, J.F. (1983b) 'Uncertain innovation and the persistence of monopoly', *American Economic Review*, 73:741–748.

Reinganum, J.F. (1984) 'Practical implications of game theoretic models of R&D', *American Economic Review*, 74:61–66.

Reinganum, J.F (1985) 'Innovation and industry evolution', *Quarterly Journal of Economics*, 81–99.

Roberts, K. and Weitzman, M.L. (1981) 'Funding criteria for research, development, and exploration projects', *Econometrica*, 49:1261–1288.

Rogerson, W.P. (1982) 'The social costs of regulation and monopoly: A game-theoretic analysis', *Bell Journal*, 13:391–401.

Salant, S.W. (1984) 'Preemptive patenting and the persistence of monopoly: Comment', *American Economic Review*, 74:247–250.

Scherer, F.M. (1967) 'Research and development resource allocation under rivalry', *Quarterly Journal of Economics*, 81:359–394.

Scherer, F.M. (1980) *Industrial market structure and economic performance*. Chicago: Rand McNally.
Schumpeter, J.A. (1942) *Capitalism, socialism and democracy*. New York: Harper & Row.
Selten, R. (1975) 'Reexamination of the perfectness concept for equilibrium points in extensive games', *International Journal of Game Theory*, 4:25–55.
Spence, A.M. (1976) 'Product selection, fixed costs and monopolistic competition', *Review of Economic Studies*, 43:217–235.
Spence, A.M. (1981) 'The learning curve and competition', *Bell Journal*, 12:49–70.
Spence, A.M. (1984) 'Cost reduction, competition and industrial performance', *Econometrica*, 52:101–121.
Stewart, M.B. (1983) 'Noncooperative oligopoly and preemptive innovation without winner-take-all', *Quarterly Journal of Economics*, 98:681–694.
Stoneman, P. (1983) *The economic analysis of technological change*. Oxford: Oxford University Press.
Tandon, P. (1984) 'Innovation, market structure, and welfare', *American Economic Review*, 74:394–403.
Telser, L.G. (1982) 'A theory of innovation and its effects', *Bell Journal*, 13:69–92.
Vickers, J. (1984) 'Notes on the evolution of market structure when there is a sequence of innovations', mimeo.

Chapter 15

THE THEORY AND THE FACTS OF HOW MARKETS CLEAR: IS INDUSTRIAL ORGANIZATION VALUABLE FOR UNDERSTANDING MACROECONOMICS?

DENNIS W. CARLTON*

University of Chicago and NBER

Contents

*I thank NSF for research support and Yakov Amihud, Reuven Brenner, Kenneth McLaughlin, Haim Mendelson, Richard Schmalensee, Margaret Sheridan, and George Stigler for helpful comments. The research reported here is part of NBER's research program in Economic Fluctuations. Any opinions expressed are those of the author and not those of NBER.

Handbook of Industrial Organization, Volume I, Edited by R. Schmalensee and R.D. Willig

1. Introduction

Industrial organization is the study of how individual industries operate. It attempts to explain how an industry reaches an equilibrium price and output and how the industry behaves over time in response to changes in either supply or demand conditions. As is typical in microeconomics, an important focus of attention has been on how price clears markets. Industrial organization, perhaps more than any other branch of microeconomics, has been well aware that the observed behavior of prices turns out to be different from that predicted by any of the simple models of market clearing. Despite this disparity between the evidence and the theory, industrial organization has not, until quite recently, made great strides toward resolving the conflict. This chapter describes some of the simple as well as more recently developed and more complicated theories of how markets clear, and presents evidence on what industrial organization economists know about how markets clear.

Aside from industrial organization economists, macroeconomists are also deeply interested in the question of how markets clear. In Keynesian macroeconomics it is assumed that for some (often unexplained) reason certain markets, typically the labor market, do not clear because a price is rigid. When prices fail to clear markets, inefficiencies develop, resources are wasted and unemployment can arise. If industrial organization economists find that certain prices are rigid, that fact should be of great interest to Keynesians since their theories depend on these price rigidities. Whether or not one is a Keynesian, understanding how markets clear over time is valuable information to a macroeconomist. If industrial organization economists can indeed predict the time path of prices, output, investments, the employment of factors, and inventories, and the transmission of shocks from one sector of the economy to the other, those predictions would be of interest to macroeconomists attempting to explain business cycles. Recent explanations of business cycles [e.g. Lucas (1981)] stress the importance of intertemporal substitution patterns, either in demand or in supply. It is these intertemporal substitution patterns that industrial organization economists can help describe.

Much of the recent work in macroeconomics emphasizes the importance of information transmission in the economy [e.g. Lucas (1981)]. For example, some current explanations for unemployment and business cycles depend upon individuals having difficulty obtaining information about the economic environment from their own observations of the marketplace. These theories, which stress the role of information, owe a great debt to Stigler's (1961) initial analysis of market behavior when search costs are positive. Recent advances in the theory of finance have emphasized how well-organized competitive auction markets, like a stock market, can facilitate the aggregation of information [see, for example, Grossman and Stiglitz (1980)]. This chapter will explain that auction markets and search markets are just two of many possible types of market organization, each of which have different properties of information transmission. This means that if industrial organization economists have theories to predict which type of market organization will develop and how information gets transmitted in each type of market organization, they could assist macroeconomists in pinpointing those sectors of the economy where information lags and information errors are most likely to occur.

One possible reason why macroeconomics has not paid more attention to industrial organization is that much of industrial organization seems fixated on answering how the behavior of markets differs as industry concentration changes. Although this is certainly an interesting question, industry concentration is only one of many ways in which markets can differ. Market liquidity, heterogeneity of product, variability in demand and supply, the ability to hold inventories, and the ability to plan are also interesting characteristics, and differences in these characteristics lead to different market behavior. Yet the effect of these other characteristics has received much less attention from industrial organization economists than the effect of differences in industry concentration. And the effects of differences in these other characteristics may well be of more importance to macroeconomists than the effects of differences in concentration. This chapter will discuss some of these other characteristics.

Although it is clear that industrial organization does have something to offer macroeconomists, it is unlikely that macroeconomists who study industrial organization will suddenly realize that they have been overlooking key insights into macroeconomics. One reason is that the attempt within the last ten to fifteen years to provide a rigorous micro-foundation for macroeconomics already represents interaction between industrial organization and macroeconomics. Another reason is that industrial organization has only recently been making progress in areas of potential interest to macroeconomists. My own assessment is that some of these new areas of research, which I describe below, do have the potential to provide a valuable contribution to macroeconomics. However, the contributions will probably be better characterized as sharpening the perspective of macroeconomists rather than as fundamentally changing how macroeconomists think.[1]

This chapter is organized as follows. Section 2 discusses some simple theories of how markets clear. These simple theories focus on price as the mechanism

[1] I do not discuss the concept of money and credit. Even here, a few industrial organization economists have done some work that might interest macroeconomists. See, for example, Telser and Higinbotham (1977) and Telser (1978, ch. 10). I also do not discuss the political theory of regulation [Stigler (1971), Peltzman (1976)] which might be used to explain fiscal and monetary policy.

used to achieve resource allocation and investigate how the price-clearing function is altered depending upon whether the market is a competitive one, an oligopoly or a monopoly. Section 3 provides evidence on what industrial economists know about price behavior. The evidence is sufficiently at variance with any of the predictions of the simple theories that it raises serious questions about the usefulness of these theories for explaining price behavior in many markets. Section 4 investigates a variety of alternative theories that go a good way, though not all the way, toward explaining some of the observed puzzles in the data on price. In particular, I present a general theory of how markets operate without relying upon price as the exclusive market clearing mechanism. In Section 5, I focus on features of market structure other than the degree of market concentration to show how market structure matters in explaining the response of various industries to shocks in either supply or demand. Section 6 presents my conclusions.

2. Simple theories of how markets clear

In this section I briefly survey the three most important simple models of how markets operate. These simple models form the background against which I will analyze the evidence on prices in the next section. Although these models are admittedly simple, it is first necessary to understand where the simple models fail in order to develop better models.

2.1. Competition

Probably the simplest and most frequently used model to evaluate industry behavior is the standard competitive model in which price adjusts so as to equate supply to demand. This model assumes that there is a well-functioning auction market in which transactions take place. There is no cost to using such a market nor is there uncertainty affecting suppliers or demanders.

The focus of the model is to explain price fluctuations as the mechanism to clear markets. Given the standard assumptions of a perfectly competitive model, it is straightforward to trace out how the market responds to shifts in either supply or demand. For example, we can write in equilibrium that

$$D(P;\alpha) = S(P;\alpha), \tag{1}$$

where D is the demand curve, S is the supply curve, P is the price, and α represents exogenous factors influencing supply or demand or both. We can rewrite equation (1) in logarithmic form (with the obvious change of variables) as in equation (2)

$$\ln D(\ln P; \ln \alpha) = \ln S(\ln P; \ln \alpha), \tag{2}$$

where $\ln \alpha$ = log of exogenous factors. We can perform comparative statistics on equation (2) to figure out how price will change in response to fluctuations in α. It is straightforward to show that the percentage change in price resulting from a 1 percent change in exogenous factors will be related inversely to the elasticities of demand and supply as given by equation (3):

$$\frac{\mathrm{d} \ln P}{\mathrm{d} \ln \alpha} \propto \frac{1}{E_{\mathrm{S}} - E_{\mathrm{D}}}, \tag{3}$$

where E = elasticity of supply (E_{S}) or demand (E_{D}).

The insights from the competitive model usually stop with (3). This means that the analyst, once he knows the elasticities of supply and demand, is done. He uses equation (3) to predict the price effects using the price elasticities. Typically not much attention is paid to the economic explanations of the likely magnitude of E_{S} or E_{D}, based upon the economic motivation of firms and individuals.

The competitive model is elegant in its simplicity and in its predictions. When either demand or supply changes, price adjusts to clear the market. The amount by which price has to adjust depends upon the supply and demand elasticities. There are no unsatisfied demanders at any instant nor any sellers who wish to sell the good but cannot. All sellers receive and all buyers pay the same price, and price changes are perfectly correlated across different buyers.

2.2. *Oligopoly models*

It has long been recognized that the competitive model will fail if there are only a few firms in the marketplace and if these few firms recognize their mutual interdependence. In such a situation, the industry supply curve will no longer equal the summation of the marginal cost curves of the firms. Instead, the amount one firm is willing to supply depends, in part, on the reactions that the firm thinks its rivals will take to its actions. There is no one model of oligopoly behavior that is uniformly accepted today. This inability to develop a single model reflects in part ignorance, but also the fact that oligopolies differ quite a bit in their behavior, and therefore it is unrealistic to expect one model to completely describe their behavior. Most simple models of oligopoly (e.g. Bertrand, Cournot, kinked demand curve) assume that however price is set, there are no unsatisfied demanders or sellers at that price, that price changes are passed

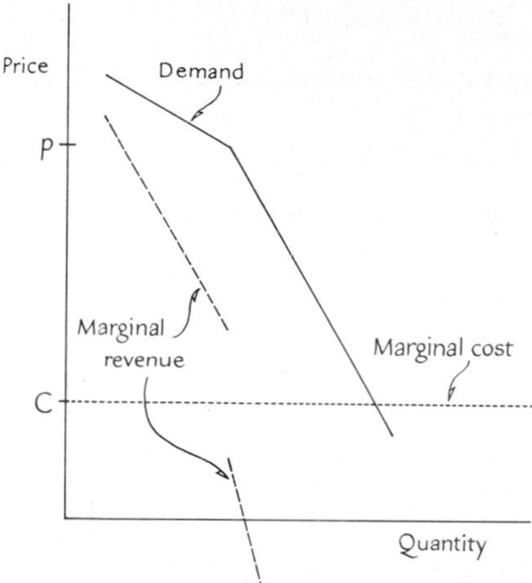

Figure 15.1. Kinked demand curve.

along to all buyers simultaneously, and that it is not costly to transact in the market.

One common theme of most models of oligopoly is that the behavior of price in an oligopoly is much different than it is in a competitive market. This insight is useless, though, unless it is possible to describe the types of differences one expects. One early attempt was to use the model of the kinked demand curve to explain oligopoly pricing.[2] As shown in Figure 15.1, under the kinked demand curve theory of oligopoly pricing, every firm faces a demand curve that is much more elastic above a price, p, and much less elastic below that price. If firms do face such demand curves, it is clear that there will be a tendency for firms to price at p for a range of different marginal costs. The marginal cost curve will go through the gap in the marginal revenue curve (see Figure 15.1). The kinked demand theory of oligopoly behavior therefore predicts that prices will tend to remain unchanged for small changes in costs.

Unfortunately, the theory is silent on how price initially gets set. The kinked demand curve is certainly not a theory to explain price levels. At best, it is a theory to explain why prices do not change in response to modest shifts in cost. (In response to large shifts in cost, the theory predicts that prices should change, although it provides no guidelines as to how the new price level will then be set.)

The property of the kinked demand curve that price is unresponsive to some cost fluctuations is preserved in most discussions of oligopoly theory whether or

[2]Other recent models yielding kinked demand curves include Salop (1979) and Schmalensee (1982).

not based on the kinked demand curve. The reasoning is that in oligopolies prices fluctuate less in response to cost changes (especially small ones) than they would otherwise in order not to disturb existing oligopolistic discipline. Anytime a price change occurs in an oligopoly, there is a risk that a price war could break out. Hence, firms are reluctant to change price.

2.3. Monopoly

The theory of monopoly like the theory of competition is exceedingly simple. The firm calculates its marginal revenue curve and equates marginal revenue to marginal cost. Again, the simple theory of monopoly does not typically analyze how the shapes of either the demand curve or marginal cost curve will be influenced by economic motivations facing consumers or the firm. The implication of the theory of monopoly is that price will exceed marginal cost. Again, as in the models of competition and oligopoly, there are no unsatisfied demanders at the market price, and the cost of allocating goods, that is the cost of using a market price to allocate goods, is assumed to be zero. The demand curve is assumed to be known and price changes across different buyers are expected to be highly correlated.

It is straightforward to use the simple theory of monopoly to explain how a monopolist will react to shifts in either supply or demand. For example, if marginal costs change, then the new price will be determined by the intersection of the new marginal cost curve with the marginal revenue curve.

It is common to see statements that a monopolist will have his price vary less than it would if the market were competitive. This intuition seems to be based upon an example in which demand curves are linear. In such a case any change in marginal costs will be translated into a change in price that is *less* than the change in marginal costs. For example, if the demand curve equals

$$Q = 9 - P, \tag{4}$$

and marginal cost equals 1, the optimal price is 5. If marginal cost rises from 1 to 3, the optimal price goes up from 5 to 6. That is, price rises by one-half of the cost increase.

With linear demand curves and constant marginal cost, it is easy to show that if costs are changing over time, then the resulting variance in cost will be *greater* than the variance in price. However, it is also possible to construct models with precisely the opposite property. For example, suppose a monopolist faces a demand curve with a constant elasticity of demand and has a constant marginal cost. Then the monopolist's price equals a constant mark up above marginal cost. Since the mark up exceeds 1, it follows that the variance of price will exceed the variance in marginal cost. For example, if the elasticity were two, the monopolist would be charging a price of $2 if marginal cost were $1. If marginal cost were to rise by $2 to $3, the optimal price would rise by $4 and become $6. The increase in price would exceed the increase in cost.

The previous examples show that the relationship of price changes to cost changes varies with the shape of the demand curve and therefore it is not possible to make any general statements about the variance of price in relation to the variance of cost based upon whether a market is competitive or monopolized. Moreover, since we know that oligopolies run the spectrum from almost competitive industries to almost monopolized industries, the simple theories do not allow any differential predictions of price flexibility for (large cost changes) that depend solely on the degree of competitiveness of the market.[3]

3. Empirical evidence on the role of price in allocating goods

Several types of evidence are available to enlighten economists on the role that price plays in clearing markets. One type of evidence is casual observation which, although not terribly scientific, is better than no observation at all. Another type of evidence relies upon surveys of prices paid, as best they can be measured, for different commodities and across time. We now review the evidence.

3.1. Casual observation

Even if an economist has never studied the actual empirical distributions of prices across markets, he has transacted in many markets himself. He knows that it is not unusual for him to go to the supermarket to buy a product and for the supermarket to be out of that product. He knows that if there are three cars ahead of him at the gas station, the price of gasoline at the pump will not rise, but rather he will have to wait to get his car filled up. In fact, for many items he commonly purchases, the price, once set, stays fixed for a while.

Newspaper articles often describe how some companies have difficulty assuring themselves of supply during periods of high demand. Histories of business, such as Alfred Chandler's *The Visible Hand* [Chandler (1977)] described in detail that many firms vertically integrate, not necessarily to get a lower price for the product, but rather simply to get the product on a reliable basis. Waiting for a good and being unable to purchase a good when one wants it are typical rather than atypical experiences in many markets. In periods of tight supply, preferred customers get delivery, while new customers often are unable to assure them-

[3] For small cost changes, the theory of oligopoly suggests that prices may remain unchanged.

selves of a supply at the same price as the steady customers. In fact, short-term customers may be unable to get the product at all.

The notion that emerges from these types of observations is that in many markets price may not be the sole mechanism used to clear the market. None of the simple theories of Section 2 are able to explain the existence of unsatisfied demanders, yet, that fact appears to be an essential feature of many markets.

3.2. Studies of price statistics

3.2.1. Early studies

One of the earliest studies regarding the flexibility and behavior of prices is the one by Frederick Mills (1927). Mills examined numerous price statistics gathered by the BLS for frequency of change and amplitude of change. His work represents an outstanding contribution to our knowledge of price behavior.

In Figure 15.2 I have reproduced some of Mills' findings regarding the frequency of price change over various time periods. The diagrams show that the distribution across markets of the frequency of price changes is U-shaped. That is, there are many products whose prices change frequently, and many products whose prices change infrequently. I am unaware of any attempt by economists to explain empirically the shape of these functions. Of course, it is possible to say that in some industries there is no need for price change, and what Mills is showing reflects simply the distribution of shocks to various supply and demand curves. So, for example, there are many markets for which shocks are frequent,

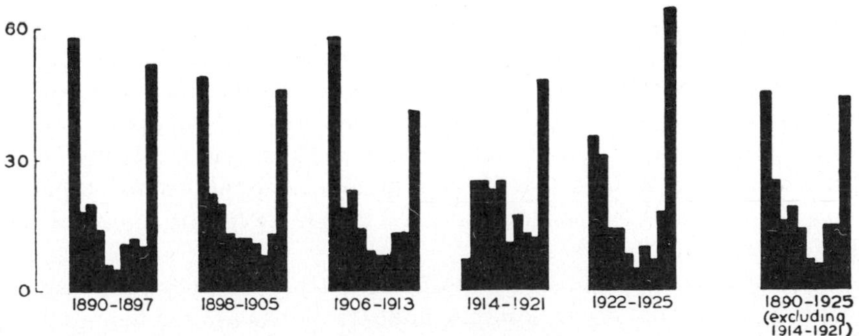

Figure 15.2. Column diagrams showing distributions of measures of frequency of price change, by periods. The horizontal axis measures frequency of price change. Frequency increases as one moves to the right. The vertical axis measures the number of commodities of any given frequency. [*Source*: Mills (1927, p. 371).]

while there are also many markets for which shocks are few. While that is one possibility, another is that there are some markets for which prices change frequently and are the exclusive device used to clear markets, while there are other markets for which price does not vary frequently and something else is going on to clear those markets.

It remained for Means (1935) to create turmoil in the profession by suggesting that the Great Depression occurred because in many markets the laws of supply and demand had been repealed and prices no longer fluctuated to clear the market. Whatever one thinks of Means' arguments, they attracted widespread attention. Here was a man claiming that the Great Depression, which was (and is) inexplicable to most economists, was caused by a breakdown in market clearing, which formed the basis for all economists' beliefs. Keynes' general theory soon came along with predictions of economic behavior that resulted from an assumed wage rigidity. Although I have never seen any analyses of wage rigidity comparable to, for example, Mills' work, my suspicion is that wage rigidity is less important than price rigidity, and the reliance by macroeconomists on wage rigidity strikes me as misplaced.[4] In any event, Means' hypotheses challenged the profession and though, as I explain later, his inferences from price rigidity are misguided, they are based on, what I believe, is a correct phenomenon, namely that none of the simple theories explain price behavior very well.

Means' theory was that in many market prices were "administered" – which meant that the laws of supply and demand no longer predicted price behavior, and instead prices were under the control of firms which, for unexplained reasons, chose not to vary prices to clear markets. Means claimed that price changes in "administered" markets were much less frequent, and, when they did occur, much larger in amplitude than those in competitive markets. According to Means, because administered markets had long stretches of rigid prices, prices were failing to clear these markets, and this faiilure caused the disequilibrium of which the Great Depression is an example.

Means seems to have resisted equating administered prices to prices in markets with high concentration, and there was confusion as to what exactly an administered price was. A voluminous and contentious literature developed to try to give structure to Means' arguments and test them.[5] The result of that literature has, I think, been to confirm that something unusual is going on in the behavior of some prices. [See, for example, Weiss (1977), but see Stigler and Kindahl (1972) for a different point of view.]

Mills' (1927) earlier work, which attracted much less attention than that of Gardiner Means, did not indicate a significant decrease in the frequency of price

[4] If prices are stickier than wages, real wages should be procyclical, while if wages are stickier than prices, real wages should be countercyclical. The evidence [see, for example, Zarnowitz (1985)] is that real wages are procyclical.

[5] The interested reader is referred to Beals (1975), Lustgarten (1975), Qualls (1979), Scherer (1980, ch. 13), Weiss (1977), and Weston and Lustgarten (1974), and the references cited therein.

changes from the 1890s to the mid-1920s (see Figure 15.2). Although I am not aware of any study that has redone Mills' analysis on price flexibility for the period of the Great Depression, my hunch is that prices did not become dramatically more rigid after 1929. That is to say, Gardiner Means may well have been right to point out that economists had inadequate theories to predict the flexibility of prices, but the phenomenon he was talking about was one that was not confined to the period of the Great Depression. Indeed, as we shall soon see, the phenomenon of rigid prices characterizes the U.S. economy today. However, Means did raise the possibility of a link between industrial structure and business cycles – a link that is only now being explored (see Subsection 2.2.3).

3.2.2. *Later studies*

The major criticism of Means' work is that it relies on price statistics gathered by the BLS. A study done by McAllister (1961) for a Congressional Committee on Price Statistics showed that the BLS data typically did not reflect price discounts. Moreover, an examination of the way in which the BLS gathered price statistics showed that the number of reporters relied upon by the BLS varied from market to market. It is a simple statistical exercise to show that the more reporters there are, the more likely it is to observe some flexibility in an average price. This is especially true when products are somewhat heterogeneous. The McAllister study showed that the flexibility of prices, as determined from BLS numbers, was closely linked to the number of reporters taking BLS surveys.

The findings of the McAllister study led to one of the most important contributions to the debate on administered prices – the work by Stigler and Kindahl (1970). Recognizing the inadequacies of BLS price statistics, Stigler and Kindahl collected data on individual transaction prices based on actual transactions between buyers and sellers. Although the Stigler–Kindahl data undoubtedly contain reporting errors, it is probably the best source of information on pricing behavior available to economists today. Stigler and Kindahl constructed indices of prices for individual commodities, and found that their price indices moved much more smoothly than those of the BLS. Price indices, when based upon actual transaction prices, were much more flexible than the price indices based on BLS data. Although Stigler and Kindahl did not explicitly claim that their findings were completely in accord with any of the simple theories of market clearing, they did suggest that their work went a long way towards explaining the unusual findings of price investigations based on BLS data. Their explanation was that the BLS data were simply misleading.

Stigler and Kindahl did recognize that there were some puzzling features even in their own data set. For example, they noted that the typical pattern of buyer–seller behavior was for buyers and sellers to remain in contact with each other for long periods of time even for transactions involving what appear to be homogeneous goods. This suggests that buyers and sellers build up some specific capital from the transactions and that this capital is valuable and must be preserved over time. As will be seen below, this insight can be used to explain a great deal of what appears to be unusual pricing behavior. Furthermore, the Stigler and Kindahl data produced a price index that was not only more flexible than the BLS index, but also had a different general trend from the BLS index during some time periods. For example, if one believes that the BLS price is more of a spot price than the Stigler–Kindahl price index,[6] which is based on long-term contract prices, then the Stigler–Kindahl data suggest that over the course of the business cycle there are systematic differences between how spot prices behave and how long-term contract prices behave. During booms, spot prices rise relative to long-term contract prices. There have been only a few attempts to explain why such differences exist.[7]

Another interesting feature noted by Stigler and Kindahl is that most of the transactions, although they last a long time and although they may be pursuant to a "contract", seem to specify neither a price nor in many cases a quantity. It is simply wrong to think of contracts as rigidly setting both the price and the quantity terms in a market place. [Williamson (1975) makes this same point.] That is, it is wrong to believe that it is the writing down of a fixed price contract that is causing rigid prices in markets. Even if buyers and sellers had the opportunity to renegotiate after they had entered a deal, it will often be the case that prices would not change in the contracts.

Means (1972) responded to the Stigler–Kindahl study by claiming that their evidence, instead of contradicting his earlier work, actually supported it. Since it is very hard to define exactly what Means' hypotheses were, it is not worth attempting to resolve this dispute here. However, Weiss (1977) did attempt to weigh the evidence of Stigler–Kindahl against the evidence put forward by Means. Although recognizing the difficulty of giving theoretical content to Means' hypothesis, Weiss concluded that the evidence on pricing did appear unusual in the sense that the simple theories do not do a good job of explaining pricing behavior.

The only other study using the Stigler–Kindahl data base is my own [Carlton (1986)]. Unlike Stigler and Kindahl, I did not construct indices of prices to examine how a price index behaved over time because indices can mask interesting behavior. For example, it is possible for an index of prices to be perfectly flexible even if most contracts are characterized by rigid prices. This could occur if new buyers simply paid a different price than old buyers. Yet, it is surely important to know whether price is being used to allocate goods to some buyers while not to others and whether some other mechanism, such as a seller's

[6]The BLS index is based on current price quotations for delivery. Therefore, it is reasonable that the BLS index will reflect fewer long-term contracts than the Stigler–Kindahl index [see Stigler and Kindahl (1970, p. 6)].

[7]See Stigler and Kindahl (1970), Carlton (1979), and Hubbard and Weiner (1986).

Table 15.1
Price rigidity by industry

Product group	Average duration of price rigidity (months)
Steel	17.9
Non-ferrous metals	7.5
Petroleum	8.3
Rubber tires	11.5
Paper	11.8
Chemicals	19.2
Cement	17.2
Glass	13.3
Truck motors	8.3
Plywood	7.5
Household appliances	5.9

Source: Carlton (1986, table 1).

knowledge of each buyer's requirements, is being used to allocate goods.[8] Instead of examining indices, I examined how prices to individual buyers change relative to each other during the course of a ten year period. I also analyzed how often a price, once set to an individual buyer, changed.

Table 15.1 presents a summary of some of my findings. It shows that the degree of price rigidity differs greatly across industries. In some industries the average price does not change for periods well over one year, while in other industries the price changes quite frequently. In fact, there are several instances of transactions in which the price paid by a buyer does not change for periods of well over 5 years. Although the evidence in Table 15.1 would conform to the simple theories under some extreme assumptions, I think it is better viewed as casting doubt on them. For example, one could argue that in industries with very rigid prices the supply and demand conditions are virtually stable over time, while in the other industries with flexible prices the supply and demand conditions are changing frequently. I find that the duration of the rigidity in some prices to individual buyers is so long that this explanation is not credible. And, further investigation (described next) reveals that such explanations are wrong.

[8]Rigid prices are troubling to an economist because they suggest that prices may not be clearing markets. However, it is not *rigidity* per se that should bother economists, but rather the inference from the rigid prices that prices are not clearing markets. Even if prices were perfectly indexed to inflation and hence were always changing, it would still be troubling if the evidence (e.g. unsatisfied buyers) indicated that price did not clear markets.

It is also important to understand that the simple models predict inefficient resource allocation when the *marginal* price fails to clear markets. A contract that specifies a fixed quantity at a fixed price is *not* a rigid price that can induce inefficiency since the marginal price of an additional unit is the price of buying that unit in the marketplace. When the quantity term is left open, as appears to be the case for the Stigler–Kindahl data, the contract price is the marginal price.

The Stigler–Kindahl data allow one to examine how price changes across different buyers of the identical commodity are correlated. In all of the simple theoretical models of market clearing, the price changes across different buyers of the same commodity should be highly correlated. Although there were some markets for which this was true, there were several markets in which price changes seem to be poorly correlated across buyers. My interpretation of these results is that the simple models which rely exclusively on price to clear markets simply fail to explain how many markets operate. It is an unsolved puzzle to explain why price changes in some markets are highly correlated across buyers, while price changes in other markets are not.

One of the findings of this study is the strong positive relationship between industry concentration and price rigidity. The more highly concentrated an industry is, the greater is the likelihood that the industry has prices that remain unchanged for long periods of time. (Recall that the simple models do not have any prediction relating price rigidity to the amount of concentration in the market.[9])

In summary, detailed examination of the Stigler–Kindahl data uncovers a number of anomalies in price behavior. These anomalies do not support any of the simple models of market clearing. As will be explained in Section 4, I think it wrong to assert that these findings necessarily prove that markets are operating inefficiently. Instead, these findings prove that the simple models of price clearing are inapplicable to certain markets.

3.2.3. Other recent studies

There have been numerous empirical investigations of the relationship between price, cost, business cycles, and concentration.[10] Although I will not describe them in great detail here, I would like to call attention to several recent studies that improve on earlier studies by using more comprehensive data.

The work of Domowitz, Hubbard and Peterson (1986a, 1986b, 1986c) examines the behavior of prices in the United States over the period 1958 to 1981 using data at the four digit SIC code level. They reached several interesting conclusions. First, price–cost margins in concentrated industries are procyclical – they rise in booms and fall in recessions.[11] Second, price–cost margins

[9]Although the theory of oligopoly can justify price rigidity in the face of small cost changes, notice that as the industry becomes more concentrated and an oligopoly becomes more powerful, the oligopoly should behave more like a monopolist for whom, according to the simple theory of monopoly, prices should not be rigid.

[10]The interested reader is referred to Scherer (1980, chs. 9 and 13) for a survey of some of these studies.

[11]Qualls (1979) also finds this procyclical effect.

in relatively unconcentrated industries "tend" to be countercyclical. Third, unionization in concentrated industries appears to keep wages in those industries relatively stable over the business cycle.

Domowitz et al. explain their finding of procyclical margins in concentrated industries by showing that costs, in particular real wages, tend to be more rigid in those industries. That is, during a boom, a firm in a concentrated industry experiences a price increase that is accompanied by only a modest cost increase so that the gap between price and (marginal) cost rises. Unions provide one explanation for the greater rigidity of wages in concentrated industries since unionization and concentration are positively correlated. Domowitz et al. find that the differential degree of unionization (not just concentration) is an important explanation for this procyclical behavior of margins in concentrated industries. A corroborating piece of evidence is that local demand effects are less important than aggregate economic activity in explaining margins. This is exactly what one would expect if price changes were relatively similar across industries but not cost changes so that differences in cost were the main variable explaining different behavior of margins across industries during the business cycle.

This finding of procyclical margins in concentrated industries is interesting for what it implies about how concentrated markets work. A monopolist (or an oligopolist trying to behave like a monopolist) will have his price–cost margin rise only if the elasticity of demand changes. I have not seen any evidence to suggest that firm demand elasticities decrease in booms.[12] Therefore, some other explanation is neeeded to explain procyclical margins in concentrated industries. Possible explanations could rely on either oligopolistic behavior [e.g. incentives to cheat (see Section 4) or the long-term relationship of the buyer or seller (see Section 4)].

There has been some work that reaches opposite conclusions to those of Domowitz et al. For example, Scherer (1980, ch. 9), in reviewing the literature, concludes that margins in concentrated industries are likely to be countercyclical. This view is based on studies that find slow adjustment of prices to cost changes in concentrated industries.

Another contradiction to the procyclical nature of margins comes from the work of Bils (1985). He finds that marginal cost is procyclical and that, in general, margins are countercyclical. He finds no effect of concentration on this relationship; however, his investigation of the concentration effect relies on fewer observations than does the work of Domowitz et al. Bils takes special care to measure marginal as opposed to average variable cost. In contrast, Domowitz et al. are forced to use average variable cost in their measure of margins. If marginal cost is rising, then the true margin (which is based on marginal cost)

[12]A systematic tendency for industry demand elasticities to decrease would be unusual because of the "adding up" constraint on the demand elasticities.

could well be unchanging or even falling over the cycle, while Domowitz et al. would measure an increasing margin. Whether this explains the discrepancy between Bils and Domowitz et al. is unclear, but it surely reconciles at least part of the discrepancy.

A final piece of possibly contradictory evidence comes from Mills (1936). Mills studied the behavior of margins during the period before and after the Great Depression and found margins to be strongly countercyclical. Although Mills did not investigate the relationship of margins to concentration, his strong finding across all industries does contrast with Domowitz et al.'s finding of a "tendency" for countercyclical behavior of margins and then only in unconcentrated industries.

Just as it is important to understand how markets in the United States clear, it is also important to understand how markets in different countries clear. There has been some work trying to describe the different price flexibilities among various countries. One of the best is the work by Encaoua and Geroski (1984).[13] They put together a detailed data base that they used to estimate the relationship between price, cost, and concentration across a wide variety of countries and commodities. They find, in general, that the higher the degree of concentration in a market, the slower is the adjustment of price to cost changes.[14] They show that the more an industry is characterized by new entry and competition (measured by imports), the more likely it is that prices rapidly adjust to cost changes. They also find that there is a difference in the flexibility of prices across countries with, for example, Japan having more flexible prices than the United States. Understanding the reasons for the differential flexibility of prices across countries remains an important task.

3.3. *Summary of evidence on prices*

The evidence on price reveals that some markets are well described by the simple models of market clearing, but others are clearly not. Markets differ greatly in how flexible prices are, with the degree of competition being an important determinant of flexibility. In some markets, price changes to one buyer may be uncorrelated with those to another buyer, suggesting that other factors, such as a seller's knowledge of a buyer, are involved. In many markets, long-term relationships between buyers and sellers appear to be important. This suggests that industrial organization must consider arrangements more complicated than those based on impersonal markets in which prices alone allocate goods.

[13] See also Gordon (1983).

[14] The empirical findings of Domberger (1979) for the United Kingdom are precisely opposite. Domberger's explanation of his results is that information should be easier to gather as concentration increases and, so, prices should respond more rapidly to cost changes. See also Eckard (1982).

4. How to explain the evidence

There are several approaches to developing theories that better explain the observed evidence. [See Tucker (1938) for an early attempt.] One approach is simply to think harder about the simple theories, improve them, and see how far we can get. That approach takes us a good distance and I will describe some of the most useful extensions to the simple theories. However, these extensions to the theories get us only part of the way and in the remainder of this section I explore alternative theories that are useful in explaining some, though perhaps not all, of the evidence. It is the development of new theories of market clearing that should receive priority in explaining the pricing anomalies and that could have some impact on macroeconomic thinking.[15]

4.1. Extensions to the simple theory – the introduction of time

The expositions of any of the simple theories stress price as the market-clearing mechanism and ignore the possibility of delaying consumption or production to a later time. However, there is nothing in the theory that prevents it from taking account of such intertemporal substitution. For example, it is a straightforward extension of the simple competitive model to date goods and treat the same good at one date as a different commodity than the same good at a different date [see Debreu (1959, ch. 7)]. Once dynamic elements are introduced in this way, it is clear that the demander faces many substitutes to consuming a product today, not only from other products consumed today, but also from products consumed in the future. Conversely, from the viewpoint of the supplying firm, the firm could substitute production today for production tomorrow by holding inventories; in fact, the supply decisions of the firm across time are based on a complicated decision problem of how to vary inventories of inputs and final output and production in such a way as to satisfy a given stream of consumption. These observations suggest that the intertemporal substitution patterns of both consumers and firms are critical to understanding the extent to which prices today must adjust in order to clear markets.

The introduction of time into any of the three simple models described in Section 2 makes those models more realistic descriptions of the world. The introduction of time emphasizes the importance of intertemporal substitution on

[15] I do not explore the importance of risk aversion in explaining price rigidity. My empirical work [Carlton (1986)] indicated it not to be important. The theoretical development of the effect of risk aversion on pricing turns out to be identical to that in my 1979 paper [Carlton (1979)]. See Polinsky (1985) for a detailed study of risk aversion and pricing. I also do not explicitly examine pricing under conditions of natural monopoly [see Hall (1984)].

both the demand side and the supply side. We now describe how each of the three simple theories gets altered by the introduction of time.

4.1.1. Competition

By employing the simple device, described above, of dating commodities, it is straightforward to introduce time into the analysis of competition. In this analysis, each commodity at each separate date is regarded as a distinct commodity that is related in both supply and demand to all other commodities. The most important new relations are among the identical physical commodity over time.

The demand curve for a product at a particular point in time depends upon consumers' perceptions about what the price of the product will be in the future. If consumers are not impatient about consuming the product, then the price today cannot deviate very far above the price expected to prevail in the future without inducing consumers to cease purchasing today. That is, the elasticity of demand (ceteris paribus) will be very high. Similarly, on the supply side, intertemporal substitution affects the willingness of firms to supply the product today at a given price. Firms recognize that an alternative to producing and selling today is to produce and sell tomorrow, or perhaps to produce today, hold the good in inventory, and sell it tomorrow. The recognition that a firm can decide on the optimal time path of production and the optimal employment of factors of production, one of which is inventory, affects the shape of the short-run marginal cost curve (ceteris paribus).

A competitive equilibrium involves a separate price for each date at which the commodity will be consumed. Anything that changes either the cost of producing today or in the future or the demand today or in the future will affect the entire vector of prices over time. This means, for example, that a shock to demand might well affect the price of the good not only today but also in the future. This raises the possibility that shocks to supply or demand today will be absorbed primarily by something other than prices today. In fact, it is quite conceivable that in response to only slight changes in the vector of prices in the future, consumers will significantly rearrange their consumption of the good over time. In such a case, increases in demand today may not increase price today by very much, but rather leave most prices today and into the future unchanged, but simply shift consumption from today to the future.

The important insight from this way of viewing competition is that even though prices are clearing markets, the necessary equilibrating price changes can be quite small. It will be quantity shifts among different goods (i.e. the same good consumed at different periods of time) that will bear the brunt of the adjustment and not price.

If there are large shifts in the timing of when goods get consumed as demand and supply conditions change, the data should reveal large swings in delivery lags (the lag between the placement and shipment of an order). Many markets do

Table 15.2
Price and delivery lag fluctuations

Industry	Standard deviation of log of price	Standard deviation of log of delivery lag	Median delivery lag (months)
Textile mill products	0.06	0.17	1.26
Paper and allied products	0.05	0.08	0.46
Steel	0.03	0.25	1.95
Fabricated metals	0.03	0.18	3.06
Non-electrical machinery	0.04	0.25	3.63
Electrical machinery	0.05	0.10	3.86

Source: Carlton (1983b, table 1).

seem to be characterized more by fluctuations in delivery dates than by fluctuations in price. For example, Table 15.2 presents the variability of price and the variability of delivery lags for several major manufacturing industries. As the table shows, the variability of delivery lags swamps the variability in price for many industries. This evidence is consistent with the theory we have just outlined of competitive market clearing. The insight of the theory is that the price fluctuations that "one expects" to clear markets may well be lower than that predicted by the simple model that ignores the importance of the time dimension.

The importance of delivery lags as a market-clearing device, in addition to price, has not been extensively studied. Zarnowitz (1962, 1973) appears to have been the first to stress the importance of delivery lags as a market-clearing phenomenon. [See also Maccini (1973) and Carlton (1983b).] In Carlton (1985b), I estimated the importance of delivery lags as a determinant of demand. Those estimates are reproduced in Table 15.3. In conjunction with Table 15.2, the results imply that for many markets the fluctuations in delivery lags are approximately as important to the equilibration of demand and supply as are fluctuations in price.

There have been several studies that estimate the time path by which firms adjust factors of production in an attempt to meet fluctuations in demand. These studies [see, for example, Nadiri and Rosen (1973), Haltwanger and Maccini (1983) and Topel (1982)] explicitly recognize that firms can vary inventories, labor, price, and other factors of production to achieve their desired sales. These studies of intertemporal substitution in production provide us with a better understanding of the shape of the (ceteris paribus) marginal cost curve at any instant in time. Obviously, if it is costless to store inventories, prices will tend to

Table 15.3
Elasticities of demand

Industry	Price	Delivery lag
Paper and allied products	−1.37 (7.9)	−0.40 (3.7)
Steel	−14.26 (2.8)	−0.78 (3.0)
Fabricated metals	−1.75 (1.8)	−0.30 (3.6)
Non-electrical machinery	−3.5 (5.4)	−0.35 (3.5)
Electrical machinery	−1.60 (2.2)	−0.64 (3.3)

t-ratios in parentheses.
Source: Carlton (1985b).

be stable. If prices were not stable, there would be an incentive to hold inventory to speculate on any expected appreciation in price.

Some recent work by Mills and Schumann (1985) has investigated the determinants of how flexible firms make their production technology. Since the flexibility of production technology is an endogenous decision [see Stigler (1939)], an understanding of this endogenous choice of flexibility will enable the analyst to better predict the likely supply responses that are available in the short run to help meet changes in demand conditions. Mills and Schumann have uncovered what appears to be a systematic difference between small firms and large firms. They found that small firms have more flexible production technologies than large firms. If true, this would suggest that the industries in which entry of small firms is difficult will be less able to expand production during booms than industries with no such difficulties.

In summary, the introduction of time into the simple competitive model goes a good way toward explaining how markets may respond to shocks without the analyst ever observing large changes in current prices. Instead of large price changes, there may be large shifts over time in quantities consumed or produced as either firms or consumers take advantage of intertemporal substitution.[16]

[16]An analysis that recognizes the quality of goods is conceptually the same as one involving time. If goods are described by a vector of characteristics, q, then in response to a perturbation in either supply or demand conditions, not only will the price of the good change, but the quality of the good, q, will change [see Rosen (1974)]. Again, this raises the possibility that, within the context of a perfectly competitive model, adjustments to demand or supply shocks can occur through changes in q as well as through changes in price. Although it appears that delivery lags are one of the most important quality components of a good that seem to fluctuate, there may well be others, depending upon the particular commodity. For example, in response to an increase in the demand for bus transportation during rush hour, a city may put on more buses, but each bus may be much more crowded than during nonrush hour. That is, a less desirable product has been substituted and prices have remained unchanged.

4.1.2. Oligopoly

The introduction of time affects oligopoly models for many of the same reasons I have already discussed in the competitive model. That is, the ability of consumers to substitute across time periods as well as the ability of firms to produce the good across different time periods will affect how the market responds to changes in the underlying conditions of supply and demand. Some recent work has shown that the introduction of time adds a new element to the analysis of oligopolies that is lacking in the analysis of static oligopoly or dynamic competition. The key insight is that firms in an oligopoly are playing a game with each other over time. They are attempting to send each other a signal about the likelihood of successful collusion.

Firms cannot communicate directly because of the antitrust laws, and therefore, any one firm has uncertainty about whether his rivals are actually coordinating their policies with him or, instead, are cheating and stealing away his customers. One way for an oligopoly to behave is for all firms to agree to charge a high price; however, whenever cheating is suspected, all firms in the industry cut price as punishment for some fixed period. This type of model, developed and refined by Porter (1983) and Green and Porter (1984), suggests that oligopolies will go through price wars. The oligopoly during good times will be characterized by high and stable prices; however, when demand starts falling for the industry, some industry members will mistakenly think that their downturn in demand is caused by rivals secretly cheating on the cartel price and taking business away from them and will cut their price as punishment. This suggests a theory in which prices fall during downturns because of a breakdown in oligopolistic coordination.

As Stigler (1964) pointed out, a breakdown in oligopolistic coordination is more likely to occur the greater the "noise" in the economy. Inflation increases the "noise" in the economy by making real prices more uncertain [see Vining and Elwertowski (1976)].[17] Therefore breakdowns in oligopolistic discipline should be more common during times of rapid price change.

Rotemberg and Saloner (1986) reach a different conclusion. In their model, oligopolies behave more competitively in booms. The reason is that, in their model, the gains from cheating on any non-competitive price are greater during a boom. Since the gains from cheating can be lowered by a lowering of price, oligopolists consciously choose a relatively low price in booms to deter cheating. The theory suggests that the margins of oligopolists should behave countercyclically, rising in lean years and falling in boom years.[18]

[17]See Carlton (1983a) for a discussion of the effects of inflation on market behavior.

[18]Rotemberg and Saloner (1985) have also explored how their model can help explain some unusual empirical facts on inventory holdings over the business cycle.

For these theories of oligopoly to have macroeconomic implications, one must presume that economy-wide fluctuations simultaneously affect many industries and account for significant fluctuations in each industry's fortunes. For example, these theories might be especially relevant during the Great Depression when the common large shock of a downturn in demand simultaneously affected a wide spectrum of the economy. Whether such theories of oligopoly are helpful in explaining cyclical behavior during the more moderate business cycles after World War II remains to be seen.

4.1.3. Monopoly

The introduction of dynamic elements into the study of monopoly raises the same issues about intertemporal substitution in demand and supply discussed above for competition. There is one additional element though that arises in the case of monopoly (or perhaps a cooperating oligopoly) but not in the case of competition. A monopolist is concerned not only with the influence of today's prices on demand today, but also with its influence on future demand. For example, an increase in the price of steel scrap may lead some steel producers to alter their plans for building a new steel furnace, and this will, in turn, affect the future demand for steel scrap. To the extent that consumers adjust their future behavior in response to price changes today, a monopolist will take that adjustment into account in setting price. In contrast, a competitive firm has no control over its price today or in the future, and therefore cannot respond to the incentives to influence future demand. This reasoning explains why a monopolist might not want to raise price for fear of inducing substitution away from his product in the long run. This suggests one reason why prices in a monopoly may be more stable over time than in a competitive industry.

To the extent that consumers are uncertain about future prices, a monopolist might use his pricing path as a signal to tell consumers what price they should expect in the future. This means that, if costs rise unexpectedly in the short run but the monopolist knows that the increase will be only temporary, the monopolist might be reluctant to raise his price and pass these temporary cost changes on to consumers for fear that they will mistake the current price increases as being permanent and react to them in the long run by substituting away from the product. Therefore, a monopolist has an incentive to absorb temporary cost changes so that the price charged today might be a good indicator to consumers of the price to be charged in the future.

A monopolist who can hold inventory takes account of the relation between the marginal revenue curves at different points in time in setting his price. By taking account of these interactions, the monopolist is lead to choose a more stable price policy than the simple models of monopoly would suggest. [See, for example, Amihud and Mendelson (1983), Blinder (1982), Philips (1981), and Reagan (1982)].

4.2. Fixed costs of changing price

If there is a fixed cost that must be incurred every time a price is changed, the firm will not continuously vary price as predicted by a simple market-clearing model under either competition or monopoly. Instead, price once set will remain fixed until the new price exceeds the old price by an amount sufficient to justify incurring the fixed costs. [See Barro (1972) for a development of a model along these lines.]

This theory clearly accounts for nominal price rigidities, but, to be believable, requires an explanation of the source of these fixed costs of changing price. For example, it may cost money to publish a new catalog, print a new menu, or remark items already on the shelf. In a setting where the firm sells many products, it might well be more costly to change price than in a setting in which only a few products are involved. For example, grocery stores sell many products one of which is cigarettes. It is not uncommon for a pack of cigarettes of one size, say regular, to sell for the same price as a pack of cigarettes of another size, say, king size, even though the wholesale price of the two packages to the individual store differs. One rationale for the common retail price is that the difficulty of training a clerk to recognize different prices for different packages of cigarettes would induce too much error into the process of checking out. Instead, price differences tend to be taken into account only when larger packages, such as cartons of cigarettes, are sold. Therefore, the probability of observing price differences on different sized cigarettes increases when the quantity purchased in a single transaction is larger.

Aside from the cost of having to relabel prices on items or send out new catalogs or print up new menus, there is another reason why a firm might be reluctant to change price and act as if it faced a fixed cost of changing price. Some customers will settle on a firm to buy from only after they have engaged in a search in which they have compared the price of this firm to the price in the rest of the market. As long as the customer believes nothing has changed, the customer will remain with the initially chosen firm. If the customer interprets a change in price by the firm as a signal that market conditions have changed, then that customer may well decide to search in order to investigate whether his chosen firm still remains the optimal supplier for him.

In Carlton (1986), I tabulated the minimum observed price change across a wide variety of products sold at the intermediate level of manufacturing. If the fixed costs of changing price are high, then small price changes will tend not to occur. I have reproduced in Table 15.4 the minimum price changes observed. Table 15.4 shows that for the large majority of commodities examined the minimum price changes are quite small. The evidence is that small price changes occur in many transactions and suggests that, at least for some transactions, the fixed cost of changing price is small.[19] A theory that postulates a uniform fixed cost to change price simply does not square very well with these facts.[20] A theory that predicts a different fixed cost to different customers could, of course, explain the facts but then one would have to explain the source of the differing fixed costs among different customers. This is in fact the approach taken by the recently developed theory of market clearing which is described in Subsection 4.4.

Whether or not there is a common large fixed cost of changing price to individual buyers, the evidence in Section 3 shows that for many markets prices do not change, at least in the short run. In such a setting, the market behavior will deviate considerably from those of any of the simple models. The new feature of models with a temporarily fixed price is that consumers run some risk of not being satisfied in their demand. The notion that consumers may find a product unavailable simply has no counterpart in the standard theory. Yet unavailability of a product is surely a fact of life and is one that our economic theories should deal with.

One of the early contributions to this literature on fixed prices and product availability is the work by Mills (1962). Mills examined the behavior of a monopolist who must set price and produce before he observes demand. The optimal inventory policy for the monopolist is to choose output in such a way that the expected price equals marginal cost. The expected price will equal the price charged times the probability that a customer will come to the firm. It is easy to show that the inventory holding policy of the firm depends on the mark-up of price above cost. The closer is price to cost, the smaller will be the inventory of the firm, and conversely the higher the mark-up of price over cost, the larger will be the inventory of the firm. The reason is that the incentive to hold inventory declines as the mark-up falls because the profit from making a sale falls, while the cost of getting stuck with unsold goods remains unchanged. What is interesting about this relationship is that the probability of stock-outs, that is shortages, increases as the market price falls to marginal cost.

[19]I use the word "suggest" because it is possible that I am observing small price changes only when the new supply and demand conditions are expected to persist for a long time. The evidence could then be consistent with a significant fixed cost of changing price that causes prices to remain rigid for temporary shifts in supply and demand, but not for permanent ones. Although this explanation is possible, I have seen no evidence to suggest it to be true.

[20]It is possible to set a *price policy* that specifies price as a function of certain variables. Price could then change when the underlying variables changed. My evidence cannot be used to determine if there is a substantial fixed cost to changing the price policy.

Table 15.4
Frequency of small price changes by product group by contract type

Product	Contract type	Fraction of price changes less than			
		1/4%	1/2%	1%	2%
Steel	Annual	0.04	0.08	0.11	0.27
	Quarterly	0.05	0.11	0.17	0.24
	Monthly	0.09	0.20	0.36	0.52
Non-ferrous metals	Annual	0.02	0.05	0.09	0.27
	Quarterly	0.02	0.05	0.12	0.25
	Monthly	0.08	0.15	0.28	0.49
Petroleum	Annual	0	0	0.08	0.24
	Quarterly	0	0	0.02	0.17
	Monthly	0.01	0.05	0.19	0.47
Rubber tires	Annual	0.12	0.21	0.30	0.44
	Quarterly	0.07	0.11	0.18	0.34
	Monthly	0.13	0.23	0.38	0.63
Paper	Annual	0.04	0.09	0.08	0.27
	Quarterly	0	0.19	0.24	0.33
	Monthly	0.13	0.23	0.43	0.62
Chemicals	Annual	0.04	0.08	0.13	0.24
	Quarterly	0	0.05	0.11	0.24
	Monthly	0.05	0.14	0.30	0.42
Cement	Annual	0.14	0.22	0.32	0.46
	Quarterly	0	0	0.01	0.19
	Monthly	0.71	0.75	0.85	0.94
Glass	Annual	0	0	0.07	0.19
	Quarterly	0	0	0.20	0.40
	Monthly	0.03	0.20	0.45	0.67
Trucks, motors	Annual	0.03	0.03	0.12	0.20
	Quarterly	0	0	0	0.08
	Monthly	0.12	0.27	0.50	.75
Plywood	Annual	—	—	—	—
	Quarterly	0.01	0.02	0.06	0.19
	Monthly	0.19	0.38	0.54	0.72
Household appliances	Annual	0	0	0	0.25
	Quarterly	—	—	—	—
	Monthly	0.22	0.44	0.70	0.95

Source: Carlton (1986, table 3).

Models analyzing the availability of goods in competitive markets have been developed in the work of Carlton (1977, 1978, 1985a, 1988), DeVany and Saving (1977), and Gould (1978). In these models, consumers value a firm not only for its pricing policies but also for its inventory policy. The commodity space now is not simply a good at a particular period of time, but rather a good consumed at a particular point of time with some probability. Inventory policy affects the probability that the firm will have the good available. Some consumers will prefer to shop at high-priced stores that run out of the good infrequently, while other consumers will prefer to shop at stores that charge low prices but may run out of the good more frequently.

Once it is realized that a firm must stock an inventory to satisfy customers, it should be obvious that the variability of consumers' demand for the product will affect the firm's costs. The cost function of the firm depends upon the demand characteristics of consumers. The simple separation between supply curves and demand curves is lost in these more complicated models.

If the consumers' variability of demand influences the firm's cost, firms will want to charge different consumers different prices based on their respective variability of demand. These price differences do not reflect price discrimination, but cost differences. Prices to consumers will differ as long as consumers have a different variability of demand from each other, even though each consumer consumes the physically identical product. This means that prices to one consumer could change at the same time that prices to another consumer remain unchanged. The result would be a low correlation of price changes across consumers – a finding that characterizes many markets (Section 3).

4.3. Asymmetric information and moral hazard

It is common in economic transactions that a buyer has different information than a seller. For example, when someone buys a house, the buyer generally knows less about the house than the seller who has lived there for a long time. When someone buys a share of IBM stock, he may know less about IBM than other investors who are employed by IBM. Does the introduction of this kind of asymmetric information affect how markets reach equilibrium? In 1970, George Akerlof showed that the answer to this question was a resounding yes. He showed that with asymmetric information equilibrium no longer requires supply to equal demand. Moreover, not only does asymmetric information affect how prices are set, asymmetric information can also cause markets to vanish completely.

Akerlof used a simple example to illustrate his point. Consider a market in which buyers are purchasing used cars that differ in quality. A buyer knows nothing about the quality of a particular used car and only knows the quality of the average car sold. The seller on the other hand knows exactly the quality of his used car. At any price, p, an owner is willing to sell his car only if the value of the car is *less than or equal to* p. If only cars whose quality is valued at p or *less* are placed on the market, then the average quality of cars offered at price p will be valued at less than p. But if the average quality of a car offered at p is not valued to be worth p, the price will fall. A simple repetition of the argument shows that no matter how low the price falls, the average quality offered in the marketplace will never be valued at the stated price. This causes the market to vanish entirely. That is, not only does the price mechanism not clear the market, there is no market left to clear. This collapse of the market can occur even though there may be buyers and sellers who, in a world of perfect information, would find it mutually beneficial to transact with each other.

It is possible to extend Akerlof's model to show how equilibrium can involve either excess demand or supply. [See, for example, Stiglitz (1976, 1984).] For example, suppose a firm wishes to hire a worker of a particular skill level. The firm obviously wants to pay as little as possible for such a worker. However, if the firm advertises a low wage, the people who apply for the job are likely to be low quality workers. The higher the wage rate offered, the higher the average quality of the applicant.[21] Therefore, when firms have difficulty measuring worker quality in advance, it might be sensible for the firm to set a sufficiently high wage in order to attract more than one applicant for the job. Although the firm would like to pay a lower wage for a given quality worker, the firm realizes that if it lowers its wage, only lower quality workers will apply for the job. Equilibrium, therefore, involves setting a high wage and having an excess supply of labor.

Akerlof's model can be recast as a problem in the principal–agent literature. In that literature there is a principal who hires an agent to perform some task. The principal can only imperfectly observe the agent's action. The problem that the principal–agent literature addresses is how to design the best contract given the constraints of asymmetric information. For example, in Akerlof's automobile example, the buyer could be regarded as the principal and the seller the agent. The seller's decision to sell the car is based on the car's quality which is unobservable to the buyer. The problem in Akerlof's model is that as the price of a car falls, the agent, that is the seller, is able to respond by choosing to withdraw the higher quality cars from the market.

Akerlof's model has been extended to a variety of circumstances using the principal–agent analogy. For example, Keeton (1979), and Stiglitz and Weiss (1981) have examined the market for loans. They observe that when a bank makes a loan, the bank is unable to perfectly monitor the riskiness of the investments that the borrower puts the money into. One response of a borrower

[21] The average quality rises with the wage because higher quality workers (in addition to the lower quality workers who applied at the lower wage) apply as the wage rises.

to a higher interest rate might be to take on riskier projects. There are instances when a bank is unwilling to raise the interest rate in the face of excess demand for loans for fear that the increased interest rate will drive borrowers to pursue riskier projects to the disadvantage of the bank. Therefore, the bank might be content to refuse to make additional loans rather than raise the interest rate. This is an example in which asymmetric information leads to an equilibrium in which supply does not equal demand and in which there is a rigidity in a price variable, namely the interest rate. In short, asymmetric information creates incentives for adverse selection (only bad workers showing up for a low paying job), and for moral hazard (borrowers choosing riskier investments in response to higher interest rates), and can, as a result, lead to either the disappearance of markets or to market equilibrium in which supply does not equal demand and in which there are rigidities in the relevant price variables.

4.4. Toward a general theory of allocation[22]

4.4.1. It is costly to create a market that clears by price alone

The key feature which most theories of market clearing ignore is that it is costly to create a market in which price equates supply to demand. In the standard theory, we usually assume that there is a fictional Walrassian auctioneer adjusting prices to clear markets. But in fact there is no such person. The markets that probably come closest to the textbook model of competitive markets are financial markets, such as futures markets. A moment's thought will reveal that it is costly to run such markets. Aside from the actual physical space that is required, there is the time cost of all the participants who are necessary to run the market. For example, at the Chicago Board of Trade, the floor traders, the employees of the brokerage firms, as well as the members of the associated clearinghouses, are all working together to produce a successful futures exchange. The people who use these futures markets must somehow pay all the people who work either directly or indirectly in making the transactions of customers.[23] These payments from the customer to the market makers can take several forms, such as direct commissions or simply bid–ask spreads.

Another important cost of making markets is the time cost of the actual customers [see Becker (1965)]. It would be very inefficient to have a market in which customers had to spend large amounts of their own time in order to transact. The purpose of a market is not merely to create transactions but rather to create transactions at the lowest cost.

[22]The theories in this section are developed in detail by Carlton (1988). See also Okun (1981) and Williamson (1975).

[23]Markets benefit non-users too by providing price information. This creates a free-rider problem.

Table 15.5
Death rates of futures markets

Age (years)	Probability of dying at the given age or less
1	0.16
2	0.25
3	0.31
4	0.37
5	0.40
10	0.50

Source: Carlton (1984, table 5).

Once one recognizes that the creation of markets is itself a productive activity that consumes resources, it makes sense to regard the "making of markets" as an industry. There has not been much research on the "making of markets" [see Carlton (1984)], but just like there is competition to produce a better mousetrap, so too is there competition to produce better and more efficient markets. The New York Stock Exchange competes with the American Stock Exchange; the Chicago Mercantile Exchange competes with the Chicago Board of Trade, and so on.

Lest one think that it is easy to create a successful futures market, one need only consult the historical record. I have presented in Table 15.5 the average failure rates of new successfully introduced futures markets based on evidence from the United States. The table indicates that about 40 percent of these futures markets fail by their fifth year. The making of successful markets is a risky activity, and as the exchanges themselves well know, it is hard to predict which markets will succeed and which will fail.

Organized[24] spot and futures markets exist for only a handful of commodities. Since we know that there are definitely social benefits to the creation of markets and since at least some of these benefits can probably be privately appropriated, the paucity of organized markets emphasizes that it must be costly to create them.

4.4.2. Heterogeneity is an important characteristic of determining how markets will clear

The heterogeneity of the product is perhaps the most critical characteristic in determining whether a market will clear by price alone. If buyers have different

[24] I use the term "organized" to mean auction markets that clear by price alone.

preferences for when they want to transact, what they want to transact (that is, the particular quality of the good), or where they want to transact, it is unlikely that a successful market can be organized that clears by price alone. Attempts to create an organized market in the face of widespread product heterogeneity will simply lead to an illiquid market that cannot support the cost of having the requisite number of traders [Telser and Higgenbotham (1977)].

Since product heterogeneity within an industry is an endogenous characteristic, the industrial organization economist should be able to predict which markets are likely to be sufficiently homogeneous so that an organized market can exist. For example, suppose each buyer is purchasing a standardized product. Each buyer is deciding whether he should continue purchasing the standardized product or whether he should customize the product to his own taste. The advantage of customizing will depend on how idiosyncratic the buyer's needs are. The disadvantage is that the buyer is forced to transact in a less liquid (higher transaction cost) market. The greater the benefits from custom designing a product to one's own specifications, the less likely it will be that a market can be created that will clear by price alone. Indeed, in the extreme case in which every buyer demands a slightly different product, it will be impossible for buyers to trade with each other and the incentive to create an organized market will be small.

4.4.3. *How do markets clear if there is no organized market?*

When an organized market does not exist, it is not possible for the firm to discover (costlessly) the market-clearing price, and the firm must rely on something else to figure out how to allocate its products to buyers. There are a wide variety of mechanisms other than the auction price mechanism that can be used to clear the market. One alternative was discussed by Stigler (1961) in his article on search theory. In Stigler's model, there is no organized market in which price equates supply to demand. Instead, buyers must search across different sellers in order to discover prices. Buyers' search costs become the resource cost of operating the market.

The notion of firms posting prices and consumers searching across firms is only one of many ways in which markets can function. An alternative is for firms to hire salesmen whose task it is to become knowledgeable about the demands of individual customers. Even if it is difficult for the firm to get the market-clearing price, it may be possible to identify those customers who should obtain the goods (i.e. the efficient allocation of goods).[25] The firm could use price to identify those buyers who want the goods the most, and then could use a second screen, based

[25]An example may help. Imagine that a firm, with a capacity of 100 units, has only two buyers who are known to be identical. If the firm is supply constrained (i.e. each buyer's demands are high at the stated price), then the efficient allocation is obvious (50–50), but the market-clearing price is not. [See Carlton (1983a, 1988) for more details.]

on the firm's own internal knowledge of each buyer's needs, to decide which of the remaining buyers should receive the goods. So, for example, it would not be uncommon during tight supply situations for steady customers to obtain delivery while new customers wait for delivery. It would also not be unusual to see buyers and sellers entering long-term relationships so that the sellers could better understand the buyers' needs and vice versa.

The importance of price diminishes once one recognizes that price alone may not be clearing markets and, instead, that price in conjunction with other mechanisms, such as a seller's knowledge of a buyer's needs, is performing that function. Indeed, if price is not the sole mechanism used to allocate goods, it becomes less interesting to observe whether price remains rigid. Although a rigid price does imply inefficiency under any of the simple models in which price alone is the exclusive mechanism used to achieve efficient resource allocation, a rigid price does not imply inefficiency in a world in which price is but one of the many methods firms are using to allocate goods to customers.

A theory that combines price with non-price methods of allocation would have the following implications.[26]

(a) The longer the buyer and seller have dealt with each other, and therefore the better they know each other, the less need there is to rely on price to allocate goods efficiently. A seller's knowledge of a buyer's need can be a substitute for an impersonal (auction) market that clears by price alone.

(b) The length of time a buyer and seller are doing business with each other becomes a characteristic of the transaction and can make one buyer different from another from the viewpoint of the seller. Therefore, observing differences in the price movements to different buyers who are purchasing the identical physical commodity may reveal nothing about allocative efficiency, since prices for different "products" should be expected to move differently from one another. The evidence in Section 3 that indices of spot prices and long-term contract prices do not always move together is consistent with this implication, as is the evidence that the correlation of price movements across buyers of the same product is often low.

(c) The pattern of a buyer's demand over the business cycle or, alternatively, the covariance of one buyer's demands with those of other buyers, will be a characteristic of interest to the seller because it will affect the difficulty of allocating goods efficiently. Again, even though two buyers purchase the identical commodity, they may be charged different prices and have their prices change differently simply because they have different buying patterns over time. The evidence on different price movements for different buyers of the same product is consistent with this observation.

[26]Additional implications regarding behavior during periods of price controls, speed of price adjustment, and behavior of price indices are discussed and tested in Carlton (1986, 1988).

(d) Rapid turnover of customers will inhibit the use of long-term relationships in which a seller's knowledge of customers is used to allocate goods. Industries with significant new entry or with customers with little "loyalty" should tend to rely on price as the primary mechanism to allocate goods.

(e) The establishment of a new futures market will distrupt the traditional pricing policies of existing firms in the industry. These firms should be expected to complain about the introduction of the new futures market. If the allocation of goods is a productive activity that requires resources, then a futures market acts as a "competitor" to the marketing department of firms in the industry. Futures markets create marketing information. Without futures markets, other agents, such as brokers or salesmen, must create this marketing information and get compensated for doing so. If a futures market is established, there is increased competition in this marketing arena and the value of marketing skills declines. Therefore, it is natural for those firms who were successfully performing the marketing function, before the introduction of the futures market, to complain about the increased competition in this activity.

There is some evidence of hostility towards the creation of new futures markets from the affected industry's members. For example, the aluminum futures market was established in the late 1970s. Aluminum producers opposed their establishment (*American Metal Market*, Jan. 6, 1978, p. 9). If marketing requires money, one possible interpretation of the complaints of the aluminum companies is that the resources they have invested to market their product are now competing with the resources of a futures market to market the product.

4.5. Summary of new theories

The development of theories of allocation that use methods in addition to price alone to clear markets is in its infancy. These theories hold the promise of explaining many of the puzzling features of price behavior.[27] They also may explain why these features of price behavior emerge from what is (at least privately) efficient behavior.

Macroeconomists have studied the properties of information transmission in search markets and have based theories of unemployment and business cycles on these properties [see, for example, Lucas (1981)]. Search markets, as I have described, are just one of many ways to allocate goods. The method chosen to allocate goods will influence how information gets transmitted, as well as how markets respond to various shocks. For this reason, the study of how markets

[27]They may also be useful in explaining some of the empirical puzzles associated with purchasing power parity, such as why prices (expressed in a common currency) of identical products in two different countries seem to differ when exchange rates change.

clear is one to which both industrial economists and macroeconomists should look for valuable insights into where information lags are likely to occur in the economy and how various industries are likely to respond to shocks.

5. Market structure means more than just the degree of concentration

Industrial economists often examine how market behavior differs as concentration in the market changes.[28] However, as the preceding section made clear, there are many other features of market structure that matter a great deal in explaining how markets behave, and, in particular, how markets will respond to shocks in either supply or demand. For example, we saw in the previous section that market operation will be significantly influenced by the ability of consumers and suppliers to substitute over time, and by the reliance the market places on price to allocate goods. Studying the importance of features other than market concentration may lead industrial organization economists to develop insights that are useful to macroeconomists. In this section, I discuss two illustrations of market characteristics that influence an industry's responses to shifts in either supply or demand:[29]

(a) whether an industry holds inventories, and
(b) whether the industry has a fixed price in the face of random demand.

5.1. Produce to order versus produce to stock

There are two basic ways an industry can be organized. It can wait for orders to come in (produce to order) and then produce, or it can produce first, hold inventories, and then hope to sell the products (produce to stock).[30] Although I have not seen much research on this topic, I expect that our economy has increased its reliance on industries that produce to order versus produce to stock, especially with the growth of the service sector in recent times.

An industry that produces to stock will be able to satisfy customers quicker, and be able to take advantage of economies of scale more than an industry that produces to order. On the other hand, an industry that produces to order will be

[28]This experiment only makes sense if concentration in a market is an exogenous variable. Recent research has suggested that concentration is an endogenous variable and is influenced by the relative efficiency of firms. [See, for example, Demsetz (1973), Peltzman (1977). See Schmalensee (1985) for a different viewpoint.]

[29]Other illustrations include the incentives the industry has to plan [Carlton (1982)], the degree of vertical integration [Carlton (1983a) and Wachter and Williamson (1978)], the importance of new products [Shleifer (1985)], and the effect of search [Lucas (1981) and Diamond (1982)]. Each of these features affect how an industry responds to shocks.

[30]See Zarnowitz (1973) and Belsley (1969).

able to avoid the cost of inventory holdings of the final good (though not necessarily of inputs), will be able to custom design products to closely match the buyer's specifications, and will perhaps be induced to adopt flexible technologies to compensate for its inability to hold inventories of the final output. The need to cut or raise prices significantly in order to clear markets will be greater in produce-to-stock industries than in produce-to-order ones. Moreover, the transmission of shocks will depend on whether the industry produces to stock (i.e. hold inventories). If either firms or final consumers are holding inventories, a temporary increase in demand will be at least partially accommodated by a decrease in inventory which, next period, will lead to an increase in production. If inventory holding is not occurring, the increase in demand may only drive current price up with little, if any, increase in production in the current or subsequent periods. Work by Amihud and Mendelson (1982) has shown how the recognition of inventory holding can justify a Lucas-type aggregate supply equation.

5.2. Transmission of shocks in industries with fixed prices

Suppose an industry is organized as described in Subsection 4.2 and that prices once set do not change for some period of time. The production of the goods must occur before demand is observed and therefore there is some risk that firms will run out of the good. It is straightforward to show that the ratio of inventory to average demand will depend on the ratio of price to cost [see, for example, Carlton (1977)]. The reason is that the opportunity cost of a lost sale rises with prices, so that the incentive to hold inventories increases with price. If price exceeds cost by a large amount, the amount of goods produced will exceed the amount demanded on average. A contrasting case would be one where price is close to cost so that inventory on hand is small relative to the average level of demand. In this second case, stock-outs will be frequent.

It is possible to show that in response to a mean-preserving increase in the riskiness of demand, firms will increase their inventory holdings in the first case, while firms will decrease their inventory holdings in the second case. In the second case, stock-outs become more frequent. Firms that operate with little extra inventory will not be able to cushion demand shocks. Therefore, when prices are temporarily unchanging, an economy is more vulnerable to disruption (i.e. stock-outs) from shocks the more competitive it is (i.e. the closer price is to marginal cost).

There has recently been interesting work linking aggregate macroeconomic activity to models involving fixed costs of price changes.[31] [See, for example,

[31] See also Drèze (1975), Fischer (1977), Hall (1978), Malinvaud (1979), Rotemberg (1982), and Phelps and Taylor (1977).

Akerlof and Yellen (1985), Mankiw (1985) and Blanchard and Kiyotaki (1987).] These papers make the interesting point that the need to adjust prices may be less important for the firm than for the economy as a whole. The reason is that firms are assumed to have market power so that there is a gap between price and marginal cost. Even if a change in price does not raise the firm's profits significantly it could, in this second-best world, significantly raise consumer welfare. This point is related to the one in public finance that in a second-best world, small shifts in one market can have significant welfare effects if price does not equal marginal cost in other markets [see, for example Harberger (1971)]. Therefore, there may be a divergence between a firm's incentive to incur a cost to change price and society's incentive to do so.[32]

6. Summary

This chapter has presented a survey of what industrial economists know about how markets clear. The evidence on price behavior is sufficiently inconsistent with the simple theories of market clearing that industrial economists should be led to explore other paradigms. The most useful extensions of the theory will be those that recognize that marketing is a costly activity, that an impersonal price mechanism is not the only device used to allocate goods, and that price methods in conjunction with non-price methods are typically used to allocate goods.

Exactly what macroeconomists can learn from all this is less clear to me. Since both macroeconomists and industrial economists are interested in the same question of how markets clear, I have no doubt that there is the potential for the two groups to influence each other's research. Whether that potential is realized depends in part on how some of the new areas of research in industrial organization develop.

References

Akerlof, G. (1970) 'The market for lemons: Qualitative uncertainty and the market mechanism', *Quarterly Journal of Economics*, 84(3):488–500.

Akerlof, G. and Yellen, J. (1985) 'A near-rational model of the business cycle with wage and price inertia', *Quarterly Journal of Economics*, 100(5):823–838.

Amihud, Y. and Mendelson, H. (1982) 'The output–inflation relationship: An inventory adjustment approach', *Journal of Monetary Economics*, 9(2):163–184.

Amihud, Y. and Mendelson, H. (1983) 'Price smoothing and inventory', *Review of Economic Studies*, 50(1):87–98.

Barro, R.J. (1972) 'A theory of monopolistic price adjustment', *Review of Economic Studies*, 39(1):17–26.

[32]A closely related point is that in the presence of distortions between price and marginal cost, the value of an output expansion can be greater to society than to the firm [see Harberger (1971)]. Hart (1982) and Hall (1988) apply this principle in a macroeconomic setting.

Beals, R. (1975) 'Concentrated industries, administered prices and inflation: A survey of empirical research', in: *Council on wage and price stability*, Washington.

Becker, G. (1965) 'A theory of allocation of time', *Economic Journal*, 75(299):493–517.

Belsley, D.A. (1969) *Industry production behavior: The order stock distinction*. Amsterdam: North-Holland.

Bils, M. (1985) 'The cyclical behavior of marginal cost of price', working paper no. 30, University of Rochester.

Blanchard, O. and Kiyotaki, N. (1987) 'Monopolistic competition and the effects of aggregate demand', *American Economic Review*, 77(4):647–666.

Blinder, A.S. (1982) 'Inventories and sticky prices: More on the microfoundations of macroeconomics', *American Economic Review*, 72(3):334–348.

Carlton, D.W. (1977) 'Uncertainty, production lags, and pricing', *American Economic Review*, 67(1):244–249.

Carlton, D.W. (1978) 'Market behavior with demand uncertainty and price inflexibility', *American Economic Review*, 68(4):571–587.

Carlton, D.W. (1979) 'Contracts, price rigidity, and market equilibrium', *Journal of Political Economy*, 87(5):1034–1062.

Carlton, D.W. (1982) 'Planning and market structure', in: J.J. McCall, ed., *The economics of information and uncertainty*. Chicago: University of Chicago Press, 47–72.

Carlton, D.W. (1983a) 'The distruptive effect of inflation on the organization of markets', in: Hall, ed., *Inflation*. Chicago: University of Chicago Press, 139–152.

Carlton, D.W. (1983b) 'Equilibrium fluctuations when price and delivery lag clear the market', *Bell Journal of Economics*, 14(2):562–572.

Carlton, D.W. (1984) 'Futures markets: Their purpose, their history, their growth, their successes and failures', *Journal of Future Markets*, 4(3):237–271.

Carlton, D.W. (1985a) *Market behavior under uncertainty*. New York: Garland.

Carlton, D.W. (1985b) 'Delivery lags as a determinant of demand', unpublished.

Carlton, D.W. (1986) 'The rigidity of prices', *American Economic Review*, 76(4):637–658.

Carlton, D.W. (1988) 'The theory of allocation and its implications for marketing and industrial structure', unpublished.

Chandler, A. (1977) *The visible hand: The managerial revolution in American business*. Cambridge, Mass.: Harvard University Press.

Debreu, G. (1959) *Theory of value*. New York: Wiley.

Demsetz, H. (1973) 'Industry structure, market rivalry, and public policy', *Journal of Law and Economics*, 16(1):1–10.

DeVany, A. and Saving, T. (1977) 'Product quality, uncertainty, and regulation: The trucking industry', *American Economic Review*, 67(4):583–594.

Diamond, P. (1982) 'Aggregate demand management in search equilibrium', *Journal of Political Economy*, 90(5):881–894.

Domberger, S. (1979) 'Price adjustment and market structure', *Economic Journal*, 89(353):96–108.

Domowitz, I., Hubbard, R.G. and Petersen, B.C. (1986a) 'Business cycles and the relationship between concentration and price-cost margins', *Rand Journal of Economics*, 17(1):1–17.

Domowitz, I., Hubbard, R.G. and Petersen, B.C. (1986b) 'Intertemproal stability of the concentration–margins relationship', *Journal of Industrial Economics*, 35(1):1–22.

Domowitz, I., Hubbard, R.G. and Petersen, B.C. (1986c) 'Oligopoly supergames: Some empirical evidence', unpublished.

Drèze (1975) 'Existence of an exchange equilibrium under price rigidities', *International Economic Review*, 16(2):301–320.

Eckard, E.W. (1982) 'Firm market share price flexibility, and imperfect information', *Economic Inquiry*, 20(3):388–392.

Encaoua, D. and Geroski, P. (1984) 'Price dynamics and competition in five countries', working paper no. 8414, University of Southampton.

Fischer, S. (1977) 'Long term contracts, rational expectations, and the optimal money supply rule', *Journal of Political Economy*, 85(1):191–205.

Gordon, R. (1983) 'A century of evidence on wage and price stickiness in the United States, the United Kingdom, and Japan', in: J. Tobin, ed., *Macroeconomics, prices and quantities: Essays in Memory of Arthur M. Oken*. Washington, D.C.: Brookings Institution, 85–134.

Gould, J. (1978) 'Inventories and stochastic demand: Equilibrium models of the firm and industry', *Journal of Business*, 51(1):1–42.

Green, E. and Porter, R. (1984) 'Noncooperative collusion under imperfect price information, *Econometrica*, 52(1):1–42.

Grossman, S. and Stiglitz, J. (1980) 'On the impossibility of informationally efficient markets', *American Economic Review*, 70(3): 393–408.

Hall, R.E. (1978) 'The macroeconomic impact of changes in income taxes in the short and medium runs', *Journal of Political Economy*, 86(2):571–585.

Hall, R.E. (1984) 'The inefficiency of marginal cost pricing and the apparent rigidity of prices', working paper no. 1347, National Bureau of Economic Research.

Hall, R.E. (1988) 'A non-competitive equilibrium model of fluctuations', working paper no. 2576, National Bureau of Economic Research.

Haltwanger, J. and Maccini, L. (1983) 'A model of inventory and layoff behavior under uncertainty', unpublished.

Harberger, A. (1971) 'Three basic postulates for cost benefit analysis', *Journal of Economic Literature*, 9(3):785–797.

Hart, O. (1982) 'A model of imperfect competition with Keynesian features', *Quarterly Journal of Economics*, 97(1):109–138.

Hubbard, G. and Weiner, R. (1986) 'Contracting and price flexibility in product markets', unpublished.

Keeton, W. (1979) *Credit rationing*. New York: Garland.

Lucas, Jr., R.E. (1981) *Studies in business-cycle theory*. Cambridge, Mass.: MIT Press.

Lustgarten, S. (1975) 'Administered pricing: A reappraisal', *Economic Inquiry*, 13(2):191–206.

Maccini, L.J. (1973) 'On optimal delivery lags', *Journal of Economic Theory*, 6(2):107–125.

Malinvaud, E. (1979) *The theory of unemployment reconsidered*. New York: Halsted.

Mankiw, N.G. (1985) 'Small menu costs and large business cycles: A macroeconomic model of monopoly', *Quarterly Journal of Economics*, 100(2):329–333.

McAllister, H. (1961) 'Government price statistics', Hearings before the Subcommittee on Economic Statistics of the Joint Economic Committee, 87th Congress, 1st session.

Means, G.C. (1935) 'Industrial prices and their relative inflexibility', Senate document 13, 74th Congress, 1st session. Washington, D.C.: U.S. Government Printing Office.

Means, G.C. (1972) 'The administered price thesis reconfirmed', *American Economic Review*, 62(3):292–307.

Mills, D.E. and Schuman, L. (1985) 'Industry structure with fluctuating demand', *American Economic Review*, 75(4):758–767.

Mills, E. (1962) *Prices, output and inventory policy*. New York: Wiley.

Mills, F.C. (1927) *The behavior of prices*. New York: National Bureau of Economic Research.

Mills, F.C. (1936) *Prices in recession and recovery*. New York: National Bureau of Economic Research.

Nadiri, M.I. and Rosen, S. (1973) *A disequilibrium model of the demand for factors of production*. New York: National Bureau of Economic Research and Columbia University Press.

Okun, A. (1981) *Prices and quantities: A macroeconomic analysis*. Washington, D.C.: The Brookings Institution.

Peltzman, S. (1976) 'Toward a more general theory of regulation', *Journal of Law and Economics*, 19(2):211–240.

Peltzman, S. (1977) 'The gains and losses from industrial concentration', *Journal of Law and Economics*, 20(2):229–263.

Phelps, E.S. and Taylor, J.B. (1977) 'Stabilizing powers of monetary policy under rational expectations', *Journal of Political Economy*, 85(1):163–190.

Phlips, L. (1981) *The economics of price discrimination*, New York: Cambridge University Press.

Polinsky, A.M. (1985) 'Fixed price versus spot price contracts: A study in risk allocation', working paper no. 20, Stanford Law School.

Porter, R. (1983) 'Optimal cartel trigger-price strategies', *Journal of Economic Theory*, 29(2):313–338.

Qualls, P.D. (1979) 'Market structure and the cyclical flexibility of price–cost margins', *Journal of Business*, 52(2):305–325.

Reagan, P. (1982) 'Inventory and price behavior', *Review of Economic Studies*, 49(1):137–142.

Rosen, S. (1974) 'Hedonic prices and implicit markets: Product differentiation in pure competition', *Journal of Political Economy*, 82(1):34–55.

Rotemberg, J. (1982) 'Sticky prices in the United States', *Journal of Political Economy*, 90(6):1187–1211.

Rotemberg, J.J. and Saloner, G. (1985) 'Strategic inventories and the excess volatility of production', working paper no. 1650-85, Sloan School of Management, MIT.

Rotemberg, J.J. and Saloner, G. (1986) 'A supergame-theoretic model of business cycles and price wars during booms', *American Economic Review*, 76(3):390–407.

Salop, S. (1979) 'Monopolistic competition with outside goods', *Bell Journal of Economics*, 10(1):141–156.

Scherer, F.M. (1980) *Industrial market structure and economic performance*. Chicago: Rand McNally.

Schmalensee, R. (1982) 'Product differentiation advantage of pioneering brands, *American Economic Review*, 79(3):349–365.

Schmalensee, R. (1985) 'Do markets differ much', *American Economic Review*, 75(3):341–351.

Shleifer, A. (1985) 'Implementation cycles', unpublished, MIT.

Stigler, G. (1939) 'Production and distribution in the short run', *Journal of Political Economy*, 47(3):305–327.

Stigler, G. (1961) 'The economics of information', *Journal of Political Economy*, 69(2):213–225.

Stigler, G. (1964) 'A theory of oligopoly', *Journal of Political Economy*, 72(1):44–61.

Stigler, G. (1971) 'The theory of economic regulation', *Bell Journal of Economics*, 2(1):3–21.

Stigler, G.J. and Kindahl, J.K. (1970) *The behavior of industrial prices*. New York: National Bureau of Economic Research.

Stigler, G.J. and Kindahl, J.K. (1972) 'Industrial prices as administered by Dr. Means', *American Economic Review*, 63(4):717–721.

Stiglitz, J. (1976) 'Prices and queues as screening devices in competitive markets', IMSS technical report no. 212, Stanford University.

Stiglitz, J. (1984) 'Price rigidities and market structure', *American Economic Review*, 74(2):350–355.

Stiglitz, J. and Weiss, A. (1981) 'Credit rationing in markets with imperfect information', *American Economic Review*, 71(3):393–410.

Telser, L. (1978) *Economic theory and the core*. Chicago: University of Chicago Press.

Telser, L. and H. Higinbotham (1977) 'Organized futures markets: The costs and benefits', *Journal of Political Economy*, 85(5):969–1000.

Topel, R.H. (1982) 'Inventories, layoffs, and the short-run demand for labor', *American Economic Review*, 72(4):769–787.

Tucker, R. (1978) 'The reasons for price rigidity', *American Economic Review*, 28(1):41–54.

Vining, D. and Elwertowski, T. (1976) 'The relationship between relative prices and the general price level', *American Economic Review*, 66(4):699–708.

Wachter, M. and Williamson, O. (1978) 'Obligational markets and the mechanics of inflation', *Bell Journal of Economics*, 9(2):549–571.

Weiss, L. (1977) 'Stigler, Kindahl and Means on administered prices', *American Economic Review*, 67(4):610–619.

Weston, F. and Lustgarten, S. (1974) 'Concentration and wage–price changes', in: H. Goldschmidt, ed., *Industrial concentration: The new learning*. Boston: Little, Brown and Co., 307–338.

Williamson, O.E. (1975) *Markets and hierarchies: Analysis and antitrust implications: A study in the economics of internal organization*. New York: Free Press.

Zarnowitz, V. (1962) 'Unfilled orders, price changes and business fluctuations', *Review of Economics and Statistics*, 44(4):367–394.

Zarnowitz, V. (1973) *Orders, production and investment*. New York: National Bureau of Economic Research.

Zarnowitz, V. (1985) 'Recent work on business cycles in historical prospective: A review of theories and evidence', *Journal of Economic Literature*, 23(2):523–580.

INDEX